TWENTY-FIRST CENTURY PROCEDURE

ASPEN CASEBOOK SERIES

TWENTY-FIRST CENTURY PROCEDURE

Christopher B. Mueller

Henry S. Lindsley Professor of Law
University of Colorado School of Law

Wolters Kluwer
Law & Business

Published by Wolters Kluwer Law & Business in New York.

Wolters Kluwer Law & Business serves customers worldwide with CCH, Aspen Publishers, and Kluwer Law International products. (www.wolterskluwerlb.com)

To contact Customer Service, e-mail customer.service@wolterskluwer.com, call 1-800-234-1660, fax 1-800-901-9075, or mail correspondence to:

Wolters Kluwer Law & Business
Attn: Order Department
PO Box 990
Frederick, MD 21705

Printed in the United States of America.

1 2 3 4 5 6 7 8 9 0

ISBN 978-1-4548-1952-3

Library of Congress Cataloging-in-Publication Data

Mueller, Christopher B.
Twenty-first century procedure/Christopher B. Mueller, Henry S. Lindsley Professor of Law, University of Colorado School of Law.
  pages cm
  ISBN 978-1-4548-1952-3
1. Civil procedure—United States. 2. I. Title. II. Title: 21st century procedure.

KF8839.M84 2013
347.73′5—dc23

2013002981

Certified Chain of Custody
Promoting Sustainable Forestry
www.sfiprogram.org
SFI-01042

SFI label applies to the text stock

About Wolters Kluwer Law & Business

Wolters Kluwer Law & Business is a leading global provider of intelligent information and digital solutions for legal and business professionals in key specialty areas, and respected educational resources for professors and law students. Wolters Kluwer Law & Business connects legal and business professionals as well as those in the education market with timely, specialized authoritative content and information-enabled solutions to support success through productivity, accuracy and mobility.

Serving customers worldwide, Wolters Kluwer Law & Business products include those under the Aspen Publishers, CCH, Kluwer Law International, Loislaw, Best Case, ftwilliam.com and MediRegs family of products.

CCH products have been a trusted resource since 1913, and are highly regarded resources for legal, securities, antitrust and trade regulation, government contracting, banking, pension, payroll, employment and labor, and healthcare reimbursement and compliance professionals.

Aspen Publishers products provide essential information to attorneys, business professionals and law students. Written by preeminent authorities, the product line offers analytical and practical information in a range of specialty practice areas from securities law and intellectual property to mergers and acquisitions and pension/benefits. Aspen's trusted legal education resources provide professors and students with high-quality, up-to-date and effective resources for successful instruction and study in all areas of the law.

Kluwer Law International products provide the global business community with reliable international legal information in English. Legal practitioners, corporate counsel and business executives around the world rely on Kluwer Law journals, looseleafs, books, and electronic products for comprehensive information in many areas of international legal practice.

Loislaw is a comprehensive online legal research product providing legal content to law firm practitioners of various specializations. Loislaw provides attorneys with the ability to quickly and efficiently find the necessary legal information they need, when and where they need it, by facilitating access to primary law as well as state-specific law, records, forms and treatises.

Best Case Solutions is the leading bankruptcy software product to the bankruptcy industry. It provides software and workflow tools to flawlessly streamline petition preparation and the electronic filing process, while timely incorporating ever-changing court requirements.

ftwilliam.com offers employee benefits professionals the highest quality plan documents (retirement, welfare and non-qualified) and government forms (5500/PBGC, 1099 and IRS) software at highly competitive prices.

MediRegs products provide integrated health care compliance content and software solutions for professionals in healthcare, higher education and life sciences, including professionals in accounting, law and consulting.

Wolters Kluwer Law & Business, a division of Wolters Kluwer, is headquartered in New York. Wolters Kluwer is a market-leading global information services company focused on professionals.

To My Wife Martha and Our Children
Gretchen and David
—CBM

SUMMARY OF CONTENTS

CONTENTS

4   SUBJECT MATTER JURISDICTION (THE COMPETENCE OF COURTS)

7 STATING CLAIMS AND DEFENSES: THE ART OF PLEADING

9   PRETRIAL DISCOVERY   911

14   BINDING EFFECT OF JUDGMENTS   1249

Twenty-First Century Procedure offers a new examination of a critical subject—the most important one in law school, in the author's opinion. The book is designed for required first-year Procedure courses, whether they are assigned four units in one semester, or five or six (hopefully in two semesters). I teach the course in four units (but would rather have five or six), and cover most of the pages in this book without unduly stressing students.

Twenty-First Century Procedure takes up all the subjects that a careful study of this subject demands—jurisdiction to joinder, pleading to appeals, discovery to post-trial motions, and the other topics in between (like pretrial, preclusion doctrines, and of course *Erie*).

There are, I think, five things that make this book different from most Procedure texts. First is the use of textual exposition that provides context and covers the basics. Too often students have to go elsewhere to get their bearings, and too often the cases they read expose doctrinal problems without imparting the sense that these doctrines do, after all, work reasonably well much of the time. Of course, I would not discourage a student from resorting to one or more of the fine treatises on the subject, but this book provides much of what students seek from such sources.

Second is the attention paid to federalism. Teaching *Erie* while ignoring three other very important aspects of federalism is a bit like telling someone about Dickens by describing *Oliver Twist* and *A Christmas Carol* without mentioning *David Copperfield, Great Expectations*, and *Bleak House*. What is ignored in most Procedure texts are the other critical aspects of federalism as it affects modern litigation, by which I mean federal pre-emption, the abstention doctrines, and antisuit injunctions. While these subjects are examined in other courses (Federal Courts and Complex Litigation come to mind), relatively few students take them, and the main focus of those courses is elsewhere.

Third, this book offers Problems as a way of getting at points that can't be adequately illuminated by description, or that benefit from the more open-textured discussion that a brief scenario followed by questions and variants can invite. Particularly in the area of discovery, where so much is left to the discretion of the trial judge and yet the Rules provide us with abundant details about the limits, uses, and mechanics of discovery, Problems can cover the ground much better than cases or descriptive materials.

Fourth, this book devotes fewer pages to federal jury entitlement and more pages to the rules and mechanics of actually impaneling a jury. Every veteran teacher knows that the jury entitlement decisions are difficult, largely inconclusive, and (worst of all) obscure and relentlessly convoluted, and that doctrine is not what students most need to grasp. What students do need to grasp, in addition to post-trial challenges to jury verdicts, is some sense of how juries are assembled and what lawyers do in this process.

Fifth and finally, this book offers Notes after the cases and Problems, but they differ from the Notes so often found in modern texts, which pile obscurity on obscurity and head off in inexplicable directions. In this book, the Notes are primarily designed to help students think about the issues raised in the cases and Problems. I do not believe that helping students in this way deprives the classroom experience of its vitality or importance: Students are encountering the subtleties of Civil Procedure for the first time in their first year of law school, and they do not immediately grasp everything that is important even when they have such help, and classroom discussion—real two-way conversation emulating the best in the Socratic tradition—can be both lively and vitally important even if students have already encountered in the Notes some of the ideas and themes that are basic to the case and sure to come out in classroom sessions. In almost 40 years of teaching, and in two runs through this book, I have never encountered a student who thought Procedure had been made too easy or boring, and have never been at a loss when it comes to engaging in useful conversations about the material.

Over many years of teaching this subject, I have used five different standard texts, all in current use. The fact that I've undertaken the present work speaks for itself, but I should pause here to say that I've learned much from the effort that others have invested in the subject. I want to single out Professor Rick Marcus, currently at Hastings, with whom I had the pleasure of serving on the Illinois faculty in the 1980s. Rick's superb writings on Procedure, and his many insights that he's shared over the years in email correspondence and personal conversations, have been invaluable and have helped shape my ideas about the subject.

Here at Colorado, I'm grateful to my colleagues Melissa Hart and Sarah Krakoff for taking the time to read and critique an early version of the beginning chapters of this book. I wish also to thank my former colleague Mike Waggoner for reacting helpfully to my puzzlements about parts of the course over the years, and my colleague Dayna Matthew, who always makes time to talk shop with me. I wish to thank my new colleague Fred Bloom, who has taken time to look at parts of this book and give me his reaction. I am grateful as well to Ed Brunet of Lewis and Clark for reading and critiquing parts of this book, and to Jim Duane at Regent for giving me extended comments about many chapters.

I wish to thank my research assistant Morgan Figuers, class of 2013, for her invaluable assistance in helping compile the statutes and Rules that go with this book, and my research assistants Laura Sturgess and Christopher Estoll, class of 2005, for their wonderful work done several years ago on this book.

Two groups of students at Colorado have used this book as they studied Procedure in my section. They are members of the CU Law classes of 2014 and 2015. I invited their comments, and students rose to the occasion, sending me questions and suggesting corrections where typos had infected the manuscript, or my own infelicities of expression, and this book is better for their efforts as well. I must especially mention Matt Montazzoli and Stacey Wong, of the class of 2014, and Kyle Moen, of the class of 2015, who were particularly conscientious and thorough in this task. Also I wish to thank Stephanie So, class of 2013, for putting together a great image of the football field, which I use to illustrate burdens of production and persuasion (it is included, with her permission, in Chapter 11). Finally, I wish to thank as well other members of the class of 2015 who pointed out typos and infelicities, including Mike Bohan, Courtney Cole, John Cook, John Guevara, Margaret Mandeville, and Andy Merchant.

The author wishes to thank as well former Dean David Getches and current Dean Phil Weiser at Colorado, who have supported work on this project over many years by summer research stipends.

My longtime colleague and coauthor of books on Evidence Law, Laird Kirkpatrick of George Washington University Law School, does not teach Civil Procedure. On this project, I sorely miss our collaboration, but I benefitted from his frequent encouragement and flexibility when work on this book overlapped with our work together on the Evidence books.

Many years of writing books have taught me that families too feel the anxieties and preoccupations of authors. I am grateful to my children Gretchen and David, and especially to my wife Martha, for their patience when I was distracted or preoccupied with the present project on weekends and evenings. After all, family is what it's all about, in so many ways.

Finally, members of the editorial staff at Wolters Kluwer, especially Troy Froebe, Eric Holt, Naomi Kornhauser, and Barbara Roth, have been exceptionally helpful and supportive in putting this book together. Before them, Nate Welch did wonderfully quick turnaround work in publishing preliminary versions of this work for use in my Procedure class in Fall 2011 and 2012. I also want to thank my friends of many years on the acquisitions side of Wolters Kluwer, Carol McGeehan and Lynn Churchill, for believing in this project and waiting patiently for me to get it done. I should mention the four unnamed reviewers who took time to examine the entire manuscript and to send in their anonymous comments to Eric Holt, who forwarded them to me. I don't know who you are, but I read and took seriously all of your comments, and the book is better for the efforts that you put in on this project.

Christopher B. Mueller
Henry S. Lindsley Professor of Law
University of Colorado
Boulder, Colorado

March 2013

The following images appear with the kind permission of the copyright holders:

Beaverhead-Deerlodge National Forest in Montana. Reproduced by permission of Chuck Haney.

Betty Boop. Reproduced by permission of the Everett Collection.

Chicago Vocation High School. Reproduced by permission of Laurence Appleton.

Children's swings in City Park in Spearfish, South Dakota. Reproduced by permission of Jana Thompson.

CIBA (now BASF) plant in McIntosh, Alabama. Reproduced by permission of Mike Kittrell / AL.COM / Landov.

Clara Barton Elementary School. Reproduced by permission of Laurence Appleton.

Dora Browning Donner and William Donner. Reproduced by permission of the Greater Monessen Historical Society.

Earl B. Dickerson. Reproduced by permission of the Daily Worker / Daily World Photographs Collection. Tamiment Library, New York University.

Eisenhower with stolen art. Reproduced by permission of the National Archives.

Erasmus L. Mottley. Reproduced by permission of the Roger D. Hunt Collection at the U.S. Army Military Institute.

Erté, Ebony on White. © Sevenarts Ltd. Reproduced by permission.

Football field diagram. Reproduced by permission of Stephanie So.

General Jackson at the Battle of New Orleans. Reproduced by permission of the Library of Congress.

Harry Tompkins before and after train accident. Originally published in the Luzerne Legal Register. Reproduced by permission.

Jeremy Bentham. Reproduced by permission of cutcaster.com.

John Mitchell. Reproduced by permission of the Library of Congress.

Judge Brandeis. Reproduced by permission of the Library of Congress.

Justice Hugo Black. By John Pelham Black, Collection of the Supreme Court of the United States. Reproduced by permission.

Justice Joseph Story. By George Peter Alexander Healy, Collection of the Supreme Court of the United States. Reproduced by permission.

Justice Robert H. Jackson. © Bettmann / CORBIS. Reproduced by permission.

Justice Sonia Sotomayor. Reproduced by permission of Steve Petteway, Collection of the Supreme Court of the United States.

Kress Store in Hattiesburg, Mississippi. Reproduced by permission of Wayne Archer.

Lord Mansfield. Reproduced by permission of The Granger Collection, New York.

Piper Aztec plane. Reproduced by permission of Martin Stephen.

Railyard at Grand Central Station in Memphis, Tennessee. Reproduced by permission of Classic Trains collection.

Robert Nicastro. Reproduced by permission of Jerry McCrea / The Star-Ledger.

Sikorsky Sea Stallion helicopter. © George Hall / CORBIS. Reproduced by permission.

Sylvester Pennoyer. Reproduced by permission of the Library of Congress.

Tropicale ship. Reproduced by permission of AP Photo / Scott Martin.

The following abbreviations are used in this book:

ACN = Advisory Committee Notes
FRAP = Federal Rules of Appellate Procedure
FRCP = Federal Rules of Civil Procedure
FRCrimP = Federal Rules of Criminal Procedure

The Problems in this book, and examples offered in Notes and text, are sometimes drawn from reported cases and sometimes from the author's imagination. Even when I rely on actual cases, however, I have changed facts for pedagogical reasons—to add human interest, to adapt a situation to classroom use, to add issues or to make them more interesting, to combine in one example issues that may have arisen in different cases. Names used in the Problems, and in examples offered in Notes and text, are inventions of the author. None of the Problems or examples should be read as referring to an actual person, and none is intended as a comment about any actual person.

CBM

TWENTY-FIRST CENTURY PROCEDURE

CHAPTER 1

Procedure and the System

INTRODUCTION

Welcome to Civil Procedure. For generations, students in their first year of legal study have taken up this subject. A sense of procedure lies at the heart of the profession: If there is anything lawyers should be able to do, it is to figure out how to treat fairly the various sides of a dispute in arriving at a sensible resolution.

Yet for entering law students, procedure is an alien subject. You come to law school with a better sense for other basic subjects: You know that contracts are agreements that both sides must honor, that a driver may be liable for running over a pedestrian, and that property rights are protected by elaborate rules and practices. But you likely have less sense of procedure: Rules of jurisdiction, pleading and joinder, discovery, issues of federalism, rules relating to pretrial disposition, appeals, and *res judicata*—all are unfamiliar terrain.

The law governing the rights of people who enter contracts, and the law that applies to drivers and pedestrians (tort law) are what we call substantive law. Other substantive areas include antitrust and unfair competition, environmental regulation, securities regulation, employment discrimination, and commercial law. In contrast to substantive law, procedural law governs the manner in which disputes are worked out. The line between substance and procedure is often clear: Whether an automaker is liable because the weakness in a car roof allowed it to collapse in a rollover accident is a matter of substantive law, but whether a complaint sufficiently alleges product defect by averring that "the roof on the car was weaker than roofs on cars made by other manufacturers" is a procedural issue.

The line between substance and procedure is not *always* so clear. Indeed, the distinction can be important in such different contexts that sometimes an issue is viewed as substantive for one purpose and procedural for another. Statutes of limitation provide an example. They look like procedural law because they allow a claimant only so much time to file suit (maybe three years, or four or six). One reason for such statutes is to keep stale claims out of court because they are, all things considered, harder to resolve than newer claims, if only because witnesses are more likely to be available for newer claims, and memories are better. These look like procedural concerns. But in the setting of the *Erie* doctrine, which requires federal courts in diversity cases (plaintiff from one state sues defendant from another) to apply *state* substantive law but *federal* procedural law, statutes of limitation are viewed as *substantive*. This result is sensible because another reason for statutes of limitations is to provide repose: Potential defendants know they cannot be sued for torts committed long ago, which seems a substantive concern.

Broadly speaking, procedural rules are usually *trans-substantive*, meaning they apply in all substantive areas. FRCP 8(c) provides, for example, that a complaint in a civil action must contain "a short and plain statement" showing that plaintiff is entitled to relief, and this standard applies as much in product liability actions as in contract suits.

Although procedure may seem an alien subject, the good news is that it rewards study. You will emerge from the course with a developed sense of practical considerations that surround dispute resolution. Mastering procedure takes you far along the road to becoming a lawyer. And there is no turning back: In the end, you might conclude that the system works and should be kept as it is. Or you may think it needs fixing or restructuring. You will likely not conclude, however, that the issues and concerns you study are unreal or can be ignored, and you will see things that you have not yet imagined.

A | WHAT IS CIVIL PROCEDURE? WHY ARE RULES OF PROCEDURE NECESSARY?

You will have the whole course to develop your own sense of the right answers to these questions, but here are some suggestions to bear in mind as you proceed.

To begin with, in a large sense procedure is about truth and justice. In any civilized society, disputes, clashes, and controversies arise, perhaps no more so than in the United States, where (as Alexis de Tocqueville observed) the issues of the day are peculiarly likely to end up in court. So we must have institutions that resolve disputes in hope of achieving truth and justice. Those institutions are our courts.

Our rules of procedure provide ways for raising and joining issues, bringing the right parties before the court, obtaining information needed to resolve the dispute, and deciding some issues or cases quickly and some only after a full-blown trial. Our rules provide the parties and the court with a set of directions: They provide a good idea of what steps must be taken, who must take them, and how much time each side has, in order to bring to the attention of the court the claims and defenses that make up civil litigation. Our rules address mechanical issues, like the manner of serving papers, preparation of jury instructions, and form of verdicts. Some rules speak with specificity (a party seeking to take a deposition must subpoena the witness, on pain of paying the expenses of the other side if no subpoena is obtained and the witness does not appear), and others speak in generalities (parties should be joined if, in their absence their interests are likely to be impaired, or those of others who are before the court, or complete relief cannot be given without them). Our rules also provide safeguards against mistaken outcomes: They allow judges to take certain cases away from juries, and to press plaintiffs to accept less than a jury has awarded (if they don't, the judge can grant a defense request for a new trial) or to press defendants to pay more than a jury has awarded (if they don't, the judge can grant a plaintiff's request for a new trial). And our rules provide for appellate review as safeguards against errors or misconduct that might have affected outcome.

If procedure is in large measure about truth and justice, it is also about *pragmatism*. Our rules recognize that litigation costs money, and we have provisions that penalize parties who abuse the system or fail to cooperate. We also empower judges to encourage settlement. We usually require each side to bear its own attorneys' fees, but sometimes shift to the loser the responsibility to pay the winner's fees. And our rules recognize that we have only so much time and so many resources to spend in resolving disputes. We know that humans and their institutions (including courts) are fallible, but they must keep working anyway, like Congress and the Chicago Cubs and the Internet. So our rules help ensure that we get to the end of things, that we achieve some sort of resolution, and move on. We think finality is better than perfection, and we can achieve the former even when we cannot achieve the latter.

Finally, and perhaps paradoxically, there are at least two senses in which truth and justice are *not* what procedure is about.

For one thing, when rules are necessary there must be penalties or costs for violating them. That is true in procedure, and violating procedural rules can mean that cases get dismissed, advanced, or limited *simply because* someone did not comply with the rules. Probably you will conclude that not complying *often* means the noncompliant party would lose even if cost were not imposed—the party lacks a good case. And probably you will conclude that failing to comply sometimes produces consequences that are richly deserved. But sometimes these conclusions are less certain. You will discover that prevailing in our system means *not only* having the facts and law on your side but complying with the rules, and sometimes noncompliance means losing even though one has a good case.

Perhaps more important, our system may not always reach the right result. One reason is that reconstructing past events is a perilous business, as human witnesses are imperfect observers, and factfinders are lay people who may simply "get it wrong" even if the witnesses accurately say what happened. You will also discover in the Evidence course that the rules of proof sometimes exclude evidence that an ideal factfinder might want to examine. There are reasons, of course, and you will consider them. For now, keep in mind that sometimes we exclude evidence because we don't trust juries, or don't think the evidence is reliable enough, or for reasons of policy that may or may not have any connection to the lawsuit.

Another reason we may not reach the right outcomes is that doing so does not *always* turn on reaching correct *factual* conclusions: In a case described later, for example, plaintiff fell while installing insulation in a new house, because his ladder toppled when a leg lodged in a hole cut in the floor for an air vent, and the question was whether this condition made a dangerous workplace for which the general contractor was responsible. The outcome turns less on being right about historical facts than on a value judgment on social responsibility. And different people, whether judges or juries, can reach different conclusions. Think about cigarette litigation: However we resolve the question whether we should allow cigarettes to be made and sold, and the question whether manufacturers knew cigarettes are hazardous to health, and whether they manipulated nicotine levels or misled the public, we still acknowledge that smokers realize they are taking health risks and bear some or all of the responsibility for the consequences.

In our system, many such questions are categorized as matters of law: Often rules or statutes (or constitutional provisions or common law) *answer* the question whether employers are responsible for workplace conditions. But many such questions are answered case by case by judges or juries sitting as factfinders: We call these "issues of fact" or "application of law to fact," as in a negligence suit where we expect the factfinder to *decide* for the case at hand (not more generally for all cases) whether conduct is "negligent." Resolving such questions seems less a matter of "finding the truth" than of "expressing ideas about social responsibility."

B   PROCEDURE AS A VALUE IN ITSELF

The very term "civil procedure" suggests a mechanism to entertain and resolve conflicting claims and defenses. In our judicial system, this mechanism entails a hearing in which competing arguments are aired, often aided by witnesses or affidavits whose function is to relate facts, usually with the aid of lawyers. Hence the term "civil procedure" suggests a *hearing* of some sort.

CAREY v. PIPHUS

Supreme Court of the United States
435 U.S. 247 (1978)

Mr. Justice POWELL delivered the opinion of the Court.

[In 1974, Reginald Brown (principal of Chicago Vocational High School) saw freshman Jarius Piphus and another student standing outside on school grounds passing back and forth "an irregularly shaped cigarette." Approaching the boys, Brown smelled what he thought was marihuana. On seeing Brown, one of them threw the cigarette into a hedge. Brown took them to the disciplinary office and told the assistant principal to impose the "usual" 20-day suspension for violating the rule against drug use. Both students protested their innocence, but to no avail.

Suspension notices were sent out, and meetings were arranged in which Piphus' mother participated, along with people from a legal aid clinic. After an "unfruitful exchange of views," Piphus and his mother (as guardian ad litem) filed suit against school officials, including Reginald Brown, the assistant principal, members of the school board, John Carey (President of the Chicago Board of Education), and the superintendent of schools. The complaint sought declaratory and injunctive relief and actual and punitive damages in the amount of $3,000. The court entered a temporary restraining order reinstating Piphus after he had been suspended for eight days.

Sixth grader Silas Brisco came to Clara Barton Elementary School in Chicago in September 1973 wearing "one small earring." The Clara Barton principal, Rudolph Jezik, had instituted a rule barring male students from wearing earrings in the belief that this practice denoted membership in street gangs and increased risks that gang members would bully or terrorize students. Reminded of the rule, Brisco refused to remove the earring, stating that it was a symbol of black pride, not gang membership.

The assistant principal at Clara Barton talked with Brisco's mother, advising her that Silas would be suspended for 20 days if he did not remove the earring. She supported her son, and he was suspended. He and his mother (as guardian ad litem) filed suit seeking declaratory and injunctive relief, and actual and punitive damages in the amount of $5,000. By order of the court, Brisco was reinstated during the pendency of the proceedings after 17 days of suspension.

The suits brought by Piphus and Brisco were both filed in federal court, and both rested on 42 USC §1983, which provides that any person acting "under color of" state law to deprive "any citizen of the United States or other person . . . to the deprivation of any rights . . . secured by the Constitution" shall be liable "in an action at law" or "suit in equity." The two suits were consolidated for trial and submitted on stipulated records. The court held that both Piphus and Brisco had been denied procedural due process. It concluded that the school officials were *not* entitled to qualified immunity from damages because they should have known that such lengthy suspensions without a hearing violate due process. Nevertheless, the court did not award damages because plaintiffs adduced "no evidence" supporting such awards. The court awarded declaratory relief and deleted the suspensions from the students' records, but did not enter orders implementing this relief, and simply dismissed.

The Seventh Circuit reversed: The court should have awarded declaratory and injunctive relief, and should have considered evidence on the economic value of days of missed school submitted later. The Seventh Circuit also addressed damage relief generally.

Defendants petitioned, and the Supreme Court granted review. Defendants argued that recovery under §1983 should "parallel" recovery for common law torts: Plaintiffs should have to prove that their rights were violated and that they were injured, and they are entitled "at most to nominal damages" without such proof. Plaintiffs claim they are entitled to "substantial damages" regardless of injury because "constitutional rights are valuable in and of themselves," and violations must be deterred. They also argue that "every violation of procedural due process" should be "presumed to cause" injury, relieving them from having to prove actual injury.]

II

A

Insofar as petitioners contend that the basic purpose of a §1983 damages award should be to compensate persons for injuries caused by the deprivation of constitutional rights, they have the better of the argument. Rights, constitutional and otherwise, do not exist in a vacuum. Their purpose is to protect persons from injuries to particular interests, and their contours are shaped by the interests they protect.

Our legal system's concept of damages reflects this view of legal rights. "The cardinal principle of damages in Anglo-American law is that of compensation for the injury caused to plaintiff by defendant's breach of duty." 2 F. Harper & F. James, Law of Torts §25.1, p. 1299 (1956). . . . The Court implicitly has recognized the applicability of this principle to actions under §1983 by stating that damages are available under that section for actions "found . . . to have been violative of . . . constitutional rights and to have caused compensable injury. . . ." Wood v. Strickland, 420 U.S., at 319. . . . The lower federal courts appear generally to agree that damages awards under §1983 should be determined by the compensation principle.

The Members of the Congress that enacted §1983 did not address directly the question of damages, but the principle that damages are designed to compensate persons for injuries caused by the deprivation of rights hardly could have been foreign to the many lawyers in Congress in 1871. Two other sections of the Civil Rights Act of 1871 appear to incorporate this principle, and no reason suggests itself for reading §1983 differently. To the extent that Congress intended that awards under §1983 should deter the deprivation of constitutional rights, there is no evidence that it meant to establish a deterrent more formidable than that inherent in the award of compensatory damages.[11]

---

[11] This is not to say that exemplary or punitive damages might not be awarded in a proper case under §1983 with the specific purpose of deterring or punishing violations of constitutional rights. . . . [T]here is no basis for such an award in this case. The District Court specifically found that petitioners did not act with malicious intention to deprive respondents of their rights or to do them other injury, and the Court of Appeals approved only the award of "non-punitive" damages. . . . We also note that the potential liability of §1983 defendants for attorney's fees [under 42 USC §1988] provides additional—and by no means inconsequential—assurance that agents of the State will not deliberately ignore due process rights. [§1988 provides that the "prevailing party" may recover its attorneys' fees.—ED.] See also 18 USC §242, the criminal counterpart of §1983.

B

It is less difficult to conclude that damages awards under §1983 should be governed by the principle of compensation than it is to apply this principle to concrete cases. But over the centuries the common law of torts has developed a set of rules to implement the principle that a person should be compensated fairly for injuries caused by the violation of his legal rights. These rules, defining the elements of damages and the prerequisites for their recovery, provide the appropriate starting point for the inquiry under §1983 as well.

It is not clear, however, that common-law tort rules of damages will provide a complete solution to the damages issue in every §1983 case. In some cases, the interests protected by a particular branch of the common law of torts may parallel closely the interests protected by a particular constitutional right. In such cases, it may be appropriate to apply the tort rules of damages directly to the §1983 action. In other cases, the interests protected by a particular constitutional right may not also be protected by an analogous branch of the common law torts. In those cases, the task will be the more difficult one of adapting common-law rules of damages to provide fair compensation for injuries caused by the deprivation of a constitutional right.

Although this task of adaptation will be one of some delicacy—as this case demonstrates—it must be undertaken. The purpose of §1983 would be defeated if injuries caused by the deprivation of constitutional rights went uncompensated simply because the common law does not recognize an analogous cause of action. In order to further the purpose of §1983, the rules governing compensation for injuries caused by the deprivation of constitutional rights should be tailored to the interests protected by the particular right in question—just as the common-law rules of damages themselves were defined by the interests protected in the various branches of tort law. We agree with Mr. Justice Harlan that "the experience of judges in dealing with private [tort] claims supports the conclusion that courts of law are capable of making the types of judgment concerning causation and magnitude of injury necessary to accord meaningful compensation for invasion of [constitutional] rights." Bivens v. Six Unknown Fed. Narcotics Agents, [403 U.S. 388], at 409 (Harlan, J., concurring in judgment). With these principles in mind, we now turn to the problem of compensation in the case at hand.

C

The Due Process Clause of the Fourteenth Amendment provides [that no state shall "deprive any person of life, liberty, or property, without due process of law."]

This Clause "raises no impenetrable barrier to the taking of a person's possessions," or liberty, or life. Procedural due process rules are meant to protect persons not from the deprivation, but from the mistaken or unjustified deprivation of life, liberty, or property. Thus, in deciding what process constitutionally is due in various contexts, the Court repeatedly has emphasized that "procedural due process rules are shaped by the risk of error inherent in the truth-finding process. . . ." Mathews v. Eldridge, 424 U.S. 319, 344 (1976). Such rules "minimize substantively unfair or mistaken deprivations of" life, liberty, or property by enabling persons to contest the basis upon which a State proposes to deprive them of protected interests. Fuentes v. Shevin, 407 U.S. 67, 81 (1972).

In this case, the Court of Appeals held that if petitioners can prove on remand that "[respondents] would have been suspended even if a proper hearing had been held," then respondents will not be entitled to recover damages to compensate them for injuries caused by the suspensions. The court thought that in such a case, the failure to accord procedural due process could not properly be viewed as the cause of the suspensions. The court suggested that in such circumstances, an award of damages for injuries caused by the suspensions would constitute a windfall, rather than compensation, to respondents. We do not understand the parties to disagree with this conclusion. Nor do we.

The parties do disagree as to the further holding of the Court of Appeals that respondents are entitled to recover substantial—although unspecified—damages to compensate them for "the injury which is 'inherent in the nature of the wrong,'" even if their suspensions were justified and even if they fail to prove that the denial of procedural due process actually caused them some real, if intangible, injury. Respondents, elaborating on this theme, submit that the holding is correct because injury fairly may be "presumed" to flow from every denial of procedural due process. Their argument is that in addition to protecting against unjustified deprivations, the Due Process Clause also guarantees the "feeling of just treatment" by the government. Anti-Fascist Committee v. McGrath, 341 U.S. 123, 162 (1951) (Frankfurter, J., concurring). They contend that the deprivation of protected interests without procedural due process, even where the premise for the deprivation is not erroneous, inevitably arouses strong feelings of mental and emotional distress in the individual who is denied this "feeling of just treatment." They analogize their case to that of defamation per se, in which "the plaintiff is relieved from the necessity of producing any proof whatsoever that he has been injured" in order to recover substantial compensatory damages.[16]

---

[16] Respondents also contend that injury should be presumed because, even if they were guilty of the conduct charged, they were deprived of the chance to present facts or arguments in mitigation to the initial decisionmaker. . . . But . . . the Court of Appeals held that respondents cannot recover damages for injuries caused by their suspensions if the District Court determines that "[respondents] would have been suspended even if a proper hearing had been held." This holding, which respondents do not challenge, necessarily assumes that the District Court can determine what the outcome would have been if respondents had received their hearing. We presume that this determination will include consideration of the likelihood that any mitigating circumstances to which respondents can point would have swayed the initial decisionmakers.

Petitioners do not deny that a purpose of procedural due process is to convey to the individual a feeling that the government has dealt with him fairly, as well as to minimize the risk of mistaken deprivations of protected interests. They go so far as to concede that, in a proper case, persons in respondents' position might well recover damages for mental and emotional distress caused by the denial of procedural due process. Petitioners' argument is the more limited one that such injury cannot be presumed to occur, and that plaintiffs at least should be put to their proof on the issue, as plaintiffs are in most tort actions.

We agree with petitioners in this respect. As we have observed in another context, the doctrine of presumed damages in the common law of defamation per se "is an oddity of tort law, for it allows recovery of purportedly compensatory damages without evidence of actual loss." Gertz v. Robert Welch, Inc., 418 U.S. 323, 349 (1974). The doctrine has been defended on the grounds that those forms of defamation that are actionable per se are virtually certain to cause serious injury to reputation, and that this kind of injury is extremely difficult to prove. Moreover, statements that are defamatory per se by their very nature are likely to cause mental and emotional distress, as well as injury to reputation, so there arguably is little reason to require proof of this kind of injury either.[18] But these considerations do not support respondents' contention that damages should be presumed to flow from every deprivation of procedural due process.

First, it is not reasonable to assume that every departure from procedural due process, no matter what the circumstances or how minor, inherently is as likely to cause distress as the publication of defamation per se is to cause injury to reputation and distress. Where the deprivation of a protected interest is substantively justified but procedures are deficient in some respect, there may well be those who suffer no distress over the procedural irregularities. Indeed, in contrast to the immediately distressing effect of defamation per se, a person may not even know that procedures were deficient until he enlists the aid of counsel to challenge a perceived substantive deprivation.

Moreover, where a deprivation is justified but procedures are deficient, whatever distress a person feels may be attributable to the justified deprivation rather than to deficiencies in procedure. But as the Court of Appeals held, the injury caused by a justified deprivation, including distress, is not properly compensable under §1983.[19] This ambiguity in causation, which is absent in

---

[18] The essence of libel per se is the publication in writing of false statements that tend to injure a person's reputation. The essence of slander per se is the publication by spoken words of false statements imputing to a person a criminal offense; a loathsome disease; matter affecting adversely a person's fitness for trade, business, or profession; or serious sexual misconduct.

[19] In this case, for example, respondents denied the allegations against them. They may well have been distressed that their denials were not believed. They might have been equally distressed if they had been disbelieved only after a full-dress hearing, but in that instance they would have no cause of action against petitioners.

the case of defamation per se, provides additional need for requiring the plaintiff to convince the trier of fact that he actually suffered distress because of the denial of procedural due process itself.

Finally, we foresee no particular difficulty in producing evidence that mental and emotional distress actually was caused by the denial of procedural due process itself. Distress is a personal injury familiar to the law, customarily proved by showing the nature and circumstances of the wrong and its effect on the plaintiff.[20] In sum, then, although mental and emotional distress caused by the denial of procedural due process itself is compensable under §1983, we hold that neither the likelihood of such injury nor the difficulty of proving it is so great as to justify awarding compensatory damages without proof that such injury actually was caused.

D

The Court of Appeals believed, and respondents urge, that cases dealing with awards of damages for racial discrimination, the denial of voting rights and the denial of Fourth Amendment rights, support a presumption of damages where procedural due process is denied. Many of the cases relied upon do not help respondents because they held or implied that some actual, if intangible, injury must be proved before compensatory damages may be recovered. Others simply did not address the issue. More importantly, the elements and prerequisites for recovery of damages appropriate to compensate injuries caused by the deprivation of one constitutional right are not necessarily appropriate to compensate injuries caused by the deprivation of another. As we have said, these issues must be considered with reference to the nature of the interests protected by the particular constitutional right in question. For this reason, and without intimating an opinion as to their merits, we do not deem the cases relied upon to be controlling.

III

Even if respondents' suspensions were justified, and even if they did not suffer any other actual injury, the fact remains that they were deprived of their right to procedural due process. "It is enough to invoke the procedural safeguards of the Fourteenth Amendment that a significant property interest is at stake, whatever the ultimate outcome of a hearing. . . ." *Fuentes.*

Common-law courts traditionally have vindicated deprivations of certain "absolute" rights that are not shown to have caused actual injury through the

---

[20] We use the term "distress" to include mental suffering or emotional anguish. Although essentially subjective, genuine injury in this respect may be evidenced by one's conduct and observed by others. Juries must be guided by appropriate instructions, and an award of damages must be supported by competent evidence concerning the injury.

award of a nominal sum of money. By making the deprivation of such rights actionable for nominal damages without proof of actual injury, the law recognizes the importance to organized society that those rights be scrupulously observed; but at the same time, it remains true to the principle that substantial damages should be awarded only to compensate actual injury or, in the case of exemplary or punitive damages, to deter or punish malicious deprivations of rights.

Because the right to procedural due process is "absolute" in the sense that it does not depend upon the merits of a claimant's substantive assertions, and because of the importance to organized society that procedural due process be observed, we believe that the denial of procedural due process should be actionable for nominal damages without proof of actual injury. We therefore hold that if, upon remand, the District Court determines that respondents' suspensions were justified, respondents nevertheless will be entitled to recover nominal damages not to exceed one dollar from petitioners.

The judgment of the Court of Appeals is reversed, and the case is remanded for further proceedings consistent with this opinion.

It is so ordered.

Mr. Justice MARSHALL concurs in the result. Mr. Justice BLACKMUN took no part in the consideration or decision of this case.

■ NOTES ON PROCEDURE AS AN INDEPENDENT VALUE

1. What do high school freshman Jarius Piphus and sixth grader Silas Brisco want the Court to do? If the system had "done right," what would it have done differently? Do you think these youngsters thought they could have been exonerated if given hearings?

2. *Piphus* involved suits against "the schools." But schools are not entities, and it is necessary to sue actual persons or entities (school boards or districts). So plaintiffs sued principals (Reginald Brown and Rudolph Jezik), assistant principals, members of the board, and superintendent John Carey (president of the Chicago Board of Education). The suits were consolidated because they were filed in the same court and raised the same issues. They were brought under 42 USC §1983, which provides civil remedies against any "person" who "under color of" state law deprives plaintiff of rights secured by the Constitution or federal law.

(a) A government entity (like a district or board) is a "person" under §1983. When an entity acts in its official capacity (or its agents do), they act "under color of" state law. Plaintiffs in *Piphus* claimed the board, acting

through officials, was in effect the State of Illinois for purposes of the Four-teenth Amendment, and that in suspending Piphus and Brisco without hear-ings the State violated their right to a public education. The language of §1983 implies that damages are appropriate ("action at law" usually means damage claim) and injunctive relief too ("suit in equity" usually involves injunctive relief).

(b) The Fourteenth Amendment, source of the right claimed by the plaintiffs, provides that no state shall "deprive any person of life, liberty, or property, without due process of law." *Piphus* assumes that a system of public education creates "property" or "liberty" rights. See Goss v. Lopez, 419 U.S. 565 (1975) (public education entails interests in "liberty" and "property").

(c) The Fourteenth Amendment requires "due process of law" if the state seeks to deprive anyone of "life, liberty or property." In its landmark decision in Goldberg v. Kelly, 397 U.S. 254 (1970), the Court concluded that terminating subsistence welfare payments requires a hearing because welfare entails property rights. But deciding that liberty or property is at stake does not answer the question whether a hearing is required: If it did, then patrons of a public library would be entitled to a hearing before they could be fined for overdue books, and a school child would be entitled to a hearing before he could be sent to the principal's office. In fact, hearings are not *always* required, even when interests in life, liberty, or property are at stake: *Goss* held, for example, only that a student is entitled to a hearing if he is suspended for more than ten days. And in *Mathews v. Eldridge,* 424 U.S. 319 (1976), the Court held that disability payments could be terminated without a hearing. See generally John E. Nowak & Ronald D. Rotunda, Constitutional Law §13.9(c) (5th ed. 1995).

3. Piphus was suspended for 20 days for possessing and maybe using marijuana. Within 8 days he won a court order entitling him to return. Brisco got a 20-day suspension for wearing an earring in violation of a rule applying to male students, but within 17 days he was back in school. Piphus and Brisco acted quickly, and the court responded quickly. Under FRCP 65(b), "temporary restraining orders" (TROs) may be awarded without notice to the other side if it is "clearly" shown that "immediate and irreparable injury" will otherwise occur. Under that rule, such orders are only effective for 14 days (the period may be extended), and the other side is entitled to appear and contest the order "at the earliest possible time." When both sides appear, the question whether to issue a continuing "preliminary injunction" pending final resolu-tion of the case usually turns on showing that plaintiff is likely to prevail (also on need to maintain the status quo and, in a modern formulation, on showing that plaintiff will be hurt more if the injunction is not granted than defendant if the injunction is granted). In a footnote edited from the opinion, *Goss* (note 2(b), supra) was read as requiring a hearing for any suspension exceed-ing ten days. Does it follow that the "likely to prevail" standard is satisfied? See Leary v. Daeschner, 228 F.3d 729 (6th Cir. 2000) (in suit by teachers claim-ing they had been wrongfully transferred in retaliation for exercising First

Chicago Vocational High School (As It Was) and Clara Barton Elementary School (Modern Picture)

Chicago Vocational High School (left, below), where freshman Jarius Piphus and a fellow student were caught allegedly passing "an irregularly shaped cigarette," is located on the South Side. It opened its doors in 1940 as a trade school, but in World War II it was turned over to the Navy, and it emphasized aviation mechanics. After the war, the school returned to the City's control, and it offered classes 24 hours a day to serve the needs of veterans. Included among the alumni of CVHS was Dick Butkus (1961), who became a linebacker for the Chicago Bears, and ultimately a Pro Football Hall of Famer. Clara Barton Elementary School (right, below), the other institution involved in the *Piphus* litigation, was named for the famous educator and humanist who ministered to wounded soldiers for the Union Army during the Civil War, and served as president of the American Red Cross. Her humanitarian efforts

extended to war-ravaged Europe too, where she helped provide relief to soldiers and displaced civilians in the 1870s. She also met Susan B. Anthony, and worked in the women's suffrage movement.

Amendment freedoms, denying preliminary injunction because plaintiffs had not shown that they were likely to prevail). Is it clear that *if* these young men were entitled to a hearing before being suspended, *then* they should be immediately reinstated? It's possible that they did not violate the rules, but doesn't it seem more likely that both are "guilty as charged"? What happens to the authority of a principal if a court orders reinstatement of suspended students who are guilty of the offenses? Would plaintiffs suffer more without an injunction than the school system suffers when the boys are reinstated?

4. When *Piphus* reaches the Supreme Court, Brisco and Piphus are reinstated and records of their suspensions have been expunged, but the trial court failed to enter an order confirming plaintiffs' entitlement to this relief.

Much of the argument entertained on appeal in *Piphus* is about damages. Consider these points:

(a) Plaintiffs argue that they are entitled to damages for wrongful denial of a hearing even if they suffered no injury. What is the basis of this argument? How does it fare?

(b) Plaintiffs argue that damages from wrongful denial of an injunction should be *presumed*. Why does the Court reject this argument?

(c) On remand, Piphus and Brisco can recover damages if they show they are innocent of the underlying infractions (hence would have prevailed if hearings had been held). How much can they recover? The per-student per-day cost of public education for missed days? The cost of alternative schooling? Even if they would not have sought or obtained such schooling, or could not get it because private schools would not admit them or would only accept students for longer periods?

(d) On remand, can Piphus and Brisco recover damages even if they committed the underlying infractions and would have been suspended after hearings? What would damages be? How could they prove damages?

(e) In its last sentence, the Court says Piphus and Brisco are entitled to "nominal damages not to exceed one dollar." Why? Consider the fee-shifting statute cited in footnote 11 of the opinion.

5. On remand, who should bear the burden of persuasion on the question whether Piphus and Brisco would have been suspended after hearings? Had hearings been held, *the school* would have to prove the boys broke the rules. Does this fact bear on the question of who has to prove this point in a trial of the constitutional claims?

6. What about punitive damages? Even if Piphus and Brisco cannot show actual damages, should they be entitled to punitive damages? On facts such as those presented here, do you think punitive damages are appropriate?

7. Piphus and Brisco sued not only the board but school officers and others. It is easy enough to see why the lawyers named the persons who suspended the youngsters. Under the statute, would *they* be liable personally to Piphus and Brisco in damages? Note that they claimed the benefit of qualified immunity, which protects officials against damage claims if they act wrongfully but in good faith, but the Court thought the principals should have known that "lengthy suspensions" without hearings were wrongful, hence that they were not entitled to qualified immunity. If they *were*, would there be any reason to name them as defendants? Consider the school board: For all intents and purposes, the Board *is* the school district, and *it* (the district) might be liable for damages, if any are awarded. Why name the *members*?

8. What kind of hearing should Piphus and Brisco have had? The decision in *Goss* requiring a hearing in cases involving suspensions lasting longer than ten days had not come down when Piphus and Brisco were suspended. *Goss* involved a class action challenging school procedures in Ohio, which allowed suspensions without a hearing. The lead plaintiffs were (a) six high school students suspended for ten days for "disruptive or disobedient conduct" (one physically attacked a police officer who was removing another from an auditorium for demonstrating while class was in session there), (b) two junior high students suspended for ten days "in connection with a disturbance in the lunchroom which involved some physical damage to school property" on an occasion when "at least 75" others were suspended, and (c) one student suspended for ten days when her school learned she had been arrested while demonstrating at another school. In *Goss,* the Supreme Court described the hearing required for students facing suspension for more than ten days in this vein:

> There need be no delay between the time "notice" is given and the time of the hearing. In the great majority of cases the disciplinarian may informally discuss the alleged misconduct with the student minutes after it has occurred. We hold only that, in being given an opportunity to explain his version of the facts at this discussion, the student first be told what he is accused of doing and what the basis of the accusation is. . . . Since the hearing may occur almost immediately following the misconduct, it follows that as a general rule notice and hearing should precede removal of the student from school. We agree with the District Court, however, that there are recurring situations in which prior notice and hearing cannot be insisted upon. Students whose presence poses a continuing danger to persons or property or an ongoing threat of disrupting the academic process may be immediately removed from school. In such cases, the necessary notice and rudimentary hearing should follow as soon as practicable, as the District Court indicated.

Goss v. Lopez, 419 U.S. 565, 581 (1975). Where a principal finds a boy like Piphus (probably about 14 years old) in possession of marijuana and a boy like Brisco (probably about 11 years old) wearing an earring, do you think an "immediate hearing" where the principal gives each a chance to tell his side is enough? Should the principal have to summon an outsider (maybe a principal at another school, or a teacher) to act as judge? A parent to speak for the student? Why do you suppose the Court did *not* require such steps?

C CUSTOMS AND INSTITUTIONS—A FIRST LOOK

1. Three Hallmarks and a New Development

American courts operate in an environment influenced by three strong traditions and one distinctly modern development. Two of these traditions—civil juries and the federal structure of governing institutions—are formally enshrined in the Constitution. Arguably the other tradition, captured in the phrase "adversary system," is *presupposed* by the Constitution. The modern development is the growing involvement of judges in *managing* cases, as opposed to merely *presiding* over them.

Consider first our adversary tradition. At its core is the practice of putting on the parties, acting through lawyers, the lion's share of responsibility for bringing, preparing, and finally trying lawsuits. This tradition, not *formally* endorsed by the Constitution, reflects the ideal of personal rights and freedom that inspired the Bill of Rights, and of self-reliance and liberty expressed in the Constitution and Declaration of Independence. The thought is that self-interested parties can do the best job of developing and presenting the case for each side, and that truth is most likely to emerge if the parties advance their interests in this way.

Jury trial entitlement is enshrined in the Seventh Amendment for civil damage suits in federal court, and similar rights are secured in state courts by state constitutions or statutes. This entitlement reflects a vision of citizens playing critical roles. Functionally, the notion is that many minds are more likely to reach sound conclusions on matters of social responsibility than any one mind. But our faith in juries is limited, and important rules let judges curb what juries do, and discard verdicts that seem flawed.

In its American form, federalism involves a national government and 50 state governments, with overlapping lawmaking power and restrictions on what each may do. In this somewhat untidy system, we have laws that are sometimes overlapping and complementary, sometimes complex or uncertain in their relationship, and sometimes conflicting. Much the same observation applies to state and federal courts: Sometimes they exercise jurisdiction that is overlapping and complementary, and sometimes their responsibilities bring them into conflict or into areas of uncertainty.

The modern development is that the role of judges in managing litigation expanded in the late twentieth and early twenty-first century, particularly in the federal system (to a lesser degree in state courts). Part of the impetus came from the demand for efficiency—for "clearing cases" to cut delays and make the work of judges more efficient. Part of it came from complexity in litigation, as seen in class actions and suits seeking institutional reform. In these settings and others, judges have been asked to play ever larger roles in fashioning strategies and remedies. Also in the mix is a suspicion that the adversary system is dysfunctionally "over-adversarial," that lawyers are letting us down, and that judicial intervention can improve justice.

2. Lawsuits in Century 21: Complexity in a Regulated Society

If your parents or other forebears went to law school, they lived in a world in which suits usually involved a car accident, product liability claim, family issues (divorce, property, custody) or breach of a private or commercial contract. Except in family cases, the typical remedy was damages. Often suits involved only a few parties, maybe one plaintiff and one defendant, or a couple of each. The typical suit invoked common law principles rather than statutes, and state rather than federal law.

Those suits are still typical, and perhaps the *prototypical* example is *still* litigation arising from accidents or product liability claims. These examples involve claims in tort law—usually "negligence," "strict liability," or "breach of warranty." In the closing half of the twentieth century, however, litigation broadened. Today we see an extraordinary *range* of issues and claims.

To a degree, modern suits reflect regional ethos and culture. In the state that is home to Sea World, for example, litigation arises out of accidents that probably don't happen anywhere else. See, e.g., Jefferson Insurance Company of New York v. Sea World of Florida, 586 So. 2d 95 (Fla. 1991) (wrongful death suit arising out of performer in "Ski Pirates" Act). In states like Montana and South Dakota, collisions between livestock and cars are serious matters, and "cow out" suits may raise the question whether a driver must compensate a rancher, or vice versa. The answer can turn on whether the accident took place on "open range," where the driver is at fault almost by definition, or where fencing is required. See, e.g., Inendi v. Workman, 899 P.2d 1085 (Mont. 1995); Horsley v. Essman, 763 N.E.2d 245 (Ohio App. 2001).

Much of the modern variety of litigation reflects changes in the world—political, social, economic, technological. In the twenty-first century, many seemingly simple lawsuits are complicated by modern legislation, state and federal, and the modern age is in some respects the Age of Statutes. Common law principles (the sort you study in tort and contract classes) are still important, but increasingly lawsuits are affected by statutes. Consider the following, which are first briefly described and then considered in more detail:[1]

(1) Ronaldo underwent heart bypass surgery in Chicago, during which he received a transfusion of blood supplied by United Blood Services (UBS), a blood bank that depends on volunteers and does not pay its donors. He contracted AIDS from this transfusion and died, and his widow Marietta sues UBS in state court in Illinois, alleging that it had not conducted proper tests.

(2) Monique cultivates walnut orchards, and she applied Guthion and Morestan to her trees to kill aphids and mites, but the pesticides damaged her trees and crops to the tune of $150,000. In state court in California,

---

[1] The examples come, respectively, from Advincula v. United Blood Services, 678 N.E.2d 1009 (Ill. 1997) (reversing judgment for $2.14 million; should have applied "professional negligence" standard); Etcheverry v. Tri-Ag Service, 993 P.2d 366 (Cal. 2000) (claims based on failure to warn are pre-empted by Federal Insecticide, Fungicide, and Rodenticide Act, coupled with EPA approval of products and labels); Perez v. Wyeth Laboratories, 734 A.2d 1245 (N.J. 1999) ("learned intermediary" doctrine plays diminished role where drug maker markets directly to consumers); Toll Brothers, Inc. v Considine, 706 A.2d 493 (Del. 1998) (reversing judgment for plaintiff; violation of OSHA regulations is not negligence per se, but counts in appraising negligence). And see generally *Developments in the Law—The Paths of Civil Litigation*, 113 Harv. L. Rev. 1752 (2000).

she sues Bayer, which made the pesticides, and Tri-Ag, which marketed them.

(3) Cheryl underwent surgical insertion of contraceptive capsules made by Wyeth Laboratories, marketed as Norplant and advertised in magazines like *Glamour*, *Mademoiselle*, and *Cosmopolitan*, and she suffered adverse effects and sues Wyeth in state court in New Jersey.

(4) Scott works for Cary, which entered into a subcontract with Toll Brothers, as general contractor in a housing development, under which Cary was to install insulation. While on the job, Scott suffered compound fractures of both wrists when one leg of the ladder he had mounted fell into an open ventilation return. Scott sues Toll Brothers in state court in Delaware, alleging an unsafe workplace under standards set by the federal Occupational Safety and Health Administration.

These modern suits bring special problems. In the first and third examples, the issues are new and the law needs time to catch up (lawyers and courts make mistakes, learn, and change). All four look like tort claims that would be decided under common law principles, but three (all but the third) were affected by legislation—statutes. That statutes should be so important reflects the point that we live in a mature and heavily regulated society, in which modern technology both *invites* new legal rules and *enables* legislative and regulatory bodies to promulgate them.

In Marietta's suit for the death of Ronaldo, the judge gave the case to the jury with instructions to determine whether defendant exercised "the care that would be used by reasonably careful blood banks." The reviewing court thought the Blood Shield Act of Illinois required blood banks to conform to a "professional standard of care" that is "higher" than the one that applies to lay persons and requires expert testimony on "recognized standards of competency" in the profession. Since plaintiff's lawyer did not introduce such testimony, the reviewing court remanded for a new trial. It wasn't that the trial court or lawyers ignored the law: Everybody knew about the statute, and the trial and appellate courts thought it imposed a standard of ordinary care of the sort given to the jury in the instructions. But the Illinois Supreme Court looked at the same statute and decided otherwise. Marietta could try her claim again, but only if she could find an expert to describe the standard that applies to blood banks. She could only hope to recover if the expert could point out some shortcoming or failing in defendant's operation which could count as negligence.

In her suit against the maker and manufacturer of pesticides, Monique encountered a different problem: Federal environmental legislation provides that pesticides must pass inspection by the Environmental Protection Agency before being marketed, and the EPA also examines labels, warnings, and instructions. The Guthion and Morestan that Monique applied to her trees had gone through this process, and the California Supreme Court held that federal law pre-empts claims asserted under state law resting on alleged inadequacy of warnings or instructions. Monique not only lost, but could not bring any claim that depended on proving that warnings or instructions were inadequate (the case went back to the Court of Appeals to decide whether claims in fraud or negligent manufacture survived).

Cheryl fared better: The drug maker invoked the "learned intermediary" doctrine, which holds that the role of doctors in prescribing certain medications has the effect of blocking claims that might otherwise be advanced against the manufacturer because doctors are expected to explain and interpret instructions and warnings provided by drug makers. Stressing that defendant advertised the product in popular magazines, the New Jersey Supreme Court concluded that the learned intermediary doctrine plays a diminished role, and that drug makers who advertise this way may be liable if they fail to alert consumers to the dangers.

Like Ronaldo, Scott learned to his sorrow that the court misapplied a statute. His lawyer had argued that the employer's violation of an OSHA safety rule amounted to negligence *per se,* and the court instructed the jury accordingly. The reviewing court concluded that the OSHA standards were "relevant," but that violating such standards was *not* negligence per se. Hence Scott's judgment based on a jury verdict was set aside, leaving him free to try the case again if he could show that the employer's conduct was negligent for reasons *apart from* violating the OSHA rule.

D CUSTOMS AND INSTITUTIONS—OUR ADVERSARY SYSTEM

1. Lawyers Take the Laboring Oar

A good way to get a sense of the importance of lawyers is to consider what they do in order to bring or defend a suit. To a larger extent than you may imagine, the course of litigation turns on the effort of lawyers. Suppose you represent Scott in the claim against Toll Brothers, which had hired Scott's employer Cary to insulate new houses.

Before you file suit on Scott's behalf, you grapple with the facts. You talk to Scott and learn his story, and you listen with care to separate elements that seem exaggerated or self-justifying or falsely accusatory from what seems objective or verifiable. You note the names of witnesses with whom you can check on Scott's story. You help him realize that you must be able to substantiate factual contentions.

If you take Scott's case, filing suit is *not* the first thing. Instead, you try to settle. Scott will likely have gone in this direction too, since an aggrieved person usually seeks a lawyer only after failing personally to work things out. Scott is likely to have sought recovery from Cary (his employer) and perhaps from Toll Brothers (general contractor), although he may not know enough about the legal system to be sure that either of them is liable for his injuries, and one reason he needs you is to figure out whether he has a claim against anyone. But settlement efforts do not end when a lawyer gets involved, and most civil cases that are actually filed settle (close to 90 percent). So you will make your own effort: A letter from you is understood as a signal that Scott is not satisfied or willing to "just go away," and the next possible step may be a lawsuit. It is common to bring home the sense of urgency by stating in such letters that if no response is had within a few weeks Scott "will seek legal recourse." You ask for a sum certain (say $200,000) and you might supply supporting documents or arguments. (In the trade, such letters are called "demands.")

Whether you take the case, and whether you sue, may depend in part on self-interest. Lawyers too must "put food on the table." One question on the lawyer's mind is whether litigating a case will be profitable. In personal injury damage suits, common practice involves a contingent fee. The client agrees to pay the lawyer a percentage—often 25 to 40 percent of any award ultimately recovered, sometimes more. This arrangement enables "ordinary human" clients, who could not pay out of their own pockets a lawyer's hourly fee, to go forward with a suit. The arrangement also enables the lawyer to take cases in which the outcome is uncertain. The percentage is high enough so that the lawyer needs only to prevail once out of four times (or even one in ten times) to come out ahead. Scott probably can't pay your fees, so you will take it for a contingent fee (or decline it).

Suppose settlement efforts break down. You have contacted Cary and Toll Brothers and sent demand letters, and they have been ignored or Cary and Toll Brothers are "stonewalling." You talk it over with Scott and agree that it is time to sue. There are no jurisdictional problems, and you think the only defendant worth suing is Toll Brothers. Here are the main steps:

Initial Pleadings. Lawyers prepare, file, and serve the "pleadings" that begin a case (complaint and answer, sometimes additional pleadings). So on behalf of Scott you prepare, file in court, and serve on Toll Brothers, a complaint setting forth allegations charging it with negligence in creating a dangerous workplace, alleging that this condition caused Scott to fall and break his wrists, and that he incurred medical expenses and endured pain and suffering, for which he seeks recovery. See FRCP 8 (complaint to be a "short and plain" statement that, among other things, shows that the plaintiff "is entitled to relief"). As Scott's lawyer, you must sign the complaint. Your signature amounts to your certification that you can back up your allegations and are not bringing them for an improper purpose. See FRCP 11(b). And see FRCP 4(d) and (e) (providing for service of the complaint by "delivering a copy" to defendant personally, and for "waiver" allowing mailed service in place of personal delivery). The lawyer for the defendant is responsible for filing a response, usually an answer that must admit or deny the charging allegations, see FRCP 8(b).

Pretrial Motions. Lawyers make pretrial motions, and usually these are made by the defense. They might seek dismissal for lack of jurisdiction or failure to state a claim on which a court can grant relief. See FRCP 12(b). As lawyer for Scott, you must be prepared to resist such motions (you have thought already of points raised by the defense, and think you can prevail). In resisting these motions, you submit written arguments or briefs arguing, for example, that the court has jurisdiction or the complaint states a proper claim. Some pretrial motions, such as the motion for summary judgment, can be "dispositive," in that prevailing means the case is over. This motion argues that there is no disagreement on any fact that counts, and that the law requires judgment for plaintiff or defendant. See FRCP 56.

Discovery. Lawyers spend substantial time in discovery. At a minimum, you as lawyer for Scott will gather his medical records and send copies to the other side, and modern rules require you to do that much without even being asked. See FRCP 26(a)(1)(B) & (C). Discovery entails both seeking and supplying documents and information. Each side can ask for documents, and can expect to have to produce documents on request by the other side. See FRCP 34. Each side can notice and take depositions of witnesses (sworn testimony given in a law office with a court reporter and the lawyers for each side), and can expect to attend depositions taken by the other side (in each deposition both sides may question the witness). See FRCP 32. And each side can propound interrogatories and must, of course, answer interrogatories from the other side. See FRCP 33. Discovery entails an obligation to cooperate with other parties in meeting and arranging the exchange of information. See FRCP 26(f). Often the process goes on for months, and consumes not only time to prepare requests and responses, but time to prepare for depositions and analyze the documents and testimony. Lawyers do it all.

Pretrial. In many civil cases, lawyers engage in planning efforts in cooperation with the court, to map out the course of discovery and pretrial motions and plan for trial itself. See FRCP 16 and 26(f). In pretrial proceedings, lawyers explore settlement possibilities (again), enter stipulations relating to facts and the genuineness of documents, and weed out claims and defenses that aren't going anywhere. Although these pretrial proceedings are held under the auspices, even the supervision, of the court, lawyers do the lion's share of the work.

Trial and After. Of course, lawyers try the case, if it is not settled. You as Scott's lawyer call and question witnesses, cross-examine witnesses called by the other side, and present an opening statement and closing argument. Behind the scenes, you have obtained and seen to the service of the subpoenas, and have prepared your questions, statements, and arguments, and you have spoken privately with your witnesses to prepare them. And you, as lawyer for Scott, are responsible for making objections if the other side asks improper questions or offers improper evidence, and making offers of proof if the other side raises successful objections to the evidence you want to introduce. See FRE 103 (requirements to object and to offer proof). You also put together and propose jury instructions. See FRCP 51.

When the trial is over, there may be post-trial motions—especially motions for "judgment as a matter of law" (which must *also* be sought before the jury retires) or for a new trial. See FRCP 50 (judgment as a matter of law) and 59 (new trial). There can also be appeals and further settlement negotiations: The loser at trial can often settle a case, even after judgment, by persuading the winner that settling is better than incurring further expense and risk in what might be a long appeal process.

2. Why an Adversary System? What Are the Drawbacks?

In an oft-quoted statement, the Supreme Court said that "accurate and just results are most likely to be obtained through the equal contest of opposed interests," and this claim has the stature of an article of faith, or perhaps bedrock belief.[2] After all, nobody has more interest in developing and presenting a case than the parties themselves, and the lawyer's motivations can be expected to reflect those of the client. The lawyer who works on retainer or for an hourly fee will try hard to earn the trust and gratitude of her client, and the lawyer working on a contingent fee knows he will be paid only if he wins. At least equally important, the lawyer preparing the case knows more about it than anyone else—including the judge.

We cannot expect outcomes to always be right. If testimony conflicts, the factfinder decides who to believe, and its decision is not scientific or certain. Appeals are possible, but the losing side cannot argue that the court made mistakes in finding facts. If, for example, the claim is that defendant was negligent because he was speeding and the factfinder concludes that he was *not* speeding, plaintiff cannot win a reversal by showing that "the jury was just wrong because the evidence shows that the defendant was speeding." The system allows for appeals only if the trial court made a *legal* mistake or some kind of misconduct occurred. The most common errors relate to rulings admitting or excluding evidence or instructing the jury. The most common misconduct involves improper argument by lawyers or misbehavior by juries. Correcting for such errors and misconduct stops short of assuring perfection.

---

[2] See Lassiter v. Department of Social Services, 452 U.S. 18, 27 (1981) (hence due process may require states to supply lawyers to parties, but not in parental termination proceedings based on criminal conviction of mother); Poe v. Ullman, 367 U.S. 497, 502 (1961) ("within the framework of our adversary system, the adjudicatory process is most securely founded when it is exercised under the impact of a lively conflict between antagonistic demands, actively pressed, which make resolution of the controverted issue a practical necessity").

Many people, including lawyers and judges, defend the adversary system, but it has detractors. Consider these arguments:

(1) The system is too expensive. Few cases are actually tried, partly because most cases settle and the system would break down if most cases *did* go to trial. Mostly, however, the cost of lawyers makes it prohibitive to try small cases: If prospective recovery is small, the contingent fee won't make it worthwhile, and claimant would not be willing to pay the rate that lawyers charge.

(2) The system distorts the truth. Judges and lawyers think perjury occurs, and that lawyer "prepping" distorts what witnesses say on the stand. The terms "sandpapering" and "woodshedding" (commonly applied to this process) conjure up images of lawyers pushing and influencing witnesses so they change their stories, perhaps without even knowing it.[3]

(3) The system may not yield truth. We lack proof that this method works better than, for instance, the continental model where judges take an active role. And what lawyers do at trial in an adversary system is to create *images* or *pictures* rather than uncover truth. The finished product may have more rhetorical than factual content, and prevailing may have more to do with resources and cleverness than with facts.[4]

Now consider two related developments that have come to the fore:

Tactical Excesses. The first development is a growing sense that the adversary system produces tactical excesses by lawyers that cannot be tolerated. To curb these, amendments to the Rules of Procedure were adopted in two important areas:

First, pleading rules were tightened in 1993. FRCP 11 now provides that a lawyer must sign every "pleading, written motion, and other paper," and that "presenting" such material in court constitutes a representation by the lawyer that (1) it is not "being presented for any improper purpose" (such as harassment or delay); (2) claims, defenses, and other legal contentions are "warranted by existing law or by a nonfrivolous argument for extending, modifying, or reversing existing law or for establishing new law"; (3) allegations and factual contentions "have evidentiary support" or are likely to have it after "reasonable opportunity for further investigation or discovery";

---

[3] See Geoffrey C. Hazard, Ethics in the Practice of Law, Ch. 9 (1976) (summarizing 1976 conference of lawyers where adversary system was "savaged").

[4] See Carrie Menkel-Meadow, *The Trouble with the Adversary System in a Postmodern, Multicultural World,* 38 Wm. & Mary L. Rev. 5, 13, 17 (1996) (litigators don't seek truth, they seek victory; if "oppositional theory" works when factfinder has "an off/on, guilt/innocence" decision to make, it will not serve when "polycentric factual findings, legal conclusions, and mixed fact/law questions are at issue," such as "comparative negligence, business necessity defenses, excuse and justification in criminal law, and best interest of the child"); Deborah Rhode, *Ethical Perspectives on Legal Practice,* 37 Stan. L. Rev. 589, 587 (1985) (defense of adversary system "presupposes combatants with roughly equal incentives").

and (4) denials of factual contentions "are warranted on the evidence" or "reasonably based on belief or a lack of information." Violating the Rule can lead to sanctions against parties and attorneys.

Second, discovery rules were tightened. Now FRCP 26(f) requires the parties to meet and discuss settlement and consult on discovery. Now FRCP 26(c) requires parties to make a good faith effort to resolve discovery disputes, including those affecting depositions. Now FRCP 26(a) provides that the parties must turn over certain materials (including lists of persons "likely to have discoverable information," copies or descriptions of documents, computations of damages, insurance agreements) without being asked. And now FRCP 26(b)(2)(B) requires parties to exchange expert reports and designate persons to be called as experts. In connection with depositions, FRCP 30(d) limits length and bars or limits certain other obstructionist tactics.

Lack of Civility. The other development, related to the first, is a growing sense that civility has declined. Included on the list of grievances are "Rambo tactics" seeking to exploit every conceivable advantage; name calling, baiting, obstructionism in discovery and elsewhere; and abuse of the sanctions system that was itself designed to *increase* cooperation. In 1991, the Seventh Circuit adopted a series of Professional Standards. Consider what kind of conduct could justify the following provisions (selected from a longer array that includes rules dealing with lawyer interactions with court personnel, behavior of judges on the bench and toward one another):

1. We will practice our profession with a continuing awareness that our role is to advance the legitimate interests of our clients. In our dealings with others we will not reflect the ill feelings of our clients. We will treat all other counsel, parties, and witnesses in a civil and courteous manner, not only in court, but also in all other written and oral communications.
2. We will not, even when called upon by a client to do so, abuse or indulge in offensive conduct directed to other counsel, parties, or witnesses. We will abstain from disparaging personal remarks or acrimony toward other counsel, parties, or witnesses. We will treat adverse witnesses and parties with fair consideration.
3. We will not encourage or knowingly authorize any person under our control to engage in conduct that would be improper if we were to engage in such conduct.
4. We will not, absent good cause, attribute bad motives or improper conduct to other counsel or bring the profession into disrepute by unfounded accusations of impropriety.
5. We will not seek court sanctions without first conducting a reasonable investigation and unless fully justified by the circumstances and necessary to protect our client's lawful interests.
6. We will adhere to all express promises and to agreements with other counsel, whether oral or in writing, and will adhere in good faith to all agreements implied by the circumstances or local customs.
7. When we reach an oral understanding on a proposed agreement or a stipulation and decide to commit it to writing, the drafter will endeavor in good faith to state

the oral understanding accurately and completely. The drafter will provide the opportunity for review of the writing to other counsel. As drafts are exchanged between or among counsel, changes from prior drafts will be identified in the draft or otherwise explicitly brought to the attention of other counsel. We will not include in a draft matters to which there has been no agreement without explicitly advising other counsel in writing of the addition.

. . .

12. We will not time the filing or service of motions or pleadings in any way that unfairly limits another party's opportunity to respond.
13. We will not request an extension of time solely for the purpose of unjustified delay or to obtain a tactical advantage.
14. We will consult other counsel regarding scheduling matters in a good faith effort to avoid scheduling conflicts.

. . .

17. We will agree to reasonable requests for extensions of time and for waiver of procedural formalities, provided our clients' legitimate rights will not be materially or adversely affected.

. . .

20. We will not engage in any conduct during a deposition that would not be appropriate in the presence of a judge.
21. We will not obstruct questioning during a deposition or object to deposition questions unless necessary under the applicable rules to preserve an objection or privilege for resolution by the court.

. . .

29. We will not ascribe a position to another counsel that counsel has not taken or otherwise seek to create an unjustified inference based on counsel's statements or conduct.
30. Unless specifically permitted or invited by the court, we will not send copies of correspondence between counsel to the court.

Final Report of the Committee on Civility of the Seventh Federal Judicial Circuit, 143 F.R.D. 441, 448-451 (1992).

An Alternative: Modify the Adversary System. In this environment, serious suggestions have been made to modify the system by changing the behavior and functions of lawyers and judges. Consider these modest suggestions advanced by Judge Marvin Frankel (then federal District Judge in the Southern District of New York), who complained that the adversary system simply does not achieve truth:

Employed by interested parties, the [adversary] process often achieves truth only as a convenience, a byproduct, or an accidental approximation. The business of the advocate, simply stated, is to win if possible without violating the law. (The phrase "if possible" is meant to modify what precedes it, but the danger of slippage is well known.) His is not the search for truth as such. To put that thought more exactly, the truth and victory are mutually incompatible for some considerable percentage of the attorneys trying cases at any given time.

· · ·

[In civil litigation,] we may say that it is the rare case in which either side yearns to have the witnesses, or anyone, give *the whole truth*. And our techniques for developing evidence feature devices for blocking and limiting such unqualified revelations.

The devices are too familiar to warrant more than a fleeting reminder. To begin with, we leave most of the investigatory work to paid partisans, which is scarcely a guarantee of thorough and detached exploration. Our courts wait passively for what the parties will present, almost never knowing—often not suspecting—what the parties have chosen not to present. The ethical standards governing counsel command loyalty and zeal for the client, but no positive obligation at all to the truth. Counsel must not knowingly break the law or commit or countenance fraud. Within these unconfining limits, advocates freely employ time-honored tricks and stratagems to block or distort the truth.

As a matter of strict logic, in the run of cases where there are flatly contradictory assertions about matters of fact, one side must be correct, the other wrong. Where the question is "Did the defendant pass a red light?" or "Does the plaintiff have a scarred retina?" . . . the "facts" are, or were, one way or the other. To be sure, honest people may honestly differ, and we mere lawyers cannot—actually must not—set ourselves up as judges of the facts. That is the great release from effective ethical inhibitions. We are not to pass judgment, but only to marshal our skills to present and test the witnesses and other evidence—the skills being to make the most of these for our side and the least for the opposition. What will out, we sometimes tell ourselves and often tell others, is the truth. And, if worse comes to worst, in the end who really knows what is truth?

There is much in this of cant, hypocrisy, and convenient overlooking. As people, we know or powerfully suspect a good deal more than we are prepared as lawyers to admit or explore further. The clearest cases are those in which the advocate has been informed directly by a competent client, or has learned from evidence too clear to admit of genuine doubt, that the client's position rests upon falsehood. It is not possible to be certain, but I believe from recollection and conversation such cases are far from rare. Much more numerous are the cases in which we manage as counsel to avoid too much knowledge. The sharp eye of the cynical lawyer becomes at strategic moments a demurely averted and filmy gaze. It may be agreeable not to listen to the client's tape recordings of vital conversations that may contain embarrassments for the ultimate goal of vindicating the client. Unfettered by the clear prohibitions [that] actual "knowledge" of the truth might impose, lawyers may be effective and exuberant in employing the familiar skills: techniques that make a witness look unreliable although the look stems only from counsel's artifice, cunning questions that stop short of discomfiting revelations, complaisant experts for whom some shopping may have been necessary. The credo that frees counsel for such arts is not a doctrine of truth-seeking.

Marvin E. Frankel, *The Search for Truth: An Umpireal View*, 123 U. Pa. L. Rev. 1031, 1037-1039 (1975).

Judge Frankel offered several suggestions, including these: First, judges can play a more active role, for example, in questioning witnesses. Second, lawyers should be committed "to the discovery or truth rather than to the advancement of the client's interest." We should consider anew the question "whether it would be an excessive price for the client to be stuck with the truth" that he tells his lawyer in confidence, under the protection of the attorney-client privilege, "rather than having counsel allied with [the client] for concealment and distortion." The latter idea seems to suggest that sometimes lawyers should not protect what their clients tell them, while not quite saying as much. See Frankel, supra, at 1053-1056.

Another Alternative: Move Toward Other Models. Consider another approach—one that would address perceived inadequacies of the adversary system by a broader reform. Here are arguments presented by Professor John Langbein to move toward what he calls the "German model" of procedure:

> My theme is that, by assigning judges rather than lawyers to investigate the facts, the Germans avoid the most troublesome aspects of our practice. But I shall emphasize that the familiar contrast between our adversarial procedure and the supposedly nonadversarial procedure of the Continental tradition has been grossly overdrawn.
>
> To be sure, since the greater responsibility of the bench for fact-gathering is what distinguishes the Continental tradition, a necessary (and welcome) correlative is that counsel's role in eliciting evidence is greatly restricted. Apart from fact-gathering, however, the lawyers for the parties play major and broadly comparable roles in both the German and American systems. Both are adversary systems of civil procedure. There as here, the lawyers advance partisan positions from first pleadings to final arguments. German litigators suggest legal theories and lines of factual inquiry, they superintend and supplement judicial examination of witnesses, they urge inferences from fact, they discuss and distinguish precedent, they interpret statutes, and they formulate views of the law that further the interests of their clients. I shall urge that German experience shows that we would do better if we were greatly to restrict the adversaries' role in fact-gathering.
>
> . . .
>
> There are two fundamental differences between German and Anglo-American civil procedure, and these differences lead in turn to many others. First, the court rather than the parties' lawyers takes the main responsibility for gathering and sifting evidence, although the lawyers exercise a watchful eye over the court's work. Second, there is no distinction between pretrial and trial, between discovering evidence and presenting it. Trial is not a single continuous event. Rather, the court gathers and evaluates evidence over a series of hearings, as many as the circumstances require.
>
> *Initiation.* The plaintiff's lawyer commences a lawsuit in Germany with a complaint. Like its American counterpart, the German complaint narrates the key facts, sets forth a legal theory, and asks for a remedy in damages or specific

relief. Unlike an American complaint, however, the German document proposes means of proof for its main factual contentions. The major documents in the plaintiff's possession that support his claim are scheduled and often appended; other documents (for example, hospital files or government records such as police accident reports or agency files) are indicated; witnesses who are thought to know something helpful to the plaintiff's position are identified. The defendant's answer follows the same pattern. It should be emphasized, however, that neither plaintiff's nor defendant's lawyer will have conducted any significant search for witnesses or for other evidence unknown to his client. Digging for facts is primarily the work of the judge.

Judicial preparation. The judge to whom the case is entrusted examines these pleadings and appended documents. He routinely sends for relevant public records. These materials form the beginnings of the official dossier, the court file. All subsequent submissions of counsel, and all subsequent evidence-gathering, will be entered in the dossier, which is open to counsel's inspection continuously.

When the judge develops a first sense of the dispute from these materials, he will schedule a hearing and notify the lawyers. He will often invite and sometimes summon the parties as well as their lawyers to this or subsequent hearings. If the pleadings have identified witnesses whose testimony seems central, the judge may summon them to the initial hearing as well.

Hearing. The circumstances of the case dictate the course of the hearing. Sometimes the court will be able to resolve the case by discussing it with the lawyers and parties and suggesting avenues of compromise. If the case remains contentious and witness testimony needs to be taken, the court will have learned enough about the case to determine a sequence for examining witnesses.

Examining and recording. The judge serves as the examiner-in-chief. At the conclusion of his interrogation of each witness, counsel for either party may pose additional questions, but counsel are not prominent as examiners. Witness testimony is seldom recorded verbatim; rather, the judge pauses from time to time to dictate a summary of the testimony into the dossier. The lawyers sometimes suggest improvements in the wording of these summaries, in order to preserve or to emphasize nuances important to one side or the other.

Since the proceedings in a difficult case may require several hearings extending across many months, these summaries of concluded testimony—by encapsulating succinctly the results of previous hearings—allow the court to refresh itself rapidly for subsequent hearings. The summaries also serve as building blocks from which the court will ultimately fashion the findings of fact for its written judgment. If the case is appealed, these concise summaries constitute the record for the reviewing court. (We shall see that the first appellate instance in German procedure involves review de novo, in which the appellate court can form its own view of the facts, both from the record and, if appropriate, by recalling witnesses or summoning new ones.)

Anyone who has had to wade through the longwinded narrative of American pretrial depositions and trial transcripts (which preserve every inconsequential utterance, every false start, every stammer) will see at once the economy of the German approach to taking and preserving evidence. Our incentives run the other way; we pay court reporters by the page and lawyers mostly by the hour.

A related source of dispatch in German procedure is the virtual absence of any counterpart to the Anglo-American law of evidence. German law exhibits expansive notions of testimonial privilege, especially for potential witnesses drawn from the family. But German procedure functions without the main chapters of our law of evidence, those rules (such as hearsay) that exclude probative evidence for fear of the inability of the trier of fact to evaluate the evidence purposely. In civil litigation German judges sit without juries . . . ; evidentiary shortcomings that would affect admissibility in our law affect weight or credit in German law.

John H. Langbein, The German Advantage in Civil Procedure, 52 U. Chi. L. Rev. 823, 830 (1985). Professor Langbein argues that the continental (or German) approach achieves important things, including these:

(1) The German system operates without "sequence rules" of American litigation, in which plaintiff proceeds first, then defendant, then plaintiff in rebuttal and defendant in rejoinder, and so forth. Instead, German procedure lets the court range "over the entire case," looking into the matter "in the fashion most likely to narrow the inquiry."

(2) The "episodic character" or "conference method" in Germany produces a "businesslike tone" that reduces "tension and theatrics" and "encourages settlement." In contrast, American trials "make for good theatre" because they bring (a) "the potential for surprise witnesses," (b) lawyerly "tricks" in questioning witnesses, and (c) the "unpredictability of juries and the mysterious opacity of their conclusory verdicts."

(3) The German system avoids "partisan preparation, examination, and cross-examination of witnesses." Lawyers speak to their clients and "nominate" witnesses, but have no out-of-court contact with nonparty witnesses.

(4) In American trials, expert witnesses are mere "saxophones" playing the tune of the lawyer, but European expertise is "neutral" because experts are selected and called by courts (parties may "nominate" experts, and if the parties agree on an expert the court must select that person). The court then "instructs" the expert on the facts and formulates the questions, and the expert prepares a report that is circulated among the litigants.

Langbein, supra, at 823, 830-841.

A study by Professor Menkel-Meadow argues for a multi-track approach that would retain the adversary model where it works (she expects disagreement on this question), while experimenting with (1) regulatory negotiation (parties "get involved in the construction of rules" governing their behavior); (2) multiparty representational conversation (different views aired under guidance of facilitator who asks participants about "gray areas," their reactions to other views, and what facts or data might move each to another view); (3) "civil inquisitorial/investigative procedures" (similar to German approach); (4) conventional forms of Alternative Dispute Resolution (ADR), such as mediation, mini-trials, settlement conferences, early neutral evaluation; and (5) third-party "neutralizing" (pairs of judges, such as a man and a woman). See Carrie Menkel-Meadow, *The Trouble with the Adversary System in a Postmodern, Multicultural World*, 38 Wm. & Mary L. Rev. 5, 32-38 (1996).

■ NOTES ON THE ADVERSARY MODEL AND THE ALTERNATIVES

1. Is a judge-directed inquiry more likely to develop truth than competing factual presentations by interested parties? Long ago Professor Fuller defended adversarial presentations, arguing that judges acting as fact gatherers and decision makers would become too quickly invested in a particular outcome: "[W]hat starts as a preliminary diagnosis designed to direct the inquiry tends, quickly and imperceptibly, to become a fixed conclusion, as all that confirms the diagnosis makes a strong imprint on the mind, while all that runs counter to it is received with diverted attention. . . . An adversary [system] seems the only effective means for combating this natural human tendency to judge too swiftly in terms of the familiar that which is not fully known." Lon Fuller, *The Adversary System, in* Talks on American Law 37, 43-44 (1971). There is some value, isn't there, in separating functions of gathering and presenting evidence from deciding the facts and applying the law?

2. Professor Langbein thinks that the German system is more efficient, with its "conference method" that explores facts without distinguishing "between trial and pretrial, between discovering evidence and presenting it." But 90 percent of cases settle in the American system too, and we have no data suggesting that German procedure is *in fact* more efficient. For a critique of the Langbein article, see Ronald J. Allen et al., *The German Advantage in Civil Procedure: A Plea for More Details and Fewer Generalities in Comparative Scholarship*, 82 Nw. U. L. Rev. 705, 730-732 (1988). See also John H. Langbein, *Trashing the German Advantage*, 82 Nw. U. L. Rev. 763 (1988) (replying to Allen et al). For another take, see Samuel R. Gross, *The American Advantage: The Value of Inefficient Litigation*, 85 Mich. L. Rev. 734 (1987) (German-style success depends on efficient judicial bureaucracy in a centralized system; countries such as Italy have similar traditions but less success; America is larger and heterogeneous, with more fragmented institutions).

3. Could a judge play a bigger part in a system that includes an entitlement to a jury trial? Does the "German advantage" suggest that we should scrap jury trials in civil litigation (which Britain has done, for the most part)? In the next section, we will think further about use of civil juries.

4. Michael Bohlander, a German-educated lawyer and jurist, agrees that German lawyers "do not normally conduct searches for evidence unknown to the client," but rely on the court to "tell them if it needs further evidence." Indeed, he says most lawyers could not handle the case "without helpful comments" from the judge. But *the parties* gather evidence in the German system too: With the court's guidance, they seek out proof, and doing so is not unethical "so long as the lawyer [does] not try to influence the witnesses or tamper with the evidence." One need not worry about the court's ability to know what is needed, Bohlander argues, since a judge knows that "every party must ... eventually prove all the facts which are necessary to justify its claim or defense." See Michael Bohlander, *The German Advantage Revisited: An Inside View of German Civil Procedure in the Nineties*, 13 Tul. Eur. & Civ. L.F. 25, 34-36 (1998). Is a judge really likely to know better than the lawyer who brings or defends a case which facts must be proved?

5. Consider the arguments that our system encourages lawyers to "win if possible," to use their skills simply "to make the most" of friendly witnesses and "the least" of unfriendly ones (Judge Frankel), leading to "theatrics" and "tricks" (Professor Langbein). Doesn't the presence of a motivated lawyer on the other side reduce temptations to take indefensible positions? It is true that lawyers question witnesses in America, but lawyers are not free to ask whatever they want, and there are limits on the ways in which lawyers can "impeach" or attack the credibility of witnesses. See generally FRE 611(a) (judges control "the mode and order of examining witnesses and presenting evidence" in the interests of "the ascertainment of truth" and to "avoid wasting time" and "protect witnesses from harassment or undue embarrassment"). And see FRE 608 (empowering courts to restrict cross-examination on bad acts relating to truthfulness) and 609 (regulating use of prior convictions to impeach).

6. In the German system, there is no verbatim transcript. The judge prepares summaries and enters a judgment that includes findings of fact. The German-trained judge quoted above says the court records statements of witnesses "as verbatim as possible, as long as the literal reading is pertinent," but that witnesses often "cannot give a coherent account" and must be "prodded" or "reined in," and that German judges "often polish their wording," apparently to spare the feelings of witnesses and "to get an intelligible account," which is "questionable but harmless" so long as the polished account "does not lead to a different meaning." Bohlander, supra, at 25, 44. The American system involves a verbatim record reflecting every word of testimony. If you were a German judge, how would you be affected by knowing that a reviewing court knows nothing more about the evidence than what you include? One study suggests that a German judge asked questions leading to "gradual restructuring" of witness erceptions, so the judge in effect "created the testimony he wanted." See Allen et al., supra, at 705, 730-732 (1988) (describing study by Professor Caesar-Wolf). Isn't this kind of thing exactly what Judge Frankel and Professor Langbein criticize as the result of questioning conducted by lawyers?

7. Compare the German practice, in which the judge conducts most of the questioning but lets parties ask follow-up questions, with the American practice where attorneys do almost all the questioning. Would it surprise you to learn that American judges *can* call and question witnesses? See FRE 614(a) (court may call witnesses); 614(b) (court may question witnesses); FRE 706 (court may call experts). Why are these powers so seldom exercised by

American judges? Does the fact that American litigants enjoy the right of trial by jury account for it? See generally John C. Reitz, *Why We Probably Cannot Adopt the German Advantage in Civil Procedure*, 75 Iowa L. Rev. 987, 991-993 (1990) (citing "cultural differences" and fact that German judges are "career bureaucrats" while American judges are political appointees and former attorneys, and stressing that in jury cases questioning by judge would carry more weight than questioning by lawyers).

E   CUSTOMS AND INSTITUTIONS—CIVIL JURIES

In the federal system, the Seventh Amendment provides that in "suits at common law" seeking more than $20, the right to trial by jury "shall be preserved" and that "no fact tried by a jury" shall be "otherwise re-examined in any Court of the United States, than according to the rules of the common law." As noted above, this language covers only cases in federal court, but civil cases litigated in state court often bring a jury trial entitlement, as a matter of state law. In both state and federal courts, it is up to a party to demand a jury trial (if neither does, the case is tried to a judge).

Reasons to Have the Jury Trial Option in Civil Cases. So many books have been written about the jury system, and juries have been praised in so many different ways, that summing up is itself a perilous business. Here are some common supporting arguments for juries (with special emphasis on civil litigation):

First, jurors are better at finding facts than judges. In depth and breadth of experience, 12 citizens bring more useful understanding to the table than any judge, and are more likely to get it right. In short, "twelve heads are better than one" as one federal judge put it, and a state judge expanded the same idea in this way:

> Judges try the same type of action day after day. Our judgment on issues of fact must always be based in part on what we, as individuals, are—the sum total of our experiences, our backgrounds, our prejudices and our limitations. There can be no "averaging out" such as there is when twelve individuals are gathered together, most of them serving as jurors only a few times in their lives. They, or at least some of them, can approach a case with a fresh outlook, without a subconscious predetermination of one sort or another about the type of case or, perhaps, the attorneys or the litigants.[5]

---

[5] See Harold R. Medina, Judge Medina Speaks 219 (1954) (commenting about "twelve heads"); Judge Howard T. Hogan, Some Thoughts on Juries in Civil Cases, 50 A.B.A. J. 752, 753 (Aug. 1964) (second quote set out above). See also Harry Kalven, Jr., *The Dignity of the Civil Jury*, 50 Va. L. Rev. 1055, 1067 (1964) ("twelve lay heads are very probably better than one").

Some commentators think juries are especially helpful in determining damages, where part of the award involves arithmetic (adding up "medical specials," meaning costs of doctors, hospitals, medicines, and prosthetic devices, and computing the value of lost wages or income), but part involves something else. As one commentator put it, allowing compensation for pain and suffering "gives the jury immediate freedom to price the injury subjectively," so the law recognizes that computing these and other damages (like lost economic opportunities) "involves a complex value judgment as well as a literal determination of fact." See Harry Kalven, Jr., *The Jury, The Law, and the Personal Injury Damage Award*, 19 Ohio St. L. Rev. 158, 161 (1958) (mentioning special cases of estimating value of housekeeping services and lives of children).

Second, juries perform an equalizing function putting powerful or wealthy citizens or entities on a more nearly equal footing with the average citizen, helping ensure that nobody is above the law. The fact that civil disputes may eventually be determined by 12 persons, who are themselves chosen after the fact and unknown to the parties prior to trial, may itself exert some effect on the behavior of wealthier and more powerful people in their dealings with others. In case you think this idea came from some modern socialist or academic liberal, think again:

> [S]ensible and upright jurymen, chosen by lot from among those of the middle rank, will be found the best investigators of truth, and the surest guardians of public justice. For the most powerful individual in the state will be cautious of committing any flagrant invasion of another's right, when he knows that the fact of his oppression must be examined and decided by twelve indifferent men, not appointed till the hour of trial; and that, when once the fact is ascertained, the law must of course redress. This ... prevents the encroachments of the more powerful and wealthy citizens.

3 William Blackstone, Commentaries on the Laws of England 501-502 (William Hammond ed., Bancroft-Whitney Co. 1890) (Blackstone lived from 1723 to 1780).

Third, jury service is an exercise in civic responsibility. It educates jurors in the ways of the law, involves them in the life of the community, and asks them to undertake the serious business of finding the just outcome in a serious matter. Consider this appraisal by Alexis de Tocqueville, done in the 1830s when only men served on American juries, but bearing on all who serve on juries today:

> [The jury] teaches men to practice equity; every man learns to judge his neighbor as he would himself be judged. And this is especially true of the jury in civil causes; for while the number of persons who have reason to apprehend a criminal prosecution is small, everyone is liable to have a lawsuit. The jury teaches every man not to recoil before the responsibility of his own actions .... It invests each citizen with a kind of magistracy; it makes them all feel the duties which they are

bound to discharge towards society and the part which they take in its government. By obliging men to turn their attention to other affairs than their own, it rubs off that private selfishness which is the rust of society.

The jury contributes powerfully to form the judgment and to increase the natural intelligence of a people; and this, in my opinion, is its greatest advantage. It may be regarded as a gratuitous public school, ever open, in which every juror learns his rights, enters into daily communication with the most learned and enlightened members of the upper classes, and becomes practically acquainted with the laws, which are brought within the reach of his capacity by the efforts of the bar, the advice of the judge, and even the passions of the parties. I think that the practical intelligence and political good sense of the Americans are mainly attributable to the long use that they have made of the jury in civil cases.

1 Alexis de Tocqueville, Democracy in America 284-285 (Alfred A. Knopf 1984).

Fourth, juries help form and shape the common law, and their role is important to the legitimacy of law. The term "common law" refers, after all, to unwritten "rules" that derive from values, practice, and custom, from civic life at the grass-roots level: If a jury decides the driver of a car going 15 miles an hour on an ice-slick street is negligent when she strikes another car stopped to pick up children at the end of the school day, this decision embodied in a verdict gives meaning to the concept of negligence. The alternative is a decision by a judge. (One drawback to verdicts, meaning what a jury says, rather than "decisions," meaning what a judge says, is that verdicts are usually "opaque" in the sense that they announce a conclusion but give no reasons, while decisions by judges come with findings of fact and conclusions of law.)

Fifth, juries provide a safeguard against official oppression and unjust laws. It is not accidental that the jury trial entitlement was enshrined in the Magna Carta in 1215 (no "freeman" will be dispossessed or imprisoned except by "the lawful judgment of his peers"). American colonists followed English cases in which juries resisted unjust laws, and a few celebrated American cases presented juries in similar light. We don't usually think of judges as oppressors, but American juries probably do play critical roles in reshaping the law to achieve better justice, as happened in moving away from the rule that contributory negligence by plaintiffs bars recovery.

There is another side to the story. Modern critics of the jury system make the following points: First, jurors are amateur factfinders, having no experience resolving conflicts in testimony or deciding important matters, while judges are professional people with deeper legal understanding and experience in performing this task. Second, a jury that can ignore or change an unjust law can also ignore or refuse to enforce a just one. Third, juries are prone to sympathy verdicts allowing excessive recovery, such as an award by a Los Angeles jury in 2001 in the amount of $3 billion dollars against a cigarette maker on account of the suffering of a single smoker. Fourth, the jury system is expensive and cumbersome, and you will get some sense of this aspect of jury trial entitlement as you proceed through the course.

Railyard of Grand Central Station in Memphis

Switchtender L.E. Haney died at night from a blow to the head while working in the rail-yard at Grand Central Station in Memphis, Tennessee. Suit was brought on behalf of his estate by Walter Lavender against J.M. Kurn and other trustees of the St. Louis-San Francisco Railway Company (better known as the Frisco) and against the Illinois Central, and part of the trial was devoted to unraveling the question who actually employed Haney and which railroad controlled that part of the yard. The court took testimony by Haney's widow, by his son Alvin Arthur Haney, who worked on the railroad with his father, and by his daughter Marjorie Haney Linsom, who described a button or badge that Haney wore that might contain the initials of his employer, or perhaps only the initials of the Brotherhood of Railroad Trainmen, which allegedly gave such buttons to members to show that they had paid their dues. Other testimony indicated that transients frequented the railyard "seeking chances to steal rides on trains" (according to the brief filed by the Illinois Central). Still other testimony described the mailhook, but most of the proof went to the position of the body, the lay of the land, and measurements taken to determine whether the mailhook could have struck Haney. Plaintiff Walter Lavender sued as "administrator de bonis non" of the Haney estate (the Latin designation is short for "de bonis non administrates," meaning "of goods not administered"): The description refers to a situation requiring a new representative to take over after the death or removal of the person who was to administer the estate.

LAVENDER v. KURN

Supreme Court of the United States
327 U.S. 645 (1946)

Mr. Justice MURPHY delivered the opinion of the Court.

The Federal Employers' Liability Act permits recovery for personal injuries to an employee of a railroad engaged in interstate commerce if such injuries result "in whole or in part from the negligence of any of the officers, agents, or employees of such carrier, or by reason of any defect or insufficiency, due to its negligence, in its cars, engines, appliances, machinery, track, roadbed, works, boats, wharves, or other equipment." 45 USC §51.

Petitioner, the administrator of the estate of L.E. Haney, brought this suit under the Act against the respondent trustees of the St. Louis-San Francisco

Railway Company (Frisco) and the respondent Illinois Central Railroad Company. It was charged that Haney, while employed as a switchtender by the respondents in the switchyard of the Grand Central Station in Memphis, Tennessee, was killed as a result of respondents' negligence. Following a trial in the Circuit Court of the City of St. Louis, Missouri, the jury returned a verdict in favor of petitioner and awarded damages in the amount of $30,000. Judgment was entered accordingly. On appeal, however, the Supreme Court of Missouri reversed the judgment, holding that there was no substantial evidence of negligence to support the submission of the case to the jury. We granted certiorari to review the propriety of the Supreme Court's action under the circumstances of this case.

It was admitted that Haney was employed by the Illinois Central, or a subsidiary corporation thereof, as a switchtender in the railroad yards near the Grand Central Station, which was owned by the Illinois Central. His duties included the throwing of switches for the Illinois Central as well as for the Frisco and other railroads using that station. For these services, the trustees of Frisco paid the Illinois Central two-twelfths of Haney's wages; they also paid two-twelfths of the wages of two other switchtenders who worked at the same switches. In addition, the trustees paid Illinois Central $1.87 1/2 for each passenger car switched into Grand Central Station, which included all the cars in the Frisco train being switched into the station at the time Haney was killed.

The Illinois Central tracks run north and south directly past and into the Grand Central Station. About 2700 feet south of the station the Frisco tracks cross at right angles to the Illinois Central tracks. A westbound Frisco train wishing to use the station must stop some 250 feet or more west of this crossing and back into the station over a switch line curving east and north. The events in issue center about the switch several feet north of the main Frisco tracks at the point where the switch line branches off. This switch controls the tracks at this point.

It was very dark on the evening of December 21, 1939. At about 7:30 P.M. a westbound interstate Frisco passenger train stopped on the Frisco main line, its rear some 20 or 30 feet west of the switch. Haney, in the performance of his duties, threw or opened the switch to permit the train to back into the station. The respondents claimed that Haney was then required to cross to the south side of the track before the train passed the switch; and the conductor of the train testified that he saw Haney so cross. But there was also evidence that Haney's duties required him to wait at the switch north of the track until the train had cleared, close the switch, return to his shanty near the crossing and change the signals from red to green to permit trains on the Illinois Central tracks to use the crossing. The Frisco train cleared the switch, backing at the rate of 8 or 10 miles per hour. But the switch remained open and the signals still were red. Upon investigation Haney was found north of the track near the switch lying face down on the ground, unconscious. An ambulance was called, but he was dead upon arrival at the hospital.

Haney had been struck in the back of the head, causing a fractured skull from which he died. There were no known eye-witnesses to the fatal blow. Although it is not clear there is evidence that his body was extended north and south, the head to the south. Apparently he had fallen forward to the south; his face was bruised on the left side from hitting the ground and there were marks indicating that his toes had dragged a few inches southward as he fell. His head was about 5 1/2 feet north of the Frisco tracks. Estimates ranged from 2 feet to 14 feet as to how far west of the switch he lay.

The injury to Haney's head was evidenced by a gash about two inches long from which blood flowed. The back of Haney's white cap had a corresponding black mark about an inch and a half long and an inch wide, running at an angle downward to the right of the center of the back of the head. A spot of blood was later found at a point 3 or 4 feet north of the tracks. The conclusion following an autopsy was that Haney's skull was fractured by "some fast moving small round object." One of the examining doctors testified that such an object might have been attached to a train backing at the rate of 8 or 10 miles per hour. But he also admitted that the fracture might have resulted from a blow from a pipe or club or some similar round object in the hands of an individual.

Petitioner's theory is that Haney was struck by the curled end or tip of a mail hook hanging down loosely on the outside of the mail car of the backing train. This curled end was 73 inches above the top of the rail, which was 7 inches high. The overhang of the mail car in relation to the rails was about 2 to 2 1/2 feet. The evidence indicated that when the mail car swayed or moved around a curve the mail hook might pivot, its curled end swinging out as much as 12 to 14 inches. The curled end could thus be swung out to a point 3 to 3 1/2 feet from the rail and about 73 inches above the top of the rail. Both east and west of the switch, however, was an uneven mound of cinders and dirt rising at its highest points 18 to 24 inches above the top of the rails. Witnesses differed as to how close the mound approached the rails, the estimates varying from 3 to 15 feet. But taking the figures most favorable to the petitioner, the mound extended to a point 6 to 12 inches north of the overhanging side of the mail car. If the mail hook end swung out 12 to 14 inches it would be 49 to 55 inches above the highest parts of the mound. Haney was 67 1/2 inches tall. If he had been standing on the mound about a foot from the side of the mail car he could have been hit by the end of the mail hook, the exact point of contact depending upon the height of the mound at the particular point. His wound was about 4 inches below the top of his head, or 63 1/2 inches above the point where he stood on the mound—well within the possible range of the mail hook end.

Respondents' theory is that Haney was murdered. They point to the estimates that the mound was 10 to 15 feet north of the rail, making it impossible for the mail hook end to reach a point of contact with Haney's head. Photographs were placed in the record to support the claim that the ground was level north of the rail for at least 10 feet. Moreover, it appears that the area immediately surrounding the switch was quite dark. Witnesses stated that it was so dark that it was impossible to see a 3-inch pipe 25 feet away. It also appears that many hoboes and tramps frequented the area at night in order to get rides on freight trains. Haney carried a pistol to protect himself. This pistol was found loose under his body by those who came to his rescue. It was testified, however, that the pistol had apparently slipped out of his pocket or scabbard as he fell. Haney's clothes were not disarranged and there was no evidence of a struggle or fight. No rods, pipes or weapons of any kind, except Haney's own pistol, were found near the scene. Moreover, his gold watch and diamond ring were still on him after he was struck. Six days later his unsoiled billfold was found on a high board fence about a block from the place where Haney was struck and near the point where he had been placed in an ambulance. It contained his social security card and other effects, but no money. His wife testified that he "never carried much money, not very much more than $10." Such were the facts in relation to respondents' theory of murder.

Finally, one of the Frisco foremen testified that he arrived at the scene shortly after Haney was found injured. He later examined the fireman's side of the train very carefully and found nothing sticking out or in disorder. In explaining why he examined this side of the train so carefully he stated that while he was at the scene of the accident "someone said they thought that train No. 106 backing in to Grand Central Station is what struck this man" and that Haney "was supposed to have been struck by something protruding on the side of the train." The foreman testified that these statements were made by an unknown Illinois Central switchman standing near the fallen body of Haney. The foreman admitted that the switchman "didn't see the accident." This testimony was admitted by the trial court over the strenuous objections of respondents' counsel that it was mere hearsay falling outside the res gestae rule.

The jury was instructed that Frisco's trustees were liable if it was found that they negligently permitted a rod or other object to extend out from the side of the train as it backed past Haney and that Haney was killed as the direct result of such negligence, if any. The jury was further told that Illinois Central was liable if it was found that the company negligently maintained an unsafe and dangerous place for Haney to work, in that the ground was high and uneven and the light insufficient and inadequate, and that Haney was injured and killed as a direct result of the said place being unsafe and dangerous. This latter instruction as to Illinois Central did not require the jury to find that Haney was killed by something protruding from the train.

The Supreme Court, in upsetting the jury's verdict against both the Frisco trustees and the Illinois Central, admitted that "It could be inferred from the facts that Haney could have been struck by the mail hook knob if he were standing on the south side of the mound and the mail hook extended out as far as 12 or 14 inches." But it held that "all reasonable minds would agree that it would be mere speculation and conjecture to say that Haney was struck by the mail hook" and that "plaintiff failed to make a submissible case on that question." It also ruled that there "was no substantial evidence that the uneven ground and insufficient light were cause or contributing causes of the death of Haney." Finally, the Supreme Court held that the testimony of the foreman as to the statement made to him by the unknown switchmen was inadmissible under the res gestae rule since the switchman spoke from what he had heard rather than from his own knowledge.

We hold, however, that there was sufficient evidence of negligence on the part of both the Frisco trustee and the Illinois Central to justify the submission of the case to the jury and to require appellate courts to abide by the verdict rendered by the jury.

The evidence we have already detailed demonstrates that there was evidence from which it might be inferred that the end of the mail hook struck Haney in the back of the head, an inference that the Supreme Court admitted could be drawn. That inference is not rendered unreasonable by the fact that Haney apparently fell forward toward the main Frisco track so that his head was 5 1/2 feet north of the rail. He may well have been struck and then wandered in a daze to the point where he fell forward. The testimony as to blood marks some distance away from his head lends credence to that possibility, indicating that he did not fall immediately upon being hit. When that is added to the evidence most favorable to the petitioner as to the height and swing-out of the hook, the height and location of the mound and the nature of Haney's duties, the inference that Haney was killed by the hook cannot be said to be unsupported by probative facts or to be so unreasonable as to warrant taking the case from the jury.

It is true that there is evidence tending to show that it was physically and mathematically impossible for the hook to strike Haney. And there are facts from which it might reasonably be inferred that Haney was murdered. But such evidence has become irrelevant upon appeal, there being a reasonable basis in the record for inferring that the hook struck Haney. The jury having made that inference, the respondents were not free to relitigate the factual dispute in a reviewing court. Under these circumstances it would be an undue invasion of the jury's historic function for an appellate court to weigh the conflicting evidence, judge the credibility of witnesses and arrive at a conclusion opposite from the one reached by the jury.

It is no answer to say that the jury's verdict involved speculation and conjecture. Whenever facts are in dispute or the evidence is such that fair-minded men may draw different inferences, a measure of speculation and conjecture is required on the part of those whose duty it is to settle the dispute by choosing what seems to them to be the most reasonable inference. Only when there is a complete absence of probative facts to support the conclusion reached does a reversible error appear. But where, as here, there is an evidentiary basis for the jury's verdict, the jury is free to discard or disbelieve whatever facts are inconsistent with its conclusion. And the appellate court's function is exhausted when that evidentiary basis becomes apparent, it being immaterial that the court might draw a contrary inference or feel that another conclusion is more reasonable.

We are unable, therefore, to sanction a reversal of the jury's verdict against Frisco's trustees. Nor can we approve any disturbance in the verdict as to Illinois Central. The evidence was uncontradicted that it was very dark at the place where Haney was working and the surrounding ground was high and uneven. The evidence also showed that this area was entirely within the domination and control of Illinois Central despite the fact that the area was technically located in a public street of the City of Memphis. It was not unreasonable to conclude that these conditions constituted an unsafe and dangerous working place and that such conditions contributed in part to Haney's death, assuming that it resulted primarily from the mail hook striking his head.

In view of the foregoing disposition of the case, it is unnecessary to decide whether the allegedly hearsay testimony was admissible under the res gestae rule. Rulings on the admissibility of evidence must normally be left to the sound discretion of the trial judge in actions under the Federal Employers' Liability Act. But inasmuch as there is adequate support in the record for the jury's verdict apart from the hearsay testimony, we need not determine whether that discretion was abused in this instance.

The judgment of the Supreme Court of Missouri is reversed and the case is remanded for whatever further proceedings may be necessary not inconsistent with this opinion.

Reversed.

THE CHIEF JUSTICE and Mr. Justice FRANKFURTER concur in the result. Mr. Justice REED dissents. Mr. Justice JACKSON took no part in the consideration or decision of this case.

■ NOTES ON GIVING CASES TO JURIES AND TAKING THEM AWAY FROM JURIES

1. Walter Lavender (administrator of Haney's estate) sued in state court in Missouri, but the complaint sought relief under a federal statute (FELA, the Federal Employers Liability Act). Such things can happen because suits under federal statutes may be brought in *either* state or federal court, unless Congress says otherwise. Ordinarily, a defendant may remove to federal court a state suit brought under a federal statute. See 28 USC §1441(b). In FELA, however, Congress blocked railroads from removing. See 28 USC §1445. Why do you suppose Congress did so?

2. Given that the Seventh Amendment does not apply to civil actions in state courts, did Missouri *have* to accord the parties a jury trial? The Missouri Constitution protects the right to a jury trial in civil cases, see Mo. Const. Art. I §22(a), but what if Missouri had abolished this right in civil cases? It is at least possible that a Missouri court would *still* have to accord the right of trial by jury because the Supreme Court has said this right is embedded in FELA itself, as a matter of federal law that state courts must honor. See, e.g., Bailey v. Central Vermont Railway, 319 U.S. 350, 355 (1943) (right of trial by jury is "part and parcel of the remedy" afforded by FELA). In one case the Supreme Court said FELA cases in state court may be tried under state rules allowing less-than-unanimous verdicts, see Minneapolis & St. Louis Ry. Co. v. Bombolis, 241 U.S. 211 (1916), but in another case the Court condemned the practice in Ohio of letting a *judge* decide whether a railroader was bound by a release that he had signed, holding that the FELA requires *that* question to be resolved by a jury, but then adding a cryptic comment that a state would not have to try FELA cases to a jury if it abolished jury trials in all negligence cases. See Dice v. Akron, Canton & Youngstown Ry. Co., 342 U.S. 359, 362 (1952) (Chapter 6B3, infra).

3. *Lavender* presented as a stark choice between two theories: Haney was killed by the mailhook or by an intruder—one of "many hoboes and tramps" (today we say "homeless persons"). If the former, the railroad could be negligent. If the latter, the railroad was not liable. (Uneven ground could count, along with the mailhook, as unsafe working conditions, but not the presence of intruders; the Missouri Court thought uneven ground could not account for Haney's death; the Supreme Court does not disagree). What's the strongest argument that Haney was struck by the mailhook? What is the strongest argument that he was attacked by an intruder?

4. Is *Lavender* the kind of case juries are better equipped to decide than judges? Why or why not? If you were on the jury, which side would you be on? In its opinion, the Missouri Supreme Court gives a fuller description of the testimony, and quotes testimony by J.E. Mee, an engineer on the train at the time:

I got a blast of 3 whistles on the air from the conductor to start backing up. I couldn't see the back end of the train from my position in the cab because of a curve. In starting the backward movement I always looked back at the movement of the train, turned and faced the rear end, in the direction we were going, and watched the movement of the train. That is my duty, to look down to the back and alongside my train as I start backing. We lean out of the window to do that. It is up to the engineer whether he leans out the side or looks through the rear vision window. The first cars I was looking at would be the mail and baggage cars, and I was looking back along the north side of them and as far back as I could see. As we made that backward movement the conductor controlled the air brake on the train from the rear end of the train. We stopped the train on that occasion before we got into the station and, with his signal which I had to get from him before I could move, I started again. I could see nothing of the rear end. It was on the curve and out of sight. After stopping and getting his signal to proceed, I backed on clear into the station. I did not see Haney or any person at that switch as I approached (backing in) and passed it. I didn't see any person lying on the ground or standing up there or anybody at all near the side of my train. I was at all times looking out of my window toward the rear and past the side of the mail and baggage cars at the head of the train. I was backing around the curve to the left and north and upgrade. We were going approximately 8 miles an hour before I got the signal to stop. I suppose we backed up about 300 feet or something like that when I was stopped.

Lavender v. Kurn, 189 S.W.2d 253, 255 (Mo. 1945). Could Haney have been struck by the mailhook on a car close to the engine without being seen by J.E. Mee?

5. Juries determine witness credibility, and courts routinely *instruct* juries to do so. See Kevin F. O'Malley, Jay E. Grenig, William C. Lee, Federal Jury Practice and Instructions §101.43 (2004) (you "may believe everything a witness says, or part of it, or none of it," and may consider the "opportunity and ability" of a witness to see or hear or know, the memory of the witness, the "appearance and manner" of the witness on the stand, as well as her "interest in the outcome," any "bias or prejudice" she may have; you may also consider "other evidence that may have contradicted" her testimony, and "the reasonableness" of that testimony "in light of all the evidence"). If you were a juror thinking about J.E. Mee's testimony in *Lavender,* would it make a difference whether he kept working for the railroad? Whether he might be blamed if the mailhook killed Haney? Are jurors better than judges in thinking about such things?

6. You will see that to "get her case to a jury" the claimant must offer sufficient evidence of the necessary facts to enable a reasonable person to conclude that they are probably true (more likely so than not). We have a procedural mechanism to enforce this rule, and the central term is "judgment as a matter of law." Thus the judge can "take the case from the jury" and award judgment as a matter of law if the evidence does not satisfy the "sufficiency" standard, which means a reasonable person could *not* find the necessary facts to be proved. Less often, the judge may take the case from the jury (and award judgment as a matter of law) if the evidence is so "cogent and compelling" that a reasonable person *must* find the necessary facts to be true. See FRCP 50, which we study in Chapter 12. In *Lavender,* the judge thought the evidence *was* sufficient to support the verdict for the plaintiff, but the Missouri Supreme Court thought otherwise. The Supreme Court agrees with the trial judge. Who is right?

7. Does *Lavender* illustrate the point that juries are useful because they put the average citizen on an equal footing with powerful entities? In the FELA statute enacted in 1908, Congress modified common law limitations that might block recovery. Thus in FELA suits plaintiff need only show that the employer's negligence was a causal factor, see 45 USC §51 (creating liability for death or injury caused "in whole or in part" by negligence). The statute adopts a comparative negligence standard, so negligence by the claimant does not necessarily block recovery. See 45 USC §53 ("contributory negligence shall not bar" recovery, but reduces it proportionately). Nor is recovery denied because the dead or injured worker *chose* a dangerous job, see 45 USC §54 (employees shall not be deemed to have "assumed the risks"). Finally, recovery is not to be denied because a "fellow servant" caused the injury, see Consolidated Rail Corp. v. Gottshall Consolidated Rail Corp., 512 U.S. 532, 542 (1994) (Congress "did away with" fellow servant rule because it blocked recovery where other workers caused death or injury). With these pro-plaintiff modifications, should courts be *more* willing to accord juries some leeway, or *less* willing to do so?

8. Does *Lavender* help make de Tocqueville's point that jury service is an exercise in civic responsibility that serves an educational function? De Tocqueville thought citizens would serve on juries once every three or four years, but one commentator studied civil jury service in Cook County, Illinois, and concluded on the basis of measurements covering the 20 years between 1959 and 1979 that the average annual likelihood of jury service was .0038, translating into serving on a jury once every 260.2 years, meaning that the average citizen has only about a one-in-five chance of serving on a civil jury once in a lifetime. See George L. Priest, *The Role of the Civil Jury in a System of Private Litigation*, 1990 U. Chi. L.F. 161, 181-190 (also jurors spend most of their time "evaluating truly routine injuries" like broken legs and arms, and only a tiny fraction of the time evaluating the exercise of governmental power; traditional justifications for civil juries are not worth the costs and delays).

F A NEW DEVELOPMENT—MANAGERIAL JUDGING

Countless movies and television dramas show lawyers taking the initiative in calling witnesses and presenting testimony. Judges are relatively passive, ruling on motions and objections (up or down, yes or no), and the roles are clear.

To some extent this picture is misleading. For a long time judges have played important roles in encouraging settlement, and judges make many decisions that are *not* binary—decisions that shape litigation. More importantly, we live in a regulated society in which laws affect broad categories of modern life. Hence litigation can be complex and sprawling, and judges exercise more control than the popular picture suggests, especially in federal courts, but also in state courts. In a landmark article, Professor Resnik gave us a term that has stuck—"managerial judging." See Judith Resnik, *Managerial Judges*, 96 Harv. L. Rev. 374 (1982).

MALONE v. UNITED STATES POSTAL SERVICE

United States Court of Appeals for the Ninth Circuit
833 F.2d 128 (9th Cir. 1987), **cert. denied,** *488 U.S. 819 (1988)*

CHOY, Senior Circuit Judge:

Ann Malone appeals the district court's decision, following Malone's violation of a pretrial order, to dismiss with prejudice her suit against the United States Postal Service. We affirm.

BACKGROUND

Ann Malone brought suit against the United States Postal Service (the "Government") for alleged violations of Title VII of the Civil Rights Act of 1964, 42 USC §§2000e et seq. The trial began in November 1984. Because Malone's attorney presented the case in a confused and inefficient manner, the district court restricted counsel's presentation of witnesses and evidence. Counsel believed that the court was treating her unfairly; on November 16, she made a motion for a mistrial. The court denied the motion, but a few hours later declared a mistrial on its own motion. The district court explained in the June 10, 1985, dismissal order at issue here that the mistrial had been declared because of lack of preparation on the part of Malone's attorney.

The district court issued a pretrial order on December 13, 1984. The order required both parties to file information with the court prior to a new trial. Among the information requested was a complete list of witnesses and a "thorough and complete list of each and every" direct question and anticipated response. The court stated that no oral argument concerning this requirement would be entertained, and that motions for continuances would not be accepted. The deadline for compliance with the order was April 25, 1985. Trial was set for June 1985. On April 23, 1985, Malone's attorney informed the Government by telephone that Malone would not be complying in any way with the order. The Government had already devoted considerable effort to complying with the pretrial order. On April 26, Malone for the first time filed objections to the pretrial order, requesting recusal of the trial judge, modification of the pretrial order, and a continuance.

On May 1, 1985, the Government moved to dismiss the action on the ground that Malone had willfully failed to comply with any aspect of the pretrial order. A hearing was held on May 16, at which Malone's attorney stated that Malone had not complied with the pretrial order because Malone lacked the financial resources to do so. The district court granted the Government's motion, and dismissed the action with prejudice on June 10, 1985.

Malone timely appeals the order of dismissal.

DISCUSSION

Malone makes three basic arguments against the district court's order of dismissal: (1) the district court abused its discretion in weighing the five factors which we have set forth to guide dismissal decisions; (2) the district court's pretrial order was invalid and therefore the court was precluded from sanctioning Malone's violation of the order; and (3) Malone has been unfairly punished for the faults of her attorney. We reject all of these arguments.

I. DISMISSAL FACTORS

The district court relied primarily on FRCP 16(f) in ordering dismissal. Rule 16(f) states that for violation of a pretrial order a judge may order sanctions as provided in FRCP 37(b)(2)(C). Rule 37(b)(2)(C) [now FRCP 37(b)(2)(A)—Ed.] provides for the sanction of dismissal. The district court also relied on FRCP 41(b), which enables a court to order dismissal "[f]or failure of the plaintiff . . . to comply with . . . any order of [the] court. . . ." The standards governing dismissal for failure to obey a court order are basically the same under either of these rules. See Price v. McGlathery, 792 F.2d 472, 474 (5th Cir. 1986).

The district court's dismissal of a case with prejudice is reviewed for abuse of discretion. "Dismissal is a harsh penalty and is to be imposed only in extreme circumstances." Henderson v. Duncan, 779 F.2d 1421, 1423 (9th Cir. 1986). Nevertheless, we will overturn a dismissal sanction only if we have a definite and firm conviction that it was clearly outside the acceptable range of sanctions.

A district court must weigh five factors in determining whether to dismiss a case for failure to comply with a court order: "(1) the public's interest in expeditious resolution of litigation; (2) the court's need to manage its docket; (3) the risk of prejudice to the defendants; (4) the public policy favoring disposition of cases on their merits; and (5) the availability of less drastic sanctions." Thompson v. Housing Authority, 782 F.2d 829, 831 (9th Cir.), cert. denied, 479 U.S. 829 (1986). It is not necessary for a district court to make explicit findings to show that it has considered these factors. We may review the record independently to determine if the district court has abused its discretion.

In the instant case, the district court did not explicitly indicate that it had considered any of the five dismissal factors in rendering its decision. The court explained its decision to dismiss as follows:

> [The Court] feels that the flagrant disobedience by plaintiff's counsel, her bad faith and her repeated failure to comply in any respect with the Court's pretrial order warrants the sanction of dismissal in this case. The Court's finding in this regard is amplified by the fact that plaintiff's counsel did not communicate in any way with the Court or opposing counsel at any time in an attempt to clarify or modify the Court's pretrial order until April 23, 1985 when plaintiff's counsel . . . informed defendants' counsel for the first time that plaintiff would not file any of the requested documents by the Court.

The court concluded that the violation of the pretrial order was deliberate and willful. The court also rejected the excuse given by counsel for refusing to comply with the order: that Malone lacked the financial means to meet the order's detailed requirements.

Because the district court did not explicitly consider the five dismissal factors set forth in *Thompson*, we must review the record independently to determine whether the order of dismissal was an abuse of discretion. Our independent evaluation of the dismissal factors convinces us that the district court's order was not an abuse of discretion.

A. THE FIRST TWO DISMISSAL FACTORS

The first two dismissal factors are the public interest in expeditious resolution of litigation and the trial court's interest in docket control. It is clear that these two factors support the district court's decision to dismiss Malone's case. Malone's dilatory conduct greatly impeded resolution of the case and prevented the district court from adhering to its trial schedule.

B. PREJUDICE TO DEFENDANT

In determining whether a defendant has been prejudiced, we examine whether the plaintiff's actions impair the defendant's ability to go to trial or threaten to interfere with the rightful decision of the case. In the instant case, the district court was primarily concerned with counsel's bad faith decision to wait until the last minute before notifying the Government that Malone was not complying with the pretrial order. While Malone did nothing to fulfill her responsibilities under the pretrial order, the Government made a diligent effort to comply with the pretrial order in a timely manner. We have no doubt that Malone's last-minute notification of her decision not to comply with the pretrial order had a prejudicial effect on the Government.

We hold that the prejudice to the Government from Malone's actions was sufficient to justify an order of dismissal. In so holding, we place particular reliance on the district court's determination that Malone's excuse for her conduct was groundless. Whether prejudice is sufficient to support an order of dismissal is in part judged with reference to the strength of the plaintiff's excuse for the default. The district court rejected the excuse that Malone lacked the financial resources to comply with the pretrial order. The court found that compliance with the pretrial order was feasible in light of the numerous depositions and interrogatories already taken by Malone's counsel and the "numerous alternatives available to [Malone]" for compliance. In addition, counsel offered no explanation as to why she waited until April 23 to inform the Government that Malone was unable to comply with the pretrial order. Malone's intentional and unjustified violation of the pretrial order prejudiced the Government in a manner which justifies dismissal.

C. CONSIDERATION OF LESS DRASTIC ALTERNATIVES

Malone argues that in ordering dismissal the district court did not consider the feasibility of alternatives to dismissal. We disagree.

"The district court abuses its discretion if it imposes a sanction of dismissal without first considering the impact of the sanction and the adequacy of less drastic sanctions." United States v. National Medical Enterprises, Inc., 792 F.2d 906, 912 (9th Cir. 1986).[1] Our case law reveals that the following factors are of particular relevance in determining whether a district court has considered alternatives to dismissal: (1) Did the court explicitly discuss the feasibility of less drastic sanctions and explain why alternative sanctions would be inadequate? (2) Did the court implement alternative methods of sanctioning or curing the malfeasance before ordering dismissal? (3) Did the court warn the plaintiff of the possibility of dismissal before actually ordering dismissal?

The district court did not explicitly discuss the feasibility of alternatives to dismissal. The Government argues that the court did explicitly consider alternatives, citing to part of the transcript of the hearing regarding whether to dismiss the case. In the passage cited by the Government, the district court discussed counsel's excuse that Malone was unable to afford the extensive preparation necessary to comply with the pretrial order. The court refused

---

[1] Alternative sanctions include: "a warning, a formal reprimand, placing the case at the bottom of the calendar, a fine, the imposition of costs or attorney fees, the temporary suspension of the culpable counsel from practice before the court, . . . dismissal of the suit unless new counsel is secured[,] . . . preclusion of claims or defenses, or the imposition of fees and costs upon plaintiff's counsel. . . ." Titus v. Mercedes Benz of North America, 695 F.2d 746, 749 n.6 (3d Cir. 1982). In addition, "[p]roviding plaintiff with a second or third chance following a procedural default is a 'lenient sanction,' which, when met with further default, may justify imposition of the ultimate sanction of dismissal with prejudice." Callip v. Harris County Child Welfare Department, 757 F.2d 1513, 1521 (5th Cir. 1985) (quoting [earlier decision]).

to accept this excuse, stating that the "alternative" suggested by counsel would be to allow every indigent plaintiff to "conduct[ ] a fishing expedition" at trial. This discussion of an "alternative" by the court is not a discussion of an alternative to dismissal. Rather, it is a justification for rejecting the proffered excuse for noncompliance with the pretrial order.

We have indicated a preference for explicit discussion by the district court of the feasibility of alternatives when ordering dismissal. However, we have never held that explicit discussion of alternatives is *necessary* for an order of dismissal to be upheld. Under the egregious circumstances present here, where the plaintiff has purposefully and defiantly violated a court order, it is unnecessary (although still helpful) for a district court to discuss why alternatives to dismissal are infeasible.

Moreover, explicit discussion of alternatives is unnecessary if the district court actually tries alternatives before employing the ultimate sanction of dismissal. We conclude that the district court's November 16, 1984, declaration of mistrial and subsequent pretrial order constituted attempts at less drastic alternatives to dismissal. The mistrial, pretrial order, and order of dismissal were *all* instituted in response to the lack of preparation on the part of Malone and her counsel. The district court's imposition of less drastic measures for lack of preparation during the aborted first trial is sufficient indication to us that alternatives were considered prior to dismissal of Malone's case for lack of preparation.

Finally, the case law suggests that warning a plaintiff that failure to obey a court order will result in dismissal can suffice to meet the "consideration of alternatives" requirement. Failure to warn has frequently been a contributing factor in our decisions to reverse orders of dismissal. Although in the instant case the district court did not explicitly warn Malone that dismissal would follow violation of the pretrial order, the court made it clear that no continuances would be accepted. Moreover, we find a warning to be unnecessary here. A plaintiff can hardly be surprised by a harsh sanction in response to willful violation of a pretrial order. Rules 16(f) and 41(b) explicitly state that dismissal may be ordered for violation of a court order.

Under the circumstances in this case, the district court satisfied the "consideration of alternatives" requirement by implementing alternative measures prior to ordering dismissal for willful failure to prepare for trial. We conclude that, pursuant to the five dismissal factors, the district court's order of dismissal was not an abuse of discretion.[2]

---

[2] We have not discussed the fifth dismissal factor: the public policy favoring disposition of cases on their merits. Although this factor weighs against dismissal, it is not sufficient to outweigh the other four factors, which in this case support dismissal.

II. ALLEGED INVALIDITY OF PRETRIAL ORDER

Malone also argues that the district court's pretrial order was invalid and therefore that her refusal to comply with the order was justified. Malone primarily contends that the court did not have the authority to require her to supply all anticipated questions and answers for the witnesses that would testify at trial. Malone concludes that the district court's order of dismissal was improper because an order of dismissal cannot be premised on the violation of an invalid order.

It is well established that "[a]n attorney who believes a court order is erroneous is not relieved of the duty to obey it." Chapman v. Pacific Telephone and Telegraph Co., 613 F.2d 193, 197 (9th Cir. 1979). We note, however, that several courts have looked to the validity of an order in deciding whether violation of that order may result in dismissal. See, e.g., Identiseal Corporation of Wisconsin v. Positive Identification Systems, Inc., 560 F.2d 298, 301 (7th Cir. 1977) (district court's dismissal based on plaintiff's failure to file court-ordered pretrial report can be upheld only if it was within court's authority to compel plaintiff to conduct discovery which would provide the facts to be contained in the pretrial report); McCargo v. Hedrick, 545 F.2d 393, 396-402 (4th Cir. 1976) (reversing dismissal in part because violated order was premised on invalid local rule); J.F. Edwards Construction Co. v. Anderson Safeway Guard Rail Corp., 542 F.2d 1318, 1325 (7th Cir. 1976) (because Rule 16 does not authorize court to order parties to stipulate facts, sanctions for failure to so stipulate are not available); see also Titus [v. Mercedes Benz of North America, 695 F.2d 746,] at 752 [(3d Cir. 1982)] (Fullam, J., concurring) (dismissal for failure to obey requirement of pretrial order is justified only if requirement is reasonable).

Even if dismissal cannot be premised on the violation of an invalid order, the district court's order of dismissal was proper because the court's pretrial order was valid under FRCP 16. Rule 16 basically enables trial courts to take steps to improve the efficiency of trials. Hitherto we have not explicitly approved a pretrial order requiring the parties to provide a list of all proposed direct questions and answers. However, we have encouraged attempts by district courts to simplify trials by requiring the parties to submit proposed testimony. See Miller v. Los Angeles County Board of Education, 799 F.2d 486, 488 (9th Cir. 1986) (order requiring plaintiff to submit proposed questions); *Chapman*, 613 F.2d at 197-98 (order requiring plaintiffs to submit written narrative of direct testimony of each witness). The pretrial order at issue here was designed in that spirit.

Malone has submitted no evidence that the pretrial order was unfair. Because both Malone and the Government were required to supply proposed questions and answers, the pretrial order imposed no special burdens or disadvantages on Malone. Nor was the pretrial order unnecessarily or excessively burdensome. We note that another circuit has cautioned that "Rule 16 should not be implemented in such a manner that the pretrial procedure itself is more difficult and time consuming than the actual trial." *McCargo,* 545 F.2d at 401. However, unlike the order at issue in *McCargo,* the pretrial order at issue served a valuable purpose by trying to organize a very disorganized case. We conclude that the pretrial order issued by the trial court in this case was valid.

III. MALONE'S RESPONSIBILITY FOR COUNSEL'S MALFEASANCE

Malone argues that the district court's order of dismissal unfairly punishes her for the misdeeds of her attorney. We have repeatedly rejected such arguments. We acknowledge that the degree of a plaintiff's personal responsibility for malfeasance is relevant to the propriety of dismissal. But in light of the egregious nature of the malfeasance at issue here, we cannot conclude that the district court abused its discretion in declining to excuse Malone for the faults of her attorney. As we stated in *Chism,* "district courts cannot function efficiently unless they can effectively require compliance with reasonable rules." *Chism,* 637 F.2d at 1332.

CONCLUSION

The district court's pretrial order was valid. The court did not abuse its discretion in ordering dismissal with prejudice for Malone's violation of the order.

Affirmed.

TANG, Circuit Judge, dissenting:
. . . I do not share the majority's view that the declaration of mistrial and the pretrial order were attempts at less drastic alternatives to dismissal. The district court imposed the extreme sanction of dismissal because of Malone's attorney's failure to comply with the court's pretrial order. The declaration of mistrial and the pretrial order were not sanctions but efforts to manage the litigation. When the attorney belatedly announced that she would or could not comply with the court's order, the court had a number of options that would not have had such a negative impact on the litigant. It could have considered sanctions against counsel. Alternatively, because it was still forty-five days before the trial was scheduled to begin, the court could have warned counsel of the possibility of dismissal if she did not immediately make an effort to comply with the order. This court has frequently required a warning prior to dismissal for proper exercise of the district court's discretion.

The majority indicates that the prejudice to the Government from Malone's late notification of her inability to comply with the order was that the Government had made a diligent effort to comply. There would have been very little prejudice had the court warned Malone and assured compliance. If the court had modified its requirements of Malone it could have reduced the prejudice to the Government of any such change by withholding from Malone full disclosure of the Government's trial strategy.

I would reverse the district court's order because the district judge's "understandable pique [does not] excuse his failure to consider alternative sanctions." Hamilton [v. Neptune Orient Lines, Ltd., 811 F.2d 498], at 500 [9th Cir. 1987)].

■ NOTES ON JUDGES AS MANAGERS

1. Judge John Vukasin and lawyer Isable Medford (counsel for Ann Malone) didn't get along. We're told that Ms. Medford asked for a mistrial, apparently because the judge "restricted [her] presentation of witnesses and evidence." Initially, the court refused, but later granted a mistrial on its own. Still later, the judge said he declared the mistrial because of Medford's "lack of preparation." In the meantime, he told *both* lawyers to submit in writing the questions they proposed to ask on direct, as well as anticipated responses, giving them four months. He refused to hear argument or grant continuances. Citing FRCP 16(f) and 37(b), the reviewing court says the judge had authority to enter this order, and to dismiss when Ms. Medford did not comply. This exercise of judicial control is extraordinary, is it not? Are there clues in the opinion that this judge has tested the outer limits of judicial authority?

2. Do you think the Rules were intended to create such authority in judges? Why does the reviewing court affirm? What else could it do? What else could Ms. Medford have done that might have worked better?

3. The reviewing court cites the "public interest in expeditious resolution" and "docket control" as reasons favoring dismissal. But the suit was one person's claim of discrimination against a government agency. Does the public interest require rapid disposition of such suits over plaintiff's objection? "Docket control" *always* cuts in favor of dismissal with prejudice, doesn't it? If Medford was unprepared, does that mean that counsel *for the government* should have to script the second trial?

4. The reviewing court says the government was prejudiced on account of counsel's "last minute notification of her decision not to comply" with the order. Did late notification prejudice the government? Apparently, the government had made an effort to comply. But if compliance is prejudice, the source is the order itself, isn't it?

5. Who bears the weight of the sanction, plaintiff or her lawyer? Is it fair to visit on the client the shortcomings of her lawyer? What other (and lesser) sanction might the judge have imposed? The reviewing court says it prefers trial judges to engage in "explicit discussion" of lesser alternatives. Why? The reviewing court faults Medford for offering "no explanation" of her refusal to comply, but it excuses the judge for failing to consider alternative sanctions expressly. What's the message here? Isn't it that lawyers must turn square corners in dealing with court orders, but that courts are given a certain leeway in applying the relevant legal criteria?

6. There is a good chance, isn't there, that *all* trials will go more smoothly if they are scripted? Why aren't such orders common? See Chapman v. Pacific Telephone and Telegraph Co., 613 F.2d 193, at 197-198 (9th Cir. 1979) (judge tells plaintiff's attorney to "submit a written narrative statement of the direct testimony of each witness," holding her in contempt and fining her when she did not comply; order contemplates "direct oral testimony" that could "supplement the written narrative statement," and also live cross-examination and redirect).

7. Suppose *Malone* had held that the order was invalid. The court suggests that such invalidity might affect the propriety of dismissal. But one of the sanctions a court may impose on a lawyer who refuses to do as instructed is an order holding the lawyer in contempt. And under the "collateral bar" rule, an order by a court having jurisdiction must be obeyed even if erroneous. During the era of civil rights demonstrations, for example, an Alabama court enjoined civil rights leaders, including Dr. Martin Luther King, Jr., from marching through Birmingham over the Easter weekend. Some demonstrators ignored the order, were convicted of criminal contempt, sentenced to five days in jail, and fined $50 apiece. The United States Supreme Court affirmed. See Walker v. City of Birmingham, 388 U.S. 307, 320-321 (1967) (respecting judicial process "is a small price to pay for the civilizing hand of law"). See generally David B. Oppenheimer, *Martin Luther King, Walker v. City of Birmingham, and the Letter from the Birmingham Jail*, 26 U.C. Davis L. Rev. 791 (1993) (describing Dr. King's decision to violate the injunction rather than see protest fail because review could not be had until too late; while in jail, Dr. King wrote one of the salient testaments of the era, known as the *Letter from the Birmingham Jail*).

8. In *Chapman* (note 6, supra), the court invoked the "collateral bar" rule in concluding that the attorney could not avoid punishment for contempt even if the order was invalid. See also In re Novak, 932 F.2d 1397, 1400 (11th Cir. 1991) (even if order directing represented party to attend pretrial personally was invalid, this fact was not a defense to contempt). The message of *Malone*, *Chapman*, and *Novak* is that lawyers must obey court directives and test them later, if the case is lost on the merits. The alternative, which would let the lawyer flout an order and avoid punishment if it was erroneous, would give lawyers more latitude. Taking this option away goes far to secure the authority of trial courts, doesn't it?

9. Bear in mind that one who violates a *statute* or *rule* has a defense if the statute or rule is invalid. In another case arising during the civil rights movement, the Supreme Court sharply distinguished *Walker*, concluding that demonstrators who marched without a permit as required by local ordinance could defend against criminal charges by arguing that the ordinance was constitutionally invalid. See Shuttlesworth v. City of Birmingham, 394 U.S. 147, 157 n.7 (1969) (*Walker* raised "quite different issues" because there was an injunction and the proper procedure involved complying and then appealing). Does it make sense to distinguish between disobeying a statute and disobeying a court order? Why or why not?

10. The collateral bar rule admits of some exceptions, which are defined in general terms that resist refinement. Consider the following description:

> There are situations . . . where the collateral bar rule is inapplicable. First, if the issuing court lacks subject-matter jurisdiction over the underlying controversy or personal jurisdiction over the parties to it, its order may be violated with impunity. "In such a case, the original order is deemed a nullity, and the accused contemnor cannot be fairly punished for violating nothing at all." In re Hern Iron Works, 881 F.2d 772, at 726-27 (9th Cir. 1989). Second, the collateral bar rule presupposes that adequate and effective remedies exist for orderly review of the challenged ruling; in the absence of such an opportunity for review, the accused contemnor may challenge the validity of the disobeyed order on appeal from his criminal contempt conviction and escape punishment if that order is deemed invalid. Third, the order must not require an irretrievable surrender of constitutional guarantees. In such a case, the only way to preserve a challenge to the validity of the order and repair the error is to violate the order and contest its validity on appeal from the district court's judgment of criminal contempt. Finally, court orders that are transparently invalid or patently frivolous need not be obeyed. This exception is based, as is the first for jurisdictional defects, on the notion that "the right of the citizen to be free of clearly improper exercises of judicial authority" demands respect.

In re Novak, 932 F.2d 1397, 1401-1402 (11th Cir. 1991).

G AMERICAN FEDERALISM

1. Introduction

We live in a federal republic. The term "federal" describes a political organization with two systems of government—in our case, a central overarching government with nationwide authority, directed by institutions in Washington DC, and multiple co-equal regional (state) governments.

Our central government (the "federal government" or simply the "government") has huge power and responsibility. It regulates the economy, including the workplace; it exercises sweeping powers in areas like environment, energy, and interstate communication (phone lines, radio and television, the internet); it provides for national security and responds to emergencies; it prosecutes crimes with interstate elements, especially drug crimes and terrorist acts. Still, the government does not—and probably cannot, under our Constitution—do everything we expect from public institutions, and in that sense it is one of limited powers. For the most part, it is not in charge of education or the regulation of families, for example, or the prosecution of most criminal offenses, from assault and malicious mischief to robbery and murder.

State governments too have limited power. They are limited by geography (the New York legislature cannot regulate Illinois contracts) and subject matter: They cannot conduct foreign relations, raise armies, coin money, or obstruct interstate commerce. As a practical matter, states can often act only if the federal government has not. In the *Lavender* case, for example, the question was what duties a railroad owes to its employee, and Congress stepped into this field by enacting FELA. State law would have controlled if Congress had not occupied the field.

The term "republic" refers to representative government, as opposed to a direct democracy in which each citizen votes on most issues. In our republic, both federal and state governments have three parts—executive, legislative, and judicial—and the role that each plays is similar in the federal and state systems. In both, the three branches operate under procedural rules: In the executive branch, state and federal agencies engage in factfinding that is sometimes conducted in hearings with the purpose of designing administrative strategies or adopting regulations. State and federal agencies also engage in quasi-judicial undertakings that involve focused factfinding, aimed at determining such matters as whether a person should receive benefits (or be cut off) or whether an employer is in compliance with workplace safety standards. In the legislative branch, Congress and state legislatures operate under rules governing the manner in which legislation is considered, composition and functions of committees, and like matters.

In Procedure, we are concerned with the rules that apply in the judicial branch. Mostly we study the Federal Rules, although you will read state decisions too. Rules and doctrine vary in state courts, and between state and federal court, but most issues you will consider arise in state and federal court, and are often resolved the same way.

2. State Courts

Most states have courts of limited jurisdiction and courts of general jurisdiction. In the former category are courts that deal with probate or juvenile justice, domestic relations, or smaller claims (like justice courts, municipal courts, or county courts, with jurisdictional limits set at amounts ranging from $5,000 to $25,000). Most states also have small claims courts of the sort made popular on television ("Judge Judy"), where people represent themselves (lawyers are not allowed, except when they appear on behalf of entities that are not natural persons).

Courts of general jurisdiction, typically called district courts,[6] hear cases of all kinds, without regard to amount at stake, except for cases assigned to specialty courts or agencies like the Workers Compensation Board (where authority overlaps, we speak of concurrent jurisdiction). These courts are set up in judicial districts, each usually comprised of one or more counties. A single judge presides in each court, but there may be many courts in a district, especially in urban areas.

State judges are usually appointed for initial terms by the governor under something called the "Missouri Plan," in which a commission of lawyers and citizens recommends candidates, inviting professional and public input. State judges who are appointed in this way then stand for "retention" (usually once every five or six years). This approach separates political payoffs from judicial appointments. The retention system tends to ensure that judges keep their seats unless actively opposed by a significant segment of the public or the bar, and it constitutes a daily reminder that judges serve at the sufferance of the voters.

Usually in the state system, cases are assigned for hearings or motions or other pretrial proceedings to whatever judge is available, and sometimes judges rotate functions: Five may be assigned to try cases, while a sixth sits at "law and motion" or in pretrial proceedings, so a case may be heard in different phases by different judges.

Appeals may be had from most trial courts. In the case of municipal and county courts, often the appeal goes to the court of general jurisdiction, where the case is essentially retried, although usually the litigants are limited to the issues argued at trial. This style is known as *de novo* review because the parties simply present the case over again, and the reviewing court simply decides the case as it deems best, without according any particular deference to the result reached originally.

Appeals from judgments by trial courts of general jurisdiction are taken to the state court of appeals or supreme court. Review proceeds "on the record," meaning that the appellate court hears argument and learns what happened at trial by looking at the record, which includes important documents filed in the case, exhibits offered at trial, and excerpts of the written verbatim transcript. Customarily, such review accords deference to the trial judge in appraising rulings on matters like admitting or excluding evidence and granting or denying motions, and still more deference to judge or jury in connection with findings of fact.

---

[6] Nomenclature is not uniform. In some states (like Florida and Missouri), the trial court of general jurisdiction is called the Circuit Court. In others (like California, Delaware, and Maryland), it is the Superior Court. Delaware differs from the rest of the country in maintaining a Court of Chancery, which hears cases dealing with corporate law, land title, commercial and contractual matters, and trusts and estates. In New York, confusingly, the trial court of general jurisdiction is the Supreme Court, and the highest court is the New York Court of Appeals. In Pennsylvania, the trial court of general jurisdiction is the Court of Common Pleas.

In most states, review is a matter of right for the party who loses at trial. The appeal goes to the court of appeal or, if the state lacks this intermediate appellate court, to the state supreme court. In states that have both, review by the state supreme court is discretionary.[7]

3. Federal Courts

Federal courts are said to be courts of "limited jurisdiction" because their authority depends on constitutional language and federal statute, and both place limits on that authority. Putting aside criminal cases, their most important areas of authority involve suits arising under federal law and suits between citizens of different states where the amount at stake exceeds $75,000 (the minimum being set by statute, and not by the Constitution), and in these suits usually federal courts are applying state law. These areas of authority are known as "federal question jurisdiction" and "diversity jurisdiction." In some specific instances like antitrust, federal question jurisdiction is exclusive in federal courts, but in others (like suits under §1983 as in *Piphus*) federal and state courts have concurrent jurisdiction.

The structure of the federal judiciary is similar to that of the states. The main federal trial court is the District Court. There are 91 districts, each being either a state or a division of a state. There is, for instance, the Federal District of Utah (whole state) and three federal districts in Florida (Northern, Central, Southern). District judges (all federal judges) enjoy life tenure, so they need not stand for retention and can be removed only by impeachment (very rare). District judges have the assistance of Magistrate Judges, who serve under long-term contracts and decide procedural matters under special statutes, including discovery disputes in civil cases.

There are also specialty courts: Bankruptcy Courts, for example, resolve issues relating to bankruptcy, governed by federal law. The Federal Court of Claims sits in Washington DC, but its judges travel and hear cases across the country. It resolves claims against the government, typically arising out of contractual relationships with suppliers and service providers. The Court of Claims also hears taxpayer suits seeking repayment of deficiency assessments (if the IRS says a taxpayer owes more, he must pay, then sue to get it back if he thinks the assessment is wrong).

In the federal system, review is conducted primarily by Circuit Courts of Appeal. There are 13, one each for the First through Eleventh Circuits, plus the Court of Appeals for the District of Columbia and the Court of Appeals for the Federal Circuit. The numbered circuits cover the 50 states: The Tenth Circuit, for example, embraces federal districts defined by the boundaries of Colorado,

---

[7] Nine states and the District of Columbia have no intermediate appellate courts. See Chapter 13, footnote 1, infra.

New Mexico, Oklahoma, Utah, and Wyoming. The number of appellate judges varies widely among the Circuits, but each Court of Appeals sits in panels of three to hear cases.

In civil suits, ordinarily appeals are taken from the District Court, after entry of final judgment, to the Circuit Court of Appeals, and review is of right. In unusual cases, extraordinary "interlocutory" appeals proceed by writ of mandamus or under special statutes or Rules, even though final judgment has not yet been entered and the case, or part of it, is still pending at the trial level.

The highest level of review in the federal system is the United States Supreme Court. Litigants disappointed in results obtained in the Circuit Court of Appeals may petition the Supreme Court for a writ of certiorari, which is discretionary. Less than 2 percent of petitions lead to review.

The Supreme Court can correct any reviewable error in cases litigated in the federal system: Federal appellate courts (Supreme Court and Circuit Courts of Appeal) have "supervisory authority" to correct mistakes. The Supreme Court can also review cases litigated in the state systems (again by writ of certiorari). For cases coming from the state system, Supreme Court review is limited to federal issues, meaning for the most part issues implicating the Constitution or federal statutes.

4. Intersystem Effects—Introduction

State law and federal law overlap one another, sometimes in complementary fashion and sometimes colliding. The operations of state and federal courts overlap one another in similar ways, complementing each other and sometimes colliding. These overlaps are a function of federalism, and they have led to legal doctrines that have important impacts on civil litigation. This book examines four of these doctrines, which go under the names of federal pre-emption, the *Erie* doctrine, abstention doctrines, and the law of antisuit injunctions (mostly the Anti-Injunction Act, 28 USC §2283). We will also look at a fifth doctrine, similar to the others in being an example of federal law having an impact on state court operations: This one, rooted in the Constitution, is captured in the phrase "full faith and credit," and it deals with recognition of final judgments.

Overlap and collision between state and federal law come about because the *lawmaking powers* of state and federal governments are extensive and overlapping, even though also limited. That these powers are limited comes as no surprise. Congress is constrained by the Bill of Rights (it cannot enact a statute barring criticism of the President, for example),[8] and by the less

---

[8] The Bill of Rights (most provisions in the first ten amendments, like the bar against laws restricting freedom of speech) was originally thought to limit only federal power (Congress), not states. But most of these provisions were "read into" the Due Process Clause of the Fourteenth Amendment, which *does* apply to states.

familiar principle that it has "enumerated" powers (it can legislate only where the Constitution says it can), which implies limits, however hard to define.[9] That these powers are nonetheless extensive also comes as no surprise. The prevailing academic view is that the implied limits do not bar Congress from acting in any particular area (the "unitary sovereignty" model holds that Congress can legislate in all areas, so long as its laws are tied to a constitutional grant of power). Thus it can regulate guns or telephones or packaged cereal, so long as it is exercising powers conferred by the Commerce Clause (Art. I §8). This model enjoys more support than the "dual sovereignty" model that would "carve out" certain areas ("enclaves") as being off limits. Even under the latter view, congressional power is extensive, and Congress can pass laws affecting liability in such common areas as contract, tort, landlord-tenant, employment, and the environment. *State* legislative power is limited too because states are *geographically* bounded, and there are other limits: States cannot, for example, unduly burden interstate commerce (they are restricted by the "dormant commerce clause," which operates to assure a national marketplace). But those limits apart, state legislatures have extensive powers, and can, like Congress, enact laws affecting liability in all the areas just mentioned.

Overlap and collision between the operations of state and federal courts come about for an analogous reason: The *judicial jurisdiction* of the federal government and that of the states are also overlapping, even though limited. As already noted, federal courts hear both federal question and diversity cases, applying federal law in the former, state law in the latter. State judicial power is limited geographically (Chapter 3 takes up the geographical "reach" of state court jurisdiction), and in other ways (Congress has decided, for example, that suits under federal patent laws are to be heard *exclusively* in federal courts; the same is true of suits under federal antitrust laws). But state courts, like federal courts, apply federal law sometimes and state law sometimes. In short, both state and federal courts apply both state and federal law.

Now let us look a little more closely at the five doctrines listed above:

(1) Federal Pre-emption. We will start here, by looking at Problem 1-A ("We're in Compliance with Federal Standards") because in some ways pre-emption is the easiest of the four doctrines to understand. Often everyone can see that federal law applies, and not state law, or vice versa. There is no doubt, for example, that Congress acted properly under the Commerce Clause in enacting FELA, and this law controls when railroaders sue their employers for injuries sustained on the job (you saw the statute in operation in the

---

[9] Beginning in the closing decade of the twentieth century, the Court tried to define limits on congressional power, overturning federal laws on grounds that they exceeded the scope of congressional power under the Commerce Clause. See, e.g., United States v. Morrison, 529 U.S. 598 (2000) (civil damage recovery; Violence Against Women Act rejected); United States v. Lopez, 514 U.S. 549 (1995) (criminal penalties for carrying firearms in school zones; Gun Free School Zones Act rejected).

Lavender case). Where federal law exists, it is the "supreme law" of the land, and state courts must apply it. See U.S. Constitution, Art. VI (the Constitution and "the Laws of the United States" are "the supreme Law of the Land" and judges in state court "shall be bound thereby"). Often everyone understands as well that state law applies, as in ordinary auto accident cases, product liability cases, or suits on contracts. Congress *could* enact federal law in some of these areas, such as product liability (most commercial products are marketed nationwide; Congress could regulate under the Commerce Clause), but Congress has not acted, so state law applies. Sometimes, however, it is less clear whether state or federal law controls, and we consider such an instance in Problem 1-A.

(2) The *Erie* Doctrine. We won't get to this subject until Chapter 6, but it may help to anticipate what you will discover there. Oversimplifying in the interest of brevity, the *Erie* doctrine holds that federal courts in diversity cases (citizen of one state suing a citizen of another) must apply state substantive law and federal procedure law. This doctrine is named after Erie Railroad Co. v. Tompkins, 304 U.S. 64 (1938), and it means that in diversity cases federal courts cannot look to a general or nationwide body of common law (there is no such thing). Instead, they look to state law (typically the state where the federal court sits), including state common law in areas like torts, contracts, and property. The substance/procedure distinction matters in state courts too. As *Lavender* illustrates, state courts sometimes apply federal legislation, but in these cases state courts apply state procedural law. Often the substance/procedure distinction is easy to figure out, but many rules seem both substantive and procedural, and we face difficult choices.

(3) Abstention Doctrines. We will get to this subject in Chapter 6 as well. Because state and federal judicial authority overlaps, the same issue can arise in state or federal court, and sometimes the same issue arises in the courts of both systems at the same time. For a variety reasons, it may be preferable to resolve such issues in one system rather than another, and federal courts sometimes accommodate state litigation by getting out of the way, or try to co-ordinate with it. There are judge-made doctrines under which federal courts "abstain" from deciding cases or from taking up legal issues, leading to orders that dismiss or put litigation on hold. Sometimes the purpose is to avoid interfering with development of state law by state courts, or to let state government carry on its business, or simply to avoid two courts going forward on parallel tracks. Sometimes the purpose is to let state courts resolve state law issues in order to avoid unnecessarily having to resolve federal issues.

(4) Law of Antisuit Injunctions. This subject too is covered in Chapter 6. When the same issue arises in state court and federal court at the same time, it is usually because of duplicative litigation going forward in both systems that can bring the courts of the two systems into awkward and unseemly collision with one another. Federal courts sometimes put a stop to state litigation by enjoining the parties against continuing to litigate in state court. Long ago, however, Congress limited the power of federal courts to block state litigation, but the Anti-Injunction Act, as it is called (28 USC §2283), contains important exceptions that enable limited interference with state suits. See Chapter 6C2.

(5) Finality and Full Faith and Credit. In Chapter 14, you will see that doctrines of claim preclusion (commonly called "*res judicata*") and issue preclusion (commonly called "collateral estoppel") operate in both federal and state systems. Briefly, and again oversimplifying for a moment, the former means that litigants cannot bring new suits once claims and defenses are finally resolved, and the latter means the litigants cannot relitigate issues once they are finally resolved ("claim preclusion").

It turns out that both federal and state judgments have preclusive effects in later suits brought in either state or federal court. Here we speak of "full faith and credit," which is the language used in Article IV of the Constitution. This provision requires state courts to honor judgments by other state courts, and empowers Congress to enact implementing legislation. The relevant statute goes further, requiring *both* state and federal courts to honor state court judgments. See 28 USC §1738. Although the textual basis for this outcome is elusive, it turns out as well that state courts must honor (give full faith and credit to) federal judgments.

5. A Particular Intersystem Effect—Federal Pre-emption

The areas of congressional competence are set forth in Article I in a list of specifics, including most importantly the power to "regulate Commerce . . . among the several States" and "make all Laws" that are "necessary and proper" in exercising its authority (Art. I §8). If, for example, Congress enacts a statute providing that minimum wage for people engaging in interstate commerce is $7.25 per hour, and if an employer pays a covered employee $6.70 per hour, the employer is subject to federal administrative sanctions and perhaps a damage suit brought by the underpaid employee (or on behalf of a class), even if state law sets the minimum wage at $6.50 per hour. See 29 USC §206 (minimum wage is $7.25 per hour as of July 25, 2009).

Congress often avoids the specificity we find in the minimum wage statute. In the National Traffic and Motor Vehicle Safety Act of 1966 (MVSA), for example, Congress instructed the Department of Transportation (DOT), in effect, to legislate safety requirements for automobiles. The statute is broad, with almost no specifics. It begins with a statement of purpose, which is "to reduce traffic accidents and deaths and injuries from traffic accidents." Hence it is necessary to set "motor vehicle safety standards" and conduct "needed safety research and development." 49 USC §30101. The statute directs the Secretary of Transportation to "prescribe motor vehicle safety standards," each of which shall be "practicable" and shall "meet the need for motor vehicle safety." See 49 USC §30111(a). In promulgating standards, the Secretary is to "consider relevant available motor vehicle safety information," and "consult" with other agencies, consider whether a standard is "reasonable, practicable, and appropriate," and consider "the extent to which" the standard will further the purposes of the law. The Secretary is to provide lead times of 180 days for each standard (unless doing otherwise "for good cause shown"). And the Secretary is to "establish and periodically review and update" a "5-year plan" for testing safety standards. See 49 USC §30111(b). The DOT has been busy. Under the leadership of many Secretaries, it has promulgated regulations on such matters as rectangular headlights, brakes, steering systems, tires, and sidelights.

Given all this activity, you may be surprised to learn that Congress has not "occupied the field" of product liability, or even suits against automakers. Yet the MVSA has had an impact in suits brought in state court against automakers. (Recall also Monique's suit against the maker of pesticides, where the California court concluded that federal law exempted defendant from a state failure-to-warn claim because defendant had gotten EPA approval of its labels (section C2, supra).) Let us consider just what the impact of federal law should be in a suit against an automaker raising issues of product defect that are addressed by federal law.

■ PROBLEM 1-A. "We're in Compliance with Federal Standards!"

While driving a 1987 Honda Accord in Washington, DC, Alexis Greer suffered serious injuries when she veered off the street and struck a large tree. Filing suit on her behalf (as she was a minor at the time), her parents alleged that the Honda was defective in that it lacked an airbag, and that this defect caused the injuries.

Honda sought dismissal of the suit, claiming that the common law product defect claim advanced by Greer was pre-empted by Standard 208, promulgated by the Department of Transportation pursuant to the MVSA. Standard 208, many pages in length, required a certain proportion of cars to have airbags, but not all cars. "We're in compliance with federal standards," Honda's lawyer told the court: "Standard 208 requires a certain proportion of our 1987 cars to have airbags, and we've done that." In other words, Honda complied with the Standard even though the car driven by Greer did not have an airbag. Honda relied on the "pre-emption clause" in the MVAS. That clause says that if a Standard is in effect, no state "shall have any authority either to establish, or to continue in effect" a safety standard relating to "the same aspect of performance" that is "not identical" to the federal standard.

Opposing Honda's position, Alexis Greer argued that compliance with Standard 208 did *not* immunize Honda from tort liability. Greer stressed that the MVSA has a "savings clause." The savings clause says that "compliance with" an applicable Standard "does not exempt any person from any liability under common law."

How do you think a court should rule on this matter? Does the pre-emption clause mean that Alexis Greer cannot recover because the state rule on product liability—and in this context the District of Columbia is considered to be a state—has been displaced (pre-empted) by federal law? Or does the savings clause mean that Alexis Greer should be allowed to go forward because her common law claim has been "saved," and compliance with federal law is no defense?

■ NOTES ON FEDERAL PRE-EMPTION OF STATE LAW

1. There is no need to keep you in suspense. The facts of Problem 1-A track a real case leading to a 5-4 opinion by the Supreme Court in which the majority concluded that pre-emption applied and that compliance with Standard 208 was a defense. See Geier v. American Honda Motor Company, 529 U.S. 861 (2000). You can look at the opinion if you're curious, but the point of this example is to get you to think about the relationship between state and federal law:

(a) We can start with the point that Congress clearly *can* regulate automobile safety because of its power under the Commerce Clause (quoted prior to the Problem). If Congress wants to, it can include language expressly saying that state law has no application to anything covered in a federal statute. In the real case, as in the Problem, Honda argued that the MVSA had done that. What are the benefits of this view?

(b) Congress can also put into statutes language that "saves" suits under state law. Why does Congress often do so? Plaintiffs in *Geier* argued that this clause controlled the case. What are the benefits of this view?

(c) Don't the pre-emption clause and the savings clause simply contradict one another? Why wouldn't a court simply conclude that they cannot both be given effect, and throw one of them out?

2. Traditionally, courts describe pre-emption issues as falling into three categories. In theory, "express" pre-emption is narrowest because it turns primarily on parsing language, which is specific. "Conflict" pre-emption is broader because it turns on assessing congressional purposes and deciding whether applying state law would undermine or defeat them. And "field" pre-emption is broadest, because it means the whole area is cut off from state law, and only federal law can apply. But the categories are not watertight, and all three turn on what Congress meant, which in turn is mainly affected by the words in the statute. Here are the categories:

(a) Express Pre-emption. Often Congress states expressly that federal law pre-empts state law, and the statute construed in *Geier* is an example (states cannot apply "any safety standard" differing from any applicable federal standard). Another example is the Cigarette Labeling and Advertising Act of 1965, which provides that "[n]o statement relating to smoking and health, other than the statement required by section 4 of this Act, shall be required" on cigarette packages or advertising. In the Public Health Cigarette Smoking Act of 1969, this clause was broadened to say that "[n]o requirement or prohibition based on smoking and health shall be imposed under State law with respect to the advertising or promotion of any cigarettes the packages of which are labeled in conformity with the provisions of this Act." See Cipollone v. Liggett Group, Inc., 505 U.S. 504, 515-517, 522-530 (1992) (these provisions pre-empt failure-to-warn claims based on labeling or advertising, but *not* claims based on breach of warranty, fraud and similar theories).

(b) Conflict Pre-emption. This kind of pre-emption does not rely on *express* language in federal statutes, but rather on the notion that state law cannot be allowed to frustrate the purpose of federal law, and the majority in *Geier* applied this notion. See also Buckman Company v. Plaintiffs' Legal Committee, 531 U.S. 341, 349-350 (2001) (invoking conflict pre-emption in blocking suit against consulting company that helped obtain FDA approval for orthopedic bone screws; suit rested on theory that defendant committed fraud against FDA, which conflicts with the "flexibility" that is a "critical component" of a statutory framework setting forth a "comprehensive scheme" for assessing such devices, along with provisions "aimed at detecting, deterring, and punishing false statements" during approval process).

(c) Field Pre-emption. "The scheme of federal regulation may be so pervasive as to make reasonable the inference that Congress left no room for the States to supplement it." See Rice v. Santa Fe Elevator Corp., 331 U.S. 218, 230, 233 (1947) ("strong language" in Warehouse Act makes it plain that federal licensee is "subject to regulation by one agency and one agency alone," eliminating dual system of regulation that previously existed). See also Norfolk Southern Railway Co. v. Shanklin, 529 U.S. 344, 354 (2000) (regulations of Secretary of Transportation specifying requirements of railway grade crossing signs, promulgated under Railroad Safety Act, cover whole subject of safety devices at federally funded grade crossings).

3. Advocates of the "law and economics" school would argue that *Geier* reached the right outcome. That approach emphasizes a "cost/benefit" analysis that can be applied with the aid of models and estimates of relative costs of different approaches. Many agree that the aim of tort law is to maximize product safety by transferring to manufacturers the costs of injuries caused by curable defects in their products. Followers of the law and economics approach would stress that letting a manufacturer "off the hook" for injuries caused by products that could be made safer will produce "underdeterrence," which lets dangerous conditions exist that could be corrected by changes in design or manufacturing, or by warnings. And they would stress that imposing liability when improvements cannot be made will produce "overdeterrence," which discourages or penalizes innovation and socially valuable goods. Finding the line between too little and too much deterrence is no easy task. Some argue that the very best way to locate that line is to look to the kind of regulation that the government produced in *Geier*. After all, if we are trying to figure out how much care is enough, peering into the future and imagining the kinds of accidents that might happen, how better to do that than to think carefully and promulgate safety regulations that try to do just that? If you compare *that* method of measuring the right amount of care with an "after-the-fact look back at an accident that has happened," isn't it clear that "hindsight" bias will affect judgment? If it is better to measure the right standard of care by "before-the-fact" regulation than by "after-the-fact" second-guessing, does it follow that *Geier* was rightly decided?

4. Opponents of the law and economics school argue that agencies often don't "get it right" *by themselves*, and that courts applying common law principles of tort law also have a role to play. In part, this view stresses that agencies are "captured" by the industry they're supposed to regulate and that the virtue of common law development is that it grows and adjusts to the realities of the world in incremental steps, and reflects practical wisdom born of experience. In *Geier*, Justice Breyer offered a lengthy account of the rulemaking process that led to the regulation in issue in that case. That process itself went on for several years, perhaps suggesting that even the legislative process can gradually accommodate and acclimate to modern realities, much like the processes of the common law.

5. Federal law has other effects on state courts: For example, the "automatic stay" provision of the Bankruptcy Code stops litigation against the bankrupt pending in any court, state and federal, when a bankruptcy petition is filed. See 11 USC §362. The purpose is to prevent other suits from depleting assets, so bankruptcy proceedings can do their job, which may involve reorganizing and adjusting debts so a company can continue in business, or perhaps dissolving it and distributing its assets among creditors and claimants. Another example is the "civil rights removal" statute, which allows certain defendants to remove, from state to federal court, a civil or criminal case brought against such defendants where they are "denied or cannot enforce" a law providing for "equal civil rights." See 28 USC §1443 (this provision is seldom used). You will also discover that the due process clause of the Fourteenth Amendment limits the "reach" of state court jurisdiction (taken up in Chapter 3).

CHAPTER 2

Remedies and Costs in Civil Suits

INTRODUCTION

One of the first things a lawyer considers in filing suit is what she should ask the court to do for her client. Sometimes the answer is obvious: We cannot restore what once was, so the only possible relief is damages. Sometimes courts provide injunctive relief—an order directing the defendant to do (or not do) something. And sometimes conduct is so bad—"malicious" or "willful," mean-spirited or purposefully harmful or uncaring—that courts (and juries) are persuaded to award punitive damages.

 ## A JUDICIAL REMEDIES

1. Provisional Remedies

In a bygone era, courts could help a plaintiff at the threshold of a lawsuit by seizing assets of the defendant on plaintiff's request. Seizure could mean freezing title or possession so defendant could not spend or convey what had been seized, or it could mean taking physical possession so defendant lost the use of it. Or seizure could involve placing a lien on property. Such "provisional remedies" were stopgap measures taken early, in anticipation that plaintiff would win (they could be undone if plaintiff abandoned the claim or defendant won). Courts can *still* enter temporary restraining orders, as happened in *Piphus* (Chapter 1B, supra), but rules governing pretrial seizure changed in the last decades of the twentieth century.

Provisional remedies in the form of property seizure intersected with doctrines relating to jurisdiction, commercial law, and property.[1] A common form of seizure involved "prejudgment attachment." Plaintiff obtained a writ, typically issued automatically by the court clerk for the asking. The writ directed the sheriff to attach property of the defendant. In the case of real property, the sheriff executed the writ by posting notice on the property and recording the writ, which appeared in title records as a lien. In the case of tangible personal property, such as an automobile, the sheriff could take physical possession and store it in a lot or warehouse. Enterprising claimants could attach intangible property, like a debt or obligation owed by an outsider to the defendant, or defendant's bank account or wages. In such cases, the writ of attachment became a writ of "garnishment," which denoted a seizure of property owned by the defendant but held by another. The writ told the outsider *not* to pay the defendant or honor his directions, but to pay the sheriff or hold the property subject to later direction.

The Court Limits Pretrial Seizures. In a series of cases, the Supreme Court decided that prejudgment seizure, without prior notice and hearing, violated due process. The first was Sniadach v. Family Finance Corp., 395 U.S. 337 (1969), which struck down a pretrial garnishment of defendant's wages. The case arose in an era of growing sensitivity to consumer rights, and the Court was impressed with the reality that debtors who borrow money from finance companies and default are likely to be out of money and in no position to resist demands for payment and penalties. Garnishment of wages, the Court said, "may as a practical matter drive a wage-earning family to the wall." Hence such garnishment, the Court concluded in *Sniadach*, is permissible only after notice and a hearing.

Sniadach left room for creditors to argue that garnishment of *wages* amounted to a special case, and that pretrial seizures of other property, without notice or hearing, could still pass muster. But in Fuentes v. Shevin, 407 U.S. 67 (1972), involving consolidated challenges to other forms of pretrial seizure, the Supreme Court extended *Sniadach*. In *Fuentes,* Firestone used a writ of "replevin" in Florida to repossess a stove and stereo bought on a conditional sales contract. In a companion case, a Pennsylvania sheriff used attachment to seize toys in the possession of his ex-wife. The Court found that these seizures, although differing on points of detail, were alike in their essential nature, so we can focus on the Florida writ of replevin. That writ required that the creditor file a complaint alleging entitlement to possession and post a security bond in the amount of double the value of the property, which would indemnify the buyer if repossession was wrongful. The

---

[1] Soon you will read landmark cases that established the principle that plaintiff may get jurisdiction over a defendant in this way. See Pennoyer v. Neff, 95 U.S. (5 Otto.) 714 (1877); Harris v. Balk, 198 U.S. 215 (1905) (Chapter 3A1, infra).

sheriff was to keep the items for three days, during which time the debtor could regain possession by posting a similar bond in the amount of double the value of the property. But there was no opportunity for preseizure notice or hearing, and failure to post a counterbond resulted in the property being delivered immediately to the creditor.

In a 4-3 decision (two Justices not participating), the Court in *Fuentes* disapproved both the Florida and the Pennsylvania procedures:

> The constitutional right to be heard is a basic aspect of the duty of government to follow a fair process of decisionmaking when it acts to deprive a person of his possessions. The purpose of this requirement is not only to ensure abstract fair play to the individual. Its purpose, more particularly, is to protect his use and possession of property from arbitrary encroachment—to minimize substantively unfair or mistaken deprivations of property, a danger that is especially great when the State seizes goods simply upon the application of and for the benefit of a private party. So viewed, the prohibition against the deprivation of property without due process of law reflects the high value, embedded in our constitutional and political history, that we place on a person's right to enjoy what is his, free of governmental interference.

> The requirement of notice and an opportunity to be heard raises no impenetrable barrier to the taking of a person's possessions. But the fair process of decision making that it guarantees works, by itself, to protect against arbitrary deprivation of property. For when a person has an opportunity to speak up in his own defense, and when the State must listen to what he has to say, substantively unfair and simply mistaken deprivations of property interests can be prevented. It has long been recognized that "fairness can rarely be obtained by secret, one-sided determination of facts decisive of rights. . . . [And n]o better instrument has been devised for arriving at truth than to give a person in jeopardy of serious loss notice of the case against him and opportunity to meet it." Joint Anti-Fascist Refugee Committee v. McGrath, 341 U.S. 123, 170-172 (Frankfurter, J., concurring).

> If the right to notice and a hearing is to serve its full purpose, then, it is clear that it must be granted at a time when the deprivation can still be prevented. At a later hearing, an individual's possessions can be returned to him if they were unfairly or mistakenly taken in the first place. Damages may even be awarded to him for the wrongful deprivation. But no later hearing and no damage award can undo the fact that the arbitrary taking that was subject to the right of procedural due process has already occurred. "This Court has not . . . embraced the general proposition that a wrong may be done if it can be undone." Stanley v. Illinois, 405 U.S. 645, 647.

> . . .

> The Florida and Pennsylvania prejudgment replevin statutes fly in the face of this principle. To be sure, the requirements that a party seeking a writ must first post a bond, allege conclusorily that he is entitled to specific goods, and open himself to possible liability in damages if he is wrong, serve to deter wholly unfounded applications for a writ. But those requirements are hardly a substitute for a prior hearing, for they test no more than the strength of the applicant's own

belief in his rights.[13] Since his private gain is at stake, the danger is all too great that his confidence in his cause will be misplaced. Lawyers and judges are familiar with the phenomenon of a party mistakenly but firmly convinced that his view of the facts and law will prevail, and therefore quite willing to risk the costs of litigation. Because of the understandable, self-interested fallibility of litigants, a court does not decide a dispute until it has had an opportunity to hear both sides—and does not generally take even tentative action until it has itself examined the support for the plaintiff's position. The Florida and Pennsylvania statutes do not even require the official issuing a writ of replevin to do that much.

The minimal deterrent effect of a bond requirement is, in a practical sense, no substitute for an informed evaluation by a neutral official. More specifically, as a matter of constitutional principle, it is no replacement for the right to a prior hearing that is the only truly effective safeguard against arbitrary deprivation of property. While the existence of these other, less effective, safeguards may be among the considerations that affect the form of hearing demanded by due process, they are far from enough by themselves to obviate the right to a prior hearing of some kind.

407 U.S. at 81-84. Elsewhere the Court concluded that even a temporary seizure was a deprivation of property under the Fourteenth Amendment, and that it made no difference that the defendants who were buyers under a conditional sales contract "lacked full legal title," since "property" for purposes of the Fourteenth Amendment "has never been interpreted to safeguard only the rights of undisputed ownership."

The *Fuentes* plurality, however, took pains to limit the holding, noting that seizure without notice and a hearing could still be justified in "extraordinary situations," citing the following examples: summary seizure to collect taxes, or "to meet the needs of a national war effort," or "to protect against the economic disaster of a bank failure," or "to protect the public from misbranded drugs and contaminated food." In these cases, the Court said, there were three distinguishing characteristics: First, seizure was "necessary to secure an important governmental or general public interest"; second, there was "a special need for very prompt action"; third, the State "kept strict control over its monopoly of legitimate force" (the person who initiated the seizure was "a government official"). The Court also said in footnotes that seizure of evidence under a search warrant was "quite a different matter" and that "attachment necessary to secure jurisdiction in state court" might also be a different matter.

Three dissenters in *Fuentes* saw the case differently. They stressed that both the buyer and the seller have interests in the property, and seemed to say that the schemes in place in Florida and Pennsylvania were fair. More

---

[13] They may not even test that much. For if an applicant for the writ knows that he is dealing with an uneducated, uninformed consumer with little access to legal help and little familiarity with legal procedures, there may be a substantial possibility that a summary seizure of property—however unwarranted—may go unchallenged, and the applicant may feel that he can act with impunity.

importantly, the dissenters argued that the likelihood of a "mistaken claim of default" was remote and that creditors have more incentive to make the transaction work than to make false claims, undertaking "the expense of instituting replevin actions and putting up bonds." In a footnote, the *Fuentes* plurality offered an answer: Perhaps it is "more efficient" to go forward without a hearing, but due process "is not intended to promote efficiency," and the Constitution "recognizes higher values than speed and efficiency." Finally, the dissenters warned that the constitutional holding could be vitiated by waiver provisions in consumer contracts, and that making repossession harder would diminish the availability of consumer credit or raise the cost.

The Court Retreats. In *Fuentes,* the Court appeared to adopt *Sniadach* across the board, making illegal virtually all pretrial seizures accomplished without notice or a hearing, unless justified by "extraordinary circumstances." That would mean civil litigants could not easily resort to such measures, except perhaps to get jurisdiction over absent defendants. In two later decisions, however, the Court retreated.

In Mitchell v. Grant, 416 U.S. 600 (1974), the Court *approved* a Louisiana procedure under which a court issued a writ of "sequestration" authorizing the sheriff to seize a refrigerator, range, and stereo without prior notice to the debtor, and without a hearing. The situation was not controlled by *Fuentes* because of certain safeguards, only one of which was in place in *Fuentes*. While *Mitchell* did not clearly say that all the safeguards are essential, the opinion mentions seven, and stresses many as critical. First, a *judge* (not a court clerk) issued the writ. Second, only a party holding a mortgage or lien could invoke the Louisiana procedure, so most sellers could use it (like Firestone in *Fuentes*), but not "unsecured claimants." Third, the Louisiana procedure was available only where the nature of the claim "clearly appear[ed] from specific facts" in a complaint or affidavit, suggesting that general allegations were not sufficient. Fourth, the Louisiana procedure was more focused than the schemes in *Fuentes,* since a Louisiana creditor could not merely *claim* defendant was at fault, but had to *show* title (which could be done with documentary proof). Fifth, the Louisiana procedure required the creditor to post a bond in double the value of the property (similar to *Fuentes*). Sixth, the Louisiana procedure *required* a hearing if defendant demanded one, in contrast to *Fuentes* (where defendants could post a counterbond, but no hearing was expressly required). If a hearing was demanded, plaintiff was required to prove "the grounds upon which the writ was issued." Seventh, there is a suggestion that the Louisiana procedure was justified by exigent circumstances—the creditor would lose its lien if the debtor sold the property while the creditor's suit was under way. (Probably, the same thing would have happened in *Fuentes,* since a consumer's sale of personal property in a noncommercial transaction destroys a security interest perfected by the party who sold the goods originally.)

In North Georgia Finishing, Inc. v. Di-Chem, 419 U.S. 601 (1975), the Court *disapproved* a Georgia garnishment. In *North Georgia Finishing*, the writ was issued by a clerk on the basis of a conclusory affidavit. The dispute involved commercial actors (not a claim by a retailer against consumers) and the amount frozen by the writ was large ($51,000 in defendant's bank account). The Georgia procedure was "vulnerable for the same reasons" as the procedures condemned in *Fuentes*, and *Mitchell* did not save it because *Mitchell* turned on the fact that the writ "was issuable only by a judge" on the filing of something "beyond merely conclusory allegations," and because the procedure approved in *Mitchell* "entitled the debtor to an immediate hearing." (Justice Stewart, who authored the opinion in *Fuentes*, complained in *Mitchell* that the Court had overruled *Fuentes*, but in *North Georgia Finishing* he added the wry comment that his report of the demise of *Fuentes* "seems to have been greatly exaggerated," citing Mark Twain's comment on reports of his own death.)

Where Are We? Taken as a whole, *Fuentes, Mitchell,* and *Di-Chem* suggest that pretrial seizures of property, without prior notice to the other side and opportunity for a hearing, can proceed only if certain formalities are observed. At the very least, it seems important that a judge issue the order and that a hearing be quickly available on demand by the defendant. Beyond these points, it is arguable that plaintiff must be required to post a bond in at least double the value of the property (a feature common to all three cases), and that supporting documents must be specific in their allegations, and perhaps the procedure must be limited to cases where the plaintiff claims a pre-existing interest in the property (as is true of secured creditors, including sellers who take a contractual security interest in the items sold, or retain title pending payment of the last installment). It is even arguable that these procedures can properly result in seizure only in exigent cases (where it appears that the defendant is likely to remove or destroy the property), but if this requirement exists, we can expect very few pretrial seizures, since it is hard to imagine that many plaintiffs can show that such a thing is likely to happen.

CONNECTICUT v. DOEHR

United States Supreme Court
501 U.S. 1 (1991)

[Justice WHITE delivered the unanimous opinion of the Court with respect to Parts I and III, and an opinion of the Court joined by all but Justice SCALIA with respect to Part II. In Part IV, Justice WHITE delivered an opinion in which Justices MARSHALL, STEVENS, and O'CONNOR join.]

This case requires us to determine whether a state statute that authorizes prejudgment attachment of real estate without prior notice or hearing, without a showing of extraordinary circumstances, and without a requirement that the person seeking the attachment post a bond, satisfies the Due Process Clause of the Fourteenth Amendment. We hold that, as applied to this case, it does not.

I

On March 15, 1988, petitioner John F. DiGiovanni submitted an application to the Connecticut Superior Court for an attachment in the amount of $75,000 on respondent Brian K. Doehr's home in Meriden, Connecticut. DiGiovanni took this step in conjunction with a civil action for assault and battery that he was seeking to institute against Doehr in the same court. The suit did not involve Doehr's real estate, nor did DiGiovanni have any pre-existing interest either in Doehr's home or any of his other property.

Connecticut law authorizes prejudgment attachment of real estate without affording prior notice or the opportunity for a prior hearing to the individual whose property is subject to the attachment. The State's prejudgment remedy statute provides, in relevant part:

> The court or a judge of the court may allow the prejudgment remedy to be issued by an attorney without hearing as provided in sections 52-278c and 52-278d upon verification by oath of the plaintiff or of some competent affiant, that there is probable cause to sustain the validity of the plaintiff's claims and (1) that the prejudgment remedy requested is for an attachment of real property. . . .

Conn. Gen. Stat. §52-278e (1991). The statute does not require the plaintiff to post a bond to insure the payment of damages that the defendant may suffer should the attachment prove wrongfully issued or the claim prove unsuccessful.

As required, DiGiovanni submitted an affidavit in support of his application. In five one-sentence paragraphs, DiGiovanni stated that the facts set forth in his previously submitted complaint were true; that "I was willfully, wantonly and maliciously assaulted by the defendant, Brian K. Doehr"; that "[s]aid assault and battery broke my left wrist and further caused an ecchymosis to my right eye, as well as other injuries"; and that "I have further expended sums of money for medical care and treatment." The affidavit concluded with the statement, "In my opinion, the foregoing facts are sufficient to show that there is probable cause that judgment will be rendered for the plaintiff."

On the strength of these submissions the Superior Court Judge, by an order dated March 17, found "probable cause to sustain the validity of the plaintiff's claim" and ordered the attachment on Doehr's home "to the value of $75,000." The sheriff attached the property four days later, on March 21. Only after this did Doehr receive notice of the attachment. He also had yet to be served with the complaint, which is ordinarily necessary for an action to commence in Connecticut. As the statute further required, the attachment notice informed Doehr that he had the right to a hearing: (1) to claim that no probable cause existed to sustain the claim; (2) to request that the attachment be vacated, modified, or dismissed or that a bond be substituted; or (3) to claim that some portion of the property was exempt from execution.

Rather than pursue these options, Doehr filed suit against DiGiovanni in Federal District Court, claiming that §52-278e(a)(1) was unconstitutional under the Due Process Clause of the Fourteenth Amendment. The District Court upheld the statute and granted summary judgment in favor of DiGiovanni. On appeal, a divided panel of the United States Court of Appeals for the Second Circuit reversed.[3] Judge Pratt, who wrote the opinion for the court, concluded that the Connecticut statute violated due process in permitting ex parte attachment absent a showing of extraordinary circumstances. "The rule to be derived from Sniadach v. Family Finance Corp., 395 U.S. 337 (1969) and its progeny, therefore, is not that postattachment hearings are generally acceptable provided that plaintiff files a factual affidavit and that a judicial officer supervises the process, but that a prior hearing may be postponed where exceptional circumstances justify such a delay, and where sufficient additional safeguards are present." This conclusion was deemed to be consistent with our decision in Mitchell v. W.T. Grant Co., 416 U.S. 600 (1974), because the absence of a preattachment hearing was approved in that case based on the presence of extraordinary circumstances.

A further reason to invalidate the statute, the court ruled, was the highly factual nature of the issues in this case. In *Mitchell,* there were "uncomplicated matters that len[t] themselves to documentary proof" and "[t]he nature of the issues at stake minimize[d] the risk that the writ [would] be wrongfully issued by a judge." Similarly, in Mathews v. Eldridge, 424 U.S. 319, 343-344 (1976), where an evidentiary hearing was not required prior to the termination of disability benefits, the determination of disability was "sharply focused and easily documented." Judge Pratt observed that in contrast the present case involved the fact-specific event of a fist fight and the issue of assault. He doubted that the judge could reliably determine probable cause when presented with only the plaintiff's version of the altercation. "Because the risk of a wrongful attachment is considerable under these circumstances, we conclude that dispensing with notice and opportunity for a hearing until after the attachment, without a showing of extraordinary circumstances, violates the requirements of due process." Judge Pratt went on to conclude that in his view, the statute was also constitutionally infirm for its failure to require

---

[3] The Court of Appeals invited Connecticut to intervene pursuant to 28 USC §2403(b) after oral argument. The State elected to intervene in the appeal and has fully participated in the proceedings before this Court.

the plaintiff to post a bond for the protection of the defendant in the event the attachment was ultimately found to have been improvident.

Judge Mahoney was also of the opinion that the statutory provision for attaching real property in civil actions, without a prior hearing and in the absence of extraordinary circumstances, was unconstitutional. He disagreed with Judge Pratt's opinion that a bond was constitutionally required. Judge Newman dissented from the holding that a hearing prior to attachment was constitutionally required and, like Judge Mahoney, disagreed with Judge Pratt on the necessity for a bond.

The dissent's conclusion accorded with the views of the Connecticut Supreme Court, which had previously upheld §52-278e(b). We granted certiorari to resolve the conflict of authority.

II

With this case we return to the question of what process must be afforded by a state statute enabling an individual to enlist the aid of the State to deprive another of his or her property by means of the prejudgment attachment or similar procedure. Our cases reflect the numerous variations this type of remedy can entail. In *Sniadach*, the Court struck down a Wisconsin statute that permitted a creditor to effect prejudgment garnishment of wages without notice and prior hearing to the wage earner. In Fuentes v. Shevin, 407 U.S. 67 (1972), the Court likewise found a due process violation in state replevin provisions that permitted vendors to have goods seized through an ex parte application to a court clerk and the posting of a bond. Conversely, the Court upheld a Louisiana ex parte procedure allowing a lienholder to have disputed goods sequestered in *Mitchell*. *Mitchell*, however, carefully noted that *Fuentes* was decided against "a factual and legal background sufficiently different . . . that it does not require the invalidation of the Louisiana sequestration statute." Those differences included Louisiana's provision of an immediate postdeprivation hearing along with the option of damages; the requirement that a judge rather than a clerk determine that there is a clear showing of entitlement to the writ; the necessity for a detailed affidavit; and an emphasis on the lienholder's interest in preventing waste or alienation of the encumbered property. In North Georgia Finishing, Inc. v. Di-Chem, 419 U.S. 601 (1975), the Court again invalidated an ex parte garnishment statute that not only failed to provide for notice and prior hearing but also failed to require a bond, a detailed affidavit setting out the claim, the determination of a neutral magistrate, or a prompt postdeprivation hearing.

These cases "underscore the truism that '[d]ue process,' unlike some legal rules, is not a technical conception with a fixed content unrelated to time, place and circumstances." Mathews v. Eldridge (quoting Cafeteria & Restaurant Workers v. McElroy, 367 U.S. 886, 895 (1961)). In *Mathews,* we drew upon our prejudgment remedy decisions to determine what process is due when the government itself seeks to effect a deprivation on its own initiative. That analysis resulted in the now familiar threefold inquiry requiring consideration of "the private interest that will be affected by the official action"; "the risk of an erroneous deprivation of such interest through the procedures used, and the probable value, if any, of additional or substitute safeguards"; and lastly "the Government's interest, including the function involved and the fiscal and administrative burdens that the additional or substitute procedural requirement would entail."

Here the inquiry is similar, but the focus is different. Prejudgment remedy statutes ordinarily apply to disputes between private parties rather than between an individual and the government. Such enactments are designed to enable one of the parties to "make use of state procedures with the overt, significant assistance of state officials," and they undoubtedly involve state action "substantial enough to implicate the Due Process Clause." Tulsa Professional Collection Services, Inc. v. Pope, 485 U.S. 478, 486 (1988). Nonetheless, any burden that increasing procedural safeguards entails primarily affects not the government, but the party seeking control of the other's property. For this type of case, therefore, the relevant inquiry requires, as in *Mathews*, first, consideration of the private interest that will be affected by the prejudgment measure; second, an examination of the risk of erroneous deprivation through the procedures under attack and the probable value of additional or alternative safeguards; and third, in contrast to *Mathews*, principal attention to the interest of the party seeking the prejudgment remedy, with, nonetheless, due regard for any ancillary interest the government may have in providing the procedure or forgoing the added burden of providing greater protections.

We now consider the *Mathews* factors in determining the adequacy of the procedures before us, first with regard to the safeguards of notice and a prior hearing, and then in relation to the protection of a bond.

III

We agree with the Court of Appeals that the property interests that attachment affects are significant. For a property owner like Doehr, attachment ordinarily clouds title; impairs the ability to sell or otherwise alienate the property; taints any credit rating; reduces the chance of obtaining a home equity loan or additional mortgage; and can even place an existing mortgage in technical default where there is an insecurity clause. Nor does Connecticut deny that any of these consequences occurs.

Instead, the State correctly points out that these effects do not amount to a complete, physical, or permanent deprivation of real property; their impact is less than the perhaps temporary total deprivation of household goods or wages. But the Court has never held that only such extreme deprivations trigger due process concern. To the contrary, our cases show that even the temporary or partial impairments to property rights that attachments, liens, and similar encumbrances entail are sufficient to merit due process protection. Without doubt, state procedures for creating and enforcing attachments, as with liens, "are subject to the strictures of due process."[4]

We also agree with the Court of Appeals that the risk of erroneous deprivation that the State permits here is substantial. By definition, attachment statutes premise a deprivation of property on one ultimate factual contingency—the award of damages to the plaintiff which the defendant may not be able to satisfy. See Ownbey v. Morgan, 256 U.S. 94, 104-105 (1921); R. Thompson & J. Sebert, Remedies: Damages, Equity and Restitution §5.01 (1983). For attachments before judgment, Connecticut mandates that this determination be made by means of a procedural inquiry that asks whether "there is probable cause to sustain the validity of the plaintiff's claim." Conn. Gen. Stat. §52-278e(a) (1991). The statute elsewhere defines the validity of the claim in terms of the likelihood "that judgment will be rendered in the matter in favor of the plaintiff." Conn. Gen. Stat. §52-278c(a)(2) (1991). What probable cause means in this context, however, remains obscure. The State initially took the position, as did the dissent below, that the statute requires a plaintiff to show the objective likelihood of the suit's success. Doehr, citing ambiguous state cases, reads the provision as requiring no more than that a plaintiff demonstrate a subjective good-faith belief that the suit will succeed. At oral argument, the State shifted its position to argue that the statute requires something akin to the plaintiff stating a claim with sufficient facts to survive a motion to dismiss.

We need not resolve this confusion since the statute presents too great a risk of erroneous deprivation under any of these interpretations. If the statute demands inquiry into the sufficiency of the complaint, or, still less, the plaintiff's good-faith belief that the complaint is sufficient, requirement of a complaint and a factual affidavit would permit a court to make these minimal determinations. But neither inquiry adequately reduces the risk of erroneous deprivation. Permitting a court to authorize attachment merely because the plaintiff believes the defendant is liable, or because the plaintiff can make out a facially valid complaint, would permit the deprivation of the defendant's

---

[4] Our summary affirmance in Spielman-Fond, Inc. v. Hanson's, Inc., 417 U.S. 901 (1974), does not control. In *Spielman-Fond*, the District Court held that the filing of a mechanic's lien did not amount to the taking of a significant property interest. A summary disposition does not enjoy the full precedential value of a case argued on the merits and disposed of by a written opinion. The facts of *Spielman-Fond* presented an alternative basis for affirmance in any event. Unlike the case before us, the mechanic's lien statute in *Spielman-Fond* required the creditor to have a pre-existing interest in the property at issue. As we explain below, a heightened plaintiff interest in certain circumstances can provide a ground for upholding procedures that are otherwise suspect.

property when the claim would fail to convince a jury, when it rested on factual allegations that were sufficient to state a cause of action but which the defendant would dispute, or in the case of a mere good-faith standard, even when the complaint failed to state a claim upon which relief could be granted. The potential for unwarranted attachment in these situations is self-evident and too great to satisfy the requirements of due process absent any countervailing consideration.

Even if the provision requires the plaintiff to demonstrate, and the judge to find, probable cause to believe that judgment will be rendered in favor of the plaintiff, the risk of error was substantial in this case. As the record shows, and as the State concedes, only a skeletal affidavit need be, and was, filed. The State urges that the reviewing judge normally reviews the complaint as well, but concedes that the complaint may also be conclusory. It is self-evident that the judge could make no realistic assessment concerning the likelihood of an action's success based upon these one-sided, self-serving, and conclusory sub-missions. And as the Court of Appeals said, in a case like this involving an alleged assault, even a detailed affidavit would give only the plaintiff's version of the confrontation. Unlike determining the existence of a debt or delinquent payments, the issue does not concern "ordinarily uncomplicated matters that lend themselves to documentary proof." *Mitchell.* The likelihood of error that results illustrates that "fairness can rarely be obtained by secret, one-sided determination of facts decisive of rights.... [And n]o better instrument has been devised for arriving at truth than to give a person in jeopardy of serious loss notice of the case against him and opportunity to meet it." Joint Anti-Fascist Refugee Comm. v. McGrath, 341 U.S. 123, 170-172 (1951) (Frankfurter, J., concurring).

What safeguards the State does afford do not adequately reduce this risk. Connecticut points out that the statute also provides an "expeditiou[s]" post-attachment adversary hearing, §52-278e(c); notice for such a hearing, §52-278e(b); judicial review of an adverse decision, §52-278l (a); and a double damages action if the original suit is commenced without probable cause, §52-568(a)(1). Similar considerations were present in *Mitchell,* where we upheld Louisiana's sequestration statute despite the lack of predeprivation notice and hearing. But in *Mitchell,* the plaintiff had a vendor's lien to protect, the risk of error was minimal because the likelihood of recovery involved uncomplicated matters that lent themselves to documentary proof, and the plaintiff was required to put up a bond. None of these factors diminishing the need for a predeprivation hearing is present in this case. It is true that a later hearing might negate the presence of probable cause, but this would not cure the temporary deprivation that an earlier hearing might have prevented. "The Fourteenth Amendment draws no bright lines around three-day, 10-day or 50-day deprivations of property. Any significant taking of property by the State is within the purview of the Due Process Clause." *Fuentes.*

Finally, we conclude that the interests in favor of an ex parte attachment, particularly the interests of the plaintiff, are too minimal to supply such a consideration here. The plaintiff had no existing interest in Doehr's real estate when he sought the attachment. His only interest in attaching the property was to ensure the availability of assets to satisfy his judgment if he prevailed on the merits of his action. Yet there was no allegation that Doehr was about to transfer or encumber his real estate or take any other action during the pendency of the action that would render his real estate unavailable to satisfy a judgment. Our cases have recognized such a properly supported claim would be an exigent circumstance permitting postponing any notice or hearing until after the attachment is effected. Absent such allegations, however, the plaintiff's interest in attaching the property does not justify the burdening of Doehr's ownership rights without a hearing to determine the likelihood of recovery.

No interest the government may have affects the analysis. The State's substantive interest in protecting any rights of the plaintiff cannot be any more weighty than those rights themselves. Here the plaintiff's interest is *de minimis*. Moreover, the State cannot seriously plead additional financial or administrative burdens involving predeprivation hearings when it already claims to provide an immediate post-deprivation hearing.

Historical and contemporary practices support our analysis. Prejudgment attachment is a remedy unknown at common law. Instead, "it traces its origin to the Custom of London, under which a creditor might attach money or goods of the defendant either in the plaintiff's own hands or in the custody of a third person, by proceedings in the mayor's court or in the sheriff's court." Ownbey [v. Morgan], 256 U.S. [94], at 104 (1921). Generally speaking, attachment measures in both England and this country had several limitations that reduced the risk of erroneous deprivation which Connecticut permits. Although attachments ordinarily did not require prior notice or a hearing, they were usually authorized only where the defendant had taken or threatened to take some action that would place the satisfaction of the plaintiff's potential award in jeopardy. Attachments, moreover, were generally confined to claims by creditors. As we and the Court of Appeals have noted, disputes between debtors and creditors more readily lend themselves to accurate ex parte assessments of the merits. Tort actions, like the assault and battery claim at issue here, do not. Finally, as we will discuss below, attachment statutes historically required that the plaintiff post a bond.

Connecticut's statute appears even more suspect in light of current practice. A survey of state attachment provisions reveals that nearly every State requires either a preattachment hearing, a showing of some exigent circumstance, or both, before permitting an attachment to take place. Twenty-seven States, as well as the District of Columbia, permit attachments only when some extraordinary circumstance is present. In such cases, preattachment hearings are not required but postattachment hearings are provided. Ten States permit attachment without the presence of such factors but require prewrit hearings unless one of those factors is shown. Six States limit attachments to extraordinary circumstance cases, but the writ will not issue prior to a hearing unless there is a showing of some even more compelling condition.[6] Three States always require a preattachment hearing. Only Washington, Connecticut, and Rhode Island authorize attachments without a prior hearing in situations that do not involve any purportedly heightened threat to the plaintiff's interests. Even those States permit ex parte deprivations only in certain types of cases: Rhode Island does so only when the claim is equitable; Connecticut and Washington do so only when real estate is to be attached, and even Washington requires a bond. Conversely, the States for the most part no longer confine attachments to creditor claims. This development, however, only increases the importance of the other limitations.

We do not mean to imply that any given exigency requirement protects an attachment from constitutional attack. Nor do we suggest that the statutory measures we have surveyed are necessarily free of due process problems or other constitutional infirmities in general. We do believe, however, that the procedures of almost all the States confirm our view that the Connecticut provision before us, by failing to provide a preattachment hearing without at least requiring a showing of some exigent circumstance, clearly falls short of the demands of due process.

IV

A

Although a majority of the Court does not reach the issue, Justices Marshall, Stevens, O'Connor, and I deem it appropriate to consider whether due process also requires the plaintiff to post a bond or other security in addition to requiring a hearing or showing of some exigency.

. . .

Without a bond, at the time of attachment, the danger that these property rights may be wrongfully deprived remains unacceptably high even with such safeguards as a hearing or exigency requirement. The need for a bond is especially apparent where extraordinary circumstances justify an attachment with no more than the plaintiff's ex parte assertion of a claim. We have already discussed how due process tolerates, and the States generally permit, the otherwise impermissible chance of erroneously depriving the defendant in such situations in light of the heightened interest of the plaintiff. Until a postattachment hearing, however, a defendant has no protection against damages

---

[6] [The Court notes that one State (Pennsylvania) has not had an attachment statute or rule since 1976.—Ed.]

sustained where no extraordinary circumstance in fact existed or the plaintiff's likelihood of recovery was nil. Such protection is what a bond can supply. Both the Court and its individual Members have repeatedly found the requirement of a bond to play an essential role in reducing what would have been too great a degree of risk in precisely this type of circumstance.

But the need for a bond does not end here. A defendant's property rights remain at undue risk even when there has been an adversarial hearing to determine the plaintiff's likelihood of recovery. At best, a court's initial assessment of each party's case cannot produce more than an educated prediction as to who will win. This is especially true when, as here, the nature of the claim makes any accurate prediction elusive. In consequence, even a full hearing under a proper probable-cause standard would not prevent many defendants from having title to their homes impaired during the pendency of suits that never result in the contingency that ultimately justifies such impairment, namely, an award to the plaintiff. Attachment measures currently on the books reflect this concern. All but a handful of States require a plaintiff's bond despite also affording a hearing either before, or (for the vast majority, only under extraordinary circumstances) soon after, an attachment takes place. Bonds have been a similarly common feature of other prejudgment remedy procedures that we have considered, whether or not these procedures also included a hearing.

The State stresses its double damages remedy for suits that are commenced without probable cause. This remedy, however, fails to make up for the lack of a bond. As an initial matter, the meaning of "probable cause" in this provision is no more clear here than it was in the attachment provision itself. Should the term mean the plaintiff's good faith or the facial adequacy of the complaint, the remedy is clearly insufficient. A defendant who was deprived where there was little or no likelihood that the plaintiff would obtain a judgment could nonetheless recover only by proving some type of fraud or malice or by showing that the plaintiff had failed to state a claim. Problems persist even if the plaintiff's ultimate failure permits recovery. At best, a defendant must await a decision on the merits of the plaintiff's complaint, even assuming that a §52-568(a)(1) action may be brought as a counterclaim. Settlement, under Connecticut law, precludes seeking the damages remedy, a fact that encourages the use of attachments as a tactical device to pressure an opponent to capitulate. An attorney's advice that there is probable cause to commence an action constitutes a complete defense, even if the advice was unsound or erroneous. Finally, there is no guarantee that the original plaintiff will have adequate assets to satisfy an award that the defendant may win.

Nor is there any appreciable interest against a bond requirement. Section 52-278e(a)(1) does not require a plaintiff to show exigent circumstances nor any pre-existing interest in the property facing attachment. A party must show more than the mere existence of a claim before subjecting an opponent to prejudgment proceedings that carry a significant risk of erroneous deprivation.

B

Our foregoing discussion compels the four of us to consider whether a bond excuses the need for a hearing or other safeguards altogether. If a bond is needed to augment the protections afforded by preattachment and postattachment hearings, it arguably follows that a bond renders these safeguards unnecessary. That conclusion is unconvincing, however, for it ignores certain harms that bonds could not undo but that hearings would prevent. The law concerning attachments has rarely, if ever, required defendants to suffer an encumbered title until the case is concluded without any prior opportunity to show that the attachment was unwarranted. Our cases have repeatedly emphasized the importance of providing a prompt postdeprivation hearing at the very least. Every State but one, moreover, expressly requires a preattachment or postattachment hearing to determine the propriety of an attachment.

The necessity for at least a prompt postattachment hearing is self-evident because the right to be compensated at the end of the case, if the plaintiff loses, for all provable injuries caused by the attachment is inadequate to redress the harm inflicted, harm that could have been avoided had an early hearing been held. An individual with an immediate need or opportunity to sell a property can neither do so, nor otherwise satisfy that need or recreate the opportunity. The same applies to a parent in need of a home equity loan for a child's education, an entrepreneur seeking to start a business on the strength of an otherwise strong credit rating, or simply a homeowner who might face the disruption of having a mortgage placed in technical default. The extent of these harms, moreover, grows with the length of the suit. Here, oral argument indicated that civil suits in Connecticut commonly take up to four to seven years for completion. Many state attachment statutes require that the amount of a bond be anywhere from the equivalent to twice the amount the plaintiff seeks. These amounts bear no relation to the harm the defendant might suffer even assuming that money damages can make up for the foregoing disruptions. It should be clear, however, that such an assumption is fundamentally flawed. Reliance on a bond does not sufficiently account for the harms that flow from an erroneous attachment to excuse a State from reducing that risk by means of a timely hearing.

If a bond cannot serve to dispense with a hearing immediately after attachment, neither is it sufficient basis for not providing a preattachment hearing in the absence of exigent circumstances even if in any event a hearing would be provided a few days later. The reasons are the same: a wrongful attachment can inflict injury that will not fully be redressed by recovery on the bond after a prompt postattachment hearing determines that the attachment was invalid.

Once more, history and contemporary practices support our conclusion. Historically, attachments would not issue without a showing of extraordinary circumstances even though a plaintiff bond was almost invariably required in addition. Likewise, all but eight States currently require the posting of a bond. Out of this 42-State majority, all but one requires a preattachment hearing, a showing of some exigency, or both, and all but one expressly require a post-attachment hearing when an attachment has been issued ex parte. This testimony underscores the point that neither a hearing nor an extraordinary circumstance limitation eliminates the need for a bond, no more than a bond allows waiver of these other protections. To reconcile the interests of the defendant and the plaintiff accurately, due process generally requires all of the above.

V

Because Connecticut's prejudgment remedy provision violates the requirements of due process by authorizing prejudgment attachment without prior notice or a hearing, the judgment of the Court of Appeals is affirmed, and the case is remanded to that court for further proceedings consistent with this opinion.

It is so ordered.

[An Appendix, charting the various state attachment statutes, is omitted.]

Chief Justice REHNQUIST, with whom Justice BLACKMUN joins, concurring in part and concurring in the judgment.

. . .

The Court's opinion is, in my view, ultimately correct when it bases its holding of unconstitutionality of the Connecticut statute as applied here on our [decisions in *Sniadach, Fuentes, Mitchell* and *Di-Chem*]. But I do not believe that the result follows so inexorably as the Court's opinion suggests. All of the cited cases dealt with personalty—bank or chattels—and each involved the physical seizure of the property itself, so that the defendant was deprived of its use. These cases, which represented something of a revolution in the jurisprudence of procedural due process, placed substantial limits on the methods by which creditors could obtain a lien on the assets of a debtor prior to judgment. But in all of them the debtor was deprived of the use and possession of the property. In the present case, on the other hand, Connecticut's prejudgment attachment on real property statute, which secures an incipient lien for the plaintiff, does not deprive the defendant of the use or possession of the property.

The Court's opinion therefore breaks new ground, and I would point out, more emphatically than the Court does, the limits of today's holding. In Spielman-Fond, Inc. v. Hanson's, Inc., 379 F. Supp. 997, 999 (Ariz. 1973), the District Court held that the filing of a mechanics' lien did not cause the deprivation of a significant property interest of the owner. We summarily affirmed that decision. Other courts have read this summary affirmance to mean that the mere imposition of a lien on real property, which does not disturb the owner's use or enjoyment of the property, is not a deprivation of property calling for procedural due process safeguards. I agree with the Court, however, that upon analysis the deprivation here is a significant one, even though the owner remains in undisturbed possession. "For a property owner like Doehr, attachment ordinarily clouds title; impairs the ability to sell or otherwise alienate the property; taints any credit rating; reduces the chance of obtaining a home equity loan or additional mortgage; and can even place an existing mortgage in technical default where there is an insecurity clause." Given the elaborate system of title records relating to real property which prevails in all of our States, a lienor need not obtain possession or use of real property belonging to a debtor in order to significantly impair its value to him.

But in *Spielman-Fond, Inc.*, supra, there was, as the Court points out, an alternative basis available to this Court for affirmance of that decision. Arizona recognized a pre-existing lien in favor of unpaid mechanics and materialmen who had contributed labor or supplies which were incorporated in improvements to real property. The existence of such a lien upon the very property ultimately posted or noticed distinguishes those cases from the present one, where the plaintiff had no pre-existing interest in the real property which he sought to attach. Materialman's and mechanic's lien statutes award an interest in real property to workers who have contributed their labor, and to suppliers who have furnished material, for the improvement of the real property. Since neither the labor nor the material can be reclaimed once it has become a part of the realty, this is the only method by which workmen or small businessmen who have contributed to the improvement of the property may be given a remedy against a property owner who has defaulted on his promise to pay for the labor and the materials. To require any sort of a contested court hearing or bond before the notice of lien takes effect would largely defeat the purpose of these statutes.

Petitioners in their brief rely in part on our summary affirmance in Bartlett v. Williams, 464 U.S. 801 (1983). That case involved a lis pendens, in which the question presented to this Court was whether such a procedure could be valid when the only protection afforded to the owner of land affected by the lis pendens was a postsequestration hearing. A notice of lis pendens is a well-established, traditional remedy whereby a plaintiff (usually a judgment creditor) who brings an action to enforce an interest in property to which the defendant has title gives notice of the pendency of such action to third parties;

the notice causes the interest which he establishes, if successful, to relate back to the date of the filing of the lis pendens. The filing of such notice will have an effect upon the defendant's ability to alienate the property, or to obtain additional security on the basis of title to the property, but the effect of the lis pendens is simply to give notice to the world of the remedy being sought in the lawsuit itself. The lis pendens itself creates no additional right in the property on the part of the plaintiff, but simply allows third parties to know that a lawsuit is pending in which the plaintiff is seeking to establish such a right. Here, too, the fact that the plaintiff already claims an interest in the property which he seeks to enforce by a lawsuit distinguishes this class of cases from the Connecticut attachment employed in the present case.

. . .

Justice SCALIA, concurring in part and concurring in the judgment.

Since the manner of attachment here was not a recognized procedure at common law, I agree that its validity under the Due Process Clause should be determined by applying the test we set forth in *Mathews*; and I agree that it fails that test. I join Parts I and III of the Court's opinion, and concur in the judgment of the Court.

■ NOTES ON PREJUDGMENT SEIZURE OF PROPERTY

1. In the state suit leading to federal litigation in *Doehr,* John DiGiovanni sought $3,422 in damages for battery. Brian Doehr and his wife Chris were flying kites in a park on a Saturday morning when DiGiovanni began hitting golf balls in their general direction. The two had words, and Doehr may have shoved DiGiovanni, who fell and sustained a broken wrist and injuries to his eye. Doehr's federal suit rested on 42 USC §1983. As you see, DiGiovanni's action in attaching Doehr's house was wrongful and violated Doehr's constitutional rights. Ultimately, Doehr recovered no damages because he couldn't persuade the court that DiGiovanni acted maliciously and without probable cause in pursuing the attachment. Doehr did recover "interim" attorneys' fees as "prevailing party" because he did prove that DiGiovanni violated the Constitution, but did not recover additional fees for litigating the damage claim that failed. See Doehr v. DiGiovanni, 863 F. Supp. 89 (D. Conn. 1994); Pinsky v. Duncan, 79 F.3d 306 (2d Cir. 1996). See also the discussion of this litigation in Robert Bone, *The Story of* Connecticut v. Doehr: *Balancing Costs and Benefits in Defining Procedural Rights, in* Civil Procedure Stories 159 (Kevin Clermont ed., 2d ed. 2008).

2. What happened in *Doehr* differs from *Fuentes* and *Mitchell* in that Brian Doehr retained possession of his home even after DiGiovanni attached it. Why isn't this difference enough to save the day for the plaintiff?

3. Think about the factors emphasized in *Mitchell* and *Di-Chem*. In *Doehr*, as in *Mitchell*, a judge issued the attachment. (Neither the statute in *Doehr* nor the Louisiana statute in *Mitchell* expressly required the judge to be personally involved.) Does this factor count in *Doehr*? In *Mitchell*, the claimant had a pre-existing property interest in the goods, but in *Doehr*, the plaintiff had no such interest. How does this factor count? In *Mitchell*, the Court stressed that detail was required in seeking the writ and the issues were narrow. How do these factors count in *Doehr*? In *Mitchell*, plaintiff had to post a bond of double the value of the property seized, but there was no such requirement in *Doehr*. How does this factor count? In *Mitchell*, defendant was entitled to a prompt post-seizure hearing, and the Connecticut statute in *Doehr* entitled the defendant to a hearing too. How does this factor count in *Doehr*?

4. In *Doehr*, only four Justices stand behind Part IV of the opinion, which concludes that due process requires plaintiff to post a bond and that a pre-attachment hearing *still* is necessary. Why both? What is the status of Part IV?

5. In *Doehr*, the Court invokes its decision in *Mathews v. Eldridge*, 424 U.S. 319, 334 (1976), which approved terminating disability benefits without a hearing. Pragmatism was the order of the day: Does administrative action require a right to be heard? The answer, according to *Mathews*, turns on (1) "the private interest that will be affected by the official action"; (2) "the risk of an erroneous deprivation of such interest through the procedures used, and the probable value, if any, of additional or substitute procedural safeguards"; and (3) "the Government's interest, including the function involved and the fiscal and administrative burdens that the additional or substitute procedural requirement would entail." Judge Richard A. Posner offers an interpretation of this three-factor standard. (Posner is one of the best known advocates of the "law and economics" school, in which legal rules are subjected to elaborate cost-benefit analyses.) Posner reads *Mathews* to mean that due process is denied whenever $B > PL$, where B refers to the burden or cost of the procedural safeguard, P refers to the probability of error without the safeguard, and L refers to the size of the loss if an error is committed. Consider these comments about the problem examined in *Mathews*:

> Of course . . . it is rarely possible (or at least efforts are not made) to quantify the terms [set out in *Mathews*]. But the formula is valuable even when used qualitatively rather than quantitatively. Suppose, for example, that the issue is whether the owner of an apparently abandoned car should be notified, and given an opportunity for a hearing, *before* the car is towed away and sold for scrap. The chance that the car wasn't really abandoned, but broke down or was stolen, is not trivial, and the cost of a hearing is modest relative to the value of the car; so maybe, as most courts have held, the owner should be entitled to a hearing. But suppose we are speaking not of abandoned but of illegally parked cars. Since the

cars are not about to be destroyed, the deprivation (L) is much less than in the case of the abandoned car. The probability of error [denoted as P in the suggested formula] is also much lower, because ordinarily the determination of whether a car is illegally parked is cut and dried. And the cost of a predeprivation hearing [denoted as B in the suggested formula] is very high; if the owner has to be notified before the car is towed, he'll remove it and the deterrent effect of towing will be eliminated. So courts hold that due process does not require a predeprivation hearing in the case of illegally parked cars.

Richard A. Posner, Economic Analysis of Law §21.1 (5th ed. 1998). See also City of Los Angeles v. David, 538 U.S. 715 (2003) (denying damage claim after plaintiff's car was towed from "no parking" zone, where plaintiff claimed that the sign was obscured by trees; plaintiff claimed he was entitled to a hearing within 5 days, but the Court concluded that a hearing 27 days after the fact was fast enough).

6. Since *Doehr* involved a private claim rather than government action, applying the *Mathews* three-factor standard requires adjustment. Thus *Doehr* refers to the "private interest" (what defendant stands to lose if the property is seized), the "risk of erroneous deprivation" (probability that the seizure is a mistake because plaintiff lacks a meritorious case), and "the interest of the party seeking the prejudgment remedy" (what plaintiff stands to gain by seizing the property). Borrowing from Posner's economic analysis, one might use a different formula to analyze *Doehr*. Allow prehearing seizure of property only if $(P_r)(EV_p) > (P_w)(EV_d)$. P_r is the probability that plaintiff is entitled to the property (seizure is right); EV_p is the economic value of seizure to the plaintiff; P_w is the probability that plaintiff is not entitled to the property (seizure is wrong), which is sometimes expressed as $1 - P_r$ (probability of being wrong is one minus the probability of being right); EV_d is the economic cost of the seizure to the defendant. See Posner, supra, §21.4. Suppose the risk of error is high: Then P_r might be .6 and P_w might be .4, meaning that 60 percent of the time plaintiffs, acting on their own and without the scrutiny of a hearing, are entitled to the property they seize, but 40 percent of the time they are wrong. Suppose the value of seizure to plaintiff is $75,000 (damages sought by the complaint in *Doehr*), since defendant has no other assets and is planning to sell the house and abscond with the proceeds. Suppose the cost of the seizure to the defendant is $120,000, which represents the value of the investment opportunity he will lose if he cannot raise the money now by selling his house. The question is whether $(P_r)(EV_p) > (P_w)(EV_d)$? Plugging the numbers in, the question is whether $(.6)(\$75,000) > (.4)(\$120,000)$, and the answer is no ($45,000 is not greater than $48,000), so the seizure should not be allowed.

7. If it is implausible to require a hearing every time a public agency takes action that has negative impact on a property right, it is hard to fault the approach of *Mathews*. As an alternative, one might give Congress or state legislatures a free hand to determine such matters, as the Court sometimes seems to do. See Ingraham v. Wright, 430 U.S. 651 (1977) (in context of corporal punishment in school, giving great weight to "legislative judgment" declining to establish safeguards). But *Mathews* obviously goes in the opposite direction, and indeed *Mathews* can be understood as inviting each Justice to adopt a subjective (arguably humane) view of relative value:

> Assume that each of three individuals alleges a violation of due process rights. The first, an electric utility, claims that it was arbitrarily deprived of ten million dollars through a decision of the regulatory agency. The second, a very successful jockey, alleges that the racing commission arbitrarily suspended him for fifteen days, thereby causing him to lose fifty thousand dollars. The third individual is an impoverished widow with four young children who argues that she was arbitrarily deprived of two hundred dollars in welfare payments.

See Richard J. Pierce, Jr., Sidney A. Shapiro & Paul R. Verkuil, Administrative Law and Process §6.3 (3d ed. 1999) (courts do not and should not resolve due process issues by valuing the utility's stake as 200 times that of the jockey and 50,000 times that of the widow; instead, courts "value the adverse impact of agency action subjectively"). Is the law and economics approach still useful if courts are to engage in "subjective" judgments about the situation of widows?

2. Damages

Often plaintiff seeks a compensatory award (damages). In personal injury suits for losses caused by tortious misconduct, like negligent driving or making defective products or committing medical malpractice, damages include economic loss and what the law calls "pain and suffering." Economic loss includes compensation for the interruption in ordinary living caused by the injury. The most common instance is lost wages or earnings, but the category also includes lost or diminished *future earning capacity* and, for people who are not employed, the value of lost or diminished productive time, which may be calculated in terms of household services or realistic opportunities in the employment market. Economic loss also includes medical expenses ("medical specials"), which include doctor and hospital bills, medication, and prosthetic devices. Pain and suffering refers to mental, emotional, and physical anguish, where deciding the amount involves a subjective judgment.

Of course, damages also include property loss. If plaintiff loses her house to fire, or her truck is damaged in an accident, she can recover for the loss of such items. If the cause of the loss is tortious misconduct (defendant negligently started the fire or negligently drove the car that destroyed plaintiff's truck), damages are computed by reference to either the "diminished value rule" or the "repair or replacement rule." Under the former, damages are the difference between the value of the land with and without the house, or the value of the truck before the accident compared with its value afterward. Under the latter, damages are the cost of repairing or building a similar house or repairing or buying a similar truck. Sometimes these measures produce the same result, but often they produce different results, and then the question arises whether plaintiff must be satisfied with the lower measure or can demand the higher. See generally 1 Dobbs, Law of Remedies §5.14 (2d ed. 1993).

Property loss may be incurred in contract cases too, as might happen if plaintiff doesn't receive parts that he ordered, or gets the parts but they do not conform to specifications, or if he hires someone to construct or repair a house or building and the job is done badly. If plaintiff doesn't receive the parts, damages are usually calculated as the difference between the contract price and the price plaintiff must pay to acquire substantially the same things elsewhere. (If plaintiff paid in advance, he can also recover the prepayment.) If he receives nonconforming parts (defective or not what the contract specifies), damages could be the difference in value between what he got and what he contracted for, or the cost of bringing the parts received up to snuff, or the cost of conforming goods if plaintiff cannot use what he got (which would ordinarily mean that plaintiff returns the defective or nonconforming parts). If defendant did not properly build the house or building, damages might be the cost of completion or the difference between the value of a properly completed house or building and the value of the one actually constructed.

In contract cases, damage recovery is often complicated by the appearance of "consequential damages." If, for example, the lost parts or badly built structure causes plaintiff to be unable to realize expected business profits (the parts were components in products that plaintiff could not make or sell when the shipment failed, or the building was to be a store or restaurant that could not be used as planned), the question arises whether plaintiff may recover these additional losses. This is the problem made famous in Hadley v. Baxendale, 9 Ex. 341, 156 Eng. Rep. 145 (1854), where the owner of a flour mill hired defendant to deliver the mill shaft to Greenwich to be used as the pattern for a new shaft. The carrier promised to make delivery the next day, but delayed for many days, and the mill could not operate, costing plaintiff his profits for that period. Even though the parties had discussed the situation, the reviewing court concluded that plaintiff could not recover for lost profits because they were not in "contemplation of the parties" at the time of contracting.

In general, the rule of *Hadley* is followed in American courts today, and it means that consequential damages are often not recoverable in breach-of-contract cases. The rule of *Hadley* stands behind the principle in FRCP 9(g), which says that claims for any "item of special damages," which clearly includes consequential damages, must be "specifically stated" in the complaint.

Damage recoveries do not end with personal injuries, pain and suffering, lost income, property loss, and consequential damages for breach of contract. There are many other kinds. Recall the *Piphus* case, where the Court approved damage recovery for deprivation of the right to be heard. Consider defamation cases, where plaintiffs recover for injury to reputation, employment discrimination suits where claimants recover for denials of promotion or job opportunities, and suits for copyright infringement, unfair competition, or antitrust violations where recoveries may be had for various kinds of lost opportunities.

Statutes in every state permit a married person to recover damages for wrongful death of a spouse. Under these statutes, survivors may sue for economic damages in the form of loss of support and services, such as providing for an education and homemaking services. While some of these statutes *only* cover such loss, most now authorize claims for loss of society: This category includes comfort and affection, companionship, moral support, and sexual intimacy.[2] Most states also have "survival" statutes, which allow suits to go forward on behalf of the estate of the deceased victim (without such statutes these claims would die with the victim) and authorize recovery of anything the victim could have recovered if he had lived. Typically, these statutes also ensure that if the *tortfeasor* has died, claims by survivors or estates of the victim can go forward against the estate of the tortfeasor.

Clearly, damage recovery is high on the list of remedies in the mind of every lawyer who tries lawsuits. The subject of damages is vast, and books and courses deal with the subject in detail. Consider now a "cutting edge" case, in which plaintiff claims that defendant committed a tort that puts the plaintiff at increased risk of ailment or death, but where it is not at all clear that the victim has incurred any *present* or *actual* damages that can be measured or assessed in the usual way.

ALEXANDER v. SCHEID

Supreme Court of Indiana
726 N.E.2d 272 (2000)

BOEHM, Justice.

[Plaintiffs JoAnn Alexander and her husband Jack sue Dr. Kevin Scheid and Orthopaedics Indianapolis [Orthopedics] for medical malpractice. The complaint alleges that Scheid failed properly to follow up on a report describing a chest X-ray of JoAnn taken in June 1993, in preparation for hip surgery. The report indicated a "density" in her lungs and suggested that "comparison with old films" would be valuable. JoAnn was then 60 years old.

In spring 1994, JoAnn began spitting up blood. She went to another doctor and had a second X-ray, which revealed "a large mass on the upper right lobe of the right lung." A biopsy in May 1994 led to a diagnosis of "non-small cell lung cancer." The cancer had metastasized to a lymph node in her chest, and to the bronchial margin, so surgery to remove the tumor could not effect a complete cure. JoAnn underwent chemotherapy and radiation treatment, and achieved remission in October 1994.

---

[2] These statutes may allow parents and children to recover for appropriate elements of loss of society. Even without such statutes, tort law often allows a spouse to recover for "loss of consortium" if the other spouse is injured by a third party, and for loss of services such as homemaking, home maintenance, and child care.

In Count 1, Joann alleged that Scheid and Orthopedics were negligent in failing to follow up on the 1993 X-ray, leading to (a) permanent injuries requiring extensive medical care, (b) increased risk of harm and decreased chance for long-term survival ("loss of chance"), including loss of the possibility of successful removal of the tumor, (c) medical expenses and loss of earning capacity, and (d) severe emotional distress. In Count 2, Jack Alexander alleged loss of consortium. JoAnn asserts that in the months following the 1993 X-ray she suffered deterioration of overall health (exhaustion, pneumonia-like symptoms, and a run-down feeling), specific symptoms (spitting up blood, increased tumor size and metastasis), damage to healthy lung tissue and lung collapse, and reduced prospect of successful treatment.

Depositions by three doctors addressed the medical situation. That testimony suggested that JoAnn's cancer was in Stage I in June 1993, but had advanced to Stage IIIa in May 1994, and the probability of long-term survival had declined significantly.

Scheid and Orthopedics moved for summary judgment, arguing that JoAnn had suffered no compensable injury in light of her remission. The trial court agreed, and awarded summary judgment for defendants. The Court of Appeals affirmed, concluding that Restatement of Torts §323 does not allow recovery for wrongs that increase the risk of harm unless that harm has come to pass. It thought that JoAnn had no present physical injury, and that in the absence of such injury the "modified impact rule" does not permit recovery for negligent infliction of emotional distress.

This case raises the question whether a claim for medical malpractice may be asserted if the injury has not come to its full potential, and may never do so. The Court concludes that such a claim may be pursued.]

This case raises four questions. (1) Does Indiana law permit JoAnn to recover for an increased risk of incurring a life shortening disease under the "loss of chance" doctrine or otherwise? (2) If so, what is the appropriate measure of damages? (3) Has JoAnn suffered an impact that would allow her to recover for negligent infliction of emotional distress under the "modified impact rule?" (4) May JoAnn maintain a cause of action for the aggravation to date of her lung cancer?

. . .

I. DECREASED LIFE EXPECTANCY

A. Issues Raised Under the Rubric "Loss of Chance"

"Loss of chance," also often referred to as "increased risk of harm," is usually traced back to this frequently quoted passage from Hicks v. United States:

> When a defendant's negligent action or inaction has effectively terminated a person's chance of survival, it does not lie in the defendant's mouth to raise conjectures as to the measure of the chances that he has put beyond the

possibility of realization. If there was any substantial possibility of survival and the defendant has destroyed it, he is answerable.

368 F.2d 626, 632 (4th Cir. 1966) (quoted in Mayhue v. Sparkman, 653 N.E.2d 1384, 1387 (Ind. 1995)). The term "loss of chance" has been applied to a number of related situations. These include: (1) an already ill patient suffers a complete elimination of an insubstantial or substantial probability of recovery from a life-threatening disease or condition; (2) a patient survives, but has suffered a reduced chance for a better result or for complete recovery; and (3) a person incurs an increased risk of future harm, but has no current illness or injury. The first of these was addressed by this Court in *Mayhue*. The Alexanders now present the second, which, like the first, typically arises in the context of a claim of negligent health care. The third commonly arises in connection with claims of exposure to toxic substances, where no adverse results have yet emerged.

These cases pose a number of separate but sometimes interrelated issues. First, many courts initially address the issue as one of causation. *Mayhue* took the view that under traditional medical malpractice theory, when a patient's chance of recovering from a disease is already less than fifty percent, it can never be said that the doctor's malpractice was the proximate cause of the ultimate death. Accordingly, recovery under traditional tort standards of causation is barred under those circumstances. This approach views the injury as the ultimate adverse result of the disease, which may be death, but may also be other conditions (paralysis, blindness, etc.).

Just as it is difficult to find causation where the harm is already more than likely to occur, it seems odd to speak of a causal relationship between a defendant's act or omission and an as yet unknown ultimate result. Although an act of malpractice may reduce a patient's chances for survival or for obtaining a better result, this is simply a statistical proposition based on the known experience of a group of persons thought to be similarly situated (in JoAnn's case, persons with four centimeter nodes in the lungs). In any given case, however, the plaintiff's ultimate injury either does or does not occur. Thus, if full recovery is awarded based on an appraisal of causation (or greater than fifty percent probability), the plaintiff who later beats the odds may be over-compensated for an injury that never ultimately emerges. Similarly, the plaintiff who has a less than fifty percent chance, but nonetheless does ultimately bear the full brunt of the disease, may be undercompensated.

One way to deal with this problem is to permit multiple suits as different injuries develop, but that approach has several shortcomings, including the generation of multiple litigation and the attendant costs of that litigation. Delaying suit is another possibility, but that fails altogether to compensate for the very real pain and distress that accompanies an uncertain but probable serious or fatal condition. Delaying suit for medical malpractice in Indiana also has a distinct disadvantage. Given the occurrence-based limitations period for Indiana's medical malpractice claims and our holding that the Indiana Constitution prohibits barring only claims that have accrued but are unknowable, a person in JoAnn's shoes may be forever barred if the claim cannot be presented until the disease recurs.

These factors argue in favor of permitting the Alexanders to bring their claims now. If this is to be done, however, there are further complexities to address. First, there is disagreement as to the elements of recoverable damages. Some courts purporting to address "loss of chance" allow recovery only for medical expenses, lost earnings, or loss of consortium, see, e.g., Roberts v. Ohio Permanente Medical Group, Inc., 668 N.E.2d 480, 484-85 (Oh. 1996) (in loss of chance cases, damages are recoverable for underlying injury or death). Others have explicitly allowed recovery for what the doctrine's name suggests: the loss of the chance itself, see United States v. Anderson, 669 A.2d 73, 76 (Del. 1995) (citing cases). If a lost chance is to be compensable, its valuation also presents issues. Damages may be assessed for the full amount of the injury, if the full extent of the physical injury is already known. See Weymers v. Khera, 563 N.W.2d 647, 653 (Mich. 1997) (citing cases from jurisdictions that assess full damages when plaintiff has established that defendant's negligence increased plaintiff's risk of harm). Other courts have attempted to assess the damages in proportion to the likelihood that the doctor's negligence caused (or will cause) an injury. See, e.g., McKellips v. Saint Francis Hosp., Inc., 741 P.2d 467, 475-76 (Okla. 1987) (holding, where decedent's fatal heart attack was misdiagnosed as gastritis, that loss of chance damages must be limited to "those proximately caused from a defendant's breach of duty").

Finally, if damages are awardable for the increased risk of an injury that has not yet occurred, the court faces the difficult task of putting a dollar amount on an as yet unknown loss. The Alexanders' claim here presents that issue as to the ultimate recurrence of the cancer. They also assert current injury in the form of the cancer's metastasizing, and the anxiety generated by the prospect of future recurrence.

B. Mayhue v. Sparkman

In *Mayhue*, this Court held that Section 323 of the Restatement of Torts was the appropriate mode of analysis of a claim for injuries that had been sustained (the patient had died), but which were more likely than not to have occurred even in the absence of any negligence (the patient's ultimate injury was more probable than not before treatment). Section 323, "Negligent Performance of Undertaking to Render Services," states:

> One who undertakes, gratuitously or for consideration, to render services to another which he should recognize as necessary for the protection of the other's

person or things, is subject to liability to the other for physical harm resulting from his failure to exercise reasonable care to perform his undertaking if,

> (a) his failure to exercise reasonable care increases the risk of such harm, or
>
> (b) the harm is suffered because of the other's reliance upon the undertaking.

Specifically, under Section 323, a jury may consider, "once the plaintiff proves negligence and an increase in the risk of harm, . . . whether the medical malpractice was a substantial factor in causing the harm suffered by the plaintiff." Section 323's formulation, by its terms, presupposes that physical harm has resulted from the negligent care. In *Mayhue*, because the patient had died, the ultimate physical harm was already known. We held that the plaintiff's spouse could . . . maintain his cause of action for loss of consortium even though the experts agreed that, in the absence of the defendant's negligence, it was still more likely than not that the plaintiff would have died. We distinguished Section 323 from what was dubbed a "pure loss of chance" doctrine, which compensates for the loss of chance itself and not for the plaintiff's physical injury that was incurred but likely even before the defendant's act or omission. . . .

Mayhue left unresolved the issue presented by the Alexanders' claim. . . . [H]ere the issue is whether a reduced chance of survival, which mathematically equates to a decrease in life expectancy, is itself a compensable injury. If it is, a plaintiff may recover for this injury, independently of whether the plaintiff has or has not actually beaten the odds to date.

C. "Loss of Chance" as an Independent Injury

Causation and injury are sometimes described together as the collective third element of a medical malpractice claim. . . . Causation and injury are distinct, however, and we are confronted with this distinction here.

We think that loss of chance is better understood as a description of the injury than as either a term for a separate cause of action or a surrogate for the causation element of a negligence claim. If a plaintiff seeks recovery specifically for what the plaintiff alleges the doctor to have caused, i.e., a decrease in the patient's probability of recovery, rather than for the ultimate outcome, causation is no longer debatable. Rather, the problem becomes one of identification and valuation or quantification of that injury. We view the issue presented by JoAnn's claim as whether a plaintiff may recover for an increased risk of harm, here a decreased life expectancy, caused by a doctor's negligence, before the ultimate consequences are known. Because in this case the ultimate injury is death, the increased risk of that result is a decrease in life expectancy. Although loss of chance could also be applied as a label for this injury, we do not view recognizing this injury as a deviation from traditional tort principles. Rather, in this context it is nothing more than valuation of an item of damages that is routinely valued in other contexts. . . . In Dayton Walther Corp. v. Caldwell, 402 N.E.2d 1252, 1256 (Ind. 1980), this Court held that the trial court did not err in overruling an objection to evidence of the increased risk of meningitis and epilepsy caused by the defendant's negligence. We concluded that: "To hold otherwise would virtually wipe out any appraisal by an expert medical witness as to an estimate of permanent future impairments." Scheid and Orthopedics attempt to distinguish *Caldwell*, noting that in *Caldwell* the plaintiff had, as of trial, already suffered one bout of meningitis. Meningitis was one of the two ultimate potential effects, and even as to meningitis the ultimate consequences were not yet known. *Caldwell* thus foreshadowed recognition of compensation for increased risk of yet unknown but serious consequences.

A number of jurisdictions allow recovery for negligence that has "increased the risk of harm," even where the full ramifications of the defendant's actions are not yet known. [The court cites many cases, including Boryla v. Pash, 960 P.2d 123, 127 (Colo. 1998) (error to direct verdict for defendant in view of evidence that three-month delay in diagnosing breast cancer could have increased risk of recurrence); Petriello v. Kalman, 576 A.2d 474, 484-485 (Conn. 1990) (approving instruction on compensation for increased likelihood that plaintiff would suffer bowel obstruction).]

More specifically, many jurisdictions have recognized a decrease in life expectancy as a cognizable injury. [The court cites many cases, including United States v. Anderson, 669 A.2d 73, at 78 (Del. 1995) (recovery for shortened life expectancy due to increased risk of a recurrence of testicular cancer); Davison v. Rini, 686 N.E.2d 278, 283-284 (Ohio App. 1996) (recognizing shortened life expectancy as cognizable injury where 85 percent chance of full recovery was reduced to 25 percent chance of surviving five years).]

Here, JoAnn has pointed to evidence that would support a finding of both present injury and increased risk of harm. We agree with the authorities that find these sufficient to maintain a cause of action for an increased risk of harm. JoAnn has characterized defendants' actions as having reduced her chance for long-term survival and extinguished the chance for successful removal of her tumor. The doctors testified that JoAnn's chances of complete recovery, sixty to eighty percent in June of 1993, had dropped to a ten to thirty percent chance of surviving five years by May of 1994. JoAnn has suffered physical injuries, including the growth of a cancerous tumor, the destruction of healthy lung tissue, and the collapse of a lung.[11] . . .

In some cases an "intangible" loss may be as great an injury as any that a plaintiff could suffer. JoAnn must live under constant fear that at any time she

---

[11] Scheid and Orthopedics maintain that the lung collapse was due to JoAnn's history as a smoker, and not lung cancer.

may suffer a recurrence of her lung cancer. If that occurs, her doctors have testified that she has no chance of survival. This is not too remote or speculative an injury to preclude recovery, and JoAnn should not be forced to wait until she has suffered a relapse to proceed with a cause of action for what is essentially a daily threat of impending death, or to wait until her husband, on her behalf, is left with a wrongful death claim. As already noted, given the occurrence-based statute of limitations for medical malpractice, these future claims may face substantial obstacles. Money is an inadequate substitute for a period of life, but it is the best a legal system can do. The alternative is to let a very real and very serious injury go uncompensated even if due to negligent treatment. Faced with that choice, we hold that JoAnn has stated a viable cause of action and presented evidence sufficient to defeat summary judgment. Specifically, . . . we hold that JoAnn may maintain a cause of action in negligence for this increased risk of harm, which may be described as a decreased life expectancy or the diminished probability of long-term survival.

Here, we also have an injury that often accompanies a delay in diagnosis—the invasion of healthy tissue by a tumor or other growth. Accordingly, this case does not present the issue whether a plaintiff must have incurred some physical injury as a result of the defendant's negligence in order to recover for an increased risk of harm. Some courts have concluded, particularly in the loss of chance context, that the loss must be "substantial" before it is compensable. We see no obvious method of quantifying that test.[14] Because we measure damages by probabilizing the injury, the likelihood that plaintiffs will bring claims for trivial reductions in chance of recovery seems small. If, in the future, we face a volume of insignificant claims, perhaps such a rule will become necessary. For now, we are content to rely on basic economics to deter resort to the courts to redress remote probabilities or insubstantial diminutions in the likelihood of recovery.

D. Valuation of the Injury

We have referred to a "reduced probability of survival" and "diminished life-expectancy" as two terms for the same concept. This requires some explanation. In the Alexanders' case, let us assume the jury concludes from the expert testimony that before the failure to diagnose she had a seventy percent chance of full recovery and a normal life expectancy. As already noted, this is a statistical proposition that seventy of 100 patients with JoAnn's initial condition will have a normal lifetime. To take the simplest example first, assume that there is a 100% chance of successful treatment if there were no negligence.

---

[14] Judge Posner, in dissent, has argued forcefully that an increased risk of harm, to any extent, should be compensable. See DePass v. United States, 721 F.2d 203, 206-10 (7th Cir. 1983). Allowing recovery for the lost chance, he argues, furthers an important goal of tort law — putting the victim in as near a position as he would have been before harmed.

Leaving aside any other individual factors, the patient's life expectancy is the median of our collective experience as to the age at death of persons of her age and gender. Otherwise stated, a life expectancy is no more than the composite of the remaining lives of a large number of people, some of whom will die the next day and some of whom will become nonagenarians.

Here, at the time of diagnosis, the expert testimony put her chance of survival for five years at approximately twenty percent. To be comparable to her pre-negligence expectancy, it must be converted, which we assume can be done, into a comparable median lifetime or expectancy. A person with a normal life expectancy has only a fifty percent chance of attaining that expectancy. Even if we reduce both the "before" and "after" numbers to comparables, the problem identified earlier remains: expectancy is itself a statistical proposition, and compensating on the basis of expectancy will either overcompensate or undercompensate depending on how long the plaintiff actually lives.

Finally, if we take as our starting point not a normal life expectancy, but the expectancy of someone with an already heightened risk, the analysis is the same, but both the "before" and "after" numbers require a conversion of probability of survival into an expectancy. Presumably we do not have statistics that permit confident evaluation of the anticipated life span of patients with many conditions to the same degree that mortality tables give those values for the general population. Despite these difficulties, and recognizing that it can produce a windfall for some and shortchange others, we have compensated for reduced life expectancy in other contexts.[16] Application of the same principles is the best we can do to value the reduced probability of a full recovery.[17] This would value the injury at the reduction of the patient's expectancy from her pre-negligence expectancy. Ultimately, the jury will have to attach a monetary amount to JoAnn's loss. In so doing, because this is JoAnn's action, the jury will be forced to consider what value to ascribe to the privilege of living. In other contexts, juries are routinely entrusted with the task of awarding damages for injuries not readily calculable. See Indianapolis Newspapers, Inc. v. Fields, 259 N.E.2d 651, 656 (Ind. 1970) (jury awarded $60,000 in libel suit); Miller v. Ryan, 706 N.E.2d 244, 247 (Ind. Ct. App. 1999) (jury awarded $325,000 in informed consent claim); Dollar Inn, Inc. v. Slone, 695 N.E.2d 185, 187 (Ind. Ct. App. 1998) (jury awarded $250,000 in emotional distress damages to plaintiff who was pricked in the thumb by a hypodermic needle concealed

---

[16] Compensation for reduced life expectancy is routinely awarded in the context of wrongful death claims, with the important caveat that the compensation ordinarily takes the form of lost earnings.

[17] The valuation of a reduced life expectancy in particular has proved difficult for the courts. Courts recognizing a reduced life expectancy have sometimes calculated damages in terms of compensable elements should the injury actually occur, and for present emotional distress associated with the injury. Other courts have merely stated that a reduced life expectancy is a cognizable injury, but provide no guidance as to how the injury should be valued. . . .

in toilet paper roll). Valuing a determinable number of years of life is no more challenging than these exercises.

II. NEGLIGENT INFLICTION OF EMOTIONAL DISTRESS

The Alexanders argue that JoAnn is entitled to maintain a cause of action for negligent infliction of emotional distress because she suffered an impact sufficient to satisfy the modified impact rule. Scheid and Orthopedics argue that JoAnn has failed to satisfy the modified impact rule because, in their words, "the failure to diagnose cancer" does not constitute an impact as required by Shuamber v. Henderson, 579 N.E.2d 452 (Ind. 1991).

In order to maintain a cause of action for negligent infliction of emotional distress under Indiana law, a plaintiff must satisfy the "impact rule." The impact rule originally consisted of three elements: (1) an impact on the plaintiff; (2) that causes physical injury to the plaintiff; (3) that in turn causes the emotional distress. This rule precluded recovery for the case in which a plaintiff experienced real mental stress in the absence of a physical injury. We recognized the policy reasons in support of relaxing the impact rule and held in *Shuamber*:

> [W]hen ... a plaintiff sustains a direct impact by the negligence of another and, by virtue of that direct involvement sustains an emotional trauma which is serious in nature and of a kind and extent normally expected to occur in a reasonable person, we hold that such a plaintiff is entitled to maintain an action to recover for that emotional trauma without regard to whether the emotional trauma arises out of or accompanies any physical injury to the plaintiff.

In *Shuamber,* this Court concluded that passengers in a car involved in an accident in which a family member was killed could recover for emotional distress that resulted from the death, even if it was unconnected to their physical injuries. In Conder v. Wood, 716 N.E.2d 432, 433 (Ind. 1999), we allowed a mental distress claim by a plaintiff who had beat on the side of a truck that was running over her co-worker, concluding that the contact between her fist and the truck satisfied the impact requirement.

Similarly, we conclude that JoAnn has satisfied the elements of negligent infliction of emotional distress under the modified impact rule. The impact does not consist, as Scheid and Orthopedics allege, of the failure to diagnose cancer. Rather, allegedly as a result of the defendants' negligence, JoAnn suffered the destruction of healthy lung tissue by a cancerous tumor. As we held in *Conder*, the purpose of the rule is to confine recovery to those with "direct involvement" in the defendant's negligent act or omission. JoAnn was treated by the defendants and has incurred a physical change as a result. This is good enough. JoAnn testified that she is now being treated with antidepressants and described the devastation surrounding her bleak prognosis. These are reasonable responses under the circumstances. . . . JoAnn is not precluded as a matter of law from proceeding with this claim.

III. EXACERBATION OR AGGRAVATION OF JOANN'S INJURIES

. . . The Alexanders correctly note that ordinarily a defendant is liable for the aggravation or exacerbation of a current injury, to the extent that the defendant's "conduct has resulted in an aggravation of the pre-existing condition, [but] not for the condition as it was." Dunn v. Cadiente, 516 N.E.2d 52, 56 (Ind. 1987). Scheid's and Orthopedics' contention that JoAnn has been unharmed runs contrary to the record. If nothing else, the past injuries JoAnn sustained are substantial. During the time JoAnn's cancer remained undiagnosed, she incurred the destruction of healthy lung tissue, the growth of a cancerous tumor, and the collapse of a lung. Thus, JoAnn could conceivably maintain a cause of action for the aggravation of her pre-existing condition. Given that these injuries are injuries for which JoAnn seeks no compensation, however, we agree with Scheid and Orthopedics that the Court of Appeals did not err in failing to address JoAnn's argument for recovering for aggravation of injury as formulated.

CONCLUSION

We grant transfer and reverse and remand to the trial court for proceedings consistent with this opinion.

■ NOTES ON RECOVERING DAMAGES FOR REDUCED LIFE EXPECTANCY

1. Assume a jury believes from the testimony that JoAnn Alexander had a 70 percent chance of survival if she had been promptly diagnosed and treated in 1993, but only a 20 percent chance because of the negligence of Kevin Scheid. Does it follow that the jury should estimate the value of living the remaining years of her life and award her 50 percent of that sum? Or would it make more sense to ask the jury to appraise the value of the lost chance itself? See James M. Fischer, Understanding Remedies §15[f] (1999) (some courts invite juries to appraise the value of loss caused by death and multiply that by the percentage reduction in chance of survival caused by tort, but some courts "attempt to measure the 'lost chance' itself under a broad evidence standard").

2. Ms. Alexander was 60 years old when Kevin Scheid got the report of her first X-ray, and mortality tables for somebody of that age in 1993 indicated life expectancy of 83 years (she would reach that age in 2016). That doesn't *mean,* however, that she would *likely* have lived 23 more years, does it? As the court commented, such estimates mean only that a person has a 50 percent probability of living that long, and a 50 percent probability of living more or fewer years. *Could* a jury reasonably conclude that JoAnn Alexander would most likely have lived to the age of 83?

3. If the case goes to the jury and it concludes that Ms. Alexander would likely have lived until 83, then it must estimate the value *to her* of 11½ years of living (50 percent of 23 years). How should it do that? In the typical personal injury suit, the jury calculates damages by computing medical expenses, estimating lost wages, and appraising pain and suffering. "Lost years" are something else, aren't they? Surely *part* of the value of "lost years" can be measured in lost earnings (JoAnn Alexander included such a claim), but a large element in recovery for "lost years" is the value of "enjoying life." In personal injury cases, compensating for medical expenses, lost wages, and pain and suffering doesn't seem to cover everything, but American courts do not often endorse recovery of "hedonic" damages—a slightly pejorative term describing the value of enjoying life. Rather, prevailing plaintiffs recover *indirectly* for loss of enjoyment of life by means of the award for pain and suffering. Compensating someone like JoAnn Alexander forces one to think about enjoyment of life in a slightly different way. It is worth considering some of the rules that have grown up, mostly in connection with claims for pain and suffering, that speak to this matter:

(a) Golden Rule Arguments. Few people would willingly endure injuries in exchange for money (think about breaking a leg or suffering a punctured spleen), so lawyers cannot very well ask jurors to think about what they would charge if invited to endure injuries or suffering. Courts condemn "Golden Rule" arguments for even broader reasons. Such arguments invite jurors to "put themselves in the position of the plaintiff," which interferes with the "objectivity" we expect from juries. See, e.g., Beagle v. Vasold, 417 P.2d 673 (Cal. 1966); DeJesus v. Flick, 7 P.3d 459 (Nev. 2000) (awarding new trial where plaintiff improperly used "Golden Rule" argument in asking jury to "allow such recovery as they would wish" in the same position).

(b) Fair and Reasonable Arguments. Lawyers often argue that a particular sum (like $4 million) is "fair and reasonable under the circumstances." One way to argue this point is to invite jurors to think about pain and suffering on a monthly, weekly, or hourly basis, which can make even astronomical sums of money seem modest. See CSX Transportation v. Beglery, 313 S.W.3d 52, 71 (Ky. 2010) (endorsing "fair and reasonable" standard; per diem figures may help find the right amount, but this method "should not be construed to imply an undue degree of precision," as plaintiffs "may or may not experience pain and suffering in a predictable pattern").

(c) Per Diem Arguments. Many states allow lawyers to *suggest* an amount to be awarded for every week, day, or hour, and to multiply that amount by the duration of expected suffering. A dollar a minute for pain and suffering, experienced during every waking hour (16 out of 24

hours), would yield a recovery of more than $3.5 million over ten years. See, e.g., *Beagle*, 417 P.2d at 673; Wilson v. Williams, 933 P.2d 757, 758 (Kan. 1997) (approving argument inviting jury to award $100,000 for loss of enjoyment of life over 36.5 years; lawyer told jury that this figure "comes out to around $8 a day or something like that"); Yates v. Wenk, 109 N.W.2d 828, 830 (Mich. 1961) (approving mathematical argument; cases disapproving such argument cite "the impossibility of evaluating pain in dollars and cents," but this is "exactly the task" juries must perform; the same "speculative quality" in estimating the value of one day's pain and suffering "exists likewise" in any verdict); Newberry v. Vogel, 379 P.2d 811, 813 (Colo. 1963) (approving per diem argument as "a course of reasoning suggested by the plaintiff for translating pain and suffering into reasonable compensation"). Some states, however, reject this approach. In New Jersey, for instance, a court rule lets lawyers argue "unliquidated damages" on a "time-unit basis" but prohibits any "reference to a specific sum" and requires courts to tell juries that such presentations are "argumentative only and do not constitute evidence." N.J. Rules of Court 1:1-7. And see Botta v. Brunner, 138 A.2d 713 (1958) (landmark case condemning per diem argument); DeHanes v. Rothman, 727 A.2d 8, 12 (N.J. 1999) (equating pain and suffering to monetary compensation remains "'elusive and subjective'" and lawyers cannot suggest "monetary time-units for evaluating an award of pain and suffering, per hour, day or week"). See generally 3 A.L.R.4th 940 (1981) (per diem or similar mathematical basis for fixing damages for pain and suffering).

(d) *Expert Testimony.* While experts are allowed to testify on such matters as lost wages and the value over time of household services, expert testimony on the value of "enjoying life" has tougher sledding. Compare Loth v. Truck-A-Way Corporation, 70 Cal. Rptr. 2d 571 (Cal. App. 1998) (expert cannot testify on this point based on (a) amount paid by society for protective devices like seat belts and smoke detectors, (b) risk premiums paid by employers for hazardous jobs, or (c) cost-benefit analysis of safety programs required by federal law; expert concluded that average value of 44-year life expectancy was $2.3 million) and Wilt v. Buracker, 443 S.E.2d 196 (W. Va. 1993) (loss of enjoyment of life may be compensated, but this element "is not subject to an economic calculation"; disapproving expert testimony based on "willingness-to-pay studies," which cannot actually measure how much Americans value life; these measure such things as spending on air bags and smoke detectors, or extra salary for people in high-risk work) with Smith v. Ingersoll-Rand Co., 214 F.3d 1235, 1244-1246 (10th Cir. 2000) (approving expert testimony describing hedonic damages, which is "premised on what we take to be the rather noncontroversial assumption that the value of an individual's life exceeds the sum of that individual's economic productivity," and categorizing hedonic damages in terms of "ability to enjoy the occupation of your choice," "activities of daily living," "social leisure activities," and "internal wellbeing").

4. When a court awards recovery to compensate for ongoing (future) losses, it may be appropriate to *reduce* the gross amount to some extent:

In the first place, a lump-sum award for future losses, payable *today,* need not be an amount equal to the sums of the future dollars. Instead, what plaintiff should recover is the "present value" of the sum of future dollars. In the second place, future losses are to some extent offset by future expenses that will *not* be incurred. If, for example, a person is not going to earn money by working, she is also not going to drive to work or pay the same amount for clothes, and so forth. If you were the lawyer for Kevin Scheid, would you argue these points? Would you call an expert to help the jury compute the present discounted value of a sum of money designed to compensate Ms. Alexander for 11½ years of lost living?

5. One reason given in *Alexander* for permitting the claim for diminished life expectancy is that Indiana has an "occurrence-based limitations period" for malpractice claims. Under the relevant statute (Ind. Code §34-18-7-1), such claims must be "filed within two (2) years after the date of the alleged act, omission, or neglect." Presumably JoAnn Alexander had to file before the end of June 1995, which marks the end of the second year after the X-ray that Dr. Scheid did not follow up on (she actually filed suit in December 1994.) In Martin v. Richey, 711 N.E.2d 1123 (Ind. 1999), the Indiana Supreme Court held that the statute violates the state constitution if applied to bar a suit filed more than two years after failure to diagnose breast cancer where the claimant did not realize within two years that she had the disease (*Alexander* comments that an occurrence-based statute of limitations is unconstitutional if it bars claims that are "accrued but unknowable"). Presumably, the concern is that a claimant like JoAnn Alexander *does* or *might* know about reduced life expectancy before disease manifests itself. In fact, JoAnn Alexander learned within a year or so that failing to follow up on the first X-ray let her lung cancer advance: If she had to wait until cancer was fully developed, her claim might be barred. What do you think of that reasoning? Isn't it circular? If there *is* a claim for reduced life expectancy, she must bring it within two years of the occurrence *if* she learns of it. If there *isn't* such a claim, she can't be barred until she gets sick and learns she has a claim for *that.* The question is whether she should have the "advanced" claim—the one for reduced life expectancy before she gets sick.

6. Suppose a jury awards JoAnn Alexander the sum of $4 million. Suppose it is clear from the arguments, the evidence, and the instructions to the jury, that this sum represents the present discounted value of damages sustained for the expected loss of 11½ years of life. Assume further that the jury believes each lost year was "worth" $800,000, so that total damages (before discounting) were $9,200,000.

(a) If JoAnn Alexander lives only eight years (two and one-half years less than the jury projected), should her estate be permitted to sue again? If so, should the earlier judgment bind the defendant, meaning that the court in the new suit should award an additional $2 million? (There would be no need to discount at this point, since death means the damages have been suffered.)

(b) If JoAnn Alexander suffers a recurrence of lung cancer in 2002 and dies in 2004 after undergoing treatment regimens and enduring pain and

suffering, could her estate sue Dr. Scheid and Orthopedics? Notice, if it is relevant, that we supposed that the original verdict in her suit for diminished life expectancy rested on a finding that she would likely live 11½ years beyond 1993, so her death in 2004 would be just about what our hypothetical jury believed would happen.

(c) You will learn that one who sues for personal injuries of the usual sort—broken limbs and the like—cannot "split her claims" by suing again when she discovers additional injuries that she didn't include in the first suit. See Chapter 14B, infra. Under principles of *res judicata*, all claims that one has on account of a single course of tortious conduct are "merged" in a judgment favoring plaintiff, or barred by an unfavorable judgment. In ordinary cases, then, additional claims that "might have been brought" can no longer be brought. Should that principle apply to JoAnn Alexander? If not, is it fair for Scheid and Orthopedics to face multiple suits by the same claimant arising out of a single course of conduct?

7. *Alexander* lets people recover *now* for ailments they will suffer later where it is *pretty clear* that those ailments are on the way. What about making defendants pay for medical monitoring of people who have been put at *increased risk* of future ailments by defendant's conduct, where it is not yet clear that they will suffer any damages? Is this situation distinguishable from what happened to JoAnn Alexander? Does *exposure itself* constitute a compensable harm? Some modern cases say yes. See, e.g., Bower v. Westinghouse Electric Corp., 522 S.E.2d 424 (W. Va. 1999) (even without physical symptoms, plaintiff may recover for medical monitoring if he or she has been "significantly exposed" to a "proven hazardous substance" and as a result suffers "increased risk of contracting a serious latent disease," such that it is "reasonably necessary" to undergo periodic diagnostic examinations that would not be necessary otherwise, where monitoring procedures exist that "make the early detection of a disease possible"). Led by the Supreme Court in its decision in Metro-North Commuter R.R. Co. v. Buckley, 521 U.S. 424 (1997), however, many courts have rejected such claims. There the Court said a plaintiff exposed to asbestos dust in the workplace (he and others were known as the "snowmen of Grand Central" because they emerged from work covered in white asbestos dust) could not recover for emotional distress under FELA. The Court emphasized problems of separating valid from trivial claims and the threat of unlimited liability, and also rejected a medical monitoring claim. See also Bourgeois v. A.P. Green Industries, Inc., 716 So. 2d 355 (La. 1998) (requiring higher than normal exposure to toxic substance that causes increased risk of contracting serious latent disease that is significantly greater than risk without exposure in order to support medical monitoring claim).

3. Injunctive and Other Equitable Relief

When this country won independence in 1786, English courts were divided into two independent and competing systems—common law courts and

Court of Chancery. The former were courts of "law" that functioned under a writ system, used juries, and generated decrees and writs that could be enforced "in rem" (against property) rather than "in personam" (against parties personally). The latter was a court of "equity," and its hallmarks were that it (a) provided remedies unknown to common law (like injunctions ordering parties to do or not do certain things), (b) operated with precursors to modern discovery, like interrogatories and subpoenas enabling parties to gather facts before trial and call witnesses to give evidence, (c) made decisions through the Chancellor alone, without juries, and (d) operated "in personam" because its commands were directed personally to the parties.

By 1786, it was understood that equitable relief was available only when legal relief was not, or was inadequate. This notion helped keep the Court of Chancery from encroaching on the common law courts.

Courts in the United States were bifurcated too, but differently. In England, the systems were separated by geography and personnel; in America they operated in the same building, in the same courtrooms, with the same judges, *but* American institutions still maintained separation: There were suits in law and suits in equity, and a single suit could not be both. The central doctrinal element that kept the two systems apart was the English notion that a court of equity could act only where legal remedies were inadequate, which found expression in statutes and decisions. See, e.g., Mo. Stat. §526.030 (authorizing injunctions where, *inter alia,* "irreparable injury to real or personal property is threatened," and "adequate remedy cannot be afforded by an action for damages"); McKay v. Wilderness Development, LLC, 221 P.3d 1184 (Mont. 2009) (in homeowner's suit alleging that maintenance building on adjacent golf course violated covenant, refusing to order removal of building because monetary damages would suffice).

Injunctive Relief. This form of relief is commonly divided into three categories, according to duration, formalities to be observed, and criteria that must be satisfied. See generally FRCP 65. Short-lived injunctive relief (ten days at most, with possibility of short extensions), commonly called a "temporary restraining order" or TRO, may be had on *ex parte* application. The purpose is to freeze the situation so the court can take a closer look. Relief for the duration of the suit may then be had after notice and a hearing, where the court can hear testimony and consider evidence, and this "preliminary injunction" can preserve or alter the situation pending final resolution of the suit. A "permanent injunction" can be awarded at the end.

Injunctions are sometimes distinguished by what they command: One that *prohibits* a person from doing something is often called a "writ of prohibition" or "cease and desist" order. One that requires a person *to do* something is often called a "writ of mandamus." It was once the case that courts could grant injunctive relief in the former category (easier to enforce), but not the latter (requiring supervision). While courts remain reluctant to become involved in supervisory roles, and are not well equipped for such tasks, this limit has largely disappeared, and injunctions requiring affirmative acts are commonplace.

Equity as Fairness: Two Doctrines. Equity is nearly synonymous with the notion of fairness. See Hilton Davis Chemical Co. v. Warner-Jenkinson Co., 62 F.3d 1512, 1521 (Fed. Cir. 1995) ("this court's allusions to equity invoke equity in its broadest sense—equity as general fairness"). A common tension in the cases involves the degree to which courts are limited by doctrinal constraints or can act more or less on their own in pursuit of fairness. See Grupo Mexicano de Desarrollo v. Alliance Bond Fund, 527 U.S. 308 (1999) (majority invokes doctrinal constraints, refusing to issue asset-freezing injunction; dissenters argue in favor of "adaptable" and "dynamic" equity jurisprudence and complain that majority is limiting equity "to the specific practices and remedies of the pre-Revolutionary Chancellor").

Two doctrines often affect suits in equity. First, one who seeks equitable relief should come to court with "clean hands," a notion sometimes expanded to the proposition that one who "seeks equity" must "do equity." Second, delaying a request for injunctive relief can result in denial if the delay is prejudicial, which usually means it would increase expenses to the defendant. This notion of delay is captured in French term "laches" (prejudicial delay). In one modern suit, for example, a homeowner tried to block a golf course developer from subdividing its parcel and building maintenance structures, invoking neighborhood covenants. The court (a) refused to stop defendants from subdividing because plaintiff had subdivided its own parcel and failed the "clean hands" test, (b) awarded injunctive relief requiring defendant to remove one structure, rejecting a claim of laches (finding that plaintiff had not delayed), and (c) refused to order removal of the other structure because monetary damages would adequately compensate plaintiff. See McKay v. Wilderness Development, LLC, 221 P.3d 1184 (Mont. 2009).

Other Equitable Remedies. Injunctions are not the only form of equitable relief. Courts of equity developed other remedies, including the following:

(a) Rescission. If mistake, impossibility, fraud or other ground entitled a party to a contract to be excused from performance, that party could initiate a suit for rescission in a court of equity. This remedy is obsolescent. Today a contracting party simply notifies the other party of rescission, and the other party can then sue under the contract, and the court decides whether rescission was justified.

(b) Reformation. If the parties have mistakenly signed a contract that does not conform to their mutual intention (as might happen if it refers to a "1010 Ford" when both parties intend to refer to a "2012 Ford"), then suit may be brought to reform the agreement to reflect what the parties intended.

(c) Specific Performance. If a party to a contract refuses to perform a specific obligation for which there is no adequate substitute, equitable relief is sometimes available in the form of a decree ordering the party to perform. Relief of this sort is often possible where the owner of land (or unique object) refuses to convey the land (or object) as required by contract, and a court directs the owner to do so.

(d) Quiet Title; Removing Cloud. Common law courts provided a remedy (ejectment) against trespassers and illegal occupiers of land from an early

date, but it was equity that developed remedies that allowed landowners to obtain court orders resolving ongoing challenges and adjudicating claims to title that did not necessarily involve hostile occupancy (like claims of easement). The "quiet title" remedy enabled the owner to win a decree—and it was said to be "good against the whole world"—resolving the state of title to the property. A somewhat related remedy ("quia timet," meaning "because he is afraid") allowed the owner to obtain a decree that would remove a cloud on title that had not yet become manifest, but might ripen in the future because of the apparent effect of some document.

(e) Constructive Trust. At an early time, equity developed this remedy to help a claimant obtain the benefits of property that rightfully belongs to him where another holds actual title to the property. When this remedy is awarded, the court orders the defendant title-holder to convey title to the plaintiff.

Modern Significance of Division Between Law and Equity. Modern practice has gone far to efface the distinction between law and equity. Under FRCP 2 there is but "one form of action to be known as 'civil action,'" so litigants may find "legal" and "equitable" relief in a single suit. Unfortunately, as you learn in Chapter 12, this "merger of law and equity" has not ended the need to distinguish the two. The reason is that trial by jury developed on the "law" side in England, and this aspect of the distinction between law and equity still counts in the United States. In both state and federal courts, litigants usually have a right to a jury trial in suits at law but not suits at equity. Where a suit has both "legal" and "equitable" elements, or resembles both "legal" and "equitable" actions of the past, the question whether the right to a jury trial attaches is important and hard to answer.

Beaverhead-Deerlodge National Forest

In Beaverhead-Deerlodge National Forest in Montana, a wildfire consumed 27,000 acres in 2007, leading to a reforestation project that included a plan to "recover and utilize timber" from dead or dying trees, which in turn led to this suit by the Alliance for Wild Rockies. According to its website, the Alliance is a nonprofit whose mission is to "secure the ecological integrity of the Wild Rockies Bioregion," which means "physiographic region of wetlands that are biologically connected" and includes "wildlands

 in parts of Idaho, Montana, Wyoming, Oregon, Washington, Alberta, and British Columbia." When this suit was filed, Jane Cottrell (named as defendant) had just been appointed temporary Regional Forester. In an interview given at the time, Ms Cottrell defended her policy of removing dead growth as an essential part of preventing wildfires.

ALLIANCE FOR THE WILD ROCKIES v. COTTRELL

United States Court of Appeals for the Ninth Circuit
632 F.3d 1127 (9th Cir. 2010)

W. FLETCHER, Circuit Judge:

Alliance for the Wild Rockies ("AWR") appeals the district court's denial of its motion for a preliminary injunction. AWR seeks to enjoin a timber salvage sale proposed by the United States Forest Service. Citing Winter v. Natural Resources Defense Council, 555 U.S. 7 (2008), the district court held that AWR had not shown the requisite likelihood of irreparable injury and success on the merits. After hearing oral argument, we issued an order reversing the district court and directing it to issue the preliminary injunction. In this opinion, we now set forth the reasons for our reversal, and we take this opportunity to clarify an aspect of the post-*Winter* standard for a preliminary injunction.

I. BACKGROUND

In August and September of 2007, the Rat Creek Wildfire burned about 27,000 acres in the Beaverhead-Deerlodge National Forest in Montana. On July 1, 2009, almost two years later, the Chief Forester of the Forest Service made an Emergency Situation Determination for the Rat Creek Salvage Project ("the Project"). The Emergency Situation Determination permitted the immediate commencement of the Project's logging without any of the delays that might have resulted from the Forest Service's administrative appeals process.

The Project permits salvage logging of trees on approximately 1,652 of the 27,000 acres that were burned. The logging will take place (and to some degree has already taken place) on thirty-five units of land ranging from 3 to 320 acres in size. The Forest Service describes the purpose of the Project as follows:

> to recover and utilize timber from trees that are dead or dying as a result of the Rat Creek Wildfire or forest insects and disease and reforest the harvested units with healthy trees appropriate for the site. The trees would supply wood to the forest products industry.

A further purpose is to cut trees infested with dwarf mistletoe to prevent transmission to new trees.

Trees to be cut are those from 4 to 15 inches in diameter at breast height ("dbh") that have died or are likely to die as a direct result of fire or insect attack. The Forest Service has provided species-specific guidelines for determining likelihood of mortality. For example, Douglas-fir trees from 4 to 15 inches dbh are to be logged if less than 40% of the pre-fire live crown remains. Other conifers are to be logged if less than 80% of the pre-fire live crown remains. The severity of insect attacks is to be determined by examining trees for signs such as pitch tubes or boring dust.

Trees that survived the fire but are infected with dwarf mistletoe are to be cut, regardless of size, unless doing so would reduce the number of live trees below the Forest Service's wildlife habitat standard. Uninfested live trees, including those with a dbh larger than 15 inches, are to be cut only if required by safety concerns.

The Project requires construction of 7 miles of temporary roads and reconditioning of about 3 miles of existing roads. After completion of the Project, the temporary roads will be obliterated, and the existing roads will be returned to their current uses, if any.

In April 2009, the Forest Service released an Environmental Assessment ("EA") of the Project for public comment.

On June 15, 2009, the Acting Forest Supervisor for the Beaverhead-Deerlodge National Forest wrote to the Regional Forester requesting that the Chief Forester make an Emergency Situation Determination ("ESD") in connection with the Rat Creek Project. The ESD request stated that the emergency resulted from "rapid deterioration and decay of trees proposed for salvage harvest," noting that "[t]rees that have died or are dying from secondary fire effects are rapidly losing their value and merchantable volume." The request stated that immediate commencement of logging would "prevent substantial economic loss to the Federal Government." The sites to be logged are typically accessible to loggers for only four to five months out of the year due to heavy snowfalls. The request stated that the logging needed to commence immediately so that it could be completed before winter arrived.

The request stated further:

> An objective for recovering the value of the fire-killed trees is to respond to local, regional, and national needs for commercial timber products. Local economies in Southwest Montana have developed with natural resource utilization as the foundation. This economic structure continues today and is becoming stressed and increasingly unstable due to higher energy prices, and reduced supply of timber from National Forest System lands. As markets decline and harvest activities on private lands decrease, the timber industry in Montana increasingly depends on National Forest System timber supply as an essential element to keep their mills operational.

On June 22, 2009, the Regional Forester forwarded the request for an ESD to the Chief Forester, noting that a "delay in implementation of activities included in the request would result in substantial loss of economic value to the Federal Government." On July 1, 2009, the Chief Forester granted the request for an ESD. She wrote:

> [A] delay to implementing the project until after any administrative appeals have been reviewed and answered will result in a substantial loss of economic

value to the government. Such a delay would push the award of timber sale contracts for the hazard tree and other salvage back to late October 2009, with winter access limitations delaying most operations until summer of 2010. By that time further deterioration of the affected trees will have resulted in a projected loss of receipts to the government of as much as $16,000 and significantly increased the likelihood of receiving no bids. An absence of bids would push the potential loss to the government to $70,000 and eliminate an opportunity to accomplish Douglas-fir planting and dwarf mistletoe control objectives.

In evaluating whether an emergency situation exists with this project, I also took note of the importance this project has to the local economy of southwest Montana. I understand the wood products yielded by this project will be a critical contributor to helping keep local mills operational.

On July 22, 2009, the Forest Service issued the final Environmental Assessment ("EA") and a Decision Notice and Finding of No Significant Impact ("DN/FONSI"). The Forest Service concluded that the Project would not have a significant effect on the quality of the human environment and that an Environmental Impact Statement ("EIS") was therefore not required. The Forest Service then initiated a bidding process for the Project. On July 30, 2009, Barry Smith Logging was declared the highest bidder.

Plaintiff AWR filed suit in federal district court alleging violations of the Appeals Reform Act ("ARA"), the National Forest Management Act ("NFMA"), and the National Environmental Protection Act ("NEPA"). In a brief order entered on August 14, 2009, the district court denied AWR's request for a preliminary injunction. After quoting *Winter*, the court wrote, "After reviewing the parties' filings, the Court is convinced Plaintiffs do not show a likelihood of success on the merits, nor that irreparable injury is likely in the absence of an injunction. This determination prevents the issuance of a preliminary injunction at this stage of the proceedings." The court did not describe or analyze the merits of AWR's claims and did not describe or analyze the harm alleged by AWR. The court denied AWR's motion for a stay and injunction pending appeal to this court.

Barry Smith Logging began work on the Project on August 21, 2009. The parties indicated at oral argument that approximately 49% of the planned logging was completed before winter conditions halted operations.

AWR timely appealed the district court's denial of its request for a preliminary injunction. Because a significant amount of the Project remains to be completed, this appeal is not moot.

II. STANDARD OF REVIEW

We review a district court's denial of a preliminary injunction for abuse of discretion. Lands Council v. McNair, 537 F.3d 981, 986 (9th Cir. 2008) (en banc). An abuse of discretion will be found if the district court based its decision "on an erroneous legal standard or clearly erroneous finding of fact." "We review conclusions of law de novo and findings of fact for clear error." We will not reverse the district court where it "got the law right," even if we "would have arrived at a different result," so long as the district court did not clearly err in its factual determinations.

III. DISCUSSION

A. "Sliding Scale" and "Serious Questions" After *Winter*

In *Winter,* the Supreme Court disagreed with one aspect of this circuit's approach to preliminary injunctions. We had held that the "possibility" of irreparable harm was sufficient, in some circumstances, to justify a preliminary injunction. *Winter* explicitly rejected that approach. Under *Winter,* plaintiffs must establish that irreparable harm is likely, not just possible, in order to obtain a preliminary injunction. The Court wrote, "A plaintiff seeking a preliminary injunction must establish that he is likely to succeed on the merits, that he is likely to suffer irreparable harm in the absence of preliminary relief, that the balance of equities tips in his favor, and that an injunction is in the public interest." "A preliminary injunction is an extraordinary remedy never awarded as of right."

The majority opinion in *Winter* did not, however, explicitly discuss the continuing validity of the "sliding scale" approach to preliminary injunctions employed by this circuit and others. Under this approach, the elements of the preliminary injunction test are balanced, so that a stronger showing of one element may offset a weaker showing of another. For example, a stronger showing of irreparable harm to plaintiff might offset a lesser showing of likelihood of success on the merits. See, e.g., Clear Channel Outdoor, Inc. v. City of Los Angeles, 340 F.3d 810, 813 (9th Cir. 2003). This circuit has adopted and applied a version of the sliding scale approach under which a preliminary injunction could issue where the likelihood of success is such that "serious questions going to the merits were raised and the balance of hardships tips sharply in [plaintiff's] favor." That test was described in this circuit as one alternative on a continuum. See, e.g., *Lands Council.* The test at issue here has often been referred to as the "serious questions" test. We will so refer to it as well.

The parties in this case have devoted substantial portions of their argument to the question of the continuing validity of the "serious questions" approach to preliminary injunctions after *Winter.* For the reasons that follow, we hold that the "serious questions" approach survives *Winter* when applied as part of the four-element *Winter* test. In other words, "serious questions going to the merits" and a hardship balance that tips sharply toward the plaintiff can support issuance of an injunction, assuming the other two elements of the *Winter* test are also met.

Justice Ginsburg explicitly noted in her dissent in *Winter* that the "Court has never rejected [the sliding scale] formulation, and I do not believe it does so today." Justice Ginsburg emphasized the importance of the sliding scale approach, writing "[f]lexibility is the hallmark of equity jurisdiction." As Justice Ginsburg noted, the majority opinion in *Winter* did not disapprove the sliding scale approach. Indeed, some of its language suggests that the approach survives. For example, the Court implied that balancing is appropriate when it indicated that "particular regard" should be paid to "the public consequences in employing the extraordinary remedy of injunction."

Our circuit has not yet directly discussed in a published opinion the post-*Winter* viability of the sliding scale approach. In our first post-*Winter* opinion, we recited the *Winter* four-part test and then wrote, "To the extent that our cases have suggested a lesser standard, they are no longer controlling, or even viable." American Trucking Ass'ns, Inc. v. City of Los Angeles, 559 F.3d 1046, 1052 (9th Cir. 2009). We discussed the holding of *Winter* that a preliminary injunction requires a showing of likely irreparable injury, but we did not discuss whether some version of the sliding scale test survived. In National Meat Association v. Brown, 599 F.3d 1093, 1097 n.3 (9th Cir. 2010), we wrote, "The district court applied our pre-*Winter* 'sliding scale' approach, which required only a 'possibility of irreparable injury' if plaintiff is likely to succeed on the merits." We then held that, although such an error might warrant remand, it was unnecessary in that case because all elements of the *Winter* test had been met.

[The court summarizes other post-*Winter* decisions in the Circuit, as well as a district court opinion, and says the Fourth Circuit has held that "the sliding scale approach is now invalid," while the Second and Seventh Circuits have held that "the sliding scale test survives *Winter*," and that "a weaker claim on the merits can still justify a preliminary injunction depending on the amount of 'net harm' that could be prevented." The court quotes Judge Easterbrook's conclusion for the Seventh Circuit that "the more net harm an injunction can prevent, the weaker the plaintiff's claim on the merits can be while still supporting some preliminary relief." The court also quotes modern Second Circuit authority to the effect that the "serious questions" standard allows a court to grant a preliminary injunction "where it cannot determine with certainty that the moving party is more likely than not to prevail," but where "the costs outweigh the benefits of not granting the injunction." The court says "dicta" from the Tenth Circuit and the District of Columbia support the sliding scale approach.]

For the reasons identified by our sister circuits and our district courts, we join the Seventh and the Second Circuits in concluding that the "serious questions" version of the sliding scale test for preliminary injunctions remains viable after the Supreme Court's decision in *Winter*. In this circuit, the test has been formulated as follows:

> A preliminary injunction is appropriate when a plaintiff demonstrates . . . that serious questions going to the merits were raised and the balance of hardships tips sharply in the plaintiff's favor.

Lands Council. Of course, plaintiffs must also satisfy the other *Winter* factors. To the extent prior cases applying the "serious questions" test have held that a preliminary injunction may issue where the plaintiff shows only that serious questions going to the merits were raised and the balance of hardships tips sharply in the plaintiff's favor, without satisfying the other two prongs, they are superseded by *Winter,* which requires the plaintiff to make a showing on all four prongs. See Miller v. Gammie, 335 F.3d 889, 900 (9th Cir. 2003) (en banc). But the "serious questions" approach survives *Winter* when applied as part of the four-element *Winter* test. That is, "serious questions going to the merits" and a balance of hardships that tips sharply towards the plaintiff can support issuance of a preliminary injunction, so long as the plaintiff also shows that there is a likelihood of irreparable injury and that the injunction is in the public interest.

B. Preliminary Injunction

Because it did not apply the "serious questions" test, the district court made an error of law in denying the preliminary injunction sought by AWR. We conclude that AWR has shown that there is a likelihood of irreparable harm; that there are at least serious questions on the merits concerning the validity of the Forest Service's Emergency Situation Determination; that the balance of hardships tips sharply in its favor; and that the public interest favors a preliminary injunction.

1. Likelihood of Irreparable Harm

Winter tells us that plaintiffs may not obtain a preliminary injunction unless they can show that irreparable harm is likely to result in the absence of the injunction. AWR's members use the Beaverhead-Deerlodge National Forest, including the areas subject to logging under the Project, for work and recreational purposes, such as hunting, fishing, hiking, horseback riding, and cross-country skiing. AWR asserts that its members' interests will be irreparably harmed by the Rat Creek Project. In particular, AWR asserts that the Project will harm its members' ability to "view, experience, and utilize" the areas in their undisturbed state.

The Forest Service responds that the Project areas represent only six percent of the acreage damaged by fire. It argues that because AWR members can "view, experience, and utilize" other areas of the forest, including other fire-damaged areas that are not part of the Project, they are not harmed by logging in the Project.

This argument proves too much. Its logical extension is that a plaintiff can never suffer irreparable injury resulting from environmental harm in a forest area as long as there are other areas of the forest that are not harmed. The Project will prevent the use and enjoyment by AWR members of 1,652 acres of the forest. This is hardly a de minimus injury.

"[T]he Supreme Court has instructed us that '[e]nvironmental injury, by its nature, can seldom be adequately remedied by money damages and is often permanent or at least of long duration, i.e., irreparable.'" *Lands Council.* Of course, this does not mean that "any potential environmental injury" warrants an injunction. But actual and irreparable injury, such as AWR articulates here, satisfies the "likelihood of irreparable injury" requirement articulated in *Winter.*

2. Likelihood of Success on the Merits

AWR's strongest argument on the merits is that the Forest Service has violated the Appeals Reform Act ("ARA") and its implementing regulations by granting the Emergency Situation Designation ("ESD"). Regulations promulgated under the ARA provide that most Forest Service decisions are appealable through an administrative process. The administrative appeals process would ordinarily be available for the Project at issue in this case. If the Forest Service decision had been appealed administratively, there would have been an opportunity for members of the public, including plaintiffs, to object to the Project on various grounds. Implementation would then have been delayed until at least "the 15th business day following the date of appeal disposition." 36 CFR §215.9(b).

The regulations provide an exception to the appeals process when the Forest Service makes an ESD. An ESD allows work to begin on a project as soon as notice of the otherwise appealable project decision is appropriately published. The regulations define an Emergency Situation as "[a] situation on National Forest System (NFS) lands for which immediate implementation of all or part of a decision is necessary for relief from hazards threatening human health and safety or natural resources on those NFS or adjacent lands; or that would result in substantial loss of economic value to the Federal Government if implementation of the decision were delayed." 36 CFR §215.2.

In granting the ESD for this Project, the Chief Forester considered three factors: (1) the loss of receipts to the government due to delayed commencement of the Project; (2) the potential loss of an "opportunity to accomplish Douglas-fir planting and dwarf mistletoe control objectives"; and (3) the "importance this project has to the local economy of southwest Montana." We hold that, at a minimum, there are "serious questions" on the merits whether these three factors are sufficient to justify the ESD. We consider in turn the three factors upon which the Chief Forester relied.

First, the potential loss of receipts to the government resulting from the delay inherent in the appeals process was not great. The Chief Forester wrote that a delay of the commencement of the project until the summer of 2010 would result in a "projected loss of receipts to the government of as much as $16,000." The Chief Forester wrote, in addition, that if the commencement of the project were delayed until 2010, this would "significantly increase[ ] the likelihood of receiving no bids." "An absence of bids would push the potential loss to the government to $70,000." With all due respect to the budgetary concerns of the Forest Service, a loss of anticipated revenues to the government of "as much as $16,000," or even a "potential loss" of $70,000 in the event of no bids, is likely not a "substantial loss . . . to the Federal Government."

Even if $70,000 might, in some contexts, constitute a "substantial loss," that figure here is highly speculative. The Chief Forester indicated that a one-year delay would "significantly increase[ ] the likelihood of receiving no bids," but we cannot know precisely what that statement means. We do know that with a 2009 commencement date, multiple bids were submitted almost immediately, and one was accepted. The likelihood of not receiving a bid in 2009 appears to have been essentially zero. An increase from a likelihood of essentially 0% to a likelihood of 10% would be a significant increase in likelihood. But a 10% risk of receiving no bids results in a risk-adjusted loss of 10% of $70,000, or $7,000. A risk-adjusted loss of $7,000 is not significant.

Second, the loss of the opportunity to "accomplish Douglas-fir planting and dwarf mistletoe objectives" would be an actual loss only if there were no successful bid on the Project. That is, the Chief Forester concluded that if there were a bid on the Project, the monetary loss to the government would be "as much as $16,000." But in that event, there would be no loss of opportunity to plant Douglas firs or to control dwarf mistletoe, for those objectives would be accomplished by means of the logging contract. Only if there were no bids on the contract would the opportunity be lost. For the reasons just discussed, the possibility of no bids appears to us to be highly speculative. In addition, the Forest Service did not even attempt to quantify the extent of its mistletoe abatement objectives that would be achieved through this Project. It is unclear from the record whether the acres selected are particularly infested with mistletoe and therefore the Project is essential to the Forest Service's goals, or if mistletoe abatement on these acres is simply a serendipitous byproduct of the Project.

Third, the Chief Forester took into account the importance of the Project to the local economy of southwest Montana. As discussed below, this factor is relevant to the public interest element of the preliminary injunction analysis. But the impact of a project on a local economy is not one of the factors the Chief Forester was permitted to consider in deciding whether to issue an ESD. Under Forest Service regulations, she was permitted to consider "hazards threatening human health and safety or natural resources" and any "substantial loss of economic value to the Federal Government." 36 CFR §215.2. Neither the regulation, nor the ARA, permits consideration of the local economy in making an ESD determination. Thus, in relying on the third factor, the Chief Forester "relied on factors Congress did not intend [her] to consider." *Lands Council.*

Finally, we note that the Forest Service has not been able to make clear to us, either in its briefing or at oral argument, why it waited so long to request an ESD. The Rat Creek fire occurred in August and September of 2007. The ESD was requested, and then issued, almost two years later. The delay in requesting an ESD obviously undermines the Chief Forester's determination in July 2009 that there was an Emergency Situation that justified the elimination of otherwise available administrative appeals.

We therefore conclude that AWR has, at a minimum, raised "serious questions" on the merits of its claim regarding the validity of the Chief Forester's Emergency Situation Determination.

3. Balance of Hardships

We conclude that the balance of hardships between the parties tips sharply in favor of AWR. When the question was before the district court, logging was contemplated on 1,652 acres of land in the Beaverhead-Deerlodge National Forest. Once those acres are logged, the work and recreational opportunities that would otherwise be available on that land are irreparably lost.

In addition, AWR was harmed by its inability to participate in the administrative appeals process, and that harm is perpetuated by the Project's approval. The administrative appeals process would have allowed AWR to challenge the Project under both NFMA and NEPA, and to seek changes in the Project before final approval by the Forest Service. Such administrative appeals sometimes result in significant changes to proposed projects.

The hardship to the Forest Service, set against the hardship to AWR, is an estimated potential foregone revenue of "as much as $16,000," and a much more speculative loss of up to $70,000. These foregone revenues are so small that they cannot provide a significant counterweight to the harm caused to AWR. In addition, as noted above, the Forest Service's opportunity to mitigate mistletoe infestation and to replant Douglas firs is tied to whether the Project occurs or not. Because we conclude that the risk that the project will not occur at all is speculative, those lost opportunities similarly cannot outweigh the harm to AWR.

The balance of the hardships here tips sharply enough in favor of AWR that a preliminary injunction is warranted in light of the serious questions raised as to the merits of its ARA claim. That decision, however, does not end our analysis, as the preliminary injunction must also be in the public interest.

4. Public Interest

In this case, we must consider competing public interests. On the side of issuing the injunction, we recognize the well-established "public interest in preserving nature and avoiding irreparable environmental injury." *Lands Council.* This court has also recognized the public interest in careful consideration of environmental impacts before major federal projects go forward, and we have held that suspending such projects until that consideration occurs "comports with the public interest." South Fork Band Council of West Shoshone of Nevada v. Department of Interior, 588 F.3d 718, 728 (9th Cir. 2009). While that public interest is most often noted in the context of NEPA cases, we see no reason why it does not apply equally to violations of the ARA. In the ARA, Congress specifically identified the process through which it wanted the Forest Service to make project decisions such as this one. It comports with the public interest for the Forest Service to comply faithfully with those procedures and to use the exceptional emergency procedures sparingly and only in compliance with its own implementing regulations.

We will not grant a preliminary injunction, however, unless those public interests outweigh other public interests that cut in favor of not issuing the injunction. See *Lands Council* ("Consistent with *Amoco Production Company,* we have held that the public interest in preserving nature and avoiding irreparable environmental injury outweighs economic concerns in cases where plaintiffs were likely to succeed on the merits of their underlying claim."). "The public interest analysis for the issuance of a preliminary injunction requires us to consider whether there exists some critical public interest that would be injured by the grant of preliminary relief." Cal. Pharmacists Ass'n v. Maxwell-Jolly, 596 F.3d 1098, 1114-15 (9th Cir. 2010) (internal quotations omitted).

The public interests that might be injured by a preliminary injunction here, however, do not outweigh the public interests that will be served. The primary public interest asserted by the Forest Service is that the Project will aid the struggling local economy and prevent job loss. The effect on the health of the local economy is a proper consideration in the public interest analysis. The Forest Service asserts that the Project would directly create 18 to 26 temporary jobs and would have indirect beneficial effects on other aspects of the local economy. The record before us reflects that the jobs in question, and, for the most part, the indirect effects, will begin and end with work on the Project which is now expected to be completed in 2010.

On these facts, we conclude that issuing the injunction is in the public interest.

CONCLUSION

We conclude that the district court erred in denying AWR's request for a preliminary injunction. AWR has established a likelihood of irreparable injury if the Project continues. AWR has also established serious questions, at the very least, on the merits of its claim under the ARA. Because AWR has done so with respect to its claim under the ARA, we do not reach its claims under NFMA and NEPA. The balance of hardships between the parties tips sharply in favor of AWR. Finally, the public interest favors a preliminary injunction.

We therefore REVERSE and REMAND for further proceedings consistent with this opinion.

MOSMAN, District Judge, concurring:

Today's holding that the "serious questions" test remains valid post-*Winter* is an important one for district courts tasked with evaluating requests for preliminary injunctions. The task is often a delicate and difficult balancing act, with complex factual scenarios teed up on an expedited basis, and supported only by limited discovery. A sliding scale approach, including the "serious questions" test, preserves the flexibility that is so essential to handling preliminary injunctions, and that is the hallmark of relief in equity.

While the Supreme Court cabined that flexibility with regard to the likelihood of harm, there are good reasons to treat the likelihood of success differently. As between the two, a district court at the preliminary injunction stage is in a much better position to predict the likelihood of harm than the likelihood of success. In fact, it is not unusual for the parties to be in rough agreement about what will follow a denial of injunctive relief. In this case, for example, the parties agree that more than 1,600 acres would be logged in the absence of an injunction. While they disagree about the implications of the logging—such as the extent of environmental impact or the value of natural recovery—the mere fact of logging is undisputed.

But predicting the likelihood of success is another matter entirely. As mentioned, the whole question of the merits comes before the court on an accelerated schedule. The parties are often mostly guessing about important factual points that go, for example, to whether a statute has been violated, whether a noncompetition agreement is even valid, or whether a patent is enforceable. The arguments that flow from the facts, while not exactly half-baked, do not have the clarity and development that will come later at summary judgment or trial. In this setting, it can seem almost inimical to good judging to hazard a prediction about which side is likely to succeed. There are, of course, obvious cases. But in many, perhaps most, cases the better question to ask is whether there are serious questions going to the merits. That question has a legitimate answer. Whether plaintiffs are likely to prevail often does not.

■ NOTES ON INJUNCTIVE RELIEF

1. The issue in *Alliance* is whether a court should grant a preliminary injunction stopping a reforestation project, to test the legality of the Forest Service emergency order cutting off the right of public groups to appeal the decision to go forward on the project. Notice four things. First, often preliminary injunctive relief is critical, and a denial can mean "the whole ball game," as is true in *Alliance* itself (denial left the Service free to continue and possibly complete the project before the case could be resolved). Second, the court acts *before it knows* who will win, on the basis of the parties' legal arguments and factual submissions. Third, FRCP 65 requires one who seeks preliminary injunctive relief to post a bond to cover defendant's costs (states often have similar requirements), which means damages (not attorneys' fees) in case relief is erroneously granted, and it is settled that the bond caps recovery that the defendant can get if the court has erred. Fourth, an order granting or denying preliminary injunctive relief is immediately appealable under a special statute (28 USC §1291(a)) *despite* the fact that "interlocutory orders" (those that are not the last act of the trial court in the case) are usually not reviewable until the case is over. Many states have similar provisions.

2. There is universal agreement that four criteria count in this context. As the Supreme Court put it in *Winter* (cited and construed in *Alliance*), "plaintiff seeking a preliminary injunction must establish that he is likely to succeed on the merits, that he is likely to suffer irreparable harm in the absence of preliminary relief, that the balance of equities tips in his favor, and that an injunction is in the public interest." Winter v. Natural Resources Defense Council, 555 U.S. 7, 20 (2008). At least implicit in the idea of harm to the plaintiff is the notion, carried forward from the English origins of equity jurisprudence, that injunctive relief is appropriate only where money damages would be inadequate, and *Alliance* takes as an article of faith the proposition that money damages cannot compensate for loss of recreational access to nature. The four criteria are broad, and in practice highly variable. See John Leubsdorf, *The Standard for Preliminary Injunctions*, 91 Harv. L. Rev. 525, 526 (1978) (describing variability, including formulations of the probability of success, sometimes framed as in terms of "reasonable certainty," sometimes "clear right," sometimes "fair question on the merits," sometimes "substantial probability of success").

3. In 1985, Judge Posner wrote an opinion in the *American Hospital Supply* case adopting Professor Leubsdorf's proposal, advanced in the article cited in the prior note, for what came to be called a "sliding scale" approach based on a cost-benefit analysis. Posner said a preliminary injunction should issue "if but only if $P \times H_p > (1 - P) H_d$,[3] which he then put into these words: Plaintiff should win a preliminary injunction "only if the harm to the plaintiff if the injunction is denied, multiplied by the probability that the denial would be an error (that the plaintiff, in other words, will win at trial), exceeds the harm to the defendant if the injunction is granted, multiplied by the probability that granting the injunction would be an error." See American Hospital Supply Corp. v. Hospital Products Ltd., 780 F.2d 589, 593 (7th Cir. 1986). This approach treats what may be the two most important factors as interrelated, so that—as the court comments in *Alliance*—"a stronger showing of one element may offset a weaker showing of another." The Ninth Circuit had framed the first factor—probability of plaintiff's success on the merits—as requiring plaintiff to raise "substantial questions," and *Alliance* holds that this version of the standard is still viable, even after the decision in *Winter* treated the factor as *independent*—as requiring plaintiff to show "likelihood of success," regardless how large or small are the parties' stakes, and even if plaintiff's stake is much larger than defendant's. Is *Alliance* convincing on this point?

4. The sliding scale standard of *American Hospital Supply* has some adherents,[4] but has also drawn criticism. See, e.g., Douglas Lichtman, *Uncertainty and the Standard for Preliminary Relief*, 70 U. Chi. L. Rev. 197 (2003) (formulaic approach depends on ability of judge to appraise the harm that parties would suffer as a result of mistake in awarding or denying preliminary injunctive relief, but courts cannot estimate these matters reliably); Linda S. Mullenix, *Burying (with Kindness) the Felicific Calculus of Civil Procedure*, 40 Vand. L. Rev. 541, 569-570 (1987) (probability assessments "work fine at the gambling table," and in connection with "actuarial assessments" in wrongful death cases, but no judge would have a sample in personal experience on which to base an estimate of probable success in a suit, and the model and probability formula "give the false impression that they eliminate subjectivity"). See also Linda J. Silberman, *Injunctions by the Numbers: Less Than the Sum of Its Parts*, 63 Chi.-Kent L. Rev. 279, 300-301 (1987) (formulaic approach encourages closer appellate scrutiny because it suggests that preliminary injunctive relief turns on resolving questions of law, but "broader appellate review" may be justified because injunctive relief is so drastic and far-reaching, and views of three judges should count for more than the views of one trial judge). In Chapter 13, you learn that appellate review of judge-tried cases observes an "abuse of discretion" standard for rulings that apply broad legal standards to facts (giving maximum leeway to the trial court), a "clear error"

[3] P means "probability that plaintiff will win," H_p means "loss or cost to plaintiff if the preliminary injunction is erroneously denied," (1 − P) means "probability that plaintiff will lose" or "probability that defendant will win," and H_d means "loss or cost to defendant if the preliminary injunction is erroneously granted."
[4] See, e.g., Arizona Association of Providers for Persons with Disabilities v. State, 219 P.3d 216 (Ariz. 2009); 7's Enterprises, Inc. v. Del Rosario, 143 P.3d 23 (Haw. 2006); DMF Leasing, Inc. v. Budget Rent-a-Car of Maryland, Inc., 871 A.2d 639 (Md. App. 2005); Ebony Lake Healthcare Center v. Texas Dep't of Human Services, 62 S.W.3d 867 (Tex. App. 2001), all endorsing this approach.

standard for findings of fact (giving some leeway), and a *de novo* standard to rulings on pure questions of law (giving no leeway). Doesn't *Alliance* announce that the "abuse of discretion" standard applies to the ruling denying injunctive relief, while actually scrutinizing the ruling far more closely (as clear error or *de novo* standard mandate)?

5. *Alliance* illustrates preliminary injunctive relief in the important modern setting of "public law" litigation—here, a challenge to official action. Resort to preliminary injunctive relief vastly expanded over the last half of the twentieth century, and is commonplace in business litigation. See, e.g., American Hospital Supply Corp. v. Hospital Products Ltd., 780 F.2d 589, 593 (7th Cir. 1986) (enjoining maker of surgical stapling equipment from terminating agreement with distributor); Ciena Corporation v. Jarrard, 203 F.3d 58 (4th Cir. 2000) (regional sales director quit and went to work for start-up that offered her ten times the salary; court entered TRO and preliminary injunction enforcing plaintiff's agreement not to work for competitor for a year). See also Douglas Laycock, *The Death of the Irreparable Injury Rule*, 103 Harv. L. Rev. 687, 713-714 (1990) (injunctive relief no longer depends on inadequacy of damages; injunctions "are a routine remedy for misappropriation of trade secrets; infringement of patents, copyrights, or trademarks," as well as "violations of antitrust laws or covenants not to compete" and cases raising claims of "interference with contract" and "other kinds of unfair competition," where damages are the remedy "only for past violations beyond the reach of injunctions"). Not everyone applauds this development. See, e.g., Anthony DiSarro, *Freeze Frame: The Supreme Court's Reaffirmation of the Substantive Principles of Preliminary Injunctions*, 47 Gonz. L. Rev. 51 (2011) (Supreme Court has sought to restore preliminary injunction to its rightful place "as a drastic provisional remedy that should be sparingly granted," and decisions "watering down" the irreparable injury and likelihood of success criteria have led to "excessive resort" to the remedy); Ofer Grosskopf & Barak Medina, *Remedies for Wrongfully-Issued Preliminary Injunctions: The Case for Disgorgement of Profits*, 32 Seattle U. L. Rev. 903 (2009) (measure of relief for erroneously granted injunctions should be a return to defendant of plaintiff's profits, rather than payment of defendant's losses). Others have argued for even further expansion of preliminary injunctive relief. See, e.g., Richard Brooks & Warren Schwartz, *Legal Uncertainty, Economic Efficiency, and the Preliminary Injunction Doctrine*, 58 Stan. L. Rev. 381 (2005) (courts should grant relief whenever plaintiff is willing to post bond, or when such relief would be the most efficient allocation of resources). But see John Leubsdorf, *Preliminary Injunctions: In Defense of the Merits*, 76 Fordham L. Rev. 33 (2007) (efficiency concerns should not count decisively; courts should try, as they do now, to avoid granting relief to parties not entitled to it).

6. Preliminary injunctive relief has long been important in disputes over title and construction projects affecting real property. See, e.g., City of Great Falls v. Forbes, 247 P.3d 1086 (Mont. 2011) (enjoining property owner from continuing construction project without permit); Cullen v. Tarini, 15 A.3d 968

(R.I. 2011) (enjoining construction of home in alleged violation of restrictive covenants designed to protect plaintiff's ocean view). And see Muratore v. Laprad, 733 A.2d 722 (R.I. 1999) (issuing TRO to block defendant from conveying property pending resolution of claim for specific performance of contract requiring defendant to sell property to plaintiff). But even temporary injunctive relief in such cases can be devastating to parties on the receiving end, and courts can decline to step in immediately out of concerns over fairness. See, e.g., Waller v. Golden, 706 S.E.2d 403 (Ga. 2011) (construction of swimming pool violated covenants, but court could find that plaintiff's delay in seeking injunction until construction was under way constituted laches that called for lifting temporary injunction; damage to defendants from continuation of injunction was plain; damage to plaintiffs was speculative); Hill v. Petrotech Resources Corp., 325 S.W.3d 302 (Ky. 2010) (disapproving injunction prohibiting investigator from making statements accusing defendants of misconduct; state and federal constitutions bar injunctive relief against defamatory speech until falsity has been "finally adjudicated"). Courts can also decline injunctive relief in favor of less disruptive remedies where "facts on the ground" suggest that injunctive relief would be more costly than other remedies. See, e.g., Proctor v. Huntington, 238 P.3d 1117 (Wash. 2010) (defendant owning 27-acre parcel adjacent to plaintiff's 30-acre parcel built house on plaintiff's parcel, by accident that neither party recognized, after being misinformed by surveyor on location of property line; instead of requiring defendant to remove house, court orders sale of part of plaintiff's property to defendant). But see Poynter Investments, Inc. v. Century Builders of Piedmont, Inc., 694 S.E.2d 15 (S.C. 2010) (cannot rewrite territorial restriction in noncompetition clause; choice is to enforce or refuse enforcement of clause as written).

7. Recall from your study of American history that injunctive relief was central in the civil rights struggles of the 1960s. Thus injunctions were used, for example, to implement desegregation after the famous decision in Brown v. Board of Education, 347 U.S. 483 (1954). In fact, injunctive relief is critical in a wide variety of "institutional reform" litigation that has become commonplace in American society and is examined more thoroughly in courses in remedies and complex litigation.

4. Punitive Damages

The possibility of punitive damage recovery is an important element of tort law. As the name suggests, the purpose is not to compensate for loss, but to penalize for misconduct. Generally, only egregious misconduct is thought to be bad enough to justify punitive damages—misconduct that could be described as malicious or wanton, reckless, outrageous, purposefully harmful, or deceitful. In other words, something more than negligence is required— something more than selling or making a product that is unfit for its intended purpose. Misconduct of the latter sort can support awards of compensatory damages, but punitive damages depend on showing that what the defendant did was worse.

Punitive damages are seldom awarded in personal injury suits arising out of automobile accidents. One reason may be that most ordinary people could not pay large punitive damage judgments, and insurance may or may not cover misconduct of the sort that could support punitive damage awards.[5]

Punitive damages can be awarded in contract cases too, but a mere breach of contract, even if "knowing" or "intentional," cannot support punitive damage claims. When a breach of contract is also a tort that could justify punitive damages, or close to that in the sense that the conduct indicates bad faith, punitive damages are possible. Thus insurance carriers may be liable for bad faith refusal to settle claims against the insured, and courts are affected by the fact that denial of coverage can be catastrophic to the insured, by the fact that carriers are repeat players in the setting of claims resolution, and perhaps by the disparity in economic power and the sheer size of the typical carrier. See generally 3 Dobbs, Law of Remedies §12.5(2) (2d ed. 1993). Sometimes, punitive damages can also be had where employers wrongfully terminate employees in egregious circumstances, as in cases of retaliatory discharge. See, e.g., Travis v. Gary Community Mental Health Center, Inc., 921 F.2d 108, 111 (7th Cir. 1990) (approving punitive damages where employee was fired for testifying against employer), *cert. denied,* 502 U.S. 812 (1990). Courts sometimes stress that employer misconduct violates statutes, hence constituting a special kind of public wrong. Indeed, some statutes, including a federal provision enacted in 1991, authorize punitive damages. See 42 USC §1981a (where employer engages "unlawful intentional discrimination," employee may recover "compensatory and punitive damages").

In terms of sheer numbers, tort cases involve punitive damage awards more often than contract cases, but studies suggest that punitive damages are awarded only in a small fraction of cases (most studies come up with numbers of 2 to 5 percent). In terms of percentages, some studies suggest that punitive damages are awarded most often in intentional tort cases, with libel cases in the lead (almost 30 percent include punitive damage awards). Contract cases involving fraud generate punitive damage awards often (studies suggest 21 percent of the time), and product liability cases, which attract the most attention, are next in line (studies estimate that about 15 percent generate punitive damage awards). See generally Neil

---

[5] Intentional misconduct is not covered by insurance, and the question whether a policy covers lesser forms of misconduct that are more egregious than negligence is a matter of interpretation and uncertainty. Beyond this difficulty, courts split on the question whether public policy should bar insurance coverage for punitive damage claims. See generally Northwestern National Casualty Co. v. McNulty, 307 F.2d 432 (5th Cir. 1962) (public policy bars insurance coverage for punitive damages); Ross Neely Systems, Inc. v. Continental Fire & Casualty Co., 196 F.3d 1347 (11th Cir. 1999) (insurance policy does not cover punitive damages). And see generally 1 Dobbs, Law of Remedies §3.11(8) (2d ed. 1993).

Vidmar & Mary R. Rose, *Punitive Damages by Juries in Florida: In Terrorem and In Reality*, 38 Harv. J. on Legis. 487 (2001); Michael L. Rustad, *Unraveling Punitive Damages: Current Data and Further Inquiry*, 1998 Wis. L. Rev. 15; Marika F.X. Litras et al., U.S. Department of Justice, Tort Trials and Verdicts in Large Counties (1996); Carol J. DeFrances, U.S. Department of Justice, Civil Jury Cases and Verdicts in Large Counties (1992).

Punitive damage claims put in play one factor that is normally out of bounds—the wealth of the defendant. The idea is that punitive damages should deter wrongful conduct, so the award must be economically painful enough to catch the attention of the wrongdoer and discourage future wrongdoing.

Perhaps not surprisingly, the subject of punitive damages is much written about, often passionately, and is highly controversial. Reports of astronomical awards, in amounts of billions of dollars, spurred tort reform measures, which include the following: (1) cap punitive damage recovery at a certain sum; (2) empower the state to share punitive damage judgments; (3) bifurcate trials so punitive damages are considered after liability and actual damages (keep from juries some of the information, such as that relating to defendant's wealth, until liability and actual damages are determined); (4) raise the standard of proof for showing malice, to something more rigorous than the preponderance standard (some states require "clear and convincing evidence," and a few states like Colorado require proof "beyond a reasonable doubt"); (5) prevent multiple punitive damage awards for a single course of conduct; (6) allocate responsibility for deciding the amount of punitive damages to the judge, rather than juries; and (7) put in place standards to be applied in post-trial motions and appellate review to ensure that punitive damage awards are proper and not excessive. See generally James R. McKown, *Punitive Damages: State Trends and Developments*, 14 Rev. Litig. 419 (1995); Jane Mallor & Barry Roberts, *Punitive Damages: Toward a Principled Approach*, 50 Hastings L.J. 969, 1001 (1999) (advocating that judges determine punitive damages, and suggesting criteria for determining punitive damages).

Increasingly, the Supreme Court has been asked to impose constitutional limits on punitive damages. In 1989, the Court reviewed an award of $6 million in a private antitrust suit, in which a small waste collection firm sued a nationwide company accusing it of predatory business practices violating the monopoly provision of the Sherman Act. The Court concluded that this award did not violate the Eighth Amendment's prohibition of "excessive fines," but did not reach the question whether it violated due process. See Browning-Ferris Industries v. Kelco Disposal, Inc., 492 U.S. 257 (1989).

Haslip Case. Two years later, the Court reached the due process question. The case involved an insurance agent who obtained medical coverage for city employees in Alabama and collected premiums from the city, but failed to remit them to the carriers, resulting in a termination of coverage that was not known by the employees nor the city. When an employee named Haslip incurred medical expenses that were not paid, she and others sued the agent and the carrier. Haslip won a verdict for a little more than $1 million, including actual damages of about $4,000 in out-of-pocket expenses (hospital and doctor bills) and $200,000 for what seems to be pain and suffering. The insurance carrier challenged the award of approximately $800,000 in punitive damages, arguing that this "product of unbridled jury discretion" violated due process. The Supreme Court disagreed, stressing that the common law approach followed by Alabama, in which a jury is told to determine the appropriate amount in light of "the gravity of the wrong and the need to deter similar wrongful conduct," comports with practice followed by American courts prior to the Constitution. The punitive award was "more than 4 times" the compensatory damages and more than "200 times the out-of-pocket expenses" and "much in excess" of the fine that could be imposed for insurance fraud under Alabama law. While "unlimited" discretion for either judges or juries "may invite extreme results that jar one's constitutional sensibilities," the award here did not "cross the line," although it "may be close." The Court also stressed that Alabama courts themselves review punitive damage awards by considering seven factors or criteria:

> (a) whether there is a reasonable relationship between the punitive damages award and the harm likely to result from the defendant's conduct as well as the harm that actually has occurred; (b) the degree of reprehensibility of the defendant's conduct, the duration of that conduct, the defendant's awareness, any concealment, and the existence and frequency of similar past conduct; (c) the profitability to the defendant of the wrongful conduct and the desirability of removing that profit and of having the defendant also sustain a loss; (d) the "financial position" of the defendant; (e) all the costs of litigation; (f) the imposition of criminal sanctions on the defendant for its conduct, these to be taken in mitigation; and (g) the existence of other civil awards against the defendant for the same conduct, these also to be taken in mitigation.

The common law method, implemented by such instructions and subject to the safeguards of review under these standards, sufficiently constrains Alabama juries in the award of punitive damages. Pacific Mutual Life Insurance Company v. Haslip, 499 U.S. 1, 21-22 (1991).

TXO **Case.** Two years after *Haslip*, the Court took a case involving business entities in a dispute relating to land title and oil royalties. TXO Production Corporation (a Texas company) had information that producing oil and gas from a thousand-acre parcel in West Virginia would be profitable, so TXO offered to buy the "Blevins tract" from Alliance Resources and others, in an arrangement involving cash for the land and oil and gas rights plus a share of royalties. The deal left TXO free to walk out if Alliance did not have title to the oil and gas rights, and apparently Alliance had previously deeded certain other rights (involving coal production) to a third person. TXO acquired these rights separately, then tried to renegotiate its arrangement with Alliance, and filed suit to clear title. Alliance counterclaimed, alleging slander of title. TXO's behavior was essentially a pretext to bring pressure on Alliance, to adjust downward the cost to TXO of developing the Blevins Tract, and Alliance recovered $19,000 in actual damages and $10 million in punitives (526 times actual damages). Arguing that the jury was left "without a yardstick," TXO challenged the award as violating due process. In split opinions, a plurality of three Justices, joined by three others concurring in the judgment, affirmed. The plurality stressed that the jury could consider not only actual harm from TXO's conduct but "the potential harm that might result," quoting this example from an earlier case:

> [A] man wildly fires a gun into a crowd. By sheer chance, no one is injured and the only damage is to a $10 pair of glasses. A jury reasonably could find only $10 in compensatory damages, but thousands of dollars in punitive damages to teach a duty of care. We would allow a jury to impose substantial punitive damages in order to discourage future bad acts.

Garnes v. Fleming Landfill, Inc., 413 S.E.2d 897, 901 (W. Va. 1992), quoted in TXO Production Corp. v. Alliance Resources Corp., 509 U.S. 443, 459-460 (1993).

***Oberg* Case.** In 1994, the Court again took a punitive damage case. There, plaintiff was injured when a three-wheeled all-terrain vehicle overturned, and he won a verdict of $919,290 in actual damages and $5 million in punitives. Honda argued on appeal that the award violated due process because it was excessive and Oregon courts had no power, on post-trial motion or appeal, to reduce or correct such verdicts. This time the Supreme Court sided with defendant. Stressing that judicial review of the size of punitive damages "has been a safeguard against excessive verdicts for as long as punitive damages have been awarded," and noting that Oregon stands alone in refusing to let judges or appellate courts order new trials if punitives are excessive, the Court found that the Oregon procedure violates due process. Honda Motor Co. v. Oberg, 512 U.S. 415, 421, 426 (1994). As sometimes happens in such situations, however, Honda had less to cheer about than meets the eye. On remand, the Oregon Supreme Court reviewed the verdict and assessed its size and found it reasonable, and refused to set it aside.

***Gore* Case.** Again, in 1996, the Supreme Court considered punitive damages. Plaintiff had purchased a new BMW for more than $40,000. He took it to a "detailer" to make it look "snazzier," where he learned that the top, hood, trunk, and quarter panels of the car had already been repainted. The manufacturer's policy was to repair pre-sale damages to cars without disclosing this fact, if the cost of repair came to less than 3 percent of the purchase price, and such a repair had been done here (the parties thought damage came from exposure to acid rain in transit between Germany and the preparation center).

A jury awarded actual damages of $4,000, corresponding to a loss in value of 10 percent of the purchase price, and $4 million in punitives, which (as plaintiffs argued) had the effect of penalizing defendant for selling 1,000 cars for more than their fair market value in similar situations. Defendant challenged the award, showing that its nondisclosure policy was consistent with the laws of about 25 states, and arguing that this policy had never been adjudged unlawful. The Alabama Supreme Court reduced the award to $2 million because it concluded that a jury could not rely on sales in other jurisdictions. The Supreme Court agreed that an Alabama court could not set punitives on the basis of conduct occurring out of state. Even so, the Court was convinced that the reduced award "transcends the constitutional limit," so it reversed with instructions to evaluate the award once more or retry the case. As "guideposts," the Court told the Alabama court to consider

> the degree of reprehensibility of the nondisclosure; the disparity between the harm or potential harm suffered by Dr. Gore and his punitive damages award; and the difference between this remedy and the civil penalties authorized or imposed in comparable cases.

BMW of North America, Inc. v. Gore, 517 U.S. 559, 574 (1996).

Haslip, TXO, Oberg, and *Gore* set the stage for the Supreme Court's next foray—its decision in *Campbell.*

STATE FARM MUTUAL INSURANCE COMPANY v. CAMPBELL

Supreme Court of the United States
538 U.S. 408 (2003)

KENNEDY, J., delivered the opinion of the Court, in which REHNQUIST, C.J., and STEVENS, O'CONNOR, SOUTER, and BREYER, JJ., joined. SCALIA, J., THOMAS, J., and GINSBURG, J., filed dissenting opinions.

We address once again the measure of punishment, by means of punitive damages, a State may impose upon a defendant in a civil case. The question is whether, in the circumstances we shall recount, an award of $145 million in punitive damages, where full compensatory damages are $1 million, is excessive and in violation of the Due Process Clause of the Fourteenth Amendment to the Constitution of the United States.

I

In 1981, Curtis Campbell (Campbell) was driving with his wife, Inez Preece Campbell, in Cache County, Utah. He decided to pass six vans traveling ahead of them on a two-lane highway. Todd Ospital was driving a small car approaching from the opposite direction. To avoid a head-on collision with Campbell, who by then was driving on the wrong side of the highway and toward oncoming traffic, Ospital swerved onto the shoulder, lost control of his automobile, and collided with a vehicle driven by Robert G. Slusher. Ospital was killed, and Slusher was rendered permanently disabled. The Campbells escaped unscathed.

In the ensuing wrongful death and tort action, Campbell insisted he was not at fault. Early investigations did support differing conclusions as to who caused the accident, but "a consensus was reached early on by the investigators and witnesses that Mr. Campbell's unsafe pass had indeed caused the crash." Campbell's insurance company, petitioner State Farm Mutual Automobile Insurance Company (State Farm), nonetheless decided to contest liability and declined offers by Slusher and Ospital's estate (Ospital) to settle the claims for the policy limit of $50,000 ($25,000 per claimant). State Farm also ignored the advice of one of its own investigators and took the case to trial, assuring the Campbells that "their assets were safe, that they had no liability for the accident, that [State Farm] would represent their interests, and that they did not need to procure separate counsel." To the contrary, a jury determined that Campbell was 100 percent at fault, and a judgment was returned for $185,849, far more than the amount offered in settlement.

At first State Farm refused to cover the $135,849 in excess liability. Its counsel made this clear to the Campbells: "'You may want to put for sale signs on your property to get things moving.'" Nor was State Farm willing to post a supersedeas bond to allow Campbell to appeal the judgment against him. Campbell obtained his own counsel to appeal the verdict. During the pendency of the appeal, in late 1984, Slusher, Ospital, and the Campbells reached an agreement whereby Slusher and Ospital agreed not to seek satisfaction of their claims against the Campbells. In exchange the Campbells agreed to pursue a bad faith action against State Farm and to be represented by Slusher's and Ospital's attorneys. The Campbells also agreed that Slusher and Ospital would have a right to play a part in all major decisions concerning the bad faith action. No settlement could be concluded without Slusher's and Ospital's approval, and Slusher and Ospital would receive 90 percent of any verdict against State Farm.

In 1989, the Utah Supreme Court denied Campbell's appeal in the wrongful death and tort actions. State Farm then paid the entire judgment, including the amounts in excess of the policy limits. The Campbells nonetheless filed a complaint against State Farm alleging bad faith, fraud, and intentional infliction of emotional distress. The trial court initially granted State Farm's motion for summary judgment because State Farm had paid the excess verdict, but that ruling was reversed on appeal. On remand State Farm moved *in limine* to exclude evidence of alleged conduct that occurred in unrelated cases outside of Utah, but the trial court denied the motion. At State Farm's request the trial court bifurcated the trial into two phases conducted before different juries. In the first phase the jury determined that State Farm's decision not to settle was unreasonable because there was a substantial likelihood of an excess verdict.

Before the second phase of the action against State Farm we decided BMW of North America, Inc. v. Gore, 517 U.S. 559 (1996), and refused to sustain a $2 million punitive damages award which accompanied a verdict of only $4,000 in compensatory damages. Based on that decision, State Farm again moved for the exclusion of evidence of dissimilar out-of-state conduct. The trial court denied State Farm's motion.

The second phase addressed State Farm's liability for fraud and intentional infliction of emotional distress, as well as compensatory and punitive damages. The Utah Supreme Court aptly characterized this phase of the trial:

> State Farm argued during phase II that its decision to take the case to trial was an "honest mistake" that did not warrant punitive damages. In contrast, the Campbells introduced evidence that State Farm's decision to take the case to trial was a result of a national scheme to meet corporate fiscal goals by capping payouts on claims company wide. This scheme was referred to as State Farm's "Performance, Planning and Review," or PP&R, policy. To prove the existence of this scheme, the trial court allowed the Campbells to introduce extensive expert testimony regarding fraudulent practices by State Farm in its nation-wide operations. Although State Farm moved prior to phase II of the trial for the exclusion of such evidence and continued to object to it at trial, the trial court ruled that such evidence was admissible to determine whether State Farm's conduct in the Campbell case was indeed intentional and sufficiently egregious to warrant punitive damages.

Evidence pertaining to the PP&R policy concerned State Farm's business practices for over 20 years in numerous States. Most of these practices bore no relation to third-party automobile insurance claims, the type of claim underlying the Campbells' complaint against the company. The jury awarded the Campbells $2.6 million in compensatory damages and $145 million in punitive damages, which the trial court reduced to $1 million and $25 million respectively. Both parties appealed.

The Utah Supreme Court sought to apply the three guideposts we identified in *Gore,* and it reinstated the $145 million punitive damages award. Relying in large part on the extensive evidence concerning the PP&R policy, the court concluded State Farm's conduct was reprehensible. The court also relied upon State Farm's "massive wealth" and on testimony indicating that "State Farm's actions, because of their clandestine nature, will be punished at most in one out of every 50,000 cases as a matter of statistical probability," and concluded that the ratio between punitive and compensatory damages was not unwarranted. Finally, the court noted that the punitive damages award was not excessive when compared to various civil and criminal penalties State Farm could have faced, including $10,000 for each act of fraud, the suspension of its license to conduct business in Utah, the disgorgement of profits, and imprisonment. We granted certiorari.

II

We recognized in Cooper Industries, Inc. v. Leatherman Tool Group, Inc., 532 U.S. 424 (2001), that in our judicial system compensatory and punitive damages, although usually awarded at the same time by the same decision-maker, serve different purposes. Compensatory damages "are intended to redress the concrete loss that the plaintiff has suffered by reason of the defendant's wrongful conduct" (citing Restatement (Second) of Torts §903, pp. 453-454 (1979)). By contrast, punitive damages serve a broader function; they are aimed at deterrence and retribution.

While States possess discretion over the imposition of punitive damages, it is well established that there are procedural and substantive constitutional limitations on these awards. *Cooper Industries, supra*; *Gore,* 517 U.S., at 559; Honda Motor Co. v. Oberg, 512 U.S. 415 (1994); TXO Production Corp. v. Alliance Resources Corp., 509 U.S. 443 (1993); [Pacific Mut. Life Ins. Co. v.] Haslip, 499 U.S. 1 (1991). The Due Process Clause of the Fourteenth Amendment prohibits the imposition of grossly excessive or arbitrary punishments on a tortfeasor. To the extent an award is grossly excessive, it furthers no legitimate purpose and constitutes an arbitrary deprivation of property.

Although these awards serve the same purposes as criminal penalties, defendants subjected to punitive damages in civil cases have not been accorded the protections applicable in a criminal proceeding. This increases our concerns over the imprecise manner in which punitive damages systems are administered. We have admonished that "[p]unitive damages pose an acute danger of arbitrary deprivation of property. Jury instructions typically leave the jury with wide discretion in choosing amounts, and the presentation of evidence of a defendant's net worth creates the potential that juries will use their verdicts to express biases against big businesses, particularly those without strong local presences." *Honda Motor, supra,* at 432. Our concerns are heightened when the decisionmaker is presented, as we shall discuss, with evidence that has little bearing as to the amount of punitive damages that should be awarded. Vague instructions, or those that merely inform the jury to avoid "passion or prejudice," do little to aid the decisionmaker in its task of assigning appropriate weight to evidence that is relevant and evidence that is tangential or only inflammatory.

In light of these concerns, in *Gore, supra,* we instructed courts reviewing punitive damages to consider three guideposts: (1) the degree of reprehensibility of the defendant's misconduct; (2) the disparity between the actual or potential harm suffered by the plaintiff and the punitive damages award; and (3) the difference between the punitive damages awarded by the jury and the civil penalties authorized or imposed in comparable cases. We reiterated the importance of these three guideposts in *Cooper Industries* and mandated appellate courts to conduct *de novo* review of a trial court's application of them to the jury's award. Exacting appellate review ensures that an award of punitive damages is based upon an "'application of law, rather than a decisionmaker's caprice.'"

III

Under the principles outlined in *Gore*, this case is neither close nor difficult. It was error to reinstate the jury's $145 million punitive damages award. We address each guidepost of *Gore* in some detail.

A

"[T]he most important indicium of the reasonableness of a punitive damages award is the degree of reprehensibility of the defendant's conduct." *Gore*. We have instructed courts to determine the reprehensibility of a defendant by considering whether: the harm caused was physical as opposed to economic; the tortious conduct evinced an indifference to or a reckless disregard of the health or safety of others; the target of the conduct had financial vulnerability; the conduct involved repeated actions or was an isolated incident; and the harm was the result of intentional malice, trickery, or deceit, or mere accident. The existence of any one of these factors weighing in favor of a plaintiff may not be sufficient to sustain a punitive damages award; and the absence of all of them renders any award suspect. It should be presumed a plaintiff has been made whole for his injuries by compensatory damages, so punitive damages should only be awarded if the defendant's culpability, after having paid compensatory damages, is so reprehensible as to warrant the imposition of further sanctions to achieve punishment or deterrence.

Applying these factors in the instant case, we must acknowledge that State Farm's handling of the claims against the Campbells merits no praise. The trial court found that State Farm's employees altered the company's records to make Campbell appear less culpable. State Farm disregarded the overwhelming likelihood of liability and the near-certain probability that, by taking the case to trial, a judgment in excess of the policy limits would be awarded. State Farm amplified the harm by at first assuring the Campbells their assets would be safe from any verdict and by later telling them, post-judgment, to put a for-sale sign on their house. While we do not suggest there was error in awarding punitive damages based upon State Farm's conduct toward the Campbells, a more modest punishment for this reprehensible conduct could have satisfied the State's legitimate objectives, and the Utah courts should have gone no further.

This case, instead, was used as a platform to expose, and punish, the perceived deficiencies of State Farm's operations throughout the country. The Utah Supreme Court's opinion makes explicit that State Farm was being condemned for its nationwide policies rather than for the conduct direct toward the Campbells. ("[T]he Campbells introduced evidence that State Farm's decision to take the case to trial was a result of a national scheme to meet corporate fiscal goals by capping payouts on claims companywide"). This was, as well, an explicit rationale of the trial court's decision in approving the award, though reduced from $145 million to $25 million. ("[T]he Campbells demonstrated, through the testimony of State Farm employees who had worked outside of Utah, and through expert testimony, that this pattern of claims adjustment under the PP&R program was not a local anomaly, but was a consistent, nationwide feature of State Farm's business operations, orchestrated from the highest levels of corporate management").

The Campbells contend that State Farm has only itself to blame for the reliance upon dissimilar and out-of-state conduct evidence. The record does not support this contention. From their opening statements onward the Campbells framed this case as a chance to rebuke State Farm for its nationwide activities. [The Court quotes these passages: "You're going to hear evidence that even the insurance commission[s] in Utah and around the country are unwilling or inept at protecting people against abuses." "[T]his is a very important case. . . . [I]t transcends the Campbell file. It involves a nationwide practice. And you, here, are going to be evaluating and assessing, and hopefully requiring State Farm to stand accountable for what it's doing across the country, which is the purpose of punitive damages."] This was a position maintained throughout the litigation. In opposing State Farm's motion to exclude such evidence under *Gore*, the Campbells' counsel convinced the trial court that there was no limitation on the scope of evidence that could be considered under our precedents. [The Court quotes the trial court's ruling: "As I read *Gore*, I was struck with the fact that a clear message in the case . . . seems to be that courts in punitive damages cases should receive more evidence, not less. And that the court seems to be inviting an even broader area of evidence than the current rulings of the court would indicate."]

A State cannot punish a defendant for conduct that may have been lawful where it occurred. Bigelow v. Virginia, 421 U.S. 809, 824 (1975) ("A State does not acquire power or supervision over the internal affairs of another State merely because the welfare and health of its own citizens may be affected when they travel to that State"); New York Life Ins. Co. v. Head, 234 U.S. 149, 161 (1914) ("[I]t would be impossible to permit the statutes of Missouri to operate beyond the jurisdiction of that State . . . without throwing down the constitutional barriers by which all the States are restricted within the orbits of their lawful authority and upon the preservation of which the Government under the Constitution depends. This is so obviously the necessary result of the Constitution that it has rarely been called in question and hence authorities directly dealing with it do not abound"); Huntington v. Attrill, 146 U.S. 657, 669 (1892) ("Laws have no force of themselves beyond the jurisdiction of the State which enacts them, and can have extra-territorial effect only by the comity of other States"). Nor, as a general rule, does a State have a legitimate concern in imposing punitive damages to punish a defendant for unlawful acts committed outside of the State's jurisdiction. Any proper adjudication of conduct that occurred outside Utah to other persons would require their inclusion, and, to those parties, the Utah courts, in the usual case, would need to apply the laws of their relevant jurisdiction. Phillips Petroleum Co. v. Shutts, 472 U.S. 797, 821-822 (1985).

Here, the Campbells do not dispute that much of the out-of-state conduct was lawful where it occurred. They argue, however, that such evidence was not the primary basis for the punitive damages award and was relevant to the extent it demonstrated, in a general sense, State Farm's motive against its insured. This argument misses the mark. Lawful out-of-state conduct may be probative when it demonstrates the deliberateness and culpability of the defendant's action in the State where it is tortious, but that conduct must have a nexus to the specific harm suffered by the plaintiff. A jury must be instructed, furthermore, that it may not use evidence of out-of-state conduct to punish a defendant for action that was lawful in the jurisdiction where it occurred. *Gore* (noting that a State "does not have the power . . . to punish [a defendant] for conduct that was lawful where it occurred and that had no impact on [the State] or its residents"). A basic principle of federalism is that each State may make its own reasoned judgment about what conduct is permitted or proscribed within its borders, and each State alone can determine what measure of punishment, if any, to impose on a defendant who acts within its jurisdiction.

For a more fundamental reason, however, the Utah courts erred in relying upon this and other evidence: The courts awarded punitive damages to punish and deter conduct that bore no relation to the Campbells' harm. A defendant's dissimilar acts, independent from the acts upon which liability was premised, may not serve as the basis for punitive damages. A defendant should be punished for the conduct that harmed the plaintiff, not for being an unsavory individual or business. Due process does not permit courts, in the calculation of punitive damages, to adjudicate the merits of other parties' hypothetical claims against a defendant under the guise of the reprehensibility analysis, but we have no doubt the Utah Supreme Court did that here. Punishment on these bases creates the possibility of multiple punitive damages awards for the same conduct; for in the usual case nonparties are not bound by the judgment some other plaintiff obtains.

The same reasons lead us to conclude the Utah Supreme Court's decision cannot be justified on the grounds that State Farm was a recidivist. Although "[o]ur holdings that a recidivist may be punished more severely than a first offender recognize that repeated misconduct is more reprehensible than an individual instance of malfeasance," *Gore,* in the context of civil actions courts must ensure the conduct in question replicates the prior transgressions.

The Campbells have identified scant evidence of repeated misconduct of the sort that injured them. Nor does our review of the Utah courts' decisions convince us that State Farm was only punished for its actions toward the Campbells. Although evidence of other acts need not be identical to have relevance in the calculation of punitive damages, the Utah court erred here because evidence pertaining to claims that had nothing to do with a third-party lawsuit was introduced at length. Other evidence concerning reprehensibility was even more tangential. For example, the Utah Supreme Court criticized State Farm's investigation into the personal life of one of its employees and, in a broader approach, the manner in which State Farm's policies corrupted its employees. The Campbells attempt to justify the courts' reliance upon this unrelated testimony on the theory that each dollar of profit made by underpaying a third-party claimant is the same as a dollar made by underpaying a first-party one. For the reasons already stated, this argument is unconvincing. The reprehensibility guidepost does not permit courts to expand the scope of the case so that a defendant may be punished for any malfeasance, which in this case extended for a 20-year period. In this case, because the Campbells have shown no conduct by State Farm similar to that which harmed them, the conduct that harmed them is the only conduct relevant to the reprehensibility analysis.

B

Turning to the second *Gore* guidepost, we have been reluctant to identify concrete constitutional limits on the ratio between harm, or potential harm, to the plaintiff and the punitive damages award. We decline again to impose a bright-line ratio which a punitive damages award cannot exceed. Our jurisprudence and the principles it has now established demonstrate, however, that, in practice, few awards exceeding a single-digit ratio between punitive and compensatory damages, to a significant degree, will satisfy due process. In *Haslip,* in upholding a punitive damages award, we concluded that an award of more than four times the amount of compensatory damages might be close to the line of constitutional impropriety. We cited that 4-to-1 ratio again in *Gore*. The Court further referenced a long legislative history, dating back over 700 years and going forward to today, providing for sanctions of double, treble, or quadruple damages to deter and punish. While these ratios are not binding, they are instructive. They demonstrate what should be obvious: Single-digit multipliers are more likely to comport with due process, while still achieving the State's goals of deterrence and retribution, than awards with ratios in range of 500 to 1, or, in this case, of 145 to 1.

Nonetheless, because there are no rigid benchmarks that a punitive damages award may not surpass, ratios greater than those we have previously upheld may comport with due process where "a particularly egregious act has resulted in only a small amount of economic damages." The converse is also true, however. When compensatory damages are substantial, then a lesser ratio, perhaps only equal to compensatory damages, can reach the outermost limit of the due process guarantee. The precise award in any case, of course, must be based upon the facts and circumstances of the defendant's conduct and the harm to the plaintiff.

In sum, courts must ensure that the measure of punishment is both reasonable and proportionate to the amount of harm to the plaintiff and to the general damages recovered. In the context of this case, we have no doubt that there is a presumption against an award that has a 145-to-1 ratio. The compensatory award in this case was substantial; the Campbells were awarded $1 million for a year and a half of emotional distress. This was complete compensation. The harm arose from a transaction in the economic realm, not from some physical assault or trauma; there were no physical injuries; and State Farm paid the excess verdict before the complaint was filed, so the Campbells suffered only minor economic injuries for the 18-month period in which State Farm refused to resolve the claim against them. The compensatory damages for the injury suffered here, moreover, likely were based on a component which was duplicated in the punitive award. Much of the distress was caused by the outrage and humiliation the Campbells suffered at the actions of their insurer; and it is a major role of punitive damages to condemn such conduct. Compensatory damages, however, already contain this punitive element. See Restatement (Second) of Torts §908, Comment *c*, p. 466 (1977) ("In many cases in which compensatory damages include an amount for emotional distress, such as humiliation or indignation aroused by the defendant's act, there is no clear line of demarcation between punishment and compensation and a verdict for a specified amount frequently includes elements of both").

The Utah Supreme Court sought to justify the massive award by pointing to State Farm's purported failure to report a prior $100 million punitive damages award in Texas to its corporate headquarters; the fact that State Farm's policies have affected numerous Utah consumers; the fact that State Farm will only be punished in one out of every 50,000 cases as a matter of statistical probability; and State Farm's enormous wealth. Since the Supreme Court of Utah discussed the Texas award when applying the ratio guidepost, we discuss it here. The Texas award, however, should have been analyzed in the context of the reprehensibility guidepost only. The failure of the company to report the Texas award is out-of-state conduct that, if the conduct were similar, might have had some bearing on the degree of reprehensibility, subject to the limitations we have described. Here, it was dissimilar, and of such marginal relevance that it should have been accorded little or no weight. The award was rendered in a first-party lawsuit; no judgment was entered in the case; and it was later settled for a fraction of the verdict. With respect to the Utah Supreme Court's second justification, the Campbells' inability to direct us to testimony demonstrating harm to the people of Utah (other than those directly involved in this case) indicates that the adverse effect on the State's general population was in fact minor.

The remaining premises for the Utah Supreme Court's decision bear no relation to the award's reasonableness or proportionality to the harm. They are, rather, arguments that seek to defend a departure from well-established constraints on punitive damages. While States enjoy considerable discretion in deducing when punitive damages are warranted, each award must comport with the principles set forth in *Gore.* Here the argument that State Farm will be punished in only the rare case, coupled with reference to its assets (which, of course, are what other insured parties in Utah and other States must rely upon for payment of claims) had little to do with the actual harm sustained by the Campbells. The wealth of a defendant cannot justify an otherwise unconstitutional punitive damages award. The principles set forth in *Gore* must be implemented with care, to ensure both reasonableness and proportionality.

C

The third guidepost in *Gore* is the disparity between the punitive damages award and the "civil penalties authorized or imposed in comparable cases." We note that, in the past, we have also looked to criminal penalties that could be imposed. The existence of a criminal penalty does have bearing on the seriousness with which a State views the wrongful action. When used to determine the dollar amount of the award, however, the criminal penalty has less utility. Great care must be taken to avoid use of the civil process to assess criminal penalties that can be imposed only after the heightened protections of a criminal trial have been observed, including, of course, its higher standards of proof. Punitive damages are not a substitute for the criminal process, and the remote possibility of a criminal sanction does not automatically sustain a punitive damages award.

Here, we need not dwell long on this guidepost. The most relevant civil sanction under Utah state law for the wrong done to the Campbells appears to be a $10,000 fine for an act of fraud, an amount dwarfed by the $145 million punitive damages award. The Supreme Court of Utah speculated about the loss of State Farm's business license, the disgorgement of profits, and possible imprisonment, but here again its references were to the broad fraudulent scheme drawn from evidence of out-of-state and dissimilar conduct. This analysis was insufficient to justify the award.

IV

An application of the *Gore* guideposts to the facts of this case, especially in light of the substantial compensatory damages awarded (a portion of which contained a punitive element), likely would justify a punitive damages award at or near the amount of compensatory damages. The punitive award of $145 million, therefore, was neither reasonable nor proportionate to the wrong committed, and it was an irrational and arbitrary deprivation of the property of the defendant. The proper calculation of punitive damages under the principles we have discussed should be resolved, in the first instance, by the Utah courts.

The judgment of the Utah Supreme Court is reversed, and the case is remanded for proceedings not inconsistent with this opinion.

It is so ordered.

Justice SCALIA, dissenting.

I adhere to the view expressed in my dissenting opinion in BMW of North America, Inc. v. Gore, 517 U.S. 559, 598-99 (1996), that the Due Process Clause provides no substantive protections against "excessive" or "'unreasonable'" awards of punitive damages. I am also of the view that the punitive damages jurisprudence which has sprung forth from BMW v. Gore is insusceptible of principled application; accordingly, I do not feel justified in giving the case *stare decisis* effect. I would affirm the judgment of the Utah Supreme Court.

Justice THOMAS, dissenting.

I would affirm the judgment below because "I continue to believe that the Constitution does not constrain the size of punitive damages awards." Cooper Industries, Inc. v. Leatherman Tool Group, Inc., 532 U.S. 424, 443. Accordingly, I respectfully dissent.

Justice GINSBURG, dissenting.

Not long ago, this Court was hesitant to impose a federal check on state-court judgments awarding punitive damages. In Browning-Ferris Industries of Vt., Inc. v. Kelco Disposal, Inc., 492 U.S. 257 (1989), the Court held that neither the Excessive Fines Clause of the Eighth Amendment nor federal common law circumscribed awards of punitive damages in civil cases between private parties. Two years later, in Pacific Mut. Life Ins. Co. v. Haslip, 499 U.S. 1 (1991), the Court observed that "unlimited jury [or judicial] discretion . . . in the fixing of punitive damages may invite extreme results that jar one's constitutional sensibilities," the Due Process Clause, the Court suggested, would attend to those sensibilities and guard against unreasonable awards. Nevertheless, the Court upheld a punitive damages award in *Haslip* "more than 4 times the amount of compensatory damages, . . . more than 200 times [the plaintiff's] out-of-pocket expenses," and "much in excess of the fine that could be imposed." And in TXO Production Corp. v. Alliance Resources Corp., 509 U.S. 443 (1993), the Court affirmed a state-court award "526 times greater than the actual damages awarded by the jury."[1] Cf. *Browning-Ferris,* 492 U.S., at 262 (ratio of punitive to compensatory damages over 100 to 1).

It was not until 1996, in BMW of North America, Inc. v. Gore that the Court, for the first time, invalidated a state-court punitive damages assessment as unreasonably large. If our activity in this domain is now "well-established," it takes place on ground not long held.

In *Gore,* I stated why I resisted the Court's foray into punitive damages "territory traditionally within the States' domain." I adhere to those views, and note again that, unlike federal habeas corpus review of state-court convictions under 28 USC §2254, the Court "work[s] at this business [of checking state courts] alone," unaided by the participation of federal district courts and courts of appeals. It was once recognized that "the laws of the particular State must suffice [to superintend punitive damages awards] until judges or legislators authorized to do so initiate system-wide change." *Haslip* (Kennedy, J., concurring in judgment). I would adhere to that traditional view.

I

The large size of the award upheld by the Utah Supreme Court in this case indicates why damage-capping legislation may be altogether fitting and proper. Neither the amount of the award nor the trial record, however, justifies this Court's substitution of its judgment for that of Utah's competent decisionmakers. In this regard, I count it significant that, on the key criterion "reprehensibility," there is a good deal more to the story than the Court's abbreviated account tells.

Ample evidence allowed the jury to find that State Farm's treatment of the Campbells typified its "Performance, Planning and Review" (PP&R) program; implemented by top management in 1979, the program had "the explicit objective of using the claims-adjustment process as a profit center." "[T]he Campbells presented considerable evidence," the trial court noted, documenting "that the PP&R program . . . has functioned, and continues to function, as an unlawful scheme . . . to deny benefits owed consumers by paying out less

---

[1] By switching the focus from the ratio of punitive to compensatory damages to the potential loss to the plaintiffs had the defendant succeeded in its illicit scheme, the Court could describe the relevant ratio in *TXO* as 10 to 1. See *Gore.*

than fair value in order to meet preset, arbitrary payout targets designed to enhance corporate profits." That policy, the trial court observed, was encompassing in scope; it "applied equally to the handling of both third-party and first-party claims."

Evidence the jury could credit demonstrated that the PP&R program regularly and adversely affected Utah residents. Ray Summers, "the adjuster who handled the Campbell case and who was a State Farm employee in Utah for almost twenty years," described several methods used by State Farm to deny claimants fair benefits, for example, "falsifying or withholding of evidence in claim files." A common tactic, Summers recounted, was to "unjustly attac[k] the character, reputation and credibility of a claimant and mak[e] notations to that effect in the claim file to create prejudice in the event the claim ever came before a jury." State Farm manager Bob Noxon, Summers testified, resorted to a tactic of this order in the Campbell case when he "instruct[ed] Summers to write in the file that Todd Ospital (who was killed in the accident) was speeding because he was on his way to see a pregnant girlfriend." In truth, "[t]here was no pregnant girlfriend." Expert testimony noted by the trial court described these tactics as "completely improper."

The trial court also noted the testimony of two Utah State Farm employees, Felix Jensen and Samantha Bird, both of whom recalled "intolerable" and "recurrent" pressure to reduce payouts below fair value. When Jensen complained to top managers, he was told to "get out of the kitchen" if he could not take the heat; Bird was told she should be "more of a team player." At times, Bird said, she "was forced to commit dishonest acts and to knowingly underpay claims." Eventually, Bird quit. Utah managers superior to Bird, the evidence indicated, were improperly influenced by the PP&R program to encourage insurance underpayments. For example, several documents evaluating the performance of managers Noxon and Brown "contained explicit preset average payout goals."

Regarding liability for verdicts in excess of policy limits, the trial court referred to a State Farm document titled the "Excess Liability Handbook"; written before the Campbell accident, the handbook instructed adjusters to pad files with "self-serving" documents, and to leave critical items out of files, for example, evaluations of the insured's exposure. Divisional superintendent Bill Brown used the handbook to train Utah employees. While overseeing the Campbell case, Brown ordered adjuster Summers to change the portions of his report indicating that Mr. Campbell was likely at fault and that the settlement cost was correspondingly high. The Campbells' case, according to expert testimony the trial court recited, "was a classic example of State Farm's application of the improper practices taught in the Excess Liability Handbook."

The trial court further determined that the jury could find State Farm's policy "deliberately crafted" to prey on consumers who would be unlikely to defend themselves. In this regard, the trial court noted the testimony of several former State Farm employees affirming that they were trained to target "the weakest of the herd"—"the elderly, the poor, and other consumers who are least knowledgeable about their rights and thus most vulnerable to trickery or deceit, or who have little money and hence have no real alternative but to accept an inadequate offer to settle a claim at much less than fair value."

The Campbells themselves could be placed within the "weakest of the herd" category. The couple appeared economically vulnerable and emotionally fragile. At the time of State Farm's wrongful conduct, "Mr. Campbell had residuary effects from a stroke and Parkinson's disease."

To further insulate itself from liability, trial evidence indicated, State Farm made "systematic" efforts to destroy internal company documents that might reveal its scheme, efforts that directly affected the Campbells. For example, State Farm had "a special historical department that contained a copy of all past manuals on claim-handling practices and the dates on which each section of each manual was changed." Yet in discovery proceedings, State Farm failed to produce any claim-handling practice manuals for the years relevant to the Campbells' bad-faith case.

State Farm's inability to produce the manuals, it appeared from the evidence, was not accidental. Documents retained by former State Farm employee Samantha Bird, as well as Bird's testimony, showed that while the Campbells' case was pending, Janet Cammack, "an in-house attorney sent by top State Farm management, conducted a meeting . . . in Utah during which she instructed Utah claims management to search their offices and destroy a wide range of material of the sort that had proved damaging in bad-faith litigation in the past—in particular, old claim-handling manuals, memos, claim school notes, procedure guides and other similar documents." "These orders were followed even though at least one meeting participant, Paul Short, was personally aware that these kinds of materials had been requested by the Campbells in this very case."

Consistent with Bird's testimony, State Farm admitted that it destroyed every single copy of claim-handling manuals on file in its historical department as of 1988, even though these documents could have been preserved at minimal expense. Fortuitously, the Campbells obtained a copy of the 1979 PP&R manual by subpoena from a former employee. Although that manual has been requested in other cases, State Farm has never itself produced the document.

"As a final, related tactic," the trial court stated, the jury could reasonably find that "in recent years State Farm has gone to extraordinary lengths to stop damaging documents from being created in the first place." State Farm kept no records at all on excess verdicts in third-party cases, or on bad-faith claims or attendant verdicts. State Farm alleged "that it has no record of its punitive damage payments, even though such payments must be reported to the [Internal Revenue Service] and in some states may not be used to justify rate increases." Regional Vice President Buck Moskalski testified that "he would not report a punitive damage verdict in [the Campbells'] case to higher management, as such reporting was not set out as part of State Farm's management practices."

State Farm's "wrongful profit and evasion schemes," the trial court underscored, were directly relevant to the Campbells' case:

> The record fully supports the conclusion that the bad-faith claim handling that exposed the Campbells to an excess verdict in 1983, and resulted in severe damages to them, was a product of the unlawful profit scheme that had been put in place by top management at State Farm years earlier. The Campbells presented substantial evidence showing how State Farm's improper insistence on claims-handling employees' reducing their claim payouts ... regardless of the merits of each claim, manifested itself ... in the Utah claims operations during the period when the decisions were made not to offer to settle the Campbell case for the $50,000 policy limits—indeed, not to make any offer to settle at a lower amount. This evidence established that high-level manager Bill Brown was under heavy pressure from the PP&R scheme to control indemnity payouts during the time period in question. In particular, when Brown declined to pay the excess verdict against Curtis Campbell, or even post a bond, he had a special need to keep his year-end numbers down, since the State Farm incentive scheme meant that keeping those numbers down was important to helping Brown get a much-desired transfer to Colorado. . . . There was ample evidence that the concepts taught in the Excess Liability Handbook, including the dishonest alteration and manipulation of claim files and the policy against posting any supersedeas bond for the full amount of an excess verdict, were dutifully carried out in this case. . . . There was ample basis for the jury to find that everything that had happened to the Campbells—when State Farm repeatedly refused in bad-faith to settle for the $50,000 policy limits and went to trial, and then failed to pay the "excess" verdict, or at least post a bond, after trial—was a direct application of State Farm's overall profit scheme, operating through Brown and others.

State Farm's "policies and practices," the trial evidence thus bore out, were "responsible for the injuries suffered by the Campbells," and the means used to implement those policies could be found "callous, clandestine, fraudulent, and dishonest." The Utah Supreme Court, relying on the trial court's record-based recitations, understandably characterized State Farm's behavior as "egregious and malicious."

II

The Court dismisses the evidence describing and documenting State Farm's PP&R policy and practices as essentially irrelevant, bearing "no relation to the Campbells' harm." It is hardly apparent why that should be so. What is infirm about the Campbells' theory that their experience with State Farm exemplifies and reflects an overarching underpayment scheme, one that caused "repeated misconduct of the sort that injured them"? The Court's silence on that score is revealing: Once one recognizes that the Campbells did show "conduct by State Farm similar to that which harmed them," [it] becomes impossible to shrink the reprehensibility analysis to this sole case, or to maintain, at odds with the determination of the trial court, that "the adverse effect on the State's general population was in fact minor."

Evidence of out-of-state conduct, the Court acknowledges, may be "probative [even if the conduct is lawful in the state where it occurred] when it demonstrates the deliberateness and culpability of the defendant's action in the State where it is tortious. . . ." "Other acts" evidence concerning practices both in and out of State was introduced in this case to show just such "deliberateness" and "culpability." The evidence was admissible, the trial court ruled: (1) to document State Farm's "reprehensible" PP&R program; and (2) to "rebut [State Farm's] assertion that [its] actions toward the Campbells were inadvertent errors or mistakes in judgment." Viewed in this light, there surely was "a nexus" between much of the "other acts" evidence and "the specific harm suffered by [the Campbells]."

III

When the Court first ventured to override state-court punitive damages awards, it did so moderately. The Court recalled that "[i]n our federal system, States necessarily have considerable flexibility in determining the level of punitive damages that they will allow in different classes of cases and in any particular case." *Gore.* Today's decision exhibits no such respect and restraint. No longer content to accord state-court judgments "a strong presumption of validity," *TXO*, the Court announces that "few awards exceeding a single-digit ratio between punitive and compensatory damages, to a significant degree, will satisfy due process."[2] Moreover, the Court adds, when compensatory damages are substantial, doubling those damages "can reach the outermost limit of the due process guarantee." In a legislative scheme or a state high court's design to cap punitive damages, the handiwork in setting single-digit and 1-to-1 benchmarks could hardly be questioned; in a judicial decree imposed on the States by this Court under the banner of substantive due process, the numerical controls today's decision installs seem to me boldly out of order.

---

[2] *TXO* noted that "[u]nder well-settled law," a defendant's "wrongdoing in other parts of the country" and its "impressive net worth" are factors "typically considered in assessing punitive damages." It remains to be seen whether, or the extent to which, today's decision will unsettle that law.

I remain of the view that this Court has no warrant to reform state law governing awards of punitive damages. *BMW v. Gore* (Ginsburg, J., dissenting). Even if I were prepared to accept the flexible guides prescribed in *BMW v. Gore,* I would not join the Court's swift conversion of those guides into instructions that begin to resemble marching orders. For the reasons stated, I would leave the judgment of the Utah Supreme Court undisturbed.

■ NOTES ON PUNITIVE DAMAGE RECOVERY

1. *Campbell* suggests that punitives exceeding the amount indicated by a "single-digit" multiplier usually won't satisfy due process, and that the "145-to-1" ratio is presumptively invalid. In *Haslip,* the Court thought an award four times higher than actual damages came "close to the line," and *BMW v. Gore* commented that $2 million was "grossly excessive" where actual damages are $4,000 (ratio of 500 to 1). But in *TXO,* the Court approved a punitive award 526 times actual damages. Do these cases give some sense of parameters? Recall Justice Kennedy's comment in *Campbell* that the case was "neither close nor difficult." That implies, doesn't it, that the Court thinks the Utah court badly misunderstood the applicable standard?

2. *Campbell* involved a "bifurcated trial." One jury decided whether State Farm was unreasonable in refusing to settle for policy limits of $50,000. Another decided whether State Farm was guilty of fraud or intentional infliction of emotional distress, and determined compensatory and punitive damages. In language tracking FRCP 42, the Utah counterpart lets a court order separate trials of "any claim" and "any separate issue" in the interests of "convenience" or to "avoid prejudice." What advantages does bifurcation bring in cases like *Campbell*? What drawbacks?

3. You will see that courts may set aside verdicts as being "against the weight of the evidence" and award new trials (Chapter 12). Sometimes courts tell plaintiffs a new trial will be awarded to defendant unless plaintiff consents to entry of judgment in an amount less than the verdict ("remittitur"). And sometimes courts grant judgment "as a matter of law," modifying or discarding an improper verdict, where the evidence overwhelmingly points toward a conclusion that differs from that reached by the jury. On remand in *BMW v. Gore,* the Alabama Supreme Court concluded that $46,000 was right for punitives, and advised plaintiff that it would order a new trial unless it filed a remittitur reducing the total damage award to $50,000. See BMW of North America, Inc. v. Gore, 701 So. 2d 507 (Ala. 1997). Thus the defendant in *BMW v. Gore* not only persuaded the Court to disapprove the approach taken in Alabama, but succeeded in sharply reducing the judgment.

4. In *BMW* and *TXO,* the fact that defendant engaged in similar conduct elsewhere took on special importance, didn't it? *TXO* had recognized that conduct in other jurisdictions might affect the assessment of what the defendant did in West Virginia. *Campbell* agrees that conduct elsewhere is relevant when it shows "the deliberateness and culpability" of acts in the forum state, but that the conduct "must have a nexus to the specific harm suffered by the plaintiff." What conduct did trial court consider in *Campbell* that failed to satisfy this standard? How could a plaintiff who sues State Farm in Utah *prove* that conduct in other states had a "nexus to the specific harm" suffered by the plaintiff?

5. The Court applies what it calls the *Gore* guideposts in analyzing the punitive damage award in *Campbell.* Consider how each of those factors fares*:*

(a) Degree of Reprehensibility. What defines the spectrum of "reprehensibility"? How reprehensible was State Farm's conduct here?

(b) Disparity Between Actual or Potential Harm and Size of the Award. The Court discusses the "ratio" between actual and punitive damages. Is there something about this case that cries out for a far lower ratio than 145 to 1?

(c) Difference Between Punitives and Possible Criminal Penalty. The Court points out that criminal fraud would carry a $10,000 fine. Is fraud the best label for what State Farm did? Wasn't its behavior in the nature of "callous disregard" for the interests of its insured?

6. In dissent, Justice Ginsburg bemoans the "foray" of the Court into an area traditionally left to states. State courts are subject to the "Due Process" Clause, aren't they? If the Court doesn't enforce that clause by taking such cases, do states have incentive to enforce it? In *Campbell,* a Utah citizen recovered punitives computed with reference to State Farm's behavior in other states. Does a Utah court have an incentive to prevent such things from happening? In *Campbell,* the lawyer for plaintiffs said the case provided a chance "to rebuke State Farm for its nationwide activities," and invited the jury to see the case as one that "transcends" the Campbells, in which the jury can hold State Farm "accountable for what it's doing across the country." In the *TXO* case ten years earlier, Justice O'Connor would have reversed a West Virginia award, in part because lawyers for plaintiff repeatedly argued *not* that defendant should pay for the harm it *might have caused,* but rather that the jury should take advantage of the opportunity to take money from a wealthy out-of-stater:

> Repeatedly [lawyers for plaintiff] reminded the jury that TXO was from another State. Repeatedly they told the jury about TXO's massive wealth. And repeatedly they told the jury that it could do anything it thought "fair." The opening line from rebuttal set the tone. "Ladies and gentleman of the jury," one attorney began, "this greedy bunch from down in Texas still doesn't understand this case." Playing on images of Texans as overrich gamblers who profit by chance rather than work, he referred to TXO shortly thereafter as a bunch of "Texas high rollers, wildcatters." Finally, counsel drove the point home yet one

more time, comparing TXO to an obviously wealthy out-of-town visitor who refuses to put money in the parking meter to help pay for community service: "Well, what is fair? . . . If someone comes to town and intentionally doesn't put a quarter in the meter, stays here all day, [in this] town that needs it to pay for the police force and the fire department, they give [him] a fine. And at the end of the day [he] may have to pay a dollar. That person reaches in his billfold at the end of the day and maybe he's got a hundred bucks in there. He doesn't want to have to pay that dollar, but he does, because he knows if he doesn't [he'll have legal problems]. . . . The town didn't take everything from the individual, didn't ruin [him], just took one percent of what that person had in cash. One percent. You can fine TXO one percent if you want, you can fine them one dollar if you want. But I submit to you a one percent fine, the same as John Doe on this street, would be fair. That's twelve and a half million dollars, based on what they had left over. And their earnings w[ere] $225,000,000.00 [per year]. I mean, yeah, their cash flow. Their surplus. So anything between twelve and a half million and twenty-two million is only one percent—the same as this poor guy who just tried to cheat a little bit. Now that's a lot of money. I hope, like I said, you don't analyze this on a lot or a little, but fair."

TXO Production Corp. v. Alliance Resources Corp., 509 U.S. 443, 492 (1993). Should lawyers be allowed to argue that juries should award large sums to local plaintiffs against out-of-state defendants? Are state courts likely to block such arguments? Does this situation explain the willingness of the Supreme Court to intervene?

7. Punitive damage cases *invite* juries to make awards based on redistributionist sentiments, don't they? Consider Justice O'Connor's account of the *TXO* case:

> That a jury might have such inclinations should come as no surprise. Courts long have recognized that jurors may view large corporations with great disfavor. Corporations are mere abstractions and, as such, are unlikely to be viewed with much sympathy. Moreover, they often represent a large accumulation of productive resources; jurors naturally think little of taking an otherwise large sum of money out of what appears to be an enormously larger pool of wealth. Finally, juries may feel privileged to correct perceived social ills stemming from unequal wealth distribution by transferring money from "wealthy" corporations to comparatively needier plaintiffs.
>
> . . .
>
> Over and over [plaintiffs' lawyers] reminded the jury that there were virtually no substantive limits on its discretion. Time and again they told the jury of TXO's great wealth and that it could take away any amount it wanted, as long as it seemed "fair." ("It isn't really whether the verdict is too large or too small, too big or too little. It's whether it's fair"); ("A two billion dollar company. Have earnings of $225,000,000.00, average. Last year [they] made $125,000,000.00 alone. Last year. Now, what's a good fine for a company like that? A hundred thousand? A million? You can do that if you think it's fair . . ."). And each time the argument found solid support in the trial court's instructions, which not only licensed the jury to

afford respondents any "additional compensation" they believed appropriate, but also encouraged them to do so based on TXO's wealth alone.

Id. at 443, 474-477, 490-491, 492-494 (jurors "are not infallible guardians of the public good," but "ordinary citizens" who are "more susceptible" to "impermissible" considerations, particularly in the area of "punitive damages" where juries receive only "vague and amorphous guidance"). Justice O'Connor has a point, doesn't she? Notice that the lawyer for the plaintiff in *TXO* equated "profits" with "cash flow" and "surplus." Those are vastly different things, aren't they? Do juries understand the difference?

8. If only a small fraction of cases (2 to 5 percent) involve punitives, should we be concerned with large awards? Consider product liability cases, where reportedly 15 percent of verdicts include punitive damages. Is there such a thing as an award that is objectively too large? What costs does such an award bring? On the basis of empirical evidence, one commentator argues that punitives do not promote safety, that their capriciousness (variability and unpredictability) reduces innovation (hence progress and perhaps safety), see W. Kip Viscusi, *The Social Costs of Punitive Damages Against Corporations in Environmental and Safety Torts,* 87 Geo L.J. 285 (1998), but others have attacked these findings as flawed and erroneous, see Theodore Eisenberg, *Measuring the Deterrent Effect of Punitive Damages,* 87 Geo. L. Rev. 347 (1998), and David Luban, *A Flawed Case Against Punitive Damages,* 87 Geo. L.J. 359 (1998).

9. Whether or not one accepts the Viscusi arguments, there is a consensus that punitives are varied and unpredictable. One study concludes that juries are apt to agree on the question whether conduct should be penalized, but are all over the lot when it comes to setting the amount of a punitive award. In lay terms, this study suggests, the problem is the one suggested by the defense in *TXO*—absence of a yardstick. Psychologists contrast choices made on "category scales" that are "bounded and anchored in verbal descriptions at both ends" and choices made on "magnitude scales" that are "unbounded" except for a "zero point" at one end. If decision makers are given a reference point ("modulus") such as 5 that attaches to a particular case, they perform more consistently in considering other cases and assigning comparative values. But magnitude scaling without a modulus "produces extremely large variability," which happens in punitive damage cases. The bad news, these authors suggest, is that the problem cannot be solved by different (or tighter) instructions, or damage "caps." See Cass R. Sunstein, Daniel Kahneman & David Schkade, *Assessing Punitive Damages (with Notes on Cognition and Valuation in Law),* 107 Yale L.J. 2071, 2106, 2113-2125 (1998) (suggesting that juries might be asked to select a number on a bounded scale, like "5," or to choose one of many calibrated scenarios that is most like the case at hand, leading either to a judge decision on the amount or to use of some predetermined amount assigned to each choice, or even eliminating juries from the role, in favor of an administrative agency determination of punitive damages).

10. Consider another possibility. It has been earnestly argued that punitive damages should be assessed in terms of economic efficiency, and by this criterion the appropriate role of punitives is to be sure that the cost of undetected violations of norms is assessed against the offending party. If an automaker, for example, sells 10,000 sedans with defective gearshifts that could cause the car suddenly to move while in idle, and if plaintiff sues when injured in an accident caused in this way, the jury should be asked to assess punitives. If the conduct involves wanton or reckless disregard of safety, the jury should estimate the number of similar accidents that do not generate similar claims and award punitives that approximate those undetected damages. See A. Mitchell Polinsky & Steven Shavell, *Punitive Damages: An Economic Analysis,* 111 Harv. L. Rev. 869 (1998). But see W. Kip Viscusi, *The Challenge of Punitive Damages Mathematics,* 30 J. Legal Stud. 313 (2001) (on basis of experiments with mock juries, reporting that jurors cannot follow instructions and formulae asking them to fix damages as recommended by Polinsky and Shavell).

11. The message of cases like *Campbell* has had an impact. See, e.g., Bennett v. Reynolds, 315 S.W.3d 867 (Tex. 2010) (in cattle rancher's suit alleging that neighboring rancher had stolen 13 head of cattle, jury awarded $5,327 in actual damages and $1.25 million in punitive damages; quoting Robert Frost's poetic observation that "good fences make good neighbors," state supreme court remands to court of appeals to adjust the punitive ratio downward, concluding that the 47:1 and 188:1 ratios exemplified in this verdict exceed constitutional maxima); Mitchell, Jr. v. Fortis Insurance Co., 686 S.E.2d 176 (S.C. 2009) ($15 million punitive damage award, when compared to "present value" of just over $1 million for treatment and costs, was constitutionally excessive; reducing punitive award to $10 million).

12. Punitive damage awards may be reduced on the basis of substantive standards found in common law tradition or statute, even without reference to constitutional limits set by the Supreme Court. See, e.g., Slovinski v. Elliot, 927 N.E.2d 1221 (Ill. 2010) (approving order reducing punitive award from $2 million to $81,600 on basis of common law standards); Perrine v. E.I. du Pont de Nemours and Co., 694 S.E.2d 815 (W. Va. 2010) (in class suit for environmental pollution, directing court to reduce by $20 million a punitive award of $196,200,000, through remittitur order that plaintiff could accept or decline in favor of new trial on punitives only).

B   ATTORNEYS' FEES

Under the "American Rule," which prevails in state and federal courts across the country, each side pays its own attorneys' fees. A plaintiff may win a judgment for $500,000, and may owe her lawyer $200,000, and the money comes out of her pocket. The "English Rule," in contrast, lets the winner collect fees from the loser. Under this tradition, a plaintiff who wins judgment for $500,000 can apply to the court for fees. If her lawyer invested $200,000 in hours litigating, and if the court considers that amount fair and reasonable, judgment can go against the defendant for $700,000.

The virtue in the English Rule is that the costs that a claimant must incur in obtaining what is rightfully hers can reasonably be considered part of damages, chargeable to the person legally responsible. The virtues in the American Rule are less obvious, but two seem important: One is that requiring each side to bear its own litigation expenses may help minimize them because the party in charge of strategy is the one who pays the costs. Second, it would often be draconian to tax the loser with the winner's fees because of the uncertainties that attend claims of legal liability. A defendant who does not pay what is demanded may be mistaken, but reasonably so in light of the facts and the law; similarly, a plaintiff may sue and lose, while being reasonable in thinking that there was liability.

The difference between the English and American Rules is real, and fee shifting is unusual in conventional litigation—each side bears its own fees most of the time, in suits for product liability, malpractice, and breach of contract, and many others. Sometimes, however, contracts include fee-shifting clauses, as is often true of promissory notes and leases. And fee shifting *does* occur in American litigation because statutes and rules authorize it in particular cases, most prominently in federal civil rights suits and antitrust litigation. Moreover, the fees of claimants in class actions (and certain other "common fund" suits) are paid from the award, spreading the burden among all the claimants. (When class suits proceed in fee-shifting areas, plaintiffs can collect a higher total award to cover fees.) Finally, the English Rule is not, so to speak, eaten as hot as it's cooked: It is simply not true that winners in British courts collect every penny they spend on their lawyers. See Charles E. Hyde & Phillip L. Williams, *Necessary Costs and Expenditure Incentives Under the English Rule,* 22 Int'l Rev. L. & Econ. 133 (2002) (analyzing effects of English Rule on actual litigation expenditures, and stressing that prevailing parties are awarded not actual costs, but reasonable costs).

You will not be surprised to learn that scholars, particularly those in the law and economics school, have a field day analyzing incentives produced by these competing approaches, but they have had a struggle in reaching solid conclusions, in part because of one salient feature in American practice, which is that *lawyers* finance so much litigation themselves through contingent fee arrangements. Think about what that means, and what you would say to clients as they walk in your door. Would you only take cases you are sure you can win? Wouldn't you take some long shots? Who actually "pays" for your losing efforts?

There are two articles of faith about the relative virtues of the English and the American Rules: One is that the American Rule does a better job of encouraging small claimants to sue powerful adversaries. The thought is that the American Rule avoids the *in terrorem* effect that a plaintiff might experience if she thought suing General Motors, for example, might leave her with no recovery and a huge bill for the other side's fees. The other is that the English Rule does a better job in weeding out frivolous cases. The thought is that a claimant would not sue if the chance of success was remote and the prospect of losing brought an obligation to pay the other side's costs. Even these two points may, however, be less certain than they appear: It is reported, for example, that English courts do not visit on losing claimants the real costs of a high-priced corporate defense team. And some scholars argue that, counter to our intuitions, the English Rule does not do well in weeding out doubtful suits. See A. Mitchell Polinsky & Daniel L. Rubinfeld, *Does the English Rule Discourage Low-Probability-of-Prevailing Plaintiffs?*, 27 J. Legal Stud. 519 (1998) (English Rule encourages low-probability plaintiffs to sue more than the American Rule).

PERDUE v. KENNY A.

Supreme Court of the United States
130 S. Ct. 1662 (2010)

Justice ALITO delivered the opinion of the Court.

This case presents the question whether the calculation of an attorney's fee, under federal fee-shifting statutes, based on the "lodestar," *i.e.*, the number of hours worked multiplied by the prevailing hourly rates, may be increased due to superior performance and results. We have stated in previous cases that such an increase is permitted in extraordinary circumstances, and we reaffirm that rule. But as we have also said in prior cases, there is a strong presumption that the lodestar is sufficient; factors subsumed in the lodestar calculation cannot be used as a ground for increasing an award above the lodestar; and a party seeking fees has the burden of identifying a factor that the lodestar does not adequately take into account and proving with specificity that an enhanced fee is justified. Because the District Court did not apply these standards, we reverse the decision below and remand for further proceedings consistent with this opinion.

I

A

[Plaintiffs] are children in the Georgia foster-care system and their next friends. They filed this class action on behalf of 3,000 children in foster care and named as defendants the Governor of Georgia and various state officials. Claiming that deficiencies in the foster-care system in two counties near Atlanta violated their federal and state constitutional and statutory rights, respondents sought injunctive and declaratory relief, as well as attorney's fees and expenses.

The United States District Court for the Northern District of Georgia eventually referred the case to mediation, where the parties entered into a consent decree, which the District Court approved. The consent decree resolved all pending issues other than the fees that respondents' attorneys were entitled to receive under 42 USC §1988.[2]

B

Respondents submitted a request for more than $14 million in attorney's fees. Half of that amount was based on their calculation of the lodestar—roughly 30,000 hours multiplied by hourly rates of $200 to $495 for attorneys and $75 to $150 for non-attorneys. In support of their fee request, respondents submitted affidavits asserting that these rates were within the range of prevailing market rates for legal services in the relevant market.

The other half of the amount that respondents sought represented a fee enhancement for superior work and results. Affidavits submitted in support of this request claimed that the lodestar amount "would be generally insufficient to induce lawyers of comparable skill, judgment, professional representation and experience" to litigate this case. Petitioners objected to the fee request, contending that some of the proposed hourly rates were too high, that the hours claimed were excessive, and that the enhancement would duplicate factors that were reflected in the lodestar amount.

The District Court awarded fees of approximately $10.5 million. The District Court found that the hourly rates proposed by respondents were "fair and reasonable," but that some of the entries on counsel's billing records were vague and that the hours claimed for many of the billing categories were excessive. The court therefore cut the non-travel hours by 15% and halved the hourly rate for travel hours. This resulted in a lodestar calculation of approximately $6 million.

The court then enhanced this award by 75%, concluding that the lodestar calculation did not take into account "(1) the fact that class counsel were required to advance case expenses of $1.7 million over a three-year period with no ongoing reimbursement, (2) the fact that class counsel were not paid on an ongoing basis as the work was being performed, and (3) the fact that class counsel's ability to recover a fee and expense reimbursement were completely contingent on the outcome of the case." The court stated that respondents' attorneys had exhibited "a higher degree of skill, commitment, dedication, and professionalism . . . than the Court has seen displayed

---

[2] [The Court quotes 42 USC §1988(b), which provides that in certain civil rights and other cases the court "in its discretion" may allow "the prevailing party . . . a reasonable attorney's fee as part of the costs."—Ed.]

by the attorneys in any other case during its 27 years on the bench." The court also commented that the results obtained were "'extraordinary'" and added that "[a]fter 58 years as a practicing attorney and federal judge, the Court is unaware of any other case in which a plaintiff class has achieved such a favorable result on such a comprehensive scale." The enhancement resulted in an additional $4.5 million fee award.

Relying on prior Circuit precedent, a panel of the Eleventh Circuit affirmed. The panel held that the District Court had not abused its discretion by failing to make a larger reduction in the number of hours for which respondents' attorneys sought reimbursement, but the panel commented that it "would have cut the billable hours more if we were deciding the matter in the first instance" and added that the hourly rates approved by the District Court also "appear[ed] to be on the generous side." On the question of the enhancement, however, the panel splintered, with each judge writing a separate opinion.

Judge Carnes concluded that binding Eleventh Circuit precedent required that the decision of the District Court be affirmed, but he opined that the reasoning in our opinions suggested that no enhancement should be allowed in this case. He concluded that the quality of the attorneys' performance was "adequately accounted for 'either in determining the reasonable number of hours expended on the litigation or in setting the reasonable hourly rates'" (quoting Pennsylvania v. Delaware Valley Citizens' Council for Clean Air, 478 U.S. 546, 565-566 (1986) (*Delaware Valley I*)). He found that an enhancement could not be justified based on delay in the recovery of attorney's fees and reimbursable expenses because such delay is a routine feature of cases brought under 42 USC §1983. And he reasoned that the District Court had contravened our holding in Burlington v. Dague, 505 U.S. 557 (1992), when it relied on "'the fact that class counsel's compensation was totally contingent upon prevailing in this action'" (quoting affidavit in support of fee request).

Judge Wilson concurred in the judgment but disagreed with Judge Carnes' view that Eleventh Circuit precedent is inconsistent with our decisions. Judge Hill also concurred in the judgment but expressed no view about the correctness of the prior Circuit precedent.

The Eleventh Circuit denied rehearing en banc over the dissent of three judges. Judge Wilson filed an opinion concurring in the denial of rehearing; Judge Carnes, joined by Judges Tjoflat and Dubina, filed an opinion dissenting from the denial of rehearing; and Judge Tjoflat filed a separate dissent, contending, among other things, that the District Court, by basing the enhancement in large part on a comparison of the performance of respondents' attorneys with all of the unnamed attorneys whose work he had observed during his professional career, had improperly rendered a decision that was effectively unreviewable on appeal and had essentially served as a witness in support of the enhancement.

We granted certiorari.

II

The general rule in our legal system is that each party must pay its own attorney's fees and expenses, see Hensley v. Eckerhart, 461 U.S. 424, 429 (1983), but Congress enacted 42 USC §1988 in order to ensure that federal rights are adequately enforced. Section 1988 provides that a prevailing party in certain civil rights actions may recover "a reasonable attorney's fee as part of the costs." Unfortunately, the statute does not explain what Congress meant by a "reasonable" fee, and therefore the task of identifying an appropriate methodology for determining a "reasonable" fee was left for the courts.

One possible method was set out in Johnson v. Georgia Highway Express, Inc., 488 F.2d 714, 717-719 (5th Cir. 1974), which listed 12 factors that a court should consider in determining a reasonable fee.[4] This method, however, "gave very little actual guidance to district courts. Setting attorney's fees by reference to a series of sometimes subjective factors placed unlimited discretion in trial judges and produced disparate results." *Delaware Valley I.*

An alternative, the lodestar approach, was pioneered by the Third Circuit in Lindy Bros. Builders, Inc. of Philadelphia v. American Radiator & Standard Sanitary Corp., 487 F.2d 161 (3d Cir. 1973), appeal after remand, 540 F.2d 102 (3d Cir. 1976), and "achieved dominance in the federal courts" after our decision in *Hensley.* Gisbrecht v. Barnhart, 535 U.S. 789, 801 (2002). "Since that time, '[t]he "lodestar" figure has, as its name suggests, become the guiding light of our fee-shifting jurisprudence.'" *Ibid.* (quoting *Dague, supra*).

Although the lodestar method is not perfect, it has several important virtues. First, in accordance with our understanding of the aim of fee-shifting statutes, the lodestar looks to "the prevailing market rates in the relevant community." *Blum.* Developed after the practice of hourly billing had become widespread, see *Gisbrecht,* the lodestar method produces an award that *roughly* approximates the fee that the prevailing attorney would have received if he or she had been representing a paying client who was billed by the hour in a comparable case. Second, the lodestar method is readily administrable, and unlike the *Johnson* approach, the lodestar calculation is "objective," *Hensley,* and thus cabins the discretion of trial judges, permits meaningful judicial review, and produces reasonably predictable results.

[4] These factors were: "(1) the time and labor required; (2) the novelty and difficulty of the questions; (3) the skill requisite to perform the legal service properly; (4) the preclusion of employment by the attorney due to the acceptance of the case; (5) the customary fee; (6) whether the fee is fixed or contingent; (7) time limitations imposed by the client or the circumstances; (8) the amount involved and the results obtained; (9) the experience, reputation, and ability of the attorneys; (10) the 'undesirability' of the case; (11) the nature and length of the professional relationship with the client; and (12) awards in similar cases." *Hensley.*

III

Our prior decisions concerning the federal fee-shifting statutes have established six important rules that lead to our decision in this case.

First, a "reasonable" fee is a fee that is sufficient to induce a capable attorney to undertake the representation of a meritorious civil rights case. Section 1988's aim is to enforce the covered civil rights statutes, not to provide "a form of economic relief to improve the financial lot of attorneys." *Delaware Valley I.*

Second, the lodestar method yields a fee that is presumptively sufficient to achieve this objective. See *Dague; Delaware Valley I; Blum;* see also *Gisbrecht.* Indeed, we have said that the presumption is a "strong" one. *Dague; Delaware Valley I.*

Third, although we have never sustained an enhancement of a lodestar amount for performance, we have repeatedly said that enhancements may be awarded in "'rare'" and "'exceptional'" circumstances. *Delaware Valley I; Blum; Hensley.*

Fourth, we have noted that "the lodestar figure includes most, if not all, of the relevant factors constituting a 'reasonable' attorney's fee," *Delaware Valley I,* and have held that an enhancement may not be awarded based on a factor that is subsumed in the lodestar calculation. We have thus held that the novelty and complexity of a case generally may not be used as a ground for an enhancement because these factors "presumably [are] fully reflected in the number of billable hours recorded by counsel." *Blum.* We have also held that the quality of an attorney's performance generally should not be used to adjust the lodestar "[b]ecause considerations concerning the quality of a prevailing party's counsel's representation normally are reflected in the reasonable hourly rate." *Delaware Valley I.*

Fifth, the burden of proving that an enhancement is necessary must be borne by the fee applicant. *Dague; Blum.*

Finally, a fee applicant seeking an enhancement must produce "specific evidence" that supports the award. This requirement is essential if the lodestar method is to realize one of its chief virtues, *i.e.,* providing a calculation that is objective and capable of being reviewed on appeal.

IV

A

In light of what we have said in prior cases, we reject any contention that a fee determined by the lodestar method may not be enhanced in any situation. The lodestar method was never intended to be conclusive in all circumstances. Instead, there is a "strong presumption" that the lodestar figure is reasonable, but that presumption may be overcome in those rare circumstances in which the lodestar does not adequately take into account a factor that may properly be considered in determining a reasonable fee.

B

In this case, we are asked to decide whether either the quality of an attorney's performance or the results obtained are factors that may properly provide a basis for an enhancement. We treat these two factors as one. When a plaintiff's attorney achieves results that are more favorable than would have been predicted based on the governing law and the available evidence, the outcome may be attributable to superior performance and commitment of resources by plaintiff's counsel. Or the outcome may result from inferior performance by defense counsel, unanticipated defense concessions, unexpectedly favorable rulings by the court, an unexpectedly sympathetic jury, or simple luck. Since none of these latter causes can justify an enhanced award, superior results are relevant only to the extent it can be shown that they are the result of superior attorney performance. Thus, we need only consider whether superior attorney performance can justify an enhancement. And in light of the principles derived from our prior cases, we inquire whether there are circumstances in which superior attorney performance is not adequately taken into account in the lodestar calculation. We conclude that there are a few such circumstances but that these circumstances are indeed "rare" and "exceptional," and require specific evidence that the lodestar fee would not have been "adequate to attract competent counsel," *Blum*.

First, an enhancement may be appropriate where the method used in determining the hourly rate employed in the lodestar calculation does not adequately measure the attorney's true market value, as demonstrated in part during the litigation. This may occur if the hourly rate is determined by a formula that takes into account only a single factor (such as years since admission to the bar) or perhaps only a few similar factors. In such a case, an enhancement may be appropriate so that an attorney is compensated at the rate that the attorney would receive in cases not governed by the federal fee-shifting statutes. But in order to provide a calculation that is objective and reviewable, the trial judge should adjust the attorney's hourly rate in accordance with specific proof linking the attorney's ability to a prevailing market rate.

Second, an enhancement may be appropriate if the attorney's performance includes an extraordinary outlay of expenses and the litigation is exceptionally protracted. As Judge Carnes noted below, when an attorney agrees to represent a civil rights plaintiff who cannot afford to pay the attorney, the attorney presumably understands that no reimbursement is likely to be received until the successful resolution of the case, and therefore enhancements to compensate for delay in reimbursement for expenses must be reserved for unusual cases. In such exceptional cases, however, an enhancement may be allowed, but the amount of the enhancement must be calculated using a method that is reasonable, objective, and capable of being reviewed on appeal, such as by applying a standard rate of interest to the qualifying outlays of expenses.

Third, there may be extraordinary circumstances in which an attorney's performance involves exceptional delay in the payment of fees. An attorney who expects to be compensated under §1988 presumably understands that payment of fees will generally not come until the end of the case, if at all. Compensation for this delay is generally made "either by basing the award on current rates or by adjusting the fee based on historical rates to reflect its present value." *Missouri v. Jenkins,* 491 U.S. 274, 282 (1989). But we do not rule out the possibility that an enhancement may be appropriate where an attorney assumes these costs in the face of unanticipated delay, particularly where the delay is unjustifiably caused by the defense. In such a case, however, the enhancement should be calculated by applying a method similar to that described above in connection with exceptional delay in obtaining reimbursement for expenses.

We reject the suggestion that it is appropriate to grant performance enhancements on the ground that departures from hourly billing are becoming more common. As we have noted, the lodestar was adopted in part because it provides a rough approximation of general billing practices, and accordingly, if hourly billing becomes unusual, an alternative to the lodestar method may have to be found. However, neither respondents nor their *amici* contend that that day has arrived. Nor have they shown that permitting the award of enhancements on top of the lodestar figure corresponds to prevailing practice in the general run of cases.

We are told that, under an increasingly popular arrangement, attorneys are paid at a reduced hourly rate but receive a bonus if certain specified results are obtained, and this practice is analogized to the award of an enhancement such as the one in this case. The analogy, however, is flawed. An attorney who agrees, at the outset of the representation, to a *reduced hourly rate* in exchange for the opportunity to earn a performance bonus is in a position far different from an attorney in a §1988 case who is compensated at the *full prevailing rate* and then seeks a performance enhancement in addition to the lodestar amount after the litigation has concluded. Reliance on these comparisons for the purposes of administering enhancements, therefore, is not appropriate.

V

In the present case, the District Court did not provide proper justification for the large enhancement that it awarded. The court increased the lodestar award by 75% but, as far as the court's opinion reveals, this figure appears to have been essentially arbitrary. Why, for example, did the court grant a 75% enhancement instead of the 100% increase that respondents sought? And why 75% rather than 50% or 25% or 10%?

The District Court commented that the enhancement was the "minimum enhancement of the lodestar necessary to reasonably compensate [respondents'] counsel." But the effect of the enhancement was to increase the top rate for the attorneys to more than $866 per hour,[7] and the District Court did not point to anything in the record that shows that this is an appropriate figure for the relevant market.

The District Court pointed to the fact that respondents' counsel had to make extraordinary outlays for expenses and had to wait for reimbursement, but the court did not calculate the amount of the enhancement that is attributable to this factor. Similarly, the District Court noted that respondents' counsel did not receive fees on an ongoing basis while the case was pending, but the court did not sufficiently link this factor to proof in the record that the delay here was outside the normal range expected by attorneys who rely on §1988 for the payment of their fees or quantify the disparity. Nor did the court provide a calculation of the cost to counsel of any extraordinary and unwarranted delay. And the court's reliance on the contingency of the outcome contravenes our holding in *Dague*.

Finally, insofar as the District Court relied on a comparison of the performance of counsel in this case with the performance of counsel in unnamed prior cases, the District Court did not employ a methodology that permitted meaningful appellate review. Needless to say, we do not question the sincerity of the District Court's observations, and we are in no position to assess their accuracy. But when a trial judge awards an enhancement on an impressionistic basis, a major purpose of the lodestar method—providing an objective and reviewable basis for fees—is undermined.

Determining a "reasonable attorney's fee" is a matter that is committed to the sound discretion of a trial judge, see 42 USC §1988 (permitting court, "in its discretion," to award fees), but the judge's discretion is not unlimited. It is essential that the judge provide a reasonably specific explanation for all aspects of a fee determination, including any award of an enhancement. Unless such an explanation is given, adequate appellate review is not feasible,

---

[7] Justice Breyer's reliance on the *average* hourly rate for all of respondents' attorneys is highly misleading. In calculating the lodestar, the District Court found that the hourly rate for each of these attorneys was "eminently fair and reasonable" and "consistent with the prevailing market rates in Atlanta for comparable work." Justice Breyer's calculation of an average hourly rate for all attorney hours reflects nothing more than the fact that much of the work was performed by attorneys whose "fair and reasonable" market rate was below the market average. There is nothing unfair about compensating these attorneys *at the very rate that they requested.*

and without such review, widely disparate awards may be made, and awards may be influenced (or at least, may appear to be influenced) by a judge's subjective opinion regarding particular attorneys or the importance of the case. In addition, in future cases, defendants contemplating the possibility of settlement will have no way to estimate the likelihood of having to pay a potentially huge enhancement. See Marek v. Chesny, 473 U.S. 1, 7 (1985) ("'[M]any a defendant would be unwilling to make a binding settlement offer on terms that left it exposed to liability for attorney's fees in whatever amount the court might fix on motion of the plaintiff'").

Section 1988 serves an important public purpose by making it possible for persons without means to bring suit to vindicate their rights. But unjustified enhancements that serve only to enrich attorneys are not consistent with the statute's aim.[8] In many cases, attorney's fees awarded under §1988 are not paid by the individuals responsible for the constitutional or statutory violations on which the judgment is based. Instead, the fees are paid in effect by state and local taxpayers, and because state and local governments have limited budgets, money that is used to pay attorney's fees is money that cannot be used for programs that provide vital public services.

. . .

For all these reasons, the judgment of the Court of Appeals is reversed, and the case is remanded for proceedings consistent with this opinion.

It is so ordered.

[Concurring opinions by Justice Kennedy and Justice Thomas are omitted.]

Justice BREYER, with whom Justice STEVENS, Justice GINSBURG, and Justice SOTOMAYOR join, concurring in part and dissenting in part.

. . .

This case well illustrates why our tiered and functionally specialized judicial system places the task of determining an attorney's fee award primarily in the district court's hands. The plaintiffs' lawyers spent eight years investigating the underlying facts, developing the initial complaint, conducting court proceedings, and working out final relief. The District Court's docket, with

---

[8] Justice Breyer's opinion dramatically illustrates the danger of allowing a trial judge to award a huge enhancement not supported by any discernible methodology. That approach would retain the $4.5 million enhancement here so that respondents' attorneys would earn as much as the attorneys at some of the richest law firms in the country. These fees would be paid by the taxpayers of Georgia, where the annual per capita income is less than $34,000, see Dept. of Commerce, Bureau of Census, Statistical Abstract of the United States: 2010 (figures for 2008), and the annual salaries of attorneys employed by the State range from $48,000 for entry-level lawyers to $118,000 for the highest paid division chief, see Brief for State of Alabama. Section 1988 was enacted to ensure that civil rights plaintiffs are adequately represented, not to provide such a windfall.

over 600 entries, consists of more than 18,000 pages. Transcripts of hearings and depositions, along with other documents, have produced a record that fills 20 large boxes. Neither we, nor an appellate panel, can easily read that entire record. Nor should we attempt to second-guess a district judge who is aware of the many intangible matters that the written page cannot reflect.

My own review of this expansive record cannot possibly be exhaustive. But those portions of the record I have reviewed lead me to conclude, like the Court of Appeals, that the District Judge did not abuse his discretion when awarding an enhanced fee. I reach this conclusion based on four considerations.

[First, the aim was "unusually important" and required "an exceptionally high degree of skill and effort." The record indicates that the system could not provide "essential medical and mental health services," leading to "illness and lifelong medical disabilities." There was understaffing, and children were physically assaulted and abused. Shelters were unsanitary, dilapidated, and overcrowded, and children abused drugs. Some tried to escape or commit suicide.

Second, the lawsuit was "lengthy and arduous," and the State offered vigorous resistance, spending $2.4 million to engage outside counsel and putting in 5,200 hours of work by its own lawyers.

Third, plaintiffs obtained "exceptional" results, winning a consent decree negotiated in mediation that required the State to take 31 steps to address deficiencies, amounting to "comprehensive reforms" of its foster care system.

Fourth, the judge said that the mediation effort "went far beyond" anything he had seen, and that counsel brought "a higher degree of skill, commitment, dedication, and professionalism to this litigation than the Court has seen displayed by the attorneys in any other case during its 27 years on the bench."]

On the basis of what I have read, I believe that assessment was correct. I recognize that the ordinary lodestar calculation yields a large fee award. But by my assessment, the lodestar calculation in this case translates to an average hourly fee per attorney of $249. (The majority's reference to an hourly fee of $866 refers to the rate associated with the *single highest* paid of the 17 attorneys under the *enhanced* fee, not the *average* hourly rate under the *lodestar*. The lay reader should also bear in mind that a lawyer's "fee" is substantially greater than his "profit," given that attorneys must sometimes cover case-specific costs (which in this case exceeded $800,000) and also must cover routine overhead expenses, which typically consume 40% of their fees.)

At $249 per hour, the lodestar would compensate this group of attorneys—whom the District Court described as extraordinary—at a rate *lower* than the *average* rate charged by attorneys practicing law in the State of Georgia, where the average hourly rate is $268. Accordingly, even the majority would seem to acknowledge that some form of an enhancement is appropriate in this case. Indeed, the fact that these exceptional results were achieved in a case where "much of the work" was performed by relatively inexperienced attorneys (who, accordingly, would be compensated by the lodestar "below the market average") is all the more reason to think that their service rendered their out-standing performance worthy of an enhancement. By comparison, the District Court's enhanced award—a special one-time adjustment unique to this excep-tional case—would compensate these attorneys, on this one occasion, at an average hourly rate of $435, which is comparable to the rates charged by the Nation's leading law firms on average on every occasion [citing news reports and scholarly articles]. Thus, it would appear that the enhanced award is wholly consistent with the purpose of §1988, which was enacted to ensure that "counsel for prevailing parties [are] paid as is traditional with attorneys compensated by a fee-paying client." S. Rep. No. 94-1011, p6 (1976); see H.R. Rep. No. 94-1558, p. 9 (1976) ("[C]ivil rights plaintiffs should not be singled out for different and less favorable treatment"); see also *Blum*.

In any event, the circumstances I have listed likely make this a "rare" or "exceptional" case warranting an enhanced fee award. And they certainly make clear that it was neither unreasonable nor an abuse of discretion for the District Court to reach that conclusion. Indeed, if the facts and circum-stances that I have described are even roughly correct, then it is fair to ask: If this is not an exceptional case, what is?

. . .

My disagreement with the Court is limited. As I stated at the outset, we are in complete agreement with respect to the answer to the question pre-sented: "[A]n increase" to the lodestar "due to superior performance and results" "is permitted in extraordinary circumstances." . . . Our prior cases make clear that enhancements are permitted in "'exceptional' cases," *Dela-ware Valley*, where the attorney achieves "exceptional success," *Hensley*; see also *Blum*. . . . And with respect to that central holding we are unanimous.

. . .

[The dissenters would "affirm the judgment below."]

■ NOTES ON FEE SHIFTING TO ENCOURAGE CERTAIN KINDS OF SUITS

1. Fee-shifting statutes play critical roles in federal litigation. In Alyeska Pipeline Service Co. v. Wilderness Society, 421 U.S. 240 (1975), the Court held that only Congress can authorize fee shifting. A year later, Congress enacted 42 USC §1988, the statute applied in *Perdue* (one of the more important fee-shifting provisions), and there are *many* others.[6] Under §1988, the "prevailing party" in many civil rights cases can recover fees "as part of costs." The statute applies in suits seeking to vindicate constitutional rights infringed by state action under 42 USC §1983, the provision involved in cases you've read (*Piphus* in Chapter 1; *Doehr* in this chapter). Similar wording is in 42 USC §2000e-5k, covering suits under the Civil Rights Act of 1964 (discrimination in employment, public accommodations, housing). Both provisions authorize "two way" fee shifting. But in two decisions, the Court found a pro-plaintiff purpose behind the latter provision, and §1988 has been construed similarly. See Christianburg Garment Co. v. EEOC, 434 U.S. 412 (1978) (in suit under Title VII for discrimination in employment, prevailing defendant can recover attorney fees *only if* suit was frivolous, unreasonable, or without foundation) (*not* true here); and Newman v. Piggie Park Enterprises, 390 U.S. 400 (1968) (under Title II, covering discrimination in public accommodations, prevailing plaintiffs should "ordinarily recover an attorney's fee unless special circumstances would render such an award unjust") (rejecting view that prevailing plaintiffs should recover only where defenses were advanced for delay and not in good faith).

2. The central task of courts applying §1988 and many of other fee-shifting provisions is to calculate the appropriate award. Three competing methodologies have emerged—a multi-factor approach described in footnote 4 of *Perdue,* a percentage approach emulating contingent fee practice, see In re Activision Securities Litigation, 723 F. Supp. 1373 (N.D. Cal. 1989), and the "lodestar" approach endorsed in *Perdue.* The lodestar approach means reasonable rate times hours. See Gisbrecht v. Barnhart, 535 U.S. 789, 792 (2002) (lodestar means "hours reasonably spent on the case times reasonable hourly rate"). What are the advantages and drawbacks of each of these approaches? After leaving the matter to the lower courts for almost 20 years, the Court entered the fray, endorsing the lodestar approach in Hensley v. Eckerhart, 461 U.S. 424 (1983) (institutional reform litigation similar to *Perdue,* challenging conditions in a state mental hospital), repeating its preference for this approach in later cases. See, e.g., Blanchard v. Bergeron, 489 U.S. 87 (1987); City of Burlington v. Dague, 505 U.S. 557 (1992).

3. In *Perdue,* plaintiffs sought $14 million in fees, half representing the lodestar "hours times rate" calculation and half representing a "fee enhancement for superior work and results." The judge cut the lodestar amount to $6 million, then awarded a 75 percent enhancement, for a total of $10.5 million.

---

[6] Some statutes make fee shifting mandatory for prevailing plaintiffs. See, e.g., 15 USC §15 (Clayton Act); 29 USC §216(b) (Fair Labor Standards Act); 7 USC §210(f) (Packers and Stockyards Act); 15 USC §1640(a) (Truth in Lending Act). Others benefit only prevailing plaintiffs, but vest discretion in the court on the question whether to shift fees. See, e.g., 5 USC §552a(g)(2)(B) (Privacy Act of 1974); 42 USC §3612(c) (Fair Housing Act). Yet others are discretionary but authorize awards to either plaintiffs or defendants. See, e.g., 15 USC §77ooo(e) (Trust Indenture Act); 15 USC §§78i(e) & 78r(a) (Securities Exchange Act); 33 USC §1365(d) (Federal Water Pollution Control Act); 42 USC §1857h-2(d) (Clean Air Act); 42 USC §4911(d) (Noise Control Act).

For the Court, Justice Alito rejects this enhancement, but Justice Breyer argues for the dissenters that the enhanced award should be upheld. Is it fair to say the majority thinks the billing rate reflects the ability of the lawyer, so success is rewarded by the lodestar alone, but the dissent thinks otherwise? The majority insists on an "objective" approach while the dissent argues for "an element of judgment" in deciding the fee award. Who's right here, and what is at stake?

4. Institutional reform litigation is often supported by nonprofit legal organizations, where attorneys work for salaries that are relatively low when compared with large private law firms. In one such case, the defense argued that the fee award should be based on the *actual cost* of legal services rather than prevailing market rates, but the Supreme Court rejected this view. See Blum v. Stenson, 465 U.S. 886, 896 (1984) ("reasonable fees" under §1988 means "prevailing market rates in the relevant community," regardless whether plaintiff is represented by "nonprofit counsel"). In *Blum* (cited in *Perdue*), the Court recognized that determining market rates is "inherently difficult" because lawyers' hourly charges "vary widely," and in other settings fees are "discussed" or "negotiated." Still, the Court thought judges can make this determination, with the assistance of the applicant who is to provide information on rates "prevailing in the community for similar services by lawyers of reasonably comparable skill, experience, and reputation." Do you think such an inquiry can be rationally undertaken?

5. The Court has said that "prevailing" requires significant relief, and one who wins "nominal damages" is not entitled to a fee. See Farrar v. Hobby, 506 U.S. 103 (1992) (if plaintiff fails to prove an "essential element" in a monetary claim, and recovers nominal damages, "the only reasonable fee is usually no fee at all"). See also Hensley v. Eckerhart, 461 U.S. 424, 435 (1983) (where work on unsuccessful claim is "unrelated" to work on a successful claim, no fees can be awarded for work on the former, but if plaintiff obtains "excellent results," lawyer should recover "a fully compensatory fee" encompassing "all hours reasonably expended," and award "should not be reduced simply because the plaintiff failed to prevail on every contention raised in the lawsuit"). But see Texas State Teachers Association v. Garland Independent School District, 489 U.S. 782 (1989) (plaintiff need not prevail on "central issue," and prevailing on any "significant issue" in resolution that "changes the legal relationship" between plaintiff and defendant entitles plaintiffs to a fee award).

6. *Perdue* is not the first case that disapproves fee enhancements. In *Blum* (cited in *Perdue*), the Court disapproved a "quality multiplier" on the ground that quality "generally is reflected in the reasonable hourly rate," see Blum v. Stenson, 465 U.S. 886, 899 (1984). In *Dague* (also cited in *Perdue*), the Court disapproved a "contingency multiplier" for similar reasons, see City of Burlington v. Dague, 505 U.S. 557, 562 (1992) (enhancement for contingency "would likely duplicate in substantial part factors already subsumed in the lodestar," either because lawyer spends more hours due to difficulty of the case or because lawyer charges higher rate). See also Pennsylvania v. Delaware Valley Citizens' Council for Clean Air, 468 U.S. 711, 726-727 (contingency multiplier would result in "a windfall for an attorney who prevailed in a difficult case").

7. Perhaps not surprisingly, a lawyer in a fee-shifting case sometimes has a contingent fee agreement. If the contingent fee is higher than the amount indicated by the lodestar, can the lawyer collect the contract sum or should she be required to accept a lower lodestar award? Does it count that it is actually the *client* who owns the right to recover the fee? See Venegas v. Mitchell, 495 U.S. 82, 87-88 (1990) (court awarded $75,000 in fees under §1988, but lawyer can collect $406,000 under contingent fee contract) (balance of $331,000 coming from client's recovery). See also Blanchard v. Bergeron, 489 U.S. 87 (1989) (client recovered $10,000; fact that contingency contract entitled lawyer to 40 percent did not bar recovery of *higher fees*).

8. Fee shifting is sometimes allowed in suits that are far from the "big ticket" or "cutting edge" variety illustrated in *Perdue*. Successful claimants for Social Security benefits, for example, can recover fees, as can successful claimants in suits against the government under the Federal Tort Claims Act, which authorizes recovery, for example, for people hurt or injured by the negligence of officials driving government vehicles. See 42 USC §406 (fee shifting for Social Security claimants); 28 USC §2412(c) (fee shifting in FTA suits). In the *Gisbrecht* case, the lawyer was successful in advancing claims for Social Security benefits, and the case was complicated by two factors: First, the statute allowed contingent fee contracts capped at 25 percent of any award, to be taken from the client's recovery. Second, the clients *also* had claims for fees under the Equal Access to Justice Act (EAJA), 28 USC §2412(c), which allows litigants suing the government to recover fees if the government's resistance is unreasonable. In *Gisbrecht,* the Court concluded that Congress intended that the lawyer receive whichever amount was higher—the percentage called for by the contract or the reasonable sum awarded under the EAJA, but recovery under the latter was to offset any amount awarded under the contract. Thus if the contract called for a $3,000 fee and the award under the EAJA was $4,000, the lawyer would receive the latter sum and the client would enjoy the full amount of his recovery. If the award under EAJA was $2,000, the lawyer would receive $3,000 and the client's recovery would be reduced by only $1,000. The Court in *Gisbrecht* also tackled the question whether the task of figuring an award of reasonable fees under the EAJA should take into account the contingency, and concluded in the affirmative. See Gisbrecht v. Barnhart, 535 U.S. 789 (2002) (in calculating award under EAJA, court should look first to contingent fee contract, then adjust it for reasonableness; Justice Scalia in dissent argues that EAJA requires court to award fair market value of services performed, and purpose of a contingent fee contract is to deal with uncertainty, not measure what is reasonable).

9. Ethical rules limit what lawyers can charge as contingent fees. See DR2-106 (lawyer shall not "enter into an agreement for, charge, or collect an illegal or clearly excessive fee," and a fee is clearly excessive "when, after a review of the facts, a lawyer of ordinary prudence would be left with a definite and firm conviction that the fee is in excess of a reasonable fee," and listing factors). Why have limits at all? Does an overarching "reasonableness" limit mean courts are drawn into the kind of *ex ante* analysis that Justice Scalia attacked in *Gisbrecht*? In tort suits against private actors (not covered by Federal Tort Claims Act or by statute), the only limit is "reasonableness." In product liability suits, for example, and suits against airlines and other common carriers for injuries and deaths, a lawyer can set the contingent fee much higher than 25 percent. Often lawyers set the fee at 33 percent, but fees can run as high as 50 percent, and sometimes contracts set variable rates depending on factors such as whether the case settles or goes to trial. See generally Herbert M. Kritzer, *The Wages of Risk: The Returns of Contingency Fee Legal Practice,* 47 DePaul L. Rev. 267, 285 (1998).

10. Do contingent-fee arrangements produce conflicts of interest between lawyer and client? Suppose a lawyer takes a case on a 40 percent contingency, and thinks the odds of winning are two to one (67 percent) and that recovery should be in the neighborhood of $500,000. Suppose he invests $10,000 in time and expenses preparing the case, and thinks going to trial will cost $30,000 more. Suppose the other side offers to settle for $300,000. The lawyer sees that settling puts him ahead by $110,000 (40 percent of $300,000, less $10,000). Going to trial could put him ahead by $160,000 (40 percent of $500,000 less $40,000), but factoring in the risk of losing suggests that the present value of the gain from trial is $94,000 (67 percent times $500,000 times 40 percent less $40,000). From the client's perspective, the settlement value is $180,000 ($300,000 less 40 percent in lawyer fees). Going to trial brings a good chance of winning $300,000 (verdict of $500,000 less $200,000 lawyer fees), and factoring in the risk of losing suggests that the present value of going to trial is $201,000 ($300,000 times 67 percent). To the extent that financial prospects drive the case, the lawyer will prefer settlement, but the client will prefer trial. Such differences are inevitable in a contingent fee situation, aren't they?

CHAPTER 3

Personal Jurisdiction: The Geographical Reach of Judicial Authority

INTRODUCTION

The judicial authority of courts—their jurisdiction—is best understood as having two branches. In one, we find doctrines and rules regulating "subject matter" jurisdiction.[1] In the other, we find doctrines and rules regulating what we call "personal jurisdiction," meaning geographical "reach," which is the topic of this chapter.

Personal jurisdiction (you will also see the Latin term "in personam" jurisdiction) describes the authority of courts to require people or entities to appear as witnesses or parties. Our focus here is on the authority of courts to require parties (usually we mean defendants) to appear and defend suits against them.

Most of us would assume that any state court of general jurisdiction can require anyone in the state to appear and defend. That is correct, although venue rules restrict the plaintiff's choice of forum: If a defendant living in Tucson, Arizona is sued in state court in Phoenix by a plaintiff living in Phoenix on account of an automobile accident in Tucson, the defendant is likely to be entitled to a "change of venue" transferring the suit to Tucson. Basic venue rules often channel the suit to a court where defendant lives. See Ariz. Stat.

---

[1] Subject matter jurisdiction, taken up in Chapter 4, describes the competence of courts, which is established by statute. In federal courts, the most common areas of competence are diversity and federal question cases.

§12-401 (providing, with exceptions, that nobody "shall be sued out of the county in which such person lives").

We would assume as well that a plaintiff living in Tucson cannot sue in Arizona a defendant who lives in New Hampshire on account of an automobile accident that happened in the latter state. That's right too, although the answer would be different if the accident was in Arizona. Prior to the adoption of the Fourteenth Amendment after the Civil War, questions of the extraterritorial reach of state court jurisdiction were resolved in accordance with principles drawn from international law, which meant that a state court had no authority, or at most very limited authority, over people beyond the boundaries of the state.

A TRADITIONAL THEORY ARISES: TERRITORIALITY AND POWER

1. The Original Idea: Presence of Person or Property

John Mitchell and Sylvester Pennoyer

Many generations of American law students began their studies, and their course in Civil Procedure, by reading Pennoyer v. Neff. A YouTube video pokes fun at the academy's devotion to this case in teaching the course, but *Pennoyer* remains an important and engaging decision: It imagined and created a world in which the authority of state courts is clearly defined, and the decision brought into equilibrium the commands of due process and full faith and credit. In some ways, as you will see, the world of *Pennoyer* still exists. John Mitchell (left, below) and Sylvester Pennoyer (right, below) were formidable men, whatever one might think of Mitchell's personal life (see the Notes after the case) and his legal strategy in suing his client Marcus Neff. Sylvester Pennoyer, who bought the land at the sheriff's sale, carried with him great resentment at losing the case to Neff, who got his land back. At the time, the land was forested, and some of it remains forested today, but much of it now contains residential neighborhoods

of Portland. John Mitchell was to serve a term as United States Senator from Oregon (1872-1878) and Sylvester Pennoyer became Governor of Oregon (1886-1895), but Marcus Neff faded from view, unlike the case to which his name is attached.

PENNOYER v. NEFF

United States Supreme Court
95 U.S. 714 (1877)

Mr. Justice FIELD delivered the opinion of the court.

[Oregon lawyer John Mitchell sued Marcus Neff, a former client, to recover legal fees. By affidavit, Mitchell averred that Neff had moved to California, that Mitchell did not know his address, and that Neff owned property in Oregon. The Oregon court authorized service on Neff by publication: Notice of suit was published once a week for six weeks in the *Pacific Christian Advocate*, a newspaper in general circulation in Multnomah County. (Where the address of the absent defendant was known, the Oregon statute required plaintiff either to obtain personal service of the summons and complaint on the defendant, or to mail them to him.)

Neff did not appear. In 1866, several months after filing suit, Mitchell obtained a default judgment for $253.14. Thereafter, Neff acquired real property in Oregon. Judgment in hand, Mitchell executed against this property and had it sold at a sheriff's sale. Mitchell himself was the buyer, paying $341.60, presumably bidding the amount of his judgment (a credit toward purchase price) and paying sheriff's costs. Days later, Mitchell conveyed title to Sylvester Pennoyer.

In 1874, Marcus Neff sued Sylvester Pennoyer in federal court in Oregon to get the land back, alleging that it was worth $15,000. He claimed Mitchell's judgment was invalid because service by publication did not confer jurisdiction.]

The Code of Oregon provides for [service by publication] when an action is brought against a nonresident and absent defendant, who has property within the State. It also provides, where the action is for the recovery of money or damages, for the attachment of the property of the non-resident. And it also declares that no natural person is subject to the jurisdiction of a court of the State, "unless he appear in the court, or be found within the State, or be a resident thereof, or have property therein; and, in the last case, only to the extent of such property at the time the jurisdiction attached." Construing this latter provision to mean, that, in an action for money or damages where a defendant does not appear in the court, and is not found within the State, and is not a resident thereof, but has property therein, the jurisdiction of the court extends only over such property, the declaration expresses a principle of general, if not universal, law. The authority of every tribunal is necessarily restricted by the territorial limits of the State in which it is established. Any attempt to exercise authority beyond those limits would be deemed in every other forum, as has been said by this court, an illegitimate assumption of power, and be resisted as mere abuse. In the case against the plaintiff, the property here in controversy sold under the judgment rendered was not attached, nor in any way brought under the jurisdiction of the court. Its first connection with the case was caused by a levy of the execution. It was not, therefore, disposed of pursuant to any adjudication, but only in enforcement of a personal judgment, having no relation to the property, rendered against a non-resident without service of process upon him in the action, or his appearance therein.

[The federal Circuit Court held that the judgment was invalid because the affidavit was executed by the editor of the newspaper, while the statute provided that the affidavit must be executed by "the printer, or his foreman, or his principal clerk." The Supreme Court concludes that the affidavit was adequate.]

If, therefore, we were confined to the rulings of the court below upon the defects in the affidavits mentioned, we should be unable to uphold its decision. But it was also contended in that court, and is insisted upon here, that the judgment in the State court against the plaintiff was void for want of personal service of process on him, or of his appearance in the action in which it was rendered and that the premises in controversy could not be subjected to the payment of the demand of a resident creditor except by a proceeding in rem; that is, by a direct proceeding against the property for that purpose. If these positions are sound, the ruling of the Circuit Court as to the invalidity of that judgment must be sustained, notwithstanding our dissent from the reasons upon which it was made. And that they are sound would seem to follow from two well-established principles of public law respecting the jurisdiction of an independent State over persons and property. The several States of the Union are not, it is true, in every respect independent, many of the right and powers which originally belonged to them being now vested in the government created by the Constitution. But, except as restrained and limited by that instrument, they possess and exercise the authority of independent States, and the principles of public law to which we have referred are applicable to them. One of these principles is, that every State possesses exclusive jurisdiction and sovereignty over persons and property within its territory. As a consequence, every State has the power to determine for itself the civil status and capacities of its inhabitants; to prescribe the subjects upon which they may contract, the forms and solemnities with which their contracts shall be executed, the rights and obligations arising from them, and the mode in which their validity shall be determined and their obligations enforced; and also to regulate the manner and conditions upon which property situated within such territory, both personal and real, may be acquired, enjoyed, and transferred. The other principle of public law referred to follows from the one mentioned; that is, that no State can exercise direct jurisdiction and authority over persons or property without its territory. Story, Conflict of Laws, ch. 2; Wheat, International Law, pt. 2, c. 2. The several States are of equal dignity and authority, and the independence of one implies the exclusion of power from all others. And so it is laid down by jurists, as an elementary principle, that the laws of one State have no operation outside of its territory, except so far as is allowed by comity; and that no tribunal established by it can extend its process beyond that territory so as to subject either persons or property to its decisions. "Any exertion of authority of this sort beyond this limit," says Story, "is a mere nullity, and incapable of binding such persons or property in any other tribunals."

But as contracts made in one State may be enforceable only in another State, and property may be held by non-residents, the exercise of the jurisdiction which every State is admitted to possess over persons and property within its own territory will often affect persons and property without it. To any influence exerted in this way by a State affecting persons resident or property situated elsewhere, no objection can be justly taken; whilst any direct exertion of authority upon them, in an attempt to give ex-territorial operation to its laws, or to enforce an ex-territorial jurisdiction by its tribunals, would be deemed an encroachment upon the independence of the State in which the persons are domiciled or the property is situated, and be resisted as usurpation.

Thus the State, through its tribunals, may compel persons domiciled within its limits to execute, in pursuance of their contracts respecting property elsewhere situated, instruments in such form and with such solemnities as to transfer the title, so far as such formalities can be complied with; and the exercise of this jurisdiction in no manner interferes with the supreme control over the property by the State within which it is situated.

So the State, through its tribunals, may subject property situated within its limits owned by non-residents to the payment of the demand of its own citizens against them; and the exercise of this jurisdiction in no respect infringes upon the sovereignty of the State where the owners are domiciled. Every State owes protection to its own citizens; and, when nonresidents deal with them, it is a legitimate and just exercise of authority to hold and appropriate any property owned by such non-residents to satisfy the claims of its citizens. It is in virtue of the State's jurisdiction over the property of the nonresident situated within its limits that its tribunals can inquire into that nonresident's obligations to its own citizens, and the inquiry can then be carried only to the extent necessary to control the disposition of the property. If the non-resident have no property in the State, there is nothing upon which the tribunals can adjudicate. . . .

If, without personal service, judgments in personam, obtained ex parte against non-residents and absent parties, upon mere publication of process, which, in the great majority of cases, would never be seen by the parties interested, could be upheld and enforced, they would be the constant instruments of fraud and oppression. Judgments for all sorts of claims upon contracts and for torts, real or pretended, would be thus obtained, under which property would be seized, when the evidence of the transactions upon which they were founded, if they ever had any existence, had perished.

Substituted service by publication, or in any other authorized form, may be sufficient to inform parties of the object of proceedings taken where property is once brought under the control of the court by seizure or some equivalent act. The law assumes that property is always in the possession of its owner, in person or by agent; and it proceeds upon the theory that its seizure will inform him, not only that it is taken into the custody of the court, but that he must look to any proceedings authorized by law upon such seizure for its condemnation and sale. Such service may also be sufficient in cases where the object of the action is to reach and dispose of property in the State, or of some interest therein, by enforcing a contract or a lien respecting the same, or to partition it among different owners, or, when the public is a party, to condemn and appropriate it for a public purpose. In other words, such service may answer in all actions which are substantially proceedings in rem. But where the entire object of the action is to determine the personal rights and obligations of the defendants, that is, where the suit is merely in personam, constructive service in this form upon a non-resident is ineffectual for any purpose. Process from the tribunals of one State cannot run into another State, and summon parties there domiciled to leave its territory and respond to proceedings against them. Publication of process or notice within the State where the tribunal sits cannot create any greater obligation upon the non-resident to appear. Process sent to him out of the State, and process published within it, are equally unavailing in proceedings to establish his personal liability.

The want of authority of the tribunals of a State to adjudicate upon the obligations of non-residents, where they have no property within its limits, is not denied by the court below: but the position is assumed, that, where they have property within the State, it is immaterial whether the property is in the first instance brought under the control of the court by attachment or some other equivalent act, and afterwards applied by its judgment to the satisfaction of demands against its owner; or such demands be first established in a personal action, and the property of the non-resident be afterwards seized and sold on execution. But the answer to this position has already been given in the statement, that the jurisdiction of the court to inquire into and determine his obligations at all is only incidental to its jurisdiction over the property. Its jurisdiction in that respect cannot be made to depend upon facts to be ascertained after it has tried the cause and rendered the judgment. If the judgment be previously void, it will not become valid by the subsequent discovery of property of the defendant, or by his subsequent acquisition of it. The judgment, if void when rendered, will always remain void: it cannot occupy the doubtful position of being valid if property be found, and void if there be none. Even if the position assumed were confined to cases where the non-resident defendant possessed property in the State at the commencement of the action, it would still make the validity of the proceedings and judgment depend upon the question whether, before the levy of the execution, the defendant had or had not disposed of the property. If before the levy the property should be sold, then, according to this position, the judgment would not be binding. This doctrine would introduce a new element of uncertainty in judicial proceedings. The contrary is the law: the validity of every judgment depends upon the jurisdiction of the court before it is rendered, not upon what may occur subsequently. . . .

The force and effect of judgments rendered against non-residents without personal service of process upon them, or their voluntary appearance, have been the subject of frequent consideration in the courts of the United States and of the several States, as attempts have been made to enforce such judgments in States other than those in which they were rendered, under the provision of the Constitution requiring that "full faith and credit shall be given in each State to the public acts, records, and judicial proceedings of every other State[,]" and the act of Congress providing for the mode of authenticating such acts, records, and proceedings, and declaring that, when thus authenticated, "they shall have such faith and credit given to them in every court within the United States as they have by law or usage in the courts of the State from which they are or shall or taken." In the earlier cases, it was supposed that the act gave to all judgments the same effect in other States which they had by law in the State where rendered. But this view was afterwards qualified so as to make the act applicable only when the court rendering the judgment had jurisdiction of the parties and of the subject-matter, and not to preclude an inquiry into the jurisdiction of the court in which the judgment was rendered, or the right of the State itself to exercise authority over the person or the subject-matter. . . .

Since the adoption of the Fourteenth Amendment to the Federal Constitution, the validity of such judgments may be directly questioned, and their enforcement in the State resisted, on the ground that proceedings in a court of justice to determine the personal rights and obligations of parties over whom that court has no jurisdiction do not constitute due process of law. Whatever difficulty may be experienced in giving to those terms a definition which will embrace every permissible exertion of power affecting private rights, and exclude such as is forbidden, there can be no doubt of their meaning when applied to judicial proceedings. They then mean a course of legal proceedings according to those rules and principles which have been established in our systems of jurisprudence for the protection and enforcement of private rights. To give such proceedings any validity, there must be a tribunal competent by its constitution—that is, by the law of its creation—to pass upon the subject-matter of the suit; and, if that involves merely a determination of the personal liability of the defendant, he must be brought within its jurisdiction by service of process within the State, or his voluntary appearance.

Except in cases affecting the personal status of the plaintiff, and cases in which that mode of service may be considered to have been assented to in advance, as hereinafter mentioned, the substituted service of process by publication, allowed by the law of Oregon and by similar laws in other States, where actions are brought against non-residents, is effectual only where, in connection with process against the person for commencing the action, property in the State is brought under the control of the court, and subjected to its disposition by process adapted to that purpose, or where the judgment is sought as a means of reaching such property or affecting some interest therein; in other words, where the action is in the nature of a proceeding in rem. As stated by Cooley in his Treatise on Constitutional Limitations, for any other purpose than to subject the property of a non-resident to valid claims against him in the State, "due process of law would require appearance or personal service before the defendant could be personally bound by any judgment rendered."

It is true that, in a strict sense, a proceeding in rem is one taken directly against property, and has for its object the disposition of the property, without reference to the title of individual claimants; but, in a larger and more general sense, the terms are applied to actions between parties, where the direct object is to reach and dispose of property owned by them, or of some interest therein. Such are cases commenced by attachment against the property of debtors, or instituted to partition real estate, foreclose a mortgage, or enforce a lien. So far as they affect property in the State, they are substantially proceedings in rem in the broader sense which we have mentioned. . . .

To prevent any misapplication of the views expressed in this opinion, it is proper to observe that we do not mean to assert, by any thing we have said, that a State may not authorize proceedings to determine the status of one of its citizens towards a non-resident, which would be binding within the State, though made without service of process or personal notice to the non-resident. The jurisdiction which every State possesses to determine the civil status and capacities of all its inhabitants involves authority to prescribe the conditions on which proceedings affecting them may be commenced and carried on within its territory. The State, for example, has absolute right to prescribe the conditions upon which the marriage relation between its own citizens shall be created, and the causes for which it may be dissolved. One of the parties guilty of acts for which, by the law of the State, a dissolution may be granted, may have removed to a State where no dissolution is permitted. The complaining party would, therefore, fail if a divorce were sought in the State of the defendant; and if application could not be made to the tribunals of the complainant's domicile in such case, and proceedings be there instituted without personal service of process or personal notice to the offending party, the injured citizen would be without redress.

Neither do we mean to assert that a State may not require a non-resident entering into a partnership or association within its limits, or making contracts enforceable there, to appoint an agent or representative in the State to receive service of process and notice in legal proceedings instituted with respect to such partnership, association, or contracts, or to designate a place where such service may be made and notice given, and provide, upon their failure, to make such appointment or to designate such place that service may be made upon a public officer designated for that purpose, or in some other prescribed way, and that judgments rendered upon such service may not be binding upon the non-residents both within and without the State.... Nor do we doubt that a State, on creating corporations or other institutions for pecuniary or charitable purposes, may provide a mode in which their conduct may be investigated, their obligations enforced, or their charters revoked, which shall require other than personal service upon their officers or members. Parties becoming members of such corporations or institutions would hold their interest subject to the conditions prescribed by law.

In the present case, there is no feature of this kind, and, consequently, no consideration of what would be the effect of such legislation in enforcing the contract of a non-resident can arise. The question here respects only the validity of a money judgment rendered in one State, in an action upon a simple contract against the resident of another, without service of process upon him, or his appearance therein.

Judgment affirmed.

[A dissenting opinion by Justice Hunt is omitted.]

■ NOTES ON DUE PROCESS AND LIMITS OF JURISDICTION

1. Technically, the Due Process Clause of the Fourteenth Amendment did not apply in *Pennoyer* because the amendment was not in effect when John Mitchell's suit went to judgment (it took effect in 1868). But *Pennoyer* tells us the standard it announces *is* the due process standard. Henceforth the validity of a judgment in state court depends on jurisdiction over the defendant; if a judgment is entered by a court that *lacks* jurisdiction, enforcing it violates defendant's due process rights. For close to 60 years, *Pennoyer* set the meaning of due process in this area.

2. Suppose Mitchell had gone to California after winning the default judgment against Neff in Oregon, and sued Neff in California. Suppose Neff owned real property there. As you probably suspect, an Oregon judgment could not be the basis in California for an attachment and execution sale, since a California sheriff does not take orders from an Oregon court, and Oregon sheriffs have no authority in California. But a plaintiff who wins a judgment in one state may *sue on* that judgment in another, and get a new judgment in the latter, and this new judgment can be executed through attachment and execution. So Mitchell could sue in California on the Oregon judgment. Why should a California court pay more attention to an Oregon judgment than a California sheriff would pay? As noted in Chapter 1G4, the answer is in another clause in the Constitution: Article IV provides that "Full Faith and Credit shall be given in each State to the . . . judicial Proceedings of every other state." And see 28 USC §1738 (containing similar language). *Pennoyer* tells us, doesn't it, that Mitchell's default judgment is invalid *even in Oregon*? That means, doesn't it, that the judgment must also be invalid in California? The answer is yes: One accomplishment of *Pennoyer* was to put due process and full faith and credit on the same level, so a state court judgment is either valid in all states or valid in none.

3. If Neff had owned Greenacre (a stand of trees in Oregon worth $15,000) when Mitchell sued, Mitchell could have attached Greenacre at the outset. To do so, Mitchell would have enlisted the services of the sheriff, which involves first getting a writ of attachment (a court order) that the sheriff serves and executes. He serves the writ by delivering or mailing a copy to the defendant. Executing the writ involves, among other things, filing in the recorder's office, which lists the writ in records relating to the property. The sheriff also goes to the property and posts written notices. A judgment obtained this way would have been valid.

4. Why does the Court in *Pennoyer* insist that attachment occur *at the outset*, rather than at the end of the case? It isn't *just* a matter of giving notice, is it?

5. *Pennoyer* implies that jurisdiction would have been good in Oregon if John Mitchell had managed to serve Marcus Neff with the necessary papers (summons and complaint) in Oregon. If that had happened in April 1865, and if Neff were still living in Oregon, Neff would be subject to the jurisdiction of the Oregon court until the case concluded, even if he moved to California in September 1865, before the case could be tried or go to judgment. What if Neff still lived in Oregon but, getting wind of Mitchell's intent to bring suit, went to California for an "extended visit"? See Milliken v. Meyer, 311 U.S. 457 (1940) (Wyoming citizen may be sued there even though staying out of state, visiting and traveling in Colorado).

6. What is the *reason* in *Pennoyer* for upholding jurisdiction if plaintiff attaches property belonging to the defendant, or serves him in the state? Admittedly, it is more convenient to be sued only in the state where one lives, and arguably it is fair to make the plaintiff go to the defendant. But if Marcus Neff lived in Truckee, California (in the Sierras close to the Nevada border), his *presence* in California would make him amenable to suit in San Francisco (about 120 miles west of Truckee) while a court in Reno, Nevada (about 20 miles east of Truckee) would lack jurisdiction. So *fairness* is really not the basis of *Pennoyer,* is it? It's the relative *power* of sovereign states in a federal union, isn't it? Should the Due Process Clause enforce notions of sovereignty? See generally Albert Ehrenzweig, *The Transient Rule of Personal Jurisdiction: The "Power" Myth and Forum Conveniens,* 65 Yale L.J. 289 (1956) (arguing that personal service within the forum state had not been thought either necessary or sufficient before *Pennoyer*).

7. If John Mitchell and Marcus Neff had lived in Oregon at all relevant times, it would be right, wouldn't it, to say that Oregon law should apply to the dispute between them over attorneys' fees? And if John Mitchell had gone to Eureka (in California, just south of the Oregon border) to sue for those fees in a California state court, serving Neff in Oregon, a default judgment rendered in California would be invalid, wouldn't it? In short, Oregon law should apply to this dispute, and Oregon courts should adjudicate it. And it makes sense to say (as *Pennoyer* says) that each state may "prescribe the subjects upon which [its inhabitants] may contract . . . and the rights and obligations arising" from such contracts, and that "the laws of one State have no operation outside of its territory." It *also* makes sense to say (as *Pennoyer* says) that "every State possesses exclusive jurisdiction and sovereignty over persons and property within its territory." If these are sensible propositions, what kind of world do they envision?

8. Unfortunately, transactions and lawsuits in a federal union are not always connected with only one state. If an Oregon resident agrees to sell lumber to a Montana resident, and the two enter into a contract by mail, or through negotiations by phone or the internet, any dispute arising from such an arrangement is not connected "exclusively" with either Oregon or Montana. *Pennoyer* still tells us that the Oregon seller can sue the Montana buyer in Oregon if the seller attaches property in Oregon belonging to the Montana buyer, or if the Montana buyer comes to Oregon and is served there. But does Oregon law apply, or Montana law? Does it make sense to say that *only* Oregon or *only* Montana can try such a dispute?

9. Justice Field's opinion in *Pennoyer* recognizes exceptions, where neither presence of the defendant nor presence of her property is required:

(a) Status. An Oregon husband may divorce his wife even if the latter has moved to California, cannot be served in Oregon, and owns no property there. And the wife, even if she deserted her husband by moving to California, may seek a divorce in California. Why have this doctrine? (In a way, it is not an "exception" to the *Pennoyer* principle that presence of person or property is necessary, as the marriage was conceptualized as a *res* or "thing" that existed wherever the marital domicile existed, which became extended to include the place where the plaintiff spouse is domiciled.) Should a spouse who leaves the marital domicile and brings divorce proceedings elsewhere be able to get *also* a decree dividing marital property, allocating child custody, or awarding support?

(b) Consent. Pennoyer says John Mitchell would have had good jurisdiction in Oregon if Marcus Neff had consented to be sued there, by "voluntary appearance." Practically speaking, Neff might appear in Oregon by hiring an

Oregon lawyer to represent him, and the lawyer could file the necessary papers (an answer to the complaint that does not object to jurisdiction). If *Pennoyer* rests on notions of state *power,* does it make sense to recognize an exception where defendant consents?

(c) *Partnership or Association. Pennoyer* says a state may require such an entity, when formed within the state by residents of another state, to "appoint an agent or representative" for service of process in the state. One difference between people and entities is that the latter have no corporeal existence, so "presence" is a harder concept to apply. It makes sense, doesn't it, to require a business entity to designate a person to receive service of process? And every entity should have such a person, shouldn't it, regardless whether put together by people from out of state?

10. *Pennoyer* is an epic case, with some legendary characters. John Mitchell, once known as John Hipple, had been a teacher in Pennsylvania when he seduced (and was forced to marry) a 15-year-old student. He became a lawyer, but left Pennsylvania for California with money belonging to clients, and a mistress. Leaving her in California, he went to Oregon and entered practice in Portland, under the name John Mitchell. Marcus Neff was an illiterate Iowa native who left home by wagon train at age 24. In 1850, he filed an application for land under the Oregon Land Donation Act, and 12 years later enlisted Mitchell's aid in processing his application. He paid Mitchell $6.50, but in 1865 Neff moved to California. Three days after purchasing Neff's land at the sheriff's sale, Mitchell gave a quitclaim deed to Sylvester Pennoyer, also a lawyer. Ten years after Neff's successful suit against Pennoyer, the latter became governor of Oregon, complaining that the decision in *Pennoyer* usurped state power. Still later, Mitchell was elected Senator from Oregon, serving until 1905 (more than 20 years). During one re-election bid, Mitchell prevailed despite disclosure of love letters to his second wife's sister during an affair. The letters were published in the Portland *Oregonian,* which was (and is) the main Portland newspaper. The notice in Mitchell's suit was published in the *Pacific Christian Advocate,* a small weekly with religious articles and essays. See Wendy Purdue, *Sin, Scandal, and Substantive Due Process: Personal Jurisdiction and* Pennoyer *Reconsidered,* 62 Wash. L. Rev. 479 (1987).

■ NOTES ON TRADITIONAL TERMS AND CATEGORIES

In *Pennoyer,* Justice Field speaks of jurisdiction *in personam* and jurisdiction *in rem.* In fact, the philosophy embodied in *Pennoyer* came to recognize even more categories, and it is useful to look briefly at all of them:

(1) In Personam *Jurisdiction.* An *in personam* judgment is said to bind the defendant personally, typically awarding a sum of money (damages) or directing the defendant to do or to *not* do something (injunctive relief). Mitchell sought money damages for breach of contract in his suit against Neff, and *in personam* jurisdiction would be an appropriate basis for such a judgment.

(2) In Rem *Jurisdiction.* This kind of jurisdiction, sometimes called "true *in rem* jurisdiction," can be used to determine the rights of all persons who claim an interest in property before the court (the judgment "binds the whole world"). Quiet title and probate are examples. Another is the libel action in admiralty, where as a matter of historical custom it was said that injured seamen could sue a shipowner by seizing the vessel. Here, seizure was an important formality that forced the owner to post sufficient bond to cover a judgment, and the idea was to make it possible for the seaman to sue and collect wherever he disembarked the ship.

Security of land titles is a critical matter, and all states have recording systems designed to help buyers and sellers (and owners and lenders) to know exactly the condition of title to real property, and to ascertain that condition by consulting the records where the property is located. In implementing any such system, it is critical that local courts have jurisdiction. Consider this account, offered by the Supreme Court more than a century ago:

> The present suit is one in ejectment, between grantees of the respective parties to the foregoing proceedings to quiet title; and the question before us . . . is whether the decree in such proceedings to quiet title . . . operated to quiet the title in the plaintiff therein. In other words, has a state the power to provide by statute that the title to real estate within its limits shall be settled and determined by a suit in which the defendant, being a non-resident, is brought into court only by publication? . . . But it is earnestly contended that no decree in such a case, rendered on service by publication only, is valid, or can be recognized in the federal courts. . . . The propositions are that an action to quiet title is a suit in equity, that equity acts upon the person, and that the person is not brought into court by service by publication alone. While these propositions are doubtless correct as statements of the general rules respecting bills to quiet title, and proceedings in courts of equity, they are not applicable or controlling here. The question is not what a court of equity . . . might do, but . . . what jurisdiction has a state over titles to real estate within its limits . . . ? If a state has no power to bring a nonresident into its courts for any purposes by publication, it is impotent to perfect the titles of real estate within its limits held by its own citizens; and a cloud cast upon such title by a claim of a nonresident will remain for all time a cloud, unless such nonresident shall voluntarily come into its courts for the purpose of having it adjudicated. But no such imperfections attend the sovereignty of the state. It has control over property within its limits; and the condition of ownership of real estate therein, whether the owner be stranger or citizen, is subjection to its rules concerning the holding, the transfer, liability to obligations, private or public, and the modes of establishing titles thereto. It cannot bring the person of a non-resident within its limits—its process goes not out beyond its borders—but it may determine the extent of his title to real estate within its limits; and, for the purpose of such determination, may provide any reasonable methods of imparting notice. The wellbeing of every community requires that the title to real estate therein shall be secure, and that there be convenient and certain methods of determining any unsettled questions respecting it. The duty of accomplishing this is local in its nature. It is not a

matter of national concern, or vested in the general government. It remains with the state; and, as this duty is one of the state, the manner of discharging it must be determined by the state, and no proceeding which it provides can be declared invalid, unless in conflict with some special inhibitions of the constitution, or against natural justice.

Arndt v. Griggs, 134 U.S. 316, 319-320 (1890).

(3) Quasi In Rem *("Type 1") Jurisdiction.* The category of *in rem* jurisdiction took on refinements. In modern usage, *quasi in rem* type 1 jurisdiction describes the setting in which a court adjudicates the rights of named parties (not "the whole world") over property before the court in a dispute whose whole focus is title or rights in the property itself. An example is a buyer's suit to compel a seller to deliver a deed to Greenacre, brought in a court where Greenacre is located. Thus a suit in Indiana by the would-be purchaser of Woodacre in Indiana would involve *quasi in rem* type 1 jurisdiction, and defendant (no matter where he resided or was served) would be subject to jurisdiction to adjudicate his rights and obligations respecting Woodacre under the contract. (If the *seller* sued in Indiana to collect the purchase price for Woodacre, the suit would be for damages. Jurisdiction over the buyer would turn on whether he was subject to personal jurisdiction in Indiana.)

(4) Quasi In Rem *("Type 2") Jurisdiction.* A court had jurisdiction of this kind if a claimant invoked the judicial process to seize property at the outset, asserting that the owner owed him money. Thus Mitchell could have gotten jurisdiction over Neff if Mitchell had been able to attach, at the outset, property belonging to Neff in Oregon, even though Neff lived in California. Here attachment is a jurisdictional hook that forces defendant to come to the forum, at risk of losing the property (or as much of its value as needed to satisfy the claim) if he stays away. This type became obsolescent under modern notions of due process,[2] but it may not be entirely gone, and the historical legacy is important to understand.

HARRIS v. BALK

United States Supreme Court
198 U.S. 215 (1905)

Mr. Justice Peckham delivered the opinion of the Court.

[Jacob Epstein of Baltimore, Maryland, claimed that B. Balk of North Carolina owed Epstein approximately $300. Isaac Harris, also of North

---

[2] There are two reasons. First, courts can no longer seize property, absent special circumstances, unless the owner first gets notice and a chance to resist in a hearing. See Fuentes v. Shevin, 407 U.S. 67 (1972) (Chapter 2A1, supra). Second, the Court has abandoned the conceptual apparatus allowing courts to obtain jurisdiction over defendants by seizing property where the dispute is unrelated to the property. See Shaffer v. Heitner, 433 U.S. 186 (1977) (Section C1, infra).

Carolina, apparently owed Balk the lesser sum of $180. In 1896, Harris went to Baltimore on business, and Epstein got wind of it and obtained a writ that was served on Harris. The writ attached the debt Harris owed to Balk. (The term that applies when a writ of attachment is served on one person X in order to seize or exercise judicial control over property in X's possession that is owned by Y, is "garnishment." Epstein "garnished" the debt Harris owed to Balk.) Along with the writ, Epstein obtained a summons and declaration against Balk pursuant to Maryland law, which were delivered to the sheriff in Baltimore and posted on the courthouse door.

Harris returned to North Carolina without contesting the writ. There he signed an affidavit saying he owed Balk $180, but that this amount had been attached by Epstein in Baltimore, and delivered the affidavit to Balk. In Baltimore, counsel for Harris consented entry of judgment against him for $180. Harris paid this sum to a lawyer for Epstein in North Carolina.

Meanwhile, Balk sued Harris in North Carolina, seeking the $180 that he claimed Harris owed him. Harris said the Maryland judgment was entitled to full faith and credit in North Carolina, barring Balk's claim. The court rejected this argument, concluding that Harris's temporary presence in North Carolina did not provide jurisdiction to seize his debt to Balk, which remained in North Carolina.]

[Balk] contends that the Maryland court obtained no jurisdiction to award the judgment of condemnation, because the garnishee, although at the time in the state of Maryland, and personally served with process therein, was a nonresident of that state, only casually or temporarily within its boundaries; that the situs of the debt due from Harris . . . was in North Carolina, and did not accompany Harris to Maryland; that, consequently, Harris, though within the state of Maryland, had not possession of any property of Balk, and the Maryland state court therefore obtained no jurisdiction over any property of Balk in the attachment proceedings, and the consent of Harris to the entry of the judgment was immaterial. [Harris], on the contrary, insists that, though the garnishee were but temporarily in Maryland, yet the laws of that state provide for an attachment of this nature if the debtor, the garnishee, is found in the state, and the court obtains jurisdiction over him by the service of process therein; that the judgment, condemning the debt from Harris to Balk, was a valid judgment, provided Balk could himself have sued Harris for the debt in Maryland. This, it is asserted, he could have done, and the judgment was therefore entitled to full faith and credit in the courts of North Carolina.

The cases holding that the state court obtains no jurisdiction over the garnishee if he be but temporarily within the state proceed upon the theory that the situs of the debt is at the domicile either of the creditor or of the debtor, and that it does not follow the debtor in his casual or temporary journey into another state, and the garnishee has no possession of any property or credit of the principal debtor in the foreign state.

We regard the contention of [Harris] as the correct one. . . .

Attachment is the creature of the local law; that is, unless there is a law of the state providing for and permitting the attachment, it cannot be levied there. If there be a law of the state providing for the attachment of the debt, then, if the garnishee be found in that state, and process be personally served upon him therein, we think the court thereby acquires jurisdiction over him, and can garnish the debt due from him to the debtor of the plaintiff, and condemn it, provided the garnishee could himself be sued by his creditor in that state. We do not see how the question of jurisdiction vel non can properly be made to depend upon the so-called original situs of the debt, or upon the character of the stay of the garnishee, whether temporary or permanent, in the state where the attachment is issued. Power over the person of the garnishee confers jurisdiction on the courts of the state where the writ issues. If, while temporarily there, his creditor might sue him there and recover the debt, then he is liable to process of garnishment, no matter where the situs of the debt was originally. We do not see the materiality of the expression "situs of the debt," when used in connection with attachment proceedings. If by situs is meant the place of the creation of the debt, that fact is immaterial. If it be meant that the obligation to pay the debt can only be enforced at the situs thus fixed, we think it plainly untrue. The obligation of the debtor to pay his debt clings to and accompanies him wherever he goes. He is as much bound to pay his debt in a foreign state when therein sued upon his obligation by his creditor, as he was in the state where the debt was contracted. We speak of ordinary debts, such as the one in this case. It would be no defense to such suit for the debtor to plead that he was only in the foreign state casually or temporarily. His obligation to pay would be the same whether he was there in that way or with an intention to remain. It is nothing but the obligation to pay which is garnished or attached. This obligation can be enforced by the courts of the foreign state after personal service of process therein, just as well as by the courts of the domicile of the debtor. If the debtor leave the foreign state without appearing, a judgment by default may be entered, upon which execution may issue, or the judgment may be sued upon in any other state where the debtor might be found. In such case the situs is unimportant. It is not a question of possession in the foreign state, for possession cannot be taken of a debt or of the obligation to pay it, as tangible property might be taken possession of. Notice to the debtor (garnishee) of the commencement of the suit, and notice not to pay to his creditor, is all that can be given, whether the garnishee be a mere casual and temporary comer, or a resident of the state where the attachment is laid. His obligation to pay to his creditor is thereby arrested, and a lien created upon the debt itself. We can see no reason why the attachment could not be thus laid, provided the creditor of the garnishee could himself sue in that state, and its laws permitted the attachment.

There can be no doubt that Balk, as a citizen of the state of North Carolina, had the right to sue Harris in Maryland to recover the debt which Harris owed him. Being a citizen of North Carolina, he was entitled to all the privileges and immunities of citizens of the several states, one of which is the right to institute actions in the courts of another state. . . .

It thus appears that Balk could have sued Harris in Maryland to recover his debt, notwithstanding the temporary character of Harris' stay there; it also appears that the municipal law of Maryland permits the debtor of the principal debtor to be garnished, and therefore if the court of the state where the garnishee is found obtains jurisdiction over him, through the service of process upon him within the state, then the judgment entered is a valid judgment. . . .

The importance of the fact of the right of the original creditor to sue his debtor in the foreign state, as affecting the right of the creditor of that creditor to sue the debtor or garnishee, lies in the nature of the attachment proceeding. The plaintiff in such proceeding in the foreign state is able to sue out the attachment and attach the debt due from the garnishee to his (the garnishee's) creditor, because of the fact that the plaintiff is really, in such proceeding, a representative of the creditor of the garnishee, and therefore if such creditor himself had the right to commence suit to recover the debt in the foreign state, his representative has the same right, as representing him, and may garnish or attach the debt, provided the municipal law of the state where the attachment was sued out permits it.

It seems to us, therefore, that the judgment against Harris in Maryland, condemning the $180 which he owed to Balk, was a valid judgment, because the court had jurisdiction over the garnishee by personal service of process within the state of Maryland.

It ought to be and it is the object of courts to prevent the payment of any debt twice over. Thus, if Harris, owing a debt to Balk, paid it under a valid judgment against him, to Epstein, he certainly ought not to be compelled to pay it a second time, but should have the right to plead his payment under the Maryland judgment. It is objected, however, that the payment by Harris to Epstein was not under legal compulsion. Harris in truth owed the debt to Balk, which was attached by Epstein. He had, therefore, as we have seen, no defense to set up against the attachment of the debt. Jurisdiction over him personally had been obtained by the Maryland court. As he was absolutely without defense, there was no reason why he should not consent to a judgment impounding the debt, which judgment the plaintiff was legally entitled to, and which he could not prevent. There was no merely voluntary payment within the meaning of that phrase as applicable here.

But most rights may be lost by negligence, and if the garnishee were guilty of negligence in the attachment proceeding, to the damage of Balk, he ought not to be permitted to set up the judgment as a defense. Thus it is recognized as the duty of the garnishee to give notice to his own creditor, if he would protect himself, so that the creditor may have the opportunity to defend himself against the claim of the person suing out the attachment. . . . While the want of notification by the garnishee to his own creditor may have no effect upon the validity of the judgment against the garnishee (the proper publication being made by the plaintiff), we think it has and ought to have an effect upon the right of the garnishee to avail himself of the prior judgment and his payment thereunder. This notification by the garnishee is for the purpose of making sure that his creditor shall have an opportunity to defend the claim made against him in the attachment suit. Fair dealing requires this at the hands of the garnishee. In this case, while neither the defendant nor the garnishee appeared, the court, while condemning the credits attached, could not, by the terms of the Maryland statute, issue the writ of execution unless the plaintiff gave bond or sufficient security before the court awarding the execution, to make restitution of the money paid if the defendant should, at any time within a year and a day, appear in the action and show that the plaintiff's claim, or some part thereof, was not due to the plaintiff. The defendant in error, Balk, had notice of this attachment, certainly within a few days after the issuing thereof and the entry of judgment thereon, because he sued the plaintiff in error to recover his debt within a few days after his (Harris') return to North Carolina, in which suit the judgment in Maryland was set up by Harris as a plea in bar to Balk's claim. Balk, therefore, had an opportunity for a year and a day after the entry of the judgment to litigate the question of his liability in the Maryland court, and to show that he did not owe the debt, or some part of it, as was claimed by Epstein. He, however, took no proceedings to that end, so far as the record shows, and the reason may be supposed to be that he could not successfully defend the claim, because he admitted in this case that he did, at the time of the attachment proceeding, owe Epstein some $344. . . .

The judgment of the Supreme Court of North Carolina must be reversed, and the cause remanded for further proceedings not inconsistent with the opinion of this court. Reversed.

■ NOTES ON QUASI-IN-REM (TYPE 2) JURISDICTION

1. Doesn't *Harris* carry *Pennoyer* to a logical conclusion? Mitchell could get jurisdiction in Oregon over the absent Neff by attaching a stand of trees in Oregon belonging to Neff, so Epstein can obtain jurisdiction in Maryland over the absent Balk by attaching a debt in Maryland that Epstein owes to Balk. But a debt has no "situs," and *Harris* says it travels with the debtor (Harris) wherever he goes. That means, doesn't it, that if Frank from Florida had an accident with Balk in North Carolina, and if Harris (Balk's debtor) wandered into Florida, Frank could sue Balk in Florida over the North Carolina accident?

2. In *Pennoyer,* attachment of a stand of trees in Oregon provided notice to Neff of Mitchell's suit. How does Balk get notice of Epstein's suit?

3. Suppose Balk wanted to contest Epstein's claim in Maryland. Recall that Epstein sought to recover $300, but the "property" garnished by Epstein was worth only $180. Could Balk appear in Maryland without submitting in full to the jurisdiction of the Maryland court? The answer is that most courts recognized a "limited appearance" that defendant could enter solely to defend his property. That would mean Balk could deny owing Epstein any money. If the matter went to trial, the two sides could present evidence, and the court would decide: Balk owes money to Epstein, or he does not. If Epstein won, he would get the $180 that Harris owed Balk. Then Epstein could bring a second suit in North Carolina for the balance. If Epstein *lost* the Maryland suit, Harris would still owe Balk the $180. Epstein could bring another suit on the debt in North Carolina. Normally, as you might suspect, a person with a single claim can only sue once: Win or lose, the claimant cannot sue another time because the doctrine of *res judicata* says his claim is extinguished in the first action. And normally a claimant cannot relitigate the same *issue* over and over again: If the court in Maryland concluded that Balk owed nothing to Epstein because Epstein had not delivered merchandise that Balk was to pay for, Epstein would not be permitted in a second suit to claim that he delivered this merchandise, because the doctrine of *collateral estoppel* would allow Epstein only one chance to prove this point. But to make a limited appearance effective under *Pennoyer* and *Harris,* courts recognized *exceptions* to *res judicata* and *collateral estoppel* that would let *either side,* after losing in the first (attachment) suit, relitigate claims, defenses, and issues in a second suit.

4. Suppose a Kentuckian named Tom goes to Arizona, and has an automobile accident with an Arizona resident named Ann. Suppose Tom learns that Ann works for United Airlines as Senior Vice President for Operations, and learns that United employees have pension plans managed by Whitney Mutual, a company incorporated in Delaware doing business nationwide, with offices in major cities, including Cleveland, Chicago, Dallas, Louisville, Los Angeles, and Seattle. Suppose the value of Ann's retirement account is $600,000. Tom sues Ann in Kentucky for $500,000, serving a writ of garnishment on Whitney in Louisville. Is there jurisdiction under *Harris*? Does it matter that Ann cannot withdraw money from her account at the time she is sued? What if the terms of her arrangement allow her to use the account as collateral to secure a bank loan?

5. As you might suspect, Epstein's claim against Balk arose from a business deal. Epstein was a Baltimore importer, Balk a dry goods retailer who bought imported goods from Epstein on credit. Harris was in the dry goods business in North Carolina, and often borrowed money from Balk. We do not know whether Harris too bought goods from Epstein, or whether Harris told Epstein about owing money to Balk, but Epstein knew Balk was lending money to Harris. See generally Andreas Lowenfeld, *In Search of the Intangible: A Comment on* Shaffer v. Heitner, 53 N.Y.U. L. Rev. 102 (1978). Balk chose not to go to Maryland to contest Epstein's claim (he had a year and a day), and yet Balk pursued Harris with vigor. Perhaps Balk knew Epstein's claim was just, and the pursuit of Harris was "personal" (as they say). In any event, the situation is common: The seller of goods (Epstein) wants to recover the purchase price from the buyer (Balk), and it is inconvenient to travel to the buyer's state to sue. Should the rules let a person like Epstein sue at home? The doctrine embraced in *Harris* makes this result possible, doesn't it? But this doctrine does not directly address the problem, since the outcome depends on the "fortuity" that a person owing money to the real defendant enters the claimant's state. And the proposition that seizing property confers jurisdiction could lead to suits like the one described in the prior note.

■ **PROBLEM 3-A. Flight 1403: Served over Arkansas**

Peter and Christine Gordon travel from their home in Little Rock, Arkansas northeastward into Tennessee to visit their daughter in Memphis. While in Tennessee, they collide with a car driven by James Martin, who lives in Tennessee. The Gordons' car is totaled, but fortunately nobody sustains serious injuries.

After their return to Little Rock, the Gordons consult a lawyer, who recommends a suit and files in Arkansas. The lawyer learns that Martin regularly flies back and forth between Memphis and Dallas, Texas, and he discovers from a friend in the travel business that Martin has a ticket on American Airlines Flight 1677, seat 6B, leaving Memphis at 4:55 P.M. and arriving at Dallas/Fort Worth at 6:35 P.M. The lawyer retains a private process server, who buys a ticket on the same flight, seat 4E. At 5:20 P.M., the process server leaves his seat, steps back two rows, introduces himself, ascertains that it is James Martin in seat 6B, and serves him with the summons and complaint. The plane is in the airspace above the state of Arkansas.

In the Gordons' Arkansas suit, James Martin moves to dismiss for lack of jurisdiction, pointing out that "at no time relevant to this suit" has Martin been in Arkansas, and that "the accident that is the subject matter of this suit took place in Memphis, within five miles of my home there, and the suit has nothing to do with Arkansas, apart from the fact that plaintiffs live here." Should the Arkansas court dismiss for lack of jurisdiction over defendant James Martin?

■ **NOTES ON JURISDICTION BASED ON PRESENCE OF DEFENDANT**

1. In the world envisioned in *Pennoyer*, it makes sense, doesn't it, to treat Martin as being present in Arkansas while he is in the airspace over Arkansas? And *Pennoyer* holds, doesn't it, that being "caught" in the jurisdiction is a sufficient basis for the exercise of jurisdiction by courts of the state?

2. In a case somewhat similar to Problem 3-A, one court sustained jurisdiction. See Grace v. MacArthur, 170 F. Supp. 442 (D.C. Ark. 1959) (federal government exercises national sovereignty over national airspace, but plane and passengers in flight from Memphis to Dallas "were within the 'territorial limits' of the State of Arkansas" under FRCP 4(f), even though "a time may come . . . when commercial aircraft will fly at altitudes so high that it would be unrealistic to consider them as being within the territorial limits" of any state). In the 1950s, most passenger flights involved propeller planes that flew at about 20,000 feet. Modern jets fly at elevations of 30,000-40,000 feet. Should that matter? In fact, there are very few reported cases like *Grace*. Why do you suppose that is?

2. The Idea Modified: Cars and Companies Stretch Theory

HESS v. PAWLOSKI

United States Supreme Court
274 U.S. 352 (1927)

Mr. Justice BUTLER delivered the opinion of the Court.

[After being struck by a car at an intersection in Worcester, Massachusetts on a pleasant September day while walking to a store, plaintiff Leo Pawloski sued the driver, H.R. Hess of Pennsylvania, in Massachusetts. In accordance with the state's Nonresident Motorist statute, Pawloski served Hess by providing copies of the summons and complaint to the registrar of motor vehicles in Massachusetts, who forwarded these by registered mail to defendant in Pennsylvania.

The statute provides that acceptance by a nonresident of the "rights and privileges" of operating a car "on a public way" in Massachusetts "shall be deemed equivalent to an appointment" of the registrar as "true and lawful attorney" upon whom service of process may be made in a suit "growing out of any accident or collision." Defendant Hess "appeared specially" and moved to dismiss.]

The question is whether the Massachusetts enactment contravenes the due process clause of the Fourteenth Amendment.

The process of a court of one state cannot run into another and summon a party there domiciled to respond to proceedings against him. Notice sent outside the state to a nonresident is unavailing to give jurisdiction in an action against him personally for money recovery. Pennoyer v. Neff, 95 U.S. 714 (1877). There must be actual service within the state of notice upon him or upon some one authorized to accept service for him. A personal judgment rendered against a nonresident, who has neither been served with process nor appeared in the suit, is without validity. McDonald v. Mabee, 243 U.S. 90 (1917). The mere transaction of business in a state by nonresident natural persons does not imply consent to be bound by the process of its courts. Flexner v. Farson, 248 U.S. 289 (1919). The power of a state to exclude foreign corporations, although not absolute, but qualified, is the ground on which such an implication is supported as to them. Pennsylvania Fire Insurance Co. v. Gold Issue Mining Co., 243 U.S. 93 (1917). But a state may not withhold from nonresident individuals the right of doing business therein. The privileges and immunities clause of the Constitution (section 2, art. 4), safeguards to the citizens of one state the right "to pass through, or to reside in any other state for purposes of trade, agriculture, professional pursuits, or otherwise." [Corfield v. Coryell, 6 Fed. Case 546 (C.C. Pa. 1823.)] And it prohibits state legislation discriminating against citizens of other states.

Motor vehicles are dangerous machines, and, even when skillfully and carefully operated, their use is attended by serious dangers to persons and property. In the public interest the state may make and enforce regulations reasonable calculated to promote care on the part of all, residents and non-residents alike, who use its highways. The measure in question operates to require a nonresident to answer for his conduct in the state where arise causes of action alleged against him, as well as to provide for a claimant a convenient method by which he may sue to enforce his rights. Under the statute the implied consent is limited to proceedings growing out of accidents or collisions on a highway in which the nonresident may be involved. It is required that he shall actually receive and receipt for notice of the service and a copy of the process. And it contemplates such continuances as may be found necessary to give reasonable time and opportunity for defense. It makes no hostile discrimination against nonresidents, but tends to put them on the same footing as residents. Literal and precise equality in respect of this matter is not attainable; it is not required. The state's power to regulate the use of its highways extends to their use by nonresidents as well as by residents. And, in advance of the operation of a motor vehicle on its highway by a nonresident, the state may require him to appoint one of its officials as his agent on whom process may be served in proceedings growing out of such use. Kane v. New Jersey, 242 U.S. 160, 167 (1916). That case recognized power of the state to exclude a nonresident until the formal appointment is made. And, having the power so to exclude, the state may declare that the use of the highway by the nonresident is the equivalent of the appointment of the registrar as agent on whom process may be served. The difference between the formal and implied appointment is not substantial, so far as concerns the application of the due process clause of the Fourteenth Amendment.

Judgment affirmed.

■ NOTES ON SOCIAL DANGERS AND SPECIAL STANDARDS

1. *Hess* suggests that "implied consent" is the basis of jurisdiction over nonresident motorists in Massachusetts. *Pennoyer* itself recognized that jurisdiction could rest on consent: Does *Hess* represent any real change?

(a) Do you think a motorist from New York could write to the Massachusetts registrar stating that he planned to drive into the state but was *not* consenting to jurisdiction? When cars were a new phenomenon, some states expected motorists *actually* to consent to jurisdiction on entering the state. See Kane v. New Jersey, 242 U.S. 160, 164-165 & n.1 (1916) (New Jersey statute requires motorists to pay a fee and file a "duly executed instrument" appointing secretary of state as agent for service of process) (statute upheld).

(b) *Hess* stops short of saying Massachusetts could exclude out-of-state motorists who refuse to consent, but the Court says a state "having the power . . . to exclude," may treat use of its highways as "equivalent" to appointing a local agent. Isn't this equation a patent fiction? What is the purpose? (In the vocabulary of the profession, we might say entering the state is "constructive consent" to appointment of a local agent.)

(c) In *Pennoyer,* the Court commented that a state could require any "nonresident entering into a partnership or association" in the state to appoint a local agent for service of process. Consider Lafayette Insurance Co. v. French, 59 U.S. 404 (1855), holding that a state can exclude a foreign corporation from conducting business unless it appoints a local agent. Does it follow that a state can exclude a nonresident motorist who refuses to consent to jurisdiction?

2. Consider Doherty & Co. v. Goodman, 294 U.S. 623 (1935), approving the exercise in Iowa of *in personam* jurisdiction over an out-of-state company selling securities. As partial justification, the Court commented that the law of Iowa treats this business as "exceptional and subjects it to special regulation." Can it be said that operating cars and selling securities have in common that they bring danger to the public? It is understandable, isn't it, that these subjects should draw special interest in the 1920s and 1930s (era of the Model T and the Great Depression)? In the twenty-first century, would we expand this list to cover, for example, consumer products and environmental pollution? What else? Should it include *everything* that could harm the public, such as adulterated foods and medicines? How about internet services?

3. Suppose we *accept* the notion that many activities bring risks to the public, so states have regulating interests. Does it follow that special jurisdictional rules should apply? In a case like *Hess,* for example, probably the tort law of Massachusetts would apply because the accident occurred there, the injured party lived there, and damage was incurred there. If Massachusetts *substantive* rules apply, does it follow that Massachusetts courts should have jurisdiction? Would the same be true in a case like *Doherty*? If so, then consent doesn't matter, does it?

4. The Massachusetts statute construed in *Hess* required the registrar to send copies of the summons and complaint by registered mail to the defendant, which means that most motorists would get actual notice. Do you think this point is critical? Apparently, the Court thought so: A year later it held that a similar statute lacking a notice provision violated due process. See *Wuchter v. Pizzutti*, 276 U.S. 13, 19 (1928) (reversing *even though* defendant got actual notice here).

5. In *Hess,* the Pennsylvania defendant "appeared specially" to contest jurisdiction. In other words, Massachusetts allowed a defendant to contest jurisdiction without at the same time *submitting to* jurisdiction. Without a "special appearance," it would be possible for a plaintiff to serve the summons and complaint on the defendant (or her lawyer) when she appears to argue the motion to dismiss. Of course, the lawyer might arrange for her client to stay home, and might even enter into a formal agreement limiting the lawyer's authority and stipulating that she is *not* authorized to take service of summons and complaint, but probably such attempts would be ineffective (they would certainly not bind the plaintiff), and the only way to *ensure* that one can contest jurisdiction without at the same time *submitting to* jurisdiction is to have some formal procedural rule that protects this option. Traditionally, a special appearance required the defendant to address *only* the jurisdictional point, and to stay clear of merits issues, and of course the jurisdictional point had to be broached at the outset, as part of the defendant's initial appearance. In modern practice, the rules are somewhat looser. While the point must be raised at the outset, it is possible to combine a jurisdictional objection with other motions. See Chapter 3E, *infra*, and FRCP 12(b).

B   MODERN THEORY ARRIVES: FAIRNESS AND CONTACTS

1. The Constitutional Shift

One can view *Hess* as signaling what modernists would call a "paradigm shift" away from the philosophy of *Pennoyer,* where power and presence were the bases of state court jurisdiction. But in *Hess* we have only a signal of such a shift, and it was not until *International Shoe* that a change in approach formally hit the scene in 1945.

Unlike *Pennoyer, Harris,* and *Hess, International Shoe* raised the jurisdictional question in the setting of a corporate defendant. This matter was traditionally addressed in terms of "consent" and "presence." Applying the idea of "presence" to the legal construct that is a corporation requires resort to fictions, since a corporation has no physical existence. And "consent" did not involve a free decision by management, but was exacted by so-called domestication statutes as a condition of gaining corporate access to commercial markets in the state.

Both "presence" and "consent" turned on whether a corporation was "doing business" in the state. "Presence" depended on evaluating activities in the state, and presence meant there was jurisdiction. "Consent" meant a corporation agreed to jurisdiction, and consent was required if the corporation did business in the state. It was harder to say whether either presence or consent opened the corporation to jurisdiction in all suits, or only in those arising out of activities in the state.

INTERNATIONAL SHOE v. WASHINGTON
United States Supreme Court
326 U.S. 310 (1945)

Mr. Chief Justice STONE delivered the opinion of the Court.

The questions for decision are (1) whether, within the limitations of the due process clause of the Fourteenth Amendment, appellant, a Delaware corporation, has by its activities in the State of Washington rendered itself amenable to proceedings in the courts of that state to recover unpaid contributions to the state unemployment compensation fund exacted by state statutes, and (2) whether the state can exact those contributions consistently with the due process clause of the Fourteenth Amendment.

The statutes in question set up a comprehensive scheme of unemployment compensation, the costs of which are defrayed by contributions required to be made by employers to a state unemployment compensation fund. The contributions are a specified percentage of the wages payable annually by each employer for his employees' services in the state. The assessment and collection of the contributions and the fund are administered by respondents. [One section] of the Act authorizes respondent Commissioner to issue an order and notice of assessment of delinquent contributions upon prescribed personal service of the notice upon the employer if found within the state, or, if not so found, by mailing the notice to the employer by registered mail at his last known address. That section also authorizes the Commissioner to collect the assessment by distraint if it is not paid within ten days after service of the notice. By [other sections] the order of assessment may be administratively reviewed by an appeal tribunal within the office of unemployment upon petition of the employer, and this determination is made subject to judicial review on questions of law by the state Superior Court, with further right of appeal in the state Supreme Court as in other civil cases.

In this case notice of assessment for the years in question was personally served upon a sales solicitor employed by appellant in the State of Washington, and a copy of the notice was mailed by registered mail to appellant at its address in St. Louis, Missouri. Appellant appeared specially before the office of unemployment and moved to set aside the order and notice of assessment on the ground that the service upon appellant's salesman was not proper service upon appellant; that appellant was not a corporation of the State of Washington and was not doing business within the state; that it had no agent within the state upon whom service could be made; and that appellant is not an employer and does not furnish employment within the meaning of the statute.

The motion was heard on evidence and a stipulation of facts by the appeal tribunal which denied the motion and ruled that respondent Commissioner was entitled to recover the unpaid contributions. That action was affirmed by the Commissioner; both the Superior Court and the Supreme Court affirmed. Appellant in each of these courts assailed the statute as applied, as a violation of the due process clause of the Fourteenth Amendment, and as imposing a constitutionally prohibited burden on interstate commerce. The cause comes here on appeal, appellant assigning as error that the challenged statutes as applied infringe the due process clause of the Fourteenth Amendment and the commerce clause.

The facts, as found by the appeal tribunal and accepted by the state Superior Court and Supreme Court, are not in dispute. Appellant is a Delaware corporation, having its principal place of business in St. Louis, Missouri, and is engaged in the manufacture and sale of shoes and other footwear. It maintains places of business in several states, other than Washington, at which its manufacturing is carried on and from which its merchandise is distributed interstate through several sales units or branches located outside the State of Washington.

Appellant has no office in Washington and makes no contracts either for sale or purchase of merchandise there. It maintains no stock of merchandise in that state and makes there no deliveries of goods in intrastate commerce. During the years from 1937 to 1940, now in question, appellant employed eleven to thirteen salesmen under direct supervision and control of sales managers located in St. Louis. These salesmen resided in Washington; their principal activities were confined to that state; and they were compensated by commissions based upon the amount of their sales. The commissions for each year totaled more than $31,000. Appellant supplies its salesmen with a line of samples, each consisting of one shoe of a pair, which they display to prospective purchasers. On occasion they rent permanent sample rooms, for exhibiting samples, in business buildings, or rent rooms in hotels or business buildings temporarily for that purpose. The cost of such rentals is reimbursed by appellant.

The authority of the salesmen is limited to exhibiting their samples and soliciting orders from prospective buyers, at prices and on terms fixed by appellant. The salesmen transmit the orders to appellant's office in St.

Louis for acceptance or rejection, and when accepted the merchandise for filling the orders is shipped f.o.b. from points outside Washington to the purchasers within the state. All the merchandise shipped into Washington is invoiced at the place of shipment from which collections are made. No salesman has authority to enter into contracts or to make collections.

The Supreme Court of Washington was of opinion that the regular and systematic solicitation of orders in the state by appellant's salesmen, resulting in a continuous flow of appellant's product into the state, was sufficient to constitute doing business in the state so as to make appellant amenable to suit in its courts. But it was also of opinion that there were sufficient additional activities shown to bring the case within the rule frequently stated, that solicitation within a state by the agents of a foreign corporation plus some additional activities there are sufficient to render the corporation amenable to suit brought in the courts of the state to enforce an obligation arising out of its activities there. [The Court cites International Harvester Co. v. Kentucky, 234 U.S. 579 (1914), and other cases.] The court found such additional activities in the salesmen's display of samples sometimes in permanent display rooms, and the salesmen's residence within the state, continued over a period of years, all resulting in a substantial volume of merchandise regularly shipped by appellant to purchasers within the state. The court also held that the statute as applied did not invade the constitutional power of Congress to regulate interstate commerce and did not impose a prohibited burden on such commerce. . . .

Appellant also insists that its activities within the state were not sufficient to manifest its "presence" there and that in its absence the state courts were without jurisdiction, that consequently it was a denial of due process for the state to subject appellant to suit. It refers to those cases in which it was said that the mere solicitation of orders for the purchase of goods within a state, to be accepted without the state and filled by shipment of the purchased goods interstate, does not render the corporation seller amenable to suit within the state. And appellant further argues that since it was not present within the state, it is a denial of due process to subject it to taxation or other money exaction. It thus denies the power of the state to lay the tax or to subject appellant to a suit for its collection.

Historically the jurisdiction of courts to render judgment in personam is grounded on their de facto power over the defendant's person. Hence his presence within the territorial jurisdiction of court was prerequisite to its rendition of a judgment personally binding him. Pennoyer v. Neff, 95 U.S. (5 Otto.) 714 (1877). But now that the capias ad respondendum has given way to personal service of summons or other form of notice, due process requires only that in order to subject a defendant to a judgment in personam, if he be not present within the territory of the forum, he have certain minimum contacts with it such that the maintenance of the suit does not offend "traditional notions of fair play and substantial justice." Milliken v. Meyer, 311 U.S. 457, 463 (1940).

Since the corporate personality is a fiction, although a fiction intended to be acted upon as though it were a fact, it is clear that unlike an individual its "presence" without, as well as within, the state of its origin can be manifested only by activities carried on in its behalf by those who are authorized to act for it. To say that the corporation is so far "present" there as to satisfy due process requirements, for purposes of taxation or the maintenance of suits against it in the courts of the state, is to beg the question to be decided. For the terms "present" or "presence" are used merely to symbolize those activities of the corporation's agent within the state which courts will deem to be sufficient to satisfy the demands of due process. Those demands may be met by such contacts of the corporation with the state of the forum as make it reasonable, in the context of our federal system of government, to require the corporation to defend the particular suit which is brought there. An "estimate of the inconveniences" which would result to the corporation from a trial away from its "home" or principal place of business is relevant in this connection.

"Presence" in the state in this sense has never been doubted when the activities of the corporation there have not only been continuous and systematic, but also give rise to the liabilities sued on, even though no consent to be sued or authorization to an agent to accept service of process has been given. Conversely it has been generally recognized that the casual presence of the corporate agent or even his conduct of single or isolated items of activities in a state in the corporation's behalf are not enough to subject it to suit on causes of action unconnected with the activities there. To require the corporation in such circumstances to defend the suit away from its home or other jurisdiction where it carries on more substantial activities has been thought to lay too great and unreasonable a burden on the corporation to comport with due process.

While it has been held in cases on which appellant relies that continuous activity of some sorts within a state is not enough to support the demand that the corporation be amenable to suits unrelated to that activity, there have been instances in which the continuous corporate operations within a state were thought so substantial and of such a nature as to justify suit against it on causes of action arising from dealings entirely distinct from those activities.

Finally, although the commission of some single or occasional acts of the corporate agent in a state sufficient to impose an obligation or liability on the corporation has not been thought to confer upon the state authority to enforce it, Rosenberg Bros. & Co. v. Curtis Brown Co., 260 U.S. 516 [1923], other such acts, because of their nature and quality and the circumstances of their commission, may be deemed sufficient to render the corporation liable to suit. True, some of the decisions holding the corporation amenable to suit have been supported by resort to the legal fiction that it has given its consent to service and suit, consent being implied from its presence in the state through the acts of its authorized agents. But more realistically it may be said that those authorized acts were of such a nature as to justify the fiction.

It is evident that the criteria by which we mark the boundary line between those activities which justify the subjection of a corporation to suit, and those which do not, cannot be simply mechanical or quantitative. The test is not merely, as has sometimes been suggested, whether the activity, which the corporation has seen fit to procure through its agents in another state, is a little more or a little less. Whether due process is satisfied must depend rather upon the quality and nature of the activity in relation to the fair and orderly administration of the laws which it was the purpose of the due process clause to insure. That clause does not contemplate that a state may make binding a judgment in personam against an individual or corporate defendant with which the state has no contacts, ties, or relations.

But to the extent that a corporation exercises the privilege of conducting activities within a state, it enjoys the benefits and protection of the laws of that state. The exercise of that privilege may give rise to obligations; and, so far as those obligations arise out of or are connected with the activities within the state, a procedure which requires the corporation to respond to a suit brought to enforce them can, in most instances, hardly be said to be undue.

Applying these standards, the activities carried on in behalf of appellant in the State of Washington were neither irregular nor casual. They were systematic and continuous throughout the years in question. They resulted in a large volume of interstate business, in the course of which appellant received the benefits and protection of the laws of the state, including the right to resort to the courts for the enforcement of its rights. The obligation which is here sued upon arose out of those very activities. It is evident that these operations establish sufficient contacts or ties with the state of the forum to make it reasonable and just according to our traditional conception of fair play and substantial justice to permit the state to enforce the obligations which appellant has incurred there. Hence we cannot say that the maintenance of the present suit in the State of Washington involves an unreasonable or undue procedure. . . .

Affirmed.

Mr. Justice Black delivered the following opinion. . . .

I believe that the Federal Constitution leaves to each State, without any "ifs" or "buts," a power to tax and to open the doors of its courts for its citizens to sue corporations whose agents do business in those States. Believing that the Constitution gave the States that power, I think it a judicial deprivation to condition its exercise upon this Court's notion of "fair play," however appealing that term may be. Nor can I stretch the meaning of due process so far as to authorize this Court to deprive a State of the right to afford judicial protection to its citizens on the ground that it would be more "convenient" for the corporation to be sued somewhere else.

There is a strong emotional appeal in the words "fair play," "justice," and "reasonableness." But they were not chosen by those who wrote the original Constitution or the Fourteenth Amendment as a measuring rod for this Court to use in invalidating State or Federal laws passed by elected legislative representatives. No one, not even those who most feared a democratic government, ever formally proposed that courts should be given power to invalidate legislation under any such elastic standards. Express prohibitions against certain types of legislation are found in the Constitution, and under the long settled practice, courts invalidate laws found to conflict with them. This requires interpretation, and interpretation, it is true, may result in extension of the Constitution's purpose. But that is no reason for reading the due process clause so as to restrict a State's power to tax and sue those whose activities affect persons and businesses within the State, provided proper service can be had. Superimposing the natural justice concept on the Constitution's specific prohibitions could operate as a drastic abridgment of democratic safeguards they embody, such as freedom of speech, press and religion, and the right to counsel. This has already happened. For application of this natural law concept, whether under the terms "reasonableness," "justice," or "fair play," makes judges the supreme arbiters of the country's laws and practices. This result, I believe, alters the form of government our Constitution provides. I cannot agree.

■ NOTES ON MINIMUM CONTACTS AND SPECIFIC JURISDICTION

1. What are the "contacts" supporting Washington's exercise of jurisdiction? Do the defendant's contacts relate to the claims made by the State? Do you think Washington would have jurisdiction in a suit brought by a *salesman* against the company to recover unpaid commissions for sales generated in the state?

2. Thirty years before *International Shoe,* the Court decided a similar case on the basis of corporate "presence." See International Harvester v. Kentucky, 234 U.S. 579 (1914), upholding jurisdiction in Kentucky to try private antitrust claims against a company that, like International Shoe, had in-state salesmen who took orders and forwarded them to the home office, but had no inventory, property, or offices in Kentucky, and operated under a system in which salesmen could collect money but not settle accounts. *International Shoe* might have been decided by simply relying on corporate presence in

Washington, but the Court didn't do that. Why, if at all, is the "new paradigm" superior to the old one?

3. *International Shoe* says a corporation that conducts activities in the forum state "enjoys the benefits and protection of the laws" of the state. How did International Shoe enjoy "benefits and protections" of the laws of Washington?

4. *International Shoe* recognizes four levels of corporate involvement or "contacts" with the forum state:

(a) At the lowest level, there are "single" or "occasional" acts that give rise to liability, but the contacts are not sufficient even to sustain jurisdiction in a suit to enforce resultant obligations. Necessarily, then, such acts would not support jurisdiction over suits unrelated to the acts.

(b) At a higher level, there are single acts whose "nature and quality" in the "circumstances of their commission" may or may not be sufficient for jurisdiction in suits arising from such acts, but they would not support jurisdiction over suits unrelated to the acts.

(c) At a still higher level are "continuous corporate operations" that are "substantial," which support jurisdiction in suits arising out of those operations. Again such jurisdiction is called "specific jurisdiction." Even these acts are "not enough," however, to sustain jurisdiction over claims "unconnected with" the acts. In common parlance, this kind of jurisdiction is usually called "specific jurisdiction."

(d) At the highest level are activities that are "continuous" and "systematic," which support jurisdiction not only in suits arising out of the acts themselves, but in suits on claims "arising from dealings entirely distinct from those activities." Such jurisdiction has come to be called "general jurisdiction."

In which category does *International Shoe* itself belong?

5. Terms like "substantial" and "occasional" and "continuous" admit of degrees. If a Florida producer sends 5,000 bushels of oranges to Georgia, this activity might be viewed as "substantial" if its total output is 15,000 bushels, because this would mean that one-third of its business involves the Georgia market. What if its output is a million bushels (the Georgia portion being one-half of 1 percent)?

6. *International Shoe* involved an enforcement suit seeking payments to a state unemployment compensation fund. Suppose the Oregon "contacts" remain the same, but the suit is of a very different kind:

(a) Portland Shoes, a retail outlet, orders 500 pairs of shoes from International Shoe after negotiations with an in-state salesman culminating in an agreement approved in St. Louis, but the shoes never come. Portland Shoes sues in Oregon to recover damages for lost sales. Good jurisdiction? What if Portland Shoes paid in advance, and seeks reimbursement?

(b) Paul, an Oregon rock climber, purchased a pair of International rock-climbing boots, but he falls on a climb because the sole detaches at a difficult moment. He sues International in Oregon for personal injuries. Does

it matter that he bought the boots from Portland Shoes rather than directly from International Shoe?

(c) Suppose the shoe is on the other foot: International Shoe shipped 500 pairs of shoes to Portland Shoes, but never received payment. International Shoe can sue Portland Shoes in Oregon, but can International Shoe sue Portland Shoes in St. Louis?

7. A corporation is not the officers and employees who run or work for it, and reverse is also true—the officers and employees are not themselves the corporation. Thus jurisdiction may exist over one but not the other. See Rush v. Savchuk, 444 U.S. 320, 332 (1977) (requirements of minimum contacts "must be met as to each defendant over whom a state court exercises jurisdiction"); Joyner v. MERS, 2010 WL 3419468 (E.D. Mich. 2010) ("where jurisdiction is to be asserted over an individual officer of a corporation," it cannot be predicated on jurisdiction over corporation) (dismissing claim against chief financial officer); Sholz Research and Development, Inc. v. Kurzke, 720 F. Supp. 710, 714 (N.D. Ill. 2989) (transient service on officer does not create jurisdiction over corporation) (officers served in state are subject to jurisdiction, but not corporation).

8. Does *International Shoe* make decisions on jurisdiction easier or harder? If the latter, does increased functionality of the new principle justify its adoption? See generally Kevin C. McMunigal, *Desert, Utility, and Minimum Contacts: Toward a Mixed Theory of Personal Jurisdiction*, 108 Yale L.J. 189, 189 (1998) ("ambiguity and incoherence have plagued the minimum contacts test"); Christopher D. Cameron & Kevin R. Johnson, *Death of a Salesman? Forum Shopping and Outcome Determination Under* International Shoe, 28 U.C. Davis L. Rev. 769, 809-815 (1995) (discussing "mysterious origins" of minimum contacts standard).

■ NOTES ON "DOMESTICATION" STATUTES AND JURISDICTION OVER OUT-OF-STATE CORPORATIONS

1. *Pennoyer* says a state may require nonresidents "entering into a partnership or association" in the state or "making contracts enforceable there," to appoint local agents on whom process may be served. "Domestication statutes," in force in many states, require a corporation doing business in the state to file information with an official or agency (often the Secretary of State or Department of Corporations) and appoint a local agent. Often the statutes provide that a corporation doing business in violation of these requirements cannot sue in the courts of the state, and impose fines and other administrative penalties. See, e.g., Conn. Gen. Stat. Ann. §§33:920:929 (out-of-state corporation must obtain "certificate of authority" from Secretary of State before transacting business; corporation shall maintain "registered office" and "registered agent" who serves as agent for "service of process" and any "notice or demand required or permitted by law").

2. More than a century ago, the Supreme Court held that a state can require corporations doing business in the state to consent to jurisdiction in local courts for *all* lawsuits, not just those arising out of corporate contacts with the state. See Pennsylvania Fire Ins. Co. v. Gold Issue Mining & Milling Co., 243 U.S. 93, 95 (1917) (approving jurisdiction in Missouri, on basis of appointing state insurance superintendent as agent, in suit arising out of fire loss in Colorado).

(a) There are, however, limits to what a state can do with its domestication statute. A state cannot, for example, deny to a noncompliant corporation a defense that would otherwise be available, see Bendix Autolite Corp. v. Midwestco Enterprises, Inc., 486 U.S. 888 (1988).

(b) It also seems that a court in a state where a noncompliant corporation is sued (it's doing business but has *not* registered) *cannot* "infer" consent if the cause does not arise out of contacts with the state. In other words, *express* consent that a state can exact under *Gold Issue* may be *broader* than "implied" consent inferred from acts by a noncompliant corporation. See *Gold Issue*, 243 U.S. at 93, 95 (where corporation does business without authority, "service on the agent whom they should have appointed" did not reach suits on claims "arising in other states").

(c) States disagree on the scope of consent indicated by compliance with domestication statutes. Compare Merriman v. Crompton Corp., 146 P.3d 162, 170 (Kan. 2006) (statute requires irrevocable consent; many courts construe consent as providing basis "for exercising general jurisdiction") with Freeman v. Second Judicial District Court, 1 P.3d 963 (Nev. 2000) (appointing insurance commissioner as local agent was *not* consent to jurisdiction in Nevada over claim arising in California). One scholar doubts the vitality of the holding in *Gold Issue* that states may use domestication statutes to exact broad consent. See, e.g., Pierre Riou, *General Jurisdiction over Foreign Corporations: All That Glitters Is Not* Gold Issue Mining, 14 Rev. Litig. 741 (1995) (general jurisdiction based on appointment of agent "has no basis in, and is in fact contrary to, Supreme Court precedent," and such jurisdiction "violates limitations on territorial sovereignty").

3. In another early decision, the Court concluded that states may *not* use domestication statutes to exact consent to local jurisdiction over individuals and partnerships. The holding rests on the Commerce Clause (Art. I §8), which says Congress can regulate this area. The Commerce Clause, even without legislation, has been read to mean that states cannot exclude corporations or people engaging in interstate commerce, which includes shipping goods into or out of a state (we speak of the "dormant Commerce Clause"). See Flexner v. Farson, 248 U.S. 289 (1919) (state lacked jurisdiction over out-of-state partners, since "consent that is said to be implied in such cases is a mere fiction, founded upon the accepted doctrine that the States could exclude foreign corporations altogether," but state "had no power to exclude the defendants"). But *Flexner* may not completely block efforts to exact consent for jurisdiction over individuals doing business in the state. See Henry L. Doherty & Co. v. Goodman, 294 U.S. 623 (1935) (upholding Iowa statute providing for service on "any agent or clerk" employed by nonresident individual doing business there, and noting that state treats "dealing in corporate securities" as "exceptional" and requiring "special regulation") (citing *Hess*).

4. To sum it up, domestication statutes affect jurisdiction, but primarily they address service of process. They provide lawyers who want to sue a corporation the information they need. Service of process is taken up in Section C1, infra (see especially Notes on Serving Companies). If a lawyer wants to file suit in Nevada against Acme Corporation, chartered in Delaware with its principal place of business in California, and if the claim arises out of an accident between a Nevada plaintiff and an Acme truck in Arizona, the lawyer can figure out who is the agent in Nevada for service of process, but having a local agent does not necessarily mean Nevada has jurisdiction to hear the claim against Acme. If the lawyer files in Arizona, where jurisdiction is likely, he can serve Acme's Arizona agent.

5. You will not be surprised to learn that corporations hire private companies to act as registered agents for service of process. One large provider is CT Corporation, but there are many others, and they can be located by internet search. (Often these companies provide additional services relating to annual reports, filings, corporate documents, and similar matters.) State governments have offices that provide information (usually on websites), lifted from corporate filings required by domestication statutes, on the identity of the agent for service of process.

McGEE v. INTERNATIONAL LIFE INSURANCE CO.

United States Supreme Court
355 U.S. 220 (1957)

Opinion of the Court by Justice BLACK, announced by Justice DOUGLAS.

[Lulu McGee obtained judgment in California state court against International Life Insurance Company ("International") on a policy insuring against accidental death. Jurisdiction rested on a statute extending jurisdiction to suits on insurance contracts with California residents, regardless where the insurance company is located. Unable to collect in California, McGee sued on the judgment in Texas, which refused to recognize the judgment on the ground that it violated due process.

The policy was issued to Lowell Franklin, who purchased it in California from Empire Mutual Insurance Corporation, an Arizona company. In 1948 (four years later), International assumed the obligations of Empire, and mailed a "reinsurance certificate" to Franklin in California offering to continue to cover him. Franklin accepted the offer, and mailed to International in Texas his premiums from then until his death in 1950. Franklin's mother Lulu McGee was the beneficiary. She sent in proof of death, but International refused to pay on the ground that Franklin had committed suicide.]

Since *Pennoyer*, this Court has held that the Due Process Clause of the Fourteenth Amendment places some limit on the power of state courts to enter binding judgments against persons not served with process within their boundaries. But just where this line of limitation falls has been the subject of prolific controversy, particularly with respect to foreign corporations. In a continuing process of evolution this Court accepted and then abandoned "consent," "doing business," and "presence" as the standard for measuring the extent of state judicial power over such corporations. More recently in *International Shoe* the Court decided that "due process requires only that in order to subject a defendant to a judgment in personam," if he be not present within the territory of the forum, he have certain minimum contacts with it such that the maintenance of the suit does not offend "traditional notions of fair play and substantial justice."

Looking back over this long history of litigation a trend is clearly discernible toward expanding the permissible scope of state jurisdiction over foreign corporations and other nonresidents. In part this is attributable to the fundamental transformation of our national economy over the years. Today many commercial transactions touch two or more States and may involve parties separated by the full continent. With this increasing nationalization of commerce has come a great increase in the amount of business conducted by mail across state lines. At the same time modern transportation and communication have made it much less burdensome for a party sued to defend himself in a State where he engages in economic activity.

Turning to this case we think it apparent that the Due Process Clause did not preclude the California court from entering a judgment binding on respondent. It is sufficient for purposes of due process that the suit was based on a contract which had substantial connection with that State. The contract was delivered in California, the premiums were mailed from there and the insured was a resident of that State when he died. It cannot be denied that California has a manifest interest in providing effective means of redress for its residents when their insurers refuse to pay claims. These residents would be at a severe disadvantage if they were forced to follow the insurance company to a distant State in order to hold it legally accountable. When claims were small or moderate individual claimants frequently could not afford the cost of bringing an action in a foreign forum—thus in effect making the company judgment proof. Often the crucial witnesses as here on the company's defense of suicide—will be found in the insured's locality. Of course there may be inconvenience to the insurer if it is held amenable to suit in California where it had this contract but certainly nothing which amounts to a denial of due process. There is no contention that respondent did not have adequate notice of the suit or sufficient time to prepare its defenses and appear.

. . .

Dora Browning Donner

Dora Browning Donner (left, in picture) came from a prominent Philadelphia family. She married William H. Donner, (right, in picture; the identity of the woman between Mr. and Mrs. Donner is unknown) from Columbus, Indiana. Ultimately, he became a wealthy steel magnate, founder of Union Steel Company (later American Steel and Wire), located in a new community called Donora, Pennsylvania (name drawn from Donner's own), southeast of Pittsburgh. An air inversion (the Donora Smog of 1948) was a lesson in the perils of pollution (reportedly killing 20 people and sickening thousands of others). The Donners had five children, including Elizabeth, Dorothy and Katherine (the latter two were adopted). After the death from cancer of their son John, William H. Donner set up a cancer research foundation that later became the William H. Donner Foundation, which supports conservation and research into public policy, has endowed major chairs in science at MIT, Harvard, Yale, Princeton, and University of Pennsylvania, as well as many causes that are viewed as conservative in nature. Dora Browning Donner died in 1952, her husband dying the next year. The opinion—of which you are reading only a heavily edited excerpt showing only the tip of the iceberg of complicated financial arrangements—is the vehicle in which the Court came up with what is still known as the critical idea of "purposeful availment" that limits the reach of the *International Shoe* "minimum contacts" standard.

HANSON v. DENCKLA

United States Supreme Court
357 U.S. 235 (1958)

Mr. Chief Justice WARREN delivered the opinion of the Court.

[Dora Browning Donner died in Florida in 1952, leaving an estate that she wanted to pass along to her children Katherine Denckla and Dorothy Stewart, and to the two children of her third daughter Elizabeth Hanson, who were named Donner Hanson (DH) and Joseph Donner Windsor (JDW).

Donner lived much of her life in Pennsylvania. She set up an *inter vivos* trust in nearby Delaware, naming Wilmington Trust Company as trustee. When she died in Florida, the trust was worth over a million dollars. Before she died, Donner executed in Florida a will providing that Denckla and Stewart would get $500,000 apiece from the Delaware Trust. In the residual clause, the will provided that anything not otherwise disposed of would also go to them. Donner also executed an "appointment" transferring $400,000 from the Delaware trust to two *other* Delaware trusts for grandchildren DH and JDW. (If things went as Donner intended, Denckla and Stewart would get half a million each, and grandsons DH and JDW, children of Elizabeth Hanson, would get $200,000 each.)

The Donner will was admitted to probate in Florida, and Elizabeth Hanson was appointed executrix. Denckla and Stewart argued that the appointment to the grandchildren was invalid under Florida law because it was testamentary, and had to be witnessed like a will. (If the appointment failed, the $400,000 intended for the grandchildren would go to Denckla and Stewart under the residuary clause.)

The Florida court sustained the position of Denckla and Stewart, who then sued in Delaware to stop the Wilmington Trust Company from conveying the $400,000 to the trust set up for the grandchildren. The Delaware court refused to honor the Florida judgment. The losers in Florida (grandchildren DH and JDW, represented by their mother Elizabeth Hanson) and the losers in Delaware (Denckla and Stewart) all sought review in the Supreme Court. The former argued that Florida lacked jurisdiction over the assets in the Wilmington Trust. The latter argued that Delaware had to recognize the Florida judgment.

The Court concludes that Florida lacked jurisdiction, so Delaware need not recognize the Florida judgment. The opinion addresses the question whether Florida had *in personam* jurisdiction over the Wilmington Trust Company.]

In personam jurisdiction. [Stewart's and Danka's] stronger argument is for in personam jurisdiction over [Wilmington Trust Company]. They urge that the circumstances of this case amount to sufficient affiliation with the State of Florida to empower its courts to exercise personal jurisdiction over this nonresident defendant. Principal reliance is placed upon *McGee*. In *McGee* the Court noted the trend of expanding personal jurisdiction over nonresidents. As technological progress has increased the flow of commerce between States, the need for jurisdiction over nonresidents has undergone a similar increase. At the same time, progress in communications and transportation has made the defense of a suit in a foreign tribunal less burdensome. In response to these changes, the requirements for personal jurisdiction over nonresidents have evolved from the rigid rule of *Pennoyer* to the flexible standard of *International Shoe*. But it is a mistake to assume that this trend heralds the eventual demise of all restrictions on the personal jurisdiction of state courts. Those restrictions are more than a guarantee of immunity from inconvenient or distant litigation. They are a consequence of territorial limitations on the power of the respective States. However minimal the burden of defending in a foreign tribunal, a defendant may not be called upon to do so unless he has had the "minimal contacts" with that State that are a prerequisite to its exercise of power over him.

We fail to find such contacts in the circumstances of this case. The defendant trust company has no office in Florida, and transacts no business there. None of the trust assets has ever been held or administered in Florida, and the record discloses no solicitation of business in that State either in person or by mail.

The cause of action in this case is not one that arises out of an act done or transaction consummated in the forum State. In that respect, it differs from *McGee* and the cases there cited. In *McGee*, the nonresident defendant solicited a reinsurance agreement with a resident of California. The offer was accepted in that state, and the insurance premiums were mailed from there until the insured's death. Noting the interest California has in providing effective redress for its residents when nonresident insurers refuse to pay claims on insurance they have solicited in that state, the Court upheld jurisdiction because the suit "was based on a contract which had substantial connection with that state." In contrast, this action involves the validity of an agreement that was entered without any connection with the forum state. The agreement was executed in Delaware by a trust company incorporated in that state and a settlor domiciled in Pennsylvania. The first relationship Florida had to the agreement was years later when the settlor became domiciled there, and the trustee remitted the trust income to her in that state. From Florida Mrs. Donner carried on several bits of trust administration that may be compared to the mailing of premiums in *McGee*.[24] But the record discloses no instance in which the trustee performed any acts in Florida that

---

[24] [The Court describes two letters from Mrs. Donner to the company, one changing the compensation of the trust advisor, the other revoking the trust as to $75,000 and returning that amount to the trustee.—ED.] To these acts may be added the execution of the two powers of appointment mentioned earlier.

bear the same relationship to the agreement as the solicitation in *McGee.* Consequently, this suit cannot be said to be one to enforce an obligation that arose from a privilege the defendant exercised in Florida. This case is also different from *McGee* in that there the State had enacted special legislation to exercise what *McGee* called its "manifest interest" in providing effective redress for citizens who had been injured by nonresidents engaged in an activity that the State treats as exceptional and subjects to special regulation.

The execution in Florida of the powers of appointment . . . does not give Florida a substantial connection with the contract on which this suit is based. It is the validity of the trust agreement, not the appointment, that is at issue here. For the purpose of applying its rule that the validity of a trust is determined by the law of the State of its creation, Florida ruled that the appointment amounted to a "republication" of the original trust instrument in Florida. For choice-of-law purposes such a ruling may be justified, but we think it an insubstantial connection with the trust agreement for purposes of determining the question of personal jurisdiction over a nonresident defendant. The unilateral activity of those who claim some relationship with a nonresident defendant cannot satisfy the requirement of contact with the forum State. The application of that rule will vary with the quality and nature of the defendant's activity, but it is essential in each case that there be some act by which the defendant purposefully avails itself of the privilege of conducting activities within the forum State, thus invoking the benefits and protections of its laws. *International Shoe.* The settlor's execution in Florida of her power of appointment cannot remedy the absence of such an act in this case.

It is urged that because the settlor and most of the appointees and beneficiaries were domiciled in Florida the courts of that State should be able to exercise personal jurisdiction over the nonresident trustees. This is a non sequitur. With personal jurisdiction over the executor, legatees, and appointees, there is nothing in federal law to prevent Florida from adjudicating concerning the respective rights and liabilities of those parties. But Florida has not chosen to do so. As we understand its law, the trustee is an indispensable party over whom the court must acquire jurisdiction before it is empowered to enter judgment in a proceeding affecting the validity of a trust. It does not acquire that jurisdiction by being the "center of gravity" of the controversy, or the most convenient location for litigation. The issue is personal jurisdiction, not choice of law. It is resolved in this case by considering the acts of the trustee. As we have indicated, they are insufficient to sustain the jurisdiction.

[The Court reverses the Florida judgment and affirms the Delaware judgment. Dissenting opinions by Justice Black, joined by Justices Burton and Brennan, are omitted, as is a separate dissenting opinion by Justice Douglas.]

■ NOTES ON MINIMUM CONTACTS AND "PURPOSEFUL AVAILING"

1. In *McGee,* International Life in Texas mailed to Lowell Franklin in California an offer of reinsurance. Franklin accepted, paid premiums, then died. International Life resists the claim by the surviving mother Lulu McGee because it thinks Franklin committed suicide.[3] Did International Life enjoy the benefits and protections of the state of California? Even if we were hard-hearted enough to put aside the anguish suffered by a mother at the loss of her son, it makes sense, doesn't it, for the beneficiary to be able to sue at home for a loss sustained there? Did Franklin and McGee enjoy the benefits and protections of the laws of *Texas*? Suppose International Life learned that Franklin had taken up bungee jumping: Could International Life sue Franklin in Texas for a declaratory judgment that Franklin's new avocation violated the terms of the policy (so Empire can cancel)?

2. *McGee* speaks of the "interest" of California. How would you describe that interest? Does the "interest" factor come from *International Shoe*?

3. *Hanson* is a hard case: If it was about the validity of the Delaware trust, does it make sense for Florida to exercise jurisdiction over the Delaware trustee merely because the settlor and her surviving children lived in Florida? If it was about the exercise in Florida of a power of appointment affecting probate of a local decedent's will, does it make sense to say Florida lacks jurisdiction because of the Delaware residence of the custodian holding the assets covered by the appointment?

4. In a dissenting opinion omitted from the edited version, Justice Black in *Hanson* argues that the majority was applying principles drawn from *Pennoyer* barring jurisdiction over nonresidents unless served in the state: The world has changed, he argues, and he cites *McGee, Hess,* and *International Shoe* for the proposition that the "old jurisdictional landmarks have been left far behind" and that "further relaxation seems certain." What we should do, Black argues, is to recognize that Florida has "sufficient interest" to apply Florida law to resolve the dispute among the Florida survivors of the Florida decedent, and that "where a transaction has as much relationship to a State as Mrs. Donner's appointment had to Florida its courts ought to have power to adjudicate" unless doing so would impose an unfairly "heavy and disproportionate burden on a nonresident defendant." Black is really making two

---

[3] Typically, there is no payout on an accidental death policy if death was by suicide. If enough time has elapsed, typically a *life* insurance policy *does* pay (regulations often say the carrier must pay if the insured lives at least a year after acquiring the policy, even if death is by suicide). Carriers often write policies with a "double indemnity" feature: The beneficiary collects the face amount if the insured dies of natural causes, or twice the amount he suffers accidental death (of course, the additional coverage costs more). Suicide is not "accident" and does not trigger the double indemnity feature, and does not lead to recovery under a policy insuring only against "accidental" death.

points—Florida law should apply, and Florida courts should have jurisdiction. How does the *Hanson* majority reply to this "center of gravity" argument? It is true, isn't it, that jurisdiction in Florida fails in *Hanson* only because the *one* party with *no real interest* cannot be sued in Florida? That party is Wilmington Trust, which will pay out the $400,000, either to the trustee for the two grandchildren or to Denckla and Stewart.

5. There is no jurisdiction in Florida over Wilmington Trust because "there must be some act by which [it] purposely avails itself of the privilege of conducting activities within the forum State." *Hanson* repeatedly cites *McGee*, which was decided only a year earlier, so it seems fair to conclude that the "purposeful availment" standard is satisfied in *McGee*, which indicates that it can be satisfied by transactions touching the state by mail. Presumably, in the new millennium, the Court would reach the same conclusion where transactions involve the internet, including email and Instant Messaging and Twitter and other digital communication (or phone or fax). Why don't the "bits of trust administration" that Donner conducted from Florida *also* satisfy the "purposeful availment" standard?

2. The Coming of Long-Arm Statutes

In the era of *Pennoyer*, the reach of state court jurisdiction was limited by the geographical boundaries of a state. Merely *creating* courts with power to issue summonses was seen as authorizing their jurisdiction over defendants served within the state. No special statute defining jurisdictional reach was needed. *International Shoe* changed all that. Now state courts could exercise jurisdiction over defendants on the basis of "minimum contacts," and statutes authorizing jurisdiction over nonresidents sprouted everywhere. (In a sense, the automobile had already changed the jurisdictional landscape, as nonresident motorist statutes are an early form of long-arm statute, although they rested on consent.)

GRAY v. STANDARD AMERICAN RADIA-TOR & STANDARD SANITARY CORP.

Supreme Court of Illinois
176 N.E.2d 761 (1961)

KLINGBIEL, Justice.

Phyllis Gray appeals from a judgment of the circuit court of Cook County dismissing her action for damages. The issues are concerned with the construction and validity of our statute providing for substituted service of process on nonresidents. Since a constitutional question is involved, the appeal is direct to this court.

The suit was brought against the Titan Valve Manufacturing Company and others, on the ground that a certain water heater had exploded and injured the plaintiff. The complaint charges, inter alia, that the Titan company, a foreign corporation, had negligently constructed the safety valve; and that the injuries were suffered as a proximate result thereof. Summons issued and was duly served on Titan's registered agent in Cleveland, Ohio. The corporation appeared specially, filing a motion to quash on the ground that it had not committed a tortious act in Illinois. Its affidavit stated that it does no business here; that it has no agent physically present in Illinois; and that it sells the completed valves to defendant, American Radiator & Standard Sanitary Corporation, outside Illinois. The American Radiator & Standard Sanitary Corporation (also made a defendant) filed an answer in which it set up a cross claim against Titan, alleging that Titan made certain warranties to American Radiator, and that if the latter is held liable to the plaintiff it should be indemnified and held harmless by Titan. The court granted Titan's motion, dismissing both the complaint and the cross claim.

Section 16 of the Civil Practice Act provides that summons may be personally served upon any party outside the State; and that as to nonresidents who have submitted to the jurisdiction of our courts, such service has the force and effect of personal service within Illinois. Under section 17(1)(b) a nonresident who, either in person or through an agent, commits a tortious act within this State submits to jurisdiction. The questions in this case are (1) whether a tortious act was committed here, within the meaning of the statute, despite the fact that the Titan corporation had no agent in Illinois; and (2) whether the statute, if so construed, violates due process of law.

The first aspect to which we must direct our attention is one of statutory construction. Under section 17(1)(b) jurisdiction is predicated on the committing of a tortious act in this State. It is not disputed, for the purpose of this appeal, that a tortious act was committed. The issue depends on whether it was committed in Illinois, so as to warrant the assertion of personal jurisdiction by service of summons in Ohio.

The wrong in the case at bar did not originate in the conduct of a servant physically present here, but arose instead from acts performed at the place of manufacture. Only the consequences occurred in Illinois. It is well established, however, that in law the place of a wrong is where the last event takes place which is necessary to render the actor liable. Restatement, Conflict of Laws, §377. A second indication that the place of injury is the determining factor is found in rules governing the time within which an action must be brought. In applying statutes of limitation our court has computed the period from the time when the injury is done. We think it is clear that the alleged negligence in manufacturing the valve cannot be separated from the resulting injury; and that for present purposes, like those of liability and limitations, the tort was committed in Illinois.

Titan seeks to avoid this result by arguing that instead of using the word "tort," the legislature employed the term "tortious act"; and that the latter refers only to the act or conduct, separate and apart from any consequences thereof. We cannot accept the argument. To be tortious an act must cause injury. The concept of injury is an inseparable part of the phrase. In determining legislative intention courts will read words in their ordinary and popularly understood sense. We think the intent should be determined less from technicalities of definition than from considerations of general purpose and effect. To adopt the criteria urged by defendant would tend to promote litigation over extraneous issues concerning the elements of a tort and the territorial incidence of each, whereas the test should be concerned more with those substantial elements of convenience and justice presumably contemplated by the legislature. As we observed in Nelson v. Miller, 143 N.E.2d 673 (Ill. 1957), the statute contemplates the exertion of jurisdiction over nonresident defendants to the extent permitted by the due-process clause.

. . .

Under modern doctrine the power of a State court to enter a binding judgment against one not served with process within the State depends upon two questions: first, whether he has certain minimum contacts with the State, and second, whether there has been a reasonable method of notification. In the case at bar there is no contention that section 16 provides for inadequate notice or that its provisions were not followed. Defendant's argument on constitutionality is confined to the proposition that applying section 17(1)(b), where the injury is defendant's only contact with the State, would exceed the limits of due process.

. . .

In the case at bar the defendant's only contact with this State is found in the fact that a product manufactured in Ohio was incorporated in Pennsylvania, into a hot water heater which in the course of commerce was sold to an Illinois consumer. The record fails to disclose whether defendant has done any other business in Illinois, either directly or indirectly; and it is argued, in reliance on the *International Shoe* test, that since a course of business here has not been shown there are no "minimum contacts" sufficient to support jurisdiction. We do not think, however, that doing a given volume of business is the only way in which a nonresident can form the required connection with this State. Since the *International Shoe* case was decided the requirements for jurisdiction have been further relaxed, so that at the present time it is sufficient if the act or transaction itself has a substantial connection with the State of the forum.

In McGee v. International Life Insurance Co., 355 U.S. 220 (1957), suit was brought in California against a foreign insurance company on a policy issued to a resident of California. The defendant was not served with process in that State but was notified by registered mail at its place of business in Texas, pursuant to a statute permitting such service in suits on insurance contracts. The contract in question was delivered in California, the premiums were mailed from there and the insured was a resident of that State when he died, but defendant had no office or agent in California nor did it solicit any business there apart from the policy sued on. After referring briefly to the *International Shoe* case the court held that "it is sufficient for purposes of due process that the suit was based on *a contract* which had substantial connection" with California. (Emphasis supplied.)

In Smyth v. Twin State Improvement Corp., 80 A.2d 664, 666 (Vt. 1951), a Vermont resident engaged a foreign corporation to re-roof his house. While doing the work the corporation negligently damaged the building, and an action was brought for damages. Service of process was made on the Secretary of State and a copy was forwarded to defendant by registered mail at its principal place of business in Massachusetts. A Vermont statute provided for such substituted service on foreign corporations committing a tort in Vermont against a resident of Vermont. In holding that the statute affords due process of law, the court discussed the principal authorities on the question and concluded, inter alia, that "continuous activity within the state is not necessary as a prerequisite to jurisdiction."

In *Nelson*, the commission of a single tort within this State was held sufficient to sustain jurisdiction under the present statute. The defendant in that case, a resident of Wisconsin, was engaged in the business of selling appliances. It was alleged that in the process of delivering a stove in Illinois, an employee of the defendant negligently caused injury to the plaintiff. In holding that the defendant was not denied due process by being required to defend in Illinois, this court observed: "The defendant sent his employee into Illinois in the advancement of his own interests. While he was here, the employee and the defendant enjoyed the benefit and protection of the laws of Illinois, including the right to resort to our courts. In the course of his stay here the employee performed acts that gave rise to an injury. The law of Illinois will govern the substantive rights and duties stemming from the incident. Witnesses, other than the defendant's employee, are likely to be found here, and not in Wisconsin. In such circumstances, it is not unreasonable to require the defendant to make his defense here."

Whether the type of activity conducted within the State is adequate to satisfy the requirement depends upon the facts in the particular case. The question cannot be answered by applying a mechanical formula or rule of thumb but by ascertaining what is fair and reasonable in the circumstances. In the application of this flexible test the relevant inquiry is whether defendant engaged in some act or conduct by which he may be said to have invoked the benefits and protections of the law of the forum. The relevant decisions since Pennoyer v. Neff, 95 U.S. 714 (1877), show a development of the concept of personal jurisdiction from one which requires service of process within the

State to one which is satisfied either if the act or transaction sued on occurs there or if defendant has engaged in a sufficiently substantial course of activity in the State, provided always that reasonable notice and opportunity to be heard are afforded. As the Vermont court recognized the *Smyth* case, the trend in defining due process of law is away from the emphasis on territorial limitations and toward emphasis on providing adequate notice and opportunity to be heard: from the court with immediate power over the defendant, toward the court in which both parties can most conveniently settle their dispute.

. . .

It is true that courts cannot "assume that this trend heralds the eventual demise of all restrictions on the personal jurisdiction of state courts." Hanson v. Denckla, 357 U.S. 235 (1958). An orderly and fair administration of the law throughout the nation requires protection against being compelled to answer claims brought in distant States with which the defendant has little or no association and in which he would be faced with an undue burden or disadvantage in making his defense. It must be remembered that lawsuits can be brought on frivolous demands or groundless claims as well as on legitimate ones, and that procedural rules must be designed and appraised in the light of what is fair and just to both sides in the dispute. Interpretations of basic rights which consider only those of a claimant are not consonant with the fundamental requisites of due process.

In the case at bar defendant does not claim that the present use of its product in Illinois is an isolated instance. While the record does not disclose the volume of Titan's business or the territory in which appliances incorporating its valves are marketed, it is a reasonable inference that its commercial transactions, like those of other manufacturers, result in substantial use and consumption in this State. To the extent that its business may be directly affected by transactions occurring here it enjoys benefits from the laws of this State, and it has undoubtedly benefited, to a degree, from the protection which our law has given to the marketing of hot water heaters containing its valves. Where the alleged liability arises, as in this case, from the manufacture of products presumably sold in contemplation of use here, it should not matter that the purchase was made from an independent middleman or that someone other than the defendant shipped the product into this State.

With the increasing specialization of commercial activity and the growing interdependence of business enterprises it is seldom that a manufacturer deals directly with consumers in other States. The fact that the benefit he derives from its laws is an indirect one, however, does not make it any the less essential to the conduct of his business; and it is not unreasonable, where a cause of action arises from alleged defects in his product, to say that the use of such products in the ordinary course of commerce is sufficient contact with this State to justify a requirement that he defend here.

As a general proposition, if a corporation elects to sell its products for ultimate use in another State, it is not unjust to hold it answerable there for any damage caused by defects in those products. Advanced means of distribution and other commercial activity have made possible these modern methods of doing business, and have largely effaced the economic significance of State lines. By the same token, today's facilities for transportation and communication have removed much of the difficulty and inconvenience formerly encountered in defending lawsuits brought in other States.

Unless they are applied in recognition of the changes brought about by technological and economic progress, jurisdictional concepts which may have been reasonable enough in a simpler economy lose their relation to reality, and injustice rather than justice is promoted. Our unchanging principles of justice, whether procedural or substantive in nature, should be scrupulously observed by the courts. But the rules of law which grow and develop within those principles must do so in the light of the facts of economic life as it is lived today. Otherwise the need for adaptation may become so great that basic rights are sacrificed in the name of reform, and the principles themselves become impaired.

The principles of due process relevant to the issue in this case support jurisdiction in the court where both parties can most conveniently settle their dispute. The facts show that the plaintiff, an Illinois resident, was injured in Illinois. The law of Illinois will govern the substantive questions, and witnesses on the issues of injury, damages and other elements relating to the occurrence are most likely to be found here. Under such circumstances the courts of the place of injury usually provide the most convenient forum for trial. See Watson v. Employers Liability Assurance Corp., 348 U.S. 66, 72 (1954). In Travelers Health Association v. Commonwealth of Virginia, 339 U.S. 643 (1950), a Nebraska insurance corporation was held subject to the jurisdiction of a Virginia regulatory commission although it had no paid agents within the State and its only contact there was a mail-order business operated from its Omaha office. The court observed, by way of dictum, that "suits on alleged losses can be more conveniently tried in Virginia where witnesses would most likely live and where claims for losses would presumably be investigated. Such factors have been given great weight in applying the doctrine of *forum non conveniens*. And prior decisions of this Court have referred to the unwisdom, unfairness and injustice of permitting policyholders to seek redress only in some distant state where the insurer is incorporated. The Due Process Clause does not forbid a state to protect its citizens from such injustice." We think a similar conclusion must follow in the case at bar.

We are aware of decisions, cited by defendant, wherein the opposite result was reached on somewhat similar factual situations. Little purpose can be served, however, by discussing such cases in detail, since the existence of sufficient "contact" depends upon the particular facts in each case. In any event we think the better rule supports jurisdiction in cases of the present kind. We conclude accordingly that defendant's association with this State is sufficient to support the exercise of jurisdiction.

We construe section 17(1)(b) as providing for jurisdiction under the circumstances shown in this case, and we hold that as so construed the statute does not violate due process of law.

■ NOTES ON STATE LONG-ARM STATUTES

1. Titan in Ohio sent its valves to American Standard in Pennsylvania, which incorporated them into water heaters and shipped some to Illinois. Under the Illinois statute, jurisdiction over Titan turns on whether Titan committed a "tortious act" in Illinois. But if Titan did something wrong in putting together the water heater, it happened in Ohio, didn't it? How does the court conclude that Titan committed a tortious act in Illinois?

2. Jurisdiction must exist at the outset of the suit. Before judgment is reached, we cannot know whether Titan committed a tortious act, can we? How can we construe a "tortious act" clause to avoid this difficulty?

3. At the time *Gray* was decided, §17 of the Civil Practice Act (the long-arm statute) provided that any person submits to jurisdiction in Illinois if he or she "in person or through an agent" engages in

(a) the transaction of any business within this State;

(b) the commission of a tortious act within this State;

(c) the ownership, use, or possession of any real estate situated in this State;

(d) contracting to insure any person, property, or risk located within this State at the time of contracting.

Other provisions authorized personal service outside the state and said the statute covers only "causes of action rising from acts enumerated" therein. Still other language said the statute reached the estate of a person who committed such acts (death of the actor would not keep plaintiff from suing her estate in Illinois).

4. Consider the following cases:

(a) An Illinois wife, left without income in Urbana when her husband moved to Dallas, Texas, sues her husband in Illinois for divorce and support. Does the statute quoted above confer jurisdiction?

(b) A Rockford, Illinois woman wishes to sue a man from Sioux City, Iowa, after she purchased from him a 1970 Cadillac, in a transaction she initiated after reading an ad he placed in an Iowa newspaper that the woman read in the library in Rockford. She called the seller, and the two agreed on a price, then she sent him a written offer that he signed in Iowa and mailed back to her. She went to Iowa, picked up the car, and paid for it. Her theories are that defendant committed fraud and breached the contract because the car has major mechanical problems that she did not discover until returning to Illinois. If the *tort* claim is covered, does it follow that the *contract* claim is also covered? What if the Iowa man had placed the ad on an internet list that the Illinois buyer accessed on her computer at home?

5. You might think *Gray* reached the best result, and one that is obvious—at least in hindsight, since the statutory phrase "tortious act within this State" is malleable in the hands of a skilled jurist. But a New York court reached the opposite result on the basis of similar language in a long-arm statute. See Feathers v. McLucas, 209 N.E.2d 68 (N.Y. 1965) (the phrase does *not* reach negligent behavior out of state). New York's legislature amended its statute to reach tortious acts outside the state if defendant "expects or should reasonably expect the act to have consequences in the state and derives substantial revenue from interstate or international commerce" *or* "regularly does or solicits business, or engages in any other persistent course of conduct, or derives substantial revenue from goods used or consumed or services rendered, in the state." See N.Y. CPLR §302.

6. The Illinois legislature amended and refined the statute several times after *Gray,* adding (among other things) the following new clauses (each item now carries a number rather than a letter):

> (5) With respect to actions of dissolution of marriage, declaration of invalidity of marriage and legal separation, the maintenance in this State of a matrimonial domicile at the time this cause of action arose or the commission in this State of any act giving rise to the cause of action;
>
> (6) With respect to actions brought under the Illinois Parentage Act of 1984, as now or hereafter amended, the performance of an act of sexual intercourse within this State during the possible period of conception;
>
> (7) The making or performance of any contract or promise substantially connected with this State;
>
> (8) The performance of sexual intercourse within this State which is claimed to have resulted in the conception of a child who resides in this State;
>
> (9) The failure to support a child, spouse or former spouse who has continued to reside in this State since the person either formerly resided with them in this State or directed them to reside in this State;
>
> (10) The acquisition of ownership, possession or control of any asset or thing of value present within this State when ownership, possession or control was acquired;
>
> (11) The breach of any fiduciary duty within this State;
>
> (12) The performance of duties as a director or officer of a corporation organized under the laws of this State or having its principal place of business within this State;
>
> (13) The ownership of an interest in any trust administered within this State; or

(14) The exercise of powers granted under the authority of this State as a fiduciary.

See Ill. Comp. Stat. §5/2-209. Item (5) covers the Urbana wife who wants to divorce the husband who moved to Dallas, and item (9) covers her claim for support. But the Rockford woman who wants to sue the Iowa seller will have a harder time: It seems a stretch to argue for jurisdiction on the basis of the "transaction of any business" clause (in the original statute; retained in the revised statute), doesn't it? How about clause (7) covering the "making or performance of any contract or promise substantially connected with" Illinois? How about the "tortious act" clause (in the original statute and construed in *Gray*; retained in the revised statute)?

7. Some states took a different approach. The California long-arm statute authorizes jurisdiction "on any basis not inconsistent with the Constitution of this state or of the United States." Cal. Code Civ. Proc. §410.10. It is apparent, isn't it, that this statute maximizes state court jurisdiction? Do specific-clause statutes like the one in Illinois risk authorizing less jurisdiction than the Constitution allows? Would a rational legislature *prefer* to limit situations where citizens may sue nonresidents?

8. The difference between the California and Illinois approaches might not be as great as it seems: Decisions in some states with Illinois-style statutes hold that the language should be construed as authorizing as much jurisdiction as the Constitution allows. And one of the amendments adopted in Illinois added yet another clause that incorporates the Constitution. In addition to the list, the Illinois statute now has a catchall: "A court may also exercise jurisdiction on any other basis now or hereafter permitted by the Illinois Constitution and the Constitution of the United States."

■ NOTES ON "STREAM OF COMMERCE"

1. In *Gray*, the court says Titan Valve's "only contact" with Illinois was that the valve, after being installed in a water heater in Pennsylvania, wound up in Illinois when the heater was sold "in the course of commerce" to an Illinois consumer. That means, doesn't it, that Titan Valve had no contact with Illinois? Or does it mean merely that Titan Valve had no "direct" contact with Illinois?

2. Apparently troubled by the absence of "direct" contact, the court says that jurisdictional requirements were "further relaxed" after *International Shoe*, then describes *McGee*. Isn't it true that there was a direct and purposeful contact between the insurance carrier and California in *McGee*, in the form of a solicitation of coverage? And the solicitation led to a contract, which led to the suit. But there is no indication that Titan Valve solicited business in Illinois, and the claim in *Gray* arose out of business that Titan conducted with American Standard in Pennsylvania. The cases aren't comparable, are they?

3. The court says Titan "does not claim" that use of its product in Illinois was "an isolated instance," and that it is a fair inference that Titan's transactions "result in substantial use and consumption" in Illinois. Really? Is it up to Titan to show how many (or how few) valves wind up in Illinois? Absent any proof of business done by Titan in Pennsylvania or by American Standard in Illinois, how can the court *assume* there are many Titan valves in Illinois?

4. Doesn't *Hanson* say contacts must be "purposeful"? Can there be "purposeful availing" when an Ohio valve maker sells valves to a Pennsylvania maker of water heaters who then ships the heaters to Illinois?

3. Immunity from Service of Process

As you have seen, jurisdiction based on personal service on a defendant who is only traveling through (or over) the forum state can result in great inconvenience. Sometimes the situation seems worse than merely inconvenient: Plaintiffs have been known to trick defendants into entering the forum state in order to serve them. And sometimes defendants enter the state temporarily to serve as witnesses in trials, or to settle lawsuits, furthering the judicial process. If such people can be served by plaintiffs trying to obtain jurisdiction in unrelated cases, others in similar situations may be deterred from entering the state even temporarily.

CANNINGTON v. CANNINGTON

Circuit Court of Virginia
50 Va. Cir. 165 (1999)

ALDEN, Judge.

[John and Jodelle Cannington married in Houston, Texas in 1988. In June 1995, they moved to Maryland and bought a house, where they lived until separating in July 1996. John moved to Virginia. Still in Maryland, Jodelle gave birth to a son. John made support payments, and was "the primary source of financial support," for Jodelle and their son. John's parents lived in Virginia too, and the son often visited them. In March 1999, John had Jodelle served with a complaint as she stepped out of a car at Dulles Airport in Virginia, seeking a divorce, determination of support obligations, division of assets, and determination of custody. Jodelle was about to board a flight to Houston. John had made the travel arrangements for her. She moved to dismiss on the ground that John "used fraud and trickery to lure her into Virginia" to serve her in the divorce action.]

Defendant contends that in order for a state to obtain *in personam* jurisdiction over a nonresident defendant, the defendant must have some minimum contacts with the state. However, where the Defendant is personally served while in the Commonwealth of Virginia, that action is sufficient to confer over her the jurisdiction of the Court.... ["Minimum contacts" under *International* Shoe] are not required when the defendant is physically present.... [The] courts of a state have jurisdiction over nonresidents who are physically present in the state, and personal service on a nonresident defendant who is present in the state does not offend "traditional notions of fair play and substantial justice." Consequently, service of process on the Defendant while she was present in Virginia, of her own volition, was sufficient for the state to obtain *in personam* jurisdiction over her.

Defendant alleges that personal service of process on her in Virginia is invalid because Complainant used fraud and trickery to induce Defendant to come into the state. Defendant contends that her presence in the state, when she accepted the travel arrangements made for her by Complainant to fly out of Dulles, was fraudulently induced. Defendant maintains that Complainant, armed with the exact time she would be at the airport, took advantage of the arrangement and had process served on her at that time.

However, the evidence presented during her testimony on June 7, 1999, does not support these contentions. The evidence showed that: (i) Defendant decided to fly to Houston and asked Complainant to make arrangements for her to do so; (ii) Complainant has paid for flights or used his frequent flyer miles for Defendant in the past; (iii) Complainant arranged and paid for Defendant's flight from Dulles to Houston on at least one prior occasion; (iv) Complainant arranged for Defendant's Dulles transportation on at least one prior occasion; (v) Defendant has visited Virginia on several occasions to conduct personal business and to leave her son with Complainant's parents; and most importantly, (vi) Defendant would have driven to Fredericksburg, Virginia to leave her son with his grandparents on March 12, 1999, had she made different travel plans. In light of this testimony, Defendant's presence in Virginia was neither contrived nor unusual, and neither fraud nor trickery was used to cause her to be present in the Commonwealth of Virginia.

Defendant relies on Tickle v. Barton, 95 S.E.2d 427 (Va. 1956), and Shaw v. Hughes, 400 S.E.2d 501 (1991), two cases in which the court declined to exercise jurisdiction over the nonresident defendant, to support her claim of trickery. However, these cases are inapposite. In *Tickle,* the plaintiff's attorney telephoned the defendant and invited him to attend a high school banquet in West Virginia, without disclosing his identity or his purpose. The defendant would not have traveled to West Virginia but for the bogus invitation. By similar contrivance, the plaintiff in *Shaw* telephoned the defendant's attorney and informed him that the defendant could retrieve his gun collection if he came to the plaintiff's home in Greenville, South Carolina. At that time, Plaintiff was in contempt of a Florida court order to release the guns into the defendant's possession. The defendant, who was served when he and his attorney arrived at the plaintiff's home, had no other business to conduct in South Carolina and would not have traveled there but for the artifice of the plaintiff.

Here, Defendant's testimony established not only that she traveled to Virginia regularly to conduct personal business and for other reasons, but that she had planned to visit Virginia the same weekend that process was served on her by Complainant. Hence, her presence in Virginia was not *induced* by the Complainant.

[Virginia has *in personam* jurisdiction, so it can "decide all issues of spousal support and equitable distribution of marital property," which plaintiff has requested. Virginia has a "legitimate interest" in these matters because the suit concerns plaintiff's "personal and financial interests," and the doctrine of *forum non conveniens* does not require transferring the case to Maryland. The court need not apply Maryland law on "issues of spousal support and equitable distribution of marital property," and can apply Virginia law. The court can determine issues of custody over the son under a statute granting jurisdiction to determine custody if (a) the child and at least one parent has "significant connections" with the state, and (b) there is substantial evidence in the state relating to the child's "present or future care, protection, training and personal relationships."]

For the reasons stated above, the Court finds that Virginia does have *in personam* jurisdiction over the Defendant and is a proper forum for deciding all issues before it related to this litigation. Accordingly, the Motion to Oppose Jurisdiction is denied and Defendant is to file responsive pleadings within 14 days of this date. An appropriate order shall be entered on this date.

■ NOTES ON TRICKERY AND OTHER REASONS FOR IMMUNITY FROM PROCESS

1. *Cannington* accepts the principle that the defendant can obtain a dismissal *if* her husband induced her to enter Virginia by means of fraud or trickery, doesn't it? Why should we make this exception to the rule that presence suffices to confer jurisdiction? What facts persuade the court *not* to dismiss?

2. If all that John Cannington wanted was a divorce from Jodelle, he could obtain that in Virginia, as state of his domicile, even without "catching" Jodelle in Virginia, couldn't he?

3. Are there other situations in which we should make exception to the usual rule that presence suffices as the basis to exercise jurisdiction over the person?

(a) Suppose John had persuaded Jodelle to come to Virginia "so we can work out our differences." If she did so and, when they could not agree, he

then had her served, would she have a good argument for dismissal? Why or why not?

(b) Suppose Jodelle had been involved in an accident during a trip to Virginia to pick up her child from his visit with John's parents, and was sued and was attending trial when John served her with the complaint in his divorce suit. Should she be immune from process so she can have free passage to defend the other suit?

(c) Suppose Jodelle simply witnessed a traffic accident in Virginia involving two Virginians. If a lawsuit ensued, and Jodelle were subpoenaed (or even persuaded to come voluntarily) to testify, should she be immune from service of process in John's divorce suit?

4. What if defendant, served in the state, could be brought in as a defendant under the state long-arm statute, consistently with the due process standard of *International Shoe*? See generally Wright & Miller, Federal Practice and Procedure §1076 (if defendant is subject to local jurisdiction under a long-arm statute, consistent with due process, "little purpose is served by giving that person immunity from process" while in the state).

C EVOLUTION OF MODERN THEORY (INTERESTS AND POLICIES)

1. Limited Jurisdiction Shrinks

SHAFFER v. HEITNER

United States Supreme Court
433 U.S. 186 (1977)

Mr. Justice MARSHALL delivered the opinion of the Court.

The controversy in this case concerns the constitutionality of a Delaware statute that allows a court of that State to take jurisdiction of a lawsuit by sequestering any property of the defendant that happens to be located in Delaware. Appellants contend that the sequestration statute as applied in this case violates the Due Process Clause of the Fourteenth Amendment both because it permits the state courts to exercise jurisdiction despite the absence of sufficient contacts among the defendants, the litigation, and the State of Delaware and because it authorizes the deprivation of defendants' property without providing adequate procedural safeguards. We find it necessary to consider only the first of these contentions.

I

Appellee Heitner, a nonresident of Delaware, is the owner of one share of stock in the Greyhound Corp., a business incorporated under the laws of Delaware with its principal place of business in Phoenix, Ariz. On May 22, 1974, he filed a shareholder's derivative suit in the Court of Chancery for New Castle County, Del., in which he named as defendants Greyhound, its wholly owned subsidiary Greyhound Lines, Inc., and 28 present or former officers or directors of one or both of the corporations. In essence, Heitner alleged that the individual defendants had violated their duties to Greyhound by causing it and its subsidiary to engage in actions that resulted in the corporations being held liable for substantial damages in a private antitrust suit[2] and a large fine in a criminal contempt action.[3] The activities which led to these penalties took place in Oregon.

Simultaneously with his complaint, Heitner filed a motion for an order of sequestration of the Delaware property of the individual defendants pursuant to Del. Code Ann., Tit. 10, §366 (1975).[4] This motion was accompanied by a supporting affidavit of counsel which stated that the individual defendants were nonresidents of Delaware. The affidavit identified the property to be sequestered as [certain common and preferred stock in Greyhound Corporation, along with options, warrants, and contract rights or debts payable by Greyhound to the defendants]. The requested sequestration order was signed the day the motion was filed. Pursuant to that order, the sequestrator "seized" approximately 82,000 shares of Greyhound common stock belonging to 19 of the defendants,[7] and options belonging to another 2 defendants. These seizures were accomplished by placing "stop transfer" orders or their equivalents on the books of the Greyhound Corp. So far as the record shows, none of the certificates representing the seized property was physically present in Delaware. The stock was considered to be in Delaware, and so subject to seizure, by virtue of Del. Code Ann., Tit. 8, §169 (1975), which makes Delaware the situs of ownership of all stock in Delaware corporations.

All 28 defendants were notified of the initiation of the suit by certified mail directed to their last known addresses and by publication in a New Castle County newspaper. The 21 defendants whose property was seized (hereafter referred to as appellants) responded by entering a special appearance for the purpose of moving to quash service of process and to vacate the sequestration

---

[2] A judgment of $13,146,090 plus attorney's fees was entered against Greyhound. . . .

[3] Greyhound was fined $100,000 and Greyhound Lines $500,000.

[4] [The Court quotes Delaware statute, which provides for seizure of property owned by any nonresident defendant, and for its release if defendant makes a "general appearance" unless plaintiff shows that releasing the property makes it less likely that any judgment will be satisfied.—ED.]

[7] The closing price of Greyhound stock on the day the sequestration order was issued was $14 3/8. Thus, the value of the sequestered stock was approximately $1.2 million.

order. They contended that the ex parte sequestration procedure did not accord them due process of law and that the property seized was not capable of attachment in Delaware. In addition, appellants asserted that under the rule of International Shoe Co. v. Washington, 326 U.S. 310 (1945), they did not have sufficient contacts with Delaware to sustain the jurisdiction of that State's courts.

The Court of Chancery rejected these arguments in a letter opinion which emphasized the purpose of the Delaware sequestration procedure. [That purpose is to "compel the personal appearance" of a nonresident, and the sequestered property is "routinely released" when the defendant appears, so the seizure is consistent with the Court's decisions in *Sniadach* and *Fuentes* and *Mitchell*. The Delaware Supreme Court affirmed.]

We noted probable jurisdiction.[12] We reverse.

II

The Delaware courts rejected appellants' jurisdictional challenge by noting that this suit was brought as a *quasi in rem* proceeding. Since *quasi in rem* jurisdiction is traditionally based on attachment or seizure of property present in the jurisdiction, not on contacts between the defendant and the State, the courts considered appellants' claimed lack of contacts with Delaware to be unimportant. This categorical analysis assumes the continued soundness of the conceptual structure founded on the century-old case of Pennoyer v. Neff, 95 U.S. 714 (1878). [The Court reviews decisions from *Pennoyer* through *International Shoe*.] Thus, the relationship among the defendant, the forum, and the litigation, rather than the mutually exclusive sovereignty of the States on which the Rules of *Pennoyer* rest, became the central concerns of the inquiry into personal jurisdiction. The immediate effect of this departure from *Pennoyer*'s conceptual apparatus was to increase the ability of the state courts to obtain personal jurisdiction over nonresident defendants.

No equally dramatic change has occurred in the law governing jurisdiction *in rem*. There have, however, been intimations that the collapse of the *in personam* wing of *Pennoyer* has not left that decision unweakened as a foundation for *in rem* jurisdiction. Well-reasoned lower court opinions have questioned the proposition that the presence of property in a State gives that State jurisdiction to adjudicate rights to the property regardless of the relationship of the underlying dispute and the property owner to the forum. [The Court cites cases.] The overwhelming majority of commentators have also rejected

---

[12] Under Delaware law, defendants whose property has been sequestered must enter a general appearance, thus subjecting themselves to in personam liability, before they can defend on the merits. Thus, if the judgment below were considered not to be an appealable final judgment, appellants would have the choice of suffering a default judgment or entering a general appearance and defending on the merits. . . . Accordingly, . . . we conclude that the judgment below is final within the meaning of [28 USC] §1257.

Pennoyer's premise that a proceeding "against" property is not a proceeding against the owners of that property. Accordingly, they urge that the "traditional notions of fair play and substantial justice" that govern a State's power to adjudicate *in personam* should also govern its power to adjudicate personal rights to property located in the State. *See, e.g.,* Von Mehren & Trautman, Jurisdiction to Adjudicate: A Suggested Analysis, 79 Harv. L. Rev. 1121 (1966) (hereafter Von Mehren & Trautman).

. . .

It is clear, therefore, that the law of state-court jurisdiction no longer stands securely on the foundation established in *Pennoyer*. We think that the time is ripe to consider whether the standard of fairness and substantial justice set forth in *International Shoe* should be held to govern actions *in rem* as well as *in personam*.

III

The case for applying to jurisdiction *in rem* the same test of "fair play and substantial justice" as governs assertions of jurisdiction *in personam* is simple and straightforward. It is premised on recognition that "(t)he phrase, 'judicial jurisdiction over a thing,' is a customary elliptical way of referring to jurisdiction over the interests of persons in a thing." Restatement (Second) of Conflict of Laws §56, Introductory Note (1971) (hereafter Restatement). This recognition leads to the conclusion that in order to justify an exercise of jurisdiction *in rem*, the basis for jurisdiction must be sufficient to justify exercising "jurisdiction over the interests of persons in a thing." The standard for determining whether an exercise of jurisdiction over the interests of persons is consistent with the Due Process Clause is the minimum contacts standard elucidated in *International Shoe*.

This argument, of course, does not ignore the fact that the presence of property in a State may bear on the existence of jurisdiction by providing contacts among the forum State, the defendant, and the litigation. For example, when claims to the property itself are the source of the underlying controversy between the plaintiff and the defendant,[24] it would be unusual for the State where the property is located not to have jurisdiction. In such cases, the defendant's claim to property located in the State would normally[25]

---

[24] This category includes true in rem actions and the first type of quasi in rem proceedings. See n.17, supra. [Footnote 17 reads as follows: "A judgment in rem affects the interests of all persons in designated property. A judgment quasi in rem affects the interests of particular persons in designated property. The latter is of two types. In one the plaintiff is seeking to secure a pre-existing claim in the subject property and to extinguish or establish the nonexistence of similar interests of particular persons. In the other the plaintiff seeks to apply what he concedes to be the property of the defendant to the satisfaction of a claim against him. Restatement, Judgments, 5-9." Hanson v. Denckla, 357 U.S. 235, 246 n.12 (1958). As did the Court in *Hanson*, we will for convenience generally use the term "in rem" in place of "in rem and quasi in rem."—ED.]

[25] In some circumstances the presence of property in the forum State will not support the inference suggested in text. *Cf.,* e.g., Restatement Second, Conflict of Laws §60, Comments c, d.

indicate that he expected to benefit from the State's protection of his interest. The State's strong interests in assuring the marketability of property within its borders and in providing a procedure for peaceful resolution of disputes about the possession of that property would also support jurisdiction, as would the likelihood that important records and witnesses will be found in the State.[28] The presence of property may also favor jurisdiction in cases such as suits for injury suffered on the land of an absentee owner, where the defendant's ownership of the property is conceded but the cause of action is otherwise related to rights and duties growing out of that ownership.[29]

It appears, therefore, that jurisdiction over many types of actions which now are or might be brought *in rem* would not be affected by a holding that any assertion of state-court jurisdiction must satisfy the *International Shoe* standard.[30] For the type of *quasi in rem* action typified by Harris v. Balk and the present case, however, accepting the proposed analysis would result in significant change. These are cases where the property which now serves as the basis for state-court jurisdiction is completely unrelated to the plaintiff's cause of action. Thus, although the presence of the defendant's property in a State might suggest the existence of other ties among the defendant, the State, and the litigation, the presence of the property alone would not support the State's jurisdiction. If those other ties did not exist, cases over which the State is now thought to have jurisdiction could not be brought in that forum.

Since acceptance of the *International Shoe* test would most affect this class of cases, we examine the arguments against adopting that standard as they relate to this category of litigation. Before doing so, however, we note that this type of case also presents the clearest illustration of the argument in favor of assessing assertions of jurisdiction by a single standard. For in cases such as *Harris* and this one, the only role played by the property is to provide the basis for bringing the defendant into court.[32] Indeed, the express purpose of the Delaware sequestration procedure is to compel the defendant to enter a personal appearance.[33] In such cases, if a direct assertion of personal jurisdiction over the defendant would violate the Constitution, it

---

[28] We do not suggest that these illustrations include all the factors that may affect the decision, nor that the factors we have mentioned are necessarily decisive.

[29] Cf. Dubin v. Philadelphia, 34 Pa. D. & C. 61 (1938). If such an action were brought under the in rem jurisdiction rather than under a long-arm statute, it would be a quasi in rem action of the second type. See n.17, supra [quoted in note 24, supra—ED.].

[30] We do not suggest that jurisdictional doctrines other than those discussed in text, such as the particularized rules governing adjudications of status, are inconsistent with the standard of fairness.

[32] The value of the property seized does serve to limit the extent of possible liability, but that limitation does not provide support for the assertion of jurisdiction. In this case, appellants' potential liability under the in rem jurisdiction exceeds $1 million.

[33] This purpose is emphasized by Delaware's refusal to allow any defense on the merits unless the defendant enters a general appearance, thus submitting to full in personam liability. See n.12, supra.

would seem that an indirect assertion of that jurisdiction should be equally impermissible.

The primary rationale for treating the presence of property as a sufficient basis for jurisdiction to adjudicate claims over which the State would not have jurisdiction if *International Shoe* applied is that a wrongdoer "should not be able to avoid payment of his obligations by the expedient of removing his assets to a place where he is not subject to an *in personam* suit." Restatement Second, Judgments §66, Comment a. This justification, however, does not explain why jurisdiction should be recognized without regard to whether the property is present in the State because of an effort to avoid the owner's obligations. Nor does it support jurisdiction to adjudicate the underlying claim. At most, it suggests that a State in which property is located should have jurisdiction to attach that property, by use of proper procedures, as security for a judgment being sought in a forum where the litigation can be maintained consistently with *International Shoe*. Moreover, we know of nothing to justify the assumption that a debtor can avoid paying his obligations by removing his property to a State in which his creditor cannot obtain personal jurisdiction over him. The Full Faith and Credit Clause, after all, makes the valid *in personam* judgment of one State enforceable in all other States.[36]

It might also be suggested that allowing *in rem* jurisdiction avoids the uncertainty inherent in the *International Shoe* standard and assures a plaintiff of a forum.[37] We believe, however, that the fairness standard of *International Shoe* can be easily applied in the vast majority of cases. Moreover, when the existence of jurisdiction in a particular forum under *International Shoe* is unclear, the cost of simplifying the litigation by avoiding the jurisdictional question may be the sacrifice of "fair play and substantial justice." That cost is too high.

We are left, then, to consider the significance of the long history of jurisdiction based solely on the presence of property in a State. Although the theory that territorial power is both essential to and sufficient for jurisdiction has been undermined, we have never held that the presence of property in a State does not automatically confer jurisdiction over the owner's interest in that

---

[36] Once it has been determined by a court of competent jurisdiction that the defendant is a debtor of the plaintiff, there would seem to be no unfairness in allowing an action to realize on that debt in a State where the defendant has property, whether or not that State would have jurisdiction to determine the existence of the debt as an original matter.

[37] This case does not raise, and we therefore do not consider, the question whether the presence of a defendant's property in a State is a sufficient basis for jurisdiction when no other forum is available to the plaintiff.

property. This history must be considered as supporting the proposition that jurisdiction based solely on the presence of property satisfies the demands of due process, cf. Ownbey v. Morgan, 256 U.S. 94, 111 (1921), but it is not decisive. "(T)raditional notions of fair play and substantial justice" can be as readily offended by the perpetuation of ancient forms that are no longer justified as by the adoption of new procedures that are inconsistent with the basic values of our constitutional heritage. The fiction that an assertion of jurisdiction over property is anything but an assertion of jurisdiction over the owner of the property supports an ancient form without substantial modern justification. Its continued acceptance would serve only to allow state-court jurisdiction that is fundamentally unfair to the defendant.

We therefore conclude that all assertions of state-court jurisdiction must be evaluated according to the standards set forth in *International Shoe* and its progeny.

IV

The Delaware courts based their assertion of jurisdiction in this case solely on the statutory presence of appellants' property in Delaware. Yet that property is not the subject matter of this litigation, nor is the underlying cause of action related to the property. Appellants' holdings in Greyhound do not, therefore, provide contacts with Delaware sufficient to support the jurisdiction of that State's courts over appellants. If it exists, that jurisdiction must have some other foundation.

Appellee Heitner did not allege and does not now claim that appellants have ever set foot in Delaware. Nor does he identify any act related to his cause of action as having taken place in Delaware. Nevertheless, he contends that appellants' positions as directors and officers of a corporation chartered in Delaware provide sufficient "contacts, ties, or relations," *International Shoe*, with that State to give its courts jurisdiction over appellants in this stockholder's derivative action. This argument is based primarily on what Heitner asserts to be the strong interest of Delaware in supervising the management of a Delaware corporation. That interest is said to derive from the role of Delaware law in establishing the corporation and defining the obligations owed to it by its officers and directors. In order to protect this interest, appellee concludes, Delaware's courts must have jurisdiction over corporate fiduciaries such as appellants.

This argument is undercut by the failure of the Delaware Legislature to assert the state interest appellee finds so compelling. Delaware law bases jurisdiction, not on appellants' status as corporate fiduciaries, but rather on the presence of their property in the State. Although the sequestration procedure used here may be most frequently used in derivative suits against officers and directors, the authorizing statute evinces no specific concern with such actions. Sequestration can be used in any suit against a nonresident, and reaches corporate fiduciaries only if they happen to own interests in a Delaware corporation, or other property in the State. But as Heitner's failure to secure jurisdiction over seven of the defendants named in his complaint demonstrates, there is no necessary relationship between holding a position as a corporate fiduciary and owning stock or other interests in the corporation. If Delaware perceived its interest in securing jurisdiction over corporate fiduciaries to be as great as Heitner suggests, we would expect it to have enacted a statute more clearly designed to protect that interest.

Moreover, even if Heitner's assessment of the importance of Delaware's interest is accepted, his argument fails to demonstrate that Delaware is a fair forum for this litigation. The interest appellee has identified may support the application of Delaware law to resolve any controversy over appellants' actions in their capacities as officers and directors.[44] But we have rejected the argument that if a State's law can properly be applied to a dispute, its courts necessarily have jurisdiction over the parties to that dispute.

> (The State) does not acquire . . . jurisdiction by being the "center of gravity" of the controversy, or the most convenient location for litigation. The issue is personal jurisdiction, not choice of law. It is resolved in this case by considering the acts of the (appellants).

Hanson v. Denckla, 357 U.S. 235, 254 (1958).

Appellee suggests that by accepting positions as officers or directors of a Delaware corporation, appellants performed the acts required by *Hanson*. He notes that Delaware law provides substantial benefits to corporate officers and directors, and that these benefits were at least in part the incentive for appellants to assume their positions. It is, he says, "only fair and just" to require appellants, in return for these benefits, to respond in the State of Delaware when they are accused of misusing their power.

But like Heitner's first argument, this line of reasoning establishes only that it is appropriate for Delaware law to govern the obligations of appellants to Greyhound and its stockholders. It does not demonstrate that appellants have "purposefully avail[ed themselves] of the privilege of conducting activities within the forum State," *Hanson*, in a way that would justify bringing them before a Delaware tribunal. Appellants have simply had nothing to do with the State of Delaware. Moreover, appellants had no reason to expect to be haled before a Delaware court. Delaware, unlike some States, has not enacted a statute that treats acceptance of a directorship as consent to jurisdiction in

---

[44] In general, the law of the State of incorporation is held to govern the liabilities of officers or directors to the corporation and its stockholders. The rationale for the general rule appears to be based more on the need for a uniform and certain standard to govern the internal affairs of a corporation than on the perceived interest of the State of incorporation.

the State. And "[i]t strains reason . . . to suggest that anyone buying securities in a corporation formed in Delaware 'impliedly consents' to subject himself to Delaware's . . . jurisdiction on any cause of action." Appellants, who were not required to acquire interests in Greyhound in order to hold their positions, did not by acquiring those interests surrender their right to be brought to judgment only in States with which they had had "minimum contacts."

The Due Process Clause "does not contemplate that a state may make binding a judgment . . . against an individual or corporate defendant with which the state has no contacts, ties, or relations." *International Shoe.* Delaware's assertion of jurisdiction over appellants in this case is inconsistent with that constitutional limitation on state power. The judgment of the Delaware Supreme Court must, therefore, be reversed.

It is so ordered.

Mr. Justice REHNQUIST took no part in the consideration or decision of this case.

Mr. Justice POWELL, concurring.

I agree that the principles of *International Shoe* should be extended to govern assertions of *in rem* as well as *in personam* jurisdiction in a state court. I also agree that neither the statutory presence of appellants' stock in Delaware nor their positions as directors and officers of a Delaware corporation can provide sufficient contacts to support the Delaware courts' assertion of jurisdiction in this case.

I would explicitly reserve judgment, however, on whether the ownership of some forms of property whose situs is indisputably and permanently located within a State may, without more, provide the contacts necessary to subject a defendant to jurisdiction within the State to the extent of the value of the property. In the case of real property, in particular, preservation of the common-law concept of *quasi in rem* jurisdiction arguably would avoid the uncertainty of the general *International Shoe* standard without significant cost to "'traditional notions of fair play and substantial justice.'"

Subject to the foregoing reservation, I join the opinion of the Court.

Mr. Justice STEVENS, concurring in the judgment.

The Due Process Clause affords protection against "judgments without notice." *International Shoe* (opinion of Black, J.). Throughout our history the acceptable exercise of *in rem* and *quasi in rem* jurisdiction has included a procedure giving reasonable assurance that actual notice of the particular claim will be conveyed to the defendant. Thus, publication, notice by registered mail, or extraterritorial personal service has been an essential ingredient of any procedure that serves as a substitute for personal service within the jurisdiction.

The requirement of fair notice also, I believe, includes fair warning that a particular activity may subject a person to the jurisdiction of a foreign sovereign. If I visit another State, or acquire real estate or open a bank account in it, I knowingly assume some risk that the State will exercise its power over my property or my person while there. My contact with the State, though minimal, gives rise to predictable risks.

Perhaps the same consequences should flow from the purchase of stock of a corporation organized under the laws of a foreign nation, because to some limited extent one's property and affairs then become subject to the laws of the nation of domicile of the corporation. As a matter of international law, that suggestion might be acceptable because a foreign investment is sufficiently unusual to make it appropriate to require the investor to study the ramifications of his decision. But a purchase of securities in the domestic market is an entirely different matter.

One who purchases shares of stock on the open market can hardly be expected to know that he has thereby become subject to suit in a forum remote from his residence and unrelated to the transaction. As a practical matter, the Delaware sequestration statute creates an unacceptable risk of judgment without notice. Unlike the 49 other States, Delaware treats the place of incorporation as the situs of the stock, even though both the owner and the custodian of the shares are elsewhere. Moreover, Delaware denies the defendant the opportunity to defend the merits of the suit unless he subjects himself to the unlimited jurisdiction of the court. Thus, it coerces a defendant either to submit to personal jurisdiction in a forum which could not otherwise obtain such jurisdiction or to lose the securities which have been attached. If its procedure were upheld, Delaware would, in effect, impose a duty of inquiry on every purchaser of securities in the national market. For unless the purchaser ascertains both the State of incorporation of the company whose shares he is buying, and also the idiosyncrasies of its law, he may be assuming an unknown risk of litigation. I therefore agree with the Court that on the record before us no adequate basis for jurisdiction exists and that the Delaware statute is unconstitutional on its face.

How the Court's opinion may be applied in other contexts is not entirely clear to me. I agree with Mr. Justice Powell that it should not be read to invalidate *quasi in rem* jurisdiction where real estate is involved. I would also not read it as invalidating other long-accepted methods of acquiring jurisdiction over persons with adequate notice of both the particular controversy and the fact that their local activities might subject them to suit. My uncertainty as to the reach of the opinion, and my fear that it purports to decide a great deal more than is necessary to dispose of this case, persuade me merely to concur in the judgment.

Mr. Justice BRENNAN, concurring in part and dissenting in part.

I join Parts I-III of the Court's opinion. I fully agree that the minimum contacts analysis developed in *International Shoe*, represents a far more sensible construct for the exercise of state-court jurisdiction than the patch-work of legal and factual fictions that has been generated from the decision in *Pennoyer*. It is precisely because the inquiry into minimum contacts is now of such overriding importance, however, that I must respectfully dissent from Part IV of the Court's opinion.

[Justice Brennan argues that the Court should not have rejected the exercise of jurisdiction in Delaware on the basis of minimum contacts, because this question was neither litigated nor determined in the Delaware court.]

Nonetheless, because the Court rules on the minimum contacts question, I feel impelled to express my view. While evidence derived through discovery might satisfy me that minimum contacts are lacking in a given case, I am convinced that as a general rule a state forum has jurisdiction to adjudicate a shareholder derivative action centering on the conduct and policies of the directors and officers of a corporation chartered by that State. Unlike the Court, I therefore would not foreclose Delaware from asserting jurisdiction over appellants were it persuaded to do so on the basis of minimum contacts.

It is well settled that a derivative lawsuit as presented here does not inure primarily to the benefit of the named plaintiff. Rather, the primary beneficiaries are the corporation and its owners, the shareholders. "The cause of action which such a plaintiff brings before the court is not his own but the corporation's. . . . Such a plaintiff often may represent an important public and stockholder interest in bringing faithless managers to book." Koster v. Lumbermens Mutual Casualty Co., 330 U.S. 518 (1947).

Viewed in this light, the chartering State has an unusually powerful interest in insuring the availability of a convenient forum for litigating claims involving a possible multiplicity of defendant fiduciaries and for vindicating the State's substantive policies regarding the management of its domestic corporations. I believe that our cases fairly establish that the States' valid substantive interests are important considerations in assessing whether it constitutionally may claim jurisdiction over a given cause of action.

In this instance, Delaware can point to at least three interrelated public policies that are furthered by its assertion of jurisdiction. First, the State has a substantial interest in providing restitution for its local corporations that allegedly have been victimized by fiduciary misconduct, even if the managerial decisions occurred outside the State. The importance of this general state interest in assuring restitution for its own residents previously found expression in cases that went outside the then-prevailing due process framework to authorize state-court jurisdiction over nonresident motorists who injure others within the State. More recently, it has led States to seek and to acquire jurisdiction over nonresident tortfeasors whose purely out-of-state activities produce domestic consequences. Second, state courts have legitimately read their jurisdiction expansively when a cause of action centers in an area in which the forum State possesses a manifest regulatory interest. *E.g.,* McGee v. International Life Ins. Co., 355 U.S. 220 (1957) (insurance regulation); Travelers Health Assn. v. Virginia, 339 U.S. 643 (1950) (blue sky laws). . . . Finally, a State like Delaware has a recognized interest in affording a convenient forum for supervising and overseeing the affairs of an entity that is purely the creation of that State's law. For example, even following our decision in *International Shoe*, New York courts were permitted to exercise complete judicial authority over nonresident beneficiaries of a trust created under state law, even though, unlike appellants here, the beneficiaries personally entered into no association whatsoever with New York. I, of course, am not suggesting that Delaware's varied interests would justify its acceptance of jurisdiction over any transaction touching upon the affairs of its domestic corporations. But a derivative action which raises allegations of abuses of the basic management of an institution whose existence is created by the State and whose powers and duties are defined by state law fundamentally implicates the public policies of that forum.

To be sure, the Court is not blind to these considerations. It notes that the State's interests "may support the application of Delaware law to resolve any controversy over appellants' actions in their capacities as officers and directors." But this, the Court argues, pertains to choice of law, not jurisdiction. I recognize that the jurisdictional and choice-of-law inquiries are not identical. Hanson v. Denckla, 357 U.S. 235, 254 (1958). But I would not compartmentalize thinking in this area quite so rigidly as it seems to me the Court does today, for both inquiries "are often closely related and to a substantial degree depend upon similar considerations" (Black, J., dissenting). In either case an important linchpin is the extent of contacts between the controversy, the parties, and the forum State. While constitutional limitations on the choice of law are by no means settled, important considerations certainly include the expectancies of the parties and the fairness of governing the defendants' acts and behavior by rules of conduct created by a given jurisdiction. See, e.g., Restatement (Second) of Conflict of Laws §6 (1971) (hereafter Restatement). These same factors bear upon the propriety of a State's exercising jurisdiction over a legal dispute. At the minimum, the decision that it is fair to bind a defendant by a State's laws and rules should prove to be highly relevant to the fairness of permitting that same State to accept jurisdiction for adjudicating the controversy.

Furthermore, I believe that practical considerations argue in favor of seeking to bridge the distance between the choice-of-law and jurisdictional inquiries. Even when a court would apply the law of a different forum, as a general rule it will feel less knowledgeable and comfortable in interpretation, and less interested in fostering the policies of that foreign jurisdiction, than would the courts established by the State that provides the applicable law. Obviously, such choice-of-law problems cannot entirely be avoided in a diverse legal system such as our own. Nonetheless, when a suitor seeks to lodge a suit in a State with a substantial interest in seeing its own law applied to the transaction in question, we could wisely act to minimize conflicts, confusion, and uncertainty by adopting a liberal view of jurisdiction, unless considerations of fairness or efficiency strongly point in the opposite direction.

This case is not one where, in my judgment, this preference for jurisdiction is adequately answered. Certainly nothing said by the Court persuades me that it would be unfair to subject appellants to suit in Delaware. The fact that the record does not reveal whether they "set foot" or committed "act[s] related to [the] cause of action" in Delaware, is not decisive, for jurisdiction can be based strictly on out-of-state acts having foreseeable effects in the forum State. I have little difficulty in applying this principle to nonresident fiduciaries whose alleged breaches of trust are said to have substantial damaging effect on the financial posture of a resident corporation. Further, I cannot understand how the existence of minimum contacts in a constitutional sense is at all affected by Delaware's failure statutorily to express an interest in controlling corporate fiduciaries. To me this simply demonstrates that Delaware did not elect to assert jurisdiction to the extent the Constitution would allow. Nor would I view as controlling or even especially meaningful Delaware's failure to exact from appellants their consent to be sued. Once we have rejected the jurisdictional framework created in *Pennoyer*, I see no reason to rest jurisdiction on a fictional outgrowth of that system such as the existence of a consent statute, expressed or implied.

I, therefore, would approach the minimum contacts analysis differently than does the Court. Crucial to me is the fact that appellants voluntarily associated themselves with the State of Delaware, "invoking the benefits and protections of its laws" by entering into a long-term and fragile relationship with one of its domestic corporations. They thereby elected to assume powers and to undertake responsibilities wholly derived from that State's rules and regulations, and to become eligible for those benefits that Delaware law makes available to its corporations' officials. E.g., Del. Code Ann., Tit. 8, §143 (1975) (interest-free loans); §145 (1975 ed. and Supp. 1976) (indemnification). While it is possible that countervailing issues of judicial efficiency and the like might clearly favor a different forum, they do not appear on the meager record before us; and, of course, we are concerned solely with "minimum" contacts, not the "best" contacts. I thus do not believe that it is unfair to insist that appellants make themselves available to suit in a competent forum that

Delaware might create for vindication of its important public policies directly pertaining to appellants' fiduciary associations with the State.

■ NOTES ON REDUCED APPLICATION OF LIMITED JURISDICTION

1. Under *Pennoyer* and *Harris,* Delaware would have jurisdiction in Heitner's derivative suit against Shaffer, wouldn't it? On the matter of *situs,* all 50 states agree that the location of shares of corporate stock is determined by the law of the state of incorporation, and Delaware law (unlike the law of the other 49 states) says the location of stock in a Delaware corporation is Delaware. (The other 49 states say the stock is located where the certificate is found.) Delaware law allowed Shaffer to defend his stock ownership rights only by submitting generally to Delaware jurisdiction (refusing to permit a "limited appearance"), but this fact would not have been fatal in the traditional scheme.

2. Look first at the big picture: *Shaffer* is constructive, isn't it, in revising our ideas about due process by insisting that jurisdiction rest on minimum contacts? The case means, doesn't it, that Epstein could not get jurisdiction in Maryland over Balk in North Carolina by garnishing the debt Harris owed Balk when Harris ventured into Maryland? And Mitchell could not sue Neff for legal fees by attaching real property that Neff owned in Oregon, although he might well be able to sue Neff based on minimum contacts? Doesn't *Shaffer* mean *quasi-in-rem* (type 2) jurisdiction is dead, at least in its most common form as a jurisdictional "hook"?

3. Like *Pennoyer* before it, *Shaffer* recognizes exceptions. Be sure you locate the passages in *Shaffer* that relate to the following:

(a) A wife in Illinois, wishes to divorce her husband. Assume that she left the marital domicile in Texas while he remained there. Can she divorce him in Illinois?

(b) A Kentucky claimant obtains in Kentucky, on the basis of personal service on the defendant there, a judgment for $500,000 on account of an accident there, and the judgment is unsatisfied. The defendant, who has never been in Arizona and has no other connections with Arizona, owns a 50-acre plot of land near Flagstaff that he inherited from his rich uncle, which can be subdivided and sold as residential lots, so its market value exceeds $2 million. The Kentucky claimant brings suit in Arizona on the Kentucky judgment, and defendant moves to dismiss for lack of minimum contacts. How should the court rule, and why?

(c) Suppose Baker of Texas hires Alden, also from Texas, to perform risky cosmetic surgery, in an operation that costs $52,000, and is not covered by insurance. The surgery performed, Baker refuses to pay and prepares to

emigrate to Scotland. He liquidates his property and deposits the proceeds in Citybank in New York. Alden files suit in Texas, seeking $70,000 (including interest and attorneys' fees under their contract) and serves Baker personally in Texas (he has not yet left). Alden also obtains a writ of garnishment in New York and serves it on Citybank, directing it to hold $70,000 of Baker's deposits. Baker seeks to dissolve the writ in New York on ground that the court there lacks jurisdiction. How should the court rule, and why? Suppose Baker argues that the attachment violates due process under the *Fuentes* line of cases because it was obtained *ex parte*. What issues does the latter argument raise?

4. Does *Shaffer* hold that Delaware cannot exercise jurisdiction over R.F. Shaffer? Shortly after *Shaffer* was decided, the Delaware legislature enacted a statute providing that every nonresident who "accepts election or appointment as a director, trustee or member of the governing body" of a Delaware corporation is "deemed thereby to have consented to the appointment of the registered agent of such corporation (or, if there is none, the Secretary of State)" for service of process in derivative suits alleging breach of duty to the corporation. See 10 Del. Code §3114. Would exercising jurisdiction in Delaware under this statute violate the minimum contacts standard? Note the comments by Justice Brennan about the benefits that nonresident directors obtain under Delaware law. And see Armstrong v. Pomerance, 423 A.2d 174 (Del. 1980), holding the statute constitutional when challenged under *Shaffer*. If it is constitutional to assert jurisdiction in Delaware over a nonresident director of a Delaware corporation based on a rifle-shot statute aimed specifically at this situation, why is it *un*constitutional to do so on the basis of seizing stock in Delaware? Does it matter that the statute applies across the board to any suit brought in the Delaware Chancery Court?

■ PROBLEM 3-B. Slip and Fall

Christine Carter, a 30-year-old woman, lives in San Francisco. In 2010, she was notified that her paternal uncle Lawrence Carter, late of Philadelphia, Pennsylvania, had died and that she was named in his will as recipient of Berwyn Farm, a 70-acre parcel of wooded land in Lower Merion Township in Pennsylvania fronting on Spring Mill Road. On advice of counsel, Carter filed the necessary papers in the Pennsylvania probate proceedings accepting the bequest.

Carter has never been in Pennsylvania or engaged in any activities connected with the state. She had met Uncle Lawrence at family gatherings in California and Massachusetts, where most of the Carter forbears resided. Apparently, comments she made to her uncle about "returning to a simpler life in natural surroundings" resonated with him, which is why he wanted her to have Berwyn Farm. Through her California lawyer, with the help of a realtor in Philadelphia, Carter arranged for a caretaker to reside in the house on Berwyn Farm to do upkeep and chores.

In the winter of 2011, Michael Mason was walking on the public sidewalk along Spring Mill Road adjacent to Berwyn Farm. Snow had fallen four days earlier, and it had turned icy and slick. The caretaker had not shoveled the walk or applied salt or de-icing compound. Mason fell and seriously injured himself.

In Superior Court in Montgomery County, Mason filed suit naming Christine Carter and the caretaker as defendants. The complaint alleged that Carter had a duty to "keep the premises safe for pedestrians," that she as owner had been negligent in failing to clear the sidewalk, resulting in "hazardous conditions that caused plaintiff's injury." A local ordinance requires owners of property to clear sidewalks of snow within three days.

Through a lawyer in Pennsylvania, Carter moved to dismiss for lack of jurisdiction. The Pennsylvania long-arm statute, 42 Pa. Cons. Stat. Ann. §5322, is similar to the Illinois statute construed in *Gray*. It authorizes jurisdiction over nonresidents on claims arising from "transacting any business" in Pennsylvania, or "having an interest in, using, or possessing real property in this Commonwealth," or causing "harm or tortious injury" by any "act or omission" in Pennsylvania or "outside this Commonwealth." The statute also has a clause authorizing Pennsylvania courts to exercise jurisdiction over nonresidents "to the fullest extent allowed" by the United States Constitution.

Is Carter subject to jurisdiction in Pennsylvania on Mason's claim? If Mason were to win judgment for an amount exceeding the proceeds from the sale of Berwyn Farm in aid of execution, would the Pennsylvania judgment be entitled to full faith and credit in California if Mason sued on the judgment in California to obtain any amount that remained unsatisfied by the sale of Berwyn Farm?

■ NOTES ON THE CONTINUING VIABILITY OF *IN REM* JURISDICTION

1. In Mason's suit against Carter in Problem 3-B, the argument favoring jurisdiction stresses Carter's ownership of Berwyn Farm, and the obligations of a landowner, doesn't it? How should the argument favoring jurisdiction be shaped, in light of *Shaffer*?

2. *Shaffer* dealt a mortal blow to *quasi-in-rem* type 2 jurisdiction of the sort exercised in *Harris*, but did not rule out *quasi-in-rem* type 1 jurisdiction, did it? And *Shaffer* even seemed to preserve what it called *quasi-in-rem* type 2 jurisdiction in suits to enforce landowner duties. See footnotes 24 and 25 of

Shaffer and accompanying text, supra. What else fits that category? See Notes on Traditional Terms and Categories (Section A1, supra).

3. What about "true" or "pure" assertions of jurisdiction *in rem*? Consider quiet title suits, where the purpose is to determine ownership and rights in real property. Consider probate proceedings, where the purpose is to wind up and distribute the assets of a decedent's estate. Or consider dissolution proceedings in bankruptcy, where the purpose is to wind up the affairs of a failed business or other debtor and distribute what is left among creditors. To secure coherent outcomes, every such suit must go forward in a single forum, and (if all the assets are in one place) the forum should be located where the assets are, shouldn't it?

4. The Anticybersquatting Protection Act of 1999 creates a cause of action for persons or businesses whose trade or business name has been in effect pirated by others in what amounts to attempts to exact ransom: The former are disabled from using their names because others have registered them as internet sites, or the registrant is conducting business that in effect sponges or steals from the former. The statute provides that the owner of a mark "may file an in rem civil action against a domain name in the judicial district" where the registrar or registry of such name is located, for the sole purpose of ordering the "forfeiture or cancellation" of the name, or its transfer "to the owner of the mark." See 15 USC §1125(d)(2)(A)-(D); Nike, Inc. v. Nike Pioneer.com, 2010 WL 4393896 (E.D. Va. 2010) (authorizing service of process by email in one such suit brought in Virginia against alleged cybersquatting names including variations of the word "Nike").

WORLD-WIDE VOLKSWAGEN CORP. v. WOODSON

United States Supreme Court
444 U.S. 286 (1980)

Mr. Justice WHITE delivered the opinion of the Court.

I

[While driving through Oklahoma in the course of moving from New York to Arizona, the Robinson family was involved in a two-car collision that severely burned Kay Robinson and her two children. Mr. and Mrs. Robinson brought a product liability suit in state court in Oklahoma. Named as defendants were the manufacturer of their car (Audi), importer Volkswagen of America (Volkswagen), regional distributor World-Wide, and the retail dealer Seaway in Messina, New York, who sold the car to the Robinsons (Seaway). The other driver "does not figure" in the suit.

Seaway, World-Wide, and Volkswagen entered special appearances seeking dismissal on the ground that exercising jurisdiction over them would violate due process under *International Shoe.* In support, the moving parties developed these points: Seaway and World-Wide are incorporated and have their principal places of business in New York. World-Wide distributes vehicles, parts, and accessories to retailers in New York, New Jersey, and Connecticut. The two are "fully independent corporations," related to one another and to Volkswagen and Audi only by contract. There is no evidence that Seaway or World-Wide does business in Oklahoma, ships to or sells products in Oklahoma, has agents to receive process in Oklahoma, or advertises in media calculated to reach Oklahoma. Indeed, there was no showing that any car sold by Seaway or World-Wide ever entered Oklahoma, aside from the vehicle involved in the present suit.

The trial court rejected the attempts by Seaway, World-Wide, and Volkswagen to get the case dismissed as to them. They filed a petition for a writ of prohibition blocking the trial court from going forward with them in the case, but the writ was denied. Seaway and World-Wide appealed to the Oklahoma Supreme Court, which rejected their claim. (Volkswagen did not pursue the matter in the Oklahoma Supreme Court. Both Volkswagen and Audi remain as defendants.)]

II

The Due Process Clause of the Fourteenth Amendment limits the power of a state court to render a valid personal judgment against a nonresident defendant. A judgment rendered in violation of due process is void in the rendering State and is not entitled to full faith and credit elsewhere. Due process requires that the defendant be given adequate notice of the suit, and be subject to the personal jurisdiction of the court, International Shoe Co. v. Washington, 326 U.S. 310 (1945). In the present case, it is not contended that notice was inadequate; the only question is whether these particular petitioners were subject to the jurisdiction of the Oklahoma courts.

As has long been settled, and as we reaffirm today, a state court may exercise personal jurisdiction over a nonresident defendant only so long as there exist "minimum contacts" between the defendant and the forum State. The concept of minimum contacts, in turn, can be seen to perform two related, but distinguishable, functions. It protects the defendant against the burdens of litigating in a distant or inconvenient forum. And it acts to ensure that the States through their courts, do not reach out beyond the limits imposed on them by their status as coequal sovereigns in a federal system.

The protection against inconvenient litigation is typically described in terms of "reasonableness" or "fairness." We have said that the defendant's contacts with the forum State must be such that maintenance of the suit "does not offend 'traditional notions of fair play and substantial justice.'" *International Shoe,* quoting *Milliken.* The relationship between the defendant and the forum must be such that it is "reasonable . . . to require the corporation to defend the particular suit which is brought there." Implicit in this emphasis on reasonableness is the understanding that the burden on the defendant, while always a primary concern, will in an appropriate case be considered in light of other relevant factors, including the forum State's interest in adjudicating the dispute, see *McGee*; the plaintiff's interest in obtaining convenient and effective relief, at least when that interest is not adequately protected by the plaintiff's power to choose the forum; the interstate judicial system's interest in obtaining the most efficient resolution of controversies; and the shared interest of the several States in furthering fundamental substantive social policies.

The limits imposed on state jurisdiction by the Due Process Clause, in its role as a guarantor against inconvenient litigation, have been substantially relaxed over the years. As we noted in *McGee*, this trend is largely attributable to a fundamental transformation in the American economy:

> Today many commercial transactions touch two or more States and may involve parties separated by the full continent. With this increasing nationalization of commerce has come a great increase in the amount of business conducted by mail across state lines. At the same time modern transportation and communication have made it much less burdensome for a party sued to defend himself in a State where he engages in economic activity.

The historical developments noted in *McGee*, of course, have only accelerated in the generation since that case was decided.

Nevertheless, we have never accepted the proposition that state lines are irrelevant for jurisdictional purposes, nor could we, and remain faithful to the principles of interstate federalism embodied in the Constitution. The economic interdependence of the States was foreseen and desired by the Framers. In the Commerce Clause, they provided that the Nation was to be a common market, a "free trade unit" in which the States are debarred from acting as separable economic entities. But the Framers also intended that the States retain many essential attributes of sovereignty, including, in particular, the sovereign power to try causes in their courts. The sovereignty of each State, in turn, implied a limitation on the sovereignty of all of its sister States—a limitation express or implicit in both the original scheme of the Constitution and the Fourteenth Amendment.

Hence, even while abandoning the shibboleth that "[t]he authority of every tribunal is necessarily restricted by the territorial limits of the State in which it is established," *Pennoyer*, we emphasized that the reasonableness of asserting jurisdiction over the defendant must be assessed "in the context of our federal system of government," *International Shoe*, and stressed that the Due Process Clause ensures not only fairness, but also the "orderly administration of the laws." As we noted in *Hanson*:

As technological progress has increased the flow of commerce between the States, the need for jurisdiction over nonresidents has undergone a similar increase. At the same time, progress in communications and transportation has made the defense of a suit in a foreign tribunal less burdensome. In response to these changes, the requirements for personal jurisdiction over nonresidents have evolved from the rigid rule of *Pennoyer* to the flexible standard of *International Shoe*. But it is a mistake to assume that this trend heralds the eventual demise of all restrictions on the personal jurisdiction of state courts. Those restrictions are more than a guarantee of immunity from inconvenient or distant litigation. They are a consequence of territorial limitations on the power of the respective States.

Thus, the Due Process Clause "does not contemplate that a state may make binding a judgment in personam against an individual or corporate defendant with which the state has no contacts, ties, or relations." *International Shoe*. Even if the defendant would suffer minimal or no inconvenience from being forced to litigate before the tribunals of another State; even if the forum State has a strong interest in applying its law to the controversy; even if the forum State is the most convenient location for litigation, the Due Process Clause, acting as an instrument of interstate federalism, may sometimes act to divest the State of its power to render a valid judgment. *Hanson*.

III

Applying these principles to the case at hand, we find in the record before us a total absence of those affiliating circumstances that are a necessary predicate to any exercise of state-court jurisdiction. Petitioners carry on no activity whatsoever in Oklahoma. They close no sales and perform no services there. They avail themselves of none of the privileges and benefits of Oklahoma law. They solicit no business there either through salespersons or through advertising reasonably calculated to reach the State. Nor does the record show that they regularly sell cars at wholesale or retail to Oklahoma customers or residents or that they indirectly, through others, serve or seek to serve the Oklahoma market. In short, respondents seek to base jurisdiction on one, isolated occurrence and whatever inferences can be drawn therefrom: the fortuitous circumstance that a single Audi automobile, sold in New York to New York residents, happened to suffer an accident while passing through Oklahoma.

It is argued, however, that because an automobile is mobile by its very design and purpose it was "foreseeable" that the Robinsons' Audi would cause injury in Oklahoma. Yet "foreseeability" alone has never been a sufficient benchmark for personal jurisdiction under the Due Process Clause. In *Hanson*, it was no doubt foreseeable that the settlor of a Delaware trust would subsequently move to Florida and seek to exercise a power of appointment there;

yet we held that Florida courts could not constitutionally exercise jurisdiction over a Delaware trustee that had no other contacts with the forum State. In Kulko v. California Superior Court, 436 U.S. 84 (1978), it was surely "foreseeable" that a divorced wife would move to California from New York, the domicile of the marriage, and that a minor daughter would live with the mother. Yet we held that California could not exercise jurisdiction in a child-support action over the former husband who had remained in New York.

If foreseeability were the criterion, a local California tire retailer could be forced to defend in Pennsylvania when a blowout occurs there, see Erlanger Mills, Inc. v. Cohoes Fibre Mills, Inc., 239 F.2d 502, 507 (4th Cir. 1956); a Wisconsin seller of a defective automobile jack could be haled before a distant court for damage caused in New Jersey, Reilly v. Phil Tolkan Pontiac, Inc., 372 F. Supp. 1205 (N.J. 1974); or a Florida soft-drink concessionaire could be summoned to Alaska to account for injuries happening there, see Uppgren v. Executive Aviation Services, Inc., 304 F. Supp. 165, 170-171 (Minn. 1969). Every seller of chattels would in effect appoint the chattel his agent for service of process. His amenability to suit would travel with the chattel. We recently abandoned the outworn rule of Harris v. Balk, 198 U.S. 215 (1905), that the interest of a creditor in a debt could be extinguished or otherwise affected by any State having transitory jurisdiction over the debtor. Shaffer v. Heitner, 433 U.S. 186 (1977). Having inferred the mechanical rule that a creditor's amenability to a quasi in rem action travels with his debtor, we are unwilling to endorse an analogous principle in the present case.[11]

This is not to say, of course, that foreseeability is wholly irrelevant. But the foreseeability that is critical to due process analysis is not the mere likelihood that a product will find its way into the forum State. Rather, it is that the defendant's conduct and connection with the forum State are such that he should reasonably anticipate being haled into court there. The Due Process Clause, by ensuring the "orderly administration of the laws," *International Shoe*, gives a degree of predictability to the legal system that allows potential defendants to structure their primary conduct with some minimum assurance as to where that conduct will and will not render them liable to suit.

When a corporation "purposefully avails itself of the privilege of conducting activities within the forum State," *Hanson*, it has clear notice that it is

---

[11] Respondents' counsel, at oral argument, sought to limit the reach of the foreseeability standard by suggesting that there is something unique about automobiles. It is true that automobiles are uniquely mobile, that they did play a crucial role in the expansion of personal jurisdiction through the fiction of implied consent, e.g., Hess v. Pawloski, 274 U.S. 352 (1927), and that some of the cases have treated the automobile as a "dangerous instrumentality." But today, under the regime of *International Shoe*, we see no difference for jurisdictional purposes between an automobile and any other chattel. The "dangerous instrumentality" concept apparently was never used to support personal jurisdiction; and to the extent it has relevance today it bears not on jurisdiction but on the possible desirability of imposing substantive principles of tort law such as strict liability.

subject to suit there, and can act to alleviate the risk of burdensome litigation by procuring insurance, passing the expected costs on to customers, or, if the risks are too great, severing its connection with the State. Hence if the sale of a product of a manufacturer or distributor such as Audi or Volkswagen is not simply an isolated occurrence, but arises from the efforts of the manufacturer or distributor to serve directly or indirectly, the market for its product in other States, it is not unreasonable to subject it to suit in one of those States if its allegedly defective merchandise has there been the source of injury to its owner or to others. The forum State does not exceed its powers under the Due Process Clause if it asserts personal jurisdiction over a corporation that delivers its products into the stream of commerce with the expectation that they will be purchased by consumers in the forum State. Cf. Gray v. American Radiator & Standard Sanitary Corp., 176 N.E.2d 761 (Ill. 1961).

But there is no such or similar basis for Oklahoma jurisdiction over World-Wide or Seaway in this case. Seaway's sales are made in Massena, New York. World-Wide's market, although substantially larger, is limited to dealers in New York, New Jersey, and Connecticut. There is no evidence of record that any automobiles distributed by World-Wide are sold to retail customers outside this tristate area. It is foreseeable that the purchasers of automobiles sold by World-Wide and Seaway may take them to Oklahoma. But the mere "unilateral activity of those who claim some relationship with a nonresident defendant cannot satisfy the requirement of contact with the forum State." *Hanson.*

In a variant on the previous argument, it is contended that jurisdiction can be supported by the fact that petitioners earn substantial revenue from goods used in Oklahoma. The Oklahoma Supreme Court so found, drawing the inference that because one automobile sold by petitioners had been used in Oklahoma, others might have been used there also. While this inference seems less than compelling on the facts of the instant case, we need not question the court's factual findings in order to reject its reasoning.

This argument seems to make the point that the purchase of automobiles in New York, from which the petitioners earn substantial revenue, would not occur but for the fact that the automobiles are capable of use in distant States like Oklahoma. Respondents observe that the very purpose of an automobile is to travel, and that travel of automobiles sold by petitioners is facilitated by an extensive chain of Volkswagen service centers throughout the country, including some in Oklahoma. However, financial benefits accruing to the defendant from a collateral relation to the forum State will not support jurisdiction if they do not stem from a constitutionally cognizable contact with that State. See *Kulko.* In our view, whatever marginal revenues petitioners may receive by virtue of the fact that their products are capable of use in Oklahoma is far too attenuated a contact to justify that State's exercise of in personam jurisdiction over them.

Because we find that petitioners have no "contacts, ties, or relations" with the State of Oklahoma, the judgment of the Supreme Court of Oklahoma is reversed.

Mr. Justice Marshall, with whom Mr. Justice Blackmun joins, dissenting. . . .

Petitioners are sellers of a product whose utility derives from its mobility. The unique importance of the automobile in today's society . . . needs no further elaboration. Petitioners know that their customers buy cars not only to make short trips, but also to travel long distances. In fact, the nationwide service network with which they are affiliated was designed to facilitate and encourage such travel. Seaway would be unlikely to sell many cars if authorized service were available only in Massena, N.Y. Moreover, local dealers normally derive a substantial portion of their revenues from their service operations and thereby obtain a further economic benefit from the opportunity to service cars which were sold in other States. It is apparent that petitioners have not attempted to minimize the chance that their activities will have effects in other States; on the contrary, they have chosen to do business in a way that increases that chance, because it is to their economic advantage to do so.

To be sure, petitioners could not know in advance that this particular automobile would be driven to Oklahoma. They must have anticipated, however, that a substantial portion of the cars they sold would travel out of New York. Seaway, a local dealer in the second most populous State, and World-Wide, one of only seven regional Audi distributors in the entire country, would scarcely have been surprised to learn that a car sold by them had been driven in Oklahoma on Interstate 44, a heavily traveled transcontinental highway. In the case of the distributor, in particular, the probability that some of the cars it sells will be driven in every one of the contiguous States must amount to a virtual certainty. This knowledge should alert a reasonable businessman to the likelihood that a defect in the product might manifest itself in the forum State—not because of some unpredictable, aberrant, unilateral action by a single buyer, but in the normal course of the operation of the vehicles for their intended purpose. . . .

The majority apparently acknowledges that if a product is purchased in the forum State by a consumer, that State may assert jurisdiction over everyone in the chain of distribution. With this I agree. But I cannot agree that jurisdiction is necessarily lacking if the product enters the State not through the channels of distribution but in the course of its intended use by the consumer. We have recognized the role played by the automobile in the expansion of our notions of personal jurisdiction. Unlike most other chattels, which may find their way into States far from where they were purchased because their owner takes them there, the intended use of the automobile is precisely as a means of traveling from one place to another. In such a case, it is highly artificial to restrict the concept of the "stream of commerce" to the chain of distribution from the manufacturer to the ultimate consumer.

. . .

[Dissenting opinion of Justice Blackmun is omitted.]

Justice BRENNAN, dissenting. . . .

The Court's opinions focus tightly on the existence of contacts between the forum and the defendant. In so doing, they accord too little weight to the strength of the forum State's interest in the case and fail to explore whether there would be any actual inconvenience to the defendant. . . .

Surely *International Shoe* contemplated that the significance of the contacts necessary to support jurisdiction would diminish if some other consideration helped establish that jurisdiction would be fair and reasonable. The interests of the State and other parties in proceeding with the case in a particular forum are such considerations. *McGee*, for instance, accorded great importance to a State's "manifest interest in providing effective means of redress" for its citizens.

Another consideration is the actual burden a defendant must bear in defending the suit in the forum. Because lesser burdens reduce the unfairness to the defendant, jurisdiction may be justified despite less significant contacts. The burden, of course, must be of constitutional dimension. Due process limits on jurisdiction do not protect a defendant from all inconvenience of travel, and it would not be sensible to make the constitutional rule turn solely on the number of miles the defendant must travel to the courtroom.[1] Instead, the constitutionally significant "burden" to be analyzed relates to the mobility of the defendant's defense. For instance, if having to travel to a foreign forum would hamper the defense because witnesses or evidence or the defendant himself were immobile, or if there were a disproportionately large number of witnesses or amount of evidence that would have to be transported at the defendant's expense, or if being away from home for the duration of the trial would work some special hardship on the defendant, then the Constitution would require special consideration for the defendant's interests.

That considerations other than contacts between the forum and the defendant are relevant necessarily means that the Constitution does not require that trial be held in the State which has the "best contacts" with the defendant. The defendant has no constitutional entitlement to the best forum or, for that matter, to any particular forum. Under even the most restrictive view of *International Shoe*, several States could have jurisdiction

---

[1] In fact, a courtroom just across the state line from a defendant may often be far more convenient for the defendant than a courtroom in a distant corner of his own State.

over a particular cause of action. We need only determine whether the forum States in these cases satisfy the constitutional minimum. . . .

[T]he interest of the forum State and its connection to the litigation is strong. The automobile accident underlying the litigation occurred in Oklahoma. The plaintiffs were hospitalized in Oklahoma when they brought suit. Essential witnesses and evidence were in Oklahoma. The State has a legitimate interest in enforcing its laws designed to keep its highway system safe, and the trial can proceed at least as efficiently in Oklahoma as anywhere else.

The petitioners are not unconnected with the forum. Although both sell automobiles within limited sales territories, each sold the automobile which in fact was driven to Oklahoma where it was involved in an accident.[8] It may be true, as the Court suggests, that each sincerely intended to limit its commercial impact to the limited territory, and that each intended to accept the benefits and protection of the laws only of those States within the territory. But obviously these were unrealistic hopes that cannot be treated as an automatic constitutional shield.[9]

An automobile simply is not a stationary item or one designed to be used in one place. An automobile is intended to be moved around. Someone in the business of selling large numbers of automobiles can hardly plead ignorance of their mobility or pretend that the automobiles stay put after they are sold. It is not merely that a dealer in automobiles foresees that they will move. The dealer actually intends that the purchasers will use the automobiles to travel to distant States where the dealer does not directly "do business." The sale of an automobile does purposefully inject the vehicle into the stream of interstate commerce so that it can travel to distant States. . . .

The Court accepts that a State may exercise jurisdiction over a distributor which "serves" that State "indirectly" by "deliver[ing] its products into the stream of commerce with the expectation that they will be purchased by consumers in the forum State." It is difficult to see why the Constitution should distinguish between a case involving goods which reach a distant State through a chain of distribution and a case involving goods which reach the same State because a consumer, using them as the dealer knew the customer would, took them there. In each case the seller purposefully injects the goods

---

[8] On the basis of this fact the state court inferred that the petitioners derived substantial revenue from goods used in Oklahoma. The inference is not without support. Certainly, were use of goods accepted as a relevant contact, a plaintiff would not need to have an exact count of the number of petitioners' cars that are used in Oklahoma.

[9] Moreover, imposing liability in this case would not so undermine certainty as to destroy an automobile dealer's ability to do business. According jurisdiction does not expand liability except in the marginal case where a plaintiff cannot afford to bring an action except in the plaintiff's own State. In addition, these petitioners are represented by insurance companies. They not only could, but did, purchase insurance to protect them should they stand trial and lose the case. The costs of the insurance no doubt are passed on to customers.

into the stream of commerce and those goods predictably are used in the forum State.[12]

Furthermore, an automobile seller derives substantial benefits from States other than its own. A large part of the value of automobiles is the extensive, nationwide network of highways. Significant portions of that network have been constructed by and are maintained by the individual States, including Oklahoma. The States, through their highway programs, contribute in a very direct and important way to the value of petitioners' businesses. Additionally, a network of other related dealerships with their service departments operates throughout the country under the protection of the laws of the various States, including Oklahoma, and enhances the value of petitioners' businesses by facilitating their customers' traveling.

Thus, the Court errs in its conclusion that "petitioners have no 'contacts, ties, or relations'" with Oklahoma. There obviously are contacts, and, given Oklahoma's connection to the litigation, the contacts are sufficiently significant to make it fair and reasonable for the petitioners to submit to Oklahoma's jurisdiction.

It may be that affirmance of the judgments in these cases would approach the outer limits of *International Shoe*'s jurisdictional principle. But that principle, with its almost exclusive focus on the rights of defendants, may be outdated. . . .

As the Court acknowledges, both the nationalization of commerce and the ease of transportation and communication have accelerated in the generation since 1957. The model of society on which the *International Shoe* Court based its opinion is no longer accurate. Business people, no matter how local their businesses, cannot assume that goods remain in the business' locality. Customers and goods can be anywhere else in the country usually in a matter of hours and always in a matter of a very few days.

In answering the question whether or not it is fair and reasonable to allow a particular forum to hold a trial binding on a particular defendant, the interests of the forum state and other parties loom large in today's world and surely are entitled to as much weight as are the interests of the defendant. The "orderly administration of the laws" provides a firm basis for according some protection to the interests of plaintiffs and States as well as of defendants. Certainly, I cannot see how a defendant's right to due process is violated if the defendant suffers no inconvenience. . . .

The Court's opinion . . . suggests that the defendant ought to be subject to a State's jurisdiction only if he has contacts with the State "such that he should reasonably anticipate being haled into court there." There is nothing unreasonable or unfair, however, about recognizing commercial reality. Given

---

[12] The manufacturer in [*Gray,*] the case cited by the Court, had no more control over which States its goods would reach than did the petitioners in this case.

the tremendous mobility of goods and people, and the inability of business-men to control where goods are taken by customers (or retailers), I do not think that the defendant should be in complete control of the geographical stretch of his amenability to suit. Jurisdiction is no longer premised on the notion that nonresident defendants have somehow impliedly consented to suit. People should understand that they are held responsible for the conse-quences of their actions and that in our society most actions have conse-quences affecting many States. When an action in fact causes injury in another State, the actor should be prepared to answer for it there unless defending in that State would be unfair for some reason other than that a state boundary must be crossed.

In effect the Court is allowing defendants to assert the sovereign rights of their home States. The expressed fear is that otherwise all limits on personal jurisdiction would disappear. But the argument's premise is wrong. I would not abolish limits on jurisdiction or strip state boundaries of all significance; I would still require the plaintiff to demonstrate sufficient contacts among the parties, the forum, and the litigation to make the forum a reasonable State in which to hold the trial.

. . .

■ FURTHER NOTES ON STREAM OF COMMERCE

1. *World-Wide* approves in dictum a version of the "stream of commerce" theory, doesn't it? The Court's statement of this theory refers to "products" in the stream of commerce (more than units) that enter the state through the "efforts" of the maker and with the "expectation" that they will wind up in the forum.

(a) At the core of *World-Wide* is the proposition that there is a critical difference between the case where one "delivers its products into the stream of commerce" expecting that they will be "purchased by consumers" in the forum state and the case where a product is bought locally and the consumer takes the goods to a distant state that becomes the forum in a suit alleging product defect. What is the difference, and why does the Court think it is important? Do you agree?

(b) It is not enough, the Court says, that it might be "foreseeable" that the products will wind up in the forum state. "Foreseeability" counts, however, when the focus is on what the defendant could anticipate from "conduct and connection with the forum state." Why isn't foreseeability enough? Note the argument of all three dissenters that cars are different. The majority (Court's footnote 11) rejects this argument, seeing no difference between a car and "any other chattel." Are cars a special case? Would it make sense to *sustain*

jurisdiction in Oklahoma when a car causes injury, but not when a ladder or hair dryer bought in New York and taken to Oklahoma causes injury?

2. *World-Wide* says the due process standard of *International Shoe* turns on five factors: burden on defendant ("primary" factor); interest of the forum state; plaintiff's interest in effective relief; judicial system's interest in efficiency; shared interests of the states in advancing fundamental policies. How do these factors play out in this case? Do they shed useful light on the standard? In dissent, Justice Brennan suggests that the standard is "outmoded." What is the key for him?

3. Justice White says the minimum contacts standard keeps states from "reach[ing] out beyond the limits imposed on them by their status as coequal sovereigns in a federal system." That's straight out of *Pennoyer,* isn't it? Is it also visible in *International Shoe*? You will see when you read the *Bauxites* decision (Section E, infra), also written by Justice White, that the Court appeared to change its mind on this point. You will also see when you read the decisions in *Asahi* and *Nicastro* (coming up next) that the idea of state "sovereignty," as an element in the jurisdictional calculus, is making a comeback. If we remove this consideration, would it nevertheless play a role because of the other elements—the "interest" of the forum, the interest of the judicial system in efficiency, and the shared interests of the states in fundamental social policies? Does this consideration also come into play because of the *Hanson* requirement of purposeful availment?

4. In *World-Wide,* only Seaway (car dealer) and World-Wide (East Coast regional distributor) resisted jurisdiction. Manufacturer Audi and importer Volkswagen did not. Presumably, both have direct contact with the forum state because Audis were being sent directly from Germany to Oklahoma, so they have commercial contact with Oklahoma even if Seaway and World-Wide do not. Still, the claims in this case don't *arise out of* the commercial contacts that Audi and Volkswagen have with Oklahoma, do they? (The Robinsons bought their car in New York and drove it to Oklahoma.) Why, then, didn't Audi and Volkswagen contest jurisdiction? Consider the decision in Buckeye Boiler Co. v. Superior Court, 458 P.2d 57 (Cal. 1969), where a California plaintiff injured in that state by an exploding boiler sued the Ohio maker in California. The boiler had been sold outside California and brought into the state by the owner, and Buckeye Boiler Company never shipped to California a boiler like the one that exploded in this case. Still, the California court upheld jurisdiction because it concluded that the risks assumed by the defendant in sending *other kinds of boilers* into the state was so similar to the risks generating this suit that there could be nothing unfair about exercising jurisdiction. If *Buckeye Boiler* is right, would it follow that Audi and Volkswagen can be sued in Oklahoma in *World-Wide*?

5. Why did the Robinsons fight so hard to keep Seaway and World-Wide in the case? Isn't it clear that Audi and Volkswagen could pay the judgment, if plaintiffs prevailed? (The answer might surprise you: The Robinsons were still New York citizens when they filed, since the rule is that a person remains a citizen of the state she leaves until she gets to the state where she intends to live, and the Robinsons had not gotten to Arizona when the accident happened. Seaway and World-Wide were New York corporations. Audi and Volkswagen were foreign corporations, so the Robinsons could have sued them in federal court under diversity jurisdiction, or "alienage jurisdiction" as it is called when a U.S. citizen sues a foreign defendant. If the suit had been brought against Audi and Volkswagen *alone* in state court, they could have *removed* it to federal court. But adding Seaway and World-Wide meant there was not *complete* diversity between the Robinsons and all defendants, so the suit could *not* be removed. The Robinsons wanted to be in state court, and keeping Seaway and World-Wide in the case insured that result.)

ASAHI METAL INDUSTRY CO. v. SUPERIOR COURT

United States Supreme Court
480 U.S. 102 (1987)

Justice O'CONNOR announced the judgment of the Court and delivered the unanimous opinion of the Court with respect to Part I, the opinion of the Court with respect to Part II-B, in which THE CHIEF JUSTICE, Justice BRENNAN, Justice WHITE, Justice MARSHALL, Justice BLACKMUN, Justice POWELL, and Justice STEVENS join, and an opinion with respect to Parts II-A and III, in which THE CHIEF JUSTICE, Justice POWELL, and Justice SCALIA join.

This case presents the question whether the mere awareness on the part of a foreign defendant that the components it manufactured, sold, and delivered outside the United States would reach the forum State in the stream of commerce constitutes "minimum contacts" between the defendant and the forum State such that the exercise of jurisdiction "does not offend 'traditional notions of fair play and substantial justice.'" International Shoe Co. v. Washington, 326 U.S. 310, 316 (1945), quoting Milliken v. Meyer, 311 U.S. 457, 463 (1940).

I

[While riding his Honda motorcycle in California, Gary Zurcher lost control and collided with a tractor. He was seriously injured and his wife, who was riding with him, was killed. Zurcher claimed the accident resulted from sudden loss of air and an explosion of the rear tire, and his product liability claim named as defendant Cheng Shin Rubber Industrial Company (maker of the inner tube) of Taiwan, along with others. Cheng Shin sought indemnity from other defendants, and from Asahi Metal Industry (maker of the valve assembly) of Japan. Zurcher's claims settled, leaving unresolved only Cheng Shin's indemnity claim against Asahi. The California Supreme Court upheld jurisdiction over Asahi in California.]

We granted certiorari, and now reverse.

II

A

... Since *World-Wide Volkswagen*, lower courts have been confronted with cases in which the defendant acted by placing a product in the stream of commerce, and the stream eventually swept defendant's product into the forum State, but the defendant did nothing else to purposefully avail itself of the market in the forum State. Some courts have understood the Due Process Clause, as interpreted in *World-Wide Volkswagen*, to allow an exercise of personal jurisdiction to be based on no more than the defendant's act of placing the product in the stream of commerce. Other courts have understood the Due Process Clause and the above-quoted language in *World-Wide Volkswagen* to require the action of the defendant to be more purposefully directed at the forum State than the mere act of placing a product in the stream of commerce.

. . .

We now find this latter position to be consonant with the requirements of due process. The "substantial connection," *Burger King*, between the defendant and the forum State necessary for a finding of minimum contacts must come about by *an action of the defendant purposefully directed toward the forum State*. The placement of a product into the stream of commerce, without more, is not an act of the defendant purposefully directed toward the forum State. Additional conduct of the defendant may indicate an intent or purpose to serve the market in the forum State, for example, designing the product for the market in the forum State, advertising in the forum State, establishing channels for providing regular advice to customers in the forum State, or marketing the product through a distributor who has agreed to serve as the sales agent in the forum State. But a defendant's awareness that the stream of commerce may or will sweep the product into the forum State does not convert the mere act of placing the product into the stream into an act purposefully directed toward the forum State.

Assuming, *arguendo,* that respondents have established Asahi's awareness that some of the valves sold to Cheng Shin would be incorporated into tire tubes sold in California, respondents have not demonstrated any action by Asahi to purposefully avail itself of the California market. Asahi does not do business in California. It has no office, agents, employees, or property in California. It does not advertise or otherwise solicit business in California. It did not create, control, or employ the distribution system that brought its valves to California. There is no evidence that Asahi designed its product in anticipation of sales in California. On the basis of these facts, the exertion of personal jurisdiction over Asahi by the Superior Court of California* exceeds the limits of due process.

B

The strictures of the Due Process Clause forbid a state court to exercise personal jurisdiction over Asahi under circumstances that would offend "'traditional notions of fair play and substantial justice.'" *International Shoe*, quoting Milliken v. Meyer.

We have previously explained that the determination of the reasonableness of the exercise of jurisdiction in each case will depend on an evaluation of several factors. A court must consider the burden on the defendant, the interests of the forum State, and the plaintiff's interest in obtaining relief. It must also weigh in its determination "the interstate judicial system's interest in obtaining the most efficient resolution of controversies; and the shared interest of the several States in furthering fundamental substantive social policies." *World-Wide Volkswagen*.

A consideration of these factors in the present case clearly reveals the unreasonableness of the assertion of jurisdiction over Asahi, even apart from the question of the placement of goods in the stream of commerce.

Certainly the burden on the defendant in this case is severe. Asahi has been commanded by the Supreme Court of California not only to traverse the distance between Asahi's headquarters in Japan and the Superior Court of California in and for the County of Solano, but also to submit its dispute with Cheng Shin to a foreign nation's judicial system. The unique burdens placed upon one who must defend oneself in a foreign legal system should have significant weight in assessing the reasonableness of stretching the long arm of personal jurisdiction over national borders.

When minimum contacts have been established, often the interests of the plaintiff and the forum in the exercise of jurisdiction will justify even the serious burdens placed on the alien defendant. In the present case, however, the interests of the plaintiff and the forum in California's assertion of jurisdiction over Asahi are slight. All that remains is a claim for indemnification asserted by Cheng Shin, a Taiwanese corporation, against Asahi. The transaction on which the indemnification claim is based took place in Taiwan; Asahi's components were shipped from Japan to Taiwan. Cheng Shin has not demonstrated that it is more convenient for it to litigate its indemnification claim against Asahi in California rather than in Taiwan or Japan.

---

* We have no occasion here to determine whether Congress could, consistent with the Due Process Clause of the Fifth Amendment, authorize federal court personal jurisdiction over alien defendants based on the aggregate of *national* contacts, rather than on the contacts between the defendant and the State in which the federal court sits.

Because the plaintiff is not a California resident, California's legitimate interests in the dispute have considerably diminished. The Supreme Court of California argued that the State had an interest in "protecting its consumers by ensuring that foreign manufacturers comply with the state's safety standards." The State Supreme Court's definition of California's interest, however, was overly broad. The dispute between Cheng Shin and Asahi is primarily about indemnification rather than safety standards. Moreover, it is not at all clear at this point that California law should govern the question whether a Japanese corporation should indemnify a Taiwanese corporation on the basis of a sale made in Taiwan and a shipment of goods from Japan to Taiwan. The possibility of being haled into a California court as a result of an accident involving Asahi's components undoubtedly creates an additional deterrent to the manufacture of unsafe components; however, similar pressures will be placed on Asahi by the purchasers of its components as long as those who use Asahi components in their final products, and sell those products in California, are subject to the application of California tort law.

World-Wide Volkswagen also admonished courts to take into consideration the interests of the "several States," in addition to the forum State, in the efficient judicial resolution of the dispute and the advancement of substantive policies. In the present case, this advice calls for a court to consider the procedural and substantive policies of other *nations* whose interests are affected by the assertion of jurisdiction by the California court. The procedural and substantive interests of other nations in a state court's assertion of jurisdiction over an alien defendant will differ from case to case. In every case, however, those interests, as well as the Federal interest in Government's foreign relations policies, will be best served by a careful inquiry into the reasonableness of the assertion of jurisdiction in the particular case, and an unwillingness to find the serious burdens on an alien defendant outweighed by minimal interests on the part of the plaintiff or the forum State. "Great care and reserve should be exercised when extending our notions of personal jurisdiction into the international field." United States v. First National City Bank, 379 U.S. 378, 404 (1965) (Harlan, J., dissenting).

Considering the international context, the heavy burden on the alien defendant, and the slight interests of the plaintiff and the forum State, the exercise of personal jurisdiction by a California court over Asahi in this instance would be unreasonable and unfair.

III

Because the facts of this case do not establish minimum contacts such that the exercise of personal jurisdiction is consistent with fair play and substantial justice, the judgment of the Supreme Court of California is reversed, and the case is remanded for further proceedings not inconsistent with this opinion.

It is so ordered.

Justice BRENNAN, with whom Justice WHITE, Justice MARSHALL, and Justice BLACKMUN join, concurring in part and concurring in the judgment.

I do not agree with the interpretation in Part II-A of the stream-of-commerce theory, nor with the conclusion that Asahi did not "purposely avail itself of the California market." I do agree, however, with the Court's conclusion in Part II-B that the exercise of personal jurisdiction over Asahi in this case would not comport with "fair play and substantial justice," *International Shoe Co.* This is one of those rare cases in which "minimum requirements inherent in the concept of 'fair play and substantial justice' . . . defeat the reasonableness of jurisdiction even [though] the defendant has purposefully engaged in forum activities." *Burger King.* I therefore join Parts I and II-B of the Court's opinion, and write separately to explain my disagreement with Part II-A.

Part II-A states that "a defendant's awareness that the stream of commerce may or will sweep the product into the forum State does not convert the mere act of placing the product into the stream into an act purposefully directed toward the forum State." Under this view, a plaintiff would be required to show "[a]dditional conduct" directed toward the forum before finding the exercise of jurisdiction over the defendant to be consistent with the Due Process Clause. I see no need for such a showing, however. The stream of commerce refers not to unpredictable currents or eddies, but to the regular and anticipated flow of products from manufacture to distribution to retail sale. As long as a participant in this process is aware that the final product is being marketed in the forum State, the possibility of a lawsuit there cannot come as a surprise. Nor will the litigation present a burden for which there is no corresponding benefit. A defendant who has placed goods in the stream of commerce benefits economically from the retail sale of the final product in the forum State, and indirectly benefits from the State's laws that regulate and facilitate commercial activity. These benefits accrue regardless of whether that participant directly conducts business in the forum State, or engages in additional conduct directed toward that State. Accordingly, most courts and commentators have found that jurisdiction premised on the placement of a product into the stream of commerce is consistent with the Due Process Clause, and have not required a showing of additional conduct.

. . .

In this case, the facts found by the California Supreme Court support its finding of minimum contacts. The court found that "[a]lthough Asahi did not design or control the system of distribution that carried its valve assemblies into California, Asahi was aware of the distribution system's operation, and it knew that it would benefit economically from the sale in California of products incorporating its components." Accordingly, I cannot join the determination in Part II-A that Asahi's regular and extensive sales of component parts to a manufacturer it knew was making regular sales of the final product in California is insufficient to establish minimum contacts with California.

Justice STEVENS, with whom Justice WHITE and Justice BLACKMUN join, concurring in part and concurring in the judgment.

The judgment of the Supreme Court of California should be reversed for the reasons stated in Part II-B of the Court's opinion. While I join Parts I and II-B, I do not join Part II-A for two reasons. First, it is not necessary to the Court's decision. . . .

Second, even assuming that the test ought to be formulated here, Part II-A misapplies it to the facts of this case. The plurality seems to assume that an unwavering line can be drawn between "mere awareness" that a component will find its way into the forum State and "purposeful availment" of the forum's market. Over the course of its dealings with Cheng Shin, Asahi has arguably engaged in a higher quantum of conduct than "[t]he placement of a product into the stream of commerce, without more. . . ." Whether or not this conduct rises to the level of purposeful availment requires a constitutional determination that is affected by the volume, the value, and the hazardous character of the components. In most circumstances I would be inclined to conclude that a regular course of dealing that results in deliveries of over 100,000 units annually over a period of several years would constitute "purposeful availment" even though the item delivered to the forum State was a standard product marketed throughout the world.

J. McINTYRE MACHINERY, LTD. v. NICASTRO

Supreme Court of the United States
131 S. Ct. 2780 (2011)

Justice KENNEDY announced the judgment of the Court and delivered an opinion, in which THE CHIEF JUSTICE, Justice SCALIA, and Justice THOMAS join.

. . .

I

This case arises from a product liability suit filed in New Jersey state court. Robert Nicastro seriously injured his hand while using a metal-shearing machine manufactured by J. McIntyre Machinery, Ltd. (J. McIntyre). The accident occurred in New Jersey, but the machine was manufactured in England, where J. McIntyre is incorporated and operates. The question here is whether the New Jersey courts have jurisdiction over J. McIntyre, notwithstanding the fact that the company at no time either marketed goods in the State or shipped them there. Nicastro was a plaintiff in the New Jersey trial court and is the respondent here; J. McIntyre was a defendant and is now the petitioner.

[When injured, Nicastro was working for Curcio Scrap Metal (CSM) in Saddle Brook, New Jersey. J. McIntyre did not sell the machine to CSM, but worked with McIntyre America, Ltd. to distribute its products in America. Although having similar names, J. McIntyre and McIntyre America had no common ownership or management, and it is not alleged that McIntyre America was "under J. McIntyre's control." At most four machines made by J. McIntyre "ended up in New Jersey" ("the record suggests only one"). McIntyre America billed itself as McIntyre UK's distributor, and McIntyre America structured its "advertising and sales efforts" in accord with J. McIntyre's directions and guidance. J. McIntyre sold some machines "on consignment" to McIntyre America.[4] J. McIntyre's officers "attended annual conventions for the scrap metal recycling industry" in the United States in order to advertise its machines, although not in New Jersey. J. McIntyre itself did not sell machines to American buyers other than McIntyre America. J. McIntyre held U.S. and European patents.]

[T]he New Jersey Supreme Court concluded that New Jersey courts could exercise jurisdiction over petitioner without contravention of the Due Process Clause. Jurisdiction was proper, in that court's view, because the injury occurred in New Jersey; because petitioner knew or reasonably should have known "that its products are distributed through a nationwide distribution system that might lead to those products being sold in any of the fifty states"; and because petitioner failed to "take some reasonable step to prevent the distribution of its products in this State."

Both the New Jersey Supreme Court's holding and its account of what it called "[t]he stream-of-commerce doctrine of jurisdiction" were incorrect, however. This Court's decision in Asahi Metal Industry Co. v Superior Court, 480 U.S. 102 [(1987)] may be responsible in part for that court's error regarding the stream of commerce, and this case presents an opportunity to provide greater clarity.

II

The Due Process Clause protects an individual's right to be deprived of life, liberty, or property only by the exercise of lawful power. This is no less true

---

[4] According to the New Jersey Supreme Court's opinion, McIntyre America "filed for bankruptcy in 2001 and has not participated in this lawsuit." See Nicastro v. McIntyre Machinery America, Ltd., 987 A.2d 575 (N.J. 2010).

with respect to the power of a sovereign to resolve disputes through judicial process than with respect to the power of a sovereign to prescribe rules of conduct for those within its sphere. As a general rule, neither statute nor judicial decree may bind strangers to the State.

A court may subject a defendant to judgment only when the defendant has sufficient contacts with the sovereign "such that the maintenance of the suit does not offend 'traditional notions of fair play and substantial justice.'" International Shoe Co. v. Washington, 326 U.S. 310, 316 (1945) (quoting Milliken v. Meyer, 311 U.S. 457, 463 (1940)). Freeform notions of fundamental fairness divorced from traditional practice cannot transform a judgment rendered in the absence of authority into law. As a general rule, the sovereign's exercise of power requires some act by which the defendant "purposefully avails itself of the privilege of conducting activities within the forum State, thus invoking the benefits and protections of its laws," Hanson v. Denckla, 357 U.S. 235 (1958), though in some cases, as with an intentional tort, the defendant might well fall within the State's authority by reason of his attempt to obstruct its laws. In product liability cases like this one, it is the defendant's purposeful availment that makes jurisdiction consistent with "traditional notions of fair play and substantial justice."

A person may submit to a State's authority in a number of ways. [The opinion goes on to cite "explicit consent" and "presence within a state" and "citizenship or domicile" or "incorporation or principal place of business," and finally "a more limited form of submission" through "contact with and activity directed at a sovereign."]

The imprecision arising from *Asahi*, for the most part, results from its statement of the relation between jurisdiction and the "stream of commerce." The stream of commerce, like other metaphors, has its deficiencies as well as its utility. It refers to the movement of goods from manufacturers through distributors to consumers, yet beyond that descriptive purpose its meaning is far from exact. This Court has stated that a defendant's placing goods into the stream of commerce "with the expectation that they will be purchased by consumers within the forum State" may indicate purposeful availment. World-Wide Volkswagen Corp. v. Woodson, 444 U.S. 286, 298 (1980) (finding that expectation lacking). But that statement does not amend the general rule of personal jurisdiction. It merely observes that a defendant may in an appropriate case be subject to jurisdiction without entering the forum—itself an unexceptional proposition—as where manufacturers or distributors "seek to serve" a given State's market. The principal inquiry in cases of this sort is whether the defendant's activities manifest an intention to submit to the power of a sovereign. In other words, the defendant must "purposefully avai[l] itself of the privilege of conducting activities within the forum State, thus invoking the benefits and protections of its laws." *Hanson*; Insurance Corp. of Ireland v. Compagnie des Bauxites de Guinee, 456 U.S.

694, 704-705 (1982) ("[A]ctions of the defendant may amount to a legal submission to the jurisdiction of the court"). Sometimes a defendant does so by sending its goods rather than its agents. The defendant's transmission of goods permits the exercise of jurisdiction only where the defendant can be said to have targeted the forum; as a general rule, it is not enough that the defendant might have predicted that its goods will reach the forum State.

In *Asahi*, an opinion by Justice Brennan for four Justices, outlined a different approach. It discarded the central concept of sovereign authority in favor of considerations of fairness and foreseeability. As that concurrence contended, "jurisdiction premised on the placement of a product into the stream of commerce [without more] is consistent with the Due Process Clause," for "[a]s long as a participant in this process is aware that the final product is being marketed in the forum State, the possibility of a lawsuit there cannot come as a surprise." It was the premise of the concurring opinion that the defendant's ability to anticipate suit renders the assertion of jurisdiction fair. In this way, the opinion made foreseeability the touchstone of jurisdiction.

The standard set forth in Justice Brennan's concurrence was rejected in an opinion written by Justice O'Connor; but the relevant part of that opinion, too, commanded the assent of only four Justices, not a majority of the Court. That opinion stated: "The 'substantial connection' between the defendant and the forum State necessary for a finding of minimum contacts must come about by an action of the defendant purposefully directed toward the forum State. The placement of a product into the stream of commerce, without more, is not an act of the defendant purposefully directed toward the forum State."

Since *Asahi* was decided, the courts have sought to reconcile the competing opinions. But Justice Brennan's concurrence, advocating a rule based on general notions of fairness and foreseeability, is inconsistent with the premises of lawful judicial power. This Court's precedents make clear that it is the defendant's actions, not his expectations, that empower a State's courts to subject him to judgment.

[Jurisdiction "is in the first instance a question of authority rather than fairness." Were] general fairness considerations the touchstone of jurisdiction, a lack of purposeful availment might be excused where carefully crafted judicial procedures could otherwise protect the defendant's interests, or where the plaintiff would suffer substantial hardship if forced to litigate in a foreign forum. That such considerations have not been deemed controlling is instructive. See, *e.g.*, *World-Wide Volkswagen*.

Two principles are implicit in the foregoing. First, personal jurisdiction requires a forum-by-forum, or sovereign-by-sovereign, analysis. The question is whether a defendant has followed a course of conduct directed at the society or economy existing within the jurisdiction of a given sovereign, so that the sovereign has the power to subject the defendant to judgment concerning that conduct. Personal jurisdiction, of course, restricts "judicial power not as a matter of sovereignty, but as a matter of individual liberty," for due process protects the individual's right to be subject only to lawful power. *Bauxites de Guinee.* But whether a judicial judgment is lawful depends on whether the sovereign has authority to render it.

The second principle is a corollary of the first. Because the United States is a distinct sovereign, a defendant may in principle be subject to the jurisdiction of the courts of the United States but not of any particular State. This is consistent with the premises and unique genius of our Constitution. Ours is "a legal system unprecedented in form and design, establishing two orders of government, each with its own direct relationship, its own privity, its own set of mutual rights and obligations to the people who sustain it and are governed by it." U.S. Term Limits, Inc. v. Thornton, 514 U.S. 779, 838 (1995) (Kennedy, J., concurring). For jurisdiction, a litigant may have the requisite relationship with the United States Government but not with the government of any individual State. That would be an exceptional case, however. If the defendant is a domestic domicil-iary, the courts of its home State are available and can exercise general juris-diction. And if another State were to assert jurisdiction in an inappropriate case, it would upset the federal balance, which posits that each State has a sover-eignty that is not subject to unlawful intrusion by other States. Furthermore, foreign corporations will often target or concentrate on particular States, subjecting them to specific jurisdiction in those forums.

It must be remembered, however, that although this case and *Asahi* both involve foreign manufacturers, the undesirable consequences of Justice Brennan's approach are no less significant for domestic producers. The owner of a small Florida farm might sell crops to a large nearby distributor, for example, who might then distribute them to grocers across the country. If foreseeability were the controlling criterion, the farmer could be sued in Alaska or any number of other States' courts without ever leaving town. And the issue of foreseeability may itself be contested so that significant expenses are incurred just on the preliminary issue of jurisdiction. Jurisdic-tional rules should avoid these costs whenever possible.

The conclusion that the authority to subject a defendant to judgment depends on purposeful availment, consistent with Justice O'Connor's opinion in *Asahi*, does not by itself resolve many difficult questions of jurisdiction that will arise in particular cases. The defendant's conduct and the economic realities of the market the defendant seeks to serve will differ across cases, and judicial exposition will, in common-law fashion, clarify the contours of that principle.

III

In this case, petitioner directed marketing and sales efforts at the United States. It may be that . . . Congress could authorize the exercise of jurisdiction in appropriate courts. That circumstance is not presented in this case, however, and it is neither necessary nor appropriate to address here any constitutional concerns that might be attendant to that exercise of power. Nor is it necessary to determine what substantive law might apply were Congress to authorize jurisdiction in a federal court in New Jersey. See *Hanson* ("The issue is personal jurisdiction, not choice of law"). A sovereign's legislative authority to regulate conduct may present considerations different from those presented by its authority to subject a defendant to judgment in its courts. Here the question concerns the authority of a New Jersey state court to exercise jurisdiction, so it is petitioner's purposeful contacts with New Jersey, not with the United States, that alone are relevant.

Respondent has not established that J. McIntyre engaged in conduct purposefully directed at New Jersey. Recall that respondent's claim of jurisdiction centers on three facts: The distributor agreed to sell J. McIntyre's machines in the United States; J. McIntyre officials attended trade shows in several States but not in New Jersey; and up to four machines ended up in New Jersey. The British manufacturer had no office in New Jersey; it neither paid taxes nor owned property there; and it neither advertised in, nor sent any employees to, the State. Indeed, after discovery the trial court found that the "defendant does not have a single contact with New Jersey short of the machine in question ending up in this state." These facts may reveal an intent to serve the U.S. market, but they do not show that J. McIntyre purposefully availed itself of the New Jersey market.

It is notable that the New Jersey Supreme Court appears to agree, for it could "not find that J. McIntyre had a presence or minimum contacts in this State—in any jurisprudential sense—that would justify a New Jersey court to exercise jurisdiction in this case." The court nonetheless held that petitioner could be sued in New Jersey based on a "stream-of-commerce theory of jurisdiction." As discussed, however, the stream-of-commerce metaphor cannot supersede either the mandate of the Due Process Clause or the limits on judicial authority that Clause ensures. The New Jersey Supreme Court also cited "significant policy reasons" to justify its holding, including the State's "strong interest in protecting its citizens from defective products." That interest is doubtless strong, but the Constitution commands restraint before discarding liberty in the name of expediency.

. . .

Due process protects petitioner's right to be subject only to lawful authority. At no time did petitioner engage in any activities in New Jersey that reveal an intent to invoke or benefit from the protection of its laws. New Jersey is without power to adjudge the rights and liabilities of J. McIntyre, and its exercise of jurisdiction would violate due process. The contrary judgment of the New Jersey Supreme Court is *Reversed.*

Justice BREYER, with whom Justice ALITO joins, concurring in the judgment.

. . .

I

. . .

The plurality seems to state strict rules that limit jurisdiction where a defendant does not "inten[d] to submit to the power of a sovereign" and cannot "be said to have targeted the forum." But what do those standards mean when a company targets the world by selling products from its Web site? And does it matter if, instead of shipping the products directly, a company consigns the products through an intermediary (say, Amazon.com) who then receives and fulfills the orders? And what if the company markets its products through popup advertisements that it knows will be viewed in a forum? Those issues have serious commercial consequences but are totally absent in this case.

But though I do not agree with the plurality's seemingly strict no-jurisdiction rule, I am not persuaded by the absolute approach adopted by the New Jersey Supreme Court and urged by respondent and his *amici*. Under that view, a producer is subject to jurisdiction for a product liability action so long as it "knows or reasonably should know that its products are distributed through a nationwide distribution system that *might* lead to those products being sold in any of the fifty states." In the context of this case, I cannot agree.

For one thing, to adopt this view would abandon the heretofore accepted inquiry of whether, focusing upon the relationship between "the defendant, the *forum,* and the litigation," it is fair, in light of the defendant's contacts *with that forum*, to subject the defendant to suit there. Shaffer v. Heitner, 433 U.S. 186, 204 (1977) (emphasis added). It would ordinarily rest jurisdiction instead upon no more than the occurrence of a product-based accident in the forum State. But this Court has rejected the notion that a defendant's amenability to suit "travel[s] with the chattel." *World-Wide Volkswagen.*

For another, I cannot reconcile so automatic a rule with the constitutional demand for "minimum contacts" and "purposefu[l] avail[ment]," each of which rest upon a particular notion of defendant-focused fairness. A rule like the New Jersey Supreme Court's would permit every State to assert jurisdiction in a product liability suit against any domestic manufacturer who sells its products (made anywhere in the United States) to a national distributor, no matter how large or small the manufacturer, no matter how distant the forum, and no matter how few the number of items that end up in the particular forum at issue. What might appear fair in the case of a large manufacturer which specifically seeks, or expects, an equal-sized distributor to sell its product in a distant State might seem unfair in the case of a small manufacturer (say, an Appalachian potter) who sells his product (cups and saucers) exclusively to a large distributor, who resells a single item (a coffee mug) to a buyer from a distant State (Hawaii). I know too little about the range of these or in-between possibilities to abandon in favor of the more absolute rule what has previously been this Court's less absolute approach.

Further, the fact that the defendant is a foreign, rather than a domestic, manufacturer makes the basic fairness of an absolute rule yet more uncertain. I am again less certain than is the New Jersey Supreme Court that the nature of international commerce has changed so significantly as to require a new approach to personal jurisdiction.

It may be that a larger firm can readily "alleviate the risk of burdensome litigation by procuring insurance, passing the expected costs on to customers, or, if the risks are too great, severing its connection with the State." *World-Wide Volkswagen.* But manufacturers come in many shapes and sizes. It may be fundamentally unfair to require a small Egyptian shirt maker, a Brazilian manufacturing cooperative, or a Kenyan coffee farmer, selling its products through international distributors, to respond to product liability tort suits in virtually every State in the United States, even those in respect to which the foreign firm has no connection at all but the sale of a single (allegedly defective) good. And a rule like the New Jersey Supreme Court suggests would require every product manufacturer, large or small, selling to American distributors to understand not only the tort law of every State, but also the wide variance in the way courts within different States apply that law.

. . .

Justice GINSBURG, with whom Justice SOTOMAYOR and Justice KAGAN join, dissenting.

A foreign industrialist seeks to develop a market in the United States for machines it manufactures. It hopes to derive substantial revenue from sales it makes to United States purchasers. Where in the United States buyers reside does not matter to this manufacturer. Its goal is simply to sell as much as it can, wherever it can. It excludes no region or State from the market it wishes to reach. But, all things considered, it prefers to avoid products liability litigation in the United States. To that end, it engages a U.S. distributor to ship its machines stateside. Has it succeeded in escaping personal jurisdiction in a State where one of its products is sold and causes injury or even death to a local user?

Under this Court's pathmarking precedent in *International Shoe,* and subsequent decisions, one would expect the answer to be unequivocally, "No." [The dissent sets out facts relating to J. McIntyre's contacts with the United States.]

II

A few points on which there should be no genuine debate bear statement at the outset. [First, J. McIntyre is not subject to general jurisdiction, so the question relates to specific jurisdiction. Second, the case does not raise issues about "fair and reasonable allocation of adjudicatory authority among the states." Third, limits on state jurisdiction "derive from considerations of due process, not state sovereignty."] Finally, in *International Shoe* itself, and decisions thereafter, the Court has made plain that legal fictions, notably "presence" and "implied consent," should be discarded, for they conceal the actual bases on which jurisdiction rests. "[T]he relationship among the defendant, the forum, and the litigation" determines whether due process permits the exercise of personal jurisdiction over a defendant, *Shaffer*, and "fictions of implied consent" or "corporate presence" do not advance the proper inquiry.

Whatever the state of academic debate over the role of consent in modern jurisdictional doctrines, the plurality's notion that consent is the animating concept draws no support from controlling decisions of this Court. Quite the contrary, the Court has explained, a forum can exercise jurisdiction when its contacts with the controversy are sufficient; invocation of a fictitious consent, the Court has repeatedly said, is unnecessary and unhelpful. See, *e.g.,* Burger King Corp. v. Rudzewicz, 471 U.S. 462, 472 (1985) (Due Process Clause permits "forum . . . to assert specific jurisdiction over an out-of-state defendant who has not consented to suit there"); McGee v. International Life Ins. Co., 355 U.S. 220, 222 (1957) ("[T]his Court [has] abandoned 'consent,' 'doing business,' and 'presence' as the standard for measuring the extent of state judicial power over [out-of-state] corporations.").[5]

III

This case is illustrative of marketing arrangements for sales in the United States common in today's commercial world.[6] A foreign-country manufacturer engages a U.S. company to promote and distribute the manufacturer's products, not in any particular State, but anywhere and everywhere in the United States the distributor can attract purchasers. The product proves defective and injures a user in the State where the user lives or works. Often, as here, the manufacturer will have liability insurance covering personal injuries caused by its products.

When industrial accidents happen, a longarm statute in the State where the injury occurs generally permits assertion of jurisdiction, upon giving proper notice, over the foreign manufacturer. For example, the State's statute might provide, as does New York's longarm statute, for the "exercise [of] personal jurisdiction over any non-domiciliary . . . who . . .

> commits a tortious act without the state causing injury to person or property within the state, . . . if he . . . expects or should reasonably expect the act to have

---

[5] But see plurality opinion (maintaining that a forum may be fair and reasonable, based on its links to the episode in suit, yet off limits because the defendant has not submitted to the State's authority). The plurality's notion that jurisdiction over foreign corporations depends upon the defendant's "submission," seems scarcely different from the long-discredited fiction of implied consent. It bears emphasis that a majority of this Court's members do not share the plurality's view.

[6] Last year, the United States imported nearly 2 trillion dollars in foreign goods. Capital goods, such as the metal shear machine that injured Nicastro, accounted for almost 450 billion dollars in imports for 2010. New Jersey is the fourth-largest destination for manufactured commodities imported into the United States, after California, Texas, and New York.

consequences in the state and derives substantial revenue from interstate or international commerce.

N.Y. Civ. Prac. Law Ann. §302(a)(3)(ii).[7] Or, the State might simply provide, as New Jersey does, for the exercise of jurisdiction "consistent with due process of law." N.J. Ct. Rule 4:4-4(b)(1) (2011).[8]

The modern approach to jurisdiction over corporations and other legal entities, ushered in by *International Shoe*, gave prime place to reason and fairness. Is it not fair and reasonable, given the mode of trading of which this case is an example, to require the international seller to defend at the place its products cause injury? Do not litigational convenience and choice-of-law considerations point in that direction? On what measure of reason and fairness can it be considered undue to require McIntyre UK to defend in New Jersey as an incident of its efforts to develop a market for its industrial machines anywhere and everywhere in the United States?[12] Is not the burden on McIntyre UK to defend in New Jersey fair, *i.e.*, a reasonable cost of transacting business internationally, in comparison to the burden on Nicastro to go to Nottingham, England to gain recompense for an injury he sustained using McIntyre's product at his workplace in Saddle Brook, New Jersey?

McIntyre UK dealt with the United States as a single market. Like most foreign manufacturers, it was concerned not with the prospect of suit in State X as opposed to State Y, but rather with its subjection to suit anywhere in the United States. See Hay, Judicial Jurisdiction Over Foreign-Country Corporate Defendants—Comments on Recent Case Law, 63 Ore. L. Rev. 431, 433 (1984) (hereinafter Hay). As a McIntyre UK officer wrote in an email to McIntyre America: "American law—who needs it?!" If McIntyre UK is answerable in the United States at all, is it not "perfectly appropriate to permit the exercise of that jurisdiction . . . at the place of injury"? See Hay 435; Degnan & Kane, The Exercise of Jurisdiction Over and Enforcement of Judgments Against Alien Defendants, 39 Hastings L.J. 799, 813-815 (1988) (noting that "[i]n the international order," the State that counts is the United States, not its component States, and that the fair place of suit within the United States is essentially a question of venue).

---

[7] This provision was modeled in part on the Uniform Interstate and International Procedure Act. Connecticut's longarm statute also uses the "derives substantial revenue from interstate or international commerce" formulation. See Conn. Gen. Stat. §52-59b(a) (2011).

[8] State longarm provisions allow the exercise of jurisdiction subject only to a due process limitation in Alabama, Arkansas, California, Colorado, Georgia, Illinois, Indiana, Iowa, Kansas, Kentucky, Louisiana, Maryland, Michigan, Minnesota, Missouri, Nevada, North Dakota, Oregon, Pennsylvania, Puerto Rico, South Carolina, South Dakota, Tennessee, Texas, Utah, Washington, and West Virginia.

[12] The plurality suggests that the Due Process Clause might permit a federal district court in New Jersey, sitting in diversity and applying New Jersey law, to adjudicate McIntyre UK's liability to Nicastro. In other words, McIntyre UK might be compelled to bear the burden of traveling to New Jersey and defending itself there under New Jersey's products liability law, but would be entitled to federal adjudication of Nicastro's state-law claim. I see no basis in the Due Process Clause for such a curious limitation.

In sum, McIntyre UK, by engaging McIntyre America to promote and sell its machines in the United States, "purposefully availed itself" of the United States market nationwide, not a market in a single State or a discrete collection of States. McIntyre UK thereby availed itself of the market of all States in which its products were sold by its exclusive distributor. "Th[e] 'purposeful availment' requirement," this Court has explained, simply "ensures that a defendant will not be haled into a jurisdiction solely as a result of 'random,' 'fortuitous,' or 'attenuated' contacts." *Burger King*. Adjudicatory authority is appropriately exercised where "actions by the defendant *himself*" give rise to the affiliation with the forum. How could McIntyre UK not have intended, by its actions targeting a national market, to sell products in the fourth largest destination for imports among all States of the United States and the largest scrap metal market? But see plurality opinion (manufacturer's purposeful efforts to sell its products nationwide are "not . . . relevant" to the personal jurisdiction inquiry).

Courts, both state and federal, confronting facts similar to those here, have rightly rejected the conclusion that a manufacturer selling its products across the USA may evade jurisdiction in any and all States, including the State where its defective product is distributed and causes injury. They have held, instead, that it would undermine principles of fundamental fairness to insulate the foreign manufacturer from accountability in court at the place within the United States where the manufacturer's products caused injury. See, *e.g.*, Tobin v. Astra Pharmaceutical Prods., Inc., 993 F.2d 528, 544 (6th Cir. 1993); A. Uberti & C. v. Leonardo, 892 P.2d 1354, 1362 (Ariz. 1995).

IV

A

While this Court has not considered in any prior case the now-prevalent pattern presented here—a foreign-country manufacturer enlisting a U.S. distributor to develop a market in the United States for the manufacturer's products—none of the Court's decisions tug against the judgment made by the New Jersey Supreme Court. McIntyre contends otherwise, citing *World-Wide Volkswagen*, and *Asahi*.

[*World-Wide Volkswagen* turned on the fact that the consumer brought the car to the forum state. The manufacturer did not object to jurisdiction, and the importer abandoned its initial objection. *World-Wide Volkswagen* indicates that their objections "would have been unavailing." The decision in *Asahi* "was not a close call," since it involved a foreign plaintiff (Taiwanese manufacturer) and foreign defendant (Japanese valve maker), in a dispute over indemnification in a transaction occurring abroad. Hence "the dueling opinions" by Justices Brennan and O'Connor "were hardly necessary." Unlike J. McIntyre, Asahi did not "seek out customers" in this country, and "engaged no distributor to promote its wares here," and "appeared at no tradeshows" here "and, of course, it had no Web site advertising its products to the world." Also, Asahi was a component part maker that had little control over the final destination of its products.] To hold that *Asahi* controls this case would, to put it bluntly, be dead wrong.[15]

B

The Court's judgment also puts United States plaintiffs at a disadvantage in comparison to similarly situated complainants elsewhere in the world. Of particular note, within the European Union, in which the United Kingdom is a participant, the jurisdiction New Jersey would have exercised is not at all exceptional. The European Regulation on Jurisdiction and the Recognition and Enforcement of Judgments provides for the exercise of specific jurisdiction "in matters relating to tort . . . in the courts for the place where the harmful event occurred." Council Reg. 44/2001, Art. 5, 2001 O.J. (L. 12) 4. The European Court of Justice has interpreted this prescription to authorize jurisdiction either where the harmful act occurred or at the place of injury. See Handelskwekerij G.J. Bier B.V. v. Mines de Potasse d'Alsace S.A., 1976 E.C.R. 1735, 1748-1749.

V

The commentators who gave names to what we now call "general jurisdiction" and "specific jurisdiction" anticipated that when the latter achieves its full growth, considerations of litigational convenience and the respective situations of the parties would determine when it is appropriate to subject a defendant to trial in the plaintiff's community. See von Mehren & Trautman, Jurisdiction to Adjudicate: A Suggested Analysis, 79 Harv. L. Rev. 1121, 1166-1179 (1966). Litigational considerations include "the convenience of witnesses and the ease of ascertaining the governing law." As to the parties, courts would differently appraise two situations: (1) cases involving a substantially local plaintiff, like Nicastro, injured by the activity of a defendant engaged in interstate or international trade; and (2) cases in which the defendant is a natural or legal person whose economic activities and legal involvements are largely home-based, *i.e.*, entities without designs to gain substantial revenue from sales in distant markets. As the attached appendix of illustrative cases indicates, courts presented with von Mehren and Trautman's first scenario—a local plaintiff injured by the activity of a manufacturer seeking to exploit a multistate or global market—have repeatedly confirmed that jurisdiction is appropriately exercised by courts of the place where the product was sold and caused injury.

. . .

---

[15] The plurality notes the low volume of sales in New Jersey. A $24,900 shearing machine, however, is unlikely to sell in bulk worldwide, much less in any given State. By dollar value, the price of a single machine represents a significant sale. Had a manufacturer sold in New Jersey $24,900 worth of flannel shirts, see Nelson v. Park Industries, Inc., 717 F.2d 1120 (7th Cir. 1983), cigarette lighters, see Oswalt v. Scripto, Inc., 616 F.2d 191 (5th Cir. 1980), or wire-rope splices, see Hedrick v. Daiko Shoji Co., 715 F.2d 1355 (9th Cir. 1983), the Court would presumably find the defendant amenable to suit in that State.

For the reasons stated, I would hold McIntyre UK answerable in New Jersey for the harm Nicastro suffered at his workplace in that State using McIntyre UK's shearing machine. While I dissent from the Court's judgment, I take heart that the plurality opinion does not speak for the Court, for that opinion would take a giant step away from the "notions of fair play and substantial justice" underlying *International Shoe*.

■ STILL FURTHER NOTES ON STREAM OF COMMERCE

1. In both *Asahi* and *Nicastro*, the Court tried to resolve the question whether putting a product into the stream of commerce confers jurisdiction where the product causes injury. In both, pluralities of four Justices were prepared to say that commercial distribution, without more, is not enough, *rejecting* at least the broadest interpretation of the Illinois decision in *Gray* (Section B2, supra) and resolving the question left open in *World-Wide*. In both cases, separate concurring opinions (Justice Stevens in *Asahi*, speaking for himself and two others; Justice Breyer in *Nicastro*, speaking for himself and Justice Alito) agree that the facts do not establish jurisdiction, but do not agree on the "black letter" rule that the plurality hopes to establish. What reasons emerge from these concurring opinions? Where do *Asahi* and *Nicastro* leave the matter? Writing after *Asahi* but before *Nicastro*, Professor Baker concluded that we still don't know. See generally Kristin R. Baker, *Product Liability Suit and the Stream of Commerce After* Asahi: World-Wide Volkswagen *Is Still the Answer*, 45 Tulsa L.J. 705, 706 (2000).

2. *Asahi* involved a component part (tire valve) that came to this country as part of a motorcycle, and the question of jurisdiction in California arose in an indemnity claim between a Taiwanese tire maker and a Japanese valve maker arising out of a contract between them. *Nicastro* involved a finished product (scrap metal shear) shipped by the UK manufacturer J. McIntyre to McIntyre America (in Ohio, according to the opinion of the New Jersey Supreme Court), from where it was shipped to CSM (plaintiff's employer) in New Jersey, and the question of jurisdiction in New Jersey arose in a New Jersey plaintiff's tort claim against the UK manufacturer. Which case is the stronger one for the exercise of jurisdiction?

3. In addition to whatever conclusion we can draw on the stream of commerce theory, consider these strands in the various opinions in *Nicastro*:

(a) Justice Kennedy's opinion advances the proposition that a manufacturer (domestic or foreign) serving a national market may be subject to jurisdiction *somewhere*, but not necessarily in the place where the product is shipped. Do Justices Breyer and Alito appear to go along? If so, we have a majority on this side of it, don't we? Clearly, Justice Ginsburg (representing the

views of three Justices) does not agree. What would these three do on this point?

(b) Justice Kennedy's opinion advances territorial concerns as an element in due process analysis. This idea surfaced in *World-Wide*, disappeared two years later in the *Bauxites* case (Section E, infra), but now resurfaces. Justices Breyer and Alito, concurring (no jurisdiction in New Jersey), do not include a territorial element, do they? How about Justice Ginsburg's opinion for the three dissenters?

(c) Justice Kennedy's opinion embraces a requirement of a strong mental element in jurisdictional analysis, speaking of defendant's *intent* to "submit to the power of the sovereign." Again Justices Breyer and Alito, while concurring and speaking of this point, don't clearly embrace a strong mental element. The dissenters *clearly* disagree on this point, don't they? Where does that leave us?

Robert Nicastro

The opinion of the New Jersey Supreme Court, sustaining jurisdiction over the British manufacturer McIntyre, states that Robert Nicastro (shown right) was injured by the Model 640 Shear that was made in Britain in 1995, and was said to be "about eight feet long and six feet high [weighing] more than three tons." Nicastro was working for Curcio Scrap Metal in Saddle Brook, New Jersey, where he had been employed for 30 years.

The record of the case indicates that Nicastro had reported for work at 7:30 A.M. and that the accident happened at 11:55 A.M. At the time, Nicastro was wearing "a Jets sweatshirt and had gloves on." He paused to help a customer, and shut off the machine. When he returned, he turned the machine on and bent down to pick up a piece of copper and aluminum tubing that was three to four feet long, and he slipped on something, which brought his right hand into the machine, when the shear blade came down. The dissenters in the Supreme Court opinion note that the machine cost $24,900. Published reports indicated that Nicastro, who was 49 years old at the time, underwent eight surgeries on his hand and ultimately lost four fingers as a result of the accident in which the machine "sliced through" those fingers. Reportedly, Nicastro said after the accident that it happened in "the bat of an eye" and that he "was in the wrong place at the right time for that blade." For academic commentary on the *Nicastro* case, see the Symposium in 63 S.C. L. Rev. 465 et seq. (2011) (with introductory comments by Professor Arthur R. Miller and articles about the case by John Vail, and by Professors Lea Brilmayer (with Matthew Smith), Paul Carrington, Rodger D. Citron, Richard D. Freer, Linda J. Silberman, Adam N. Steinman, Howard B. Stravitz, and Wendy Collins Purdue, along with articles about the *Goodyear Dunlop* case by Meir Feder, Collyn A. Peddie, and Professor Allan R. Stein).

4. Not surprisingly, lower courts after *Nicastro* are divided on the question whether manufacturers are subject to jurisdiction in states where their products wind up in the course of commercial distribution. Compare Graham v. Hamilton, 2012 WL 893748 (W.D. La. 2012) (good jurisdiction in Louisiana over GM Canada, which sold car to GM Corporation in Louisiana, where it was resold to plaintiff and allegedly caused injury and death; unlike *Nicastro*, where defendant "likely sold only a single machine" that wound up in the forum, here "GM Canada places over 800,000 vehicles into the US market each year") and Dierig v. Lees Leisure Industries, Ltd., 2012 WL 669968 (E.D. Ky. 2012) (good jurisdiction in Kentucky over Canadian manufacturer of motorcycle tent-trailer, which plaintiff purchased from South Carolina distributor in South Carolina; plaintiff was injured while towing trailer in Canada; defendant placed "national advertisements in Wing World magazine," had commercial website, published "testimonial of a Kentucky resident" and established "apparent agency relationship" with distributor; defendant made "clear effort . . . directly and through its apparent agent, to attract Kentucky residents to purchase their Kentuckian-approved products"), with Askue v. Aurora Corp. of America, 2012 WL 843939 (N.D. Ga. 2012) (no jurisdiction in Georgia over Taiwanese maker of paper shredder that allegedly caused personal injury in Georgia; as in *Nicastro*, defendant here sold its product to U.S. distributor, and "only a small number of machines wound up in the forum state") (defendant had fewer contacts with forum than defendant in *Nicastro*; no purposeful availment).

2. Specific Jurisdiction Expands

BURGER KING v. RUDZEWICZ

United States Supreme Court
471 U.S. 462 (1985)

Justice BRENNAN delivered the opinion of the Court.

The State of Florida's long-arm statute extends jurisdiction to "[a]ny person, whether or not a citizen or resident of this state," who, inter alia, "[b]reach[es] a contract in this state by failing to perform acts required by the contract to be performed in this state," so long as the cause of action arises from the alleged contractual breach. Fla. Stat. §48.193(1)(g) (Supp. 1984). The United States District Court for the Southern District of Florida, sitting in diversity, relied on this provision in exercising personal jurisdiction over a Michigan resident who allegedly had breached a franchise agreement with a Florida corporation by failing to make required payments in Florida. The question presented is whether this exercise of long-arm jurisdiction offended "traditional conception[s] of fair play and substantial justice" embodied in the Due Process Clause of the Fourteenth Amendment. International Shoe Co. v. Washington, 326 U.S. 310 (1945).

I

A

Burger King Corporation is a Florida corporation whose principal offices are in Miami. It is one of the world's largest restaurant organizations, with over 3,000 outlets in the 50 States, the Commonwealth of Puerto Rico, and 8 foreign nations. Burger King conducts approximately 80% of its business through a franchise operation that the company styles the "Burger King System"—"a comprehensive restaurant format and operating system for the sale of uniform and quality food products." Burger King licenses its franchisees to use its trademarks and service marks for a period of 20 years and leases standardized restaurant facilities to them for the same term. In addition, franchisees acquire a variety of proprietary information concerning the "standards, specifications, procedures and methods for operating a Burger King Restaurant." They also receive market research and advertising assistance; ongoing training in restaurant management;[2] and accounting, cost-control, and inventory-control guidance. By permitting franchisees to tap into Burger King's established national reputation and to benefit from proven procedures for dispensing standardized fare, this system enables them to go into the restaurant business with significantly lowered barriers to entry.

In exchange for these benefits, franchisees pay Burger King an initial $40,000 franchise fee and commit themselves to payment of monthly royalties, advertising and sales promotion fees, and rent computed in part from monthly gross sales. Franchisees also agree to submit to the national organization's exacting regulation of virtually every conceivable aspect of their operations.[4] Burger King imposes these standards and undertakes its rigid regulation out of conviction that "[u]niformity of service, appearance, and

---

[2] Mandatory training seminars are conducted at Burger King University in Miami and at Whopper College Regional Training Centers around the country.

[4] [These include "quality, appearance, size, taste, and processing" of menu items; "standards of service and cleanliness," hours of operation, "official mandatory restaurant operating standards, specifications and procedures," building layout, displays, equipment, vending machines, service, uniforms, advertising, and promotion; employee training; accounting and auditing requirements; insurance requirements. Burger King "also imposes extensive standards governing franchisee liability, assignments, defaults, and termination."—ED.]

quality of product is essential to the preservation of the Burger King image and the benefits accruing therefrom to both Franchisee and Franchisor."

Burger King oversees its franchise system through a two-tiered administrative structure. The governing contracts provide that the franchise relationship is established in Miami and governed by Florida law, and call for payment of all required fees and forwarding of all relevant notices to the Miami headquarters. The Miami headquarters sets policy and works directly with its franchisees in attempting to resolve major problems. Day-to-day monitoring of franchisees, however, is conducted through a network of 10 district offices which in turn report to the Miami headquarters.

The instant litigation grows out of Burger King's termination of one of its franchisees, and is aptly described by the franchisee as "a divorce proceeding among commercial partners." The appellee John Rudzewicz, a Michigan citizen and resident, is the senior partner in a Detroit accounting firm. In 1978, he was approached by Brian MacShara, the son of a business acquaintance, who suggested that they jointly apply to Burger King for a franchise in the Detroit area. MacShara proposed to serve as the manager of the restaurant if Rudzewicz would put up the investment capital; in exchange, the two would evenly share the profits. Believing that MacShara's idea offered attractive investment and tax-deferral opportunities, Rudzewicz agreed to the venture.

Rudzewicz and MacShara jointly applied for a franchise to Burger King's Birmingham, Michigan, district office in the autumn of 1978. Their application was forwarded to Burger King's Miami headquarters, which entered into a preliminary agreement with them in February 1979. During the ensuing four months it was agreed that Rudzewicz and MacShara would assume operation of an existing facility in Drayton Plains, Michigan. MacShara attended the prescribed management courses in Miami during this period, and the franchisees purchased $165,000 worth of restaurant equipment from Burger King's Davmor Industries division in Miami. Even before the final agreements were signed, however, the parties began to disagree over site-development fees, building design, computation of monthly rent, and whether the franchisees would be able to assign their liabilities to a corporation they had formed.[6] During these disputes Rudzewicz and MacShara negotiated both with the Birmingham district office and with the Miami headquarters.[7] With some misgivings, Rudzewicz and MacShara finally obtained limited concessions

---

[6] [On the matters of rent and assigning the liabilities of Rudzewicz and MacShara to a corporation, the parties had disagreements. On both points, the District Court found in favor of Burger King, concluding that the position of Rudzewicz and MacShara on rent was "incredible," and that testimony on oral assurances relating to assignability was barred by the parol evidence rule.—ED.]

[7] Although Rudzewicz and MacShara dealt with the Birmingham district office on a regular basis, they communicated directly with the Miami headquarters in forming the contracts; moreover, they learned that the district office had "very little" decisionmaking authority and accordingly turned directly to headquarters in seeking to resolve their disputes.

from the Miami headquarters, signed the final agreements, and commenced operations in June 1979. By signing the final agreements, Rudzewicz obligated himself personally to payments exceeding $1 million over the 20-year franchise relationship.

The Drayton Plains facility apparently enjoyed steady business during the summer of 1979, but patronage declined after a recession began later that year. Rudzewicz and MacShara soon fell far behind in their monthly payments to Miami. Headquarters sent notices of default, and an extended period of negotiations began among the franchisees, the Birmingham district office, and the Miami headquarters. After several Burger King officials in Miami had engaged in prolonged but ultimately unsuccessful negotiations with the franchisees by mail and by telephone,[9] headquarters terminated the franchise and ordered Rudzewicz and MacShara to vacate the premises. They refused and continued to occupy and operate the facility as a Burger King restaurant.

B

Burger King commenced the instant action in the United States District Court for the Southern District of Florida in May 1981, invoking that court's diversity jurisdiction pursuant to 28 USC §1332(a) and its original jurisdiction over federal trademark disputes pursuant to §1338(a). Burger King alleged that Rudzewicz and MacShara had breached their franchise obligations "within [the jurisdiction of] this district court" by failing to make the required payments "at plaintiff's place of business in Miami, Dade County, Florida," and also charged that they were tortiously infringing its trademarks and service marks through their continued, unauthorized operation as a Burger King restaurant. Burger King sought damages, injunctive relief, and costs and attorney's fees. Rudzewicz and MacShara entered special appearances and argued, inter alia, that because they were Michigan residents and because Burger King's claim did not "arise" within the Southern District of Florida, the District Court lacked personal jurisdiction over them. The District Court denied their motions after a hearing, holding that, pursuant to Florida's long-arm statute, "a nonresident Burger King franchisee is subject to the personal jurisdiction of this Court in actions arising out of its franchise agreements." Rudzewicz and MacShara then filed an answer and a counterclaim seeking damages for alleged violations by Burger King of Michigan's Franchise Investment Law, Mich. Comp. Laws §445.1501 et seq. (1979).

---

[9] Miami's policy was to "deal directly" with franchisees when they began to encounter financial difficulties, and to involve district office personnel only when necessary. In the instant case, for example, the Miami office handled all credit problems, ordered cost-cutting measures, negotiated for a partial refinancing of the franchisees' debts, communicated directly with the franchisees in attempting to resolve the dispute, and was responsible for all termination matters.

After a 3-day bench trial, the court again concluded that it had "jurisdiction over the subject matter and the parties to this cause." Finding that Rudzewicz and MacShara had breached their franchise agreements with Burger King and had infringed Burger King's trademarks and service marks, the court entered judgment against them, jointly and severally, for $228,875 in contract damages. The court also ordered them "to immediately close Burger King Restaurant Number 775 from continued operation or to immediately give the keys and possession of said restaurant to Burger King Corporation," found that they had failed to prove any of the required elements of their counterclaim, and awarded costs and attorney's fees to Burger King.

Rudzewicz appealed to the Court of Appeals for the Eleventh Circuit.[11] A divided panel of that Circuit reversed the judgment, concluding that the District Court could not properly exercise personal jurisdiction over Rudzewicz pursuant to Fla. Stat. §48.193(1)(g) because "the circumstances of the Drayton Plains franchise and the negotiations which led to it left Rudzewicz bereft of reasonable notice and financially unprepared for the prospect of franchise litigation in Florida." Accordingly, the panel majority concluded that "[j]urisdiction under these circumstances would offend the fundamental fairness which is the touchstone of due process." . . .

II

A

The Due Process Clause protects an individual's liberty interest in not being subject to the binding judgments of a forum with which he has established no meaningful "contacts, ties, or relations." *International Shoe.*[13] By requiring that individuals have "fair warning that a particular activity may subject [them] to the jurisdiction of a foreign sovereign," Shaffer v. Heitner, 433 U.S. 186, 218 (1977) (Stevens, J., concurring in judgment), the Due Process Clause "gives a degree of predictability to the legal system that allows potential defendants to structure their primary conduct with some minimum assurance as to where that conduct will and will not render them liable to suit," World-Wide Volkswagen Corp. v. Woodson, 444 U.S. 286, 297 (1980).

---

[11] MacShara did not appeal his judgment. In addition, Rudzewicz entered into a compromise with Burger King and waived his right to appeal the District Court's finding of trademark infringement and its entry of injunctive relief. Accordingly, we need not address the extent to which the tortious act provisions of Florida's long-arm statute may constitutionally extend to out-of-state trademark infringement. Cf. Calder v. Jones, 465 U.S. 783, 788-789 (1984) (tortious out-of-state conduct); Keeton v. Hustler Magazine, Inc., 465 U.S. 770 (1984) (same).

[13] Although this protection operates to restrict state power, it "must be seen as ultimately a function of the individual liberty interest preserved by the Due Process Clause" rather than as a function "of federalism concerns." Insurance Corp. of Ireland v. Compagnie des Bauxites de Guinee, 456 U.S. 694, 702-703, n.10 (1982).

Where a forum seeks to assert specific jurisdiction over an out-of-state defendant who has not consented to suit there, this "fair warning" requirement is satisfied if the defendant has "purposefully directed" his activities at residents of the forum, Keeton v. Hustler Magazine, Inc., 465 U.S. 770, 774 (1984), and the litigation results from alleged injuries that "arise out of or relate to" those activities, Helicopteros Nacionales de Colombia, S.A. v. Hall, 466 U.S. 408, 414 (1984).[15] . . . And with respect to interstate contractual obligations, we have emphasized that parties who "reach out beyond one state and create continuing relationships and obligations with citizens of another state" are subject to regulation and sanctions in the other State for the consequences of their activities. Travelers Health Assn. v. Virginia, 339 U.S. 643, 647 (1950). See also McGee v. International Life Insurance Co., 355 U.S. 220, 222-223 (1957).

We have noted several reasons why a forum legitimately may exercise personal jurisdiction over a nonresident who "purposefully directs" his activities toward forum residents. A State generally has a "manifest interest" in providing its residents with a convenient forum for redressing injuries inflicted by out-of-state actors. Moreover, where individuals "purposefully derive benefit" from their interstate activities, it may well be unfair to allow them to escape having to account in other States for consequences that arise proximately from such activities; the Due Process Clause may not readily be wielded as a territorial shield to avoid interstate obligations that have been voluntarily assumed. And because "modern transportation and communications have made it much less burdensome for a party sued to defend himself in a State where he engages in economic activity," it usually will not be unfair to subject him to the burdens of litigating in another forum for disputes relating to such activity. *McGee.*

Notwithstanding these considerations, the constitutional touchstone remains whether the defendant purposefully established "minimum contacts" in the forum State. . . . [T]he Court frequently has drawn from the reasoning of Hanson v. Denckla, 357 U.S. 235, 253 (1958), [source of the "purposeful availment" standard that] ensures that a defendant will not be haled into a jurisdiction solely as a result of "random," "fortuitous," or "attenuated" contacts, or of the "unilateral activity of another party or a third person." Jurisdiction is proper, however, where the contacts proximately result from actions by the defendant himself that create a "substantial connection" with the forum State. Thus where the defendant "deliberately" has engaged in significant activities within a State, or has created "continuing obligations" between himself and

---

[15] "Specific" jurisdiction contrasts with "general" jurisdiction, pursuant to which "a State exercises personal jurisdiction over a defendant in a suit not arising out of or related to the defendant's contacts with the forum." Helicopteros Nacionales de Colombia, S.A. v. Hall, 466 U.S., at 414, n.9; see also Perkins v. Benguet Consolidated Mining Co., 342 U.S. 437 (1952).

residents of the forum, he manifestly has availed himself of the privilege of conducting business there, and because his activities are shielded by "the benefits and protections" of the forum's laws it is presumptively not unreasonable to require him to submit to the burdens of litigation in that forum as well.

Jurisdiction in these circumstances may not be avoided merely because the defendant did not physically enter the forum State. Although territorial presence frequently will enhance a potential defendant's affiliation with a State and reinforce the reasonable foreseeability of suit there, it is an inescapable fact of modern commercial life that a substantial amount of business is transacted solely by mail and wire communications across state lines, thus obviating the need for physical presence within a State in which business is conducted. So long as a commercial actor's efforts are "purposefully directed" toward residents of another State, we have consistently rejected the notion that an absence of physical contacts can defeat personal jurisdiction there.

Once it has been decided that a defendant purposefully established minimum contacts within the forum State, these contacts may be considered in light of other factors to determine whether the assertion of personal jurisdiction would comport with "fair play and substantial justice." *International Shoe.* Thus courts in "appropriate case[s]" may evaluate "the burden on the defendant," "the forum State's interest in adjudicating the dispute," "the plaintiff's interest in obtaining convenient and effective relief," "the interstate judicial system's interest in obtaining the most efficient resolution of controversies," and the "shared interest of the several States in furthering fundamental substantive social policies." *World-Wide Volkswagen.* These considerations sometimes serve to establish the reasonableness of jurisdiction upon a lesser showing of minimum contacts than would otherwise be required. On the other hand, where a defendant who purposefully has directed his activities at forum residents seeks to defeat jurisdiction, he must present a compelling case that the presence of some other considerations would render jurisdiction unreasonable. Most such considerations usually may be accommodated through means short of finding jurisdiction unconstitutional. For example, the potential clash of the forum's law with the "fundamental substantive social policies" of another State may be accommodated through application of the forum's choice-of-law rules. Similarly, a defendant claiming substantial inconvenience may seek a change of venue. Nevertheless, minimum requirements inherent in the concept of "fair play and substantial justice" may defeat the reasonableness of jurisdiction even if the defendant has purposefully engaged in forum activities. *World-Wide Volkswagen;* see also Restatement (Second) of Conflict of Laws §§36-37 (1971). As we previously have noted, jurisdictional rules may not be employed in such a way as to make litigation "so gravely difficult and inconvenient" that a party unfairly is at a "severe disadvantage" in comparison to his opponent.

B

(1)

Applying these principles to the case at hand, we believe there is substantial record evidence supporting the District Court's conclusion that the assertion of personal jurisdiction over Rudzewicz in Florida for the alleged breach of his franchise agreement did not offend due process. At the outset, we note a continued division among lower courts respecting whether and to what extent a contract can constitute a "contact" for purposes of due process analysis. If the question is whether an individual's contract with an out-of-state party alone can automatically establish sufficient minimum contacts in the other party's home forum, we believe the answer clearly is that it cannot. The Court long ago rejected the notion that personal jurisdiction might turn on "mechanical" tests, *International Shoe Co.*, or on "conceptualistic . . . theories of the place of contracting or of performance," Hoopeston Canning Co. v. Cullen, 318 U.S., at 316. Instead, we have emphasized the need for a "highly realistic" approach that recognizes that a "contract" is "ordinarily but an intermediate step serving to tie up prior business negotiations with future consequences which themselves are the real object of the business transaction." It is these factors—prior negotiations and contemplated future consequences, along with the terms of the contract and the parties' actual course of dealing—that must be evaluated in determining whether the defendant purposefully established minimum contacts within the forum.

In this case, no physical ties to Florida can be attributed to Rudzewicz other than MacShara's brief training course in Miami.[22] Rudzewicz did not maintain offices in Florida and, for all that appears from the record, has never even visited there. Yet this franchise dispute grew directly out of "a contract which had a substantial connection with that State." *McGee.* Eschewing the option of operating an independent local enterprise, Rudzewicz deliberately "reach[ed] out beyond" Michigan and negotiated with a Florida corporation for the purchase of a long-term franchise and the manifold benefits that would derive from affiliation with a nationwide organization. Upon approval, he entered into a carefully structured 20-year relationship that envisioned continuing and wide-reaching contacts with Burger King in Florida. In light

---

[22] . . . [W]e have previously noted that when commercial activities are "carried on in behalf of" an out-of-state party those activities may sometimes be ascribed to the party, at least where he is a "primary participan[t]" in the enterprise and has acted purposefully in directing those activities. Because MacShara's matriculation at Burger King University is not pivotal to the disposition of this case, we need not resolve the permissible bounds of such attribution.

of Rudzewicz' voluntary acceptance of the long-term and exacting regulation of his business from Burger King's Miami headquarters, the "quality and nature" of his relationship to the company in Florida can in no sense be viewed as "random," "fortuitous," or "attenuated." Rudzewicz' refusal to make the contractually required payments in Miami, and his continued use of Burger King's trademarks and confidential business information after his termination, caused foreseeable injuries to the corporation in Florida. For these reasons it was, at the very least, presumptively reasonable for Rudzewicz to be called to account there for such injuries.

The Court of Appeals concluded, however, that in light of the supervision emanating from Burger King's district office in Birmingham, Rudzewicz reasonably believed that "the Michigan office was for all intents and purposes the embodiment of Burger King" and that he therefore had no "reason to anticipate a Burger King suit outside of Michigan." This reasoning overlooks substantial record evidence indicating that Rudzewicz most certainly knew that he was affiliating himself with an enterprise based primarily in Florida. The contract documents themselves emphasize that Burger King's operations are conducted and supervised from the Miami headquarters, that all relevant notices and payments must be sent there, and that the agreements were made in and enforced from Miami. Moreover, the parties' actual course of dealing repeatedly confirmed that decisionmaking authority was vested in the Miami headquarters and that the district office served largely as an intermediate link between the headquarters and the franchisees. When problems arose over building design, site-development fees, rent computation, and the defaulted payments, Rudzewicz and MacShara learned that the Michigan office was powerless to resolve their disputes and could only channel their communications to Miami. Throughout these disputes, the Miami headquarters and the Michigan franchisees carried on a continuous course of direct communications by mail and by telephone, and it was the Miami headquarters that made the key negotiating decisions out of which the instant litigation arose.

Moreover, we believe the Court of Appeals gave insufficient weight to provisions in the various franchise documents providing that all disputes would be governed by Florida law. The franchise agreement, for example, stated:

> This Agreement shall become valid when executed and accepted by BKC at Miami, Florida; it shall be deemed made and entered into in the State of Florida and shall be governed and construed under and in accordance with the laws of the State of Florida. The choice of law designation does not require that all suits concerning this Agreement be filed in Florida.

The Court of Appeals reasoned that choice-of-law provisions are irrelevant to the question of personal jurisdiction, relying on *Hanson* for the proposition that "the center of gravity for choice-of-law purposes does not necessarily confer the sovereign prerogative to assert jurisdiction." This reasoning misperceives the import of the quoted proposition. The Court in *Hanson* and subsequent cases has emphasized that choice-of-law analysis—which focuses on all elements of a transaction, and not simply on the defendant's conduct—is distinct from minimum contacts jurisdictional analysis—which focuses at the threshold solely on the defendant's purposeful connection to the forum. Nothing in our cases, however, suggests that a choice-of-law provision should be ignored in considering whether a defendant has "purposefully invoked the benefits and protections of a State's laws" for jurisdictional purposes. Although such a provision standing alone would be insufficient to confer jurisdiction, we believe that, when combined with the 20-year interdependent relationship Rudzewicz established with Burger King's Miami headquarters, it reinforced his deliberate affiliation with the forum State and the reasonable foreseeability of possible litigation there. As Judge Johnson argued in his dissent below, Rudzewicz "purposefully availed himself of the benefits and protections of Florida's laws" by entering into contracts expressly providing that those laws would govern franchise disputes.[24]

(2)

Nor has Rudzewicz pointed to other factors that can be said persuasively to outweigh the considerations discussed above and to establish the unconstitutionality of Florida's assertion of jurisdiction. We cannot conclude that Florida had no "legitimate interest in holding [Rudzewicz] answerable on a claim related to" the contacts he had established in that State. *McGee* (noting that State frequently will have a "manifest interest in providing effective means of redress for its residents").[25] Moreover, although Rudzewicz has argued at some length that Michigan's Franchise Investment Law governs many aspects of this franchise relationship, he has not demonstrated how Michigan's acknowledged interest might possibly render jurisdiction in

---

[24] In addition, the franchise agreement's disclaimer that the "choice of law designation does not require that all suits concerning this Agreement be filed in Florida," reasonably should have suggested to Rudzewicz that by negative implication such suits could be filed there. The lease also provided for binding arbitration in Miami of certain condemnation disputes, and Rudzewicz conceded the validity of this provision at oral argument. Although it does not govern the instant dispute, this provision also should have made it apparent to the franchisees that they were dealing directly with the Miami headquarters and that the Birmingham district office was not "for all intents and purposes the embodiment of Burger King."

[25] Complaining that "when Burger King is the plaintiff, you won't 'have it your way' because it sues all franchisees in Miami," Rudzewicz contends that Florida's interest in providing a convenient forum is negligible given the company's size and ability to conduct litigation anywhere in the country. We disagree. Absent compelling considerations, a defendant who has purposefully derived commercial benefit from his affiliations in a forum may not defeat jurisdiction there simply because of his adversary's greater net wealth.

Florida unconstitutional. Finally, the Court of Appeals' assertion that the Florida litigation "severely impaired [Rudzewicz'] ability to call Michigan witnesses who might be essential to his defense and counterclaim," is wholly without support in the record. And even to the extent that it is inconvenient for a party who has minimum contacts with a forum to litigate there, such considerations most frequently can be accommodated through a change of venue. Although the Court has suggested that inconvenience may at some point become so substantial as to achieve constitutional magnitude, *McGee*, this is not such a case.

The Court of Appeals also concluded, however, that the parties' dealings involved "a characteristic disparity of bargaining power" and "elements of surprise," and that Rudzewicz "lacked fair notice" of the potential for litigation in Florida because the contractual provisions suggesting to the contrary were merely "boilerplate declarations in a lengthy printed contract." Rudzewicz presented many of these arguments to the District Court, contending that Burger King was guilty of misrepresentation, fraud, and duress; that it gave insufficient notice in its dealings with him; and that the contract was one of adhesion. After a 3-day bench trial, the District Court found that Burger King had made no misrepresentations, that Rudzewicz and MacShara "were and are experienced and sophisticated businessmen," and that "at no time" did they "ac[t] under economic duress or disadvantage imposed by" Burger King. FRCP 52(a) requires that "[f]indings of fact shall not be set aside unless clearly erroneous," and neither Rudzewicz nor the Court of Appeals has pointed to record evidence that would support a "definite and firm conviction" that the District Court's findings are mistaken. To the contrary, Rudzewicz was represented by counsel throughout these complex transactions and, as Judge Johnson observed in dissent below, was himself an experienced accountant "who for five months conducted negotiations with Burger King over the terms of the franchise and lease agreements, and who obligated himself personally to contracts requiring over time payments that exceeded $1 million." Rudzewicz was able to secure a modest reduction in rent and other concessions from Miami headquarters; moreover, to the extent that Burger King's terms were inflexible, Rudzewicz presumably decided that the advantages of affiliating with a national organization provided sufficient commercial benefits to offset the detriments.[28]

---

[28] We do not mean to suggest that the jurisdictional outcome will always be the same in franchise cases. Some franchises may be primarily intrastate in character or involve different decisionmaking structures, such that a franchisee should not reasonably anticipate out-of-state litigation. Moreover, commentators have argued that franchise relationships may sometimes involve unfair business practices in their inception and operation. For these reasons, we reject Burger King's suggestion for "a general rule, or at least a presumption, that participation in an interstate franchise relationship" represents consent to the jurisdiction of the franchisor's principal place of business.

III

Notwithstanding these considerations, the Court of Appeals apparently believed that it was necessary to reject jurisdiction in this case as a prophylactic measure, reasoning that an affirmance of the District Court's judgment would result in the exercise of jurisdiction over "out-of-state consumers to collect payments due on modest personal purchases" and would "sow the seeds of default judgments against franchisees owing smaller debts." We share the Court of Appeals' broader concerns and therefore reject any talismanic jurisdictional formulas; "the facts of each case must [always] be weighed" in determining whether personal jurisdiction would comport with "fair play and substantial justice." Kulko v. California Superior Court.[29] The "quality and nature" of an interstate transaction may sometimes be so "random," "fortuitous," or "attenuated" that it cannot fairly be said that the potential defendant "should reasonably anticipate being haled into court" in another jurisdiction. We also have emphasized that jurisdiction may not be grounded on a contract whose terms have been obtained through "fraud, undue influence, or overweening bargaining power" and whose application would render litigation "so gravely difficult and inconvenient that [a party] will for all practical purposes be deprived of his day in court." Just as the Due Process Clause allows flexibility in ensuring that commercial actors are not effectively "judgment proof" for the consequences of obligations they voluntarily assume in other States, so too does it prevent rules that would unfairly enable them to obtain default judgments against unwitting customers.

For the reasons set forth above, however, these dangers are not present in the instant case. Because Rudzewicz established a substantial and continuing relationship with Burger King's Miami headquarters, received fair notice from the contract documents and the course of dealing that he might be subject to suit in Florida, and has failed to demonstrate how jurisdiction in that forum would otherwise be fundamentally unfair, we conclude that the District Court's exercise of jurisdiction pursuant to Fla. Stat. §48.193(1)(g) (Supp. 1984) did not offend due process. The judgment of the Court of Appeals is accordingly reversed, and the case is remanded for further proceedings consistent with this opinion.

It is so ordered.

Justice POWELL took no part in the consideration or decision of this case.

---

[29] This approach does, of course, preclude clear-cut jurisdictional rules. But any inquiry into "fair play and substantial justice" necessarily requires determinations "in which few answers will be written 'in black and white. The greys are dominant and even among them the shades are innumerable.'" Kulko v. California Superior Court.

Justice STEVENS, with whom Justice WHITE joins, dissenting.

In my opinion there is a significant element of unfairness in requiring a franchisee to defend a case of this kind in the forum chosen by the franchisor. It is undisputed that appellee maintained no place of business in Florida, that he had no employees in that State, and that he was not licensed to do business there. Appellee did not prepare his French fries, shakes, and hamburgers in Michigan, and then deliver them into the stream of commerce "with the expectation that they [would] be purchased by consumers in" Florida. To the contrary, appellee did business only in Michigan, his business, property, and payroll taxes were payable in that State, and he sold all of his products there.

Throughout the business relationship, appellee's principal contacts with appellant were with its Michigan office. Notwithstanding its disclaimer, the Court seems ultimately to rely on nothing more than standard boilerplate language contained in various documents, to establish that appellee "'purposefully availed himself of the benefits and protections of Florida's laws.'" Such superficial analysis creates a potential for unfairness not only in negotiations between franchisors and their franchisees but, more significantly, in the resolution of the disputes that inevitably arise from time to time in such relationships. . . .

■ NOTES ON JURISDICTION IN CONTRACT SUITS

1. Few Supreme Court cases decided after *International Shoe* involve contract claims. *International Shoe* involved a government claim for employer contributions to an unemployment compensation program; *Hanson* was a will case or a trust case; *Shaffer* was a derivative suit for breach of fiduciary duty; *World-Wide*, *Asahi*, and *Nicastro* were product liability cases. *McGee* was a contract case of sorts, although the plaintiff there was what we would call a third-party beneficiary (mother of the insured) rather than a contracting party, and *Asahi* morphed into a contract case (dispute between Chinese tire maker and Japanese valve maker). Do contract suits differ in some important way from the others?

2. The contract in *Rudzewicz* contained a choice-of-law clause stating that Florida law would govern any dispute. Such provisions are commonplace in agreements between parties residing in different states. As you will see when you read *Carnival Cruise*, another commonplace provision is a "forum selection" clause stating that any dispute shall be litigated in a particular state or court. Who do you suppose put the choice-of-law clause in the contract? Why wasn't there also a forum selection clause designating Florida?

3. The Court says Rudzewicz "reached out" beyond Michigan and entered into a "deliberate affiliation with" Florida, hence "purposefully availed himself of the benefits and protections of Florida's laws," so jurisdiction in Florida satisfied the constitutional standard. Given that Rudzewicz never set foot in Florida, conducted negotiations with Burger King in Michigan, performed under the contract solely by operating the restaurant in Michigan, and dealt primarily with Burger King's Michigan office, is the conclusion announced by Justice Brennan justified?

4. The Court says that once the minimum contacts standard is satisfied, the court may consider "other factors" to determine whether the exercise of jurisdiction "comports with fair play and substantial justice," which may make it reasonable to exercise jurisdiction on "a lesser showing of minimum contacts than would otherwise be required." Does this language mean jurisdiction may rest on something *less than* minimum contacts? Recall that Justice Brennan called for the abolition of the minimum contacts standard in his opinion in *Shaffer*. Did he achieve in *Rudzewicz* what he could not in *Shaffer*? You saw in *World-Wide* that the Court lists five factors as critical in determining whether the minimum contacts standard is satisfied: There the five factors seemed to be *synonymous* with minimum contacts, didn't they? In *Asahi*, Justice O'Connor cited the same five factors in suggesting that sometimes jurisdiction should *not* be exercised, even though there were minimum contacts. But in *Rudzewicz* Justice Brennan seems to use the same factors not as *synonymous* with minimum contacts, nor as *reducing* the reach of jurisdiction, but as *expanding* its reach, doesn't he?

■ NOTES ON *IN PERSONAM* JURISDICTION IN FEDERAL COURT

1. Burger King sued MacShara and Rudzewicz in federal court in Florida, and sought, among other things, damages and injunctive relief for breach of contract. In other words, this part of the suit brought a state law claim, and the federal court had subject matter jurisdiction because of diversity. For personal jurisdiction, the court looked to the Florida long-arm statute. Why does personal jurisdiction in a *federal* court involve a *state* long-arm statute? This matter was not even raised on appeal because it is settled that state long-arm statutes do apply in diversity suits. It follows, doesn't it, that a litigant suing somebody from another state cannot "get around" the limits of long-arm statutes by going to federal court?

2. Having decided that the long-arm statute authorized jurisdiction in Florida, the Court took up the due process standard. It is not surprising that the Constitution limits not only what *state* courts may do, but what *federal* courts may do. But the "Due Process" Clause applied in *International Shoe* is in the Fourteenth Amendment, which says no *state* shall deprive "any person of life, liberty, or property, without due process of law." It says nothing about the *federal government*. There is, however, a *second* Due Process Clause, found in the Fifth Amendment, which contains similar language, and this provision *does* apply to the federal government.

(a) Assuming that the two provisions mean the same thing, it is arguable that the *reach* of federal court jurisdiction cannot be longer than the reach of state court jurisdiction. See generally Maryellen Fullerton, *Constitutional Limits on Nationwide Personal Jurisdiction in the Federal Courts*, 79 Nw. U. L. Rev. 1 (1994).

(b) It is far from certain, however, that *in personam* jurisdiction in federal court is limited in this way. What *International Shoe* requires is "minimum contacts" between defendant and the forum state, which could be translated for federal courts to mean that what is required is "minimum contacts" with the *country*. At least in *federal question* cases, where the relevant federal statute authorizes nationwide service of process, federal courts often take this view. See, e.g., Action Embroidery Corp. v. Atlantic Embroidery, Inc., 368 F.3d 1174, 1181 (9th Cir. 2004) (minimum contacts with United States is what due process requires). It is even arguable that in other cases, where the federal statute is silent on the matter of jurisdiction, federal courts have nationwide jurisdiction: After all, state courts have statewide jurisdiction even without statutes so providing.

(c) Part of the uncertainty stems from the fact that Congress never enacted a federal long-arm statute. The question whether it *could* do so, or whether doing so would violate any constitutional principle, has never been resolved. It was once argued that Federal Rule 4, governing service of process, displaced state law on the reach of jurisdiction, but this argument was rejected on the theory that the Rule governs *mechanics* of service, not *reach* of federal jurisdiction. In fact, absent a statutory authorization of nationwide jurisdiction, FRCP 4(k)(1)(A) requires federal courts to apply state long-arm statutes, even in federal question cases, often leading to a due process inquiry under the minimum contacts standard. See, e.g., Attachmate Corp. v. Public Health Trust of Miami-Dade County, 686 F. Supp. 2d 1140, 1146 (W.D. Wash. 2010) (copyright infringement suit; court must apply state long-arm statute because there is no federal statute on personal jurisdiction).

3. Exceptional Cases: Domestic Relations and Libel

a. Domestic Relations Cases

From the beginning, you have seen that domestic relations suits stand by themselves. In *Pennoyer*, the Court said every state "has the power to determine for itself the civil *status* and capacities of its inhabitants," which means that one spouse may divorce another even if the latter has left the state and cannot be served there. In *Shaffer,* the Court abolished jurisdiction based on seizure of property unrelated to the cause of action, but did not displace "other" jurisdictional doctrines, "such as the particularized rules governing adjudications of status."

American courts practice what is called "divisible divorce." The term refers to the fact that a state may award a divorce to any of its domiciliaries, even if the defendant spouse is not in the state, has never set foot in the state, and has no contacts with the state. Domicile ordinarily means that plaintiff has resided in the forum state for some significant period (often six months, sometimes as long as several years or as short as six weeks). Obviously, this system serves important interests. But issues of spousal support, child support, division of property, and child custody are also important, and *these* matters are *not* governed by the jurisdictional rule that applies to divorce itself.

The days are long gone when one spouse could divorce another only if the latter was guilty of infidelity or "extreme cruelty," and American jurisdictions have gone in the direction of "no-fault divorce," meaning that a spouse who wants to end a marriage can do so even if the other has "done nothing wrong." Perhaps it is not surprising that "fault" still seems to play a role in divorce proceedings, and in disputes over custody, support, and division of property, but officially it is irrelevant. In its modern formulation, the most common ground for divorce is that the couple has "irreconcilable differences" or the marriage is "irretrievably broken," and often a significant element in the proof is that the parties are living apart.

The *jurisdictional* significance of these developments is that spouses who want to end their marriages no longer have much reason to travel to distant states, which diminishes the number of cases in which jurisdictional issues arise. On the other side of the ledger is the fact that divorce is commonplace, and in an increasingly mobile society divorce may lead one or the other spouse to move out of state. Bear in mind that divorce is *always* litigated in state courts, and the Supreme Court has said more than once that federal courts lack subject matter jurisdiction in the area of domestic relations.

KULKO v. KULKO

United States Supreme Court
436 U.S. 84 (1978)

Mr. Justice MARSHALL delivered the opinion of the Court.

I

[New Yorkers Ezra and Sharon Kulko married in California in 1959 while Ezra was en route to Korea to serve in the armed forces. Sharon returned to New York, and in due course Ezra returned from Korea. They resided in

New York as husband and wife. In 1961 and 1962, Sharon Kulko bore a son Darwin and a daughter Ilsa, but ten years later husband and wife separated. By mutual agreement, she moved to California and the children stayed in New York with Ezra during the school year, spending summers in California with Sharon. Ezra paid Sharon $3,000 per year in child support for the time the children spent in California.

Sharon Kulko went to Haiti, where she obtained a divorce decree that incorporated the terms of the separation agreement. She then remarried, and took the name Hern. In 1973, the parents agreed that Ilsa would stay in California during the school year, and spend vacations in New York. Without Ezra's knowledge, Sharon later arranged for Darwin to join her in California too. When he arrived, Sharon filed suit in California to establish the Haitian divorce as a California judgment, and to increase Ezra's support obligations. Ezra appeared, objected to jurisdiction, but lost. On appeal, the California Supreme Court concluded that California had jurisdiction. Noting that the long-arm statute authorizes jurisdiction on any basis "not inconsistent with the Constitution," the California Court concluded that Ezra "purposefully availed himself of the benefits and protections" of California law by sending Ilsa to the state, and it was "fair and reasonable" to exercise jurisdiction over Ezra in a suit for support of *both* children.]

II

... We cannot accept the proposition that appellant's acquiescence in Ilsa's desire to live with her mother conferred jurisdiction over appellant in the California courts in this action. A father who agrees, in the interests of family harmony and his children's preferences, to allow them to spend more time in California than was required under a separation agreement can hardly be said to have "purposefully availed himself" of the "benefits and protections" of California's laws. See Shaffer v. Heitner, 433 U.S. 186, 216 (2977).[7]

Nor can we agree with the assertion of the court below that the exercise of in personam jurisdiction here was warranted by the financial benefit appellant derived from his daughter's presence in California for nine months of the year. This argument rests on the premise that, while appellant's liability for support payments remained unchanged, his yearly expenses for supporting the child in

---

[7] The court below stated that the presence in California of appellant's daughter gave appellant the benefit of California's "police and fire protection, its school system, its hospital services, its recreational facilities, its libraries and museums. . . ." But, in the circumstances presented here, these services provided by the State were essentially benefits to the child, not the father, and in any event were not benefits that appellant purposefully sought for himself.

New York decreased. But this circumstance, even if true, does not support California's assertion of jurisdiction here. Any diminution in appellant's household costs resulted, not from the child's presence in California, but rather from her absence from appellant's home. Moreover, an action by appellee Horn [Sharon Kulko] to increase support payments could now be brought, and could have been brought when Ilsa first moved to California, in the State of New York;[8] a New York court would clearly have personal jurisdiction over appellant and, if a judgment were entered by a New York court increasing appellant's child-support obligations, it could properly be enforced against him in both New York and California. Any ultimate financial advantage to appellant thus results not from the child's presence in California, but from appellee's failure earlier to seek an increase in payments under the separation agreement.[10] The argument below to the contrary, in our view, confuses the question of appellant's liability with that of the proper forum in which to determine that liability.

In light of our conclusion that appellant did not purposefully derive benefit from any activities relating to the State of California, it is apparent that the California Supreme Court's reliance on appellant's having caused an "effect" in California was misplaced. This "effects" test is derived from the American Law Institute's Restatement (Second) of Conflict of Laws §37 (1971), which provides:

> A state has power to exercise judicial jurisdiction over an individual who causes effects in the state by an act done elsewhere with respect to any cause of action arising from these effects unless the nature of the effects and of the individual's relationship to the state make the exercise of such jurisdiction unreasonable.

While this provision is not binding on this Court, it does not in any event support the decision below. As is apparent from the examples accompanying §37 in the Restatement, this section was intended to reach wrongful activity outside of the State causing injury within the State, see, e.g., Comment a (shooting bullet from one State into another), or commercial activity affecting state residents. Even in such situations, moreover, the Restatement recognizes

---

[8] Under the separation agreement, appellant is bound to "indemnify and hold [his] Wife harmless from any and all attorney fees, costs and expenses which she may incur by reason of the default of [appellant] in the performance of any of the obligations required to be performed by him pursuant to the terms and conditions of this agreement." To the extent that appellee Horn seeks arrearages, her litigation expenses, presumably including any additional costs incurred by her as a result of having to prosecute the action in New York, would thus be borne by appellant.

[10] It may well be that, as a matter of state law, appellee Horn could still obtain through New York proceedings additional payments from appellant for Ilsa's support from January 1974, when a de facto modification of the custody provisions of the separation agreement took place, until the present. See H. Clark, Domestic Relations §15.2, p. 500 (1968).

that there might be circumstances that would render "unreasonable" the assertion of jurisdiction over the nonresident defendant.

The circumstances in this case clearly render "unreasonable" California's assertion of personal jurisdiction. There is no claim that appellant has visited physical injury on either property or persons within the State of California. The cause of action herein asserted arises, not from the defendant's commercial transactions in interstate commerce, but rather from his personal, domestic relations. It thus cannot be said that appellant has sought a commercial benefit from solicitation of business from a resident of California that could reasonably render him liable to suit in state court; appellant's activities cannot fairly be analogized to an insurer's sending an insurance contract and premium notices into the State to an insured resident of the State. Furthermore, the controversy between the parties arises from a separation that occurred in the State of New York; appellee Horn seeks modification of a contract that was negotiated in New York and that she flew to New York to sign. As in Hanson v. Denckla, 357 U.S. 235 (1958), the instant action involves an agreement that was entered into with virtually no connection with the forum State.

Finally, basic considerations of fairness point decisively in favor of appellant's State of domicile as the proper forum for adjudication of this case, whatever the merits of appellee's underlying claim. It is appellant who has remained in the State of the marital domicile, whereas it is appellee who has moved across the continent. Appellant has at all times resided in New York State, and, until the separation and appellee's move to California, his entire family resided there as well. As noted above, appellant did no more than acquiesce in the stated preference of one of his children to live with her mother in California. This single act is surely not one that a reasonable parent would expect to result in the substantial financial burden and personal strain of litigating a child-support suit in a forum 3,000 miles away, and we therefore see no basis on which it can be said that appellant could reasonably have anticipated being "haled before a [California] court," Shaffer v. Heitner, 433 U.S., at 216. To make jurisdiction in a case such as this turn on whether appellant bought his daughter her ticket or instead unsuccessfully sought to prevent her departure would impose an unreasonable burden on family relations, and one wholly unjustified by the "quality and nature" of appellant's activities in or relating to the State of California. International Shoe v. Washington, 326 U.S. 310 (1945).

III

In seeking to justify the burden that would be imposed on appellant were the exercise of in personam jurisdiction in California sustained, appellee argues that California has substantial interests in protecting the welfare of its minor residents and in promoting to the fullest extent possible a healthy and sup-portive family environment in which the children of the State are to be raised. These interests are unquestionably important. But while the presence of the children and one parent in California arguably might favor application of California law in a lawsuit in New York, the fact that California may be the "'center of gravity'" for choice-of-law purposes does not mean that California has personal jurisdiction over the defendant. *Hanson.* And California has not attempted to assert any particularized interest in trying such cases in its courts by, e.g., enacting a special jurisdictional statute. *Cf.* McGee v. International Life Ins. Co., 355 U.S. 220, 223-224 (1957).

California's legitimate interest in ensuring the support of children resident in California without unduly disrupting the children's lives, moreover, is already being served by the State's participation in the Revised Uniform Reci-procal Enforcement of Support Act of 1968. This statute provides a mecha-nism for communication between court systems in different States, in order to facilitate the procurement and enforcement of child-support decrees where the dependent children reside in a State that cannot obtain personal jurisdic-tion over the defendant. California's version of the Act essentially permits a California resident claiming support from a nonresident to file a petition in California and have its merits adjudicated in the State of the alleged obligor's residence, without either party's having to leave his or her own State. Cal. Civ. Proc. Code Ann. §1650.[13] New York State is a signatory to a similar Act.

Thus, not only may plaintiff-appellee here vindicate her claimed right to additional child support from her former husband in a New York court, but also the Uniform Acts will facilitate both her prosecution of a claim for addi-tional support and collection of any support payments found to be owed by appellant.

It cannot be disputed that California has substantial interests in protect-ing resident children and in facilitating child-support actions on behalf of those children. But these interests simply do not make California a "fair forum" [under *Shaffer*] in which to require appellant, who derives no personal

---

[13] In addition to California, 24 other States are signatories to this Act. Under the Act, an "obligee" may file a petition in a court of his or her State (the "initiating court") to obtain support. 9 ULA §§11, 14 (1973). If the court "finds that the [petition] sets forth facts from which it may be determined that the obligor owes a duty of support and that a court of the responding state may obtain jurisdiction of the obligor or his property," it may send a copy of the petition to the "responding state." §14. This has the effect of requesting the responding State "to obtain jurisdiction over the obligor." §18(b). If jurisdiction is obtained, then a hearing is set in a court in the responding State at which the obligor may, if he chooses, contest the claim. The claim may be litigated in that court, with deposition testimony submitted through the initiating court by the initiating spouse or other party. §20. If the responding state court finds that the obligor owes a duty of support pursuant to the laws of the State where he or she was present during the time when support was sought, §7, judgment for the petitioner is entered. §24. If the money is collected from the spouse in the responding State, it is then sent to the court in the initiating State for distribution to the initiating party. §28.

or commercial benefit from his child's presence in California and who lacks any other relevant contact with the State, either to defend a child-support suit or to suffer liability by default.

IV

We therefore believe that the state courts in the instant case failed to heed our admonition that "the flexible standard of *International Shoe*" does not "heral[d] the eventual demise of all restrictions on the personal jurisdiction of state courts." *Hanson.* In *McGee,* we commented on the extension of in personam jurisdiction under evolving standards of due process, explaining that this trend was in large part "attributable to the . . . increasing nationalization of commerce . . . [accompanied by] modern transportation and communication [that] have made it much less burdensome for a party sued to defend himself in a State where he engages in economic activity." But the mere act of sending a child to California to live with her mother is not a commercial act and connotes no intent to obtain or expectancy of receiving a corresponding benefit in the State that would make fair the assertion of that State's judicial jurisdiction.

Accordingly, we conclude that the appellant's motion to quash service, on the ground of lack of personal jurisdiction, was erroneously denied by the California courts. The judgment of the California Supreme Court is, therefore, Reversed.

[The dissenting opinion of Mr. Justice Brennan, with whom Mr. Justice WHITE and Mr. Justice Powell join, is omitted.]

■ NOTES ON JURISDICTION IN DOMESTIC RELATIONS CASES

1. What is the strongest argument that Sharon Kulko can make in favor exercising jurisdiction in California over Ezra Kulko? Does the Court in *Kulko* disapprove the exercise of jurisdiction in California because Ezra Kulko lacked minimum contacts with the forum state, or because the Court does not want to discourage cooperation between parents? Is the latter concern a legitimate constitutional basis for the decision?

2. Much has changed since *Kulko* was decided. Already in 1974, Congress had entered the fray, setting up a federal Office of Child Support Enforcement and requiring states to establish enforcement programs when custodial parents are receiving state support. In 1992, Congress criminalized nonpayment of interstate child support, and required all states to enact the Uniform Interstate Family Support Act (UIFSA), which is similar to the Reciprocal

Enforcement of Support Act described in *Kulko*. UIFSA authorizes courts in the responding jurisdiction to "register" support orders from other jurisdictions, in which case they become enforceable as local judgments, see UIFSA §§601-604, and to issue and modify support orders and, among other things, to "order income withholding," and "place liens and order execution on the obligor's property," see UIFSA §305. See generally Ann Laquer Estin, *Sharing Governance: Family Law in Congress and the States*, 18 Cornell J.L. & Pub. Pol'y 267, 283-286 (2009).

3. UIFSA includes jurisdictional provisions. One authorizes the exercise of jurisdiction over an absent parent who once "resided with the child" in the forum state, and another authorizes jurisdiction over an absent parent if "the child resides in this State as a result of the acts or directives" of the parent. See UIFSA §201(a) (2001). Would this provision authorize jurisdiction in California over Ezra Kulko? If so, would it comport with due process?

4. In response to the argument that California has a special interest, the Court comments that California "has not attempted to assert any particularized interest" by "enacting a special jurisdictional statute." Does this argument resemble the point made in *Shaffer* that Delaware had not enacted a statute authorizing the exercise of jurisdiction over officers of Delaware corporations?

5. What if Sharon Kulko had written or telephoned Ezra to urge him to "pay some attention to your children"? (In today's world, she might do so by email or voicemail.) If Ezra took the point seriously and came to California to spend time with Ilsa or Darwin, and if Sharon served him when he came to her door to pick the children up, should he win a dismissal on grounds that he is immune from service of process? What if Sharon spoke truthfully in saying that Ilsa or Darwin "needed some contact with their father," but her motive was to serve Ezra in her suit for increased support payments? Recall the decision in the *Cannington* case, supra. You will have a chance to revisit this question when you read *Burnham*, infra.

6. *Support Obligations. Kulko* involves child support payments. It illustrates the broader point that a spouse seeking *either* child support or spousal support must obtain personal jurisdiction over the defendant. Recall the days of *Harris*, where the presence in the forum of a person who owed money to the defendant conferred jurisdiction over the defendant: The theory was that the debtor represented property owned by the defendant, and its presence in the forum provided jurisdiction to determine ownership of that debt.

(a) A New York husband once sought to turn this doctrine to his advantage. At the time, New York allowed divorce only for adultery, so this husband went to Nevada and established domicile (only six weeks were required). His wife had already obtained a separate maintenance decree in New York, but the husband got a Nevada divorce decree, and later sought in New York to terminate her rights to continued support. There was a colorable argument that the Nevada decree could have this effect, since it was then settled law, as the Supreme Court recognized, that jurisdiction over a

debtor "is sufficient to give the State of his domicile some control over the debt which he owes." Arguably, then, the Nevada decree cut off the husband's obligation to his stay-at-home spouse in New York. But the Supreme Court refused to go along: The husband could not use the Nevada decree this way, because it would amount to "an attempt to exercise an in personam jurisdiction over a person not before the court." Nevada "had no power to adjudicate" the wife's rights in her New York judgment, and New York "need not give full faith and credit to that phase" of what Nevada did. See Estin v. Estin, 334 U.S. 541 (1948). A later case extended *Estin* to the situation in which there was no prior decree. See Vanderbilt v. Vanderbilt, 354 U.S. 416 (1957).

(b) Estin and *Vanderbilt* mean jurisdiction to award a divorce does not bring with it jurisdiction to resolve support rights. Many state long-arm statutes authorize jurisdiction over an absent spouse who maintained "a matrimonial domicile" in the state. See, e.g., Colo. Rev. Stat. §13-1-124(1)(e). Obviously, support obligations come to life where the spouses live together, and a spouse who leaves the state is likely to remain subject to suit in that state, just as a nonresident motorist remains subject to suit for torts committed in the state. Does a provision like this "assert" the interest of the state so as to remove the objection in *Kulko* to proceeding under California's more general statute?

7. *Division of Property.* All American states recognize that both spouses have certain rights in property acquired by the efforts of either spouse during marriage, although states differ in the ways and theories by which they implement this idea. Under the principle recognized in *Estin* and *Vanderbilt,* a forum having jurisdiction *only* because it is the domicile of the plaintiff cannot, as an incident of divorce, divide marital property. The court can do so, however, if the defendant is subject to personal jurisdiction, as would happen if the long-arm statute of the state is satisfied and the defendant has minimum contacts with the state, or if the defendant appears and consents to jurisdiction.

With respect to real property, the state where the property is located has jurisdiction to divide it in a divorce situation. Such a suit, like a quiet title suit, is one in which the forum state has substantial interest and complete regulatory control, and such a suit generally fits into the category of *quasi-in-rem* type 1 that was left intact by *Shaffer.* Pretty clearly, the same result obtains in connection with tangible personal property, such as automobiles and household furniture, and also intangible property, like stock and bank accounts, subject to the problem noted in *Shaffer* that assigning a *locus* to such property is sometimes difficult.

8. *Custody of Children.* Because any state in which a minor child may be found has an interest in her welfare, it was once the "rule" that jurisdiction in child custody disputes "followed the child." Unfortunately, children can become pawns in disputes between parents, and the traditional rule let a parent "kidnap" her child, travel to whatever state suited the parent's purpose, and there seek a custody decree. See May v. Anderson, 345 U.S. 548 (1953) (refusing to require Ohio, where mother had taken her children, to honor a decree by Wisconsin court, domicile of children, awarding custody to father). There have been two major modern reform efforts in this area.

(a) First, many states adopted the Uniform Child Custody Jurisdiction Act (UCCJA), later replaced by the Uniform Child Custody Jurisdiction and Enforcement Act (UCCJEA). These statutes sought to channel child custody disputes to the most appropriate forum and to block courts from going forward in such cases when a child had been brought into the forum state by a "kidnapping" parent or guardian, and the UCCJEA seeks to give priority to the child's "home state" and to secure the exclusive authority of that state to enter custody orders. See generally Patricia M. Hoff, *The ABC's of the UCCJEA: Interstate Child Custody Practice Under the New Act,* 32 Fam. L.Q. 267 (1998).

(b) Second, Congress entered the fray with the Parental Kidnapping Prevention Act of 1980 (PKPA), which also seeks to discourage parental abductions and to encourage state courts to recognize and give effect to custody decrees by courts in states with substantial connections with a marriage and a child. See 28 USC §1738A. The PKPA overlaps with state legislation, but Congress did not intend to displace state law completely, and reportedly the UCCJEA has largely succeeded in harmonizing state and federal law. If conflicts do arise between the UCCJA and PKPA, the latter controls. See generally Estin, supra note 2, at 307-308.

9. *The "Status" Exception Revisited.* It has long been understood that the so-called status exception to the rule requiring personal jurisdiction over an absent defendant reaches divorce cases. Does it reach further? See, e.g., In re Termination of Parental Rights to Thomas J.R., 663 N.W.2d 734 (Wis. 2003) ("status exception" to UCCJA allows court to terminate parental rights of absent person without minimum contacts, and doing so is constitutional).

b. Libel Cases

Particularly in the internet age, but really beginning earlier in the twentieth century as newspapers and magazines achieved nationwide circulation, libel and slander rose in importance as occasions for the exercise of jurisdiction for acts committed by persons or companies located outside the forum state.

CALDER v. JONES

Supreme Court of the United States
465 U.S. 783 (1984)

Justice REHNQUIST delivered the opinion of the Court.

... Respondent [Shirley Jones] lives and works in California. She and her husband brought this suit [in California] against the National Enquirer, Inc., its local distributing company, and petitioners for libel, invasion of privacy, and intentional infliction of emotional harm. The Enquirer is a Florida corporation with its principal place of business in Florida. It publishes a national weekly newspaper with a total circulation of over 5 million. About 600,000 of those copies, almost twice the level of the next highest State, are sold in California. Respondent's and her husband's claims were based on an article that appeared in the Enquirer's October 9, 1979 issue. Both the Enquirer and the distributing company answered the complaint and made no objection to the jurisdiction of the California court.

Petitioner South is a reporter employed by the Enquirer. He is a resident of Florida, though he frequently travels to California on business.[3] South wrote the first draft of the challenged article, and his byline appeared on it. He did most of his research in Florida, relying on phone calls to sources in California for the information contained in the article.[4] Shortly before publication, South called respondent's home and read to her husband a draft of the article so as to elicit his comments upon it. Aside from his frequent trips and phone calls, South has no other relevant contacts with California.

Petitioner Calder is also a Florida resident. He has been to California only twice—once, on a pleasure trip, prior to the publication of the article and once after to testify in an unrelated trial. Calder is president and editor of the Enquirer. He "oversee[s] just about every function of the Enquirer." He reviewed and approved the initial evaluation of the subject of the article and edited it in its final form. He also declined to print a retraction requested by respondent. Calder has no other relevant contacts with California.

In considering petitioners' motion to quash service of process, the superior court surmised that the actions of petitioners in Florida, causing injury to respondent in California, would ordinarily be sufficient to support an assertion of jurisdiction over them in California. But the court felt that special solicitude was necessary because of the potential "chilling effect" on reporters and editors which would result from requiring them to appear in remote jurisdictions to answer for the content of articles upon which they worked. The court also noted that respondent's rights could be "fully satisfied" in her suit against the publisher without requiring petitioners to appear as parties. The superior court, therefore, granted the motion.

The California Court of Appeal reversed. The court agreed that neither petitioner's contacts with California would be sufficient for an assertion of jurisdiction on a cause of action unrelated to those contacts. But the court

---

[3] South stated that during a four-year period he visited California more than 20 times. A friend estimated that he came to California from 6 to 12 times each year.

[4] The superior court found that South made at least one trip to California in connection with the article. South hotly disputes this finding, claiming that an uncontroverted affidavit shows that he never visited California to research the article. Since we do not rely for our holding on the alleged visit, we find it unnecessary to consider the contention.

concluded that a valid basis for jurisdiction existed on the theory that petitioners intended to, and did, cause tortious injury to respondent in California. The fact that the actions causing the effects in California were performed outside the State did not prevent the State from asserting jurisdiction over a cause of action arising out of those effects. The court rejected the superior court's conclusion that First Amendment considerations must be weighed in the scale against jurisdiction.

[The case has not been tried, and came up for review in unusual circumstances. The Court grants petition of John South and Iain Calder for certiorari.]

The Due Process Clause of the Fourteenth Amendment to the United States Constitution permits personal jurisdiction over a defendant in any State with which the defendant has "certain minimum contacts ... such that the maintenance of the suit does not offend 'traditional notions of fair play and substantial justice.' Milliken v. Meyer, 311 U.S. 457, 463 (1940)." *International Shoe.* In judging minimum contacts, a court properly focuses on "the relationship among the defendant, the forum, and the litigation." Shaffer v. Heitner, 433 U.S. 186, 204 (1977). The plaintiff's lack of "contacts" will not defeat otherwise proper jurisdiction, but they may be so manifold as to permit jurisdiction when it would not exist in their absence. Here, the plaintiff is the focus of the activities of the defendants out of which the suit arises.

The allegedly libelous story concerned the California activities of a California resident. It impugned the professionalism of an entertainer whose television career was centered in California.[9] The article was drawn from California sources, and the brunt of the harm, in terms both of respondent's emotional distress and the injury to her professional reputation, was suffered in California. In sum, California is the focal point both of the story and of the harm suffered. Jurisdiction over petitioners is therefore proper in California based on the "effects" of their Florida conduct in California. World-Wide Volkswagen Corp. v. Woodson, 444 U.S. 286, 297-298 (1980); Restatement (Second) of Conflicts of Law §37.

Petitioners argue that they are not responsible for the circulation of the article in California. A reporter and an editor, they claim, have no direct economic stake in their employer's sales in a distant State. Nor are ordinary employees able to control their employer's marketing activity. The mere fact that they can "foresee" that the article will be circulated and have an effect in California is not sufficient for an assertion of jurisdiction. They do not "in effect appoint the [article their] agent for service of process." *World-Wide Volkswagen Corp.* Petitioners liken themselves to a welder employed in

---

[9] The article alleged that respondent drank so heavily as to prevent her from fulfilling her professional obligations.

Florida who works on a boiler which subsequently explodes in California. Cases which hold that jurisdiction will be proper over the manufacturer, Buckeye Boiler Co. v. Superior Court, 458 P.2d 57 (Cal. 1969); Gray v. American Radiator & Standard Sanitary Corp., 176 N.E.2d 761 (Ill. 1961), should not be applied to the welder who has no control over and derives no direct benefit from his employer's sales in that distant State.

Petitioners' analogy does not wash. Whatever the status of their hypothetical welder, petitioners are not charged with mere untargeted negligence. Rather, their intentional, and allegedly tortious, actions were expressly aimed at California. Petitioner South wrote and petitioner Calder edited an article that they knew would have a potentially devastating impact upon respondent. And they knew that the brunt of that injury would be felt by respondent in the State in which she lives and works and in which the *National Enquirer* has its largest circulation. Under the circumstances, petitioners must "reasonably anticipate being haled into court there" to answer for the truth of the statements made in their article. *World-Wide Volkswagen Corp.*; *Kulko*; *Shaffer*. An individual injured in California need not go to Florida to seek redress from persons who, though remaining in Florida, knowingly cause the injury in California.

Petitioners are correct that their contacts with California are not to be judged according to their employer's activities there. On the other hand, their status as employees does not somehow insulate them from jurisdiction. Each defendant's contacts with the forum State must be assessed individually. See Rush v. Savchuk, 444 U.S. 320, 332 (1980) ("The requirements of *International Shoe* ... must be met as to each defendant over whom a state court exercises jurisdiction"). In this case, petitioners are primary participants in an alleged wrongdoing intentionally directed at a California resident, and jurisdiction over them is proper on that basis.

We also reject the suggestion that First Amendment concerns enter into the jurisdictional analysis. The infusion of such considerations would needlessly complicate an already imprecise inquiry. Moreover, the potential chill on protected First Amendment activity stemming from libel and defamation actions is already taken into account in the constitutional limitations on the substantive law governing such suits. See New York Times, Inc. v. Sullivan, 376 U.S. 254 (1964); Gertz v. Robert Welch, Inc., 418 U.S. 323 (1974). To reintroduce those concerns at the jurisdictional stage would be a form of double counting. We have already declined in other contexts to grant special procedural protections to defendants in libel and defamation actions in addition to the constitutional protections embodied in the substantive laws.

We hold that jurisdiction over petitioners in California is proper because of their intentional conduct in Florida calculated to cause injury to respondent in California. The judgment of the California Court of Appeal is *Affirmed.*

■ NOTES ON JURISDICTION IN LIBEL (AND OTHER INTENTIONAL TORT) CASES

1. *Calder* is an easy case, isn't it? The National Enquirer has long been in the business of exposing—accurately or not—details of the lives of well-known people, and this publication and others are on sale at supermarket checkout counters everywhere. Often the stories, even if true (perhaps especially then) are embarrassing and sometimes damaging to the persons described. John South and Iain Calder could have had no doubt, could they, that a story saying that Shirley Jones "drank so heavily as to prevent her from fulfilling her professional obligations" would cause embarrassment and professional harm? Add the fact that the National Enquirer had a large circulation in California, and that California is the place where damages would be most acutely felt, and it is easy to see why a California court should hear the case, and why, whatever the inconvenience to Messrs. South and Calder, they should have to defend in California.

2. Suppose less egregious facts: Shirley Jones sues in Idaho (far from home, in a smaller state where the Enquirer enjoys fewer sales). Or suppose she names as defendants the "fact checkers" who did not write or create the story, but checked up on whatever facts are set out in the article.

(a) Consider Keeton v. Hustler, 465 U.S. 770 (1984), handed down the same day as *Calder.* There a former executive of Hustler Magazine sued for libel and invasion of privacy (the magazine ran an insinuating cartoon of her, and nude photographs of another woman identifying plaintiff as the subject): Kathy Keeton won a verdict of $2 million, but many facts supporting jurisdiction in *Calder* were absent. Keeton was from New York, but she sued in New Hampshire to take advantage of its six-year statute of limitations (longer than any in the country), New Hampshire being the *only* state where her libel claim was not barred.[4] Only 1 percent of the magazine's circulation was in New Hampshire; there was no indication that anyone involved in the story had contact with New Hampshire. Still the Court found that the forum state had "sufficient" interest to exercise jurisdiction, and that plaintiff was suing "at least in part" for "damages suffered in New Hampshire," suggesting that false statements damage "both the subject ... *and* the readers," and New Hampshire may "employ its libel laws to discourage the deception of its

---

[4] Keeton first sued in Ohio (the magazine's state of incorporation), but the court dismissed the libel claim as barred by Ohio's statute of limitations, and her privacy claim as barred by New York's statute. In her later suit in New Hampshire, she brought only the libel claim: Not only was New Hampshire the only state where the statute had not run, but it had no "borrowing" statute (that would apply the shorter Ohio or New York statute). Usually, when a court applies its own limitations statute, a dismissal is "procedural," allowing suit elsewhere. Usually, when it applies another state's statute, the dismissal is on the merits, barring later suit.

citizens."[5] The Court rejected any notion that "minimum contacts" requires a connection between *plaintiff* and the forum, even though plaintiff's residence is not "completely irrelevant" to the jurisdictional inquiry, which "focuses on the relations among the defendant, the forum and the litigation." Hustler Magazine, the Court concluded, "continuously and deliberately exploited the New Hampshire market," so it could "reasonably anticipate being haled into court there in a libel action based on the contents of its magazine," and it must anticipate that such a suit will seek "nationwide damages." Keeton v. Hustler Magazine, Inc., 465 U.S. 770 (1984).

    (b) Should it make a difference that 1 percent of the magazine's circulation in *Keeton* amounted to 10,000-15,000 copies—seemingly a nontrivial amount, even if small in proportion to its total circulation? Would the case come out the same way if only five copies of the offending publication had been sold there?

    3. Other courts have been far less generous in recognizing jurisdiction in libel cases in plaintiff's home state, based on the effects test and the idea of targeted wrongdoing. See, e.g., Davis v. Simon, 2012 WL 649098 (Ind. App. 2012) (no jurisdiction in Indiana to hear local plaintiff's suit against California defendant, whose allegedly libelous comments were made over the telephone to a radio reporter; radio station "initiated the contact" and defendant "did *nothing more* than simply respond to WHTR's inquiry [that] it initiated").

    4. If one concern in cases like *Keeton* is that allegedly libelous material can travel far and wide quickly, potentially subjecting defendants to jurisdiction in distant fora on the basis of what seem to be minor contacts, the internet age has clearly magnified this risk. See, e.g., cases cited in note 4(d) in Notes on Jurisdiction over Internet Claims, in Section C6, infra.

4. General Jurisdiction and Presence

In the *International Shoe* era, "general jurisdiction" continues as a theoretical possibility: *International Shoe* itself suggests that sometimes "continuous corporate operations" in a state are "so substantial" and "of such a nature" that they support jurisdiction even when the claims arise out of "dealings entirely distinct from those activities." See also uBid v. GoDaddy Group, Inc., 623 F.3d 421 (7th Cir. 2010) (contacts may be "so extensive" that defendant is subject to "general personal jurisdiction" and can be sued "for any cause of action arising in any place").

---

[5] The "single publication" rule holds that a libel claimant may recover in one suit all damages caused by *every* publication of the defaming matter (an exception to the rule that each separate publication is a separate tort), so Ms. Keeton could (and ultimately did) recover judgment in New Hampshire for all her damages.

GOODYEAR DUNLOP TIRES OPERATIONS, S.A. v. BROWN

Supreme Court of the United States
131 S. Ct. 2846 (2011)

Justice GINSBURG delivered the opinion of the Court.

This case concerns the jurisdiction of state courts over corporations organized and operating abroad. We address, in particular, this question: Are foreign subsidiaries of a United States parent corporation amenable to suit in state court on claims unrelated to any activity of the subsidiaries in the forum State?

A bus accident outside Paris that took the lives of two 13-year-old boys from North Carolina gave rise to the litigation we here consider. Attributing the accident to a defective tire manufactured in Turkey at the plant of a foreign subsidiary of The Goodyear Tire and Rubber Company (Goodyear USA), the boys' parents commenced an action for damages in a North Carolina state court; they named as defendants Goodyear USA, an Ohio corporation, and three of its subsidiaries, organized and operating, respectively, in Turkey, France, and Luxembourg. Goodyear USA, which had plants in North Carolina and regularly engaged in commercial activity there, did not contest the North Carolina court's jurisdiction over it; Goodyear USA's foreign subsidiaries, however, maintained that North Carolina lacked adjudicatory authority over them.

. . .

A court may assert general jurisdiction over foreign (sister-state or foreign-country) corporations to hear any and all claims against them when their affiliations with the State are so "continuous and systematic" as to render them essentially at home in the forum State. Specific jurisdiction, on the other hand, depends on an "affiliatio[n] between the forum and the underlying controversy," principally, activity or an occurrence that takes place in the forum State and is therefore subject to the State's regulation. von Mehren & Trautman, Jurisdiction to Adjudicate: A Suggested Analysis, 79 Harv. L. Rev. 1121, 1136 (1966) (hereinafter von Mehren & Trautman); see Brilmayer et al., A General Look at General Jurisdiction, 66 Texas L. Rev. 721, 782 (1988) (hereinafter Brilmayer). In contrast to general, all-purpose jurisdiction, specific jurisdiction is confined to adjudication of "issues deriving from, or connected with, the very controversy that establishes jurisdiction." von Mehren & Trautman 1136.

Because the episode-in-suit, the bus accident, occurred in France, and the tire alleged to have caused the accident was manufactured and sold abroad, North Carolina courts lacked specific jurisdiction to adjudicate the controversy. The North Carolina Court of Appeals so acknowledged. Were the foreign subsidiaries nonetheless amenable to general jurisdiction in North Carolina courts? Confusing or blending general and specific jurisdictional inquiries, the North Carolina courts answered yes. Some of the tires made abroad by Goodyear's foreign subsidiaries, the North Carolina Court of Appeals stressed, had reached North Carolina through "the stream of commerce"; that connection, the Court of Appeals believed, gave North Carolina courts the handle needed for the exercise of general jurisdiction over the foreign corporations.

A connection so limited between the forum and the foreign corporation, we hold, is an inadequate basis for the exercise of general jurisdiction. Such a connection does not establish the "continuous and systematic" affiliation necessary to empower North Carolina courts to entertain claims unrelated to the foreign corporation's contacts with the State.

I

On April 18, 2004, a bus destined for Charles de Gaulle Airport overturned on a road outside Paris, France. Passengers on the bus were young soccer players from North Carolina beginning their journey home. Two 13-year-olds, Julian Brown and Matthew Helms, sustained fatal injuries. The boys' parents, respondents in this Court, filed a suit for wrongful death damages in the Superior Court of Onslow County, North Carolina, in their capacity as administrators of the boys' estates. Attributing the accident to a tire that failed when its plies separated, the parents alleged negligence in the "design, construction, testing, and inspection" of the tire.

Goodyear Luxembourg Tires, SA (Goodyear Luxembourg), Goodyear Lastikleri TAS (Goodyear Turkey), and Goodyear Dunlop Tires France, SA (Goodyear France), petitioners here, were named as defendants. Incorporated in Luxembourg, Turkey, and France, respectively, petitioners are indirect subsidiaries of Goodyear USA, an Ohio corporation also named as a defendant in the suit. Petitioners manufacture tires primarily for sale in European and Asian markets. Their tires differ in size and construction from tires ordinarily sold in the United States. They are designed to carry significantly heavier loads, and to serve under road conditions and speed limits in the manufacturers' primary markets.[1]

In contrast to the parent company, Goodyear USA, which does not contest the North Carolina courts' personal jurisdiction over it, petitioners are not registered to do business in North Carolina. They have no place of business, employees, or bank accounts in North Carolina. They do not design, manufacture, or advertise their products in North Carolina. And they do not solicit business in North Carolina or themselves sell or ship tires to North Carolina customers. Even so, a small percentage of petitioners' tires

---

[1] Respondents portray Goodyear USA's structure as a reprehensible effort to "outsource" all manufacturing, and correspondingly, tort litigation, to foreign jurisdictions. Yet Turkey, where the tire alleged to have caused the accident-in-suit was made, is hardly a strange location for a facility that primarily supplies markets in Europe and Asia.

(tens of thousands out of tens of millions manufactured between 2004 and 2007) were distributed within North Carolina by other Goodyear USA affiliates. These tires were typically custom ordered to equip specialized vehicles such as cement mixers, waste haulers, and boat and horse trailers. Petitioners state, and respondents do not here deny, that the type of tire involved in the accident, a Goodyear Regional RHS tire manufactured by Goodyear Turkey, was never distributed in North Carolina.

[Goodyear Turkey and Goodyear France moved to dismiss for lack of jurisdiction, but the trial court denied the motion and the North Carolina Court of Appeals affirmed. It recognized that the question was whether these defendants had sufficient contacts to confer general jurisdiction, and concluded in the affirmative because they put the tires "in the stream of interstate commerce without any limitation" preventing sale in North Carolina. The tires reached the state through a "highly-organized distribution process" involving other Goodyear subsidiaries, and the tire involved in the Paris accident confirmed to standards imposed by the U.S. Department of Transportation (DOT). These markings "do not necessarily show" that the tires were destined for sale in this country, as DOT "encourages other countries" to treat compliance with DOT standards and markings as evidence of safe manufacture. The state has an interest in providing relief for its citizens, the North Carolina Court of Appeals said. The North Carolina Supreme Court declined review.]

II

A

The Due Process Clause of the Fourteenth Amendment sets the outer boundaries of a state tribunal's authority to proceed against a defendant. The canonical opinion in this area remains *International Shoe,* in which we held that a State may authorize its courts to exercise personal jurisdiction over an out-of-state defendant if the defendant has "certain minimum contacts with [the State] such that the maintenance of the suit does not offend 'traditional notions of fair play and substantial justice'" (quoting *Meyer*).

Endeavoring to give specific content to the "fair play and substantial justice" concept, the Court in *International Shoe* classified cases involving out-of-state corporate defendants. First, as in *International Shoe* itself, jurisdiction unquestionably could be asserted where the corporation's in-state activity is "continuous and systematic" and *that activity gave rise to the episode-in-suit.* Further, the Court observed, the commission of certain "single or occasional acts" in a State may be sufficient to render a corporation answerable in that State with respect to those acts, though not with respect to matters unrelated to the forum connections. The heading courts today use to encompass these two *International Shoe* categories is "specific jurisdiction." See von Mehren &

Trautman 1144-1163. Adjudicatory authority is "specific" when the suit "aris[es] out of or relate[s] to the defendant's contacts with the forum." Helicopteros Nacionales de Colombia, S.A. v. Hall, 466 U.S. 408, 414 n.8 (1984).

International Shoe distinguished from cases that fit within the "specific jurisdiction" categories, "instances in which the continuous corporate operations within a state [are] so substantial and of such a nature as to justify suit against it on causes of action arising from dealings entirely distinct from those activities." Adjudicatory authority so grounded is today called "general jurisdiction." For an individual, the paradigm forum for the exercise of general jurisdiction is the individual's domicile; for a corporation, it is an equivalent place, one in which the corporation is fairly regarded as at home. See Brilmayer 728 (identifying domicile, place of incorporation, and principal place of business as "paradig[m]" bases for the exercise of general jurisdiction).

Since *International Shoe*, this Court's decisions have elaborated primarily on circumstances that warrant the exercise of specific jurisdiction, particularly in cases involving "single or occasional acts" occurring or having their impact within the forum State. As a rule in these cases, this Court has inquired whether there was "some act by which the defendant purposefully avail[ed] itself of the privilege of conducting activities within the forum State, thus invoking the benefits and protections of its laws." Hanson v. Denckla, 357 U.S. 235, 253 (1958). [The Court cites and quotes its decisions in *World-Wide, Rudzewicz*, and *Asahi*.] See also Twitchell, The Myth of General Jurisdiction, 101 Harv. L. Rev. 610, 628 (1988) (in the wake of *International Shoe*, "specific jurisdiction has become the centerpiece of modern jurisdiction theory, while general jurisdiction plays a reduced role").

In only two decisions postdating *International Shoe* has this Court considered whether an out-of-state corporate defendant's in-state contacts were sufficiently "continuous and systematic" to justify the exercise of general jurisdiction over claims unrelated to those contacts: Perkins v. Benguet Consol. Mining Co., 342 U.S. 437 (1952) (general jurisdiction appropriately exercised over Philippine corporation sued in Ohio, where the company's affairs were overseen during World War II); and *Helicopteros* (helicopter owned by Colombian corporation crashed in Peru; survivors of U.S. citizens who died in the crash, the Court held, could not maintain wrongful-death actions against the Colombian corporation in Texas, for the corporation's helicopter purchases and purchase-linked activity in Texas were insufficient to subject it to Texas court's general jurisdiction).

B

To justify the exercise of general jurisdiction over petitioners, the North Carolina courts relied on the petitioners' placement of their tires in the "stream of commerce." The stream-of-commerce metaphor has been invoked frequently in lower court decisions permitting "jurisdiction in products liability cases in which the product has traveled through an extensive chain of distribution before reaching the ultimate consumer." 18 W. Fletcher, Cyclopedia of the Law of Corporations §8640.40, p. 133 (rev. ed. 2007). Typically, in such cases, a nonresident defendant, acting *outside* the forum, places in the stream of commerce a product that ultimately causes harm *inside* the forum. See generally Dayton, Personal Jurisdiction and the Stream of Commerce, 7 Rev. Litigation 239, 262-268 (1988) (discussing origins and evolution of the stream-of-commerce doctrine).

Many States have enacted longarm statutes authorizing courts to exercise specific jurisdiction over manufacturers when the events in suit, or some of them, occurred within the forum state. For example, the "Local Injury; Foreign Act" subsection of North Carolina's longarm statute authorizes North Carolina courts to exercise personal jurisdiction in "any action claiming injury to person or property within this State arising out of [the defendant's] act or omission outside this State," if, "in addition[,] at or about the time of the injury," "[p]roducts ... manufactured by the defendant were used or consumed, within this State in the ordinary course of trade." N.C. Gen. Stat. Ann. §10-75.4(4)(b). As the North Carolina Court of Appeals recognized, this provision of the State's longarm statute "does not apply to this case," for both the act alleged to have caused injury (the fabrication of the allegedly defective tire) and its impact (the accident) occurred outside the forum.[4]

The North Carolina court's stream-of-commerce analysis elided the essential difference between case-specific and all-purpose (general) jurisdiction. Flow of a manufacturer's products into the forum, we have explained, may bolster an affiliation germane to *specific* jurisdiction. See, *e.g.*, *World-Wide Volkswagen* (where "the sale of a product ... is not simply an isolated occurrence, but arises from the efforts of the manufacturer or distributor to serve ... the market for its product in [several] States, it is not unreasonable to subject it to suit in one of those States if its allegedly defective merchandise *has there been the source of injury to its owner or to others*" (emphasis added)). But ties serving to bolster the exercise of specific jurisdiction do not warrant a determination that, based on those ties, the forum has *general* jurisdiction over a defendant. See, *e.g.*, Stabilisierungsfonds Fur Wein v. Kaiser Stuhl Wine Distributors Pty. Ltd., 647 F.2d 200, 203, n.5 (D.C. Cir. 1981) (defendants' marketing arrangements, although "adequate to permit litigation of claims relating to [their] introduction of ... wine into the United States stream of

---

[4] The court instead relied on N.C. Gen. Stat. Ann. §1-75.4(1)(d), which provides for jurisdiction, "whether the claim arises within or without [the] State," when the defendant "[i]s engaged in substantial activity within this State, whether such activity is wholly interstate, intrastate, or otherwise." This provision, the North Carolina Supreme Court has held, was "intended to make available to the North Carolina courts the full jurisdictional powers permissible under federal due process." Dillon v. Numismatic Funding Corp., 231 S.E.2d 629, 630 (N.C. 1977).

commerce, . . . would not be adequate to support general, 'all purpose' adjudicatory authority").

A corporation's "continuous activity of some sorts within a state," *International Shoe* instructed, "is not enough to support the demand that the corporation be amenable to suits unrelated to that activity." Our 1952 decision in *Perkins* remains "[t]he textbook case of general jurisdiction appropriately exercised over a foreign corporation that has not consented to suit in the forum." Donahue v. Far Eastern Air Transport Corp., 652 F.2d 1032, 1037 (D.C. Cir. 1981).

Sued in Ohio, the defendant in *Perkins* was a Philippine mining corporation that had ceased activities in the Philippines during World War II. To the extent that the company was conducting any business during and immediately after the Japanese occupation of the Philippines, it was doing so in Ohio: The corporation's president maintained his office there, kept the company files in that office, and supervised from the Ohio office "the necessarily limited wartime activities of the company." Although the claim-in-suit did not arise in Ohio, this Court ruled that it would not violate due process for Ohio to adjudicate the controversy.

We next addressed the exercise of general jurisdiction over an out-of-state corporation over three decades later, in *Helicopteros*. In that case, survivors of United States citizens who died in a helicopter crash in Peru instituted wrongful-death actions in a Texas state court against the owner and operator of the helicopter, a Colombian corporation. The Colombian corporation had no place of business in Texas and was not licensed to do business there. "Basically, [the company's] contacts with Texas consisted of sending its chief executive officer to Houston for a contract-negotiation session; accepting into its New York bank account checks drawn on a Houston bank; purchasing helicopters, equipment, and training services from [a Texas enterprise] for substantial sums; and sending personnel to [Texas] for training." These links to Texas, we determined, did not "constitute the kind of continuous and systematic general business contacts . . . found to exist in *Perkins*," and were insufficient to support the exercise of jurisdiction over a claim that neither "ar[o]se out of . . . no[r] related to" the defendant's activities in Texas.

Helicopteros concluded that "mere purchases [made in the forum State], even if occurring at regular intervals, are not enough to warrant a State's assertion of [general] jurisdiction over a nonresident corporation in a cause of action not related to those purchase transactions." We see no reason to differentiate from the ties to Texas held insufficient in *Helicopteros*, the sales of petitioners' tires sporadically made in North Carolina through intermediaries. Under the sprawling view of general jurisdiction urged by respondents and embraced by the North Carolina Court of Appeals, any substantial manufacturer or seller of goods would be amenable to suit, on any claim for relief, wherever its products are distributed. But cf. *World-Wide Volkswagen* (every seller of chattels does not, by virtue of the sale, "appoint the chattel his agent for service of process").

Measured against *Helicopteros* and *Perkins*, North Carolina is not a forum in which it would be permissible to subject petitioners to general jurisdiction. Unlike the defendant in *Perkins*, whose sole wartime business activity was conducted in Ohio, petitioners are in no sense at home in North Carolina. Their attenuated connections to the State fall far short of the "the continuous and systematic general business contacts" necessary to empower North Carolina to entertain suit against them on claims unrelated to anything that connects them to the State.[5]

C

Respondents belatedly assert a "single enterprise" theory, asking us to consolidate petitioners' ties to North Carolina with those of Goodyear USA and other Goodyear entities. In effect, respondents would have us pierce Goodyear corporate veils, at least for jurisdictional purposes. See Brilmayer & Paisley, Personal Jurisdiction and Substantive Legal Relations: Corporations, Conspiracies, and Agency, 74 Cal. L. Rev. 1, 14, 29-30 (1986) (merging parent and subsidiary for jurisdictional purposes requires an inquiry "comparable to the corporate law question of piercing the corporate veil"). [The Court notes that the North Carolina Court of Appeals in this case "understood that petitioners are 'separate corporate entities . . . not directly responsible for the presence in North Carolina of tires that they had manufactured.'"] Neither below nor in their brief in opposition to the petition for certiorari did respondents urge disregard of petitioners' discrete status as subsidiaries and treatment of all Goodyear entities as a "unitary business," so that jurisdiction over the parent would draw in the subsidiaries as well.[6] Respondents have therefore forfeited this contention, and we do not address it.

---

[5] As earlier noted, the North Carolina Court of Appeals invoked the State's "well-recognized interest in providing a forum in which its citizens are able to seek redress for injuries that they have sustained." But "[g]eneral jurisdiction to adjudicate has in [United States] practice never been based on the plaintiff's relationship to the forum. There is nothing in [our] law comparable to . . . Article 14 of the Civil Code of France (1804) under which the French nationality of the plaintiff is a sufficient ground for jurisdiction." von Mehren & Trautman 1137; see Clermont & Palmer, Exorbitant Jurisdiction, 58 Me. L. Rev. 474, 492-495 (2006) (French law permitting plaintiff-based jurisdiction is rarely invoked in the absence of other supporting factors). When a defendant's act outside the forum causes injury in the forum, by contrast, a plaintiff's residence in the forum may strengthen the case for the exercise of *specific jurisdiction*. See Calder v. Jones, 465 U.S. 783, 788 (1984); von Mehren & Trautman 1167-1173.

[6] In the brief they filed in the North Carolina Court of Appeals, respondents stated that petitioners were part of an "integrated worldwide efforts to design, manufacture, market and sell *their tires* in the United States, including in North Carolina." Read in context, that assertion was offered in support of a narrower proposition: The distribution of petitioners' tires in North Carolina, respondents maintained, demonstrated petitioners' own "calculated and deliberate efforts to take advantage of the North Carolina market." As already explained, even regularly occurring sales of a product in a State do not justify the exercise of jurisdiction over a claim unrelated to those sales.

. . .

For the reasons stated, the judgment of the North Carolina Court of Appeals is *Reversed.*

■ NOTES ON GENERAL JURISDICTION

1. There are three straightforward situations in which it has long been thought that "general jurisdiction" exists—in which, in other words, the defendant may be sued on any claim:

(a) First, individual defendants are subject to general jurisdiction in the state where they live (domicile). In an early case, the Supreme Court sustained jurisdiction over a defendant sued in Wyoming, state of his domicile, although he was actually served in Colorado. See Milliken v. Meyer, 311 U.S. 457, 461-462 (1940) (domicile alone brings absent defendant within state's jurisdiction for purposes of personal judgment). The coming of "minimum contacts," and the broad idea that jurisdictional issues should be resolved on fairness grounds, raised doubt on this point. See Restatement (Second) of Conflict of Laws §29 (1988 revision) (although domicile supports jurisdiction, there may be "highly unusual cases" where such jurisdiction is unreasonable). In *Nicastro* (Section C1, supra), handed down the same day as *Goodyear,* the Court reaffirmed the traditional notion, saying citizenship or domicile "indicates general submission to a State's powers."

(b) Second, a corporation is suable in the state that issued its charter. See Restatement (Second) of Conflict of Laws §11, Comment l (state that charters a corporation may "exercise judicial jurisdiction over it and regulate its corporate activities") and §41, Comment b (chartering state has "a basis for the exercise of personal jurisdiction over the corporation in any action that may there be brought against it"). This notion is seldom put to any real test. Still, the Supreme Court approved this idea in *Nicastro* too ("by analogy" to personal citizenship or domicile, "incorporation or principal place of business" indicates for corporations "general submission to a State's powers").

(c) Third, general jurisdiction may be exercised over any person who is physically served in the forum state. In the *Burnham* case, which you are about to read, a California wife served her New Jersey husband with a summons and complaint in California, seeking divorce, division of property, child support, and a decree determining parental rights. But for the fact that her husband was *served* in California while he was visiting the state, it is not at all clear that she would have been able to adjudicate anything *other than* marital status (divorce) in California. But inasmuch as she served her husband in the forum state, jurisdiction was sustained. See also Goodin v. Department of Human Services, 772 So. 2d 1051, 1055 (Miss. 2000) (ex-husband, served in

Mississippi, was subject to jurisdiction there, in suit by state agency on behalf of wife seeking enforcement of Arizona child support order; under *Burnham,* a nonresident "is subject to the jurisdiction of that State's courts if properly served process while physically present in that state").

2. Goodyear USA did not contest jurisdiction in North Carolina: But the tire that exploded in France was manufactured in Turkey by Goodyear Turkey (a subsidiary of Goodyear USA). Should Goodyear USA have contested jurisdiction?

3. Courts seldom address the question of general jurisdiction. Why? Three well-known opinions *did* address general jurisdiction prior to *Goodyear.*

(a) First is Perkins v. Benguet Consolidated Mining Co., 342 U.S. 437 (1952), described in *Goodyear.* There the Court approved jurisdiction in Ohio over a Philippine mining company, where plaintiff sought stock dividends and shares in the corporation, based on claims having no connection with Ohio. The corporation, however, had moved its headquarters to Ohio as a temporary expedient during World War II, and the company president was served there:

> The company's . . . operations [in the Philippines] were completely halted during the occupation of the Islands by the Japanese. During that interim the president, who was also the general manager and principal stockholder of the company, returned to his home in Clermont County, Ohio. There he maintained an office in which he conducted his personal affairs and did many things on behalf of the company. He kept there office files of the company. He carried on their correspondence relating to the business of the company and to its employees. He drew and distributed there salary checks on behalf of the company, both in his own favor as president and in favor of two company secretaries who worked there with him. He used and maintained in Clermont County, Ohio, two active bank accounts carrying substantial balances of company funds. A bank in Hamilton County, Ohio, acted as transfer agent for the stock of the company. Several directors' meetings were held at his office or home in Clermont County. From that office he supervised policies dealing with the rehabilitation of the corporation's properties in the Philippines and he dispatched funds to cover purchases of machinery for such rehabilitation. Thus he carried on in Ohio a continuous and systematic supervision of the necessarily limited wartime activities of the company. He there discharged his duties as president and general manager. . . . While no mining properties in Ohio were owned or operated by the company, many of its wartime activities were directed from Ohio and were being given the personal attention of its president in that State at the time he was served with summons.

Id. at 437, 448-449. *Perkins* is a rare case, isn't it? How often will a corporation mainly doing business abroad be so connected with one American state?

(b) Second is the *Helicopteros* case, also described in *Goodyear,* where the question was whether survivors of American citizens killed in a helicopter crash in Peru could sue in Texas the Colombian owner/operator of the helicopter, when its only connection with that state involved negotiation and the purchase

there of helicopters, and sending pilots for training in Texas. These contacts were not enough, the Court said, to sustain *general* jurisdiction in Texas, but the Court declined to consider the question whether *specific* jurisdiction in Texas would have been proper because the parties did not argue it. See Helicopteros Nacionales de Colombia, S.A. v. Hall, 466 U.S. 408 (1984).

(c) Third was the state decision in *Bryant v. Finnish National Airline*, where a New York appellate court upheld jurisdiction in that state in a suit by a local plaintiff injured by defendant's negligence in a Paris airport. Defendant operated no flights into or out of the United States, but maintained a small office in New York City, with three full-time and some part-time employees, who took reservations for travel in Europe on Finnair. To say the least, the outcome in *Bryant* is surprising. See Bryant v. Finnish National Airline, 308 N.E.2d 439 (N.Y. 1965).

4. Some other Supreme Court decisions include comments that general jurisdiction remains a viable concept. In Keeton v. Hustler, 465 U.S. 770, 779 (1984), the Court approved jurisdiction in New Hampshire in a defamation suit by a New York plaintiff against a "skin" magazine on the basis that defendant sold 10,000-15,000 copies there. But the Court said defendant's activities in New Hampshire "may not be so substantial as to support jurisdiction over a cause of action unrelated to those activities" and stressed that defendant carried on "part of its general business" in New Hampshire and that the claim arose "out of the very activity being conducted, in part, in New Hampshire." In Rush v. Savchuk, 444 U.S. 430, 439 (1980), the Court refused to sustain jurisdiction in Minnesota over an Indiana motorist, where plaintiff had tried to obtain *quasi-in-rem* type 2 jurisdiction by attaching the Indiana motorist's insurance policy in Minnesota. The Court commented that State Farm (insurer of the Indiana driver) could be " 'found,' in the sense of doing business, in all 50 states and the District of Columbia." This comment sounds like a suggestion that plaintiff could sue defendant's *insurer* in any state, which suggests that a tort claimant's suit against a nationwide insurance carrier can be brought in the state where the claimant lives, regardless of where the claim arose. (Of course, such suits usually cannot be brought at all for another reason: In most states, the tort claimant must sue the alleged tortfeasors, and cannot directly sue their insurance carriers. Only Louisiana and Wisconsin authorize "direct actions" against the carrier.)

BURNHAM v. SUPERIOR COURT

Supreme Court of the United States
495 U.S. 604 (1990)

SCALIA, J., announced the judgment of the Court and delivered an opinion, in which REHNQUIST, C.J., and KENNEDY, J., joined, and in which WHITE, J., joined as to Parts I, II-A, II-B, and II-C. WHITE, J., filed an opinion concurring in part and concurring in the judgment. BRENNAN, J., filed an opinion concurring in the judgment, in which MARSHALL, BLACKMUN, and O'CONNOR, JJ., joined. STEVENS, J., filed an opinion concurring in the judgment.

The question presented is whether the Due Process Clause of the Fourteenth Amendment denies California courts jurisdiction over a nonresident, who was personally served with process while temporarily in that State, in a suit unrelated to his activities in the State.

I

Petitioner Dennis Burnham married Francie Burnham in 1976 in West Virginia. In 1977 the couple moved to New Jersey, where their two children were born. In July 1987 the Burnhams decided to separate. They agreed that Mrs. Burnham, who intended to move to California, would take custody of the children. Shortly before Mrs. Burnham departed for California that same month, she and petitioner agreed that she would file for divorce on grounds of "irreconcilable differences."

In October 1987, petitioner filed for divorce in New Jersey state court on grounds of "desertion." Petitioner did not, however, obtain an issuance of summons against his wife and did not attempt to serve her with process. Mrs. Burnham, after unsuccessfully demanding that petitioner adhere to their prior agreement to submit to an "irreconcilable differences" divorce, brought suit for divorce in California state court in early January 1988.

In late January, petitioner visited southern California on business, after which he went north to visit his children in the San Francisco Bay area, where his wife resided. He took the older child to San Francisco for the weekend. Upon returning the child to Mrs. Burnham's home on January 24, 1988, petitioner was served with a California court summons and a copy of Mrs. Burnham's divorce petition. He then returned to New Jersey.

Later that year, petitioner made a special appearance in the California Superior Court, moving to quash the service of process on the ground that the court lacked personal jurisdiction over him because his only contacts with California were a few short visits to the State for the purposes of conducting business and visiting his children. The Superior Court denied the motion, and the California Court of Appeal denied mandamus relief, rejecting petitioner's contention that the Due Process Clause prohibited California courts from asserting jurisdiction over him because he lacked "minimum contacts" with the State. The court held it to be "a valid jurisdictional predicate for *in personam* jurisdiction" that the "defendant [was] present in the forum state and personally served with process." We granted certiorari.

II

A

The proposition that the judgment of a court lacking jurisdiction is void traces back to the English Year Books, see Bowser v. Collins, 145 Eng. Rep. 97 (Ex. Ch. 1482), and was made settled law by Lord Coke in Case of the Marshalsea, 77 Eng. Rep. 1027, 1041 (K.B. 1612). Traditionally that proposition was embodied in the phrase *coram non judice,* "before a person not a judge"—meaning, in effect, that the proceeding in question was not a *judicial* proceeding because lawful judicial authority was not present, and could therefore not yield a *judgment.* American courts invalidated, or denied recognition to, judgments that violated this common law principle long before the Fourteenth Amendment was adopted. In *Pennoyer,* we announced that the judgment of a court lacking personal jurisdiction violated the Due Process Clause of the Fourteenth Amendment as well.

To determine whether the assertion of personal jurisdiction is consistent with due process, we have long relied on the principles traditionally followed by American courts in marking out the territorial limits of each State's authority. That criterion was first announced in *Pennoyer,* in which we stated that due process "mean[s] a course of legal proceedings according to those rules and principles which have been established in our systems of jurisprudence for the protection and enforcement of private rights," including the "well-established principles of public law respecting the jurisdiction of an independent State over persons and property." In what has become the classic expression of the criterion, we said in *International Shoe* that a state court's assertion of personal jurisdiction satisfies the Due Process Clause if it does not violate "'traditional notions of fair play and substantial justice.'" Since *International Shoe,* we have only been called upon to decide whether these "traditional notions" permit States to exercise jurisdiction over absent defendants in a manner that deviates from the rules of jurisdiction applied in the 19th century. We have held such deviations permissible, but only with respect to suits arising out of the absent defendant's contacts with the State.[1] See, *e.g.,* Helicopteros Nacionales de Colombia v. Hall, 466 U.S. 408, 414 (1984). The

---

[1] We have said that "[e]ven when the cause of action does not arise out of or relate to the foreign corporation's activities in the forum State, due process is not offended by a State's subjecting the corporation to its *in personam* jurisdiction when there are sufficient contacts between the State and the foreign corporation." *Helicopteros Nacionales.* Our only holding supporting that statement, however, involved "regular service of summons upon [the corporation's] president while he was in [the forum State] acting in that capacity." See Perkins v. Benguet Consolidated Mining Co., 342 U.S. 437, 440 (1952). It may be that whatever special rule exists permitting "continuous and systematic" contacts to support jurisdiction with respect to matters unrelated to activity in the forum applies *only* to corporations, which have never fitted comfortably in a jurisdictional regime based primarily upon "de facto power over the defendant's person." *International Shoe.* We express no views on these matters—and, for simplicity's sake, omit reference to this aspect of "contacts"—based jurisdiction in our discussion.

question we must decide today is whether due process requires a similar connection between the litigation and the defendant's contacts with the State in cases where the defendant is physically present in the State at the time process is served upon him.

B

Among the most firmly established principles of personal jurisdiction in American tradition is that the courts of a State have jurisdiction over non-residents who are physically present in the State. The view developed early that each State had the power to hale before its courts any individual who could be found within its borders, and that once having acquired jurisdiction over such a person by properly serving him with process, the State could retain jurisdiction to enter judgment against him, no matter how fleeting his visit. That view had antecedents in English common law practice, which sometimes allowed "transitory" actions, arising out of events outside the country, to be maintained against seemingly nonresident defendants who were present in England. Justice Story believed the principle, which he traced to Roman origins, to be firmly grounded in English tradition: "[B]y the common law[,] personal actions, being transitory, may be brought in any place, where the party defendant may be found," for "every nation may ... rightfully exercise jurisdiction over all persons within its domains." J. Story, Commentaries on the Conflict of Laws §§554, 543 (1846). See also *id.*, §§530-538.

Recent scholarship has suggested that English tradition was not as clear as Story thought, see Hazard, A General Theory of State-Court Jurisdiction, 1965 S. Ct. Rev. 241, 253-260; Ehrenzweig, The Transient Rule of Personal Jurisdiction: The "Power" Myth and Forum Conveniens, 65 Yale L.J. 289 (1956). Accurate or not, however, judging by the evidence of contemporaneous or near-contemporaneous decisions, one must conclude that Story's understanding was shared by American courts at the crucial time for present purposes: 1868, when the Fourteenth Amendment was adopted. ...

Decisions in the courts of many States in the 19th and early 20th centuries held that personal service upon a physically present defendant sufficed to confer jurisdiction, without regard to whether the defendant was only briefly in the State or whether the cause of action was related to his activities there. [The Court cites decisions handed down between 1814 and 1936 in California, Connecticut, Florida, Iowa, Louisiana, Missouri, New York, Oregon, Pennsylvania, Texas, and West Virginia.] Although research has not revealed a case deciding the issue in every State's courts, that appears to be because the issue was so well settled that it went unlitigated. Opinions from the courts of other States announced the rule in dictum. [The Court cites decisions handed down between 1842 and 1905 in Colorado, Indiana, Kentucky, Mississippi, Nebraska,

New Hampshire, Rhode Island, and Vermont.] Most States, moreover, had statutes or common law rules that exempted from service of process individuals who were brought into the forum by force or fraud, or who were there as a party or witness in unrelated judicial proceedings. These exceptions obviously rested upon the premise that service of process conferred jurisdiction. Particularly striking is the fact that, as far as we have been able to determine, *not one* American case from the period (or, for that matter, not one American case until 1978) held, or even suggested, that in-state personal service on an individual was insufficient to confer personal jurisdiction. Commentators were also seemingly unanimous on the rule.

This American jurisdictional practice is, moreover, not merely old; it is continuing. It remains the practice of, not only a substantial number of the States, but as far as we are aware *all* the States and the Federal Government—if one disregards (as one must for this purpose) the few opinions since 1978 that have erroneously said, on grounds similar to those that petitioner presses here, that this Court's due process decisions render the practice unconstitutional. We do not know of a single state or federal statute, or a single judicial decision resting upon state law, that has abandoned in-state service as a basis of jurisdiction. Many recent cases reaffirm it. [The Court cites cases decided between 1963 and 1989 in Florida, Georgia, Kansas, Illinois, Massachusetts, Mississippi, Minnesota, Nevada, New Jersey, North Carolina, West Virginia, Wisconsin, and Wyoming.]

C

Despite this formidable body of precedent, petitioner contends, in reliance on our decisions applying the *International Shoe* standard, that in the absence of "continuous and systematic" contacts with the forum, a nonresident defendant can be subjected to judgment only as to matters that arise out of or relate to his contacts with the forum. This argument rests on a thorough misunderstanding of our cases.

[The Court summarizes the law of jurisdiction as set out in *Pennoyer*, which required personal service in the forum state in order to obtain *in personam* jurisdiction. The Court then turns to the "weakening of the *Pennoyer* rule culminating in the decision in *International Shoe* and the "minimum contacts" standard that "may take the place" of service within the jurisdiction.]

Nothing in *International Shoe* or the cases that have followed it, however, offers support for the very different proposition petitioner seeks to establish today: that a defendant's presence in the forum is not only unnecessary to validate novel, nontraditional assertions of jurisdiction, but is itself no longer sufficient to establish jurisdiction. That proposition is unfaithful to both elementary logic and the foundations of our due process jurisprudence. The distinction between what is needed to support novel procedures and what is needed to sustain traditional ones is fundamental, as we observed over a century ago:

> [A] process of law, which is not otherwise forbidden, must be taken to be due process of law, if it can show the sanction of settled usage both in England and in this country; but it by no means follows that nothing else can be due process of law. . . . [That which], in substance, has been immemorially the actual law of the land . . . therefor[e] is due process of law. But to hold that such a characteristic is essential to due process of law, would be to deny every quality of the law but its age, and to render it incapable of progress or improvement. It would be to stamp upon our jurisprudence the unchangeableness attributed to the laws of the Medes and Persians.

Hurtado v. California, 110 U.S. 516, 528-529 (1884).

The short of the matter is that jurisdiction based on physical presence alone constitutes due process because it is one of the continuing traditions of our legal system that define the due process standard of "traditional notions of fair play and substantial justice." That standard was developed by *analogy* to "physical presence," and it would be perverse to say it could now be turned against that touchstone of jurisdiction.

D

Petitioner's strongest argument, though we ultimately reject it, relies upon our decision in *Shaffer*. [The Court summarizes the *Shaffer* case.]

It goes too far to say, as petitioner contends, that *Shaffer* compels the conclusion that a State lacks jurisdiction over an individual unless the litigation arises out of his activities in the State. *Shaffer,* like *International Shoe,* involved jurisdiction over an *absent defendant,* and it stands for nothing more than the proposition that when the "minimum contact" that is a substitute for physical presence consists of property ownership it must, like other minimum contacts, be related to the litigation. Petitioner wrenches out of its context our statement in *Shaffer* that "all assertions of state-court jurisdiction must be evaluated according to the standards set forth in *International Shoe* and its progeny." When read together with the two sentences that preceded it, the meaning of this statement becomes clear:

> The fiction that an assertion of jurisdiction over property is anything but an assertion of jurisdiction over the owner of the property supports an ancient form without substantial modern justification. Its continued acceptance would serve only to allow state-court jurisdiction that is fundamentally unfair to the defendant.
>
> We *therefore conclude* that all assertions of state-court jurisdiction must be evaluated according to the standards set forth in *International Shoe* and its progeny. (Emphasis added.)

Shaffer was saying, in other words, not that all bases for the assertion of *in personam* jurisdiction (including, presumably, in-state service) must be treated alike and subjected to the "minimum contacts" analysis of *International Shoe;* but rather that *quasi in rem* jurisdiction, that fictional "ancient form," and *in personam* jurisdiction, are really one and the same and must be treated alike—leading to the conclusion that *quasi in rem* jurisdiction, *i.e.,* that form of *in personam* jurisdiction based upon a "property ownership" contact and by definition unaccompanied by personal, in-state service, must satisfy the litigation-relatedness requirement of *International Shoe.* The logic of *Shaffer's* holding—which places all suits against absent nonresidents on the same constitutional footing, regardless of whether a separate Latin label is attached to one particular basis of contact—does not compel the conclusion that physically present defendants must be treated identically to absent ones. As we have demonstrated at length, our tradition has treated the two classes of defendants quite differently, and it is unreasonable to read *Shaffer* as casually obliterating that distinction. *International Shoe* confined its "minimum contacts" requirement to situations in which the defendant "be not present within the territory of the forum," and nothing in *Shaffer* expands that requirement beyond that.

It is fair to say, however, that while our holding today does not contradict *Shaffer,* our basic approach to the due process question is different. We have conducted no independent inquiry into the desirability or fairness of the prevailing in-state service rule, leaving that judgment to the legislatures that are free to amend it; for our purposes, its validation is its pedigree, as the phrase "*traditional notions* of fair play and substantial justice" makes clear. *Shaffer* did conduct such an independent inquiry, asserting that "'traditional notions of fair play and substantial justice' can be as readily offended by the perpetuation of ancient forms that are no longer justified as by the adoption of new procedures that are inconsistent with the basic values of our constitutional heritage." Perhaps that assertion can be sustained when the "perpetuation of ancient forms" is engaged in by only a very small minority of the States. Where, however, as in the present case, a jurisdictional principle is both firmly approved by tradition and still favored, it is impossible to imagine what standard we could appeal to for the judgment that it is "no longer justified." While in no way receding from or casting doubt upon the holding of *Shaffer* or any other case, we reaffirm today our time-honored approach. For new procedures, hitherto unknown, the Due Process Clause requires analysis to determine whether "traditional notions of fair play and substantial justice" have been offended. *International Shoe.* But a doctrine of personal jurisdiction that dates back to the adoption of the Fourteenth Amendment and is still generally observed unquestionably meets that standard.

III

A few words in response to Justice Brennan's opinion concurring in the judgment: It insists that we apply "contemporary notions of due process" to determine the constitutionality of California's assertion of jurisdiction. But our analysis today comports with that prescription, at least if we give it the only sense allowed by our precedents. The "contemporary notions of due process" applicable to personal jurisdiction are the enduring "traditional notions of fair play and substantial justice" established as the test by *International Shoe*. By its very language, that test is satisfied if a state court adheres to jurisdictional rules that are generally applied and have always been applied in the United States.

But the concurrence's proposed standard of "contemporary notions of due process" requires more: It measures state-court jurisdiction not only against traditional doctrines in this country, including current state-court practice, but also against each Justice's subjective assessment of what is fair and just. Authority for that seductive standard is not to be found in any of our personal jurisdiction cases. It is, indeed, an outright break with the test of "traditional notions of fair play and substantial justice," which would have to be reformulated "*our* notions of fair play and substantial justice."

The subjectivity, and hence inadequacy, of this approach becomes apparent when the concurrence tries to explain *why* the assertion of jurisdiction in the present case meets its standard of continuing-American-tradition-plus-innate-fairness. Justice Brennan lists the "benefits" Mr. Burnham derived from the State of California—the fact that, during the few days he was there, "[h]is health and safety [were] guaranteed by the State's police, fire, and emergency medical services; he [was] free to travel on the State's roads and waterways; he likely enjoy[ed] the fruits of the State's economy." Three days' worth of these benefits strike us as powerfully inadequate to establish, as an abstract matter, that it is "fair" for California to decree the ownership of all Mr. Burnham's worldly goods acquired during the 10 years of his marriage, and the custody over his children. We daresay a contractual exchange swapping those benefits for that power would not survive the "unconscionability" provision of the Uniform Commercial Code. Even less persuasive are the other "fairness" factors alluded to by Justice Brennan. It would create "an asymmetry," we are told, if Burnham were *permitted* (as he is) to appear in California courts as a plaintiff, but were not *compelled* to appear in California courts as defendant; and travel being as easy as it is nowadays, and modern procedural devices being so convenient, it is no great hardship to appear in California courts. The problem with these assertions is that they justify the exercise of jurisdiction over *everyone, whether or not* he ever comes to California. The only "fairness" elements setting Mr. Burnham apart from the rest of the world are the three days' "benefits" referred to above—and even those, do not set him apart from many other people who have enjoyed three days in the Golden State (savoring the fruits of its economy, the availability of its roads and police services) but who were fortunate enough not to be served with process while they were there and thus are not (simply by reason of that savoring) subject to the general jurisdiction of California's courts. In other words, even if one agreed with Justice Brennan's conception of an equitable bargain, the "benefits" we have been discussing would explain why it is "fair" to assert general jurisdiction over Burnham-returned-to-New-Jersey-after-service only at the expense of proving that it is also "fair" to assert general jurisdiction over Burnham-returned-to-New-Jersey-without-service—which we *know* does not conform with "contemporary notions of due process."

[Justice Brennan speaks of one's "reasonable expectation" of being subject to suit wherever he goes, which may seem like a "fairness" consideration, but it is in fact "just tradition masquerading as 'fairness,'" and Justice Brennan has taken a "circular" journey relying completely on "the very factor he sought to avoid," which is the "continuing tradition" authorizing jurisdiction in such case. Justice Brennan's approach is framed in terms of a "rule," but what if "elements of fairness" point away from the conclusion that exercising jurisdiction would be fair? If Mr. Burnham were "impecunious" and could not take advantage of "modern means of transportation," would jurisdiction still exist? In fact Justice Brennan's rule is just a "totality of the circumstances" test that brings the very "uncertainty" that the territorial principle avoids.]

The difference between us and Justice Brennan has nothing to do with whether "further progress [is] to be made" in the "evolution of our legal system." It has to do with whether changes are to be adopted as progressive by the American people or decreed as progressive by the Justices of this Court. Nothing we say today prevents individual States from limiting or entirely abandoning the in-state-service basis of jurisdiction. And nothing prevents an overwhelming majority of them from doing so, with the consequence that the "traditional notions of fairness" that this Court applies may change. But the States have overwhelmingly declined to adopt such limitation or abandonment, evidently not considering it to be progress.[5] The question is whether, armed with no authority other than individual Justices' perceptions of fairness that conflict with both past and current practice, this Court can

---

[5] I find quite unacceptable as a basis for this Court's decisions Justice Brennan's view that "the *raison d'etre* of various constitutional doctrines designed to protect out-of-staters, such as the Art. IV Privileges and Immunities Clause and the Commerce Clause" entitles this Court to brand as "unfair," and hence unconstitutional, the refusal of all 50 States "to limit or abandon bases of jurisdiction that have become obsolete." "Due process" (which is the constitutional text at issue here) does not mean that process which shifting majorities of this Court feel to be "due"; but that process which American society—self-interested American society, which expresses its judgments in the laws of self-interested States—has traditionally considered "due." The notion that the Constitution, through some penumbra emanating from the Privileges and Immunities Clause and the Commerce Clause, establishes this Court as a Platonic check upon the society's greedy adherence to its traditions can only be described as imperious.

compel the States to make such a change on the ground that "due process" requires it. We hold that it cannot.

Because the Due Process Clause does not prohibit the California courts from exercising jurisdiction over petitioner based on the fact of in-state service of process, the judgment is

Affirmed.

Justice WHITE, concurring in part and concurring in the judgment.

I join Parts I, II-A, II-B, and II-C of Justice Scalia's opinion and concur in the judgment of affirmance. The rule allowing jurisdiction to be obtained over a nonresident by personal service in the forum State, without more, has been and is so widely accepted throughout this country that I could not possibly strike it down, either on its face or as applied in this case, on the ground that it denies due process of law guaranteed by the Fourteenth Amendment. Although the Court has the authority under the Amendment to examine even traditionally accepted procedures and declare them invalid, there has been no showing here or elsewhere that as a general proposition the rule is so arbitrary and lacking in common sense in so many instances that it should be held violative of due process in every case. Furthermore, until such a showing is made, which would be difficult indeed, claims in individual cases that the rule would operate unfairly as applied to the particular nonresident involved need not be entertained. At least this would be the case where presence in the forum State is intentional, which would almost always be the fact. Otherwise, there would be endless, fact-specific litigation in the trial and appellate courts, including this one. Here, personal service in California, without more, is enough, and I agree that the judgment should be affirmed.

Justice BRENNAN, with whom Justice MARSHALL, Justice BLACKMUN, and Justice O'CONNOR join, concurring in the judgment.

. . .

I

I believe that the approach adopted by Justice Scalia's opinion today—reliance solely on historical pedigree—is foreclosed by our decisions in *International Shoe* and *Shaffer*. In *International Shoe*, we held that a state court's assertion of personal jurisdiction does not violate the Due Process Clause if it is consistent with "'traditional notions of fair play and substantial justice.'"[2] In *Shaffer*, we

---

[2] Our reference in *International Shoe* to "'traditional notions of fair play and substantial justice'" meant simply that those concepts are indeed traditional ones, not that, as Justice Scalia's opinion suggests, their specific *content* was to be determined by tradition alone. We recognized that contemporary societal norms must play a role in our analysis. See, *e.g.,* 326 U.S., at 317 (considerations of "reasonable[ness], in the context of our federal system . . . of government").

stated that "*all* assertions of state-court jurisdiction must be evaluated according to the standards set forth in *International Shoe* and its progeny." The critical insight of *Shaffer* is that all rules of jurisdiction, even ancient ones, must satisfy contemporary notions of due process. No longer were we content to limit our jurisdictional analysis to pronouncements that "[t]he foundation of jurisdiction is physical power," McDonald v. Mabee, 243 U.S. 90, 91 (1917), and that "every State possesses exclusive jurisdiction and sovereignty over persons and property within its territory." *Pennoyer*. While acknowledging that "history must be considered as supporting the proposition that jurisdiction based solely on the presence of property satisfie[d] the demands of due process," we found that this factor could not be "decisive." We recognized that "'[t]raditional notions of fair play and substantial justice' can be as readily offended by the perpetuation of ancient forms that are no longer justified as by the adoption of new procedures that are inconsistent with the basic values of our constitutional heritage."

. . .

II

Tradition, though alone not dispositive, is of course *relevant* to the question whether the rule of transient jurisdiction is consistent with due process.[7] Tradition is salient not in the sense that practices of the past are automatically reasonable today; indeed, under such a standard, the legitimacy of transient jurisdiction would be called into question because the rule's historical "pedigree" is a matter of intense debate. [In brief textual assertions and long footnotes, Justice Brennan argues that the rule of transient jurisdiction was "a stranger to the common law" and was "rather weakly implanted in American jurisprudence," and was not widely recognizes or observed until well after *Pennoyer*.]

[The historical background is relevant] because, however murky the jurisprudential origins of transient jurisdiction, the fact that American courts have announced the rule for perhaps a century (first in dicta, more recently in holdings) provides a defendant voluntarily present in a particular State *today* "clear notice that [he] is subject to suit" in the forum. *World-Wide Volkswagen*. Regardless of whether Justice Story's account of the rule's genesis is mythical, our common understanding *now*, fortified by a century of judicial practice, is that jurisdiction is often a function of geography. The transient

---

[7] I do not propose that the "contemporary notions of due process" to be applied are no more than "each Justice's subjective assessment of what is fair and just." Rather, the inquiry is guided by our decisions beginning with *International Shoe*, and the specific factors that we have developed to ascertain whether a jurisdictional rule comports with "traditional notions of fair play and substantial justice." This analysis may not be "mechanical or quantitative," *International Shoe*, but neither is it "freestanding" or dependent on personal whim. Our experience with this approach demonstrates that it is well within our competence to employ.

rule is consistent with reasonable expectations and is entitled to a strong presumption that it comports with due process. "If I visit another State, ... I knowingly assume some risk that the State will exercise its power over my property or my person while there. My contact with the State, though minimal, gives rise to predictable risks." *Shaffer,* 433 U.S., at 218 (Stevens, J., concurring in judgment); see also Burger King Corp. v. Rudzewicz, 471 U.S. 462, 476 (1985) ("Territorial presence frequently will enhance a potential defendant's affiliation with a State and reinforce the reasonable foreseeability of suit there"); Glen, An Analysis of "Mere Presence" and Other Traditional Bases of Jurisdiction, 45 Brooklyn L. Rev. 607, 611-612 (1979). Thus, proposed revisions to the Restatement (Second) of Conflict of Laws §28, p. 39 (1986), provide that "[a] state has power to exercise judicial jurisdiction over an individual who is present within its territory unless the individual's relationship to the state is so attenuated as to make the exercise of such jurisdiction unreasonable."[11]

By visiting the forum State, a transient defendant actually "avail[s]" himself, *Burger King,* of significant benefits provided by the State. His health and safety are guaranteed by the State's police, fire, and emergency medical services; he is free to travel on the State's roads and waterways; he likely enjoys the fruits of the State's economy as well. Moreover, the Privileges and Immunities Clause of Article IV prevents a state government from discriminating against a transient defendant by denying him the protections of its law or the right of access to its courts. Subject only to the doctrine of *forum non conveniens,* an out-of-state plaintiff may use state courts in all circumstances in which those courts would be available to state citizens. Without transient jurisdiction, an asymmetry would arise: A transient would have the full benefit of the power of the forum State's courts as a plaintiff while retaining immunity from their authority as a defendant.

The potential burdens on a transient defendant are slight. "'[M]odern transportation and communications have made it much less burdensome for a party sued to defend himself'" in a State outside his place of residence. *Burger King,* quoting McGee v. International Life Ins. Co., 355 U.S. 220, 223 (1957). That the defendant has already journeyed at least once before to the forum—as evidenced by the fact that he was served with process there—is an indication that suit in the forum likely would not be prohibitively inconvenient. Finally, any burdens that do arise can be ameliorated by a variety of

---

[11] As the Restatement suggests, there may be cases in which a defendant's involuntary or unknowing presence in a State does not support the exercise of personal jurisdiction over him. The facts of the instant case do not require us to determine the outer limits of the transient jurisdiction rule.

procedural devices.[13] For these reasons, as a rule the exercise of personal jurisdiction over a defendant based on his voluntary presence in the forum will satisfy the requirements of due process.

I note, moreover, that the dual conclusions of Justice Scalia's opinion create a singularly unattractive result. Justice Scalia suggests that when and if a jurisdictional rule becomes substantively unfair or even "unconscionable," this Court is powerless to alter it. Instead, he is willing to rely on individual States to limit or abandon bases of jurisdiction that have become obsolete. This reliance is misplaced, for States have little incentive to limit rules such as transient jurisdiction that make it *easier* for their own citizens to sue out-of-state defendants. That States are more likely to expand their jurisdiction is illustrated by the adoption by many States of longarm statutes extending the reach of personal jurisdiction to the limits established by the Federal Constitution. Out-of-staters do not vote in state elections or have a voice in state government. We should not assume, therefore, that States will be motivated by "notions of fairness" to curb jurisdictional rules like the one at issue here. The reasoning of Justice Scalia's opinion today is strikingly oblivious to the *raison d'etre* of various constitutional doctrines designed to protect out-of-staters, such as the Art. IV Privileges and Immunities Clause and the Commerce Clause.

In this case, it is undisputed that petitioner was served with process while voluntarily and knowingly in the State of California. I therefore concur in the judgment.

Justice STEVENS, concurring in the judgment.

As I explained in my separate writing, I did not join the Court's opinion in Shaffer v. Heitner, 433 U.S. 186 (1977), because I was concerned by its unnecessarily broad reach. The same concern prevents me from joining either Justice Scalia's or Justice Brennan's opinion in this case. For me, it is sufficient to note that the historical evidence and consensus identified by Justice Scalia, the considerations of fairness identified by Justice Brennan, and the common sense displayed by Justice White, all combine to demonstrate that this is, indeed, a very easy case.* Accordingly, I agree that the judgment should be affirmed.

---

[13] For example, in the federal system, a transient defendant can avoid protracted litigation of a spurious suit through a motion to dismiss for failure to state a claim or through a motion for summary judgment. FRCP 12(b)(6) and 56. He can use relatively inexpensive methods of discovery, such as oral deposition by telephone (Rule 30(b)(7)), deposition upon written questions (Rule 31), interrogatories (Rule 33), and requests for admission (Rule 36), while enjoying protection from harassment (Rule 26(c)), and possibly obtaining costs and attorney's fees for some of the work involved (Rules 37(a)(4), (b)-(d)). Moreover, a change of venue may be possible. 28 USC §1404. In state court, many of the same procedural protections are available, as is the doctrine of *forum non conveniens*, under which the suit may be dismissed.

* Perhaps the adage about hard cases making bad law should be revised to cover easy cases.

■ NOTES ON THE CONTINUING VITALITY OF PRESENCE AS BASIS FOR JURISDICTION

1. On the question whether California has jurisdiction over Dennis Burnham, all nine Justices say yes. They disagree on the reasons: Led by Justice Scalia, four Justices (maybe five, counting Justice Stevens) think presence confers jurisdiction as a matter of tradition that remains intact after *International Shoe* and *Shaffer.* Led by Justice Brennan, four others (maybe five, counting Justice Stevens) think jurisdiction exists because a fairness standard based on minimum contacts is satisfied, and that *International Shoe,* as interpreted in *Shaffer,* did not merely *extend* jurisdiction *in personam* to cases where defendant was not present, but *required* application of a fairness standard even if defendant *was* present. As a matter of construction, which side has the stronger argument? As a matter of policy, which approach is better? Given that the minimum contact standard is somewhat vague, is there something to be said for a "bright line" rule?

2. As pointed out in the notes after *Goodyear Dunlop,* supra, Francie Burnham sought not only a divorce, but a decree resolving issues of child custody, support, and division of property. The divorce posed no difficulties: She could obtain a California divorce on the basis of her own domicile. The other matters—division of property, support obligations, and child custody—are different. In fact, the two spouses had entered into a marital settlement agreement before Francie Burnham left New Jersey, but she claimed that the agreement had been coerced and was procured by fraud, and was unfair to her. Which state's courts should resolve such matters—New Jersey's or California's? Should she have to go to New Jersey to obtain relief? Should he have to go to California to enforce it?

3. Do the opinions in *Burnham* mean that California could constitutionally exercise jurisdiction over Francie Burnham's claims if she had persuaded Dennis Burnham to come to California by falsely telling him that one of their children had been injured and was in the hospital? What if she had served him while on an airplane flight from Denver to Honolulu?

5. Jurisdiction by Consent: Private Contract

CARNIVAL CRUISE LINES, INC. v. SHUTE

United States Supreme Court
499 U.S. 585 (1991)

Justice BLACKMUN delivered the opinion of the Court.

[Eulala and Russell Shute bought passage on a seven-day cruise on the *Tropicale,* paying the fare to a travel agent in Arlington, Washington, who forwarded payment to Carnival Cruise headquarters in Miami, Florida. Carnival then mailed the tickets to the Shutes. On the face of each ticket was a legend stating that one who accepts the ticket as passenger "shall be deemed" to accept the "terms and conditions," including the proposition that "all disputes" shall be litigated in a court in Florida (without specifying state or federal).

The Shutes boarded the *Tropicale* in Los Angeles, and sailed to Puerto Vallarta, Mexico, then back to Los Angeles. While the *Tropicale* was in international waters off the Mexican coast, Eulala Shute slipped on a deck mat during a guided tour of the galley. On their return, the Shutes filed suit against Carnival in the federal district court in Washington, claiming that Eulala Shute's injuries were caused by the negligence of Carnival and its employees.

On motion by Carnival, the court dismissed the suit. The Ninth Circuit Court of Appeals initially reversed, ruling that the forum selection clause was unreasonable and unenforceable, but the opinion was withdrawn and the Court certified to the Washington Supreme Court the question whether the state's long-arm statute would confer personal jurisdiction. After the Washington Supreme Court answered in the affirmative, the Ninth Circuit again concluded that the forum selection clause was unenforceable, and remanded for trial in federal district court in Washington.]

We granted certiorari to address the question whether the Court of Appeals was correct in holding that the District Court should hear respondents' tort claim against petitioner. Because we find the forum-selection clause to be dispositive of this question, we need not consider petitioner's constitutional argument as to personal jurisdiction.

[This suit arises in admiralty, so federal law governs the enforceability of the forum selection clause. The Shutes "have conceded that they had notice" of the substance of that provision. The question is whether it is unenforceable because it was not freely bargained for.]

[The Shutes'] passage contract was purely routine and doubtless nearly identical to every commercial passage contract issued by petitioner and most other cruise lines. In this context, it would be entirely unreasonable for us to assume that respondents—or any other cruise passenger—would negotiate with petitioner the terms of a forum-selection clause in an ordinary commercial cruise ticket. Common sense dictates that a ticket of this kind will be a form contract the terms of which are not subject to negotiation, and that an individual purchasing the ticket will not have bargaining parity with the cruise line. . . .

In evaluating the reasonableness of the forum clause at issue in this case, we must refine the analysis of *The Bremen* to account for the realities of form passage contracts. As an initial matter, we do not adopt the Court of Appeals' determination that a nonnegotiated forum-selection clause in a form ticket contract is never enforceable simply because it is not the subject of bargaining. Including a reasonable forum clause in a form contract of this kind well may be permissible for several reasons: First, a cruise line has a special interest in limiting the fora in which it potentially could be subject to suit. Because a cruise ship typically carries passengers from many locales, it is not unlikely that a mishap on a cruise could subject the cruise line to litigation in several different fora. Additionally, a clause establishing *ex ante* the forum for dispute resolution has the salutary effect of dispelling any confusion about where suits arising from the contract must be brought and defended, sparing litigants the time and expense of pretrial motions to determine the correct forum and conserving judicial resources that otherwise would be devoted to deciding those motions. Finally, it stands to reason that passengers who purchase tickets containing a forum clause like that at issue in this case benefit in the form of reduced fares reflecting the savings that the cruise line enjoys by limiting the fora in which it may be sued.

. . .

It bears emphasis that forum-selection clauses contained in form passage contracts are subject to judicial scrutiny for fundamental fairness. In this case, there is no indication that petitioner set Florida as the forum in which disputes were to be resolved as a means of discouraging cruise passengers from pursuing legitimate claims. Any suggestion of such a bad-faith motive is belied by two facts: Petitioner has its principal place of business in Florida, and many of its cruises depart from and return to Florida ports. Similarly, there is no evidence that petitioner obtained respondents' accession to the forum clause by fraud or overreaching. Finally, respondents have conceded that they were given notice of the forum provision and, therefore, presumably retained the option of rejecting the contract with impunity. In the case before us, therefore, we conclude that the Court of Appeals erred in refusing to enforce the forum-selection clause.

[The dissenting opinion by Justice Stevens and Justice Marshall is omitted.]

■ NOTES ON CHOOSING THE FORUM BY PRIVATE AGREEMENT

1. In a bygone era, courts bridled at forum selection clauses, on the ground that parties should not "oust a court" of jurisdiction by clauses specifying that suits should be brought in a particular court. But the modern attitude is different. See Restatement (Second) of Conflict of Laws §11 (agreement about choice of forum "will be given effect unless it is unfair or unreasonable"). See also The Bremen v. Zapata Off-Shore Co., 407 U.S. 1 (1972), upholding enforcement of such a clause in an agreement between an American corporation and a German corporation under which the latter was to tow the former's ocean-going drilling rig from Louisiana to the Adriatic Sea near Italy, designating London as the location for any suit. A storm damaged the rig off the Florida coast, and the owner sued the towing company in federal court in Florida (invoking admiralty jurisdiction). Defendant moved to dismiss on the ground that the suit should be brought in London. The Court concluded that the forum selection clause was enforceable, stressing that it was a vital part of the agreement and that London was a reasonable choice because of its expertise in admiralty and its location midway between the parties' domiciles.

2. Eulala and Russell Shute bought tickets through a Washington travel agent for a seven-day cruise to Puerto Vallarta in 1986. Defendant Carnival Cruise owned and operated the *Tropicale*, then a modern ship in its fifth year of service, which left from and returned to Los Angeles. Mrs. Shute fell during a guided tour of the galley while the *Tropicale* was off the coast of Mexico. The Court's decision means the Shutes must litigate their claim against Carnival Cruise in Florida, doesn't it? In this case, unlike *The Bremen*, the forum selection clause was not negotiated, was it? Are there factors that suggest that such clauses are good things, from the standpoint of the orderly and fair administration of civil justice? Is Florida a reasonable choice? Or should every passenger be entitled to sue where she lives?

Carnival Cruise Lines' *Tropicale*

Not surprisingly, cruise lines take advantage of the opportunity provided by the contract that passengers enter into when they purchase tickets of passage. Shown at right is the *Tropicale*, on which the Shutes were passengers when Mrs. Shute was injured. The forum selection clause addressed in *Carnival Cruise* was not the only restriction contained in the tickets purchased by the Shutes.  Those tickets also stated that Carnival Cruise "shall not be liable for any loss of life or personal injury or delay whatsoever," but federal law does not permit cruise lines to limit their liability for "personal injury or death caused by the negligence or fault of the owner [of the vessel] or the owner's employees or agents." See 46 USC §30509. Perhaps in recognition of this fact, the tickets bought by the Shutes also stated that notice in writing of any claim had to be given "within 185 days," and such clauses are often enforceable (like the forum selection clause enforced in *Carnival Cruise*). The statute, however, expressly allows cruise lines to limit their liability for infliction of emotional distress, and the statute does not cover cruises that do not touch United States ports, see Wallis v. Princess Cruises, Inc., 306 F.3d 827 (9th Cir. 2002) (statute does not apply, but liability-limiting clause was unenforceable because it failed "reasonable communicativeness" standard).

---

3. There are other ways, less certain and more problematic, to affect the locus of disputes arising out of contracts. One involves designating a local agent for service of process. See National Equipment Rental, Ltd. v. Szukhent, 375 U.S. 311 (1964) (enforcing, in equipment rental agreement between New York lessor and Michigan farmer-lessee, an appointment in New York of Florence Weinberg, the wife of an officer of the rental company, as agent for the Michigan farmer, so New York suit filed by lessor could resolve the dispute). Another, both draconian and unusual, involves appointment of a local person to "confess judgment" in a suit against a contract debtor. See Overmyer v. Frick, 405 U.S. 174 (1972) (allowing this mechanism in commercial context).

4. Parties to a contract often choose not only one particular *forum* to hear any dispute, but a particular state's (or nation's) *law* to govern the rights of the parties. It is common to include *both* a forum selection clause and a choice-of-law clause, and common to choose to litigate in the same state or country whose law is to apply. Thus in *The Bremen,* the parties selected London as the forum and probably understood that British law would apply. Recall that in *Rudzewicz* (Section C2 supra), the parties chose to be governed by Florida law, but the contract did *not* say litigation was to go forward in Florida. In *Carnival Cruise,* the parties did just the opposite: The back of the ticket said the parties were to litigate in Florida but said nothing about which law applied.

5. *Carnival Cruise* is not the only case where tourists injured during their travels have found themselves bound by forum selection clauses. Hotels and or other vacation vendors use such clauses too. See Krenkel v. Kerzner International Hotels, Ltd., 579 F.3d 1279 (11th Cir. 2009) (New Jersey resident allegedly injured in slip-and-fall on path in "pool lagoon area" sued Bahamian hotel in federal court in Florida, which dismissed under clause selecting "The Supreme Court of the Bahamas as the exclusive venue" for such litigation). For a case reaching a similar result on the basis of a forum selection clause in an informed consent agreement in a medical malpractice case, see Rivera v. Centro Medico de Turabo, Inc., 575 F.3d 10 (1st Cir. 2009).

6. Brave New World: Jurisdiction and the Internet

Computers and other electronic devices (smartphones to iPads), coupled with the growth of the internet, have brought new challenges to the minimum contacts standard, in part because the internet makes it easier for businesses, government agencies, and individuals to have instant visibility and impact on a national (indeed, global) basis, and to conduct business and deliver messages seen by many or few, with keyboard or voice technology, and modern "apps."

Longstanding national legislation, such as statutes protecting copyright and trade names, antitrust statutes, and newer legislation like the Cybersquatting Consumer Protection Act, 15 USC §1125(d), have led to new types of litigation involving internet activities, bringing additional jurisdictional challenges.

Erté (*Ebony on White*) and Betty Boop (with Pudgy)

The Erté image (left, below) is the one involved in the *Dudnikov* suit; the Betty Boop image (right, below) is not the alleged infringing image, but it provides a good idea of her—a cartoonish character out of the flapper era of the 1920s. In the allegedly infringing image, Betty Boop appears in a flowing white gown with a fur on one arm, with long extenders draped behind her and suspended with the other arm, which also holds a leash connected to her little dog Pudgy. Copyright law protects not only against literal copying, but also nonliteral adaptation of copyrighted material, so it is at least possible that this case, had the litigation persisted, would have wound up before a jury or judge acting as decision maker on the merits. The "fair use" defense would likely be raised, in which the argument would be that a parody of an image amounts to a fair use. Other claims could be brought in such cases, such as trademark infringement, in which the argument would be that the Betty Boop image confuses consumers about its origins. In the *Dudnikov* case, plaintiffs seized the initiative and represented themselves (they filed a pro se complaint). When the trial court dismissed their case, they enlisted the help of the Public Citizen Litigation Group in Washington, D.C. in taking the appeal. Despite prevailing on the jurisdictional point in the Tenth Circuit, they elected to settle shortly thereafter. As of 2012, they maintained a website at www.tabberone.com setting forth information about products that they sell out

of their shop in Hartsell, Colorado, as well as a "Trademark & Copyright Abusers' Hall of Shame" containing information and opinions about litigation initiated by copyright holders similar to SevenArts and Chalk & Vermilion in this case.

DUDNIKOV v. CHALK & VERMILION FINE ARTS, INC.

United States Court of Appeals for the Tenth Circuit
514 F.3d 1063 (2008)

Before McConnell, Ebel, and Gorsuch, Circuit Judges.

Gorsuch, Circuit Judge.

Plaintiffs are eBay "power sellers." Through the Internet auction site, they sell a variety of fabrics from their home in Colorado. This case concerns two of plaintiffs' prints, both of which play on famous images by the artist Erté,

Symphony in Black and *Ebony on White.* While Erté's images depict elegant women walking aquiline dogs, plaintiffs' prints portray Betty Boop next to her aptly named canine companion, Pudgy.

Defendants, owners of the rights to the Erté images, saw plaintiffs' eBay auction page (which disclosed plaintiffs' Colorado location), and came to the conclusion that plaintiffs' prints infringed their copyrights. Defendants promptly contacted eBay in California and successfully suspended plaintiffs' auction, an action that allegedly had adverse consequences for plaintiffs' business and future dealings with the auction site. By e-mail, defendants also threatened plaintiffs with suit in federal court. Before defendants could carry out that threat, however, plaintiffs initiated this action in federal district court in Colorado seeking a declaratory judgment that their prints do not infringe defendants' copyrights. Defendants responded with a motion to dismiss, arguing that the court lacked personal jurisdiction over them. The district court concurred and dismissed plaintiffs' complaint. For reasons we explore below, we reverse.

I

Taken in the light most favorable to plaintiffs, as they must be at this stage in the litigation, the facts of this case establish that Karen Dudnikov and Michael Meadors, a husband-and-wife team, operate a small and unincorporated Internet-based business from their home in Colorado. Together, they sell fabric and handmade crafts such as aprons, blankets, and placemats under the name "Tabber's Temptations." The majority of their income is derived from selling these products on eBay, whose operations are based in California. Tabber's Temptations is described by eBay as a "power seller," and has received over 6,000 "feedback messages" in the past year from its eBay customers, and over 13,000 positive feedback messages since 1998. Ms. Dudnikov's and Mr. Meadors' eBay auction pages clearly list the location of their merchandise as Hartsel, Colorado, and link to their personal website which contains more information about their business, including its location in Colorado.

In October 2005, Ms. Dudnikov and Mr. Meadors launched an auction on eBay offering fabric for sale with the imprint of the cartoon character Betty Boop wearing various gowns. One of these gowns, Ms. Dudnikov and Mr. Meadors concede for purposes of defendants' motion to dismiss, is easily recognizable as a design of the artist known as Erté, a 20th century Russian-born French artist and fashion designer. In Erté's original works, *Symphony in Black* and *Ebony on White*, a tall, slender woman is pictured wearing a floor length form-fitting dress that trails her feet, and holding the leash of a thin, regal dog. The fabric offered for sale by Ms. Dudnikov and Mr. Meadors replaced the rather elegant woman in Erté's images with the rather less elegant Betty Boop, and substituted Erté's svelte canine with Betty Boop's pet, Pudgy.

[A British company (SevenArts) owns the copyright to the Erté works, and a Delaware company (Chalk & Vermilion or "C&V") is SevenArts' agent. C&V participates in eBay's Verified Rights Owner (VeRO) program, which allows a member to terminate an auction on receiving a verified notice of claimed infringement (NOCI). C&V sent such a notice to eBay in California, claiming the Betty Boop image infringed the Erté copyright. Under the VeRO program, the auction is terminated for ten days. The auction is reinstated if the targeted seller files a counter-notice contesting the validity of the claim, unless the complaining party files suit within the ten days.

On receiving the NOCI from eBay, and being told that the auction of the Betty Boop fabric pattern was suspended, Dudnikov contacted C&V and SevenArts by email asking that the NOCI be withdrawn and offering to refrain from relisting the disputed pattern. Dudnikov expressed fear that the NOCI put her business "in danger of going under" ("Nothing to you perhaps but everything to me"). SevenArts declined to withdraw the NOCI. Dudnikov and Meadors then filed a counter-notice. SevenArts replied that it intended to file suit in federal court. Before SevenArts did so, Dudnikov and Meadors filed a pro se suit in federal court in Colorado seeking a declaratory judgment of noninfringement and an injunction barring defendants from further interference with their business.]

II

[On motion by SevenArts and C&V, the district court dismissed the case for lack of jurisdiction, and plaintiffs (now represented by counsel) appealed. The reviewing court concludes that neither federal statute (Copyright Act and Declaratory Judgment Act) provides for nationwide service of process, hence that FRCP 4(k)(1)(A) controls, hence that the Colorado long-arm statute applies, which confers the "maximum jurisdiction" permitted by due process.]

In this arena, the Supreme Court has instructed that the "minimum contacts" standard requires, first, that the out-of-state defendant must have "purposefully directed" its activities at residents of the forum state, and second, that the plaintiff's injuries must "arise out of" defendant's forum-related activities. Burger King Corp. v. Rudzewicz, 471 U.S. 462, 472 (1985). Additionally, exercising personal jurisdiction over defendants must always be consonant with traditional notions of fair play and substantial justice. While these elements afford some shape to the due process inquiry, each is, as we shall see, not without its own interpretative difficulties.

III

The first element can appear in different guises. In the tort context, we often ask whether the nonresident defendant "purposefully directed" its activities at the forum state; in contract cases, meanwhile, we sometimes ask whether the defendant "purposefully availed" itself of the privilege of conducting activities or consummating a transaction in the forum state. In all events, the shared aim of "purposeful direction" doctrine has been said by the Supreme Court to ensure that an out-of-state defendant is not bound to appear to account for merely "random, fortuitous, or attenuated contacts" with the forum state. *Burger King.*

Because this rule of law is more aspirational than self-defining, courts have often retreated to analogizing individual cases to discrete Supreme Court personal jurisdiction precedents. Indeed, this feature of due process personal jurisdiction litigation has led many commentators to complain of the lack of predictability and certainty in this area of law. *See International Shoe* (Black, J. concurring in the judgment) (referring to the majority's approach to jurisdiction as consisting of "elastic standards" and "vague Constitutional criteria"); *see also* C. Douglas Floyd and Shima Baradaran-Robinson, *Toward a Unified Test of Personal Jurisdiction in an Era of Widely Diffused Wrongs: The Relevance of Purpose and Effects,* 81 Ind. L.J. 601, 638 (2006). Happily, at least in this case, plaintiffs have fixed their focus on a single precedential analogy that, they argue, controls the outcome of the "purposeful direction" inquiry in this case: the Supreme Court's disposition in Calder v. Jones, 465 U.S. 783 (1984). While we do not imagine that *Calder* necessarily describes the only way to satisfy the purposeful direction test, because plaintiffs assert it provides the key to unlocking the courthouse door for them, we are able to limit our attention in this case to *Calder*'s demands.

[The court summarizes the facts of *Calder*.]

Distilling *Calder* to its essence, we thus understand the Court to have found purposeful direction there because of the presence of (a) an intentional action (writing, editing, and publishing the article), that was (b) expressly aimed at the forum state (the article was about a California resident and her activities in California; likewise it was drawn from California sources and widely distributed in that state), with (c) knowledge that the brunt of the injury would be felt in the forum state (defendants knew Ms. Jones was in California and her career revolved around the entertainment industry there). At plaintiffs' invitation, we turn our attention to examining the presence or absence of these same factors in their case.

A

1

In *Calder*, the Court emphasized in the first instance that the defendants undertook "intentional, and allegedly tortious, actions. . . ." Plaintiffs argue, and defendants do not dispute, that the sending of the NOCI was an intentional act. However, the parties disagree over whether under *Calder* plaintiffs must also allege that the act itself was wrongful or tortious in some sense, and whether in this case plaintiffs have done so successfully.

[The decision in Yahoo! Inc. v. La Ligue Contre le Racisme et L'Antisemitisme, 433 F.3d 1199 (9th Cir. 2006) (*en banc*) suggests that *Calder* does not necessarily require that "all (or even any) jurisdictionally relevant effects have been caused by wrongful acts," which would "improperly conflate the jurisdictional analysis with the merits." *Calder* itself supports this view in rejecting claims that "First Amendment concerns" affect jurisdictional analysis, even though they affect the substantive standard. Other decisions, however, suggest that *Calder* applies only if the intentional act is tortious.]

As it happens, we are able to avoid entering this thicket. Even if *Calder* can be properly read as requiring some form of "wrongful" intentional conduct, we agree with plaintiffs that their complaint complies. Plaintiffs allege that defendants intentionally sent a letter to eBay invoking the VeRO procedures. They allege that defendants took this action with the intent of terminating plaintiffs' auction—thereby causing them lost business and a damaged business reputation. They further allege that defendants took this action on the basis of an erroneous copyright claim, asserting that the fabric in question was perfectly lawful in light of the fair use doctrine, and that defendants were well aware of this fact. Finally, plaintiffs allege that, in light of the foregoing, defendants' claim that they were innocently seeking to protect their copyright was "simply a smoke-screen attempt to justify unwarranted interference in the lawful sale of an item." . . . [C]rediting the complaint as true as we must at this stage of the litigation, and further giving it the solicitous construction due a *pro se* filing, the facts described above are sufficient to permit an inference that defendants tortiously interfered with plaintiffs' business. Plaintiffs' allegations . . . include facts detailing what defendants did (sending the NOCI), what they knew would happen when they sent the NOCI (the cancellation of plaintiffs' auction and its ramifications for plaintiffs' business), and the basis for that knowledge (the specifics of the VeRO program and defendants' participation in that program).

2

Defendants separately object that plaintiffs seek jurisdiction based not on defendants' intentional actions, as they must, but instead based on plaintiffs' own, unilateral conduct. In this vein, defendants emphasize it was plaintiffs who chose to sell allegedly infringing material through eBay, and they remind us of our legion case law holding that "the unilateral activity of another party 'is not an appropriate consideration when determining whether a defendant has sufficient contacts with a forum State to justify an assertion of jurisdiction.'" Doe v. Nat'l Med. Servs., 974 F.2d 143, 146 (10th Cir. 1992) (quoting Helicopteros Nacionales de Colombia, S.A. v. Hall, 466 U.S. 408, 417 (1984)).

Unilateral acts, however, occur in at least two analytically distinct ways. First, as in *World-Wide Volkswagen,* a plaintiff might purchase a product in one forum and carry it into another forum. Absent at least the seller's foreknowledge that the buyer was going to take the product into a particular forum, the defendant cannot reasonably be said to have purposefully directed its activities at the forum. The defendant's only contact, the presence of its product in the forum, is the result of the act of someone else and not the defendant's own intentional conduct. A second type of unilateral activity appears where the defendant *has* purposefully directed its activities at the forum, but the plaintiff's injury nonetheless "arises out of" the plaintiff's or a third party's unilateral acts, rather than the defendant's. *See, e.g.,* Kuenzle v. HTM Sport-Und Freizeitgeräte AG, 102 F.3d 453, 456-57 (10th Cir. 1996) (holding that "[r]egardless of any contacts that exist between [the defendant] and the forum," the suit arose from the activities of the plaintiff). We believe this second sort of unilateral act, with something of a supervening causation flavor to it, is more appropriately addressed at the second ("arising out of") stage of the minimum contacts inquiry, and so we defer discussion of it until then.

With respect to the first type of unilateral act, we have no difficulty determining that plaintiffs have alleged an intentional and wrongful act by defendants on which jurisdiction may permissibly be founded. Plaintiffs do not argue, and we do not remotely hold, that jurisdiction is proper simply based on plaintiffs' decision to hold an eBay auction of materials that allegedly infringe upon defendants' copyrights.[8] Rather, it is essential to our analysis that it was defendants who in this case took the intentional action of sending a NOCI specifically designed to terminate plaintiffs' auction, and defendants who followed that act with an express threat to sue within 10 days in order to prevent the revival of plaintiffs' auction.

B

Calder, of course, required more than an intentional action. It also stressed that the defendants' conduct was "expressly aimed at California." In the sentences immediately following its introduction of this concept, the Court emphasized that California was the "focal point" of the allegedly tortious story.[9] ... [T]he "express aiming" test focuses ... on a defendant's intentions—where was the

---

[8] In Marschke v. Wratislaw, 743 N.W.2d 402 (S.D. 2007), the South Dakota Supreme Court held that exercising personal jurisdiction in South Dakota over a Montana car dealer who had posted a car for sale on eBay that was subsequently bought by the South Dakota plaintiff violated due process. In Winfield Collection, Ltd. v. McCauley, 105 F. Supp. 2d 746 (E.D. Mich. 2000), the court held similarly in a case involving a defendant who sold crafts through eBay that used patterns allegedly infringing the plaintiff's copyrights.

[9] Some courts have held that the "expressly aimed" portion of *Calder* is satisfied when the defendant "individually target[s] a known forum resident." *See* Bancroft & Masters, Inc. v. Augusta National, Inc., 223 F.3d 1082, 1087 (9th Cir. 2000). We have taken a somewhat more restrictive approach, holding that the

"focal point" of its purposive efforts . . . —where was the alleged harm actually felt by the plaintiff.

Defendants submit that plaintiffs have failed to meet the "expressly aiming" standard, pointing to the uncontested fact that they sent their NOCI invoking eBay's VeRO procedures not to plaintiffs in Colorado but to eBay in California. Such focus on the physical direction of defendants' NOCI, however, does not tell the whole story. It overlooks, for example, the fact that eBay's VeRO procedures allow a NOCI filer to terminate another party's auction automatically, as well as plaintiffs' allegation that defendants intended to halt their auction. It overlooks, too, the fact that the NOCI at issue in this case itself attests to this alleged intent: the NOCI explicitly requests eBay to "act expeditiously to remove or disable access to the material or items claimed to be infringing." . . . And when plaintiffs did not acquiesce, defendants emailed plaintiffs directly in Colorado threatening them with suit in federal court to prevent the future sales of the fabric in question.

Thus, while, as defendants emphasize, the NOCI formally traveled only to California, it can be fairly characterized as an intended means to the further intended end of canceling plaintiffs' auction in Colorado. In this way, it is something like a bank shot in basketball. A player who shoots the ball off of the backboard intends to hit the backboard, but he does so in the service of his further intention of putting the ball into the basket. Here, defendants intended to send the NOCI to eBay in California, but they did so with the ultimate purpose of canceling plaintiffs' auction in Colorado. Their "express aim" thus can be said to have reached into Colorado in much the same way that a basketball player's express aim in shooting off of the backboard is not simply to hit the backboard, but to make a basket.

. . .

In *Bancroft*, a case perhaps even more analogous to ours, a small California company that sold computer and networking products and services, Bancroft & Masters, registered the domain name masters.com with Network Solutions Inc. ("NSI"), a company based in Virginia. Augusta National, which operates the Augusta National Golf Club and sponsors the Masters golf tournament, sent a letter from its headquarters in Georgia to NSI in Virginia, asserting that Bancroft & Masters had violated its trademark. Much as under the VeRO procedures at issue here, Augusta National's complaint had the effect, under NSI policy, of prohibiting Bancroft & Masters from retaining its domain name unless it obtained a declaratory judgment that it was not infringing on Augusta National's marks. Bancroft & Masters brought such a suit in California and our sister circuit held that, because Augusta National's purpose was specifically to target a known

---

forum state itself must be the "focal point of the tort." *See* Far West Capital, Inc. v. Towne, 46 F.3d 1071, 1080 (10th Cir. 1995) (internal quotations omitted). Any difference between these standards is immaterial to the resolution of this case, however, as plaintiffs succeed under either.

California business, it satisfied *Calder*'s "express aiming" test despite the fact that letter was formally sent to Virginia rather than California. Precisely the same reasoning applies here.

Informative in its contrast, Schwarzenegger v. Fred Martin Motor Co., 374 F.3d 797 (9th Cir. 2004), dealt with a car dealer in Ohio whose local Akron advertisements encouraged potential buyers to "terminate" their current car leases in favor of a new Martin auto. The advertisement featured a photograph of Arnold Schwarzenegger in *The Terminator* (1984), one of his most popular film roles in which he appears as a murderous cyborg, "(a cybernetic organism; i.e., a robot whose mechanical parts are encased in living tissue . . .)." When Mr. Schwarzenegger sought to sue the car dealership in California for the unauthorized use of his likeness, the Ninth Circuit refused jurisdiction, stressing that, unlike the defendants in *Calder,* the car dealership's advertisements were not "expressly aimed" at Mr. Schwarzenegger in the forum state (California). While Mr. Martin perhaps *knew* Mr. Schwarzenegger lived in California, this was insufficient to convey jurisdiction there because the *intentions* behind his advertisement was solely to entice local market Ohioans, not Californians, "to buy or lease cars from Fred Martin." By contrast, defendants in our case *are* alleged to have *intended* their extra-forum conduct to reach and affect plaintiffs' business operations in Colorado.

[The defendants deny knowing that plaintiffs' business was in Colorado, but the complaint alleges the contrary, based on "well-pled and record facts." Plaintiff's business location appears on their auction page, where it is noted that Colorado residents must pay Colorado sales tax, and "presumably seeing this page" is what persuaded defendants to contact eBay.]

C

In assessing the question of "purposeful direction," *Calder* stressed the fact that the *Enquirer* defendants "knew that the brunt of th[e] injury would be felt" in the forum state. . . . [P]laintiffs have satisfied their burden of establishing, at this stage, that defendants knew plaintiffs' business and auction were based in Colorado, and therefore knew the effects of the NOCI would be felt there.

Defendants . . . contend, just as the unsuccessful defendants in *Calder* did, that the "mere foreseeability" that the NOCI would have effects in Colorado is insufficient to support jurisdiction, and that plaintiffs have failed to allege the "something more" than foreseeability required to establish personal jurisdiction, *see, e.g.,* Asahi Metal Indus. Co., Ltd. v. Superior Court, 480 U.S. 102, 111 (1987) (O'Connor, J.) (plurality opinion). We surely agree that under *Calder* the mere foreseeability of causing an injury in the forum state is, standing alone, insufficient to warrant a state exercising its sovereignty over an out-of-state defendant. But under the *Calder* test plaintiffs have invoked, they must establish, and have established for purposes of a motion to dismiss decided on the pleadings and affidavits, not only that defendants foresaw (or knew) that the effects of their conduct would be felt in the forum state, but also that defendants undertook *intentional actions that were expressly aimed at that forum state*. That is, in satisfying *Calder*'s first two prongs, plaintiffs have established that defendants acted with more than foresight (or knowledge) that effects would be felt in Colorado.

Indeed, at the end of the day our case is an easier one than *Calder* itself. There, the defendants intended to write an article, the "focal point" of which was California, for the *Enquirer* to publish and distribute in California. Yet, the effects of which the plaintiff complained likely were not bound up in the defendants' intentions. The defendant writer and editor were professionals presumably interested chiefly in the sale of newspapers, not in doing *intentional* harm to Ms. Jones; that is, while they *knew* their article would have adverse effects on her in California, those effects were to them perhaps no more than foreseeable side-effects. By contrast, defendants here more than foresaw or knew the harm alleged to have befallen forum residents; indeed, they do not dispute that they *intended* to cause the cancellation of plaintiffs' auction, and it is that precise alleged harm that plaintiffs seek to have redressed through this suit. As our sister circuit has said, actions that "are performed for the very purpose of having their consequences felt in the forum state" are more than sufficient to support a finding of purposeful direction under *Calder*. Finley v. River North Records, Inc., 148 F.3d 913, 916 (8th Cir. 1998) (quotation omitted) (holding jurisdiction proper where an out-of-state defendant sent fraudulent material into the forum state with the purpose of inducing plaintiff's reliance, and such reliance was the harmful effect for which plaintiff sought redress).

IV

Having determined that defendants "purposefully directed" their activities at the forum state, due process requires us next to ask whether plaintiffs' injuries "arise out of" defendants' contacts with the forum jurisdiction. Many courts have interpreted this language to require some sort of causal connection between a defendant's contacts and the suit at issue. Of course, as Prosser and Keeton have noted, "[t]here is perhaps nothing in the entire field of law which has called forth more disagreement, or upon which the opinions are in such a welter of confusion," as causation doctrine, Prosser and Keeton on the Law of Torts 263 (5th ed., 1984), and this arena is no exception. Some courts have interpreted the phrase "arise out of" as endorsing a theory of "but-for" causation, *see, e.g.,* Mattel, Inc. v. Greiner and Hausser GmbH., 354 F.3d 857, 864 (9th Cir. 2003), while other courts have required proximate cause to support the exercise of specific jurisdiction, *see, e.g.,* Massachusetts School of Law at Andover, Inc. v. American Bar Association, 142 F.3d 26, 35 (1st Cir. 1998). Under the former approach, any event in the causal chain leading to the plaintiff's injury is sufficiently related to the claim to support the exercise of specific jurisdiction. The latter approach, by contrast, is considerably more restrictive and calls for courts to "examine whether any of the defendant's contacts with the forum are relevant to the merits of the plaintiff's claim." O'Connor v. Sandy Lane Hotel Co., 496 F.3d 312, 319 (3d Cir. 2007). Yet a third approach, departing somewhat from these causation-based principles, instead asks whether there is a "substantial connection" or "discernible relationship" between the contacts and the suit. Under this theory, the relationship between the contacts and the suit can be weaker when the contacts themselves are more extensive. *See* Shoppers Food Warehouse v. Moreno, 746 A.2d 320, 335-36 (D.C. 2000).

The parties point us to no case in which we have had occasion to announce a test as to when a contact is sufficiently related to a claim to support the exercise of jurisdiction, but we agree with our sister circuit that the "substantial connection" test inappropriately blurs the distinction between specific and general personal jurisdiction. General jurisdiction is based on an out-of-state defendant's "continuous and systematic" contacts with the forum state, and does not require that the claim be related to those contacts. Specific jurisdiction, on the other hand, is premised on something of a *quid pro quo:* in exchange for "benefiting" from some purposive conduct directed at the forum state, a party is deemed to consent to the exercise of jurisdiction for claims related to those contacts. A relatedness inquiry that varies the required connection between the contacts and the claims asserted based on the number of the contacts improperly conflates these two analytically distinct approaches to jurisdiction. By eliminating the distinction between contacts that are sufficient to support any suit and those that require the suit be related to the contact, it also undermines the rationale for the relatedness inquiry: to allow a defendant to anticipate his jurisdictional exposure based on his own actions. *See* Linda Sandstrom Simard, *Meeting Expectations: Two Profiles For Specific Jurisdiction,* 38 Ind. L. Rev. 343, 366 (2005).

As between the remaining but-for and proximate causation tests, we have no need to pick sides today. On the facts of this case, we are satisfied that either theory adopted by our sister circuits would support a determination that plaintiffs' cause of action arises from the defendants' contact with Colorado. That defendants' contact with Colorado, the sending of the NOCI to eBay and the ensuing e-mail exchange in which defendants threatened plaintiffs with suit, is a but-for cause of this action is clear. After all, if defendants had not claimed that plaintiffs were infringing their copyright, plaintiffs would have had no reason to seek a declaratory judgment that their actions did not run afoul of defendants' rights. The NOCI was also the cause in fact of the real world harm that plaintiffs seek to have remedied: the cancellation of their auction and the black mark on their eBay record. In the absence of the NOCI, plaintiffs would not have had to contend with either of those effects, and thus would have had no reason to attempt to hale defendants into court.

We believe that the NOCI can also fairly be considered the proximate cause of plaintiffs' claim. In the NOCI, defendants swore under penalty of perjury that they had a good faith belief that plaintiffs' auction infringed their rights. The merits of plaintiffs' declaratory judgment action addresses the exact same question, and their claim for injunctive relief seeks to prevent future interference with plaintiffs' business, interference which defendants have threatened. More specifically, plaintiffs argue that defendants' infringement claim contained in the NOCI is incorrect, and that therefore their auction was improperly cancelled and their sales record erroneously smeared. The NOCI is thus at the very core of plaintiffs' suit.

Defendants' chief argument against finding plaintiffs' suit sufficiently related to the NOCI is (once again) that plaintiffs' suit is based on plaintiffs' unilateral conduct. Even if the NOCI was purposefully directed at Colorado, defendants argue that because plaintiffs are seeking a judgment that their own actions are legal, their claim does not arise out of any activity of defendants. This argument, however, neglects the fact that plaintiffs filed suit in direct response to defendants' suppression of their auction and threat to bring a suit in less than two weeks. While plaintiffs' actions are admittedly also a but-for cause of this suit, that does not change the fact that what plaintiffs seek is relief from defendants' actions and the ensuing consequences following directly from those actions.

Our case is, in this respect, akin to Red Wing Shoe Co. v. Hockerson-Halberstadt, Inc., 148 F.3d 1355, 1360 (Fed. Cir. 1998), and CompuServe v. Patterson, 89 F.3d 1257 (6th Cir. 1996). In *Red Wing Shoe,* the Federal Circuit held the threat of an infringement suit carried by a cease-and-desist letter acts as a restraint on the free flow of goods, and a declaratory judgment action by the purveyor of allegedly non-infringing goods arises from (and is an attempt to eliminate) that restraint.[10] Neither is the restraint here based on threats alone, although defendants did indeed threaten litigation; rather, defendants affirmatively interfered with plaintiffs' business, and this suit arises directly from that interference.

Similarly, in *CompuServe,* a Texas defendant had threatened to sue an Ohio corporation for trademark infringement if it did not pay him $100,000

---

[10] To be sure, *Red Wing Shoe* ultimately held that jurisdiction was inappropriate on the reasonableness prong of our due process analysis because of policy concerns unique to the intellectual property context, a question we take up in Part V, *infra.* But for purposes of the relatedness prong of our analysis, plaintiffs' suit attacks the very type of restraint that *Red Wing Shoe* held gives rise to a suit seeking a declaration of non-infringement.

to settle his claim. The Ohio corporation thereafter filed a preemptive declaratory judgment suit in Ohio. After holding that the defendant's threat constituted a contact with Ohio, the court applied a proximate cause standard to determine whether the plaintiff's claim arose from that contact. The court noted that there, as here, the defendant's actions threatened harm to the economic livelihood of the plaintiff, and it was that threat the plaintiff sought to eliminate through its suit. Indeed, the instant case is an even clearer case for jurisdiction than *CompuServe* because Ms. Dudnikov and Mr. Meadors seek relief not merely from threats, but from actual restraints on their business resulting from defendants' NOCI.

V

Having determined that plaintiffs met their burden, at this stage of the litigation, of establishing "minimum contacts"—that defendants' conduct was "purposefully directed" at Colorado and that this lawsuit arose out of defendants' contacts with Colorado—we must still inquire whether the exercise of personal jurisdiction would "offend traditional notions of fair play and substantial justice." *International Shoe* (internal quotation omitted). In doing so, we are cognizant of the fact that, with minimum contacts established, it is incumbent on defendants to "present a compelling case that the presence of some other considerations would render jurisdiction unreasonable." Pro Axess, Inc. v. Orlux Distributors, Inc., 428 F.3d 1270 (10th Cir. 2005) (internal quotation omitted).

In making such an inquiry courts traditionally consider factors such as these:

> (1) the burden on the defendant, (2) the forum state's interests in resolving the dispute, (3) the plaintiff's interest in receiving convenient and effectual relief, (4) the interstate judicial system's interest in obtaining the most efficient resolution of controversies, and (5) the shared interest of the several states [or foreign nations] in furthering fundamental social policies.

OMI Holdings, Inc. v. Royal Ins. Co. of Canada, 149 F.3d 1086, 1095 (10th Cir. 2005). *But see* International Shoe *and the Legacy of Legal Realism*, 2001 Sup. Ct. Rev. 347, 368 (2001) (arguing that considering factors such as these "imposes all of the costs of case-by-case adjudication without conferring any benefits in the form of predictable outcomes").

None of these factors, separately or in combination, seems to weigh definitively in favor of defendants. With respect to the burden on them associated with litigating in Colorado, defendants' threat to litigate in federal court indicates a willingness to litigate in some federal court in the United States. As far as we can tell, there are a finite number of possible fora in this country in which this case might be litigated, including perhaps Connecticut or Delaware, Chalk & Vermilion's home state and state of incorporation; Colorado, the plaintiffs' home state; or California, eBay's home state.

California has virtually nothing to do with this litigation: eBay is not a party to this suit, we have been pointed to no specific witnesses or evidence located in California, and the merits of this dispute are wholly unrelated to California substantive law. Thus, we are left to consider the burden on the parties of litigating this suit in Colorado rather than, say, Connecticut or Delaware. As in any case in which the parties reside in different fora, one side must bear the inconvenience of litigating "on the road." While admittedly a burden, defendants have not indicated that their defense of this case would be hindered by the territorial limits on the Colorado district court's power to subpoena relevant witnesses, or indeed hampered in any other significant way.

. . .

The only traditional factor that does loom large for either side in this case is the potential policy interests of a foreign nation. [Substantive British policies are not implicated even though C&V is a named defendant, since nobody disputes that federal copyright law applies, and the only claim is a violation of U.S. law. Moreover, SevenArts itself threatened to file suit in federal court. In fact, the interests of the United States in adjudicating this case "do[] weigh strongly in [plaintiffs'] favor." In *Red Wing Shoe,* a Louisiana company sent a cease-and-desist notice to a Minnesota company claiming patent infringement, which sufficed to create jurisdiction in Minnesota when the recipient sued. Here the NOCI "went well beyond providing notice" of a claimed infringement, and in fact "purposefully caused the cancellation of [plaintiffs'] auction."]

. . .

Defendants sent a NOCI to eBay expressly intending (and effectually acting) to suspend plaintiffs' auction in Colorado. Plaintiffs' suit arises from, and is indeed an effort to reverse, the intended consequences of defendants' NOCI which they incurred in Colorado. For purposes of this motion, moreover, we must assume defendants knew plaintiffs' business was located in Colorado. And defendants point us to no basis in traditional notions of fair play or substantial justice that would preclude suit in that forum. Accordingly, the judgment of the district court is reversed, and this case is remanded for further proceedings not inconsistent with this opinion.

So ordered.

■ NOTES ON JURISDICTION OVER INTERNET CLAIMS

1. In a sense, *Dudnikov* brings nothing new: Defendants allegedly committed a wrongful act outside Colorado by sending a complaint to eBay that, "like a bank shot in basketball," bounced from California into Colorado when eBay terminated plaintiffs' auction of the Betty Boop fabric pattern. As in

Calder, the behavior was verbal, and defendant "intended" to have an impact in the forum state (we can speak of a "target").

(a) The court asks whether conduct must be "wrongful" to support jurisdiction. How does it resolve this point? It also asks whether the suit was really about plaintiffs' or defendants' conduct. How does it resolve this one?

(b) To satisfy the *Calder* version of "purposeful availment," the conduct must be intentional and aimed at the forum. Was that true in this case?

(c) The court says the injuries or claims must "arise out of" defendants' conduct. How does the court interpret this requirement? Do you agree that it is satisfied here?

(d) Finally, the opinion asks whether exercising jurisdiction comports with traditional notions of fair play, and invokes the five-factor standard that came originally from *World-Wide*. This approach looks very much like the approach taken in *Asahi*, which looked first at minimum contacts and then at the five-factor standard. How does the court deal with the five factors here?

2. Consider this case: Plaintiff uBid auctioned excess inventory over the internet. In federal court in Illinois, uBid sued GoDaddy, a Texas company, alleging that it was registering (for a fee) domain names "confusingly similar" to plaintiff's. Registrants would "squat" (hold names without using them, except for advertising that paid the holder for every hit) or build websites and profit from hits by customers looking for plaintiff's website. In uBid's suit, the court addressed the question whether "hundreds of thousands" of sales in Illinois were sufficiently "related" to plaintiff's claims to sustain jurisdiction over GoDaddy. The court concluded that neither "but for" nor "proximate" causation was the right standard: The former was "vastly overinclusive" by haling defendants into court "even if they gained nothing" from local conducts and the "tacit quid pro quo" underlying the minimum contacts standard would break down. But requiring proximate causation would exclude "too many claims." Without trying further to define relatedness, the Seventh Circuit concluded that the relationship between Illinois sales and the claim was "close enough to make the relatedness quid pro quo balanced and reasonable." See uBid, Inc. v. GoDaddy Group, Inc., 623 F.3d 421 (7th Cir. 2010).

(a) Does *uBid* make sense in applying an undefined standard that is *looser* than proximate cause? Recall that *Dudnikov* rejected a looser standard as blurring the line between specific and general jurisdiction.

(b) *uBid* was a federal question case, and *Dudnikov* was probably a federal question case too. In a passage edited from the case, *Dudnikov* explained that FRCP 4(k)(1)(A) required it to apply the state long-arm statute, which led to the minimum contacts analysis. The same thing happened in *uBid*. In both cases, state law (and the minimum contacts standard) limited federal jurisdiction.

3. Among internet jurisdiction cases, an early district court opinion in the *Zippo* case has proved influential. The court divided internet contacts among highly interactive websites ("knowing and repeated transmission of computer files over the internet," where one can "conduct business throughout the world entirely from a desktop"), modestly interactive websites (user "can exchange information with the host computer"), and passive websites (that do "little more than make information available"). *Zippo* said that operating highly interactive websites, like sending products directly into the forum, often suffices for jurisdiction, but that operating passive websites is not reason enough to exercise jurisdiction in another state from which the site is accessed. Among websites in the middle of the range (modestly interactive), jurisdiction turns on "examining the level of interactivity and commercial nature of the exchange." See Zippo Mfg. Co. v. Zippo Dot Com, Inc., 952 F. Supp. 1119 (W.D. Pa. 1997) (sustaining jurisdiction in Pennsylvania in trademark dilution and infringement suit by maker of Zippo lighters against California corporation operating internet website using Zippo in its title with users in Pennsylvania).

4. Internet jurisdiction cases often fall into four major categories:

(a) Unfair Competition, Trademark Infringement, and Related Claims. Like *Dudnikov,* many cases involve claims that defendant is infringing plaintiff's trademark or trade name, or using a name that is the same as (or unfairly similar to) plaintiff's, or stealing content from plaintiff's website. The decisions are mixed, some finding jurisdiction, some coming out the other way. Compare CollegeSource, Inc. v. AcademyOne, Inc., 2011 WL 3437040 (9th Cir. 2011) (no jurisdiction in federal court in California to hear claim by CollegeSource that AcademyOne was stealing web content; both parties were in business of facilitating college transfers); be2LLC v. Ivanov, 2011 WL 1565490 (7th Cir. 2011) (no jurisdiction in Illinois where matchmaking service "be2.com" sued *I* for allegedly using "be2.net" to run competing service in New Jersey; record did not show that *I* "deliberately targeted or exploited the Illinois market") with Mavrix Photo, Inc. v. Brand Technologies, Inc., 2011 WL 3437047 (9th Cir. 2011) (in California, celebrity photo agency could sue Ohio corporation for copyright infringement after plaintiff's photos appeared on defendant's celebrity gossip website) *and* uBid, Inc. v. GoDaddy Group, Inc., 623 F.3d 421 (7th Cir. 2010) (described in note 2, supra).

(b) Internet Services. Many cases involve disputes with providers of internet services, where jurisdictional issues connect with the activities of the provider or the contacts that a customer has with the provider's "home" state. See, e.g., BroadVoice, Inc. v. TP Innovations, LLC, 723 F. Supp. 2d 219 (D. Mass. 2010) (internet phone service provider sues customer in provider's home state alleging defamation and related claims arising from postings on customer's website) (case dismissed; website did not constitute purposeful availment of forum state).

(c) Libel. Many cases involve claims that defendant posted a defamatory comment on a website (or wrote defamatory emails) that injured plaintiff where he resides, and the question is whether jurisdiction exists under *Calder.* Often the answer has been no. See, e.g., Shrader v Biddinger, 633 F.3d 1235

(10th Cir. 2011) (Oklahoma author brought suit at home alleging that out-of-state defendants sent defamatory email and posted contents on website explaining why defendants and plaintiff had "parted ways," but there was no jurisdiction in Oklahoma; posting information on internet does not subject poster to jurisdiction wherever posting can be accessed; Oklahoma was not the "focal point" of the email, "either in terms of its audience or its content") (no general jurisdiction either); Best Van Lines v. Walker, 490 F.3d 239 (2d Cir. 2007) (Iowa blogger posted on website "MovingScam.com" derogatory comments about Best Van Lines, operating out of Brooklyn; Best brought suit in New York, and defendant moved to dismiss; state's long-arm statute did *not* reach situation; defendant was not "transacting business" in New York, and comments were *not* "purposefully directed to New Yorkers rather than a nationwide audience") (only "interactive" feature of the website was that it accepted donations). See also the discussion of jurisdiction in libel cases in Section C3b, supra.

(d) Internet Sales. As in the *Marschke* case (described in footnote 8 in *Dudnikov*), most decisions conclude that the buyer who purchases an item on eBay cannot sue at home on claims that the seller misrepresented the item. See, e.g., Hinners v. Robey, 336 S.W.3d 891 (Ky. 2011) (no jurisdiction in Kentucky to hear Kentucky buyer's fraud claim against Missouri eBay seller; buyer had traveled to Missouri to take title and delivery).

5. See, e.g., Danielle Keats Citron, *Minimum Contacts in a Borderless World: Voice Over Internet Protocol and the Coming Implosion of Personal Jurisdiction Theory,* 39 U.C. Davis L. Rev. 1481 (2006).

D   THE REQUIREMENT OF REASONABLE NOTICE

1. The Constitutional Standard

MULLANE v. CENTRAL HANOVER BANK & TRUST CO.

Supreme Court of the United States
339 U.S. 306 (1950)

Mr. Justice JACKSON delivered the opinion of the Court.

This controversy questions the constitutional sufficiency of notice to beneficiaries on judicial settlement of accounts by the trustee of a common trust fund established under the New York Banking Law. . . .

Common trust fund legislation is addressed to a problem appropriate for state action. Mounting overheads have made administration of small trusts undesirable to corporate trustees. In order that donors and testators of moderately sized trusts may not be denied the service of corporate fiduciaries, the District of Columbia and some thirty states other than New York have permitted pooling small trust estates into one fund for investment administration. The income, capital gains, losses and expenses of the collective trust are shared by the constituent trusts in proportion to their contribution. By this plan, diversification of risk and economy of management can be extended to those whose capital standing alone would not obtain such advantage.

Statutory authorization for the establishment of such common trust funds is provided in the New York Banking Law. Under this Act a trust company may, with approval of the State Banking Board, establish a common fund and, within prescribed limits, invest therein the assets of an unlimited number of estates, trusts or other funds of which it is trustee. Each participating trust shares ratably in the common fund, but exclusive management and control is in the trust company as trustee, and neither a fiduciary nor any beneficiary of a participating trust is deemed to have ownership in any particular asset or investment of this common fund. The trust company must keep fund assets separate from its own, and in its fiduciary capacity may not deal with itself or any affiliate. Provisions are made for accountings twelve to fifteen months after the establishment of a fund and triennially thereafter. The decree in each such judicial settlement of accounts is made binding and conclusive as to any matter set forth in the account upon everyone having any interest in the common fund or in any participating estate, trust or fund.

In January, 1946, Central Hanover Bank and Trust Company established a common trust fund in accordance with these provisions, and in March, 1947, it petitioned the Surrogate's Court for settlement of its first account as common trustee. During the accounting period a total of 113 trusts, approximately half inter vivos and half testamentary, participated in the common trust fund, the gross capital of which was nearly three million dollars. The record does not show the number or residence of the beneficiaries, but they were many and it is clear that some of them were not residents of the State of New York.

The only notice given beneficiaries of this specific application was by publication in a local newspaper in strict compliance with the minimum requirements of N.Y. Banking Law §100-c(12) [the Court quotes statute]. Thus the only notice required, and the only one given, was by newspaper publication setting forth merely the name and address of the trust company, the name and the date of establishment of the common trust fund, and a list of all participating estates, trusts or funds.

At the time the first investment in the common fund was made on behalf of each participating estate, however, the trust company, pursuant to the requirements of §100-c(9), had notified by mail each person of full age and sound mind whose name and address was then known to it and who was "entitled to share in the income therefrom . . . (or) . . . who would be entitled to share in the principal if the event upon which such estate, trust or fund will become distributable should have occurred at the time of sending such notice." Included in the notice was a copy of those provisions of the Act relating to the sending of the notice itself and to the judicial settlement of common trust fund accounts.

Upon the filing of the petition for the settlement of accounts, appellant [Kenneth Mullane] was, by order of the court pursuant to §100-c(12), appointed special guardian and attorney for all persons known or unknown not otherwise appearing who had or might thereafter have any interest in the income of the common trust fund; and appellee [James] Vaughan was appointed to represent those similarly interested in the principal. There were no other appearances on behalf of anyone interested in either interest or principal.

Appellant appeared specially, objecting that notice and the statutory provisions for notice to beneficiaries were inadequate to afford due process under the Fourteenth Amendment, and therefore that the court was without jurisdiction to render a final and binding decree. Appellant's objections were entertained and overruled, the Surrogate holding that the notice required and given was sufficient. A final decree accepting the accounts has been entered, affirmed by the Appellate Division of the Supreme Court, and by the Court of Appeals of the State of New York.

The effect of this decree, as held below, is to settle "all questions respecting the management of the common fund." We understand that every right which beneficiaries would otherwise have against the trust company, either as trustee of the common fund or as trustee of any individual trust, for improper management of the common trust fund during the period covered by the accounting is sealed and wholly terminated by the decree.

We are met at the outset with a challenge to the power of the State—the right of its courts to adjudicate at all as against those beneficiaries who reside without the State of New York. It is contended that the proceeding is one in personam in that the decree affects neither title to nor possession of any res, but adjudges only personal rights of the beneficiaries to surcharge their trustee for negligence or breach of trust. Accordingly, it is said, under the strict doctrine of *Pennoyer v. Neff*, the Surrogate is without jurisdiction as to nonresidents upon whom personal service of process was not made.

Distinctions between actions in rem and those in personam are ancient and originally expressed in procedural terms what seems really to have been a distinction in the substantive law of property under a system quite unlike our own. The legal recognition and rise in economic importance of incorporeal or intangible forms of property have upset the ancient simplicity of property law and the clarity of its distinctions, while new forms of proceedings have confused the old procedural classification. American courts have sometimes classed certain actions as in rem because personal service of process was not required, and at other times have held personal service of process not required because the action was in rem.

Judicial proceedings to settle fiduciary accounts have been sometimes termed in rem, or more indefinitely quasi in rem, or more vaguely still, "in the nature of a proceeding in rem." It is not readily apparent how the courts of New York did or would classify the present proceeding, which has some characteristics and is wanting in some features of proceedings both in rem and in personam. But in any event we think that the requirements of the Fourteenth Amendment to the Federal Constitution do not depend upon a classification for which the standards are so elusive and confused generally and which, being primarily for state courts to define, may and do vary from state to state. Without disparaging the usefulness of distinctions between actions in rem and those in personam in many branches of law, or on other issues, or the reasoning which underlies them, we do not rest the power of the State to resort to constructive service in this proceeding upon how its courts or this Court may regard this historic antithesis. It is sufficient to observe that, whatever the technical definition of its chosen procedure, the interest of each state in providing means to close trusts that exist by the grace of its laws and are administered under the supervision of its courts is so insistent and rooted in custom as to establish beyond doubt the right of its courts to determine the interests of all claimants, resident or nonresident, provided its procedure accords full opportunity to appear and be heard.

Quite different from the question of a state's power to discharge trustees is that of the opportunity it must give beneficiaries to contest. Many controversies have raged about the cryptic and abstract words of the Due Process Clause but there can be no doubt that at a minimum they require that deprivation of life, liberty or property by adjudication be preceded by notice and opportunity for hearing appropriate to the nature of the case.

In two ways this proceeding does or may deprive beneficiaries of property. It may cut off their rights to have the trustee answer for negligent or illegal impairments of their interests. Also, their interests are presumably subject to diminution in the proceeding by allowance of fees and expenses to one who, in their names but without their knowledge, may conduct a fruitless or uncompensatory contest. Certainly the proceeding is one in which they may be deprived of property rights and hence notice and hearing must measure up to the standards of due process.

Personal service of written notice within the jurisdiction is the classic form of notice always adequate in any type of proceeding. But the vital interest of the State in bringing any issues as to its fiduciaries to a final settlement can be served only if interests or claims of individuals who are outside of the State can somehow be determined. A construction of the Due Process

Clause which would place impossible or impractical obstacles in the way could not be justified.

Against this interest of the State we must balance the individual interest sought to be protected by the Fourteenth Amendment. This is defined by our holding that "The fundamental requisite of due process of law is the opportunity to be heard." Grannis v. Ordean, 234 U.S. 385, 394 (1914). This right to be heard has little reality or worth unless one is informed that the matter is pending and can choose for himself whether to appear or default, acquiesce or contest.

The Court has not committed itself to any formula achieving a balance between these interests in a particular proceeding or determining when constructive notice may be utilized or what test it must meet. Personal service has not in all circumstances been regarded as indispensable to the process due to residents, and it has more often been held unnecessary as to nonresidents. We disturb none of the established rules on these subjects. No decision constitutes a controlling or even a very illuminating precedent for the case before us. But a few general principles stand out in the books.

An elementary and fundamental requirement of due process in any proceeding which is to be accorded finality is notice reasonably calculated, under all the circumstances, to apprise interested parties of the pendency of the action and afford them an opportunity to present their objections. The notice must be of such nature as reasonably to convey the required information, and it must afford a reasonable time for those interested to make their appearance. But if with due regard for the practicalities and peculiarities of the case these conditions are reasonably met the constitutional requirements are satisfied. "The criterion is not the possibility of conceivable injury, but the just and reasonable character of the requirements, having reference to the subject with which the statute deals." American Land Co. v. Zeiss, 219 U.S. 47, 67 (1911).

But when notice is a person's due, process which is a mere gesture is not due process. The means employed must be such as one desirous of actually informing the absentee might reasonably adopt to accomplish it. The reasonableness and hence the constitutional validity of any chosen method may be defended on the ground that it is in itself reasonably certain to inform those affected, compare Hess v. Pawloski, 274 U.S. 352 (1927) with Wuchter v. Pizzutti, 276 U.S. 13 (1928), or, where conditions do not reasonably permit such notice, that the form chosen is not substantially less likely to bring home notice than other of the feasible and customary substitutes.

It would be idle to pretend that publication alone as prescribed here, is a reliable means of acquainting interested parties of the fact that their rights are before the courts. It is not an accident that the greater number of cases reaching this Court on the question of adequacy of notice have been concerned with actions founded on process constructively served through local newspapers. Chance alone brings to the attention of even a local resident an advertisement in small type inserted in the back pages of a newspaper, and if he makes his home outside the area of the newspaper's normal circulation the odds that the information will never reach him are large indeed. The chance of actual notice is further reduced when as here the notice required does not even name those whose attention it is supposed to attract, and does not inform acquaintances who might call it to attention. In weighing its sufficiency on the basis of equivalence with actual notice we are unable to regard this as more than a feint.

Nor is publication here reinforced by steps likely to attract the parties' attention to the proceeding. It is true that publication traditionally has been acceptable as notification supplemental to other action which in itself may reasonably be expected to convey a warning. The ways of an owner with tangible property are such that he usually arranges means to learn of any direct attack upon his possessory or proprietary rights. Hence, libel of a ship, attachment of a chattel or entry upon real estate in the name of law may reasonably be expected to come promptly to the owner's attention. When the state within which the owner has located such property seizes it for some reason, publication or posting affords an additional measure of notification. A state may indulge the assumption that one who has left tangible property in the state either has abandoned it, in which case proceedings against it deprive him of nothing, or that he has left some caretaker under a duty to let him know that it is being jeopardized. As phrased long ago by Chief Justice Marshall in The Mary, 9 Cranch 126 (1815), "It is the part of common prudence for all those who have any interest in (a thing), to guard that interest by persons who are in a situation to protect it."

In the case before us there is, of course, no abandonment. On the other hand these beneficiaries do have a resident fiduciary as caretaker of their interest in this property. But it is their caretaker who in the accounting becomes their adversary. Their trustee is released from giving notice of jeopardy, and no one else is expected to do so. Not even the special guardian is required or apparently expected to communicate with his ward and client, and, of course, if such a duty were merely transferred from the trustee to the guardian, economy would not be served and more likely the cost would be increased.

This Court has not hesitated to approve of resort to publication as a customary substitute in another class of cases where it is not reasonably possible or practicable to give more adequate warning. Thus it has been recognized that, in the case of persons missing or unknown, employment of an indirect and even a probably futile means of notification is all that the situation permits and creates no constitutional bar to a final decree foreclosing their rights.

Those beneficiaries represented by appellant whose interests or whereabouts could not with due diligence be ascertained come clearly within this category. As to them the statutory notice is sufficient. However great the odds that publication will never reach the eyes of such unknown parties, it is not in the typical case much more likely to fail than any of the choices open to legislators endeavoring to prescribe the best notice practicable.

Nor do we consider it unreasonable for the State to dispense with more certain notice to those beneficiaries whose interests are either conjectural or future or, although they could be discovered upon investigation, do not in due course of business come to knowledge of the common trustee. Whatever searches might be required in another situation under ordinary standards of diligence, in view of the character of the proceedings and the nature of the interests here involved we think them unnecessary. We recognize the practical difficulties and costs that would be attendant on frequent investigations into the status of great numbers of beneficiaries, many of whose interests in the common fund are so remote as to be ephemeral; and we have no doubt that such impracticable and extended searches are not required in the name of due process. The expense of keeping informed from day to day of substitutions among even current income beneficiaries and presumptive remaindermen, to say nothing of the far greater number of contingent beneficiaries, would impose a severe burden on the plan, and would likely dissipate its advantages. These are practical matters in which we should be reluctant to disturb the judgment of the state authorities.

Accordingly we overrule appellant's constitutional objections to published notice insofar as they are urged on behalf of any beneficiaries whose interests or addresses are unknown to the trustee.

As to known present beneficiaries of known place of residence, however, notice by publication stands on a different footing. Exceptions in the name of necessity do not sweep away the rule that within the limits of practicability notice must be such as is reasonably calculated to reach interested parties. Where the names and post office addresses of those affected by a proceeding are at hand, the reasons disappear for resort to means less likely than the mails to apprise them of its pendency.

The trustee has on its books the names and addresses of the income beneficiaries represented by appellant, and we find no tenable ground for dispensing with a serious effort to inform them personally of the accounting, at least by ordinary mail to the record addresses. Certainly sending them a copy of the statute months and perhaps years in advance does not answer this purpose. The trustee periodically remits their income to them, and we think that they might reasonably expect that with or apart from their remittances word might come to them personally that steps were being taken affecting their interests.

We need not weigh contentions that a requirement of personal service of citation on even the large number of known resident or nonresident beneficiaries would, by reasons of delay if not of expense, seriously interfere with the proper administration of the fund. Of course personal service even without the jurisdiction of the issuing authority serves the end of actual and personal notice, whatever power of compulsion it might lack. However, no such service is required under the circumstances. This type of trust presupposes a large number of small interests. The individual interest does not stand alone but is identical with that of a class. The rights of each in the integrity of the fund and the fidelity of the trustee are shared by many other beneficiaries. Therefore notice reasonably certain to reach most of those interested in objecting is likely to safeguard the interests of all, since any objections sustained would inure to the benefit of all. We think that under such circumstances reasonable risks that notice might not actually reach every beneficiary are justifiable. "Now and then an extraordinary case may turn up, but constitutional law, like other mortal contrivances, has to take some chances, and in the great majority of instances, no doubt, justice will be done." Blinn v. Nelson, 222 U.S. 1, 7 (1911).

The statutory notice to known beneficiaries is inadequate, not because in fact it fails to reach everyone, but because under the circumstances it is not reasonably calculated to reach those who could easily be informed by other means at hand. However it may have been in former times, the mails today are recognized as an efficient and inexpensive means of communication. Moreover, the fact that the trust company has been able to give mailed notice to known beneficiaries at the time the common trust fund was established is persuasive that postal notification at the time of accounting would not seriously burden the plan.

In some situations the law requires greater precautions in its proceedings than the business world accepts for its own purposes. In few, if any, will it be satisfied with less. Certainly it is instructive, in determining the reasonableness of the impersonal broadcast notification here used, to ask whether it would satisfy a prudent man of business, counting his pennies but finding it in his interest to convey information to many persons whose names and addresses are in his files. We are not satisfied that it would. Publication may theoretically be available for all the world to see, but it is too much in our day to suppose that each or any individual beneficiary does or could examine all that is published to see if something may be tucked away in it that affects his property interests. We have before indicated in reference to notice by publication that, "Great caution should be used not to let fiction deny the fair play that can be secured only by a pretty close adhesion to fact." McDonald v. Mabee, 243 U.S. 90 (1917).

We hold the notice of judicial settlement of accounts required by the New York Banking Laws 100-c(12) is incompatible with the requirements of the Fourteenth Amendment as a basis for adjudication depriving known persons whose whereabouts are also known of substantial property rights.

Accordingly the judgment is reversed and the cause remanded for further proceedings not inconsistent with this opinion.

Reversed.

[Justice Douglas did not take part in deciding this case. Justice Burton dissented.]

■ NOTES ON THE REQUIREMENT OF NOTICE

1. Does *Mullane* hold that notice *must be given* in order to bring parties into a suit? If not, then what is required? See, e.g. Dusenbery v. United States, 534 U.S. 161 (2002) (rejecting D's claim that government failed properly to notify him of pending destruction of firearm and drug paraphernalia seized from his trailer, leading to charges and guilty plea; government sent written notice to prison where D was incarcerated, and to his trailer, and to the address of his mother, and published notice in newspaper; under *Mullane*, government satisfied its burden of showing that it provided notice "reasonably calculated under all the circumstances" to apprise intended recipient of intended action, even if letter was not delivered).

2. *Mullane* is a little bit unusual, because plaintiff was not seeking money damages, or any kind of affirmative or coercive relief. What would the judgment do if plaintiff got all it wanted? Should *Mullane* be characterized as an *in personam* suit, or as some kind of *in rem* or *quasi in rem* case? Doesn't *Mullane* say its conclusion would be the same regardless which category applies? If it *is* an *in personam* suit, the minimum contact standard applies. Is it satisfied here? Does *Mullane* throw out *Pennoyer*'s seizure-as-notice notion?

3. The "gold standard" for notice is personal service, meaning "delivery in hand" of hard-copy documents, and this matter is taken up below. The Court has sometimes disapproved of lesser forms of notice, see Green v. Lindsey, 456 U.S. 444 (1982) (disapproving eviction notice posted on the door in public housing project, where tenant showed that such notices were often torn off and removed).

4. In the *Jones* case in 2006, the Court revisited the *Mullane* standard. There, the state of Arkansas sold a residence in Little Rock for nonpayment of taxes, after sending a certified letter to Jones notifying him that the property would be sold in two years if he did not redeem the property by paying the amount owed. The letter was not delivered and was not retrieved at the post office later. After an attempted public sale yielded no bids, the Commissioner of Lands negotiated a private sale to Flowers, and again tried unsuccessfully to notify Jones by certified letter of his last opportunity to redeem the property. The Court found that the attempts to notify Jones were insufficient: One who "actually desired to inform a real property owner of an impending tax sale of a house" would not "do nothing" when a certified letter is returned unclaimed. The adequacy of a notice procedure is assessed "*ex ante* rather than *post hoc*," but if the government chooses a procedure that "provides additional information" on the effectiveness of the notice, then "what the government does with that information" counts in assessing the adequacy of the notice. While Jones "should have been more diligent" in taking care of his property, the state "should have taken additional reasonable steps to notify Jones," such as resending the notice by regular mail or posting notice on the front door. See Jones v. Flowers, 547 U.S. 220, 234-235 (2006) (reversing judgment for Flowers and Lands Commissioner).

5. The entitlement to notice should not be a matter of formalism—failing to serve papers in exactly the form prescribed by rules should not be fatal if the substance of the necessary information is made known to the party entitled to notice. See United Student Aid Funds, Inc. v. Espinosa, 130 S. Ct. 1367, 1378 (2010) (approving discharge of student loan in bankruptcy despite alleged failure to serve summons and complaint as required by Bankruptcy Rules; creditor "received *actual* notice of the filing and contents of [the debtor's] plan," which "more than satisfied" due process under *Mullane*); Grable & Sons Metal Products, Inc. v. Darue Engineering & Mfg., 545 U.S. 308 (2005) (lower court rejects taxpayer's challenge, based on fact that government gave notice by certified mail rather than personal service, on sale of property to satisfy tax lien; ground was that substantial conformance with notice provision was sufficient).

6. You will see that notice is a key element in other procedural settings. One example is a class suit seeking money damages, FRCP 23(b)(3), where the defining characteristic is "common questions," class members have the right to "opt out," and the Court has held that class members are entitled to "personal notice." See Eisen v. Carlisle, 417 U.S. 156 (1974) (rejecting strategy of allowing personal notice to a small fraction of a class comprised of six million persons) (Chapter 8H7, infra). Similarly, the Court has found that some nonparties are entitled to notice, as a matter of due process, in the unusual situation in which a decision is to have *res judicata* (or claim preclusive) effect on such parties. See Richards v. Jefferson County, 517 U.S. 793, 803-804) (judgment in suit rejecting challenge to state occupational tax did not bar later suit by second taxpayer challenging tax; states may adopt remedial schemes foreclosing relitigation by nonparties, as in probate and bankruptcy, but scheme must satisfy due process; where citizen challenges tax as invalid expenditure, such a scheme could be deployed; where citizen claims tax is invalid as applied to him specifically, he may not be foreclosed by prior suit if he has not received notice and was not adequately represented).

2. Service in the Digital Age

We cannot yet say that defendants may be summoned to respond to claims against them—or for that matter that persons may be subpoenaed to give testimony—by email or text message or other ways of instant communications in the Digital Age. As noted, the "gold standard" for personal service at the commencement of a suit is service in hand, and the same is true of subpoenas for witnesses.

How does plaintiff start a suit? Rule 3 says suit is "commenced" by "filing a complaint with court." In Chapter 7, you will learn what goes into a complaint, but basically a complaint sketches the claims made by the plaintiff. Rule 4(b) says plaintiff is responsible for serving a summons and a copy of the complaint on the defendant. A summons is a court-issued document informing defendant that "a lawsuit has been filed" against her, and saying she "must serve" an answer or a preliminary motion on plaintiff's attorney, or else "judgment by default" will be entered against her. For the text of a summons, see Form 3 (back of the Rules).

Under FRCP 4(c), the summons and a copy of the complaint must be "served" on the defendant by a person who is "not a party" to the suit or by an officer of the court (U.S. marshal in the federal system, normally a sheriff in state systems).

Now for the good part: In the ordinary case, service is to be made by "delivering" the summons and a copy of the complaint "personally" to the defendant, or by "leaving" them at defendant's "dwelling or usual place of abode with someone of suitable age and discretion who resides there" or by delivering these to "an agent authorized by appointment or by law" to receive service of process. See FRCP 4(e).

Defendants are not thrilled to be sued, and if they know in advance what is coming, they may evade the process server—locking the door or hiding or refusing to answer the doorbell. There are amusing stories about defendants trying such tactics, and about countermeasures to which process servers resort. An internet site found by the author in April 2011 gives advice on "How to Hide from a Process Server," which includes things like staying close to home, skipping "unnecessary trips to the grocery store," staying away from "that coffee shop near your office," and changing one's personal appearance.

■ PROBLEM 3-C. "Would You Please Give This to Your Dad?"

After an intersection collision in Kansas City, Kansas, Julie Page decides to sue Daniel D. Diller, the other driver. At the accident scene, they exchanged information on insurance, addresses, and phone numbers. Page's car is an expensive Lexus only a few weeks old. As it happens, she had just purchased a valuable Ming vase at a charity auction, for which she paid in excess of $60,000, all going to support Habitat for Humanity, and the vase was shattered in the accident.

Unable to work out a settlement with Diller or his insurance carrier, Page sees a lawyer who files suit on her behalf. Page lives in Hyde Park in Kansas City, Missouri (across the river from the accident scene), and her suit is filed in federal court in Kansas on the basis of diversity jurisdiction (she and Diller are from different states). She seeks recovery in the amount of $80,000.

Page's lawyer learns that Diller lives in the Mission Hills area of the City and is a wealthy entrepreneur who is worth suing (he has sufficient assets to pay a judgment regardless of whether he is covered by insurance). The lawyer retains QuickServe of Kansas City to effect service. The process server finds Diller's home and rings the bell. An adult baby-sitter answers and says that neither Diller nor his wife is at home, as they have gone for the weekend to a convention in Chicago. The babysitter is caring for Diller's seven-year-old daughter Madison.

The process server leaves the summons and complaint with Madison, noting on the "return of service" (form affidavit at bottom of summons) that he "handed the complaint and service to Madison Diller, daughter of Daniel D. Diller, at 7735 Mission Woods Drive." Defendant's lawyer moves to quash service under FRCP 12(b), arguing that Madison is not a person of "suitable age and discretion" under FRCP 4(e) so service was improper. How should the court rule, and why? Should it matter whether Madison or the sitter delivered the papers to Diller on his return?

■ NOTES ON SERVING PEOPLE

1. Is a seven-year-old child a person of "suitable age and discretion" under FRCP 4(e)? Does it matter that she is in the care of an adult babysitter? See Trammel v. National Bank of Georgia, 285 S.E.2d 590, 591-592 (Ga. App. 1981) (under state rule, 12-year-old daughter qualified; defendant received papers, which was "some indication" that service was reasonable); Miebach v. Colasurdo, 685 P.2d 1074, 1080 (Wash. 1984) (approving service on defendant's 15-year-old foster daughter, even though she was "troubled and rebellious" with below-par academic achievements; she was "talented, familiar with the court system, and had an appreciation for the consequences of violating the law" (!)).

2. Given the vagueness of the term "suitable age and discretion," would it be better simply to specify a minimum age, such as "over 18 years"? Does it make sense to require such a person to "reside" in the abode or dwelling of the defendant?

3. Consider the requirement that the recipient of process, if the defendant is not personally served, "reside there." A minor child living with parents satisfies this standard. How about a maid or household employee? A mother-in-law staying there? A landlord? Temporary caretaker? See Polo Fashions, Inc. v. B. Bowman & Co., 102 F.R.D. 905, 908 (D.C.N.Y. 1984) (disapproving service on housekeeper working in home during day but not staying there); Hasenfus v. Corporate Air Services, 700 F. Supp. 58, 66 (D.D.C. 1988) (disapproving service on defendant's part-time secretary in the abode but not living there); Magazine v. Bedoya, 475 So. 2d 1035 (Fla. App. 1985) (approving service on mother-in-law staying with defendant for six weeks recuperating from leg surgery); Salts v. Estes, 943 P.2d 275, 276-277 (Wash. 1997) (disapproving service on woman looking after defendant's home, feeding dog, taking in mail, and taking care of similar matters, spending one to two hours at home during period of defendant's absence).

4. Suppose the process server rings the doorbell, hears a voice on an intercom ("who's there?"), and identifies himself. The door is not opened but the server sees an adult male near the side-panel window. The server says, "I have papers for you," but the door is still not opened, so the server says, "consider yourself served," leaving the papers on the porch, covered partly by the doormat to keep them from blowing away. Has the defendant been served? See Travelers Casualty and Surety Co. v. Brenneke, 551 F.3d 1132, 1134 (9th Cir. 2009) (yes; server tried four times, saw that people were home, left notes asking them to call; "good faith effort to comply" with FRCP 4(e) is sufficient where it led to "placement of the summons and complaint within the defendant's immediate proximity" and further compliance is only prevented by defendant's "knowing and intentional actions to evade service"); Errion v. Connell, 236 F.2d 447, 457 (9th Cir. 1956) (server "pitched the papers through a hole in the screen door" after seeing defendant and telling her he was serving her; she had "ducked behind a door") (sufficient).

5. Many people live in "gated communities" or apartments or condominium complexes to which outsiders have access only if admitted by a guard, manager, or concierge. Since job security for people in these lines of work depends partly on keeping residents happy, such gatekeepers are unlikely to admit process servers who announce themselves as such. Nor is it easy to create a false cover story that will persuade a gatekeeper to admit a process server. Suppose a server succeeds in such a ruse: He gains entry by offering a false story ("Hello, I'm from Caruso's Flowers, with a delivery for Mr. and Mrs. Tarewa in 834"). Should service be quashed? Is it different from the situations discussed in *Cannington* (Section B3, supra), where defendant is tricked into entering the forum state? Do situations like this one show that we should provide for alternatives to personal service? See, e.g., Colo. RCP 4(g) (if "due diligence" to effect personal service proves unavailing, plaintiff can seek court permission to serve by "registered or certified mail").

6. What if defendant, in business dealings with plaintiff, has provided an address that turns out to be a hotel? Does the hotel count as defendant's "dwelling" or "abode"? Is the manager a person of "suitable age and discretion"? See Howard Johnson International, Inc. v. Wang, 7 F. Supp. 336 (S.D.N.Y. 1998) (answering both questions yes). The manager would not likely "reside" at the hotel, would he? Does this matter? Compare Lennon v. McClory, 3 F. Supp. 2d 1461, 1462 (D.C. C. 1998) (receptionist in building where defendant lives does not qualify; she does not reside there) with Churchill v. Barach, 863 F. Supp. 1266, 1271 (D. Nev. 1994) (doorman of defendant's department building resided therein for purposes of FRCP 4; courts construe this requirement "liberally," and doorman acknowledged that his regular duties include accepting messages and packages for delivery to tenants).

7. In thinking about making service of process difficult, consider these points: The losing side is liable for "costs" to the prevailing side, see FRCP 54(d). In ordinary suits, costs do not include attorneys' fees, but do include money spent on service of process, fees to the reporter for making necessary transcripts, docket fees, and witness fees. See generally Wright & Miller, Federal Practice and Procedure §1670; 28 USC §1920 (defining taxable costs). Thus driving up the cost of service is not necessarily a good idea.

8. Are we still right to insist on personal service? Beginning in 1993, FRCP 4(d) has allowed defendants to waive personal service and accept service by mail. Under this provision, plaintiff can mail to defendant ("by first-class mail or other reliable means") a copy of the complaint with a form waiving service of process. This material is to include an advisement that defendant has "reasonable time" (at least 30 days) to return the waiver, and at least 60 days to answer (compared with 21 days if defendant is served in person). Defendant is also to be told that failing to waive "without good cause" can result in becoming liable for "reasonable costs" incurred by the plaintiff in making personal service, plus expenses and attorneys' fees if plaintiff must make a motion to collect such costs.

(a) For years this technique has been used in federal courts, but it is not authorized or frequently used in most states. Isn't this approach preferable?

(b) Does the arrival of the digital age mean that still more efficient means of service should be allowed? What about service by email? Text message? Facebook? Does the fact that some lack access to these mechanisms mean that they should not be used even where defendants *do* have such access? See Nike, Inc. v. NikePioneer.com, 2010 WL 4393896 (E.D. Va. 2010) (authorizing service by email in Virginia suit against alleged cybersquatting names, including variations of the word "Nike"). Decisions in suits against foreign defendants approve service by email. Here FRCP 4 authorizes courts to permit alternative forms of service, so long as they are "internationally agreed" to, or "reasonably calculated to give notice," or otherwise approved by the court and "not prohibited by international agreement." See Rio Properties, Inc. v. Rio International Interlink, 284 F.3d 1007 (9th Cir. 2002) (approving service by email on foreign internet gambling entity that had no physical address other than that of its "international currier (*sic*)" that was not authorized to accept service; email service was "reasonably calculated" to apprise defendant of suit and provide opportunity to respond and was "the method of service most likely to reach" defendant); Gucci America, Inc. v.

Wang Huoqing, 2011 WL 31191 (N.D. Cal. 2011) (authorizing service by email on foreign defendant).

■ NOTES ON SERVING COMPANIES

1. Serving a company that is a corporation normally proceeds in one of three ways. First, a company can be asked to waive service and accept what amounts to service by mail under FRCP 4(d) (which applies not only to individuals, but to any "corporation or association"). Second, under FRCP 4(h) a corporation may be served by delivering a copy of the summons and complaint to "an officer" or "managing or general agent." Third, under FRCP 4(h) a corporation may be served by delivering a copy of the summons and complaint to "any other agent authorized by appointment or by law to receive service of process." This language commonly applies when plaintiff seeks to serve an out-of-state corporation that maintains a "registered agent" under a domestication statute. (See Notes on "Domestication" Statutes and Jurisdiction over Out-of-State Corporations in Section B1, supra.)

2. Associations as well as other business organizations, such as partnerships and limited liability companies, may be served under FRCP 4(h) by personal delivery of summons and complaint to an officer, managing, or general agent. See, e.g., CapFinancial Properties CV1, LLC v. Highway 210 LLC, 2011 WL 1303323 (D. Kan. 2011) (FRCP 4(h) applies to limited liability companies); Sokolow v. Palestine Liberation Organization, 2011 WL 11345086 (S.D.N.Y. 2011) (approving service on PLO by personal delivery of summons and complaint to Hassan Abdel Rahman at his home; "overwhelming competent evidence" showed that he was the "Chief Representative of the Palestine Liberation Organization and the Palestinian Authority in the United States").

3. As in the case of FRCP 4(e) governing service on individual defendants, the personal delivery contemplated in FRCP 4(h) for serving corporations or other organizations does not mean "mailing the summons and complaint" to an officer or a managing or general agent. See Williams v. Citibank, 2011 WL 289955 (D. Colo. 2011) (mailing did not accomplish service under FRCP 4(h)).

4. In FRCP 4(h), the terms "officer" or "managing" or "general" agent does not reach every employee, even if she is a responsible person. See Turpin v. Wellpoint Companies, Inc., 2011 WL 1086482 (E.D. Va. 2011) (corporation not served by delivery of summons and complaint to Staci Hoover, an administrative assistant); Mason v. Republic Services, Inc., 2011 WL 283310 (D. Nev. 2011) ("human resources employee" was not an officer, manager, or general agent).

■ NOTES ON SERVING PUBLIC AGENCIES

1. Rule 4(i) has special provisions governing service of process on the United States as a party, and other provisions for service on government agencies.

(a) Serving the United States entails (i) delivering the summons and complaint to the U.S. Attorney in the district where suit is brought, or sending copies "by registered or certified mail" to the "civil-process clerk" at the U.S. Attorney's office, or (ii) sending copies by registered or certified mail to the Attorney General in Washington DC, or (iii) if the suit "challenges an order of a nonparty agency or officer," sending copies by registered or certified mail to the agency or officer.

(b) Serving a federal agency entails serving the United States, as indicated above, and also sending copies of the summons and complaint by registered or certified mail to the agency.

2. Service on state and local officials in state court systems is of course governed by state rules of procedure. Typical are provisions authorizing service on the state by personal delivery of the summons and complaint to the attorney general; also provisions allowing service on cities or towns by delivering the summons and complaint to the mayor, city manager, clerk, or deputy clerk. Service on counties can be accomplished by delivering copies of summons and complaint to the county clerk, deputy, or county commissioner. Service on school districts entails serving the superintendent. Serving state agencies entails serving officers or agents, with copies delivered to the attorney general. See Colo. Rule 4(e)(6)-(10).

E LITIGATING JURISDICTION

In Chapter 7C1, you will learn that certain defenses, including lack of jurisdiction over the person, must be raised at the outset, normally by motion filed by the defendant before answering the complaint, or in the answer itself as an "affirmative defense." Failing to raise the point in one of these ways means the issue is lost and the court can proceed to decide the case, with binding effect on the defendant.

INSURANCE CORP. OF IRELAND, LTD. v. COMPAGNIE DES BAUXITES DE GUINEE

Supreme Court of the United States
456 U.S. 694 (1982)

Justice WHITE delivered the opinion of the Court.

[Compagnie des Bauxites de Guinee (CBG) brought suit in federal court in Pennsylvania to collect on certain business interruption insurance covering its operations in the Republic of Guinea. Insurance Company of America provided half the coverage, and did not object to jurisdiction. The other half, described as "excess" coverage, was provided by other companies operating in London, in response to an offer placed on behalf of CBG in "the London insurance market," and these carriers raised the issue of lack of *in personam* jurisdiction, which they pressed in the form of a motion for summary judgment that also advanced other defenses to the suit.

In response, plaintiffs sought copies of "all business interruption insurance policies" issued by these defendants during the previous five years. Defendants objected to this request, and plaintiff sought an order compelling production. Later plaintiffs "narrowed" their request, seeking only policies that were "delivered" or "covered risks" in Pennsylvania. The court ordered production of this material, and then allowed additional time, and finally defendants offered to make available some four million files for inspection in London. Plaintiffs made another motion to compel production, and the court warned the defendants that if they did not produce the material it would impose as a sanction a finding of good jurisdiction. Some months later, the court made good on its threat and held that defendants were subject to jurisdiction in Pennsylvania.]

... The requirement that a court have personal jurisdiction flows not from Art. III, but from the Due Process Clause. The personal jurisdiction requirement recognizes and protects an individual liberty interest. It represents a restriction on judicial power not as a matter of sovereignty, but as a matter of individual liberty.[10] ...

Because the requirement of personal jurisdiction represents first of all an individual right, it can, like other such rights, be waived. In McDonald v. Mabee, 243 U.S. 90 (1917), the Court indicated that regardless of the power of the State to serve process, an individual may submit to the jurisdiction of the court by appearance. A variety of legal arrangements have been taken to represent express or implied consent to the personal jurisdiction of the court. In National Equipment Rental, Ltd. v. Szukhent, 375 U.S. 311, 316 (1964), we stated that "parties to a contract may agree in advance to submit to the jurisdiction of a given court," and in Petrowski v. Hawkeye-Security Co., 350 U.S. 495 (1956), the Court upheld the personal jurisdiction of a District Court on the basis of a stipulation entered into by the defendant. In addition, lower federal courts have found such consent implicit in agreements to arbitrate. Furthermore, the Court has upheld state procedures which find constructive consent to the personal jurisdiction of the state court in the voluntary use of certain state procedures.

---

[10] It is true that we have stated that the requirement of personal jurisdiction, as applied to state courts, reflects an element of federalism and the character of state sovereignty vis-à-vis other States. ... The restriction on state sovereign power described in *World-Wide Volkswagen Corp.* [Section 3C1, supra], however, must be seen as ultimately a function of the individual liberty interest preserved by the Due Process Clause. That Clause is the only source of the personal jurisdiction requirement and the Clause itself makes no mention of federalism concerns. Furthermore, if the federalism concept operated as an independent restriction on the sovereign power of the court, it would not be possible to waive the personal jurisdiction requirement: Individual actions cannot change the powers of sovereignty, although the individual can subject himself to powers from which he may otherwise be protected.

See Adam v. Saenger, 303 U.S. 59, 67-68 (1938) ("There is nothing in the Four-teenth Amendment to prevent a state from adopting a procedure by which a judgment *in personam* may be rendered in a cross-action against a plaintiff in its courts. . . . It is the price which the state may exact as the condition of open-ing its courts to the plaintiff"); Chicago Life Ins. Co. v. Cherry, 244 U.S. 25, 29-30 (1917) ("[W]hat acts of the defendant shall be deemed a submission to [a court's] power is a matter upon which States may differ"). Finally, unlike subject-matter jurisdiction, which even an appellate court may review *sua sponte*, under FRCP 12(h), "[a] defense of lack of jurisdiction over the person . . . is waived" if not timely raised in the answer or a responsive pleading.

In sum, the requirement of personal jurisdiction may be intentionally waived, or for various reasons a defendant may be estopped from raising the issue. These characteristics portray it for what it is—a legal right protect-ing the individual. The plaintiff's demonstration of certain historical facts may make clear to the court that it has personal jurisdiction over the defendant as a matter of law—*i.e.,* certain factual showings will have legal consequences—but this is not the only way in which the personal jurisdiction of the court may arise. The actions of the defendant may amount to a legal submission to the jurisdiction of the court, whether voluntary or not.

The expression of legal rights is often subject to certain procedural rules: The failure to follow those rules may well result in a curtailment of the rights. Thus, the failure to enter a timely objection to personal jurisdiction consti-tutes, under Rule 12(h)(1), a waiver of the objection. A sanction under Rule 37(b)(2)(A) consisting of a finding of personal jurisdiction has precisely the same effect. As a general proposition, the Rule 37 sanction applied to a finding of personal jurisdiction creates no more of a due process problem than the Rule 12 waiver. Although "a court cannot conclude all persons interested by its mere assertion of its own power," Chicago Life Ins. Co. v. Cherry, not all rules that establish legal consequences to a party's own behavior are "mere assertions" of power.

. . .

Petitioners argue that a sanction consisting of a finding of personal juris-diction differs from all other instances in which a sanction is imposed, . . . because a party need not obey the orders of a court until it is established that the court has personal jurisdiction over that party. If there is no obligation to obey a judicial order, a sanction cannot be applied for the failure to comply. Until the court has established personal jurisdiction, moreover, any assertion of judicial power over the party violates due process.

This argument again assumes that there is something unique about the requirement of personal jurisdiction, which prevents it from being established or waived like other rights. A defendant is always free to ignore the judicial proceedings, risk a default judgment, and then challenge that judgment on jurisdictional grounds in a collateral proceeding. See Baldwin v. Traveling Men's Assn., 283 U.S. 522, 525 (1931). By submitting to the jurisdiction of the court for the limited purpose of challenging jurisdiction, the defendant agrees to abide by that court's determination on the issue of jurisdiction: That decision will be res judicata on that issue in any further proceedings. As demonstrated above, the manner in which the court determines whether it has personal jurisdiction may include a variety of legal rules and presumptions, as well as straightforward factfinding. . . . [T]he mere use of procedural rules does not in itself violate the defendant's due process rights.

■ NOTES ON APPEARING VERSUS "STAYING HOME"

1. It makes sense, doesn't it, to require objections for lack of jurisdiction over the person to be raised at the outset? *Pennoyer* stressed that a court must have a basis for exercising jurisdiction before it may go forward. You will see that FRCP 12(b), adopted some 60 years later, requires defendants to raise personal jurisdiction early, either in the answer or by motion filed with the answer or before.

2. In early practice, a defendant who wished to argue lack of jurisdiction over the person had to take care to address *only* jurisdiction. He needed to make a "special appearance" to avoid "consenting" to jurisdiction. Filing an answer denying (or admitting) the charging allegations was viewed as conceding jurisdiction (a form of consent). Occasionally, state courts did not even permit special appearances, and the Supreme Court approved. See York v. Texas, 137 U.S. 15 (1890) (if defendant in Texas "asks the court to determine any question, even that of service [of process], he submits himself wholly to its jurisdiction," and Fourteenth Amendment does not require opportunity "to raise the question of jurisdiction, in the first instance, in the court in which suit is pending") (it is enough that defendant who does not appear can deny validity of judgment later). Modern jurisdictions let defendants appear and contest jurisdiction without *submitting* to jurisdiction, and (like the federal system) let them also answer the complaint at the same time. Still, the "special appearance" rubric has continued, and states vary in their strictness about what else a defendant may do without waiving objection to jurisdiction. See, e.g., Tex. Civ. Rule 120a (allowing "special appearance" to object to jurisdiction, which must be done "prior to" motions to transfer venue or other pleadings, but these "may be contained in the same instrument," and every appearance prior to judgment that is "not in compliance" with this Rule is a "general appearance").

3. Suppose that Frieda, who lives in Florida, sues Orlin, who lives in Oregon, in a state court in Florida on account of an automobile accident in Kansas. Orlin has two choices:

(a) First, Orlin can appear in Florida and move to dismiss for lack of jurisdiction, and the motion will likely be granted unless he has adequate

contacts with Florida or is served there. If the Florida court *denies* Orlin's motion to dismiss, can he seek immediate review? In Florida, the answer is yes (see Fla. R. App. P. 9.130), but federal courts and many states do *not* allow immediate appeal from such rulings. Where immediate appeal is not allowed, defendant must litigate the whole case, and *then* (in case of a loss on the merits) seek review of the ruling on jurisdiction. If defendant loses because the reviewing court in Florida concludes that jurisdiction is good, defendant is bound. Then if Frieda sues Orlin on the Florida judgment in Oregon, the Oregon court must give it full faith and credit, must it not? See, e.g., Baldwin v. Iowa State Traveling Men's Association, 283 U.S. 522 (1931) (defendant who litigates jurisdiction and loses is estopped later from claiming that court lacked jurisdiction). In other words, Orlin cannot argue in Oregon that the judgment should *not* be given full faith and credit because the Florida court made a mistake, either on a jurisdictional point or on the merits, isn't that so? Burns v. Baldwin, 65 P.3d 502 (Idaho 2003) (Idaho court would not review defense claim that California judgment was erroneous) (defendant litigated there).

(*b*) Second, if Orlin stays home and the Florida court enters a default judgment for Frieda, she can sue on the judgment in Oregon. What can Orlin argue? What will the Oregon court likely do? Suppose instead that the facts are less clearcut: Frieda sues Orlin in Florida because Orlin posted something on a website that Frieda considers slanderous. If Orlin is not sure whether Florida has good jurisdiction, what should he do? What would be the cost to Orlin if he "stays home," and Frieda gets a default judgment that she later uses as the basis for suit in Oregon, if the Oregon court thinks Florida *did* have good jurisdiction?

4. As *Compagnie des Bauxites* makes clear, the jurisdictional analysis required as a constitutional matter by *International Shoe* can lead the court into a detailed factual inquiry. The question whether a court has jurisdiction is for the judge to decide, and plaintiff bears the burden of proving by a preponderance of the evidence that jurisdiction exists. See Mylan Laboratories, Inc. v. Arzo, N.V., 2 F.3d 56, 59-60 (4th Cir. 1993). The question raised by *Compagnie des Bauxites* is whether a defendant who appears and raises the point must cooperate in the inquiry. If the court lacks jurisdiction, because no facts support a finding of jurisdiction, how can the court force defendant to cooperate?

5. At what point did the London "excess" insurance carriers become subject to jurisdiction in Pennsylvania? Did they have any other choice, realistically speaking, than to appear in Pennsylvania and contest jurisdiction? Of course, the Full Faith and Credit Clause and the statute that goes with it (Const. Art. IV §1, and 28 USC §1738) do not apply to courts in London or other places outside the United States, but principles of "comity" are observed by most courts around the world, and they honor judgments if the legal system that produced them merits respect and if the exercise of jurisdiction appears to be reasonable.

CHAPTER 4

Subject Matter Jurisdiction (The Competence of Courts)

INTRODUCTION

You know that the United States has a dual system of courts, and that many cases are (and must be) litigated in state court—examples include most suits in tort or contract between citizens of a single state. And you know that courts of "general jurisdiction" are in the state systems: State district courts are usually the ones that can hear any civil case, no matter how big or small. (These courts go by other names as well: In some states they are the circuit courts; in others they are the superior courts. Yet other names can be found: In New York, trial courts with general jurisdiction are known as state supreme courts.)

In the federal system, the courts have limited jurisdiction, and their most important areas of authority are diversity cases, meaning suits "between citizens of different states" seeking recovery of more than $75,000 (usually invoking state law), and federal question cases, meaning suits "arising under" federal law, regardless of citizenship or amount in controversy. See U.S. Const. Art. III §2 and 28 USC §§1331 and 1332.

States too have courts of limited jurisdiction, like county courts that often have jurisdiction up to $25,000. Here, however, issues of subject matter jurisdiction are less complex. Generally, plaintiffs having claims exceeding the jurisdictional limit of county courts may waive recovery of anything that exceeds that amount and gain entry to such courts, which is sometimes attractive because of simplified procedure and shorter dockets. Defendants with counterclaims that exceed the jurisdictional limit of such courts generally have the choice of "removing" to a court of general jurisdiction within the state system, waiving anything above the jurisdictional maximum, or reserving their claims to bring in a separate suit, in which case facts underlying these "counterclaims" may sometimes be advanced by way of defense. We will not spend further time on these matters.

 # DIVERSITY JURISDICTION (SUITS "BETWEEN CITIZENS OF DIFFERENT STATES")

1. A First Look

It may come as a surprise that diversity jurisdiction is the older and more established branch of civil jurisdiction in the federal system. For the first century of our history, most civil litigation in the federal system consisted of diversity cases, and only in the modern era did federal question cases catch up and ultimately surpass diversity cases. To give you some idea of scale, the Federal Judicial Center reports that in fiscal year 2008, there were 267,257 civil cases filed in federal district courts, of which 88,457 were diversity cases (about a third).[1]

Diversity litigation can span a wide range of controversies, including suits advancing almost any kind of contract or tort claim. There are, however, some "unwritten" limits. Thus one cannot get a divorce, or litigate child custody disputes, or seek spousal support in federal court, even if the spouses are citizens of different states. See Ankenbrandt v. Richards, 504 U.S. 689, 701 (1992) (domestic relations exception "divests the federal courts of power to issue divorce, alimony, and child custody decrees," because this restriction has long been recognized, "without any expression of congressional dissatisfaction").

Complete Diversity? Early in our history, the question arose whether the diversity requirement required *each and every* claimant to be diverse from *each and every* defendant. In the simplest cases, the question takes these forms: Is the diversity requirement satisfied if a Florida plaintiff sues a Georgia defendant and a Florida defendant? Is it satisfied if a Florida plaintiff and a Georgia plaintiff sue a Georgia defendant? In larger cases, the question takes these forms: Is the diversity requirement satisfied if plaintiffs from Florida, Georgia, South Carolina, Mississippi, and Alabama sue defendants from Texas, New Mexico, Oklahoma, and Alabama? In these situations, we have "minimal" diversity because at least one claimant is diverse from at least one defendant, but not "complete" diversity because at least one plaintiff is a citizen of the same state as at least one defendant.

When this question first arose, the Court in an opinion by Chief Justice John Marshall concluded that "complete diversity" was required, so *none* of

---

[1] See www.uscourts.gov/judbus2008/JudicialBus2008pdf (viewed Aug. 17, 2009).

the examples described in the previous paragraph involve complete diversity. See Strawbridge v. Curtiss, 3 Cranch 267 (1806) (diversity requirement not satisfied in suit by Massachusetts citizens against citizens of Massachusetts and Vermont; "each distinct interest should be represented by persons, all of whom are entitled to sue, or may be sued, in the federal courts"). *Strawbridge* cited only the statute (now 28 USC §1332), not the constitutional provision. Still, the fact that both the statute and the Constitution refer to suits between "citizens of different states" (the same phrase) raised the question whether it is *only* the statute that requires complete diversity, or whether the Constitution *also* requires it. The Court answered that question more than a century later, concluding that *Strawbridge* was construing *only* the statute, and that the Constitution is satisfied with *minimal* diversity. See State Farm Fire & Casualty Co. v. Tashire, 386 U.S. 523 (1967) (Chapter 8F, infra).

Taken together, *Strawbridge* and *Tashire* have great salience. On the one hand, *Tashire*'s holding that the *Constitution* does not require complete diversity means Congress can change the requirement any time it wants. On the other hand, the fact that *Strawbridge* is written by Chief Justice John Marshall, a pivotal figure in shaping American constitutional history, means that the "complete diversity" requirement is firmly enshrined as the definitive interpretation of the basic diversity statute (28 USC §1332). The stature of this interpretive convention has led courts to be cautious in allowing any departure from this standard—at least until the Court decided the *Exxon* case (Section C2 infra).

In *Tashire*, the question was whether minimal diversity sufficed in an interpleader suit. Interpleader is a rare kind of litigation in which typically plaintiff is an insurance carrier. If a married woman covered by life insurance dies, and a surviving husband and two former husbands approach the carrier, each claiming exclusive entitlement to the proceeds, the carrier can bring an interpleader suit inviting each to prove his case. Usually one wins and the other loses, and the carrier can pay the winner while resting secure in the knowledge that losers cannot later sue. Under the interpleader statute, federal courts can proceed as long as there is "minimal diversity" among claimants.[2] See 28 USC §1335 (providing for federal jurisdiction if amount exceeds $500 and there are "two or more adverse claimants"). The effect is that jurisdiction exists if any claimant is diverse from any other, even if one or more come from the same state as another and even if one or more shares the same citizenship as the nominal plaintiff (the insurance carrier, in our example). The interpleader statute confers jurisdiction, and the statute, according to *Tashire*, is constitutional.

In the twenty-first century, Congress went further in taking advantage of the opening that *Tashire* provided, enacting statutes requiring only minimal diversity in situations that exist far more often than those giving rise to

---

[2] The statute also allows nationwide service of process. If one claimant is in Florida, another in California, and the third in Alaska, the carrier can interplead all three in any of those places. See 28 USC §§1335 and 1337. Probably, a state court could not do the same thing because of the problem of getting jurisdiction over distant claimants with no connection to the forum.

interpleader suits. In 2002 came the Multiparty, Multiforum Trial Jurisdiction Act, codified as 28 USC §1369. This complex provision cannot be easily summarized, but its aim is to enable federal courts to hear "single accident" cases resulting in the deaths of "at least 75 natural persons" on the basis of "minimal diversity" among adverse parties, subject to qualifications aimed at denying jurisdiction over local controversies where most claimants and defendants hale from one state. In 2005 came the Class Action Fairness Act, which added subsection (d) to §1332 (and did other things), expanding diversity jurisdiction in class actions in ways discussed further below.

Amount in Controversy. As noted above, the Constitution provides that the federal judicial power extends to cases "between citizens of different states," U.S. Const. Art. III §2. The Constitution says nothing about amount in controversy, but its jurisdictional provisions are not "self-executing," and Congress chose from the beginning to limit diversity jurisdiction to cases seeking more than a certain minimum. The Judiciary Act of 1789 set the minimum at "more than $500," and it stayed there for most of a century. In 1887, the amount was increased to $2,000. The "more than" amounts went to $3,000 in 1911, $10,000 in 1958, $50,000 in 1988, and $75,000 in 1996. See 28 USC §1332, and see generally Wright & Kane, Law of Federal Courts §32 (7th ed. 2011).

Often the amount-in-controversy requirement poses no problem. If a claimant who sustained serious bodily injury sues a defendant on a tort law claim, few would doubt that plaintiff, if he prevails, will be entitled to more than $75,000. That suffices to satisfy the amount-in-controversy requirement, even if plaintiff loses and ultimately recovers nothing, or wins but recovers less. As you can see, what counts is substantial allegations that, if proved, could support recovery exceeding the minimum—not actually prevailing or winning more than that.

In addition, it can be said that many questions surrounding this requirement have been answered. Let's dispose of some of these. To begin with, if plaintiff brings multiple claims against a single defendant, the amount-in-controversy requirement can be satisfied if the claims in aggregate could plausibly lead to judgment for more than the minimum. In such cases, it does not matter whether the claims are similar (such as personal injuries) or arise out of the same transaction or rest on the same theory, or instead differ (personal injuries can be combined with property damages), or arise out of different transactions, or rest on different theories. If a single plaintiff sues two defendants, seeking $40,000 from each, however, or if two plaintiffs sue a single defendant and each plaintiff seeks $40,000, the amounts *cannot* be combined to get above the jurisdictional minimum. Here is a rule of thumb that summarizes these points: Claims can be added to reach the jurisdictional minimum, but not claims and parties.

Unfortunately, it is not always so easy. Many questions in administering the amount-in-controversy requirement can arise, and some questions remain shrouded in doubt. We take up these matters in detail below.

2. What Does "Citizenship" Mean?

Citizenship for purposes of diversity jurisdiction has long been defined, for individuals, as domicile. For entities like corporations and partnerships, citizenship or domicile is artificial, and is determined by statute and judicial interpretation.

For individuals, domicile refers to the place where a person lives or "hangs his hat." Thus domicile (hence citizenship) changes if a person moves from one place to another. See Sun Printing & Publishing Association v. Edwards, 194 U.S. 377, 383 (1904) ("to effect a change of one's legal domicile, two things are indispensable," namely "residence in a new domicil" and "intention to remain"); Restatement (Second) of Conflict of Laws §18 (1971) (to acquire domicile of choice in a certain place, one "must intend to make that place his home for the time at least").

Often this definition of citizenship for persons works well, and many points of detail have been worked out. Thus we know, for example, that if a Florida citizen sues a Maryland citizen in federal court in March, a diversity suit can continue even if plaintiff moves to Maryland in April. Citizenship at the date of filing is what counts, and post-filing changes do not count, either in creating or in defeating jurisdiction (so if the plaintiff resided in Maryland in March, then moved to Florida later, the case could still be dismissed for lack of jurisdiction). See Grupo Dataflux v. Atlas Global Group, L.P., 541 U.S. 567, 571 (2004) (referring to "time-of-filing rule" as "hornbook law (quite literally) taught to first-year law students in any basic course in federal civil procedure") (challenges to subject matter jurisdiction test "the state of facts that existed at the time of filing").

Consider the *Schwerzler* case, where citizenship is hard to determine.

JANE DOE v. SCHWERZLER

United States District Court for the District of New Jersey
2008 WL 1781986 (D.N.J. 2008)

HILLMAN, District Judge.

This matter originally came before the Court on Defendant Robert Taffet's motion to dismiss Plaintiff's Complaint, as well as Gloucester County Institute of Technology's [GCIT] motion to dismiss Plaintiff's Complaint. Defendants Trish Green and Daniel Green had joined in on GCIT's motion. In the Court's previous Opinion and Order, Defendants' motions to dismiss Plaintiff's Complaint for lack of subject matter jurisdiction were denied without prejudice to allow Plaintiff another opportunity to submit proofs evidencing that when she filed her Complaint on August 1, 2006 she was a citizen of Kentucky, and not a citizen of New Jersey. Plaintiff submitted such proofs, and oral argument was held, during which Plaintiff was ordered to submit additional documents. Plaintiff complied, and the issue of subject matter jurisdiction is now ripe for decision.

Plaintiff, proceeding as Jane Doe, filed a Complaint against the Defendants for claims arising out of a sexual relationship Plaintiff had with her swim coach, Defendant John Schwerzler. According to Plaintiff's Complaint, Schwerzler initiated a sexual relationship with Plaintiff in 1998, when she was thirteen years old, and it lasted until 2004, when she was nineteen. Plaintiff claims that Defendants violated the New Jersey Law Against Discrimination because of their various roles in the inappropriate sexual relationship.

Plaintiff brought her action in this Court pursuant to 28 USC §1332. In order for the Court to have jurisdiction over Plaintiff's action under §1332, there must be complete diversity of the parties—that is, the citizenship of Plaintiff must be diverse from the citizenship of each Defendant. Defendants have argued that Plaintiff, now a student at a university in Kentucky but who grew up in New Jersey and whose parents live in New Jersey, is a citizen of New Jersey. Defendants have argued that because they are also citizens of New Jersey, complete diversity is lacking, and the case must be dismissed.

Plaintiff has countered, however, that she is a citizen of Kentucky, and, therefore, complete diversity exists, and her case is properly before this Court. Because it is the citizenship of the parties at the time the action is commenced which is controlling, it must be determined what state Plaintiff was a citizen of when she filed her Complaint on August 1, 2006. As set forth in the Court's prior Opinion, the Third Circuit has provided a standard for determining the citizenship of a party.

> The party asserting diversity jurisdiction bears the burden of proof. A party generally meets this burden by proving diversity of citizenship by a preponderance of the evidence.
>
> Citizenship is synonymous with domicile, and "the domicile of an individual is his true, fixed and permanent home and place of habitation. It is the place to which, whenever he is absent, he has the intention of returning." In determining an individual's domicile, a court considers several factors, including "declarations, exercise of political rights, payment of personal taxes, house of residence, and place of business." Other factors to be considered may include location of brokerage and bank accounts, location of spouse and family, membership in unions and other organizations, and driver's license and vehicle registration.
>
> An individual can change domicile instantly. To do so, two things are required: "[h]e must take up residence at the new domicile, and he must intend to remain there." But "[a] domicile once acquired is presumed to continue until it is shown to have been changed." This principle gives rise to a presumption favoring an established domicile over a new one.

McCann v. Newman Irrevocable Trust, 458 F.3d 281, 286-87 (3d Cir. 2006) (internal citations omitted).

In a case where a party with a claimed new domicile is the proponent of federal jurisdiction, the burden of production regarding domicile and the burden of persuasion regarding federal jurisdiction both fall on that party. First, the party must rebut the presumption in favor of an established domicile. If the party does so, the presumption falls out of the case and the party is then required to carry the burden of persuasion by proving that a change of domicile occurred, creating diversity of citizenship. For both assertions, the appropriate standard of proof is preponderance of the evidence.

. . .

Plaintiff has asserted in her Complaint that her domicile is Kentucky. In the prior Opinion, the Court characterized Kentucky as Plaintiff's "claimed new domicile" because Plaintiff is a college student and Defendants had raised a substantial question about the status of Plaintiff's domicile. *See* Bradley v. Zissimos, 721 F. Supp. 738, 740 (E.D. Pa. 1989) ("It is generally presumed that a student who attends a university in a state other than the student's 'home' state intends to return 'home' upon completion of studies"); Alicea-Rivera v. SIMED, 12 F. Supp. 2d 243, 246 (D. Puerto Rico 1998) (holding that although the college student had a driver's license, voter's registration, and part-time job in Ohio, he was still considered a citizen of Puerto Rico because Plaintiff did not own or rent any property, did not pay a telephone or utilities bill, did not have any post-graduate commitments in Ohio, or any job in Ohio that would indicate steps towards a permanent career); *see also* Scoggins v. Pollock, 727 F.2d 1025 (11th Cir. 1984); Bair v. Peck, 738 F. Supp. 1354, 1357 (D. Kan. 1990).

The Court then noted that Plaintiff was required to first produce some evidence to demonstrate that she had a new domicile . . . , and once she had done that, she was required, by the preponderance of the evidence, to meet her burden of persuasion to demonstrate that this Court has jurisdiction to hear her case.

As directed by the Court, Plaintiff has submitted various proofs with regard to her claims that even though she had been a citizen of New Jersey, she is now a citizen of Kentucky, and was a citizen of Kentucky when she filed her Complaint. Some of this proof arises after the date of her Complaint, does not indicate a date, or are statements with regard to her future intentions. Other proof consists of statements from her family members and friends indicating their understanding of Plaintiff's intentions to remain a citizen of Kentucky. All of this proof, however, has no bearing on the status of her citizenship at the time she filed her Complaint.

The remainder of Plaintiff's proof is dispositive on the issue of her citizenship at the time she filed her Complaint. As of August 1, 2006, Plaintiff has shown that: (1) she had registered to vote in Kentucky;[2] (2) she had a Kentucky driver's license and she had surrendered her New Jersey driver's license; (3) she leased property in Kentucky; (4) she had an open bank account in Kentucky; (5) she paid utilities in Kentucky; and (6) she paid Kentucky state income taxes for the 2006 tax year.[3]

Based on this evidence, the Court finds that Plaintiff has met . . . her burden of persuasion regarding jurisdiction—that is, Plaintiff's proof is sufficient to demonstrate that she was a citizen of Kentucky, and not New Jersey, as of August 1, 2006. Accordingly, because Plaintiff was a citizen of Kentucky when she filed her Complaint, diversity of citizenship exists between the parties. Consequently, this Court has subject matter jurisdiction to hear Plaintiff's case.

An appropriate Order will issue.

■ NOTES ON CITIZENSHIP FOR DIVERSITY PURPOSES

1. As plaintiff, "Jane Doe" bears the burden of proving subject matter jurisdiction. See also Slaughter v. Toye Bros. Yellow Cab Co., 359 F.3d 954, 956 (5th Cir. 1996) (burden of proving diversity rests with plaintiff). Indeed, a plaintiff in federal court must allege in her complaint the ground of jurisdiction, and "Jane Doe" alleged that her domicile was Kentucky. FRCP 8(a). Whether she has established jurisdiction is for the judge to decide, and she normally decides such things on submissions in the form of affidavits—sworn statements bearing a notarial seal—setting forth facts like those submitted in this case. In resolving such matters, the judge is not "bound by the rules of evidence," and can consider anything she considers probative. It is possible, although rare, to hold a full-fledged hearing on such points, where plaintiff or other knowledgeable witnesses could be sworn and could testify and submit to questioning and cross-examination. Most such motions, however, are resolved as this one was, on affidavits.

2. "Jane Doe" lived in Kentucky on August 1, 2006 (date of filing), and defendants lived in New Jersey (they were "domiciled" there, making them New Jersey citizens for diversity purposes), so why is there any question at all? In putting the burden of proof on "Jane Doe" to show that the court has jurisdiction, the court says she must carry a "burden of production" and a

---

[2] Defendants point out that Plaintiff voted in New Jersey in 2004. This would be relevant to her citizenship as of 2004, but because there is no evidence that she voted in New Jersey since that time, it does not defeat her claim that she was a citizen of Kentucky as of August 1, 2006.

[3] The Court finds that even though Plaintiff's parents claimed her as a dependent on their 2006 tax returns, the Court credits Plaintiff's statement that she was unaware of this. Additionally, the Court does not find the actions of Plaintiffs' parents to be dispositive to Plaintiff's citizenship as of August 1, 2006.

"burden of persuasion." We will look more closely at these in Chapters 11A (on summary judgment) and 12E (on judgment as a matter of law). The court also invokes a "presumption" favoring "an established domicile," referring to New Jersey (her family home). Apparently, this presumption came into play because Jane Doe, who'd left New Jersey and reached Kentucky, was a student there, and leaving a parental home to study elsewhere does not indicate an intent to live permanently in the new place. In federal court (and many states), presumptions in civil cases affect "the burden of production" and not "the burden of persuasion." See FRE 301. Hence putting the burdens of production and persuasion on "Jane Doe" already does everything that this presumption does. She produced evidence that she'd moved permanently to Kentucky, making the presumption "fall[ ] out of the case," which is equivalent to saying she carried her burden of production. The court concludes that she carried her burden of persuasion too. How did she do it? Are you persuaded? What other kinds of proof would help her?

3. Judging from the opinion and the allegations, "Jane Doe" was 19 years old in 2004, so she must have been 21 years old, or nearly so, on August 1, 2006 when she filed suit. Under the laws of New Jersey and Kentucky, she attained majority at age 18, when presumptively she was no longer under the supervision of her parents and they no longer had a legal obligation to support her. See N.J. Stat. Ann. §9:17B-3 (with exceptions "every person 18 or more years of age shall . . . be deemed to be an adult"); Ky. Rev. Stat. §405.020 (with qualifications, parents "have the joint custody, nurture, and education of their children who are under the age of eighteen"). Does this factor count on the matter of citizenship at the time of filing?

4. Suppose a Michigan native moves to Florida in search of warmer weather, but finds that he prefers the Midwest to the supposed benefits of a southern climate, and he longs to return home and decides to do so some day. Is he still a Floridian for purposes of diversity jurisdiction? See Garcia Perez v. Santaella, 364 F.3d 348 (court erred in dismissing claim against Puerto Rican defendant on testimony that plaintiff, who had moved to Florida from Puerto Rico, thought "just about every other day" of returning; "vague and noncommittal" language stating intent to "return to a former domicile at some unspecified future date" is a mere "floating intention" and does not prevent a party from having acquired a domicile in the place to which he has moved).

5. Diversity jurisdiction extends to suits between U.S. citizens and foreign citizens, but not to suits involving only foreign citizens, and not (under language added to the statute in 2011) to a suit between a U.S. citizen of, let us say, New York, and a foreign citizen "lawfully admitted for permanent residence" in the same state. See 28 USC §1332(a)-(d). The idea that citizenship means domicile leads to the odd result that a U.S. citizen who moves out of the country and retains no domestic domicile is "stateless," hence not diverse from anyone, which means that she cannot sue or be sued in federal court on the basis of diversity. See King v. Cessna Aircraft Co., 505 F.3d 1160, 1170 (11th

Cir. 2007) (U.S. citizen "with no domicile in any state of his country is 'stateless' and cannot satisfy the complete diversity requirement when she, or her estate, files an action against a US citizen"). The *Mas* case managed to combine the question whether an adult student changes her domicile when she goes to another state to study—the same question that came up in *Schwerzler*—and the possibility of treating a U.S. citizen as stateless. *Mas* involved an American woman and her French-born husband, who sued a Louisiana landlord in federal court in Louisiana for allegedly spying on them in their bedroom during the early months of their marriage. Did Ms. Mas retain the citizenship of her family (Mississippi), acquire citizenship in Louisiana (where she had come to study), or acquire the domicile of her husband (which would make her a French domiciliary, hence stateless and unable to invoke diversity jurisdiction)? See Mas v. Perry, 489 F.2d 1396 (5th Cir. 1974) (Ms. Mas retained domicile of her family in Mississippi; there was good diversity jurisdiction).

6. As noted in the introduction, citizenship *at the time of filing* counts, but there are some departures from this rule. Compare Caterpillar Inc. v. Lewis, 519 U.S. 61 (1996) (in removed case, dismissal of nondiverse party created diversity that did not exist at filing, which sufficed) (limiting holding to situation in which "neither the parties nor the judge raise the error until after a jury verdict has been rendered, or a dispositive ruling has been made by the court" *and* where jurisdictional defect was cured "before the verdict is rendered, or [dispositive] ruling [was] issued") with Grupo Dataflux v. Atlas Global Group, L.P., 541 U.S. 567 (2004) (refusing to extend *Caterpillar* to situation where post-filing change in citizenship of party created diversity; *Caterpillar* "broke no new ground" because curing defect by dismissal of party is "an exception to the time-of-filing rule") (5-4 opinion).

7. Suppose an Ohio plaintiff sues three citizens of West Virginia, two citizens of Indiana, and a citizen of Ohio. If one defendant moves to dismiss because the complete diversity requirement is not satisfied, can plaintiff move to dismiss the claims against the Ohio citizen to cure the problem? See FRCP 21 (on motion or *sua sponte,* court may "add or drop a party" on terms that are "just," and may take such action "at any time"); Newman-Green, Inc. v. Alfonzo-Larrain, 490 U.S. 826, 832 (1989) ("Rule 21 invests district courts with authority to allow a dispensable nondiverse party to be dropped at any time, even after judgment has been rendered," and Courts of Appeal may do the same thing).

8. Since citizenship is what counts, does it matter if plaintiff changes domicile *for the purpose of* creating diversity in order to sue in federal court? In an early case, W (West Virginia married woman) brought a divorce suit against her husband H, and then moved to Virginia. She then sued O, a West Virginia woman, alleging that O and H had been having an affair. The parties agreed that W had gone to Virginia "with the intention of making her home in that state for an indefinite time" in order to sue the other woman in federal court. Still, W became a Virginia citizen after the move. The "essential fact" that changes domicile is "the absence of any intention to live elsewhere," and W "did not then contemplate an end" to living in Virginia. She "had a right to select her domicil for any reason that seemed good to her." Williamson v. Osenton, 232 U.S. 619 (1914).

9. It seems to have been understood from the beginning that parties might use the device of *transferring* or *assigning* claims to others as a way of creating or defeating diversity jurisdiction. So the First Congress enacted a statute to prevent parties from creating diversity jurisdiction in this way. Today the statute is broader. See 28 USC §1359 (district courts shall not have jurisdiction where "any party, by assignment or otherwise, has been improperly or collusively made or joined to invoke [federal] jurisdiction"). In the *Kramer* case, the Supreme Court concluded that this provision barred suit brought by a plaintiff who had acquired by assignment the entire claim of one corporation against another, with a separate agreement in which plaintiff was to return to the corporation 95 percent of any recovery. See Kramer v. Caribbean Mills, Inc., 394 U.S. 823, 829 (1969) (if this mechanism could create federal jurisdiction, "then a vast quantity of ordinary contract and tort litigation could be channeled into the federal courts at the will of one of the parties"). Notice that the statute does not bar attempts to *defeat* diversity jurisdiction.

10. In the case of corporations, the matter of citizenship is addressed by statute. Since 1958, the basic diversity statute has stated that a corporation is "a citizen of any State by which it has been incorporated and of the State where it has its principal place of business." See 28 USC §1332(c)(1). Thus corporations have at least "dual" citizenship, sometimes multiple citizenship (in rare instances, corporations are chartered by more than one state).

(a) In early days, the corporate form was virtually unknown. Chief Justice Marshall took the view that a corporation was a "mere legal entity" that could not be a citizen, hence that the citizenship of the owners of a corporation is what counts. See Bank of the United States v. Deveaux, 5 Cranch 61 (1809). Later the Court ruled that a corporation was a citizen of the chartering state, see Louisville, C. & C.R.R. Co. v. Letson, 2 How. 497, 555 (1844). Still later the Court again altered its approach, returning to the notion that a corporate entity could not be a citizen but adding the wrinkle that its human owners should conclusively be presumed to be citizens of the chartering state, see Marshall v. Baltimore & Ohio Railroad Co., 16 How. 314 (1853).

(b) Now the corporate form is commonplace. *Corporations* as such, not simply their human owners, can be the object of local prejudice if *individuals* can be, so it makes sense to treat corporations *as if* they are citizens for purposes of diversity jurisdiction. To the extent "citizenship" implies civic responsibility, it seems appropriate to apply this label to corporations too, and to hope and expect that corporate entities contribute to the lives of communities in ways that go beyond self-interest, much in the way that such expectations apply to individuals.

(c) Modern corporations often have no connection with their chartering state. Sometimes the lack of connection is accidental, as a corporation chartered in one state may find that it conducts much of its business elsewhere because of shifting economic trends and opportunities. Often, however, the lack of connection stems from the fact that Delaware specializes in issuing corporate charters and regulating the internal affairs of entities chartered there (usually the law of the state of incorporation governs relations between shareholders and corporation and the obligations of directors and managers). To allow a corporation chartered in Delaware but doing all its work in, let us say, Texas, to be treated in Texas as an out-of-state citizen for purposes of litigation there does not make much sense. It is for that reason that §1332 was changed in 1958 to establish dual citizenship for corporations.

(d) What is a corporation's "principal place of business"? Sometimes it is obvious. Microsoft, for instance, has its principal place of business in Redmond, Washington (it is also incorporated in that state), and there we find its corporate campus and most of its employees and research facilities. Other times it may be less obvious. Union Pacific runs a railroad system covering the western third of the country, reaching as far east as Milwaukee, Chicago, St. Louis, Memphis, Little Rock, and New Orleans, and as far west as Los Angeles, San Francisco, Portland, and Seattle. Its principal place of business is Omaha, Nebraska (it is incorporated in Delaware). How can a court figure these things out? It is not a matter of declaration or registration—corporations are not asked to *say* that their principal place of business is one place rather than another, or to file papers or obtain any kind of certificate that resolves the question.

(e) For years, courts addressed this question by applying either of two tests: One asked where the "nerve center" or central decision-making authority was located; the other asked where the corporation conducts most of its business ("activities" test). Sometimes courts used these tests as alternatives. See, e.g., Davis v. HSBC Bank Nevada, N.A., 557 F.3d 1026 (9th Cir. 2009) (principal place of business is either (a) the state that contains "a substantial predominance of corporate operations" or (b), if no state satisfies this standard, the "nerve center"); MacGinnitie v. Hobbs Group, LLC, 420 F.3d 1234 (11th Cir. 2005) (endorsing "total activities" test that involves "a somewhat subjective analysis to choose between the results of the nerve center and place of activities tests, if they differ").

(f) In 2010, the Supreme Court addressed this matter, reviewing a decision by the Ninth Circuit that Hertz Corporation, being sued in federal court in California for alleged violations of state wage and hour laws, was a citizen of California because of the volume of business Hertz conducts there. In *Hertz*, the Court adopted a version of the "nerve center test" and rejected the "activities" test:

> We conclude that "principal place of business" is best read as referring to the place where a corporation's officers direct, control, and coordinate the

corporation's activities [which reviewing courts] have called the corporation's "nerve center." And in practice it should normally be the place where the corporation maintains its headquarters—provided that the headquarters is the actual center of direction, control, and coordination, i.e., the "nerve center," and not simply an office where the corporation holds its board meetings (for example, attended by directors and officers who have traveled there for the occasion).

Three sets of considerations, taken together, convince us that this approach, while imperfect, is superior to other possibilities. First, the statute's language supports the approach. The statute's text deems a corporation a citizen of the "State where it has its principal place of business." 28 USC §1332(c)(1). The word "place" is in the singular, not the plural. The word "principal" requires us to pick out the "main, prominent" or "leading" place. 12 Oxford English Dictionary 495 (2d ed. 1989) (def.(A)(I)(2)). Cf. Commissioner v. Soliman, 506 U.S. 168, 174 (1993) (interpreting "principal place of business" for tax purposes to require an assessment of "whether any one business location is the 'most important, consequential, or influential' one"). And the fact that the word "place" follows the words "State where" means that the "place" is a place within a State. It is not the State itself.

A corporation's "nerve center," usually its main headquarters, is a single place. The public often (though not always) considers it the corporation's main place of business. And it is a place within a State. By contrast, the application of a more general business activities test has led some courts, as in the present case, to look, not at a particular place within a State, but incorrectly at the State itself, measuring the total amount of business activities that the corporation conducts there and determining whether they are "significantly larger" than in the next-ranking State.

This approach invites greater litigation and can lead to strange results, as the Ninth Circuit has since recognized. Namely, if a "corporation may be deemed a citizen of California on th[e] basis" of "activities [that] roughly reflect California's larger population . . . nearly every national retailer—no matter how far flung its operations—will be deemed a citizen of California for diversity purposes." Davis v. HSBC Bank Nev., N.A., 557 F.3d 1026, 1029-1030 (2009). But why award or decline diversity jurisdiction on the basis of a State's population, whether measured directly, indirectly (say proportionately), or with modifications?

Second, administrative simplicity is a major virtue in a jurisdictional statute. Complex jurisdictional tests complicate a case, eating up time and money as the parties litigate, not the merits of their claims, but which court is the right court to decide those claims. Complex tests produce appeals and reversals, encourage gamesmanship, and, again, diminish the likelihood that results and settlements will reflect a claim's legal and factual merits. Judicial resources too are at stake. Courts have an independent obligation to determine whether subject-matter jurisdiction exists, even when no party challenges it. So courts benefit from straightforward rules under which they can readily assure themselves of their power to hear a case.

Simple jurisdictional rules also promote greater predictability. Predictability is valuable to corporations making business and investment decisions.

Predictability also benefits plaintiffs deciding whether to file suit in a state or federal court.

A "nerve center" approach, which ordinarily equates that "center" with a corporation's headquarters, is simple to apply comparatively speaking. The metaphor of a corporate "brain," while not precise, suggests a single location. By contrast, a corporation's general business activities more often lack a single principal place where they take place. That is to say, the corporation may have several plants, many sales locations, and employees located in many different places. If so, it will not be as easy to determine which of these different business locales is the "principal" or most important "place."

Third, the statute's legislative history, for those who accept it, offers a simplicity-related interpretive benchmark. The Judicial Conference provided an initial version of its proposal that suggested a numerical test. A corporation would be deemed a citizen of the State that accounted for more than half of its gross income. The Conference changed its mind in light of criticism that such a test would prove too complex and impractical to apply. That history suggests that the words "principal place of business" should be interpreted to be no more complex than the initial "half of gross income" test. A "nerve center" test offers such a possibility. A general business activities test does not.

Hertz Corp. v. Friend, 130 S. Ct. 1181 (2010) (remanding to allow plaintiff to address jurisdictional question in light of new standard, but noting that Hertz submitted "unchallenged declaration" that nerve center is in New Jersey) (if so, diversity exists and case was properly removed).

11. What is the citizenship of a partnership or other unincorporated association, for purposes of diversity of citizenship? By longstanding tradition, the answer is that any unincorporated association is a citizen of every state in which its members are citizens, so a partnership comprised of people who are citizens of Colorado, New Jersey, and Georgia is itself a citizen of those states. See Carden v. Arkoma Associates, 494 U.S. 185, 195-196 (1996) (for purposes of diversity jurisdiction, an unincorporated entity or association is a citizen of every state in which its members are citizens); Harvey v. Grey Wolf Drilling Co., 542 F.3d 1077 (5th Cir. 2008) (same is true of limited liability corporation, which is like partnership rather than corporation, for purposes of diversity). Often the result of treating the citizenship of unincorporated associations this way is to make it hard for them to invoke diversity jurisdiction: They cannot get into federal courts as plaintiffs because multiple citizenship makes them co-citizens with at least some defendants, and cannot *remove* state suits to federal courts for the same reason. Consider the following:

(a) Two of the salient differences between "classical" business partnerships and corporations are that only the latter offered protection against personal liability and only the latter allowed centralized governance (there are other differences, including the manner in which earnings are taxed). Modern "hybrid" membership organizations resemble corporations in offering limited liability for partners.

(b) Some modern businesses are LLCs rather than corporations. One example is PriceWaterhouseCoopers, a professional services firm specializing in accounting and business consulting, which is set up as a LLC. Are such organizations *less likely* than corporate entities like Microsoft and Union Pacific to suffer local prejudice if they must sue and be sued in state courts because they so seldom satisfy the diversity requirement?

(c) Do these points mean we should change the rules on diversity jurisdiction for unincorporated associations—at least when they resemble corporations? Commentators have long been critical of the current state of the law. See, e.g., Peter Oh, *A Jurisdictional Approach to Collapsing Corporate Distinctions*, 55 Rutgers L. Rev. 389, 474 (2003) (citing our approach to citizenship for associations as "a classic illustration of how the doctrine of stare decisis can perpetuate outmoded rules"); Debra R. Cohen, *Citizenship of Limited Liability Companies for Diversity Jurisdiction*, 6 J. Small & Emerging Bus. L. 435, 476 (2001) (as business organizations evolve to reflect "changing needs of the economic community," rules for determining citizenship for purposes of diversity jurisdiction have "stagnated," and current law has proven "more and more deficient" as "more hybrid organizations [now] resemble corporations"); Christine M. Kailus, *Diversity Jurisdiction and Unincorporated Businesses: Collapsing The Doctrinal Wall*, 2007 U. Ill. L. Rev. 1543 (2007) (arguing for amendment to §1332 that would treat unincorporated associations the same way as corporations, for diversity purposes).

(d) The Class Action Fairness Act (CAFA), which goes far to *increase* the availability of diversity jurisdiction in class actions, contains a clause that applies only in cases covered by CAFA (not ordinary diversity suits), which treats an unincorporated association the same as a corporation. See 28 USC §1332(c)(10) (in CAFA suits, an unincorporated association "shall be deemed to be a citizen of the State where it has its principal place of business and the State under whose laws it is organized"). Should this provision be broadened to ordinary diversity suits?

12. Federal law provides that the "legal representative of the estate of a decedent" is "deemed" to have the same citizenship as the decedent. In wrongful death cases, citizenship of decedent at the moment of death is what counts. See 28 USC §1332(c)(2). See King v. Cessna Aircraft Co., 505 F.3d 1160, 1171 (11th Cir. 2007). Prior to the enactment of this provision, it was easy to appoint executors or administrators of the estates of deceased persons in ways that would create (or sometimes destroy) diversity of citizenship with respect to persons who were to be sued, or who were likely plaintiffs. Sometimes local appointment of representatives is necessary in order to bring suit or carry on the task of administering estates. The statute removes opportunities to manipulate diversity jurisdiction in this setting, but doesn't reach as far as it might. See, e.g., Steinlage ex rel. Smith v. Mayo Clinic Rochester, 435 F.3d 913 (Minn. 2006) (wrongful death trustee was not personal representative of estate; trustee's citizenship counts, not decedent's). And issues arise as to the domicile of someone who has become incompetent to act and is moved by a relative to another state to obtain better care or a better living circumstance. See Acridge v. Evangelical Lutheran Good Samaritan Society, 334 F.3d 444 (Tex. 2003) (one who acts in "best interests" of incompetent may change domicile of incompetent; wife moved husband from New Mexico retirement center to one in Texas; he became Texas domiciliary; even though she lived in Colorado, she was deemed to be Texas citizen for purposes of suing Texas retirement center) (dismissing for lack of diversity).

3. Amount-in-Controversy Requirement Revisited

Recall that the amount-in-controversy requirement is not satisfied if multiple plaintiffs bring undersized claims against one defendant, even if the claims in aggregate exceed the minimum. Recall too that the requirement is not satisfied if one plaintiff brings undersized claims against multiple defendants, even if the claims in aggregate exceed the minimum. Suppose two Missouri citizens sue an Arkansas citizen, and one of the two plaintiffs seeks $80,000 while the other seeks $40,000. Or suppose the other side of this question arises: One Missouri citizen sues two Arkansas citizens, seeking $80,000 from one and $40,000 from the other. In these cases, is the amount-in-controversy requirement satisfied because one claim satisfies it, even though another does not? For years, it appeared that the answer in both cases was no, which is consistent with the rule of thumb suggested above—one adds claims to get above the minimum, but not claims and parties.

You will discover that this matter is made complicated by the supplemental jurisdiction statute, 28 USC §1367. Construing this provision, the *Exxon* case holds that in the first of these cases (one of two claimants seeks more than the minimum; another seeks less) the amount-in-controversy requirement *is* satisfied. Because of the wording of the statute, however, the amount-in-controversy requirement is *not* satisfied in the second case (one claimant seeks more than the minimum against one defendant, less than the minimum against another).

■ NOTES ON ADMINISTERING THE AMOUNT-IN-CONTROVERSY REQUIREMENT

1. Suppose plaintiff falls on alighting from an escalator and sustains a simple fracture of her arm that is quickly set, leading to full and speedy recovery. Medical damages are less than $10,000. There are no lost wages, and pain and suffering are nominal. There is no indication of recklessness by the defendant, and no claim is made for punitive damages. Can plaintiff satisfy the amount-in-controversy requirement by alleging that damages exceed $75,000? If so, the requirement can be easily skirted. If not, how does a court decide whether the requirement is met? See McMillian v. Sheraton

Chicago Hotels & Towers, 657 F.3d 839 (7th Cir. 2009) (in suit against hotel for injuries allegedly sustained when escalator jerked, one plaintiff's claim based on laceration on leg and sprained knee did not satisfy minimum; neither did second plaintiff's claim for meniscus tear in knee that did not require surgery; neither did third plaintiff's claim for separated shoulder and scalp lacerations). *McMillian* invokes the rule long followed by courts, which is that good faith allegations of the amount in controversy are accepted unless it appears "to a legal certainty" that a claim is really for a lesser amount. See St. Paul Mercury Indemnity Co. v. Red Cab Co., 303 U.S. 283 289 (1938) ("unless the law gives a different rule, the sum claimed by the plaintiff controls if the claim is apparently made in good faith," and dismissal is justified only if it appears "to a legal certainty" that the claim is "really less than the jurisdictional amount," and plaintiff's "inability to recover" the minimum does not by itself show bad faith, nor does the fact that the complaint itself "discloses a valid defense").

2. Suppose plaintiff seeks injunctive or declaratory relief, rather than a money judgment. How is the amount-in-controversy requirement to be administered? See Hunt v. Washington State Apple Advertising Commission, 432 U.S. 333 (1977) (in suits seeking declaratory or injunctive relief, amount in controversy is "measured by the value of the object of the litigation," which in this case is the value of the right of plaintiffs [Washington growers] to carry on business in North Carolina free from interference by challenged statute; testimony on lost sales and diminished profits exceeding $2 million supported finding that requirement was satisfied) (minimum at the time was $10,000).

(a) Unfortunately, the *Hunt* rule has not gone far to solve the amount-in-controversy problem in suits seeking declaratory or injunctive relief, and the circuits split over two competing rules. One turns on the estimated cost or value *to the plaintiff* of the sought-after recovery. See Garcia v. Koch Oil Co. of Texas, Inc., 351 F.3d 636, 640 n.4 (5th Cir. 2003). The other turns on the estimated cost or value to *either* plaintiff *or* defendant. See In re Ford Motor Co./Citybank (South Dakota), N.A., 264 F.3d 952 (9th Cir. 2001) (requirement turns on "the pecuniary result to either party" that judgment "would directly produce," but this rule cannot be applied in class suits).

(b) Suppose a lender is threatened with suit by a borrower for charging usurious interest under state law, and the lender sues the borrower to compel arbitration of their dispute, arguing that the amount-in-controversy requirement is met because otherwise the lender would be threatened with a class suit that could result in recovery far exceeding $75,000. Should the risks of losing a class suit be counted in applying the amount-in-controversy requirement? See Advance America Servicing of Arkansas, Inc. v. McGinnis, 526 F.3d 1170, 1173 (8th Cir. 2008) (no).

4. Class Suits

Both the diversity and amount-in-controversy requirements have raised challenges in class suits brought in federal court on the basis of diversity jurisdiction. For a long time, it has been settled that only the citizenship of the named plaintiff ("standard bearer") counts in deciding the diversity issue, not the citizenship of members of the class. Thus a New Jersey standard bearer may bring a class suit against a Connecticut defendant even if members of the class are also citizens of Connecticut, although a Connecticut standard bearer could not bring this suit. See Supreme Tribe of Ben Hur v. Cauble, 255 U.S. 356 (1921).

As to the amount-in-controversy requirement, the Court decided in the *Snyder* case that the claims of class members could not be aggregated, see Snyder v. Harris, 394 U.S. 332 (1969), and in the *Zahn* case that *every member* of a plaintiff class had to satisfy the jurisdictional minimum, see Zahn v. International Paper Co., 414 U.S. 291 (1973). *Zahn* made it hard to bring class suits based on diversity jurisdiction in federal court, but you will see in the *Exxon* case, decided in 2005, that the Court has decided that the supplemental jurisdiction statute allows diversity class suits if the standard bearer satisfies the jurisdictional minimum even if class members do not.

The Class Action Fairness Act (CAFA) had a huge impact on jurisdiction in class suits. Where the matter in controversy exceeds $5 million, it expands jurisdiction to let federal courts hear class suits advancing claims under state law even when the standard bearer is not diverse from all defendants, while limiting the expansion by barring federal jurisdiction over "local controversies," where most members of the class and at least one major defendant is a citizen of the forum state. This limitation puts into play the citizenship of corporate defendants, which counts not only in administering the basic diversity requirement, but the "local controversy" limit. See §1332(d). See also Davis v. HSBC Bank Nevada, N.A., 557 F.3d 1026 (9th Cir. 2009) (refusing to remand class suit to state court under "local controversy" exception; although defendant Best Buy's California operations "predominate" over those in other states, they do not "substantially predominate," and Best Buy is "no more familiar to Californians than it is to Texans or Illinoisans, and hence no less likely to suffer prejudice in California than elsewhere") (Best Buy is *not* a California citizen, so "local controversy" exception does not apply).

5. Reasons for Diversity Jurisdiction—An Ongoing Debate

Why do we have diversity jurisdiction? Should we keep it? *Both* these questions have generated a huge debate among scholars, practitioners and judges.

Why Do We Have It? In favor of diversity jurisdiction, the traditional primary justification is that it helps assure fairness to out-of-state litigants. In an early opinion, Chief Justice Marshall made this point in diplomatic language. Even if state courts are as impartial as federal courts, "it is not less true that the constitution itself either entertains apprehensions on this subject, or views with such indulgence the possible fears and apprehensions of suitors, that it has established national tribunals for the decision of controversies between aliens and a citizen, or between citizens of different states." Bank of United States v. Deveaux, 5 Cranch 61, 87 (1809). Constitutional framers, including James Madison, thought diversity jurisdiction in federal courts was important as a way of avoiding local prejudice. See 10 Documentary History of the Constitution 1414 (John P. Kaminski & Gaspare Saladino eds., 1993) ("strong prejudice may arise in some States, against the citizens of others, who may have claims against them"). Modern pronouncements of the Court accept this rationale. See, e.g., Exxon Mobil Corp. v. Allapattah Services, Inc., 545 U.S. 546 (2005) (diversity jurisdiction provides federal forum "for important disputes where state courts might favor, or be perceived as favoring, home-state litigants"); Jerome B. Grubart, Inc. v. Great Lakes Dredge Dock Co., 513 U.S. 527, 546 n.6 (1995) (citing "local bias" as "presupposition" of diversity jurisdiction). See also Regis Associates v. Rank Hotels (Management) Ltd., 894 F.2d 193, 196 (6th Cir. 1990) ("some litigants perceive certain 'home court' advantages in litigating in a state court," which is "one of the reasons why diversity jurisdiction still exists").

Fear of local bias may be the first and primary reason for diversity jurisdiction, but other reasons have a long provenance in debates on the subject:

A second reason is that diversity jurisdiction serves the interests of creditors, and this argument may have had special salience when the young nation was growing in a westerly direction, encouraging the spread of capital during that expansionist era. See JP Morgan Chase Bank v. Traffic Stream (BVI) Infrastructures Ltd., 536 U.S. 88 (2002) ("state courts were notoriously frosty to British creditors trying to collect debts from American citizens," and proponents of Constitution made it clear that eliminating or ameliorating difficulties with credit was the main reason for alienage and diversity jurisdictions, and one of the main reasons for federal courts), quoting Holt, *"To Establish Justice": Politics, the Judiciary Act of 1789, and the Invention of the Federal Courts*, 1989 Duke L.J. 1421, 1448-1449. One scholar has argued that the real fear was state legislatures rather than state courts. See Henry J. Friendly, *The Historic Basis of Diversity Jurisdiction*, 41 Harv. L. Rev. 483, 492-494, 495 (1928) (creditors' fear was "not of state courts so much as of state legislatures").

A third reason, sometimes paired with the second, is that diversity jurisdiction encourages uniformity of law across the nation. Justice Marshall voiced this view, see Bank of United States v. Deveaux, supra (one "great object" of diversity jurisdiction is to "obtain a uniformity of decision in cases of a commercial nature"). This argument, however, proceeds on an obsolete premise, which is that in diversity cases federal courts apply what amounts to federal law, or "national law," rather than the law of any particular state. Except in areas covered by statute (in the early days statutes were few and modest) and in the area of land titles, federal courts in diversity cases *did* for the most part apply their own idea of law, but in 1938 the *Erie* doctrine put an end to that. *Erie* voiced the opinion that the aspiration toward national uniformity had not achieved its goal. Under *Erie,* federal courts in diversity cases apply state substantive law. See Erie R. Co. v. Tomkins, 404 U.S. 64 (1938). You will read about the *Erie* doctrine in Chapter 6.

A fourth reason is that diversity jurisdiction has a cross-fertilizing effect that has several dimensions. It may be that the judges in the two systems, conscious that they have overlapping areas of responsibility in applying state law, will try harder to "get it right." In doing so, they may influence each other and raise the quality of interpretive conventions. As you will discover, the Federal Rules of Civil Procedure became the model for rules of procedure followed in most states, and the ongoing work of state and federal rules committees in amending and "tweaking" the rules may result in constructive cross-influences that benefit both systems. A somewhat harsh—and certainly impolitic—version of this argument maintains that federal courts are simply better than state courts in delivering civil justice to litigants, leading to the conclusion that as much litigation as possible should be channeled to the federal system, or perhaps to the less radical conclusion that federal courts will play the leading role in the cross-system influences. See generally Wright & Kane, Law of Federal Courts §23 (6th ed. 2002).

There are other accounts of the genesis of diversity jurisdiction. One scholar, focusing less on policy arguments or justifications, looks instead at the politics of constitutional formation. He argues that diversity jurisdiction was an avenue in which federal officials could exercise more power, in order to "transform the federal courts into a superior forum" that was "more aligned with the values and perspectives of the Framers than the state courts." See Robert L. Jones, *Finishing a Friendly Argument: The Jury and the Historical Origins of Diversity Jurisdiction,* 82 N.Y.U. L. Rev. 997, 1005, 1050 (2007) ("control over the composition of federal juries meant that the Framers and their political allies would be in a position to influence, if not dictate, the outcome of federal litigation") (reporting that in New York federal marshals "were free to hand-select jury panels").

Should We Keep It? Consider these facts: First, diversity jurisdiction creates a situation in which *both* state and federal courts are available, and *both* state and federal courts are *necessarily* involved in developing and interpreting state law. The effect of diversity litigation in the federal system is to separate legislative and executive authority from judicial authority—federal judges are not impeachable by state legislatures and not responsive to state governors. Does diversity jurisdiction represent an extravagance and a distortion of democracy? These matters are pursued further below, in the Notes on the Diversity Jurisdiction Controversy.

Diversity Jurisdiction and Political Realities. In the 1970s and 1980s, it looked as though diversity jurisdiction might be on its way out. Over many years, prominent Justices on the Supreme Court have suggested that diversity jurisdiction be abolished.[3] Already in 1968, the American Law Institute proposed to reduce diversity jurisdiction by measures that would block plaintiffs from invoking it when bringing suit in their own home states.[4] In 1968, the House of Representatives passed a bill that would have abolished diversity jurisdiction more or less completely, and Congress did trim it slightly (raising the minimum and limiting time for removal from state to federal court). Congress also commissioned a blue-ribbon committee, which in 1990 recommended abolishing diversity jurisdiction, with a few narrow exceptions.[5] But the Senate never voted on the 1968 bill, and neither the recommendations of the ALI nor the recommendations of the blue-ribbon study committee was ever adopted. See generally James M. Underwood, *The Late, Great Diversity Jurisdiction*, 57 Case W. Res. L. Rev. 179 (2006).

Realistically, the matter has dropped from the political agenda. It seems unlikely that diversity jurisdiction will be abolished soon. In a nutshell, trial lawyers want it and politicians have been unwilling to tackle the matter.

■ NOTES ON THE DIVERSITY JURISDICTION CONTROVERSY

1. Does the "local bias" argument hold water today? Consider these points:

(a) State judges are elected or appointed—taking office by applying to a judicial nominating commission or being appointed or elected, and in any event standing for "retention" periodically. Federal judges are appointed by the President, who customarily seeks the advice of the Senator or Senators representing the state where a district court vacancy appears, or the states in the Circuit where an appellate appointment is to be made. Do these processes suggest that state judges will be more biased toward outsiders than federal judges? Are federal judges likely to be free of "local bias" when they take a position in the federal judiciary?

---

[3] These include Justices Felix Frankfurter and Robert Jackson, and Chief Justices Warren, Burger, and Rehnquist. See Burford v. Sun Oil Co., 319 U.S. 315, 337 (1943) (Frankfurter, J., dissenting); Robert H. Jackson, The Supreme Court in the American System of Government 38 (1955); 36th Meeting, ALI Proceedings 27-33 (1959) (Chief Justice Warren); Annual Report on the State of the Judiciary, 62 A.B.A. J. 443, 444 (1976) (Chief Justice Burger); William Rehnquist, *Reforming Diversity Jurisdiction and Civil RICO*, 21 St. Mary's L. Rev. 5, 7-9 (1989).

[4] ALI, Study of the Division of Jurisdiction Between State and Federal Courts (1969).

[5] 101st Cong. Report of the Federal Courts Study Committee 31-39 (1990) ("no other class of cases has a weaker claim on federal judicial resources" and "no other step will do anywhere nearly as much" to reduce case load pressures). Important exceptions are "alienage" cases involving suits between U.S. and foreign citizens, and interpleader, where restrictions on state jurisdiction can leave stakeholders without a remedy. You will encounter interpleader in Chapter 8.

(b) Federal juries are drawn from district-wide venires, usually coming from larger geographic areas than counties that define the venires of state courts. Do these differences matter in terms of fairness to "outsiders"? Although the geographic area from which federal jurors are drawn is district-wide, how many jurors in, for example, Colorado do you think a federal judge in sitting in Denver would empanel from Pueblo (132 miles away) or Durango (332 miles away)?

(c) As a society, we are conscious of bias—and especially conscious of *claims* of bias—in connection with race, gender, ethnicity, religion, age, physical appearance, disabilities, and sexual orientation. Do we hear much talk about bias against people from other states? Does the lack of talk prove that it doesn't exist, or just that we just don't talk about it? Some modern commentators doubt that local bias was *ever* the reason for diversity jurisdiction, despite the fact that influential men like John Marshall and James Madison said it was. See, e.g., Friendly, supra, at 483, 492-493 ("the very form in which the argument is stated throws doubts on the sincerity of those pro-pounding it") (no examples of local prejudice in state courts were given in debates, and sample of state cases involving out-of-state litigants produces no instances of such prejudice); Richard A. Posner, The Federal Courts: Crisis and Reform 141 (1981) (substance of jurisdiction statute suggests that bias played smaller role creating federal judiciary than is assumed).

(d) Almost all federal courts are in larger urban areas. Should we be concerned, in western states and all states with substantial rural populations, that diversity jurisdiction introduces another kind of bias—a bias against rural people? For an argument that federal courts have this bias, and that it is a serious enough problem to justify doing away with diversity jurisdiction, see Debra Lyn Bassett, *The Hidden Bias in Diversity Jurisdiction*, 81 Wash. U. L.Q. 119 (2003).

2. Consider the "cross-fertilization" argument, and the more edgy "better justice" argument:

(a) A state trial judge is not "bound" by federal opinions on matters of state law, but a federal trial judge *is* bound, in a special sense of that term, by state opinions construing the law she is applying (a federal trial judge in a diversity case is supposed to follow authoritative pronouncements from state courts on the meaning of state law). But in another sense, a federal trial judge is not "bound" by state decisions (the judgment of a federal court cannot be appealed to state court). Does it matter, in terms of cross-fertilization, whether decisions in the other system are binding? To the extent that judges from the two systems pay attention to one another, how likely is it that a better end product will emerge?

(b) State and federal rule-making committees exist, but they are appointed by officials in the different systems and do not work together. The federal judicial conference appoints federal rule makers, and typically state supreme courts appoint state rule makers. Federal rule makers address problems that arise in the federal system, state rule makers address problems in the state systems. How much attention are they likely to pay to one another?

3. Consider the principal argument *against* diversity jurisdiction—that it is an extravagance and is wasteful of judicial resources:

(a) If federal decisions on matters of state law do not bind state judges, doesn't the expenditure of time and energy by federal courts in resolving such issues represent a waste? Similar time and energy spent on the state court system generates precedent that binds later judges.

(b) Is the motivation to "get it right" sufficient to ensure that state judges will consider what their federal counterparts have decided on matters of state law?

(c) On the other side of the arguments suggested above, *both* federal and state judges apply the law of the other system, at least sometimes. State judges, after all, are limited by clauses in the Constitution, including the "Due Process" and "Equal Protection" Clauses of the Fourteenth Amendment, and some federal legislation, such as the FELA statute, must be applied in state court when suits under such statutes are brought there. And federal courts, in addition to applying state law in diversity cases, must apply state law in suits against federal officials under the Federal Tort Claims Act, which incorporates state tort law as the rule of decision. Is it a good thing that judges from each system must know something about the law of the other system?

B FEDERAL QUESTION JURISDICTION (SUITS "ARISING UNDER" FEDERAL LAW)

1. Threshold Matters

As suggested above, "arising under" jurisdiction is a relative latecomer. For nearly the first hundred years of American history, diversity litigation was far more common in federal courts than federal question litigation. In part, the reason is that the extensive federal legislation that exists in the first decades of the twenty-first century did not exist for most of the first hundred years of American history.

Much has changed: We live in an era of federal legislation, regulating such areas as collective bargaining and rights of union members; sale of securities; discrimination in employment, public accommodations, and housing; protection of the environment; and safety in the workplace. And there was earlier legislation that continues to generate arising under cases. Examples include federal antitrust laws, securities law, environmental regulation, employment discrimination law, and civil rights statutes.

The existence of federal legislation does not *necessarily* mean we should have federal courts with jurisdiction at the trial level. State courts must follow and apply federal law, and it would be possible to leave to state courts the matter of litigating federal claims. Consider, however, what this course of action would entail: The source of much lawmaking (Congress, agencies) would be separated from the institutional authority for interpreting and applying rules (courts); there are 50 states, giving rise to the possibility of 50 different interpretive conventions; state judges would have to master not only state law, but federal law; *federal* appellate guidance and correction would come only from the Supreme Court, in the rare cases in which that Court grants review. The existence of federal arising under jurisdiction, in contrast, provides extensive institutional involvement of judges appointed by the same (federal) authority that is the source of the law being applied, and enables reviewing courts (Circuit Courts of Appeal) to have extensive involvement in guiding and correcting the interpretation of federal law.

As a general rule, arising under cases can brought in *either* federal *or* state court, which is to say that state and federal courts have "concurrent jurisdiction." Unless Congress specifies otherwise, jurisdiction is concurrent.[6] Thus, for example, suits under §1983 (the civil rights statute) can proceed in state or federal court. Three areas in which Congress *has* specified otherwise are copyright suits, antitrust, and suits under the Securities Exchange Act of 1934. See 15 USC §§15 & 26 (antitrust); 28 USC §1338(a) (copyright); 15 USC §78aa (Securities Exchange Act). Despite the fact that jurisdiction of state and federal courts is often concurrent, *most* federal question claims are brought in federal court.

In a few cases, Congress has provided that plaintiffs who choose to bring federal question claims in state court can *keep* the litigation there. As you will discover at the end of this chapter, defendants generally can remove to federal court those suits commenced in state court that *could have been brought originally* in federal court. In FELA cases like Lavender v. Kurn, 327 U.S. 645 (1946) (Chapter 1E, supra), however, the statute confers jurisdiction on state and federal courts (*Lavender* was in state court), *and* the FELA statute bars defendants from removing state-filed cases to federal courts. The same is true of Jones Act suits.

The "Colorable Claim" Principle. Arising under jurisdiction presents a special kind of problem in some cases: Suppose a complaint asserts rights that turn on legal requirements in federal law, but there is no private right of action?

If arising under jurisdiction depended on whether plaintiff actually has a right to sue, or for that matter on the question whether plaintiff prevails after a trial on the merits, then a decision that plaintiff cannot sue (or a decision against plaintiff on the merits) would lead to dismissal rather than resolution of the case. Hence courts developed the "colorable claim" principle, which holds that arising under jurisdiction exists if plaintiff states such a claim—one that is at least plausible in the known state of the law, even if the court ultimately decides that plaintiff does *not* have a federal right. See, e.g., Bell v.

---

[6] States cannot *refuse* to entertain federal question cases, as long as they have courts that are competent to hear comparable state law claims. See, e.g., Haywood v. Drown, 129 S. Ct. 2108 (2009) (New York cannot refuse to entertain suit under 42 USC §1983 against state correctional officer; state statute depriving states courts of jurisdiction to hear damage suits against correctional officers acting in scope of duties was invalid as applied to suits under federal statute).

Hood, 327 U.S. 678, 682 (jurisdiction is not lost "by the possibility that the averments might fail to state a cause of action," which "calls for a judgment on the merits and not for a dismissal for want of jurisdiction") (plaintiffs sought recovery from FBI agents for violations of Fourth and Fifth Amendments); Bivens v. Six Unknown Named Agents of Federal Bureau of Narcotics, 403 U.S. 388 (1971) (recognizing private right of action for violations of Fourth Amendment by federal agents). Thus the Court has referred to a federal claim having "substance sufficient to confer subject matter jurisdiction," see United Mine Workers of America v. Gibbs, 383 US. 715, 715 (1986).

Here is a good place to pause for a related point: Years ago, the Supreme Court was often ready to construe federal legislation as "implying" private rights to sue. See, e.g., Case v. Borak, 377 U.S. 426 (1964) (implied private right to sue for securities fraud under Rule 10b-5); Cannon v. University of Chicago, 441 U.S. 667 (1979) (Title IX creates private right of action for sex discrimination in federally assisted programs). These precedents still stand, but the modern Court has been reluctant to infer private rights to sue, and has taken the position that this matter is up to Congress, and if Congress is silent there is probably *not* a private right to sue. We look more closely at this point in Chapter 7B3, infra (note 6 in the Notes on the Conventions of Rules Pleading).

2. The "Well-Pleaded Complaint" Principle

Often it is easy to tell that arising under jurisdiction exists under 28 USC §1331. Many cases readily fit a maxim coined by Justice Holmes in the *American Well Works* case almost a century ago: "A suit arises under the law that creates the cause of action." See American Well Works Co. v. Layne & Bowler Co., 241 U.S. 257, 260 (1916) (suit alleging that defendants engaged in false and malicious libel by claiming that plaintiff's pump infringed defendant's patent did not arise under federal law; seeking damages from threats to sue under patent law "is not itself a suit under the patent law").

Although the claim in *American Well Works* did not fit Justice Holmes's maxim, you have seen cases that do fit: In Carey v. Piphus, 435 U.S. 247 (1978) (Chapter 1), plaintiffs sued under 42 USC §1983, which authorizes damage suits for violations of constitutional rights by officials acting under color of state law; in *Lavender,* a railroader allegedly died when struck by a protrusion on a railroad car, and suit was brought under the FELA statute, which provides that a railroad engaged in interstate commerce is "liable in damages to any person suffering injury while . . . employed" by such railroad (see 45 USC §51). You will read many other cases that similarly fit Justice Holmes's definition as you go through this book.

Suppose, however, that federal issues appear in a case as a matter of defense rather than as part of plaintiff's claim, or *in refutation* of a defense. Such circumstances arise more often than you might think, as you will see as you read the foundational case on arising under jurisdiction—the venerable *Mottley* case.

Colonel Erasmus L. Mottley

Plaintiff Erasmus L. Mottley (shown at left) was 33 years old in 1871, when he and his wife Annie E. Mottley took a lifetime free pass on the railroad in settlement of their claims for personal injuries. The agreement specified that the Mottleys "released [the Railroad] from all damages or claims for damages for injuries received by them on the 7th of September, 1871, in consequence of a collision of trains" at Randolph's Station, and specified further that the Railroad "agrees to issue free passes on said Railroad and branches now existing or to exist [to the Mottleys] for the remainder of the present year, and thereafter, to renew said passes annually during the lives of said Mottley and wife or either of them." Colonel Mottley served in the Union Army in the Civil War, and his family traced its origins to England (one of his forbears reportedly immigrated to America in 1600). Colonel Mottley served under Generals Buell, Grant, and Sherman and participated in the battles of Shiloh, Perryville, Stone's River, and was present when Atlanta fell. Discharged from the Army in 1865, he took a job as collector of Internal Revenue for the government and moved to Bowling Green, Kentucky. In that year he married Anna Hawkins, of Bowling Green, and the couple had four children. Mottley ran for Congress in 1876 as a Republican, but was defeated, and he later ran unsuccessfully for Mayor of Bowling Green.

LOUISVILLE & NASHVILLE RAILROAD COMPANY v. MOTTLEY

Supreme Court of the United States
211 U.S. 149 (1908)

Mr. Justice MOODY delivered the opinion of the Court:

The appellees (husband and wife), being residents and citizens of Kentucky, brought this suit in equity in the circuit court of the United States for the western district of Kentucky against the appellant, a railroad company and a citizen of the same state. The object of the suit was to compel the specific performance of [a contract entered into in 1871, under which the Mottleys released the railroad from all claims for injuries that the Mottleys sustained in a collision of trains while the Mottleys were riding a train run by the defendant, in exchange for defendant's promise to issue annual "free passes" allowing the Mottleys to ride on trains operated by the defendant during their lives, or the lives of either of them].

The bill alleged that . . . the contract was performed by the defendant up to January 1, 1907, when the defendant declined to renew the passes. The bill then alleges that the refusal to comply with the contract was based solely upon that part of the act of Congress of June 29, 1906, which forbids the giving of free passes or free transportation. The bill further alleges: First, that the act of Congress referred to does not prohibit the giving of passes under the circumstances of this case; and, second, that, if the law is to be construed as prohibiting such passes, it is in conflict with the 5th Amendment of the Constitution, because it deprives the plaintiffs of their property without due process of law. The defendant demurred to the bill. The judge of the circuit court overruled the demurrer, entered a decree for the relief prayed for, and the defendant appealed directly to this court.

Two questions of law were raised by the demurrer to the bill, were brought here by appeal, and have been argued before us. They are, first, whether that part of the act of Congress of June 29, 1906 which forbids the giving of free passes or the collection of any different compensation for transportation of passengers than that specified in the tariff filed, makes it unlawful to perform a contract for transportation of persons who, in good faith, before the passage of the act, had accepted such contract in satisfaction of a valid cause of action against the railroad; and, second, whether the statute, if it should be construed to render such a contract unlawful, is in violation of the 5th Amendment of the Constitution of the United States. We do not deem it necessary, however, to consider either of these questions, because, in our opinion, the court below was without jurisdiction of the cause. Neither party has questioned that jurisdiction, but it is the duty of this court to see to it that the jurisdiction of the circuit court, which is defined and limited by statute, is not exceeded. This duty we have frequently performed of our own motion.

There was no diversity of citizenship, and it is not and cannot be suggested that there was any ground of jurisdiction, except that the case was a "suit . . . arising under the Constitution or laws of the United States." [The Court cites the statute that is now codified as 28 USC §1331.] It is the settled interpretation of these words, as used in this statute, conferring jurisdiction, that a suit arises under the Constitution and laws of the United States only when the plaintiff's statement of his own cause of action shows that it is based upon those laws or that Constitution. It is not enough that the plaintiff alleges some anticipated defense to his cause of action, and asserts that the defense is invalidated by some provision of the Constitution of the United States. Although such allegations show that very likely, in the course of the litigation, a question under the Constitution would arise, they do not show that the suit, that is, the plaintiff's original cause of action, arises under the Constitution. In *Tennessee v. Union & Planters' Bank*, 152 U.S. 454 (1894), . . . [the state of Tennessee] brought suit in the circuit court of the United States to recover from the defendant certain taxes alleged to be due under the laws of the state. The plaintiff alleged that the defendant claimed an immunity from the taxation by virtue of its charter, and that therefore the tax was void, because in violation of the provision of the Constitution of the United States, which forbids any state from passing a law impairing the obligation of contracts. The cause was held to be beyond the jurisdiction of the circuit court, the court saying, by Mr. Justice Gray: "A suggestion of one party, that the other will or may set up a claim under the Constitution or laws of the United States, does not make the suit one arising under that Constitution or those laws." Again, in Boston & M. Consol. Copper & S. Min. Co. v. Montana Ore Purchasing Co. 188 U.S. 632 (1903), the plaintiff brought suit in the circuit court of the United States for the conversion of copper ore and for an injunction against its continuance. The plaintiff then alleged, for the purpose of showing jurisdiction, in substance, that the defendant would set up in defense certain laws of the United States. The cause was held to be beyond the jurisdiction of the circuit court, the court saying, by Mr. Justice Peckham: "It would be wholly unnecessary and improper, in order to prove complainant's cause of action, to go into any matters of defense which the defendants might possibly set up, and then attempt to reply to such defense, and thus, if possible, to show that a Federal question might or probably would arise in the course of the trial of the case. To allege such defense and then make an answer to it before the defendant has the opportunity to itself plead or prove its own defense is inconsistent with any known rule of pleading, so far as we are aware, and is improper. . . ."

The interpretation of the act which we have stated was first announced in Metcalf v. Watertown, 128 U.S. 586 (1888), and has since been repeated and applied in [many additional cases that the Court collects here]. The application of this rule to the case at bar is decisive against the jurisdiction of the circuit court.

It is ordered that the judgment be reversed and the case remitted to the circuit court with instructions to dismiss the suit for want of jurisdiction.

■ NOTES ON THE WELL-PLEADED COMPLAINT RULE

1. *Mottley* is different from *Piphus* and *Lavender*. What is the theory of the complaint in *Mottley*? What is the source of the law under which plaintiffs proceed? There are issues of federal law in *Mottley*. How did they get there? Apparently, *Mottley* is not an arising under case—and yet the Court must resolve federal issues: Does it follow that sometimes federal issues must be resolved in state court?

2. *Mottley* is associated with the "well-pleaded complaint" rule, even though the term does not appear in the opinion. In what sense does *Mottley* stand for this rule, and what is the rule, exactly? Why should it matter whether the complaint is "well pleaded?" See, e.g., Taylor v. Anderson, 234 U.S. 74, 75 (1914) (whether suit arises under federal law is determined by "what necessarily appears" in complaint); Gully v. First National Bank in Meridian, 299 U.S. 109, 112 (1936) (claim alleged in complaint "must be such that it will be supported if the Constitution or laws of the United States are given one construction or effect, and defeated if they receive another"). You will see in Chapter 7 that modern procedure doctrine de-emphasizes pleadings, so distinguishing between a complaint that is "well pleaded" and one that is "ill pleaded" is not always easy.

3. Not only federal defenses, but some federal counterclaims (brought by defendants against plaintiffs) must be resolved in state courts, because federal counterclaims do not create arising under jurisdiction, see Holmes Group, Inc. v. Vornado Air Circulation Systems, Inc., 535 U.S. 826 (2002) (compulsory counterclaims do not pave the way for arising under jurisdiction). Because some such cases seem to be mostly *about* federal law—the whole dispute turns on resolution of federal issues—it has long been suggested that Congress should *expand* arising under jurisdiction by amending §1331. See American Law Institute, Study of the Division of Jurisdiction Between State and Federal Courts §1312 (1969) (legislation would count responsive pleadings raising federal issues that might be dispositive in deciding whether arising under jurisdiction exists). As the Court laconically noted, however, Congress "has not responded to these suggestions," Vaden v. Discover Bank, 556 U.S. 49, 61 n.11 (2009).

4. In the Declaratory Judgment Act, Congress authorized federal courts, in any "actual controversy" (but with certain exceptions) to "declare the rights and other legal relations" of the parties, which declaration has "the force and effect of a final judgment." The Act also authorizes federal courts to provide such further relief as may be "necessary and proper." See 28 USC §2201. Here is how one modern court summed up the impact of the federal Declaratory Judgment Act:

> The Declaratory Judgment Act allows a party . . . who expects to eventually be sued, to determine his rights and liabilities without waiting for his adversary, the presumptive plaintiff, to bring suit. That act, however, is not an independent grant of federal subject-matter jurisdiction, so jurisdiction depends upon the nature of the anticipated claims. Thus, although the presence or absence of a federal question normally turns on an examination of the face of the plaintiff's complaint, in an action for declaratory judgment the positions of the parties are reversed: The declaratory-judgment plaintiff would have been the defendant in the anticipated suit whose character determines the district court's jurisdiction.

DeBartolo v. Healthsouth Corp., 569 F.3d 736, 741 (7th Cir. 2009). The language quoted above envisions a potential defendant striking first, coming to court as plaintiff to launch litigation that would pre-empt or block an expected suit by the other side (one can imagine the railroad suing the Mottleys for declaratory relief). But the statute can also work the other way: Instead of suing for damages and perhaps injunctive relief for breach of contract, or in addition to such claims, the Mottleys too could seek declaratory relief under the Act. Whichever party sues in this setting, wouldn't a complaint for declaratory relief *necessarily* raise federal law issues? It would seek a declaration of rights and obligations under the contract, given the newly enacted federal statute. The complaint would satisfy the well-pleaded complaint rule, hence apparently the arising under standard, and a declaratory judgment could become the basis for injunctive relief or damage claims.

(a) Seeing that the Declaratory Judgment Act could become an easy "end run around" the *Mottley* rule, the Court decided in the *Skelly Oil* case that the Declaratory Judgment Act is "procedural only." Congress "enlarged the range of remedies" available in federal court, but "did not extend" federal jurisdiction. Hence a plaintiff cannot, by "artful pleading" of a claim under the Declaratory Judgment Act, "anticipate a defense based on federal law" to invoke arising under jurisdiction. Skelly Oil Co. v. Phillips Petroleum Co., 339 U.S. 667, 671 (1950). Because of the *Skelly Oil* interpretation of the Declaratory Judgment Act, the court in the *DeBartolo* case concluded that the claim before it belonged in state court:

> [The complaint, filed by a surgeon as limited partner against general partners who were allegedly trying to buy him out,] invokes the Anti-Kickback Act [forbidding doctors from taking fees for patient referrals but containing "safe harbor" for practices authorized by the Secretary for Health and Human Services] as a defense to his partners' anticipated state-law contract action to enforce their rights under the partnership agreement, [but plaintiff's claims] cannot be a source of federal jurisdiction. . . . After all, a federal defense does not establish federal question jurisdiction. In the context of this action for a declaratory judgment, therefore, the allegations in [the] complaint must demonstrate that the defendants could file a federal claim. The defendants, however, have not attempted to identify any federal claim they might have brought, and we can think of none. [This] lawsuit has belonged in state court all along, and it must be pursued in that forum if at all.

DeBartolo, supra, 569 F.3d at 736, 741 (acknowledging that a contrary result might be indicated if the Anti-Kickback "statutory defense" raised "a pure question of federal law of the caliber at stake in Grable & Sons Metal Products, Inc. v. Darue Engineering & Manufacturing, 545 U.S. 308 (2005), which, even the defendants concede, it does not") (you will read *Grable* next). Under *Skelly Oil,* then, federal courts may entertain declaratory judgment suits on federal issues only if they would have jurisdiction to entertain claims for damages or injunctive relief, sometimes together called "coercive" judgments. Since we learn from *Mottley* that there is no arising under jurisdiction to grant the Mottleys injunctive relief or damages, the Declaratory Judgment Act would not enable the Mottleys to sue the railroad in federal court, nor enable the railroad to sue the Mottleys in federal court either.

(b) It turns out that a declaratory judgment suit can go forward if *either of the two parties* has a federal claim for damages or injunctive relief. To use the late Professor Charles Wright's example, suppose Jones Company wants to establish its patent rights against Smith, an alleged infringer. Clearly, Jones Company could sue Smith in federal court for damages and injunctive relief, arguing that it holds a valid patent and that Smith is infringing it. It is but a short step to the conclusion that Jones Company could also sue Smith in federal court for a declaratory judgment that its patent is valid and that Smith is infringing it. This suit is not viewed as enlarging federal jurisdiction because Jones could sue for damages. Now take it a step further: Suppose Jones Company merely threatens Smith instead. Now Smith "will have a lively interest" in figuring out whether the patent is valid. Even though Smith could not sue Jones Company *without* the Declaratory Judgment Act, *nevertheless* he can sue Jones Company for declaratory relief *without* violating the *Skelly Oil* rule: Since Jones Company could bring a coercive suit, it is said that there is no violation of *Skelly Oil* for Smith to anticipate this suit and bring a claim for declaratory relief. See Wright & Kane, Federal Courts §19 (6th ed. 2002); Franchise Tax Board of State of California v. Construction Laborers Vacation Trust, 463 U.S. 1, 18 n.19 (1983) ("federal courts have consistently adjudicated suits by alleged patent infringers to declare a patent invalid, on the theory that an infringement suit by the alleged declaratory judgment defendant would raise a federal question over which the federal courts have exclusive jurisdiction").

5. Similar to the Declaratory Judgment Act, in terms of deciding whether arising under jurisdiction exists in federal court, is the federal Arbitration Act. This statute authorizes federal courts to order parties in a written contract to submit their dispute to arbitration, if the contract so provides, but only if the federal district court would, "save for the arbitration agreement, have jurisdiction . . . of the subject matter of a suit arising out of the controversy." See 9 USC §4. And see Moses H. Cone Memorial Hosp. v. Mercury Construction Corp., 460 U.S. 1, 26 n.32 (1983) (Arbitration Act is "something of an anomaly" because it creates "a body of federal substantive law" relating to the duty to honor an arbitration agreement, "yet it does not create any independent federal-question jurisdiction"). See also Vaden v. Discover Bank, 129 S. Ct. 1262 (2009) (federal court can "look through" plaintiff's claim and assume jurisdiction if court would have jurisdiction over substantive controversy, but may not assume jurisdiction merely because counterclaim filed by defendant rests on federal law).

■ NOTES ON LITIGATING SUBJECT MATTER JURISDICTION

1. Note that the Court in *Mottley* "reached out" to decide the question of subject matter jurisdiction, as *neither party* raised it. See Arbaugh v. Y&H Corp., 546 U.S. 500, 507 (2006) ("courts, including this Court, have an independent obligation to determine whether subject-matter jurisdiction exists, even in the absence of a challenge"). Why should this matter be of such concern?

2. Not only do courts sometimes raise subject matter jurisdiction on their own, and sometimes late in the game, but parties can do so as well. Under FRCP 12(h)(3), parties may raise subject matter jurisdiction "at any time," which contrasts sharply with the approach to jurisdiction over the person, which defendants must raise in the answer or by pre-answer motion under FRCP 12(b) and 12(h)(1). See Chapter 3E, supra. *Even though* issues of subject matter jurisdiction may be raised "at any time," isn't it far preferable to resolve these issues at the outset? Doesn't the *Mottley* "well-pleaded complaint" principle serve this end?

3. If any party may raise subject matter jurisdiction any time, is there anything to stop a plaintiff, if he loses at trial, from taking an appeal that argues that the court lacked subject matter jurisdiction—the court that the plaintiff *chose* in which to sue? Is there anything, for that matter, to stop a *defendant* who loses at trial from taking an appeal raising this point? As you can imagine, legal doctrines readily available in the profession, like "estoppel" (preventing a party who has taken a particular position from changing position in ways that disadvantage others) and "waiver" could easily be invoked in this setting. In fact, however, they are not, and a plaintiff or defendant who loses a case, or even just *fears that she is losing*, can raise the issue of subject matter jurisdiction and get a dismissal if the point has merit. See, e.g., Capron v. Van Noorden, 6 U.S. (2 Cranch) 126 (1804) (after losing trespass suit in federal court, plaintiff appealed and argued that there was no diversity—actually "alienage"—jurisdiction, so the judgment should be set aside; Court sets aside judgment).

4. Suppose the Mottleys litigated their case to the end and won in the District Court (as did happen), but either (a) no appeal was taken and the judgment in the Mottleys' favor became final or (b) appeals were taken and their victory was sustained, and *nobody ever noticed* that subject matter jurisdiction was lacking. Suppose the railroad eventually refused to issue passes to the Mottleys, and they came back to court, suing on the judgment, to obtain a new order requiring the railroad to comply. Suppose the railroad *now* raises the claim that the original court lacked subject matter jurisdiction because the Mottleys' claim did not qualify for arising under jurisdiction. Should the court *now* refuse to honor the judgment in the original suit? See Des Moines Navigation & R. Co. v. Iowa Homestead Co., 123 U.S. 552, 557 (1887) (error to refuse to recognize judgment for lack of subject matter jurisdiction; judgments may be "erroneous" for lack of such jurisdiction, but they are not "nullities," and they "bind the parties until reversed or otherwise set aside"); Durfee v. Duke, 375 U.S. 106 (1963) (Nebraska court determined that it had jurisdiction to resolve title dispute over bottom land on Missouri river, in suit brought by GD against JD; then JD sued GD in Missouri raising the same issue; Missouri court erred in refusing to recognize Nebraska judgment; doctrine of "jurisdictional finality" requires that "once the matter has been fully litigated and judicially determined," it cannot be retried in another state).

■ NOTES ON THE BREADTH OF ARISING UNDER JURISDICTION

1. After the Supreme Court, in the opinion you read, threw out the judgment that the Mottleys had won, they repaired to a Kentucky state court, brought another suit, and won again. The trial court ordered the railroad to continue issuing free passes. For the second time, the case went to the United States Supreme Court. This time the Court reached the merits, holding that the federal statute *did* bar the railroad from continuing to perform under the contract, and that applying the statute this way did not unconstitutionally interfere with the rights of the Mottleys. See Louisville & N.R. Co. v. Mottley, 219 U.S. 467 (1911).

(a) The Constitution spells out the extent of federal question jurisdiction in *all* federal courts using a single phrase. It says states that the "judicial power" of the United States "shall extend to all Cases, in Law and Equity, arising under this Constitution [or] the Laws of the United States." U.S. Const. Art. III §2. The statute that defines the authority of federal district courts in this setting uses the very same "arising under" phrase. See 28 USC §1331.

(b) It follows from these facts that the arising under phrase in the Constitution means something different from the same phrase in the statute. It follows as well that arising under jurisdiction of federal courts authorized by the Constitution is *broader* than the authority that Congress conferred on federal district courts to hear such cases. See Verlinden B.V. v. Central Bank of Nigeria, 461 U.S. 480, 494-495 (1983) ("'arising under' jurisdiction is broader than federal-question jurisdiction under §1331"). Thus the Mottleys' suit is *not* an arising under case for purposes of 28 USC §1331, and it cannot be tried in federal district court. But their suit *is* an arising under case for purposes of Supreme Court review of the decision reached in the state courts of Kentucky. What is the indicated conclusion? It is that Congress has not conferred on federal trial courts as much jurisdiction as the Constitution allows?

(c) Exactly how much broader the *constitutional* grant of arising under jurisdiction is than the *statutory* grant of arising under jurisdiction in federal district courts is hard to say. For a close look, see Anthony J. Bellia, *The Origins of Article III "Arising Under" Jurisdiction*, 57 Duke L.J. 263, 341 (2007) (Article III's grant of arising under jurisdiction was designed to secure the

supremacy of federal law, and the scope of appellate arising under jurisdiction may embrace all cases litigated originally in federal court, but only those cases from state court in which "federal law would be determinative of a right or title" advanced by the appellant).

2. You have seen something similar before. Recall that the phrase "between citizens of different States" appears *both* in the Constitution and in a jurisdictional statute. See U.S. Const. Art. III §2 (federal courts have jurisdiction in suits "between Citizens of different States"); 28 USC §1332 (district courts have jurisdiction to try cases for more than $75,000 between "citizens of different States"). Recall that the *Tashire* case concluded that the *constitutional* phrase requires only "minimum diversity" but that the same statutory phrase requires "complete diversity" (see Section A1, supra).

3. Arising Under Jurisdiction in Cases of Special Federal Concern

Would that the *Mottley* "well-pleaded complaint" rule told us all we need to know about arising under jurisdiction. It does not. If you think about it, we have seen two tests for arising under jurisdiction. One came from Justice Holmes in *American Well Works*: Arising under jurisdiction exists if federal law "creates the cause of action," see American Well Works Co. v. Layne & Bowler Co., 241 U.S. 257, 260 (1916). The other came from *Mottley*: Arising under jurisdiction exists if the federal issue appears on the face of a well-pleaded complaint.

American Well Works Test Too Narrow. As it turns out, the definition in *American Well Works* seems too narrow. It works well as a test of *inclusion*, less well as a test of *exclusion*. That is to say, if federal law creates the cause of action, almost certainly arising under jurisdiction exists, as was true in *Piphus* and *Lavender* (Chapter 1, supra), and *American Well Works* leads to the right outcome.

Even if federal law does *not* create the cause of action, however, the Court sometimes finds that arising under jurisdiction exists (so *American Well Works* sometimes leads to the wrong result). In the *Kansas City Title* case, for example, a shareholder brought a derivative suit, claiming the corporation could not legally buy bonds issued by the government because they were unconstitutional. Missouri law supplied the cause of action, but the suit was brought in federal court and the Supreme Court concluded that arising under jurisdiction existed. In a broad statement, the Court said there is arising under jurisdiction if it "appears from the [complaint] that the right to relief depends upon the construction or application" of federal law. See Smith v. Kansas City Title & Trust Co., 255 U.S. 180, 199 (1921).

Mottley Test Too Broad. In contrast to the *American Well Works* test, the *Mottley* test seems too broad. It works well as a test of *exclusion*, less well as a test of *inclusion*. That is to say, if the federal issue does *not* appear in a well-pleaded complaint—or to put it another way, if the federal element does not enter the suit as part of plaintiff's case—probably arising under jurisdiction does not exist.

But even if the federal element *does* enter the suit as part of plaintiff's case, federal jurisdiction does not *always* exist (so *Mottley* sometimes leads to the wrong result). This point arose in the *Moore* and *Merrell Dow* cases. In *Moore*, one count of plaintiff's complaint alleged claims against his employer under Kentucky law, and invoked a federal statute (Safety Appliance Act), "reproduced in substance, and with almost literal exactness," in the Kentucky statute under which plaintiff sued. But, the Court concluded, this claim "is not to be regarded as one arising under the laws of the United States." See Moore v. Chesapeake & Ohio Ry. Co., 291 U.S. 205, 217 (1934). In *Merrell Dow*, plaintiffs brought suit in state court alleging claims against a drug manufacturer under state law (Ohio), including a claim that the drug was misbranded in violation of the federal Food, Drug, and Cosmetic Act (FDCA), which allegedly gave rise to a "rebuttable presumption of negligence" under Ohio law. Defendant removed the case to federal court, arguing *not* that plaintiff had a federal right to sue, but that plaintiff's *state law claim* supported arising under jurisdiction because of the embedded federal law element. Again the Court concluded that arising under jurisdiction did not exist. See Merrell Dow Pharmaceuticals v. Thompson, 478 U.S. 804 (1986).

Where Are We? We have *three* imperfect tests, if one counts the broad statement in *Kansas City Title* as another test. We have *American Well Works* (arising under jurisdiction exists if federal law creates the claim for relief); *Mottley* (arising under jurisdiction exists if the federal issue appears in a well-pleaded complaint, or enters the suit as part of plaintiff's case); *Kansas City Title* (arising under jurisdiction exists if the outcome turns on a federal issue).

GRABLE & SONS METAL PRODUCTS, INC. v. DARUE ENGINEERING & MANUFACTURING

Supreme Court of the United States
545 U.S. 308 (2005)

Justice SOUTER delivered the opinion of the Court.

The question is whether want of a federal cause of action to try claims of title to land obtained at a federal tax sale precludes removal to federal court of a state action with nondiverse parties raising a disputed issue of federal title law. We answer no, and hold that the national interest in providing a federal forum for federal tax litigation is sufficiently substantial to support the exercise of federal-question jurisdiction over the disputed issue on removal, which would not distort any division of labor between the state and federal courts, provided or assumed by Congress.

I

In 1994, the Internal Revenue Service seized Michigan real property belonging to petitioner Grable & Sons Metal Products, Inc., to satisfy Grable's federal tax delinquency. Title 26 USC §6335 required the IRS to give notice of the seizure, and there is no dispute that Grable received actual notice by certified mail before the IRS sold the property to respondent Darue Engineering & Manufacturing. Although Grable also received notice of the sale itself, it did not exercise its statutory right to redeem the property within 180 days of the sale, §6337(b)(1), and after that period had passed, the Government gave Darue a quitclaim deed, §6339.

Five years later, Grable brought a quiet title action in state court, claiming that Darue's record title was invalid because the IRS had failed to notify Grable of its seizure of the property in the exact manner required by §6335(a), which provides that written notice must be "given by the Secretary to the owner of the property [or] left at his usual place of abode or business." Grable said that the statute required personal service, not service by certified mail.

Darue removed the case to Federal District Court as presenting a federal question, because the claim of title depended on the interpretation of the notice statute in the federal tax law. The District Court declined to remand the case at Grable's behest after finding that the "claim does pose a 'significant question of federal law,'" and ruling that Grable's lack of a federal right of action to enforce its claim against Darue did not bar the exercise of federal jurisdiction. On the merits, the court granted summary judgment to Darue, holding that although §6335 by its terms required personal service, substantial compliance with the statute was enough.

The Court of Appeals for the Sixth Circuit affirmed. On the jurisdictional question, the panel thought it sufficed that the title claim raised an issue of federal law that had to be resolved, and implicated a substantial federal interest (in construing federal tax law). The court went on to affirm the District Court's judgment on the merits. We granted certiorari on the jurisdictional question alone, to resolve a split within the Courts of Appeals on whether Merrell Dow Pharmaceuticals Inc. v. Thompson, 478 U.S. 804 (1986), always requires a federal cause of action as a condition for exercising federal-question jurisdiction. We now affirm.

II

Darue was entitled to remove the quiet title action if Grable could have brought it in federal district court originally, 28 USC §1441(a), as a civil action "arising under the Constitution, laws, or treaties of the United States," §1331. This provision for federal-question jurisdiction is invoked by and large by plaintiffs pleading a cause of action created by federal law (e.g., claims under 42 USC §1983). There is, however, another longstanding, if less frequently encountered, variety of federal "arising under" jurisdiction, this Court having recognized for nearly 100 years that in certain cases federal-question jurisdiction will lie over state-law claims that implicate significant federal issues. E.g., Hopkins v. Walker, 244 U.S. 486, 490-491 (1917). The doctrine captures the commonsense notion that a federal court ought to be able to hear claims recognized under state law that nonetheless turn on substantial questions of federal law, and thus justify resort to the experience, solicitude, and hope of uniformity that a federal forum offers on federal issues, see ALI, Study of the Division of Jurisdiction Between State and Federal Courts 164-166 (1968).

The classic example is Smith v. Kansas City Title & Trust Co., 255 U.S. 180 (1921), . . . [which] held, in a somewhat generous statement of the scope of the doctrine, that a state-law claim could give rise to federal-question jurisdiction so long as it "appears from the [complaint] that the right to relief depends upon the construction or application of [federal law]."

The *Smith* statement has been subject to some trimming to fit earlier and later cases recognizing the vitality of the basic doctrine, but shying away from the expansive view that mere need to apply federal law in a state-law claim will suffice to open the "arising under" door. As early as 1912, this Court had confined federal-question jurisdiction over state-law claims to those that "really and substantially involv[e] a dispute or controversy respecting the validity, construction or effect of [federal] law." Shulthis v. McDougal, 225 U.S. 561, 569 (1912). This limitation was the ancestor of Justice Cardozo's later explanation that a request to exercise federal-question jurisdiction over a state action calls for a "common-sense accommodation of judgment to [the] kaleidoscopic situations" that present a federal issue, in "a selective process which picks the substantial causes out of the web and lays the other ones aside." Gully v. First Nat. Bank in Meridian, 299 U.S. 109, 117-118 (1936). It has in fact become a constant refrain in such cases that federal jurisdiction demands not only a contested federal issue, but a substantial one, indicating a serious federal interest in claiming the advantages thought to be inherent in a federal forum.

But even when the state action discloses a contested and substantial federal question, the exercise of federal jurisdiction is subject to a possible veto. For the federal issue will ultimately qualify for a federal forum only if federal jurisdiction is consistent with congressional judgment about the sound division of labor between state and federal courts governing the application of §1331. Thus, Franchise Tax Board of State of California v. Construction Laborers Vacation Trust, 463 U.S. 1, 21-22 (1983), explained that the appropriateness of a federal forum to hear an embedded issue could be evaluated only after considering the "welter of issues regarding the interrelation of federal and state authority and the proper management of the federal judicial system." Because arising-under jurisdiction to hear a state-law claim always raises the possibility of upsetting the state-federal line drawn (or at least assumed) by Congress, the presence of a disputed federal issue and the ostensible importance of a federal forum are never necessarily dispositive; there must always be an assessment of any disruptive portent in exercising federal jurisdiction.

These considerations have kept us from stating a "single, precise, all-embracing" test for jurisdiction over federal issues embedded in state-law claims between nondiverse parties. Christianson v. Colt Industries Operating Corp., 486 U.S. 800, 821 (1988) (Stevens, J., concurring). We have not kept them out simply because they appeared in state raiment, as Justice Holmes would have done, see *Smith, supra* (dissenting opinion), but neither have we treated "federal issue" as a password opening federal courts to any state action embracing a point of federal law. Instead, the question is, does a state-law claim necessarily raise a stated federal issue, actually disputed and substantial, which a federal forum may entertain without disturbing any congressionally approved balance of federal and state judicial responsibilities.

III

A

This case warrants federal jurisdiction. Grable's state complaint must specify "the facts establishing the superiority of [its] claim," Mich. Ct. Rule 3.411(B)(2)(c), and Grable has premised its superior title claim on a failure by the IRS to give it adequate notice, as defined by federal law. Whether Grable was given notice within the meaning of the federal statute is thus an essential element of its quiet title claim, and the meaning of the federal statute is actually in dispute; it appears to be the only legal or factual issue contested in the case. The meaning of the federal tax provision is an important issue of federal law that sensibly belongs in a federal court. The Government has a strong interest in the "prompt and certain collection of delinquent taxes," United States v. Rodgers, 461 U.S. 677, 709 (1983), and the ability of the IRS to satisfy its claims from the property of delinquents requires clear terms of notice to allow buyers like Darue to satisfy themselves that the Service has touched the bases necessary for good title. The Government thus has a direct interest in the availability of a federal forum to vindicate its own administrative action, and buyers (as well as tax delinquents) may find it valuable to come before judges used to federal tax matters. Finally, because it will be the rare state title case that raises a contested matter of federal law, federal jurisdiction to resolve genuine disagreement over federal tax title provisions will portend only a microscopic effect on the federal-state division of labor. See n.3, *infra.*

This conclusion puts us in venerable company, quiet title actions having been the subject of some of the earliest exercises of federal-question jurisdiction over state-law claims. In *Hopkins, supra,* the question was federal jurisdiction over a quiet title action based on the plaintiffs' allegation that federal mining law gave them the superior claim. Just as in this case, "the facts showing the plaintiffs' title and the existence and invalidity of the instrument or record sought to be eliminated as a cloud upon the title are essential parts of the plaintiffs' cause of action."[3] As in this case again, "it is plain that a controversy respecting the construction and effect of the [federal] laws is involved and is sufficiently real and substantial." This Court therefore upheld federal jurisdiction in *Hopkins,* as well as in the similar quiet title matters of Northern Pacific R. Co. v. Soderberg, 188 U.S. 526, 528 (1903), and Wilson Cypress Co. v. Del Pozo y Marcos, 236 U.S. 635, 643-644 (1915). Consistent with those cases, the recognition of federal jurisdiction is in order here.

B

Merrell Dow Pharmaceuticals v. Thompson, 478 U.S. 804 (1986), on which Grable rests its position, is not to the contrary. *Merrell Dow* considered a state tort claim resting in part on the allegation that the defendant drug company had violated a federal misbranding prohibition, and was thus presumptively negligent under Ohio law. The Court assumed that federal law would have to be applied to resolve the claim, but after closely examining the strength of the federal interest at stake and the implications of opening the federal forum, held federal jurisdiction unavailable. Congress had not provided a private federal cause of action for violation of the federal branding requirement, and the Court found "it would . . . flout, or at least undermine, congressional intent to conclude that federal courts might nevertheless exercise federal-question jurisdiction and provide remedies for violations of that federal statute solely because the violation . . . is said to be a . . . 'proximate cause' under state law."

Because federal law provides for no quiet title action that could be brought against Darue, Grable argues that there can be no federal jurisdiction here, stressing some broad language in *Merrell Dow* (including the passage just

---

[3] The quiet title cases also show the limiting effect of the requirement that the federal issue in a state-law claim must actually be in dispute to justify federal-question jurisdiction. In Shulthis v. McDougal, 225 U.S. 561 (1912), this Court found that there was no federal-question jurisdiction to hear a plaintiff's quiet title claim in part because the federal statutes on which title depended were not subject to "any controversy respecting their validity, construction, or effect." As the Court put it, the requirement of an actual dispute about federal law was "especially" important in "suit[s] involving rights to land acquired under a law of the United States," because otherwise "every suit to establish title to land in the central and western states would so arise [under federal law], as all titles in those States are traceable back to those laws."

quoted) that on its face supports Grable's position, see Note, Mr. Smith Goes to Federal Court: Federal Question Jurisdiction over State Law Claims Post-*Merrell Dow*, 115 Harv. L. Rev. 2272, 2280-2282 (2002) (discussing split in Courts of Appeals over private right of action requirement after *Merrell Dow*). But an opinion is to be read as a whole, and *Merrell Dow* cannot be read whole as overturning decades of precedent, as it would have done by effectively adopting the Holmes dissent in *Smith*, and converting a federal cause of action from a sufficient condition for federal-question jurisdiction[5] into a necessary one.

In the first place, *Merrell Dow* disclaimed the adoption of any bright-line rule, as when the Court reiterated that "in exploring the outer reaches of §1331, determinations about federal jurisdiction require sensitive judgments about congressional intent, judicial power, and the federal system." The opinion included a lengthy footnote explaining that questions of jurisdiction over state-law claims require "careful judgments" about the "nature of the federal interest at stake" (emphasis deleted). And as a final indication that it did not mean to make a federal right of action mandatory, it expressly approved the exercise of jurisdiction sustained in *Smith*, despite the want of any federal cause of action available to *Smith*'s shareholder plaintiff. *Merrell Dow* then, did not toss out, but specifically retained, the contextual enquiry that had been *Smith*'s hallmark for over 60 years. At the end of *Merrell Dow*, Justice Holmes was still dissenting.

Accordingly, *Merrell Dow* should be read in its entirety as treating the absence of a federal private right of action as evidence relevant to, but not dispositive of, the "sensitive judgments about congressional intent" that §1331 requires. The absence of any federal cause of action affected *Merrell Dow*'s result two ways. The Court saw the fact as worth some consideration in the assessment of substantiality. But its primary importance emerged when the Court treated the combination of no federal cause of action and no pre-emption of state remedies for misbranding as an important clue to Congress's conception of the scope of jurisdiction to be exercised under §1331. The Court saw the missing cause of action not as a missing federal door key, always required, but as a missing welcome mat, required in the circumstances, when exercising federal jurisdiction over a state misbranding action would have attracted a horde of original filings and removal cases raising other state claims with embedded federal issues. For if the federal labeling standard without a federal cause of action could get a state claim into federal court, so could any other federal standard without a federal cause of action. And that would have meant a tremendous number of cases.

One only needed to consider the treatment of federal violations generally in garden variety state tort law. "The violation of federal statutes and regulations is commonly given negligence per se effect in state tort

---

[5] For an extremely rare exception to the sufficiency of a federal right of action, see Shoshone Mining Co. v. Rutter, 177 U.S. 505, 507 (1900).

proceedings."[6] Restatement (Third) of Torts §14, Reporters' Note, Comment *a*, p. 195 (Tent. Draft No. 1, Mar. 28, 2001). See also W. Keeton, D. Dobbs, R. Keeton, & D. Owen, Prosser and Keeton on Law of Torts §36, p. 221 n.9 (5th ed. 1984) ("[T]he breach of a federal statute may support a negligence per se claim as a matter of state law" (collecting authority)). A general rule of exercising federal jurisdiction over state claims resting on federal mislabeling and other statutory violations would thus have heralded a potentially enormous shift of traditionally state cases into federal courts. Expressing concern over the "increased volume of federal litigation," and noting the importance of adhering to "legislative intent," *Merrell Dow* thought it improbable that the Congress, having made no provision for a federal cause of action, would have meant to welcome any state-law tort case implicating federal law "solely because the violation of the federal statute is said to [create] a rebuttable presumption [of negligence] . . . under state law" (internal quotation marks omitted). In this situation, no welcome mat meant keep out. *Merrell Dow*'s analysis thus fits within the framework of examining the importance of having a federal forum for the issue, and the consistency of such a forum with Congress's intended division of labor between state and federal courts.

As already indicated, however, a comparable analysis yields a different jurisdictional conclusion in this case. Although Congress also indicated ambivalence in this case by providing no private right of action to Grable, it is the rare state quiet title action that involves contested issues of federal law. Consequently, jurisdiction over actions like Grable's would not materially affect, or threaten to affect, the normal currents of litigation. Given the absence of threatening structural consequences and the clear interest the Government, its buyers, and its delinquents have in the availability of a federal forum, there is no good reason to shirk from federal jurisdiction over the dispositive and contested federal issue at the heart of the state-law title claim.[7]

IV

The judgment of the Court of Appeals, upholding federal jurisdiction over Grable's quiet title action, is affirmed.

It is so ordered.

---

[6] Other jurisdictions treat a violation of a federal statute as evidence of negligence or, like Ohio itself in *Merrell Dow*, as creating a rebuttable presumption of negligence. Either approach could still implicate issues of federal law.

[7] At oral argument Grable's counsel espoused the position that after *Merrell Dow*, federal-question jurisdiction over state-law claims absent a federal right of action could be recognized only where a constitutional issue was at stake. There is, however, no reason in text or otherwise to draw such a rough line. As *Merrell Dow* itself suggested, constitutional questions may be the more likely ones to reach the level of substantiality that can justify federal jurisdiction. But a flat ban on statutory questions would mechanically exclude significant questions of federal law like the one this case presents.

Justice THOMAS, concurring.

[Justice Thomas indicates his willingness, in "an appropriate case" and with "better evidence as to the original meaning" of §1331, to adopt Justice Holmes's rule from *American Well Works*, limiting §1331 jurisdiction to cases where federal law creates the claim pleaded in the complaint.]

■ **NOTES ON CASES OF SPECIAL FEDERAL CONCERN**

1. After the IRS seized Grable's real property in Eaton Rapids and sold it to Darue, Grable sued Darue in state court in Michigan, where appellate precedent suggested that in serving Grable by certified mail (rather than personally) the IRS had not done enough. Darue removed to federal court, which was proper only if the suit could originally have been brought there. Grable's was a "quiet title" suit, "which is a generally a state law cause of action," as the Sixth Circuit acknowledged, but Grable alleged that the quitclaim deed did not convey title because the IRS notice did not satisfy the federal standard. See Grable & Sons Metal Products, Inc. v. Darue Engineering & Manufacturing, 377 F.3d 582, 594 (6th Cir. 2004). Arguably, the federal issue in *Grable* rightly appeared in the complaint, even though the claim rested on state law, thus apparently passing the *Mottley* (but not the *American Well Works*) test.

2. Ignoring *Mottley* and looking instead to *Kansas City Title,* the Court concludes that Grable's claim supports the exercise of arising under jurisdiction: The claim "necessarily raise[s] a stated federal issue" that is "actually disputed and substantial," and a federal court can hear the case "without disturbing any congressionally approved balance of federal and state judicial responsibilities." Do both *Kansas City Title* and *Grable* involve important federal interests? What might happen to those interests if the cases could not be litigated in federal court?

3. In *Merrell Dow*, described before (and quoted in) *Grable*, plaintiffs from Canada and Scotland brought product liability claims against Merrell Dow, alleging birth defects from their mothers' use of Bendectin (anti-nausea drug taken during pregnancy). They sued in Ohio state court specifically to *avoid* federal court, because related federal diversity suits filed elsewhere had been consolidated and transferred to New Jersey under the multidistrict venue transfer statute (28 USC §1407).[7] Merrell Dow removed, not admitting that plaintiffs had claims authorized by federal law, but arguing instead that *state*

---

[7] Defendant in *Merrell Dow* was an Ohio corporation, and a local citizen cannot remove on the basis of diversity, as you will see when you look at 28 USC §1441 (Chapter 4D, infra). It could remove if arising under jurisdiction exists.

law claims satisfied the arising under standard because Ohio law incorporated a *federal* standard drawn from the FDCA. The Court assumed that Merrell Dow was correct on this point, and concluded that there was no arising under jurisdiction. If the FDCA did not create a private right to sue, "some combination of the following factors" must be present:

> (1) the plaintiffs are not part of the class for whose special benefit the statute was passed; (2) the indicia of legislative intent reveal no congressional purpose to provide a private cause of action; (3) a federal cause of action would not further the underlying purposes of the legislative scheme; and (4) the respondents' cause of action is a subject traditionally relegated to state law.

Merrell Dow Pharmaceuticals v. Thompson, 478 U.S. 804, 810 (1986) (so "Congress did not intend a private remedy" under its statute). Does *Merrell Dow* implicate federal interests as much as *Kansas City Title* and *Grable* do? In *Merrell Dow* and cases like it, what is the worst that could happen if they must stay in state court?

4. The Court in *Grable* was also troubled by the *Franchise Tax Board* decision. There, the California Franchise Tax Board (Tax Board) sued the Construction Laborers Vacation Trust (CLVT) in state court, seeking a declaratory judgment that CLVT was obligated by California law to withhold state income tax from union member earnings deposited with CLVT, and to make payments to the Tax Board. CLVT removed, claiming that arising under jurisdiction existed because the federal Employee Retirement Income Security Act of 1974 (ERISA) pre-empted state power to levy on funds held in trust by CLVT. As it was to do five years later in *Merrell Dow*, the Court concluded that the Tax Board's suit did *not* qualify for arising under jurisdiction. The claim for declaratory relief revealed the federal issue on the face of the complaint, but "fidelity to [the] spirit" of *Skelly Oil* required that *state* declaratory judgment suits be treated the same way as *federal* declaratory judgment suits (federal jurisdiction exists only if suit satisfies arising under standard without regard to declaratory judgment count). In a surprising turn, the Court acknowledged that ERISA "specifically grants" trustees "a cause of action for injunctive relief when their rights and duties under ERISA are at issue," but the Court *still* concluded that arising under jurisdiction did not exist:

> We have always interpreted what *Skelly Oil* called "the current of jurisdictional legislation since the [1875 enactment of the arising under statute, now 28 USC §1331]" with an eye to practicality and necessity. "What is needed is something of that common-sense accommodation of judgment to kaleidoscopic situations which characterizes the law in its treatment of causation . . . a selective process which picks the substantial causes out of the web and lays the other ones aside." Gully v. First National Bank, 299 U.S., at 117-118 (1936). There are good reasons why the federal courts should not entertain suits by the States to declare the validity of their regulations despite possibly conflicting federal law. States are not significantly prejudiced by an inability to come to federal court for a

declaratory judgment in advance of a possible injunctive suit by a person subject to federal regulation. They have a variety of means by which they can enforce their own laws in their own courts, and they do not suffer if the preemption questions such enforcement may raise are tested there. The express grant of federal jurisdiction in ERISA is limited to suits brought by certain parties, as to whom Congress presumably determined that a right to enter federal court was necessary to further the statute's purposes. It did not go so far as to provide that any suit against such parties must also be brought in federal court when they themselves did not choose to sue. The situation presented by a State's suit for a declaration of the validity of state law is sufficiently removed from the spirit of necessity and careful limitation of district court jurisdiction that informed our statutory interpretation in *Skelly Oil* and *Gully* to convince us that, until Congress informs us otherwise, such a suit is not within the original jurisdiction of the United States district courts. Accordingly, the same suit brought originally in state court is not removable either.

Franchise Tax Board of State of California v. Construction Laborers Vacation Trust, 463 U.S. 1, 21-22 (1983).

5. Creating rights to sue, and enacting statutes that apply in suits governed by state law (as in *Grable* and *Kansas City Title*), are not the *only* sources of arising under jurisdiction. Consider the following examples:

(a) Statutes that confer jurisdiction in federal court—what one might call "procedural" statutes, at least on their surface—are sometimes construed as supporting arising under jurisdiction. An example is the Labor Management Relations Act of 1947 (LMRA), which authorizes suits in federal court for violations of collective bargaining agreements. This provision *not only* confers jurisdiction, but also authorizes federal courts to fashion federal common law to resolve disputes. See 28 USC §185 (suits for violation of contracts between employer and labor organization may be brought in federal district court), construed in Textile Workers Union of America v. Lincoln Mills of Alabama, 353 U.S. 448, 451 (1957) (LMRA "authorizes federal courts to fashion a body of federal law" in enforcing collective bargaining agreements). Of course, the basic diversity jurisdiction statute (28 USC §1332) does *not* authorize federal courts to create federal common law, as you will see in Chapter 6 on the *Erie* doctrine.

(b) Where Congress creates a federal entity and authorizes it to sue in federal court, arising under jurisdiction often exists. In the *Osborn* case in 1824, Chief Justice John Marshall took up this question in connection with the Bank of the United States, and concluded that federal courts have arising under jurisdiction to entertain suits by the Bank even if they involve only state law claims. See Osborn v. Bank of the United States, 22 U.S. 738 (1824) (federal courts can be given jurisdiction where federal question "forms an ingredient of the original cause"). The *Osborn* doctrine is usually described as espousing a theory of "protective jurisdiction" in which federal courts are available to federal officials to protect federal authority. It is not, however, commonly invoked, nor as broad as may appear. See Anthony J. Bellia, *The Origins of Article III "Arising Under" Jurisdiction*, 57 Duke L.J. 263, 342 (2007) ("seemingly

boundless theories of protective jurisdiction" should *not* derive from *Osborn*, which rests on view that "an actual federal law must be demonstrably determinative of the legal relations of the parties"). And see generally James Pfander, *Protective Jurisdiction, Aggregate Litigation, and the Limits of Article III*, 95 Cal. L. Rev. 1423, 1428-1429 (2007) (describing three theories of protective jurisdiction).

(c) Perhaps surprisingly, arising under jurisdiction has been found to exist where a claimant seeks a declaratory judgment that federal law completely pre-empts state law claims that another seeks to advance. In the *Verizon Maryland* case, Verizon as a "local exchange carrier" (LEC) under the Telecommunications Act of 1996 (TCA) decided that the statute, which obliged it to work with competitors by sharing its networks and arranging mutual compensation with other entrants in the field, did not apply to calls that Verizon customers placed to Internet Service Providers (ISPs) because such calls connected users to distant internet sites and were therefore not "local" calls. As a competitor entitled to compensation under a sharing agreement with Verizon, WorldCom filed a complaint with the Maryland Public Service Commission (the TCA contemplates that such disputes are to be adjudicated in this manner), which ruled in favor of WorldCom. Verizon then sued WorldCom in federal court, claiming that the Commission's order was unlawful and that the TCA pre-empts state regulation of nonlocal calls. The Court rejected WorldCom's objection to federal jurisdiction: "We have no doubt that federal courts have jurisdiction under §1331 to entertain such a suit" because Verizon seeks relief from the order "on the ground that such regulation is preempted by a federal statute which, by virtue of the Supremacy Clause of the Constitution, must prevail," so Verizon's claim "presents a federal question" over which federal courts have jurisdiction under §1331. Verizon Maryland Inc. v. Public Service Commission of Maryland, 535 U.S. 635, 642 (2002).

6. Suppose a suit identical to *Mottley* were brought in federal court today. If the railroad moved to dismiss, could the Mottleys argue that there is a special federal interest in resolving the question whether the statute construed in that case does or does not block the continuation of contracts obligating the railroad to provide free passes in settlement of a lawsuit, hence that the case arises under federal law, after all?

7. As the text comments prior to *Grable*, the *American Well Works* test is narrow and, "if federal law creates the cause of action, almost certainly arising under jurisdiction exists." *Sometimes,* however, even this *narrow* test for federal jurisdiction can be satisfied, and yet arising under jurisdiction does not exist. Footnote 5 in *Grable* cites *Shoshone Mining* as an "extremely rare exception" to the general rule. There, Congress authorized mining companies to sue adverse claimants to determine mining rights, without specifying state or federal court, but stating that suits should be resolved by applying "local customs or rules." Hence, the Court decided, even the authorization to sue did not confer arising under jurisdiction. See Shoshone Mining Co. v. Rutter, 177 U.S. 505, 507 (1900).

FEDERAL SUPPLEMENTAL JURISDICTION

Courts decide "cases" (or "controversies"), not issues. In the federal system, this definition (or "limit") of judicial power is stated in the Constitution, which provides that federal judicial power extends, *inter alia,* to "all Cases" arising under federal law, and "Controversies" between citizens of different states. U.S. Const. Art. III §2.

Inevitably, then, two large questions arise, both stemming from the twin requirements in diversity cases that (a) claimant and defendant must be of diverse citizenship, and (b) amount in controversy must exceed $75,000. The former requirement is in Article III, Section 2. The latter is *not* in the Constitution and is purely statutory (see 28 USC §1331). Here are the two questions:

First, to what extent can federal courts *in federal question cases* (those arising under federal law) decide claims governed by state law if, for example, the parties do not satisfy the diversity or amount-in-controversy requirement? Perhaps you are thinking something like the following thoughts: "Why should there be any such problem? By definition, federal question cases involve claims arising under federal law. Why should we worry about state law claims?" The answer, as you will discover when you get to Chapter 8, is that modern procedural law invites (sometimes *requires*) parties to bring all the claims they have that arise out of "the same transaction." Plaintiffs often have both state and federal claims that satisfy this criterion, and defendants often have counterclaims based on state law that can (sometimes must) be brought in the suit. Also state claims appear in federal question cases in virtue of provisions like FRCP 14 (allowing defendants to *implead* other parties who may be liable defendants for any sums for which they are found liable to plaintiffs). You will study this provision in Chapter 8.

Thus, to draw from the facts in *American Well Works,* suppose a patent holder sues for infringement (an arising under claim) and wants to add claims for libel because defendant claimed that *plaintiff* has no right to make or sell the item in question. If plaintiff and defendant are from the same state, or the claim does not satisfy the jurisdictional minimum for diversity cases, can the libel claim be joined with the patent claim? See American Well Works Co. v. Layne & Bowler Co., 241 U.S. 257 (1916) (the case is described in Section B3, supra).

Second, to what extent can federal courts *in diversity cases* decide claims governed by state law that do not *themselves* satisfy jurisdictional requirements? If, for example, an Idaho plaintiff sues a New Hampshire defendant in federal court in New Hampshire for injuries sustained there in a car accident, seeking recovery of $200,000, can defendant bring a counterclaim for damages to her car, if they are not enough to satisfy the minimum? Can the New Hampshire defendant bring, in the same suit, a claim against *another* New Hampshire citizen (a third party involved in the accident) on the theory that the third party was the "real" cause, and should pay defendant any moneys that the court says defendant must pay plaintiff? (FRCP 14 authorizes "impleader" claims of this sort.)

In today's world, these questions are mostly answered by a statute enacted by Congress in 1990, see 28 USC §1367, and the term in the statute for jurisdiction over claims associated with claims covered by the basic jurisdiction statutes is "supplemental jurisdiction."

1. Common Law Doctrines of Ancillary and Pendent Jurisdiction

The supplemental jurisdiction statute was enacted against a background of common law doctrines setting the parameters of what courts called "ancillary" and "pendent" jurisdiction. The concepts are related: "Ancillary" jurisdiction developed mostly in diversity cases, while "pendent" jurisdiction was mostly associated with federal question cases. We need to look at this background before reading the Court's definitive treatment of the statute itself.

The beginning point is the Court's opinion in Osborn v. Bank of the United States, 22 U.S. 738 (1874), where Chief Justice John Marshall approved federal jurisdiction in the Bank's suit to recover money levied by a state official seeking to enforce state-created tax obligations. Marshall wrote in *Osborn* that a suit may turn on "several questions of fact and law," some of which "may depend on the construction of [federal] law" while "others [may depend] on principles unconnected with that law." If federal jurisdiction exists, the court may decide the federal issues and "all the other questions" that are "incidental to this," as such other questions "cannot arrest the proceedings" and doing otherwise would mean that federal judicial power "never can be extended to a whole case."

Pendent Jurisdiction. In 1933, the Court ruled that what had come to be called "pendent jurisdiction" extended to claims based on state law in which it can be said that "two distinct grounds," one state and one federal, support "a single cause of action," even though only one is federal in nature. Hurn v. Oursler, 289 U.S. 238, 589 (1933) (jurisdiction extends to state claim for unfair competition in which the same acts supporting recovery for that tort also support the claim for copyright infringement). In a landmark decision in the *Gibbs* case more than 50 years later, the Supreme Court went further. A trucker named Gibbs had sued a labor union in federal court, alleging that its activities in a dispute with mine operators interfered with Gibbs's right to perform contractual services, and that the activities of the defendant violated the federal Labor Management Relations Act and constituted tortious interference with contract under state law. Finding the *Hurn* test "unnecessarily grudging," the Court adopted a new and broader standard:

> Pendent jurisdiction, in the sense of judicial power, exists whenever there is a claim "arising under (the) Constitution, the Laws of the United States, and Treaties made, or which shall be made, under their Authority . . . ," U.S. Const., Art. III §2, and the relationship between that claim and the state claim permits the conclusion that the entire action before the court comprises but one

constitutional "case." The federal claim must have substance sufficient to confer subject matter jurisdiction on the court. The state and federal claims must derive from a common nucleus of operative fact. But if, considered without regard to their federal or state character, a plaintiff's claims are such that he would ordinarily be expected to try them all in one judicial proceeding, then, assuming substantiality of the federal issues, there is power in federal courts to hear the whole.

United Mine Workers of America v. Gibbs, 383 U.S. 715, 725 (1966).

Gibbs went on to say that pendent jurisdiction is "a doctrine of discretion, not of plaintiff's right." In other words, the fact that federal courts have constitutional power to resolve related claims does not mean they must exercise that power. The question *whether to exercise* pendent jurisdiction over related claims turns on "considerations of judicial economy, convenience and fairness to litigants." Issues of "jury confusion in treating divergent legal theories of relief" count in deciding whether to exercise pendent jurisdiction, and federal courts should avoid "needless decisions of state law." *Gibbs* commented that if the federal claims are dismissed before trial, state claims "should be dismissed as well," and if state issues "substantially predominate, whether in terms of proof, of the scope of the issues raised, or of the comprehensiveness of the remedy sought, the state claims may be dismissed without prejudice" for resolution in state courts. The contrary conclusion is indicated if a state claim is "closely tied" to federal policy questions.

Gibbs became the foundation for the supplemental jurisdiction statute. Justice Brennan was not a shrinking violet when it came to expansive interpretations of judicial power, but even if that comment is taken as a criticism, it is fair to say that *Gibbs* was a formative and landmark case, and its influence is very much seen in the supplemental jurisdiction statute itself.

After *Gibbs*, it was only a matter of time before plaintiffs tried to use pendent jurisdiction as a means of adding not only *claims* but *parties*. (Pendent jurisdiction extended to cases in which a *defendant* brought in a third party, as could happen if a defendant sued under federal law claimed, on state law grounds, that another party should reimburse him for any federal liability to the plaintiff.) The question whether plaintiffs could use this doctrine in this way reached the Supreme Court in Aldinger v. Howard, 427 U.S. 1 (1976), and again in Finley v. United States, 490 U.S. 545 (1989). In *Aldinger,* plaintiff sued individual defendants under 42 USC §1983 for allegedly violating her constitutional rights, and tried to join a *state law* claim against the County (at the time, federal claims against counties could not be brought, but the law has since changed, and now the contrary is true): The Court held that there was no pendent jurisdiction over claims against the County because the statute conferring jurisdiction over §1983 claims (28 USC §1343) did not authorize pendent-party claims. In *Finley,* plaintiff sued the United States under the Federal Tort Claims Act (FTCA), seeking damages for negligence by the Federal Aviation Administration in operating runway lights. She tried to add claims against other defendants who could not be sued under the statute (it authorizes suits only against the government), and there was no independent basis for federal jurisdiction over these claims. Again the Court concluded that there was no pendent jurisdiction, and again the Court cited the jurisdiction-conferring statute—this time the statute conferring jurisdiction over FTA claims (28 USC §1346)—and concluded that it did not authorize joining additional parties.

Finley was the more drastic decision, in consequences for litigants: Claims under the FTA can *only* be brought in federal court (jurisdiction is *exclusively* federal), so *Finley* meant that plaintiffs in a similar position must bring two suits. *Aldinger* did not have that consequence, since §1983 claims can be brought in federal or state court. *Aldinger* and *Finley* put the decision whether to broaden jurisdiction to allow joinder of additional parties squarely into the lap of Congress.

One other critical decision affected the contours of ancillary and pendent jurisdiction—the *Kroger* case. In contrast with *Gibbs, Aldinger,* and *Finley, Kroger* was a diversity suit in which an Iowa woman sued for the death of her husband, who was electrocuted while walking next to a crane that came into contact with a power line. Defendant OPPD was a Nebraska corporation, and OPPD filed a third-party impleader complaint under FRCP 14 against Owen Equipment and Erection Co. (Owen), alleging that its operation of the crane caused the accident. Plaintiff amended her complaint to add a claim against Owen, and OPPD won summary judgment dismissing the claim against it. Plaintiff went to trial against Owen alone. The amended complaint alleged that Owen was a Nebraska corporation, and Owen had admitted as much, but in a strange turn of events Owen disclosed at trial that it was in fact an Iowa corporation, which means that plaintiff and Owen were co-citizens.[8] The trial court denied Owen's motion to dismiss, and rendered judgment against it. The Court of Appeals affirmed, but the Supreme Court disagreed. There was no "independent basis" for federal jurisdiction, and the fact that the Rules authorize both the impleader by which OPPD brought Owen into the case to begin with, and the amended complaint by which plaintiff asserted her claim against Owen, did not affect the issue ("the [Rules] do not create or withdraw federal jurisdiction"). While the *Gibbs* doctrine of "pendent jurisdiction" was another "species of the same generic problem," which is to decide when federal courts may "hear and decide state law claims arising between citizens of the same state," nevertheless jurisdiction did not exist here.

Invoking *Aldinger* and other cases, the Court concluded as follows:

> It is a fundamental precept that federal courts are courts of limited juris-diction. The limits upon federal jurisdiction, whether imposed by the

---

[8] The Missouri River (boundary between Nebraska and Iowa) had changed course in a rapid manner, moving eastward. When a river changes course quickly, it is called "avulsion" ("accretion" describes gradual change). Sensibly enough, a sudden change in a boundary river does *not* change political boundaries. This physical change put a piece of Iowa on the *west* side of the river, so it looked like part of Nebraska. But legally Crater Lake, Iowa (site of the accident; state where Owen was incorporated) remained in Iowa.

Constitution or by Congress, must be neither disregarded nor evaded. Yet under the reasoning of the Court of Appeals in this case, a plaintiff could defeat the statutory requirement of complete diversity by the simple expedient of suing only those defendants who were of diverse citizenship and waiting for them to implead nondiverse defendants.[17] If, as the Court of Appeals thought, a "common nucleus of operative fact" were the only requirement for ancillary jurisdiction in a diversity case, there would be no principled reason why the respondent in this case could not have joined her cause of action against Owen in her original complaint as ancillary to her claim against OPPD. Congress' requirement of complete diversity would thus have been evaded completely.

It is true, as the Court of Appeals noted, that the exercise of ancillary jurisdiction over nonfederal claims has often been upheld in situations involving impleader, cross-claims or counterclaims.[18] But in determining whether jurisdiction over a nonfederal claim exists, the context in which the nonfederal claim is asserted is crucial. See *Aldinger*. And the claim here arises in a setting quite different from the kinds of nonfederal claims that have been viewed in other cases as falling within the ancillary jurisdiction of the federal courts.

First, the nonfederal claim in this case was simply not ancillary to the federal one in the same sense that, for example, the impleader by a defendant of a third-party defendant always is. A third-party complaint depends at least in part upon the resolution of the primary lawsuit. Its relation to the original complaint is thus not mere factual similarity but logical dependence. The respondent's claim against the petitioner, however, was entirely separate from her original claim against OPPD, since the petitioner's liability to her depended not at all upon whether or not OPPD was also liable. Far from being an ancillary and dependent claim, it was a new and independent one.

Second, the nonfederal claim here was asserted by the plaintiff, who voluntarily chose to bring suit upon a state-law claim in a federal court. By contrast, ancillary jurisdiction typically involves claims by a defending party haled into court against his will, or by another person whose rights might be irretrievably lost unless he could assert them in an ongoing action in a federal court. A plaintiff cannot complain if ancillary jurisdiction does not encompass all of his possible claims in a case such as this one, since it is he who has chosen the federal rather than the state forum and must thus accept its limitations. "[T]he efficiency

---

[17] This is not an unlikely hypothesis, since a defendant in a tort suit such as this one would surely try to limit his liability by impleading any joint tortfeasors for indemnity or contribution. Some commentators have suggested that the possible abuse of third-party practice could be dealt with under 28 USC §1359, which forbids collusive attempts to create federal jurisdiction. The dissenting opinion today also expresses this view. But there is nothing necessarily collusive about a plaintiff's selectively suing only those tortfeasors of diverse citizenship, or about the named defendants' desire to implead joint tortfeasors. Nonetheless, the requirement of complete diversity would be eviscerated by such a course of events. [Footnote by the Court—ED.]

[18] The ancillary jurisdiction of the federal courts derives originally from cases such as Freeman v. Howe, 24 How. 450 (1860), which held that when federal jurisdiction "effectively controls the property or fund under dispute, other claimants thereto should be allowed to intervene in order to protect their interests, without regard to jurisdiction." *Aldinger*. More recently, it has been said to include cases that involve multiparty practice, such as compulsory counterclaims, impleader, crossclaims, or intervention as of right. [Footnote by the Court—ED.]

plaintiff seeks so avidly is available without question in the state courts." Kenrose Mfg. Co. v. Fred Whitaker Co., 512 F.2d 890, 894 (4th Cir. 1972).

It is not unreasonable to assume that, in generally requiring complete diversity, Congress did not intend to confine the jurisdiction of federal courts so inflexibly that they are unable to protect legal rights or effectively to resolve an entire, logically entwined lawsuit. Those practical needs are the basis of the doctrine of ancillary jurisdiction. But neither the convenience of litigants nor considerations of judicial economy can suffice to justify extension of the doctrine of ancillary jurisdiction to a plaintiff's cause of action against a citizen of the same State in a diversity case. Congress has established the basic rule that diversity jurisdiction exists under 28 USC §1332 only when there is complete diversity of citizenship. "The policy of the statute calls for its strict construction." Healy v. Ratta, 292 U.S. 263, 270 (1934). To allow the requirement of complete diversity to be circumvented as it was in this case would simply flout the congressional command.

Owen Equipment & Erection Co. v. Kroger, 437 U.S. 365, 374-377 (1978).

2. The Supplemental Jurisdiction Statute

Now read the supplemental jurisdiction statute (28 USC §1367). It is, as you will see, a provision of considerable subtlety.

To begin with, subdivision (a) creates the broadest possible federal jurisdiction, extending it as far as the Constitution allows. Thus federal courts have jurisdiction over "all other claims" joined with the claim that supported jurisdiction originally—over claims joined with claims satisfying the federal question statute (28 USC §1331) or diversity statute (28 USC §1332)—so long as the add-on claims "are so related" to the original claim "that they form part of the same case or controversy" under Article III. Do you recognize the *Gibbs* formulation? *Gibbs* described Article III jurisdiction as extending to any claim that "permits the conclusion that the entire action before the court comprises but one constitutional 'case.'" *Gibbs* went on to describe claims that are part of that single "constitutional case" as those claims that "derive from a common nucleus of operative fact," and there is every reason to believe that the statute means the same thing.

For purposes of ease in discussion, let us invent a shorthand term that *means* those claims that "comprise but one constitutional case" under the statute, or "derive from a common nucleus of operative fact" under *Gibbs*. Let us simply refer to them as "connected claims."

Now notice that subsection (a) begins with the phrase "Except as provided" in subsections (b) and (c), which warns us that there are exceptions to the broad general rule extending jurisdiction to connected claims. Subsection (b) "carves out" exceptions in diversity cases, and section (c) is a discretion clause echoing thoughts expressed in *Gibbs*. In short, subsection (a) giveth, but (b) and (c) taketh away.

We will take up points of detail after the *Exxon* case. For the moment, however, let's start with three additional broad observations:

Federal Question Cases. First, the statute *extends* federal jurisdiction to fill the gaps created in the *Aldinger* and *Finley* decisions. *Aldinger* rejected "pendent party" jurisdiction in federal question cases, and *Finley* rejected it in the special setting of the Federal Tort Claims Act, where *only* a federal court could hear the main claim. But the supplemental jurisdiction statute has *no* carve-outs in federal question cases, so *Aldinger* and *Finley* would both come out the other way today. If Abby (from Vermont) brings a federal question suit against Bob in federal court, and if she joins her related state law claims against Carl (another Vermont citizen), the federal court has supplemental jurisdiction to hear connected claims against Carl. Of course, a federal court may *decline to exercise* jurisdiction over these connected claims under subsection (c) for any of the concerns spelled out there. Still, the supplemental jurisdiction statute takes the Court up on the invitation extended in *Aldinger* and *Finley*. Congress, the Court said in those cases, had not extended jurisdiction far enough to cover such claims. Now Congress has done so.

Second, the supplemental jurisdiction statute *codifies* the exception to ancillary jurisdiction that the Court described in *Kroger*. Recall that *Kroger* said ancillary jurisdiction did not reach a claim by the original plaintiff in a diversity case against an impleaded third-party defendant brought in by the original defendant. A plaintiff may not advance such a claim (jurisdiction is lacking) if she and the impleaded third-party defendant are co-citizens, or the amount-in-controversy requirement is not met. Looking at the statute, we see that supplemental jurisdiction extends to all connected claims, but under subsection (b) such jurisdiction does *not* extend, in diversity cases, to "claims by plaintiffs against persons made parties under Rule 14." If the two are citizens of different states and the amount exceeds the jurisdictional minimum, of course, jurisdiction exists and there is no need to invoke the statute.

Third, the discretion authorized in subsection (c) matches the *Gibbs* account of discretion in some ways, but differs from *Gibbs* in others. Both *Gibbs* and the statute speak of exercising discretion to dismiss any state law claim that "substantially predominates" over claims that are the original basis for the federal suit, and both speak of dismissing state law claims if the court has dismissed claims that are the basis for the original federal suit. Only *Gibbs* mentions dismissal of state law claims on account of jury confusion, however, and only *Gibbs* mentions dismissing state law claims in order to avoid needless decisions of state law. Of course, subsection (c) has a catchall "exceptional circumstances" clause, which seems broad enough to bring in the other factors expressed in *Gibbs,* and others besides.

EXXON MOBIL CORPORATION v. ALLAPATTAH SERVICES, INC.

Supreme Court of the United States
545 U.S. 546 (2005)

KENNEDY, J., delivered the opinion of the Court, in which REHNQUIST, C.J., and SCALIA, SOUTER, and THOMAS, JJ., joined. STEVENS, J., filed a dissenting opinion, in which BREYER, J., joined. GINSBURG, J., filed a dissenting opinion, in which STEVENS, O'CONNOR, and BREYER, JJ., joined.

[This case presents a consolidated appeal from decisions in the *Exxon* case handed down by the Eleventh Circuit and the *Rosario Ortega* case handed down by the First Circuit.

In the *Exxon* case, some 10,000 Exxon dealers sued Exxon Corporation in a class action in federal court in Florida, based on diversity jurisdiction, for alleged systematic overcharges for fuel, and won a jury verdict. The trial court, which had yet to determine damages for each member of the class, certified for interlocutory appeal the question whether each member of the class had to satisfy the $75,000 jurisdictional minimum. The Eleventh Circuit concluded that §1367 rejects the *Zahn* rule, under which each member of the class did have to satisfy the minimum.

In the *Rosario Ortega* case, nine-year-old Beatriz Blanc-Ortega sued Star Kist in federal court in Puerto Rico after she cut her little finger badly on a can of tuna. She sought recovery for personal injuries, and her parents and sister brought related claims for emotional distress and, in her mother's case, for medical expenses as well. The trial court thought none of the claims satisfied the jurisdictional minimum of $75,000, and dismissed them all. The First Circuit thought the claims of Beatriz satisfied the minimum, but not those of her parents or sister, concluding that supplemental jurisdiction did not cover the latter claims.]

We hold that, where the other elements of jurisdiction are present and at least one named plaintiff in the action satisfies the amount-in-controversy requirement, §1367 does authorize supplemental jurisdiction over the claims of other plaintiffs in the same Article III case or controversy, even if those claims are for less than the jurisdictional amount specified in the statute setting forth the requirements for diversity jurisdiction. We affirm the judgment of the Court of Appeals for the Eleventh Circuit in [the *Exxon* case], and we reverse the judgment of the Court of Appeals for the First Circuit in [the *Rosario Ortega* case].

. . .

II

A

The district courts of the United States, as we have said many times, are "courts of limited jurisdiction. They possess only that power authorized by Constitution and statute." . . .

Although the district courts may not exercise jurisdiction absent a statutory basis, it is well established—in certain classes of cases—that, once a court has original jurisdiction over some claims in the action, it may exercise supplemental jurisdiction over additional claims that are part of the same case or controversy. The leading modern case for this principle is Mine Workers v. Gibbs, 383 U.S. 715 (1966). . . .

We have not . . . applied *Gibbs'* expansive interpretive approach to [certain] aspects of the jurisdictional statutes. For instance, we have consistently interpreted §1332 as requiring complete diversity: In a case with multiple plaintiffs and multiple defendants, the presence in the action of a single plaintiff from the same State as a single defendant deprives the district court of original diversity jurisdiction over the entire action. Strawbridge v. Curtiss, 3 Cranch 267 (1806); Owen Equipment & Erection Co. v. Kroger, 437 U.S. 365, 375 (1978). The complete diversity requirement is not mandated by the Constitution, State Farm Fire & Casualty Co. v. Tashire, 386 U.S. 523, 530-531 (1967), or by the plain text of §1332(a). The Court, nonetheless, has adhered to the complete diversity rule in light of the purpose of the diversity requirement, which is to provide a federal forum for important disputes where state courts might favor, or be perceived as favoring, home-state litigants. The presence of parties from the same State on both sides of a case dispels this concern, eliminating a principal reason for conferring §1332 jurisdiction over any of the claims in the action. The specific purpose of the complete diversity rule explains both why we have not adopted *Gibbs'* expansive interpretive approach to this aspect of the jurisdictional statute and why *Gibbs* does not undermine the complete diversity rule. In order for a federal court to invoke supplemental jurisdiction under *Gibbs,* it must first have original jurisdiction over at least one claim in the action. Incomplete diversity destroys original jurisdiction with respect to all claims, so there is nothing to which supplemental jurisdiction can adhere.

In contrast to the diversity requirement, most of the other statutory prerequisites for federal jurisdiction, including the federal-question and amount-in-controversy requirements, can be analyzed claim by claim. True, it does not follow by necessity from this that a district court has authority to exercise supplemental jurisdiction over all claims provided there is original jurisdiction over just one. Before the enactment of §1367, the Court declined in contexts other than the pendent-claim instance to follow *Gibbs'* expansive approach to interpretation of the jurisdictional statutes. The Court took a more restrictive view of the proper interpretation of these statutes in so-called pendent-party cases involving supplemental jurisdiction over claims involving additional parties—plaintiffs or defendants—where the district courts would lack original jurisdiction over claims by each of the parties standing alone.

Thus, with respect to plaintiff-specific jurisdictional requirements, the Court held in Clark v. Paul Gray, Inc., 306 U.S. 583 (1939), that every plaintiff must separately satisfy the amount-in-controversy requirement. Though *Clark* was a federal-question case, at that time federal-question jurisdiction had an amount-in-controversy requirement analogous to the amount-in-controversy requirement for diversity cases. "Proper practice," *Clark* held, "requires that where each of several plaintiffs is bound to establish the jurisdictional amount with respect to his own claim, the suit should be dismissed as to those who fail to show that the requisite amount is involved." The Court reaffirmed this rule, in the context of a class action brought invoking §1332(a) diversity jurisdiction, in Zahn v. International Paper Co., 414 U.S. 291 (1973). It follows "inescapably" from *Clark*, the Court held in *Zahn*, that "any plaintiff without the jurisdictional amount must be dismissed from the case, even though others allege jurisdictionally sufficient claims."

The Court took a similar approach with respect to supplemental jurisdiction over claims against additional defendants that fall outside the district courts' original jurisdiction. [The Court discusses *Aldinger, Finley, Zahn,* and *Kroger.*]

As the jurisdictional statutes existed in 1989, then, here is how matters stood: First, the diversity requirement in §1332(a) required complete diversity; absent complete diversity, the district court lacked original jurisdiction over all of the claims in the action. *Strawbridge; Kroger.* Second, if the district court had original jurisdiction over at least one claim, the jurisdictional statutes implicitly authorized supplemental jurisdiction over all other claims between the same parties arising out of the same Article III case or controversy. *Gibbs.* Third, even when the district court had original jurisdiction over one or more claims between particular parties, the jurisdictional statutes did not authorize supplemental jurisdiction over additional claims involving other parties. *Clark; Zahn; Finley.*

B

In *Finley* we emphasized that "[w]hatever we say regarding the scope of jurisdiction conferred by a particular statute can of course be changed by Congress." In 1990, Congress accepted the invitation. It passed the Judicial Improvements Act, which enacted §1367, the provision which controls these cases.

[The Court quotes 28 USC §1367(a) and (b).]

All parties to this litigation and all courts to consider the question agree that §1367 overturned the result in *Finley*. There is no warrant, however, for assuming that §1367 did no more than to overrule *Finley* and otherwise to codify the existing state of the law of supplemental jurisdiction. We must not give jurisdictional statutes a more expansive interpretation than their text warrants, but it is just as important not to adopt an artificial construction that is narrower than what the text provides. No sound canon of interpretation requires Congress to speak with extraordinary clarity in order to modify the rules of federal jurisdiction within appropriate constitutional bounds. Ordinary principles of statutory construction apply. In order to determine the scope of supplemental jurisdiction authorized by §1367, then, we must examine the statute's text in light of context, structure, and related statutory provisions.

Section 1367(a) is a broad grant of supplemental jurisdiction over other claims within the same case or controversy, as long as the action is one in which the district courts would have original jurisdiction. The last sentence of §1367(a) makes it clear that the grant of supplemental jurisdiction extends to claims involving joinder or intervention of additional parties. The single question before us, therefore, is whether a diversity case in which the claims of some plaintiffs satisfy the amount-in-controversy requirement, but the claims of other plaintiffs do not, presents a "civil action of which the district courts have original jurisdiction." If the answer is yes, §1367(a) confers supplemental jurisdiction over all claims, including those that do not independently satisfy the amount-in-controversy requirement, if the claims are part of the same Article III case or controversy. If the answer is no, §1367(a) is inapplicable and, in light of our holdings in *Clark* and *Zahn*, the district court has no statutory basis for exercising supplemental jurisdiction over the additional claims.

We now conclude the answer must be yes. When the well-pleaded complaint contains at least one claim that satisfies the amount-in-controversy requirement, and there are no other relevant jurisdictional defects, the district court, beyond all question, has original jurisdiction over that claim. The presence of other claims in the complaint, over which the district court may lack original jurisdiction, is of no moment. If the court has original jurisdiction over a single claim in the complaint, it has original jurisdiction over a "civil action" within the meaning of §1367(a), even if the civil action over which it has jurisdiction comprises fewer claims than were included in the complaint. Once the court determines it has original jurisdiction over the civil action, it can turn to the question whether it has a constitutional and statutory basis for exercising supplemental jurisdiction over the other claims in the action.

[Summarizing §1367, the Court concludes that there is no "meaningful" or "substantive" distinction between ancillary and pendent jurisdiction.]

If §1367(a) were the sum total of the relevant statutory language, our holding would rest on that language alone. The statute, of course, instructs us to examine §1367(b) to determine if any of its exceptions apply, so we proceed to that section. While §1367(b) qualifies the broad rule of §1367(a), it does not withdraw supplemental jurisdiction over the claims of the additional parties at issue here. The specific exceptions to §1367(a) contained in §1367(b), moreover, provide additional support for our conclusion that §1367(a) confers supplemental jurisdiction over these claims. Section 1367(b), which applies only to diversity cases, withholds supplemental jurisdiction over the claims of plaintiffs proposed to be joined as indispensable parties under Federal Rule of Civil Procedure 19, or who seek to intervene pursuant to Rule 24. Nothing in the text of §1367(b), however, withholds supplemental jurisdiction over the claims of plaintiffs permissively joined under Rule 20 (like the additional plaintiffs in [*Rosario Ortega*]) or certified as class-action members pursuant to Rule 23 (like the additional plaintiffs in [*Exxon*]). The natural, indeed the necessary, inference is that §1367 confers supplemental jurisdiction over claims by Rule 20 and Rule 23 plaintiffs. This inference, at least with respect to Rule 20 plaintiffs, is strengthened by the fact that §1367(b) explicitly excludes supplemental jurisdiction over claims against defendants joined under Rule 20.

We cannot accept the view, urged by some of the parties, commentators, and Courts of Appeals, that a district court lacks original jurisdiction over a civil action unless the court has original jurisdiction over every claim in the complaint. As we understand this position, it requires assuming either that all claims in the complaint must stand or fall as a single, indivisible "civil action" as a matter of definitional necessity—what we will refer to as the "indivisibility theory"—or else that the inclusion of a claim or party falling outside the district court's original jurisdiction somehow contaminates every other claim in the complaint, depriving the court of original jurisdiction over any of these claims—what we will refer to as the "contamination theory."

The indivisibility theory is easily dismissed, as it is inconsistent with the whole notion of supplemental jurisdiction. If a district court must have original jurisdiction over every claim in the complaint in order to have "original jurisdiction" over a "civil action," then in *Gibbs* there was no civil action of which the district court could assume original jurisdiction under §1331, and so no basis for exercising supplemental jurisdiction over any of the claims. The indivisibility theory is further belied by our practice—in both federal-question and diversity cases—of allowing federal courts to cure jurisdictional defects by dismissing the offending parties rather than dismissing the entire action. *Clark,* for example, makes clear that claims that are jurisdictionally defective as to amount in controversy do not destroy original jurisdiction over other claims. *Clark* (dismissing parties who failed to meet the amount-in-controversy requirement but retaining jurisdiction over the remaining party). If the presence of jurisdictionally problematic claims in the complaint meant the district court was without original jurisdiction over the single, indivisible civil action before it, then the district court would have to dismiss the whole action rather than particular parties.

We also find it unconvincing to say that the definitional indivisibility theory applies in the context of diversity cases but not in the context of federal-question cases. The broad and general language of the statute does not permit this result. The contention is premised on the notion that the phrase "original jurisdiction of all civil actions" means different things in §§1331 and 1332. It is implausible, however, to say that the identical phrase means one thing (original jurisdiction in all actions where at least one claim in the complaint meets the following requirements) in §1331 and something else (original jurisdiction in all actions where every claim in the complaint meets the following requirements) in §1332.

The contamination theory, as we have noted, can make some sense in the special context of the complete diversity requirement because the presence of nondiverse parties on both sides of a lawsuit eliminates the justification for providing a federal forum. The theory, however, makes little sense with respect to the amount-in-controversy requirement, which is meant to ensure that a dispute is sufficiently important to warrant federal-court attention. The presence of a single nondiverse party may eliminate the fear of bias with respect to all claims, but the presence of a claim that falls short of the minimum amount in controversy does nothing to reduce the importance of the claims that do meet this requirement.

It is fallacious to suppose, simply from the proposition that §1332 imposes both the diversity requirement and the amount-in-controversy requirement, that the contamination theory germane to the former is also relevant to the latter. There is no inherent logical connection between the amount-in-controversy requirement and §1332 diversity jurisdiction. After all, federal-question jurisdiction once had an amount-in-controversy requirement as well. If such a requirement were revived under §1331, it is clear beyond peradventure that §1367(a) provides supplemental jurisdiction over federal-question cases where some, but not all, of the federal-law claims involve a sufficient amount in controversy. In other words, §1367(a) unambiguously overrules the holding and the result in *Clark*. If that is so, however, it would be quite extraordinary to say that §1367 did not also overrule *Zahn*, a case that was premised in substantial part on the holding in *Clark*.

. . .

We also reject the argument . . . that while the presence of additional claims over which the district court lacks jurisdiction does not mean the civil action is outside the purview of §1367(a), the presence of additional parties does. The basis for this distinction is not altogether clear, and it is in considerable tension with statutory text. Section 1367(a) applies by its terms to any civil action of which the district courts have original jurisdiction, and the last sentence of §1367(a) expressly contemplates that the court may have supplemental jurisdiction over additional parties. So it cannot be the case that the presence of those parties destroys the court's original jurisdiction, within the meaning of §1367(a), over a civil action otherwise properly before it. Also, §1367(b) expressly withholds supplemental jurisdiction in diversity cases over claims by plaintiffs joined as indispensable parties under Rule 19. If joinder of such parties were sufficient to deprive the district court of original jurisdiction over the civil action within the meaning of §1367(a), this specific limitation on supplemental jurisdiction in §1367(b) would be superfluous. The argument that the presence of additional parties removes the civil action from the scope of §1367(a) also would mean that §1367 left the *Finley* result undisturbed. *Finley,* after all, involved a Federal Tort Claims Act suit against a federal defendant and state-law claims against additional defendants not otherwise subject to federal jurisdiction. Yet all concede that one purpose of §1367 was to change the result reached in *Finley.*

Finally, it is suggested that our interpretation of §1367(a) creates an anomaly regarding the exceptions listed in §1367(b): It is not immediately obvious why Congress would withhold supplemental jurisdiction over plaintiffs joined as parties "needed for just adjudication" under Rule 19 but would allow supplemental jurisdiction over plaintiffs permissively joined under Rule 20. The omission of Rule 20 plaintiffs from the list of exceptions in §1367(b) may have been an "unintentional drafting gap." If that is the case, it is up to Congress rather than the courts to fix it. The omission may seem odd, but it is not absurd. An alternative explanation for the different treatment of Rules 19 and 20 is that Congress was concerned that extending supplemental jurisdiction to Rule 19 plaintiffs would allow circumvention of the complete diversity rule: A nondiverse plaintiff might be omitted intentionally from the original action, but joined later under Rule 19 as a necessary party. The contamination theory described above, if applicable, means this ruse would fail, but Congress may have wanted to make assurance double sure. More generally, Congress may have concluded that federal jurisdiction is only appropriate if the district court would have original jurisdiction over the claims of all those plaintiffs who are so essential to the action that they could be joined under Rule 19.

To the extent that the omission of Rule 20 plaintiffs from the list of §1367(b) exceptions is anomalous, moreover, it is no more anomalous than the inclusion of Rule 19 plaintiffs in that list would be if the alternative view of §1367(a) were to prevail. If the district court lacks original jurisdiction over a civil diversity action where any plaintiff's claims fail to comply with all the requirements of §1332, there is no need for a special §1367(b) exception for Rule 19 plaintiffs who do not meet these requirements. Though the omission of Rule 20 plaintiffs from §1367(b) presents something of a puzzle on our view of the statute, the inclusion of Rule 19 plaintiffs in this section is at least as difficult to explain under the alternative view.

And so we circle back to the original question. When the well-pleaded complaint in district court includes multiple claims, all part of the same case or controversy, and some, but not all, of the claims are within the court's original jurisdiction, does the court have before it "any civil action of which the district courts have original jurisdiction"? It does. Under §1367, the court has original jurisdiction over the civil action comprising the claims for which there is no jurisdictional defect. No other reading of §1367 is plausible in light of the text and structure of the jurisdictional statute. Though the special nature and purpose of the diversity requirement mean that a single nondiverse party can contaminate every other claim in the lawsuit, the contamination does not occur with respect to jurisdictional defects that go only to the substantive importance of individual claims.

It follows from this conclusion that the threshold requirement of §1367(a) is satisfied in cases, like those now before us, where some, but not all, of the plaintiffs in a diversity action allege a sufficient amount in controversy. We hold that §1367 by its plain text overruled *Clark* and *Zahn* and authorized supplemental jurisdiction over all claims by diverse parties arising out of the same Article III case or controversy, subject only to enumerated exceptions not applicable in the cases now before us.

C

The proponents of the alternative view of §1367 insist that the statute is at least ambiguous and that we should look to other interpretive tools, including the legislative history of §1367, which supposedly demonstrate Congress did not intend §1367 to overrule *Zahn.* We can reject this argument at the very outset simply because §1367 is not ambiguous. For the reasons elaborated above, interpreting §1367 to foreclose supplemental jurisdiction over plaintiffs in diversity cases who do not meet the minimum amount in controversy is inconsistent with the text, read in light of other statutory provisions and our established jurisprudence. Even if we were to stipulate, however, that the reading these proponents urge upon us is textually plausible, the legislative history cited to support it would not alter our view as to the best interpretation of §1367.

Those who urge that the legislative history refutes our interpretation rely primarily on the House Judiciary Committee Report on the Judicial Improvements Act. This Report explained that §1367 would "authorize jurisdiction in a case like *Finley,* as well as essentially restore the pre-*Finley* understandings of the authorization for and limits on other forms of supplemental jurisdiction." The Report stated that §1367(a) "generally authorizes the district court to exercise jurisdiction over a supplemental claim whenever it forms part of the same constitutional case or controversy as the claim or claims that provide the basis of the district court's original jurisdiction," and in so doing codifies *Gibbs* and fills the statutory gap recognized in *Finley.* The Report then remarked that

§1367(b) "is not intended to affect the jurisdictional requirements of [§1332] in diversity-only class actions, as those requirements were interpreted prior to *Finley*," citing, without further elaboration, *Zahn* and Supreme Tribe of Ben-Hur v. Cauble, 255 U.S. 356 (1921). The Report noted that the "net effect" of §1367(b) was to implement the "principal rationale" of *Kroger*, effecting only "one small change" in pre-*Finley* practice with respect to diversity actions: §1367(b) would exclude "Rule 23(a) plaintiff-intervenors to the same extent as those sought to be joined as plaintiffs under Rule 19." (It is evident that the report here meant to refer to Rule 24, not Rule 23.)

As we have repeatedly held, the authoritative statement is the statutory text, not the legislative history or any other extrinsic material. Extrinsic materials have a role in statutory interpretation only to the extent they shed a reliable light on the enacting Legislature's understanding of otherwise ambiguous terms. Not all extrinsic materials are reliable sources of insight into legislative understandings, however, and legislative history in particular is vulnerable to two serious criticisms. First, legislative history is itself often murky, ambiguous, and contradictory. Judicial investigation of legislative history has a tendency to become, to borrow Judge Leventhal's memorable phrase, an exercise in "'looking over a crowd and picking out your friends.'" See Wald, Some Observations on the Use of Legislative History in the 1981 Supreme Court Term, 68 Iowa L. Rev. 195, 214 (1983). Second, judicial reliance on legislative materials like committee reports, which are not themselves subject to the requirements of Article I, may give unrepresentative committee members—or, worse yet, unelected staffers and lobbyists—both the power and the incentive to attempt strategic manipulations of legislative history to secure results they were unable to achieve through the statutory text. We need not comment here on whether these problems are sufficiently prevalent to render legislative history inherently unreliable in all circumstances, a point on which Members of this Court have disagreed. It is clear, however, that in this instance both criticisms are right on the mark.

First of all, the legislative history of §1367 is far murkier than selective quotation from the House Report would suggest. The text of §1367 is based substantially on a draft proposal contained in a Federal Court Study Committee working paper, which was drafted by a Subcommittee chaired by Judge Posner. See also Judicial Conference of the United States, Report of the Federal Courts Study Committee 47-48 (Apr. 2, 1990) (Study Committee Report) (echoing, in brief summary form, the Subcommittee Working Paper proposal and noting that the Subcommittee Working Paper "contains additional material on this subject"); House Report ("[Section 1367] implements a recommendation of the Federal Courts Study Committee found on pages 47 and 48 of its Report"). While the Subcommittee explained, in language echoed by the House Report, that its proposal "basically restores the law as it existed prior to *Finley*," it observed in a footnote that its proposal would overrule

Zahn and that this would be a good idea. Although the Federal Courts Study Committee did not expressly adopt the Subcommittee's specific reference to *Zahn*, it neither explicitly disagreed with the Subcommittee's conclusion that this was the best reading of the proposed text nor substantially modified the proposal to avoid this result. Therefore, even if the House Report could fairly be read to reflect an understanding that the text of §1367 did not overrule *Zahn*, the Subcommittee Working Paper on which §1367 was based reflected the opposite understanding. The House Report is no more authoritative than the Subcommittee Working Paper. The utility of either can extend no further than the light it sheds on how the enacting Legislature understood the statutory text. Trying to figure out how to square the Subcommittee Working Paper's understanding with the House Report's understanding, or which is more reflective of the understanding of the enacting legislators, is a hopeless task.

Second, the worst fears of critics who argue legislative history will be used to circumvent the Article I process were realized in this case. The telltale evidence is the statement, by three law professors who participated in drafting §1367, see House Report, that §1367 "on its face" permits "supplemental jurisdiction over claims of class members that do not satisfy section 1332's jurisdictional amount requirement, which would overrule [*Zahn*]. [There is] a disclaimer of intent to accomplish this result in the legislative history. . . . It would have been better had the statute dealt explicitly with this problem, and the legislative history was an attempt to correct the oversight." Rowe, Burbank, & Mengler, Compounding or Creating Confusion About Supplemental Jurisdiction? A Reply to Professor Freer, 40 Emory L.J. 943, 960, n.90 (1991). The professors were frank to concede that if one refuses to consider the legislative history, one has no choice but to "conclude that section 1367 has wiped *Zahn* off the books." So there exists an acknowledgment, by parties who have detailed, specific knowledge of the statute and the drafting process, both that the plain text of §1367 overruled *Zahn* and that language to the contrary in the House Report was a *post hoc* attempt to alter that result. One need not subscribe to the wholesale condemnation of legislative history to refuse to give any effect to such a deliberate effort to amend a statute through a committee report.

In sum, even if we believed resort to legislative history were appropriate in these cases—a point we do not concede—we would not give significant weight to the House Report. The distinguished jurists who drafted the Subcommittee Working Paper, along with three of the participants in the drafting of §1367, agree that this provision, on its face, overrules *Zahn*. This accords with the best reading of the statute's text, and nothing in the legislative history indicates directly and explicitly that Congress understood the phrase "civil action of which the district courts have original jurisdiction" to exclude cases in which some but not all of the diversity plaintiffs meet the amount-in-controversy requirement.

No credence, moreover, can be given to the claim that, if Congress understood §1367 to overrule *Zahn*, the proposal would have been more controversial. We have little sense whether any Member of Congress would have been particularly upset by this result. This is not a case where one can plausibly say that concerned legislators might not have realized the possible effect of the text they were adopting. Certainly, any competent legislative aide who studied the matter would have flagged this issue if it were a matter of importance to his or her boss, especially in light of the Subcommittee Working Paper. There are any number of reasons why legislators did not spend more time arguing over §1367, none of which are relevant to our interpretation of what the words of the statute mean.

D

Finally, we note that the Class Action Fairness Act (CAFA) enacted this year, has no bearing on our analysis of these cases. Subject to certain limitations, the CAFA confers federal diversity jurisdiction over class actions where the aggregate amount in controversy exceeds $5 million. It abrogates the rule against aggregating claims, a rule this Court recognized in *Ben-Hur* and reaffirmed in *Zahn*. The CAFA, however, is not retroactive, and the views of the 2005 Congress are not relevant to our interpretation of a text enacted by Congress in 1990. The CAFA, moreover, does not moot the significance of our interpretation of §1367, as many proposed exercises of supplemental jurisdiction, even in the class-action context, might not fall within the CAFA's ambit. The CAFA, then, has no impact, one way or the other, on our interpretation of §1367.

. . .

The judgment of the Court of Appeals for the Eleventh Circuit is affirmed. The judgment of the Court of Appeals for the First Circuit is reversed, and the case is remanded for proceedings consistent with this opinion.

It is so ordered.

[The dissenting opinion of Justice Stevens, with whom Justice Breyer joins, is omitted.]

Justice GINSBURG, with whom Justice STEVENS, Justice O'CONNOR, and Justice BREYER join, dissenting.

. . .

The Court adopts a plausibly broad reading of §1367, a measure that is hardly a model of the careful drafter's art. There is another plausible reading, however, one less disruptive of our jurisprudence regarding supplemental jurisdiction. If one reads §1367(a) to instruct, as the statute's text suggests, that the district court must first have "original jurisdiction" over a "civil action" before supplemental jurisdiction can attach, then *Clark* and *Zahn* are preserved, and supplemental jurisdiction does not open the way for joinder of plaintiffs, or inclusion of class members, who do not independently meet the amount-in-controversy requirement. For the reasons that follow, I conclude that this narrower construction is the better reading of §1367.

. . .

II

A

Section 1367, by its terms, operates only in civil actions "of which the district courts have original jurisdiction." The "original jurisdiction" relevant here is diversity-of-citizenship jurisdiction, conferred by §1332. The character of that jurisdiction is the essential backdrop for comprehension of §1367.

The Constitution broadly provides for federal-court jurisdiction in controversies "between Citizens of different States." This Court has read that provision to demand no more than "minimal diversity," *i.e.,* so long as one party on the plaintiffs' side and one party on the defendants' side are of diverse citizenship, Congress may authorize federal courts to exercise diversity jurisdiction. Further, the Constitution includes no amount-in-controversy limitation on the exercise of federal jurisdiction. But from the start, Congress, as its measures have been construed by this Court, has limited federal-court exercise of diversity jurisdiction in two principal ways. First, unless Congress specifies otherwise, diversity must be "complete," *i.e.,* all parties on plaintiffs' side must be diverse from all parties on defendants' side. Strawbridge v. Curtiss, 3 Cranch 267 (1806). Second, each plaintiff's stake must independently meet the amount-in-controversy specification: "When two or more plaintiffs, having separate and distinct demands, unite for convenience and economy in a single suit, it is essential that the demand of each be of the requisite jurisdictional amount." Troy Bank v. G.A. Whitehead & Co., 222 U.S. 39, 40 (1911).

The statute today governing federal-court exercise of diversity jurisdiction in the generality of cases, §1332, like all its predecessors, incorporates both a diverse-citizenship requirement and an amount-in-controversy specification.[5] As to the latter, the statute reads: "The district courts shall have original

---

[5] Endeavoring to preserve the "complete diversity" rule first stated in *Strawbridge* (1806), the Court's opinion drives a wedge between the two components of 28 USC §1332, treating the diversity-of-citizenship requirement as essential, the amount-in-controversy requirement as more readily disposable. Section 1332 itself, however, does not rank order the two requirements. What "[o]rdinary principl[e] of statutory construction" or "sound canon of interpretation," allows the Court to slice up §1332 this way? In partial explanation, the Court asserts that amount in controversy can be analyzed claim by claim, but the diversity requirement cannot. It is not altogether clear why that should be so. The cure for improper joinder of a nondiverse party is the same as the cure for improper joinder of a plaintiff who does not satisfy the jurisdictional amount. In both cases, original jurisdiction can be preserved by dismissing the nonqualifying party. See Caterpillar Inc. v. Lewis, 519 U.S. 61, 64 (1996) (diversity); Newman-Green, Inc. v. Alfonzo-Larrain, 490 U.S. 826, 836-838 (1989) (same); *Zahn,* 414 U.S., at 295 (amount in controversy); Clark v. Paul Gray, Inc., 306 U.S. 583, 590 (1939) (same).

jurisdiction [in diversity-of-citizenship cases] where the matter in controversy exceeds the sum . . . of $75,000." §1332(a). This Court has long held that, in determining whether the amount-in-controversy requirement has been satisfied, a single plaintiff may aggregate two or more claims against a single defendant, even if the claims are unrelated. But in multiparty cases, including class actions, we have unyieldingly adhered to the nonaggregation rule stated in *Troy Bank.*

This Court most recently addressed "[t]he meaning of [§1332's] 'matter in controversy' language" in *Zahn. Zahn,* like Snyder v. Harris, 394 U.S. 332 (1969), decided four years earlier, was a class action. In *Snyder,* no class member had a claim large enough to satisfy the jurisdictional amount. But in *Zahn,* the named plaintiffs had such claims. Nevertheless, the Court declined to depart from its "longstanding construction of the 'matter in controversy' requirement of §1332." . . . The rule that each plaintiff must independently satisfy the amount-in-controversy requirement, unless Congress expressly orders otherwise, was thus the solidly established reading of §1332 when Congress enacted [§1367].

B

These cases present the question whether Congress abrogated the nonaggregation rule long tied to §1332 when it enacted §1367. In answering that question, "context [should provide] a crucial guide." [The dissent quotes the appellate court opinion in *Rosario.*] The Court should assume, as it ordinarily does, that Congress legislated against a background of law already in place and the historical development of that law. Here, that background is the statutory grant of diversity jurisdiction, the amount-in-controversy condition that Congress, from the start, has tied to the grant, and the nonaggregation rule this Court has long applied to the determination of the "matter in controversy."

[The dissent quotes 28 USC §1367(a).]

The Court is unanimous in reading §1367(a) to permit pendent-party jurisdiction in federal-question cases, and thus, to overrule *Finley.* The basic jurisdictional grant, §1331, provides that "[t]he district courts shall have original jurisdiction of all civil actions arising under the Constitution, laws, or treaties of the United States." Since 1980, §1331 has contained no amount-in-controversy requirement. Once there is a civil action presenting a qualifying claim arising under federal law, §1331's sole requirement is met. District courts, we have held, may then adjudicate, additionally, state-law claims "deriv[ing] from a common nucleus of operative fact." *Gibbs.* Section 1367(a) enlarges that category to include not only state-law claims against the defendant named in the federal claim, but also "[state-law] claims that involve the joinder or intervention of additional parties."

The Court divides, however, on the impact of §1367(a) on diversity cases controlled by §1332. Under the majority's reading, §1367(a) permits the joinder of related claims cut loose from the nonaggregation rule that has long attended actions under §1332. Only the claims specified in §1367(b) would be excluded from §1367(a)'s expansion of §1332's grant of diversity jurisdiction. And because §1367(b) contains no exception for joinder of plaintiffs under Rule 20 or class actions under Rule 23, the Court concludes, *Clark* and *Zahn* have been overruled.[8]

The Court's reading is surely plausible, especially if one detaches §1367(a) from its context and attempts no reconciliation with prior interpretations of §1332's amount-in-controversy requirement. But §1367(a)'s text, as the First Circuit held, can be read another way, one that would involve no rejection of *Clark* and *Zahn.*

As explained by the First Circuit in *Rosario Ortega* . . . §1367(a) addresses "civil action[s] of which the district courts have original jurisdiction," a formulation that, in diversity cases, is sensibly read to incorporate the rules on joinder and aggregation tightly tied to §1332 at the time of §1367's enactment. On this reading, a complaint must first meet that "original jurisdiction" measurement. If it does not, no supplemental jurisdiction is authorized. If it does, §1367(a) authorizes "supplemental jurisdiction" over related claims. In other words, §1367(a) would preserve undiminished, as part and parcel of §1332 "original jurisdiction" determinations, both the "complete diversity" rule and the decisions restricting aggregation to arrive at the amount in controversy.[9] Section 1367(b)'s office, then, would be "to prevent the erosion of the complete diversity [and amount-in-controversy] requirement[s] that might otherwise result from an expansive application of what was once termed the doctrine of ancillary jurisdiction." See Pfander, Supplemental Jurisdiction and Section 1367: The Case for a Sympathetic Textualism, 148 U. Pa. L. Rev. 109, 114 (1999). In contrast to the Court's construction of §1367, which draws a sharp line between the diversity and amount-in-controversy components of §1332, the interpretation presented here does not sever the two jurisdictional requirements.

The more restrained reading of §1367 just outlined would yield affirmance of the First Circuit's judgment in *Rosario Ortega,* and reversal of the Eleventh Circuit's judgment in *Exxon.* It would not discard entirely, as the Court does, the judicially developed doctrines of pendent and ancillary jurisdiction as they

---

[8] Under the Court's construction of §1367, Beatriz Ortega's family members can remain in the action because their joinder is merely permissive, see FRCP 20. If, however, their presence was "needed for just adjudication," Rule 19, their dismissal would be required. The inclusion of those who may join, and exclusion of those who should or must join, defies rational explanation. . . .

[9] On this reading of §1367(a), it is immaterial that §1367(b) "does not withdraw supplemental jurisdiction over the claims of the additional parties at issue here." Because those claims would not come within §1367(a) in the first place, Congress would have had no reason to list them in §1367(b).

existed when *Finley* was decided. Instead, it would recognize §1367 essentially as a codification of those doctrines, placing them under a single heading, but largely retaining their substance, with overriding *Finley* the only basic change: Supplemental jurisdiction, once the district court has original jurisdiction, would now include "claims that involve the joinder or intervention of additional parties." §1367(a).

Pendent jurisdiction, as earlier explained, applied only in federal-question cases and allowed plaintiffs to attach nonfederal claims to their jurisdiction-qualifying claims. Ancillary jurisdiction applied primarily, although not exclusively, in diversity cases and "typically involve[d] claims *by a defending party* haled into court against his will." *Kroger.* As the First Circuit observed [in the *Rosario Ortega* case], neither doctrine permitted a plaintiff to circumvent the dual requirements of §1332 (diversity of citizenship and amount in controversy) "simply by joining her [jurisdictionally inadequate] claim in an action brought by [a] jurisdictionally competent diversity plaintiff."

. . .

The less disruptive view I take of §1367 also accounts for the omission of Rule 20 plaintiffs and Rule 23 class actions in §1367(b)'s text. If one reads §1367(a) as a plenary grant of supplemental jurisdiction to federal courts sitting in diversity, one would indeed look for exceptions in §1367(b). Finding none for permissive joinder of parties or class actions, one would conclude that Congress effectively, even if unintentionally, overruled *Clark* and *Zahn*. But if one recognizes that the nonaggregation rule delineated in *Clark* and *Zahn* forms part of the determination whether "original jurisdiction" exists in a diversity case, then plaintiffs who do not meet the amount-in-controversy requirement would fail at the §1367(a) threshold. Congress would have no reason to resort to a §1367(b) exception to turn such plaintiffs away from federal court, given that their claims, from the start, would fall outside the court's §1332 jurisdiction. See Pfander, *supra,* at 148.

. . .

What is the utility of §1367(b) under my reading of §1367(a)? Section 1367(a) allows parties other than the plaintiff to assert reactive claims once entertained under the heading ancillary jurisdiction. [Justice Ginsburg lists "claims, including compulsory counterclaims and impleader claims, over which federal courts routinely exercised ancillary jurisdiction."] As earlier observed, §1367(b) stops plaintiffs from circumventing §1332's jurisdictional requirements by using another's claim as a hook to add a claim that the plaintiff could not have brought in the first instance. *Kroger* is the paradigm case. There, the Court held that ancillary jurisdiction did not extend to a plaintiff's claim against a nondiverse party who had been impleaded by the defendant under Rule 14. Section 1367(b), then, is corroborative of §1367(a)'s coverage of claims formerly called ancillary, but provides exceptions to ensure that accommodation of added claims would not fundamentally alter "the jurisdictional requirements of section 1332." See Pfander, 148 U. Pa. L. Rev., at 135-137.

While §1367's enigmatic text defies flawless interpretation,[13] the precedent-preservative reading, I am persuaded, better accords with the historical and legal context of Congress' enactment of the supplemental jurisdiction statute, and the established limits on pendent and ancillary jurisdiction. It does not attribute to Congress a jurisdictional enlargement broader than the one to which the legislators adverted, cf. *Finley,* and it follows the sound counsel that "close questions of [statutory] construction should be resolved in favor of continuity and against change," Shapiro, Continuity and Change in Statutory Interpretation, 67 N.Y.U. L. Rev. 921, 925 (1992).

. . .

For the reasons stated, I would hold that §1367 does not overrule *Clark* and *Zahn.* I would therefore affirm the judgment of the Court of Appeals for the First Circuit and reverse the judgment of the Court of Appeals for the Eleventh Circuit.

■ NOTES ON FEDERAL SUPPLEMENTAL JURISDICTION AFTER *EXXON*

1. As you can tell from this 5-4 opinion and the vigor of the arguments, *Exxon* presented an exceptionally difficult issue. The stakes were thought to be high. It is easier to describe the effect of the opinion than to explain the reasoning: First, in an ordinary diversity suit, if the complete diversity requirement is satisfied, and one plaintiff has a claim against a defendant that exceeds the jurisdictional minimum, there is supplemental jurisdiction to hear "undersized claims" by another plaintiff against the same defendant (claims that do not satisfy the amount-in-controversy requirement). This is the *Rosario Ortega* case. Second, in a class suit in federal court on diversity jurisdiction, if the diversity requirement is satisfied (standard bearer diverse from defendants), and if the standard bearer's claim satisfies the amount-in-controversy requirement, there is supplemental jurisdiction to hear undersized claims by class members. This is the *Exxon* case.

---

[13] If §1367(a) itself renders unnecessary the listing of Rule 20 plaintiffs and Rule 23 class actions in §1367(b), then it is similarly unnecessary to refer, as §1367(b) does, to "persons proposed to be joined as plaintiffs under Rule 19." On one account, Congress bracketed such persons with persons "seeking to intervene as plaintiffs under Rule 24" to modify pre-§1367 practice. Before enactment of §1367, courts entertained, under the heading ancillary jurisdiction, claims of Rule 24(a) intervenors "of right," see *Kroger,* but denied ancillary jurisdiction over claims of "necessary" Rule 19 plaintiffs. Congress may have sought simply to underscore that those seeking to join as plaintiffs, whether under Rule 19 or Rule 24, should be treated alike, *i.e.,* denied joinder when "inconsistent with the jurisdictional requirements of section 1332." See 370 F.3d, at 140, and n.15.

2. Why the problem in *Exxon* and *Rosario Ortega*? Is it because §1367(a) confers jurisdiction over connected claims, subject in diversity cases *only* to "carve-outs" in §1367(b) *and* there is no carve-out for "claims by persons proposed to be joined as plaintiffs under Rule 20 or members of plaintiff class under Rule 23"? The statute *does* include carve-outs for "persons proposed to be joined as plaintiffs under Rule 19 . . . or seeking to intervene as plaintiffs under Rule 24." You have not yet looked at FRCP 19, 20, or 24 (see Chapter 8C2, infra). FRCP 19 applies to plaintiffs who *must be included* to make "complete relief" possible, or because their interests might be "impair[ed] or impede[d]" by the outcome, or their absence would expose parties in the suit to substantial risks of "incurring double, multiple, or otherwise inconsistent obligations." Loosely speaking, such plaintiffs are "necessary" or "indispensable," and *must be* joined. Similarly, FRCP 24 applies to persons entitled to "intervene" because their interests may be "impair[ed] or impede[d]." Loosely speaking, such plaintiffs are "intervenors of right." FRCP 20 applies to plaintiffs with claims "arising out of the same transaction, occurrence, or series of transactions or occurrences" in the suit, where "questions of law or fact common to all" arise. Loosely speaking, these are "optional" plaintiffs, who *can be* joined, but are not necessary. Read *literally,* the statute says there *is* supplemental jurisdiction for claims by optional plaintiffs, but *not* for claims by indispensable plaintiffs or intervenors of right. Does this result make sense?

(a) Should supplemental jurisdiction reach more essential parties, rather than less essential ones? Note Justice Ginsburg's comment (footnote 8): "The inclusion of those who may join, and exclusion of those who should or must join, defies rational explanation." If she's right, the statute has it backward.

(b) Is it possible that the statute is *right* in barring supplemental jurisdiction for claims by the more essential plaintiffs? Is it wiser to apply the concept of supplemental jurisdiction to claims and parties only if, before considering those, we already have a "whole lawsuit" that could go forward on its own? If we allowed use of supplemental jurisdiction to create a suit that could not be in federal court *without it,* wouldn't we be making a huge hole in the complete diversity and amount-in-controversy requirements? See, e.g., Picciotto v. Continental Cas. Co., 512 F.3d 9, 20-21 (1st Cir. 2009) ("the Rule 19(b) indispensability determination means there is no viable lawsuit without the missing party," and "plain language" of 1367 "incorporates this well established requirement that there be a viable action over which the district court has 'original jurisdiction' before supplemental jurisdiction may be considered").

(c) Could the statute contain a mistake—what the Court calls a "drafting gap"? The framers carved out an exception barring supplemental jurisdiction in diversity cases for plaintiffs named under FRCP 19 or 24 (already in statute), but accidentally *left out* a reference to FRCP 20 by oversight? If so,

should the Court do what the framers *meant*, or apply the language of the statute?

3. The *Rosario Ortega* case asks whether, in an ordinary suit where the complete diversity requirement is satisfied and at least one claimant seeks more than the jurisdictional minimum from a defendant, there is supplemental jurisdiction over undersized claims by other claimants against the same defendant. The majority opinion says yes. Recall that §1367 answers the *other side* of this question: If one plaintiff sues two defendants, advancing a claim that satisfies the amount-in-controversy requirement against the first defendant and an undersized claim against the second, there is no supplemental jurisdiction over the latter. See 28 USC §1367(b) (carving out exception in diversity cases for "claims by plaintiffs against persons made parties under Rule . . . 20"). Does it make sense to say yes in one case and no in the other?

4. On their facts, the cases reviewed in *Exxon* did not present problems with the "complete diversity" rule. All plaintiffs were diverse from all defendants (one defendant in *Exxon,* more than one in *Rosario Ortega*). Suppose Mason (Ohio) and Neva (Indiana) sue Oswald (Indiana), each seeking more than $75,000, and join as plaintiffs because the suit involves a single automobile accident. Does §1367 create supplemental jurisdiction to hear Neva's claim?

(a) Under the "plain meaning" approach (the majority in *Exxon* says "the authoritative statement is the statutory text"), the statute *does not* withhold supplemental jurisdiction over Neva's claims against Oswald—if there were a carve-out in §1367(b) for "claims by persons proposed to be joined as plaintiffs under Rule 20," then we would know Neva could not join because she is a citizen of Indiana and her presence would destroy complete diversity (no supplemental jurisdiction). Recall that it is the absence of this language that led to the conclusion that an undersized claim is covered by supplemental jurisdiction (note 2, supra).

(b) Despite the conclusion indicated above as the product of the plain meaning approach, the majority in *Exxon* says the "complete diversity" requirement survives! It comments that *Gibbs's* "expansive approach" has not been applied to modify the "complete diversity" rule. The majority then says a court must "first have" original jurisdiction over "at least one claim," and incomplete diversity "destroys original jurisdiction with respect to all claims, so there is nothing to which supplemental jurisdiction can adhere."

(c) If the "complete diversity" requirement survives, but the amount-in-controversy requirement was changed, the opinion "drives a wedge between the two components," doesn't it? Justice Ginsburg makes this charge. It's even worse than that, isn't it? The majority takes a plain meaning approach to the amount-in-controversy requirement (which it calls "readily disposable"), but a policy-based approach to the complete diversity requirement (which it calls "essential"), and it is for *that* reason that the missing

carve-out described above changes the amount-in-controversy requirement but not the complete diversity requirement.

(d) Is complete diversity more fundamental than amount in controversy? A diversity requirement (although not a *complete* diversity requirement) is in the Constitution (Art. III §2), but the amount-in-controversy requirement is not. Before *Exxon,* the Court had construed the *complete diversity* requirement in class suits as meaning that diversity is necessary only between standard bearer(s) and defendant(s), see Supreme Tribe of Ben Hur v. Cauble, 255 U.S. 356 (1921), while concluding that *every member of the plaintiff class* had to satisfy the amount-in-controversy requirement, see Zahn v. International Paper Co., 414 U.S. 291 (1973). Which of the two traditional requirements is the more fundamental, once again?

5. Justice Ginsburg's "less disruptive" interpretation would disapprove *both* the attempt in *Rosario Ortega* to add a claimant seeking less than the minimum to a suit by another claimant seeking more than the minimum (preserving the prior decision in the *Carter v. Paul Gray, Inc.* case) *and* the attempt in *Exxon* to go forward with a class suit where the standard bearer satisfies the jurisdictional minimum but class members do not (preserving the prior decision in the *Zahn*). She reaches that result by adopting what the majority calls the "indivisibility" theory, under which the question of supplemental jurisdiction arises only *after* a court has jurisdiction over "every claim in the complaint."

(a) Under the Ginsburg view, the trial court in *Rosario Ortega* did *not* have jurisdiction over every claim because only the injured nine-year-old girl could claim damages exceeding $75,000. Her family members could not, so the question of supplemental jurisdiction does not arise, and the case should have been dismissed (at least the undersized claims). The absence from §1367(b) of a carve-out" for claims joined under FRCP 20 makes sense—there is no carve-out because there would not have been supplemental jurisdiction *anyway.*

(b) Under the Ginsburg view, the court in *Exxon* also did not have jurisdiction. Why? Apparently, because the *Zahn* interpretation of the jurisdictional requirements for class suits means that there was no original jurisdiction in *Exxon,* and once again the question of supplemental jurisdiction does not arise, and the suit should have been dismissed. Again, the absence from §1367 of a carve-out for claims joined under FRCP 23 makes sense—there is no carve-out because there would not have been supplemental jurisdiction *anyway.*

(c) Note the majority's response to Ginsburg: The "indivisibility" theory is "inconsistent with the whole notion of supplemental jurisdiction." If a court must *first* have jurisdiction over *all* claims *before* one invokes supplemental jurisdiction, then how does one account for cases like *Gibbs,* where a plaintiff who did not satisfy the diversity requirement (co-citizen with some defendants) made federal and state law claims? And if the presence of claims that could not be brought by themselves destroys jurisdiction over the whole case, how does one account for the practice of dismissing those

claims that don't meet jurisdictional requirements, as opposed to dismissing the whole case?

6. It is worth pondering for a moment the areas where §1367 clearly authorizes supplemental jurisdiction, and you will revisit this point when you come to various procedural devices that are covered in Chapter 7, infra. Supplemental jurisdiction exists

(a) Over *at least some* counterclaims made by defendant against plaintiff. As a rule of thumb, such jurisdiction exists over most if not all "compulsory counterclaims," which arise out of "the [same] transaction or occurrence" underlying plaintiff's claim. Such jurisdiction probably does *not* exist over *most* "permissive" counterclaims, which do *not* arise out of that transaction. See FRCP 13(a) and (b) (Chapter 7C5, infra). Do you see why §1367 allows jurisdiction over the first but not the second?

(b) Over impleader claims, which *defendant* makes against a third-party defendant, in which the former claims that if he is liable to the plaintiff, then the third-party defendant is liable to defendant ("pass through" liability). See FRCP 14 (Chapter 8D, infra).

(c) Over claims by impleaded third-party defendant against the defendant, or against the plaintiff. See FRCP 14 (Chapter 8D, infra).

(d) Over cross-claims that one defendant makes against another, again if they arise out of "the [same] transaction or occurrence" as the plaintiff's claims against the defendants. See FRCP 13(g) (Chapter 8E, infra).

In all these cases, the beginning point is that supplemental jurisdiction covers every claim that is part of "the same case or controversy." If that criterion is satisfied, the next question is whether the claim in question is the subject of one of the carve-outs in §1367(b). Supplemental jurisdiction exists if the claim is *not* carved out. Recall that in federal question cases there are *no* carve-outs, *and* that even in diversity cases there is no need for "supplemental" jurisdiction if the opposing parties are diverse and the amount-in-controversy requirement is satisfied.

D   FEDERAL REMOVAL JURISDICTION

Like diversity jurisdiction, federal "removal" jurisdiction has existed since the earliest days of the republic. As codified in 28 USC §1441, removal is a device that enables a defendant sued in state court on claims that *could have been brought* in federal court to *remove* the suit from state to federal court. The statute contemplates removal of both federal question and diversity cases.

You have looked at supplemental jurisdiction, so you know federal question cases can include claims based on state law, regardless whether they could be brought by themselves in federal court. And you know diversity cases can include claims that could not be brought by themselves in federal court. The wording of 28 USC §1367 leaves room to suppose that it applies only to cases *originally filed* in federal court (it speaks of cases where district courts "have original jurisdiction," not cases *removed to* district courts), but a 2011 amendment to the removal statute confirms what the cases had already concluded, which is that §1367 applies in removed cases too. See 28 USC §1441(c). Hence such cases can include claims that would not by themselves support federal jurisdiction if they were the only ones, just as suits *originally* filed in federal court can properly include such claims.

Removal of Suits with State Law Claims. Removal based on diversity of citizenship cannot properly occur "if any of the parties in interest properly joined and served as defendants" is a citizen of the state where the action was brought, but this limit does not apply to cases that qualify for arising under jurisdiction. See 28 USC §1441(c). It makes sense, doesn't it, to bar local defendants from invoking diversity jurisdiction by removing state-filed cases? Recall that the basic diversity jurisdiction statute (28 USC §1332) has been criticized as overbroad because it lets local *plaintiffs* sue in federal court, even in the state where they live. The removal statute is more carefully tailored to serve situations for which diversity jurisdiction exists. That much conceded, does it make sense to bar nonlocal defendants from removing diversity cases just because *one* defendant is from the forum state?

Removal of Suits with Federal Claims. Suits that include federal claims are all removable. Recall that the supplemental jurisdiction statute (28 USC §1367) contains no carve-outs in federal question cases, with the result that federal courts can hear state law claims that are joined with federal claims as long as all are part of "the same case or controversy." As amended in 2011, the removal statute authorizes removal of cases raising federal question claims along with *any kind* of state law claims, even those that *do not satisfy* the "same case or controversy" criterion, but the statute goes on to say that a federal court should then remand state law claims that do not satisfy this criterion. See 28 USC §1441(c).

As noted in the introductory material on arising under jurisdiction, Congress has specified that certain suits that can be brought in *either* federal *or* state court cannot be removed. These include FELA suits by railroaders or their widows, such as you saw in Lavender v. Kurn (Chapter 1, supra), and Jones Act suits by or on behalf of sailors. See 28 USC §1445(a) (barring removal of FELA cases); 46 USC §30104 (incorporating into Jones Act laws "regulating recovery for personal injury to, or death of, a railway employee," which includes nonremovability under 28 USC §1445). Compare Breuer v. Jim's Concrete of Brevard, Inc., 538 U.S. 691 (2003) (suit under Labor Standards Act, which can be brought in state or federal court, can be removed; nothing in statute bars removal).

Reasons for Removal Jurisdiction; Basic Mechanics. Why do we have removal jurisdiction? The answer stems partly from the main reasons underlying the two big branches of federal jurisdiction: If arising under cases had to stay in state court when plaintiffs file them there, *defendants* would be deprived of the advantages that might accrue from having such cases heard by judges appointed by the authority that is the source of the law being applied. And if a defendant, who is sued away from home on claims that could be brought in federal court under diversity jurisdiction, were powerless to remove, he would be deprived of the opportunity to avoid local prejudice.

Removal is accomplished by filing and serving a "notice of removal" in federal district court, see 28 USC §1446(a), so a defendant need not make a motion or obtain a ruling first. Once the notice is filed and served, the suit is removed. State jurisdiction ends and the case is now in federal court, where plaintiff can raise the question whether removal was proper and seek a remand to state court if it was not.

1. Scope of the Doctrine

The propriety of removal turns on whether plaintiff's claims, as set forth in the complaint, could properly be brought in federal court. Recall from *Mottley* that federal defenses do not satisfy the arising under criterion for cases originally filed in federal court, although they do satisfy that criterion when it comes to jurisdiction in the Supreme Court to review state court decisions. Recall as well, from the Notes after *Mottley,* that federal *counterclaims* do not support removal. As we are about to discover, even federal *defenses* do not generally support removal jurisdiction either.

CATERPILLAR, INC. v. WILLIAMS

Supreme Court of the United States
482 U.S. 386 (1987)

Justice BRENNAN delivered the opinion of the Court.

The question for decision is whether respondents' state-law complaint for breach of individual employment contracts is completely pre-empted by §301 of the Labor Management Relations Act of 1947 (LMRA), and therefore removable to Federal District Court.

I

At various times between 1956 and 1968, Caterpillar Tractor Company (Caterpillar) hired respondents to work at its San Leandro, California, facility. Initially, each respondent filled a position covered by the collective bargaining agreement between Caterpillar and Local Lodge No. 284, International Association of Machinists (Union). Each eventually became either a managerial or a weekly salaried employee, positions outside the coverage of the collective bargaining agreement. Respondents held the latter positions for periods ranging from 3 to 15 years; all but two respondents served 8 years or more.

Respondents allege that, "[d]uring the course of [their] employment, as management or weekly salaried employees," Caterpillar made oral and written representations that "they could look forward to indefinite and lasting employment with the corporation and that they could count on the corporation to take care of them." More specifically, respondents claim that, "while serving Caterpillar as managers or weekly salaried employees, [they] were assured that if the San Leandro facility of Caterpillar ever closed, Caterpillar would provide employment opportunities for [them] at other facilities of Caterpillar, its subsidiaries, divisions, or related companies."[1] Respondents maintain that these "promises were continually and repeatedly made," and that they created "a total employment agreement wholly independent of the collective bargaining agreement pertaining to hourly employees." In reliance on these promises, respondents assert, they "continued to remain in Caterpillar's employ rather than seeking other employment."

Between May 1980 and January 1984, Caterpillar downgraded respondents from managerial and weekly salaried positions to hourly positions covered by the collective bargaining agreement. Respondents allege that, at the time they were downgraded to unionized positions, Caterpillar supervisors orally assured them that the downgrades were temporary. On December 15, 1983, Caterpillar notified respondents that its San Leandro plant would close and that they would be laid off.

On December 17, 1984, respondents filed an action based solely on state law in California state court, contending that Caterpillar "breached [its] employment agreement by notifying [respondents] that the San Leandro plant would be closed and subsequently advising [respondents] that they would be terminated" without regard to the individual employment contracts. Caterpillar then removed the action to federal court, arguing that removal was proper because any individual employment contracts made with respondents "were, as a matter of federal substantive labor law, merged into and superseded by the . . . collective bargaining agreements." Respondents denied that they alleged any federal claim and immediately sought remand of the action to the state court. In an oral opinion, the District Court held that removal to

---

[1] The complaint also avers that Caterpillar "made clear . . . its intention to employ [respondents] indefinitely by promoting them from entry level hourly positions to mid-level technical or weekly positions and to management positions," and by giving respondents "favorable performance evaluations," "payment increases and bonuses," and "training . . . to provide additional job security." Written representations with respect to job security were allegedly contained in employment memoranda, manuals, brochures, handbooks, and in Caterpillar's "Code of Worldwide Business Conduct and Operating Principles."

federal court was proper, and dismissed the case when respondents refused to amend their complaint to attempt to state a claim under §301 of the LMRA.

The Court of Appeals for the Ninth Circuit reversed, holding that the case was improperly removed. The court determined that respondents' state-law claims were not grounded, either directly or indirectly, upon rights or liabilities created by the collective bargaining agreement. Caterpillar's claim that its collective bargaining agreement with the Union superseded and extinguished all previous individual employment contracts alleged by respondents was deemed irrelevant. The court labeled this argument a "defensive allegation," "raised to defeat the [respondents'] claims grounded in those independent contracts." Since respondents' cause of action did not require interpretation or application of the collective bargaining agreement, the court concluded that the complaint did not arise under §301 and was not removable to federal court.[4]

We granted certiorari, and now affirm.

II

A

. . .

Only state-court actions that originally could have been filed in federal court may be removed to federal court by the defendant. Absent diversity of citizenship, federal question jurisdiction is required. The presence or absence of federal question jurisdiction is governed by the "well-pleaded complaint rule," which provides that federal jurisdiction exists only when a federal question is presented on the face of the plaintiff's properly pleaded complaint. The rule makes the plaintiff the master of the claim; he or she may avoid federal jurisdiction by exclusive reliance on state law.

Ordinarily federal pre-emption is raised as a defense to the allegations in a plaintiff's complaint. Before 1887, a federal defense such as pre-emption could provide a basis for removal, but, in that year, Congress amended the removal statute. We interpret that amendment to authorize removal only where original federal jurisdiction exists. Thus, it is now settled law that a case

---

[4] The Court of Appeals also appears to have held that a case may not be removed to federal court on the ground that it is completely pre-empted unless the federal cause of action relied upon provides the plaintiff with a remedy. This analysis is squarely contradicted by our decision in Avco Corp. v. Machinists, 390 U.S. 557 (1968). We there held that a §301 claim was properly removed to federal court although, at the time, the relief sought by the plaintiff could be obtained only in state court. We reasoned as follows:

> The nature of the relief available after jurisdiction attaches is, of course, different from the question whether there is jurisdiction to adjudicate the controversy. . . . [T]he breadth or narrowness of the relief which may be granted under federal law in §301 cases is a distinct question from whether the court has jurisdiction over the parties and the subject matter.

Thus, although we affirm the Court of Appeals' judgment, we reject its reasoning insofar as it is inconsistent with *Avco.*

may *not* be removed to federal court on the basis of a federal defense, including the defense of pre-emption, even if the defense is anticipated in the plaintiff's complaint, and even if both parties concede that the federal defense is the only question truly at issue.

There does exist, however, an "independent corollary" to the well-pleaded complaint rule, known as the "complete pre-emption" doctrine. On occasion, the Court has concluded that the pre-emptive force of a statute is so "extraordinary" that it "converts an ordinary state common-law complaint into one stating a federal claim for purposes of the well-pleaded complaint rule." *Metropolitan Life Insurance Co.*[8] Once an area of state law has been completely pre-empted, any claim purportedly based on that pre-empted state law is considered, from its inception, a federal claim, and therefore arises under federal law.

The complete pre-emption corollary to the well-pleaded complaint rule is applied primarily in cases raising claims pre-empted by §301 of the LMRA. Section 301 provides:

> Suits for violation of contracts between an employer and a labor organization representing employees in an industry affecting commerce as defined in this chapter, or between any such labor organizations, may be brought in any district court of the United States having jurisdiction of the parties, without respect of the amount in controversy or without regard to the citizenship of the parties.

29 USC §185(a).

In *Avco Corp. v. Machinists*, the Court of Appeals decided that "[s]tate law does not exist as an independent source of private rights to enforce collective bargaining contracts." In affirming, we held that, when "[t]he heart of the [state law] complaint [is] a . . . clause in the collective bargaining agreement," that complaint arises under federal law:

> [T]he pre-emptive force of §301 is so powerful as to displace entirely any state cause of action "for violation of contracts between an employer and a labor organization." Any such suit is purely a creature of federal law, notwithstanding the fact that state law would provide a cause of action in the absence of §301.

B

Caterpillar asserts that respondents' state-law contract claims are in reality completely pre-empted §301 claims, which therefore arise under federal law. We disagree. Section 301 governs claims founded directly on rights created by

---

[8] See, e.g., Metropolitan Life Insurance Co. v. Taylor (state contract and tort claims completely pre-empted by §§502(a)(1)(B) and 502(f) of the Employee Retirement Income Security Act of 1974); Oneida Indian Nation v. County of Oneida, 414 U.S. 661, 675 (1974) (state-law complaint that alleges a present right to possession of Indian tribal lands necessarily "asserts a present right to possession under federal law," and is thus completely pre-empted and arises under federal law); *Avco,* supra (discussed infra).

collective bargaining agreements, and also claims "substantially dependent on analysis of a collective bargaining agreement." Electrical Workers v. Hechler, 481 U.S. 851, 859, n.3 (1987); see also Allis-Chalmers Corp. v. Lueck, 471 U.S. 202, 220 (1985). Respondents allege that Caterpillar has entered into and breached *individual* employment contracts with them. Section 301 says nothing about the content or validity of individual employment contracts. It is true that respondents, bargaining unit members at the time of the plant closing, possessed substantial rights under the collective agreement, and could have brought suit under §301. As masters of the complaint, however, they chose not to do so.

Moreover, contrary to Caterpillar's assertion, respondents' complaint is not substantially dependent upon interpretation of the collective bargaining agreement. It does not rely upon the collective agreement indirectly, nor does it address the relationship between the individual contracts and the collective agreement.[9] As the Court has stated, "it would be inconsistent with congressional intent under [§301] to pre-empt state rules that proscribe conduct, or establish rights and obligations, independent of a labor contract." *Allis-Chalmers Corp., supra.*

Caterpillar next relies on this Court's decision in J.I. Case Co. v. NLRB, 321 U.S. 332 (1944), arguing that when respondents returned to the collective bargaining unit, their individual employment agreements were subsumed into, or eliminated by, the collective bargaining agreement. Thus, Caterpillar contends, respondents' claims under their individual contracts actually *are* claims under the collective agreement and pre-empted by §301.

Caterpillar is mistaken. First, *Case* does not stand for the proposition that all individual employment contracts are subsumed into, or eliminated by, the collective bargaining agreement. In fact, the Court there held:

> Individual contracts cannot subtract from collective ones, and whether under some circumstances they may add to them in matters covered by the collective bargain, we leave to be determined by appropriate forums under the law of contracts applicable, and to the Labor Board if they constitute unfair labor practices.

---

[9] Caterpillar contends for example, that, under California law governing implied contracts of employment, the state court will have to examine the collective bargaining agreement as part of its evaluation of the "totality of the parties' relationship." But respondents rely on contractual agreements made while they were in managerial or weekly salaried positions—agreements in which the collective bargaining agreement played no part. The irrelevance of the collective bargaining agreement to these individual employment contracts is illustrated by the District Court's disposition of the claim of Mr. Chambers, who was not in the bargaining unit at the time he was laid off. His claim was deemed solely a matter of state law (and, by implication, not intertwined with the collective bargaining agreement), and thus was remanded to state court. Moreover, it is unclear whether an examination of the collective bargaining agreement is truly required by California law. See Youngman v. Nevada Irrigation Dist., 70 Cal. 2d 240, 246-247 (Cal. 1969) ("In pleading a cause of action on an agreement implied from conduct, only the facts from which the promise is implied must be alleged").

Thus, individual employment contracts are not inevitably superseded by any subsequent collective agreement covering an individual employee, and claims based upon them may arise under state law. Caterpillar's basic error is its failure to recognize that a plaintiff covered by a collective bargaining agreement is permitted to assert legal rights *independent* of that agreement, including state-law contract rights, so long as the contract relied upon is *not* a collective bargaining agreement.[10] Caterpillar impermissibly attempts to create the prerequisites to removal by ignoring the set of facts (*i.e.,* the individual employment contracts) presented by respondents, along with their legal characterization of those facts, and arguing that there are different facts respondents might have alleged that would have constituted a federal claim. In sum, Caterpillar does not seek to point out that the contract relied upon by respondents is in fact a collective agreement; rather it attempts to justify removal on the basis of facts not alleged in the complaint. The "artful pleading" doctrine cannot be invoked in such circumstances.[11]

Second, if an employer wishes to dispute the continued legality or viability of a pre-existing individual employment contract because an employee has taken a position covered by a collective agreement, it may raise this question in state court. The employer may argue that the individual employment contract has been pre-empted due to the principle of exclusive representation in §9(a) of the National Labor Relations Act (NLRA), 29 USC §159(a). Or the employer may contend that enforcement of the individual employment contract arguably would constitute an unfair labor practice under the NLRA, and is therefore pre-empted. The fact that a defendant might ultimately prove that a plaintiff's claims are pre-empted under the NLRA does not establish that they are removable to federal court.

Finally, Caterpillar argues that §301 pre-empts a state-law claim even when the employer raises only a defense that requires a court to interpret or apply a collective bargaining agreement. Caterpillar asserts such a defense

---

[10] Section 301 does not, as Caterpillar suggests, require that all "employment-related matters involving unionized employees" be resolved through collective bargaining and thus be governed by a federal common law created by §301. The Court has stated that "not every dispute concerning employment, or tangentially involving a provision of a collective bargaining agreement, is pre-empted by §301 or other provisions of the federal labor law." *Allis-Chalmers Corp. supra.* Claims bearing no relationship to a collective bargaining agreement beyond the fact that they are asserted by an individual covered by such an agreement are simply not pre-empted by §301. See also *Franchise Tax Board v. Construction Laborer's Trust,* 463 U.S. 1, 23 (1983) ("[E]ven under §301 we have never intimated that any action merely relating to a contract within the coverage of §301 arises exclusively under that section. For instance, a state battery suit growing out of a violent strike would not arise under §301 simply because the strike may have been a violation of an employer-union contract").

[11] Cf. *Federated Department Stores, Inc. v. Moitie,* 452 U.S. 394, 410, n.6 (1981) (Brennan, J., dissenting) (Although "occasionally the removal court will seek to determine whether the real nature of the claim is federal, regardless of plaintiff's characterization, . . . most of them correctly confine this practice to areas of the law pre-empted by federal substantive law") (internal quotations omitted).

claiming that, in its collective bargaining agreement, its unionized employees waived any pre-existing individual employment contract rights.[13]

It is true that when a defense to a state claim is based on the terms of a collective bargaining agreement, the state court will have to interpret that agreement to decide whether the state claim survives. But the presence of a federal question, even a §301 question, in a defensive argument does not overcome the paramount policies embodied in the well-pleaded complaint rule—that the plaintiff is the master of the complaint, that a federal question must appear on the face of the complaint, and that the plaintiff may, by eschewing claims based on federal law, choose to have the cause heard in state court. When a plaintiff invokes a right created by a collective bargaining agreement, the plaintiff has *chosen* to plead what we have held must be regarded as a federal claim, and removal is at the defendant's option. But a *defendant* cannot, merely by injecting a federal question into an action that asserts what is plainly a state-law claim, transform the action into one arising under federal law, thereby selecting the forum in which the claim shall be litigated. If a defendant could do so, the plaintiff would be master of nothing. Congress has long since decided that federal defenses do not provide a basis for removal.

III

Respondents' claims do not arise under federal law and therefore may not be removed to federal court. The judgment of the Court of Appeals is
Affirmed.

■ NOTES ON SCOPE OF THE REMOVAL DOCTRINE

1. In *Caterpillar*, as in *Mottley*, defendant raised the federal issue in response to a state law claim. In *Mottley*, plaintiffs chose federal court and nobody objected until the Supreme Court raised the issue, but in *Caterpillar* defendants wanted to get the case into federal court. Under *Mottley*'s well-pleaded complaint principle, even a defense of federal *pre-emption* doesn't create arising under jurisdiction. It made sense in *Mottley* to insist that arising under jurisdiction is determined by the complaint because the matter should be resolved at the outset. Does it make sense to apply this rule in removal cases? We *know* there is a federal defense if it is the basis of removal, don't we? But in a suit like *Mottley*, we do *not* know there will be a federal issue.

---

[13] We intimate no view on the merits of this or any of the pre-emption arguments discussed above. These are questions that must be addressed in the first instance by the state court in which respondents filed their claims.

See Study of the Division of Jurisdiction Between State and Federal Courts 187-188 (1969) (removal should be allowed on basis of federal defenses and compulsory counterclaims resting on federal law).

2. *Caterpillar* says plaintiff is "the master of the claim." From what principle does this statement derive? Defendants in *Caterpillar* invoked what amounts to an exception to this proposition—namely the "artful pleading" doctrine. As employed in *Caterpillar,* this doctrine holds that the absence from the complaint of any indication that plaintiff is relying on federal law, and even an allegation that plaintiff is relying on *state* law, cannot defeat arising under jurisdiction if the allegations support recovery *only* under federal law. Recall *Skelly Oil* (note 4(a) in Notes on the Well-Pleaded Complaint Rule), which holds that plaintiffs cannot invoke arising under jurisdiction by bringing suit under the Declaratory Judgment Act, where a federal question appears on the face of a well-pleaded complaint, which it would *not* in an "ordinary" civil damage suit. In *Skelly Oil,* the Court spoke of "artful pleading" in describing the case in which plaintiff was using the declaratory judgment tactic to anticipate a defense. That's *not* involved in *Caterpillar,* is it?

3. The "artful pleading" doctrine refers to an attempt to obtain recovery that *only* federal law can provide. Plaintiff in *Caterpillar* sought recovery under state contract law. The defense argued that federal law of collective bargaining agreements *completely* pre-empts state contract remedies, so there is no room for state law to operate. Recall *Lincoln Mills* (described in Section 4B3, supra), where the Court concluded that the statute authorizing federal courts to adjudicate disputes under collective bargaining agreements impliedly authorizes them to create federal common law to resolve such disputes. See Textile Workers Union of America v. Lincoln Mills of Alabama, 353 U.S. 448, 451 (1957) (construing 28 USC §185). And note the decision in Avco Corp. v. Machinists, 390 U.S. 557 (1968), mentioned in *Caterpillar,* which held that federal law of collective bargaining agreements completely pre-empts state law claims. The Court continues to adhere to this form of the "artful pleading" doctrine. See, e.g., Beneficial National Bank v. Anderson, 539 U.S. 1, 8 (2003) (state law claim may be removed in two circumstances—"when Congress expressly so provides, such as in the Price-Anderson Act [allowing removal of claims arising out of nuclear accidents, even when they rest on state law] or when a federal statute wholly displaces the state law cause of action through complete preemption"); Rivet v. Regions Bank of Louisiana, 522 U.S. 470, 475 (1998) (if plaintiff has "artfully pleaded" claims that can only advance under federal law, case may be removed; court "may uphold removal even though no federal question appears on the face of complaint . . . where federal law completely preempts a plaintiff's state law claim").

4. The artful pleading doctrine has proved difficult of application:

(a) In the *Davila* case, the Supreme Court concluded that state tort or contract claims against a health care plan regulated by the Employee Retirement Income Security Act of 1974 (ERISA) *are* "completely preempted" by the federal statute, and that such claims support removal jurisdiction.

See Aetna Health Inc. v. Davila, 542 U.S. 200 (2004) (approving removal of suit alleging that refusal of health care plan administrator to approve treatment caused injuries; suit rested on state statute, but claims sought to remedy denial of benefits under plan covered by ERISA, and these "fall within the scope of, and are completely preempted by" ERISA, hence being "removable to federal district court").

(b) In the *Pollitt* case, however, the Seventh Circuit concluded that a federal employee's suit seeking recovery from Health Care Service Corporation for medical expenses incurred by plaintiff's son was *not* completely pre-empted by federal law, so removal was improper. See Pollitt v. Health Care Service Corp., 558 F.3d 615, 616 (7th Cir. 2009) (pre-emption was a defense, not ground for removal). Similarly, in the *Moore-Thomas* case, the Ninth Circuit concluded that claims that Alaska Airlines violated state law in failing to pay former employees all wages that they were due on termination were *not* completely pre-empted by federal law. See Moore-Thomas v. Alaska Airlines, Inc., 553 F.3d 1241 (9th Cir. 2009) (contrasting "complete" against "ordinary" pre-emption and concluding that Railway Labor Act does not provide for "exclusive federal cause of action," but requires disputes to be submitted to "internal dispute-resolution processes" and then to National Adjustment Board or to arbitration; hence state-filed case could not be removed).

(c) Recall the somewhat curious cases interpreting the well-pleaded complaint rule, which approve the exercise of arising under jurisdiction when plaintiffs seek declaratory or injunctive relief on the ground that federal law completely pre-empts a claim that the defendants are threatening to prosecute (note 5 in the Notes on Cases of Special Federal Concern, supra). Recall too that ordinary pre-emption claims do *not* satisfy the well-pleaded complaint rule. The Supreme Court has held that in such settings, if the person with the pre-empted claim sues on it in state court, the defendant indeed *can* remove.

(d) Given these cases, and especially given the decisions in *Lincoln Mills* and *Avco,* why did defendants in *Caterpillar* lose the pre-emption argument? What would have happened if they had won? Can this kind of argument be resolved in a preliminary stage of the proceedings when the propriety of removal is determined?

5. Can removal rights be waived by contract? See Ensco International, Inc. v. Certain Underwriters at Lloyd's, 579 F.3d 442 (5th Cir. 2009) (yes; contract provision requiring any dispute between parties to be resolved in state court in Texas foreclosed removal of suit brought there).

6. Plaintiffs in *Caterpillar* thought they had a better shot at recovery by emphasizing a "culture of job security" in a statement aimed at encouraging loyalty, than they would have by suing under the collective bargaining agreement. There is nothing wrong with letting plaintiffs make such a choice, is there? Consider the damage that can be done when courts *ignore* this principle: In the *Moitie* case that arose in California, plaintiffs challenged pricing practices of retailers of women's clothing, suing in state court and alleging only *state law* claims. Defendants removed on the theory that the claims "were really disguised federal antitrust claims," and ultimately plaintiffs *lost* because they had brought an earlier suit (also removed to federal court). The earlier suit rejected the claims (construed as federal) because plaintiffs did not suffer damage to "business or property." In the second suit (again in state court, again removed), the Ninth Circuit agreed that the state law claims were removable because they were "really" federal. Thus plaintiffs ultimately recovered nothing because of the earlier holding that federal law did not allow recovery for personal economic loss (as opposed to damages to "business or property"), even though this construction of federal law had been determined to be erroneous and other plaintiffs who brought federal claims and appealed from the earlier decision were allowed to prevail. See Moitie v. Federated Department Stores, Inc., 611 F.2d 1267 (9th Cir. 1980) (state claims were "federal in nature" but plaintiffs were not bound by earlier loss), *rev'd sub nom.* Federated Department Stores, Inc. v. Moitie, 452 U.S. 394 (1981) (failure to appeal earlier loss meant plaintiffs were bound; fact that others with federal claims did appeal and win reversal does not mean nonappealing plaintiffs should benefit from reversal).

2. Procedural Details and Tactical Maneuvers

Removal is a litigation-provoking tactic, partly because it is surrounded by complicated rules, partly because defendants are willing to fight hard to remove, and plaintiffs are willing to fight hard to prevent removal, and partly because removal is open to manipulation by both sides.

From a defense perspective, removal may be attractive just *because* it enables the defendant to seize the initiative. Even before filing an answer, and without waiving objection to jurisdiction over the person, the defense can file in federal district court, and serve on plaintiff, a "notice of removal" along with a "short and plain statement of the grounds for removal," and this step *in itself* removes the case and leaves the state court powerless. "Promptly" after filing the notice, the defense must "give written notice thereof" to the other parties and "file a copy of the notice" in the state court. See 28 USC §1446(a) and (d).

A defendant may also find removal attractive just *because* plaintiff prefers litigating in state court (that's usually why an arguably removable case was filed in state court to begin with)—anything to oppose (and make life difficult for) the other side. And it is worth remembering that federal jurisdiction exists for some good reasons that may appeal to defendants—getting federal issues adjudicated by judges appointed in the same system whose law is being applied, which tends to assure sympathetic and thoughtful application of federal law, and avoiding local prejudice in diversity cases. Finally, as noted further below, there is good reason to think that defendants benefit from removal in terms of likely outcome of the suit.

From the plaintiff's perspective, there may be good reasons to prefer state court. To speak broadly, one modern study has found marked differences in the rate of success for plaintiffs between state and federal court. This study concludes that plaintiffs suffer "a precipitous drop" in "win rate" when cases are removed: The overall "win rate" for plaintiffs in federal court is 57.97 percent, but for removed cases their win rate is 36.7 percent. In other words, plaintiffs win about a third fewer cases after suffering removal from state to federal court. See Kevin M. Clermont & Theodore Eisenberg, *Do Case Outcomes Really Reveal Anything About the Legal System? Win Rates and Removal Jurisdiction*, 83 Cornell L. Rev. 581, 593 (1998).

There may be other reasons why plaintiffs prefer state court. Although such sentiments are seldom voiced, practitioners hint at a kind of aloofness in federal court. They sometimes find state procedural rules more congenial than federal rules, and sometimes find that federal judges are more bent on controlling cases and achieving efficiencies that get in the way of the agenda of plaintiffs' lawyers. Consider the following comments voiced by one practitioner:

> Plaintiff attorneys' preference for state courts is undisputed and understandable. Reasons for avoiding federal court range from the mundane (greater familiarity with state procedure) to the strategic (greater likelihood of securing justice for clients).
>
> In most states, local judges are elected by the very people whose disputes they will hear, motivating speedy and fair adjudication. Federal judges are appointed for life, and their courts are clogged with criminal cases. The so-called war on drugs has so overburdened the federal judiciary that getting a civil case tried at all in many federal courts is nearly impossible.
>
> To reduce their burgeoning dockets, federal courts have increasingly engaged in stringent control of discovery, aggressive encouragement of settlement, and more frequent granting of summary judgment. As a result, litigation in federal court is more expensive and time-consuming. Moreover, plaintiffs whose cases are removed to federal court are substantially less successful than those who originally file there. Finally, but significantly, lawsuits in federal court are increasingly being consolidated into multidistrict, pretrial litigation proceedings, where they often languish for years.

Erik B. Walker, *Keep Your Case in State Court*, Trial, Sept. 2004, at 22.

Note that the removal statute says "defendant or defendants" shall file the removal petition: It has long been understood that if there are multiple defendants, all must agree to the removal, see Chicago, Rock Island & Pac. Ry. Co. v. Martin, 178 U.S. 245, 248 (1900) (all defendants must join in application), and in 2011 the statute was amended to make this requirement express. See 28 USC §1446(b)(2)(A) ("all defendants who have been properly joined and served must join in or consent to the removal"). Contrast this provision with the CAFA removal provision, which lets one defendant remove a class action.

See 28 USC §1453(b) (class actions satisfying 28 USC §1332(d) "may be removed by any defendant without the consent of all").

■ PROBLEM 4-A. "I Hurt My Hand"

Alden Peck, who lives in Columbus, Ohio, was building a gazebo in his backyard in September 2011. He was sawing 2×8 redwood beams for floor joists, using a Back & Deckler circular saw, when he accidentally brushed his wrist against the blade and sustained serious injuries. "I hurt my hand," Peck told his frightened wife Jane when he rushed to the house gripping his left wrist. She drove him to the Mount Carmel Hospital emergency room. Doctors reconnected nerves and tendons and saved his hand. Medical insurance paid his expenses, and he made a full recovery.

Alden Peck is an auditor who works for the Ohio Department of Education. His injury caused him to miss work, but did not impair his abilities to continue his employment. He did not suffer loss in salary (absence was covered by sick leave).

Peck does not know whether he has any viable claims, but he asks around and ultimately goes to a product liability lawyer named Jeff Bracey, who agrees to represent him. After discussing the matter and examining the saw, Bracey thinks there is a design flaw because the blade guard, designed to roll back as the saw proceeds along a cut, does not sufficiently cover the rotating blade as the cut begins. He thinks Peck has a product liability claim against Back & Deckler, and against Zittler Hardware of Columbus, which sold the saw to Peck.

Bracey ascertains that Peck's medical expenses come to $45,500. He thinks Peck has a plausible claim for pain and suffering in an amount exceeding $50,000. Even though medical insurance paid all but $3,500 of Peck's medicals, Bracey knows that under the collateral source doctrine Peck is entitled, if he can prove liability, to collect all his medical expenses. (You will read more about this doctrine in Chapters 7B5 and 8A4, infra.)

Back & Deckler is incorporated in Maryland and has its principal place of business there. The company can be sued in Ohio because it shipped to Ohio the saw that Peck bought (it ships many such saws to Ohio). Zittler Hardware is a family-run business set up under Ohio law, and can be sued under that name.

(A) If Bracey wants to keep the suit in state court while suing only Back & Deckler, he might consider a few strategies. He could try to forestall removal by naming "John Doe" defendants who are allegedly citizens of Ohio, and by leaving out any specification of damages. He would still allege that Peck sustained injuries, and something about their nature, and that Peck had medicals and endured pain and suffering, but he might leave out any "bottom line," and might even allege that he seeks "not more than $75,000." Should these tactics prevent removal?

(B) Bracey might sue in state court naming only Back & Deckler and seeking recovery for Peck exceeding $75,000, just to see whether the defense removes. He thinks removal will happen soon, if at all. He might have to act quickly himself to get the case remanded, but he could add Zittler as defendant, and *then* seek remand. What about this approach?

(C) Suppose Bracey, acting on behalf of Peck, does name both Back & Deckler and Zittler Hardware as defendants, and files in state court on January 17, 2013, alleging damages of $95,000. If Bracey works out a settlement for $10,000 with Zittler in February, and if Peck dismisses the claim against Zittler on February 18th, can Back & Deckler remove the suit to federal court? By what date must Back & Deckler act if it wants to remove after Zittler is dismissed?

(D) Bracey might reflect on the trend in modern tort law, which is to apportion liability among joint tortfeasors according to degree of fault: If this principle applies, recovery against Zittler might be difficult if Zittler played no role in designing or manufacturing the saw. Indeed, some states bar suits against sellers on account of design defects if, as is often true, plaintiff can get good jurisdiction locally over the manufacturer (note 5(d), infra). In such a state, Bracey might ponder what would happen if he named Zittler in order to block removal but was unable to state a colorable claim against Zittler. Would inclusion of a local defendant against whom no colorable claim exists still block removal?

(E) If Back and Deckler removes Peck's suit despite the presence of Zittler as a defendant and Bracey considers making a motion in federal court to remand, Bracey will likely consider whether he can get sanctions for improper removal, and whether any decision on the remand motion can itself be appealed.

■ NOTES ON PROCEDURAL DETAILS OF REMOVAL AND TACTICAL OPTIONS

1. Before going too far into the complications, bear in mind that Bracey may be able to choose either state or federal court, and take steps to ensure that the case stays in the court of his choice. He can, for example, ensure federal jurisdiction for Peck's claim by filing in federal court and naming Back & Deckler alone as defendants. Or Bracey might be able to ensure that the suit stays in state court, by naming both Back & Deckler and Zittler as defendants, or naming as additional defendants a local doctor or hospital if there are possible claims of malpractice.

2. Bracey will conclude that Option A is not promising:

(a) Federal courts disregard "John Doe" defendants, so naming them and alleging that they are Ohio citizens won't help. See McPhail v. Deere & Co., 529 F.3d 947 (10th Cir. 2008) (presence of "John Doe" defendants creates no impediment to removal); 28 USC §1441(b)(1) (citizenship of defendants "sued under fictitious name" is "disregarded").

(b) Seeking less than the federal minimum is more promising, assuming such a choice is realistic. As amended in 2011, the statute addresses this issue: The amount sought in the complaint controls, so long as it is "demanded in good faith." But "information relating to the amount in controversy in the record of the State proceeding," or developed "in responses to discovery," may generate a right to remove later. And in states where the amount in the complaint does not limit plaintiff's recovery, defendant may allege in the notice of removal that the amount-in-controversy requirement is satisfied, and can prevail if the federal court finds "by the preponderance of the evidence" that indeed the requirement is satisfied. (This same procedure can be used in other situations, including cases where plaintiff seeks only "nonmonetary relief" or where state practice "does not permit a demand for a specific sum.") See 28 USC §1446(c)(2).

(c) Federal judges are suspicious of the stated intentions of a plaintiff in a case that seems big enough to satisfy the amount-in-controversy requirement. See In re 1994 Exxon Chemical Fire, 558 F.3d 378, 389 (5th Cir. 2009) (in suit arising out of chemical fire, fact that complaint sought less than minimum did *not* prevent removal; defendant established that amount exceeded minimum, since claims included "individual and familial suffering" and "injuries to physical and mental health" caused by toxic exposure; under Louisiana law, claimant may recover relief to which he is entitled, regardless whether he has demanded it; Louisiana "anti-removal provision," requiring specific allegation of damages if necessary to establish "lack" of federal jurisdiction, does not "irrevocably" bind plaintiff).

(d) On the other hand, where a defendant removes a case in which plaintiff has *not* stated the amount sought, it is often said that *defendant* bears the burden of proving that the amount-in-controversy requirement is met. See Ellenburg v. Spartan Motors Chassis, Inc., 519 F.3d 192, 200 (4th Cir. 2008) (defendant alleges in notice of removal that jurisdictional minimum is met; court may inquire, and impose on defendant "the burden of demonstrating jurisdiction"); Miedema v. Maytag Corp., 450 F.3d 1322, 1330 (11th Cir. 2006) (where complaint does not allege that minimum is satisfied, defendant must show it is).

3. In connection with Option B, Bracey is right that removal will happen, if at all, pretty fast, and he may have time then to add a nondiverse defendant and get the case remanded, but this option too is less than a sure thing.

(a) Like most states, Ohio observes the rule that a suit is commenced by filing, and requires that plaintiff serve defendant with a summons and copy of the complaint. The statute allows 30 days from the date of service to

remove: If Peck files on Tuesday, January 22, 2013, and serves defendant Back & Deckler the same day, the latter has 30 days from then to remove. Observing the usual rules about counting days, Back & Deckler has until Thursday, February 21 to file its removal petition. See FRCP 5 and 6 (setting out counting rules), and see 28 USC §1446(b). "Promptly after filing" the petition, Back & Deckler must "give written notice" to Peck (to "all adverse parties") and file a copy of the notice in state court. See 28 USC §1446(d).

(b) Timing for removal is more complicated if there are multiple defendants who are served at different times. Suppose, for example, Bracey decided to sue both Back & Deckler and Carson Component, a company that made one of the parts. And suppose Back & Deckler is served on January 22, 2013, but Carson is not served until Friday February 1. Under §1446(b)(1) as amended in 2011, each defendant has 30 days, after being served, to remove. Prior to the amendment, the statute was opaque on this point, leading some courts to follow a "first-served defendant rule," under which the 30-day period began when the first defendant is served, while others followed the "last-served defendant rule." See United Steel etc. Union v. Shell Oil Co., 549 F.3d 1204, 1208 (9th Cir. 2008) (noting split among circuits between those following first-served and last-served rule). And see 14A Wright, Miller, Cooper & Steinman, Federal Practice and Procedure §3732 (first-served rule deprives later-served defendants of "opportunity to persuade the first defendant to join in the notice of removal").

(c) If removal were improper, Peck would have 30 days (from date of "filing of the notice of removal") to make a "motion to remand the case" to state court. See 28 USC §1447. If the removal petition had been filed on February 7, 2013, then Peck would have until Monday, March 11, 2013 to act (the 30th day falls on the weekend, so time is extended to the next Monday), or perhaps until Thursday, March 14 (a party gets three extra days if served by mail or electronically, so if Back & Deckler serves Peck with notice of removal by mailing the document to Bracey or using electronic means, Peck has 33 days from February 7 to make the motion to remand). See FRCP 6(d).

(d) On the facts, removal seems proper: The amount-in-controversy requirement is met and Back & Deckler is a citizen of Maryland, not Ohio, so the complete diversity requirement is satisfied and it is an out-of-state defendant who removed. If Bracey, acting on Peck's behalf, *now* wants to add Zittler as defendant, which would destroy diversity jurisdiction, then Bracey must make a motion asking permission to amend the complaint. See FRCP 15. The court might grant permission and remand because *at this time* removal has become improper. See 28 USC §1447(e) (if plaintiff "seeks to join additional defendants" after removal, and the result destroys subject matter jurisdiction, court may "deny joinder, or permit joinder and remand" to state court). See Schur v. L.A. Weight Loss Centers, Inc., 577 F.3d

752 (7th Cir. 2009) (court has two choices; one is to allow joinder and remand; the other is to deny joinder; in choosing, court should consider plaintiff's motive in seeking joinder, and whether motive was to defeat federal jurisdiction, timeliness of request to add new party, whether plaintiff will be "significantly injured" if joinder is not allowed; and "any other equitable considerations"); Curry v. U.S. Bulk Transport, Inc., 462 F.3d 536 (6th Cir. 2006) (plaintiff substituted nondiverse defendants for unnamed "does," but court kept whole case and awarded summary judgment against plaintiff, which was error; court should have remanded; there was no dispute that plaintiff "engaged in a good-faith effort" to identify "Doe" defendants "at the earliest possible time," and he was unable to do so until discovery was under way; court should have remanded).

(e) The 30-day limit for moving to remand an improperly removed case does not apply to motions to remand a removed case for reasons *other than* a defect in the removal procedure itself. See Kamm v. ITEX Corp., 568 F.3d 752, 755 (9th Cir. 2009) (remanding under forum selection clause does not involve a "defect" in removal under the statute; 30-day limit does not apply).

4. In connection with Option C, note that under 28 USC §1441(b) a defendant can remove a case that was "not removable" when originally filed by filing a notice of removal within 30 days after "receipt . . . through service or otherwise" of a copy of "an amended pleading, motion, order or other paper" from which it "may first be ascertained" that the suit is removable. If Bracey settles Peck's claim against Zittler and files a dismissal on February 18, 2013, Back and Deckler has 30 days from then to remove (until Wednesday, March 20th). Note, however, that a diversity case cannot be removed under this provision "more than 1 year after commencement of the action." See 28 USC §1446(c). Hence a settlement leading to dismissal more than a year after commencement cannot lead to removal.

5. In connection with Option D, there are at least two good reasons why a lawyer would hesitate to name additional defendants in order to block removal if the legal basis to bring claims against them is thin:

(a) First, FRCP 11 requires an attorney of record to sign every pleading and motion, and provides that by "signing, filing, [or] submitting" such a document, or even "advocating" a position set out in such a document, an attorney "certifies" that to the best of his or her "knowledge, information, and belief" the document "is not being presented for any improper purpose" and that the "claims, defenses, and other legal contentions" are "warranted by existing law or by a nonfrivolous argument for extending, modifying, or reversing existing law" *and* that any factual contentions "have evidentiary support" or will likely have it. Violating this provision can lead to sanctions against the attorney (see Chapter 7E, infra).

(b) Second, courts recognize something called improper or fraudulent joinder. This doctrine turns on showing either that plaintiff misstated jurisdictional facts relating to a defendant, or failed to state a colorable claim against her. See In re 1994 Exxon Chemical Fire, 558 F.3d 378, 386 (5th Cir. 2009) (in suit arising out of chemical fire, claims against local employees did not prevent Exxon from removing on basis of diversity; under state law, employees could not be personally liable; person who headed valve replacement team lacked knowledge of condition of valve that failed; other individual defendants "had even less connection" to valve and were not members of replacement team) (removal proper despite these nondiverse defendants); Campbell v. Stone Ins., Inc., 509 F.3d 665 (5th Cir. 2005) (under "narrow exception" to complete diversity rule, fraudulent joinder of nondiverse party against whom plaintiff is unable to establish claim does not block removal). But see Florence v. Crescent Resources, LLC, 484 F.3d 1293, 1299 (11th Cir. 2007) (since it was not clear whether plaintiffs could recover against nondiverse defendants, joinder was not fraudulent; dismissal was not required). Can the "fraudulent joinder" doctrine apply to defendants added *after* removal? See Schur v. L.A. Weight Loss Centers, Inc., 577 F.3d 752 (7th Cir. 2009) (decedent's administrator sued company operating diet and weight loss program; after defendant removed, plaintiff added local employees and moved to remand; "fraudulent joinder" doctrine can apply to post-removal addition of defendants, but joinder was not fraudulent here; court should have remanded) (vacating judgment for defendants and remanding).

(c) Third, modern tort reform legislation makes it harder than it used to be to bring product liability claims against *sellers* as opposed to manufacturers. Ohio has a statute, and many states have similar statutes, sharply limiting liability of sellers of mass-produced products for defects leading to injury. See, e.g., Ohio Rev. Code §2307.78 (limiting liability of sellers in product liability suits where claimant can sue manufacturer directly).

6. In connection with Option E, improper removal can result in the imposition of costs and attorneys' fees under §1447(c). See Martin v. Franklin Capital Corp., 546 U.S. 132, 146 (2005) (rejecting argument that there should be "a strong presumption in favor of awarding fees," but affirming that fees may be awarded if defendant "lacked an objectively reasonable basis for seeking removal"). It may also be possible to seek sanctions for wrongful removal under FRCP 11. See, e.g., Ballard's Service Center, Inc. v. Transue, 865 F.2d 447 (1st Cir. 1989) (invoking FRCP 11 and affirming award of sanctions against *plaintiff* for improperly removing state-filed case on basis of contention that defendant's counterclaim, based on state law, was actually a federal claim).

(a) Usually a decision *denying* a motion to remand on the ground the case was improperly removed cannot be appealed because it is not a final order. See 28 USC §1291 (conferring appellate jurisdiction in courts of appeal to review "all final decisions" of federal district courts). You will see in Chapter 13 that there are exceptions to the final judgment rule, but these are few and far between.

(b) A decision *granting* a motion to remand *is* a final order because it is the last thing a federal court does in a removed suit. But the removal statute provides that such an order cannot be appealed. See 28 USC §1447(d) (remand order "is not reviewable on appeal or otherwise"). The statute embraces the situation where plaintiff moves to remand on the ground that the case was not removable under §1441 because it does not satisfy the requirements of the removal statute itself (28 USC §1441). So if Peck sued Zittler in state court on the claim arising from the accident, and if Zittler removed to federal court and Peck moved to remand on ground that an Ohio defendant cannot remove a diversity case, and if the court grants the motion (as it should), Zittler could not appeal the decision to remand.

(c) Appeal possibilities are different if a decision to remand is based on something other than "defect" in removal. In 2009, the Supreme Court held that the bar against appealing a remand order does *not* apply where the reason for remand is that the case involves claims that depend on supplemental jurisdiction and the federal court has decided in its discretion not to hear them. See Carlsbad Technology, Inc. v. HIF Bio, Inc., 556 U.S. 635 (2009) (defendant removed case involving claimed violations of state and federal law relating to patent dispute; case was remanded, and defendant appealed; bar against appeal did not apply where remand rested on discretionary refusal to hear claims within supplemental jurisdiction). Similarly, the bar does not apply where the order to remand rests on a decision to abstain from deciding state law issues. See Quackenbush v. Allstate Insurance Co., 517 U.S. 706 (1996) (bar against appealing remand order does not apply to remand based on abstention). What if the remand rests on a forum selection clause stating that any dispute will be litigated in state court? See Kamm v. ITEX Corp., 568 F.3d 752 (9th Cir. 2009) (bar against review does not apply, nor 30-day limit on motion to remand) (failure to comply with removal time limit is a "defect" subject to nonreviewability provision in §1447(c), as is removal that violates prohibition against removing workers' compensation cases, and requirement that no defendant in case removed for diversity be citizen of state where suit was brought).

(d) Note that one way in which CAFA expands federal jurisdiction is in enabling courts of appeal to review orders remanding cases removed under CAFA. See Hertz Corp. v. Friend, 130 S. Ct. 1181 (2010) (under 28 USC §1453(c), order remanding removed class suit can be reviewed).

3. Broadened Removal Opportunities

Modern statutory reforms designed to broaden federal jurisdiction come with special provisions making removal easier. Thus the Multiparty, Multiforum Trial Jurisdiction Act (28 USC §1369) enacted in 2002 has a provision letting any defendant remove a suit that "is or could have been brought" under the Act, which means that one defendant may remove (the concurrence of all is not required), and may do so even if the defendant is a citizen of the forum state. See 28 USC §1441(e)(1). Similarly, the Class Action Fairness Act of 2005, which expands federal diversity jurisdiction to cover large cases (seeking more than $5 million in damages) in which there is *some* diversity of citizenship but not *complete* diversity, has a provision that expands removal possibilities. See 28 USC §1453, discussed in Pallisades Collections LLC v. Shorts, 552 F.3d 327, 331-332 (4th Cir. 2008) (§1453(b) eliminates limitations barring local citizen from removing, requiring all defendants to join, and restricting removal to one year from date of filing).

CHAPTER 5

The Right Court: Venue and Transfer

INTRODUCTION

All American states, and the federal system too, have venue rules for civil litigation. Venue rules reflect the fact that plaintiff may obtain jurisdiction in more than one court, but recognize that plaintiffs don't always make the best choice, and give voice to the conviction that defendants ought to have a say in the matter. The New Mexico Supreme Court put it this way:

> Plaintiffs initiating an action in New Mexico must look to the venue statute to determine the proper county in which to bring their suit. Our "venue statute is expansive and provides plaintiffs with broad discretion in choosing where to bring an action." Baker v. BP Am. Prod. Co., 110 P.3d 1071 (N.M. 2005). Nonetheless, plaintiffs do not enjoy an unfettered right to bring an action wherever they please. Instead, their choice of forum is limited by our venue rules, which "reflect an attempt to balance the common-law right of a defendant to be sued in [the] most convenient forum (usually the county of [defendant's] residence) with the right of the plaintiff to choose the forum in which to sue." Team Bank v. Meridian Oil, Inc., 879 P.2d 779, 782 (N.M. 1994).

Blancett v. Dial Oil Co., 176 P.3d 1100, 1102 (N.M. 2008). Hence defendants may raise "venue objections" and, if they prevail, get the case transferred from the court chosen by the plaintiff to a court where venue is proper.

A   HOW VENUE RULES OPERATE

In a manner of speaking, venue rules *presuppose* jurisdiction. If a court lacks jurisdiction over a defendant, the more likely defense tactic is to move to dismiss. This tactic is more attractive because it can force plaintiff to start over again and may mean the suit cannot go forward at all if the statute of limitations has run.

In state systems, courts of general jurisdiction can usually hear cases brought against any defendant who lives (or is served) in the state. If an Arizona plaintiff sues an Arizona defendant in the state superior court in Flagstaff, for example, and if defendant lives and was served in Phoenix and the suit involves an automobile accident in Phoenix, the court has *jurisdiction*, but venue is not proper in Flagstaff. If the Flagstaff court hears the case, its judgment is valid and enforceable even *if* it was the wrong venue, and even if this point was raised and a defense motion to transfer venue was denied in error. See Ariz. Rev. Stat. §§12-401 (with some exceptions, venue to be laid where defendant "resides") and §12-404 (if suit "is not brought in the proper county, the court shall nevertheless have jurisdiction").

In the federal system, much the same thing is true. Venue *presupposes* jurisdiction. Unlike state systems, however, where every court of general jurisdiction has statewide power and authority, it is not quite clear whether federal district courts have nationwide power and authority. In diversity cases, as you saw in Chapter 3, federal courts apply (and are limited by) state long-arm statutes and the "minimum contacts" doctrine (and at least sometimes they are similarly limited in federal question cases). Hence the "reach" of jurisdiction in a diversity case for a federal District Court sitting in San Francisco is the same as the "reach" of jurisdiction for a California Superior Court sitting in San Francisco. In both federal question and diversity cases, Congress occasionally authorizes federal courts to exercise power on a nationwide basis,[1] but in diversity cases, at least, the general rule is otherwise, and federal courts do not have nationwide jurisdiction.

In the *Goldlawr* case, however, the Court blurred the distinction between jurisdiction and venue in federal courts. There it held that a federal court lacking jurisdiction over defendant can still *transfer* the case to a court where both venue and jurisdiction are proper. See Goldlawr v. Heiman, 369 U.S. 463, 466-467 (1962) (citing hardship that plaintiff would suffer from dismissal; statute of limitations had run on some claims). In 2007, the Court reaffirmed this approach, ruling in *Sinochem* that a federal court can bypass

---

[1] The interpleader statute authorizes federal courts located where any claimant resides to exercise power over all claimants (most interpleader actions are governed by state law and go forward as diversity suits). See 28 USC §§1335 and 1397. The antitrust statutes authorize nationwide service of process too. See Action Embroidery Corp. v. Atlantic Embroidery, Inc., 368 F.3d 1174, 1180 (9th Cir. 2004) (Clayton Act provides for "nationwide service of process," and minimum contacts with nation suffices).

not only issues of personal jurisdiction, but issues of subject matter jurisdiction, and dismiss for *forum non conveniens*. See Sinochem International Co. Ltd. v. Malaysia International Shipping Corp., 549 U.S. 422, 432 (2007) (district court "may dispose of an action by a *forum non conveniens* dismissal, bypassing questions of subject-matter and personal jurisdiction, when considerations of convenience, fairness, and judicial economy so warrant").

Typical Venue Provisions. Venue statutes vary, and some jurisdictions have many different statutes tailored to particular situations. In that sense, there is no typical venue statute. Still, many venue statutes include these elements:

(a) Defendant's residence is almost always a choice that is allowed, if not preferred. The matter is complicated if there is more than one defendant and they reside in different places. Venue provisions commonly deal with this situation by allowing venue where *any* defendant resides, to avoid "multiplicity of suits," see Zappala v. Brandolini Property Management, Inc., 909 A.2d 1272, 2180 (Pa. 2006).

(b) Many statutes allow venue where the acts or events giving rise to the suit occurred, but phrasing varies. See, e.g., 735 Ill. Comp. Stat. 5/2-101 (venue laid where any defendant resides or where "transaction or some part thereof occurred").

(c) Many statues allow venue, in suits against corporations or other entities, where defendant has an office or place of business, or where it conducts business, or where the entity has its principal place of business. See, e.g., Kan. Stat. Ann. §60-604(3) (corporation may be sued where it is "transacting business"). Many such statutes allow suit against an out-of-state corporation to be brought in *any* county, because it is assumed that for such entities there is little difference in convenience as between one county and another. See Mo. Stat. §508.010 (when all defendants are nonresidents, "suit may be brought in any county in this state").

(d) Many statutes allow venue to be laid where the plaintiff resides, but only in limited situations or if other venue provisions cannot be satisfied. See, e.g., Ohio Civ. R. 3(b)(7) and 4.3 (in suits brought against nonresidents, venue may be laid "in the county where plaintiff resides").

Let us look at an example. Here is the basic venue provision for Texas:

(a) Except as otherwise provided by [various provisions], all lawsuits shall be brought:
(1) in the county in which all or a substantial part of the events or omissions giving rise to the claim occurred;
(2) in the county of defendant's residence at the time the cause of action accrued if defendant is a natural person;
(3) in the county of the defendant's principal office in this state, if the defendant is not a natural person; or

(4) if Subdivisions (1), (2), and (3) do not apply, in the county in which the plaintiff resided at the time of the accrual of the cause of action.

Tex. Code Ann. Civ. Prac. & Rem. §15.002. A related statute provides that in cases against multiple defendants, there is good venue for "all defendants in all claims or actions arising out of the same transaction, occurrence, or series of transactions or occurrences" if plaintiff "has established proper venue against [any one] defendant." Tex. Code Ann. Civ. Prac. & Rem. §15.005.

Forum Non Conveniens. Even suits brought in a proper venue may be transferred for reasons of convenience — on grounds of *forum non conveniens,* which is in many states a common law doctrine. We will explore this doctrine in the federal system, where it is now recognized by statute, in Section C, infra. Transfer on account of *forum non conveniens* presupposes that there is another court where the action could have been filed (and one that is more convenient), but it is commonly said that venue should *not* be changed as "wrong" merely because another venue is also proper. See Jeter v. South Carolina Dep't of Transportation, 633 S.E.2d 143, 148 (S.C. 2006) (where multiple venues are proper, defendant does not have a right to transfer suit to its county of residence merely because it too would be proper).

Local Actions. Many states have "venue" provisions stating that actions affecting real property must be brought where the property is located. Until 2011, federal courts also observed this principle, but in that year the provision was repealed. The accompanying congressional report stated that the rule had caused problems because courts were applying it in "disputes over suits for damages due to trespass," but that the court where the land is located might lack jurisdiction over the defendant, adding the comment that the local action rule serves no useful function. See H.R. Rep. 112-10, Federal Courts Jurisdiction and Venue Clarification Act of 2011, at 18 (2011).

There actually is a good reason to litigate disputes involving *land title* in courts where the land is located — namely, to enable lawyers (and title companies) to search local records, including county title records and court records, and be certain of finding information relating to deeds, mortgages and other liens, and "clouds" affecting title, including such things as judgments, attachments, and notices of "*lis pendens*" ("suit pending"). The security of titles is diminished if proceedings in, for example, Montezuma County, Colorado (southwest corner of state) could adjudicate title to Greenacre in Boulder County (north central part of state), which would make title searches in Boulder (county seat) less certain.

In practice, "local actions" are thought to include not only suits that affect title directly and necessarily, like quiet title suits and suits for specific performance of agreements to convey land, but also trespass and other suits that may entail damages to real property. See, e.g., Piven v. Comcast Corp., 916 A.2d 984 (Md. 2007) (under local action statute, cannot bring class trespass suit against internet service providers alleging damages to property in different counties). It is in these cases that commentators argue that the rule is obsolete, which is why it was abolished in the federal system.

Raising Venue Issues. For obvious reasons, venue issues must be raised early. Under FRCP 12(b), for example, venue objections are waived if not raised by answer or pre-answer motion, and also waived if defendant makes *any* motion under FRCP 12 and fails to raise the point. See FRCP 12(b)(3), 12(g)(2), and 12(h)(1).

■ **PROBLEM 5-A. "You Can't Add My Clients If Venue Is Wrong"**

BankSouth is a regional bank with its place of business in Mobile, Alabama (in Mobile County) in the southwest corner of the state. The bank extends credit to Fred's Pretty Good Grocery, Inc., lending the sum of $300,000. Fred's Grocery operates two stores in Alabama, a large one in Mobile and a smaller store in Brewton, just east of Mobile in Escambia County. The documents, which require payments on the loan to be made to BankSouth at its office, were signed at a table in Wendy's Restaurant in Dothan, Alabama. An agent of BankSouth met there with Fred Alston, who signed the promissory note on behalf of Fred's, and also signed as personal guarantor of the loan. Dothan is in Houston County, in the southeast corner of Alabama, 165 miles east of Mobile.

Thereafter, BankSouth obtained the signatures of John and Sally Landforth as additional guarantors. The bank officer went to the Landforths' home in Baldwin County to obtain their signature. Baldwin County is located across Mobile Bay, between Mobile and Brewton. The Landforths were willing to sign because they are the parents-in-law of Fred Alston, who also resides in Baldwin County.

Fred's Grocery ran into trouble when Giant Foods opened megastores in the area, and sold the same goods cheaper. Ultimately, Fred's defaulted.

BankSouth brought suit in state court in Houston County, where Fred Alston signed the note and guarantee. The suit named Fred's Grocery and Fred personally as defendants. Defendants filed answers denying the charging allegations, and neither raised the matter of venue. BankSouth moved for summary judgment, and neither Fred's Grocery nor Fred appeared. The court ruled in favor of BankSouth.

BankSouth then moved to amend the complaint to add John and Sally Landforth. They appeared, objected to the motion, and moved to dismiss or transfer the suit to Baldwin County. "You can't add my clients to this lawsuit, your honor, if venue is wrong. And venue *is* wrong here. Suits in contract must be brought where one or more of the defendants reside. *None* of the defendants resides here."

BankSouth's lawyer replies in this way: "Neither Fred's Grocery nor Fred Alton raised a venue objection. By answering on the merits they waived venue issues under Alabama Rule 12, which reads the same as Federal Rule 12. If venue is proper at the beginning of the suit, it is proper all the way through, and the later addition of new defendants cannot make it improper. Even if Fred Alston had objected, he would have lost. Venue is proper in Houston County for our claim against Fred's Grocery, which can be sued where a 'substantial part of the events' occurred, and they did occur in Houston County, since that's where Fred's signed the note."

Two statutes and a Rule are relevant to the issues:

(1) One statute says suits "against individuals" on contracts "must be commenced in the county in which the defendant or one of the defendants resides." See Ala. Code §6-3-2(a)(2).

(2) Another statute provides that a corporation is to be sued where it has its "principal office" or where "a substantial part of the events or omissions giving rise to the claim occurred" or (if these provisions do not apply) "in any county in which the corporation was doing business." See Ala. Code §6-3-7.

(3) Alabama Civil Rule 82 says this: "Where several claims or parties have been joined, the suit may be brought in any county in which any one of the claims could properly have been brought. Whenever an action has been commenced in a proper county, additional claims and parties may be joined . . . as ancillary thereto, without regard to whether that county would be a proper venue for an independent action on such claims or against such parties." Ala. RCP 82(c).

Was venue proper in Houston County in the suit against Fred's Grocery and Fred Alton? When neither of them raised the venue issue, could the court proceed? What about the argument of the Landforths that they cannot be added because venue is improper as to them?

■ NOTES ON MOTIONS TO CHANGE VENUE

1. One of the issues in Problem 5-A is commonplace: What is to be done when multiple venue provisions apply, and point in different directions? For a case that wrestles with these questions in a jurisdiction lacking a provision like Alabama Rule 82, see Morris v. Crown Equipment Corp., 633 S.E.2d 292, 356 (W. Va. 2006) (product liability suit could go forward on behalf of Virginia plaintiff, injured in Virginia by forklift manufactured by defendant Crown in Ohio and sold by defendant Jefferd in West Virginia, despite statute allowing nonresident to sue only if a substantial part of acts or events occurred in West Virginia; if venue was proper for claim against Jefferd, "venue-giving defendant principle" made venue proper for claims against Ohio manufacturer subject to jurisdiction here).

2. Many states provide for venue on terms similar to those in the Alabama statute — where "a substantial part of the events or omissions occurred," or where "the cause of action arose," or where the tort was committed. Does signing a promissory note or guarantee constitute "a substantial part" of the events? Where do "omissions" occur? Consider some related problems:

(a) In a wrongful death suit based on malpractice, does the claim "arise" where a doctor or hospital treated the decedent, or where he died? See, e.g., Howell v. Willamette Urology, P.C., 178 P.3d 220, 221-222 (Or. 2008) (for purposes of venue, claim "arose" in county where "the negligence that caused the wrongful death occurred") (requiring transfer to county where treatment was given).

(b) If venue can be laid "where the tort was committed," what happens if multiple tortfeasors act in different counties? See, e.g., Hernandez v. Downing, 154 P.3d 1068, 1071 (Colo. 2007) (in wrongful death suit alleging malpractice by doctor who performed exploratory surgery in one county and medical center that provided post-surgical care in another, Colorado rule laying venue where tort occurred conflicted with statute requiring death claims to be brought in single suit; "so long as venue as proper as to one defendant in a wrongful death action, it is proper at to all other codefendants").

3. Some statutes say venue may be laid "in the county in which the injury or damage is sustained," or use similar language. See, e.g., Iowa Code §616.18. If plaintiff suffers damage to her business, does the statute let her sue where the business is located? See, e.g., Addison Ins. Co. v. Knight, Hoppe, Kurnik & Knight, L.L.C., 734 N.W.2d 473, 479 (Iowa 2007) (yes; in suit against Illinois law firm alleging malpractice in Illinois suit, Iowa insurance carrier could lay venue in its county of residence) (court had jurisdiction under long-arm statute); Circle S Seeds of Montana, Inc. v. Montana Merchandising, Inc., 157 P.3d 671, 675 (Mont. 2006) (in suit under state law for trademark infringement, venue could be laid in Gallatin County as plaintiff's principal place of business, under provision setting venue where tort was committed; "the arrow hit its mark" where plaintiff was damaged).

4. A ruling that denies a motion to change venue is not a final order that would ordinarily pave the way for appeal, and the same is true of rulings granting a change of venue. Some states, however, routinely review decisions on change-of-venue motions by entertaining interlocutory appeals.

(a) For examples of the usual attitude, in state courts and the federal system, see, e.g., Van Cauwenberghe v. Biard, 486 U.S. 517, 537-530 (2007) (denial of motion to dismiss on ground of *forum non conveniens* is *not* within collateral order exception allowing appeal); In re LimitNone, L.L.C., 551 F.3d 572, 575 (7th Cir. 2008) (refusing interlocutory review of order changing venue, sought in petition for mandamus; must show that ruling cannot be effectively

reviewed after trial because it would inflict irreparable harm, and was usurpative) (relief denied); Tex. RCP 87(6) ("no interlocutory appeals" from venue
determination); In re Team Rocket, L.P., 256 S.W.3d 257, 259 (Tex. 2008) (disappointed litigant cannot take nonsuit and refile to overcome venue determination; can review after trial).

(b) For examples of less common approaches, see Ex Parte Movie Gallery, Inc., 31 So. 3d 104 (Ala. 2009) (can review denial of change of venue in a
civil action by petition for writ of mandamus); State ex rel. Selminovic v. Dier-
ker, 246 S.W.3d 931, 932 (Mo. 2008) (mandamus can be used to compel change
of venue); Hedgepeth v. Johnson, 975 So. 2d 235 (Miss. 2008) (granting plaintiff's petition for interlocutory appeal to review order granting defense motion
to transfer venue).

(c) Some states more readily entertain appeals where a court *denies* a
motion to change venue than where a court *grants* the motion, on the ground
that in the former instance the court may be exercising power that it lacks
(venue being likened to jurisdiction) while in the latter case it may be declining to exercise power that it has. Compare Evans v. Blankenship, 286 S.W.3d
137, 140 (Ark. 2008) (court granted motion to transfer case to proper venue;
can only review ruling on venue after a final appealable order issues) with
Centerpoint Energy, Inc. v. Miller County Circuit Court, 276 S.W.3d 231, 354
(Ark. 2008) ("this court has a long history of granting the writ [of prohibition]
when venue is improper as to a party" because court "characterizes the venue
issue as one of jurisdiction over the person").

5. Motions to change venue raise the question whether, when the suit is
transferred, or is dismissed and a new one is filed in the proper venue, the
statute of limitations was "tolled" (clock stops ticking) by the original filing.

(a) Some states observe a rule that filing tolls the statute of limitations
even if venue is changed, either because the transferred suit continues the
original suit or because the statute was tolled while the suit was pending
in the first court, so this period can be "tacked on" to the date of dismissal,
leaving that much time to file in the right court. See, e.g., Bertonazzi v.
Hillman, 216 A.2d 723 (Md. 1966) (in tort suit against estate, where statute
of limitations required suit within six months after appointment of administrator, filing in wrong county tolled statute; plaintiff had 44 days, representing
time between filing and dismissal, to file in new county); Oltman v. Holland
America Line, Inc., 538 F.3d 1271 (9th Cir. 2008) (state court dismissed suit
under forum selection clause specifying federal court as venue for resolution
of disputes relating to trip on cruise ship; filing in state court tolled statute of
limitations; plaintiff acted promptly after dismissal in filing federal suit);
Booth v. Darnival Corp., 522 F.3d 1143 (11th Cir. 2008) (similar to *Oltman*).

(b) Some states have "savings statutes" providing that in case of dismissal for improper venue, plaintiff has some fixed period to refile, and then
the new suit relates back to the date of the original suit for purposes of the
statute of limitations. See., e.g., Kan. R. Stat. §413.270 (if plaintiff files "in due
time and in good faith," and court dismisses for lack of "jurisdiction," new

action may be commenced within 90 days); Dollar General Stores, Ltd. v. Smith, 237 S.W.3d 162 (Ky. 2007) (venue is not the same as jurisdiction, but savings statute applies to dismissal for improper venue, including *forum non conveniens*; transfer is preferable to dismissal).

6. Some states have taken what seems to be a flexible and progressive approach to venue. Indiana, for example, has a venue rule that lists "preferred" venues for different suits. Thus Indiana Trial Procedure Rule 75 lists as "preferred" venues the following counties: (1) "where the greater percentage" of defendants resides or, if there is such place, then "the place where any individual defendant" resides, or (2) where the land is located if the complaint includes a claim for injuries to the land or for quiet title, or (3) where the accident or collision occurred, or (4) where the principal office of a "defendant organization" is located, or "that office or agency of a defendant," or (5) where "one or more individual plaintiffs reside" or where "the principal office of a governmental organization" named as defendant is located, or (6) where all the parties agree to proceed on the basis of "written stipulations," or (7) where a person is held in custody or restrained, if the suit seeks relief relating to this matter, or (8) where any statute authorizes plaintiff to sue, or (9) where "all or some of the property is located or can be found" if the suit seeks only "judgment in rem" or (10) where any plaintiff resides or where any plaintiff organization or government organization is located, if the other provision do not apply. The Indiana Supreme Court has ruled that a suit filed in a "preferred venue" should not be transferred, see Meridian Mutual Ins. Co. v. Harter, 671 N.E.2d 861, 863 (Ind. 1996), but sometimes multiple counties count as "preferred," and the Court said that among "preferred" venues the place where plaintiff resides has "secondary status"! See R & D Transport, Inc. v. A.H., 859 N.E.2d 332 (Ind. 2006) (in suit arising out of car-truck collision, plaintiff sued in her own county of residence; trial court erred in refusing to change venue to county where defendant resided or accident occurred).

B   FEDERAL VENUE LAW

In federal courts, the basic venue statute, which was revised in 2011 to resolve mostly technical problems, provides two primary choices for both diversity and federal question cases, and a third possibility if either of the first two won't work:

(1) Venue may be laid in "a judicial district where any defendant resides, if all defendants reside in the same state," and
(2) Venue may be laid in "a judicial district in which a substantial part of the events or omissions giving rise to the claim occurred, or a substantial part of the property that is the subject of the action is situated," and

(3) If neither of these provisions can be satisfied in any court, then venue may be laid in "any judicial district in which any defendant is subject to personal jurisdiction."

See 28 USC §1391(b). The statute goes on to provide that for venue purposes a corporation or other entity "with the capacity to sue and be sued in its common name" is "deemed to reside, if a defendant, in any judicial district in which such defendant is subject to the court's personal jurisdiction," and is deemed to reside, "if a plaintiff, only in the judicial district in which it maintains its principal place of business." 28 USC §1391(c).

■ NOTES ON THE BASIC FEDERAL VENUE PROVISIONS

1. Many federal statutes contain their own venue provisions, raising the question whether these are "restrictive," so suits under the statutes *must be brought* in these venues, or "permissive," so under those statutes suits may *also* be bought in venues allowed by §1391. See Cortez Byrd Chips, Inc. v. Bill Harbert Construction Co., 529 U.S. 193 (2000) (clause in Federal Arbitration Act, allowing venue where award was made, is permissive; may also lay venue as provided by §1391).

2. The basic venue transfer statute provides that a court should either transfer or dismiss a suit brought in the wrong venue. See 28 USC §1406. Dismissing would mean plaintiff would have to begin over, and might raise issues under the statute of limitations, although it is commonplace to view the original filing as tolling the statute of limitations. See Minette v. Time Warner, 997 F.2d 1023, 1026-1027 (2d Cir. 1993) (transferring to proper venue a pro se claim for sex discrimination; filing followed by dismissal does not toll 90-day limitation period that begins when EEOC issues right-to-sue letter; transfer rather than dismissal serves interest of justice).

■ PROBLEM 5-B. "It Happened So Fast!"

While riding his new Harker-Diamond V-Rod motorcycle on a hilly road in Arkansas, Ron Patten encountered a motorist named Bill Morton coming toward him. Exactly how it happened is not entirely clear, but a collision ensued and Patten was seriously injured. "It happened so fast!" Patten told his lawyer several weeks later, while recuperating at Methodist Hospital in Memphis, Tennessee, where he lives. Patten had purchased the motorcycle at a dealer in Memphis, who had in turn acquired the motorcycle directly from Harker-Diamond.

On Patten's behalf, the lawyer files suit in Federal District Court for the Western District of Tennessee, naming as defendants Harker-Diamond Company, Dunrap Tire Company, and Bill Morton, who turns out to be an Arkansas citizen. Harker-Diamond manufactured the motorcycle in Milwaukee, Wisconsin. Dunrap made the tire at its plant in Buffalo, New York, and shipped it to Milwaukee. Both companies are incorporated in Delaware, and their principal places of business are in the locations of the factories just mentioned.

Both Harker-Diamond and Dunrap send their products to retailers in all 50 states, and both do substantial business in Tennessee. Although Bill Morton lives in Arkansas, he travels occasionally to Tennessee to shop or enjoy recreational opportunities in Memphis, and he was served with process while in Memphis.

Morton moves to dismiss for lack of jurisdiction over the person, and in the alternative seeks a change of venue to Arkansas, invoking 28 USC §1406 (statute authorizing such motion when venue is improper). He argues that jurisdiction is improper in Tennessee because the accident happened in Arkansas and Morton "has no contacts with Tennessee except occasional trips to Memphis for reasons having nothing to do with the suit." Invoking the *Burnham* case (Chapter 3C4, *supra*), the court *denies* the motion to dismiss for lack of jurisdiction. (Neither Harker-Diamond nor Dunrap move to dismiss, recognizing that Tennessee has a California-style long-arm statute under which its courts can exercise jurisdiction, *inter alia*, on "any basis not inconsistent with the constitution of this state or of the United States," and understanding that a federal court in Tennessee will apply that statute. See Tenn. Code §20-2-225.)

Morton argues that "venue cannot be properly laid in Tennessee because he lives in Arkansas and the events or omissions giving rise to the claim occurred in Arkansas." How should the court rule on the motion to transfer venue to Arkansas, and why?

■ NOTES ON THE FEDERAL VENUE STATUTE

1. Can venue be laid in Tennessee under §1391(a)(1), authorizing suit in the district where "any defendant resides," if all defendants "are residents of the State" where the district is located? Notice that residency of a *corporate defendant* is defined as "any judicial district in which such defendant is subject to the court's personal jurisdiction." See 28 USC §1391(c)(2). The two corporate defendants (Harker-Diamond and Dunrap) are subject to jurisdiction in Tennessee, so they reside there. But Morton does not, so this provision of the statute is not satisfied. Notice, however, that, for corporate defendants at least, jurisdiction over the person *is* pretty nearly equivalent to venue.

2. How about laying venue in Tennessee under the second part of the statute — the provision in §1391(a)(2) allowing venue to be laid where "a substantial part of the events or omissions giving rise to the claim" occurred. Does the fact that Patten bought the motorcycle in Tennessee count? Notice, however, that the products were made elsewhere (Wisconsin and New York) and the accident happened in Arkansas. It would be easier to make this argument if the accident happened in Tennessee, wouldn't it? Then the "last necessary act" happened in Tennessee, and federal courts often find that this act satisfies the "substantial part" standard. See, e.g., Bates v. C&S Adjusters, Inc., 980 F.2d 865 (2d Cir. 1992) (receipt of allegedly abusive debt collection notice in New York was a "substantial part of the events giving rise to a claim" under federal Fair Debt Collection Practices Act, even though defendant was located in Pennsylvania, and mailed the notice to plaintiff's then-address in Pennsylvania) (notice was later forwarded to plaintiff in New York).

3. Could venue be laid in Tennessee under the third part of the statute—allowing venue to be laid in a district where "any defendant is subject to personal jurisdiction," provided that there is "no district in which the action may otherwise be brought"? This "fallback" provision requires the court to look at other districts, doesn't it? Could the suit be brought in Wisconsin? New York? Arkansas?

4. Recall that corporate entities have "dual citizenship" for purposes of diversity jurisdiction (each is a citizen of its state of incorporation and state of its principal place of business). The matter is covered in Chapter 4A, supra. Now you know that corporate *defendants* have "multiple residences" for purposes of venue, and residence is defined *very broadly* in this setting, to mean simply "subject to personal jurisdiction."

5. Notice that a corporate *plaintiff* has only one residence for purposes of venue — that of "its principal place of business." See §1391(c)(2). Since there is no provision in §1391, however, that authorizes venue to be laid where *plaintiff* resides, the purpose of this limiting definition of the domicile of a corporate plaintiff is to implement other venue statutes, which sometimes do authorize suit where plaintiff resides. See, e.g., 28 USC §1402(a)(1) (authorizing venue in taxpayer refund suits to be laid "in the judicial district where the plaintiff resides").

6. For individuals (but obviously not corporations), recall that "domicile" determines "citizenship" when it comes to subject matter jurisdiction in diversity cases. You read Jane Doe v. Schwerzler, 2008 WL 1781986 (D.N.J. 2008) (Chapter 4A2, supra). In that setting, domicile means essentially the place where one "hangs his hat," or sometimes "residence" plus "intent to remain." In the setting of venue, "residence" is the critical concept, and residence means essentially the same thing as domicile, but with perhaps less stress on "intent to remain." See, e.g., United States v. Arango, 2012 WL 89184 (9th Cir. 2012) (in denaturalization case, equating "residence" with "place of general abode"); Crawley v. Advocacy Alliance, 2012 WL 707001 (E.D. Pa. 2012) (for venue purposes "the residence of an individual is equivalent to his or her legal domicile," which in turn is established by "residence and an intent to make the place of residence one's home").

C *FORUM NON CONVENIENS* AND FORUM SELECTION CLAUSES

As you have seen, venue statutes operate as more-or-less mandatory provisions that defendants can invoke if plaintiff has chosen to bring suit in an "improper" court. There is also a longstanding tradition, in the federal system and many states, of changing venue in civil cases if the court chosen by the plaintiff is "proper" but is less convenient than some other court. See 28 USC §1404.

"Forum non conveniens" venue transfer, as it is known, is discretionary and involves, as you will see when you read *Piper Aircraft*, a mix of factors relating to private interests of the litigants and public interests of courts, witnesses, juries, and administration of justice. In contrast to objections to "improper venue," which defendant must raise at the outset (see FRCP 12(b)(3)), motions for a change of venue on grounds of *forum non conveniens* can be made at any time, although delay is likely to count *against* a change on this ground.

Contracting parties often include provisions pledging to litigate any dispute in a particular forum. In *Burger King*, you saw a choice-of-law provision, and in *Carnival Cruise* (both in Chapter 3) you saw a forum selection clause in operation.

It is to these branches of the subject of venue that we now turn.

1. "Forum Non Conveniens" Venue Transfer

PIPER AIRCRAFT COMPANY v. REYNO
United States Supreme Court
454 U.S. 235 (1981)

Justice MARSHALL delivered the opinion of the Court.

These cases arise out of an air crash that took place in Scotland. Respondent, acting as representative of the estates of several Scottish citizens killed in the accident, brought wrongful-death actions against petitioners that were ultimately transferred to the United States District Court for the Middle District of Pennsylvania. Petitioners moved to dismiss on the ground of forum non conveniens. After noting that an alternative forum existed in Scotland, the District Court granted their motions. The United States Court of Appeals for the Third Circuit reversed. The Court of Appeals based its decision, at least in part, on the ground that dismissal is automatically barred where the law of the alternative forum is less favorable to the plaintiff than the law of the forum chosen by the plaintiff. Because we conclude that the possibility of an unfavorable change in law should not, by itself, bar dismissal, and because we conclude that the District Court did not otherwise abuse its discretion, we reverse.

I

A

In July 1976, a small commercial aircraft crashed in the Scottish highlands during the course of a charter flight from Blackpool to Perth. The pilot and five passengers were killed instantly. The decedents were all Scottish subjects and residents, as are their heirs and next of kin. There were no eyewitnesses to the accident. At the time of the crash the plane was subject to Scottish air traffic control.

The aircraft, a twin-engine Piper Aztec, was manufactured in Pennsylvania by petitioner Piper Aircraft Co. (Piper). The propellers were manufactured in Ohio by petitioner Hartzell Propeller, Inc. (Hartzell). At the time of the crash the aircraft was registered in Great Britain and was owned and maintained by Air Navigation and Trading Co., Ltd. (Air Navigation). It was operated by McDonald Aviation, Ltd. (McDonald), a Scottish air taxi service. Both Air Navigation and McDonald were organized in the United Kingdom. The wreckage of the plane is now in a hangar in Farnsborough, England.

The British Department of Trade investigated the accident shortly after it occurred. A preliminary report found that the plane crashed after developing a spin, and suggested that mechanical failure in the plane or the propeller was responsible. At Hartzell's request, this report was reviewed by a three-member Review Board, which held a 9-day adversary hearing attended by all interested parties. The Review Board found no evidence of defective equipment and indicated that pilot error may have contributed to the accident. The pilot, who had obtained his commercial pilot's license only three months earlier, was flying over high ground at an altitude considerably lower than the minimum height required by his company's operations manual.

In July 1977, a California probate court appointed respondent Gaynell Reyno administratrix of the estates of the five passengers. Reyno is not related to and does not know any of the decedents or their survivors; she was a legal secretary to the attorney who filed this lawsuit. Several days after her appointment, Reyno commenced separate wrongful-death actions against Piper and Hartzell in the Superior Court of California, claiming negligence and strict liability. Air Navigation, McDonald, and the estate of the pilot are not parties to this litigation. The survivors of the five passengers whose estates are represented by Reyno filed a separate action in the United Kingdom against Air Navigation, McDonald, and the pilot's estate.[2] Reyno candidly admits that the action against Piper and Hartzell was filed in the United States because its

---

[2] The pilot's estate has also filed suit in the United Kingdom against Air Navigation, McDonald, Piper, and Hartzell.

laws regarding liability, capacity to sue, and damages are more favorable to her position than are those of Scotland. Scottish law does not recognize strict liability in tort. Moreover, it permits wrongful-death actions only when brought by a decedent's relatives. The relatives may sue only for "loss of support and society."

On petitioners' motion, the suit was removed to the United States District Court for the Central District of California. Piper then moved for transfer to the United States District Court for the Middle District of Pennsylvania, pursuant to 28 USC §1404(a). Hartzell moved to dismiss for lack of personal jurisdiction, or in the alternative, to transfer.[5] In December 1977, the District Court quashed service on Hartzell and transferred the case to the Middle District of Pennsylvania. Respondent then properly served process on Hartzell.

B

In May 1978, after the suit had been transferred, both Hartzell and Piper moved to dismiss the action on the ground of *forum non conveniens.* The District Court granted these motions in October 1979. It relied on the balancing test set forth by this Court in Gulf Oil Corp. v. Gilbert, 330 U.S. 501 (1947), and its companion case, Koster v. Lumbermens Mut. Cas. Co., 330 U.S. 518 (1947). In those decisions, the Court stated that a plaintiff's choice of forum should rarely be disturbed. However, when an alternative forum has jurisdiction to hear the case, and when trial in the chosen forum would "establish . . . oppressiveness and vexation to a defendant . . . out of all proportion to plaintiff's convenience," or when the "chosen forum [is] inappropriate because of considerations affecting the court's own administrative and legal problems," the court may, in the exercise of its sound discretion, dismiss the case. *Koster.* To guide trial court discretion, the Court provided a list of "private interest factors" affecting the convenience of the litigants, and a list of "public interest factors" affecting the convenience of the forum.[6]

---

[5] The District Court concluded that it could not assert personal jurisdiction over Hartzell consistent with due process. However, it decided not to dismiss Hartzell because the corporation would be amenable to process in Pennsylvania.

[6] The factors pertaining to the private interests of the litigants included the "relative ease of access to sources of proof; availability of compulsory process for attendance of unwilling, and the cost of obtaining attendance of willing, witnesses; possibility of view of premises, if view would be appropriate to the action; and all other practical problems that make trial of a case easy, expeditious and inexpensive." *Gilbert.* The public factors bearing on the question included the administrative difficulties flowing from court congestion; the "local interest in having localized controversies decided at home"; the interest in having the trial of a diversity case in a forum that is at home with the law that must govern the action; the avoidance of unnecessary problems in conflict of laws, or in the application of foreign law; and the unfairness of burdening citizens in an unrelated forum with jury duty.

After describing our decisions in *Gilbert* and *Koster*, the District Court analyzed the facts of these cases. It began by observing that an alternative forum existed in Scotland; Piper and Hartzell had agreed to submit to the jurisdiction of the Scottish courts and to waive any statute of limitations defense that might be available. It then stated that plaintiff's choice of forum was entitled to little weight. The court recognized that a plaintiff's choice ordinarily deserves substantial deference. It noted, however, that Reyno "is a representative of foreign citizens and residents seeking a forum in the United States because of the more liberal rules concerning products liability law," and that "the courts have been less solicitous when the plaintiff is not an American citizen or resident, and particularly when the foreign citizens seek to benefit from the more liberal tort rules provided for the protection of citizens and residents of the United States."

The District Court next examined several factors relating to the private interests of the litigants, and determined that these factors strongly pointed towards Scotland as the appropriate forum. Although evidence concerning the design, manufacture, and testing of the plane and propeller is located in the United States, the connections with Scotland are otherwise "overwhelming." The real parties in interest are citizens of Scotland, as were all the decedents. Witnesses who could testify regarding the maintenance of the aircraft, the training of the pilot, and the investigation of the accident—all essential to the defense—are in Great Britain. Moreover, all witnesses to damages are located in Scotland. Trial would be aided by familiarity with Scottish topography, and by easy access to the wreckage.

The District Court reasoned that because crucial witnesses and evidence were beyond the reach of compulsory process, and because the defendants would not be able to implead potential Scottish third-party defendants, it would be "unfair to make Piper and Hartzell proceed to trial in this forum." The survivors had brought separate actions in Scotland against the pilot, McDonald, and Air Navigation. "[I]t would be fairer to all parties and less costly if the entire case was presented to one jury with available testimony from all relevant witnesses." Although the court recognized that if trial were held in the United States, Piper and Hartzell could file indemnity or contribution actions against the Scottish defendants, it believed that there was a significant risk of inconsistent verdicts.[7]

The District Court concluded that the relevant public interests also pointed strongly towards dismissal. The court determined that Pennsylvania law would apply to Piper and Scottish law to Hartzell if the case were tried in

---

[7] The District Court explained that inconsistent verdicts might result if petitioners were held liable on the basis of strict liability here, and then required to prove negligence in an indemnity action in Scotland. Moreover, even if the same standard of liability applied, there was a danger that different juries would find different facts and produce inconsistent results.

the Middle District of Pennsylvania.[8] As a result, "trial in this forum would be hopelessly complex and confusing for a jury." In addition, the court noted that it was unfamiliar with Scottish law and thus would have to rely upon experts from that country. The court also found that the trial would be enormously costly and time-consuming; that it would be unfair to burden citizens with jury duty when the Middle District of Pennsylvania has little connection with the controversy; and that Scotland has a substantial interest in the outcome of the litigation.

In opposing the motions to dismiss, respondent contended that dismissal would be unfair because Scottish law was less favorable. The District Court explicitly rejected this claim. It reasoned that the possibility that dismissal might lead to an unfavorable change in the law did not deserve significant weight; any deficiency in the foreign law was a "matter to be dealt with in the foreign forum."

C

On appeal, the United States Court of Appeals for the Third Circuit reversed and remanded for trial. The decision to reverse appears to be based on two alternative grounds. First, the Court held that the District Court abused its discretion in conducting the *Gilbert* analysis. Second, the Court held that dismissal is never appropriate where the law of the alternative forum is less favorable to the plaintiff.

The Court of Appeals began its review of the District Court's *Gilbert* analysis by noting that the plaintiff's choice of forum deserved substantial weight, even though the real parties in interest are nonresidents. It then rejected the District Court's balancing of the private interests. It found that Piper and Hartzell had failed adequately to support their claim that key witnesses would be unavailable if trial were held in the United States: they had never specified the witnesses they would call and the testimony these witnesses would provide. The Court of Appeals gave little weight to the fact that Piper and Hartzell would not be able to implead potential Scottish third-party defendants, reasoning that this difficulty would be "burdensome" but not "unfair."[9] Finally, the court stated that resolution of the suit would not be significantly aided by familiarity with Scottish topography, or by viewing the wreckage.

[8] Under Klaxon v. Stentor Electric Mfg. Co., 313 U.S. 487 (1941), a court ordinarily must apply the choice-of-law rules of the State in which it sits. However, where a case is transferred pursuant to 28 USC §1404(a), it must apply the choice-of-law rules of the State from which the case was transferred. Van Dusen v. Barrack, 376 U.S. 612 (1946). Relying on these two cases, the District Court concluded that California choice-of-law rules would apply to Piper, and Pennsylvania choice-of-law rules would apply to Hartzell. It further concluded that California applied a "governmental interests" analysis in resolving choice-of-law problems, and that Pennsylvania employed a "significant contacts" analysis. The court used the "governmental interests" analysis to determine that Pennsylvania liability rules would apply to Piper, and the "significant contacts" analysis to determine that Scottish liability rules would apply to Hartzell.

[9] The court claimed that the risk of inconsistent verdicts was slight because Pennsylvania and Scotland both adhere to principles of res judicata.

The Court of Appeals also rejected the District Court's analysis of the public interest factors. It found that the District Court gave undue emphasis to the application of Scottish law: "'the mere fact that the court is called upon to determine and apply foreign law does not present a legal problem of the sort which would justify the dismissal of a case otherwise properly before the court'" (quoting Hoffman v. Goberman, 420 F.2d 427 (3d Cir. 1970)). In any event, it believed that Scottish law need not be applied. After conducting its own choice-of-law analysis, the Court of Appeals determined that American law would govern the actions against both Piper and Hartzell.[10] The same choice-of-law analysis apparently led it to conclude that Pennsylvania and Ohio, rather than Scotland, are the jurisdictions with the greatest policy interests in the dispute, and that all other public interest factors favored trial in the United States.

In any event, it appears that the Court of Appeals would have reversed even if the District Court had properly balanced the public and private interests. . . . [The Court of Appeals] decided that dismissal is automatically barred if it would lead to a change in the applicable law unfavorable to the plaintiff.

We granted certiorari in these cases to consider the questions they raise concerning the proper application of the doctrine of *forum non conveniens.*

II

The Court of Appeals erred in holding that plaintiffs may defeat a motion to dismiss on the ground of *forum non conveniens* merely by showing that the substantive law that would be applied in the alternative forum is less favorable to the plaintiffs than that of the present forum. The possibility of a change in substantive law should ordinarily not be given conclusive or even substantial weight in the *forum non conveniens* inquiry.

We expressly rejected the position adopted by the Court of Appeals in our decision in Canada Malting Co. v. Paterson Steamships, Ltd., 285 U.S. 413 (1932). That case arose out of a collision between two vessels in American waters. The Canadian owners of cargo lost in the accident sued the Canadian owners of one of the vessels in Federal District Court. The cargo owners chose an American court in large part because the relevant American liability rules were more favorable than the Canadian rules. The District Court dismissed on grounds of *forum non conveniens.* The plaintiffs argued that dismissal was

---

[10] The Court of Appeals agreed with the District Court that California choice-of-law rules applied to Piper, and that Pennsylvania choice-of-law rules applied to Hartzell, see n.8, *supra.* It did not agree, however, that California used a "governmental interests" analysis and that Pennsylvania used a "significant contacts" analysis. Rather, it believed that both jurisdictions employed the "false conflicts" test. Applying this test, it concluded that Ohio and Pennsylvania had a greater policy interest in the dispute than Scotland, and that American law would apply to both Piper and Hartzell.

inappropriate because Canadian laws were less favorable to them. This Court nonetheless affirmed:

> We have no occasion to enquire by what law the rights of the parties are governed, as we are of the opinion that, under any view of that question, it lay within the discretion of the District Court to decline to assume jurisdiction over the controversy.... "[T]he court will not take cognizance of the case if justice would be as well done by remitting the parties to their home forum" (quoting Charter Shipping Co. v. Bowring, Jones & Tidy, 281 U.S. 515, 517 (1930)).

The Court further stated that "[t]here was no basis for the contention that the District Court abused its discretion."

It is true that *Canada Malting* was decided before *Gilbert*, and that the doctrine of *forum non conveniens* was not fully crystallized until our decision in that case. However, *Gilbert* in no way affects the validity of *Canada Malting*. Indeed, by holding that the central focus of the *forum non conveniens* inquiry is convenience, *Gilbert* implicitly recognized that dismissal may not be barred solely because of the possibility of an unfavorable change in law. Under *Gilbert*, dismissal will ordinarily be appropriate where trial in the plaintiff's chosen forum imposes a heavy burden on the defendant or the court, and where the plaintiff is unable to offer any specific reasons of convenience supporting his choice.[15] If substantial weight were given to the possibility of an unfavorable change in law, however, dismissal might be barred even where trial in the chosen forum was plainly inconvenient.

The Court of Appeals' decision is inconsistent with this Court's earlier *forum non conveniens* decisions in another respect. Those decisions have repeatedly emphasized the need to retain flexibility. In *Gilbert*, the Court refused to identify specific circumstances "which will justify or require either grant or denial of remedy." Similarly, in *Koster*, the Court rejected the contention that where a trial would involve inquiry into the internal affairs of a foreign corporation, dismissal was always appropriate. "That is one, but only one, factor which may show convenience." And in Williams v. Green Bay & Western R. Co., 326 U.S. 549, 557 (1946), we stated that we would not lay down a rigid rule to govern discretion, and that "[e]ach case turns on its facts." If central emphasis were placed on any one factor, the *forum non conveniens* doctrine would lose much of the very flexibility that makes it so valuable.

In fact, if conclusive or substantial weight were given to the possibility of a change in law, the *forum non conveniens* doctrine would become virtually

---

[15] In other words, *Gilbert* held that dismissal may be warranted where a plaintiff chooses a particular forum, not because it is convenient, but solely in order to harass the defendant or take advantage of favorable law. This is precisely the situation in which the Court of Appeals' rule would bar dismissal.

useless. Jurisdiction and venue requirements are often easily satisfied. As a result, many plaintiffs are able to choose from among several forums. Ordinarily, these plaintiffs will select that forum whose choice-of-law rules are most advantageous. Thus, if the possibility of an unfavorable change in substantive law is given substantial weight in the *forum non conveniens* inquiry, dismissal would rarely be proper.

Except for the court below, every Federal Court of Appeals that has considered this question after *Gilbert* has held that dismissal on grounds of *forum non conveniens* may be granted even though the law applicable in the alternative forum is less favorable to the plaintiff's chance of recovery. Several courts have relied expressly on *Canada Malting* to hold that the possibility of an unfavorable change of law should not, by itself, bar dismissal.

The Court of Appeals' approach is not only inconsistent with the purpose of the *forum non conveniens* doctrine, but also poses substantial practical problems. If the possibility of a change in law were given substantial weight, deciding motions to dismiss on the ground of *forum non conveniens* would become quite difficult. Choice-of-law analysis would become extremely important, and the courts would frequently be required to interpret the law of foreign jurisdictions. First, the trial court would have to determine what law would apply if the case were tried in the chosen forum, and what law would apply if the case were tried in the alternative forum. It would then have to compare the rights, remedies, and procedures available under the law that would be applied in each forum. Dismissal would be appropriate only if the court concluded that the law applied by the alternative forum is as favorable to the plaintiff as that of the chosen forum. The doctrine of *forum non conveniens*, however, is designed in part to help courts avoid conducting complex exercises in comparative law. As we stated in *Gilbert*, the public interest factors point towards dismissal where the court would be required to "untangle problems in conflict of laws, and in law foreign to itself."

Upholding the decision of the Court of Appeals would result in other practical problems. At least where the foreign plaintiff named an American manufacturer as defendant,[17] a court could not dismiss the case on grounds of *forum non conveniens* where dismissal might lead to an unfavorable change in law. The American courts, which are already extremely attractive to foreign

---

[17] In fact, the defendant might not even have to be American. A foreign plaintiff seeking damages for an accident that occurred abroad might be able to obtain service of process on a foreign defendant who does business in the United States. Under the Court of Appeals' holding, dismissal would be barred if the law in the alternative forum were less favorable to the plaintiff — even though none of the parties are American, and even though there is absolutely no nexus between the subject matter of the litigation and the United States.

plaintiffs,[18] would become even more attractive. The flow of litigation into the United States would increase and further congest already crowded courts.[19]

The Court of Appeals based its decision, at least in part, on an analogy between dismissals on grounds of *forum non conveniens* and transfers between federal courts pursuant to §1404(a). In Van Dusen v. Barrack, 376 U.S. 612 (1964), this Court ruled that a §1404(a) transfer should not result in a change in the applicable law. Relying on dictum in an earlier Third Circuit opinion interpreting *Van Dusen,* the court below held that that principle is also applicable to a dismissal on *forum non conveniens* grounds. However, §1404(a) transfers are different than dismissals on the ground of *forum non conveniens.*

Congress enacted §1404(a) to permit change of venue between federal courts. Although the statute was drafted in accordance with the doctrine of *forum non conveniens*, it was intended to be a revision rather than a codification of the common law. District courts were given more discretion to transfer under §1404(a) than they had to dismiss on grounds of *forum non conveniens.*

The reasoning employed in *Van Dusen* is simply inapplicable to dismissals on grounds of *forum non conveniens.* That case did not discuss the common-law doctrine. Rather, it focused on "the construction and application" of §1404(a). Emphasizing the remedial purpose of the statute, *Barrack* concluded that Congress could not have intended a transfer to be accompanied by a change in law. The statute was designed as a "federal housekeeping measure," allowing easy change of venue within a unified federal system. The Court feared that if a change in venue were accompanied by a change in law,

---

[18] First, all but 6 of the 50 American States — Delaware, Massachusetts, Michigan, North Carolina, Virginia, and Wyoming — offer strict liability. Rules roughly equivalent to American strict liability are effective in France, Belgium, and Luxembourg. West Germany and Japan have a strict liability statute for pharmaceuticals. However, strict liability remains primarily an American innovation. Second, the tort plaintiff may choose, at least potentially, from among 50 jurisdictions if he decides to file suit in the United States. Each of these jurisdictions applies its own set of malleable choice-of-law rules. Third, jury trials are almost always available in the United States, while they are never provided in civil law jurisdictions. Even in the United Kingdom, most civil actions are not tried before a jury. Fourth, unlike most foreign jurisdictions, American courts allow contingent attorney's fees, and do not tax losing parties with their opponents' attorney's fees. Fifth, discovery is more extensive in American than in foreign courts.

[19] In holding that the possibility of a change in law unfavorable to the plaintiff should not be given substantial weight, we also necessarily hold that the possibility of a change in law favorable to defendant should not be considered. Respondent suggests that Piper and Hartzell filed the motion to dismiss, not simply because trial in the United States would be inconvenient, but also because they believe the laws of Scotland are more favorable. She argues that this should be taken into account in the analysis of the private interests. We recognize, of course, that Piper and Hartzell may be engaged in reverse forum-shopping. However, this possibility ordinarily should not enter into a trial court's analysis of the private interests. If the defendant is able to overcome the presumption in favor of plaintiff by showing that trial in the chosen forum would be unnecessarily burdensome, dismissal is appropriate — regardless of the fact that defendant may also be motivated by a desire to obtain a more favorable forum.

forum-shopping parties would take unfair advantage of the relaxed standards for transfer. The rule was necessary to ensure the just and efficient operation of the statute.

We do not hold that the possibility of an unfavorable change in law should *never* be a relevant consideration in a *forum non conveniens* inquiry. Of course, if the remedy provided by the alternative forum is so clearly inadequate or unsatisfactory that it is no remedy at all, the unfavorable change in law may be given substantial weight; the district court may conclude that dismissal would not be in the interests of justice.[22] In these cases, however, the remedies that would be provided by the Scottish courts do not fall within this category. Although the relatives of the decedents may not be able to rely on a strict liability theory, and although their potential damages award may be smaller, there is no danger that they will be deprived of any remedy or treated unfairly.

III

The Court of Appeals also erred in rejecting the District Court's *Gilbert* analysis. The Court of Appeals stated that more weight should have been given to the plaintiff's choice of forum, and criticized the District Court's analysis of the private and public interests. However, the District Court's decision regarding the deference due plaintiff's choice of forum was appropriate. Furthermore, we do not believe that the District Court abused its discretion in weighing the private and public interests.

A

The District Court acknowledged that there is ordinarily a strong presumption in favor of the plaintiff's choice of forum, which may be overcome only when the private and public interest factors clearly point towards trial in the alternative forum. It held, however, that the presumption applies with less force when the plaintiff or real parties in interest are foreign.

The District Court's distinction between resident or citizen plaintiffs and foreign plaintiffs is fully justified. In *Koster*, the Court indicated that a

---

[22] At the outset of any *forum non conveniens* inquiry, the court must determine whether there exists an alternative forum. Ordinarily, this requirement will be satisfied when the defendant is "amenable to process" in the other jurisdiction. *Gilbert*. In rare circumstances, however, where the remedy offered by the other forum is clearly unsatisfactory, the other forum may not be an adequate alternative, and the initial requirement may not be satisfied. Thus, for example, dismissal would not be appropriate where the alternative forum does not permit litigation of the subject matter of the dispute. Cf. Phoenix Canada Oil Co. Ltd. v. Texaco, Inc., 78 F.R.D. 445 (Del. 1978) (court refuses to dismiss, where alternative forum is Ecuador, it is unclear whether Ecuadorean tribunal will hear the case, and there is no generally codified Ecuadorean legal remedy for the unjust enrichment and tort claims asserted).

plaintiff's choice of forum is entitled to greater deference when the plaintiff has chosen the home forum.[23] When the home forum has been chosen, it is reasonable to assume that this choice is convenient. When the plaintiff is foreign, however, this assumption is much less reasonable. Because the central purpose of any *forum non conveniens* inquiry is to ensure that the trial is convenient, a foreign plaintiff's choice deserves less deference.

Respondent argues that since plaintiffs will ordinarily file suit in the jurisdiction that offers the most favorable law, establishing a strong presumption in favor of both home and foreign plaintiffs will ensure that defendants will always be held to the highest possible standard of accountability for their purported wrongdoing. However, the deference accorded a plaintiff's choice of forum has never been intended to guarantee that the plaintiff will be able to select the law that will govern the case.

B

The *forum non conveniens* determination is committed to the sound discretion of the trial court. It may be reversed only when there has been a clear abuse of discretion; where the court has considered all relevant public and private interest factors, and where its balancing of these factors is reasonable, its decision deserves substantial deference. *Gilbert.* Here, the Court of Appeals expressly acknowledged that the standard of review was one of abuse of discretion. In examining the District Court's analysis of the public and private interests, however, the Court of Appeals seems to have lost sight of this rule, and substituted its own judgment for that of the District Court.

(1)

In analyzing the private interest factors, the District Court stated that the connections with Scotland are "overwhelming." This characterization may be somewhat exaggerated. Particularly with respect to the question of relative ease of access to sources of proof, the private interests point in both directions. As respondent emphasizes, records concerning the design, manufacture, and testing of the propeller and plane are located in the United States. She would have greater access to sources of proof relevant to her strict

---

[23] In *Koster,* we stated that "[i]n any balancing of conveniences, a real showing of convenience by a plaintiff who has sued in his home forum will normally outweigh the inconvenience the defendant may have shown." As the District Court correctly noted in its opinion, the lower federal courts have routinely given less weight to a foreign plaintiff's choice of forum. A citizen's forum choice should not be given dispositive weight, however. Citizens or residents deserve somewhat more deference than foreign plaintiffs, but dismissal should not be automatically barred when a plaintiff has filed suit in his home forum. As always, if the balance of conveniences suggests that trial in the chosen forum would be unnecessarily burdensome for the defendant or the court, dismissal is proper.

liability and negligence theories if trial were held here.[25] However, the District Court did not act unreasonably in concluding that fewer evidentiary problems would be posed if the trial were held in Scotland. A large proportion of the relevant evidence is located in Great Britain.

The Court of Appeals found that the problems of proof could not be given any weight because Piper and Hartzell failed to describe with specificity the evidence they would not be able to obtain if trial were held in the United States. It suggested that defendants seeking *forum non conveniens* dismissal must submit affidavits identifying the witnesses they would call and the testimony these witnesses would provide if the trial were held in the alternative forum. Such detail is not necessary. Piper and Hartzell have moved for dismissal precisely because many crucial witnesses are located beyond the reach of compulsory process, and thus are difficult to identify or interview. Requiring extensive investigation would defeat the purpose of their motion. Of course, defendants must provide enough information to enable the District Court to balance the parties' interests. Our examination of the record convinces us that sufficient information was provided here. Both Piper and Hartzell submitted affidavits describing the evidentiary problems they would face if the trial were held in the United States.[27]

The District Court correctly concluded that the problems posed by the inability to implead potential third-party defendants clearly supported holding the trial in Scotland. Joinder of the pilot's estate, Air Navigation, and McDonald is crucial to the presentation of petitioners' defense. If Piper and Hartzell can show that the accident was caused not by a design defect, but rather by the negligence of the pilot, the plane's owners, or the charter company, they will be relieved of all liability. It is true, of course, that if Hartzell and Piper were found liable after a trial in the United States, they could institute an action for indemnity or contribution against these parties in Scotland. It would be far more convenient, however, to resolve all claims in one trial. The Court of Appeals rejected this argument. Forcing petitioners to rely on actions for indemnity or contributions would be "burdensome" but not "unfair." Finding that trial in the plaintiff's chosen forum would be burdensome, however, is sufficient to support dismissal on grounds of *forum non conveniens.*

(2)

The District Court's review of the factors relating to the public interest was also reasonable. On the basis of its choice-of-law analysis, it concluded that if the case were tried in the Middle District of Pennsylvania, Pennsylvania law would

---

[25] In the future, where similar problems are presented, district courts might dismiss subject to the condition that defendant corporations agree to provide the records relevant to the plaintiff's claims.

[27] The affidavit provided to the District Court by Piper states that it would call the following witnesses: the relatives of the decedents; the owners and employees of McDonald; the persons responsible for the training and licensing of the pilot; the persons responsible for servicing and maintaining the aircraft; and two or three of its own employees involved in the design and manufacture of the aircraft.

apply to Piper and Scottish law to Hartzell. It stated that a trial involving two sets of laws would be confusing to the jury. It also noted its own lack of familiarity with Scottish law. Consideration of these problems was clearly appropriate under *Gilbert*; in that case we explicitly held that the need to apply foreign law pointed towards dismissal. The Court of Appeals found that the District Court's choice-of-law analysis was incorrect, and that American law would apply to both Hartzell and Piper. Thus, lack of familiarity with foreign law would not be a problem. Even if the Court of Appeals' conclusion is correct, however, all other public interest factors favored trial in Scotland.

Scotland has a very strong interest in this litigation. The accident occurred in its airspace. All of the decedents were Scottish. Apart from Piper and Hartzell, all potential plaintiffs and defendants are either Scottish or English. As we stated in *Gilbert*, there is "a local interest in having localized controversies decided at home." Respondent argues that American citizens have an interest in ensuring that American manufacturers are deterred from producing defective products, and that additional deterrence might be obtained if Piper and Hartzell were tried in the United States, where they could be sued on the basis of both negligence and strict liability. However, the incremental deterrence that would be gained if this trial were held in an American court is likely to be insignificant. The American interest in this accident is simply not sufficient to justify the enormous commitment of judicial time and resources that would inevitably be required if the case were to be tried here.

IV

The Court of Appeals erred in holding that the possibility of an unfavorable change in law bars dismissal on the ground of *forum non conveniens*. It also erred in rejecting the District Court's *Gilbert* analysis. The District Court properly decided that the presumption in favor of the respondent's forum choice applied with less than maximum force because the real parties in interest are foreign. It did not act unreasonably in deciding that the private interests pointed towards trial in Scotland. Nor did it act unreasonably in deciding that the public interests favored trial in Scotland. Thus, the judgment of the Court of Appeals is
Reversed.

Justice POWELL took no part in the decision of these cases.

Justice O'CONNOR took no part in the consideration or decision of these cases.

Justice WHITE, concurring in part and dissenting in part.
I join Parts I and II of the Court's opinion. However, like Justice Brennan and Justice Stevens, I would not proceed to deal with the issues addressed in Part III. To that extent, I am in dissent.

Justice Stevens, with whom Justice Brennan joins, dissenting.

[The dissenters agree that a motion to dismiss for *forum non conveniens* need not be denied if the law of the alternate forum is less favorable to recovery, but would remand the case to consider the question whether the court "correctly decided that Pennsylvania was not a convenient forum in which to litigate a claim against a Pennsylvania company that a plane was defectively designed and manufactured in Pennsylvania."]

■ NOTES ON *FORUM NON CONVENIENS*

1. How and why does such a suit get filed in an American court? The case involved a crash in Scotland of a plane owned by a British company, operated by a Scottish air taxi service, in a flight between one point in Scotland and another, and all the victims were Scottish citizens. Gaynell Reyno, who appears as plaintiff, was legal secretary to the lawyer who filed the suit, and had no connection to the victims, parties, or transaction. Why was she appointed administratrix of the estates of five Scottish decedents?

Twin Engine Piper Aztec Plane

This 1976 Piper Aztec plane resembles the one that crashed in Scotland, giving rise to the litigation in the *Piper Aircraft* case. It was no accident that the Scottish plaintiffs wound up contacting lawyer Daniel Cathcart of Los Angeles: He was known for his expertise in aviation litigation. It is not only aircraft litiga-

tion that draws foreign plaintiffs to American courts. In one case, a Brazilian consumer who allegedly suffered permanent loss of sight after using a drug developed and patented in the United States, but made and marketed in Brazil, sued Lederle Laboratories in the United States. See De Melo v. Lederle Laboratories, 801 F.2d 1058 (8th Cir. 1986) (dismissing on finding that Brazilian forum would be more convenient). And after the disastrous release of gas from a chemical plant in Bhopal, India, American lawyers representing Indian claimants filed suit in federal court in the Southern District of New York. Ultimately, the Second Circuit approved dismissal of the case, on condition that American defendants agree to jurisdiction in India, to waive defenses based on the statute of limitations, to enforcement of any eventual judgment entered by an Indian court, and to make discovery under the provisions of the Federal Rules. See In re Union Carbide Corp. Gas Plant Disaster at Bhopal, India, 809 F.2d 195 (2d Cir. 1987).

2. Was venue proper in federal court in California? Why or why not? Note that 28 USC §1441(a) provides that suits may be removed from state court "to the district court of the United States for the district and division embracing the place where such action is pending." In this case, suit was filed in state court in Los Angeles and removed to the federal district court in the Southern District of California, which encompasses Los Angeles. Note too that 28 USC §1441(e)(6) provides that the federal court to which a suit is removed may "transfer or dismiss an action" for *forum non conveniens.*

3. Piper (manufacturer of plane) and Hartzell (manufacturer of propeller) moved *both* to dismiss for lack of jurisdiction *and* to transfer venue to Pennsylvania, invoking the *forum non conveniens* statute, 28 USC §1404(a). For years, this provision allowed transfer to a federal court where the suit "might have been brought," and was interpreted as limiting transfers to courts in which both personal jurisdiction and venue would have been proper initially. See Hoffman v. Blaski, 363 U.S. 335 (1960). In 2011, however, the provision was expanded to permit transfer also to a court "to which all parties have consented." In *Piper Aircraft,* the suit probably could have been brought originally in Pennsylvania — jurisdiction would have been good with respect to Piper itself, and probably would have existed over Hartzell because it sent the propeller into Pennsylvania. Venue would have been good in Pennsylvania *both* because Piper and Hartzell "reside" there and because "a substantial part of the events" giving rise to suit happened there. Recall that the residence of a corporate defendant, for venue purposes, is any place that has good *in personam* jurisdiction. See 28 USC §1391(a) and (c). Today, we can add that venue could be transferred from California to Pennsylvania under §1404 because both defendants wanted the case transferred to Pennsylvania.

4. *Piper Aircraft* is made complicated by choice-of-law considerations. In Chapter 6, you will encounter Klaxon Co. v. Stentor Electric Mfg. Co., 313 U.S. 487 (1941), under which federal courts in diversity cases apply *state* choice-of-law rules. Such rules are just what they sound like, although they are complex and give rise to much disagreement: They are rules that courts use to decide which substantive law to apply — on the facts of *Piper Aircraft,* we are talking about which body of product liability law to apply. One could imagine applying California law, at least with respect to Piper, because Gaynell Reyno is from California (although that seems a thin basis for choosing California law, inasmuch as she represented foreign decedents), and Piper does business there. One could also imagine applying Pennsylvania law, again with respect to Piper, because that is where Piper has its principal place of business and manufactured the plane. One could also imagine applying the law of Ohio, at least with respect to Hartzell, because that is where Hartzell has its principal place of business and made the propeller. Finally, one could imagine applying the law of Scotland to all these issues, because that is where the crash occurred, where the flight began and was to have ended, where plaintiff's decedents resided before they were killed, and perhaps (although this fact is not given) the place where Piper sold the plane. *Piper Aircraft* presents major issues in choice of law, and the reason for saying that "one could imagine" the law of California, Ohio, Pennsylvania, and Scotland applying is that there are different approaches to choice of law, as the case illustrates, and room for disagreement and debate.

5. In Van Dusen v. Barrack, 376 U.S. 612 (1966), plaintiffs filed in federal court in Pennsylvania a suit against Eastern Air Lines arising out of the crash in Boston Harbor of a commercial airliner that had just taken off from Logan Airport on a flight to Philadelphia. Apparently, the crash was caused by the ingestion of birds into the turbo prop engines. The principal defendants were Eastern, Lockheed (manufacturer of the plane), and General Motors (manufacturer of the engines). Defendants moved to transfer venue to federal court in Massachusetts, invoking the *forum non conveniens* statute, see 28 USC §1404(a).[2] Plaintiffs opposed the move, arguing that transferring the case would result in application of the Massachusetts statute limiting recovery to $20,000. The Supreme Court disagreed. Citing appellate opinions that were "strongly inclined to protect plaintiffs against the risk that transfer might be accompanied by a prejudicial change in applicable state laws," the Court in *Van Dusen* concluded that "in cases such as the present, where the defendants seek transfer, the transferee district court must be obligated to apply the state law that would have been applied if there had been no change of venue." See also Ferens v. John Deere Co., 494 U.S. 516 (1990) (applying *Van Dusen* principle even where *plaintiff* moves to transfer venue).

6. Look at footnotes 8 and 10 in *Piper Aircraft*, which say the federal court in Pennsylvania thought California choice-of-law rules would apply to Piper, but Pennsylvania choice-of-law rules would apply to Hartzell, and that the Third Circuit agreed about which choice-of-law rules applied, but disagreed on the question of which state's law was selected by these rules. Why should California's choice-of-law rule apply to claims against Piper while Pennsylvania's choice-of-law rule applies to the claims against Hartzell? Why doesn't *Van Dusen* apply when the *Piper Aircraft* suit is dismissed and refiled in Scotland? Does *Piper Aircraft* mean that when the suit is litigated in Scotland, the court might apply Scottish law?

7. Although *Piper Aircraft* involved a *dismissal* so a new suit could be "refiled" in Scotland, rather than *transfer of venue* under §1404(a), the Court treats the underlying criteria as being the same, and they include reference to public interest factors and private interest factors. What public interest factors support transfer from the United States to Scotland? What private interest factors?

---

[2] At the time, the basic venue statute provided that venue in diversity cases could be laid "only in the judicial district where all plaintiffs or all defendants reside." Thus Pennsylvania was a proper venue for suits by Pennsylvanians who survived and suits by Pennsylvania representatives on behalf of passengers who died. The citizenship of the personal representative was her own personal citizenship, and her *residence* was usually the same, which counted when they were plaintiffs in diversity cases because §1391 let them lay venue at home. Today, §1391 no longer provides for venue in diversity cases at the residence of the plaintiff, and §1332(c)(2) provides that "the legal representative of the estate of a decedent" is "deemed to be" a citizen of the state in which the decedent was a citizen.

8. In *Piper Aircraft*, the federal court in Pennsylvania conditioned dismissal on defendants' waiving defenses in Scotland based on claims of lack of jurisdiction or the statute of limitations. Note the suggestion in footnote 25 in *Piper Aircraft* that a court might condition a *forum non conveniens* dismissal on the agreement of defendants to "provide the records relevant to the plaintiff's claims." What other conditions might a court impose? If Scotland had a statute limiting damage recovery, like the Massachusetts statute in *Van Dusen*, might the court in *Piper Aircraft* condition a dismissal on waiving the damage limit?

9. Professor Clermont says of *Piper Aircraft* that "[n]o procedural doctrine is so encapsulated in a single opinion that is so ill-conceived." The California lawyer representing plaintiff in *Piper Aircraft* admitted that he'd filed in the United States because "prospective recovery in the courts of the United States is much greater than in those of Scotland," see Brief for Respondent Gaynell Reyno 24 (1981). Professor Clermont argues, then, that the "real motive" in seeking dismissal on ground of *forum non conveniens* in such cases is the "substantive impact" on outcome, and that we should "overlook" this factor only if we can "somehow neutralize it," as the Court did in transfers under §1404(a) in *Van Dusen*. Professor Clermont argues further that it is "hard to see" why this *one* factor should be viewed as irrelevant, and that it is "illogical" to say that a change in applicable law is irrelevant if a court in ordering dismissal so a case can be refiled is to consider the adequacy of the remedy offered in the court that is to try the case. See Kevin M. Clermont, *The Story of* Piper: *Forum Matters, in* Civil Procedure Stories 199, 215-216 (Kevin M. Clermont ed., 2d ed. 2008). What do you think of this argument?

2. Forum Selection Clauses

Recall the *Carnival Cruise* case (Chapter 3C6), where the Court enforced a clause in a ticket requiring suits against the cruise ship company to be litigated in Florida, and the *Bremen* case where the Court honored the agreement between American and German companies to litigate in London. As it happens, both *Carnival Cruise* and *Bremen* were suits in admiralty, and the Court was applying admiralty law (a particular area of federal common law). For a more recent example, see Holland America Lines v. Wartsila North America, Inc., 485 F.3d 450 (9th Cir. 2009) (under forum selection clause, shipowner must sue French classification society in France, in claims arising out of loss in Caribbean of cruise ship due to fire).

Shipping companies and cruise lines are not the only parties who find forum selection clauses useful. See, e.g., Ginter ex rel. Ballard v. Belcher, Prendergast & Lapore, 536 F.3d 439 (5th Cir. 2008) (dismissing suit filed in federal court by clients of lawyer under clause in lawyer-client agreement specifying Louisiana state court as venue for dispute); Abbott Laboratories v. Takeda Pharmaceutical Co. Ltd., 476 F.3d 421 (7th Cir. 2007) (in suit by American party to joint venture against Japanese party, clause requiring suit in Japan was enforceable; suit dismissed).

Forum selection clauses can be used to avoid litigating in state courts or in federal courts. See, e.g., Ocwen Orlando Holdings Corp. v. Harvard Property Trust, LLC, 526 F.3d 1379 (11th Cir. 2008) (clause in real estate purchase agreement permitting either party to sue in state court and waiving other party's right to transfer to "any other court" waived defendant's right to remove from state to federal court); Oltman v. Holland America Line USA, Inc., 178 P.3d 981 (Wash. 2008) (passenger obliged to litigate claim against cruise line in federal court; passenger's nontraveling spouse was not bound, and could litigate claim for loss of consortium in state court); Pee Dee Health Care, P.A. v. Sanford, 509 F.3d 204 (4th Cir. 2007) (forum selection clause can require claimant to litigate even federal question claim in state court; dismissing federal suit brought under §1983 on basis of clause requiring suit between parties to be brought in state court).

At least one state does not accept forum selection clauses, and sometimes statutes make them unenforceable in particular settings. See Fog Motorsports No. 3, Inc. v. Arctic Cat Sales Inc., 982 A.2d 963 (N.H 2009) (refusing to enforce clause requiring snowmobile dealership to sue manufacturer in Minnesota; Dealership Act renders "unenforceable" any forum selection clause that would block dealer from suing under Act); Regal-Beloit Corp. v. Kawasaki Kisen Kaisha Ltd., 557 F.3d 985 (9th Cir. 2009) (under Carmack Amendment to Interstate Commerce Act, governing rail and motor carriers, venue is limited, and "forum selection clauses are generally forbidden," but COGSA (Carriage of Goods by Sea Act) does not contain venue restrictions that prohibit forum selection clauses); Doe 1 v. AOL LLC, 552 F.3d 1077 (9th Cir. 2009) (refusing to enforce forum selection clause in member agreement of internet service provider; it violated Consumer Legal Remedies Act).

Forum selection clauses can have the effect of consenting to jurisdiction in fora where defendants could not otherwise be sued. See National Equipment Rental, Ltd. v. Szukhent, 375 U.S. 311, 315-316 (1964) ("parties to a contract may agree in advance to submit to the jurisdiction of a given court"); Consulting Engineers Corp. v. Geometric Ltd., 561 F.3d 273, 282 n.11 (4th Cir. 2009) (forum selection clause "may act as a waiver [of] objections to personal jurisdiction").

■ NOTES ON FORUM SELECTION CLAUSES

1. Bringing suit in the "wrong court" in violation of a forum selection clause may breach a contract, but does not deprive the court of jurisdiction, and the matter can be raised in the answer by way of defense. See Gabbanelli Accordions & Imports, L.L.C. v. Gabbanelli, 575 F.3d 693, 695 (7th Cir. 2009); Reiner, Reiner and Bendett, P.C. v. The Cadle Co., 897 A.2d 58 (Conn. 2006) (Connecticut court had jurisdiction in suit by Ohio lawyers against

Connecticut clients, despite clause selecting Ohio as proper court; clients defaulted; clause did not divest Connecticut court of jurisdiction or render judgment void).

2. Contractual forum selection clauses often cover some claims, but not every claim that a party might make. If a suit is not covered by the clause, plaintiff can sue in a different court. See Altvater Gessler-J.A. Baczewski International (USA) Inc. v. Sobieski, 572 F.3d 86, 89 (2d Cir. 2009) (claims did not sound in contract, but in unfair competition, trademark dilution and infringement, deceptive trade practices, and unjust enrichment, and were *not* subject to clause specifying venue in Poland) (defense must show the clause was "reasonably communicated" to plaintiff, was "mandatory and not merely permissive," and that "claims and parties" in suit are subject to it; establishing these points "shifts to the party resisting enforcement" the burden to "rebut the presumption of enforceability" by showing that enforcement would be "unreasonable or unjust" or that the clause was "invalid for such reasons as fraud or overreaching"); Phillips v. Audio Active Ltd., 494 F.3d 378 (2d Cir. 2007) (forum selection clause covered claims based on breach of contract, which must be brought in UK, even though result is to split suit; copyright and state law claims are not covered). See also Oltman v. Holland America Line USA, Inc., 178 P.3d 981 (Wash. 2008) (in suit against cruise line, nonpassenger wife could bring claim for loss of consortium in state court; she was not bound by clause as she did not travel). But see F.L. Crane & Sons, Inc. v. Malouf Construction Corp., 953 So. 2d 366 (Ala. 2006) (where condominium association sued construction contractor, who filed third-party claims against subcontractors, refusing to enforce forum selection clauses that would result in severing third-party claims from main suit).

3. Under the *Erie* doctrine (covered in Chapter 6), federal courts apply state substantive law in diversity cases but federal law on matters of procedure. For years there has been a lively debate whether forum selection clauses raise issues of substance or procedure. See Piper Aircraft Co. v. Reyno, 454 U.S. 235, n.13 (1981) (whether state or federal law governs *forum non conveniens* in diversity cases remains unresolved) (Section B1, supra). And compare Alliance Health Group, LLC v. Bridging Health Options, LLC, 553 F.3d 397, 399 (5th Cir. 2008) (federal law determines enforceability of forum selection clauses); Jones v. Weibrecht, 901 F.2d 17, 19 (2d Cir. 1990) (venue and enforcement of forum selection clauses are procedural matters); Manetti-Farrow, Inc. v. Gucci America, Inc., 858 F.3d 509, 513 (9th Cir. 1988) ("federal procedural issues raised by forum selection clauses significantly outweigh the state interests") with Preferred Capital, Inc. v. Sarasota Kennel Club, Inc., 489 F.3d 303, 307 (6th Cir. 2007) (forum selection clause purported to confer jurisdiction in Ohio, as principal place of business of assignee of contract rights; validity of clause is determined by reference to *state* law).

4. Forum selection clauses can be the basis of a motion to remand a case removed to federal court. The question arises whether a remand motion must be made within 30 days of removal (limit established by removal statute for motions to remand on ground of "defect in removal procedure," see 28 USC §1447(c)). For the same reason that forum selection clauses do not destroy subject matter jurisdiction, their violation should *not* be considered a "defect in removal procedure," so the 30-day limit should not apply. See, e.g., Kamm v. ITEX Corp., 568 F.3d 752, 756 (9th Cir. 2009) (forum selection clause "operates outside of the various requirements for removal," so existence of clause does not render removal "defective" under statute).

5. On motions to transfer for *forum non conveniens,* defendants bear the burden of showing that another court is more appropriate, and plaintiff's choice of forum is entitled to respect. See, e.g., Langenhorst v. Norfolk Southern Ry. Co., 848 N.E.2d 927 (Ill. 2006) (can reverse decision denying transfer on this ground only if defendants show that court abused discretion in balancing factors) (denying railroad's motion to transfer wrongful death suit, brought in St. Clair County where nonresident railroad's agent for service of process was located, to Clinton County where fatal grade-crossing accident occurred and plaintiff resided).

6. Courts disagree on the right way to invoke forum selection clauses as a means of forcing a venue transfer.

(a) One might treat forum selection clauses as raising issues of subject matter jurisdiction under FRCP 12(b)(1). Consider this approach. Are there time limits to moving to dismiss on this ground? Would the *court* be obliged to raise issues under such clauses? See FRCP 12(h)(3).

(b) One might treat forum selection clauses as raising issues of venue under FRCP 12(b)(3). Consider this approach. Would it mean that rights under such clauses must be raised by answer or pre-answer motion? See FRCP 12(h)(1).

(c) One might treat forum selection clauses as raising the question whether plaintiff stated a claim for relief under FRCP 12(b)(6), thus becoming a basis for a motion to dismiss for judgment on the pleadings. Consider this approach. Would it mean that rights under such clauses could be raised at trial? Would it mean that pleadings had to be taken as true and courts could not make factual inquiries?

(d) Most courts treat these matters under FRCP 12(b)(3) as raising the defense of improper venue. See Ferrell v. Allstate Ins. Co., 188 P.3d 1156, 1174 (N.M. 2008) (most decisions treat the matter as defense to be raised by motion or answer under FRCP 12(b)(3), and opting for this approach); Polk County Recreational Association v. Susquehanna Patriot Commercial Leasing Co., 734 N.W.2d 750, 757 (Neb. 2007) (enforcement of forum selection clause is by motion to dismiss, rather than motion claiming lack of jurisdiction over person; court "engages in a procedure similar to ruling on a motion to dismiss for lack of subject matter jurisdiction," and may base decision "solely on the complaint" or may need to make findings of fact); Sucampo Pharmaceuticals, Inc. v. Astellas Pharma, Inc., 471 F.3d 544, 549-550 (4th Cir. 2006) (rejecting 12(b)(1) because it forces "legal fiction" that forum selection clause affects "power of the court to adjudicate" and brings "practical

difficulties" of requiring court to raise the matter *sua sponte* and making it nonwaivable; rejecting 12(b)(6) because it would require court to treat pleadings as true and allow motion any time before trial; preferring 12(b)(3) because it presses defense to raise issue in first responsive pleading). But see Langley v. Prudential Mortgage Capital Co., L.L.C., 546 F.3d 365, 370-371 (6th Cir. 2008) (in suit removed from state to federal court, venue is by definition proper in court to which suit was removed; defense based on forum selection clause is not raised by motion under FRCP 12(b)(3), and should be made by motion under 28 USC §1404(a)).

7. Where defendant in a state court seeks a change of forum to another state, the court cannot transfer, simply because each state is sovereign, and a court in one state need not accept anything from a court of another state. (As *Piper Aircraft* illustrates, American courts cannot simply transfer a case to a court in another country either.) Thus a state court can only accommodate a motion invoking *forum non conveniens* to move the suit to another state by dismissing, leaving plaintiffs to file in the other state. To avoid problems, state courts commonly dismiss subject to what amounts to conditions subsequent, including requirements that defendant waive defenses based on lack of jurisdiction or statute of limitations. See, e.g., Gianocostas v. Interface Group-Massachusetts, Inc., 881 N.E.2d 134, 143 (Mass. 2008) (wrongful death suit on behalf of American tourist who died vacationing in Dominican Republic, based on allegations of malpractice arising out of medical treatment there and alleged negligent misrepresentations by tour operator, should be dismissed for *forum non conveniens*; dismissal conditioned on defendant's written agreement to waive defenses based on statute of limitations or lack of personal jurisdiction, and to waive any requirement that plaintiffs post bond, and on further condition that the court in the Dominican Republic give effect to such waivers).

8. Forum selection clauses are not enforceable under conditions of hardship. See, e.g., Carnival Cruise Lines, Inc. v. Shute, 499 U.S. 585, 595 (1991) (such clauses "are subject to judicial scrutiny for fundamental fairness," and claims of "fraud or overreaching" may be considered); Calix-Chacon v. Global International Marine, Inc., 493 F.3d 507 (2007) (court may decline to enforce forum selection clause if (a) it was included through "fraud or overreaching," (b) party seeking to avoid clause will for all practical purposes be deprived of his day in court because of "grave inconvenience or unfairness" of selected forum, (c) "fundamental unfairness" of chosen law deprives plaintiff of remedy, or (d) enforcement would "contravene a strong public policy" of forum). See also Nagrampa v. MailCoups, Inc., 469 F.3d 1257, 1289-1293 (9th Cir. 2006) (refusing to enforce clause requiring California franchisee of mail coupon advertising company to arbitrate dispute in Boston; court cites "unequal" bargaining power; clause required plaintiff to travel 3,000 miles to forum a few miles from defendant's home; language was misleading, and clause was unconscionable, not entered into freely or voluntarily).

9. Decisions enforcing forum selection clauses, at least when they lead to dismissal, are final judgments that can be appealed. Should decisions refusing to enforce such clauses be immediately reviewable? See In re Lyon Financial Services, Inc., 257 S.W.2d 228 (Tex. 2008) (mandamus is available to enforce forum selection clause; no adequate remedy by appeal if trial court refuses to enforce such clauses); In re Pirelli Tire, LLC, 247 S.W.3d 670, 678 (Tex. 2007) (erroneous denial of motion based on *forum non conveniens* is "closely analogous" to refusals to enforce forum selection clauses; mandamus is appropriate).

10. Suppose a contract includes a "floating" forum selection clause tied to an assignment clause. One party anticipates assigning rights under the contract to a third party some day, and the contract says any dispute will be litigated in the principal place of business of one of the parties, "or in the principal place of business of the assignee of rights under this contract." Compare Preferred Capital, Inc. v. Sarasota Kennel Club, Inc., 489 F.3d 303, 307 (6th Cir. 2007) (floating forum selection clause put jurisdiction in Ohio, as principal place of business of assignee) with Preferred Capital, Inc. v. Power Engineering Group, Inc., 860 N.E.2d 741 (Ohio 2007) (when NorVergence, as lessor of equipment, allegedly "failed to provide" promised savings, out-of-state lessees stopped paying; Preferred Capital, as assignee of lessor's rights, sued in Ohio under floating forum selection clause; court dismisses; "when one party to a contract containing a floating forum-selection clause possesses undisclosed information of its intent to assign its interest in the contract almost immediately to a company in a foreign jurisdiction, the forum-selection clause is unreasonable and against public policy absent a clear showing that the second party knowingly waived personal jurisdiction and assented to litigate in any forum").

CHAPTER 6

Modern Federalism: *Erie*, Abstention, and Related Doctrines

INTRODUCTION: FEDERALISM REVISITED

In the introductory chapter, you read a description of our federal system, which has a central government with overarching national authority and state governments having regional authority. In Chapter 1G, supra, the discussion was laid out in four parts dealing with (1) the substance-procedure distinction, (2) the supremacy of federal law and federal pre-emption of state law, (3) judicial coordination and accommodation, and (4) finality of judgments and full faith and credit.

In this chapter, we examine more closely the first and third parts of this subject—the substance-procedure distinction and the judicial coordination and accommodation. We look closely at the substance-procedure distinction, particularly as it applies in federal courts in diversity cases, and in state courts entertaining suits under federal substantive law. We also look at the judicial coordination and accommodation from the perspective of federal courts, particularly abstention doctrines and the Anti-Injunction Act.

We looked at the second part of the subject in Chapter 1. Recall that Problem 1-A ("We're in Compliance with Federal Law") dealt with pre-emption, and the question was whether the federal Motor Vehicle Safety Act displaced state common law tort claims (the answer was no, and state law does continue to apply). We take up the fourth part of the subject (finality and full faith and credit) in Chapter 14.

STATE LAW IN FEDERAL COURTS: THE *ERIE* DOCTRINE

From the beginning, Congress has told federal courts to apply state law, except where federal law applies.

The statute containing this directive, found in the First Judiciary Act of 1789, is known as the "Rules of Decision Act" (RDA), and it is mercifully short: "The laws of the several states, except where the Constitution or treaties of the United States or Acts of Congress otherwise require or provide, shall be regarded as rules of decision in civil actions in the courts of the United States, in cases where they apply." 28 USC §1652. Sounds almost too simple, perhaps tautological, doesn't it? If state law applies, it *must be* the "rule[] of decision," mustn't it? And as the rule of decision, surely it must "apply."

The reference to federal law seems to be a truism. Federal law, if it exists, *always* takes precedence over state law. See U.S. Const. Art. VI (federal law is "the supreme Law of the Land" and "judges in every State shall be bound thereby").

Despite these points, the RDA has proved to be a text of some subtlety, and its meaning has changed over time. And knowing *when* to apply state law, and *which* state law to apply, has proved more difficult than you might suspect.

1. The Era of *Swift*

Prior to 1938, the RDA was not the only statute directing federal courts to apply state law. There was another, called the Conformity Act. This statute told federal courts that "the practice, pleadings, and forms and modes of proceeding" in civil suits in federal courts were to "conform as near as may be" to the rules "existing at the time in the courts of record of the state" where the federal court sits. See 28 USC §724 (now repealed).

The directive to follow state procedural law ended in 1938 when the Federal Rules of Civil Procedure were adopted. These Rules were promulgated under yet another statute—the Rules Enabling Act of 1934 (REA), codified today as 28 USC §§2071-2077.

Perhaps surprisingly, while federal courts followed state procedural law under the Conformity Acts and a lot of other state law under the RDA, still federal courts did not feel bound to apply the *unwritten* or *common* law of the states, except in limited situations. The *Swift* doctrine, as it is known, provides an opportunity to look at where we came from in arriving at the world we see today.

Justice Joseph Story

Joseph Story of Marblehead, Massachusetts (1779-1845) was a lawyer, educator, legislator, scholar, and Supreme Court Justice. His father was one of the Sons of Liberty who participated in the Boston Tea Party in 1773. Joseph went to Harvard, graduating second in his class, and read law in Salem, Massachusetts. Appointed to the Supreme Court in 1832 at the age of 32 (still the youngest to be seated on the Court at the time of appointment), he served for 33 years. While on the Court, he gave a public speech opposing
slavery, and he wrote the Court's opinion in La Amistad de Rues, 18 U.S. 385 (1820), resulting in the freeing of blacks held as slaves who had rebelled on a ship at sea. (In the Steven Spielberg movie *Amistad*, Justice Harry Blackmun appears as Justice Story.) Justice Story also wrote the opinion in Martin v. Hunter's Lessee, 14 U.S. 304 (1816), which was an important decision during the time of Justice John Marshall's leadership, holding that the Court determines the meaning of federal treaties, and its decisions on such points are binding on the states, contributing significantly to the uniformity of federal law. In 1833, he published his Commentaries on the Constitution of the United States, and he wrote many other books on law, including his Commentaries on the Conflict of Laws, which you saw cited in *Pennoyer* and *Burnham*. Story was a highly successful author, earning significant income from books.

SWIFT v. TYSON

Supreme Court of the United States
41 U.S. 1 (1842)

STORY, Justice, delivered the opinion of the court.

[In May 1836, Nathaniel Norton and Jairus Keith agreed to sell to George Tyson property in Maine. Tyson was to make payment by accepting a "bill of exchange" drawn by Norton and Keith on Tyson in the amount of $1,536.30.

The bill of exchange was made payable "to the order of" Norton. Tyson accepted the bill. Norton endorsed it and turned it over the plaintiff John Swift, to pay him for having covered a debt owed by Norton and Keith. Swift presented the bill to Tyson for payment, but Tyson refused. Tyson claimed Norton and Keith never had title to the land in Maine and that it had no value anyway, so Tyson got nothing from Norton and Keith and did not have to pay the bill of exchange when Swift presented it.

Swift argued that he was what we call a "holder in due course" and was entitled to collect the bill, augmented by unpaid interest (the amount had risen to $1,862.06), regardless whether Tyson had defenses against Norton and Keith. (One reason why negotiable instruments are valuable is that they are almost as liquid as cash, and holders in due course are entitled to payment even if an original obligor like Tyson would have a defense against the original payee—Norton.)

The critical question was whether Swift qualified as a holder in due course. The argument was that he took the bill from Norton *after* covering the debt that Norton and Keith owed. Hence Swift got the note for antecedent consideration, not present consideration, and was *not* a holder in due course (hence *was* subject to defenses that Tyson could raise against Norton). Since Swift sued Tyson in federal court on the basis of diversity jurisdiction, a further critical question arose: What law resolves the question whether Swift qualified as holder in due course?]

At the trial, the acceptance and endorsement of the bill were admitted, and the plaintiff there rested his case. . . . The defendant then offered to prove, that the bill was accepted by [Tyson], as part consideration for the purchase of certain lands in the state of Maine, which Norton & Keith represented themselves to be the owners of, and also represented to be of great value, and contracted to convey a good title thereto; and that the representations were in every respect fraudulent and false, and Norton & Keith had no title to the lands, and that the same were of little or no value. [Swift] objected to the admission of such testimony, or of any testimony, as against him, impeaching or showing a failure of the consideration, on which the bill was accepted, under the facts admitted by [Tyson], and those proved by [Swift], by reading the [his] answer . . . to the bill of discovery. The judges of the circuit court thereupon divided in opinion upon the following point or question of law—Whether, under the facts last mentioned, [Tyson] was entitled to the same defense to the action, as if the suit was between the original parties to the bill, that is to say, Norton, or Norton & Keith, and the defendant; and whether the evidence so offered was admissible as against the [Swift]. And this is the question certified to us for our decision.

There is no doubt, that a *bona fide* holder of a negotiable instrument, for a valuable consideration, without any notice of facts which impeach its validity, as between the antecedent parties, if he takes it under an endorsement made before the same becomes due, holds the title unaffected by these facts, and may recover thereon, although, as between the antecedent parties, the transaction may be without any legal validity. This is a doctrine so long and so well established, and so essential to the security of negotiable paper, that it is laid up among the fundamentals of the law, and requires no authority or reasoning to be now brought in its support. As little doubt is there, that the holder of any negotiable paper, before it is due, is not bound to prove that he is a *bona fide* holder for a valuable consideration, without notice; for the law will presume, that, in the absence of all rebutting proofs, and therefore, it is incumbent upon the defendant to establish by way of defense, satisfactory proofs of the contrary, and thus to overcome the *prima facie* title of the plaintiff.

In the present case, the plaintiff is a *bona fide* holder, without notice, for what the law deems a good and valid consideration, that is, for a preexisting debt; and the only real question in the cause is, whether, under the circumstances of the present case, such a pre-existing debt constitutes a valuable consideration, in the sense of the general rule applicable to negotiable instruments. We say, under the circumstances of the present case, for the acceptance having been made in New York, the argument on behalf of the defendant is, that the contract is to be treated as a New York contract, and therefore, to be governed by the laws of New York, as expounded by its courts, as well upon general principles, as by the express provisions of the 34th section of the judiciary act of 1789 [the RDA, now 28 USC §1652]. And then it is further contended, that by the law of New York, as thus expounded by its courts, a pre-existing debt does not constitute, in the sense of the general rule, a valuable consideration applicable to negotiable instruments.

[The Court surveys the law of New York. Early cases held that one could be a holder in due course, even though taking a negotiable instrument for antecedent consideration. Later cases cast doubt on that point. Still later cases may have restored the earlier doctrine, but the matter remains uncertain.]

But . . . it remains to be considered, whether [New York law] is obligatory upon this court, if it differs from the principles established in the general commercial law. It is observable, that the courts of New York do not found their decisions upon this point, upon any local statute, or positive, fixed or ancient local usage; but they deduce the doctrine from the general principles of commercial law. It is, however, contended, that the 34th section of the judiciary act of 1789 furnishes a rule obligatory upon this court to follow the decisions of the state tribunals in all cases to which they apply. That section provides that "the laws of the several states, except where the constitution, treaties or statutes of the United States shall otherwise require or provide, shall be regarded as rules of decision, in trials at common law, in the courts of the United States, in cases where they apply." In order to maintain the argument, it is essential, therefore, to hold, that the word "laws" in this section, includes within the scope of its meaning, the decisions of the local tribunals. In the ordinary use of language, it will hardly be contended, that the decisions of courts constitute laws. They are, at most, only evidence of what the laws are, and are not, of themselves, laws. They are often re-examined, reversed and qualified by the courts themselves, whenever they are found to be either defective, or ill-founded, or otherwise incorrect. The laws of a state are more usually understood to mean the rules and enactments promulgated by the legislative authority thereof, or long-established local customs having the force of laws. In all the various cases, which have hitherto come before us for decision, this court have uniformly supposed, that the true interpretation of the 34th section limited its application to state laws, strictly local, that is to say, to the positive statutes of the state, and the construction thereof adopted by the local tribunals, and to rights and titles to things having a permanent locality, such as the rights and titles to real estate, and other matters immovable and intra-territorial in their nature and character. It never has been supposed by us, that the section did apply, or was designed to apply, to questions of a more general nature, not at all dependent upon local statutes or local usages of a fixed and permanent operation, as, for example, to the construction of ordinary contracts or other written instruments, and especially to questions of general commercial law, where the state tribunals are called upon to perform the like functions as ourselves, that is, to ascertain, upon general reasoning and legal analogies, what is the true exposition of the contract or instrument, or what is the just rule furnished by the principles of commercial law to govern the case. And we have not now the slightest difficulty in holding, that this section, upon its true intendment and construction, is strictly limited to local statutes and local usages of the character before stated, and does not extend to contracts and other instruments of a commercial nature, the true interpretation and effect whereof are to be sought, not in the decisions of the local tribunals, but in the general principles and doctrines of commercial jurisprudence. Undoubtedly, the decisions of the local tribunals upon such subjects are entitled to, and will receive, the most deliberate attention and respect of this court; but they cannot furnish positive rules, or conclusive authority, by which our own judgments are to be bound up and governed. The law respecting negotiable instruments may be truly declared in the languages of Cicero, adopted by Lord Mansfield in Luke v. Lyde, 2 Burr. 883, 887, to be in a great measure, not the law of a single country only, but of the commercial world. *Non erit alia lex Romae, alia Athenis; alia nunc, alia posthac; sed et apud omnes gentes, et omni tempore una eademque lex obtinebit.*[1]

It becomes necessary for us, therefore, upon the present occasion, to express our own opinion of the true result of the commercial law upon the question now before us. And we have no hesitation in saying, that a pre-existing debt does constitute a valuable consideration, in the sense of the general rule already stated, as applicable to negotiable instruments. . . . It is for the

---

[1] ["Nor will it be one law for Rome and another for Athens; one thing today and another tomorrow; but it is a law eternal and unchangeable for all people and in every age." See Republic of Cicero 256-257 (Hardingham ed., 1884). See also Arthur E. Sunderland, *The Flag, the Constitution, and International Agreements,* 68 Harv. L. Rev. 1374, 1381 (1955), commenting on this use of this passage.—ED.]

benefit and convenience of the commercial world, to give as wide an extent as practicable to the credit and circulation of negotiable paper, that it may pass not only as security for new purchases and advances, made upon the transfer thereof, but also in payment of, and as security for, pre-existing debts. The creditor is thereby enabled to realize or to secure his debt, and thus may safely give a prolonged credit, or forbear from taking any legal steps to enforce his rights. The debtor also has the advantage of making his negotiable securities of equivalent value to cash. But establish the opposite conclusion, that negotiable paper cannot be applied in payment of, or as security for, pre-existing debts, without letting in all the equities between the original and antecedent parties, and the value and circulation of such securities must be essentially diminished, and the debtor driven to the embarrassment of making a sale thereof, often at a ruinous discount, to some third person, and then, by circuity, to apply the proceeds to the payment of his debts. What, indeed, upon such a doctrine, would become of that large class of cases, where new notes are given by the same or by other parties, by way of renewal or security to banks, in lieu of old securities discounted by them, which have arrived at maturity? Probably, more than one-half of all bank transactions in our country, as well as those of other countries, are of this nature. The doctrine would strike a fatal blow at all discounts of negotiable securities for pre-existing debts.

[The Court defends and elaborates its conclusion for several more pages.]

■ NOTES ON *SWIFT* AND FEDERAL COMMON LAW

1. Tyson's position was that he should not have to accept the bill of exchange (pay the sum set out in it) because Norton and Keith did not deliver proper title. If so, *and* if Tyson had not signed a negotiable instrument and was instead dealing only with Norton and Keith, who sued Tyson for the price, their claims would fail, wouldn't they? Not conveying good title would be a defense in their suit for the price. But the conclusion here is that Swift, as holder in due course of the bill of exchange drawn against Tyson, was entitled to collect the sum set out in the bill (plus interest) from Tyson. Why should Swift prevail if Norton and Keith could not?

2. The question, according to the Court, is whether Swift is a "holder in due course" of the bill of exchange drawn against Tyson. Being a holder in due course means, among other things, not knowing about problems in the transaction that induced the obligor (Tyson) to agree to accept the bill of exchange, and indeed Swift apparently did *not* know of any such problems. We're also told that Swift received the bill of exchange in payment for a "*pre-existing* debt" ("antecedent debt," as it is usually called). If Swift had parted with "present value" for the bill of exchange—if he had conveyed to Norton and Keith a team of horses and took the bill of exchange as payment, his status as holder in due course would have been assured. Having no knowledge of problems in the sale to Tyson, and having given present value, Swift would have won, hands down. So negotiability is a concept that deprives obligors of defenses when instruments are negotiated in later transactions—defenses that would be available against the original parties (available against Norton and Keith). Why is negotiability useful? Why should it matter whether Swift gave up "present value" when he took Tyson's bill of exchange?

3. In answering the question before the Court, Justice Story looks to the law of New York, but decides that the New York rule is uncertain. He then concludes that the RDA does not require a federal court to apply New York law. Why not? If the reference to "the laws of the several states" in the RDA does *not* embrace New York's law on who qualifies as a holder in due course, what does it embrace?

4. Justice Story says court decisions are not laws "of themselves," but only "evidence of what the laws are." What is he talking about? Consider the following account by Professor Ides describing lawmaking as practiced in *Swift*:

> One can read *Swift* as a reflection of a natural law philosophy that places the judiciary at the forefront of discovering the transcendent principles of an omnipresent and omniscient common law. Under this view the common law is not subdivided by state boundaries, but is, like the laws of physics or mathematics, a national or even international phenomenon that embraces certain fundamental a priori principles that can be discovered through careful reasoning and scientific analysis. Furthermore, federal and state judges are equally competent to discover the true meaning of the common law, and section thirty-four of the Judiciary Act was designed to accommodate this possibility. Certainly, the surface of the opinion in *Swift* . . . lends itself to such an interpretation, although Story was not, in fact, a proponent of natural law theory.
>
> Another, and perhaps more modern, way of viewing the *Swift* decision is through the lens of legal realism. From this perspective, Story's interpretation of the word "laws" is nothing more than a plausible textual argument designed to vest the federal judiciary with the power to make policy judgments regarding the proper scope of commercial law. Such a reading is far from inconsistent with Story's status as the preeminent protégé of Chief Justice John Marshall. And the opinion in *Swift* is largely based on a federalist-flavored policy judgment regarding the practical need for a uniform body of laws in the commercial sphere. Story was, of course, a strong advocate of the adoption of uniform laws throughout the United States. This realist perspective places the transcendence of the common law in a somewhat cynical light; homage to that transcendence is merely the means through which a non-transcendent policy can be adopted.

Alan Ides, *The Supreme Court and the Law to Be Applied in Diversity Cases: A Critical Guide to the Development and Application of the* Erie *Doctrine and Related Problems*, 163 F.R.D. 19, 23-24 (1995).

2. The Arrival of *Erie*

Justice Louis Brandeis

Justice Louis Brandeis served on the Court for 23 years (1916-1939). He had begun his career by working as a lawyer for social causes, fighting corporations and representing clients without fee in order to feel more comfortable stressing larger social interests. He became famous for the "Brandeis Brief," in which he incorporated arguments by experts. Joining forces with his Harvard classmate Samuel Warren after completing law school, Brandeis became a litigator. He and Warren authored scholarly articles, including a classic pathbreaking piece on the right of privacy. See Samuel Warren & Louis Brandeis, *Right to Privacy*, 4 Harv L. Rev. 193 (1890). By the early 1900s, Brandeis had become a crusader against monopolies and in favor of legislation regulating the workplace: In Mueller v. Oregon, 208 U.S. 412 (1908), he filed an enormous brief collecting empirical data on the impact of long working hours on women, helping the State defend its limitation of the hours that women could work against a challenge that the law infringed on freedom of contract. On the Court, Justice Brandeis opposed much of the New Deal agenda of President Roosevelt. He also defended the right of privacy that he had advanced in his earlier article, and he opposed the President's "Court-packing plan." The Court's decision in Erie Railroad Co. v. Tompkins was the last important opinion that he wrote.

ERIE R. CO. v. TOMPKINS

Supreme Court of the United States
304 U.S. 64 (1938)

Mr. Justice Brandeis delivered the opinion of the Court.

The question for decision is whether the oft-challenged doctrine of Swift v. Tyson shall now be disapproved.

Tompkins, a citizen of Pennsylvania, was injured on a dark night by a passing freight train of the Erie Railroad Company while walking along its right of way at Hughestown in that state. He claimed that the accident occurred through negligence in the operation, or maintenance, of the train; that he was rightfully on the premises as licensee because on a commonly used beaten footpath which ran for a short distance alongside the tracks; and that he was struck by something which looked like a door projecting from one of the moving cars. To enforce that claim he brought an action in the federal court for Southern New York, which had jurisdiction because the company is a corporation of that state. It denied liability; and the case was tried by a jury.

The Erie insisted that its duty to Tompkins was no greater than that owed to a trespasser. It contended, among other things, that its duty to Tompkins, and hence its liability, should be determined in accordance with the Pennsylvania law; that under the law of Pennsylvania, as declared by its highest court, persons who use pathways along the railroad right of way—that is, a longitudinal pathway as distinguished from a crossing—are to be deemed trespassers; and that the railroad is not liable for injuries to undiscovered trespassers resulting from its negligence, unless it be wanton or willful. Tompkins denied that any such rule had been established by the decisions of the Pennsylvania courts; and contended that, since there was no statute of the state on the subject, the railroad's duty and liability is to be determined in federal courts as a matter of general law.

The trial judge refused to rule that the applicable law precluded recovery. The jury brought in a verdict of $30,000; and the judgment entered thereon was affirmed by the Circuit Court of Appeals, which held that it was unnecessary to consider whether the law of Pennsylvania was as contended, because the question was one not of local, but of general, law, and that "upon questions of general law the federal courts are free, in absence of a local statute, to exercise their independent judgment as to what the law is; and it is well settled that the question of the responsibility of a railroad for injuries caused by its servants is one of general law. . . . Where the public has made open and notorious use of a railroad right of way for a long period of time and without objection, the company owes to persons on such permissive pathway a duty of care in the operation of its trains. . . . It is likewise generally recognized law that a jury may find that negligence exists toward a pedestrian using a permissive path on the railroad right of way if he is hit by some object projecting from the side of the train."

The Erie had contended that application of the Pennsylvania rule was required, among other things, by section 34 of the Federal Judiciary Act of September 24, 1789, 28 U.S.C. §725 [now 28 USC §1652], which provides: "The laws of the several States, except where the Constitution, treaties, or statutes of the United States otherwise require or provide, shall be regarded as rules of decision in trials at common law, in the courts of the United States, in cases where they apply."

Because of the importance of the question whether the federal court was free to disregard the alleged rule of the Pennsylvania common law, we granted certiorari.

First. Swift v. Tyson, 16 Pet. 1, 18, held that federal courts exercising jurisdiction on the ground of diversity of citizenship need not, in matters of general jurisprudence, apply the unwritten law of the state as declared by its highest court; that they are free to exercise an independent judgment as to what the common law of the state is—or should be; and that, as there stated by Mr. Justice Story, "the true interpretation of the 34th section limited its application to state laws, strictly local, that is to say, to the positive statutes of the state, and the construction thereof adopted by the local tribunals, and to rights and titles to things having a permanent locality, such as the rights and titles to real estate, and other matters immovable and intra-territorial in their nature and character. It never has been supposed by us, that the section did apply, or was designed to apply, to questions of a more general nature, not at all dependent upon local statutes or local usages of a fixed and permanent operation, as, for example, to the construction of ordinary contracts or other written instruments, and especially to questions of general commercial law, where the state tribunals are called upon to perform the like functions as ourselves, that is, to ascertain, upon general reasoning and legal analogies, what is the true exposition of the contract or instrument, or what is the just rule furnished by the principles of commercial law to govern the case."

The Court in applying the rule of section 34 to equity cases, in Mason v. United States, 260 U.S. 545, 559, said: "The statute, however, is merely declarative of the rule which would exist in the absence of the statute." The federal courts assumed, in the broad field of "general law," the power to declare rules of decision which Congress was confessedly without power to enact as statutes. Doubt was repeatedly expressed as to the correctness of the construction given section 34, and as to the soundness of the rule which it introduced. But it was the more recent research of a competent scholar, who examined the original document, which established that the construction given to it by the Court was erroneous; and that the purpose of the section was merely to make certain that, in all matters except those in which some federal law is controlling, the federal courts exercising jurisdiction in diversity of citizenship cases would apply as their rules of decision the law of the state, unwritten as well as written.[5]

Criticism of the doctrine became widespread after the decision of Black & White Taxicab & Transfer Co. v. Brown & Yellow Taxicab & Transfer Co., 276 U.S. 518 (1928). There, Brown & Yellow, a Kentucky corporation owned by Kentuckians, and the Louisville & Nashville Railroad, also a Kentucky corporation, wished that the former should have the exclusive privilege of soliciting passenger and baggage transportation at the Bowling Green, Ky., Railroad station; and that the Black & White, a competing Kentucky corporation, should be prevented from interfering with that privilege. Knowing that such a contract would be void under the common law of Kentucky, it was arranged that the Brown & Yellow reincorporate under the law of Tennessee, and that the contract with the

---

[5] Charles Warren, New Light on the History of the Federal Judiciary Act of 1789 (1923), 37 Harv. L. Rev. 49, 51-52, 81-88, 108.

railroad should be executed there. The suit was then brought by the Tennessee corporation in the federal court for Western Kentucky to enjoin competition by the Black & White; an injunction issued by the District Court was sustained by the Court of Appeals; and this Court, citing many decisions in which the doctrine of Swift v. Tyson had been applied, affirmed the decree.

Second. Experience in applying the doctrine of Swift v. Tyson, had revealed its defects, political and social; and the benefits expected to flow from the rule did not accrue. Persistence of state courts in their own opinions on questions of common law prevented uniformity; and the impossibility of discovering a satisfactory line of demarcation between the province of general law and that of local law developed a new well of uncertainties.[8]

On the other hand, the mischievous results of the doctrine had become apparent. Diversity of citizenship jurisdiction was conferred in order to prevent apprehended discrimination in state courts against those not citizens of the state. Swift v. Tyson introduced grave discrimination by noncitizens against citizens. It made rights enjoyed under the unwritten "general law" vary according to whether enforcement was sought in the state or in the federal court; and the privilege of selecting the court in which the right should be determined was conferred upon the noncitizen.[9] Thus, the doctrine rendered impossible equal protection of the law. In attempting to promote uniformity of law throughout the United States, the doctrine had prevented uniformity in the administration of the law of the state.

The discrimination resulting became in practice far-reaching. This resulted in part from the broad province accorded to the so-called "general law" as to which federal courts exercised an independent judgment. In addition to questions of purely commercial law, "general law" was held to include the obligations under contracts entered into and to be performed within the state, the extent to which a carrier operating within a state may stipulate for exemption from liability for his own negligence or that of his employee; the liability for torts committed within the state upon persons resident or property located there, even where the question of liability depended upon the scope of a property right conferred by the state; and the right to exemplary or punitive damages. Furthermore, state decisions construing local deeds, mineral conveyances, and even devises of real estate, were disregarded.

In part the discrimination resulted from the wide range of persons held entitled to avail themselves of the federal rule by resort to the diversity of

---

[8] Compare 2 Warren, The Supreme Court in United States History, Rev. Ed. 1935, 89: "Probably no decision of the Court has ever given rise to more uncertainty as to legal rights; and though doubtless intended to promote uniformity in the operation of business transactions, its chief effect has been to render it difficult for business men to know in advance to what particular topic the Court would apply the doctrine." The Federal Digest . . . lists nearly 1,000 decisions involving the distinction between questions of general and of local law.

[9] It was even possible for a nonresident plaintiff defeated on a point of law in the highest court of a State nevertheless to win out by taking a nonsuit and renewing the controversy in the federal court.

citizenship jurisdiction. Through this jurisdiction individual citizens willing to remove from their own state and become citizens of another might avail themselves of the federal rule. And, without even change of residence, a corporate citizen of the state could avail itself of the federal rule by reincorporating under the laws of another state, as was done in the Taxicab Case.

The injustice and confusion incident to the doctrine of Swift v. Tyson have been repeatedly urged as reasons for abolishing or limiting diversity of citizenship jurisdiction. Other legislative relief has been proposed.[21] If only a question of statutory construction were involved, we should not be prepared to abandon a doctrine so widely applied throughout nearly a century. But the unconstitutionality of the course pursued has now been made clear, and compels us to do so.

Third. Except in matters governed by the Federal Constitution or by acts of Congress, the law to be applied in any case is the law of the state. And whether the law of the state shall be declared by its Legislature in a statute or by its highest court in a decision is not a matter of federal concern. There is no federal general common law. Congress has no power to declare substantive rules of common law applicable in a state whether they be local in their nature or "general," be they commercial law or a part of the law of torts. And no clause in the Constitution purports to confer such a power upon the federal courts. . . .

The fallacy underlying the rule declared in Swift v. Tyson is made clear by Mr. Justice Holmes.[23] The doctrine rests upon the assumption that there is "a transcendental body of law outside of any particular State but obligatory within it unless and until changed by statute," that federal courts have the power to use their judgment as to what the rules of common law are; and that in the federal courts "the parties are entitled to an independent judgment on matters of general law":

> But law in the sense in which courts speak of it today does not exist without some definite authority behind it. The common law so far as it is enforced in a State, whether called common law or not, is not the common law generally but the law of that State existing by the authority of that State without regard to what it may have been in England or anywhere else.
>
> The authority and only authority is the State, and if that be so, the voice adopted by the State as its own (whether it be of its Legislature or of its Supreme Court) should utter the last word.

Thus the doctrine of Swift v. Tyson is, as Mr. Justice Holmes said, "an unconstitutional assumption of powers by the Courts of the United States which no lapse of time or respectable array of opinion should make us hesitate to correct."

---

[21] Thus, bills which would abrogate the doctrine of Swift v. Tyson have been introduced. . . . State statutes on conflicting questions of "general law" have also been suggested.

[23] Kuhn v. Fairmont Coal Co., 215 U.S. 349, 370-372 (1910); Black & White Taxicab, etc., Co. v. Brown & Yellow Taxicab, etc., Co., 276 U.S. 518, 532-536 (1928).

In disapproving that doctrine we do not hold unconstitutional section 34 of the Federal Judiciary Act of 1789 or any other act of Congress. We merely declare that in applying the doctrine this Court and the lower courts have invaded rights which in our opinion are reserved by the Constitution to the several states.

Fourth. The defendant contended that by the common law of Pennsylvania as declared by its highest court in Falchetti v. Pennsylvania R. Co., 160 A. 859 (Pa. 1932), the only duty owed to the plaintiff was to refrain from willful or wanton injury. The plaintiff denied that such is the Pennsylvania law.[24] In support of their respective contentions the parties discussed and cited many decisions of the Supreme Court of the state. The Circuit Court of Appeals ruled that the question of liability is one of general law; and on that ground declined to decide the issue of state law. As we hold this was error, the judgment is reversed and the case remanded to it for further proceedings in conformity with our opinion.

Reversed.

Mr. Justice CARDOZO took no part in the consideration or decision of this case.

Mr. Justice BUTLER (dissenting).

["No constitutional question was suggested or argued," and the Court here changes a rule "in force since the foundation of the government," where it should instead "move cautiously, seek assistance of counsel, [and] act only after ample deliberation." What the Court did violates what is now 28 USC §2403, under which the Attorney General is to be notified, to allow the government to intervene if the court considers a challenge to a federal statute.]

. . .

Mr. Justice MCREYNOLDS, concurs in this opinion.

Mr. Justice REED (concurring in part).

[*Swift* should be discarded, but all that is necessary is to interpret the word "laws" in the RDA to include "the decisions of the local tribunals," and it is not necessary "to go further and declare that the 'course pursued' was 'unconstitutional,' instead of merely erroneous." It's not clear whether federal courts, if there had been no statute, "would be compelled to follow state decisions," and there was "sufficient doubt" on this score in 1789 to persuade Congress to pass the RDA. "The line between procedural and substantive law is hazy, but no one doubts federal power over procedure."]

---

[24] Tompkins also contended that the alleged rule of the *Falchetti* Case is not in any event applicable here because he was struck at the intersection of the longitudinal pathway and a transverse crossing. The court below found it unnecessary to consider this contention, and we leave the question open.

■ NOTES ON THE COMING OF THE *ERIE* DOCTRINE

1. The decision in *Erie* came as a surprise to observers. The railroad did not argue for abandoning *Swift*. Why not? Tompkins didn't either. Why not?

2. Tompkins, who lived in Pennsylvania and was injured near Hughestown in that state while walking alongside the tracks, sued the Erie in New York. The Supreme Court says that the Federal District Court for the Southern District of New York is to resolve the question of Tompkins's rights against the railroad by applying state law. Which state's law does the Court have in mind?

3. Consider the argument that *Swift* misconstrued the RDA—the "First" or "statutory" argument. Citing the work of Charles Warren, the Court says "laws of the several states" in the RDA was intended to refer to "unwritten as well as written" laws (except when federal law controls). If you look at the Warren article, you find that he argues that the phrase bears this broader meaning because an earlier draft of the statute referred to "the Statute law of the several states in force for the time being and their unwritten or common law now in use." It is *these* laws—the "Statute law" *and* the "common law"—that were to be "regarded as rules of decision." The conclusion Warren reached was that the shorter phrase ultimately adopted was intended to mean the same thing as longer phrase. Are you persuaded? See Charles Warren, *New Light on the History of the Federal Judiciary Act of 1789,* 37 Harv. L. Rev. 49, 85-86 (1923).

4. Consider the argument that the benefits expected from *Swift* "did not accrue"—the "Second" or "policy" argument. This argument seems to have three different parts.

(a) For one thing, national "uniformity" did not come from applying *Swift*. Why didn't *Swift* produce uniformity? What benefits would uniformity produce? Brandeis stops short of suggesting that variation in common law among the states would be good. Would it be?

(b) Another drawback, perhaps the most serious policy objection to *Swift*, is that the doctrine produced "mischievous results." Brandeis says the purpose of diversity jurisdiction is to protect out-of-staters against discrimination favoring locals, which has some truth to it, but *Swift* turned this idea upside down (introducing "grave discrimination by noncitizens against citizens")? The poster child for this point is the *Black & White Taxicab* case. But this example is just the tip of the iceberg, and Brandeis was making a larger point. Does it make sense if suits between citizens of different states reach different outcomes in federal court on account of different substantive rules than would be reached in state courts if the suit went forward there? This part of the opinion relates to the policy consideration of "fairness" or "equitable administration."

(c) Finally, the distinction drawn in *Swift* between statutory law and real property law, on the one hand, and "general law" on the other, has given

rise to great uncertainty, with "nearly 1,000 decisions" addressing the matter (Court's footnote 8).

5. Consider the argument that *Swift* is unconstitutional—the "Third" argument. "There is no federal general common law," Justice Brandeis writes. Congress lacks power to "declare substantive rules of common law" and federal courts lack that power too. Hence *Swift* amounted to "an unconstitutional assumption of power," in the words of Justice Holmes, whom Brandeis quotes. But Brandeis does not cite any provision. Consider these possibilities:

(a) *Erie* might rest on Article I §8, where the Constitution sets forth the powers of Congress. These include, *inter alia,* regulating "Commerce . . . among the several States," and creating courts "inferior to the supreme Court" (the Constitution created the Supreme Court, but left to Congress the creation of other federal courts). Congressional power also includes making laws "necessary and proper" for "carrying into Execution" the other powers. As we usually say it, Congress has "enumerated" powers, and by implication no others. Could Congress pass a statute regulating the relationship between railroads like the Erie and "longitudinal trespassers" like Tompkins? Recall that Congress *has* enacted legislation regulating the relationship between railroads and their employees (FELA), as we saw in the *Lavender* case (Chapter 1E).

(b) Does it follow that Congress can enact any statute it wants, regulating any aspect of life? Let us remove from consideration laws that would violate the Bill of Rights: Everyone agrees that Congress cannot enact, for example, a statute that says "public criticism of the President and Congress is illegal." Such a statute would violate the free speech provision of the First Amendment. *Apart from such limits,* is congressional power limited in any way? This question is surprisingly hard to answer. In academic circles, the dominant model of federalism, as respects the relative authority of Congress and the states, is the "unitary sovereignty" model, which holds that Congress can legislate in any area, so long as the legislation is grounded in one of the specific clauses in Section 8, such as the Commerce Clause. In other words, there is no subject or area that is off limits to Congress. But some speak of a "dual sovereignty" model, in which Section 8 removes from congressional power certain areas of legislation.[1] Suffice it to say that the "dual sovereignty" model is out of favor in academic and most legal discourse, and it only occasionally appears as a working description or hypothesis in delineating congressional power.[2]

[1] A common example of an area thought to be beyond the power of Congress to regulate is the institution of marriage, and more generally domestic relations. While Congress has *not* tried to occupy this field, the Defense of Marriage Act in 1996 shows that Congress thinks it can legislate in this area. See 1 USC §7.
[2] For a modern case recognizing limits on congressional power implied in Article I, see United States v. Lopez, 514 U.S. 549 (1995) (Congress lacks power under Commerce Clause to impose criminal penalties for carrying firearms in school zones). For a case referring to the "dual sovereignty" model, see Printz v. United States, 521 U.S. 898 (1997) (Congress cannot impose on local sheriffs a duty to conduct background checks on handgun purchasers).

(c) Erie could rest on Article III, which defines the "judicial Power of the United States." This article creates the Supreme Court (but not any other court), and defines the power of all federal courts, including those that Congress creates, such as Federal District Courts and the Circuit Courts of Appeal. This power includes authority to decide diversity cases—"all Cases . . . between Citizens of different States" (Art. III §2), which Congress implemented by enacting the diversity jurisdiction statute (28 USC §1332).

(d) Does *Erie* mean that the existence of diversity jurisdiction does not authorize federal courts to create common law to resolve diversity cases? Probably, *Erie* does mean *at least* this much. Whether Congress *could* constitutionally authorize federal courts to behave in this manner is another question—and one that need not be faced. One word of caution is appropriate: Some statutes conferring jurisdiction *do* authorize federal courts to fashion federal common law. The National Labor Relations Act, which gives federal courts jurisdiction to resolve disputes under collective bargaining agreements, has been interpreted in this way. See Textile Workers Union of America v. Lincoln Mills of Alabama, 353 U.S. 448 (1957) (Taft-Hartley Act modifying Labor Management Relations Act authorizes federal courts to determine contract disputes in industries affecting commerce and to "fashion a body of federal law" in resolving these disputes).

(e) Erie might rest on the Tenth Amendment (powers "not delegated to the United States by the Constitution, nor prohibited by it to the States, are reserved to the States respectively, or to the people"). This provision too is sometimes cited as the basis of *Erie,* but it has so little force in decided cases and has been so long ignored, that one cannot embrace this view with any confidence.

(f) Since *Erie* cites *none* of these provisions, should it be taken seriously as resting on the Constitution at all? Commentators disagree. Compare Wright & Kane, Federal Courts §56 (6th ed. 2002) (if the Court thinks it is deciding a constitutional question, "it is wise to suppose that the constitutional question has been decided") and Bradford R. Clark, Erie's *Constitutional Source,* 95 Cal. L. Rev. 1289 (2007) (*Erie* implements constitutional separation-of-powers doctrines) and Paul J. Mishkin, *Some Further Last Words on* Erie *—The Thread,* 87 Harv. L. Rev. 1682, 1688 (1974) (*Erie* rests on constitutional principles restraining "the power of the federal courts to intrude upon the states' determination of substantive policy in areas which the Constitution and Congress have left to state competence"), with Craig Green, *Repressing* Erie's *Myth,* 96 Cal. L. Rev. 595, 603, 607 (2008) (*Erie* reflects an outmoded "dual sovereignty" theory); John B. Corr, *Thoughts on the Validity of* Erie, 41 Am. U. L. Rev. 1087, 1089 (1992) (*Erie* "is not mandated constitutionally," and *Swift* is a "preferred alternative").

(g) Perhaps you're wondering, given the statement in *Erie* that *Swift* "rendered impossible equal protection of the law," whether Brandeis was referring to the Equal Protection Clause. This provision is in the Fourteenth Amendment, and it says "no state" shall deprive anyone of the equal protection of the laws. The problem is that no *state* was doing anything—*Erie* was

brought in federal court, which was applying federal law. So Brandeis could not have had that clause in mind. It may be of interest that years after *Erie* was decided, the Court found that the Equal Protection Clause does bind the federal government. The context was a challenge to racial segregation in schools of the District of Columbia, which arose *after* the Court had struck down segregation in state schools under the Equal Protection Clause. See Bolling v. Sharpe, 347 U.S. 497 (1954) ("reading in" the Equal Protection Clause of the Fourteenth Amendment, which binds only states, to the Due Process Clause of the Fifth Amendment, which binds the federal government).[3] Can *Erie*'s reference to "equal protection" *now* be understood as a constitutional reference? See Green, supra, at 595, 603, 607 (arguing that there is no constitutional bar against applying different law in federal courts than state courts would apply).

6. *Erie* says there is "no federal general common law" (a statement of fact, not just a proscription for the future). Yet on *the very same day* that *Erie* was decided, Justice Brandeis penned another opinion, in which the issues at hand were resolved by applying "federal common law." See Hinderlider v. La Plata River & Cherry Creek Ditch Co., 304 U.S. 92 (1938) (dispute over rights in interstate stream raise question of federal common law). In short, there apparently exist *specific areas* of federal common law, even if there is no "federal general common law."

7. Consider for a moment the setting in which *Erie* arose.

(a) In 1938, the country had emerged from a deep depression; the New Deal was drawing to a close. Europe was headed toward a war that would engulf the world and engage the emerging power of the United States. President Roosevelt's Court-packing plan had been averted as the Supreme Court had begun upholding major legislation regulating the economy. The country had moved toward an urbanized and industrialized society in which corporations were major players.

(b) Suits like Harry Tompkins's were hard to bring because each corporation was viewed as a citizen of its chartering state, and often a corporate defendant could remove a state-filed suit to federal courts. Doing so brought a hardship for individual plaintiffs because federal courts are fewer and farther between than state courts. (Recall that Congress exempted FELA and Jones Act cases from removal, to allow railroaders and seamen, and often their widows, to sue in state court without fearing that the defendant, by removing, would force them to travel to cities to pursue their cases. Harry Tompkins

---

[3] *Bolling* is a "reverse incorporation" case. In one chapter of constitutional history, the Court "incorporated" most of protections in the "Bill of Rights" (first six amendments), which seemingly limits only actions by the federal government, into the Due Process Clause of the Fourteenth Amendment, thus binding states as well. *Bolling* is a "reverse" incorporation case because it did the opposite—it incorporated the Fourteenth Amendment's Equal Protection Clause into the Fifth Amendment's Due Process Clause, so it too applies to both federal and state action. (There are Due Process Clauses in both the Fifth and the Fourteenth Amendments.)

wasn't covered by FELA because he did not work for the railroad and was not injured on the job.)

(c) Harry Tompkins lived in Hughestown in northeastern Pennsylvania, which had been badly hurt by the depression that was ongoing in 1934 when his accident occurred. He was walking only a short distance to his home. Here is a modern account of what happened, drawing from the transcript of the trial:

> On the fateful night, he had been visiting his sick mother-in-law, who lived some five or six miles away. Shortly after midnight he left her house and walked several miles along the road until a car pulled over and a fellow iron molder from the foundry offered him a ride. Ferrying him the last mile or so to Hughestown, the co-worker dropped him off a couple of hundred feet from his house, at the familiar footpath along the tracks that would lead him homeward. As Tompkins headed down the path, he heard the whistle and saw the headlight of an oncoming train. "I kept right on walking," he recalled. "I had walked [along the path] plenty of times and I wasn't a bit afraid." The engine steamed by, and he glanced up at the rushing cars. Suddenly, "something came up in front of me, a black object that looked like a door." Tompkins tried to react. "I went to put my hands up and I guess before I got them up I was hit," he explained." "I didn't have a chance." Slammed in the head, he was knocked unconscious and hurled to the ground, his right arm flung under the passing cars. Hours later he awoke in a hospital.

Edward A. Purcell, Jr., *The Story of* Erie: *How Litigants, Lawyers, Judges, Politics, and Social Change Reshape the Law, in* Civil Procedure Stories 21, 37-38 (Kevin M. Clermont ed., 2d ed. 2008). According to Purcell, Tompkins's treatment included amputation of his entire right arm (he became known as "Lefty"), and he immediately sought legal advice by calling a lawyer in New York City to whom friends referred him (about 130 miles away from Hughestown). In the end, Tompkins recovered nothing on account of his accident, and his disability made it hard for him to find work. He died at the age of 54.

(d) If it is harder for people like Harry Tompkins to sue in federal than in state court, you might wonder why he chose federal court—and why he chose federal court in another state to boot. The answer, which is at least hinted in *Erie* itself, is that Pennsylvania law was likely to preclude recovery because Tompkins was a trespasser, and showing negligence would not suffice (he would have to show recklessness or wanton negligence). But a federal court applying a more generous common law rule might allow recovery on a showing of negligence. Tompkins's lawyers concluded that federal court in New York would be a better bet. Jurisdiction existed in both places—the railroad was headquartered and chartered in New York and could be sued there; it was doing business in Pennsylvania, and could be sued there too. Venue was proper in both places—New York because the railroad "resided" there, and Pennsylvania because the accident happened there. But New York was

in the Second Circuit, which was more expansive in following up *Swift's* invitation to apply general common law, and Pennsylvania is in the Third Circuit, which was more prone to treat issues of landowner liability as matters of "local" (state) law under *Swift*. So federal court in New York was chosen and—but for the Supreme Court's review and opinion—the choice would have paid off.

Harry Tompkins

Harry Tompkins was just under 27 years old when he was struck by something protruding from a moving car on the train. He is shown here prior to the accident in the early 1930s, and with his wife Edith later in life. Reportedly the Erie offered Tompkins $22,000 in settlement of the judgment, but Bernard Nemeroff and his partner Kaufman (also with the first name of Bernard), who represented  Tompkins at trial and in the later appeals, persuaded him not to take it. Indeed, they encouraged him to stay for a time on Long Island, close to Nemeroff's home, to hide him from the railroad's lawyers. It was not anticipated that the Supreme Court would grant review and reverse, and a young law student at Columbia named Aaron Danzig had helped persuade Nemeroff that Tompkins could prevail by suing in federal court, where the *Swift* doctrine would let them avoid the Pennsylvania rule, in favor of a more lenient rule followed in most states that would allow recovery on a showing of ordinary negligence. The Supreme Court did take the case, however, and its reversal of the judgment left Tompkins with no recovery. For a time he was unable to work, and depended on welfare. During the manpower shortage caused by World War II, he eventually did work again, but the end of the war brought a flood of men back into the workforce, and Tompkins did not work thereafter. Reportedly Nemeroff sent him small sums of money occasionally. Tompkins died in a local hospital 1961, at the age of fifty-four. In 1997, the Pennsylvania Historical Museum and others joined to erect a historical marker, close to the accident scene, that commemorates the case. In 2007, to mark the centennial of Tompkins' birth, a local bar association created the "Erie v. Tompkins-Maysie Bicycle Program" to provide bicycles to needy children, giving 14 bicycles away in its first year. For these and other details, see Edward A. Purcell, Jr., The Story of *Erie*: How Litigants, Lawyers, Judges, Politics, and Social Change Reshape the Law, in Civil Procedure Stories 21 (Kevin M. Clermont ed., 2d ed. 2008).

8. The intellectual basis of the Brandeis opinion in *Erie* is a theory generally described as "legal positivism." Justice Holmes, who had retired from the Court but remained a close friend of Brandeis, had deployed this theory earlier in his own attack on *Swift*. Legal positivism stresses that law has a political source or origin, such as legislative enactments, and that law is associated with political and enforcement powers. More than 20 years before *Erie*, Holmes had written: "The common law is not a brooding omnipresence in the sky, but the articulate voice of some sovereign or quasi sovereign that can be identified," by which he meant that it "always is the law of some state" that a court applies. See Southern Pacific Co. v. Jensen, 244 U.S. 205, 222 (1917) (Holmes, J., dissenting). Recall Professor Ides's description of the lawmaking in *Swift*, set out in note 4 in Notes on *Swift* and Federal Common Law. And compare Larry Kramer, *The Lawmaking Power of the Federal Courts*, 12 Pace L. Rev. 263, 283 (1992) (today we refer to "the authority of judges to make positive law," and *Erie*'s real significance is in rejecting the view that laws comprised "principles" that judges "merely interpreted"), with Jack Goldsmith & Steven Walt, Erie *and the Irrelevance of Legal Positivism*, 84 Va. L. Rev. 673 (1998) (denying that *Erie* is a decision about the nature of law, and arguing that it reflects "a particular time-bound set of constitutional and policy priorities").

9. Did Brandeis have an unspoken agenda? Some have thought so. See Purcell, Jr., supra, at 21 (Brandeis saw *Erie* as an opportunity to curb corporate power by lessening incentives to remove to federal court in pursuit of friendlier judges and laws more favorable to commercial interests, and Brandeis didn't let on that he had such purposes in mind; also he saw an opportunity to strike a blow for legislative authority and state power in an era when the Court was increasingly sustaining congressional power to centralize regulation of the economy).

GUARANTY TRUST CO. v. YORK

Supreme Court of the United States
326 U.S. 99 (1945)

Mr. Justice FRANKFURTER delivered the opinion of the Court.

[Van Sweringen Corporation issued notes in the amount of $30 million in May 1930. Guaranty Trust assumed, as trustee for noteholders, the power and duty to enforce their rights in the assets of the corporation and the Van Sweringen brothers. Thereafter, Guaranty Trust made advances to companies controlled by the brothers, and later when it became apparent that the Corporation could not meet its obligations under the notes, Guaranty Trust cooperated in a plan to exchange notes for cash in the amount of 50 percent of face value plus stock in the Van Sweringen Corporation.

Grace York received $6,000 worth of the notes as a gift in 1934, from someone who had not participated in the exchange program. In April 1940, three noteholders who had *accepted* the offer of exchange sued Guaranty Trust, alleging fraud and misrepresentation. York sought unsuccessfully to intervene. Guaranty Trust won dismissal of the suit on motion for summary judgment. York then brought the present suit, as a class action on behalf of nonaccepting noteholders, suing in federal court on the basis of diversity of citizenship.

Guaranty Trust again won summary judgment, but the Court of Appeals held that the earlier suit did not block York's suit, concluding as well that the state statute of limitations did not apply, on the ground that an equity suit in federal court is not required by the *Erie* doctrine to apply state law on this matter.]

Our starting point must be the policy of federal jurisdiction which *Erie* embodies. In overruling *Swift*, *Erie* did not merely overrule a venerable case. It overruled a particular way of looking at law which dominated the judicial process long after its inadequacies had been laid bare. Law was conceived as a "brooding omnipresence" of Reason, of which decisions were merely evidence and not themselves the controlling formulations. Accordingly, federal courts deemed themselves free to ascertain what Reason, and therefore Law, required wholly independent of authoritatively declared State law, even in cases where a legal right as the basis for relief was created by State authority and could not be created by federal authority and the case got into a federal court merely because it was "between Citizens of different States" under Art. III of the Constitution of the United States.

. . .

[T]he *Swift* doctrine was congenial to the jurisprudential climate of the time. Once established, judicial momentum kept it going. Since it was conceived that there was "a transcendental body of law outside of any particular State but obligatory within it unless and until changed by statute," Black & White Taxicab & Transfer Co. v. Brown & Yellow Taxicab & Transfer Co., 276 U.S. 518, 532-533 (1928), State court decisions were not "the law" but merely someone's opinion—to be sure an opinion to be respected—concerning the content of this all-pervading law. Not unnaturally, the federal courts assumed power to find for themselves the content of such a body of law. The notion was stimulated by the attractive vision of a uniform body of federal law. To such sentiments for uniformity of decision and freedom from diversity in State law the federal courts gave currency, particularly in cases where equitable remedies were sought, because equitable doctrines are so often cast in terms of universal applicability when close analysis of the source of legal enforceability is not demanded.

In exercising their jurisdiction on the ground of diversity of citizenship, the federal courts, in the long course of their history, have not differentiated in their regard for State law between actions at law and suits in equity. Although §34 of the Judiciary Act of 1789, directed that the "laws of the several States ... shall be regarded as rules of decision in trials of common law," this was deemed, consistently for over a hundred years, to be merely declaratory of what would in any event have governed the federal courts and therefore was equally applicable to equity suits. Indeed, it may fairly be said that the federal courts gave greater respect to State-created "substantive rights," Pusey & Jones Co. v. Hanssen, 261 U.S. 491, 498 (1923), in equity than they gave them on the law side, because rights at law were usually declared by State courts and as such increasingly flouted by extension of the doctrine of *Swift*, while rights in equity were frequently defined by legislative enactment and as such known and respected by the federal courts.

Partly because the States in the early days varied greatly in the manner in which equitable relief was afforded and in the extent to which it was available, Congress provided that "the forms and modes of proceeding in suits ... of equity" would conform to the settled uses of courts of equity. 28 USC §723. But this enactment gave the federal courts no power that they would not have had in any event when courts were given "cognizance," by the first Judiciary Act, of equity. From the beginning there has been a good deal of talk in the cases that federal equity is a separate legal system. And so it is, properly understood. The suits in equity of which the federal courts have had "cognizance" ever since 1789 constituted the body of law which had been transplanted to this country from the English Court of Chancery. But this system of equity "derived its doctrines, as well as its powers, from its mode of giving relief." Langdell, Summary of Equity Pleading (1877) xxvii. In giving federal courts "cognizance" of equity suits in cases of diversity jurisdiction, Congress never gave, nor did the federal courts ever claim, the power to deny substantive rights created by State law or to create substantive rights denied by State law.

This does not mean that whatever equitable remedy is available in a State court must be available in a diversity suit in a federal court, or conversely, that a federal court may not afford an equitable remedy not available in a State court. Equitable relief in a federal court is of course subject to restrictions: The suit must be within the traditional scope of equity as historically evolved in the English Court of Chancery; a plain, adequate and complete remedy at law must be wanting; explicit Congressional curtailment of equity powers must be respected; the constitutional right to trial by jury cannot be evaded. That a State may authorize its courts to give equitable relief unhampered by any or all such restrictions cannot remove these fetters from the federal courts. State law cannot define the remedies which a federal court must give simply because a federal court in diversity jurisdiction is available as an alternative tribunal to the State's courts. Contrariwise, a federal court may afford an equitable remedy for a substantive right recognized by a State even though a State court cannot give it. Whatever contradiction or confusion may be produced by a medley of judicial phrases severed from their environment, the body of adjudications concerning equitable relief in diversity cases leaves no doubt that the federal courts enforced State-created substantive rights if the mode of proceeding and remedy were consonant with the traditional body of equitable remedies, practice and procedure, and in so doing they were enforcing rights created by the States and not arising under any inherent or statutory federal law.

Inevitably, therefore, the principle of *Erie*, an action at law, was promptly applied to a suit in equity. Ruhlin v. New York Life Ins. Co., 304 U.S. 202 (1938).

And so this case reduces itself to the narrow question whether, when no recovery could be had in a State court because the action is barred by the statute of limitations, a federal court in equity can take cognizance of the suit because there is diversity of citizenship between the parties. Is the outlawry, according to State law, of a claim created by the States a matter of "substantive rights" to be respected by a federal court of equity when that court's jurisdiction is dependent on the fact that there is a State-created right, or is such statute of "a mere remedial character," Henrietta Mills v. Rutherford Co., 281 U.S. 121, 128 (1930), which a federal court may disregard?

Matters of "substance" and matters of "procedure" are much talked about in the books as though they defined a great divide cutting across the whole domain of law. But, of course, "substance" and "procedure" are the same key words to very different problems. Neither "substance" nor "procedure" represents the same invariants. Each implies different variables depending upon the particular problem for which it is used. See Home Ins. Co. v. Dick, 281 U.S. 397, 409 (1930). And the different problems are only distantly related at best, for the terms are in common use in connection with situations turning on such different considerations as those that are relevant to questions pertaining to ex post facto legislation, the impairment of the obligations of contract, the enforcement of federal rights in the State courts and the multitudinous phases of the conflict of laws.

Here we are dealing with a right to recover derived not from the United States but from one of the States. When, because the plaintiff happens to be a nonresident, such a right is enforceable in a federal as well as in a State court, the forms and mode of enforcing the right may at times, naturally enough, vary because the two judicial systems are not identic. But since a federal court adjudicating a state-created right solely because of the diversity of citizenship of the parties is for that purpose, in effect, only another court of the State, it cannot afford recovery if the right to recover is made unavailable by the State nor can it substantially affect the enforcement of the right as given by the State.

And so the question is not whether a statute of limitations is deemed a matter of "procedure" in some sense. The question is whether such a statute concerns merely the manner and the means by which a right to recover, as recognized by the State, is enforced, or whether such statutory limitation is a matter of substance in the aspect that alone is relevant to our problem, namely, does it significantly affect the result of a litigation for a federal court or disregard a law of a State that would be controlling in an action upon the same claim by the same parties in a State court?

It is therefore immaterial whether statutes of limitation are characterized either as "substantive" or "procedural" in State court opinions in any use of those terms unrelated to the specific issue before us. *Erie* was not an endeavor to formulate scientific legal terminology. It expressed a policy that touches vitally the proper distribution of judicial power between State and federal courts. In essence, the intent of that decision was to insure that, in all cases where a federal court is exercising jurisdiction solely because of the diversity of citizenship of the parties, the outcome of the litigation in the federal court should be substantially the same, so far as legal rules determine the outcome of a litigation, as it would be if tried in a State court. The nub of the policy that underlies *Erie* is that for the same transaction the accident of a suit by a nonresident litigant in a federal court instead of in a State court a block away, should not lead to a substantially different result. And so, putting to one side abstractions regarding "substance" and "procedure," we have held that in diversity cases the federal courts must follow the law of the State as to burden of proof, Cities Service Oil Co. v. Dunlap, 308 U.S. 208 (1939), as to conflict of laws, Klaxon Co. v. Stentor Co., 313 U.S. 487 (1941), as to contributory negligence, Palmer v. Hoffman, 318 U.S. 109, 117 (1943). *Erie* has been applied with an eye alert to essentials in avoiding disregard of State law in diversity cases in the federal courts. A policy so important to our federalism must be kept free from entanglements with analytical or terminological niceties.

Plainly enough, a statute that would completely bar recovery in a suit if brought in a State court bears on a State-created right vitally and not merely formally or negligibly. As to consequences that so intimately affect recovery or nonrecovery a federal court in a diversity case should follow State law. The fact that under New York law a statute of limitations might be lengthened or shortened, that a security may be foreclosed though the debt be barred, that a barred debt may be used as a setoff, are all matters of local law properly to be respected by federal courts sitting in New York when their incidence comes into play there. Such particular rules of local law, however, do not in the slightest change the crucial consideration that if a plea of the statute of limitations would bar recovery in a State court, a federal court ought not to afford recovery.

. . .

Diversity jurisdiction is founded on assurance to nonresident litigants of courts free from susceptibility to potential local bias. The Framers of the

Constitution, according to Marshall, entertained "apprehensions" lest distant suitors be subjected to local bias in State courts, or, at least, viewed with "indulgence the possible fears and apprehensions" of such suitors. And so Congress afforded out-of-state litigants another tribunal, not another body of law. The operation of a double system of conflicting laws in the same State is plainly hostile to the reign of law. Certainly, the fortuitous circumstance of residence out of a State of one of the parties to a litigation ought not to give rise to a discrimination against others equally concerned but locally resident. The source of substantive rights enforced by a federal court under diversity jurisdiction, it cannot be said too often, is the law of the States. Whenever that law is authoritatively declared by a State, whether its voice be the legislature or its highest court, such law ought to govern in litigation founded on that law, whether the forum of application is a State or a federal court and whether the remedies be sought at law or may be had in equity.

Dicta may be cited characterizing equity as an independent body of law. To the extent that we have indicated, it is. But insofar as these general observations go beyond that, they merely reflect notions that have been replaced by a sharper analysis of what federal courts do when they enforce rights that have no federal origin. . . .

The judgment is reversed and the case is remanded for proceedings not inconsistent with this opinion.

So ordered.

Reversed.

Mr. Justice ROBERTS and Mr. Justice DOUGLAS took no part in the consideration or decision of this case.

[A dissenting opinion by Justice Rutledge, joined by Justice Murphy, is omitted.]

■ NOTES ON *ERIE*'S FIRST 20 YEARS

1. In its most basic aspects, *York* tells us two things. First, the *Erie* doctrine applies on the "equity" side of the docket as much as the "law" side—it applies to suits seeking injunctive relief, for example, or reformation or specific performance of a contract, as much as it applies to suits for damages in tort or contract suits, for example. Second, statutes of limitation are among the laws of the states that federal courts are bound to apply.

2. *Erie* never said that "substance" and "procedure" might be different, did it? *York,* in contrast, takes as an article of faith that *Erie* requires federal courts to apply state substantive law and federal procedural law. Consider the question raised in *Erie:* What rights, if any, does a "longitudinal trespasser" have against a landowner on whose property the plaintiff suffered injury? That seems "substantive" in every possible way, doesn't it? Knowing who has what rights goes to the heart of the transaction in suit—to the out-of-court behavior of the parties. In contrast, consider one of the questions raised in the Court's earlier decision in the *Palmer* case (cited in *York*): That question was, who has to plead contributory negligence, plaintiff or defendant? This question seems "procedural" in every possible sense, doesn't it? Knowing "who has to plead what" is tied up with the process of litigation, and it has to do with the behavior of lawyers bringing and defending the case. In these polar-opposite settings, the substance-procedure dichotomy is clear, isn't it? *Palmer* comments that this issue relating to "manner of pleading" is governed by FRCP 8(c), indicating that in diversity cases *federal* pleading standards apply. See Palmer v. Hoffman, 318 U.S. 109, 117 (1943).

3. Distinguishing substance from procedure is not always so easy, as *York* shows: Is a statute of limitations (or "laches" doctrine) substantive or procedural?

(a) One way to approach this question is to ask about the purposes and effects of laws or doctrines. Do they affect the out-of-court behavior of the parties? Do they affect the way litigation is conducted? If they affect both out-of-court behavior and the way litigation is conducted, are they *both* substantive *and* procedural? See generally Paul Carrington, *"Substance" and "Procedure" in the Rules Enabling Act*, 1989 Duke L.J. 281, 290-291 (1989). In effect *York* concludes that statutes of limitation are substantive, doesn't it? On what ground?

(b) *York* is not the only case that construes *Erie* as requiring federal courts to apply a state rule that seems both substantive and procedural. In *Dunlap* (another case decided between *Erie* and *York*), the question was whether the state rule allocating burden of persuasion applies in federal diversity cases (the state rule *does* apply). See Cities Service Oil Co. v. Dunlap, 308 U.S. 208 (1939). And *Klaxon* (yet another case decided between *Erie* and *York*) raised the question whether state choice-of-law rules apply in federal court (the answer once again is yes). See Klaxon Co. v. Stentor Elec. Mfg. Co., 313 U.S. 487 (1941).

4. The *Klaxon* decision covers choice-of-law rules: You saw this doctrine in the background of the *Piper* case on *forum non conveniens* venue transfer (Chapter 5C1), and it may be puzzling to you. Suppose Knox, who lives in Reno, Nevada, crosses into California near Lake Tahoe to go skiing at the Heavenly ski resort. There he falls and breaks his leg. He is taken to Arcadia Hospital in Truckee, California, where doctors set the leg. Things go wrong, and Knox undergoes an amputation. Home in Reno, Knox consults a lawyer, who thinks Knox has a malpractice claim against Arcadia. Suppose Arcadia is a health maintenance provider that operates clinics in California, Nevada, Oregon, Washington, and Idaho, including the one in Truckee where Knox was treated. Suppose further that Knox is a member of Arcadia One, a health coverage plan, and the home office for his coverage is in Reno. On these facts, Knox can probably sue Arcadia in either California or Nevada. Suppose, finally, that California has a statute limiting recovery for noneconomic loss in the amount of $250,000, but Nevada has no similar limit. On facts such as these, it is a difficult question whether the California damage limit statute should apply, or the Nevada no-limit rule.

(a) Under a traditional territorial approach, embodied in the first Restatement of Conflicts of Law (1934), many states followed a choice-of-law rule that usually required application of the law of the place of the wrong. Since California is the place of the alleged tort, a court that followed this approach would likely apply California's damage limit.

(b) In the middle of the twentieth century, choice of law underwent something of a revolution. Brainerd Currie of the University of Chicago developed an approach that he called "interest analysis." Currie concluded that some conflicts of law were in fact "false conflicts" because only one of two jurisdictions whose laws seemed to conflict had some actual interest or concern in applying its law.[4] Under this more modern approach, taking into account the policies and interests underlying the competing legal rules, states might well differ on which law to choose.

(c) On our facts, a court might conclude that California law was designed to protect California residents from overexposure to liability, and Arcadia's presence in California, coupled with the fact that it treated Knox there, might suggest that California law should apply. But the relationship between Knox and Arcadia is centered in Nevada, so a court might conclude that Nevada has the larger interest: It was fortuitous that Knox broke his leg in California and was treated there, and Nevada has the greater interest (its no-limit rule should apply).

(d) What *Klaxon* means is that a federal court in Nevada should follow Nevada's choice-of-law rule, and a federal court in California should follow California's choice of law rule. If the choice-of-law rule in one of these states would select Nevada law as governing, while the choice-of-law rule in the

---

[4] The foundational case involved two New Yorkers who went on a trip to the Province of Ontario in Canada, where they had a single-car accident in which the passenger was injured. Back in New York, the passenger sued the driver and the question was whether New York's rule allowing such suits should prevail, or the Canadian rule barring claims by guests against drivers. The New York Court of Appeals concluded that New York's interest is "unquestionably the greater and more direct," and that "the interest of Ontario is at best minimal." Hence New York law applied to the question whether the guest could sue the driver. See Babcock v. Jackson, 191 N.E.2d 279 (N.Y. 1963).

When *Babcock* came down, the American Law Institute was at work on the Restatement (Second) of Conflicts of Law, approved in 1969 and published in 1971. Like *Babcock*, the Second Restatement abandoned the territorial approach in favor of one that is more flexible. The Second Restatement adopts the principle that the law of the state of "most significant relationship" should govern, and this state can be identified with reference to particular issues, rather than for the case as a whole. "Principles" and "contacts" are key elements, and the "interest analysis" pioneered by Brainerd Currie finds expression in the Restatement's "principles."

Thus in all cases (apart from those where "statutory directive" tells a court which law to apply), courts are to consider "the needs of the interstate and international systems," the "relevant policies" of the forum, the "relevant policies of other interested states," the "protection of justified expectations," the "basic policies" underlying particular fields of law, "certainty, predictability and uniformity of result," and "ease in the determination and application of the law." See Restatement (Second) of Conflicts of Laws, §6 (setting out "principles").

other state would choose California law as governing, then it would be advantageous for Knox to sue in the former. Under *Klaxon,* it may matter a lot whether Knox's suit proceeds in California or Nevada, but it doesn't matter much whether the suit goes forward in state or federal court. In short, *Klaxon* promotes "vertical" uniformity, but not "horizontal" uniformity. A court in California, state or federal, applies California's choice-of-law rule, and a court in Nevada, state or federal, applies Nevada's choice-of-law rule (vertical uniformity).

5. *York* makes no mention of the Constitution, does it? Instead, it stresses that the "outcome" of litigation in federal court "should be substantially the same, so far as legal rules determine the outcome of litigation, as it would be if tried in a state court." This "outcome determinative" test is forever associated with *York,* and it is the one expression of the *Erie* doctrine that *everyone* remembers, even though in some respects it is the *least satisfactory* explanation of *Erie.*

6. *Erie* was decided on April 25, 1938, and the Federal Rules of Civil Procedure took effect less than five months later—on September 16, 1938. Their content was known to the Court when it decided *Erie* (the Rules had been submitted late in 1937, and the Court approved and forwarded them to Congress in December 1937), and of course their content was known to the Court seven years later when it decided *York.* Hence the Court could not have thought when it decided *Erie,* let alone *York,* that it was thwarting the new Rules. The Justices must have had at least some notion that procedure and substance were separate. And yet many if not all procedural rules could "affect outcome." Consider, for example, a possible difference between state and federal law on the time allowed to answer a complaint. FRCP 12(b) requires a defendant to file an answer within 21 days, but suppose the state counterpart allows 28 days. Not filing a timely answer can lead to a default judgment: Must federal courts allow 28 days to file an answer in diversity cases? Surely the answer is no—yet it is arguable that the state rule is outcome determinative. Justice Frankfurter cannot have intended in *York* to be taken quite that literally, can he?

7. Four years after *York,* the Supreme Court again addressed *Erie* issues in a trio of cases decided on the same day, all raising problems located close to the intersection between substance and procedure:

(a) In the *Ragan* case, the question was whether a plaintiff who filed suit late in the two-year limitations period prescribed by Kansas law had to serve the complaint on defendant within the time that Kansas law allowed for service. Suits must normally be "commenced" within the limitation period, and FRCP 3 defines "commencement" as the date of *filing.* Under Kansas law, however, a suit commences on filing only if service is made within 60 days. You guessed it: Plaintiff in *Ragan* did not serve defendant until several weeks *after* the 60-day period had run. The question was whether FRCP 3 governed "commencement" for purposes of the limitation period, or Kansas law. The Court of Appeals relied heavily on *York* and the Supreme Court

seemed to agree: A suit may not have "longer life in the federal court than it would have had in the state court without adding something to the cause of action," which one cannot do, "consistently with *Erie*." Ragan v. Merchants Transfer & Warehouse Co., 337 U.S. 530, 533 (1949).

(b) In the *Cohen* case, the question was whether a federal court had to apply New Jersey law requiring plaintiff in a derivative suit to post a litigation expense bond, which protected defendants if they prevailed by paying their costs of suit. (A derivative suit is brought by a stockholder on behalf of the corporation. Typically, defendants are officers or directors, and the claim is that they violated duties to the corporation. Any recovery goes not to plaintiff personally, but to the corporation.) One Rule addresses derivative suits in the federal system (today it is FRCP 23.1), and there is no provision for a bond. Writing that procedural rules "do not always exhaust their effect by regulating procedure," the Court concluded that the New Jersey law was "not merely a regulation of procedure" because "it creates a new liability where none existed before," and the federal provision dealing with derivative suits does not "conflict with the [New Jersey] statute," so both "may be observed." See Cohen v. Beneficial Industrial Loan Corp., 337 U.S. 541, 555-556 (1949) (plaintiff must post bond).

(c) In the *Woods* case, the question was whether a Tennessee corporation, which had not complied with the domestication statute of Mississippi, could sue a Mississippi citizen in the federal court of that state. Under Mississippi law, an out-of-state corporation not in compliance with the domestication statute cannot sue in the courts of the state. The Court concluded that the federal court had to apply the Mississippi statute. See Woods v. Interstate Realty Co., 337 U.S. 535 (1949).

(d) What can we make of *Ragan, Cohen*, and *Woods*? Does it seem that everything that *could be* decided in favor of conforming federal practice to state rules regulating something resembling procedure *is* being decided that way? Do these cases call into question the viability of the Federal Rules? See, e.g., Edward L. Merrigan, *Erie* to *York* to *Ragan*—A Triple Play on the Federal Rules, 3 Vand. L. Rev. 711 (1950).

8. In the *Bernhardt* case in 1956, the Court addressed *Erie* issues in a case raising the question whether a federal court in a diversity case had to apply a Vermont rule allowing contracting parties to abrogate the part of their agreement committing to resolve by arbitration any differences between them. Holding that the federal Arbitration Act applies only to transactions involving interstate commerce or a maritime transaction, that neither was involved here, and that arbitration involves substantive rights, the Court concluded that the federal court had to apply the Vermont rule. Arbitration "substantially affects the cause of action" created by state law, as the "nature of the tribunal" involves "an important part of the parcel of rights" and changing from a court to an arbitration panel might "make a radical difference in ultimate result." Arbitration carries no right to a jury trial, and arbitrators "do not have the benefit of judicial instruction on the law," and the "nub of the policy" underlying *Erie* is that "for the same transaction" there should not be a different outcome in state versus federal court. Bernhardt v. Polygraphic Co. of America, Inc., 350 U.S. 198, 204-205 (1956). Later the Court seemed to change course, in a suit on a contract clearly affecting commerce, finding that the Arbitration Act applies even in state court, see Southland v. Keating, 465 U.S. 1 (1984) (federal Arbitration Act applies in state courts), and that it applies in connection with claims for fraud in the inducement, see Prima Paint Corp. v. Flood & Conklin Mfg. Co., 388 U.S. 395 (1967).

3. The *Erie* Doctrine Comes of Age

BYRD v. BLUE RIDGE RURAL ELECTRIC COOPERATIVE

Supreme Court of the United States
356 U.S. 525 (1958)

Mr. Justice BRENNAN delivered the opinion of the Court.

[James Earl Byrd, working as lineman on the crew of a construction contractor in rural South Carolina, was injured while putting up 24 miles of new power lines. His employer R.H. Bouligny, Inc. had contracted with Blue Ridge Rural Electric to do the work, which included building two substations and a breaker station. Byrd was seriously burned while connecting power lines to one of the new substations.

In federal district court in South Carolina, Byrd sued Blue Ridge for negligence and won a jury verdict. The Fourth Circuit reversed and directed entry of judgment for Blue Ridge, which had raised as an affirmative defense the proposition that South Carolina law barred Byrd from suing in tort. This defense rested on the claim that Byrd, as an actual employee of Bouligny, was a "statutory employee" of Blue Ridge because the kind of work that Bouligny contracted to perform for Blue Ridge was also the kind of work that Blue Ridge employees did.

The Court says that the case raises two questions, which are "(1) whether the Court of Appeals erred in directing judgment for respondent without a remand to give [Byrd] an opportunity to introduce further evidence; and (2) whether [Byrd], state practice notwithstanding, is entitled to a jury determination of the factual issues raised by this defense."

The Court concludes that Byrd should indeed have an opportunity to produce further evidence.]

A question is also presented as to whether on remand the factual issue is to be decided by the judge or by the jury. The respondent argues on the basis of the decision of the Supreme Court of South Carolina in Adams v. Davison-

Paxon Co., 96 S.E.2d 566 (S.C. 1957), that the issue of immunity should be decided by the judge and not by the jury. That was a negligence action brought in the state trial court against a store owner by an employee of an independent contractor who operated the store's millinery department. The trial judge denied the store owner's motion for a directed verdict made upon the ground that [the statute] barred the plaintiff's action. The jury returned a verdict for the plaintiff. The South Carolina Supreme Court reversed, holding that it was for the judge and not the jury to decide on the evidence whether the owner was a statutory employer, and that the store owner had sustained his defense. The court rested its holding on decisions . . . involving judicial review of the Industrial Commission and said:

> Thus the trial court should have in this case resolved the conflicts in the evidence and determined the fact of whether (the independent contractor) was performing a part of the "trade, business or occupation" of the department store-appellant and, therefore, whether (the employee's) remedy is exclusively under the Workmen's Compensation Law.

The respondent argues that this state court decision governs the present diversity case and "divests the jury of its normal function" to decide the disputed fact question of the respondent's immunity under [the statute]. This is to contend that the federal court is bound under *Erie* to follow the state court's holding to secure uniform enforcement of the immunity created by the State.

First. It was decided in *Erie* that the federal courts in diversity cases must respect the definition of state-created rights and obligations by the state courts. We must, therefore, first examine the rule in *Adams* to determine whether it is bound up with these rights and obligations in such a way that its application in the federal court is required.

The Workmen's Compensation Act is administered in South Carolina by its Industrial Commission. The South Carolina courts hold that, on judicial review of actions of the Commission under [the statute], the question whether the claim of an injured workman is within the Commission's jurisdiction is a matter of law for decision by the court, which makes its own findings of fact relating to that jurisdiction. The South Carolina Supreme Court states no reasons in *Adams* why, although the jury decides all other factual issues raised by the cause of action and defenses, the jury is displaced as to the factual issue raised by the affirmative defense under [the statute]. The decisions cited to support the holding are . . . concerned solely with defining the scope and method of judicial review of the Industrial Commission. A State may, of course, distribute the functions of its judicial machinery as it sees fit. The decisions relied upon, however, furnish no reason for selecting the judge rather than the jury to decide this single affirmative defense in the negligence action. They simply reflect a policy that administrative determination of "jurisdictional facts" should not be final but subject to judicial review. The conclusion is inescapable that the *Adams* holding is grounded in the practical consideration that the question had theretofore come before the South Carolina courts from the Industrial Commission and the courts had become accustomed to deciding the factual issue of immunity without the aid of juries. We find nothing to suggest that this rule was announced as an integral part of the special relationship created by the statute. Thus the requirement appears to be merely a form and mode of enforcing the immunity, *York,* and not a rule intended to be bound up with the definition of the rights and obligations of the parties. The situation is therefore not analogous to that in Dice v. Akron, C. & Y. R. Co., 342 U.S. 359 (1952), where this Court held that the right to trial by jury is so substantial a part of the cause of action created by the Federal Employers' Liability Act that the Ohio courts could not apply, in an action under that statute, the Ohio rule that the question of fraudulent release was for determination by a judge rather than by a jury.

Second. But cases following *Erie* have evinced a broader policy to the effect that the federal courts should conform as near as may be—in the absence of other considerations—to state rules even of form and mode where the state rules may bear substantially on the question whether the litigation would come out one way in the federal court and another way in the state court if the federal court failed to apply a particular local rule. Concededly the nature of the tribunal which tries issues may be important in the enforcement of the parcel of rights making up a cause of action or defense, and bear significantly upon achievement of uniform enforcement of the right. It may well be that in the instant personal-injury case the outcome would be substantially affected by whether the issue of immunity is decided by a judge or a jury. Therefore, were "outcome" the only consideration, a strong case might appear for saying that the federal court should follow the state practice.

But there are affirmative countervailing considerations at work here. The federal system is an independent system for administering justice to litigants who properly invoke its jurisdiction. An essential characteristic of that system is the manner in which, in civil common law actions, it distributes trial functions between judge and jury and, under the influence—if not the command[10]—of the Seventh Amendment, assigns the decisions of disputed questions of fact to the jury.[11] The policy of uniform enforcement of state-created rights and obligations, see, e.g., *York,* cannot in every case exact

---

[10] Our conclusion makes unnecessary the consideration of—and we intimate no view upon—the constitutional question whether the right of jury trial protected in federal courts by the Seventh Amendment embraces the factual issue of statutory immunity when asserted, as here, as an affirmative defense in a common law negligence action.

[11] The Courts of Appeals have expressed varying views about the effect of *Erie* on judge-jury problems in diversity cases. Federal practice was followed in [some cases]. State practice was followed in [others].

compliance with a state rule[12]—not bound up with rights and obligations—which disrupts the federal system of allocating functions between judge and jury. Herron v. Southern Pacific Co., 283 U.S. 91 (1931). Thus the inquiry here is whether the federal policy favoring jury decisions of disputed fact questions should yield to the state rule in the interest of furthering the objective that the litigation should not come out one way in the federal court and another way in the state court.

We think that in the circumstances of this case the federal court should not follow the state rule. It cannot be gainsaid that there is a strong federal policy against allowing state rules to disrupt the judge-jury relationship in the federal courts. In *Herron*, the trial judge in a personal-injury negligence action brought in the District Court for Arizona on diversity grounds directed a verdict for the defendant when it appeared as a matter of law that the plaintiff was guilty of contributory negligence. The federal judge refused to be bound by a provision of the Arizona Constitution which made the jury the sole arbiter of the question of contributory negligence. This Court sustained the action of the trial judge, holding that "state laws cannot alter the essential character or function of a federal court" because that function "is not in any sense a local matter, and state statutes which would interfere with the appropriate performance of that function are not binding upon the federal court under either the Conformity Act or the Rules of Decision Act." Perhaps even more clearly in light of the influence of the Seventh Amendment, the function assigned to the jury "is an essential factor in the process for which the Federal Constitution provides." Concededly the *Herron* case was decided before *Erie*, but even when *Swift* was governing law and allowed federal courts sitting in diversity cases to disregard state decisional law, it was never thought that state statutes or constitutions were similarly to be disregarded. Yet *Herron* held that state statutes and constitutional provisions could not disrupt or alter the essential character or function of a federal court.

Third. We have discussed the problem upon the assumption that the outcome of the litigation may be substantially affected by whether the issue of immunity is decided by a judge or a jury. But clearly there is not present here the certainty that a different result would follow, cf. *York*, or even the strong possibility that this would be the case, cf. Bernhardt v. Polygraphic Co., 350 U.S. 198 (1956). There are factors present here which might reduce that possibility. The trial judge in the federal system has powers denied the judges of many States to comment on the weight of evidence and credibility of witnesses, and discretion to grant a new trial if the verdict appears to him to be against the weight of the evidence. We do not think the likelihood of a different result is so strong as to require the federal practice of jury

---

[12] This Court held in Sibbach v. Wilson & Co., 312 U.S. 1 (1941), that FRCP 35 [court-ordered physical examinations] should prevail over a contrary state rule.

determination of disputed factual issues to yield to the state rule in the interest of uniformity of outcome.

The Court of Appeals did not consider other grounds of appeal raised by the respondent because the ground taken disposed of the case. We accordingly remand the case to the Court of Appeals for the decision of the other questions, with instructions that, if not made unnecessary by the decision of such questions, the Court of Appeals shall remand the case to the District Court for a new trial of such issues as the Court of Appeals may direct.

Reversed and remanded.

[The opinion of Justice Whittaker, concurring in part and dissenting in part, is omitted. The dissenting opinion by Justice Frankfurter, whom Mr. Justice Harlan joins, is also omitted.]

■ NOTES ON *BYRD* AND THE AGENDA OF THE COURT

1. James Byrd brought a tort suit against his employer in federal court, invoking diversity jurisdiction. After he prevailed in a jury trial, his employer appealed and won a reversal on the ground that the tort suit was barred by the state statutory scheme relegating his claims to the workers' compensation system. The Court applies *Erie* in deciding whether state or federal law determines when or whether a particular question is to be resolved by a judge or by a jury in federal court. The Court acknowledges that the South Carolina Supreme Court in the *Adams* case treated the question at issue in *Byrd* as one for the judge to decide. But Justice Brennan says *Adams* provided "no reason for selecting the judge rather than the jury," and the choice was merely one of "form and mode of enforcing the [workers' compensation] immunity," hence that federal courts need not take the same path. And "countervailing considerations" are at work—federal courts are "an independent system for administering justice," and the federal court system should be able to apply its own rules in allocating trial functions between judge and jury ("an essential characteristic" of the federal system).

2. Is it fair to say that *Byrd* put in place a "balancing test," where the question is whether the policy behind the state rule or the policy behind the federal is the more weighty? In the *Charneski* case, Allstate Insurance brought a diversity suit in federal court seeking a declaratory judgment that it did not insure the car driven by defendant Leonard Charneski that was involved in an accident with a car driven by defendant LaVerne Gehrt. Wisconsin permits "direct actions" *against* insurance carriers, which means Gehrt could sue Allstate "directly," rather than suing Charneski (actual alleged tortfeasor). Under Wisconsin decisional law, however, the direct action statute foreclosed a declaratory suit by the carrier. The notion was that the carrier should not be allowed to "isolate one defense against an injured plaintiff and try it in advance." The federal court in *Charneski* concluded that the "federal interest" was "slight," citing the "general interest of a court in controlling its own procedure" and the "general policy" of the federal Declaratory Judgments Act. In contrast, the interest of Wisconsin is considerable: "The cause of action arising from the accident, the issue of coverage of the policy, and the rights of the insured, the insurer and the injured parties are intimately connected with Wisconsin law." Allstate Insurance Co. v. Charneski, 286 F.2d 238, 244 (7th Cir. 1960) ("no overriding federal interest" at stake). Does *Charneski* represent an appropriate balancing of state versus federal interests under *Byrd*?

3. The Seventh Amendment provides that in "suits at common law" the right to trial by jury "shall be preserved" (see Chapter 12A, infra). In the *Herron* case, quoted in *Byrd*, the Court had concluded 27 years earlier that a federal court was *not* bound by state standards on the question whether a verdict could be "directed" on a defense (whether the defense could be taken from the jury) for lack of evidence. It would be astonishing, would it not, if state law decided what questions go to a jury and what questions go to a judge in a civil case litigated in federal court? Yet *Byrd* is coy about the impact of the Constitution—citing "the influence—if not the command—of the Seventh Amendment"! Wasn't the case a whole lot easier than the Court made it out to be?

4. The Court comments in *Byrd* that South Carolina decisions on "the issue of immunity" from tort suits (because plaintiff is covered by workers' compensation) treat the matter as raising questions of law, and the Court says "no reason" is given for "displac[ing]" the jury on "the factual issue" raised by this "affirmative defense." Can you think why one might assign this matter to the judge? When, in a tort suit, should this issue be resolved—during pretrial motions before a jury is assembled, or during trial? What sort of question is being asked? Is it the sort of question a jury should answer? South Carolina is not the only state that thinks questions of this sort are for the trial judge to decide. See Bass v. National Super Markets, Inc., 911 S.W.2d 617, 621 (Mo. 1995) ("where the facts are not in dispute as to the nature of the agreement and the work required by it, the existence or absence of statutory employment is a question of law for the courts to decide"). Doesn't Justice Brennan seem myopic when it comes to the logic behind the choice made in South Carolina to allocate to a judge the question whether the claimant must proceed in the workers' compensation system rather than in tort? If indeed these questions *should be* answered by a judge rather than a jury, and if federal courts would do the same thing, then Justice Brennan's excursion into *Erie* issues was unnecessary, wasn't it? Notice that *Byrd* does not actually say a federal jury should resolve the issue—only that federal law determines whether a judge or jury gets the issue.

5. Given that there are good reasons to assign to a judge the question whether the claimant was a "statutory employee," and that the case could easily have been resolved by holding that the Seventh Amendment governs the matter, why did *Byrd* go in the direction that it does? Can you figure out the Court's unspoken agenda here?

HANNA v. PLUMER

Supreme Court of the United States
380 U.S. 460 (1965)

Mr. Chief Justice WARREN delivered the opinion of the Court.

The question to be decided is whether, in a civil action where the jurisdiction of the United States district court is based upon diversity of citizenship between the parties, service of process shall be made in the manner prescribed by state law or that set forth in FRCP 4(d)(1).

[On February 6, 1963, Eddie Hanna of Ohio sued the estate of Louise Plumer Osgood of Massachusetts for personal injuries resulting from an accident in South Carolina. She served Edward Plumer, who was Mrs. Osgood's executor and a Massachusetts citizen, accomplishing service by leaving copies of the summons and complaint with Edward Plumer's wife at the place where the two resided.

This means of service complied with FRCP 4(d)(1), which authorized service by "delivering a copy of the summons and of the complaint" to the defendant "personally" or by "leaving copies thereof at his dwelling house or usual place of abode with some person of suitable age and discretion then residing therein." (Substantially the same option now appears as FRCP 4(e)(2).)

Plumer's answer alleged that the suit could not be maintained because it had been brought "contrary to and in violation of" a Massachusetts statute, which required that an action against an executor must be "by delivery in hand upon such executor or administrator or service thereof accepted by him."

The District Court awarded summary judgment for the defendant in October 1963 on the ground that service was inadequate, citing Ragan v. Merchants Transfer & Warehouse Co., 337 U.S. 530 (1949), and *York*.]

We conclude that the adoption of Rule 4(d)(1), designed to control service of process in diversity actions, neither exceeded the congressional mandate embodied in the Rules Enabling Act nor transgressed constitutional bounds, and that the Rule is therefore the standard against which the District Court should have measured the adequacy of the service. Accordingly, we reverse the decision of the Court of Appeals.

The Rules Enabling Act, 28 U.S.C. §2072, provides, in pertinent part:

> The Supreme Court shall have the power to prescribe, by general rules, the forms of process, writs, pleadings, and motions, and the practice and procedure

of the district courts of the United States in civil actions. Such rules shall not abridge, enlarge or modify any substantive right and shall preserve the right of trial by jury. . . .

Under the cases construing the scope of the Enabling Act, Rule 4(d)(1) clearly passes muster. Prescribing the manner in which a defendant is to be notified that a suit has been instituted against him, it relates to the "practice and procedure of the district courts."

> The test must be whether a rule really regulates procedure,—the judicial process for enforcing rights and duties recognized by substantive law and for justly administering remedy and redress for disregard or infraction of them.

Sibbach v. Wilson, 312 U.S. 1, 14 (1941).

. . .

Thus were there no conflicting state procedure, Rule 4(d)(1) would clearly control. However, respondent, focusing on the contrary Massachusetts rule, calls to the Court's attention another line of cases, a line which—like the Federal Rules—had its birth in 1938. *Erie*, overruling *Swift*, held that federal courts sitting in diversity cases, when deciding questions of "substantive" law, are bound by state court decisions as well as state statutes. The broad command of *Erie* was therefore identical to that of the Enabling Act: Federal courts are to apply state substantive law and federal procedural law. However, as subsequent cases sharpened the distinction between substance and procedure, the line of cases following *Erie* diverged markedly from the line construing the Enabling Act. *York* made it clear that *Erie*-type problems were not to be solved by reference to any traditional or common-sense substance-procedure distinction[.]

> And so the question is not whether a statute of limitations is deemed a matter of "procedure" in some sense. The question is . . . does it significantly affect the result of a litigation for a federal court to disregard a law of a State that would be controlling in an action upon the same claim by the same parties in a State court?

Respondent, by placing primary reliance on *York* and *Ragan*, suggests that the *Erie* doctrine acts as a check on the Federal Rules of Civil Procedure, that despite the clear command of Rule 4(d)(1), *Erie* and its progeny demand the application of the Massachusetts rule. Reduced to essentials, the argument is: (1) *Erie*, as refined in *York*, demands that federal courts apply state law whenever application of federal law in its stead will alter the outcome of the case. (2) In this case, a determination that the Massachusetts service requirements obtain will result in immediate victory for respondent. If, on the other hand, it should be held that Rule 4(d)(1) is applicable, the litigation will continue, with possible victory for petitioner. (3) Therefore, *Erie* demands application of the Massachusetts rule. The syllogism possesses an appealing simplicity, but is for several reasons invalid.

In the first place, it is doubtful that, even if there were no Federal Rule making it clear that in-hand service is not required in diversity actions, the *Erie* rule would have obligated the District Court to follow the Massachusetts procedure. "Outcome-determination" analysis was never intended to serve as a talisman. *Byrd.* Indeed, the message of *York* itself is that choices between state and federal law are to be made not by application of any automatic, "litmus paper" criterion, but rather by reference to the policies underlying the *Erie* rule. *York.*

The *Erie* rule is rooted in part in a realization that it would be unfair for the character of result of a litigation materially to differ because the suit had been brought in a federal court. [The Court quotes passage from *Erie*.]

The decision was also in part a reaction to the practice of "forum-shopping" which had grown up in response to the rule of *Swift*.[8] That the *York* test was an attempt to effectuate these policies is demonstrated by the fact that the opinion framed the inquiry in terms of "substantial" variations between state and federal litigation. Not only are nonsubstantial, or trivial, variations not likely to raise the sort of equal protection problems which troubled the Court in *Erie*; they are also unlikely to influence the choice of a forum. The "outcome-determination" test therefore cannot be read without reference to the twin aims of the *Erie* rule: discouragement of forum-shopping and avoidance of inequitable administration of the laws.[9]

The difference between the conclusion that the Massachusetts rule is applicable, and the conclusion that it is not, is of course at this point "outcome-determinative" in the sense that if we hold the state rule to apply, respondent prevails, whereas if we hold that Rule 4(d)(1) governs, the litigation will continue. But in this sense every procedural variation is "outcome-determinative." For example, having brought suit in a federal court, a plaintiff cannot then insist on the right to file subsequent pleadings in accord with the

---

[8] Cf. Black & White Taxicab & Transfer Co. v. Brown & Yellow Taxicab & Transfer Co., 276 U.S. 518 (1928).

[9] The Court of Appeals seemed to frame the inquiry in terms of how "important" [the statute] is to the State. In support of its suggestion that [the statute] serves some interest the State regards as vital to its citizens, the court noted that something like [it] has been on the books in Massachusetts a long time, that [the statute] has been amended a number of times and that [it] is designed to make sure that executors receive actual notice. The apparent lack of relation among these three observations is not surprising, because it is not clear to what sort of question the Court of Appeals was addressing itself. One cannot meaningfully ask how important something is without first asking "important for what purpose?" *Erie* and its progeny make clear that when a federal court sitting in a diversity case is faced with a question of whether or not to apply state law, the importance of a state rule is indeed relevant, but only in the context of asking whether application of the rule would make so important a difference to the character or result of the litigation that failure to enforce it would unfairly discriminate against citizens of the forum State, or whether application of the rule would have so important an effect upon the fortunes of one or both of the litigants that failure to enforce it would be likely to cause a plaintiff to choose the federal court.

time limits applicable in state courts, even though enforcement of the federal timetable will, if he continues to insist that he must meet only the state time limit, result in determination of the controversy against him. So it is here. Though choice of the federal or state rule will at this point have a marked effect upon the outcome of the litigation, the difference between the two rules would be of scant, if any, relevance to the choice of a forum. Petitioner, in choosing her forum, was not presented with a situation where application of the state rule would wholly bar recovery; rather, adherence to the state rule would have resulted only in altering the way in which process was served.[11] Moreover, it is difficult to argue that permitting service of defendant's wife to take the place of in-hand service of defendant himself alters the mode of enforcement of state-created rights in a fashion sufficiently "substantial" to raise the sort of equal protection problems to which the *Erie* opinion alluded.

There is, however, a more fundamental flaw in respondent's syllogism: the incorrect assumption that the rule of *Erie* constitutes the appropriate test of the validity and therefore the applicability of a Federal Rule of Civil Procedure. The *Erie* rule has never been invoked to void a Federal Rule. It is true that there have been cases where this Court has held applicable a state rule in the face of an argument that the situation was governed by one of the Federal Rules. But the holding of each such case was not that *Erie* commanded displacement of a Federal Rule by an inconsistent state rule, but rather that the scope of the Federal Rule was not as broad as the losing party urged, and therefore, there being no Federal Rule which covered the point in dispute, *Erie* commanded the enforcement of state law.

> Respondent contends in the first place that the charge was correct because of the fact that Rule 8(c) of the Rules of Civil Procedure makes contributory negligence an affirmative defense. We do not agree. Rule 8(c) covers only the manner of pleading. The question of the burden of establishing contributory negligence is a question of local law which federal courts in diversity of citizenship cases (*Erie*) must apply.

Palmer v. Hoffman, 318 U.S. 109, 117 (1943).[12] (Here, of course, the clash is unavoidable; Rule 4(d)(1) says—implicitly, but with unmistakable clarity—that in-hand service is not required in federal courts.) At the same time, in cases adjudicating the validity of Federal Rules, we have not applied the *York* rule or

---

[11] We cannot seriously entertain the thought that one suing an estate would be led to choose the federal court because of a belief that adherence to Rule 4(d)(1) is less likely to give the executor actual notice than [the statute], and therefore more likely to produce a default judgment. Rule 4(d)(1) is well designed to give actual notice, as it did in this case.

[12] To the same effect, see Ragan v. Merchants Transfer & Warehouse Co., 337 U.S. 530 (1949); Cohen v. Beneficial Indus. Loan Corp., 337 U.S. 541 (1949) (Douglas, J., dissenting); cf. Bernhardt v. Polygraphic Co., 388 U.S. 395 (1956); Iovino v. Watson, 274 F.2d 41, 47-48 (2d Cir. 1959) [allowing appointment of out-of-state administrator, appointed by court, in place of defendant who had died, despite state law requiring appointment of in-state person in that capacity—Ed.].

other refinements of *Erie,* but have to this day continued to decide questions concerning the scope of the Enabling Act and the constitutionality of specific Federal Rules in light of the distinction set forth in *Sibbach.* E.g., Schlagenhauf v. Holder, 379 U.S. 104 (1964).

Nor has the development of two separate lines of cases been inadvert. The line between "substance" and "procedure" shifts as the legal context changes. "Each implies different variables depending upon the particular problem for which it is used." *York.* It is true that both the Enabling Act and the *Erie* rule say, roughly, that federal courts are to apply state "substantive" law and federal "procedural" law, but from that it need not follow that the tests are identical. For they were designed to control very different sorts of decisions. When a situation is covered by one of the Federal Rules, the question facing the court is a far cry from the typical, relatively unguided *Erie* Choice: The court has been instructed to apply the Federal Rule, and can refuse to do so only if the Advisory Committee, this Court, and Congress erred in their prima facie judgment that the Rule in question transgresses neither the terms of the Enabling Act nor constitutional restrictions.

We are reminded by the *Erie* opinion that neither Congress nor the federal courts can, under the guise of formulating rules of decision for federal courts, fashion rules which are not supported by a grant of federal authority contained in Article I or some other section of the Constitution; in such areas state law must govern because there can be no other law. But the opinion in *Erie,* which involved no Federal Rule and dealt with a question which was "substantive" in every traditional sense (whether the railroad owed a duty of care to Tompkins as a trespasser or a licensee), surely neither said nor implied that measures like Rule 4(d)(1) are unconstitutional. For the constitutional provision for a federal court system (augmented by the Necessary and Proper Clause) carries with it congressional power to make rules governing the practice and pleading in those courts, which in turn includes a power to regulate matters which, though falling within the uncertain area between substance and procedure, are rationally capable of classification as either. Neither *York* nor the cases following it ever suggested that the rule there laid down for coping with situations where no Federal Rule applies is coextensive with the limitation on Congress to which *Erie* had adverted. Although this Court has never before been confronted with a case where the applicable Federal Rule is in direct collision with the law of the relevant State, courts of appeals faced with such clashes have rightly discerned the implications of our decisions. [The Court quotes the *Lumbermen's* case indicating that "shaping purpose" of the Federal Rules was "to bring about uniformity in the federal courts." Lumbermen's Mutual Casualty Co. v. Wright, 322 F.2d 759, 764 (5th Cir. 1963).]

Erie and its offspring cast no doubt on the long-recognized power of Congress to prescribe housekeeping rules for federal courts even though some of those rules will inevitably differ from comparable state rules. . . . Thus, though a court, in measuring a Federal Rule against the standards contained in the Enabling Act and the Constitution, need not wholly blind itself to the degree to which the Rule makes the character and result of the federal litigation stray from the course it would follow in state courts, *Sibbach,* it cannot be forgotten that the *Erie* rule, and the guidelines suggested in *York,* were created to serve another purpose altogether. To hold that a Federal Rule of Civil Procedure must cease to function whenever it alters the mode of enforcing state-created rights would be to disembowel either the Constitution's grant of power over federal procedure or Congress' attempt to exercise that power in the Enabling Act. Rule 4(d)(1) is valid and controls the instant case.

Reversed.

Mr. Justice BLACK concurs in the result.

Mr. Justice HARLAN, concurring.

It is unquestionably true that up to now *Erie* and the cases following it have not succeeded in articulating a workable doctrine governing choice of law in diversity actions. I respect the Court's effort to clarify the situation in today's opinion. However, in doing so I think it has misconceived the constitutional premises of *Erie* and has failed to deal adequately with those past decisions upon which the courts below relied.

Erie was something more than an opinion which worried about "forum-shopping and avoidance of inequitable administration of the laws," although to be sure these were important elements of the decision. I have always regarded that decision as one of the modern cornerstones of our federalism, expressing policies that profoundly touch the allocation of judicial power between the state and federal systems. *Erie* recognized that there should not be two conflicting systems of law controlling the primary activity of citizens, for such alternative governing authority must necessarily give rise to a debilitating uncertainty in the planning of everyday affairs. And it recognized that the scheme of our Constitution envisions an allocation of law-making functions between state and federal legislative processes which is undercut if the federal judiciary can make substantive law affecting state affairs beyond the bounds of congressional legislative powers in this regard. Thus, in diversity cases *Erie* commands that it be the state law governing primary private activity which prevails.

The shorthand formulations which have appeared in some past decisions are prone to carry untoward results that frequently arise from over-simplification. The Court is quite right in stating that the "outcome-determinative" test of *York,* if taken literally, proves too much, for any rule, no matter how clearly "procedural," can affect the outcome of litigation if it is not obeyed. In turning from the "outcome" test of *York* back to the unadorned forum-shopping rationale of *Erie,* however, the Court falls prey to like oversimplification, for a simple forum-shopping rule also proves too much; litigants often choose a federal forum merely to obtain what they consider the advantages of the Federal Rules of Civil Procedure or to try their cases before a supposedly more favorable judge. To my mind the proper line of approach in determining whether to apply a state or a federal rule, whether "substantive" or "procedural," is to stay close to basic principles by inquiring if the choice of rule would substantially affect those primary decisions respecting human conduct which our constitutional system leaves to state regulation. If so, *Erie* and the Constitution require that the state rule prevail, even in the face of a conflicting federal rule.

The Court weakens, if indeed it does not submerge, this basic principle by finding, in effect, a grant of substantive legislative power in the constitutional provision for a federal court system (compare *Swift*), and through it, setting up the Federal Rules as a body of law inviolate. "(T)he constitutional provision for a federal court system . . . carries with it congressional power . . . to regulate matters which, though falling within the uncertain area between substance and procedure, are rationally capable of classification as either."

So long as a reasonable man could characterize any duly adopted federal rule as "procedural," the Court, unless I misapprehend what is said, would have it apply no matter how seriously it frustrated a State's substantive regulation of the primary conduct and affairs of its citizens. Since the members of the Advisory Committee, the Judicial Conference, and this Court who formulated the Federal Rules are presumably reasonable men, it follows that the integrity of the Federal Rules is absolute. Whereas the unadulterated outcome and forum-shopping tests may err too far toward honoring state rules, I submit that the Court's "arguably procedural, ergo constitutional" test moves too fast and far in the other direction.

The courts below relied upon this Court's decisions in *Ragan* and *Cohen*. Those cases deserve more attention than this Court has given them, particularly *Ragan* which, if still good law, would in my opinion call for affirmance of the result reached by the Court of Appeals. Further, a discussion of these two cases will serve to illuminate the "diversity" thesis I am advocating.

In *Ragan* a Kansas statute of limitations provided that an action was deemed commenced when service was made on the defendant. Despite Federal Rule 3 which provides that an action commences with the filing of the complaint, the Court held that for purposes of the Kansas statute of limitations a diversity tort action commenced only when service was made upon the defendant. The effect of this holding was that although the plaintiff had filed his federal complaint within the state period of limitations, his action was barred because the federal marshal did not serve a summons on the defendant until after the limitations period had run. I think that the decision was wrong. At most, application of the Federal Rule would have meant that potential Kansas tort defendants would have to defer for a few days the satisfaction of knowing that they had not been sued within the limitations period. The choice of the Federal Rule would have had no effect on the primary stages of private activity from which torts arise, and only the most minimal effect on behavior following the commission of the tort. In such circumstances the interest of the federal system in proceeding under its own rules should have prevailed.

Cohen held that a federal diversity court must apply a state statute requiring a small stockholder in a stockholder derivative suit to post a bond securing payment of defense costs as a condition to prosecuting an action. Such a statute is not "outcome determinative"; the plaintiff can win with or without it. The Court now rationalizes the case on the ground that the statute might affect the plaintiff's choice of forum, but as has been pointed out, a simple forum-shopping test proves too much. The proper view of *Cohen* is in my opinion, that the statute was meant to inhibit small stockholders from instituting "strike suits," and thus it was designed and could be expected to have a substantial impact on private primary activity. Anyone who was at the trial bar during the period when *Cohen* arose can appreciate the strong state policy reflected in the statute. I think it wholly legitimate to view Federal Rule 23 as not purporting to deal with the problem. But even had the Federal Rules purported to do so, and in so doing provided a substantially less effective deterrent to strike suits, I think the state rule should still have prevailed. That is where I believe the Court's view differs from mine; for the Court attributes such overriding force to the Federal Rules that it is hard to think of a case where a conflicting state rule would be allowed to operate, even though the state rule reflected policy considerations which, under *Erie,* would lie within the realm of state legislative authority.

It remains to apply what has been said to the present case. The Massachusetts rule provides that an executor need not answer suits unless in-hand service was made upon him or notice of the action was filed in the proper registry of probate within one year of his giving bond. The evident intent of this statute is to permit an executor to distribute the estate which he is administering without fear that further liabilities may be outstanding for which he could be held personally liable. If the Federal District Court in Massachusetts applies Rule 4(d) instead of the Massachusetts service rule, what effect would that have on the speed and assurance with which estates are distributed? As I see it, the effect would not be substantial. It would mean simply that an executor would have to check at his own house or the federal courthouse as well as the registry of probate before he could distribute the estate with impunity. As this does not seem enough to give rise to any real impingement on the vitality of the state policy which the Massachusetts rule is intended to serve, I concur in the judgment of the Court.

■ NOTES ON *HANNA* AND THE "ARMOR-PLATED" FEDERAL RULES

1. The question in *Hanna* is whether a federal court in a diversity suit brought in Massachusetts against Edward Plumer (administrator of estate of Louise Plumer Osgood), for injuries arising out of a South Carolina accident, must follow the Massachusetts rule requiring in-hand service of process, despite a federal rule allowing "abode" service—leaving the summons and copy of complaint at the home of the defendant with a person of "suitable age and discretion." The answer is no—complying with the federal rule suffices. This issue fits comfortably into the "procedural" category, doesn't it? Hence *Hanna* is simple. Could it be that Justice Warren in *Hanna* (like Justice Brennan in *Byrd*) had an agenda? What was it?

2. *Hanna* came seven years after *Byrd.* Shouldn't *Hanna* have balanced the federal interest in efficient service of process against the state interest in making sure the administrator of a decedent's estate gets actual notice of suit? Consider the comment in footnote 9 of *Hanna*, criticizing the Court of Appeals for inquiring into the Massachusetts rule. The "importance" of a state rule, the Court says, is only relevant in asking whether applying it would make such a difference in "the character or result" of the suit that *failing* to apply it would "unfairly discriminate" against locals or cause plaintiff "to choose the federal court." What does this comment say about the viability of the *Byrd* approach?

3. In *Erie, York,* and *Byrd,* the only statute that the Court cites is the RDA, but *Hanna* cites the REA—Rules Enabling Act, now 28 USC §§2071-2077. The REA has undergone changes since *Hanna*, but its basic features have carried forward to the present time. The REA authorizes the Court to "prescribe general rules of practice and procedure and rules of evidence" for cases litigated in federal courts. A committee (once appointed by the Court, now by the Judicial Conference) comprised of "members of the bench and the professional bar, and trial and appellate judges," drafts proposed rules. (Today, the committee holds public hearings, but this element was not in the original legislation.) The Court then considers the Rules—and in practice almost always approves them as proposed, and transmits them to Congress, which has seven months to block rules from taking effect—an option rarely exercised. Under the "supersession" clause, a Rule promulgated under the REA displaces federal statutes (when a Rule is promulgated, "all laws in conflict with [it] shall be of no further force or effect").

(a) Note that the REA authorizes the Court to make Rules regulating "procedure" (including "evidence"), not to make Rules of a "substantive" nature. The REA has one more important feature: Rules under it "shall not abridge, enlarge or modify any substantive right." See 28 USC §2072. This "substantive right clause" seems critical, doesn't it? A Federal Rule, promulgated under the Enabling Act, might well provide that defendants *must* or *may* bring counterclaims against plaintiffs. A Rule, however, should not determine

whether the "fellow servant" doctrine enables a railroad to avoid liability to a railroader injured on the job. Such an issue should be resolved by reference to common law or statute (if there is one), and a Rule speaking to this subject would run afoul of the substantive right clause.

(b) In the *Sibbach* case, an early decision in the *Erie* line of cases, the Court rejected a claim that FRCP 35 (which authorizes court-ordered physical and mental examinations) affected substantive rights in violation of the REA. A Rule that governs "important and substantial rights" does not necessarily violate the substantive right clause, at least if the Rule is "reasonably necessary to maintain the integrity of the system of federal practice and procedure." This comment surely foreshadows the still-broader position taken in *Hanna.* In *Sibbach,* the Court also commented that the "test" is "whether a rule really regulates procedure" (plaintiff had admitted this point, and that was enough, the Court decided, to ensure the validity of the Rule under the REA). In dissent in *Sibbach,* Justice Frankfurter (who wrote the decision in *York* four years later) spoke for many when he argued that a power to change public policy "in a matter deeply touching the sensibilities of people" should not be drawn out of a "general authorization to formulate rules" for civil litigation. See Sibbach v. Wilson & Co., 312 U.S. 1, 13 (1941).

4. Consider the first part of *Hanna*—what we might call *Hanna 1.* Here the Court asks whether compliance with the state service-in-hand requirement would have been necessary *if there were no* federal rule (the "relatively unguided *Erie* Choice"), and answers in the negative. *Hanna 1* is dictum, but it is critical. Here the Court replies to the simplest argument—the one based on *York* that says we must follow state law whenever it controls "outcome." The outcome standard, the Court tells us in *Hanna 1,* must be applied in light of the "twin aims" of the *Erie* doctrine, which are discouraging "forum shopping" and avoiding "inequitable administration." Hence the "outcome" test asks *not* the backward-looking question whether a federal litigant who followed the federal rule would *lose* if one *later* applied the state rule in assessing what he had done—an "*ex post*" question. *Rather,* the right question is a forward-looking query: We ask whether, if a litigant was trying to decide between state and federal court, the differing rule in federal court would affect his choice because it would affect outcome—an "*ex ante*" question. Viewed in *this* light, the "outcome" test makes sense, and we know how it comes out: A litigant would *not* choose the federal forum to avoid having to do in-hand service. Hence the state rule is *not* outcome determinative in the right sense.

5. Consider the second part of the opinion—*Hanna 2.* Here the Court comes to the nub of it, and *Hanna 2* is the *holding.* The question is what to do when a Federal Rule applies, and it conflicts with a state rule that would apply if the suit were in state court. Here the Court provides an answer by indirection: *Erie* "has never been invoked to void a Federal Rule," and a court can "refuse" to apply the Rules "only if the Advisory Committee, this Court, and Congress [have] erred in their prima facie judgment" that they transgress "neither the terms of the Enabling Act nor constitutional restrictions." Suppose, however, a Rule implicated the "twin aims" of *Erie*: Suppose a Rule would encourage "forum shopping" and lead to "inequitable administration"? Again *Hanna 2* gives an indirect answer: "Congressional power to make rules" governing practice in federal courts "includes a power to regulate matters which, though falling within the uncertain area between substance and procedure, are rationally capable of classification as either." Apparently, then, a Rule that is *both* procedural and substantive can *still* pass muster: In other words, an "arguably procedural rule *is* procedural." By eloquent indirection, isn't *Hanna 2* telling us that every Federal Rule is what we might call "armor-plated"? In other words, every Rule is, at the very least, "presumptively valid." Professor Wright paraphrased *Hanna 2* this way: The Rules are valid *not* just because "wise men made them, but because wise men thought carefully before making them"! See Charles A. Wright, *Procedural Reform: Its Limitations and Its Future*, 1 Ga. L. Rev. 563, 571-574 (1967) (quoting the late Ronan E. Degnan). What judge, after reading *Hanna 2,* would ever say, "Well, we have a Federal Rule in point, but it's substantive and *Erie* requires me to apply the state rule instead"? It seems, doesn't it, that Chief Justice Warren finished the job Justice Brennan started in *Byrd*—saving federal procedural law from over-application of the *Erie* doctrine?

6. But wait. Justice Harlan has yet to be heard from. *Erie* is *not* just a case about forum shopping and inequitable administration. *Erie* is a "cornerstone" of modern federalism. What does he mean? Equally important, Justice Harlan says the real question is whether "the choice of [federal or state] rule would substantially affect those primary decisions respecting human conduct which our constitutional system leaves to state regulation."[5] Putting aside the troubled question whether the Constitution does or does not carve out some areas of substantive regulation that only states can occupy, is Harlan's point that the substance-procedure distinction turns on whether a rule regulates out-of-court conduct? Judge Posner put it this way later in the *Healy* case. See S.E. Healy Co. v. Milwaukee Metropolitan Sewerage District, 60 F.3d 305, 310 (7th Cir. 1995) ("substantive" laws are those laws "designed to shape conduct outside the courtroom and not just improve the accuracy or lower the cost of the judicial process"), cited with approval in Gasperini v. Center for Humanities, Inc., 518 U.S. 415 (1996) (Section A6, infra).

(a) Notice that Justice Harlan would throw out *Ragan*—the case that held that a summons and complaint had to be served in a federal suit within 60 days of filing (time allowed by state law) *if* the suit was to be viewed as "commenced" for purposes of the statute of limitations on the date of filing. *Ragan,* in Justice Harlan's view, is the poster child for overly enthusiastic application of *Erie*. Why?

---

[5] In a footnote edited out of this book, Justice Harlan credits a text on federal courts for his reference to "primary decisions respecting human conduct." The current version of that text continues to discuss this expression. See Hart & Wechsler, The Federal Courts and the Federal System 589 (6th ed. 2009).

(b) In contrast, Justice Harlan thinks *Cohen* was *right* in insisting that a federal court in a derivative suit apply the state rule requiring a cost bond. Why? (We should note that Justice Harlan, as a lawyer before joining the Court, argued *Cohen* for Beneficial, the party that prevailed and benefitted from the bond.)

7. In a sense, *Hanna* adds finishing touches to a picture the Court had painted in rough outline in *Erie*, to which the Court had added color and detail in *York* and *Byrd*. Underlying the *Erie* doctrine, as we know it now, are considerations grounded in the Constitution, statute, and public policy. Not surprisingly, given the complexity of federalism, the various concerns of these categories are dualities that point sometimes toward state law and sometimes toward federal:

(a) As a constitutional matter, some clauses point toward state law: *Erie* itself *seemed* to rest (it cited no specific provision) on notions of *limited federal power* that emerge in Article I (Congress has "enumerated powers," not "general powers"), Article III (federal courts hear diversity cases, but don't create federal law in deciding them), and the Tenth Amendment (powers not delegated to the federal government nor reserved to the people are left to the states). But other clauses point toward federal law: *Byrd* says the Seventh Amendment (its "influence" if not its "command") entitles parties to jury trials in suits at law, so details over implementing this right must be controlled by federal law. And *Hanna* reminds us that Congress has constitutional power to create a federal court system, and can enact laws "necessary and proper" to operate that system, including the REA, under which the Court (with congressional acquiescence) adopted the Rules.

(b) As a matter of statute, we have the RDA (28 USC §1652), which points toward state law—the laws of the states are "rules of decision in civil actions in [federal courts], in cases where they apply." And we have the REA (28 USC §§2071-2077), which points toward federal law—the Court can promulgate "general rules of practice and procedure and rules of evidence" for cases litigated in federal court.

(c) As a matter of policy, we can begin with *Erie*'s concern over what we have called fairness or equitable administration. We should not apply one body of law to disputes heard in federal court because of diversity, while a different body of law applies to disputes between citizens of a single state. This salient concern points often toward application of state law. *York* can be seen as reformulating this point—the "outcome" in federal court in a suit based on diversity should be the same as the outcome of the same suit in state court—at least "so far as legal rules determine the outcome." But there are policies favoring federal law too: First, as *Byrd* says, the federal judiciary is "an independent system for administering justice to litigants," which implies at least that it can devise such rules as it needs to achieve this purpose. And at least implicitly *Hanna* takes this point a step further—the Rules, crafted under

statutory authority and examined by a professional committee, by the Court, and by Congress, should not be lightly overturned or cast aside in favor of state law—at least such rules as are "rationally capable of classification as either" substance or procedure.

■ **PROBLEM 6-A. "The Brakes Didn't Hold"**

Al Flanders purchased a Honda motorcycle. In a fall afternoon in October 2011 he was riding on the Valhalla ATV (All Terrain Vehicle) trail in Bayfield County in Wisconsin when he found himself going too fast and he applied his brakes to slow down. Honda motorcycles boast a CBS (combined braking system), under which simultaneous use of the right handlebar lever and the pedal engage the front and back brakes simultaneously to obtain greater effectiveness in stopping while avoiding the "nosedive" tendency that appears when too much relative pressure is applied to the front brake.

The motorcycle did nose over, and Flanders was thrown against a tree, sustaining serious injuries.

In a Wisconsin court, Flanders sued American Honda, seeking recovery of medical expenses and pain and suffering in an amount exceeding $1 million. Honda removed the suit to the Federal District Court for the Western District of Wisconsin, invoking the removal and diversity statutes, pointing out correctly that Flanders is a citizen of Wisconsin and American Honda is a citizen of California.

At trial, counsel for Flanders seeks to prove that within months after the accident Honda altered the CBS design in similar motorcycles. Flanders argues that this alteration was evidence that the prior design was defective, and was important in establishing strict liability. Honda invokes FRE 407, which bars proof of "subsequent measures" when offered to prove "negligence" or "culpable conduct" or "a defect in a product or its design," or "a need for warning or instruction." Counsel for Flanders replies by pointing out that Wisconsin Rule 407 only applies to proof of subsequent measures when offered to prove "negligence or culpable conduct," and that "under Wisconsin caselaw, proof of subsequent measures is admissible to prove product defect." He cites Chart v. General Motors Corp., 258 N.W.2d 680 (Wis. 1977), and D.L. by Friederichs v. Huebner, 329 N.W. 890 (Wis. 1983), which hold that design changes *are* admissible under Wisconsin Rule 407 in product liability cases, whether based on strict liability, negligence, or breach of warranty. How should the court rule, and why?

■ NOTES ON "SUBSTANTIVE" EVIDENCE RULES

1. Suppose Flanders can win if he can show that Honda changed the design of the braking system after his accident, but not if this proof is excluded. If the suit had gone forward in Wisconsin state court, Flanders wins; in federal court, he loses. Thus removal changed the result just because Honda American is a citizen of California who can get the suit into federal court. Doesn't the situation remind you of the *Black & White Taxicab* case cited in *Erie* and raised in the Notes after *Erie*?

2. Recall *Byrd*'s reference to federal courts as "an independent system for administering justice." Doesn't independence mean there is a strong federal interest in operating federal courts in the best possible way to achieve a proper balance between providing justice for litigants and operating efficiently? That interest could easily justify following a broad array of federal "procedural" rules, even where state rules conflict. Does it also justify applying federal evidence law? See Monarch Insurance Co. of Ohio v. Spach, 281 F.2d 401 (5th Cir. 1960) (citing *Byrd* and concluding that federal evidence law controls in a diversity suit, even in the face of a conflicting state statute).

(a) You will discover in the Evidence course that most evidence rules aim at assuring accurate factfinding, as is true, for instance, of rules about hearsay and relevance, including in the latter category very important rules regulating use of "character" evidence. Strongly influenced by pathbreaking articles arguing that evidence rules are mostly "procedural," committees appointed by the Court promulgated what became the Federal Rules of Evidence in 1975. See Ronan Degnan, *The Law of Federal Evidence Reform*, 76 Harv. L. Rev. 275 (1962); Jack B. Weinstein, *The Uniformity-Conformity Dilemma Facing Draftsmen of Federal Rules of Evidence*, 69 Colum. L. Rev. 353 (1969).

(b) Some evidence rules have other aims. For example, privilege rules protect relationships among people outside of court. Thus the attorney-client privilege bars use of confidential statements by clients to lawyers, and the marital confidences privilege excludes private conversations among spouses. In both cases, the purpose is to protect privacy, thus to encourage those relationships.

(c) In the areas of presumptions, privileges, and competency of witnesses, the framers of the Rules of Evidence recognized that they were dealing with law that has substantive dimensions. Here the Rules of Evidence require federal courts to apply *state* law in diversity cases. See FRE 301, 501, and 601. By way of explanation, presumptions are substantive in civil cases because they affect burdens of production or persuasion, and the Court has always viewed burden of persuasion as substantive. Privilege rules are viewed as substantive for the reasons noted above. Competency rules are less obviously substantive, but in one area arguably they are: So-called dead man's statutes in most states block or limit use of statements by deceased persons, when suit

is brought against their estate, for the substantive purpose of preserving assets of estates (protect "widows and orphans").

3. Rule 407, the provision governing proof of subsequent measures invoked in the Problem, does *not* tell federal courts to apply state law in diversity cases. Why do we have this provision? Should it apply in product liability cases? It turns out that the reason for excluding proof of subsequent measures is *mostly* to encourage (avoid discouraging) people from making conditions better (safer) after accidents, and the various states are divided on the question whether the rule is needed in product cases. That is a *substantive* function, is it not? Recall Justice Harlan's concurrence in *Hanna*.

(a) Nobody doubts that Congress could enact legislation setting nationwide standards for product liability cases. Does the fact that Congress enacted the Rules of Evidence mean that FRE 407 can properly apply in diversity cases?[6] Surely the majority in *Hanna* supports this argument—the Evidence Rules are as much armor-plated as the Rules of Civil Procedure, maybe more so because Congress *enacted* the Evidence Rules.

(b) Did Congress *mean* to govern product liability law by enacting the Evidence Rules? Does that matter? Could one take the position that FRE 407 applies in federal question cases but not in diversity cases? You will see that in some cases the Court has given narrow construction to Rules of Procedure to avoid conflict with state law.

(c) Before Rule 407 was amended in 1997, it read the same as the Wisconsin Rule reads today—FRE 407 barred use of subsequent measures to prove "negligence or culpable conduct" and did not mention product cases. Decisions in federal and state courts split on the question whether FRE 407, and identical state counterparts, applied in product cases. Some federal courts thought FRE 407 could not bar proof of subsequent measures in product liability cases brought on the basis of diversity jurisdiction, see Moe v. Avions Marcel Dassault-Breguet Aviation, 727 F.2d 917 (10th Cir. 1984), but most thought the Rule *did* apply because it was "arguably procedural" under *Hanna*, see Flaminio v. Honda Motor Co., Ltd., 733 F.2d 463 (7th Cir. 1984).

4. Rule 407 is not the only place where the Rules of Evidence do *not* make way for state law to operate in situations in which arguably state law *should* be honored. Many states, for instance, have mandatory seatbelt statutes, and some bar proof of the use or nonuse of seatbelts in trials. Issues arise as to whether these statutes apply in product cases litigated in federal court: On the

---

[6] By accident, the Evidence Rules went to Congress as the Watergate scandal was erupting. Sensitized on the questions of the balance of powers between the executive and legislative branches, Congress saw the Evidence Rules as a further challenge to its prerogatives. So Congress did not let them become law through inaction, but held hearings, changed them in many places, and finally enacted them. Thus they are technically statutes, although Congress also amended the Enabling Act to allow the Court to appoint an Evidence Committee and to amend any Rule *except* in the area of privileges in the usual way (by Committee and Court action, followed by submission of proposed changes to Congress, which can reject or modify a proposal or do nothing, in which case the change takes effect).

one hand, it is often true that negligence by claimants is no defense (so not wearing a seatbelt would be irrelevant even if there were no statute). On the other hand, nonuse of a seatbelt could bear on the amount of damages for which defendant is liable. Here, as in the case of FRE 407, federal authority conflicts. Compare Hodges v. Mack Trucks, Inc., 474 F.3d 188, 199-202 (5th Cir. 2006) (applying Texas seatbelt statute in product suit as substantive under *Erie* but concluding that statute does *not* exclude proof of nonuse of seatbelt on question of causation), and Forrest v. Beloit Corp., 424 F.3d 244, 254 n.7 (3d Cir. 2005) (state rules governing proof of nonuse of seatbelts are "arguably inter-twined with the manner in which states seek to regulate primary behavior" and "as such may fall on the substantive side of the substance/procedure dichot-omy"), and Potts v. Benjamin, 882 F.2d 1320 (8th Cir. 1989) (in suit arising out of car-truck collision, excluding proof of failure of plaintiffs to place children in child restraint seats; Arkansas statute excluding such proof is "substantive law," enacted as part of Child Passenger Protection Act, and binds federal courts under *Erie*), and Milbrand v. DaimlerChrysler Corp., 105 F. Supp. 2d 601 (E.D. Tex. 2000) (in product liability case, Texas statute barring proof of nonuse of seatbelts is substantive under *Erie* and applies), with Sims v. Great American Life Ins. Co., 469 F.3d 870, 883-884 (10th Cir. 2006) (in suit on accidental death policy, carrier claimed death resulted from suicide; court excluded proof that decedent had not buckled up, applying Oklahoma statute; applying federal evidence law "without any regard for state substantive policy" would create "considerable tension with notions of federalism," but *Erie* is "inapplicable" because Evidence Rules were enacted by Congress; *still* federal relevancy rules respect state policies, by defining "elements and defenses" in diversity cases, requiring court to consider whether Oklahoma statute was "procedural" or "substantive") (statute does not apply in suits against insurance carriers; also excluding evidence was harmless error).

4. *Erie* in the Modern Era: *Hanna* and the Ascendancy of Federal Procedure

Modern decisions applying *Erie* (and a few old ones) approve the application of federal statutes, Federal Rules, and federal common law doctrines relating to procedure. Often the Court construes these provisions and doctrines broadly. It is apparent that *Hanna 2* succeeded in "armor-plating" the Federal Rules and some statutes, and that *Hanna 1* provides room for federal common law doctrines.

Consider these decisions rejecting *Erie*-based challenges to the application of federal *statutes* relating to procedure:

(1) In the *Ricoh* case, plaintiff sued in federal court in Alabama, on con-tract and antitrust claims. The contract had a forum selection clause pointing to New York, but such clauses were "contrary to public policy" under Alabama

law. Defendant moved to transfer to New York, invoking the *forum non conveniens* venue statute (28 USC §1404) and the venue transfer statute (28 USC §1406), arguing that Alabama was an improper venue. The question, said the Court, involves "a considerably less intricate analysis" than is necessary in the "relatively unguided *Erie* choice" where we have neither statute nor Rule. When there is a statute, "the first and chief question" is whether it controls, which "involves a straightforward exercise in statutory interpretation." If the statute "covers the point," the question is whether it represents "a valid exercise of Congress' authority under the Constitution." The *forum non conveniens* statute "does cover the point," and tells courts to "weigh in the balance a number of case-specific factors," including the forum selection clause and the fact that it is unenforceable under Alabama law, and also such factors as convenience of witnesses and "public-interest factors of systemic integrity and fairness." This statute is, in the words of *Hanna 2*, "capable of classification as a procedural rule," so it "falls comfortably within Congress' powers under Article III as augmented by the Necessary and Proper Clause." Stewart Organization, Inc. v. Ricoh Corp., 487 U.S. 22, 29-32 (1988).

(2) In the *Jinks* case, a prisoner in state custody died of complications associated with withdrawal from alcohol, and his widow sued in federal court under §1983, claiming violation of constitutional rights, joining wrongful death and survival claims under state law. The §1983 claim was dismissed, and the court dismissed the state law claims, declining to exercise supplemental jurisdiction under 28 USC §1367(c)(3). The widow filed the remaining claims in state court, but they were dismissed when the state court refused to honor the provision in the federal statute tolling the limitation period for state claims while the case is in federal court "and for a period of 30 days after it is dismissed." See 28 USC §1367(d). Invoking the "Necessary and Proper" Clause, the Court concluded that the tolling provision passes muster as "conducive to the [federal] administration of justice" because it provides "an alternative to the unsatisfactory options" otherwise facing federal courts—conditioning dismissal of state claims on waiver of a limitations defense, retaining jurisdiction over state claims that should be heard in state court, or letting plaintiff reopen the federal case if the state court refused to hear the state claims. Also, the tolling provision "eliminates a serious impediment to access to the federal courts" for those pursuing mixed federal and state claims. See Jinks v. Richland County, South Carolina, 538 U.S. 456 (2003).

Consider as well these decisions rejecting *Erie*-based challenges to the application of *Federal Rules* relating to procedure:

(3) In the *Burlington Northern* case, the question was whether, in a diversity case leading to judgment for plaintiff and an appeal by the defendant, the federal court had to apply a state rule imposing a mandatory penalty against the appellant in the amount of 10 percent of the judgment if it was affirmed on appeal. There is a federal rule on point. FRAP 38 provides that a reviewing court may "award just damages and single or double costs" to the prevailing

party on appeal. The Court rejected the argument that a court could apply both, awarding a mandatory 10 percent penalty *and also* costs and damages under FRAP 38. Quoting the phrase from *Hanna* that a Rule is valid if it regulates matters "falling within the uncertain area between substance and procedure," but are nevertheless "rationally capable of classification as either," the Court concluded that FRAP 38 applies. Nor did it violate the substantive rights clause in the Enabling Act because "Rules which incidentally affect litigants' substantive rights" are all right "if reasonably necessary to maintain the integrity of [the federal] system of rules." See Burlington Northern R. Co. v. Woods, 480 U.S. 1, 5 (1987).

(4) In the *Business Guides* case, a plaintiff seeking to block distribution of a competing business list was sanctioned under FRCP 11, which then provided that a party who signs a document submitted to the court certifies that it is "well grounded in fact" on the basis of the signer's "knowledge, information, and belief formed after reasonable inquiry." (FRCP 11 was later amended in ways that do not affect the issue here.) In affidavits submitted in support of its application for a TRO, plaintiff claimed to have discovered that defendant violated its copyright because it had planted "seeds" in its own directory (fictional or erroneous information) and some of these were found in defendant's competing publication. But plaintiff's internal editing processes had corrected misinformation in the seeds, and defendant's competing products contained no mistaken data. Plaintiff was sanctioned to the tune of more than $13,000 to reimburse defendant for its out-of-pocket costs. On the question whether FRCP 11 violated the REA in authorizing sanctions against a party, the Court quoted *Hanna 2*'s "armor-plating" language (one can challenge a federal rule only if "the Advisory Committee, this Court, and Congress" have made a mistake), then quoted *Burlington Northern*'s language that Rules "incidentally affecting" substantive rights are valid, and rejected the challenge. See Business Guides, Inc. v. Chromatic Communications Enterprises, 498 U.S. 533, 552 (1991).

Finally, consider this decision rejecting an *Erie*-based challenge to federal *common law doctrine* relating to procedure:

(5) In *Chambers*, the question was whether a federal court could impose sanctions for bad faith conduct by a party in a diversity case, who took manipulative steps designed to deprive the federal court of jurisdiction. State courts could not take such steps, and FRCP 11 did not reach much of the conduct in issue (today it is broader). The federal statute relating to sanctions (28 USC §1927) did not reach misconduct by a *party* (and was not aimed at the conduct that occurred here), but the Court concluded that federal courts have "implied" or "inherent" powers to sanction misconduct. Drawing on *Hanna 1's* reference to the "twin aims" of *Erie* (avoiding forum shopping and inequitable administration), the Court concluded that this uncodified federal common law doctrine applies. See Chambers v. NASCO, 501 U.S. 32 (1991) (a vigorous dissent argued that "prelitigation misconduct" was a matter of "primary behavior" that only states could regulate under *Erie*).

5. Unraveling *Erie*: One Doctrine, or More?

As we have seen, the *Erie* doctrine is many-faceted and multi-layered, and it is easy to get lost. Even the Supreme Court acknowledges that its attempts to elucidate this doctrine have been only partly successful. Let us look now at efforts by commentators to bring order out of chaos.

We begin with Professor John Hart Ely's insight that *Erie* itself is really a group of doctrines, and that answers to *Erie* issues emerge in different ways in different situations. Here is how he put it in his seminal article, written in 1974:

> My suggestion . . . will be that the indiscriminate admixture of all questions respecting choices between federal and state law in diversity cases, under the single rubric of "the *Erie* doctrine" or "the *Erie* problem," has served to make a major mystery out of what are really three distinct and rather ordinary problems of statutory and constitutional interpretation. Of course there will be occasions with respect to all three on which reasonable persons will differ, but that does not make the problems mysterious or even very unusual. The United States Constitution, I shall argue, constitutes the relevant text only where Congress has passed a statute [or the Court has adopted a Rule] creating law for diversity actions, and it is in this situation alone that [*Hanna 2*'s] "arguably procedural" test controls. Where a [common law] rule is involved, the Constitution necessarily remains in the background, but is functionally irrelevant because the applicable statutes are significantly more protective of the prerogatives of state law. Thus, where there is no relevant Federal Rule of Civil Procedure or other Rule promulgated pursuant to the Enabling Act and the federal [common law] rule in issue is therefore wholly judge-made, whether state or federal law should be applied is controlled by the Rules of Decision Act, the statute construed in *Erie* and *York*. Where the matter in issue is covered by a Federal Rule, however, the Enabling Act—and not the Rules of Decision Act itself or the line of cases construing it—constitutes the relevant standard. To say that, however, and that is [what *Hanna 2*] said, is by no means to concede the validity of all Federal Rules, for the Enabling Act contains significant limiting language of its own. The Court has correctly sensed that that language cannot be construed to protect state prerogatives as strenuously as the Rules of Decision Act protects them in the absence of a Federal Rule. However, the Court's recent appreciation that the Enabling Act constitutes the only check on the Rules—that "*Erie*" does not stand there as a backstop—should lead it in an appropriate case to take the Act's limiting language more seriously than it has in the past.

John Hart Ely, *The Irrepressible Myth of* Erie, 87 Harv. L. Rev. 693, 697-698 (1974).

Left out of Professor Ely's threefold approach is consideration of what we might call "purely constitutional" constraints on federal procedure. Let us add that category and then examine the remainder of Professor Ely's threefold approach:

(1) *Purely Constitutional Constraints.* It is at least possible to read *Erie* as directly applying a constitutional command. Whatever part of the Constitution *Erie* rests on, at the very least *Erie* indicates that in diversity cases the *Constitution* requires federal courts to apply state substantive law, and the *Constitution* means there is no "federal general common law." The Seventh Amendment also operates directly on federal courts, as *Byrd* recognized (citing its "influence" if not its "command"). The Seventh Amendment ensures the right to jury trial in "suits at common law," and this right applies in diversity suits as well as federal question cases. See, e.g., Simler v. Conner, 273 U.S. 221, 222 (1963) ("the right to a jury trial in the federal courts is to be determined as a matter of federal law in diversity as well as other actions" under the Seventh Amendment).

(2) *Federal Statutes.* Surely Professor Ely is right that when a federal statute comes into play, the question of validity under *Erie* (can a federal statute do what this one does, or apply as this one is being applied?) must be addressed by looking at congressional power under the Constitution. In *Ricoh* and *Jinks*, described in the previous section, the statutes passed constitutional muster. *Ricoh* concluded that the *forum non conveniens* venue statute (28 USC §1404) is constitutional, and it overcomes objections to transfer under a state rule unfriendly to forum selection clauses. And *Jinks* held that the tolling provision of the supplemental jurisdiction statute is constitutional, and applies and overcomes state law that would *not* toll the state statute of limitations while the federal suit was pending.

In speaking of the constitutionality of a federal statute, however, we should not forget to take another important step—and normally this step is taken *prior to* reaching the constitutional question. The *prior step* is to decide whether the statute applies at all. The statute construed in *Ricoh*, for example, has this to say: "For the convenience of parties and witnesses, in the interest of justice, a district court may transfer any civil action to any other district or division where it might have been brought." See 28 USC §1404(a). *Does* this provision say anything about a clause in a contract providing that suit should be brought in New York, as opposed to Alabama (where the suit in *Ricoh* was filed)? We cannot say yes merely by reading the words of the statute, so the Court's conclusion involved an act of interpretation.

(3) Erie *and Federal Rules.* Surely Professor Ely is right that when a Federal Rule comes into play, the question of validity under *Erie* (can a Rule do what this one does, or apply as this one is being applied?) must be addressed by looking at the Rules Enabling Act. In relevant part, this Act says Court-promulgated Rules can regulate "practice and procedure" (including "evidence") in federal court, so long as they do not "abridge, enlarge or modify any substantive right." See 28 USC §2072. In the *Sibbach* case (described in the Notes on *Hanna* and the Armor-Plated Federal Rules), and in *Burlington Northern* and *Business Guides* (described in the previous section), Rules on physical examinations, monetary

penalties for frivolous appeals, and sanctions for filing false pleadings—all survived muster.

In speaking of the validity of any particular Federal Rule, however, we should once again remember another important step—and this step is normally taken prior to considering questions of validity, whether measured against the REA or the Constitution. The prior step is to determine whether the Rule applies at all. Remember the *Ragan* decision, which came early in the *Erie* line (described in the Notes after *Erie*). There the question was whether a diversity suit was "commenced" by filing under FRCP 3 ("a civil action is commenced by filing") for purposes of a state statute of limitations in a case in which a *state* rule required *service* within 60 days of filing if the suit was to be viewed as tolling the statute of limitations on the filing date. *Ragan* said FRCP 3 did not answer the question.

In the *Armco Steel* case, the Court revisited this issue in the *Hanna* era. This time, plaintiff surely thought, the Court would say that FRCP 3 controlled, and that setting the moment a suit "commenced" for purposes of the statute of limitations is a matter of procedure. (Justice Harlan in *Hanna* thought *Ragan* was wrong.) In *Armco Steel*, however, the Court continued in the same direction it had taken in *Ragan*. Again the Court decided that FRCP 3 "governs [only] the date from which various timing requirements" begin to run, and "does not affect state statutes of limitation." Remarkably, the Court acknowledged that this provision *does* govern date of commencement for purposes of the statute of limitation in *federal question* cases. See West v. Conrail, 481 U.S. 35, 39 (1987) ("when the underlying cause of action is based on federal law and the absence of an express federal statute of limitations makes it necessary to borrow a limitations period from another statute, the action is not barred if it has been 'commenced' in compliance with Rule 3 within the borrowed period"); Sentry Corp. v. Harris, 802 F.2d 229, 231 (7th Cir. 1985) ("in cases involving federal rights for which Congress has expressly provided a federal limitations period, FRCP 3 directly governs the issue of when an action is commenced for statute of limitations purposes"). It is *not* that the Rules should be "narrowly construed in order to avoid a 'direct collision' with state law," the Court went on to say—they should be "given their plain meaning," and if they *then* collide with state law, they control under *Hanna*. If *Armco Steel* doesn't construe the Rule narrowly, at least it endorses what we might call a moderate and restrained construction of the Rule. See Walker v. Armco Steel Corp., 446 U.S. 740 (1980).

(4) Erie *and Federal Common Law Rules.* Professor Ely is once again surely right that *here* answering the question of validity under the *Erie* doctrine (can federal common law do what this doctrine does or apply as this one is being applied?) *begins* with the Rules of Decision Act. Recall that this statute says that "the laws of the several states" control in federal courts "in cases where they apply." See 28 USC §1652. And here the REA does not protect federal doctrine—common law rules are not "armor plated" against suggestions that they go too far toward affecting the result of litigation.

Still, we saw in *Byrd* that federal common law procedural doctrines exist. They implement a policy of ensuring that federal courts remain "independent"—*Byrd* dealt with a rule on dividing responsibility between judge and jury. And we learn in *Hanna 1* that *Erie* would not require a federal court to follow a state rule unless it would be seen *from the beginning* or *ex ante*—as a lawyer contemplating the choice between suing in federal court and suing in state court—that following the federal rule would likely affect outcome. In *Hanna 1,* the Court said nobody would choose between state and federal court on the basis that "in hand" service was required in state court but "abode" service sufficed in federal court.

We should be careful in considering Professor Ely's claim that the Constitution is "functionally irrelevant." His point is *not* that the Constitution has nothing to say about federal judicial lawmaking. Rather, his suggestion rests on his conclusion that the Rules of Decision Act is more restrictive than the Constitution. He may be right about that, but it is hard to be sure. Recall that the Court in *Erie* did say its decision was compelled by the Constitution.

■ NOTES ON APPROACHES TO *ERIE* ISSUES

1. In connection with *Erie* challenges to federal statutes (item 2 in the list above), we can sum it up this way: Arguments that federal statutes exceed the constitutional power of Congress to legislate, or do not apply in the situation at hand, have generally failed. In *Jinks* and *Ricoh,* for example, the Court found federal statutes to be dispositive, displacing state law (in *Jinks,* the supplemental jurisdiction statute tolled the state statutes of limitations; in *Ricoh,* the *forum non conveniens* venue statute displaced a state rule hostile to forum selection clauses). And in *Bernhardt* in 1956 (described in the Notes after *York,* supra), the Court initially agreed that the federal Arbitration Statute did not apply in diversity cases, but later the Court changed course and held that it applies and displaces state law.

2. In connection with *Erie* challenges to Federal Rules (item 3 in the list above), our summary looks similar. Challenges failed in *Sibbach, Burlington Northern,* and *Business Guides,* and of course in *Hanna.* The nearest thing to a successful challenge was *Armco Steel,* where the Court construed the Federal Rule to avoid conflict with state law. Here is a good place to look at Professor Ely's noble effort to describe an approach to these matters under the REA, and to take note of two cases where the "substantive right" clause of that statute has some effect:

(a) Professor Ely begins by recognizing that "substance" and "procedure" are sometimes hard to distinguish, but argues that we should not give up on the theory that these terms "have no meaning at all." In fact, he says, we have a "moderately clear notion" of what makes a procedural rule. It is a rule "designed to make the process of litigation a fair and efficient mechanism for the resolution of disputes," in order to promote "efficiency of the process." In

contrast, *substantive* rules regulate people's conduct "at the stage of primary private activity," which includes "the fostering and protection of certain state of mind" like "the feeling of release" and "the assurance that the possibility of ordeal has passed" (an obvious reference to statutes of limitation and rules of immunity). Where a Rule has *mixed purposes,* it may be procedural and thus satisfy the first sentence of the REA, but it does not satisfy the second sentence because it has an additional substantive purpose. See Ely, supra, at 693, 727. His argument, in other words, is that a substantive effect in a Rule (and presumably therefore a substantive *purpose*) brings it into conflict with the REA.

(b) The Court seems *not* to have taken Professor Ely's approach, stressing instead the "twin aims" of the *Erie* doctrine (avoiding incentives to forum shop and inequitable administration) and the notion from *Hanna 2* that if a rule can be said to regulate procedure, then it is valid even if it implements substantive policies too. This attitude is visible in *Business Guides.* See Business Guides, Inc. v. Chromatic Communications Enterprises, 498 U.S. 533, 552 (1991) (sanctions for misconduct by litigants does not violate REA restriction against altering substantive rights because "Rule 11 is reasonably necessary to maintain the integrity" of the federal court system, and "any effect on substantive rights is incidental").

(c) In two cases, however, the Court treated the REA's limit as important if not dispositive. The *Semtek* case, which you will read in Chapter 14 because it is a major pronouncement on *res judicata,* held that FRCP 41 (which says certain dismissals operate as "adjudication[s] on the merits") does not preclude refiling the same suit elsewhere. *Semtek* involved dismissal of a diversity suit on the ground that it was barred by California's statute of limitations. The Court ruled that *if* FRCP 41 operated to bar plaintiff from filing elsewhere while a *state* court dismissal in California *would not* have that effect, then FRCP 41 "would seem to violate" the substantive right clause of the REA. See Semtek International v. Lockheed Martin Corp., 531 U.S. 497 (2001). See also Ortiz v. Fibreboard Corp., 527 U.S. 815 (1999) (rejecting use of FRCP 23(b)(1)(B), the "limited fund" class suit lacking opt-out rights, as a means of achieving "global settlement" of asbestos claims; the REA "underscores the need for caution," so this category of class actions should stay "close to the practice preceding adoption" of this provision). *Semtek* and *Ortiz* suggest that the REA has bite in limiting application of the Rules.

3. A brief glance at indexes to legal literature reveals no dearth of articles taking up the question what *Erie* means. Even citing a sample of the available literature is a daunting undertaking, but here are two analyses that seem helpful:

(a) Professor Doernberg argues that *Erie* has always embodied a "balancing" standard. Pointing out that in the beginning of the Republic there was *no* federal common law, and no effective federal judicial system, Doernberg suggests that state courts and state law, including state common law, were all there was or could be. The attempt under *Swift* to create a new body of

common law failed because the idea of "natural law" as a body of moral principles that could be discovered had already fallen into disrepute, and law was understood more as Holmes understood it—as a body of law rooted in the power to enforce it and for that reason rooted in political systems. Doernberg suggests that decisions in the *Erie* line can be understood as resting on a presumption that state law applies, but the presumption is dislodged or overcome whenever a dominant federal interest appears, and such an interest can appear in a statute (which courts are prone to interpret generously, as in *Ricoh*) or a Rule (where courts are prone to interpret them in a moderate and restrained fashion, if not narrowly, as in *Ragan* and *Armco Steel*), or even a common law doctrine (as in *Byrd,* where judge-made law allocated responsibility between judge and jury). But there is *no* dominant federal interest in general principles of tort (as in *Erie*) or limitation periods for bringing suits based on state law (as in *York*). Doernberg cautions that his approach can explain many *Erie* outcomes, but cannot be taken as the basis for *Erie* arguments because it does not capture doctrine as we have it. See Donald L. Doernberg, *The Unseen Track of* Erie Railroad: *Why History and Jurisprudence Suggest a More Straightforward Form of* Erie *Analysis,* 109 W. Va. L. Rev. 611 (2007).

(*b*) In his commentary on federal courts, Professor Chemerinsky suggests the following approach to *Erie* issues:

> [I]f there is a conflict between federal and state law, in deciding whether to apply state or federal law, a three-step inquiry is used. First, is there a valid federal statute or Rule of Civil Procedure or Appellate Procedure on point? If so, the federal law is to be applied by the federal court deciding a diversity action. If there is not a valid, on point federal law, the second inquiry is whether the application of the state law is likely to determine the outcome of the litigation. If state law is not outcome determinative, then federal law is applied. But once it is concluded that state law is likely to determine the results, then the third question is whether there is an overriding federal interest. If so, then federal law controls; otherwise, the state law that is outcome determinative is applied. Of course, at each step there are unanswered questions, and federal courts possess discretion to decide what constitutes an on point federal law in a particular case, when a state law is outcome determinative, and what federal interests outweigh the need to use state law.

Erwin Chemerinsky, Federal Jurisdiction §5.3 (5th ed. 2007).

6. *Erie* Today: Accommodationist Strategies

Despite the decisions described above, federal procedural rules, statutes, or procedural conventions do not always win out in the end. Particularly in the *Gasperini* case, one can detect a movement toward greater respect for state law.

verdicts: courts would not disturb an award unless the amount was so exorbitant that it "shocked the conscience of the court."

. . .

In both state and federal courts, trial judges made the excessiveness assessment in the first instance, and appellate judges ordinarily deferred to the trial court's judgment.

In 1986, as part of a series of tort reform measures,[3] New York codified a standard for judicial review of the size of jury awards. Placed in CPLR §5501(c), the prescription reads:

> In reviewing a money judgment . . . in which it is contended that the award is excessive or inadequate and that a new trial should have been granted unless a stipulation is entered to a different award, the appellate division shall determine that an award is excessive or inadequate if it deviates materially from what would be reasonable compensation.

As stated in Legislative Findings and Declarations accompanying New York's adoption of the "deviates materially" formulation, the lawmakers found the "shock the conscience" test an insufficient check on damage awards; the legislature therefore installed a standard "invit[ing] more careful appellate scrutiny." At the same time, the legislature instructed the Appellate Division, in amended §5522, to state the reasons for the court's rulings on the size of verdicts, and the factors the court considered in complying with §5501(c). In his signing statement, then-Governor Mario Cuomo emphasized that the CPLR amendments were meant to ratchet up the review standard: "This will assure greater scrutiny of the amount of verdicts and promote greater stability in the tort system and greater fairness for similarly situated defendants throughout the State."

New York state-court opinions confirm that §5501(c)'s "deviates materially" standard calls for closer surveillance than "shock the conscience" oversight. [The Court cites state and federal cases and a treatise.]

Although phrased as a direction to New York's intermediate appellate courts, §5501(c)'s "deviates materially" standard, as construed by New York's courts, instructs state trial judges as well. [The Court describes state cases.] Application of §5501(c) at the trial level is key to this case.

To determine whether an award "deviates materially from what would be reasonable compensation," New York state courts look to awards approved in similar cases. Under New York's former "shock the conscience" test, courts also referred to analogous cases. The "deviates materially" standard, however, in design and operation, influences outcomes by tightening the range of tolerable awards.

---

[3] The legislature sought, particularly, to curtail medical and dental malpractice, and to contain "already high malpractice premiums."

III

In cases like Gasperini's, in which New York law governs the claims for relief, does New York law also supply the test for federal-court review of the size of the verdict? The Center answers yes. The "deviates materially" standard, it argues, is a substantive standard that must be applied by federal appellate courts in diversity cases. The Second Circuit agreed. Gasperini, emphasizing that §5501(c) trains on the New York Appellate Division, characterizes the provision as procedural, an allocation of decisionmaking authority regarding damages, not a hard cap on the amount recoverable. Correctly comprehended, Gasperini urges, §5501(c)'s direction to the Appellate Division cannot be given effect by federal appellate courts without violating the Seventh Amendment's re-examination clause.

As the parties' arguments suggest, CPLR §5501(c), appraised under *Erie* and decisions in *Erie*'s path, is both "substantive" and "procedural": "substantive" in that §5501(c)'s "deviates materially" standard controls how much a plaintiff can be awarded; "procedural" in that §5501(c) assigns decisionmaking authority to New York's Appellate Division. Parallel application of §5501(c) at the federal appellate level would be out of sync with the federal system's division of trial and appellate court functions, an allocation weighted by the Seventh Amendment. The dispositive question, therefore, is whether federal courts can give effect to the substantive thrust of §5501(c) without untoward alteration of the federal scheme for the trial and decision of civil cases.

A

Federal diversity jurisdiction provides an alternative forum for the adjudication of state-created rights, but it does not carry with it generation of rules of substantive law. As *Erie* read the Rules of Decision Act: "Except in matters governed by the Federal Constitution or by Acts of Congress, the law to be applied in any case is the law of the State." Under the *Erie* doctrine, federal courts sitting in diversity apply state substantive law and federal procedural law.

Classification of a law as "substantive" or "procedural" for *Erie* purposes is sometimes a challenging endeavor.[7] *York,* an early interpretation of *Erie,* propounded an "outcome-determination" test: "[D]oes it significantly affect the

---

[7] Concerning matters covered by the Federal Rules of Civil Procedure, the characterization question is usually unproblematic: It is settled that if the Rule in point is consonant with the Rules Enabling Act, 28 USC §2072, and the Constitution, the Federal Rule applies regardless of contrary state law. See Hanna v. Plumer, 380 U.S. 460, 469-474 (1965); Burlington Northern R. Co. v. Woods, 480 U.S. 1, 4-5 (1987). Federal courts have interpreted the Federal Rules, however, with sensitivity to important state interests and regulatory policies. See, *e.g.,* Walker v. Armco Steel Corp., 446 U.S. 740, 750-752 (1980) (reaffirming decision in *Ragan* that state law rather than Rule 3 determines when a diversity action commences for the purposes of tolling the state statute of limitations; Rule 3 makes no reference to the tolling of state limitations, the

result of a litigation for a federal court to disregard a law of a State that would be controlling in an action upon the same claim by the same parties in a State court?" Ordering application of a state statute of limitations to an equity proceeding in federal court, the Court said in *York*: "[W]here a federal court is exercising jurisdiction solely because of the diversity of citizenship of the parties, the outcome of the litigation in the federal court should be substantially the same, so far as legal rules determine the outcome of a litigation, as it would be if tried in a State court." See also Ragan v. Merchants Transfer & Warehouse Co., 337 U.S. 530, 533 (1949) (when local law that creates the cause of action qualifies it, "federal court must follow suit," for "a different measure of the cause of action in one court than in the other [would transgress] the principle of *Erie*"). A later pathmarking case, qualifying *York*, explained that the "outcome-determination" test must not be applied mechanically to sweep in all manner of variations; instead, its application must be guided by "the twin aims of the *Erie* rule: discouragement of forum-shopping and avoidance of inequitable administration of the laws." Hanna v. Plumer, 380 U.S. 460, 468 (1965).

Informed by these decisions, we address the question whether New York's "deviates materially" standard ... is outcome affective in this sense: Would "application of the [standard] ... have so important an effect upon the fortunes of one or both of the litigants that failure to [apply] it would [unfairly discriminate against citizens of the forum State, or] be likely to cause a plaintiff to choose the federal court"?

We start from a point the parties do not debate. Gasperini acknowledges that a statutory cap on damages would supply substantive law for *Erie* purposes. Although CPLR §5501(c) is less readily classified, it was designed to provide an analogous control.

New York's Legislature codified in §5501(c) a new standard, one that requires closer court review than the common-law "shock the conscience" test. More rigorous comparative evaluations attend application of §5501(c)'s "deviates materially" standard. To foster predictability, the legislature required the reviewing court, when overturning a verdict under §5501(c), to state its reasons, including the factors it considered relevant. We think it a fair conclusion that CPLR §5501(c) differs from a statutory cap principally in that the maximum amount recoverable is not set forth by statute, but rather is determined by case law. In sum, §5501(c) contains a procedural instruction, but the State's objective is manifestly substantive.

It thus appears that if federal courts ignore the change in the New York standard and persist in applying the "shock the conscience" test to damage

---

Court observed, and accordingly found no "direct conflict"); S.A. Healy Co. v. Milwaukee Metropolitan Sewerage Dist., 60 F.3d 305, 310-312 (7th Cir. 1995) (state provision for offers of settlement by plaintiffs is compatible with FRCP 68, which is limited to offers by defendants).

awards on claims governed by New York law, "'substantial' variations between state and federal [money judgments]" may be expected. See *Hanna.* We therefore agree with the Second Circuit that New York's check on excessive damages implicates what we have called *Erie*'s "twin aims."[12] Just as the *Erie* principle precludes a federal court from giving a state-created claim "longer life . . . than [the claim] would have had in the state court," *Ragan,* so *Erie* precludes a recovery in federal court significantly larger than the recovery that would have been tolerated in state court.

B

CPLR §5501(c) . . . is phrased as a direction to the New York Appellate Division. Acting essentially as a surrogate for a New York appellate forum, the Court of Appeals reviewed Gasperini's award to determine if it "deviate[d] materially" from damage awards the Appellate Division permitted in similar circumstances. The Court of Appeals performed this task without benefit of an opinion from the District Court, which had denied "without comment" the Center's Rule 59 motion. Concentrating on the authority §5501(c) gives to the Appellate Division, Gasperini urges that the provision shifts fact-finding responsibility from the jury and the trial judge to the appellate court. Assigning such responsibility to an appellate court, he maintains, is incompatible with the Seventh Amendment's Reexamination Clause, and therefore, Gasperini concludes, §5501(c) cannot be given effect in federal court. Although we reach a different conclusion than Gasperini, we agree that the Second Circuit did not attend to "[a]n essential characteristic of [the federal court] system," *Byrd,* when it used §5501(c) as "the standard for [federal] appellate review."

That "essential characteristic" was described in *Byrd,* a diversity suit for negligence in which a pivotal issue of fact would have been tried by a judge were the case in state court. The *Byrd* Court held that, despite the state practice, the plaintiff was entitled to a jury trial in federal court. In so ruling, the Court said that the *Guaranty Trust* "outcome-determination" test was an insufficient guide in cases presenting countervailing federal interests. The Court described the countervailing federal interests present in *Byrd* this way:

> The federal system is an independent system for administering justice to litigants who properly invoke its jurisdiction. An essential characteristic of that system is the manner in which, in civil common-law actions, it distributes trial functions between judge and jury and, under the influence—if not the command—of the Seventh Amendment, assigns the decisions of disputed questions of fact to the jury.

---

[12] For rights that are state created, state law governs the amount properly awarded as punitive damages, subject to an ultimate federal constitutional check for exorbitancy. An evenhanded approach would require federal court deference to endeavors like New York's to control compensatory damages for excessiveness.

The Seventh Amendment, which governs proceedings in federal court, but not in state court, bears not only on the allocation of trial functions between judge and jury, the issue in *Byrd;* it also controls the allocation of authority to review verdicts, the issue of concern here. The Amendment reads: "In Suits at common law, where the value in controversy shall exceed twenty dollars, the right of trial by jury shall be preserved, and no fact tried by a jury, shall be otherwise re-examined in any Court of the United States, than according to the rules of the common law."

Byrd involved the first Clause of the Amendment, the "trial by jury" Clause. This case involves the second, the "Reexamination" Clause. In keeping with the historic understanding, the Re-examination Clause does not inhibit the authority of trial judges to grant new trials "for any of the reasons for which new trials have heretofore been granted in actions at law in the courts of the United States." FRCP 59(a). That authority is large. . . . "The trial judge in the federal system," we have reaffirmed, "has . . . discretion to grant a new trial if the verdict appears to [the judge] to be against the weight of the evidence." *Byrd*. This discretion includes overturning verdicts for excessiveness and ordering a new trial without qualification, or conditioned on the verdict winner's refusal to agree to a reduction (remittitur). See Dimick v. Schiedt, 293 U.S. 474, 486-487 (1935) (recognizing that remittitur withstands Seventh Amendment attack, but rejecting additur as unconstitutional).

In contrast, appellate review of a federal trial court's denial of a motion to set aside a jury's verdict as excessive is a relatively late, and less secure, development. Such review was once deemed inconsonant with the Seventh Amendment's re-examination clause. [The Court notes that it has taken cases raising this question, but ultimately resolved them on other grounds.]

Before today, we have not "expressly [held] that the Seventh Amendment allows appellate review of a district court's denial of a motion to set aside an award as excessive." Browning-Ferris Industries of Vt., Inc. v. Kelco Disposal, Inc., 492 U.S. 257, 279, n.25 (1989). [The Court says such appellate review is constitutional.]

C

In *Byrd,* the Court faced a one-or-the-other choice: trial by judge as in state court, or trial by jury according to the federal practice.[21] In the case before us, a choice of that order is not required, for the principal state and federal interests can be accommodated. The Second Circuit correctly recognized that when New York substantive law governs a claim for relief, New York law

---

[21] The two-trial rule posited by Justice Scalia surely would be incompatible with the existence of "[t]he federal system [as] an independent system for administering justice," *Byrd*. We discern no disagreement on such examples among the many federal judges who have considered this case.

and decisions guide the allowable damages. But that court did not take into account the characteristic of the federal court system that caused us to reaffirm: "The proper role of the trial and appellate courts in the federal system in reviewing the size of jury verdicts is . . . a matter of federal law." Donovan v. Penn Shipping Co., 429 U.S. 648, 649 (1977) (per curiam).

New York's dominant interest can be respected, without disrupting the federal system, once it is recognized that the federal district court is capable of performing the checking function, *i.e.*, that court can apply the State's "deviates materially" standard in line with New York case law evolving under CPLR §5501(c).[22] We recall, in this regard, that the "deviates materially" standard serves as the guide to be applied in trial as well as appellate courts in New York.

Within the federal system, practical reasons combine with Seventh Amendment constraints to lodge in the district court, not the court of appeals, primary responsibility for application of §5501(c)'s "deviates materially" check. Trial judges have the "unique opportunity to consider the evidence in the living courtroom context," Taylor v. Washington Terminal Co., 409 F.2d 145, 148 (D.C. Cir. 1969), while appellate judges see only the "cold paper record."

District court applications of the "deviates materially" standard would be subject to appellate review under the standard the Circuits now employ when inadequacy or excessiveness is asserted on appeal: abuse of discretion. In light of *Erie*'s doctrine, the federal appeals court must be guided by the damage-control standard state law supplies,[23] but as the Second Circuit itself has said: "If we reverse, it must be because of an abuse of discretion. . . . The very nature of the problem counsels restraint. . . . We must give the benefit of every doubt to the judgment of the trial judge." Dagnello v. Long Island R. Co., 289 F.2d 797, 806 (2d Cir. 1961).

IV

It does not appear that the District Court checked the jury's verdict against the relevant New York decisions demanding more than "industry standard" testimony to support an award of the size the jury returned in this case. As the

---

[22] Justice Scalia finds in FRCP 59 a "federal standard" for new trial motions in "'direct collision'" with, and "'leaving no room for the operation of,'" a state law like CPLR §5501(c). The relevant prescription, Rule 59(a), has remained unchanged since the adoption of the Federal Rules by this Court in 1937. Rule 59(a) is as encompassing as it is uncontroversial. It is indeed "Hornbook" law that a most usual ground for a Rule 59 motion is that "the damages are excessive." See C. Wright, Law of Federal Courts 676-677 (5th ed. 1994). Whether damages are excessive for the claim-in-suit must be governed by *some law*. And there is no candidate for that governance other than the law that gives rise to the claim for relief—here, the law of New York.

[23] If liability and damage-control rules are split apart here, as Justice Scalia says they must be to save the Seventh Amendment, then Gasperini's claim and others like it would be governed by a most curious "law." The sphinx-like, damage-determining law he would apply to this controversy has a state forepart, but a federal hindquarter. The beast may not be brutish, but there is little judgment in its creation.

Court of Appeals recognized, the uniqueness of the photographs and the plaintiff's earnings as photographer—past and reasonably projected—are factors relevant to appraisal of the award. Accordingly, we vacate the judgment of the Court of Appeals and instruct that court to remand the case to the District Court so that the trial judge, revisiting his ruling on the new trial motion, may test the jury's verdict against CPLR §5501(c)'s "deviates materially" standard.

It is so ordered.

Justice STEVENS, dissenting.

[New York law does govern the sizes of the damage award, and that law does apply in diversity cases governed by New York law. The Re-examination Clause of the Seventh Amendment does not prevent federal appellate courts from reviewing jury awards for excessiveness, and applying New York's damage limit does not involve a re-examination of facts, and for that reason the case need not be remanded to the district court, and the Second Circuit's disposition of the case should be affirmed.]

Justice SCALIA, with whom THE CHIEF JUSTICE and Justice THOMAS join, dissenting.

[This decision "overrules a longstanding and well-reasoned line of precedent that has for years prohibited federal appellate courts from reviewing refusals by district courts to set aside civil jury awards as contrary to the weight of the evidence." The Court also holds that "a state practice that relates to the division of duties between state judges and juries must be followed by federal courts in diversity cases," which is "contrary" to prior law. The judgment of the Court of Appeals in this case should be reversed.

In applying the New York standard, the Court of Appeals here "engaged in a two-step process," first determining the reasonable range of compensation and then deciding whether the jury award materially deviated from that range. The first step "plainly requires" a court to "re-examine a factual matter tried by the jury," and the second step "establishes the degree of judicial tolerance." Neither of these steps is appropriate for a federal appellate court, in diversity cases or others.

The New York statute "may reflect a sound understanding of the capacities of modern juries and trial judges," but in federal court an examination at the appellate level of facts found by a jury is "precisely what the People of the Several States considered *not* to be good legal policy in 1791." The Seventh Amendment was a congressional response to "one of the principal objections" to the Constitution raised by the Anti-Federalists. The re-examination clause responded to the concern that a trial court might re-examine facts found by a jury. Under common law tradition, judgments could only be examined "on writ of error, limited to questions of law." The "proper measure of damages" involves a question of fact, which federal appellate judges "are constitutionally forbidden to entertain."

The claim that English appellate judges could grant a new trial on the ground that a jury award was contrary to the weight of the evidence "simply does not withstand examination." While trials could be held in the countryside before "a single itinerant judge," such "*nisi prius* trial" involved a jury decision of the facts in dispute, which was entered on the record and returned to "the en banc court at Westminster." Requests for new trials were made to the latter, but the en banc court was *not* an appellate body, and it would order a new trial "only if the *nisi prius* judge certified that he was dissatisfied with the verdict."

Hence our prior cases are right that only the trial court could engage in "re-examination" of the facts found by a jury. The Court draws from the *Dagnello* case in stating that reviewing a denial of a new trial motion, "if conducted under a sufficiently deferential standard, poses only 'a question of law.'" That, however, "is not the test that the Seventh Amendment sets forth." Whether or not an appeal from a denial of a new trial raises a "legal question," it cannot be resolved without re-examining the facts in a manner "'otherwise' than allowed at common law."]

II

The Court's holding that federal courts of appeals may review district-court denials of motions for new trials for error of fact is not the only novel aspect of today's decision. The Court also directs that the case be remanded to the District Court, so that it may "test the jury's verdict against CPLR §5501(c)'s 'deviates materially' standard." This disposition contradicts the principle that "[t]he proper role of the trial and appellate courts in the federal system in reviewing the size of jury verdicts is . . . a matter of federal law." Donovan v. Penn Shipping Co., 429 U.S. 648, 649 (1977) (per curiam).

The Court acknowledges that state procedural rules cannot, as a general matter, be permitted to interfere with the allocation of functions in the federal court system. Indeed, it is at least partly for this reason that the Court rejects direct application of §5501(c) at the appellate level as inconsistent with an "'essential characteristic'" of the federal court system—by which the Court presumably means abuse-of-discretion review of denials of motions for new trials. But the scope of the Court's concern is oddly circumscribed. The "essential characteristic" of the federal jury, and, more specifically, the role of the federal trial court in reviewing jury judgments, apparently counts for little. . . . [C]hanging the standard by which trial judges review jury verdicts *does* disrupt the federal system, and is plainly inconsistent with the "strong federal policy against allowing state rules to disrupt the judge-jury relationship in federal court." *Byrd*. The Court's opinion does not even acknowledge, let alone address, this dislocation.

. . .

I do not see how [the New York law can be a damage cap]. It seems to me quite wrong to regard this provision as a "substantive" rule for *Erie* purposes. The "analog[y]" to "a statutory cap on damages" fails utterly. There is an absolutely fundamental distinction between a *rule of law* such as that, which would ordinarily be imposed upon the jury in the trial court's instructions, and a *rule of review,* which simply determines how closely the jury verdict will be scrutinized for compliance with the instructions. A tighter standard for reviewing jury determinations can no more plausibly be called a "substantive" disposition than can a tighter appellate standard for reviewing trial-court determinations. The one, like the other, provides additional assurance *that the law has been complied with;* but the other, like the one, *leaves the law unchanged.*

The Court commits the classic *Erie* mistake of regarding whatever changes the outcome as substantive. That is not the only factor to be considered. . . . Outcome determination "was never intended to serve as a talisman," *Hanna*, and does not have the power to convert the most classic elements of the *process* of assuring that the law is observed into the substantive law itself. The right to have a jury make the findings of fact, for example, is generally thought to favor plaintiffs, and that advantage is often thought significant enough to be the basis for forum selection. But no one would argue that *Erie* confers a right to a jury in federal court wherever state courts would provide it; or that, were it not for the Seventh Amendment, *Erie* would require federal courts to dispense with the jury whenever state courts do so.

In any event, the Court exaggerates the difference that the state standard will make. It concludes that different outcomes are likely to ensue depending on whether the law being applied is the state "deviates materially" standard of §5501(c) or the "shocks the conscience" standard. Of course it is not the federal *appellate* standard but the federal *district-court* standard for granting new trials that must be compared with the New York standard to determine whether substantially different results will obtain—and it is far from clear that the district-court standard *ought* to be "shocks the conscience."[11] Indeed, it is not even clear (as the Court asserts) that "shocks the conscience" *is* the standard (erroneous or not) actually applied by the district courts of the Second Circuit. The Second Circuit's test for reversing a grant of a new trial for an excessive verdict is whether the award was "*clearly* within the maximum limit of a reasonable range," so any district court

---

[11] That the "shocks the conscience" standard was not the traditional one would seem clear from the opinion of Justice Story, quoted approvingly by the Court, to the effect that remittitur should be granted "if it should clearly appear that the jury . . . have given damages excessive in relation to the person or the injury." Blunt v. Little, 3 F. Cas. 760, 761-762 (No. 1,578) (C.C. Mass. 1822).

that uses that standard will be affirmed. [While trial court decisions "express the 'shocks the conscience' criterion," some use other standards, and some apply "a rule much less stringent."] In sum, it is at least highly questionable whether the consistent outcome differential claimed by the Court even exists. What seems to me far more likely to produce forum shopping is the consistent difference between the state and federal *appellate* standards, which the Court leaves untouched. Under the Court's disposition, the Second Circuit reviews only for abuse of discretion, whereas New York's appellate courts engage in a *de novo* review for material deviation, giving the defendant a double shot at getting the damages award set aside. The only result that would produce the conformity the Court erroneously believes *Erie* requires is the one adopted by the Second Circuit and rejected by the Court: *de novo* federal appellate review under the §5501(c) standard.

To say that application of §5501(c) in place of the federal standard will not consistently produce disparate results is not to suggest that the decision the Court has made today is not a momentous one. The *principle* that the state standard governs is of great importance, since it bears the potential to destroy the uniformity of federal practice and the integrity of the federal court system. Under the Court's view, a state rule that directed courts "to determine that an award is excessive or inadequate if it deviates *in any degree* from *the proper measure of compensation*" would have to be applied in federal courts, effectively requiring federal judges to determine the amount of damages *de novo*, and effectively taking the matter away from the jury entirely. Or consider a state rule that allowed the defendant a second trial on damages, with judgment ultimately in the amount of the lesser of two jury awards. Under the reasoning of the Court's opinion, even such a rule as that would have to be applied in the federal courts.

The foregoing describes why I think the Court's *Erie* analysis is flawed. But in my view, one does not even reach the *Erie* question in this case. The standard to be applied by a district court in ruling on a motion for a new trial is set forth in FRCP 59, which provides that "[a] new trial may be granted ... for any of the reasons for which new trials have heretofore been granted in actions at law *in the courts of the United States*." (Emphasis added.) That is undeniably a federal standard.[12] Federal District Courts in the Second Circuit have interpreted that standard to permit the granting of new trials where "'it is quite clear that the jury has reached a seriously erroneous result'" and letting the verdict stand would result in a "'miscarriage of justice.'"

---

[12] I agree with the Court's entire progression of reasoning in its footnote 22, leading to the conclusion that *state* law must determine "[w]hether damages are excessive." But the question whether damages are excessive is quite separate from the question of when a jury award may be set aside for excessiveness. It is the latter that is governed by Rule 59; as Browning-Ferris [Industries v. Kelco Disposal, Inc., 492 U.S. 2577 (1989)] said, district courts are "to determine, by reference to *federal standards developed under Rule 59*, whether a new trial or remittitur should be ordered" (emphasis added).

Koerner v. Club Mediterranee, S.A., 833 F. Supp. 327, 331 (S.D.N.Y. 1995) (quoting Bevevino v. Saydjari, 574 F.2d 676, 684 (2d Cir. 1978)). Assuming (as we have no reason to question) that this is a correct interpretation of what Rule 59 requires, it is undeniable that the Federal Rule is "'sufficiently broad' to cause a 'direct collision' with the state law or, implicitly, to 'control the issue' before the court, thereby leaving no room for the operation of that law." Burlington Northern R. Co. v. Woods, 480 U.S. 1, 4-5 (1987). It is simply not possible to give controlling effect both to the federal standard and the state standard in reviewing the jury's award. That being so, the court has no choice but to apply the Federal Rule, which is an exercise of what we have called Congress's "power to regulate matters which, though falling within the uncertain area between substance and procedure, are rationally capable of classification as either," *Hanna*.

. . .

There is no small irony in the Court's declaration today that appellate review of refusals to grant new trials for error of fact is "a control necessary and proper to the fair administration of justice." It is objection to *precisely* that sort of "control" by federal appellate judges that gave birth to the Reexamination Clause of the Seventh Amendment. Alas, those who drew the Amendment, and the citizens who approved it, did not envision an age in which the Constitution means whatever this Court thinks it ought to mean or indeed, whatever the courts of appeals have recently thought it ought to mean.

When there is added to the revision of the Seventh Amendment the Court's precedent-setting disregard of Congress's instructions in Rule 59, one must conclude that this is a bad day for the Constitution's distinctive Article III courts in general, and for the role of the jury in those courts in particular. I respectfully dissent.

■ NOTES ON *GASPERINI* AND THE REVIVAL OF THE "BALANCING" TEST

1. Is the New York "deviates materially" statute a damage cap? The Court says it is: The statute requires "closer court review" of damage awards, thus resembling a damage cap except that no upper-bound maximum is stated (it is to be "determined by case law"), making the provision "manifestly substantive." The federal statute on which the Court hangs its hat is the RDA (for provision applied in *Erie*), not the REA (for provision applied in *Hanna*). The Court did not find the answer to the question of how to treat the "deviates materially" standard in FRCP 59 (the provision authorizing new trial motions in federal court). Instead, *Gasperini* found the answer in an assessment of the purpose of the "deviates materially" statute, which was to "curtail medical and dental malpractice" (a reference to damage awards) and to "contain" malpractice premiums (Court's footnote 3). Does this objective, and the likely effect of applying the standard, make it substantive? Is the New York law substantive in the sense that Justice Harlan stressed in his *Hanna* concurrence, in speaking of laws affecting "primary activities"?

2. Wait a minute: Is it so clear that the statute is a damage cap? In Chapter 12C, you will learn about motions for new trials on grounds that the verdict is "against the weight of the evidence," which usually refers to awards that are unreasonably high or low. Rule 59 addresses this subject, stating that a new trial may be granted "for any reason for which a new trial has heretofore been granted in an action at law in federal courts." Couldn't the "deviates materially" standard be described as one that defines the role of a judge in deciding whether a verdict is too high (or, less often, too low)? If so, why doesn't FRCP 59 apply? Didn't *Hanna 2* say that if a federal rule applies, then it is, as we have said, "armor-plated" and presumptively valid under the Constitution and the REA? Of course, a Rule *might* not answer the question being asked, and we would expect an explanation. But the Court does not find the answer in FRCP 59 and does not offer an explanation, does it? Consider Justice Scalia's dissent: Under *Browning-Ferris* (which considered limits on punitive damages), a federal district court determines whether the verdict is "within the confines set by state law," and then decides, "by reference to federal standards developed under Rule 59," whether a new trial or remittitur (reduction in the award) should be ordered. Consider the Court's reply in footnote 22: Whether damages are excessive "must be governed by *some law,*" and the only law that could apply is "the law of New York." Who has the better of this argument?

3. Taking the Court at its word that the statute is a damage cap, why shouldn't a Court of Appeal be just as empowered to enforce it as a federal District Court in ruling on new trial motions? In Chapter 12C2, you will learn that trial courts are vested with responsibility for deciding, in the first instance, whether a verdict is against the weight of the evidence in being too high (or sometimes too low). Indeed, it was also long thought that a ruling by a federal trial court *denying* such a motion was unreviewable on appeal because the Seventh Amendment vests in trial judges *exclusive* authority to set aside verdicts on this ground. In a passage that has been edited out, however, *Gasperini* holds that the Seventh Amendment does *not* block appellate court review of decisions refusing to set aside verdicts on this ground. The issue here is less connected with *Erie* than with the Seventh Amendment. See, e.g., Geoffrey C. Hazard, *Has the* Erie *Doctrine Been Repealed by Congress?,* 156 U. Pa. L. Rev. 1629, 1637 (2008) (*Gasperini* "could have straightforwardly applied the Seventh Amendment with certain modernizations authorized by Congress").

4. The Court says the Rules are interpreted "with sensitivity to important state interests and regulatory policies," citing *Armco Steel* (the case that gave a moderate and restrained interpretation of FRCP 3 to avoid collision with a state rule). You didn't see anything like this attitude in *Byrd* or *Hanna,* did you? Elsewhere, *Gasperini* comments that *Byrd* forced a "one-or-the-other choice" between state or federal law in allocating functions between judge and jury, but the situation at hand does not require a similar choice, so "state and federal interests can be accommodated." These references to "sensitivity" and "accommodation" sound a new note. There was no hint of such deference to state concerns in *Hanna 2,* was there? It is not quite clear that these comments have anything to do with construing FRCP 59 (neither is in Part IIIB, where the Court talks about FRCP 59), so we cannot be sure that the Court was using these ideas in construing this Rule.

5. Doesn't *Gasperini* revive *Byrd*'s balancing approach? See Donald L. Doernberg, *The Unseen Track of* Erie Railroad: *Why History and Jurisprudence Suggest a More Straightforward Form of* Erie *Analysis,* 109 W. Va. L. Rev. 611, 665 (2007) ("*Gasperini* is a first-rate example of interest-balancing and *dépeçage* working together") (defining *dépeçage* to mean applying state laws to some issues and federal laws to others); Richard D. Freer, *Some Thoughts on the State of* Erie *After* Gasperini, 76 Tex. L. Rev. 1637, 1660 (1998) (*Gasperini*'s mandate to read federal law "with sensitivity toward state substantive policies is a good step away from heavy-handed use of *Hanna,*" and it "shows that *Byrd* survives *Hanna*"). But see Adam N. Steinman, *What Is the* Erie *Doctrine? (and What Does It Mean for the Contemporary Politics of Judicial Federalism?),* 84 Notre Dame L. Rev. 245, 267-268 (2008) (*Gasperini*'s endorsement of *Byrd* balancing is "ambivalent at best," as *Gasperini* cited *Byrd* only in connection with the standard that appellate courts use to review a ruling on a motion for a new trial, a function of the Seventh Amendment rather than *Erie*); Thomas D. Rowe, Jr., *Not Bad for Government Work: Does Anyone Else Think the Supreme Court Is Doing a Halfway Decent Job in Its* Erie-Hanna *Jurisprudence,* 73 Notre Dame L. Rev. 963, 999-1000 (1998) (*Gasperini* rests more on *Hanna*'s "twin aims" modification of *York* than on *Byrd*-style balancing in construing damage cap as substantive).

6. The trial court, on remand, revised the remittitur to $375,000 (asking plaintiff to accept that amount or a new trial). Recall that originally the trial court had refused a remittitur and entered judgment on the jury's verdict for $450,000, and that the Second Circuit had ordered a new trial unless plaintiff agreed to a remitted amount of $100,000. Again defendant appealed, and the Second Circuit concluded, depending on how ten of the transparencies were valued, that the correct sum was between $359,000 and $372,000 (plaintiff should accept the lesser amount, allow the judge to recalculate the value of 300 slides, or face a new trial). See Gasperini v. Center for Humanities, Inc., 972

F. Supp. 765 (S.D.N.Y. 1997), *vacated*, 149 F.3d 137, 144 (2d Cir. 1998) ("we leave it to Gasperini to decide whether he wishes to leave the ring now, or whether this potential difference of $13,000 plus prejudgment interest is worth a third round in the district court").

7. In the *Newsham* case, the question arose whether a federal court should apply the State of California's "Anti-SLAPP" statute. The acronym stands for Strategic Lawsuits Against Public Participation, and the statute tries to blunt the use of lawsuits to intimidate citizens acting as whistle-blowers or otherwise exercising constitutionally protected rights. *Newsham* was a whistleblower suit brought in federal court under the federal False Claim Act (FCA): As "relators," former employees alleged that Lockheed submitted false claims of millions of dollars for excessive and nonproductive labor on government projects. (In such "qui tam" suits, plaintiffs are called "relators," and recovery is split between them and the government, which has a right to join the suit if it chooses.) Lockheed filed a counterclaim alleging that the relators had breached "duties imposed by fiduciary obligations and loyalty, as well as contract and statute, and breached the implied covenant of good faith." The trial court dismissed the counterclaim, but denied as well the relators' motion seeking attorneys' fees based on California's Anti-SLAPP statute. The question addressed on appeal was whether a federal court should apply this California statute, and the court concluded in the affirmative:

> In determining whether the relevant provisions of California's Anti-SLAPP statute may properly be applied in federal court, we begin by asking whether such an application would result in a "direct collision" with the Federal Rules. According to [Lockheed], California's statutory regime necessarily collides with Rules 8, 12, and 56. We disagree.
>
> Only two aspects of California's Anti-SLAPP statute are at issue: the special motion to strike, Cal. Civ. P. Code §425.16(b), and the availability of fees and costs, Cal. Civ. P. Code §425.16(c). We conclude that these provisions and Rules 8, 12, and 56 "can exist side by side . . . each controlling its own intended sphere of coverage without conflict." Walker v. Armco Steel. A *qui tam* plaintiff, for example, after being served in federal court with counterclaims like those brought by LMSC, may bring a special motion to strike pursuant to §425.16(b). If successful, the litigant may be entitled to fees pursuant to §425.16(c). If unsuccessful, the litigant remains free to bring a Rule 12 motion to dismiss, or a Rule 56 motion for summary judgment. We fail to see how the prior application of the anti-SLAPP provisions will directly interfere with the operation of Rule 8, 12, or 56. In summary, there is no "direct collision" here.
>
> [Lockheed] correctly points out that the Anti-SLAPP statute and the Federal Rules do, in some respects, serve similar purposes, namely the expeditious weeding out of meritless claims before trial. This commonality of purpose, however, does not constitute a "direct collision"—there is no indication that Rules 8, 12, and 56 were intended to "occupy the field" with respect to pretrial procedures aimed at weeding out meritless claims. *Cf.* Cohen v. Beneficial Indus. Loan Corp.,

337 U.S. 541, 556 (1949) (holding that a state law requiring posting of bond in shareholder derivative suits could be enforced in addition to, and consistently with, Rule 23). The Anti-SLAPP statute, moreover, is crafted to serve an interest not directly addressed by the Federal Rules: the protection of "the constitutional rights of freedom of speech and petition for redress of grievances." Cal. Civ. P. Code §425.16(a).

In the absence of a "direct collision" between a state enactment and the Federal Rules, we must make the "typical, relatively unguided *Erie* choice." *Hanna*, 380 U.S. at 471. First, we note that [Lockheed] has not identified any federal interests that would be undermined by application of the anti-SLAPP provisions urged by the relators here. *See Byrd* (balancing state and federal interests in deciding whether to apply state law requiring that immunity question must go to judge, rather than jury). On the other hand, as noted earlier, California has articulated the important, substantive state interests furthered by the Anti-SLAPP statute. *See* Cal. Civ. P. Code §425.16(a); *cf. Gasperini* (in applying state law in diversity action, finding that while the state law at issue was plainly procedural, its objective was manifestly substantive).

We also conclude that the twin purposes of the *Erie* rule—"discouragement of forum-shopping and avoidance of inequitable administration of the law"—favor application of California's Anti-SLAPP statute in federal cases. *Hanna*; see also *Gasperini*. Although Rules 12 and 56 allow a litigant to test the opponent's claims before trial, California's "special motion to strike" adds an additional, unique weapon to the pretrial arsenal, a weapon whose sting is enhanced by an entitlement to fees and costs. Plainly, if the anti-SLAPP provisions are held not to apply in federal court, a litigant interested in bringing meritless SLAPP claims would have a significant incentive to shop for a federal forum. Conversely, a litigant otherwise entitled to the protections of the Anti-SLAPP statute would find considerable disadvantage in a federal proceeding. This outcome appears to run squarely against the "twin aims" of the *Erie* doctrine.

For these reasons, we hold that the district court erred in finding that subsections (b) and (c) of California's Anti-SLAPP statute could not be applied to [Lockheed's] counterclaims. Because the district court concluded that the Anti-SLAPP statute was inapplicable, it did not rule on the relators' motion to strike, nor on their motion for fees and costs. We remand to the district court so that it may rule on these issues.

United States ex rel. Newsham v. Lockheed Missiles & Space Company, 190 F.3d 963, 972-973 (9th Cir. 1999), *cert. denied*, 530 U.S. 1203 (2000).

8. In the *Shady Grove* case decided in 2009, the Supreme Court held that plaintiff could bring a federal class suit under FRCP 23 seeking "statutory damages" as provided by a New York statute (set at 2 percent interest for overdue insurance reimbursements), even though a separate statute provided that a suit to recover a "penalty" or "minimum measure of recovery" could not proceed "as a class action." In the Court's opinion, Justice Scalia wrote that FRCP 23 applies, rejecting any distinction between "eligibility" to sue and "certifiability" or "remedy." FRCP 23 "permits all class actions that meet its requirements," and a state cannot limit federal class suits by imposing "additional requirements." Justice Stevens wrote separately to state his support for the accommodationist approach: Federal Rules, he said, do not always "displace state law," and "must be interpreted with some degree of 'sensitivity to important state interests and regulatory policies'" (quoting *Gasperini*). Rather, a court must ask whether the Federal Rule even applies and, if so, whether is valid or whether it improperly alters substantive rights. FRCP 23 does apply, Justice Stevens concluded, and it does not violate the Enabling Act to apply it here. Justice Ginsburg, for herself and three others, warned against "immoderate interpretations" of the Rules and stressed "sensitivity to important state interests" (quoting *Gasperini*), which in this case was to "block class action proceedings for statutory damages" in service of a "manifestly substantive end," namely limiting liability to "prevent the exorbitant inflation of [statutory] penalties." Federal Rule 23 merely "describes a method of enforcing a claim," while the New York statute "defines the dimensions of the claim itself." A federal court in a diversity case "can accord due respect to both state and federal prescriptions." Pointing out that allowing class action treatment here could lead to relief ten thousand times greater than could be recovered in state court (converting the suit from one worth "no more than $500" to one seeking damages of "more than $5,000,000"), Justice Ginsburg commented thus:

> By finding a conflict without considering whether Rule 23 rationally should be read to avoid any collision, the Court unwisely and unnecessarily retreats from the federalism principles undergirding *Erie*. Had the Court reflected on the respect for state regulatory interests endorsed in our decisions, it would have found no cause to interpret Rule 23 so woodenly—and every reason not to do so.

Shady Grove Orthopedic Associates v. Allstate Insurance Co., 130 S. Ct. 1431, 1468-1469 (2009) (5-4 opinion).

9. If you find these cases bewildering, here are some thoughts that might be comforting: For better or worse, the United States is a federal republic, and the boundaries between state and federal authority are permeable, indistinct, and shifting. As Professor Wright commented in his analysis of *Erie*, "federalism is not a tidy concept," and the incoherence of which Justice Harlan complained is "inevitable in the nature of the *Erie* problem." Charles A. Wright, Federal Courts 387, 412 (6th ed. 1990). Professor Freer adds this thought: "To a degree, confusion is to be expected, because [cases selecting between state and federal law under *Erie*] reflect the ongoing, delicate process by which we allocate power between federal and state courts," and this process "will never, and should never, yield clear, litmus-test answers in all cases." Richard Freer, Erie*'s Mid-Life Crisis*, 63 Tul. L. Rev. 1087, 1090 (1989).

7. How Do Federal Courts Apply State Law?

At one level, the answer to the question of how federal courts apply state law is straightforward: They do what judges always do, which is to apply the applicable law as best they can, sometimes making doctrine to fill in gaps in statutes or in common law doctrine, and to resolve tensions and conflicts that appear among statutes and common law doctrines.

Yet in complying with *Erie*, it is usually said that federal judges act "like" state judges in a slightly different way. They try to put themselves in the shoes of a state judge and in effect to "imitate" state judges by ruling as they think state judges would rule. Early on, Judge Frank put it this way: A federal judge following the *Erie* mandate must try to reach the same decision that "reasonable intelligent lawyers" would reach if they were "fully conversant" with the law of the state and "sitting as judges of the highest . . . court" in the state. See Cooper v. American Airlines, 149 F.2d 355, 359 (2d Cir. 1945). Where uncertainty arises, a federal judge must still try to figure out what the law is, just as a state judge would do. See Meredith v. City of Winter Haven, 320 U.S. 228, 234-235 (1943) (diversity jurisdiction exists "to afford to suitors an opportunity" to be in federal court; absent "some recognized public policy or defined principle," denying this opportunity "merely because the answers to the questions of state law are difficult or uncertain or have not yet been given by the highest court of the state" is not an option).

The matter has proved difficult. It was once thought that federal trial judges applying state law should be given more deference on appeal, presumably because they come from backgrounds in practice in the state and know more about state law than reviewing courts, and perhaps because figuring out state law is, in this setting, less clearly a function of lawmaking and closer to factfinding. But the Supreme Court rejected this approach in 1991. See Salve Regina College v. Russell, 499 U.S. 225, 231-232 (1991) ("independent appellate review of legal issues" serves goals of "doctrinal coherence and economy of judicial administration," and reviewing courts are "structurally suited to the collaborative judicial process that promotes decisional accuracy," and have benefits of briefs and time for study and reflection).

Sometimes federal judges chafe at the *Erie* burden. Judge Frank once commented that *Erie* makes federal judges "play the role of ventriloquist's dummy to the courts of [the] state," see Richardson v. C.I.R., 126 F.2d 562, 567 (2d Cir. 1942), and Judge Friendly wryly said his *Erie*-based task was "to determine what the New York courts would think the California courts would think on an issue about which neither has thought," see Nolan v. Transocean Air Lines, 276 F.2d 280 (2d Cir. 1960) (diversity case; federal court in New York was trying to apply New York statute that "borrowed" California limitations period).

Champs de Blé à Vétheuil (Claude Monet)

The picturesque town of Vétheuil is located on the Seine about 33 miles from Paris. This painting, which became the celebrated focal point of a dispute between Gerda DeWeerth and Edith Baldinger, is signed by Claude Monet and dated 1879. Mrs. DeWeerth's father bought the painting in 1908, or about that time, and kept it in his home at Bad Godesberg, West Germany. Mrs. DeWeerth inherited the painting on his death in 1922, and kept it hanging in her residence in Wuppertal-Elberfeld from 1922 through 1943, when she sent it to her sister in Oberbalzheim for safekeeping. Her sister reported the painting missing in 1945, after American soldiers were quartered in the house, but there was no proof of the cause of the disappearance. Many artworks in European homes were stolen or confiscated during World War II, some by the Nazis in connection with the persecution of the Jewish population and the invasions of neighboring countries, some by Soviet troops, and some by American troops (sources say American thievery was done on an individual basis, but that Nazi and Soviet thefts were systematic and thorough). It was not only works by Monet that were stolen: Works by other artists, including Paul Cézanne, Edward Degas, Gustav Klimt, Egon Schiele, Vincent van Gogh, and Johannes Vermeer were also stolen. In a famous post-war photograph, Generals Dwight Eisenhower, Omar Bradley, and George Patton are seen inspecting stolen artworks discovered in a salt mine in the district of Thuringia in Germany.

Occasionally, dramatic examples appear in which the *Erie* doctrine seems to have gone awry because federal judges err in giving voice to state law. In a famous case involving a signed painting by Claude Monet ("Champs de Blé à Vétheuil") stolen from a castle in Germany during World War II, one Gerda DeWeerth brought suit against one Edith Baldinger in federal court in New York to recover the painting. DeWeerth claimed she had owned it during the 1940s when it was stolen, and Baldinger claimed to be a good faith purchaser who bought it from Wildenstein & Co., a New York art gallery, in 1957, paying $30,900 for it. (Its estimated value at the time of the suit in the late 1980s was more than $500,000.) The trial judge found in favor of DeWeerth and ordered the painting returned. On appeal, the Second Circuit reversed, in a long and thoughtful opinion by Judge Newman, on the ground that New York law required an owner seeking to retrieve property from a good faith purchaser to exercise due diligence, and in this case the claim was barred by New York's three-year statute of limitations. Judge Newman noted that the beginning point of the three-year period is the date of the theft if the owner sues the thief, but it is the date of the demand to return the property if suit is brought against a good faith possessor.

Ms. DeWeerth did not learn that Ms. Baldinger had the painting until 1981, and then she promptly demanded its return. The Second Circuit faulted Ms. DeWeerth for failing "to conduct any search for 24 years from 1957 to 1981," while acknowledging that she did search for the painting immediately after the war. Had she been more diligent after 1957, she might have learned that a 1974 catalogue of Monet's works stated that the painting had been sold by the Wildenstein gallery in 1957, and that the same gallery had displayed the painting (on loan from its purchaser) in 1970:

> This Court's role in exercising its diversity jurisdiction is to sit as another court of the state. Guaranty Trust Co. v. York, 326 U.S. 99, 108 (1945). When presented with an absence of controlling state authority, we must "make an estimate of what the state's highest court would rule to be its law." In making that determination, this Court may consider all of the resources that the New York Court of Appeals could use, including New York's stated policies and the law of other jurisdictions. We determine that in an action for the recovery of stolen personal property, the New York Court of Appeals would not make an exception to the unreasonable delay rule for plaintiff's actions prior to learning the identity of the current possessor. Rather, we believe that the New York courts would impose a duty of reasonable diligence in attempting to locate stolen property, in addition to the undisputed duty to make a demand for return within a reasonable time after the current possessor is identified.

DeWeerth v. Baldinger, 836 F.2d 103 (2d Cir. 1987).

You can guess what happened next. In a different case decided in 1991, New York's highest court *rejected* the idea that an owner had a duty of due diligence in demanding the return of stolen property, concluding that the "demand and refusal rule" is the one that "affords the most protection to the true owners of stolen property." Solomon R. Guggenheim Foundation v. Lubell, 569 N.E.2d 426, 430 (N.Y. 1991). Armed with the decision in the *Guggenheim Foundation* case, Ms. DeWeerth again went to federal court, seeking relief under FRCP 60(b), which authorizes a court to set aside a judgment on account of such things as "mistake" on the part of lawyers, "newly discovered evidence" and certain other grounds, and also for "any other reason justifying relief" (see Chapter 12E, infra). Again the trial court sided with plaintiff: *Erie* "placed the primary responsibility for developing and interpreting state law upon a locally chosen judiciary," and denying plaintiff's motion would "raise serious questions about the relationship between the state and federal courts under *Erie*, resulting in a denial of rights which would have flowed to the plaintiff under state law." See DeWeerth v. Baldinger, 804 F. Supp. 539, 546, 551 (S.D.N.Y. 1992).

Again, however, the Second Circuit disagreed. In an opinion by a three-judge panel that did not include Judge Newman, the Second Circuit concluded that *Erie* does not stand for the proposition that a plaintiff is entitled to reopen a federal court case that has been closed for several years" to gain the benefit of a new decision. In his prior "comprehensive opinion," Judge Newman had done just what *Erie* required. He had decided that New York would impose a "due diligence" requirement, and that *not* doing so would produce the "incongruity" of giving more protection to thieves than to good faith purchasers. Judge Newman might have been "wrong," but in choosing to sue in federal court Ms. DeWeerth "assumed the risk" that a federal judge would decide any "open question of state law." DeWeerth v. Baldinger, 38 F.3d 1266, 1273-1274 (2d Cir. 1994).

■ NOTES ON FEDERAL COURT APPLICATION OF STATE LAW

1. Let us admit that there are oddities in the arrangement required by *Erie:*

(a) Federal trial courts are not subject to review by state appellate courts, as state trial courts are, so federal decisions applying state law are not reviewed by judges operating in the state system and responsive to its concerns. In *DeWeerth*, plaintiff could not, after losing because Judge Newman thought the claim was barred, obtain review from New York's highest court. Is it an answer that she *chose* the federal forum? Suppose Ms. Baldinger had lost because the federal court thought plaintiff was *not* subject to due diligence, and suppose the New York court had ruled in *Guggenheim* that there *was* such a requirement. Then Ms. Baldinger would have "wrongfully" lost the federal suit, and *she* did not choose the federal forum. Are we comfortable with a system that can produce such results?

(b) Federal decisions on matters of state law are not "binding" on judges in the state system. Perhaps one reason why state courts take them less seriously is the reason noted above—they are outside the channels of review in the state system. In a certain sense, then, federal judges applying state law are not "making" state law in the way state judges are. To this extent, isn't it true that a system asking federal judges to perform this role is wasteful of judicial resources?

(c) One reason why *Erie* abandoned *Swift* is that federal decisions applying "federal common law" failed to achieve national uniformity because state courts did not accept federal decisions as authoritative. In *Erie's* system of "vertical uniformity" (state and federal courts in the same state apply the same law), federal courts *still* don't "make law" in diversity cases on a par with state courts, do they?

2. If it is slightly odd to ask federal judges to apply state law, should we also take into account the fact that we ask something similar of state judges? *Erie* requires federal judges to apply the law of "the other system," and the Supremacy Clause (plus the congressional decision to let state courts—or perhaps require is the better word—hear federal question claims) has the effect of requiring state judges to apply the law of the "other system." If state judges must apply federal law, is it all that odd that federal judges have to apply state law? State decisions applying federal law *can* be reviewed by a federal forum, but the Supreme Court (ordinarily the federal forum that reviews such decisions) does not take many of these cases, and the likelihood of federal review is *very* small.

3. Some have thought that the so-called certification process can help. When questions of state law seem unresolved, federal courts in 43 states can certify to the state supreme court a question of state law, under statutes authorizing this procedure. See Bradford R. Clark, *Ascertaining the Laws of the Several States: Positivism and Judicial Federalism After* Erie, 145 U. Pa. L. Rev. 1459, 1548 n.472 (1997) (collecting the statutes). In *Guggenheim*, the New York court pointedly commented that Judge Newman had declined to certify the question before him. See *Guggenheim Foundation*, supra, 569 N.E.2d at 426, 429 (Judge Newman had commented that the issue arises infrequently; the New York court retorts that it has arisen three times in the in the five years since he was writing). Can you think of a reason why a state supreme court might be reluctant to answer a question certified by a federal court? Can you think of a reason why an answer by a state supreme court might be less than satisfactory?

4. In a series of opinions, the Supreme Court endorsed abstention as a way of dealing with unsettled questions of state law.

(a) In the *Thibodaux* case, a Louisiana municipality sought to take certain land and buildings belonging to a Florida power company. The latter removed the state-filed action to federal court. The Supreme Court found that the case raised questions of "the nature and extent of the delegation of the power of eminent domain" between city and state, that the relevant statute "has never been interpreted" in a similar situation, and concluded that the district court should let Louisiana adjudicate this matter. This course would *not* represent an "abnegation of judicial duty," as the matter can return to the federal court after the Louisiana court speaks, so holding back is only a "postponement of decision," and eventually the federal court "will award compensation if the taking is sustained." If the Louisiana court does not issue a "declaratory judgment" within a reasonable time, however, the federal court can decide the case. See Louisiana Power & Light Co. v. City of Thibodaux, 360 U.S. 25, 29-30 (1959).

(b) Early in the *Erie* line is the *Burford* case, where the Supreme Court embraced abstention in the face of conflicting claims based on state law in a dispute over state regulatory policy and processes. The Texas Railroad

Commission had granted Burford a permit to drill in an East Texas oilfield, but Sun Oil sued the Commission and Burford in federal court, seeking cancellation of the permit and an injunction against drilling, raising issues under both state and federal law. The federal court should have abstained, largely because the case involved "questions of regulation of the industry" by a state agency, raising "basic problems of Texas policy" that a Texas court should resolve in the first instance, and the involvement of federal courts would be "dangerous to the success of state policies." See Burford v. Sun Oil Co., 319 U.S. 315, 333-334 (1943).

(c) Just three years after *Erie,* the Supreme Court in the *Thompson* case saw abstention as appropriate in some cases. There the question was whether a federal bankruptcy court should determine a disputed question of land title in Illinois. The Court emphasized that the bankruptcy court had control over the land, but instructed the bankruptcy court to order the trustee to litigate the title question in state court. See Thompson v. Magnolia Petroleum Co., 309 U.S. 478, 483 (1940) (given "unsettled questions of State property law. . . . , it is desirable to have the litigation proceed in the State courts of Illinois," lest the "accident of federal jurisdiction" lead to a decision "contrary to the law of the State").

5. One study concludes that, in cases where state law is uncertain, the *Erie* doctrine pushes federal courts toward two choices, both of which are unpalatable. One option is to follow a "predictive" model, somewhat like the description that Judge Frank offered in the *Cooper* case (quoted at the beginning of this section): They try creatively to figure out the content of state law. In this "static approach," Professor Clark argues, federal judges "adhere to the status quo," and "refrain from making the significant policy choices [that are] necessary." The effect is to perpetuate "outmoded principles of state law by simultaneously drawing cases into federal court and depriving state courts of opportunities to adopt novel rules of states law." The other option is to try to figure out what state law really is: This approach, Professor Clark argues, often involves choosing among "competing policy considerations," and conscientious federal judges exercise "policymaking discretion" that is "the essence of judicial lawmaking." Under *Erie,* however, this function belongs to state institutions. See Clark, supra, at 1459, 1499, 1536-1541 (criticizing abstention as a solution and favoring certification process).

6. The litigation in the *Mason* case suggests reason for greater optimism about federal court application of state law. *Mason* involved a Mississippi citizen who sued American Emery Wheel Works, maker of a wheel used on a bench grinder that shattered and injured plaintiff. Mason sued in federal court in Rhode Island, where defendant was located, but the court sought to apply Mississippi law. Mississippi had not yet abandoned the "privity" requirement, under which consumers and other end users could not sue manufacturers because they had not dealt with them. The trial court dismissed the claim, but the First Circuit took up the question whether Mississippi, if it had the case to decide then, would follow the principle of the landmark decision in the *MacPherson* case, which had long since abandoned privity. See MacPherson v. Buick, III N.E. 1050 (N.Y. 1916). The Mississippi Supreme Court had criticized privity almost 30 years earlier, and in a decision only three years earlier managed to avoid the issue by deciding the case on another ground, commenting that the *MacPherson* rule "seems now to be well established" and that many authorities support the "modern doctrine" allowing recovery without privity. The First Circuit reversed the dismissal in *Mason*, ruling that Mississippi law does not require privity. See Mason v. American Emery Wheel Works, 241 F.2d 906 (1st Cir. 1957). Nine years later, Mississippi did abandon privity, without even citing *Mason*. See State Stove Manufacturing Co. v. Hodges, 189 So. 2d 113 (Miss. 1966). Doesn't *State Stove* prove that *Mason* was right?

B FEDERAL COMMON LAW (IN STATE AND FEDERAL COURTS)

1. Federal Statutes and the Supremacy Clause

By now the present topic is familiar territory. Early in the game, you read the decision in *Lavender*, where a widow sued a railroad for the death of her husband (switchman Haney), who was found dead after being hit on the head. She sued in *state* court under FELA, the federal legislation designed to compensate for injuries or deaths suffered by railroaders on the job.

You know as well that suits under federal statutes often satisfy the "arising under" standard of the Constitution and the basic federal question statute, so they can be brought in federal court. See U.S. Const. Art. III §2, and 28 USC §1331. And you will recall that federal legislation that creates private rights of action *generally* comes with *concurrent jurisdiction*, meaning that suits under such legislation may be brought in state court as well as federal court. You may recall as well that Congress can, and sometimes does, restrict jurisdiction to federal courts ("exclusive federal jurisdiction"). Finally, you may recall that while many federal question suits may be brought in state court, defendants may *remove* them to federal court in most instances (although FELA suits, and a few others, are nonremovable and must stay in state court if brought there initially).

State courts not only *hear* federal question cases, but are *obliged* to entertain them. This obligation comes with the Supremacy Clause. See U.S. Const. Art. VI §2, and see Testa v. Katt, 330 U.S. 386 (1947) (Rhode Island state court cannot refuse to entertain suit for refund, brought by automobile buyer under Emergency Price Control Act, which capped the price of automobiles during the Second World War, even if statute was not in harmony with state policy).

2. Federal Common Law

Recall Justice Brandeis's famous line in *Erie*, stating that there is "no federal *general* common law" (emphasis added), and recall that on the same day that *Erie* was decided the Court also decided Hinderlider v. La Plata River & Cherry Creek Ditch Co., 304 U.S. 92 (1938), which held that a dispute over rights in an interstate stream raised a question to be resolved by applying federal common law. So there is no federal *general* common law, but there are special areas in which federal common law exists and must be applied.[7]

Federal Common Law Merchant. In the *Clearfield Trust* case in 1943, the Supreme Court took up the question whether to apply state or federal law in resolving a dispute over a government-issued check. Apparently, a thief had forged the endorsement of the payee (Clair Barner, who had rendered services to the Works Progress Administration) and negotiated the check at a JC Penney store in Pennsylvania. JC Penney's bank, Clearfield Trust, honored the check and presented it for payment to the Federal Reserve Bank in Philadelphia. When the theft was discovered, the government sued Clearfield Trust for the amount of the check, basing its claim on Clearfield's endorsement guaranteeing prior endorsements (including that of the thief). JC Penney intervened: If Clearfield lost, then Clearfield would subtract the amount from JC Penney's account (JC Penney too had guaranteed prior endorsements by depositing the check). The trial court ruled against the government on ground that it had "unreasonably delayed giving notice of the forgery" under the law of Pennsylvania.

The Third Circuit Court of Appeals reversed, on ground that the matter was to be resolved by applying federal common law, under which the government could recover even if it had not given notice and acted promptly. The Supreme Court agreed with the Third Circuit:

> The rights and duties of the United States on commercial paper which it issues are governed by federal rather than local law. When the United States disburses its funds or pays its debts, it is exercising a constitutional function or power. This check was issued for services performed under the Federal Emergency Relief Act of 1935. The authority to issue the check had its origin in the Constitution and the statutes of the United States and was in no way dependent on the laws of Pennsylvania or of any other state. The duties imposed upon the United States and the rights acquired by it as a result of the issuance find their roots in the same federal sources. In absence of an applicable Act of Congress it is

---

[7] See also Virginia v. Maryland, 540 U.S. 56, 74 n.9 (2003) (federal common law "governs interstate bodies of water, ensuring that the water is equitably apportioned between the States and that neither State harms the other's interest in the river"); Colorado v. New Mexico, 459 U.S. 176, 183 (1982) (equitable apportionment of waters in interstate stream is a matter of federal common law governing disputes on such matters between states).

for the federal courts to fashion the governing rule of law according to their own standards. . . .

In our choice of the applicable federal rule we have occasionally selected state law. But reasons which may make state law at times the appropriate federal rule are singularly inappropriate here. The issuance of commercial paper by the United States is on a vast scale and transactions in that paper from issuance to payment will commonly occur in several states. The application of state law, even without the conflict of laws rules of the forum, would subject the rights and duties of the United States to exceptional uncertainty. It would lead to great diversity in results by making identical transactions subject to the vagaries of the laws of the several states. The desirability of a uniform rule is plain. And while the federal law merchant developed for about a century under the [*Swift* regime] represented general commercial law rather than a choice of a federal rule designed to protect a federal right, it nevertheless stands as a convenient source of reference for fashioning federal rules applicable to these federal questions.

Clearfield Trust Co. v. United States, 318 U.S. 363, 365-367 (1943).

A decade later in the *Parnell* case a question about rights in commercial paper issued by the United States arose in a purely private dispute. Parnell had exchanged federal bonds for cash at the bank, which sued him because the bonds had been stolen from the bank in the first place. One question was whether the bonds were overdue, and another was whether Parnell or the bank had the burden of proof on the issue whether Parnell was in good faith. The Court decided that the first question (whether the bonds were overdue) was to be decided under federal law because this matter related to rights created by the bonds themselves, but the second question was to be governed by state law because it related more closely to a private transaction. See Bank of America National Trust & Savings Association v. Parnell, 352 U.S. 29 (1956).

Twenty-three years after *Parnell*, the Court took up a complicated question of lien priorities that pitted a federal agency (Small Business Administration) against a commercial lender. Both had lent money to a grocery store that ultimately went out of business, and both loans were secured by inventories in the store that were coming in and going out as the store took deliveries and sold food. The winner in this contest was the one whose security interest first became "cohate." The SBA argued that federal law controlled, and the competing lender argued for application of Texas law. Acknowledging the clear federal interest at stake, the Court nevertheless decided that the SBA was playing a role so similar to that of private lenders that it should be governed by the same rules as the latter:

Undoubtedly, federal programs that "by their nature are and must be uniform in character throughout the Nation" necessitate formulation of controlling federal rules. Conversely, when there is little need for a nationally uniform body of law, state law may be incorporated as the federal rule of decision. Apart from considerations of uniformity, we must also determine whether application of state law would frustrate specific objectives of the federal programs. If so, we must fashion special rules solicitous of those federal interests. Finally, our choice-of-law inquiry must consider the extent to which application of a federal rule would disrupt commercial relationships predicated on state law.

Thus federal law did control, but the content of federal law was the state rule. That the SBA would then have to take into account the rule of each state in which it operates would not be an undue burden, and the offices in each state could manage to do business in the same way as banks and other private lenders. See United States v. Kimbell Foods, Inc., 440 U.S. 715, 726-729 (1979) (commercial lender wins).

Other Areas of Federal Common Law. Building on the *Clearfield Trust* line of cases, the Supreme Court has fashioned federal common law in other areas of federal interest. Thus the Court has said that federal common law governs some tort claims, in suits involving government officers or employees. In the *Howard* case, for example, a Captain in the Navy and Commander of the Boston Naval Shipyard was sued for libel by two civilian Shipyard employees. The statement at issue was in a letter from the Commander to a higher officer in the Navy, which the Commander also released to newspapers and wire services and to the state congressional delegation. The Court held that the question whether a defense of privilege covered publication of the statements to the congressional delegation is to be resolved by federal law. See Howard v. Lyons, 360 U.S. 593, 597 (1959) (authority of federal officer "derives from federal sources," and privilege for statements made in course of duty promotes "effective functioning" of federal government, and is thus a matter of "peculiarly federal concern"). In the *Feres* case, the Court held, as a matter of federal common law, that a member of the armed services cannot sue the United States for personal injuries incurred in the course of duties. See Feres v. United States, 340 U.S. 135 (1950).

Two-Part Test. Commentators have sometimes thought the Court's pronouncements can be characterized as stating a two-part standard: (1) Does the issue at hand fall within the appropriate exercise of federal power, and specifically within the appropriate scope of common law doctrine? (2) What should the content of that doctrine be? Nowhere does the Court state such a standard, however, and the commentators who think the standard is implicit in the Court's approach are critical of it. See, e.g., Erwin Chemerinsky, Federal Jurisdiction §6.2 (5th ed. 2007); Martha A. Field, *Sources of Law: The Scope of Federal Common Law*, 99 Harv. L. Rev. 881, 886 (1986) (arguing that the first part of the test is meaningless because there are no definable areas or "enclaves" beyond reach of federal power).

In any event, the supposed two-part standard does not carry us far. Consider this matter in light of the *Boyle* decision.

Sikorsky CH-53D Helicopter (Sea Stallion)

A Sikorsky Sea Stallion helicopter resembling this one crashed in the ocean, leading to the death of David Boyle, to the lawsuit and judgment for $725,000 that was reversed on appeal, and to the Supreme Court opinion that sustains the reversal. The Fourth Circuit had invoked the *Feres* doctrine, which blocks tort suits against the government on account of injuries sustained by members of the armed services, but the Supreme Court prefers the military contractor defense. In the *Agent Orange* litigation that came to the fore after the Vietnam War, the military contractor defense

was to play an important role. In a class suit brought by Vietnam veterans against the manufacturers of Agent Orange, which was handled by distinguished jurist Jack Weinstein in the Southern District of New York, the parties settled under pressure by the court in the eleventh hour, for what then seemed the enormous sum of $180 million (later class suits have settled for larger sums). Some veterans had opted out, but Judge Weinstein invited them back

into the suit, and some participated in the settlement. Ultimately, this arrangement was sustained on an appeal. See In re Agent Orange Product Liability Litigation, 818 F.2d 145 (2d Cir. 1987). Some opt-out claimants later brought their own class suit, however, and Judge Weinstein ultimately ruled against them on the basis of the military contractor defense and failure to prove causation. This ruling too was affirmed on appeal, on both grounds. See id. at 187. The extraordinary story of this litigation is chronicled in an excellent book. See Peter Shuck, Agent Orange on Trial (1987).

BOYLE v. UNITED TECHNOLOGIES CORP.

Supreme Court of the United States
487 U.S. 500 (1988)

Scalia, J., delivered the opinion of the Court, in which Rehnquist, C.J., and White, O'Connor, and Kennedy, JJ., joined. Brennan, J., filed a dissenting opinion, in which Marshall and Blackmun, JJ., joined. Stevens, J., filed a dissenting opinion.

This case requires us to decide when a contractor providing military equipment to the Federal Government can be held liable under state tort law for injury caused by a design defect.

I

On April 27, 1983, David A. Boyle, a United States Marine helicopter copilot, was killed when the CH-53D helicopter in which he was flying crashed off the coast of Virginia Beach, Virginia, during a training exercise. Although Boyle survived the impact of the crash, he was unable to escape from the helicopter and drowned. Boyle's father, petitioner here, brought this diversity action in Federal District Court against the Sikorsky Division of United Technologies Corporation (Sikorsky), which built the helicopter for the United States.

At trial, petitioner presented two theories of liability under Virginia tort law that were submitted to the jury. First, petitioner alleged that Sikorsky had defectively repaired a device called the servo in the helicopter's automatic flight control system, which allegedly malfunctioned and caused the crash. Second, petitioner alleged that Sikorsky had defectively designed the copilot's emergency escape system: the escape hatch opened out instead of in (and was therefore ineffective in a submerged craft because of water pressure), and access to the escape hatch handle was obstructed by other equipment. The jury returned a general verdict in favor of petitioner and awarded him $725,000. The District Court denied Sikorsky's motion for judgment notwithstanding the verdict.

The Court of Appeals reversed and remanded with directions that judgment be entered for Sikorsky. It found, as a matter of Virginia law, that Boyle had failed to meet his burden of demonstrating that the repair work performed by Sikorsky, as opposed to work that had been done by the Navy, was responsible for the alleged malfunction of the flight control system. It also found, as a matter of federal law, that Sikorsky could not be held liable for the allegedly defective design of the escape hatch because, on the evidence presented, it satisfied the requirements of the "military contractor defense," which the court had recognized the same day in Tozer v. LTV Corp., 792 F.2d 403 (4th Cir. 1986).

Petitioner sought review here, challenging the Court of Appeals' decision on three levels: First, petitioner contends that there is no justification in federal law for shielding Government contractors from liability for design defects in military equipment. Second, he argues in the alternative that even if such a defense should exist, the Court of Appeals' formulation of the conditions for its application is inappropriate. Finally, petitioner contends that the Court of Appeals erred in not remanding for a jury determination of whether the elements of the defense were met in this case. We granted certiorari.

II

Petitioner's broadest contention is that, in the absence of legislation specifically immunizing Government contractors from liability for design defects, there is no basis for judicial recognition of such a defense. We disagree. In most fields of activity, to be sure, this Court has refused to find federal preemption of state law in the absence of either a clear statutory prescription or a direct conflict between federal and state law. But we have held that a few areas, involving "uniquely federal interests," Texas Industries, Inc. v. Radcliff Materials, Inc., 451 U.S. 630, 640 (1981), are so committed by the Constitution and laws of the United States to federal control that state law is pre-empted and replaced, where necessary, by federal law of a content prescribed (absent explicit statutory directive) by the courts—so-called "federal common law." See, *e.g.,* United States v. Kimbell Foods, Inc., 440 U.S. 715, 726-729 (1979); Banco Nacional v. Sabbatino, 376 U.S. 398, 426-427 (1964); Howard v. Lyons, 360 U.S. 593, 597 (1959); Clearfield Trust Co. v. United States, 318 U.S. 363, 366-367 (1943); D'Oench, Duhme & Co. v. FDIC, 315 U.S. 447, 457-458 (1942).

The dispute in the present case borders upon two areas that we have found to involve such "uniquely federal interests." We have held that obligations to and rights of the United States under its contracts are governed exclusively by federal law. The present case does not involve an obligation to the United States under its contract, but rather liability to third persons. That liability may be styled one in tort, but it arises out of performance of the contract—and traditionally has been regarded as sufficiently related to the contract that until 1962 Virginia would generally allow design defect suits only by the purchaser and those in privity with the seller.

Another area that we have found to be of peculiarly federal concern, warranting the displacement of state law, is the civil liability of federal officials for actions taken in the course of their duty. We have held in many contexts that the scope of that liability is controlled by federal law. The present case involves an independent contractor performing its obligation under a procurement contract, rather than an official performing his duty as a federal employee, but there is obviously implicated the same interest in getting the Government's work done.

We think the reasons for considering these closely related areas to be of "uniquely federal" interest apply as well to the civil liabilities arising out of the performance of federal procurement contracts. ...

[I]t is plain that the Federal Government's interest in the procurement of equipment is implicated by suits such as the present one—even though the dispute is one between private parties. It is true that where "litigation is purely between private parties and does not touch the rights and duties of the United States," Bank of America Nat. Trust & Sav. Assn. v. Parnell, 352 U.S. 29, 33 (1956), federal law does not govern. Thus, for example, in Miree v. DeKalb

County, 433 U.S. 25, 30 (1977), which involved the question whether certain private parties could sue as third-party beneficiaries to an agreement between a municipality and the Federal Aviation Administration, we found that state law was not displaced because "the operations of the United States in connection with FAA grants such as these ... would [not] be burdened" by allowing state law to determine whether third-party beneficiaries could sue, and because "any federal interest in the outcome of the [dispute] before us '[was] far too speculative, far too remote a possibility to justify the application of federal law to transactions essentially of local concern.'" But the same is not true here. The imposition of liability on Government contractors will directly affect the terms of Government contracts: either the contractor will decline to manufacture the design specified by the Government, or it will raise its price. Either way, the interests of the United States will be directly affected.

That the procurement of equipment by the United States is an area of uniquely federal interest does not, however, end the inquiry. That merely establishes a necessary, not a sufficient, condition for the displacement of state law.[3] Displacement will occur only where, as we have variously described, a "significant conflict" exists between an identifiable "federal policy or interest and the [operation] of state law," Wallis v. Pan American Petroleum Corp., 384 U.S. 63, 68 (1966), or the application of state law would "frustrate specific objectives" of federal legislation, *Kimbell Foods.* The conflict with federal policy need not be as sharp as that which must exist for ordinary pre-emption when Congress legislates "in a field which the States have traditionally occupied." Rice v. Santa Fe Elevator Corp., 331 U.S. 218, 230 (1947). Or to put the point differently, the fact that the area in question *is* one of unique federal concern changes what would otherwise be a conflict that cannot produce pre-emption into one that can. But conflict there must be. In some cases, for example where the federal interest requires a uniform rule, the entire body of state law applicable to the area conflicts and is replaced by federal rules. See, *e.g.,* Clearfield Trust Co. v. U.S., 318 U.S. 363, 366-367 (1943) (rights and obligations of United States with respect to commercial paper must be governed by uniform federal rule). In others, the conflict is more narrow, and only particular elements of state law are superseded. See, *e.g.,* Little Lake Misere Land Co., 412 U.S. 580, 595 (1973) (even assuming state law should generally govern federal land acquisitions, particular

---

[3] We refer here to the displacement of state law, although it is possible to analyze it as the displacement of federal-law reference to state law for the rule of decision. Some of our cases appear to regard the area in which a uniquely federal interest exists as being entirely governed by federal law, with federal law deigning to "borro[w]," United States v. Little Lake Misere Land Co., 412 U.S. 580, 594 (1973), or "incorporat[e]" or "adopt," United States v. Kimbell Foods, Inc., 440 U.S. 715, 728, 729, 730 (1979), state law except where a significant conflict with federal policy exists. We see nothing to be gained by expanding the theoretical scope of the federal pre-emption beyond its practical effect, and so adopt the more modest terminology. If the distinction between displacement of state law and displacement of federal law's incorporation of state law ever makes a practical difference, it at least does not do so in the present case.

state law at issue may not); Howard v. Lyons, 360 U.S. 593, 597 (1959) (state defamation law generally applicable to federal official, but federal privilege governs for statements made in the course of federal official's duties).

In Miree v. DeKalb County, Ga., 433 U.S. 25 (1977), the suit was not seeking to impose upon the person contracting with the Government a duty contrary to the duty imposed by the Government contract. Rather, it was the contractual duty *itself* that the private plaintiff (as third-party beneficiary) sought to enforce. Between *Miree* and the present case, it is easy to conceive of an intermediate situation, in which the duty sought to be imposed on the contractor is not identical to one assumed under the contract, but is also not contrary to any assumed. If, for example, the United States contracts for the purchase and installation of an air conditioning unit, specifying the cooling capacity but not the precise manner of construction, a state law imposing upon the manufacturer of such units a duty of care to include a certain safety feature would not be a duty identical to anything promised the Government, but neither would it be contrary. The contractor could comply with both its contractual obligations and the state-prescribed duty of care. No one suggests that state law would generally be pre-empted in this context.

The present case, however, is at the opposite extreme from *Miree*. Here the state-imposed duty of care that is the asserted basis of the contractor's liability (specifically, the duty to equip helicopters with the sort of escape-hatch mechanism petitioner claims was necessary) is precisely contrary to the duty imposed by the Government contract (the duty to manufacture and deliver helicopters with the sort of escape-hatch mechanism shown by the specifications). Even in this sort of situation, it would be unreasonable to say that there is always a "significant conflict" between the state law and a federal policy or interest. If, for example, a federal procurement officer orders, by model number, a quantity of stock helicopters that happen to be equipped with escape hatches opening outward, it is impossible to say that the Government has a significant interest in that particular feature. That would be scarcely more reasonable than saying that a private individual who orders such a craft by model number cannot sue for the manufacturer's negligence because he got precisely what he ordered.

In its search for the limiting principle to identify those situations in which a "significant conflict" with federal policy or interests does arise, the Court of Appeals, in the lead case upon which its opinion here relied, identified as the source of the conflict the *Feres* doctrine, under which the Federal Tort Claims Act (FTCA) does not cover injuries to Armed Services personnel in the course of military service. See Feres v. United States, 340 U.S. 135 (1950). Military contractor liability would conflict with this doctrine, the Fourth Circuit reasoned, since the increased cost of the contractor's tort liability would be added to the price of the contract, and "[s]uch pass-through costs would . . . defeat the purpose of the immunity for military accidents conferred upon the government itself." *Tozer.* . . . We do not adopt this analysis because it seems to us that the *Feres* doctrine, in its application to the present problem, logically produces results that are in some respects too broad and in some respects too narrow. Too broad, because if the Government contractor defense is to prohibit suit against the manufacturer whenever *Feres* would prevent suit against the Government, then even injuries caused to military personnel by a helicopter purchased from stock (in our example above), or by any standard equipment purchased by the Government, would be covered. Since *Feres* prohibits all service-related tort claims against the Government, a contractor defense that rests upon it should prohibit all service-related tort claims against the manufacturer—making inexplicable the three limiting criteria for contractor immunity (which we will discuss presently) that the Court of Appeals adopted. On the other hand, reliance on *Feres* produces (or logically should produce) results that are in another respect too narrow. Since that doctrine covers only service-related injuries, and not injuries caused by the military to civilians, it could not be invoked to prevent, for example, a civilian's suit against the manufacturer of fighter planes, based on a state tort theory, claiming harm from what is alleged to be needlessly high levels of noise produced by the jet engines. Yet we think that the character of the jet engines the Government orders for its fighter planes cannot be regulated by state tort law, no more in suits by civilians than in suits by members of the Armed Services.

There is, however, a statutory provision that demonstrates the potential for, and suggests the outlines of, "significant conflict" between federal interests and state law in the context of Government procurement. In the FTCA, Congress authorized damages to be recovered against the United States for harm caused by the negligent or wrongful conduct of Government employees, to the extent that a private person would be liable under the law of the place where the conduct occurred. 28 USC §1346(b). It excepted from this consent to suit, however, "[a]ny claim . . . based upon the exercise or performance or the failure to exercise or perform a discretionary function or duty on the part of a federal agency or an employee of the Government, whether or not the discretion involved be abused." 28 USC §2680(a). We think that the selection of the appropriate design for military equipment to be used by our Armed Forces is assuredly a discretionary function within the meaning of this provision. It often involves not merely engineering analysis but judgment as to the balancing of many technical, military, and even social considerations, including specifically the trade-off between greater safety and greater combat effectiveness. And we are further of the view that permitting "second-guessing" of these judgments through state tort suits against contractors would produce the same effect sought to be avoided by the FTCA exemption. The financial burden of judgments against the contractors would ultimately be passed through, substantially if not totally, to the United States itself, since defense contractors will predictably raise their prices to cover, or to insure against, contingent liability for the Government-ordered designs. To put the point differently: It makes little sense to insulate the Government against financial liability for the judgment that a particular feature of military equipment is necessary when the Government produces the equipment itself, but not when it contracts for the production. In sum, we are of the view that state law which holds Government contractors liable for design defects in military equipment does in some circumstances present a "significant conflict" with federal policy and must be displaced.

. . .

[The Fourth Circuit's opinion can be read to mean that it "was assessing on its own whether the defense had been established," which would be error, or to mean that no reasonable jury could find for plaintiff by rejecting the defense, which would be permissible.] Accordingly, the judgment is vacated and the case is remanded. [On remand, the Fourth Circuit said that it meant to say that no reasonable jury could find for the plaintiff, and thus dismissed the case. See Boyle v. United Technologies Corp., 857 F.2d 1468 (4th Cir. 1988) (per curiam).]

So ordered.

Justice BRENNAN, with whom Justice MARSHALL and Justice BLACKMUN join, dissenting.

. . .

If respondent's immunity "bore the legitimacy of having been prescribed by the people's elected representatives," we would be duty bound to implement their will, whether or not we approved. Congress, however, has remained silent—and conspicuously so, having resisted a sustained campaign by Government contractors to legislate for them some defense. The Court—unelected and unaccountable to the people—has unabashedly stepped into the breach to legislate a rule denying Lt. Boyle's family the compensation that state law assures them. This time the injustice is of this Court's own making.

Worse yet, the injustice will extend far beyond the facts of this case, for the Court's newly discovered Government contractor defense is breathtakingly sweeping. It applies not only to military equipment like the CH-53D helicopter, but (so far as I can tell) to any made-to-order gadget that the Federal Government might purchase after previewing plans—from NASA's Challenger space shuttle to the Postal Service's old mail cars. The contractor may invoke the defense in suits brought not only by military personnel like Lt. Boyle, or Government employees, but by anyone injured by a Government contractor's negligent design, including, for example, the children who might have died had respondent's helicopter crashed on the beach. It applies even if the Government has not intentionally sacrificed safety for other interests like speed or efficiency, and, indeed, even if the equipment is not of a type that is typically considered dangerous; thus, the contractor who designs a Government building can invoke the defense when the elevator cable snaps or the walls collapse. And the defense is invocable regardless of how blatant or easily remedied the defect, so long as the contractor missed it and the specifications approved by the Government, however unreasonably dangerous, were "reasonably precise."

In my view, this Court lacks both authority and expertise to fashion such a rule, whether to protect the Treasury of the United States or the coffers of industry. Because I would leave that exercise of legislative power to Congress, where our Constitution places it, I would reverse the Court of Appeals and reinstate petitioner's jury award.

. . .

Congress has not decided to supersede state law here (if anything, it has decided not to) and the Court does not pretend that its newly manufactured "Government contractor defense" fits within any of the handful of "narrow areas," Texas Industries v. Radcliff Materials, Inc., 451 U.S. 630, 641 (1981) of "uniquely federal interests" in which we have heretofore done so. Rather, the Court creates a new category of "uniquely federal interests" out of a synthesis of two whose origins predate *Erie* itself: the interest in administering the "obligations to and rights of the United States under its contracts," and the interest in regulating the "civil liability of federal officials for actions taken in the course of their duty." This case is, however, simply a suit between two private parties. We have steadfastly declined to impose federal contract law on relationships that are collateral to a federal contract, or to extend the federal employee's immunity beyond federal employees. . . .

The proposition that federal common law continues to govern the "obligations to and rights of the United States under its contracts" is nearly as old as *Erie* itself. Federal law typically controls when the Federal Government is a party to a suit involving its rights or obligations under a contract, whether the contract entails procurement, a loan, a conveyance of property, or a commercial instrument issued by the Government, or assigned to it. . . . But it is by now established that our power to create federal common law controlling the *Federal Government's* contractual rights and obligations does not translate into a power to prescribe rules that cover all transactions or contractual relationships collateral to Government contracts.

In *Miree,* for example, the county was contractually obligated under a grant agreement with the Federal Aviation Administration (FAA) to "'restrict the use of land adjacent to . . . the Airport to activities and purposes compatible with normal airport operations including landing and takeoff of aircraft.'" At issue was whether the county breached its contractual obligation by operating a garbage dump adjacent to the airport, which allegedly attracted the swarm of birds that caused a plane crash. Federal common law would undoubtedly have controlled in any suit by the Federal Government to enforce the provision against the county or to collect damages for its violation. The diversity suit, however, was brought not by the Government, but by assorted private parties injured in some way by the accident. We observed that "the operations of the United States in connection with FAA grants such as these are undoubtedly of considerable magnitude," and that "the United States has a substantial interest in regulating aircraft travel and promoting air travel safety." Nevertheless, we held that state law should govern the claim because "only the rights of private litigants are at issue here," and the claim against the county "will have *no direct effect upon the United States or its Treasury*" (emphasis added).

. . .

Here, as in *Miree* [and other cases], a Government contract governed by federal common law looms in the background. But here, too, the United States is not a party to the suit and the suit neither "touch[es] the rights and duties of the United States," Bank of America National Trust & Savings Association v. Parnell, 352 U.S. 29, 33 (1956), nor has a "direct effect upon the United States or its Treasury," *Miree*. The relationship at issue is at best collateral to the Government contract.[3] We have no greater power to displace state law governing the collateral relationship in the Government procurement realm than we had to dictate federal rules governing equally collateral relationships in the areas of aviation, Government-issued commercial paper, or federal lands.

That the Government might have to pay higher prices for what it orders if delivery in accordance with the contract exposes the seller to potential liability does not distinguish this case. Each of the cases just discussed declined to extend the reach of federal common law despite the assertion of comparable interests that would have affected the terms of the Government contract—whether its price or its substance—just as "directly" (or indirectly). Third-party beneficiaries can sue under a county's contract with the FAA, for example, even though—as the Court's focus on the absence of "*direct* effect on the United States or its Treasury" suggests—counties will likely pass on the costs to the Government in future contract negotiations. Similarly, we held that state law may govern the circumstances under which stolen federal bonds can be recovered. . . . As in each of the cases declining to extend the traditional reach of federal law of contracts beyond the rights and duties of the *Federal Government*, "any federal interest in the outcome of the question before us 'is far too speculative, far too remote a possibility to justify the application of federal law to transactions essentially of local concern.'" *Miree*.

. . .

---

[3] True, in this case the collateral relationship is the relationship between victim and tortfeasor, rather than between contractors, but that distinction makes no difference. We long ago established that the principles governing application of federal common law in "contractual relations of the Government . . . are equally applicable . . . where the relations affected are noncontractual or tortious in character." United States v. Standard Oil Co., 332 U.S. 301, 305 (1947).

At bottom, the Court's analysis is premised on the proposition that any tort liability indirectly absorbed by the Government so burdens governmental functions as to compel us to act when Congress has not. That proposition is by no means uncontroversial. The tort system is premised on the assumption that the imposition of liability encourages actors to prevent any injury whose expected cost exceeds the cost of prevention. If the system is working as it should, Government contractors will design equipment to avoid certain injuries (like the deaths of soldiers or Government employees), which would be certain to burden the Government. The Court therefore has no basis for its assumption that tort liability will result in a net burden on the Government (let alone a clearly excessive net burden) rather than a net gain.

Perhaps tort liability is an inefficient means of ensuring the quality of design efforts, but "[w]hatever the merits of the policy" the Court wishes to implement, "its conversion into law is a proper subject for congressional action, not for any creative power of ours." United States v. Standard Oil Co. of California, 332 U.S. 301, 314-315 (1947). It is, after all, "Congress, not this Court or the other federal courts, [that] is the custodian of the national purse. By the same token [Congress] is the primary and most often the exclusive arbiter of federal fiscal affairs. And these comprehend, as we have said, securing the treasury or the Government against financial losses *however inflicted*...." If Congress shared the Court's assumptions and conclusion it could readily enact "A BILL [t]o place limitations on the civil liability of government contractors to ensure that such liability does not impede the ability of the United States to procure necessary goods and services," H.R. 4765, 99th Cong., 2d Sess. (1986); see also S. 2441, 99th Cong., 2d Sess. (1986). It has not.

Were I a legislator, I would probably vote against any law absolving multibillion dollar private enterprises from answering for their tragic mistakes, at least if that law were justified by no more than the unsupported speculation that their liability might ultimately burden the United States Treasury. Some of my colleagues here would evidently vote otherwise (as they have here), but that should not matter here. We are judges not legislators, and the vote is not ours to cast.

I respectfully dissent.

Justice STEVENS, dissenting.

[When asked to engage in judicial lawmaking, they should consider whether they are as well equipped as a legislative body to perform the task. When "the novel question of policy involves a balancing of the conflicting interests in the efficient operation of a massive governmental program and the protection of the rights of the individual, . . . we should defer to the expertise of the Congress."]

■ NOTES ON REASONS FOR AND SCOPE OF FEDERAL COMMON LAW

1. *Boyle* involves claims arising out of the death of a Marine Corps officer on a military helicopter, based on a product liability theory. In a 5-4 opinion, the majority concludes a defense based on federal common law—the "military contractor" defense—precludes recovery. The Court says the claim pits the manufacturer's duty under product liability law against the manufacturer's contractual duty to the government.

(a) What does the Court think would happen if the suit went forward and claimants like Lt. Boyle's father could recover damages caused by product defects in military helicopters and similar equipment? Justice Brennan says he would oppose any law "absolving multibillion dollar enterprises from answering for their tragic mistakes." Is *that* what *Boyle* is about?

(b) Does the holding extend, as the dissent contends, to "any made-to-order gadget that the federal government might purchase after reviewing plans," whether related to military uses or not? In a similar suit involving a military helicopter that crashed in Afghanistan, the Ninth Circuit said *Boyle*'s military contractor defense applies only if "the government approved 'reasonably precise specifications'" relating to the equipment in question, and that "more than a cursory 'rubber stamp'" is required. See Getz v. Boeing Co., 2011 WL 3275957 (9th Cir. 2011). And see In re Katrina Canal Breaches Litigation, 620 F.3d 455 (5th Cir. 2010) (*Boyle* did not bar suit against engineering services under contract to Army Corps of Engineers, brought on account of flooding from alleged negligent backfilling; *Boyle* applies only if there are "reasonably precise specifications," the equipment "conformed to those specifications" and the supplier "warned" government about dangers known to supplier but not to government; contract referred to backfill material, but Corps "neither mandated the composition of the backfill material nor established precise procedures to test material for its suitability"). Do these elaborations of the *Boyle* doctrine adequately respond to Justice Brennan's argument that the defense is too broad?

(c) Should the *Boyle* doctrine extend to government procurement contracts generally, even those unconnected with military activities? Compare Bennett v. MIS Corp., 607 F.3d 1076 (6th Cir. 2010) (noting conflict among federal cases but concluding that claim of this defense in this setting is at least plausible), and Carley v. Wheeled Coach, 991 F.2d 117, 1123 (3d Cir. 1993) (defense available to nonmilitary contractors) with In re Hawaii Federal Asbestos Cases, 960 F.2d 806, 810-812 (9th Cir. 1992) (defense available only to military contractors).

(d) In the *Miree* case, decided 11 years before *Boyle* and described by both the majority and the dissent, the Court *allowed* survivors of a plane crash at a small airport to sue the County for failing to fulfill its obligation under a contract with the Federal Aviation Administration to ensure that the use of

adjacent lands was compatible with operation of the airport. Allegedly, the County permitted operation of a garbage dump nearby, giving rise to swarming birds, which caused the crash when they were ingested into jet engines of an airplane. Does *Miree* support the position of the majority, or that of the dissent?

2. There is no doubt, is there, that state courts must apply the *Boyle* doctrine in the event that they are called upon to adjudicate similar cases? See, e.g., Arnhold v. McDonnell Douglas Corp., 992 S.W.2d 346 (Mo. App. 1999) (applying *Boyle* doctrine in dismissing landowner's claim for property damage allegedly caused by government contractor's conduct of supersonic aircraft test flights); Miller v. United Technologies Corp., 660 A.2d 810 (Conn. 1995) (applying *Boyle* doctrine in suit by administrators of estate of Egyptian military personnel killed in crash of military plane supplied by United States to Egyptian forces). Some states recognize similar defenses for contractors performing services or supplying equipment under state contract. Compare Burgess v. Colorado Serum Co., 772 F.2d 844 (11th Cir. 1985) (applying state contractor defense under Alabama law) with Connor v. Quality Coach, Inc., 750 A.2d 823 (Pa. 2000) (rejecting state contractor defense patterned after *Boyle,* in suit against maker of automotive hand control mechanism under contract with state, after plaintiff was injured in accident allegedly because mechanism was defective).

3. Although it does not rely directly on any statute, the majority in *Boyle* cites an exemption in the Federal Tort Claims Act that makes the federal government liable in tort for negligent or wrongful conduct by government employees, but not for errors in "discretionary functions" (even careless ones).

(a) How does the FTCA bear on the issues in *Boyle*? Justice Brennan argues that there is no relevant federal statute. Who has the better of this argument?

(b) Professor Field argues that federal courts should not act *without* a federal statute that can be read as "authorizing" creation of a common law rule. See Martha Field, *Sources of the Law: The Scope of Federal Common Law,* 99 Harv. L. Rev. 881 (1986). Does the exemption in the Federal Tort Claims Act satisfy this standard?

(c) Professor Larry Kramer argues that courts *must* make common law ("judge-made law is unavoidable"), in part because there is no clear line between "making" law and "applying" law—"between commands that are clear on the face of a statute and those made through an exercise of judgment and creativity." Just as important, we would not want courts to refrain from these undertakings, because "one function of independent adjudication is to relieve legislators of having to anticipate and deal with every possible contingency," and it makes no sense for courts to "return every uncertainty to the legislature." See Larry Kramer, *The Lawmaking Power of the Federal Courts,* 12 Pace L. Rev. 263 (1992). Was *Boyle* right in reading some kind of "command" into the Federal Tort Claims Act, or acting so as to avoid forcing Congress to

"anticipate and deal with" the question whether it should be possible to sue military contractors?

4. The relationship between federal common law and federal legislation is many-faceted and complex.

(a) In an early post-*Erie* excursion into the area of federal common law, the Court concluded that the matter in suit was suitable for federal regulation, but *in the absence of* federal legislation there could be no right of recovery. Congress reacted 15 years later by passing a statute creating the right that the Court would not create on its own. The suit involved a government effort to collect from a private tortfeasor the cost of medical treatment caused by injuries sustained by a serviceman stationed in Los Angeles who was run over by defendant's truck. See United States v. Standard Oil Co. of California, 332 U.S. 301, 314 (1947) (acknowledging "the law's capacity for growth" and "the creative work of judges" in this process, and commenting that without such judicial power "all law would become antiquated strait jacket and then dead letter," but the role of the federal judiciary "outside the constitutional area" is "more modest than that of state courts," and the matter at hand is "a proper subject for congressional action"); 42 USC §2651 (where government furnishes or pays for hospital, medical, surgical, or dental care and treatment, it can recover from tortfeasor or its insurer "the reasonable value" of a treatment) (Medical Care Recovery Act in 1962).

(b) In litigation brought by the State of Illinois against Milwaukee and three other cities in Wisconsin, plaintiff claimed that defendants were discharging raw or inadequately treated sewage into Lake Michigan. The Court concluded that federal common law governs interstate pollution, and the claims in this case supported arising under jurisdiction in federal district court under 28 USC §1331. Within a year, however, Congress stepped into this area and enacted legislation addressing these issues. See Illinois v. City of Milwaukee, 406 U.S. 91, 99 (1972) (federal common law covers "air and water in their ambient or interstate aspects," and polluting interstate or navigable waters "creates actions arising under the 'laws' of the United States within the meaning of §1331(a)"); City of Milwaukee v. States of Illinois and Michigan, 451 U.S. 304 (1981) (in enacting Federal Water Pollution Control Act Amendments of 1972, Congress "occupied the field through the establishment of a comprehensive regulatory program" supervised by an agency, leaving no room for courts to formulate standards "through application of often vague and indeterminate nuisance concepts and maxims of equity jurisprudence").

(c) Sometimes legislation conferring jurisdiction in federal courts to hear disputes is construed as authorizing federal courts to create federal common law. See, e.g., Textile Workers v. Lincoln Mills, 353 U.S. 448, 456-457 (1957) (Labor Management Relations Act confers jurisdiction in federal courts to hear suits for violation of collective bargaining contracts between employer and labor organization, "furnishes some substantive law," and evinces a policy *rejecting* common law rule against enforcing promises to

arbitrate disputes, but then leaves the matter of substantive law to federal courts to "fashion from the policy of our national labor laws"). See also Pilot Life Ins. Co. v. Dedeaux, 481 U.S. 41, 56 (1987) (Employment Retirement Income Security Act (ERISA) pre-empts all but a few state claims, displaces entirely any state claims for violation of contracts between employer and labor organization; suits brought under ERISA raise federal questions to be governed by a body of substantive law developed by courts).

5. In the *Kimbell Foods* case, described in the text prior to *Boyle,* the Court concluded that federal law could absorb and in effect "federalize" the state rule. In other words, the rule applied in that case on the issue of lien priority was a "federal rule," but its content was the rule embodied in state law. That means, doesn't it, that federal law of lien priority, at least in the context of competing claims by the SBA and private lenders, varies from state to state—it can be one thing in Texas, another in Illinois? Is anything gained by absorbing state law into the fabric of federal law? Why not just say that state law governs?

6. The literature on federal common law is vast. Among the better modern treatments are these: Richard A. Epstein, *Federal Preemption, and Federal Common Law, in Nuisance Cases,* 102 Nw. U. L. Rev. 551 (2008); Pamela J. Stephens, *Spinning* Sosa: *Federal Common Law, the Alien Tort Statute, and Judicial Restraint,* 25 B.U. Int'l L.J. 1 (2007); Jay Tidmarsh & Brian J. Murray, *A Theory of Federal Common Law,* 100 Nw. U. L. Rev. 585 (2006); Anthony Bellia, Jr., *State Courts and the Making of Federal Common Law,* 153 U. Pa. L. Rev. 825 (2005); Abner J. Mikva & James E. Pfander, *On the Meaning of Congressional Silence: Using Federal Common Law to Fill the Gaps in Congress's Residual Statute of Limitations,* 107 Yale L.J. 393 (1997); Curtis A. Bradley & Jack L. Goldsmith, *Customary International Law as Federal Common Law: A Critique of the Modern Position,* 110 Harv. L. Rev. 815 (1997); Bradford R. Clark, *Federal Common Law: A Structural Interpretation,* 144 U. Pa. L. Rev. 1245 (1996); David E. Seidelson, *Federal Common Law: Whose Baby Are You,* 5 Widener J. Pub. L. 365 (1996); Martin H. Redish, *Federal Common Law, Political Legitimacy, and the Interpretive Process: An "Institutionalist" Perspective,* 83 Nw. L. Rev. 761 (1989).

3. Federal "Procedure" in State Courts ("Reverse-*Erie*" Issues)

Given the determination that you saw in decisions like *Byrd* and *Hanna* to protect, respectively, federal common law procedures and federal procedural Rules, you may be surprised to learn that *sometimes* the Supreme Court has seemed to impose on state courts an obligation to follow at least *some* federal procedural conventions.

DICE v. AKRON, CANTON & YOUNGSTOWN R. CO.

Supreme Court of the United States
342 U.S. 359 (1952)

Opinion of the Court by Mr. Justice BLACK, announced by Mr. Justice DOUGLAS.

Petitioner, a railroad fireman, was seriously injured when an engine in which he was riding jumped the track. Alleging that his injuries were due to respondent's negligence, he brought this action for damages under the Federal Employers' Liability Act, 45 USC §51 et seq., in an Ohio court of common pleas. Respondent's defenses were (1) a denial of negligence and (2) a written document signed by petitioner purporting to release respondent in full for $924.63. Petitioner admitted that he had signed several receipts for payments made [to] him in connection with his injuries but denied that he had made a full and complete settlement of all his claims. He alleged that the purported release was void because he had signed it relying on respondent's deliberately false statement that the document was nothing more than a mere receipt for back wages.

After both parties had introduced considerable evidence the jury found in favor of petitioner and awarded him a $25,000 verdict. The trial judge later entered judgment notwithstanding the verdict. In doing so he reappraised the evidence as to fraud, found that petitioner had been "guilty of supine negligence" in failing to read the release, and accordingly held that the facts did not "sustain either in law or equity the allegations of fraud by clear, unequivocal and convincing evidence." This judgment notwithstanding the verdict was reversed by the Court of Appeals of Summit County, Ohio, on the ground that under federal law, which controlled, the jury's verdict must stand because there was ample evidence to support its finding of fraud. The Ohio Supreme Court, one judge dissenting, reversed the Court of Appeals' judgment and sustained the trial court's action, holding that: (1) Ohio, not federal, law governed; (2) under that law petitioner, a man of ordinary intelligence who could read, was bound by the release even though he had been induced to sign it by the deliberately false statement that it was only a receipt for back wages; and (3) under controlling Ohio law factual issues as to fraud in the execution of this release were properly decided by the judge rather than by the jury. We granted certiorari because the decision of the Supreme Court of Ohio appeared to deviate from previous decisions of this Court that federal law governs cases arising under the Federal Employers' Liability Act.

First. We agree with the Court of Appeals of Summit County, Ohio, and the dissenting judge in the Ohio Supreme Court and hold that validity of releases under FELA raises a federal question to be determined by federal rather than state law. Congress in §1 of the Act granted petitioner a right to recover against his employer for damages negligently inflicted. State laws are not controlling in determining what the incidents of this federal right shall be. Manifestly the federal rights affording relief to injured railroad employees under a federally declared standard could be defeated if states were permitted to have the final say as to what defenses could and could not be properly interposed to suits under the Act. Moreover, only if federal law controls can the federal Act be given that uniform application throughout the country essential to effectuate its purposes. Releases and other devices designed to liquidate or defeat injured employees' claims play an important part in the federal Act's administration. Their validity is but one of the many interrelated questions that must constantly be determined in these cases according to a uniform federal law.

Second. In effect the Supreme Court of Ohio held that an employee trusts his employer at his peril, and that the negligence of an innocent worker is sufficient to enable his employer to benefit by its deliberate fraud. Application of so harsh a rule to defeat a railroad employee's claim is wholly incongruous with the general policy of the Act to give railroad employees a right to recover just compensation for injuries negligently inflicted by their employers. And this Ohio rule is out of harmony with modern judicial and legislative practice to relieve injured persons from the effect of releases fraudulently obtained. We hold that the correct federal rule is that announced by the Court of Appeals of Summit County, Ohio, and the dissenting judge in the Ohio Supreme Court—a release of rights under the Act is void when the employee is induced to sign it by the deliberately false and material statements of the railroad's authorized representatives made to deceive the employee as to the contents of the release. The trial court's charge to the jury correctly stated this rule of law.

Third. Ohio provides and has here accorded petitioner the usual jury trial of factual issues relating to negligence. But Ohio treats factual questions of fraudulent releases differently. It permits the judge trying a negligence case to resolve all factual questions of fraud "other than fraud in the factum." The factual issue of fraud is thus split into fragments, some to be determined by the judge, others by the jury.

It is contended that since a state may consistently with the Federal Constitution provide for trial of cases under the Act by a nonunanimous verdict, Minneapolis & St. Louis R. Co. v. Bombolis, 241 U.S. 211 (1916), Ohio may lawfully eliminate trial by jury as to one phase of fraud while allowing jury trial as to all other issues raised. The *Bombolis* case might be more in point had Ohio abolished trial by jury in all negligence cases including those arising under the federal Act. But Ohio has not done this. It has provided jury trials for cases arising under the federal Act but seeks to single out one phase of the question of fraudulent releases for determination by a judge rather than by a jury. Compare Testa v. Katt, 330 U.S. 386 (1947).

We have previously held that "The right to trial by jury is 'a basic and fundamental feature of our system of federal jurisprudence' and that it is 'part and parcel of the remedy afforded railroad workers under the Employers' Liability Act.'" Bailey v. Central Vermont R. Co., 319 U.S. 350, 354 (1943). We also recognized in that case that to deprive railroad workers of the benefit of a jury trial where there is evidence to support negligence "is to take away a goodly portion of the relief which Congress has afforded them." It follows that the right to trial by jury is too substantial a part of the rights accorded by the Act to permit it to be classified as a mere "local rule of procedure" for denial in the manner that Ohio has here used. Brown v. Western R. Co., 338 U.S. 294 (1949).

The trial judge and the Ohio Supreme Court erred in holding that petitioner's rights were to be determined by Ohio law and in taking away petitioner's verdict when the issues of fraud had been submitted to the jury on conflicting evidence and determined in petitioner's favor. The judgment of the Court of Appeals of Summit County, Ohio, was correct and should not have been reversed by the Supreme Court of Ohio. The cause is reversed and remanded to the Supreme Court of Ohio for further action not inconsistent with this opinion.

It is so ordered.

Reversed and remanded with directions.

Mr. Justice FRANKFURTER, whom Mr. Justice REED, Mr. Justice JACKSON and Mr. Justice BURTON join, concurring for reversal but dissenting from the Court's opinion.

Ohio . . . maintains the old division between law and equity as to the mode of trying issues, even though the same judge administers both. . . . Thus, in all cases in Ohio, the judge is the trier of fact on this issue of fraud, rather than the jury. It is contended that FELA requires that Ohio courts send the fraud issue to a jury in the cases founded on that Act. To require Ohio to try a particular issue before a different factfinder in negligence actions brought under FELA from the factfinder on the identical issue in every other negligence case disregards the settled distribution of judicial power between Federal and State courts where Congress authorizes concurrent enforcement of federally-created rights.

. . .

In 1916 the Court decided without dissent that States in entertaining actions under FELA need not provide a jury system other than that established for local negligence actions. States are not compelled to provide the jury required of Federal courts by the Seventh Amendment. Minneapolis & St. L.R. Co. v. Bombolis, 241 U.S. 211 (1916). In the thirty-six years since this early decision after the enactment of FELA, the *Bombolis* case has often been cited by this Court but never questioned. Until today its significance has been to leave to States the choice of the fact-finding tribunal in all negligence actions, including those arising under the Federal Act. . . .

Ohio and her sister States with a similar division of functions between law and equity are not trying to evade their duty under FELA; nor are they trying to make it more difficult for railroad workers to recover, than for those suing under local law. The States merely exercise a preference in adhering to historic ways of dealing with a claim of fraud; they prefer the traditional way of making unavailable through equity an otherwise valid defense. The State judges and local lawyers who must administer FELA in State courts are trained in the ways of local practice; it multiplies the difficulties and confuses the administration of justice to require, on purely theoretical grounds, a hybrid of State and Federal practice in the State courts as to a single class of cases. Nothing in the Employers' Liability Act or in the judicial enforcement of the Act for over forty years forces such judicial hybridization upon the States. The fact that Congress authorized actions under FELA to be brought in State as well as in Federal courts seems a strange basis for the inference that Congress overrode State procedural arrangements controlling all other negligence suits in a State, by imposing upon State courts to which plaintiffs choose to go the rules prevailing in the Federal courts regarding juries. Such an inference is admissible, so it seems to me, only on the theory that Congress included as part of the right created by FELA an assumed likelihood that trying all issues to juries is more favorable to plaintiffs. At least, if a plaintiff's right to have all issues decided by a jury rather than the court is "part and parcel of the remedy afforded railroad workers under the Employers Liability Act," the *Bombolis* case should be overruled explicitly instead of left as a derelict bound to occasion collisions on the waters of the law. We have put the questions squarely because they seem to be precisely what will be roused in the minds of lawyers properly pressing their clients' interests and in the minds of trial and appellate judges called upon to apply this Court's opinion. It is one thing not to borrow trouble from the morrow. It is another thing to create trouble for the morrow.

. . .

■ NOTES ON FEDERAL PROCEDURAL CONVENTIONS IN STATE COURTS

1. At one level, the question in *Dice* is whether creation of a federal right to relief carries with it, as a sort of "penumbra" of associated rights, a federal standard governing the validity of a release of claims. The Court answers this question clearly, doesn't it? Should *all* federal remedial legislation be construed as authorizing federal courts to create federal common law governing this matter?

2. In a famous article, Professor Henry Hart commented that Congress can require state courts to hear federal question cases, but should leave state procedure alone. "The general rule, bottomed deeply in belief in the importance of state control of state judicial procedure, is that federal law takes the state courts as it finds them." See Henry Hart, *The Relations Between State and Federal Law*, 54 Colum. L. Rev. 489, 509 (1954). See also Felder v. Casey, 487 U.S. 131, 138 (1988) (one who chooses to vindicate a congressionally created right in state court "must abide by the State's procedures," as states "retain the authority under the Constitution to prescribe the rules and procedures that govern actions in their own tribunals"). Isn't it surprising that *Dice* says the validity of the release is to be decided by the jury *and* the right to a jury trial is "part and parcel" of FELA rights? The Court does not cite the Seventh Amendment because this provision applies only in federal courts. It does not cite language in FELA: The right is "implied" by FELA. Does the mere fact that Congress chose to let railroaders and surviving spouses bring FELA suits in state courts justify requiring them to adopt federal procedures, like rules allocating responsibility between judge and jury?

3. Long before *Dice*, the Supreme Court had required state courts hearing FELA cases to comply with other federal procedural requirements. In the *White* case, the Court held that state courts must put on defendants the burden of proof on contributory negligence. See Central Vermont Railway Co. v. White, 238 U.S. 507, 512 (1915) ("it is a misnomer to say that the question as to the burden of proof as to contributory negligence is a mere matter of state procedure," and Congress in passing FELA intended to follow federal practice of putting this burden on defendant). In the *Dunlap* case, decided just a year after *Erie*, the Court had held that burden of proof is a substantive matter (hence federal courts in diversity cases apply state rules governing burden of proof), which seems consistent with the approach taken in *White* when state courts apply federal law. See Cities Service Oil Co. v. Dunlap, 308 U.S. 208 (1939) (cited in the Court's decision in *York*, Section A2, supra). Perhaps more surprisingly, the Court has even faulted state courts for using their own pleading rules in FELA claims, at least implicitly suggesting that the adequacy of a complaint in a FELA suit must be determined under federal standards. See Brown v. Western Ry. of Alabama, 338 U.S. 294 (1949) (noting the "troublesome question" of the "extent" to which rule of practice and procedure may "dig into" substantial rights, Court construes the pleading itself and concludes that it states a FELA claim and should not have been dismissed in state court on a demurrer; "strict local rules of pleading" cannot be allowed to "impose unnecessary burdens" on claimants asserting rights protected by federal statute).

4. Questions about the degree to which state courts can observe their own procedural conventions in hearing federal question cases have arisen in a bewildering variety of situations. Consider these opinions, both holding that states could *not* follow their own procedural conventions in federal question suits:

(a) In the *Haywood* case, the question was whether a state could channel a prisoner's claim, brought under §1983, to a state Court of Claims that was set up specifically to hear damage suits against correctional department employees. The Court held, in a 5-4 opinion, that "federal law is as much the law of the several States as are the laws passed by their legislatures," that there is a strong federal presumption of "concurrency" of jurisdiction between federal and state courts, and that states can only defeat this presumption by means of a "neutral" rule governing its own court administration. Here the state statute shields a "narrow class of defendants" from damage liability, but the state cannot ("no matter how evenhanded it may appear") escape the obligation to apply federal law unless its rule reflects concerns of "power over the person" and "competence over the subject matter." Since New York has "courts of general jurisdiction that regularly sit to entertain analogous suits," New York cannot "shut the courthouse door" to similar federal claims. See Haywood v. Drown, 129 S. Ct. 2108 (2009).

(b) In the *Felder* case, quoted above in note 2, the question was whether a state "notice of claim" statute could apply in a suit charging police brutality, based on alleged violations of constitutional rights and brought under §1983. The statute required plaintiffs to provide written notice of their claim within 120 days, and to submit an itemized statement of relief sought. The statute also required suit to be brought within six months after receiving notice that the claim was disallowed. The Court thought the state statute was "patently incompatible with the compensatory goals" of §1983, and that "burdening" the federal right in this way *cannot* be viewed as "the natural or permissible consequence of an otherwise neutral, uniformly applicable state rule" even though the notice-of-claim statute did not "discriminate between state and federal causes of action." The crucial point is that the notice-of-claim statute protects "the very persons and entities" that are the targets of the federal statute, and thus the notice-of-claim provision does discriminate against the federal claim. See Felder v. Casey, 487 U.S. 131, 144-145 (1988).

5. Consider now some cases that go the other direction—that *permit* states to follow their own procedural conventions in entertaining federal question cases.

(a) In one case, the question was whether a state court in Idaho entertaining a §1983 claim had to allow interlocutory appeal from a ruling rejecting a defense of qualified immunity. A state official sued in *federal* court under §1983 has a right to an immediate appeal, in part because qualified immunity is viewed not only as a defense to liability claims, but as a right not even to have to stand trial, and a ruling rejecting this defense is viewed as a final judgment under the federal statute governing appeals. See 28 USC §1291, and see Johnson v. Jones, 515 U.S. 304 (1995). In Johnson v. Fankell, 520 U.S. 911 (1997), however, the Court concluded that state officials do not have a federally secured right to immediate appeal, when sued in state court on §1983 claims. The Idaho rule was a "neutral state Rule regarding the administration of the state courts," and even though the immunity defense "has its source in" §1983, the purpose of immunity is "to protect the State and its officials from overenforcement of federal rights," and the Idaho rule is not so much an "interference" with federal interests as a judgment about "how best to balance the competing *state* interests of limiting interlocutory appeals and providing state officials with immediate review of the merits of their defense."

(b) In another case, an injured seaman sued in Louisiana state court, seeking damages under the Jones Act. He had been injured while working on a tugboat in the Delaware River, and defendant was a Pennsylvania corporation with its principal place of business in New Jersey. The seaman returned to his home in Mississippi after the accident, and the question was whether Louisiana could apply its rule making unavailable any *forum non conveniens* argument in Jones Act cases. The Court concluded that Louisiana could indeed exempt Jones Act claims from transfer under that doctrine, *despite* the existence of a federal doctrine of *forum non conveniens* codified in 28 USC §1404. Finding that this doctrine is "nothing more or less than a supervening venue provision" that "goes to process rather than substantive rights," the Court concluded that the doctrine is not a "characteristic feature" of admiralty, hence that applying it is not necessary in maintaining the "proper harmony" of admiralty law. See American Dredging Co. v. Miller, 510 U.S. 443, 447, 453 (1994).

6. *Dice* seems almost the mirror image of *Byrd*, doesn't it? In *Byrd*, the question was whether federal or state law governs allocation of responsibility between judge and jury in a federal court in a diversity case, and the answer was that federal law controls. In *Dice*, the question was whether state or federal law governs allocation of responsibility between judge and jury in state court in a federal question case, and the answer was that *federal* law controls (once again). Let's see now, should we conclude that the matter of allocating judge-jury responsibility is substantive when rights under federal law are at stake (so state courts must follow federal practice), but only procedural when rights under state law are at stake (so federal courts can ignore state practice)? Or are the cases distinguishable? *Byrd* came along six years after *Dice*, and Justice Brennan wrote both opinions. He said in *Byrd* that the cases were "not analogous" because jury trial entitlement was a "substantial" part of rights under FELA, while the state rule allocating to the judge the decision whether a claimant had to proceed under the workers' compensation statute (as opposed to a common law tort claim) was simply a matter of procedural expediency.

(a) Is that convincing? Would an employer in South Carolina, who stands to benefit from a decision that the workers' compensation system applies, view the right to have a judge decide this issue as a mere procedural convention?

(b) Didn't *Byrd* also rest on the idea that federal courts comprise "an independent system for administering justice," and that one "essential characteristic" of the system is the manner in which it "distributes trial functions between judge and jury"? Isn't the manner in which Ohio distributes trial functions between judge and jury an essential part of the Ohio court system?

7. Consider Professor Bellia's attempt to summarize the cases described above: "Congress may require state courts to enforce federal claims if they are competent to do so; Congress may require state courts to enforce federal procedural rules that are 'part and parcel' of a federal right of action; and Congress may, by implication, require state courts to follow federal procedural rules when application of a state procedural rule would unnecessarily burden a federal right." Anthony Bellia, *Federal Regulation of State Court Procedures*, 110 Yale L.J. 947, 962 (2001) (arguing generally that Congress has gone further in trying to regulate state court procedure even in state law cases, that states should have exclusive authority in this area, and that Congress should understand that state procedural law, as recognized in conflict-of-laws principles, should apply even in connection with federal question adjudication in state courts).

8. Assuming that a *federal* forum is more likely than a state forum to be sympathetic to federal rights, such as those found in §1983 and FELA, *and* that federal rights can only be effectively administered if federal procedures are followed, is there a problem in *making sure* that those procedures are followed? When federal question cases are litigated in federal court, a losing litigant is assured at least one level of federal review, and two if the Supreme Court agrees to hear the case, which is rare. But when federal question cases are litigated in state court, there is no federal review unless the Supreme Court agrees to hear the case. How effective can federal courts be in developing and enforcing rules like the ones that emerge in *Dice, White, Brown, Haywood,* and *Felder*?

C | INTERSYSTEM EFFECTS—FEDERAL DEFERENCE TO STATE COURTS

1. Abstention Doctrines

In our federal system, you have seen that federal courts are often called upon to resolve issues of state law, and (somewhat less often) state courts are called upon to resolve issues of federal law. As you will see in the next section, sometimes the very same issues—of either state or federal law—arise in more than one lawsuit.

In part because of the awkwardness of a system in which federal courts resolve issues of state law without being responsive to review by any state court, and in the knowledge that federal precedent on such matters does not bind state courts, federal courts sometimes abstain from resolving issues of state law. Sometimes "abstention" has to do as well with avoiding unnecessary decisions on such points, or with leaving room for state systems to resolve those issues, or with avoiding the spectacle of federal courts interfering with ongoing state litigation. Consider now a particularly challenging situation in which a decision to abstain had huge financial consequences.

PENNZOIL COMPANY v. TEXACO, INC.
Supreme Court of the United States
481 U.S. 1 (1987)

Justice POWELL delivered the opinion of the Court.

The principal issue in this case is whether a federal district court lawfully may enjoin a plaintiff who has prevailed in a trial in state court from executing the judgment in its favor pending appeal of that judgment to a state appellate court.

I

[By agreement, Pennzoil was to purchase more than 40 percent of Getty Oil's outstanding shares for $110/share. In the end, Texaco bought the shares for $128/share. In state court in Texas, Pennzoil (headquartered in Texas) sued Texaco (headquartered in New York), alleging that Texaco tortiously induced Getty to breach its contract with Pennzoil. After a jury verdict for Pennzoil in November 1985, the Texas court entered judgment in the amount of $7.53 *billion* in actual damages and $3 *billion* in punitive damages. With interest, the total judgment exceeded $11 billion.

The day before the Texas court entered its judgment, Texaco sued Pennzoil in Federal District Court in New York, alleging that the Texas proceedings denied Texaco's rights under the Constitution and federal statutes. Texaco asked the court to enjoin Pennzoil from enforcing the Texas judgment. One week later, the New York federal court issued a temporary restraining to this effect. This order was extended, and a preliminary injunction issued several weeks later.

The problem for Texaco was that the Texas judgment gave Pennzoil "significant" rights: Pennzoil could record the judgment in any Texas county, thus obtaining liens on Texaco's real property, and 30 days after entry of judgment Pennzoil could obtain writs of execution, allowing it to take possession of Texaco's assets. Texaco could suspend execution of the judgment by filing a "supersedeas" bond in the amount of the judgment plus interest and costs ($13 billion), but the bond would not prevent immediate creation of liens against real property. Texaco could delay execution of the judgment by filing a motion for a new trial, but denial of the motion would allow plaintiff to proceed, and inaction on the motion would delay enforcement for only 75 days (after that, the motion would be deemed denied). In fact, Texaco did file a motion for a new trial, and the trial court did not act, so 75 days later it was deemed denied.

Texaco could not raise enough money to post the supersedeas bond. The value of its stock "dropped markedly." Texaco "had difficulty obtaining credit," and its bond rating was lowered. Its trading partners refused to sell crude oil to Texaco on the usual market credit terms.

In its federal suit, brought under 42 USC §1983, Texaco claimed a violation of its federal constitutional rights under the Due Process and Equal Protection Clauses. The District Court issued the preliminary injunction, finding that Texaco had shown a "clear probability of success" on this claim. Although the preliminary injunction was not final, Pennzoil appealed. (See 28 USC §1292(a)(1), which authorizes appeals from interlocutory orders "granting, continuing, modifying, refusing or dissolving injunctions.") The Second Circuit Court of Appeals affirmed.

The issue that proved decisive was not the validity of the Texas bond and lien provisions, but the propriety of federal intervention. On this point, there were three main questions: First was the question whether the Anti-Injunction Act blocked the federal court in New York from acting. (This issue is taken up after the *Negrete* case in the next section of this chapter.) Second was the question whether the suit in New York violated the *Rooker/Feldman* doctrine, named after decisions in Rooker v. Fidelity Trust Co., 263 U.S. 413 (1923), and District of Columbia Court of Appeals v. Feldman, 460 U.S. 462 (1983). The Court decided that this doctrine did not apply. Third was the question whether the federal court should have abstained from deciding the issues under the decisions in Railroad Commission of Texas v. Pullman Co., 312 U.S. 496 (1941) and Younger v. Harris, 401 U.S. 37 (1971).]

Pennzoil filed a jurisdictional statement in this Court. . . . We reverse.

II

The courts below should have abstained under the principles of federalism enunciated in *Younger*. Both the District Court and the Court of Appeals failed to recognize the significant interests harmed by their unprecedented intrusion into the Texas judicial system. Similarly, neither of those courts applied the appropriate standard in determining whether adequate relief was available in the Texas courts.

A

The first ground for the *Younger* decision was "the basic doctrine of equity jurisprudence that courts of equity should not act, and particularly should not act to restrain a criminal prosecution, when the moving party has an adequate remedy at law." The Court also offered a second explanation for its decision:

> This underlying reason . . . is reinforced by an even more vital consideration, the notion of "comity," that is, a proper respect for state functions, a recognition of the fact that the entire country is made up of a Union of separate state

governments, and a continuance of the belief that the National Government will fare best if the States and their institutions are left free to perform their separate functions in their separate ways. . . . The concept does not mean blind deference to "States' Rights" any more than it means centralization of control over every important issue in our National Government and its courts. The Framers rejected both these courses. What the concept does represent is a system in which there is sensitivity to the legitimate interests of both State and National Governments, and in which the National Government, anxious though it may be to vindicate and protect federal rights and federal interests, always endeavors to do so in ways that will not unduly interfere with the legitimate activities of the States.

This concern mandates application of *Younger* abstention not only when the pending state proceedings are criminal, but also when certain civil proceedings are pending, if the State's interests in the proceeding are so important that exercise of the federal judicial power would disregard the comity between the States and the National Government. *E.g.,* Huffman v. Pursue, Ltd., 420 U.S. 592, 603-605 (1975).

Another important reason for abstention is to avoid unwarranted determination of federal constitutional questions. When federal courts interpret state statutes in a way that raises federal constitutional questions, "a constitutional determination is predicated on a reading of the statute that is not binding on state courts and may be discredited at any time—thus essentially rendering the federal-court decision advisory and the litigation underlying it meaningless." Moore v. Sims, 442 U.S. 415, 428 (1979). See Trainor v. Hernandez, 431 U.S. 434, 445 (1977).[9] This concern has special significance in this case. Because Texaco chose not to present to the Texas courts the constitutional claims asserted in this case, it is impossible to be certain that the governing Texas statutes and procedural rules actually raise these claims. Moreover, the Texas Constitution contains an "open courts" provision, Art. I, §13,[10] that appears to address Texaco's claims more specifically than the Due Process Clause of the Fourteenth Amendment. Thus, when this case was filed in federal court, it was entirely possible that the Texas courts would have resolved this case on state statutory or constitutional grounds, without reaching the federal constitutional questions Texaco raises in this case. As we

---

[9] In some cases, the probability that any federal adjudication would be effectively advisory is so great that this concern alone is sufficient to justify abstention, even if there are no pending state proceedings in which the question could be raised. Because appellant has not argued in this Court that *Pullman* abstention is proper, we decline to address Justice Blackmun's conclusion that *Pullman* abstention is the appropriate disposition of this case. We merely note that considerations similar to those that mandate *Pullman* abstention are relevant to a court's decision whether to abstain under *Younger.* The various types of abstention are not rigid pigeonholes into which federal courts must try to fit cases. Rather, they reflect a complex of considerations designed to soften the tensions inherent in a system that contemplates parallel judicial processes.

[10] Article I, §13, provides: "All courts shall be open, and every person for an injury done him, in his lands, goods, person or reputation, shall have remedy by due course of law."

have noted, *Younger* abstention in situations like this "offers the opportunity for narrowing constructions that might obviate the constitutional problem and intelligently mediate federal constitutional concerns and state interests." Moore v. Sims, *supra,* 442 U.S., at 429-430 (1979).

Texaco's principal argument against *Younger* abstention is that exercise of the District Court's power did not implicate a "vital" or "important" state interest. This argument reflects a misreading of our precedents. This Court repeatedly has recognized that the States have important interests in administering certain aspects of their judicial systems. In Juidice v. Vail, 430 U.S. 327 (1977), we held that a federal court should have abstained from adjudicating a challenge to a State's contempt process. The Court's reasoning in that case informs our decision today:

> A State's interest in the contempt process, through which it vindicates the regular operation of its judicial system, so long as that system itself affords the opportunity to pursue federal claims within it, is surely an important interest. Perhaps it is not quite as important as is the State's interest in the enforcement of its criminal laws, *Younger, supra,* or even its interest in the maintenance of a quasi-criminal proceeding such as was involved in *Huffman, supra.* But we think it is of sufficiently great import to require application of the principles of those cases.

Our comments on why the contempt power was sufficiently important to justify abstention also are illuminating: "Contempt in these cases, serves, of course, to vindicate and preserve the private interests of competing litigants, . . . but its purpose is by no means spent upon purely private concerns. It stands in aid of the authority of the judicial system, so that its orders and judgments are not rendered nugatory." *Id.,* at n.12.

The reasoning of *Juidice* controls here. That case rests on the importance to the States of enforcing the orders and judgments of their courts. There is little difference between the State's interest in forcing persons to transfer property in response to a court's judgment and in forcing persons to respond to the court's process on pain of contempt. Both *Juidice* and this case involve challenges to the processes by which the State compels compliance with the judgments of its courts.[12] Not only would federal injunctions in such cases interfere with the execution of state judgments, but they would do so on grounds that challenge the very process by which those judgments were obtained. So long as those challenges relate to pending state proceedings, proper respect for the ability of state courts to resolve federal questions

---

[12] Thus, contrary to Justice Stevens' suggestion, the State of Texas has an interest in this proceeding "that goes beyond its interest as adjudicator of wholly private disputes." Our opinion does not hold that *Younger* abstention is always appropriate whenever a civil proceeding is pending in a state court. Rather, as in *Juidice,* we rely on the State's interest in protecting "the authority of the judicial system, so that its orders and judgments are not rendered nugatory."

presented in state-court litigation mandates that the federal court stay its hand.[13]

B

Texaco also argues that *Younger* abstention was inappropriate because no Texas court could have heard Texaco's constitutional claims within the limited time available to Texaco. But the burden on this point rests on the federal plaintiff to show "that state procedural law barred presentation of [its] claims." Moore v. Sims, 442 U.S., at 432. . . .

Moreover, denigrations of the procedural protections afforded by Texas law hardly come from Texaco with good grace, as it apparently made no effort under Texas law to secure the relief sought in this case. Article VI of the United States Constitution declares that "the Judges in every State shall be bound" by the Federal Constitution, laws, and treaties. We cannot assume that state judges will interpret ambiguities in state procedural law to bar presentation of federal claims. Accordingly, when a litigant has not attempted to present his federal claims in related state-court proceedings, a federal court should assume that state procedures will afford an adequate remedy, in the absence of unambiguous authority to the contrary.

The "open courts" provision of the Texas Constitution, Article I, §13, has considerable relevance here. This provision has appeared in each of Texas' six Constitutions, dating back to the Constitution of the Republic of Texas in 1836. According to the Texas Supreme Court, the provision "guarantees all litigants . . . the right to their day in court." LeCroy v. Hanlon, 713 S.W.2d 335, 341 (Tex. 1986). "The common thread of [the Texas Supreme Court's] decisions construing the open courts provision is that the legislature has no power to make a remedy by due course of law contingent on an impossible condition." Nelson v. Krusen, 678 S.W.2d 918, 921 (Tex. 1984). In light of this demonstrable and long-standing commitment of the Texas Supreme Court to provide access to the state courts, we are reluctant to conclude that Texas courts would have construed state procedural rules to deny Texaco an effective opportunity to raise its constitutional claims.

Against this background, Texaco's submission that the Texas courts were incapable of hearing its constitutional claims is plainly insufficient. Both of the courts below found that the Texas trial court had the power to consider constitutional challenges to the enforcement provisions. The

---

[13] Texaco also suggests that abstention is unwarranted because of the absence of a state judicial proceeding with respect to which the Federal District Court should have abstained. Texaco argues that "the Texas judiciary plays no role" in execution of judgments. We reject this assertion. There is at least one pending judicial proceeding in the state courts; the lawsuit out of which Texaco's constitutional claims arose is now pending before a Texas Court of Appeals in Houston, Texas. As we explain *infra*, we are not convinced that Texaco could not have secured judicial relief in those proceedings.

Texas Attorney General filed a brief in the proceedings below, arguing that such relief was available in the Texas courts. Texaco has cited no statute or case clearly indicating that Texas courts lack such power.[15] Accordingly, Texaco has failed to meet its burden on this point.[16]

In sum, the lower courts should have deferred on principles of comity to the pending state proceedings. They erred in accepting Texaco's assertions as to the inadequacies of Texas procedure to provide effective relief. It is true that this case presents an unusual fact situation, never before addressed by the Texas courts, and that Texaco urgently desired prompt relief. But we cannot say that those courts, when this suit was filed, would have been any less inclined than a federal court to address and decide the federal constitutional claims. Because Texaco apparently did not give the Texas courts an opportunity to adjudicate its constitutional claims, and because Texaco cannot demonstrate that the Texas courts were not then open to adjudicate its claims, there is no basis for concluding that the Texas law and procedures were so deficient that *Younger* abstention is inappropriate. Accordingly, we conclude that the District Court should have abstained.

III

In this opinion, we have addressed the situation that existed on the morning of December 10, 1985, when this case was filed in the United States District Court for the Southern District of New York. We recognize that much has transpired in the Texas courts since then. Later that day, the Texas trial court entered judgment. On February 12 of this year, the Texas Court of Appeals substantially affirmed the judgment. We are not unmindful of the unique importance to Texaco of having its challenges to that judgment authoritatively considered and resolved. We of course express no opinion on the merits of those challenges. Similarly, we express no opinion on the claims Texaco has raised in this case against the Texas bond and lien provisions, nor on the possibility that Texaco now could raise these claims in the Texas courts. Today we decide only that it was inappropriate for the District

---

[15] [Texaco argues that there is no exception to the bond requirement, and an appellant must post bond in the full amount of the judgment. But the language] suggests that a trial court could suspend the bond requirement if it concluded that application of the bond requirement would violate the Federal Constitution. Rule 364(a) provides: "*Unless otherwise provided by law* or these rules, an appellant may suspend the execution of the judgment by a good and sufficient bond" (emphasis added). Texaco has failed to demonstrate that Texas courts would not construe the phrase "otherwise provided by law" to encompass claims made under the Federal Constitution. We cannot assume that Texas courts would refuse to construe the Rule, or to apply their inherent powers, to provide a forum to adjudicate substantial federal constitutional claims.

[16] We recognize that the trial court no longer has jurisdiction over the case. Thus, relief is no longer available to Texaco from the trial court. But Texaco cannot escape *Younger* abstention by failing to assert its state remedies in a timely manner. In any event, the Texas Supreme Court and the Texas Court of Appeals arguably have the authority to suspend the supersedeas requirement to protect their appellate jurisdiction.

Court to entertain these claims. If, and when, the Texas courts render a final decision on any federal issue presented by this litigation, review may be sought in this Court in the customary manner.

IV

The judgment of the Court of Appeals is reversed. The case is remanded to the District Court with instructions to vacate its order and dismiss the complaint. The judgment of this Court shall issue forthwith.

It is so ordered.

Justice SCALIA, with whom Justice O'CONNOR joins, concurring.

I join the opinion of the Court. I write separately only to indicate that I do not believe that the so-called *Rooker-Feldman* doctrine deprives the Court of jurisdiction to decide Texaco's challenge to the constitutionality of the Texas stay and lien provisions. In resolving that challenge, the Court need not decide any issue either actually litigated in the Texas courts or inextricably intertwined with issues so litigated. Under these circumstances, I see no jurisdictional bar to the Court's decision in this case.

Justice BRENNAN, with whom Justice MARSHALL joins, concurring in the judgment.

Texaco's claim that the Texas bond and lien provisions violate the Fourteenth Amendment is without merit. While Texaco cannot, consistent with due process and equal protection, be arbitrarily denied the right to a meaningful opportunity to be heard on appeal, this right can be adequately vindicated even if Texaco were forced to file for bankruptcy.

I believe that the Court should have confronted the merits of this case. I wholeheartedly concur with Justice Stevens' conclusion that a creditor's invocation of a State's postjudgment collection procedures constitutes action under color of state law within the meaning of 42 USC §1983.

I also agree with his conclusion that the District Court was not required to abstain under the principles enunciated in *Younger*. I adhere to my view that *Younger* is, in general, inapplicable to civil proceedings, especially when a plaintiff brings a §1983 action alleging violation of federal constitutional rights.

The State's interest in this case is negligible. The State of Texas—not a party in this appeal—expressly represented to the Court of Appeals that it "has no interest in the outcome of the state-court adjudication underlying this cause," except in its fair adjudication. The Court identifies the State's interest as enforcing "'the authority of the judicial system, so that its orders and judgments are not rendered nugatory.'" Yet, the District Court found that "Pennzoil has publicly admitted that Texaco's assets are sufficient to satisfy the

Judgment even without liens or a bond" (District Court findings). "Thus Pennzoil's interest in protecting the full amount of its judgment during the appellate process is reasonably secured by the substantial excess of Texaco's net worth over the amount of Pennzoil's judgment" (Second Circuit opinion).

Indeed, the interest in enforcing the bond and lien requirement is privately held by Pennzoil, not by the State of Texas. The Court of Appeals correctly stated that this "is a suit between two private parties stemming from the defendant's alleged tortious interference with the plaintiff's contract with a third private party." Pennzoil was free to waive the bond and lien requirements under Texas law, without asking the State of Texas for permission. . . . The State's decision to grant private parties unilateral power to invoke, or not invoke, the State's bond and lien provisions demonstrates that the State has no independent interest in the enforcement of those provisions.

Texaco filed this §1983 suit claiming only violations of *federal* statutory and constitutional law. In enacting §1983, Congress "created a specific and unique remedy, enforceable in a federal court of equity, that could be frustrated if the federal court were not empowered to enjoin a state court proceeding." Mitchum v. Foster, 407 U.S. 225, 237 (1972). Today the Court holds that this §1983 suit should be filed instead in Texas courts, offering to Texaco the unsolicited advice to bring its claims under the "open courts" provision of the Texas Constitution. This "'blind deference to 'States' Rights''" hardly shows "'sensitivity to the legitimate interests of *both* State *and National* Governments.'"

Furthermore, I reject Pennzoil's contention that [the *Rooker/Feldman* doctrine forbids] collateral review in this instance. In *Rooker* and *Feldman,* the Court held that lower federal courts lack jurisdiction to engage in appellate review of state-court determinations. In this case, however, Texaco filed the §1983 action only to protect its federal constitutional right to a meaningful opportunity for appellate review, not to challenge the merits of the Texas suit. Texaco's federal action seeking a stay of judgment pending appeal is therefore an action "'separable from and collateral to'" the merits of the state-court judgment. National Socialist Party v. Skokie, 432 U.S. 43, 44 (1977) (quoting Cohen v. Beneficial Loan Corp. 337 U.S. 541, 546 (1949)).

While I agree with Justice Stevens that Texaco's claim is "plainly without merit," my reasons for so concluding are different. Since Texas has created an appeal as of right from the trial court's judgment, it cannot infringe on this right to appeal in a manner inconsistent with due process or equal protection. While "a cost requirement, valid on its face, may offend due process because it operates to foreclose a particular party's opportunity to be heard," Boddie v. Connecticut, 401 U.S. 371, 380 (1971), in this case, Texaco clearly could exercise its right to appeal in order to protect its corporate interests even if it were forced to file for bankruptcy. . . . Texaco, or its successor in interest, could go forward with the appeal, and if it did prevail on its appeal in Texas courts, the bankruptcy proceedings could be terminated. Texaco simply fails to show how the initiation of corporate reorganization activities would prevent it from obtaining meaningful appellate review. . . .

Justice Marshall, concurring in the judgment.

[Federal District Court in New York was the wrong venue because the claim did not arise there. Also, the court lacked jurisdiction under *Rooker/Feldman* because a review of a state court judgment can go forward only in the Supreme Court. Issuance of the injunction turned on finding that Texaco had "significant claims" in its state court appeal, which "*necessarily* involved some review of the merits" of the state court appeal. If this case had involved "the sole proprietor of a small Texas grocery" that sued in New York to facilitate review of a Texas state court judgment, the result in the New York court would have been different. The principles that "would have governed with $10,000 at stake should also govern when thousands have become billions," as that is "the essence of equal justice under law."]

Justice Blackmun, concurring in the judgment.

[This case is not barred by the *Rooker/Feldman* doctrine, and the trial court was correct in going forward, as Younger v. Harris abstention does not apply here. But it is possible that the Texas bond requirement violates due process, as an inflexible requirement for a bond in order to lift a lien can in some circumstances amount to a confiscation that violates due process. This case presents one of those special situations in which abstention is proper under Railroad Comm'n of Texas v. Pullman Co., 312 U.S. 496 (1941), as this case is one in which unsettled questions of state law should be resolved before we reach constitutional issues.]

Justice Stevens, with whom Justice Marshall joins, concurring in the judgment.

[Texaco's attack on the Texas bond requirement is "plainly without merit." Texaco did state a claim under 42 USC §1983, and the *Rooker/Feldman* doctrine does not stand in the way. Moreover, abstention under *Younger* is improper, and today's decision "cuts the *Younger* doctrine adrift from its original doctrinal moorings." Yet Texaco did not claim that the bond requirement made appeal impossible, even though Texaco's options were unattractive (post bond, risking bankruptcy, or suffer execution of the judgment).

There is no "federal constitutional right" to be free of a bond requirement. Texaco claims that denying a stay without bond is arbitrary because (1) Texaco cannot obtain such a bond, (2) posting security for appeal would have a "devastating effect" on its financial position, and (3) neither a bond nor security is necessary because Texaco's "vast resources" guarantee that Pennzoil can collect its judgment. It would be "wise policy" for Texas to grant an exception here, but refusing is not "arbitrary in the constitutional sense." Texas has a "rational basis" for a "consistent rule" refusing to stay execution pending appeal unless bond is posted.

Texaco makes a "sympathetic argument," in light of the "adverse impact" of this suit on "its employees, its suppliers, and the community at large," but the "exceptional magnitude" of the consequences is "the product of the vast size of Texaco itself."]

■ NOTES ON ABSTENTION PENDING RESOLUTION OF STATE SUITS

1. You saw in Chapter 4D that state suits can sometimes be removed to federal courts, but that removal cannot be had merely because a federal issue appears, like the validity of bond and lien provisions in this case. The loser in a state suit may challenge these provisions in state court, asking that they be set aside as violating the Constitution. But someone in the position of Texaco, whose grievance is that state procedure violates federal rights, often thinks the chance of success is better if this claim can be raised in federal court. Once a suit has gone through the state system (to the state court of appeals, if any, and the state supreme court), a dissatisfied party can petition the United States Supreme Court to review the judgment by considering federal issues in the case. But seeking Supreme Court review is "iffy" because the Court agrees to hear only a small fraction of the cases that come its way. So Texaco brought a federal suit in hope of getting further in its claim of federal rights.

2. In *Pennzoil*, the Court applies *Younger* abstention as justification for not interfering with Pennzoil's threat to execute on its $11 billion judgment. Professors Wright and Kane have written that there is "no more controversial doctrine in the federal courts today than the doctrine of 'Our Federalism'" that describes the decision in *Younger*. While *Younger* "seems to be a special application of the abstention doctrines," they continue, the case has taken on "such a robust life of its own" as to merit special consideration. See Wright & Kane, Federal Courts §52A (6th ed. 2002).

(a) Younger came down in 1971, and represented a sudden retreat from the decision just six years earlier in Dombrowski v. Pfister, 380 U.S. 479 (1965). In *Dombrowski*, the Court approved an antisuit injunction in Louisiana, blocking state prosecution of plaintiffs, who had been involved in registration drives encouraging black citizens to vote, under a state subversive activities law. The Court concluded (in an opinion by Justice Brennan) that defending against state charges "will not assure adequate vindication of constitutional rights," and prosecution under statutes "regulating expression" and having "an overbroad sweep" could lead "too readily to denial" of

constitutional rights. *Younger* was similar, but the setting was California and plaintiffs were members of the Progressive Labor Party advocating replacement of capitalism with socialism and seeking to abolish "the profit system of production in this country." Invoking *Dombrowski,* a three-judge panel issued the injunction, and the Supreme Court (on direct appeal under now-abandoned procedure) reversed:

> Since the beginning of this country's history Congress has, subject to few exceptions, manifested a desire to permit state courts to try state cases free from interference by federal courts. [The Court quotes and traces history of Anti-Injunction Act.]
>
> The precise reasons for this longstanding public policy against federal court interference with state court proceedings have never been specifically identified but the primary sources of the policy are plain. One is the basic doctrine of equity jurisprudence that courts of equity should not act, and particularly should not act to restrain a criminal prosecution, when the moving party has an adequate remedy at law and will not suffer irreparable injury if denied equitable relief. The doctrine may originally have grown out of circumstances peculiar to the English judicial system and not applicable in this country, but its fundamental purpose of restraining equity jurisdiction within narrow limits is equally important under our Constitution, in order to prevent erosion of the role of the jury and avoid a duplication of legal proceedings and legal sanctions where a single suit would be adequate to protect the rights asserted. This underlying reason for restraining courts of equity from interfering with criminal prosecutions is reinforced by an even more vital consideration, the notion of "comity," that is, a proper respect for state functions, a recognition of the fact that the entire country is made up of a Union of separate state governments, and a continuance of the belief that the National Government will fare best if the States and their institutions are left free to perform their separate functions in their separate ways. This, perhaps for lack of a better and clearer way to describe it, is referred to by many as "Our Federalism," and one familiar with the profound debates that ushered our Federal Constitution into existence is bound to respect those who remain loyal to the ideals and dreams of "Our Federalism." The concept does not mean blind deference to "States' Rights" any more than it means centralization of control over every important issue in our National Government and its courts. The Framers rejected both these courses. What the concept does represent is a system in which there is sensitivity to the legitimate interests of both State and National Governments, and in which the National Government, anxious though it may be to vindicate and protect federal rights and federal interests, always endeavors to do so in ways that will not unduly interfere with the legitimate activities of the States. It should never be forgotten that this slogan, "Our Federalism," born in the early struggling days of our Union of States, occupies a highly important place in our Nation's history and its future.

Younger v. Harris, 401 U.S. 37, 43-44 (1971). For a modern example of *Younger* abstention in the criminal setting, see Moore v. City of Asheville, N.C., 396 F.3d 385 (4th Cir. 2005) (invoking *Younger* in declining to decide claim of street preacher that enforcement of noise ordinance violated his constitutional rights, and seeking injunctive relief against enforcement of ordinance against him).

(b) The significance of *Pennzoil* is that the decision recognized that *Younger's* idea of federalism bears on proper respect for the work of state courts in civil cases. In the *Juidice* case, described in *Pennzoil*, the Court applied *Younger* abstention to contempt proceedings against judgment debtors, which led to fines and imprisonment. The "nonintervention" principles of *Younger* "are not confined," the Court wrote in *Juidice*, to "the state criminal process," but rest on notions of "comity" and "proper respect for state functions" (quoting language from *Huffman*, also cited in *Younger*). The state has "an important interest" in its contempt process that is "of sufficiently great import" to bring *Younger* into play. *Juidice* involved quasi-criminal enforcement— contempt citations are viewed sometimes as criminal processes, particularly when a court holds a person in contempt for purposes of punishment, and sometimes as civil processes, particularly when a court holds a person in contempt in order to force compliance with a court order. But *Pennzoil* involved nothing resembling criminal processes.

(c) Why were Justice Brennan, Marshall, and Stevens, while concurring in the judgment, so opposed to the extension of *Younger* to federal challenges to state civil processes? Can it possibly be right, as Justice Brennan argues (joined by Justice Marshall), that a state has only "negligible" interest in civil enforcement proceedings and that *Younger's* concept of "Our Federalism" is "in general, inapplicable" to civil cases?

3. *Pennzoil* is far from being the only case in which federal courts have invoked *Younger* in declining to interfere with state civil proceedings.

(a) In the *Health Net* case, three state-appointed receivers sued Health Net in Louisiana state court to enforce an agreement, and recovered judgments in combined amounts exceeding $100 million. Thereafter, Health Net learned that all three receivers had *ex parte* communications with the judge. It took an appeal and also sought a federal injunction declaring the judgment a nullity under Louisiana law because it had been obtained by "fraud or ill practices." The Fifth Circuit found that the claim was barred by the Anti-Injunction Act (taken up below) and that *Younger* abstention was appropriate: As in *Pennzoil*, *Health Net* involved a challenge to post-judgment proceedings in state court, implicating "important state interests similar to those in *Pennzoil*." *Younger* abstention was also appropriate "to avoid interpreting state laws" that would lead to unnecessary resolution of constitutional questions. Louisiana "offers a forum for Health Net's challenge and ought to have the opportunity" to interpret its laws to determine "whether they infringe on the right to a fair trial by necessitating *ex parte* communication." Health Net, Inc. v. Wooley, 534 F.3d 487, 494-495 (5th Cir. 2008).

(b) In the *Rossi* case, a plumbing company filed a mechanic's lien enforcement proceeding in state court, and the Rossis as defendants

challenged the lien statute as unconstitutional. As the case wound through the state system, the Rossis, after prevailing at trial only to suffer reversal on appeal, filed a federal suit challenging the lien statute (actually two, naming different defendants). Invoking *Younger,* the federal judge dismissed the federal actions, and the First Circuit agreed:

> The *Younger* doctrine is based on principles of comity, and unless there are extraordinary circumstances, it instructs federal courts not to "interfere with ongoing state-court litigation, or, in some cases, with state administrative proceedings." Maymó-Meléndez v. Alvarez-Ramírez, 364 F.3d 27, 31 (1st Cir. 2004). Although the doctrine is frequently associated with state criminal prosecutions, it has been extended to certain "coercive" civil cases. We have articulated the basic analytical framework for *Younger* abstention. Abstention is appropriate when the requested relief would interfere (1) with an ongoing state judicial proceeding (2) that implicates an important state interest, and (3) that provides an adequate opportunity for the federal plaintiff to advance his federal constitutional challenge.

Rossi v. Gemma, 489 F.3d 26, 34 (1st Cir. 2007). In this case, granting relief to the Rossis would "substantially interfere with the lien enforcement proceeding," because obtaining a return of their funds from the state court would deprive it of its ability to satisfy any claim that the plumbing company might have. There is indeed an "ongoing judicial proceeding" in state court that "provides an adequate forum" to hear the constitutional challenge. The "state interest" requirement is satisfied as well because the case involves challenges to the processes by which state courts enforce their judgments. *Pennzoil* involved a bond requirement and this case involves funds deposited in the court registry that "act as security for [the plumbing company's] anticipated successful claims." Even though this case involves a "pre-judgment process," it is still an appropriate case for *Younger* abstention.

4. The *Rooker/Feldman* doctrine blocks litigants, for whom mechanisms like removal and appeal to the Supreme Court are unavailing, from suing in federal court to obtain federal review of state judgments. Justice Marshall thought *Rooker/Feldman* applied, but none of the other Justices agreed. Which side do you think has the better argument?

5. As the Court says, abstention doctrines exist in a handful of shapes and forms, and each is usually described by reference to the case it derives from:

(a) Pullman *Abstention.* Here the idea is that a federal court should not resolve a constitutional issue in a suit also raising state law issues that might be determinative, because it is unnecessary to resolve the constitutional issue, hence wiser not to. In this situation, a federal court retains jurisdiction but stays the suit, to allow a state suit to go forward. If the state suit is *not* finally resolved on some state law ground, the federal court can go forward after all. In *Pullman* itself, a railroad sought a federal injunction blocking enforcement of an order by the Texas Railroad Commission that passenger trains with

sleeping cars must have at least one conductor aboard (in addition to any porter), on the ground that the order violated equal protection (conductors being white, porters being black). The Supreme Court held that the federal court should abstain so a state suit could be filed, and the matter litigated there, where it might be resolved by a decision that the state statute did not authorize the order. See Railroad Commission of Texas v. Pullman, 312 U.S. 496 (1941). Justice Blackmun argued in *Pennzoil* that *Pullman* abstention should be applied there.

(b) Burford *Abstention.* Here the idea is that state administrative machinery, typically involving a complex code or regulations and an agency or commission with supervisory and enforcement powers, should be allowed to move forward without interference or interruption by a federal judge from whom one of the parties in the state case seeks injunctive relief. See Burford v. Sun Oil Co., 319 U.S. 315 (1943).

(c) Colorado River *Abstention.* Here the idea is that pending state litigation should be allowed to go its full course, rather than being interrupted by a federal suit involving the same parties and issues. The purpose is to avoid duplicative judicial efforts and the awkwardness of intersystem conflicts. See Colorado River Water Conservation District v. United States, 424 U.S. 800 (1976).

6. In *Pennzoil*, the Court comments that the abstention doctrines "are not rigid pigeonholes" (footnote 9 in the opinion), but only two years later the Court commented that "policy considerations supporting *Burford* and *Younger* are sufficiently distinct to justify independent analysis." See New Orleans Public Service, Inc. v. Council of City of New Orleans, 491 U.S. 350, 358 (1989).

7. Critics of abstention doctrines are perhaps *least* fond of *Colorado River* and *Younger* abstentions. They claim that federal courts *should* decide federal issues, especially constitutional issues, and they have in mind cases where threatened state criminal charges might infringe freedoms secured by the First Amendment. In *Younger*, for example, the law under challenge was at best constitutionally suspect for violating the principle of free speech, and critics of *Younger* argue that federal courts *should* decide such issues because state courts cannot be trusted to resolve them fairly, and the only other avenue of federal review would involve a petition for certiorari to the United States Supreme Court after a conviction and appeals in the state system, which is too expensive and time-consuming and likely to be unavailing simply because the Court takes few cases presented to it. What do you think of these criticisms?

8. You might be interested to learn that after the Court issued its opinion in the case, the Texas Supreme Court turned down Texaco's request for relief from the bond requirement. Thereafter, the parties negotiated for almost eight months, and finally settled the case for $3 billion. Among other things, the *Pennzoil* litigation brought to light the somewhat shocking fact that Joseph Jamail, who took on the representation of Pennzoil in the Texas trial court, had made a donation of $10,000 to the re-election campaign of the trial judge (Anthony Farris) two days *after* the latter was assigned to the case. For blow-by-blow accounts of the dispute between Pennzoil and Texaco over the acquisition of Getty Oil, see Robert M. Lloyd, *Pennzoil v. Texaco, Twenty Years After: Lessons for Business Lawyers,* 6 Transactions: The Tennessee Journal of Business Law 321 (2005).

2. Anti-Injunction Act

It may come as a surprise that one trial court would ever order another not to do something, but in fact such things happen. Usually, the order is not formally directed to another court or judge. You can imagine the reluctance that judges must feel about giving direct orders to other judges ("colleagues in arms"). Instead, courts order *litigants* (meaning *counsel* for litigants) to take or not to take certain steps.

When litigants ask federal courts to enjoin proceedings in state courts, issues of federalism arise. Long ago Congress passed what is known as the Anti-Injunction Act (1793), which is designed to limit federal court interference in state proceedings. The statute is a short one. Here is what it says today: "A court of the United States may not grant an injunction to stay proceedings in a State court except as expressly authorized by Act of Congress, or where necessary in aid of its jurisdiction, or to protect or effectuate its judgments." 28 USC §2283. It is settled that this statute blocks not only injunctions directed to state courts, but those directed to parties telling them to stop litigating in state court.

NEGRETE v. ALLIANZ LIFE INSURANCE COMPANY

United States Court of Appeals
523 F.3d 1091 (9th Cir. 2008)

Harry Pregerson, D.W. Nelson, and Ferdinand F. Fernandez, Circuit Judges.

Fernandez, Circuit Judge:

Vida F. Negrete filed this class action lawsuit against Allianz Life Insurance Company of North America. Allianz appeals a district court order that effectively prevents it from proceeding with any settlement negotiations on similar class action claims raised in any federal or state court without first obtaining permission from Negrete's Co-Lead Counsel, and from finalizing a settlement in any other court "that resolves, in whole or in part, the claims brought in [the Negrete] action," without first obtaining the district court's approval. We reverse.

BACKGROUND

On September 21, 2005, Vida F. Negrete filed a class action lawsuit against Allianz, an insurance corporation, in which she challenged the sale of Allianz's fixed deferred annuities. Negrete, acting as conservator for Everett E. Ow, alleges that Ow was "sold an unsuitable financial product" because the maturity date exceeded his life expectancy and restricted his access to principal without surrender charges. The complaint asserted claims for violations of the Racketeer Influenced and Corrupt Organizations Act, 18 USC §§1961-1968 ("RICO"), breach of fiduciary duty, aiding and abetting breach of fiduciary duty, unjust enrichment, and violation of California statutes.

In November 2006, the district court certified a nationwide class on the RICO claims only and a California-purchaser-only class as to the California statutory claims. The district court's certification order on the RICO claims covered all Allianz's deferred annuities purchased by individuals aged 65 or older within the applicable statutes of limitations.[3] This was not the only action against Allianz regarding its sales of annuities; several similar cases have been filed in various federal and state courts.

[Four parallel suits have been filed: (1) The *Iorio* suit is pending in Federal District Court for the Southern District of California, brought on behalf of "a California class" of people who bought "bonus annuity products." The class has been certified, and "partially overlaps the *Negrete* class." (2) The *Mooney* suit is pending in Federal District Court in Minnesota, brought on behalf of a "nationwide class" of people who bought "bonus annuities," making claims under a Minnesota statute and an unjust enrichment theory. This class too has been certified, and apparently many of the transactions at issue in *Mooney* "overlap those in *Negrete.*" (3) The *Castello* suit is pending in state court in Minnesota, brought on behalf of a nationwide class comprised of persons who bought Allianz "cash bonus" annuities. (4) The *AG Action* is pending in state court in Minnesota, brought by the Minnesota Attorney General and seeking relief under Minnesota law for Minnesota residents who bought Allianz "fixed deferred annuity products," which may "partially overlap" the *Negrete* class.]

On February 28, 2007, the parties in *Castello* participated in a hearing in which the court asked the parties to address settlement issues. Allianz indicated that it would be willing to engage in mediation discussions only if the discussions included possible settlement of *Mooney* and *The AG Action.* The parties in *Castello,* the *AG Action* and *Mooney* were amenable to that settlement plan, and on March 13, 2007, they met with a mediator to commence settlement discussions. Negrete Counsel was neither informed of nor included in that mediation session, but learned of the proceedings from a

---

[3] In certifying the class, the district court carved out the nationwide class certified in [the Minnesota state court in the *Castello* case].

third party. Believing that settlement negotiations in *Mooney* could "possibly extend to and extinguish the claims of the class in Negrete," and that Allianz might be engaged in a collusive reverse auction, Negrete Counsel contacted Allianz and requested assurances that [the *Castello, AG,* and *Mooney* negotiations would not "address any of the claims or damages asserted on behalf of the *Negrete* class," but Allianz "declined to provide those assurances."]

[Negrete's lawyer then asked the court for an order directing Allianz not to settle in those other suits any of the claims also pending in this case without approval of this court. Believing that such an order is not authorized, the judge declined to enter it. On March 19, however, the judge stated that any settlement discussions that "would affect any claims brought in this [Negrete] litigation," apart from claims of "an individual plaintiff or class member" must be conducted by plaintiff's counsel, and that any proposed settlement must be submitted to the court for approval.]

Allianz appealed that [March 19] order on April 18, 2007.

[In a September status conference, the trial court ordered Negrete and Allianz to commence mediation. The court said it would not enforce the March 19 order, but did not rescind the order. Later, the judge said that he "conferred with the judges presiding over the *Mooney* and *Iorio* cases" and that he told them he did not intend in any way to "impede their ability to go forward and set settlement conferences." Still, the court did not rescind its own order.]

Allianz, which is still bound by the district court's order, has continued with this appeal.

[The March 19 order amounted to an interlocutory injunction. It was not a mere scheduling order, nor was it the kind of temporary order that may be entered under FRCP 65 (covering TROs—temporary restraining orders—and preliminary injunctions, which can stay in place only for a short time). Because it amounted to an interlocutory injunction, the party bound by it can take an immediate appeal, and the appellate court has jurisdiction over such appeals under 28 USC §1291 (authorizing appeals over "interlocutory orders . . . granting, continuing, modifying, refusing, or dissolving injunctions"). An appellate court is "not bound by what a district court chooses to call an order," and can look instead to the "substantial effect" of an order. The March 19 order "enjoins Allianz from even discussing settlements" in the other pending cases if they "could affect any claims in this litigation," without obtaining permission from plaintiff's counsel or allowing plaintiff's counsel "to actually conduct the discussions," so it was in "practical effect" an injunction, "enforceable by contempt."]

DISCUSSION

Allianz argues that the injunction in question was not proper under the All Writs Act (28 USC §1651) and, even if it was, it was barred by the Anti-

Injunction Act (28 USC §2283) as far as state court proceedings are concerned. Both of those arguments depend on a determination that the injunction was directed against proceedings in other courts. Plainly it was.

Here, again, the mere form of the injunction does not describe its true reach. In form, it is directed to Allianz and Allianz's attorneys. In substance, it interferes with proceedings in other courts. As the Supreme Court stated in a case where a district court directed an injunction at a party but, in effect, stayed proceedings in a state court: "It is settled that the prohibition of §2283 cannot be evaded by addressing the order to the parties or prohibiting utilization of the results of a completed state proceeding." Atlantic Coast Line R.R. Co. v. Brotherhood of Locomotive Engineers, 398 U.S. 281 (1970). And, in response to an argument that the Anti-Injunction Act did not apply "because the district court order enjoins [a party] rather than the Tennessee proceeding itself" we replied that "[o]rdering the parties not to proceed is tantamount to enjoining the proceedings." Bennett v. Medtronic, Inc., 285 F.3d 801, 805 (9th Cir. 2002). The same is true here, and, while the cited cases apply to the Anti-Injunction Act, the principle is perfectly general. It applies to the All Writs Act as well, for it is the restraint on other court proceedings that is problematic.

With that said, the specific issues can now be considered.

A. THE ALL WRITS ACT

The All Writs Act provides that: "The Supreme Court and all courts established by Act of Congress may issue all writs necessary or appropriate in aid of their respective jurisdictions and agreeable to the usages and principles of law." 28 USC §1651(a). That is a broad, but not unlimited, grant of authority to federal courts, including the district court. As we have already noted, we review the district court's decision for an abuse of discretion. We are constrained to find that there was abuse here.

Much of what has been said in the Anti-Injunction Act area regarding state court cases, an area we discuss in part B of this opinion, applies here as well, and there is precious little authority dealing with injunctions directed by a district court to a court of equal dignity—another federal district court. A recent decision of the Third Circuit Court of Appeals says it all. There, a district court had enjoined proceedings in another district court. The court of appeals commented on the fact that injunctions of that nature directed at another district court, as opposed to a state court, are not typical. Indeed, they appear to be rarae aves; like us, the Third Circuit did not find any other appellate decisions on point. It said:

> Indeed, the lack of cases in which the All Writs Act has been used to enjoin settlement efforts in another federal court is telling. It is clear that the Act is generally used to prohibit activities in another court that threaten to undermine a pending settlement in the enjoining court. When the Act has been used to

block settlement efforts in another court, it is typically because a party was deliberately using that forum to circumvent a pending settlement agreement in the enjoining court.

Grider v. Keystone Health Plan Central, Inc., 500 F.3d 322, 330 (3d Cir. 2007) (citations omitted). The court then concluded:

> Based on the limited precedent in this area, there does not appear to be any basis for the injunction in this case. Although significant resources have been invested in [this] litigation to this point, there is simply no support for the proposition that a court may enjoin parties from participating in or reaching a bona fide settlement in another federal court that may dispose of claims before it—particularly when there is no pending settlement in the enjoining court and the other federal court is . . . charged with attempting to reach a global settlement.

Id. at 331 (footnote omitted).

We agree with that assessment and find that it has even more bite here. No settlement was directly in prospect in this case, and it could not, therefore, be said that a settlement was being circumvented or co-opted.[13] More than that, there were no facts before the district court that supported the notion that some kind of collusion was afoot. Negrete Counsel floated out the specter of a reverse auction, but brought forth no facts to give that eidolon more substance. A reverse auction is said to occur when "the defendant in a series of class actions picks the most ineffectual class lawyers to negotiate a settlement with in the hope that the district court will approve a weak settlement that will preclude other claims against the defendant." Reynolds v. Beneficial Nat'l Bank, 288 F.3d 277, 282 (7th Cir. 2002). It has an odor of mendacity about it. Even supposing that would be enough to justify an injunction of one district court by another one, there is no evidence of underhanded activity in this case. That being so, if Negrete's argument were accepted, the "reverse auction argument would lead to the conclusion that no settlement could ever occur in the circumstances of parallel or multiple class actions—none of the competing cases could settle without being accused by another of participating in a collusive reverse auction." Rutter & Wilbanks Corp. v. Shell Oil Co., 314 F.3d 1180, 1189 (10th Cir. 2002) (internal quotation marks omitted).

In short, the district court's order must be set aside. There simply was no proper support for the district court's enjoining of proceedings in other courts.

B. ANTI-INJUNCTION ACT

The district court's error in issuing the injunction was exacerbated by its reaching proceedings pending in the courts of Minnesota, and having the

---

[13] Incidentally, the mere fact that some other court might complete its proceedings before the district court was able to complete the proceedings in this case does not justify an injunction. See Vendo Co. v. Lektro-Vend Corp., 433 U.S. 623, 641-42 (1977).

potential of reaching proceedings in other state courts, if any are filed. That caused a further clash of jurisdictions that must be resolved.

The authority conferred upon federal courts by the All Writs Act is restricted by the Anti-Injunction Act, which is designed to preclude unseemly interference with state court proceedings. It declares that: "A court of the United States may not grant an injunction to stay proceedings in a State court except as expressly authorized by Act of Congress, or where necessary in aid of its jurisdiction, or to protect or effectuate its judgments." 28 USC §2283. Therefore, unless one of the exceptions applies, the district court erred when it issued the injunction in question here.[14]

At the outset, it is important to note that the Anti-Injunction Act restriction is based upon considerations of federalism and speaks to a question of high public policy. It is not a minor revetment to be easily overcome; it is a fortress which may only be penetrated through the portals that Congress has made available. As the Supreme Court has explained:

> On its face the present [Anti-Injunction] Act is an absolute prohibition against enjoining state court proceedings, unless the injunction falls within one of three specifically defined exceptions. The respondents here have intimated that the Act only establishes a "principle of comity," not a binding rule on the power of the federal courts. The argument implies that in certain circumstances a federal court may enjoin state court proceedings even if that action cannot be justified by any of the three exceptions. We cannot accept any such contention. In 1955 when this Court interpreted this statute, it stated: "This is not a statute conveying a broad general policy for appropriate *ad hoc* application. Legislative policy is here expressed in a clearcut prohibition qualified only by specifically defined exceptions." Amalgamated Clothing Workers v. Richman Bros., 348 U.S. 511, 515-516 (1955). Since that time Congress has not seen fit to amend the statute and we therefore adhere to that position and hold that any injunction against state court proceedings otherwise proper under general equitable principles must be based on one of the specific statutory exceptions to §2283 if it is to be upheld. Moreover since the statutory prohibition against such injunctions in part rests on the fundamental constitutional independence of the States and their courts, the exceptions should not be enlarged by loose statutory construction. Proceedings in state courts should normally be allowed to continue unimpaired by intervention of the lower federal courts, with relief from error, if any, through the state appellate courts and ultimately this Court.

Atlantic Coast Line R. Co. v. Brotherhood of Locomotive Engineers, 398 U.S. 281, 286-287 (1970). And, as the Supreme Court further stated, "[a]ny doubts as to the propriety of a federal injunction against state court proceedings should

---

[14] The phrase "proceedings in a State court" is, as the Supreme Court has said, "comprehensive. It includes all steps taken or which may be taken in the state court. . . ." Hill v. Martin, 296 U.S. 393, 403 (1935). Particularly in this day and age, that includes settlement proceedings, mediation proceedings, and the like.

be resolved in favor of permitting the state courts to proceed in an orderly fashion to finally determine the controversy." *Atlantic Coast Line.*

But is there an exception for this piece of class action litigation? Neither party contends that there is, or might be, an exception founded on an express authorization by Congress (there is no such authorization) or upon a need to protect or effectuate a judgment of the district court (there is no such judgment). That leaves the question of whether an injunction was necessary in aid of the district court's jurisdiction. *See* 28 USC §2283.

In general, the necessary-in-aid-of-jurisdiction exception applies to in rem proceedings where the federal court has jurisdiction over the res and the state court proceedings might interfere with that. But that principle does not authorize interference with parallel in personam state actions merely because the state courts might reach a conclusion before the district court does. The Court *has* said that there are times when "some federal injunctive relief may be necessary to prevent a state court from so interfering with a federal court's consideration or disposition of a case as to seriously impair the federal court's flexibility and authority to decide that case." *Atlantic Coast Line.* But, even then, the Court went on to point out that in the case before it "the state and federal courts had concurrent jurisdiction . . . , and neither court was free to prevent either party from simultaneously pursuing claims in both courts."

Nothing in this case changed that alchemy. In this proceeding, as in others, the mere fact that the actions of a state court might have some effect on the federal proceedings does not justify interference. As the Second Circuit has pointed out:

> Any time parallel state and federal actions are proceeding against the same defendant, it is conceivable that occurrences in the state action will cause delay in the federal action, by provoking motion practice in federal court regarding the effects of state court rulings, or simply by diverting the attention of the defendant. Such a rule [a rule that would allow an injunction to avoid delay] would in effect create an additional exception to the Anti-Injunction Act for circumstances where a federal court finds it *convenient* to enjoin related state proceedings—an approach contrary to the Supreme Court's direction that we construe doubts about the permissibility of an injunction "in favor of permitting the state courts to proceed in an orderly fashion to finally determine the controversy."

Retirement Systems of Alabama v. J.P. Morgan Chase & Co., 386 F.3d 419, 430 (2d Cir. 2004). And the mere fact that a state court may reach a conclusion that differs from what a federal court would prefer does not change the result. See Royal Insurance Co. of America v. Quinn-L Capital Corp., 960 F.2d 1286, 1298 (5th Cir. 1992). We see nothing in this case that would militate for a different determination here.

Courts have held that the existence of advanced federal in personam litigation may, in some instances, permit an injunction in aid of jurisdiction. That is a fairly common theme.[16] See In re Diet Drugs Products Liability Litigation, 282 F.3d 220, 239 (3d Cir. 2002) (MDL class action where class provisionally certified and settlement preliminarily approved); Hanlon v. Chrysler Corp., 150 F.3d 1011, 1018, 1024-1025 (9th Cir. 1998) (class action settlement preliminarily approved and state court action would opt out a whole subclass); In re Baldwin-United Corp., 770 F.2d 328, 337-338 (2d Cir. 1985) (MDL class action where class certified, settlement agreements reached, and only district court approval of those remained); Carlough v. Amchem Prods., Inc., 10 F.3d 189, 195, 202-204 (3d Cir. 1993) (class action where settlement imminent) [some case descriptions omitted].

But in less advanced cases, courts have been more chary about issuing injunctions, as, indeed, they should have been. For example, the Third Circuit has confronted an MDL action case where a state court was entertaining a settlement of a class action covering a class of General Motors truck owners, who alleged defective placement of fuel tanks, at the same time as an MDL class action on the same subject was before the district court. In re General Motors Corp. Pick-Up Truck Fuel Tank Products Liability Litigation, 134 F.3d 133, 137 (3d Cir. 1998). The court of appeals pointed out that no settlement had yet been approved by the MDL court, no provisional settlement was in hand, and no conditional class certification was extant. Therefore, the state court proceeding was not the kind of interference that could justify an injunction. The Second Circuit reached the same result in a similar, but more advanced, piece of litigation. There the district court was handling an MDL securities class action arising out of the collapse of WorldCom. See Retirement Systems of Alabama v. J.P. Morgan Chase & Co., 386 F.3d 419, 421 (2d Cir. 2004). The district court enjoined class action proceedings in an Alabama court arising out of the same collapse. That case had been moving toward trial, and the district court enjoined it from proceeding until after there was a trial in the federal class action. No class settlement in the MDL case was imminent, but the injunction was issued on the basis that district court trial dates should be protected. The court of appeals declared that the district court "has no interest—no interest that can be vindicated by the exercise of the federal injunction power—in being the *first* court to hold a trial on the merits." It, therefore, overturned the injunction. Retirement Systems of Alabama v. J.P. Morgan Chase & Co., 386 F.2d 419, 431 (2d Cir. 2004).

Here, none of the considerations that have induced courts to issue injunctions despite the strictures of the Anti-Injunction Act was present. This was not an MDL case; discovery was not complete; no class settlement was

---

[16] As the ensuing citations indicate, that has often arisen in multidistrict litigation (MDL) cases, which the case at hand is not.

imminent, in fact, as far as the record shows no serious settlement progress had been made; and, finally, there was no evidence of collusive procedures, reverse auction or otherwise, even assuming that the existence of those would justify an injunction of state proceedings.

CONCLUSION

The district court was troubled by the fact that settlements in other courts might draw the fangs from at least a portion of the class action case that it was then considering. Perhaps they will. But in this instance it was improper for the district court to react by issuing an injunction against other federal and state court proceedings.

Rather, the district court must live with the vicissitudes and consequences of our elegantly messy federal system. The restrictions inherent in the All Writs Act and explicit in the Anti-Injunction Act have helped to concinnate the elements of our national polity; this is not the time to disrupt the harmony.

REVERSED.

■ NOTES ON THE ANTI-INJUNCTION ACT

1. You have not looked at class suits (you will in Chapter 8), but you need to know a few things to appreciate what is happening in *Negrete*. First, class suits can lead to judgments that bind everyone in the class, even though only one (the "standard bearer") is actually a "party" in the full sense of the term. Second, class suits can only proceed as such if approved, or "certified," by the court. Third, the lawyer representing the class can negotiate a settlement, but court approval is required, and "fairness" hearings are necessary. If approval is given, the court enters judgment on the settlement. Fourth, the class lawyer's fee is paid out of any recovery. The court sets the fee, and its size depends at least in part on the result achieved. Fifth, multiple class suits can be filed, in state and federal courts in different locations, and these may duplicate one another or "overlap" in claims and class membership. In *Negrete*, such overlap appeared with the *Mooney* class in federal court in Minnesota and the *AG* class in state court in Minnesota.

2. Multiple and duplicative litigation is a fact of life in a country with 50 state court systems and a federal court system, where jurisdiction among states, and between the state and federal courts, often overlaps. The Supreme Court recognizes this fact in the *Vendo* case, invoked in *Negrete*.

(a) In *Vendo*, a company that acquired another company recovered a money judgment in state court against the controlling shareholder in the acquired company. The judgment rested on findings that he violated a

noncompetition agreement. Shortly after the state suit was brought, and while it was pending, the shareholder brought a reactive suit in federal court, claiming the noncompetition agreement violated federal antitrust law. The federal suit lay dormant, but after the state judgment was handed down the shareholder obtained an injunction in the federal suit barring enforcement of the state judgment. The Supreme Court reversed, applying the Anti-Injunction Act: "The traditional notion is that *in personam* actions in federal and state court may proceed concurrently, without interference from either court," and the Court has "never viewed parallel in personal actions as interfering with the jurisdiction of either court." Vendo Company v. Lectro-Vend Corp., 433 U.S. 623, 641 (1977) (plurality opinion).

(b) The Court in *Vendo* quoted earlier language from the *Kline* case expressing a similar sentiment: A suit to enforce personal liability "does not tend to impair or defeat the jurisdiction of the court in which a prior action for the same cause is pending," and each court is "free to proceed in its own way and in its own time, without reference to proceedings in the other court." The Court added that if one court enters judgment, a party in the other suit can notify the court and claim that the judgment blocks the other suit, and "the effect of that judgment is to be determined by application of the principles of res judicata." See Kline v. Burke Construction Co., 260 U.S. 226, 230 (1922). You will study *res judicata* (also called "claim preclusion") in Chapter 14, but basically the doctrine means that a judgment in one suit can block claims in another suit if they are the same, or arose out of the same transaction.

(c) In a federal system, in which state judicial jurisdiction overlaps with federal, the basic rules described in *Vendo* and *Kline* are almost to be expected. Would it be better to say the second-filed suit divests the court in the first suit of jurisdiction? Or to go the other way and say the first-filed suit blocks any other court from taking jurisdiction of the same suit later? If we opted for rules such as these, what would we do if, as in *Negrete*, the parties in the various suits overlapped but were not all the same (some suits included parties that were not in other suits)?

(d) To avoid some of these difficulties, courts sometimes take steps to *avoid* interfering with other litigation. Notice that the trial judge in *Negrete* certified a class in California, but "carved out the nationwide class certified in *Castello*." The court doesn't examine this point closely, but it means *at least* that some claims or parties brought in the *Castello* suit are not also being considered in the *Negrete* suit. Recall as well the abstention doctrine applied in *Pennzoil*, which similarly avoided a conflict between federal and state litigation.

3. In *Negrete*, a federal district court in California certified a nationwide federal question class suit challenging the practices of an insurance company in selling deferred annuities, invoking the RICO statute, and a statewide class action advancing claims under California statutes. Although the court avoided overlap with *Castello*, the certified classes overlapped classes in the *Mooney* suit in federal court in Minnesota and the *AG* suit in state court there. If those cases settled and judgments were entered on the settlements, those judgments would lead to motions to throw out some or all claims in the California suit, and would likely undermine the position of plaintiff's lawyer to negotiate a settlement in *Negrete* itself.

4. What if the shoe were on the other foot, so to speak? Suppose *defendant* in a federal class suit that is about to settle wants to stop *plaintiff* in a state suit from pursuing strategies that might derail the settlement? In the *Diet Drugs* case invoked in *Negrete*, for example, a nationwide federal class suit in Pennsylvania was on the verge of settlement when plaintiffs in a competing class suit in Texas state court asked the judge there to "opt out" those members of the Texas class that were also in the Pennsylvania nationwide class. Acting quickly, defendant in the Pennsylvania suit obtained an injunction barring the Texas plaintiffs from pursuing this motion, and the reviewing court approved. See In re Diet Drugs Product Liability Litigation, 282 F.3d 220 (3d Cir. 2002) (noting the extent to which suits can become enmeshed in "procedural entanglements," reviewing court approves injunction, invoking the exception in the AIA for injunctions "in aid of jurisdiction").

5. The court here considers the All Writs Act, codified as 28 USC §1651, which authorizes federal courts to "issue all writs necessary or appropriate in aid of their respective jurisdictions and agreeable to the usages and principles of law." The court treats this statute as authoritative in appraising the court's order as it impacts the *federal* suit in Minnesota, and concludes that the statute doesn't authorize the order. Why not?

6. The court also considers the AIA (28 USC §2283). The court treats this statute as authoritative in appraising the trial judge's order insofar as it impacts the *state* suit in Minnesota, and again concludes that the order is not authorized.[8] Why not?

7. *First Exception—Injunctions "Expressly Authorized."* As noted in the text prior to *Negrete*, this exception can apply (despite use of the word "expressly" in the AIA) even if the statute makes no reference to injunctions or to the AIA.

(a) A statute that you have often seen at work (42 USC §1983, which was the basis for the *Piphus* suit at the beginning of Chapter 1) fits the "expressly authorized" exception. See Mitchum v. Foster, 407 U.S. 225 (1972), which said that the critical question is whether a statute "clearly creating a federal right or remedy enforceable in a federal court of equity, could

---

[8] Originally, the statute made exception only for injunctions "authorized by any law relating to proceedings in bankruptcy" but courts did not think the statute barred antisuit injunctions where, as in *Negrete*, duplicative or reactive state litigation interfered with federal litigation. In the *Toucey* case in 1941, however, the Court concluded that the statute bars federal antisuit injunctions across the board, except where Congress authorized them expressly or where federal court jurisdiction entails possession of a *res* (and state litigation would undermine or interfere). See Toucey v. New York Life Ins. Co., 314 U.S. 118 (1941). *Toucey* prompted Congress to amend the statute by adopting the current wording. Post-amendment decisions interpreted the new exceptions broadly (lower courts treated the statute as embodying a loose notion of comity) until the Court in 1970 returned to a tough stance. In the *Atlantic Coast Line* case, the Court said that §2283 is "an absolute prohibition against enjoining state-court proceedings, unless the injunction falls within one of three specifically defined exceptions." Atlantic Coast Line R. Co. v. Brotherhood of Locomotive Engineers, 398 U.S. 281, 287 (1970).

be given its intended scope only by the stay of a state court proceeding." This interpretation paved the way for the federal court in New York in *Pennzoil* (Section C1, supra) to enjoin enforcement of the Texas judgment: Texaco had brought suit in New York under §1983, and the AIA did not block this injunction, although *Younger*-style abstention did.

(b) The interpleader act is another provision that has been construed as an "expressly authorized" exception. See 28 USC §2361. The purpose of interpleader, as you will learn in Chapter 8, is to enable a stakeholder to force all claimants seeking the same property or the same sum of money to fight it out between themselves in a single proceeding. You will read a case in which an insurance carrier obtained an injunction that blocked passengers injured in a collision involving a bus and a pickup truck from bringing separate suits against the various alleged tortfeasors. Ultimately, the Supreme Court ruled that the interpleader statute could not be used in this way, but the point here is that the interpleader statute would allow a federal court to enjoin ongoing state proceedings. See State Farm & Casualty Co. v. Tashire, 386 U.S. 523 (1967) (Chapter 8F, infra).

(c) In the *Vendo* case, the Court could not agree on the question whether a provision in the antitrust statutes authorizing private suits seeking "injunctive" and other relief was an express exception to the AIA. Two out of five in the majority thought the statute *sometimes* fit the exception, and four dissenters thought it always did, so apparently the statute *is* an exception but the criteria for being an exception remain unclear. See Vendo Co. v. Lektro-Vend Corp., 433 U.S. 623 (1977) (construing 15 USC §26).

8. *Second Exception—Injunctions "Necessary in Aid of [Federal Court] Jurisdiction."* It is this provision that the court construes in *Negrete,* and you see the result. An injunction is necessary in aid of jurisdiction only in cases *in rem,* where possession of a *res* is necessary to the work of the federal court. See Kline v. Burke Construction Co., 260 U.S. 226, 229 (1922) (in *in rem* suit where a federal court has "possession or control, actual or potential, of the res, and the exercise by the state court of jurisdiction over the same res necessarily impairs, and may defeat, the jurisdiction of the federal court," then the federal court may enjoin parties from proceeding in state court). And see Lankenau v. Coggeshall & Hicks, 350 F.3d 61 (1965) (enjoining state suit brought by creditor of broker because federal receiver had been appointed to take charge of assets of broker). In other cases, however, the exception has left courts in something of a quandary.

(a) In cases that do not involve court possession of property, if a federal court *cannot* enjoin the parties from going forward in state court, the fear is that a huge investment of energy in settling a suit may be frustrated. In addition to *Diet Drugs,* another case acting on this fear, also cited in *Negrete,* is In re Baldwin-United Corp., 770 F.2d 328, 337-338 (2d Cir. 1985) (enjoining state proceedings to protect class action formed after consolidation under multidistrict litigation statute, where federal class had been certified, and

parties had reached settlement agreements; and only district court approval remained).

(b) As a counter to this fear, one might reasonably ask, why shouldn't state litigation go forward? If the federal suit settles all the claims, the settlement can be pleaded in the state suit, can't it? If a state court reaches judgment first, can't the matter be pleaded in the federal suit as well? Or is the key in this situation that ongoing massive litigation is simply wasteful of judicial and private resources?

(c) Some have thought that the Class Action Fairness Act has the effect of making federal courts into the preferred forum or venue for large class suits, and that in this setting and some others it is time to rethink the scope of the exception. See Samuel Issacharoff & Richard A. Nagareda, *Class Settlements Under Attack*, 156 U. Pa. L. Rev. 1649 (2008) (federal judgments in class suits under CAFA should have greater preclusive effect, as federal courts represent the "congressionally preferred forum," and the possibility of antisuit injunctions make federal courts even more attractive for litigating large class suits).

9. *Third Exception—"To Protect or Effectuate [Federal Court] Judgments."* In three opinions, the Supreme Court gave a narrow construction to what is sometimes called the "relitigation exception" to the AIA.

(a) In *Parsons Steel* in 1986, plaintiffs in state court in Alabama were Parsons Steel and Jim and Melba Parsons. They sued a bank and one of its officers, alleging that the bank fraudulently induced plaintiffs to let a third person take control of a subsidiary of Parsons Steel. Plaintiffs later brought a parallel suit in federal court, alleging a claim under the Bank Holding Company Act. This suit went to trial, and the court entered judgment as a matter of law for defendants. The Alabama court, however, denied that the federal judgment was binding, and awarded plaintiffs $4 million. Defendants went back to federal court and got an injunction against enforcing the state judgment, but the Supreme Court reversed:

> [T]he Anti-Injunction Act and the Full Faith and Credit Act can be construed consistently, simply by limiting the relitigation exception of the Anti-Injunction Act to those situations in which the state court has not yet ruled on the merits of the res judicata issue. Once the state court has finally rejected a claim of res judicata, then the Full Faith and Credit Act becomes applicable and federal courts must turn to state law to determine the preclusive effect of the state court's decision.
>
> We hold, therefore, that the Court of Appeals erred by refusing to consider the possible preclusive effect, under Alabama law, of the state-court judgment. Even if the state court mistakenly rejected respondents' claim of res judicata, this does not justify the highly intrusive remedy of a federal-court injunction against the enforcement of the state-court judgment. Rather, the Full Faith and Credit Act requires that federal courts give the state-court judgment, and particularly the state court's resolution of the res judicata issue, the same preclusive effect it

would have had in another court of the same State. Challenges to the correctness of a state court's determination as to the conclusive effect of a federal judgment must be pursued by way of appeal through the state-court system and certiorari from this Court.

Parsons Steel, Inc. v. First Alabama Bank, 474 U.S. 518, 524-525 (1986). This decision means a litigant is bound, on principles of *res judicata,* by a state court holding (even if erroneous) that a prior federal judgment is not binding. It follows, does it not, that taking advantage of the relitigation exception to the AIA requires fast work by the victorious federal litigant? See Fernandez-Vargas v. Pfizer, 522 F.3d 55, 68 (1st Cir. 2008) (enjoining state proceedings; state court's rejection of preclusion defense would, under *Parsons Steel,* bar injunction later).

(b) Two years later, in the *Chick Kam Choo* case, the Court again considered the relitigation exception. This time the question was whether a federal court in Texas, after dismissing a suit by a resident of Singapore, could enjoin plaintiff from suing on the same claim in Texas state court. The federal dismissal rested on a decision that Singapore law applied (not state or federal law), and on the federal doctrine of *forum non conveniens.* Defendant argued that this *forum non conveniens* doctrine pre-empted state law as part of "federal maritime law." The Court brushed aside this claim, holding that defendant must *first* raise it in state court because the federal court had not decided the pre-emption issue. The federal court *did* decide, however, that Singapore law governed, so a *narrower* injunction might issue. In sum, the Court said that "an essential prerequisite for applying the relitigation exception is that the claims or issues which the federal injunction insulates from litigation in state proceedings actually have been decided by the federal court." See Chick Kam Choo v. Exxon Corp., 486 U.S. 140, 148, 150 (1988).

(c) In the *Bayer* case in 2011, the Supreme Court again took up the relitigation exception. Plaintiffs had brought a class action that was removed from state to federal court on the basis of diversity jurisdiction, alleging that defendant made and sold a defective drug. The suit was originally filed in West Virginia, but was consolidated after removal in federal court in Minnesota. Ultimately, the Minnesota federal court refused certification under FRCP 23 on the ground that the class of West Virginia consumers did not meet the requirement that common questions "predominate." A similar suit remained pending in West Virginia state court (unremovable because it included non-diverse defendants), and plaintiff sought class certification under West Virginia Rule 23, which (like its federal counterpart) required that common questions predominate. The Minnesota federal court ordered the West Virginia plaintiffs not to "relitigate" the certification question in West Virginia, on the ground that it was the same question resolved in the Minnesota federal court. The Supreme Court reversed, concluding that even though the federal and state standard for class certification were substantially identical, the West Virginia standard had been interpreted as meaning something different from

the federal standard, so the question being litigated in West Virginia state court was *not* the same as the question resolved in federal court in Minnesota. See Smith v. Bayer Corp., 131 S. Ct. 2368 (2011). The Seventh Circuit had done something similar in the *Bridgestone* case, but the Court in *Bayer* expressly disapproved the holding in *Bridgestone.* See Bridgestone/Firestone, Inc. Prods. Liab. Litig, 333 F.3d 763 (7th Cir. 2003) (injunction blocking plaintiffs from filing similar class suit in state court after federal court had held class treatment inappropriate).

(*d*) Ever since the decision in *Chick Kam Choo,* federal courts have split on the question whether the relitigation exception can be invoked to enforce *res judicata* in its broad dimensions (claim preclusion), or only to enforce what we usually call "collateral estoppel" (issue preclusion), which is much narrower. You will look at these doctrines in Chapter 14, but for the moment you should understand that *res judicata* bars a litigant from raising claims that *could have been* part of the first suit because they arose from the "same transaction," while collateral estoppel operates only to bar a litigant from relitigating *facts actually found* in the first suit. Invoking the phrase in *Chick Kam Choo* referring to "claims or issues" that "actually have been decided," most courts think *Chick Kam Choo* carries the latter meaning. Compare Jones v. St. Paul Companies, Inc., 495 F.3d 888 (8th Cir. 2007) (plaintiff lost race discrimination claim against employer in federal court, then sued in state court alleging tortious interference with contractual relations; court declines to enjoin state suit, adopting "narrower construction" in which relitigation exception covers only claims actually decided) with Western Systems, Inc. v. Ulloa, 958 F.3d 864, 870 (9th Cir. 1992) (to adopt the narrow reading of *Chick Kam Choo* is "to read res judicata entirely out of section 2283").

10. The Anti-Injunction Act applies *only* to federal court injunctions against state court proceedings, and does not regulate efforts by a state court to block litigation in another court of the same or another state, nor efforts by a federal court to block litigation in other federal courts.

(*a*) State courts do enjoin litigants from proceeding with suits in other jurisdictions, and in foreign countries. See, e.g., Golden Rule Ins. Co. v. Harper, 925 S.W.2d 649, 651 (Tex. 1996) (antisuit injunction is appropriate to "address a threat to the court's jurisdiction" or to "prevent the evasion of important public policy" or to "prevent a multiplicity of suits," or to "protect a party from vexatious or harassing litigation") (injunction against litigating in Illinois).

(*b*) Federal courts do much the same thing. See, e.g., William Gluckin & Co. v. International Playtex Corp., 407 F.2d 177, 178 (2d Cir. 1969) (federal court in New York enjoins Playtex, which had brought patent infringement suit in Georgia, from continuing to press the Georgia suit).

(*c*) In general, courts follow a "first-in-time" rule under which the court that first gets a case continues with it. Other courts stay proceedings filed later, or the first court enjoins the continuation of later-filed proceedings. But the first-filed rule admits of exceptions too. See generally Employers Insurance of Wausau v. Fox Entertainment Group, Inc., 522 F.3d 271, 275

(2d Cir. 2008) (court reviews district court's decision "to apply or depart from the first-filed rule for an abuse of discretion," and relevant factors include plaintiff's choice of forum, convenience of witnesses, location of relevant documents and ease of access to proof, convenience of parties, locus of operative facts, availability of process to compel attendance of witnesses, and relative means of the parties).

11. Courts are reluctant to interfere in each other's business. See, e.g., Grider v. Keystone Health Plan Central, Inc., 500 F.3d 322, 331 (3d Cir. 2007) (judge in class suit under federal statute in federal court in Pennsylvania erred in enjoining defendants from settling overlapping class suit pending in federal court in Florida; although "significant resources" have been expended in the Pennsylvania case, "there is simply no support for the proposition that a court may enjoining parties from participating in or reaching a bona fide settlement in another federal court that may dispose of the claims before it—particularly when there is no pending settlement in the enjoining court and the other court is an MDL court charged with attempting to reach a global settlement").

 ## D INTERSYSTEM EFFECTS—STATE DEFERENCE TO FEDERAL COURTS

Recall what you have already learned, in Chapter 1 and this chapter, about the effects on state courts of federal law and federal court decrees.

In connection with the substance-procedure distinction, recall that state courts in applying federal law must *sometimes* also apply certain federal procedures. You read the *Dice* case in this chapter, which deals with this subject. In connection with the second point (supremacy/pre-emption), recall that state courts must often apply federal substantive law, as in the *Lavender* case in Chapter 1 and for that matter the *Dice* case in this chapter: Both suits were brought in state court under FELA. And you looked at Problem 1-A ("We're in Compliance with Federal Law"), where the question was whether state law could operate even in an environment largely regulated by the federal Motor Vehicle Safety Act (the answer was yes). We will take up the matter of finality/full faith (the fourth point in the conversation) in Chapter 14.

There remains for us the matter of intersystem coordination or accommodation, as it appears in state courts. Not surprisingly, there are few examples of state courts attempting to enjoin litigants from proceeding in the federal system. But sometimes it happens.

In litigation arising out of a project to enlarge Love Field (municipal airport in Dallas), for example, a state court rejected challenges by adjacent property owners. Plaintiffs filed a similar suit in federal court, and the defense moved to dismiss on ground of *res judicata* arising from the state court judgment. Simultaneously, however, defendant asked the Texas Court of Civil Appeals for an injunction restraining plaintiffs from proceeding in federal court. That court denied the request, thinking it lacked power to enjoin litigants from proceeding in federal court. On appeal, however, the Texas Supreme Court held to the contrary, and the Court of Appeals then did issue the injunction. The case then went to the United States Supreme Court, which decided that the Texas Court of Appeals was right the first time:

> Early in the history of our country a general rule was established that state and federal courts would not interfere with or try to restrain each other's proceedings. That rule has continued substantially unchanged to this time. An exception has been made in cases where a court has custody of property, that is, proceedings in rem or quasi in rem. In such cases this Court has said that the state or federal court having custody of such property has exclusive jurisdiction to proceed. Princess Lida v. Thompson, 305 U.S. 456, 465-468 (1939). In *Princess Lida* this Court said "where the judgment sought is strictly in personam, both the state court and the federal court, having concurrent jurisdiction, may proceed with the litigation at least until judgment is obtained in one of them which may be set up as res judicata in the other." See also Kline v. Burke Construction Co., 260 U.S. 226 (1922). It may be that a full hearing in an appropriate court would justify a finding that the state-court judgment in favor of Dallas in the first suit barred the issues raised in the second suit, a question as to which we express no opinion. But plaintiffs in the second suit chose to file that case in the federal court. They had a right to do this, a right which is theirs by reason of congressional enactments passed pursuant to congressional policy. And whether or not a plea of res judicata in the second suit would be good is a question for the federal court to decide. While Congress has seen fit to authorize courts of the United States to restrain state-court proceedings in some special circumstances, it has in no way relaxed the old and well-established judicially declared rule that state courts are completely without power to restrain federal-court proceedings in in personam actions like the one here. And it does not matter that the prohibition here was addressed to the parties rather than to the federal court itself.

Donovan v. City of Dallas, 377 U.S. 408, 412-423 (1964). See also General Atomic Power v. Feltner, 434 U.S. 12 (1977) (error for state court to enjoin General Atomic Company from filing and prosecuting actions against United Nuclear Corp. in federal court; "the rights conferred by Congress to bring *in personam* actions in federal courts are not subject to abridgment by state-court injunctions," regardless whether federal suit is pending or not); General Atomic Power v. Feltner, 436 U.S. 493 (1978) (state court "has again done precisely what we held that it lacked the power to do" in the prior *General Atomic* opinion; Supreme Court here assumes that state court "will now conform to our previous judgment by promptly vacating or modifying its order," and for that reason will not "at present" issue a writ of mandamus).

■ NOTES ON STATE COURT INTERFERENCE WITH FEDERAL PROCEEDINGS

1. It is easier to express a "gut feeling" that state courts lack power to enjoin litigation in federal court than it is to explain why. How would you explain it? By saying the Supremacy Clause means state courts cannot behave in this way? The Supremacy Clause covers federal *law,* doesn't it, not litigation? Or does the Supremacy Clause "get in the back door," so to speak, because *Congress* authorized federal suits when the requirements of diversity or federal question litigation are satisfied? In the first of the two decisions in the *Feltner* case, cited above, the Court invoked the Supremacy Clause. See General Atomic Power v. Feltner, 434 U.S. 12, 15 (1977) (state court injunction "is in direct conflict with [*Donovan*] and the Supremacy Clause"). There are problems with enforcing injunctions if they purport to govern behavior outside the state, but that issue didn't arise in *Donovan* because the federal litigation was also in Texas. In fact, James Donovan was the lawyer for plaintiffs, and he served 20 days in a Texas jail for *refusing* to abide by the order of the Texas Court of Appeals (prior to the reversal by the Supreme Court in the opinion quoted above). In *Donovan,* 86 other litigants were fined $200 apiece for violating the injunction (a total of $17,200).

2. In *Donovan,* there was a dissenting opinion. Justice Harlan, writing for himself and Justices Clark and Stewart, thought a court of equity could always enjoin litigants from vexatiously pursuing collateral litigation elsewhere. See *Donovan,* 377 U.S. at 408, 415 (power of court in equity to enjoin parties before it from conducting "vexatious and harassing" litigation elsewhere "has not been doubted until now").

3. *Donovan* acknowledged an "exception" to the general rule against enjoining proceedings in other courts for cases where a court "has custody of property," which it describes as "proceedings in rem or quasi in rem." Apparently, *Donovan* means that this exception is also an exception to the general principle against state injunctions of ongoing federal litigation. For a couple of exceptional and rare instances where state appellate courts upheld injunctions in this setting, see Commissioner of Insurance v. Arcilio, 561 N.W.2d 412 (Mich. App. 1997) (in connection with reorganization of insolvent company, enjoining class actions in federal court); Meridian Investing & Dev. Corp. v. Suncoast Highland, 388 So. 2d 8 (Fla. App. 1980) (where holder of federal judgment brought suit on judgment in Florida state court, and sought to enforce it by suing in federal court, state court enjoined plaintiff from doing so; the action is "at least quasi in rem," and state court therefore "acquired exclusive jurisdiction over the creditor's assets with power to shield them from forays originating in all other forums"). See also Princess Lida of Thurn and Traxis v. Thompson, 305 U.S. 456, 465-466 (1939) (two *in rem* suits cannot go forward at once, and "the jurisdiction of one court must yield to that of the other," which applies "to both federal and state courts," and the first to obtain jurisdiction "may maintain and exercise that jurisdiction to the exclusion of the other"). It may be that insurance cases are special in this connection, as federal law contains what is sometimes described as a "reverse-pre-emption" clause barring federal interference with state regulation of insurance. See 15 USC §1012 (no federal statute "shall be construed to invalidate, impair, or supersede any law enacted by any State for the purpose of regulating the business of insurance"). But see Appleton Papers, Inc. v. Home Indemnity Co., 612 N.W.2d 760 (Wis. App. 2000) (refusing to issue injunction in insurance litigation despite statute quoted above).

CHAPTER 7

Stating Claims and Defenses: The Art of Pleading

INTRODUCTION

Pleading in its modern usage refers to the documents that frame a lawsuit at the outset of litigation. The plaintiff files a complaint setting out his claims, the defendant an answer setting out her defenses. As you will discover, there was a trend in American procedure for almost a century to de-emphasize pleading, in the belief that decisions "on the merits" (at least "later in the game") are preferable to early decisions on pleadings alone. In the last decades, however, there has been a shift back toward stricter pleading requirements.

More importantly, pleadings have not been abolished, and they count for a number of reasons. First, cases are sometimes won or lost at the pleading stage. Second, careful pleading can map out a lawsuit so lawyers and courts can quickly learn what is at issue. Third, effective pleading of claims or defenses based on modern statutes or theories is a task that presents considerable challenge. Fourth, in an important development in the closing decades of the last century, concerns over cost led to new emphasis on the obligations of lawyers and parties (backed by sanctions) to ensure that pleadings are well founded. Finally, as noted above, there has been renewed interest in disposing of some cases early by enforcing stricter pleading requirements.

A   PRE-RULES TRADITIONS

Modern American pleading conventions descend from the common law writ system. That system began in England about a century before the Norman Conquest in 1066 and developed gradually for centuries after that.

The writ system came with the king's courts. Originally, the Curia Regis (King's Council) consisted of a group of lords, advisors, and other hangers-on who traveled with the King and served administrative functions. In its earliest days, the Curia Regis did not function as a court deciding what we would call lawsuits. Civil and criminal cases were heard in communal and manorial courts, the former organized along the lines of towns or counties (hundreds or shires) and the latter run by wealthy landowners in the feudal system. Gradually, the Curia Regis grew into the precursors of treasury (Exchequer), legislature (Parliament) and judicial system (Chancery).

In the beginning, the Chancellor prepared documents, granted land titles and privileges, and conducted other administrative functions, but even before the Conquest he handled some criminal matters through local sheriffs. By the middle of the thirteenth century, the King had established both a central court (Chancery) and what we might call a visitorial court system run by circuit-traveling judges who met in special "assizes" (or sittings) to resolve problems or disputes.

In the Norman period (eleventh century forward), royal authority in visitorial courts was routinized. First in criminal matters tried at what came to be called King's Bench, then also in civil cases tried at what came to be called Common Pleas, the King's courts gradually displaced communal and manorial courts. This process was complete by the time of Edward I (1272-1307). Behavior leading to criminal and civil disputes came to be understood as involving breaches of the King's Peace, and the judges of the King's courts came to be professional men with experience and education as subordinate officers of the Chancellor. With the Conquest came the beginnings of what we now call trial by jury. While the earliest juries were people we would now call witnesses (summoned not to find or determine facts, but to give evidence), these beginnings led to the modern factfinding jury, which was in place in the common law courts by the fifteenth century.

1. The Writ System: Pigeon Holes and Technicality

With the coming of the Norman Kings, litigants began to seek writs from the King (or his Chancellor) directing communal or manorial courts to do justice in the matter that had arisen. The writ came to be a formal requirement, and it was directed to the King's courts. In crucial innovations by Henry II (1154-1189), actions involving rights to land came to be tried in special or grand assizes commenced by specific writs.

The salient feature of the system was that each writ dealt specifically with a particular cause, and Henry's property writs were the beginning. Afterwards came writs for the following: (1) trespass, which was designed not only for intrusions on land, but to secure damages for injury to person or property caused by direct or immediate force (like hitting or burning), (2) case (or trespass on the case), which was the precursor of the modern negligence suit where injuries to person or property resulted indirectly from defendant's action (leaving an obstruction on the road causing an accident), (3) covenant, under which one could recover damages for breach of a contract under seal, (4) debt, which supported recovery of a specific sum under an express agreement, (5) general assumpsit, which was a suit for damages from nonperformance of what we would now call an implied promise in an unsealed (usually oral understanding), where the purpose was to prevent unjust enrichment, (6) special assumpsit, which was a suit for not performing an express promise in an unsealed (usually oral) understanding, (7) detinue, which was a suit to recover chattels from one who had lawfully acquired them but retained them without right, (8) replevin, which was an action to recover goods unlawfully taken, and (9) trover, which was a suit for damages for finding and converting another's goods.

Pleadings existed even before the writ system appeared. The earliest pleadings involved oral disputations that were formalized and formulaic. Before the Conquest in 1066, court clerks began to record these pleadings, and pleaders learned to speak words that produced the record they wanted. With the writs and common law forms of action came technicality and formalism. The writ began and shaped the suit, and pleadings fleshed it out: Plaintiff made a declaration that had to fit the relief contemplated by the writ (a task that grew more complicated as the number of writs increased and boundaries blurred), and had to attain a certain level of particularity while avoiding certain pitfalls.

Defendant could reply in various ways. By *special demurrer*, he could argue that a crucial detail (like quantity of goods sold) had been omitted. By a *dilatory plea*, defendant could raise such technicalities as whether the action was in the right court. By a *plea in abatement*, defendant could claim that plaintiff lacked capacity to sue, or erred in misjoinder or nonjoinder of parties (naming parties who didn't belong or omitting parties who did). By a *peremptory plea* (or plea in bar), defendant could attack the heart of the claim by suggesting, for example, that the matter had been heard and already decided. One such plea was the *general demurrer*, which asserted that a crucial element was missing and that plaintiff could not recover at all, even assuming the truth of the declaration. Another was the *traverse*, which denied a crucial allegation (special traverse) or denied all the allegations (general traverse). Finally, defendant could make a *plea of confession and avoidance*, which assumed that the declaration was correct but raised some new point that should block recovery (like statute of limitations).

Formalism lay at the heart of the writ system and evolving conventions of pleading, which was already a high art in the fifteenth century. See Littleton,

Tenures §534 (1481) (extolling "science of well-pleading," author counsels son "especially to employ thy courage and care to learn it"). In their pleadings, litigants were to produce a single triable issue, and this reductive task led to more and more technical requirements:

The dominant precept developed to effectuate this objective was that the "facts" be alleged with certainty. Three subordinate rules—that pleadings not be duplicitous, repugnant, or stated in the alternative—tended to the "chief object," which was that "the parties be brought to issue, and that the issue be material, single and certain in its quality." Apologists supported the requirement with arguments about economy and expedience: The decision of one material issue would dispose of the controversy, so it was unnecessary to consider more.[1]

The rule against "duplicitous" pleading meant that one could not seek the same relief on different grounds. That meant, for example, that a plaintiff who hired workers to perform a task and was damaged because the work was done carelessly might sue for breach of contract, but could not also advance a claim for negligence—at least not in the same suit. The requirement to avoid "repugnance" meant that a pleading was bad if it contained contradictions. The rule against alternative pleadings meant that a claimant could not allege that one or another thing happened. Thus it was unacceptable to plead that the defendant ran over the plaintiff either because defendant was going too fast or because he wasn't looking where he was going. A similar prohibition said that "hypothetical" pleading was no good. Plaintiff could not allege that "if" the reins were loose, defendant's horse went too fast, or that if defendant wasn't watching where he was going, he didn't rein in the horse in time.

Important ensuing developments proceeded along three lines:

First, as early as the fifteenth century, the Chancellor began to exercise equity jurisdiction, providing alternatives where common law writs were unsatisfactory. In areas like trusts or "uses" (where the original purpose was to avoid outmoded feudal dues or taxes when a landowner died), enforcing contracts by remedies like specific performance; granting relief from contractual and other obligations on ground of fraud, mistake, or accident; providing remedies that required an accounting of a series of transactions; and ordering parties to do or not to do things (injunctions), equity grew in influence and importance.[2]

Procedure in equity differed sharply from common law procedure in three particulars, one having continuing importance. In the first place, pleading in equity was simpler than its common law counterpart, and it was possible to

---

[1] Roy W. McDonald, *Alternative Pleading*, 48 Mich. L. Rev. 311, 314-315 (1948) (quoting 1945 treatise, and adding ruefully that the supposed virtues of this system could be accepted only if one "did not inquire too closely" into justness of outcome).

[2] Omitted from this bland account is a description of feuds and conflicts between the Chancellor and common law judges, which came to a head in the seventeenth century in the fight between Lords Coke and Ellesmere.

join parties more or less freely. Pleading equitable causes involved what was called a *bill* alleging facts and seeking relief. The parties needed not craft their pleadings in accord with the forms of common law writs, nor worry as much about misjoinder or nonjoinder of parties, nor reduce their dispute to a single issue. In the second place, parties in equitable suits could file bills requesting depositions (sworn statements by parties and witnesses), which was the beginning of modern discovery. In this way, parties could come to trial armed with factual information developed under the auspices of the court, which forced parties to be more forthcoming. In the third place, equitable suits were tried to a judge (originally the Chancellor, whose name is still invoked as a veritable synonym for equitable jurisprudence). There was no right to a jury trial in suits tried in equity, and this distinction between what we call legal and equitable causes still figures in American law (see Chapter 12).

A second major development was the appearance of common counts. In what were seen as simple oft-repeated situations, claimants could resort to abbreviated pleadings. These included money counts (money lent to defendant; money paid on his behalf), debt counts (goods sold and delivered; work done for a price), and value counts in "quantum meruit" (seeking reasonable value of work) or "quantum valebant" (seeking reasonable value of goods).

The third major development was modern reforms. As early as 1585, an Elizabethan statute required defendants challenging defects in the form of a declaration to be specific and provided that failing to challenge formal defects waived objection to them. While the earliest conventions allowed plaintiffs to combine in one suit only those claims that rested on the same form of action, eventually it became possible to combine different forms of action by way of separate counts. Similar choices of defenses became available, at least when defendants filed separate pleas. And the Hilary Rules in 1834 sought to end the general traverse by requiring particular denials.

If success in pleading reform means simplification and removal of obstacles to trial, these reforms did not accomplish their task. Writing in 1852, Charles Dickens in *Bleak House* issues an indictment of a system that allowed a fictional will contest in Jarndyce v. Jarndyce to drag on for 34 years, bankrupting the estate while enriching only the lawyers.

2. Code Pleading: The Modern Cause of Action

English procedural conventions came with the colonists to America. In both state and federal systems, courts were divided between law and equity. On both continents, by the eighteenth century this division did not mean different buildings or judges (as it originally meant in England), but it meant suits were either legal or equitable (one suit could not be both). And in this country a complaint (new name for the declaration) still had to satisfy formal standards drawn from English common law tradition: It had to reflect a particular legal theory, attain a certain level of particularity, and avoid uncertainty and inconsistency.

The first of the two great American reform efforts began in New York, which adopted the Field Code in 1848. The Field Code merged law and equity into one system, which meant a single suit could involve claims and defenses in both law and equity. The Code continued the emphasis on pleadings as a way of controlling and defining the dispute, but also sought to simplify pleadings and allow limited use of depositions to gather information. Many states followed New York, and in the twenty-first century some of the largest states (New York, Illinois, Texas, and California) are still "Code jurisdictions."

As originally conceived, Code pleading reflected the rationalist spirit of the Enlightenment. Plaintiffs were to allege "facts" comprising a "cause of action," not "conclusions" or "evidence." Two aims lay behind these bland words: One was to discard technicalities and formalism in favor of simplicity and directness. The other was to discard the preference for separate pleading conventions, each relating to a specific kind of claim, in favor of what we now call a "trans-substantive" standard that applies to all pleadings.

In one sense the Field Code fell short, for distinguishing between facts and conclusions or evidence was virtually impossible. Consider an example: In a negligence case, an allegation that defendant drove his blue Ford Fusion car faster than the posted limit of 35 mph could be viewed as alleging fact, evidence, or conclusion. Such allegations have the particularity that the term "fact" suggests. But driving faster than the speed limit could be called "evidence" of negligence, and identifying the car seems also to be evidence—one would expect a witness to describe the car by make, model, color, and appearance, but these points do not bear on the merits of the claim. The allegation of speed also seems "conclusory" in that it embodies (appears to embody) a subjective judgment on speed (presumably plaintiff can only give an estimate). And can you think of a way to allege proximate cause that does not use a conclusory term like "cause" or "result"?

The Code categories (facts, evidence, conclusions) depend on the observer's vantage point, and it is hard to locate the right perspective. Also, the categories overlap and cannot be assigned bright lines (perhaps that's just another way to make the same point). In various ways during the first half of the twentieth century, commentators argued that the lines marked out by Code pleading were illusory. Compare Clarence Morris, *Law and Fact*, 55 Harv. L. Rev. 1303, 1329 (1942) (propositions of fact are "descriptive," propositions of law "dispositive," since one is a statement of history and the other assigns "legal significance" to history; useful propositions of fact must be relevant, and relevancy "depends on legal considerations," so distinction "is not as easy as it seems") with Walter W. Cook, *Statements of Fact in Pleading Under the Codes*, 21 Colum. L. Rev. 416, 416-419, 422 (1921) (facts that count are specific rather than generic, but pleading facts specifically would be called pleading evidence; one may err by pleading evidence, but that just means pleading too specifically; there is no logical distinction between what courts call facts and what they call conclusions, the latter being too generic as gauged by notions of fairness and convenience).

Consider now a case raising the question whether plaintiff has adequately pled that defendant owed a duty of care.

REILLY v. HIGHMAN

Supreme Court of Kansas
345 P.2d 652 (1959)

PRICE, Justice.

This appeal is from an order sustaining a demurrer to a petition in an action for damage to an automobile.

Defendant Lawrence lives on Louisiana Street in Lawrence. Defendant Highman was engaged in removing a tree from Lawrence's yard. It fell into the street just as plaintiff's son drove by in plaintiff's automobile. It struck the car causing damage. Plaintiff sued both Lawrence and Highman.

Because of the question involved, the petition, omitting formal parts, is set out in full:

Comes now the plaintiff and for his cause of action alleges:

1. That he is a resident of Leavenworth County, Kansas and resides at Leavenworth, Kansas; that the defendant James Highman is a resident of Douglas County, Kansas and resides at 1047 1/2 Delaware Street, Lawrence, Kansas; that the defendant George W. Lawrence is a resident of Douglas County, Kansas, and resides as 2101 Louisiana Street, Lawrence, Kansas.

2. That at all the times hereinafter mentioned the plaintiff was the owner of a 1956 Mercury car.

3. Plaintiff states that on May 8, 1957, the defendant Highman was engaged in removing trees from the front yard of the premises owned by the defendant Lawrence at 2101 Louisiana Street in Lawrence, Kansas. Plaintiff further states that about 2:45 P.M. on said day his son was driving plaintiff's car west on Louisiana Street and that as he was driving past the Lawrence premises, the defendant Highman, his agents and employees felled a tree in the front yard of the Lawrence premises and said tree fell out into Louisiana and onto the passing car of the plaintiff, causing severe damage to plaintiff's vehicle.

4. Plaintiff states that the proximate cause of the accident and damage to plaintiff's vehicle was due to the negligence of the defendant Highman in the following respects:

(a) Failing to have men or road signs out on Louisiana Street so as to warn passing motorists and the plaintiff's driver in particular, of the danger.

(b) By causing said tree to fall into the street when he knew or should have known it would strike plaintiff's passing vehicle.

(c) Failing to use sufficient men and equipment so as to fall said tree away from the street instead of into it, when they knew or should have known it would strike plaintiff's vehicle.

5. That because of the intrinsically dangerous work, to wit: removing and falling large trees right near the public streets the owner of the premises, the defendant Lawrence, was obligated to see that said work was carefully performed and because of the fact that said work was not carefully performed in a workmanlike manner, defendant Lawrence is also liable to this plaintiff for the negligence of the defendant Highman.

6. That as a result of the negligence of the defendants, plaintiff's vehicle was damaged in the amount of $269.39.

Wherefore, the plaintiff prays for judgment against the defendant for $269.39 and costs.

Defendant Lawrence demurred to the petition on the ground it failed to state a cause of action as to him.

This demurrer was sustained and plaintiff was given fifteen days in which to amend. Instead of amending he has appealed.

The record is silent as to any pleadings being filed by defendant Highman, and he is not a party to this appeal. . . . [T]he real question is whether this petition states a cause of action against defendant Lawrence, the owner of the premises from which the tree was being removed by defendant Highman.

As noted by the trial court, and we think it will be conceded, Lawrence could be obligated, if at all, only in the event he had employed Highman in some capacity to remove the tree. For all the petition alleges, Highman may have been an employee of the city engaged in removing a diseased tree, or, for that matter, may have been a trespasser. The petition of course "assumes" some sort of employment relationship between Lawrence and Highman, but that is as far as it goes.

In his brief plaintiff concedes the petition does not allege the relationship of agent, servant or employee, but contends it does allege that of employer and independent contractor—that is, Lawrence was the contractee and Highman the contractor. We will, for purposes of discussion, assume that such is the fact.

. . .

In the leading case of Laffery v. United States Gypsum Co., 111 P. 498 (Kan. 1910), it was held:

> The general rule is that when a person lets out work to another, the contractee reserving no control over the work or workmen, the relation of contractor and contractee exists, and not that of master and servant, and the contractee is not liable for the negligence or improper execution of the work by the contractor.
>
> To the foregoing rule there are many exceptions and limitations, one of which is that an owner, or a contractee is responsible for injuries to a third party, caused by work done by an independent contractor where the contract

directly requires the performance of work intrinsically dangerous, however skillfully done.

The rule of the *Laffery* case has been recognized and adhered to in numerous later decisions. [The court cites five Kansas decisions.]

Starting, then, with the premise as contended for by plaintiff—that the relationship of contractee and contractor is pleaded—application of the rule means that Lawrence, the contractee, would not be liable to plaintiff for the negligence of Highman, the contractor, unless the employment related to work which was inherently and intrinsically dangerous.

On the question of what type of work is or is not considered to be inherently or intrinsically dangerous, courts have found no rule of universal application by which they may abstractly draw a line of classification in every case. Generally speaking, the proper test is whether danger "inheres" in performance of the work, and important factors to be understood and considered are the contemplated conditions under which the work is to be done and the known circumstances attending it. It is not enough that it may possibly produce injury. Stated another way, intrinsic danger in an undertaking is one which inheres in the performance of the contract and results directly from the work to be done—not from the collateral negligence of the contractor.

To the same effect is the *Laffery* case, above, where, in considering the test, it was held:

> The mere liability to injury from doing the work contracted for cannot be the test, for injuries may happen in any undertaking, and many are attended with great danger if carelessly managed, although with proper care they are not specially hazardous.
>
> The intrinsic danger of the undertaking upon which the exception is based is a danger which inheres in the performance of the contract, resulting directly from the work to be done, and not from the collateral negligence of the contractor.

So much for the basic rule and mentioned exception—in cases where third parties are injured by the alleged negligence of an independent contractor.

The question here—assuming, for the sake of argument, the relationship of contractee and contractor is pleaded—is whether plaintiff has pleaded sufficient facts to bring himself within the exception relating to work inherently and intrinsically dangerous.

Paragraph 5 of the petition merely refers to "removing and falling large trees right near the public streets" as being "intrinsically dangerous work," which, standing alone, amounts to nothing more than a conclusion. The mere statement that doing a certain thing is "intrinsically dangerous" does not constitute a factual statement which justifies the conclusion. As was said in the *Laffery* case and other authorities cited above, an undertaking cannot be termed inherently dangerous merely because it may *possibly* produce injury—rather, the intrinsic danger of the work upon which the exception is based is danger which *inheres* in its performance resulting directly from the work to be done, and not from the negligence of the contractor.

Our code (G.S. 1949, 60-704) provides that a petition must contain a statement of the *facts* constituting the cause of action in ordinary and concise language. In Preston v. Shields, 156 P.2d 543 (Kan. 1945), it was held that it is the duty of the pleader to state the premises in clear and concise language, and that it is the province of the court to declare the conclusions.

With respect to the point here involved, allegations of the petition are clearly insufficient to state a cause of action against defendant Lawrence and his demurrer was properly sustained.

The judgment is affirmed.

■ NOTES ON PLEADING A CAUSE OF ACTION UNDER THE CODE

1. In *Reilly,* the defendant George Lawrence filed a *demurrer* to the complaint. What is the function of a demurrer? Consider this description:

> When a pleading meets with a demurrer, predicated upon a contention of insufficient facts, it is accepted as a true statement of the controversy, and thereupon the sole judicial labor that remains to be performed is to apply the law to the facts set forth in the pleading. But a party who elects to submit his case upon his pleading must make certain that his house is in order and that his pleading is couched in language which conforms to the established rules of pleading. Those rules do not tolerate conclusions. Conclusions are terms which do not delineate the facts; they go no further than to recite the pleader's reactions to, or the inferences he draws from, undisclosed facts. Conclusions are ignored when a pleading is tested by a demurrer. They are deemed by the courts as unsafe premises upon which to base judicially-awarded relief. When a pleading is tested in that manner, there are counted in its favor only the facts that are well pleaded. Although we said that a demurrer tests the pleading, it, in truth, tests the pleader's alleged facts, and in that test nothing passes as a fact unless it is expressed in 'plain and concise language.' A conclusion is not deemed plain language.

Baker Community Hotel Co. v. Hotel & Restaurant Employees & Bartenders International League, Local 161, 207 P.2d 1129, 1131 (Or. 1949). In *Reilly,* the court seems to be looking for properly alleged "facts," giving short shrift to the allegation that tree trimming was "intrinsically dangerous" because that is just a "conclusion." Did Edward Reilly's lawyer make a mistake? What would you add?

2. Why require specificity in a complaint? Consider these possibilities:

(a) As a matter of respect and decency, the defendant should have a good understanding of the claim against him, and the plaintiff who invokes the process of the court should provide it.

(b) The defendant (or counsel for the defendant) needs such information in order to deal constructively with the case, which may mean preparing for trial or making settlement offers.

(c) The court needs such information, either to go forward with a trial or to apply the law to the facts quickly and perhaps dispose of the suit without the need for trial.

Courts applying Code pleading conventions seem to have all three aims in mind. See Dansby v. Dansby, 133 N.E.2d 358, 360 (Ohio 1956) ("apprise the defendant of the charges against which he must defend"); Nelson v. Wolfgram, 173 N.W.2d 571, 574 (Iowa 1970) ("inform" defendant so he "may know how to prepare his defense" and "enable the court to say whether, if [the facts alleged] are proved, a good cause of action is established"); Neutauter v. Reiner, 254 N.E.2d 66, 69 (Ill. App. 1969) ("enable the court to apply the law and the adverse party to meet the issues"); Glens Falls Indemnity Co. v. Cottlieb, 44 S.E.2d 706, 710 (Ga. Ct. App. 1947) ("inform the defendant" and "enable the court to declare distinctly the law of the case," so the jury can "find an intelligible and complete verdict"). Which purpose does the court have in mind in *Reilly*? Do you think a lawyer representing George Lawrence would be confused about Edward Reilly's claims? What else should plaintiff have alleged on the matter of inherent danger? Do you think a court could not adequately "apply the law" because the complaint was too vague?

3. In a classic Code pleading case, the North Carolina Supreme Court rejected a complaint alleging that defendant Goodyear and its agents "without cause or just excuse and maliciously came upon and trespassed upon the premises occupied by the plaintiff as a residence" and "assaulted" her with "harsh and threatening language and physical force." The defense demurred, successfully challenging the complaint as insufficient, and the state supreme court agreed:

> The complaint states no facts upon which these legal conclusions may be predicated [referring to claims of malicious trespass without cause or excuse, and assault]. Plaintiff's allegations do not disclose what occurred, when it occurred, where it occurred, who did what, the relationships between defendants and plaintiff or of defendants inter se, or any other factual data that might identify the occasion or describe the circumstances of the alleged wrongful conduct of defendants.

Gillispie v. Goodyear Service Stores, 128 S.E.2d 762 (N.C. 1963). What did the court want in *Gillispie*? Names of those who came to plaintiff's house? Descriptions of their job responsibilities? Allegations that they entered the yard without permission, or the house without knocking or invitation?

Allegations describing what each said and did, in terms of grabbing or accosting plaintiff?

4. Suppose George Lawrence had hired a teen-aged boy to mow his front lawn, that the youngster used his own power mower, and that the mower hurled a stone that struck and injured a woman walking on the sidewalk. Can she recover from Lawrence? Cooley v. Benson Motor Co. of New Orleans, 695 So. 2d 1049 (La. Ct. App. 1997) (grass cutting is not intrinsically dangerous; pedestrian cannot recover from auto dealership that hired a person to cut lawn). Is the problem in *Reilly* that tree cutting just doesn't fit the category of "intrinsically dangerous activity"? Compare Kinsey v. Spann, 533 S.E.2d 487, 492 (N.C. 2000) (tree cutting in residential neighborhood is hazardous) with McCubbin v. Walker, 896 P.2d 790, 804 (Kan. 1994) (plaintiff did not offer evidence that tree trimming is dangerous; there is a "remote possibility" that "highly unusual and aggravated set of facts" would support contrary decision).

5. In *Reilly,* the court assumed that plaintiff was alleging that George Lawrence hired James Highman to cut the trees. But the assumed allegation was that Highman was hired as an independent contractor rather than a servant or agent. For the most part, an independent contractor is someone hired for a short or fixed period, often to do some specific and finite task. For the most part, an agent or employee is hired for a long or indefinite period, often to perform varied and ongoing tasks. However, the hallmark that distinguishes independent contractors from agents or servants is that the hiring party does not control or direct the work of an independent contractor. A tree trimmer is likely to be an independent contractor. A desk clerk in an office is almost always a servant or agent. Hence the court's assumption about Highman was reasonable, wasn't it?

6. What happens now in *Reilly*? Does plaintiff get another chance to amend the complaint? Didn't the trial judge offer him that opportunity? If plaintiff "stands on the complaint" by refusing to amend, and the case is then dismissed and plaintiff appeals and *loses* because the judge was right, shouldn't that end the case? On this point, whether you're in a Code jurisdiction or a Rules jurisdiction doesn't matter much. What matters is the view that the appellate court takes of the matter. Compare Player v. Village of Bensenville, 722 N.E.2d 792 (Ill. Ct. App. 1999) (one who "appeals the dismissal of a complaint stands on the complaint and foregoes the right to file an amended complaint") with Semerenko v. Cedant Corp., 223 F.3d 165, 173 (3d Cir. 2000) (plaintiff refused opportunity to amend and appealed, but now can amend to satisfy FRCP 9(c)'s particularity requirement in fraud case), *cert. denied,* 531 U.S. 1149 (2001). Most jurisdictions agree with *Player,* rather than *Semerenko.* Which is the better approach, and why? See also In re Westinghouse Securities Litigation, 90 F.3d 696 (3d Cir. 1995) (approving dismissal of some claims as inadequately stated, remanding for further proceedings on other claims).

7. For examples of decisions concluding that the person hiring an independent contractor may be liable for the latter's negligence, see

Jones v. Power Cleaning Contractors, 551 So. 2d 996, 999 (Ala. 1989) (applying paint remover; one drop caused blindness in worker's eye); Cash v. Otis Elevator Co., 684 P.2d 1041 (Mont. 1984) (installing elevator, leading to death when plaintiff's decedent stepped into shaft after door opened); Garden of the Gods Village, Inc. v. Hellman, 294 P.2d 597, 601 (Colo. 1956) (blasting operations damaging pottery kiln on nearby property); Roush v. Johnson, 80 S.E.2d 857, 873 (W. Va. 1954) (installing compressor unit for cooler in store, where independent contractor left unit "so negligently defective as to be imminently dangerous," leading to death by electrocution); Alexander v. Seaboard Air Line R. Co., 71 S.E.2d 299, 304 (S.C. 1952) (spraying weeds on railroad right-of-way, destroying adjacent cotton crop); Law v. Phillips, 68 S.E.2d 452 (W. Va. 1951) (excavating land causing subsidence in nearby building). For decisions that activities of independent contractor were *not* intrinsically dangerous, see Spitzer v. Kings Plaza Shopping Center, 713 N.Y.S.2d 68 (N.Y. Sup. Ct. 2000) (floor mopping, leading to slip-and-fall); King v. Lens Creek Limited Partnership, 483 S.E.2d 265, 271 (W. Va. 1996) (operating empty logging truck, leading to injury); Smith v. P.&.B. Corp., 386 N.E.2d 1232, 1237 (Ind. App. 1979) (excavation of sewer trench, leading to injury of worker in trench); Jones v. Indianapolis Power & Light Co., 304 N.E.2d 337 (Ind. 1973) (installation of steam generating equipment utilizing "hoist car," leading to death of operator); Silvia v. Woodhouse, 248 N.E.2d 260 (Mass. 1969) (wrestling matchmaker, after wrestler fell from ring and injured patron watching match) (auditorium owner was liable in placing seats too close to ring); McCoy v. Cohen, 140 S.E.2d 427 (W. Va. 1965) (drilling and fracturing natural gas well, leading to pollution of domestic water wells); Phillips Pipe Line Company v. Kansas Cold Storage, Inc., 389 P.2d 766 (Kan. 1964) (removing silt from drainage ditch near gasoline pipelines, leading to loss of product and damage to lines); Boulch v. John B. Gutmann Construction Co., 366 S.W. 21 (Mo. 1963) (street excavation and hauling dirt and debris, leading to slip-and-fall); Brewer v. Appalachian Constructors, 76 S.E.2d 916, 924 (W. Va. 1953) (delivering gasoline to tank in building containing burning coal stove, leading to explosion and personal injuries).

8. The question whether a complaint states a cause of action is for the judge to decide, isn't it? In ordinary parlance, the question is one of "law" rather than "fact." If the judge concludes that the complaint *does* allege an "intrinsically dangerous" activity and the complaint survives, the case might go to trial. At that point, when evidence is presented, does the *jury* get to decide whether the activity is "intrinsically hazardous"? Or does the jury simply decide whether the independent contractor was negligent (and whether there was proximate cause and damages)? Compare Saiz v. Belen School District, 827 P.2d 102, 112 (N.M. 1992) (whether contractor is engaged in inherently dangerous activity is "pure question of law") and East Coast Collision & Restoration, Inc. v. Allyn, 742 A.2d 273, 276 (R.I. 1999) (judge should not have let jury find building owner liable to tenant for fire started by electrical work that was performed badly; no basis for concluding that electrical work constituted inherently dangerous activity) with Woodson v. Rowland, 407 S.E.2d

222, 237 (some activities are or are not dangerous as a matter of law, but situations between the extremes "appropriately require a jury to decide the inherently dangerous issue"), Ballet Fabrics, Inc. v. Four Dee Realty Co., 314 N.E.2d 1 (R.I. 1974) (jury decides whether using rooting equipment to unplug drains is inherently dangerous), and Ledbetter-Johnson Company, 103 So. 2d 748 (Ala. 1958) (in homeowner's suit against prime contractor for damages to home from work by subcontractor in blasting operations, jury decides whether those operations were inherently dangerous). Suppose it is true, as one court remarked, that "there is a spectrum of activities, some of which are never inherently dangerous" and "some of which are always inherently dangerous," see Lilley v. Blue Ridge Electric Membership Corp., 515 S.E.2d 483, 486 (N.C. 1999) (setting up utility poles on a mountainside falls at neither end of the spectrum). Does it follow that juries should get the issue? Or could the matter still fall to the judge?

9. Suppose plaintiff is an "invitee" on business premises, and he is injured in a slip-and-fall because of negligence by an independent contractor. Even if the work is *not* "intrinsically dangerous," shouldn't the owner of the premises owe a duty to the plaintiff? See Borden v. Consumer Warehouse Foods, Inc., 601 So. 2d 976, 979 (Ala. 1985) (avoiding question whether cleaning floors in store was hazardous activity, and allowing suit on theory that storekeeper has "duty to warn invitees of a dangerous condition").

■ PROBLEM 7-A. "The Roof Was Leaking"

While watching a movie in Century Theater during a rainstorm, Carolyn Martin hears the noise of falling plaster and dripping water behind her. She leaps from her seat, banging her shins and knees against the chair in front. She hurts her right knee seriously, and breaks her left tibia (shinbone). She sues, alleging that Century "negligently failed to maintain a safe theater and auditorium, in that the roof was leaking and in bad repair."

At trial, Carolyn offers evidence that the theater had a main floor and balcony, that a restroom on the balcony level had a clogged drain and leaking toilet, that water gradually collected on the bathroom floor until it leaked into the lounge, and eventually the water soaked through the carpet and penetrated the floor and ceiling above the rear part of the auditorium, causing the ceiling to give way.

"Move to dismiss, your Honor," says counsel for Century after plaintiff rested her case at trial, "Ms. Martin has not proved that the roof leaked, which is what she alleged in her complaint; instead her evidence suggests that the ceiling leaked because of overflow from a nearby bathroom." What kinds of "technical" arguments would you expect the lawyers to make? What kinds of "real" objections and responses could they make?

■ NOTES ON PROBLEMS OF CODE PLEADING

1. In systems that emphasize pleadings, it is not surprising that a serious "variance" between allegations in a complaint and facts proved at trial could lead to dismissal. Is the variance in Martin's suit serious enough to justify this result? Modern Code jurisdictions like California invite courts to distinguish a minor disparity between allegations and proof from a more serious "failure of proof." See Cal. Code Civ. Proc. §§469-471 (variance is not material "unless it has actually misled the adverse party to his prejudice," and even so the court may allow the pleader to amend "upon such terms as may be just"; if variance is immaterial, court may allow the fact to be found as the evidence suggests or permit amendment; if allegation is unproved in "general scope and meaning," there is a "failure of proof," not a mere variance). If they applied, would these directives help resolve the dispute between Carolyn Martin and Century?

2. Should parties claiming negligence be required to describe specific acts? What about making do with simple allegations that the other fellow drove "negligently"? Under such an approach, a plaintiff like Carolyn Martin could allege that Century "negligently maintained its premises," couldn't she? If that were enough, could such a plaintiff still get in trouble if she alleged both that Century was negligent in maintaining the theater and that the roof leaked, but succeeded only in proving that the ceiling leaked?

3. Not only was plaintiff expected to match her evidence to her complaint, but she was also expected to embody a "theory of the case" in her complaint, and to stick with that theory at trial. Insisting on theory seemed less justified than the doctrine of variance, in part because claimants could often plead multiple counts that embodied different theories. Hence the "theory of the case" doctrine did not take hold everywhere, and is now discredited. Compare Kewaunee County v. Decker, 30 Wis. 624, 629-630 (1872) (complaint cannot be so uncertain that it might be construed as making claim in contract or in tort; when defense raises challenge, court must determine what theory is advanced, and appraise sufficiency of complaint accordingly) with Knapp v. Walker, 47 A. 655 (Conn. 1900) (allowing plaintiff who apparently pled fraud in horse swap to recover in contract).

4. Suppose defendant in *Reilly* never challenged the complaint. Suppose the suit went to trial, leading to verdict and judgment for plaintiff. If defendant took an appeal and showed that the complaint failed to allege something crucial, should the case be thrown out or tried over again, or is it too late? See St. Clair v. Jelinek, 210 P.2d 563, 566 (Or. 1949) (affirming judgment for plaintiff even though complaint was "not a model of the legal draftsman's art" and was "defective" in failing to allege that tree trimmer was acting "in the course and within the scope" of employment; nobody was misled, and finding of fact "cures all formal defects in the complaint").

B RULES PLEADING: THE COMPLAINT

After the Field Code had supplanted English common law tradition, the second American reform came with the Federal Rules of Civil Procedure in 1938. For nearly a century and a half, federal courts in civil damage suits had followed state procedural conventions under a federal statute requiring conformity to state practice. In 1935, Congress passed the Rules Enabling Act, authorizing the Court to adopt rules governing practice and procedure in the federal system. See 28 USC §§2071-2077 (today's broader lineal descendant of the original statute). The Court appointed an Advisory Committee headed by Judge Charles E. Clark (scholar of procedure on the Second Circuit, formerly a law professor), and in the space of several years the Committee drafted the Rules. As contemplated by the Enabling Act, the Court approved them and transmitted them to Congress, to become law in 180 days unless Congress amended them or blocked adoption. There was no opposition, and in 1938 they took effect.

This quiet revolution was important and influential. Broadly speaking, the Rules go further than the Field Code toward being functional rather than formal. They are short and simple in content and style (about 85 provisions that take about 100 pages in print) and largely free of technical language, cross-referencing, and interlocking provisions. They have been outstandingly successful, having been adopted (with considerable local variation) in more than half the states.[3] In 2010, a "restyling" project changed the wording and arrangement of many provisions, but the intent was to make the Rules consistent in style and language, and to simplify their organization by eliminating subsections. Many of the cases you will be reading refer to or quote older verbiage, while remaining authoritative as to the meaning of the current Rules. It should be noted that developments pioneered by the Rules are often adopted in states that retain the Field Code as well.

1. The "Short and Plain Statement" Standard: Formalism Reduced

At the heart of Rules pleading is the requirement to set forth "a short and plain statement of the claim showing that the pleader is entitled to relief." Note the use of the word "claim" in place of "cause of action," and note that

---

[3] One modern survey lists these 25 states (plus District of Columbia) as following rules that amount to "systematic replication" of the Federal Rules, or at least "strong affinity" for the "content and organization" of the Federal Rules: Alabama, Alaska, Arizona, Colorado, District of Columbia, Hawaii, Idaho, Indiana, Kentucky, Maine, Massachusetts, Michigan, Minnesota, Montana, New Mexico, North Dakota, Ohio, Rhode Island, South Dakota, Tennessee, Utah, Vermont, Washington, West Virginia, Wisconsin, and Wyoming. See John B. Oakley & Arthur F. Coon, *The Federal Rules in State Courts: A Survey of State Court Systems of Civil Procedure*, 61 Wash. L. Rev. 1367, 1377 (1986).

there is no requirement to plead "facts." The shift in terminology was intended to mean something important: At the very least, it means that formalism counts for little—among other things, we need not distinguish facts from evidence or conclusions.

Under interpretive conventions that prevailed until the Court's decision in the *Twombly* case in 2007 (which you will read after the *Swierkiewicz* case), this shift in terminology meant that complaints were still less important in setting out the parameters of the dispute, and that claimants enjoyed even greater liberality at the pleading stage, than before. Still, less formalism and greater liberality are words of degree, and pleading requirements did not disappear. It is useful to look at how little was asked under the new pleading standard.

Two classic opinions shed light on this matter. One by Judge Clark himself confronted a home-drawn complaint. The case was a suit by a man who imported "medicinal tonic," and the complaint implied that a customs collector impounded crates of the tonic, that he lost or destroyed two of them ("saying they had leaked, which could never be true in the manner they were bottled") and that he improperly sold another part of the shipment (selling "my merchandise to another bidder with my price of $110 and not his price of $120"). While the complaint did not "make wholly clear" how the collector acquired the goods, and the court said some claims were "inadequate or inadequately stated" and that plaintiff's amended complaint supplied more "volubility" than "clarity," the Second Circuit concluded:

> It would seem, however, that [plaintiff] has stated enough to withstand a mere formal motion, directed only to the face of the complaint, and here is another instance of judicial haste which in the long run makes waste. Under the new rules of civil procedure, there is no pleading requirement of stating "facts sufficient to constitute a cause of action," but only that there be "a short and plain statement of the claim showing that the pleader is entitled to relief," and the motion for dismissal under Rule 12(b) is for failure to state "a claim upon which relief can be granted."
>
> . . .
>
> [H]owever inartistically they may be stated, the plaintiff has disclosed his claims that the collector has converted or otherwise done away with two of his cases of medicinal tonics and has sold the rest in a manner incompatible with the public auction he had announced [as required by statute and regulation]. As to the latter claim, it may be that the collector's only error is a failure to collect an additional ten dollars from [the other bidder], but giving the plaintiff the benefit of reasonable intendments in his allegations (as we must on this motion), the claim appears to be in effect that he was actually the first bidder at the price for which they were sold, and hence was entitled to the merchandise. Of course, defendant did not need to move on the complaint alone; he could have disclosed the facts from his point of view, in advance of trial if he chose, by asking for a pretrial hearing or by moving for a summary judgment with supporting affidavits. But, as it stands, we do not see how the plaintiff may properly be deprived of his day in court to show what he obviously so firmly believes and what for present purposes defendant must be taken as admitting.

Dioguardi v. Durning, 139 F.2d 774, 775 (2d Cir. 1944) (noting plaintiff's "limited ability to write and speak English" and warning that it would be hard to do justice unless he accepts legal assistance; he would be "ill advised" to resist a summary judgment motion without legal advice).

The other classic statement came from the Supreme Court by way of alternate holding:

> [T]he Federal Rules of Civil Procedure do not require a claimant to set out in detail the facts upon which he bases his claim. To the contrary, all the Rules require is "a short and plain statement of the claim" that will give the defendant fair notice of what the plaintiff's claim is and the grounds upon which it rests. The illustrative forms appended to the Rules plainly demonstrate this. Such simplified "notice pleading" is made possible by the liberal opportunity for discovery and the other pretrial procedures established by the Rules to disclose more precisely the basis of both claim and defense and to define more narrowly the disputed facts and issues.

Conley v. Gibson, 355 U.S. 41, 46-48 (1958) (also commenting that "a complaint should not be dismissed for failure to state a claim unless it appears beyond doubt that the plaintiff can prove no set of facts in support of his claim which would entitle him to relief").

In some respects, *Dioguardi* and *Conley* are unsatisfactory. To begin with, no lawyer would plead as sloppily as the claimant in *Dioguardi,* and no lawyer can expect to be treated as gently as that pro se claimant. So loose and forgiving did the Rule 8 standard seem to practitioners that at least one suggested that the standard was laughable. See O.L. McCaskill, *The Modern Philosophy of Pleading: A Dialogue Outside the Shades*, 38 A.B.A. J. 123 (1952) (in humorous account, practicing lawyer argues in favor of Code pleading but later discovers how much easier life is under *Dioguardi*, confessing that he took advantage of the new regime, without even looking into the facts, by having his secretary hastily draw up a complaint). Let us look now at a modern case that is at least somewhat more realistic in applying the Rule 8 standard.

SWIERKIEWICZ v. SOREMA

United States Supreme Court
534 U.S. 506 (2002)

Justice THOMAS delivered the opinion of the Court.

This case presents the question whether a complaint in an employment discrimination lawsuit must contain specific facts establishing a prima facie case of discrimination under the framework set forth by this Court in McDonnell Douglas Corp. v. Green, 411 U.S. 792 (1973). We hold that an employment discrimination complaint need not include such facts and instead must contain only "a short and plain statement of the claim showing that the pleader is entitled to relief." FRCP 8(a)(2).

I

Petitioner Akos Swierkiewicz is a native of Hungary, who at the time of his complaint was 53 years old. In April 1989, petitioner began working for respondent Sorema N.A., a reinsurance company headquartered in New York and principally owned and controlled by a French parent corporation. Petitioner was initially employed in the position of senior vice president and chief underwriting officer (CUO). Nearly six years later, Francois M. Chavel, respondent's Chief Executive Officer, demoted petitioner to a marketing and services position and transferred the bulk of his underwriting responsibilities to Nicholas Papadopoulo, a 32-year-old who, like Mr. Chavel, is a French national. About a year later, Mr. Chavel stated that he wanted to "energize" the underwriting department and appointed Mr. Papadopoulo as CUO. Petitioner claims that Mr. Papadopoulo had only one year of underwriting experience at the time he was promoted, and therefore was less experienced and less qualified to be CUO than he, since at that point he had 26 years of experience in the insurance industry.

Following his demotion, petitioner contends that he "was isolated by Mr. Chavel . . . excluded from business decisions and meetings and denied the opportunity to reach his true potential at SOREMA." Petitioner unsuccessfully attempted to meet with Mr. Chavel to discuss his discontent. Finally, in April 1997, petitioner sent a memo to Mr. Chavel outlining his grievances and requesting a severance package. Two weeks later, respondent's general counsel presented petitioner with two options: He could either resign without a severance package or be dismissed. Mr. Chavel fired petitioner after he refused to resign.

Petitioner filed a lawsuit alleging that he had been terminated on account of his national origin in violation of Title VII of the Civil Rights Act of 1964, 42 USC §2000e *et seq.*, and on account of his age in violation of the Age Discrimination in Employment Act of 1967 (ADEA), 29 USC §621 *et seq.* The United States District Court for the Southern District of New York dismissed petitioner's complaint because it found that he "ha[d] not adequately alleged a prima facie case, in that he ha[d] not adequately alleged circumstances that support an inference of discrimination." The United States Court of Appeals for the Second Circuit affirmed the dismissal, relying on its settled precedent, which requires a plaintiff in an employment discrimination complaint to allege facts constituting a prima facie case of discrimination under the framework set forth by this Court in *McDonnell Douglas, supra.* The Court of Appeals held that petitioner had failed to meet his burden because his allegations were "insufficient as a matter of law to raise an inference of discrimination." We granted certiorari to resolve a split among the Courts of Appeals concerning the proper pleading standard for employment discrimination cases,[2] and now reverse.

II

Applying Circuit precedent, the Court of Appeals required petitioner to plead a prima facie case of discrimination in order to survive respondent's motion to dismiss. In the Court of Appeals' view, petitioner was thus required to allege in his complaint: (1) membership in a protected group; (2) qualification for the job in question; (3) an adverse employment action; and (4) circumstances that support an inference of discrimination. Cf. *McDonnell Douglas*, 411 U.S., at 802; Texas Dept. of Community Affairs v. Burdine, 450 U.S. 248, 253-254, n.6 (1981).

The prima facie case under *McDonnell Douglas*, however, is an evidentiary standard, not a pleading requirement. In *McDonnell Douglas*, this Court made clear that "[t]he critical issue before us concern[ed] the order and allocation *of proof* in a private, non-class action challenging employment discrimination." 411 U.S., at 800 (emphasis added). In subsequent cases, this Court has reiterated that the prima facie case relates to the employee's burden of presenting evidence that raises an inference of discrimination. See *Burdine, supra*, at 252-253 ("In [*McDonnell Douglas*,] we set forth the basic allocation of burdens and order of presentation of proof in a Title VII case alleging discriminatory treatment. First, the plaintiff has the burden of proving by the preponderance of the evidence a prima facie case of discrimination" (footnotes omitted)); 450 U.S., at 255, n.8 ("This evidentiary relationship between the presumption created by a prima facie case and the consequential burden of production placed on the defendant is a traditional feature of the common law").

This Court has never indicated that the requirements for establishing a prima facie case under *McDonnell Douglas* also apply to the pleading standard that plaintiffs must satisfy in order to survive a motion to dismiss. For instance, we have rejected the argument that a Title VII complaint requires greater "particularity," because this would "too narrowly constric[t] the role of the pleadings." McDonald v. Santa Fe Trail Transp. Co., 427 U.S. 273, 283, n.11 (1976). Consequently, the ordinary rules for assessing the sufficiency of a complaint apply.

In addition, under a notice pleading system, it is not appropriate to require a plaintiff to plead facts establishing a prima facie case because the *McDonnell Douglas* framework does not apply in every employment

---

[2] The majority of Courts of Appeals have held that a plaintiff need not plead a prima facie case of discrimination under *McDonnell Douglas* in order to survive a motion to dismiss. Others, however, maintain that a complaint must contain factual allegations that support each element of a prima facie case. . . .

discrimination case. For instance, if a plaintiff is able to produce direct evidence of discrimination, he may prevail without proving all the elements of a prima facie case. Under the Second Circuit's heightened pleading standard, a plaintiff without direct evidence of discrimination at the time of his complaint must plead a prima facie case of discrimination, even though discovery might uncover such direct evidence. It thus seems incongruous to require a plaintiff, in order to survive a motion to dismiss, to plead more facts than he may ultimately need to prove to succeed on the merits if direct evidence of discrimination is discovered.

Moreover, the precise requirements of a prima facie case can vary depending on the context and were "never intended to be rigid, mechanized, or ritualistic." Furnco Constr. Corp. v. Waters, 438 U.S. 567, 577 (1978). Before discovery has unearthed relevant facts and evidence, it may be difficult to define the precise formulation of the required prima facie case in a particular case. Given that the prima facie case operates as a flexible evidentiary standard, it should not be transposed into a rigid pleading standard for discrimination cases.

Furthermore, imposing the Court of Appeals' heightened pleading standard in employment discrimination cases conflicts with FRCP 8(a)(2), which provides that a complaint must include only "a short and plain statement of the claim showing that the pleader is entitled to relief." Such a statement must simply "give the defendant fair notice of what the plaintiff's claim is and the grounds upon which it rests." Conley v. Gibson, 355 U.S. 41, 47 (1957). This simplified notice pleading standard relies on liberal discovery rules and summary judgment motions to define disputed facts and issues and to dispose of unmeritorious claims. "The provisions for discovery are so flexible and the provisions for pretrial procedure and summary judgment so effective, that attempted surprise in federal practice is aborted very easily, synthetic issues detected, and the gravamen of the dispute brought frankly into the open for the inspection of the court." 5 C. Wright & A. Miller, Federal Practice and Procedure §1202, p.76 (2d ed. 1990).

Rule 8(a)'s simplified pleading standard applies to all civil actions, with limited exceptions. Rule 9(b), for example, provides for greater particularity in all averments of fraud or mistake. This Court, however, has declined to extend such exceptions to other contexts. In Leatherman v. Tarrant County Narcotics Intelligence and Coordination Unit, 507 U.S. 163 (1993)], we stated: "[T]he Federal Rules do address in Rule 9(b) the question of the need for greater particularity in pleading certain actions, but do not include among the enumerated actions any reference to complaints alleging municipal liability under §1983. *Expressio unius est exclusio alterius.*" Just as Rule 9(b) makes no mention of municipal liability under 42 USC §1983, neither does it refer to employment discrimination. Thus, complaints in these cases, as in most others, must satisfy only the simple requirements of Rule 8(a).[4]

Other provisions of the Federal Rules of Civil Procedure are inextricably linked to Rule 8(a)'s simplified notice pleading standard. Rule 8(e)(1) states that "[n]o technical forms of pleading or motions are required," and Rule 8(f) provides that "[a]ll pleadings shall be so construed as to do substantial justice." Given the Federal Rules' simplified standard for pleading, "[a] court may dismiss a complaint only if it is clear that no relief could be granted under any set of facts that could be proved consistent with the allegations." Hishon v. King & Spalding, 467 U.S. 69, 73 (1984) [citing the *Conley* case—ED.]. If a pleading fails to specify the allegations in a manner that provides sufficient notice, a defendant can move for a more definite statement under Rule 12(e) before responding. Moreover, claims lacking merit may be dealt with through summary judgment under Rule 56. The liberal notice pleading of Rule 8(a) is the starting point of a simplified pleading system, which was adopted to focus litigation on the merits of a claim. See *Conley,* supra ("The Federal Rules reject the approach that pleading is a game of skill in which one misstep by counsel may be decisive to the outcome and accept the principle that the purpose of pleading is to facilitate a proper decision on the merits").

Applying the relevant standard, petitioner's complaint easily satisfies the requirements of Rule 8(a) because it gives respondent fair notice of the basis for petitioner's claims. Petitioner alleged that he had been terminated on account of his national origin in violation of Title VII and on account of his age in violation of the ADEA. His complaint detailed the events leading to his termination, provided relevant dates, and included the ages and nationalities of at least some of the relevant persons involved with his termination. These allegations give respondent fair notice of what petitioner's claims are and the grounds upon which they rest. In addition, they state claims upon which relief could be granted under Title VII and the ADEA.

Respondent argues that allowing lawsuits based on conclusory allegations of discrimination to go forward will burden the courts and encourage disgruntled employees to bring unsubstantiated suits. Whatever the practical merits of this argument, the Federal Rules do not contain a heightened pleading standard for employment discrimination suits. A requirement of greater specificity for particular claims is a result that "must be obtained by the process of amending the Federal Rules, and not by judicial interpretation." *Leatherman,* at 168. Furthermore, Rule 8(a) establishes a pleading standard without regard

---

[4] These requirements are exemplified by the Federal Rules of Civil Procedure Forms, which "are sufficient under the rules and are intended to indicate the simplicity and brevity of statement which the rules contemplate." FRCP 84. For example, Form 9 sets forth a complaint for negligence in which plaintiff simply states in relevant part: "On June 1, 1936, in a public highway called Boylston Street in Boston, Massachusetts, defendant negligently drove a motor vehicle against plaintiff who was then crossing said highway." [Form 9 is now Form 11, and it has been revised to delete geographical references.—ED.]

to whether a claim will succeed on the merits. "Indeed it may appear on the face of the pleadings that a recovery is very remote and unlikely but that is not the test." Scheuer [v. Rhodes, 416 U.S. 232, 236 (1974)].

For the foregoing reasons, we hold that an employment discrimination plaintiff need not plead a prima facie case of discrimination and that petitioner's complaint is sufficient to survive respondent's motion to dismiss. Accordingly, the judgment of the Court of Appeals is reversed, and the case is remanded for further proceedings consistent with this opinion.

It is so ordered.

■ NOTES ON STATING A CLAIM FOR RELIEF

1. The operative language in Title VII of the Civil Rights Act of 1964, better known for its role in race discrimination suits, is short and simple: It is "unlawful" for an employer "to fail or refuse to hire or to discharge any individual, or otherwise to discriminate against any individual with respect to his compensation, terms, conditions, or privileges of employment, because of such individual's race, color, religion, sex, or national origin." See 42 USC §2000e-2. Similar language appears in the Age Discrimination statute. See 29 USC §623. In his complaint against Sorema, set forth in a joint Appendix submitted to the Court, Akos Swierkiewicz alleged that he was Hungarian, that he was 49 years old at the time, that his supervisor and the person later given his position were French, that the latter was 32 years old at the time and had less experience, that the supervisor wanted to "energize" the department "clearly implying that plaintiff was too old," and that his termination was "on account of his national origin and his age." The Court holds that these allegations suffice, doesn't it?

2. It was a "disparate treatment" case: Swierkiewicz claimed he was treated badly because of ethnicity or national origin. Only rarely can claimants muster "direct proof" of disparate treatment by showing overt animus or hostility based on membership in a protected class (being black or Hungarian, for example). Far more often the proof is circumstantial: It is likely to be "anecdotal" evidence, like comments disparaging the class or members of it, or statistical proof that persons in the class fail in disproportionate numbers to advance or find jobs. (The other large category involves claims of "disparate impact," which typically proceed on a showing that employment qualifications serve no business-related purpose, and their impact falls more heavily on one group than another. Again, proof in such cases is usually statistical.) The Second Circuit, which found the complaint in *Swierkiewicz* inadequate, took its cue from McDonnell Douglas Corp. v. Green, 411 U.S. 792, 802 (1973). There the Court said the claimant in a Title VII case must "carry the initial burden" of proving "(i) that he belongs to a racial minority; (ii) that he applied and was qualified for a job for which the employer was seeking applicants; (iii) that, despite his qualifications, he was rejected; and (iv) that, after his rejection, the position remained open and the employer continued to seek applicants from persons of complainant's qualifications." Apart from rare cases involving direct proof of mistreatment, the *McDonnell Douglas* framework applies to almost all cases based on disparate treatment. Given this fact, wouldn't it make sense to require claimant to plead elements that would satisfy the *McDonnell Douglas* framework? He's going to have to offer proof of such points at trial: Why not allege them?

3. As the opinion reflects, the Court had already rejected an effort to enforce a specificity requirement in a different area. *Leatherman* involved damage claims brought under §1983 that a state narcotics unit violated the Fourth Amendment by forced entry into homes seeking drugs, based on odors. One homeowner claimed that agents assaulted him in the search; another claimed they killed her dogs. Enforcing a Fifth Circuit rule requiring that complaints against government officials allege claims "with factual detail and particularity," to show why a defense of "qualified immunity" does not apply, the trial court dismissed the complaint, and the Fifth Circuit approved. The Supreme Court disagreed, concluding that it is "impossible to square" a "heightened pleading standard" with FRCP 8(a)(2) as construed in *Conley*, and noting that FRCP 9(b) "does impose a particularity requirement" in claims alleging "fraud or mistake." Invoking an old Latin principle ("expressio unius est exclusio alterius," meaning that "expressly covering one thing means other things are excluded"), the Court concluded that one cannot create special pleading standards in this way. Leatherman v. Tarrant County Narcotics Intelligence and Coordination Unit, 507 U.S. 163, 168 (1993). That's about the same position that *Swierkiewicz* takes, isn't it?

4. Public entities are not responsible for "constitutional torts" by their agents on the same "respondeat superior" theory that applies to ordinary torts by "servants or agents" of private companies.[4] Assume K works as a deliveryman for furniture seller L, and in delivering a table to buyer J at her home, K negligently injures her. J can sue both K and L. If K was negligent, J can obtain judgment against K because K committed a tort and is personally liable for it. J can also recover from L in like amount under respondeat superior, which makes L liable for K's tort. If, on the other hand, homeowner M suffers physical injuries, indignities, and invasion of privacy when state narcotics officer N, acting within the scope of his employment for County O, breaks down M's door in a drug sweep, different principles apply,

---

[4] "Constitutional torts" include things like assaults by law enforcement officers during a search as in *Leatherman,* and denying students a hearing, as in Carey v. Piphus, 435 U.S. 247 (1978) (Chapter 1, supra). For the most part, constitutional torts can only be committed by public officials, or persons acting in concert or agreement with them. The Constitution protects citizens against government overreaching, not against ordinary torts or crimes by other citizens.

particularly if M seeks damages for violation of his *constitutional* rights. Again, M can sue both the individual and the employer—both N and County O. As to N, recovery requires showing that N used unnecessary force in pursuing the search. But N can raise a "qualified immunity" defense, which shields him from liability if he reasonably thought his actions did not violate any rights. As to County O, respondeat superior does not apply. M can recover only by showing that County O had a practice or policy that allowed or encouraged people like M to act as he did. County O also has a defense of qualified immunity if it can show that it took reasonable steps to train M in proper procedures. See Monell v. Department of Social Services of City of New York, 436 U.S. 658, 691 (1978) (City is liable under §1983 only if agent acted "pursuant to official municipal policy of some nature" in committing this "constitutional tort").

(a) Are there reasons to prefer higher pleading standards in such suits? First, should the difference in liability standards matter for purposes of pleading? Second, what about the fact that performance of official duties is important and also likely to be annoying if not damaging to people on the receiving end? Third, should it matter that, in the case of suits against state officials (or municipal or county officials), the claim exists because of *federal* rights often implemented by federal courts, so there is an element of federal *imposition* on state officials? Fourth, what about the fact that many constitutional torts depend on proving improper motive on the part of an official? In fact, the *Leatherman* case, noted above, is but one of many cases where courts sought to implement heightened pleading standards. See generally Richard L. Marcus, *The Revival of Fact Pleading Under the Federal Rules of Civil Procedure*, 86 Colum. L. Rev. 433 (1986); Richard L. Marcus, *The Puzzling Persistence of Pleading Practice*, 76 Tex. L. Rev. 1749 (1998); Christopher M. Fairman, *Heightened Pleading*, 81 Tex. L. Rev. 551 (2002).

(b) In the *Crawford-El* case, the Court noted the last-mentioned point and said judges have a special duty to protect officials against unfounded claims:

> When a plaintiff files a complaint against a public official alleging a claim that requires proof of wrongful motive, the trial court must exercise its discretion in a way that protects the substance of the qualified immunity defense. It must exercise its discretion so that officials are not subjected to unnecessary and burdensome discovery or trial proceedings. The district judge has two primary options prior to permitting any discovery at all. First, the court may order a reply to the defendant's or a third party's answer under FRCP 7(a), or grant the defendant's motion for a more definite statement under Rule 12(e). Thus, the court may insist that the plaintiff "put forward specific, nonconclusory factual allegations" that establish improper motive causing cognizable injury in order to survive a prediscovery motion for dismissal or summary judgment. This option exists even if the official chooses not to plead the affirmative defense of qualified immunity. Second, if the defendant does plead the immunity defense, the district court should resolve that threshold question before permitting discovery. To do so, the court must determine whether, assuming the truth of the plaintiff's

allegations, the official's conduct violated clearly established law. Because the former option of demanding more specific allegations of intent places no burden on the defendant-official, the district judge may choose that alternative before resolving the immunity question, which sometimes requires complicated analysis of legal issues.

Crawford-El v. Britton, 523 U.S. 574 (1998). *Crawford-El* involved a claim by an inmate that officials purposefully mishandled his belongings (including his files) when he was transferred from one prison to another, delaying their delivery to him by months. He was a litigious prisoner whom authorities doubtless found annoying. Does it make more sense to require that plaintiff file a reply containing "specific, nonconclusory factual allegations" of motive than to impose a heightened pleading standard in the first instance? Does it make more sense to grant a defense motion for more definite statement?

(c) Following *Crawford-El,* some courts insist that when defendants raise qualified immunity, plaintiffs file a reply to meet this defense. See Rippy v. Hattaway, 270 F.3d 416, 419 (6th Cir. 2001) (when defendant in §1983 suit raises qualified immunity, plaintiff bears "additional burden of pleading facts that, if taken as true, establish not only the violation of his rights, but also that these rights were so clearly established when the acts were committed that any official in the defendant's position, measured objectively, would have clearly understood that he was under an affirmative duty to refrain from the conduct").

(d) The Court has taken pains to make qualified immunity easier to establish on the merits. A perennial problem with immunity defenses is that immunity from *liability* doesn't ensure immunity from *being sued*: A defendant who escapes liability and wins a favorable judgment at the end of a case has still endured the distractions, expense, and aggravation of suit. To improve the protection, the Court in the *Harlow* case held that qualified immunity applies as "an affirmative defense that must be pleaded," but is an "objective" standard involving "a presumptive knowledge of and respect for" basic and unquestioned constitutional rights. (Plaintiff in *Harlow* claimed White House officials conspired to get him unlawfully discharged from employment in the Air Force Department.) The Court noted that earlier efforts to implement a dual standard having *both* objective *and* subjective elements had made it hard to resolve immunity issues by affidavits before trial. Hence the Court adopted a unitary objective standard:

> [W]e conclude today that bare allegations of malice should not suffice to subject government officials either to the costs of trial or to the burdens of broad-reaching discovery. We therefore hold that government officials performing discretionary functions generally are shielded from liability for civil damages insofar as their conduct does not violate clearly established statutory or constitutional rights of which a reasonable person would have known.

Reliance on the objective reasonableness of an official's conduct, as measured by reference to clearly established law, should avoid excessive disruption of government and permit the resolution of many insubstantial claims on summary judgment. On summary judgment, the judge appropriately may determine, not only the currently applicable law, but whether that law was clearly established at the time an action occurred. If the law at that time was not clearly established, an official could not reasonably be expected to anticipate subsequent legal developments, nor could he fairly be said to "know" that the law forbade conduct not previously identified as unlawful. Until this threshold immunity question is resolved, discovery should not be allowed. If the law was clearly established, the immunity defense ordinarily should fail, since a reasonably competent public official should know the law governing his conduct. Nevertheless, if the official pleading the defense claims extraordinary circumstances and can prove that he neither knew nor should have known of the relevant legal standard, the defense should be sustained. But again, the defense would turn primarily on objective factors.

Harlow v. Fitzgerald, 457 U.S. 800, 817-819 (1982). Does changing the substantive law of immunity so it becomes easier for immunity defenses to be resolved prior to trial make more sense than a heightened pleading requirement?

5. It may have occurred to you to wonder what happened to sovereign immunity? Why isn't a public agency *completely* immune from liability? The answer, to simplify the matter, is that sovereign immunity has been largely abolished in many areas. When you read *Hedel-Ostrowski* (the last case in this chapter), you will see that sovereign immunity has been abolished for so-called proprietary torts, meaning torts of the garden-variety kinds like automobile accidents and medical malpractice. If an official negligently runs over someone, or a doctor on the staff of a public hospital commits malpractice, the injured party can likely sue the city or the hospital, and recovery could rest on the same theory that would apply if the defendant worked for a private company or hospital. In connection with "constitutional torts," like violations of Fourth Amendment rights, recovery is less certain, and it is denied altogether in the area of "discretionary functions" (like declining to upgrade warning signs at a railroad crossing). See generally Richard A. Epstein, Torts, Chapter 22 (1999).

2. The "Short and Plain Statement" Standard: New Rigor?

Cases like *Leatherman,* discussed in the notes after *Swierkiewicz,* supra, are reminders that courts and lawyers alike seek ways to dispose of some cases at the pleading stage. Consistently, however, the Supreme Court resisted efforts to move in this direction. Then came the decision in *Twombly.*

BELL ATLANTIC CORPORATION v. TWOMBLY

Supreme Court of the United States
550 U.S. 544 (2007)

Justice SOUTER delivered the opinion of the Court.

Liability under §1 of the Sherman Act, 15 USC §1, requires a "contract, combination . . . , or conspiracy, in restraint of trade or commerce." The question in this putative class action is whether a §1 complaint can survive a motion to dismiss when it alleges that major telecommunications providers engaged in certain parallel conduct unfavorable to competition, absent some factual context suggesting agreement, as distinct from identical, independent action. We hold that such a complaint should be dismissed.

I

The upshot of the 1984 divestiture of the American Telephone & Telegraph Company's (AT&T) local telephone business was a system of regional service monopolies (variously called "Regional Bell Operating Companies," "Baby Bells," or "Incumbent Local Exchange Carriers" (ILECs)), and a separate, competitive market for long-distance service from which the ILECs were excluded. More than a decade later, Congress withdrew approval of the ILECs' monopolies by enacting the Telecommunications Act of 1996 (1996 Act), which "fundamentally restructure[d] local telephone markets" and "subject[ed] [ILECs] to a host of duties intended to facilitate market entry." AT&T Corp. v. Iowa Utilities Bd., 525 U.S. 366, 371 (1999). In recompense, the 1996 Act set conditions for authorizing ILECs to enter the long-distance market. See 47 USC §271.

"Central to the [new] scheme [was each ILEC's] obligation . . . to share its network with competitors," Verizon Communications Inc. v. Law Offices of Curtis V. Trinko, LLP, 540 U.S. 398, 402 (2004), which came to be known as "competitive local exchange carriers" (CLECs). A CLEC could make use of an ILEC's network in any of three ways: by (1) "purchas[ing] local telephone services at wholesale rates for resale to end users," (2) "leas[ing] elements of the [ILEC's] network 'on an unbundled basis,'" or (3) "interconnect[ing] its own facilities with the [ILEC's] network." *Iowa Utilities Bd., supra* (quoting 47 USC §251(c)). Owing to the "considerable expense and effort" required to make unbundled network elements available to rivals at wholesale prices, the ILECs vigorously litigated the scope of the sharing obligation imposed by the 1996 Act, with the result that the Federal Communications Commission (FCC) three times revised its regulations to narrow the range of network elements to be shared with the CLECs.

Respondents William Twombly and Lawrence Marcus (hereinafter plaintiffs) represent a putative class consisting of all "subscribers of local telephone and/or high speed internet services ... from February 8, 1996 to present." In this action against petitioners, a group of ILECs,[1] plaintiffs seek treble damages and declaratory and injunctive relief for claimed violations of §1 of the Sherman Act, which prohibits "[e]very contract, combination in the form of trust or otherwise, or conspiracy, in restraint of trade or commerce among the several States, or with foreign nations."

The complaint alleges that the ILECs conspired to restrain trade in two ways, each supposedly inflating charges for local telephone and high-speed Internet services. Plaintiffs say, first, that the ILECs "engaged in parallel conduct" in their respective service areas to inhibit the growth of upstart CLECs. Their actions allegedly included making unfair agreements with the CLECs for access to ILEC networks, providing inferior connections to the networks, overcharging, and billing in ways designed to sabotage the CLECs' relations with their own customers. According to the complaint, the ILECs' "compelling common motivatio[n]" to thwart the CLECs' competitive efforts naturally led them to form a conspiracy; "[h]ad any one [ILEC] not sought to prevent CLECs ... from competing effectively ... , the resulting greater competitive inroads into that [ILEC's] territory would have revealed the degree to which competitive entry by CLECs would have been successful in the other territories in the absence of such conduct."

Second, the complaint charges agreements by the ILECs to refrain from competing against one another. These are to be inferred from the ILECs' common failure "meaningfully [to] pursu[e]" "attractive business opportunit[ies]" in contiguous markets where they possessed "substantial competitive advantages," and from a statement of Richard Notebaert, chief executive officer (CEO) of the ILEC Qwest, that competing in the territory of another ILEC "'might be a good way to turn a quick dollar but that doesn't make it right.'"

The complaint couches its ultimate allegations this way:

> In the absence of any meaningful competition between the [ILECs] in one another's markets, and in light of the parallel course of conduct that each engaged in to prevent competition from CLECs within their respective local telephone and/or high speed internet services markets and the other facts and market circumstances alleged above, Plaintiffs allege upon information and belief that [the ILECs] have entered into a contract, combination or conspiracy to prevent competitive entry in their respective local telephone and/or high speed

---

[1] The 1984 divestiture of AT&T's local telephone service created seven Regional Bell Operating Companies. Through a series of mergers and acquisitions, those seven companies were consolidated into the four ILECs named in this suit: BellSouth Corporation, Qwest Communications International, Inc., SBC Communications, Inc., and Verizon Communications, Inc. (successor-in-interest to Bell Atlantic Corporation). Together, these ILECs allegedly control 90 percent or more of the market for local telephone service in the 48 contiguous States.

internet services markets and have agreed not to compete with one another and otherwise allocated customers and markets to one another.

The United States District Court for the Southern District of New York dismissed the complaint for failure to state a claim upon which relief can be granted. The District Court... understood that allegations of parallel business conduct ["conscious parallelism"—ED.], taken alone, do not state a claim under §1; plaintiffs must allege additional facts that "ten[d] to exclude independent self-interested conduct as an explanation for defendants' parallel behavior." The District Court found plaintiffs' allegations of parallel ILEC actions to discourage competition inadequate because "the behavior of each ILEC in resisting the incursion of CLECs is fully explained by the ILEC's own interests in defending its individual territory." As to the ILECs' supposed agreement against competing with each other, the District Court found that the complaint does not "alleg[e] facts... suggesting that refraining from competing in other territories as CLECs was contrary to [the ILECs'] apparent economic interests, and consequently [does] not rais[e] an inference that [the ILECs'] actions were the result of a conspiracy."

The Court of Appeals for the Second Circuit reversed, holding that the District Court tested the complaint by the wrong standard. It held that "plus factors are not *required* to be pleaded to permit an antitrust claim based on parallel conduct to survive dismissal" (emphasis in original). Although the Court of Appeals took the view that plaintiffs must plead facts that "include conspiracy among the realm of 'plausible' possibilities in order to survive a motion to dismiss," it then said that "to rule that allegations of parallel anticompetitive conduct fail to support a plausible conspiracy claim, a court would have to conclude that there is no set of facts that would permit a plaintiff to demonstrate that the particular parallelism asserted was the product of collusion rather than coincidence."

We granted certiorari to address the proper standard for pleading an antitrust conspiracy through allegations of parallel conduct, and now reverse.

II

A

Because §1 of the Sherman Act "does not prohibit [all] unreasonable restraints of trade... but only restraints effected by a contract, combination, or conspiracy," Copperweld Corp. v. Independence Tube Corp., 467 U.S. 752, 775 (1984), "[t]he crucial question" is whether the challenged anticompetitive conduct "stem[s] from independent decision or from an agreement, tacit or express," Theatre Enterprises v. Paramount Film Distributing Corp., 346 U.S. 537 (1954). While a showing of parallel "business behavior is admissible circumstantial evidence from which the fact finder may infer agreement," it falls short of "conclusively establish[ing] agreement or . . . itself constitut[ing] a Sherman Act offense." Even "conscious parallelism," a common reaction of "firms in a concentrated market [that] recogniz[e] their shared economic interests and their interdependence with respect to price and output decisions" is "not in itself unlawful." Brooke Group Ltd. v. Brown & Williamson Tobacco Corp., 509 U.S. 209, 227 (1993); see 6 P. Areeda & H. Hovenkamp, Antitrust Law ¶ 1433a, p. 236 (2d ed. 2003) (hereinafter Areeda & Hovenkamp) ("The courts are nearly unanimous in saying that mere interdependent parallelism does not establish the contract, combination, or conspiracy required by Sherman Act §1"); Turner, The Definition of Agreement Under the Sherman Act: Conscious Parallelism and Refusals to Deal, 75 Harv. L. Rev. 655, 672 (1962) ("[M]ere interdependence of basic price decisions is not conspiracy").

The inadequacy of showing parallel conduct or interdependence, without more, mirrors the ambiguity of the behavior: consistent with conspiracy, but just as much in line with a wide swath of rational and competitive business strategy unilaterally prompted by common perceptions of the market. Accordingly, we have previously hedged against false inferences from identical behavior at a number of points in the trial sequence. An antitrust conspiracy plaintiff with evidence showing nothing beyond parallel conduct is not entitled to a directed verdict, see *Theatre Enterprises;* proof of a §1 conspiracy must include evidence tending to exclude the possibility of independent action, see Monsanto Co. v. Spray-Rite Service Corp., 465 U.S. 752 (1984); and at the summary judgment stage a §1 plaintiff's offer of conspiracy evidence must tend to rule out the possibility that the defendants were acting independently, see Matsushita Elec. Industrial Co. v. Zenith Radio Corp., 475 U.S. 574 (1986).

B

This case presents the antecedent question of what a plaintiff must plead in order to state a claim under §1 of the Sherman Act. FRCP 8(a)(2) requires only "a short and plain statement of the claim showing that the pleader is entitled to relief," in order to "give the defendant fair notice of what the . . . claim is and the grounds upon which it rests," Conley v. Gibson, 355 U.S. 41, 47 (1957). While a complaint attacked by a Rule 12(b)(6) motion to dismiss does not need detailed factual allegations, a plaintiff's obligation to provide the "grounds" of his "entitle[ment] to relief" requires more than labels and conclusions, and a formulaic recitation of the elements of a cause of action will not do, see Papasan v. Allain, 478 U.S. 265, 286 (1986) (on a motion to dismiss, courts "are not bound to accept as true a legal conclusion couched as a factual allegation"). Factual allegations must be enough to raise a right to relief above the speculative level, see 5 C. Wright & A. Miller, Federal Practice and Procedure §1216, pp. 235-236 (3d ed. 2004) (hereinafter Wright & Miller) ("[T]he pleading must contain something more . . . than . . . a statement of facts that merely creates a suspicion [of] a legally cognizable right of action"),[3] on the assumption that all the allegations in the complaint are true (even if doubtful in fact).

In applying these general standards to a §1 claim, we hold that stating such a claim requires a complaint with enough factual matter (taken as true) to suggest that an agreement was made. Asking for plausible grounds to infer an agreement does not impose a probability requirement at the pleading stage; it simply calls for enough fact to raise a reasonable expectation that discovery will reveal evidence of illegal agreement.[4] And, of course, a well-pleaded complaint may proceed even if it strikes a savvy judge that actual proof of those facts is improbable, and "that a recovery is very remote and unlikely." In identifying facts that are suggestive enough to render a §1 conspiracy plausible, we have the benefit of the prior rulings and considered views of leading commentators, already quoted, that lawful parallel conduct fails to bespeak unlawful agreement. It makes sense to say, therefore, that an allegation of parallel conduct and a bare assertion of conspiracy will not suffice. Without more, parallel conduct does not suggest conspiracy, and a conclusory allegation of agreement at some unidentified point does not supply facts adequate to show illegality. Hence, when allegations of parallel conduct are set out in order to make a §1 claim, they must be placed in a context that raises a suggestion of a preceding agreement, not merely parallel conduct that could just as well be independent action.

The need at the pleading stage for allegations plausibly suggesting (not merely consistent with) agreement reflects the threshold requirement of Rule 8(a)(2) that the "plain statement" possess enough heft to "sho[w] that the pleader is entitled to relief." A statement of parallel conduct, even conduct consciously undertaken, needs some setting suggesting the agreement

---

[3] The dissent greatly oversimplifies matters by suggesting that the Federal Rules somehow dispensed with the pleading of facts altogether. . . . Rule 8(a)(2) still requires a "showing," rather than a blanket assertion, of entitlement to relief. Without some factual allegation in the complaint, it is hard to see how a claimant could satisfy the requirement of providing not only "fair notice" of the nature of the claim, but also "grounds" on which the claim rests. See 5 Wright & Miller §1202, at 94, 95 (Rule 8(a) "contemplate[s] the statement of circumstances, occurrences, and events in support of the claim presented" and does not authorize a pleader's "bare averment that he wants relief and is entitled to it").

[4] Commentators have offered several examples of parallel conduct allegations that would state a §1 claim under this standard. See, *e.g.,* 6 Areeda & Hovenkamp ¶ 1425, at 167-185 (discussing "parallel behavior that would probably not result from chance, coincidence, independent responses to common stimuli, or mere interdependence unaided by an advance understanding among the parties"); Blechman, Conscious Parallelism, Signaling and Facilitating Devices: The Problem of Tacit Collusion Under the Antitrust Laws, 24 N.Y.L. S. L. Rev. 881, 899 (1979) (describing "conduct [that] indicates the sort of restricted freedom of action and sense of obligation that one generally associates with agreement"). The parties in this case agree that "complex and historically unprecedented changes in pricing structure made at the very same time by multiple competitors, and made for no other discernible reason" would support a plausible inference of conspiracy.

necessary to make out a §1 claim; without that further circumstance pointing toward a meeting of the minds, an account of a defendant's commercial efforts stays in neutral territory. An allegation of parallel conduct is thus much like a naked assertion of conspiracy in a §1 complaint: it gets the complaint close to stating a claim, but without some further factual enhancement it stops short of the line between possibility and plausibility of "entitle[ment] to relief." Cf. DM Research, Inc. v. College of Am. Pathologists, 170 F.3d 53, 56 (1st Cir. 1999) ("[T]erms like 'conspiracy,' or even 'agreement,' are border-line: they might well be sufficient in conjunction with a more specific allegation— for example, identifying a written agreement or even a basis for inferring a tacit agreement, . . . but a court is not required to accept such terms as a sufficient basis for a complaint").[5]

We alluded to the practical significance of the Rule 8 entitlement requirement in Dura Pharmaceuticals, Inc. v. Broudo, 544 U.S. 336 (2005), when we explained that something beyond the mere possibility of loss causation must be alleged, lest a plaintiff with "'a largely groundless claim'" be allowed to "'take up the time of a number of other people, with the right to do so representing an *in terrorem* increment of the settlement value.'" So, when the allegations in a complaint, however true, could not raise a claim of entitlement to relief, "this basic deficiency should . . . be exposed at the point of minimum expenditure of time and money by the parties and the court." 5 Wright & Miller §1216, at 233-234 (quoting Daves v. Hawaiian Dredging Co., 114 F. Supp. 643, 645 (D. Hawaii 1953)).

Thus, it is one thing to be cautious before dismissing an antitrust complaint in advance of discovery, but quite another to forget that proceeding to antitrust discovery can be expensive. . . . That potential expense is obvious enough in the present case: plaintiffs represent a putative class of at least 90 percent of all subscribers to local telephone or high-speed Internet service in the continental United States, in an action against America's largest telecommunications firms (with many thousands of employees generating reams and gigabytes of business records) for unspecified (if any) instances of antitrust violations that allegedly occurred over a period of seven years.

It is no answer to say that a claim just shy of a plausible entitlement to relief can, if groundless, be weeded out early in the discovery process through "careful case management," given the common lament that the success of judicial supervision in checking discovery abuse has been on the modest side. See, e.g., Easterbrook, Discovery as Abuse, 69 B.U. L. Rev. 635, 638 (1989) ("Judges can do little about impositional discovery when parties control the legal claims to be presented and conduct the discovery themselves"). And it is self-evident that the problem of discovery abuse cannot be solved by "careful scrutiny of evidence at the summary judgment stage," much less "lucid instructions to juries"; the

---

[5] The border in *DM Research* was the line between the conclusory and the factual. Here it lies between the factually neutral and the factually suggestive. Each must be crossed to enter the realm of plausible liability.

threat of discovery expense will push cost-conscious defendants to settle even anemic cases before reaching those proceedings. Probably, then, it is only by taking care to require allegations that reach the level suggesting conspiracy that we can hope to avoid the potentially enormous expense of discovery in cases with no "'reasonably founded hope that the [discovery] process will reveal relevant evidence'" to support a §1 claim.[6]

Plaintiffs do not, of course, dispute the requirement of plausibility and the need for something more than merely parallel behavior . . . and their main argument against the plausibility standard at the pleading stage is its ostensible conflict with an early statement of ours construing Rule 8. Justice Black's opinion for the Court in *Conley* spoke not only of the need for fair notice of the grounds for entitlement to relief but of "the accepted rule that a complaint should not be dismissed for failure to state a claim unless it appears beyond doubt that the plaintiff can prove no set of facts in support of his claim which would entitle him to relief." This "no set of facts" language can be read in isolation as saying that any statement revealing the theory of the claim will suffice unless its factual impossibility may be shown from the face of the pleadings; and the Court of Appeals appears to have read *Conley* in some such way when formulating its understanding of the proper pleading standard.

On such a focused and literal reading of *Conley*'s "no set of facts," a wholly conclusory statement of claim would survive a motion to dismiss whenever the pleadings left open the possibility that a plaintiff might later establish some "set of [undisclosed] facts" to support recovery. So here, the Court of Appeals specifically found the prospect of unearthing direct evidence of conspiracy sufficient to preclude dismissal, even though the complaint does not set forth a single fact in a context that suggests an agreement. It seems fair to

---

[6] The dissent takes heart in the reassurances of plaintiffs' counsel that discovery would be "phased" and "limited to the existence of the alleged conspiracy and class certification." But determining whether some illegal agreement may have taken place between unspecified persons at different ILECs (each a multibillion dollar corporation with legions of management level employees) at some point over seven years is a sprawling, costly, and hugely time-consuming undertaking not easily susceptible to the kind of line drawing and case management that the dissent envisions. Perhaps the best answer to the dissent's optimism that antitrust discovery is open to effective judicial control is a more extensive quotation of the authority just cited, a judge with a background in antitrust law. Given the system that we have, the hope of effective judicial supervision is slim: "The timing is all wrong. The plaintiff files a sketchy complaint (the Rules of Civil Procedure discourage fulsome documents), and discovery is launched. A judicial officer does not know the details of the case the parties will present and in theory *cannot* know the details. Discovery is used to find the details. The judicial officer always knows less than the parties, and the parties themselves may not know very well where they are going or what they expect to find. A magistrate supervising discovery does not—cannot—know the expected productivity of a given request, because the nature of the requester's claim and the contents of the files (or head) of the adverse party are unknown. Judicial officers cannot measure the costs and benefits to the requester and so cannot isolate impositional requests. Requesters have no reason to disclose their own estimates because they gain from imposing costs on rivals (and may lose from an improvement in accuracy). The portions of the Rules . . . calling on judges to trim back excessive demands, therefore, have been, and are doomed to be, hollow. We cannot prevent what we cannot detect; we cannot detect what we cannot define; we cannot define 'abusive' discovery except in theory, because in practice we lack essential information." Easterbrook, Discovery as Abuse, 69 B.U. L. Rev. 635, 638-639 (1989).

say that this approach to pleading would dispense with any showing of a "'reasonably founded hope'" that a plaintiff would be able to make a case; Mr. Micawber's optimism would be enough.

Seeing this, a good many judges and commentators have balked at taking the literal terms of the *Conley* passage as a pleading standard. *See, e.g., . . .* Hazard, From Whom No Secrets Are Hid, 76 Tex. L. Rev. 1665, 1685 (1998) (describing *Conley* as having "turned Rule 8 on its head"); Marcus, The Revival of Fact Pleading Under the Federal Rules of Civil Procedure, 86 Colum. L. Rev. 433, 463-465 (1986) (noting tension between *Conley* and subsequent understandings of Rule 8).

We could go on, but there is no need to pile up further citations to show that *Conley*'s "no set of facts" language has been questioned, criticized, and explained away long enough. To be fair to the *Conley* Court, the passage should be understood in light of the opinion's preceding summary of the complaint's concrete allegations, which the Court quite reasonably understood as amply stating a claim for relief. But the passage so often quoted fails to mention this understanding on the part of the Court, and after puzzling the profession for 50 years, this famous observation has earned its retirement. The phrase is best forgotten as an incomplete, negative gloss on an accepted pleading standard: once a claim has been stated adequately, it may be supported by showing any set of facts consistent with the allegations in the complaint. *Conley,* then, described the breadth of opportunity to prove what an adequate complaint claims, not the minimum standard of adequate pleading to govern a complaint's survival.

[Precedents from the 1940s cited by the dissent stand only for] the unobjectionable proposition that, when a complaint adequately states a claim, it may not be dismissed based on a district court's assessment that the plaintiff will fail to find evidentiary support for his allegations or prove his claim to the satisfaction of the factfinder.

III

When we look for plausibility in this complaint, we agree with the District Court that plaintiffs' claim of conspiracy in restraint of trade comes up short. To begin with, the complaint leaves no doubt that plaintiffs rest their §1 claim on descriptions of parallel conduct and not on any independent allegation of actual agreement among the ILECs. Although in form a few stray statements speak directly of agreement, on fair reading these are merely legal conclusions resting on the prior allegations. Thus, the complaint first takes account of the alleged "absence of any meaningful competition between [the ILECs] in one another's markets," "the parallel course of conduct that each [ILEC] engaged in to prevent competition from CLECs," "and the other facts and market circumstances alleged [earlier]"; "in light of" these, the complaint concludes "that [the ILECs] have entered into a contract, combination or conspiracy to prevent competitive entry into their . . . markets and have agreed not to compete with one another."[10] The nub of the complaint, then, is the ILECs' parallel behavior, consisting of steps to keep the CLECs out and manifest disinterest in becoming CLECs themselves, and its sufficiency turns on the suggestions raised by this conduct when viewed in light of common economic experience.

We think that nothing contained in the complaint invests either the action or inaction alleged with a plausible suggestion of conspiracy. As to the ILECs' supposed agreement to disobey the 1996 Act and thwart the CLECs' attempts to compete, we agree with the District Court that nothing in the complaint intimates that the resistance to the upstarts was anything more than the natural, unilateral reaction of each ILEC intent on keeping its regional dominance. The 1996 Act did more than just subject the ILECs to competition; it obliged them to subsidize their competitors with their own equipment at wholesale rates. The economic incentive to resist was powerful, but resisting competition is routine market conduct, and even if the ILECs flouted the 1996 Act in all the ways the plaintiffs allege, there is no reason to infer that the companies had agreed among themselves to do what was only natural anyway; so natural, in fact, that if alleging parallel decisions to resist competition were enough to imply an antitrust conspiracy, pleading a §1 violation against almost any group of competing businesses would be a sure thing.

The complaint makes its closest pass at a predicate for conspiracy with the claim that collusion was necessary because success by even one CLEC in an ILEC's territory "would have revealed the degree to which competitive entry by CLECs would have been successful in the other territories." But, its logic aside, this general premise still fails to answer the point that there was just no need for joint encouragement to resist the 1996 Act; as the District Court said, "each ILEC has reason to want to avoid dealing with CLECs" and "each ILEC would attempt to keep CLECs out, regardless of the actions of the other ILECs."[12]

---

[10] If the complaint had not explained that the claim of agreement rested on the parallel conduct described, we doubt that the complaint's references to an agreement among the ILECs would have given the notice required by Rule 8. Apart from identifying a seven-year span in which the §1 violations were supposed to have occurred (*i.e.*, "[b]eginning at least as early as February 6, 1996, and continuing to the present"), the pleadings mentioned no specific time, place, or person involved in the alleged conspiracies. This lack of notice contrasts sharply with the model form for pleading negligence, Form 9 [now Form 11]. . . . Whereas the model form alleges that the defendant struck the plaintiff with his car while plaintiff was crossing a particular highway at a specified date and time, the complaint here furnishes no clue as to which of the four ILECs (much less which of their employees) supposedly agreed, or when and where the illicit agreement took place. A defendant wishing to prepare an answer in the simple fact pattern laid out in [Form 11] would know what to answer; a defendant seeking to respond to plaintiffs' conclusory allegations in the §1 context would have little idea where to begin.

[12] From the allegation that the ILECs belong to various trade associations, the dissent playfully suggests that they conspired to restrain trade, an inference said to be "buttressed by the common sense of Adam Smith." If Adam Smith is peering down today, he may be surprised to learn that his tongue-in-cheek remark

Plaintiffs' second conspiracy theory rests on the competitive reticence among the ILECs themselves in the wake of the 1996 Act, which was supposedly passed in the "'hop[e] that the large incumbent local monopoly companies . . . might attack their neighbors' service areas, as they are the best situated to do so.'" Contrary to hope, the ILECs declined "'to enter each other's service territories in any significant way,'" and the local telephone and high speed Internet market remains highly compartmentalized geographically, with minimal competition. Based on this state of affairs, and perceiving the ILECs to be blessed with "especially attractive business opportunities" in surrounding markets dominated by other ILECs, the plaintiffs assert that the ILECs' parallel conduct was "strongly suggestive of conspiracy."

But it was not suggestive of conspiracy, not if history teaches anything. In a traditionally unregulated industry with low barriers to entry, sparse competition among large firms dominating separate geographical segments of the market could very well signify illegal agreement, but here we have an obvious alternative explanation. In the decade preceding the 1996 Act and well before that, monopoly was the norm in telecommunications, not the exception. The ILECs were born in that world, doubtless liked the world the way it was, and surely knew the adage about him who lives by the sword. Hence, a natural explanation for the noncompetition alleged is that the former Government-sanctioned monopolists were sitting tight, expecting their neighbors to do the same thing.

In fact, the complaint itself gives reasons to believe that the ILECs would see their best interests in keeping to their old turf. Although the complaint says generally that the ILECs passed up "especially attractive business opportunit[ies]" by declining to compete as CLECs against other ILECs, it does not allege that competition as CLECs was potentially any more lucrative than other opportunities being pursued by the ILECs during the same period,[13] and the complaint is replete with indications that any CLEC faced nearly insurmountable barriers to profitability owing to the ILECs' flagrant resistance to the network sharing requirements of the 1996 Act. Not only that, but even without a monopolistic tradition and the peculiar difficulty of mandating

---

would be authority to force his famous pinmaker to devote financial and human capital to hire lawyers, prepare for depositions, and otherwise fend off allegations of conspiracy; all this just because he belonged to the same trade guild as one of his competitors when their pins carried the same price tag.

[13] The complaint quoted a reported statement of Qwest's CEO, Richard Notebaert, to suggest that the ILECs declined to compete against each other despite recognizing that it "'might be a good way to turn a quick dollar'" (quoting Chicago Tribune, Oct. 31, 2002, Business Section, p. 1). This was only part of what he reportedly said, however, and the District Court was entitled to take notice of the full contents of the published articles referenced in the complaint, from which the truncated quotations were drawn. See FRE 201. Notebaert was also quoted as saying that entering new markets as a CLEC would not be "a sustainable economic model" because the CLEC pricing model is "just . . . nuts." Another source cited in the complaint quotes Notebaert as saying he thought it "unwise" to "base a business plan" on the privileges accorded to CLECs under the 1996 Act because the regulatory environment was too unstable. Chicago Tribune, Dec. 19, 2002, Business Section, p. 2.

shared networks, "[f]irms do not expand without limit and none of them enters every market that an outside observer might regard as profitable, or even a small portion of such markets." Areeda & Hovenkamp ¶ 307d, at 155 (Supp. 2006) (commenting on the case at bar). The upshot is that Congress may have expected some ILECs to become CLECs in the legacy territories of other ILECs, but the disappointment does not make conspiracy plausible. We agree with the District Court's assessment that antitrust conspiracy was not suggested by the facts adduced under either theory of the complaint, which thus fails to state a valid §1 claim.[14]

Plaintiffs say that our analysis runs counter to *Swierkiewicz*, which held that "a complaint in an employment discrimination lawsuit [need] not contain specific facts establishing a prima facie case of discrimination under the framework set forth in McDonnell Douglas Corp. v. Green, 411 U.S. 792 (1973)." They argue that just as the prima facie case is a "flexible evidentiary standard" that "should not be transposed into a rigid pleading standard for discrimination cases," *Swierkiewicz*, "transpos[ing] 'plus factor' summary judgment analysis woodenly into a rigid Rule 12(b)(6) pleading standard . . . would be unwise." As the District Court correctly understood, however, "*Swierkiewicz* did not change the law of pleading, but simply re-emphasized . . . that the Second Circuit's use of a heightened pleading standard for Title VII cases was contrary to the Federal Rules' structure of liberal pleading requirements." Even though Swierkiewicz's pleadings "detailed the events leading to his termination, provided relevant dates, and included the ages and nationalities of at least some of the relevant persons involved with his termination," the Court of Appeals dismissed his complaint for failing to allege certain additional facts that Swierkiewicz would need at the trial stage to support his claim in the absence of direct evidence of discrimination. We reversed on the ground that the Court of Appeals had impermissibly applied what amounted to a heightened pleading requirement by insisting that Swierkiewicz allege "specific facts" beyond those necessary to state his claim and the grounds showing entitlement to relief.

Here, in contrast, we do not require heightened fact pleading of specifics, but only enough facts to state a claim to relief that is plausible on its face. Because the plaintiffs here have not nudged their claims across the line from conceivable to plausible, their complaint must be dismissed.

---

[14] In reaching this conclusion, we do not apply any "heightened" pleading standard, nor do we seek to broaden the scope of FRCP 9, which can only be accomplished "'by the process of amending the Federal Rules, and not by judicial interpretation.'" Swierkiewicz v. Sorema N.A., 534 U.S. 506, 515 (2002) (quoting Leatherman v. Tarrant County Narcotics Intelligence and Coordination Unit, 507 U.S. 163, 168 (1993)). On certain subjects understood to raise a high risk of abusive litigation, a plaintiff must state factual allegations with greater particularity than Rule 8 requires. FRCP 9(b)-(c). Here, our concern is not that the allegations in the complaint were insufficiently "particular[ized]"; rather, the complaint warranted dismissal because it failed *in toto* to render plaintiffs' entitlement to relief plausible.

. . .

The judgment of the Court of Appeals for the Second Circuit is reversed, and the cause is remanded for further proceedings consistent with this opinion.

It is so ordered.

Justice STEVENS, with whom Justice GINSBURG joins except as to Part IV, dissenting. . . .

Does a judicial opinion that the charge is not "plausible" provide a legally acceptable reason for dismissing the complaint? I think not.

Respondents' amended complaint describes a variety of circumstantial evidence and makes the straightforward allegation that petitioners entered into a contract, combination or conspiracy to prevent competitive entry in their respective local telephone and/or high speed internet services markets and have agreed not to compete with one another and otherwise allocated customers and markets to one another.

The complaint explains that, contrary to Congress' expectation when it enacted the 1996 Telecommunications Act, and consistent with their own economic self-interests, petitioner Incumbent Local Exchange Carriers (ILECs) have assiduously avoided infringing upon each other's markets and have refused to permit nonincumbent competitors to access their networks. The complaint quotes Richard Notebaert, the former CEO of one such ILEC, as saying that competing in a neighboring ILEC's territory "might be a good way to turn a quick dollar but that doesn't make it right." Moreover, respondents allege that petitioners "communicate amongst themselves" through numerous industry associations. In sum, respondents allege that petitioners entered into an agreement that has long been recognized as a classic *per se* violation of the Sherman Act.

Under rules of procedure that have been well settled . . . a judge ruling on a defendant's motion to dismiss a complaint, "must accept as true all of the factual allegations contained in the complaint" *Swierkiewicz*. But instead of requiring knowledgeable executives such as Notebaert to respond to these allegations by way of sworn depositions or other limited discovery—and indeed without so much as requiring petitioners to file an answer denying that they entered into any agreement—the majority permits immediate dismissal based on the assurances of company lawyers that nothing untoward was afoot. . . .

The Court and petitioners' legal team are no doubt correct that the parallel conduct alleged is consistent with the absence of any contract, combination, or conspiracy. But that conduct is also entirely consistent with the *presence* of the illegal agreement alleged in the complaint. And the charge that petitioners "agreed not to compete with one another" is not just one of "a few stray statements"; it is an allegation describing unlawful conduct. As such, the

Federal Rules, our longstanding precedent, and sound practice mandate that the District Court at least require some sort of response from petitioners before dismissing the case.

Two practical concerns presumably explain the Court's dramatic departure from settled procedural law. Private antitrust litigation can be enormously expensive, and there is a risk that jurors may mistakenly conclude that evidence of parallel conduct has proved that the parties acted pursuant to an agreement when they in fact merely made similar independent decisions. Those concerns merit careful case management, including strict control of discovery, careful scrutiny of evidence at the summary judgment stage, and lucid instructions to juries; they do not, however, justify the dismissal of an adequately pleaded complaint without even requiring the defendants to file answers denying a charge that they in fact engaged in collective decisionmaking. More importantly, they do not justify an interpretation of FRCP 12(b)(6) that seems to be driven by the majority's appraisal of the plausibility of the ultimate factual allegation rather than its legal sufficiency.

I . . .

Under the relaxed pleading standards of the Federal Rules, the idea was not to keep litigants out of court but rather to keep them in. The merits of a claim would be sorted out during a flexible pretrial process and, as appropriate, through the crucible of trial. . . . The pleading paradigm under the new Federal Rules was well illustrated by the inclusion in the appendix of [Form 11], a complaint for negligence. As relevant, the Form [11] complaint states only: "On June 1, 1936, in a public highway called Boylston Street in Boston, Massachusetts, defendant negligently drove a motor vehicle against plaintiff who was then crossing said highway." The complaint then describes the plaintiff's injuries and demands judgment. The asserted ground for relief—namely, the defendant's negligent driving—would have been called a "'conclusion of law'" under the code pleading of old. But that bare allegation suffices under a system that "restrict[s] the pleadings to the task of general notice-giving and invest[s] the deposition-discovery process with a vital role in the preparation for trial." Hickman v. Taylor, 329 U.S. 495, 501 (1947).

II . . .

Today's majority calls *Conley's* "'no set of facts'" language "an incomplete, negative gloss on an accepted pleading standard: once a claim has been stated adequately, it may be supported by showing any set of facts consistent with the allegations in the complaint." This is not and cannot be what the *Conley* Court meant. First, as I have explained, and as the *Conley* Court well knew, the pleading standard the Federal Rules meant to codify does not require, or even invite, the pleading of facts. The "pleading standard" label the majority gives to what it reads into the *Conley* opinion—a statement of the permissible factual support for an adequately pleaded complaint—would not, therefore, have impressed the *Conley* Court itself. Rather, that Court would have understood the majority's remodeling of its language to express an *evidentiary* standard, which the *Conley* Court had neither need nor want to explicate. Second, it is pellucidly clear that the *Conley* Court was interested in what a complaint *must* contain, not what it *may* contain. In fact, the Court said without qualification that it was "appraising the *sufficiency* of the complaint." It was, to paraphrase today's majority, describing "the minimum standard of adequate pleading to govern a complaint's survival."

. . .

Everything today's majority says would therefore make perfect sense if it were ruling on a Rule 56 motion for summary judgment and the evidence included nothing more than the Court has described. But it should go without saying in the wake of *Swierkiewicz* that a heightened production burden at the summary judgment stage does not translate into a heightened pleading burden at the complaint stage. The majority rejects the complaint in this case because—in light of the fact that the parallel conduct alleged is consistent with ordinary market behavior—the claimed conspiracy is "conceivable" but not "plausible." I have my doubts about the majority's assessment of the plausibility of this alleged conspiracy. But even if the majority's speculation is correct, its "plausibility" standard is irreconcilable with Rule 8 and with our governing precedents. As we made clear in *Swierkiewicz* and *Leatherman*, fear of the burdens of litigation does not justify factual conclusions supported only by lawyers' arguments rather than sworn denials or admissible evidence.

. . .

III . . .

I would dispute the Court's suggestion that any inference of agreement from petitioners' parallel conduct is "implausible." Many years ago a truly great economist perceptively observed that "[p]eople of the same trade seldom meet together, even for merriment and diversion, but the conversation ends in a conspiracy against the public, or in some contrivance to raise prices." A. Smith, An Inquiry Into the Nature and Causes of the Wealth of Nations, in 39 Great Books of the Western World 55 (R. Hutchins & M. Adler eds. 1952). I am not so cynical as to accept that sentiment at face value, but I need not do so here. Respondents' complaint points not only to petitioners' numerous opportunities to meet with each other, but also to Notebaert's curious statement that encroaching on a fellow incumbent's territory "might be a good way to turn a quick dollar but that doesn't make it right." What did he mean by that? One possible (indeed plausible) inference is that he meant that while it would be in his company's economic self-interest to compete with its brethren, he had agreed with his competitors not to do so. According to the complaint, that is how the Illinois Coalition for Competitive Telecom construed Notebaert's statement (calling the statement "evidence of potential collusion among regional Bell phone monopolies to not compete against one another and kill off potential competitors in local phone service"), and that is how Members of Congress construed his company's behavior (describing a letter to the Justice Department requesting an investigation into the possibility that the ILECs' "very apparent non-competition policy" was coordinated).

Perhaps Notebaert meant instead that competition would be sensible in the short term but not in the long run. That's what his lawyers tell us anyway. But I would think that no one would know better what Notebaert meant than Notebaert himself. Instead of permitting respondents to ask Notebaert, however, the Court looks to other quotes from that and other articles and decides that what he meant was that entering new markets as a CLEC would not be a "'sustainable economic model.'" Never mind that—as anyone ever interviewed knows—a newspaper article is hardly a verbatim transcript; the writer selects quotes to package his story, not to record a subject's views for posterity. But more importantly the District Court was required at this stage of the proceedings to construe Notebaert's ambiguous statement in the plaintiffs' favor. The inference the statement supports—that simultaneous decisions by ILECs not even to attempt to poach customers from one another once the law authorized them to do so were the product of an agreement—sits comfortably within the realm of possibility. That is all the Rules require.

To be clear, if I had been the trial judge in this case, I would not have permitted the plaintiffs to engage in massive discovery based solely on the allegations in this complaint. On the other hand, I surely would not have dismissed the complaint without requiring the defendants to answer the charge that they "have agreed not to compete with one another and otherwise allocated customers and markets to one another." Even a sworn denial of that charge would not justify a summary dismissal without giving the plaintiffs the opportunity to take depositions from Notebaert and at least one responsible executive representing each of the other defendants.

Respondents in this case proposed a plan of "'phased discovery'" limited to the existence of the alleged conspiracy and class certification. Two petitioners rejected the plan. Whether or not respondents' proposed plan was sensible, it was an appropriate subject for negotiation.[13] Given the charge in the complaint—buttressed by the common sense of Adam Smith—I cannot say

---

[13] The potential for "sprawling, costly, and hugely time-consuming" discovery is no reason to throw the baby out with the bathwater. The Court vastly underestimates a district court's case-management arsenal. Before discovery even begins, the court may grant a defendant's Rule 12(e) motion; Rule 7(a) permits a trial court to order a plaintiff to reply to a defendant's answer, see Crawford-El v. Britton, 523 U.S. 574, 598

that the possibility that joint discussions and perhaps some agreements played a role in petitioners' decisionmaking process is so implausible that dismissing the complaint before any defendant has denied the charge is preferable to granting respondents even a minimal opportunity to prove their claims. See Clark, New Federal Rules 977 ("[T]hrough the weapons of discovery and summary judgment we have developed new devices, with more appropriate penalties to aid in matters of *proof*, and do not need to force the pleadings to their less appropriate function").

I fear that the unfortunate result of the majority's new pleading rule will be to invite lawyers' debates over economic theory to conclusively resolve antitrust suits in the absence of any evidence. It is no surprise that the antitrust defense bar—among whom "lament" as to inadequate judicial supervision of discovery is most "common"—should lobby for this state of affairs. But "we must recall that their primary responsibility is to win cases for their clients, not to improve law administration for the public." Clark, Special Pleading in the Big Case 152. As we did in our prior decisions, we should have instructed them that their remedy was to seek to amend the Federal Rules—not our interpretation of them.

IV . . .

The transparent policy concern that drives the decision is the interest in protecting antitrust defendants—who in this case are some of the wealthiest corporations in our economy—from the burdens of pretrial discovery. Even if it were not apparent that the legal fees petitioners have incurred in arguing the merits of their Rule 12(b) motion have far exceeded the cost of limited discovery, or that those discovery costs would burden respondents as well as

---

(1998); and Rule 23 requires "rigorous analysis" to ensure that class certification is appropriate. Rule 16 invests a trial judge with the power, backed by sanctions, to regulate pretrial proceedings via conferences and scheduling orders, at which the parties may discuss, *inter alia*, "the elimination of frivolous claims or defenses," Rule 16(c)(1); "the necessity or desirability of amendments to the pleadings," Rule 16(c)(2); "the control and scheduling of discovery," Rule 16(c)(6); and "the need for adopting special procedures for managing potentially difficult or protracted actions that may involve complex issues, multiple parties, difficult legal questions, or unusual proof problems," Rule 16(c)(12). Subsequently, Rule 26 confers broad discretion to control the combination of interrogatories, requests for admissions, production requests, and depositions permitted in a given case; the sequence in which such discovery devices may be deployed; and the limitations imposed upon them. Indeed, Rule 26(c) specifically permits a court to take actions "to protect a party or person from annoyance, embarrassment, oppression, or undue burden or expense" by, for example, disallowing a particular discovery request, setting appropriate terms and conditions, or limiting its scope.

In short, the Federal Rules contemplate that pretrial matters will be settled through a flexible process of give and take, of proffers, stipulations, and stonewalls, not by having trial judges screen allegations for their plausibility *vel non* without requiring an answer from the defendant. And should it become apparent over the course of litigation that a plaintiff's filings bespeak an *in terrorem* suit, the district court has at its call its own *in terrorem* device, in the form of a wide array of Rule 11 sanctions. See Rules 11(b), (c) (authorizing sanctions if a suit is presented "for any improper purpose, such as to harass or to cause unnecessary delay or needless increase in the cost of litigation").

petitioners, that concern would not provide an adequate justification for this law-changing decision. For in the final analysis it is only a lack of confidence in the ability of trial judges to control discovery, buttressed by appellate judges' independent appraisal of the plausibility of profoundly serious factual allegations, that could account for this stark break from precedent.

If the allegation of conspiracy happens to be true, today's decision obstructs the congressional policy favoring competition that undergirds both the Telecommunications Act of 1996 and the Sherman Act itself. More importantly, even if there is abundant evidence that the allegation is untrue, directing that the case be dismissed without even looking at any of that evidence marks a fundamental-and unjustified-change in the character of pretrial practice.

Accordingly, I respectfully dissent.

■ NOTES ON *TWOMBLY* AND TIGHTER PLEADING STANDARDS

1. In substance, the complaint in *Twombly* says the "Baby Bells" conspired to deny market opportunities to the upstart competitive local exchange carriers (CLECs), and refrained from competing with one another, thus maintaining competitive strength and dividing up the market. The trial court granted the motion to dismiss for failure adequately to allege conspiracy. Doesn't it look like the allegations would satisfy the "short and plain statement" requirement of FRCP 8(a) as it was interpreted prior to *Twombly*? Yet the Court *reverses* the appellate decision, which thought the complaint was adequate. Why did the complaint come up short?

2. The other two pleading cases that you've read (*Reilly* and *Swierkiewicz*) didn't raise a plausibility problem, did they? In *Reilly*, the problem was either that plaintiff left out an allegation that was *formally* necessary to satisfy a Code pleading standard *or* that the Court simply didn't think tree felling is intrinsically dangerous. In *Swierkiewicz*, the Court held that plaintiff did not have to structure the complaint to conform to the *McDonnell-Douglas* schema for trials of discrimination cases based on circumstantial evidence. Both cases involved pleadings that would satisfy the plausibility standard that *Twombly* announces. Why is the complaint in *Twombly* deficient in this regard?

3. *Twombly* does not set out a special rule for antitrust cases, does it? See Ashcroft v. Iqbal, 556 U.S. 662 (2009) (rejecting claim that *Twombly* applies only to antitrust claims). Yet *Twombly* repeatedly refers to claims under §1 of the Sherman Act (barring conspiracies "in restraint of trade").

(a) Is there something about economic conspiracies that calls for a pleading rule that applies differently from the way it applies in more ordinary

cases, like claims for breach of contract or negligent driving? Is there also something different from ordinary cases when we come to the behavior of law enforcement officers causing damage as they search a residence for drugs (as in *Leatherman,* described in note 3 of the Notes after *Swierkiewicz*) or the behavior of high school principals in suspending students for disciplinary infractions (as in *Piphus,* in Chapter 1B)?

(b) In dissent, Justice Stevens says that Form 11, which is offered in the Rules as an example of a complaint for negligence, states only that "defendant negligently drove a motor vehicle against plaintiff" on "a public highway called Boylston Street" in Boston on a certain date, as plaintiff "was then crossing said highway." (Since *Twombly,* Form 11 has been amended to remove the reference to Boylston Street, substituting the word "place" for the more colorful original terms.) Can the plausibility standard be squared with allegations of negligence in Form 11?

(c) In Erickson v. Pardus, 551 U.S. 89 (2007), decided two weeks after *Twombly,* the Court upheld a complaint against prison officials under §1983, in a per curiam opinion. The complaint alleged a failure to deliver medical treatment for hepatitis C and charged that officials were "deliberately indifferent" to plaintiff prisoner's needs. Allegedly, officials discontinued his treatment because they suspected he had stolen and modified a syringe and used it to take illegal drugs. The trial court dismissed for failing to allege "substantial harm," and the Tenth Circuit affirmed, but the Supreme Court reversed. Without ruling on the sufficiency of the complaint "in all respects," the Court found that it could not be thrown out because allegations of harm were "too conclusory." Is *Erickson* consistent with *Twombly*?

4. The 2009 decision in *Iqbal,* cited in the prior note, gave the Court a chance to explain *Twombly. Iqbal* was a suit brought under the *Bivens* doctrine, which allows damage claims against *federal* officials even though no statute authorizes such suits in the manner in which §1983 authorizes suits against *state* officials. Plaintiff in *Iqbal* claimed he was detained illegally in a maximum security facility in the wake of the 9/11 attacks because he was a Muslim and a citizen of Pakistan. He pled guilty, served a prison term, and was removed to Pakistan. The Attorney General and FBI Director moved to dismiss on ground of immunity, and the trial court denied the motion. In an unusual interlocutory appeal (denials of motions to dismiss are not ordinarily appealable), the Court of Appeals affirmed. The Supreme Court reversed, finding that the complaint did not satisfy the *Twombly* standard:

> To survive a motion to dismiss, a complaint must contain sufficient factual matter, accepted as true, to "state a claim to relief that is plausible on its face." A claim has facial plausibility when the plaintiff pleads factual content that allows the court to draw the reasonable inference that the defendant is liable for the misconduct alleged. The plausibility standard is not akin to a "probability requirement," but it asks for more than a sheer possibility that a defendant has

acted unlawfully. Where a complaint pleads facts that are "merely consistent with" a defendant's liability, it "stops short of the line between possibility and plausibility of 'entitlement to relief.'"

Two working principles underlie our decision in *Twombly*. First, the tenet that a court must accept as true all of the allegations contained in a complaint is inapplicable to legal conclusions. Threadbare recitals of the elements of a cause of action, supported by mere conclusory statements, do not suffice. (Although for the purposes of a motion to dismiss we must take all of the factual allegations in the complaint as true, we "are not bound to accept as true a legal conclusion couched as a factual allegation" (internal quotation marks omitted)). Rule 8 marks a notable and generous departure from the hyper-technical, code-pleading regime of a prior era, but it does not unlock the doors of discovery for a plaintiff armed with nothing more than conclusions. Second, only a complaint that states a plausible claim for relief survives a motion to dismiss. Determining whether a complaint states a plausible claim for relief will, as the Court of Appeals observed, be a context-specific task that requires the reviewing court to draw on its judicial experience and common sense. But where the well-pleaded facts do not permit the court to infer more than the mere possibility of misconduct, the complaint has alleged—but it has not "show[n]"—"that the pleader is entitled to relief." FRCP 8(a)(2).

In keeping with these principles a court considering a motion to dismiss can choose to begin by identifying pleadings that, because they are no more than conclusions, are not entitled to the assumption of truth. While legal conclusions can provide the framework of a complaint, they must be supported by factual allegations. When there are well-pleaded factual allegations, a court should assume their veracity and then determine whether they plausibly give rise to an entitlement to relief.

. . .

Under *Twombly's* construction of Rule 8, we conclude that respondent's complaint has not "nudged [his] claims" of invidious discrimination "across the line from conceivable to plausible."

We begin our analysis by identifying the allegations in the complaint that are not entitled to the assumption of truth. Respondent pleads that petitioners "knew of, condoned, and willfully and maliciously agreed to subject [him]" to harsh conditions of confinement "as a matter of policy, solely on account of [his] religion, race, and/or national origin and for no legitimate penological interest." The complaint alleges that Ashcroft was the "principal architect" of this invidious policy, and that Mueller was "instrumental" in adopting and executing it. These bare assertions, much like the pleading of conspiracy in *Twombly*, amount to nothing more than a "formulaic recitation of the elements" of a constitutional discrimination claim, namely, that petitioners adopted a policy "'because of,' not merely 'in spite of,' its adverse effects upon an identifiable group." As such, the allegations are conclusory and not entitled to be assumed true. To be clear, we do not reject these bald allegations on the ground that they are unrealistic or non-sensical. We do not so characterize them any more than the Court in *Twombly* rejected the plaintiffs' express allegation of a "'contract, combination or conspiracy to prevent competitive entry,'" because it thought that claim too chimerical to be maintained. It is the conclusory nature of respondent's allegations, rather than their extravagantly fanciful nature, that disentitles them to the presumption of truth.

We next consider the factual allegations in respondent's complaint to determine if they plausibly suggest an entitlement to relief. The complaint alleges that "the [FBI], under the direction of Defendant Mueller, arrested and detained thousands of Arab Muslim men . . . as part of its investigation of the events of September 11." It further claims that "[t]he policy of holding post-September-11th detainees in highly restrictive conditions of confinement until they were 'cleared' by the FBI was approved by Defendants Ashcroft and Mueller in discussions in the weeks after September 11, 2001." Taken as true, these allegations are consistent with petitioners' purposefully designating detainees "of high interest" because of their race, religion, or national origin. But given more likely explanations, they do not plausibly establish this purpose.

The September 11 attacks were perpetrated by 19 Arab Muslim hijackers who counted themselves members in good standing of al Qaeda, an Islamic fundamentalist group. Al Qaeda was headed by another Arab Muslim—Osama bin Laden—and composed in large part of his Arab Muslim disciples. It should come as no surprise that a legitimate policy directing law enforcement to arrest and detain individuals because of their suspected link to the attacks would produce a disparate, incidental impact on Arab Muslims, even though the purpose of the policy was to target neither Arabs nor Muslims. On the facts respondent alleges the arrests Mueller oversaw were likely lawful and justified by his non-discriminatory intent to detain aliens who were illegally present in the United States and who had potential connections to those who committed terrorist acts. As between that "obvious alternative explanation" for the arrests, and the purposeful, invidious discrimination respondent asks us to infer, discrimination is not a plausible conclusion.

But even if the complaint's well-pleaded facts give rise to a plausible inference that respondent's arrest was the result of unconstitutional discrimination, that inference alone would not entitle respondent to relief. It is important to recall that respondent's complaint challenges neither the constitutionality of his arrest nor his initial detention in the MDC. Respondent's constitutional claims against petitioners rest solely on their ostensible "policy of holding post-September-11th detainees" in the ADMAX SHU [Administrative Maximum Special Housing Unit—ED.] once they were categorized as "of high interest." To prevail on that theory, the complaint must contain facts plausibly showing that petitioners purposefully adopted a policy of classifying post-September-11 detainees as "of high interest" because of their race, religion, or national origin.

This the complaint fails to do. Though respondent alleges that various other defendants, who are not before us, may have labeled him a person of "of high interest" for impermissible reasons, his only factual allegation against petitioners accuses them of adopting a policy approving "restrictive conditions of confinement" for post-September-11 detainees until they were "'cleared' by the FBI." Accepting the truth of that allegation, the complaint does not show, or even intimate, that petitioners purposefully housed detainees in the ADMAX SHU due to their race, religion, or national origin. All it plausibly suggests is that the Nation's top law enforcement officers, in the aftermath of a devastating terrorist attack, sought to keep suspected terrorists in the most secure conditions available until the suspects could be cleared of terrorist activity. Respondent does not argue, nor can he, that such a motive would violate petitioners' constitutional obligations. He would need to allege more by way of factual content to "nudg[e]" his claim of purposeful discrimination "across the line from conceivable to plausible."

Ashcroft v. Iqbal, 556 U.S. 662, 678-683 (2009).

5. *Twombly* expresses the concern that "proceeding to antitrust discovery can be expensive," and indicates reluctance to let an antitrust case go forward to discovery on a complaint that would satisfy the pleading standard hitherto imposed under FRCP 8. You will see that courts have authority to control the nature, sequence, and extent of discovery (see Chapter 9, infra). Under FRCP 26(c), a court may protect against, *inter alia,* "undue burden or expense" in discovery by limiting or "forbidding" it. Before *Twombly,* arguments that pleading standards should be tightened because discovery is expensive typically failed on the theory that courts could supervise discovery to prevent undue burdens, and Justice Stevens takes this view in *Twombly.* What convinces the majority otherwise? Why does the majority also reject another common argument against stricter pleading standards, which is that losers can be weeded out by summary judgment (see Chapter 11, infra)?

6. The majority in *Twombly* backs away from *Conley*—the famous decision described in the introduction to this section, which says a complaint satisfies FRCP 8 unless there is "no set of facts" that plaintiff might prove that could lead to recovery. Taken "literally," as the Court says in *Twombly, Conley* would do away with any standard of clarity or completeness or content for complaints ("Mr. Micawber's optimism would be enough"). Even before *Twombly,* most courts did *not* take it literally. As a leading treatise commented, a complaint satisfies FRCP 8 only if it contains "direct allegations on every material point" or "allegations from an inference fairly may be drawn that evidence on these material points will be introduced at trial." 5 Wright & Miller, Federal Practice and Procedure §1216 (3d ed. 2004) (adding that a complaint must contain "something more by way of a claim for relief than a bare averment that the pleader wants compensation and is entitled to it or a statement of facts that merely creates a suspicion that the pleader might have a right of action"). The Wright & Miller treatise also quotes a pre-*Conley* opinion as coming closer to the mark than *Conley.* See Daves v. Hawaiian Dredging Co., 114 F. Supp. 643, 644 (D. Haw. 1953) ("it seems to be the purpose of Rule 8 to relieve the pleader from the niceties of the dotted i and the crossed t and the uncertainties of distinguishing in advance between evidentiary and ultimate facts, while still requiring, in a practical and sensible way, that he set out sufficient factual matter to outline the elements of his cause of action or claim, proof of which is essential to his recovery" so that "if a pleader cannot allege definitely and in good faith the existence of an essential element of his claim, it is difficult to see why this basic deficiency should not be exposed at the point of minimum expenditure of time and money by the parties and the court"). *Twombly* points toward the same conclusion, doesn't it, by simply burying *Conley*?

7. Academic commentary on *Twombly* is divided. For critical arguments, see Scott Dodson, *Pleading Standards After Bell Atlantic Corp. v. Twombly*, 93 Va. L. Rev. in Brief 135 (2007) (using pleading standards as safeguard against "meritless strike suits" is "problematic"; *Twombly* "encourages defendants to file motions to dismiss" and will "spawn years of increased litigation"); Benjamin Spencer, *Pleading Civil Rights Claims in the Post-*Conley *Era*, 52 Howard L.J. 99 (2008) (a *Twombly* dismissal is "nothing more than a speculative assessment that the plaintiff is unlikely—in the view of the court—to be able to identify facts through discovery that will support a claim," and allowing such an assessment at the pleading stage is "too harsh"). But *Twombly* has also attracted support. See Robert Bone, Twombly, *Pleading Rules, and the Regulation of Court Access*, 94 Iowa L. Rev. 873, 886 (2009) (explaining *Twombly*'s plausibility standard as one that requires allegations of behavior that departs "in some significant way from what usually occurs" in a way that "supports a higher probability of wrongdoing than is ordinarily associated with baseline conduct," which is why the complaint in *Twombly* failed but a similarly vague complaint complying with the Form for a negligence case should pass muster); Douglas Smith, *The* Twombly *Revolution*, 36 Pepp. L. Rev. 1063, 1088 (2009) (interpreting plausibility standard as requiring "logical coherence" and welcoming this shift as appropriate in light of costs that come with defending a claim in federal court; this standard is "consistent with common sense" and aptly expresses FRCP 8's requirement that plaintiff make a "showing" of liability in the complaint). And see Richard Epstein, *Bell Atlantic v. Twombly: How Motions to Dismiss Become (Disguised) Summary Judgments*, 25 Wash. U. J.L. & Pol'y 61 (2007) (defending *Twombly* as "welcome" and "right" for reasons that do not appear in the case; the Rules were "designed in an earlier era" for litigation that was "on average" far simpler; in antitrust cases, plaintiffs should not go forward where they advance only "public sources" suggesting collusion and defendants show from similar sources that there is no triable issue). Finally, see Donald Elliott, Twombly *in Context: Why Federal Rule of Civil Procedure 4(b) Is Unconstitutional*, 64 Fla. L. Rev. 895 (2012) (arguing that *Twombly* gets at a real problem, but that it is not located in pleading standards but in Rule 4(b), which lets private plaintiffs invoke official power to force defendants to defend suits without any prior scrutiny of the merits of plaintiff's claim).

3. Elements in a Claim for Relief

Lest you emerge from cases like *Swierkiewicz* and *Twombly* with the idea that the art of pleading is arcane and plagued by hidden traps for the unwary, it should be said that in the vast majority of cases pleading a claim is a simple matter. The importance or general applicability of *Twombly*'s "plausibility" standard should not be minimized, but *Twombly* and *Iqbal* were exceptional cases in which pleadings are most likely to receive close attention—and there are other situations, such as class actions challenging official conduct or seeking enormous sums in damages, where similar pressures are likely to be felt.

When a lawyer is preparing a complaint and needs to know what elements must be alleged to state a claim for relief under FRCP 8, she can generally find a practice guide written for her own state, or one for the federal system. Here she will find the elements of the most common claims spelled out. Short of that, the lawyer can resort to an electronic search of cases. There are also Restatements of the Law, and particularly in the area of torts the practitioner can find laundry lists of the elements of various torts. See Restatement (Second) of Torts (1965). Whatever the source, she will discover that the elements of the most common claims are well settled by the case law, and preparing the complaint is an easy matter.

If you had already completed your study of substantive areas of law affecting civil liability (torts, contracts, property, and securities law, to name a few), you would know that it would make no sense to require everything that bears on civil liability to be set out in the complaint. We don't require plaintiffs in contract suits, for example, to allege that the contract is legal or the parties had the capacity to contract. Rather, we abstract from the full picture a few of the most important factors, and these must appear in the complaint.

Four considerations seem to shape pleading requirements:[5]

(1) *Public Policy.* To some extent, what we expect in a complaint is shaped by public policy—typically a purpose of making it easier or harder for the plaintiff to bring a claim or for defendant to resist a claim. The classic example is the negligence suit. Theoretically, recovery is harder if plaintiffs must plead that they exercised due care, easier if defendants must raise this point by pleading that plaintiff was contributorily negligent. American jurisdictions were once split on this point, but no longer. Everywhere now, defendants must plead contributory negligence. (Also, proving contributory negligence used to block recovery. Now it only reduces recovery, at least where plaintiff was less than 50 percent responsible.)

(2) *Intrinsic Probabilities.* Pleading requirements are partly shaped by what we think is likely true. There is a high likelihood, for example, that any given contract is legal and both parties had capacity to contract. Restrictions on capacity are few and far between—children and insane persons lack such capacity—so any given contract is unlikely to raise this issue. And while it is possible to imagine an infinite number of contracts to commit crimes, seldom would a lawyer bring such an arrangement to court. We can also be confident that if the contract is illegal or a party lacks capacity, the *defense* will raise such points.

---

[5] For good discussions of these matters, see Edward W. Cleary, *Presuming and Pleading: An Essay on Juristic Immaturity*, 12 Stan. L. Rev. 5 (1959); James, Hazard & Leubsdorf, Civil Procedure §3.11 (5th ed. 2001).

(3) *Access to Proof.* Pleading burdens are affected by estimates of relative access to proof. In contract cases, defendants are expected to plead "payment" as a defense. See FRCP 8(c). The idea is that defendant's financial records will reflect payment, and defendant has access to them and can easily prove the point. Plaintiff could testify that he received no payment, but "proving a negative" by such testimony is harder and less satisfactory.

(4) *Practical Realities.* Again, in contract cases, we ask plaintiffs to allege that the conditions precedent to defendant's obligation have occurred, and we say that these may be "generally" alleged. If defendant thinks some crucial condition has *not* occurred, he is expected to raise this point in his answer "specifically and with particularity." See FRCP 9(c). The thinking here is that a plaintiff is unlikely to sue for breach of contract if none of the conditions precedent has occurred (or few have), so plaintiff alleges generally that all have occurred and the burden is then on the defendant to say which ones have not.

Practical realities include considerations peculiar to the process of pleading. Usually, for example, pleading burdens are more or less complementary, meaning that either plaintiff or defendant is expected to raise any particular point. Not always, however. Sometimes *both* parties must include allegations on an aspect of the case. In libel suits, for example, plaintiff is expected to allege that defendant's statement is false, but if defendant contends the statement is true, then *he too* must address the point in his answer (by claiming truth). The reason plaintiff is expected to allege falsity is that a complaint would seem incomplete without it: A complaint that defendant "stated that plaintiff is a thief" would seem oddly inconsequential (the reason for suing becomes clear if plaintiff alleges that defendant "falsely stated that plaintiff is a thief"). Much the same is true in contract cases seeking payment: A complaint alleging that the contract requires defendant "to pay $50,000" would seem oddly inconsequential unless it also alleged that defendant "has not paid that sum." Hence we expect plaintiff to include these allegations, but we *also* expect defendants to address the same point: Defendants in contract cases must allege "payment" in their answer if they expect to argue the point at trial. Under FRCP 8(c), these are "affirmative defense[s]." (FRCP 8(c) includes "payment" in the list, but the list is exemplary rather than exhaustive, and case law establishes that "truth" is among the "other matter[s]" that are also in this category.)

■ NOTES ON THE CONVENTIONS OF RULES PLEADING

1. Look now at some common claims, and the lists of elements that would be common, with only slight variations, among most courts across the country:

(a) Breach of Contract. Most courts expect claimants to allege agreement, plaintiff's performance (or more generally, the happening of "conditions

precedent"), defendant's breach, and damages. Remember from Chapter 2 that plaintiffs are normally entitled to what we might call "ordinary damages" (the cost or value of what plaintiff would have gotten if defendant had not breached his obligation), but not usually "consequential damages," such as lost business opportunities or lost profits. That is the famous rule of Hadley v. Baxendale, 9 Ex. 341, 156 Eng. Rep. 145 (1854). Notice now that FRCP 9(g) (any claim for "an item of special damage" must be "specifically stated" in the complaint), which is designed to require allegations that the parties contemplated the possibility of consequential damages when they entered into their contract. On the elements in claim for damages for breach of contract, see Brown v. Harms, 467 S.E.2d 805, 807 (Va. 1996) (elements in claim for breach of contract are "legal obligation of a defendant to the plaintiff," a "violation or breach" of that right or duty, and "consequential injury or damage") and Southern Medical Health Systems, Inc. v. Vaughn, 669 So. 2d 98, 99 (Ala. 1995) (in ordinary suit for breach of contract, claimant must prove "(1) the existence of a valid contract binding the parties in the action, (2) his own performance under the contract, (3) the defendant's nonperformance, and (4) damages").

(b) Negligence. Most jurisdictions expect negligence claims to include allegations of duty, breach, proximate cause, and injury. See, e.g., Bobo v. State, 697 A.2d 1371, 1375 (Me. Ct. App. 1996) (elements of negligence claim are "(1) a duty or obligation under which the defendant is to protect the plaintiff from injury; (2) breach of that duty; and (3) actual loss or injury to the plaintiff proximately resulting from the breach"). See also Form 11 (in the Appendix of Forms of the Rules of Civil Procedure), which *omits* any allegation of duty and *includes* only the bare conclusion "negligently" and does not even use the word "cause" in describing what defendant did. If an accident happened on July 17, 2012 on Valmont Avenue in Boulder, Colorado, would a complaint that added the date and geographical reference but otherwise used the same language as Form 11 suffice? The fact that Form 11 is included in the Rules indicates that the answer is yes. Leaving nothing to chance, the framers gave us Rule 84 (the Forms "are sufficient under the rules and are intended to indicate the simplicity and brevity of statement which the rules contemplate"). Yet the *Bobo* case (and most modern authority) says the claimant should allege duty, and breach of duty, and proximate cause. Is there any point at all in going into further detail than Form 11 requires?

(c) Interference with Contract. Here are some cases that consider the elements in this claim: Quelimane Co. v. Stewart Title Guaranty Co., 960 P.2d 513, 530 (Cal. 1998) (elements in cause of action for intentional interference with contractual relations are "(1) a valid contract between plaintiff and a third party; (2) defendant's knowledge of this contract; (3) defendant's intentional acts designed to induce a breach or disruption of the contractual relationship; (4) actual breach or disruption of the contractual relationship; and (5) resulting damage"). Compare Pasco Industries, Inc. v. Talco Recycling, Inc., 985 P.2d 535, 547 (Ariz. Ct. App. 1998) (including requirement that plaintiff

allege that defendant "acted improperly"); Mayes v. Sturdy Northern Sales, Inc., 154 Cal. Rptr. 43, 48 (Cal. App. 1979) (including requirement that breach occur "as a proximate result" of defendant's "wrongful" or "unjustified" or "unprivileged" conduct).

(d) *Attorney Malpractice.* Here are some cases that consider the elements in this claim: Nichols v. Keller, 19 Cal. Rptr. 2d 601, 607 (Cal. App. 1993) (legal malpractice consists of "the same basic elements" as other kinds of negligence, including "duty, breach of duty, causation, and damage," and elements of claim for negligence are "(1) the duty of the professional to use such skill, prudence and diligence as other members of the profession commonly possess and exercise; (2) breach of that duty; (3) a causal connection between the negligent conduct and the resulting injury; and (4) actual loss").

2. Does the "short and plain statement" required by FRCP 8(a) mean a claimant must state a "prima facie case" (or "every element in the claim") in the complaint? The best answer to that question, and the one that most courts would give, is yes—yes *despite* the "anything goes" signals that came from decisions like *Conley.* Usually, the expression "prima facie case" (or "every element in the claim") is just another way of saying that "if everything plaintiff alleges is true, and there are no unexpected facts or special reasons to deny relief," plaintiff should win if he proves what he alleges. Here is how one commentator explained it:

> [I]f the suit is on a contract and we require plaintiff to establish the existence or nonexistence, as may be appropriate, of every concept treated in Corbin and Williston, then the responsibility of plaintiff becomes burdensome indeed and the lawsuit itself may include a large amount of unnecessary territory. Actually, of course, the responsibility for dealing with every element is not placed on plaintiff. Instead we settle for a "prima facie case" or "cause of action," consisting of certain selected elements which are regarded as sufficient to entitle plaintiff to recover, if he proves them and unless defendant in turn establishes other elements which would offset them.

Cleary, supra, at 5, 9-14. See also 5 Wright & Miller, supra, §1216 (complaint must contain "either direct allegations on every material point necessary to sustain a recovery" or at least "allegations from which an inference fairly may be drawn that evidence on these material points will be introduced").

3. Plaintiffs are not supposed to advance allegations for which they have no basis. Often, the client who becomes a plaintiff can supply the lawyer, on the basis of personal knowledge, with all the facts necessary for a complaint. Sometimes, however, the lawyer herself gathers evidence by talking with people or doing original research. If a lawyer thinks there is evidence that will support critical allegations, she can craft a complaint advancing such allegations on "information and belief," which is a signal that the lawyer does not have all the proof she needs (she has not found witnesses who can testify to all the necessary facts), but she has learned from credible sources that the proof can be found somewhere somehow. The Rules do not expressly authorize such allegations, but FRCP 8(b) permits *defendants* to base denials on lack of "knowledge or information," and this provision has been read as implying that plaintiffs can do something similar. The passage from the complaint that is quoted in the first part of the opinion in *Twombly* contains averments based "upon information and belief." See also 5 Wright & Miller, supra, §1224 (even though the Rules contain no "express authorization" for allegations based on "information and belief," they are permitted on basis of FRCP 8(b)'s authorization of denials in this form).

4. Problem 7-A ("The Roof Was Leaking") examines one pitfall in pleading a claim (or cause of action) in specific detail: If the complaint is wrong on the details and the proof at trial departs materially from them, the "variance" may lead to dismissal. Suppose, however, plaintiff in an automobile accident case knows what happened—defendant ran the light and struck plaintiff as he was driving through the intersection, and running the light was the negligent act. If the attorney is confident of such facts, would it do any good to *be* specific? Consider that a lawyer may file a complaint in June and might not look at the file again until September, and in the meantime he may have filed ten other lawsuits, tried three others, and settled another nine. Consider that the other lawyer will actually read the complaint, if only because she must file an answer for her client. And the judge might read the complaint too, at least the first time he opens the file, to figure out what the case is about. Do these prospects suggest any reasons to prefer a carefully drawn complaint that alleges the operative details in some way?

5. An over-long complaint is objectionable under FRCP 8(a), just as it was at common law. Not surprisingly, however, the reason has nothing to do with the older formalist objection against "pleading evidence." Instead, the modern objection is that plaintiffs should not burden courts and defendants with long and undigested recitations. Consider this comment on over-long complaints:

> Some complaints are windy but understandable. Surplusage can and should be ignored. Instead of insisting that the parties perfect their pleadings, a judge should bypass the dross and get on with the case. A district court is not "authorized to dismiss a complaint merely because it contains repetitious and irrelevant matter, a disposable husk around a core of proper pleading." Davis v. Ruby Foods, Inc., 269 F.3d 818, 820 (7th Cir. 2001). But although "[f]at in a complaint can be ignored," Bennett v. Schmidt, 153 F.3d 516, 518 (7th Cir. 1998), "dismissal of a complaint on the ground that it is unintelligible is unexceptionable." *Davis.* Length may make a complaint unintelligible, by scattering and concealing in a morass of irrelevancies the few allegations that matter. Three other circuits have held that length and complexity may doom a complaint by obfuscating the claim's essence. See In re Westinghouse Securities Litigation, 90 F.3d 696, 702-03 (3d Cir. 1996) (600 paragraphs spanning 240 pages); Kuehl v. FDIC, 8 F.3d 905, 908-09 (1st Cir. 1993) (358 paragraphs in "only" 43 pages); Michaelis v. Nebraska State Bar Association, 717 F.2d 437, 439 (8th Cir. 1983) (144 paragraphs in 98

pages). At 400 paragraphs covering 155 pages, and followed by 99 attachments, Garst's distended pleadings join that unsavory company. A concise statement of the claim illustrated by 400 concrete examples of fraud would be one thing, but 400 variations on the kind of paragraph we have quoted are quite another. Complaints like this are pestilential, and the district court showed great restraint in wading through four iterations plus one "more definite statement" before giving up. Garst received more judicial attention than his pleadings deserved.

United States ex rel. Garst v. Lockheed-Martin Corp., 328 F.3d 374, 378 (7th Cir.), *cert. denied*, 540 U.S. 968 (2003). See also Vicom, Inc. v. Harbridge Merchant Services, Inc., 20 F.3d 771 (7th Cir. 1994) (upholding dismissal of RICO suit for failing to state claim, while denying leave to amend; 119-page complaint with 385 paragraphs was "less-than-coherent," making it hard for defendant to respond and for court to "conduct orderly litigation"). However extreme these examples might be, bear in mind that the RICO statute is vague and complex, so complexity can flow from the nature of the underlying substantive rules.

6. Whether or not a cause of action exists is itself sometimes problematic. This question has often arisen in federal litigation in which plaintiffs brought suit under modern remedial legislation. See, e.g., J.I. Case Co. v. Borak, 377 U.S. 426, 432 (1964) (implied private right to sue for securities fraud); Cannon v. University of Chicago, 441 U.S. 667 (1979) (implied private right to sue under Title IX for sex discrimination in federally assisted programs). Modern decisions stress that it is up to Congress whether to create private claims. The 1975 decision in *Cort* sets out the criteria that continue to apply:

> In determining whether a private remedy is implicit in a statute not expressly providing one, several factors are relevant. First, is the plaintiff "one of the class for whose especial benefit the statute was enacted" [quoting 1916 decision]—that is, does the statute create a federal right in favor of the plaintiff? Second, is there any indication of legislative intent, explicit or implicit, either to create such a remedy or to deny one? Third, is it consistent with the underlying purposes of the legislative scheme to imply such a remedy for the plaintiff? And finally, is the cause of action one traditionally relegated to state law, in an area basically the concern of the States, so that it would be inappropriate to infer a cause of action based solely on federal law?

Cort v. Ash, 422 U.S. 66, 78 (1975) (concluding that Federal Elections Campaign Act Amendments of 1975 does not create private cause of action in derivative suit claiming that corporation violated said Act). See also Alexander v. Sandoval, 542 U.S. 275 (2001) ("private rights of action to enforce federal law must be created by Congress," and statutory intent is "determinative"). Similar issues arise in suits brought in state court. See, e.g., Reynolds v. Diamond Foods & Poultry, Inc., 79 S.W.3d 907, 908-909 (Mo. 2002) (federal statute protecting "privacy interests of residential telephone subscribers" and stating that one may sue in state court for any violation of the statute "if otherwise permitted by the laws or rules of a court of a State" authorized private claim even in absence of state enabling legislation).

4. Pleading Special Matters: The "Strong Inference" Standard in Securities Fraud

FRCP 9 imposes heightened pleading requirements in connection with claims of "fraud or mistake." Under FRCP 9(b), such claims must include allegations of "the circumstances," and these must be set forth "with particularity." Essentially, the purpose is to shield defendants from careless or malicious suits: Merely accusing someone of fraud, perhaps especially if defendant is a professional person such as a lawyer or accountant, or anyone whose livelihood depends on attracting customers or clients, can cause serious damage. If fraud must be pled "with particularity," the theory goes, at least some claims will not be brought, and others will be dismissed at the pleading stage (preventing or minimizing damage to the defendant).

What does it take to state a claim in fraud? Consider the following:

> In order to recover damages in an action for fraud or deceit, a plaintiff must prove (1) that the defendant made a false representation to the plaintiff, (2) that its falsity was either known to the defendant or that the representation was made with reckless indifference as to its truth, (3) that the misrepresentation was made for the purpose of defrauding the plaintiff, (4) that the plaintiff relied on the misrepresentation and had the right to rely on it, and (5) that the plaintiff suffered compensable injury resulting from the misrepresentation.

Nails v. S&R, Inc., 639 A.2d 660, 668 (Md. 1994). Compare K-Tel In re International Securities Litigation, 300 F.3d 881, 887 (8th Cir. 2002) (fraud under Rule 10b-5 and Securities Act of 1933 consists of "(1) misrepresentations or omissions of material fact or acts that operated as a fraud or deceit in violation of the rule; (2) causation, often analyzed in terms of materiality and reliance; (3) scienter on the part of the defendants; and (4) economic harm caused by the fraudulent activity occurring in connection with the purchase and sale of a security").

Claims of "mistake" provide a mechanism to reformulate obligations created by contract. Such relief is hard to come by, in part because it threatens to undermine settled expectations, which contract law seeks to protect. Fraud and mistake often appear together in complaints attacking contractual arrangements. A leading treatise describes the purpose of FRCP 9(b) in these terms:

> It has been said that the requirement is necessary to safeguard potential defendants from lightly made claims charging commission of acts that involve some degree of moral turpitude. Allegations of fraud or mistake frequently are

advanced only for their nuisance or settlement value and with little hope that they will be successful. Further, since assertions of fraud or mistake often are involved in attempts to reopen completed transactions or set aside previously issued judicial orders, courts are unwilling to entertain charges of this type unless they are based on allegations that are sufficient to show whether the alleged injustice is severe enough to warrant the risks and difficulties inherent in a re-examination of old and settled matters. Also, fraud and mistake embrace such a wide variety of potential conduct that a defendant needs a substantial amount of particularized information about plaintiff's claim in order to enable him to understand it and effectively prepare his response. Finally, as has been pointed out by the commentators, the old cliché that actions or defenses based upon fraud are disfavored and are scrutinized by the courts with great care because they often form the basis for "strike suits" still retains considerable vitality.

5 Wright & Miller, supra, §1296.

There are many other kinds of suits in which allegations can bring embarrassment that may be damaging to defendants in many ways. Rule 9 is narrow and selective in the kinds of suits that require more detailed pleadings. Consider divorce and custody disputes, as well as suits for libel, malpractice, and product liability, where Rule 9 is silent.

In some areas, Congress has intervened to raise pleading standards. Consider, for example, the Prison Litigation Reform Act of 1996, which requires courts *on their own* to scrutinize complaints in suits challenging prison conditions "as soon as practicable," and to dismiss claims that are inadequately pleaded. See 28 USC §1915A and 42 USC §1997e(c)(1), construed in Baxter v. Rose, 305 F.3d 486 (6th Cir. 2002). Now consider the Public Securities Litigation Reform Act of 1995 (PSLRA), which goes even further than FRCP 9(b).

TELLABS, INC. v. MAKOR ISSUES & RIGHTS, LTD.

United States Supreme Court
551 U.S. 308 (2007)

Justice GINSBURG delivered the opinion of the Court.

This Court has long recognized that meritorious private actions to enforce federal antifraud securities laws are an essential supplement to criminal prosecutions and civil enforcement actions brought, respectively, by the Department of Justice and the Securities and Exchange Commission (SEC). See, e.g., Dura Pharmaceuticals, Inc. v. Broudo, 544 U.S. 336, 345 (2005); J.I. Case Co. v. Borak, 377 U.S. 426, 432 (1964). Private securities fraud actions, however, if not adequately contained, can be employed abusively to impose substantial costs on companies and individuals whose conduct conforms to the law. As a check against abusive litigation by private parties, Congress enacted the Private Securities Litigation Reform Act of 1995 (PSLRA).

Exacting pleading requirements are among the control measures Congress included in the PSLRA. The Act requires plaintiffs to state with particularity both the facts constituting the alleged violation, and the facts evidencing scienter, *i.e.*, the defendant's intention "to deceive, manipulate, or defraud." Ernst & Ernst v. Hochfelder, 425 U.S. 185, 194, and n.12 (1976); see 15 USC §78u-4(b)(1), (2). This case concerns the latter requirement. As set out in §21D (b)(2) of the PSLRA, plaintiffs must "state with particularity facts giving rise to a strong inference that the defendant acted with the required state of mind." 15 USC §78u-4(b)(2).

Congress left the key term "strong inference" undefined, and Courts of Appeals have divided on its meaning. In the case before us, the Court of Appeals for the Seventh Circuit held that the "strong inference" standard would be met if the complaint "allege[d] facts from which, if true, a reasonable person could infer that the defendant acted with the required intent." That formulation, we conclude, does not capture the stricter demand Congress sought to convey in §21D(b)(2). It does not suffice that a reasonable factfinder plausibly could infer from the complaint's allegations the requisite state of mind. Rather, to determine whether a complaint's scienter allegations can survive threshold inspection for sufficiency, a court governed by §21D(b)(2) must engage in a comparative evaluation; it must consider, not only inferences urged by the plaintiff, as the Seventh Circuit did, but also competing inferences rationally drawn from the facts alleged. An inference of fraudulent intent may be plausible, yet less cogent than other, nonculpable explanations for the defendant's conduct. To qualify as "strong" within the intendment of §21D(b)(2), we hold, an inference of scienter must be more than merely plausible or reasonable—it must be cogent and at least as compelling as any opposing inference of nonfraudulent intent.

I

Petitioner Tellabs, Inc., manufactures specialized equipment used in fiber optic networks. During the time period relevant to this case, petitioner Richard Notebaert was Tellabs' chief executive officer and president. Respondents (Shareholders) are persons who purchased Tellabs stock between December 11, 2000, and June 19, 2001. They accuse Tellabs and Notebaert (as well as several other Tellabs executives) of engaging in a scheme to deceive the investing public about the true value of Tellabs' stock.

Beginning on December 11, 2000, the Shareholders allege, Notebaert (and by imputation Tellabs) "falsely reassured public investors, in a series of statements . . . that Tellabs was continuing to enjoy strong demand for its products and earning record revenues," when, in fact, Notebaert knew the opposite was true. From December 2000 until the spring of 2001, the Shareholders claim, Notebaert knowingly misled the public in four ways. First, he made statements indicating that demand for Tellabs' flagship networking device, the TITAN 5500, was continuing to grow, when in fact demand for that product was waning. Second, Notebaert made statements indicating that the TITAN 6500, Tellabs' next-generation networking device, was available for delivery, and that demand for that product was strong and growing, when in truth the product was not ready for delivery and demand was weak. Third, he falsely represented Tellabs' financial results for the fourth quarter of 2000 (and, in connection with those results, condoned the practice of "channel stuffing," under which Tellabs flooded its customers with unwanted products). Fourth, Notebaert made a series of overstated revenue projections, when demand for the TITAN 5500 was drying up and production of the TITAN 6500 was behind schedule. Based on Notebaert's sunny assessments, the Shareholders contend, market analysts recommended that investors buy Tellabs' stock.

The first public glimmer that business was not so healthy came in March 2001 when Tellabs modestly reduced its first quarter sales projections. In the next months, Tellabs made progressively more cautious statements about its projected sales. On June 19, 2001, the last day of the class period, Tellabs disclosed that demand for the TITAN 5500 had significantly dropped. Simultaneously, the company substantially lowered its revenue projections for the second quarter of 2001. The next day, the price of Tellabs stock, which had reached a high of $67 during the period, plunged to a low of $15.87.

On December 3, 2002, the Shareholders filed a class action in the District Court for the Northern District of Illinois. Their complaint stated, *inter alia,* that Tellabs and Notebaert had engaged in securities fraud in violation of §10(b) of the Securities Exchange Act of 1934 and SEC Rule 10b-5, also that Notebaert was a "controlling person" under §20(a) of the 1934 Act, and therefore derivatively liable for the company's fraudulent acts. Tellabs moved to dismiss the complaint on the ground that the Shareholders had failed to plead their case with the particularity the PSLRA requires. The District Court agreed, and therefore dismissed the complaint without prejudice.

The Shareholders then amended their complaint, adding references to 27 confidential sources and making further, more specific, allegations concerning Notebaert's mental state. The District Court again dismissed, this time with prejudice. The Shareholders had sufficiently pleaded that Notebaert's statements were misleading, the court determined, but they had insufficiently alleged that he acted with scienter.

The Court of Appeals for the Seventh Circuit reversed in relevant part. Like the District Court, the Court of Appeals found that the Shareholders had pleaded the misleading character of Notebaert's statements with sufficient particularity. Unlike the District Court, however, the Seventh Circuit concluded that the Shareholders had sufficiently alleged that Notebaert acted with the requisite state of mind.

The Court of Appeals recognized that the PSLRA "unequivocally raise[d] the bar for pleading scienter" by requiring plaintiffs to "plea[d] sufficient facts to create a strong inference of scienter" (internal quotation marks omitted). In evaluating whether that pleading standard is met, the Seventh Circuit said, "courts [should] examine all of the allegations in the complaint and then . . . decide whether collectively they establish such an inference." "[W]e will allow the complaint to survive," the court next and critically stated, "if it alleges facts from which, if true, a reasonable person could infer that the defendant acted with the required intent. . . . If a reasonable person could not draw such an inference from the alleged facts, the defendants are entitled to dismissal."

In adopting its standard for the survival of a complaint, the Seventh Circuit explicitly rejected a stiffer standard adopted by the Sixth Circuit, *i.e.*, that "plaintiffs are entitled only to the most plausible of competing inferences." The Sixth Circuit's standard, the court observed, because it involved an assessment of competing inferences, "could potentially infringe upon plaintiffs' Seventh Amendment rights." We granted certiorari to resolve the disagreement among the Circuits on whether, and to what extent, a court must consider competing inferences in determining whether a securities fraud complaint gives rise to a "strong inference" of scienter.

II

Section 10(b) of the Securities Exchange Act of 1934 forbids the "use or employ, in connection with the purchase or sale of any security . . . , [of] any manipulative or deceptive device or contrivance in contravention of such rules and regulations as the [SEC] may prescribe as necessary or appropriate in the public interest or for the protection of investors." SEC Rule 10b-5 implements §10(b) by declaring it unlawful:

> (a) To employ any device, scheme, or artifice to defraud,
>
> (b) To make any untrue statement of a material fact or to omit to state a material fact necessary in order to make the statements made . . . not misleading, or
>
> (c) To engage in any act, practice, or course of business which operates or would operate as a fraud or deceit upon any person, in connection with the purchase or sale of any security.

Section 10(b), this Court has implied from the statute's text and purpose, affords a right of action to purchasers or sellers of securities injured by its violation. See, e.g., *Dura Pharmaceuticals*, 544 U.S., at 341, 345 ("The securities statutes seek to maintain public confidence in the marketplace . . . by deterring fraud, in part, through the availability of private securities fraud actions."); *Borak*, 377 U.S., at 432 (private securities fraud actions provide "a most effective weapon in the enforcement" of securities laws and are "a necessary supplement to Commission action"). To establish liability under §10(b) and Rule 10b-5, a private plaintiff must prove that the defendant acted with scienter, "a mental state embracing intent to deceive, manipulate, or defraud." *Ernst & Ernst*, 425 U.S., at 193-194, and n.12.

In an ordinary civil action, the Federal Rules of Civil Procedure require only "a short and plain statement of the claim showing that the pleader is entitled to relief." FRCP 8(a)(2). Although the rule encourages brevity, the complaint must say enough to give the defendant "fair notice of what the plaintiff's claim is and the grounds upon which it rests." *Dura Pharmaceuticals*. Prior to the enactment of the PSLRA, the sufficiency of a complaint for securities fraud was governed not by Rule 8, but by the heightened pleading standard set forth in Rule 9(b). Rule 9(b) applies to "all averments of fraud or mistake"; it requires that "the circumstances constituting fraud . . . be stated with particularity" but provides that "[m]alice, intent, knowledge, and other condition of mind of a person, may be averred generally."

Courts of Appeals diverged on the character of the Rule 9(b) inquiry in §10(b) cases: Could securities fraud plaintiffs allege the requisite mental state "simply by stating that scienter existed," or were they required to allege with particularity facts giving rise to an inference of scienter? . . . The Second Circuit's formulation was the most stringent. Securities fraud plaintiffs in that Circuit were required to "specifically plead those [facts] which they assert give rise to a *strong inference* that the defendants had" the requisite state of mind. Ross v. A.H. Robins Co., 607 F.2d 545, 558 (2d Cir. 1979) (emphasis added). The "strong inference" formulation was appropriate, the Second Circuit said, to ward off allegations of "fraud by hindsight." See, e.g., Shields v. Citytrust Bancorp, Inc., 25 F.3d 1124, 1129 (2d Cir. 1994) (quoting Denny v. Barber, 576 F.2d 465, 470 (2d Cir. 1978) (Friendly, J.)).

Setting a uniform pleading standard for §10(b) actions was among Congress' objectives when it enacted the PSLRA. Designed to curb perceived abuses of the §10(b) private action—"nuisance filings, targeting of deep-pocket defendants, vexatious discovery requests and manipulation by class action lawyers"—the PSLRA installed both substantive and procedural controls. Notably, Congress prescribed new procedures for the appointment of lead plaintiffs and lead counsel. This innovation aimed to increase the likelihood that institutional investors—parties more likely to balance the interests of the class with the long-term interests of the company—would serve as lead plaintiffs. Congress also "limit[ed] recoverable damages and attorney's fees, provide[d] a 'safe harbor' for forward-looking statements, . . . mandate[d] imposition of sanctions for frivolous litigation, and authorize[d] a stay of discovery pending resolution of any motion to dismiss." Merrill Lynch, Pierce, Fenner & Smith v. Dabit, 547 U.S. 71, 81 (2006). And in §21D(b) of the PSLRA,

Congress "impose[d] heightened pleading requirements in actions brought pursuant to §10(b) and Rule 10b-5."

Under the PSLRA's heightened pleading instructions, any private securities complaint alleging that the defendant made a false or misleading statement must: (1) "specify each statement alleged to have been misleading [and] the reason or reasons why the statement is misleading," 15 USC §78u-4(b)(1); and (2) "state with particularity facts giving rise to a strong inference that the defendant acted with the required state of mind," §78u-4(b)(2). In the instant case, . . . the District Court and the Seventh Circuit agreed that the Shareholders met the first of the two requirements: The complaint sufficiently specified Notebaert's alleged misleading statements and the reasons why the statements were misleading. But those courts disagreed on whether the Shareholders, as required by §21D(b)(2), "state[d] with particularity facts giving rise to a strong inference that [Notebaert] acted with [scienter]."

The "strong inference" standard "unequivocally raise[d] the bar for pleading scienter," and signaled Congress' purpose to promote greater uniformity among the Circuits. But "Congress did not . . . throw much light on what facts . . . suffice to create [a strong] inference," or on what "degree of imagination courts can use in divining whether" the requisite inference exists. While adopting the Second Circuit's "strong inference" standard, Congress did not codify that Circuit's case law interpreting the standard. With no clear guide from Congress other than its "inten[tion] to strengthen existing pleading requirements," Courts of Appeals have diverged again, this time in construing the term "strong inference." Among the uncertainties, should courts consider competing inferences in determining whether an inference of scienter is "strong"? Our task is to prescribe a workable construction of the "strong inference" standard, a reading geared to the PSLRA's twin goals: to curb frivolous, lawyer-driven litigation, while preserving investors' ability to recover on meritorious claims.

III

A

We establish the following prescriptions: *First,* faced with a Rule 12(b)(6) motion to dismiss a §10(b) action, courts must, as with any motion to dismiss for failure to plead a claim on which relief can be granted, accept all factual allegations in the complaint as true. See Leatherman v. Tarrant County Narcotics Intelligence and Coordination Unit, 507 U.S. 163, 164 (1993). On this point, the parties agree.

Second, courts must consider the complaint in its entirety, as well as other sources courts ordinarily examine when ruling on Rule 12(b)(6) motions to dismiss, in particular, documents incorporated into the complaint by reference, and matters of which a court may take judicial notice. The inquiry, as several Courts of Appeals have recognized, is whether *all* of the facts alleged, taken collectively, give rise to a strong inference of scienter, not whether any individual allegation, scrutinized in isolation, meets that standard.

Third, in determining whether the pleaded facts give rise to a "strong" inference of scienter, the court must take into account plausible opposing inferences. The Seventh Circuit expressly declined to engage in such a comparative inquiry. A complaint could survive, that court said, as long as it "alleges facts from which, if true, a reasonable person could infer that the defendant acted with the required intent"; in other words, only "[i]f a reasonable person could not draw such an inference from the alleged facts" would the defendant prevail on a motion to dismiss. But in §21D(b)(2), Congress did not merely require plaintiffs to "provide a factual basis for [their] scienter allegations," *i.e.*, to allege facts from which an inference of scienter rationally *could* be drawn. Instead, Congress required plaintiffs to plead with particularity facts that give rise to a "strong"—*i.e.*, a powerful or cogent—inference. See American Heritage Dictionary 1717 (4th ed. 2000) (defining "strong" as "[p]ersuasive, effective, and cogent"); 16 Oxford English Dictionary 949 (2d ed. 1989) (defining "strong" as "[p]owerful to demonstrate or convince" (definition 16b)); cf. 7 *id.*, at 924 (defining "inference" as "a conclusion [drawn] from known or assumed facts or statements"; "reasoning from something known or assumed to something else which follows from it").

The strength of an inference cannot be decided in a vacuum. The inquiry is inherently comparative: How likely is it that one conclusion, as compared to others, follows from the underlying facts? To determine whether the plaintiff has alleged facts that give rise to the requisite "strong inference" of scienter, a court must consider plausible nonculpable explanations for the defendant's conduct, as well as inferences favoring the plaintiff. The inference that the defendant acted with scienter need not be irrefutable, *i.e.*, of the "smoking-gun" genre, or even the "most plausible of competing inferences." Recall in this regard that §21D(b)'s pleading requirements are but one constraint among many the PSLRA installed to screen out frivolous suits, while allowing meritorious actions to move forward. Yet the inference of scienter must be more than merely "reasonable" or "permissible"—it must be cogent and compelling, thus strong in light of other explanations. A complaint will survive, we hold, only if a reasonable person would deem the inference of scienter cogent and at least as compelling as any opposing inference one could draw from the facts alleged.[5]

---

[5] Justice Scalia objects to this standard on the ground that "[i]f a jade falcon were stolen from a room to which only A and B had access," it could not *"possibly* be said there was a 'strong inference' that B was the thief." I suspect, however, that law enforcement officials as well as the owner of the precious falcon would

B

Tellabs contends that when competing inferences are considered, Notebaert's evident lack of pecuniary motive will be dispositive. The Shareholders, Tellabs stresses, did not allege that Notebaert sold any shares during the class period. While it is true that motive can be a relevant consideration, and personal financial gain may weigh heavily in favor of a scienter inference, we agree with the Seventh Circuit that the absence of a motive allegation is not fatal. As earlier stated, allegations must be considered collectively; the significance that can be ascribed to an allegation of motive, or lack thereof, depends on the entirety of the complaint.

Tellabs also maintains that several of the Shareholders' allegations are too vague or ambiguous to contribute to a strong inference of scienter. For example, the Shareholders alleged that Tellabs flooded its customers with unwanted products, a practice known as "channel stuffing." But they failed, Tellabs argues, to specify whether the channel stuffing allegedly known to Notebaert was the illegitimate kind (*e.g.,* writing orders for products customers had not requested) or the legitimate kind (*e.g.,* offering customers discounts as an incentive to buy). We agree that omissions and ambiguities count against inferring scienter, for plaintiffs must "state with particularity facts giving rise to a strong inference that the defendant acted with the required state of mind." We reiterate, however, that the court's job is not to scrutinize each allegation in isolation but to assess all the allegations holistically. In sum, the reviewing court must ask: When the allegations are accepted as true and taken collectively, would a reasonable person deem the inference of scienter at least as strong as any opposing inference?

IV

Accounting for its construction of §21D(b)(2), the Seventh Circuit explained that the court "th[ought] it wis[e] to adopt an approach that [could not] be misunderstood as a usurpation of the jury's role." In our view, the Seventh Circuit's concern was undue. A court's comparative assessment of plausible

---

find the inference of guilt as to B quite strong—certainly strong enough to warrant further investigation. Indeed, an inference at least as likely as competing inferences can, in some cases, warrant recovery. See Summers v. Tice, 33 Cal. 2d 80, 84-87, 199 P.2d 1, 3-5 (1948) (*en banc*) (plaintiff wounded by gunshot could recover from two defendants, even though the most he could prove was that each defendant was at least as likely to have injured him as the other). In any event, we disagree with Justice Scalia that the hardly stock term "strong inference" has only one invariably right ("natural" or "normal") reading—his.

Justice Alito agrees with Justice Scalia, and would transpose to the pleading stage "the test that is used at the summary-judgment and judgment-as-a-matter-of-law stages." But the test at each stage is measured against a different backdrop. It is improbable that Congress, without so stating, intended courts to test pleadings, unaided by discovery, to determine whether there is "no genuine issue as to any material fact." See FRCP 56(c). And judgment as a matter of law is a post-trial device, turning on the question whether a party has produced evidence "legally sufficient" to warrant a jury determination in that party's favor. See Rule 50(a)(1).

inferences, while constantly assuming the plaintiff's allegations to be true, we think it plain, does not impinge upon the Seventh Amendment right to jury trial.[8]

Congress, as creator of federal statutory claims, has power to prescribe what must be pleaded to state the claim, just as it has power to determine what must be proved to prevail on the merits. It is the federal lawmaker's prerogative, therefore, to allow, disallow, or shape the contours of—including the pleading and proof requirements for—§10(b) private actions. No decision of this Court questions that authority in general, or suggests, in particular, that the Seventh Amendment inhibits Congress from establishing whatever pleading requirements it finds appropriate for federal statutory claims. Cf. Swierkiewicz v. Sorema N.A., 534 U.S. 506, 512-513 (2002); *Leatherman*, 507 U.S., at 168 (both recognizing that heightened pleading requirements can be established by Federal Rule, citing FRCP 9(b), which requires that fraud or mistake be pleaded with particularity).[9]

. . .

In the instant case, provided that the Shareholders have satisfied the congressionally "prescribe[d] . . . means of making an issue," the case will fall within the jury's authority to assess the credibility of witnesses, resolve any genuine issues of fact, and make the ultimate determination whether Notebaert and, by imputation, Tellabs acted with scienter. We emphasize, as well, that under our construction of the "strong inference" standard, a plaintiff is not forced to plead more than she would be required to prove at trial. A plaintiff alleging fraud in a §10(b) action, we hold today, must plead facts rendering an inference of scienter *at least as likely as* any plausible opposing inference. At trial, she must then prove her case by a "preponderance of the evidence." Stated otherwise, she must demonstrate that it is *more likely* than not that the defendant acted with scienter.

. . .

While we reject the Seventh Circuit's approach to §21D(b)(2), we do not decide whether, under the standard we have described, the Shareholders' allegations warrant "a strong inference that [Notebaert and Tellabs] acted with the required state of mind." Neither the District Court nor the Court of Appeals had the opportunity to consider the matter in light of the

---

[8] In numerous contexts, gatekeeping judicial determinations prevent submission of claims to a jury's judgment without violating the Seventh Amendment. See, *e.g.*, Daubert v. Merrell Dow Pharmaceuticals, Inc., 509 U.S. 579, 589 (1993) (expert testimony can be excluded based on judicial determination of reliability); Neely v. Martin K. Eby Constr. Co., 386 U.S. 317, 321 (1967) (judgment as a matter of law); Pease v. Rathbun-Jones Engineering Co., 243 U.S. 273, 278 (1917) (summary judgment).

[9] Any heightened pleading rule, including FRCP 9(b), could have the effect of preventing a plaintiff from getting discovery on a claim that might have gone to a jury, had discovery occurred and yielded substantial evidence. In recognizing Congress' or the Federal Rule makers' authority to adopt special pleading rules, we have detected no Seventh Amendment impediment.

prescriptions we announce today. We therefore vacate the Seventh Circuit's judgment so that the case may be reexamined in accord with our construction of §21D(b)(2). The judgment of the Court of Appeals is vacated, and the case is remanded for further proceedings consistent with this opinion.

It is so ordered.

Justice SCALIA, concurring in the judgment.

I fail to see how an inference that is merely "at least as compelling as any opposing inference," can conceivably be called what the statute here at issue requires: a "strong inference." If a jade falcon were stolen from a room to which only A and B had access, could it possibly be said there was a "strong inference" that B was the thief? I think not, and I therefore think that the Court's test must fail. In my view, the test should be whether the inference of scienter (if any) is more plausible than the inference of innocence.*

The Court's explicit rejection of this reading rests on two assertions. The first (doubtless true) is that the statute does not require that "[t]he inference that the defendant acted with scienter . . . be irrefutable, *i.e.,* of the 'smoking-gun' genre." It is up to Congress, however, and not to us, to determine what pleading standard would avoid those extremities while yet effectively deterring baseless actions. Congress has expressed its determination in the phrase "strong inference"; it is our job to give that phrase its normal meaning. And if we are to abandon text in favor of unexpressed purpose, as the Court does, it is inconceivable that Congress's enactment of stringent pleading requirements in the PSLRA somehow manifests the purpose of giving plaintiffs the edge in close cases.

The Court's second assertion (also true) is that "an inference at least as likely as competing inferences can, in some cases, warrant recovery" (citing Summers v. Tice). *Summers* is a famous case, however, because it sticks out of the ordinary body of tort law like a sore thumb. It represented "a relaxation" of "such proof as is ordinarily required" to succeed in a negligence action. There is no indication that the statute at issue here was meant to relax the ordinary rule under which a tie goes to the defendant. To the contrary, it explicitly strengthens that rule by extending it to the pleading stage of a case.

One of petitioners' *amici* suggests that my reading of the statute would transform the text from requiring a "strong" inference to requiring the "strongest" inference. . . . It is certainly true that, if Congress had wanted to adopt

---

* The Court suggests that "the owner of the precious falcon would find the inference of guilt as to B quite strong." If he should draw such an inference, it would only prove the wisdom of the ancient maxim "*aliquis non debet esse Judex in propria causa*"—no man ought to be a judge of his own cause. *Dr. Bonham's Case*, 77 Eng. Rep. 638, 646, 652 (C.P. 1610). For it is quite clear (from the dispassionate perspective of one who does not own a jade falcon) that a *possibility*, even a strong possibility, that B is responsible is not a strong *inference* that B is responsible. "Inference" connotes "belief" in what is inferred, and it would be impossible to form a strong belief that it was B and not A, or A and not B.

my standard with even greater clarity, it could have restructured the entire provision—to require, for example, that the plaintiff plead "facts giving rise to *an inference of scienter that is more compelling than the inference that the defendant acted with a nonculpable state of mind.*" But if one is to consider the possibility of total restructuring, it is equally true that, to express the Court's standard, Congress could have demanded "*an inference of scienter that is at least as compelling as the inference that the defendant acted with a nonculpable state of mind.*" Argument from the possibility of saying it differently is clearly a draw. We must be content to give "strong inference" its normal meaning. I hasten to add that, while precision of interpretation should always be pursued for its own sake, I doubt that in this instance what I deem to be the correct test will produce results much different from the Court's. How often is it that inferences are precisely in equipoise? All the more reason, I think, to read the language for what it says.

. . .

Justice ALITO, concurring in the judgment.

[Justice Scalia is right that the strong inference standard requires "an inference that is more likely than not correct." The Court's standard cannot be distinguished from "normal pleading review," under which less weight is "naturally" given to allegations plagued by "omissions and ambiguities" and more weight is given to allegations stating "particularized facts." "Strong inference" standard means "an inference that is stronger than the inference that the defendant lacked the required state of mind." Justice Scalia's approach would "align the pleading test" under the PSLRA with "the test that is used at the summary-judgment and judgment-as-a-matter-of-law stages." In contrast, the majority introduces a test "previously unknown in civil litigation." Congress probably meant to adopt "a known quantity," which is Justice Scalia's approach.]

Justice STEVENS, dissenting. . . .

The basic purpose of the heightened pleading requirement in the context of securities fraud litigation is to protect defendants from the costs of discovery and trial in unmeritorious cases. Because of its intrusive nature, discovery may also invade the privacy interests of the defendants and their executives. Like citizens suspected of having engaged in criminal activity, those defendants should not be required to produce their private effects unless there is probable cause to believe them guilty of misconduct. Admittedly, the probable-cause standard is not capable of precise measurement, but it is a concept that is familiar to judges. As a matter of normal English usage, its meaning is roughly the same as "strong inference." Moreover, it is most unlikely that Congress intended us to adopt a standard that makes it more difficult to commence a civil case than a criminal case.

In addition to the benefit of its grounding in an already familiar legal concept, using a probable-cause standard would avoid the unnecessary conclusion that "in determining whether the pleaded facts give rise to a 'strong' inference of scienter, the court *must* take into account plausible opposing inferences." There are times when an inference can easily be deemed strong without any need to weigh competing inferences. For example, if a known drug dealer exits a building immediately after a confirmed drug transaction, carrying a suspicious looking package, a judge could draw a strong inference that the individual was involved in the aforementioned drug transaction without debating whether the suspect might have been leaving the building at that exact time for another unrelated reason.

If, using that same methodology, we assume (as we must) the truth of the detailed factual allegations attributed to 27 different confidential informants described in the complaint, and view those allegations collectively, I think it clear that they establish probable cause to believe that Tellabs' chief executive officer "acted with the required intent," as the Seventh Circuit held.[2]

Accordingly, I would affirm the judgment of the Court of Appeals.

■ NOTES ON THE PSLRA AND THE "STRONG INFERENCE" STANDARD

1. The PSLRA contains three provisions about pleading:

(a) A complaint alleging "an untrue statement of a material fact" or the omission of a fact "necessary in order to make" an actual statement "not misleading," must "specify each statement alleged to have been misleading" and "the reason or reasons why the statement is misleading." See 15 USC §78u-4(b)(1). This language is consistent with, but more specific than, language in the first sentence of FRCP 9(b), which requires "circumstances constituting fraud" to be alleged "with particularity."

(b) The complaint must "state with particularity facts giving rise to a strong inference that the defendant acted with the required state of mind," 15 USC §78u-4(b)(2). In the case of "forward-looking" statements, the PSLRA requires "actual knowledge" that the statement is false or misleading, 15 USC §78u-5(c)(1)(B), but for other statements (on which statutes are silent) the Supreme Court has said the required mental state is "intent to deceive,

---

[2] The "channel stuffing" allegations . . . are particularly persuasive. Contrary to petitioners' arguments that respondents' allegations of channel stuffing "are too vague or ambiguous to contribute to a strong inference of scienter," this portion of the complaint clearly alleges that Notebaert himself had specific knowledge of illegitimate channel stuffing during the relevant time period. If these allegations are actually taken as true and viewed in the collective, it is hard to imagine what competing inference could effectively counteract the inference that Notebaert and Tellabs "'acted with the required state of mind.'"

manipulate, or defraud," see Ernest & Ernest v. Hochfelder, 425 U.S. 185, 193 (1976), leaving open (as the Court comments in *Tellabs*) the possibility that "recklessness" suffices. *Tellabs* addresses the meaning of the "strong inference" standard, which seems to differ sharply from FRCP 9(b), where the second sentence says state of mind "may be averred generally." The PSLRA came later than FRCP 9, and was enacted by Congress rather than adopted by the Court as rulemaker, so the statute controls, and displaces this provision in the Rule. It is notable, however, that the Second Circuit had already adopted a "strong inference" standard requiring detail in pleading "scienter" (knowledge of falsity) *despite* the language in FRCP 9(b), see Ross v. A.H. Robins Co., 607 F.2d 545, 558 (2d Cir. 1979) (cited in *Tellabs*) and Kalnit v. Eichler, 264 F.3d 131 (2d Cir. 2001) (PSLRA "echoed this Court's scienter standard"). Note too, however, that the Court in *Tellabs* says the PSLRA does not "codify" the Second Circuit's "case law interpreting the standard," which left the Court free in *Tellabs* to adopt its own view of the standard's meaning.

(c) A court must "dismiss the complaint" if particularity requirements are not met. And "all discovery and other proceedings" are to be stayed "during the pendency of any motion to dismiss" unless the court concludes on motion that "particularized discovery is necessary to preserve evidence or to prevent undue prejudice." See 15 USC §78u-4(b)(3)(A) and (B). Discovery costs were on the mind of Congress in enacting the PSLRA, as they were on the Court's mind in *Twombly*.

2. How does the Court interpret the "strong inference" standard in *Tellabs*? Note Justice Scalia's argument that in a case in which there is an equal possibility that A or B did a particular deed, one cannot say there is a "strong inference" that A did it, as opposed to B, or vice versa (claiming that Justice Ginsburg relaxes "the ordinary rule that a tie goes to the defendant"). Justice Ginsburg replies in footnote 5. Who has the better of the argument?

(a) If a "strong inference" can be drawn even if an alternative is equally likely, is the "strong inference" distinguishable from the "plausibility" standard in *Twombly*? Can it be distinguished from the Seventh Circuit standard that the Court disapproves in *Tellabs*, under which a "strong inference" is one that a "reasonable person" could draw?

(b) For an argument that *Tellabs* sets a two-part standard, under which an inference favorable to the plaintiff must be both "cogent" and "at least as compelling as any opposing inference," see Geoffrey P. Miller, *Pleading After* Tellabs, Wis. L. Rev. 507, 511-512 (2009) (if friend does not keep restaurant engagement, possible reasons include that "he is blowing me off" or "he forgot" or "he was unavoidably delayed" or "I got the date wrong," each of which might appear equally likely; if only the inference that he blew me off could generate a claim, the inference satisfies the *second* part of the standard, but does not satisfy *Tellabs* because it is not "cogent" in light of the fact that the other possibilities in combination outweigh it).

3. *Tellabs* involved a class suit on behalf of people who bought stock in Tellabs over a six-month period from December 2000 through mid-June 2001, against Tellabs (maker of equipment for fiber optic networks), and Richard Notebaert as chief executive. The claim is that Notebaert falsely stated that (1) there was strong demand for the Titan 5500 networking device, and (2) the Titan 6500 (next generation of the product) was available and much in demand (the Seventh Circuit, on remand in *Tellabs,* reports that Notebaert spoke of having signed a "multiyear, $100 million contract"), (3) the company was enjoying good financial results in the fourth quarter of 2000, which rested on "channel stuffing" (supplying unwanted products to customers in hope of boosting sales), and (4) revenue projections were good, although demand for Titan 5500 was drying up and production of Titan 6500 was behind schedule. Given the falsity of these statements, the question is how to allege "scienter"— how to allege that defendants knew the statements were false, or were "reckless" in failing to know.

(a) In the absence of any special standard, a plaintiff could allege scienter by asserting that "defendant knew" the statements were false or misleading, or was "reckless" in failing to know. Such allegations would satisfy FRCP 8's "plain statement" standard, and are consistent with FRCP 9(b)'s provision allowing states of mind to be alleged "generally," although some courts had begun to require more detail on this point before enactment of the PSLRA.

(b) Under the "strong inference" standard, plaintiffs must allege more. In *Tellabs,* plaintiffs alleged that the Titan 5500 was the company's "principal product" that accounted for "more than half its sales," and that "no sales [of the successor Titan 6500] pursuant to the [Spring] contract closed" until after June 2001. (The complaint also alleged that the company reduced sales projections, and that in June 2001, the end of the period covered by the complaint, the company announced that revenues for 2001 were 35 percent lower than the year before and profit was down by 125 percent.) On remand, the Seventh Circuit concluded that the "strong inference" standard, as interpreted by the Supreme Court in the opinion, was met:

> Another possible, though again very unlikely, example of innocent misunderstanding is the charge of "channel stuffing." The term refers to shipping to one's distributors more of one's product than one thinks one can sell. A certain amount of channel stuffing could be innocent and might not even mislead—a seller might have a realistic hope that stuffing the channel of distribution would incite his distributors to more vigorous efforts to sell the stuff lest it pile up in inventory. Channel stuffing becomes a form of fraud only when it is used, as the complaint alleges, to book revenues on the basis of goods shipped but not really sold because the buyer can return them. They are in effect sales on consignment, and such sales "cannot be booked as revenue. Neither condition of revenue recognition has been fulfilled—ownership and its attendant risks have not been transferred, and since the goods might not even be sold, there can be no certainty of getting paid. But those strictures haven't stopped some managers from using consigned goods to fatten the top line—that is, the revenue line—of the corporate income statement." H. David Sherman et al., *Profits You Can Trust, Spotting &*

Surviving Accounting Landmines 30 (Financial Times Prentice Hall 2003). (Similarly, Tellabs could not properly record revenue on its contract with Sprint before actually transferring title to 6500 systems to Sprint.) The huge number of returns of 5500 systems is evidence that the purpose of the stuffing was to conceal the disappointing demand for the product rather than to prod distributors to work harder to attract new customers, and the purpose would have been formed or ratified at the highest level of management.

All this is not to say that the plaintiffs could name "management" as a defendant or, less absurdly, name each corporate officer. . . . But it is possible to draw a strong inference of corporate scienter without being able to name the individuals who concocted and disseminated the fraud. Suppose General Motors announced that it had sold one million SUVs in 2006, and the actual number was zero. There would be a strong inference of corporate scienter, since so dramatic an announcement would have been approved by corporate officials sufficiently knowledgeable about the company to know that the announcement was false.

Against all this the defendants argue that they could have had no motive to paint the prospects for the 5500 and 6500 systems in rosy hues because within months they acknowledged their mistakes and disclosed the true situation of the two products, and because there is no indication that Notebaert or anyone else who may have been in on the fraud profited from it financially. The argument confuses expected with realized benefits. Notebaert may have thought that there was a chance that the situation regarding the two key products would right itself. If so, the benefits of concealment might exceed the costs. Investors do not like to think they're riding a roller coaster. Prompt disclosure of the truth would have caused Tellabs's stock price to plummet, as it did when the truth came out a couple of months later. Suppose the situation had corrected itself. Still, investors would have discovered that the stock was more volatile than they thought, and risk-averse investors (who predominate) do not like volatility and so, unless it can be diversified away, demand compensation in the form of a lower price; consequently the stock might not recover to its previous level. The fact that a gamble—concealing bad news in the hope that it will be overtaken by good news—fails is not inconsistent with its having been a considered, though because of the risk a reckless, gamble. It is like embezzling in the hope that winning at the track will enable the embezzled funds to be replaced before they are discovered to be missing.

So the inference of corporate scienter is not only as likely as its opposite, but more likely. And is it cogent? Well, if there are only two possible inferences, and one is *much* more likely than the other, it must be cogent. Suppose a person woke up one morning with a sharp pain in his abdomen. He thought it was due to a recent operation to remove his gall bladder, but realized it could equally well have been due to any number of other things. The inference that it was due to the operation could not be thought cogent. But suppose he went to a doctor who performed tests that ruled out any cause other than the operation or a duodenal ulcer and told the patient that he was 99 percent certain that it was the operation. The plausibility of an explanation depends on the plausibility of the alternative explanations. United States v. Beard, 354 F.3d 691, 692-93 (7th Cir. 2004); Ronald J. Allen, *Factual Ambiguity and a Theory of Relevance,* 88 Nw. U. L.

Rev. 604 (1994). As more and more alternatives to a given explanation are ruled out, the probability of that explanation's being the correct one rises. . . . Because in our abdominal-pain example all other inferences had been ruled out except the 1 percent one, the inference that the pain was due to the operation would be cogent. This case is similar. Because the alternative hypotheses—either a cascade of innocent mistakes, or acts of subordinate employees, either or both resulting in a series of false statements—are far less likely than the hypothesis of scienter at the corporate level at which the statements were approved, the latter hypothesis must be considered cogent.

And at the top of the corporate pyramid sat Notebaert, the CEO. The 5500 and the 6500 were his company's key products. Almost all the false statements that we quoted emanated directly from him. Is it conceivable that he was unaware of the problems of his company's two major products and merely repeating lies fed to him by other executives of the company? It is conceivable, yes, but it is exceedingly unlikely.

Makor Issues & Rights, Ltd. v. Tellabs Inc., 513 F.3d 702, 709-711 (7th Cir. 2008).

4. Suppose arson is suspected in a college dorm fire on September 13, and several reports of arson are made afterward. Gail Minger, mother of Michael Minger (student living in dorm) calls the university a few days later. The Housing Director tells her the fire was "minor" and "nothing to worry about," and residents are safe. Five days later another fire starts, and Michael dies of smoke inhalation (only student killed). In a complaint against the university, Gail Minger alleges in substance that the Housing Director (a) "never revealed that arson was suspected in the September 13 fire," (b) "discouraged Gail Minger from investigating the fire," and (c) knew or should have known that Gail and Michael Minger would rely on the Director's statements and "refrain from taking further steps to protect Michael," and that (d) these statements were a "substantial factor in causing Michael to suffer fatal injuries." The case is *not* governed by the PSLRA (alleged fraud does not involve securities). Do these allegations satisfy FRCP 9(b)? See Minger v. Green, 239 F.3d 793, 799 (6th Cir. 2001) (yes; complaint states with particularity "the circumstances" of Gail Minger's conversation with the Housing Director "and her subsequent reliance," and the complaint "averred generally" the Director's intent). Would the allegations in *Minger* satisfy the PSLRA, if it applied in this case?

5. For an argument that the problem in securities litigation is not so much a matter of procedural shortcomings that can be solved by detailed pleadings, and that damage remedies do not efficiently regulate securities markets, see Janet Cooper Alexander, *Rethinking Damages in Securities Class Actions*, 48 Stan. L. Rev. 1487 (1996). See also Janet Cooper Alexander, *Do the Merits Matter? A Study of Settlements in Securities Class Actions*, 43 Stan. L. Rev. 497, 596 (1991) (in setting of securities class actions, arguing that "structural incentives" conflict with assumption that parties will achieve settlements that "closely approximate mutually expected trial outcomes," and "expected trial outcomes seem to have little if any influence" on settlements; defendants are risk-averse and claimants in class actions do not adequately monitor performance of class counsel; similar situation may obtain in context of shareholder derivative suits).

6. Putting aside the question whether *Tellabs* correctly interpreted the PSLRA, does this kind of heightened pleading standard, in conjunction with the provision in the Act deferring discovery, have a negative impact on securities law enforcement? Consider this argument:

> Another potential consequence of the enhanced pleading requirement relates to the problem of ensuring competent management. This task is formally assigned to state rather than federal law. Yet, securities class-action lawsuits can have a role. Well-performing companies are unlikely to get sued for securities fraud. Since inadequate managers tend (we assume) to work at poorly performing companies, the threat of a securities-fraud lawsuit provides an additional incentive for managers to perform well. Moreover, the process of discovery tends to reveal the dirty linen inside a company, imposing possible reputational sanctions on managers as well as exposing them to potential derivative lawsuits.
>
> The PSLRA's heightened pleading standards arguably reduce the role of securities class-action lawsuits to encourage competent performance by managers. If a complaint is thrown out for insufficient pleading, the plaintiff will have no opportunity to investigate facts that bear on corporate mismanagement. Even if a defendant's extrajudicial admissions of mismanagement come to the court's attention at the motion to dismiss stage, these will not save a defective securities-fraud complaint and may actually enhance the probability the complaint will be dismissed since they tend to rebut scienter.

Miller, supra, at 507, 530-531 (adding that bar against discovery before satisfying pleading standard "puts a plaintiff in a vise," and that plaintiff hoping to get past a motion to dismiss "is well advised to conduct a private investigation," which may be costly, with the result that "established firms" have "an even greater advantage over new entrants").

7. Particularly in light of discovery restrictions in the PSLRA, plaintiffs in securities cases often rely on private informants in the company. Arguably, such reliance implicates the particularity requirement, in which case it should suffice that a complaint discloses that the suit rests on such information, accompanied by a description of the source as one who has or had a position in the company and had access to the crucial information. Does it also implicate the "strong inference" requirement as interpreted in *Tellabs*? Compare Higginbotham v. Baxter International, Inc., 495 F.3d 753, 756-757 (7th Cir. 2007) (*Tellabs* requires court to "discount allegations that the complaint attributes to five 'confidential witnesses,'" which include ex-employee of Brazilian subsidiary, two ex-employees of Baxter's headquarters and two consultants, as it is "hard to see how information from anonymous sources could be deemed 'compelling' or how we could take account of plausible opposing inferences") (these sources may have "axes to grind" or may be "lying" or perhaps "don't even exist") with In re MBIA, Inc., Securities Litigation, 700 F. Supp. 2d 566, 590 (S.D.N.Y. 2010) (use of confidential sources implicates particularity requirement, but not strong inference requirement as it later came to be interpreted in *Tellabs*) and Novak v. Casaks, 216 F.3d 300, 313 (2d Cir. 2000) (plaintiffs need not reveal identity of confidential sources at pleading stage, although they may be compelled to reveal them later). See also Michael J. Kaufman & John M. Wunderlich, *Resolving the Continuing Controversy Regarding Confidential Informants in Private Securities Fraud Litigation*, 19 Cornell J.L. & Pub. Pol'y 637, 690 (2010) (right question is whether there is a "probability that the source had the information" put in the complaint; *Tellabs* did not mention this point, and "emerging trend" exemplified in *Baxter* rests on "fundamental misunderstanding" of relationship between confidential sources and PSLRA).

5. Alternative and Inconsistent Allegations

Like most other humans, civil claimants usually lack perfect knowledge of the facts. The motorist suddenly injured in an accident may be convinced he was driving with due care and the "other guy" must be at fault because the accident would not have happened otherwise, but knowing this much does not pin down the nature of the other guy's negligence. Was he speeding? Inattentive? Did his brakes fail? Sometimes the facts suggest alternative and mutually inconsistent explanations.

■ PROBLEM 7-B. Was It the Bartender or the Driver of the Truck?

While driving her car, motorist Laura Mack collided at an intersection with a truck owned and driven by Larry Kopp. After incurring more than $100,000 in hospital bills that were paid by Jefferson Insurance Company on a medical insurance policy, Laura Mack talks with a lawyer retained by Jefferson. After investigation undertaken by his staff, the lawyer advises Laura that she has claims against Kopp and the Red Wolf Bar and Grill, where Laura Mack had spent two hours just before the accident having cocktails with friends from work. (Kopp himself carries $500,000 in liability coverage through Everystate Insurance Company, and the Red Wolf Bar and Grill has a net worth large enough to make it worth suing.)

Laura Mack agrees to sue. The state in which she lives has adopted the Federal Rules, and she sues in state court. In Count 1, her complaint alleges that Kopp "negligently drove his truck into the left side of the car driven by plaintiff Laura Mack at the intersection of Third and Main on May 17, 2010, directly and proximately causing the injuries and property damage hereinafter set forth." Count 2 alleges that "agents for Red Wolf negligently and wrongfully allowed Laura Mack to consume three cocktails in the space of two hours, causing her to be so impaired that she drove negligently, which proximately and directly caused a collision with a truck driven by defendant Larry Kopp, which in turn proximately and directly caused the property damage and injuries hereinafter set forth."

Before trial, Kopp moved to dismiss the claim against him (Count 1), arguing that "the allegation that Kopp caused the accident is contradicted by the allegation in Count 2 that Red Wolf caused the accident." The court denied the motion. At trial, Kopp again raised an objection, asking that plaintiff be "required to elect whether to claim that Kopp caused the accident or to claim that Red Wolf caused the accident." The court declined to impose such a requirement.

Are Counts 1 and 2 inconsistent? If so, does it matter? Why might Laura's lawyer even want to pursue both claims? If Laura Mack can properly plead both, does it follow that she can go all the way through trial, offering evidence and seeking recovery on both claims? Look carefully at FRCP 8(d)(2) and (3).

■ NOTES ON ALTERNATIVE AND INCONSISTENT ALLEGATIONS

1. Should a jury be allowed to choose between imposing full liability on Kopp or on Red Wolf, or concluding that both are liable in some degree, or that neither is (hence that Laura Mack should recover nothing)? Until the enactment of reform legislation nearly everywhere in the 1970s and 1980s, each of two joint tortfeasors could be fully liable. That did not mean plaintiff could collect twice, but that she could execute a judgment against either or both until she got full recovery (joint and several liability). The trend, however, is to apportion fault among tortfeasors, each being liable for some percentage of the total (several liability).

2. Suppose that in Count 2, the complaint alleged in a single sentence that Red Wolf "either served Laura Mack three cocktails knowing that she planned to leave by car or served her enough alcohol to make her noticeably impaired." Suppose the first possibility is inadequate as the predicate fact for "dram shop liability" but the second suffices. Should the complaint be viewed as inadequate, since plaintiff might prove the first alternative and recover nothing?

3. A person in Laura's position would likely sue for two reasons. One is to get more money. Another is that an insurance policy covering medical expenses for injuries sustained in accidents may contain a cooperation clause obligating the beneficiary to assist by suing the tortfeasor. And there are two other important practical points: One is that such a policy may have a subrogation clause that lets the carrier assert the rights of its insured and keep enough of any recovery to repay itself the benefits paid on the policy. The other is that the collateral source doctrine (recognized almost everywhere) entitles claimants like Laura Mack to recover full medical expenses, so a tortfeasor cannot reduce what he owes by taking "credit" for sums that a claimant collects on the policy. (Mack can also bar evidence or mention of the sums recovered from Jefferson.) Can you see the reasons behind the contract clauses and legal doctrines? We will revisit these matters in the chapter on "shaping the suit," where we consider whether insurance carriers should be formally named as parties to such suits (Chapter 8A4, infra).

4. Alternative pleading is a commonplace phenomenon, and courts have been indulgent in letting plaintiffs take this course. See, e.g., United Technologies v. Mazer, 556 F.3d 1260, 1273-1274 (11th Cir. 2009) (plaintiff could plead that defendant M "acted both personally and on behalf of West-Hem" [company of which plaintiff was president and part owner] despite "a degree of ambiguity" as to whether M "acted for himself, for West-Hem, or for both") (FRCP 8(d) allows "alternative and inconsistent claims"); PAE Government Services, Inc. v. MPRI, Inc., 514 F.3d 856, 585-859 (9th Cir. 2007) (when filing, claimants are "often uncertain about the facts and the law," and yet they are encouraged to file by "a statute of limitations, laches, the need to preserve evidence and other such concerns," so we "do not require complaints to be verified" and "we allow pleadings in the alternative—even if the alternatives are mutually exclusive").

5. Normally, what a person says, and what an agent for a person says, can be admitted against the person (a lawyer is an agent for his client). You will study this matter in Evidence. FRE 801(d)(2) sets out the "admissions" doctrine, under which statements by a party are admissible against him or her, as well as many statements by agents of the party. Thus FRE 801(d)(2)(A) paves the way to admit "against a party . . . the party's own statement," and FRE 801(d)(2)(C) paves the way to admit "against a party . . . a statement by a person authorized by the party to make a statement."

(a) Does it follow that Kopp should be able to read to the jury Count 2 of Mack's complaint? See 2004 Stuart Moldow Trust v. XE L.I.F., LLC, 2009 WL 2222935 (S.D.N.Y. 2008) (FRCP 8 permits alternative pleading, so a pleading cannot be construed as an admission by a party). Why not allow a defendant to offer against plaintiff her alternative pleading?

(b) Suppose Laura amends her complaint to drop Red Wolf, and presents at trial only evidence that Kopp failed to yield the right of way. Now can Kopp introduce (or read to the jury from) Count 2, which claims Mack was intoxicated? See Garman v. Griffin, 666 F.2d 1156 (8th Cir. 1982) (no).

6. Pleading Damages; Prayer for Relief

FRCP 8(a) requires a complaint to include "a demand for the relief sought," and FRCP 9(g) requires any "item of special damages" to be "specifically stated." Customarily, the demand comes at the end of a complaint. Sometimes, lawyers set out an itemized list, separately monetizing each item, and of course listing or describing whatever orders the claimant may want. But the demand can also be short and sweet: "Wherefore plaintiff demands judgment in the amount of $250,000, plus recoverable costs and interest." Except in cases where defendant fails to appear and a default judgment is entered, the sum specified in a demand does not limit recovery, and a plaintiff can get relief that is not mentioned in the complaint. See FRCP 54(c) (judgment shall provide relief to which one is entitled, even if a party "has not demanded" it, but default judgment "shall not be different in kind from or exceed in amount" that sought in the demand).

The specific statement requirement for special damages may seem like an attempt to provide extra warning for defendants on items of damage that might not be obvious. In fact, however, the requirement turns less on assessing what might come as a surprise and more on established legal conventions. In contract cases, it is usually said that special damages are those that would not necessarily or ordinarily result from the breach: In a contract suit alleging that defendant failed to deliver widgets as agreed, ordinary damages include the market value of the widgets and special damages would include losses caused by plaintiff's inability to sell or otherwise use the widgets that didn't arrive. In personal injury actions, special damages include everything other than pain and suffering, like medical costs and lost wages. The specific statement requirement ordinarily means that the body of the complaint should have one or more numbered paragraphs that allege and identify items of special damages.

■ NOTES ON PLEADING DAMAGES AND DEMANDING JUDGMENT

1. Suppose plaintiff alleges in a numbered paragraph in the body of the complaint that as a result of the car accident she "sustained injuries to my neck, back, spine, and nervous system, and was otherwise injured and impaired, requiring hospitalization and surgery, continuing care and convalescence, and preventing me from gainful employment." Under such allegations, can she show that the accident led to fetal death that required her to undergo an abortion? Should such allegations pave the way for proof that she had to abandon a promising career as a dancer? Compare Ziervogel v. Royal Packing Co., 225 S.W.2d 798 (Mo. 1949) (allegations that plaintiff suffered injury to neck, back, spine, nervous system, and was "otherwise injured" did not entitle her to prove she suffered from elevated blood pressure) with Ephrem v. Phillips, 99 So. 2d 257 (Fla. App. 1957) (allegations of injuries to head, body, and limbs justified proof that plaintiff required an abortion).

2. In many state systems, claimants are forbidden from naming a dollar sum in the prayer. See, e.g., Colo. RCP 8(a) ("no dollar amount" shall be "stated in the prayer or demand"); Kan. Stat. Ann. §60-208(a) (complaint seeking more than $10,000 shall allege only that the amount sought exceeds that sum "without demanding any specific amount of money," except in contract cases). What accounts for such provisions? Does a bar against mentioning a dollar sum in the demand mean no sum may be mentioned in charging allegations in numbered paragraphs in the body of the complaint? Why is there no similar provision in the Federal Rules?

C   RULES PLEADING: THE RESPONSE TO THE COMPLAINT

When the complaint has been filed and served, the baton passes to the defendant, who must hire a lawyer and make a response. Broadly speaking, defendants can pursue three different strategies.

One involves filing what we might call a preliminary motion to dismiss, raising one or more of what we might call "procedural" objections that are listed in FRCP 12(b). Put aside for a moment the motion to dismiss for failure to "state a claim upon which relief can be granted." Note the many grounds for this motion: Suing in the wrong court accounts for three listed items, including lack of jurisdiction over the person or subject matter and improper venue. Two other grounds relate to the formalities of service: Defendant can seek dismissal for "insufficiency of process" (lack of a court summons or some irregularity in the summons) or "insufficiency of service of process" (the complaint was not served or was not served properly). Finally, the defense can move to dismiss for "failure to join a party under Rule 19," which basically means that defendant claims that the suit either cannot go forward unless plaintiff names some additional party (either as plaintiff or as defendant).

The second strategy involves attacking the complaint itself. The most common mechanism is a motion to dismiss under FRCP 12(b)(6) for failure "to state a claim upon which relief can be granted." But there are other mechanisms: Defendant can seek a "more definite statement" under Rule 12(e), or move to strike "redundant or impertinent" or "insufficient" claims under Rule 12(f). Finally, defendant may seek "judgment on the pleadings" under Rule 12(c).

The third strategy involves meeting the claim head-on by filing an answer that would normally deny at least some critical allegations in the complaint. This strategy sometimes involves raising "affirmative defenses" such as the statute of limitations that ordinary "denials" would not suggest, and these affirmative defenses are set out separately in the answer as positive averments rather than responses to what the complaint alleges. And this strategy may also involve bringing claims against the plaintiff ("counterclaims"), and perhaps even claims against other parties, like codefendants or outsiders who should for some reason bear the loss in the event that plaintiff recovers against defendant (a category that may include indemnitors who have agreed to assume such responsibilities).

1. Preliminary Defense Motions Under Rule 12(b)

If you read FRCP 12(b), (g), and (h) with care, you will conclude that some of the defenses listed in the former must be raised by answer or by motion filed with the answer or before—what we will call a "pre-answer motion" because it is ordinarily made before the answer is filed, and some of these defenses are actually lost if omitted from an answer (so a motion made later comes too late to raise them).

A close reading of these provisions will also lead you to conclude that some other defenses, particularly "lack of jurisdiction over the subject matter," to use the phrase in FRCP 12(b)(1), are essentially *never* lost, at least during the pendency of the suit. Recall from the note 4 in Notes on Litigating Subject Matter Jurisdiction (Chapter 4B2, supra) that ordinarily this point cannot be raised in a later lawsuit.

■ PROBLEM 7-C. Student versus Professor

In federal court in Kansas where he lives, a history graduate student named Miguel sues Shannon, serving her in Ohio where she is a visiting professor in a university. The complaint seeks to make a claim for libel, alleging that Shannon lied about Miguel in a letter of reference that Miguel had asked her to write, and that in consequence Miguel was not hired for a job that he wanted badly.

(1) If, as her opening move, Shannon files an answer denying the charging allegations of the complaint but raising no other matters, can she later file a motion alleging that she was never given a copy of the summons as required by FRCP 4(c)(1)? Why or why not, and why does FRCP 12 handle this question as it does?

(2) If, as her opening move, Shannon files a motion to dismiss for lack of jurisdiction over the person, but the motion is denied, can she file a second motion to transfer on ground of improper venue? Can she raise the issue of venue in her answer? Again, why or why not, and why does FRCP 12 handle this question as it does?

(3) If, as her opening move, Shannon files a motion to dismiss for failure to join a party who must be joined under FRCP 19, but the motion is denied, can she then file an answer denying the charging allegations and

alleging that the complaint fails to state a claim on which relief can be granted? After filing an answer, can she raise this point by motion? Again, why or why not, and why does FRCP 12 handle these matters as it does?

(4) Suppose Shannon makes and loses a motion to dismiss on grounds that the court lacks personal jurisdiction over her, and she then files an answer denying the charging allegations of the complaint, but judgment is entered against her after a trial on the merits. Can she then make a motion to set aside the judgment on the ground that the court lacks subject matter jurisdiction because Shannon and Miguel are both citizens of Kansas? See FRCP 50(b) (allowing motions for judgment as a matter of law to be made within ten days after entry of judgment) and 60(b)(4) (allowing "reasonable time" for motions to set aside a judgment that is "void").

■ NOTES ON RULE 12(b) MOTIONS

1. Recall from Chapter 3E that courts used to recognize something called a "special appearance," where defendant could come to court and move to dismiss for lack of jurisdiction over his person. Traditionally, defendants who took this course needed to be careful *not* to address the merits, on pain of *waiving* their objection to jurisdiction. It has been said that there is "no such thing as a limited appearance under Rule 12." In what sense is this comment correct? In what sense is it wrong?

2. You will see in Chapter 8 that sometimes FRCP 19(a) and (b) *require* joinder of certain parties in the suit. Oversimplifying for a moment, that provision means that plaintiff may be required to join a second defendant if, in the absence of the missing party, a judgment in the suit would "as a practical matter impair or impede" the interests of that party or would leave defendant already in the suit "at substantial risk of incurring double, multiple, or otherwise inconsistent obligations," or if "complete relief" cannot be had in the absence of the missing party. Notice that under FRCP 12(h)(2) this defense can be raised even if defendant omitted it from a pre-answer motion raising other defenses. Indeed, this defense gets "favored treatment" almost as much as the defense of lack of jurisdiction over the subject matter. Why do you suppose that is?

3. The argument that a complaint fails to state a claim also receives "favored treatment" in FRCP 12(h)(2). Why do you suppose it does? Recall, if it be relevant, that the philosophy of Rules pleading is to *de-emphasize* pleadings. What would happen if this particular defense could be easily waived?

2. Attacking the Sufficiency of the Complaint Under Rule 12(b) and Related Provisions

Instead of simply denying the charging allegations, defendant may elect to attack those allegations as inadequate or improper. FRCP 12 envisions at least four such attacks: First and most fundamental is the motion to dismiss. You have already seen this mechanism in action: In Problem 7-C, it's one of the things Shannon did in opposing Miguel. It also happened in *Swierkiewicz* in Section B1, supra. In *Reilly* in Section A, you saw the Code counterpart of this motion (the demurrer), which worked in the same fashion. Remember that the question here is *not* whether the judge believes what plaintiff says. Rather, the question is whether, *assuming that plaintiff proves what is alleged,* she would be entitled to relief. See, e.g., Neitzke v. Williams, 490 U.S. 319, 327 (1989) (FRCP 12(b)(6) "does not countenance . . . dismissals based on a judge's disbelief of a complaint's factual allegations"); Scheuer v. Rhodes, 416 U.S. 232, 236 (1974) (a well-pleaded complaint survives even if it appears that "recovery is very remote and unlikely").

Second, FRCP 12(e) authorizes defendants to move for a more definite statement if the complaint is "so vague or ambiguous" that defendant "cannot reasonably be required to frame a responsive pleading."

Third, FRCP 12(c) authorizes defendants to seek "judgment on the pleadings." This motion is really a deferred motion to dismiss for failure to state a claim, since the idea is that it can be filed "after the pleadings are closed" rather than prior to or contemporaneously with the filing of the answer.

Fourth, FRCP 12(f) authorizes motions to strike "any insufficient defense or any redundant, immaterial, impertinent, or scandalous matter."

■ NOTES ON MOTIONS ATTACKING THE COMPLAINT

1. What happens when a judge grants a motion to dismiss for failure to state a claim? Almost always the answer is that plaintiff is given "leave to amend" for some fixed period (like 21 days, which is the time that FRCP 12 provides for defendants to file an answer after being served with the complaint). Indeed, you can see if you read FRCP 15(a)(1) that plaintiff is *entitled* to amend within 21 days after service of the answer or a pre-answer motion filed under Rule 12. And if a plaintiff does *not* amend under FRCP 15(a)(1), a judge almost always give leave to amend even if she rules in favor of a defendant who challenges the complaint as failing to state a claim. As FRCP 15(a)(2) says, the court should "freely give leave when justice so requires."

2. Are there risks in amending a complaint when the trial judge invites plaintiff to do so? Suppose plaintiff in *Reilly* had amended by adding an allegation that "trimming trees in a residential neighborhood is necessarily dangerous." More generally, suppose a complaint contains four charging allegations, and on motion by the defendant the court dismisses (with leave to amend) because a fifth is required. Usually, the burden of pleading and burdens of production and persuasion coincide, but nobody is quite sure whether pleading burdens follow burdens of proof or vice versa.[6] In this environment, mightn't a trial court assign to the plaintiff the burden of persuasion on a point *simply because* she put it in her complaint?

3. What's the plaintiff's other choice? He can "stand on the complaint" by "refusing to amend." Recall that courts split on the question whether he can amend later, if he declines the trial court's invitation to do so, takes an appeal (he "stands on the complaint"), and loses. See Notes on Pleading a Cause of Action Under the Code, note 3 (Section A2, supra).

4. Under what conditions does it make sense to refuse an invitation to amend? Suppose Tyler, sitting in his living room, looks out the window and sees his five-year-old son Darin being attacked by neighbor Sandra's dog. The dog abandons the attack when Sandra intervenes, but not before Darin has been hurt, with scratches and bite marks on his upper body and legs, which require stitches and hospitalization. Tyler sues Sandra: Count 1 alleges claims as Darin's "next friend" for personal injuries suffered by Darin and for his pain and suffering. Count 2 alleges a claim for mental distress suffered by Tyler personally: This count alleges that Sandra knew the dog was dangerous, allowed the dog to run loose, and did not control the dog, that the dog attacked and injured Darin as Tyler was watching, and that Tyler suffered "pain and distress of mind in seeing the dog attack my son." Invoking the rule that plaintiff can only recover for negligent infliction of mental distress if he was "in the zone of danger," Sandra moves to dismiss, which would be understood as meaning that the court should strike Count 2. Suppose the judge agrees with Sandra, but offers plaintiff leave "to add an allegation that Tyler too was endangered by the dog's behavior."

(a) Suppose Tyler and his lawyer know Tyler was in his house when the attack occurred, and that Sandra and her dog were 100 feet away by the time Tyler got to Darin, and she was leading the dog by leash toward her house. It wouldn't make sense to amend, would it? Tyler should refuse to amend, and could argue on appeal that the rule requiring him to be in the zone of danger should be discarded. He will win or lose on this point, and this

---

[6] Compare McCormick on Evidence §337, at 509 (J. Strong ed., 5th ed. 1999) (usually "the party who has the burden of pleading a fact will have the burdens of producing evidence and of persuading the jury of its existence") with J. Cound, J. Friedenthal, A. Miller & J. Sexton, Civil Procedure Cases and Materials 584 (10th ed. 2009) (burden of pleading an issue "usually is assigned to the party who has the burden of producing evidence on that issue at trial"). The evidence people want the procedure people to bear the laboring oar, and vice versa. It seems more sensible for burden of pleading to follow burden of persuasion. There are some notable departures from the proposition that these burdens coincide: Thus plaintiff must plead nonpayment, but defendant must plead payment, and plaintiff must plead that libel was untruthful, but defendant must plead truth. In these cases, *both* parties have pleading burdens, but defendant bears the burden of persuasion.

course will be constructive for him because he can get an answer without first going through trial.

(b) If the reviewing court *agrees* with Tyler, the complaint is adequate and does not require amendment. The case goes back to the judge for trial. The trial judge may not be entirely happy with this course of events, but the appellate court has clarified the law (perhaps changed it), and the case goes forward to trial.

5. An old saw, often repeated by lawyers for defendants, is that moving to dismiss for failure to state a claim is a waste of time: "We're just going to educate the plaintiff," is the common refrain. Much the same point is often made about motions for more definite statement or motions to strike pleadings. What do you think of this suggestion? Are defendants better off if they remain silent on defects in a complaint? Suppose we change the facts, but not the complaint: The true facts are that Tyler ran into the yard while the dog was on the attack. Between them, Sandra and Tyler got the dog away from Darin. Tyler suffered no physical injuries, but was for a time in the "zone of danger." If Sandra does *not* move to dismiss (because she doesn't want to educate Tyler), and Tyler does not amend, what will happen at trial? If Tyler offers evidence that he arrived at the scene while the attack was ongoing and if Sandra objects that the evidence is "irrelevant" to the claims alleged in the complaint, what should the court do? Carefully read FRCP 15(b). Does this provision suggest that the old saw is right (don't educate the plaintiff by moving to dismiss for failure to allege crucial elements)? Or does it suggest that the old saw is wrong?

6. Suppose the court grants a motion to dismiss or denies a motion to amend, and the suit is thereafter dismissed. Can plaintiff refile substantially the same claim in another court, or does the dismissal block a second suit under the doctrine of *res judicata*? With the caveat that it may be hard to tell whether a new complaint states the same claim as the dismissed complaint, or a claim "arising out of the same transaction" to use the common phrase describing the reach of *res judicata*, the answer is that a dismissal on this ground *is res judicata*, and ordinarily a second suit is barred. See Professional Management Associates, Inc. v. KPMG, LLP, 345 F.3d 1030, 1032 (8th Cir. 2003) ("denial of a motion to amend a complaint in one action is a final judgment on the merits barring the same complaint in a later action"); Northern Assurance Co. v. Square D Co., 201 F.3d 84, 87 (2d Cir. 1999) (where court refuses to let plaintiff amend to add claims, "normal principles of claim preclusion" apply and the new claims "have been forfeited due to a plaintiff's failure to pursue all claims against a particular defendant in one suit"). We revisit this matter in Chapter 14B2 in connection with the *res judicata* doctrine. See Problem 14-A (*"They're Picking on Me"*), infra.

7. A complaint may be dismissed *simply* because it is too long. Recall United States ex rel. Garst v. Lockheed-Martin Corp., 328 F.3d 374, 378 (7th Cir.), *cert. denied,* 540 U.S. 968 (2003) (described in note 7 in the Notes on the Conventions of Rules Pleading, supra). In the *Westinghouse* case, for example, the district court dismissed a complaint that "rambles for more than 600 paragraphs and 240 pages, including a 50-plus page 'overview' of the alleged wrongful conduct." In re Westinghouse Securities Litigation, 90 F.3d 696, 703 (3d Cir. 1995).

8. Sometimes, the problem with a complaint is not that it fails to state a claim, but that it is confusing or downright incomprehensible. Here the remedy for the defense is a motion for a more definite statement under FRCP 12(e), or sometimes a motion to strike under FRCP 12(f). Courts send mixed signals about such motions, but the dominant strain is that they are disfavored and not often granted. Consider these points:

(a) Courts often comment that the parties should pursue discovery rather than fight over pleadings, and the function of the motion is to address problems of intelligibility rather than add detail. See Home & Nature Inc. v. Sherman Specialty Co., 322 F. Supp. 2d 260 (E.D.N.Y. 2004) (Rules discourage motions for more definite statements and encourage discovery); Castillo v. Norton, 219 F. Supp. 155, 163 (D. Ariz. 2003) (seeking more definite statement is appropriate when pleading suffers from unintelligibility, but not from want of detail).

(b) Motions for a more definite statement are preferable to motions to dismiss for failure to state a claim, and can be used when the complaint leaves the basis for the claim murky. See, e.g., Hall v. Tyco International Ltd., 2004 WL 1763218 (M.D.N.C. 2004) (plaintiff "may have intended to assert a contract claim of some sort," but complaint was "utterly devoid of any supporting facts," and court could not "discern the nature" of the claim; court on its own orders plaintiffs to produce a more definite statement); Nelson v. Long Lines Ltd., 2003 WL 21356081, *6 (N.D. Iowa 2003) (granting motion for more definite statement describing time period when alleged discrimination occurred); Clark v. McDonald's Corp., 213 F.R.D. 198 (D.N.J. 2003) (in class suit alleging that McDonald's chain violated Americans with Disabilities Act, granting defense motion requiring plaintiffs to specify which restaurants were not in compliance; plaintiffs visited 150 out of 3,000 restaurants, finding violations in one-third of them; complaint "makes no allowance for nonoffending restaurants" and "shotgun approach" left defendant "to guess" which restaurants allegedly violated Act).

(c) Sometimes courts even criticize defendants for *failing* to attack a confusing complaint under FRCP 12(e). See Byrne v. Nezhat, 261 F.3d 1075, 1128 (11th Cir. 2001) (complaints were vague and ambiguous, but defendants did not seek more definite statements, and instead answered and raised affirmative defenses; "eschewing a Rule 12(e) motion" had the effect of joining plaintiff "in setting the stage for the immense and unnecessary expenditure of resources").

(d) Requiring a more definite statement can help determine whether a pleading is to be judged by standards in the Rules, or by heightened standards set by statute. See Flamenbaum v. Orient Lines, Inc., 2004 WL 1773207, *14 (S.D. Fla. 2004) (agreeing with defense claim that plaintiffs must state whether

they are making claims for common law fraud or asserting statutory cause of action "because each cause of action contains distinct elements and provides different remedies").

9. Motions to strike are often used to dispose of claims or defenses that are insufficient or time-barred. See Barnes v. Erie Insurance Exchange, 576 S.E.2d 681, 687 (N.C. 2003) (striking third-party complaint against impleaded third-party defendant as barred by statute of limitations). A motion to strike can come in handy for reasons having nothing to do with the pleadings. See DeMelo v. Zompa, 844 A.2d 174 (R.I. 2004) (granting defendant's motion to strike plaintiff's post-trial memorandum that "incorporated several documents that had not been introduced at trial, as well as an exhibit that had been marked only for identification at trial," which was proper under Rule 12(f) even though it applies "only to pleadings").

10. On rare occasions, courts strike allegations on the ground that they are "impertinent" or "scandalous." See Roman Catholic Diocese of Lexington v. Noble, 92 S.W.2d 724 (Ky. 2002) (in suit alleging sexual abuse by priests, striking and removing from record scandalous allegations on ground that they were "irrelevant" as well as "impertinent and scandalous"); Talbot v. Robert Matthews Distributing Co., 961 F.3d 654, 664 (7th Cir. 1992) (in suit alleging violations of labor laws, striking as "scandalous" certain allegations that defendants "intentionally caused the salmonella outbreak" that closed a dairy whose products plaintiffs delivered, where court concluded that these allegations were "devoid of any factual basis").

3. Getting to the Merits—Denying or Admitting Allegations in the Complaint

FRCP 8(b) requires defendant to "state in short and plain terms its defenses to each claim" and to "admit or deny the allegations" in the complaint. Denials "must fairly respond to the substance" of the allegations, and should "specifically deny designated allegations" unless the intent is to deny "all the allegations." Under FRCP 8(b)(6), allegations that are not denied in the answer are "admitted."

Suppose the usual case in which defendant thinks some allegations are true and others false, and that some paragraphs contain both true and false statements. Under FRCP 8(b), defendant has several choices. One is to select the truthful allegations and admit them, denying the rest. Another approach is to deny particular allegations, while expressly admitting or saying nothing about the rest (thus admitting the rest). That is, defendant may "specifically deny designated allegations" or "generally deny all [allegations] except those specifically admitted."

Note that FRCP 8(b) allows a defendant who lacks necessary information to deny allegations on that ground alone. If, for instance, plaintiff alleges that "as a result of the accident plaintiff's arm was broken in two places," then defendant may answer that he lacks "knowledge or information sufficient to form a belief about the truth of the allegation that plaintiff's arm was broken in two places, or that these injuries resulted from the accident." This averment denies those allegations.

Finally, note the bar against general denials. In a sense, of course, a complaint alleging ten points that is wrong on one of them is wrong, period. In that sense, an answer that "denies the allegations of the complaint" is accurate in pointing out that the complaint is wrong on some point. But FRCP 8(b) imposes a heavier burden: Defendants are not to stand on any "general denial" unless the intent really is to deny all the allegations, "including the jurisdictional grounds."

■ PROBLEM 7-D. Who Ran the Cement Truck?

On June 15, 2010, while working on road construction for Empire Paving, Frank Zoller was struck and seriously injured when the pouring slide on a cement mixer truck hit him on the shoulder. The truck was owned by Quality Ready-Mix, as a painted logo on the mixer barrel proclaimed, and was being operated by Sid Jameson. Zoller brought a negligence suit against Jameson and Quality, filing his complaint on May 20, 2013. The statute of limitations requires personal injury suits to be filed within three years. The complaint against Jameson includes the following paragraph:

> 3. Sid Jameson was an employee of defendant Quality Ready-Mix at all relevant times, and he carelessly and negligently backed the mixer truck with the pouring slide extended but not properly braced, with the result that said slide violently came into contact with the plaintiff, striking him in the shoulder and causing serious injuries.

On being served, the general manager of Quality forwarded the summons and complaint to its liability insurer, Industrial Accident and Indemnity Company ("Industrial"). In the accompanying letter, the manager wrote as follows:

> Sid Jameson is not one of ours. We leased several of our trucks temporarily to the Dura Span Company for use on the interstate project, and I believe Jameson is one of their concrete drivers. Shouldn't Dura Span be named in this matter instead of us? Please handle as per your procedures.

Counsel retained by Industrial filed an answer on behalf of Quality that includes the following paragraph: "3. Answering the allegations in paragraph 3 of the complaint, defendant Quality denies said allegations."

During the deposition of Sid Jameson in July 2013, counsel for Zoller learned for the first time that Jameson worked for Dura Span, not Quality, and that Quality rented the truck to Dura Span. Because it seems too late to file a new suit or amend the complaint to substitute Dura Span as defendant, Zoller moves under FRCP 12(f) to strike paragraph 3 of the answer "insofar as said paragraph denies that Quality Ready-Mix is the employer of Sid Jameson." What are the best arguments for and against this motion? How should the court rule, and why?

■ NOTES ON PLEADING DENIALS

1. Usually, defendants deny negligence and causation, and in the typical case such denials are proper. The parties disagree and their memories and accounts of the accident conflict. The general denial of "the allegations in paragraph 3" thus seems proper as a way of taking issue with the claims of negligence and causation, doesn't it? Of course, the general denial also reaches the claim that Sid Jameson "was an employee of Quality Ready-Mix," but Quality means to deny this point, doesn't it? Negligence claimants usually name the right employer, so on this point Quality's denial is unusual. If Zoller's lawyer assumed the only reason for the general denial was to take issue with the charging allegations (negligence and causation), and that Quality would not seriously contest employment, does the lawyer—and really the defendant—deserve to lose? See Zielinski v. Philadelphia Piers, Inc., 139 F. Supp. 408 (E.D. Pa. 1956) (on similar facts, answer raised "ineffective denial" that forklift driver was defendant's agent; defendant should have filed "a more specific answer" warning plaintiff that he sued the wrong party).

2. Suppose a complaint alleges that defendant "drove at an excessive speed and failed to keep a proper lookout" and the answer "denies that defendant drove at an excessive speed and failed to keep a proper lookout." Such a conjunctive denial, as it is called, can be read strictly against the pleader as denying that he did both things but failing to deny that he did either one. Thus read, the answer admits negligence (driving too fast or failing to watch out). The best way of avoiding this trap is to deny the charging allegations separately: Defendant "denies that he drove at an excessive speed, and further denies that he failed to keep a proper lookout." Separate denials would remove any doubt that defendant in the Zoller suit intended to deny employment, wouldn't they?

3. Suppose a complaint alleges that defendant "caused plaintiff to incur medical expenses in the amount of $17,837," and that defendant "denies that plaintiff incurred medical expenses in the amount of $17,837." Construing the answer strictly against the defendant, one could say it denies only medical expenses in that sum but fails to deny expenses of $17,836. Or suppose a complaint alleges that defendant breached an obligation to pay a promissory note, that defendant owes the amount of the note and "reasonable attorneys' fees in the amount of $600" under a fee-shifting clause, but that defendant simply "denies the allegations" in that paragraph of the complaint. Such denials too could be considered so specific that they concede the general point (that defendant does owe reasonable attorneys' fees). Under what is known as the "negative pregnant" doctrine, defendants could be penalized for answering in these ways. See Wingfoot California Homes Co. v. Valley National Bank, 294 P.2d 370 (Ariz. 1956) (construing denial of paragraph claiming attorneys' fees in specific amount as "negative pregnant" that "implies an affirmative" and thus admits owing fees; plaintiff wins summary judgment for fees in amount less than alleged). Fortunately, the wooden-headed attitude that produces these results has gone out of fashion. See 5 Wright & Miller, Federal Practice and Procedure §1267 (1990) (only one modern federal decision applies this "anachronistic" concept). Can you see, however, why lawyers craft denials to avoid even the possibility of being charged with pleading a negative pregnant? Can you see the solution?

4. "Argumentative denials" are also sometimes considered ineffective. Such a denial simply avers the opposite of whatever is alleged, thus denying by implication but not expressly. If plaintiff claims defendant "was speeding" and defendant answers by claiming that he "was driving in a moderate and proper rate of speed," the denial is argumentative rather than direct. While penalizing such pleading seems inappropriate, lawyers usually know better than to couch denials in this form. See 5 Wright & Miller, supra, §1268 (such pleas should be upheld; if they make it unclear what allegations are being contested, motion to strike might be granted).

5. On the facts of the Problem, Jameson is not a defendant, and individual working persons seldom have enough money to pay a tort judgment. But lawyers often name as defendants both the individual and the company because doing so may bring procedural advantages: Venue possibilities may be broader (often suit may be laid in the district where any defendant resides); discovery may be easier (parties may be deposed on notice, without subpoena; parties must answer written interrogatories; nonparty witnesses need not); evidence may be more freely admissible (statements by an employee are often admissible against the employer, but sometimes what one says is admissible only against the speaker).

4. Getting to the Merits—Affirmative Defenses

Under FRCP 8(c), defendants must "affirmatively state" certain defenses, which means that these defenses cannot be raised simply by replying to (or denying) allegations in the complaint. Customarily, such defenses are set forth in numbered paragraphs in the answer under a separate heading after the denials. Contributory negligence and the bar of the statute of limitations are common affirmative defenses, and FRCP 8(c) provides a list that is useful but not exhaustive.

It is said that affirmative defenses are those that raise "new matter" that courts and lawyers would not pick up by reading the complaint and ordinary denials, hence that affirmative pleading is necessary to avoid surprise. Arguably, these observations apply to many affirmative defenses, including contributory negligence and the statute of limitations. It is not so clear, however, that this explanation accounts for all defenses for which courts require affirmative pleading.

GOMEZ v. TOLEDO

Supreme Court of the United States
446 U.S. 635 (1980)

Mr. Justice MARSHALL delivered the opinion of the Court.

The question presented is whether, in an action brought under 42 USC §1983 against a public official whose position might entitle him to qualified immunity, a plaintiff must allege that the official has acted in bad faith in order to state a claim for relief or, alternatively, whether the defendant must plead good faith as an affirmative defense.

I

Petitioner Carlos Rivera Gomez brought this action against respondent, the Superintendent of the Police of the Commonwealth of Puerto Rico, contending that respondent had violated his right to procedural due process by discharging him from employment with the Police Department's Bureau of Criminal Investigation.[1] . . . [P]etitioner alleged the following facts in his complaint. Petitioner had been employed as an agent with the Puerto Rican police since 1968. In April 1975, he submitted a sworn statement to his supervisor in which he asserted that two other agents had offered false evidence for use in a criminal case under their investigation. As a result of this statement, petitioner was immediately transferred from the Criminal Investigation Corps for the Southern Area to Police Headquarters in San Juan, and a few weeks later to the Police Academy in Gurabo, where he was given no investigative authority. In the meantime respondent ordered an investigation of petitioner's claims, and the Legal Division of the Police Department concluded that all of petitioner's factual allegations were true.

In April 1976, while still stationed at the Police Academy, petitioner was subpoenaed to give testimony in a criminal case arising out of the evidence

---

[1] The complaint originally named the Commonwealth of Puerto Rico and the police of the Commonwealth of Puerto Rico as additional defendants, but petitioner consented to their dismissal from the action.

that petitioner had alleged to be false. At the trial petitioner, appearing as a defense witness, testified that the evidence was in fact false. As a result of this testimony, criminal charges, filed on the basis of information furnished by respondent, were brought against petitioner for the allegedly unlawful wiretapping of the agents' telephones. Respondent suspended petitioner in May 1976 and discharged him without a hearing in July. In October, the District Court of Puerto Rico found no probable cause to believe that petitioner was guilty of the allegedly unlawful wiretapping and, upon appeal by the prosecution, the Superior Court affirmed. Petitioner in turn sought review of his discharge before the Investigation, Prosecution, and Appeals Commission of Puerto Rico, which, after a hearing, revoked the discharge order rendered by respondent and ordered that petitioner be reinstated with back pay.

Based on the foregoing factual allegations, petitioner brought this suit for damages, contending that his discharge violated his right to procedural due process, and that it had caused him anxiety, embarrassment, and injury to his reputation in the community. In his answer, respondent denied a number of petitioner's allegations of fact and asserted several affirmative defenses. Respondent then moved to dismiss the complaint for failure to state a cause of action, see FRCP 12(b)(6), and the District Court granted the motion. Observing that respondent was entitled to qualified immunity for acts done in good faith within the scope of his official duties, it concluded that petitioner was required to plead as part of his claim for relief that, in committing the actions alleged, respondent was motivated by bad faith. The absence of any such allegation, it held, required dismissal of the complaint. The United States Court of Appeals for the First Circuit affirmed.

We granted certiorari to resolve a conflict among the Courts of Appeals. We now reverse.

II

Section 1983 provides a cause of action for "the deprivation of any rights, privileges, or immunities secured by the Constitution and laws" by any person acting "under color of any statute, ordinance, regulation, custom, or usage, or any State or Territory." This statute, enacted to aid in "'the preservation of human liberty and human rights,'" Owen v. City of Independence, 445 U.S. 622, 636, (1980), quoting Cong. Globe, 42d Cong., 1st Sess., App. 68 (1871) (Rep. Shellabarger), reflects a congressional judgment that a "damages remedy against the offending party is a vital component of any scheme for vindicating cherished constitutional guarantees." As remedial legislation, §1983 is to be construed generously to further its primary purpose.

In certain limited circumstances, we have held that public officers are entitled to a qualified immunity from damages liability under §1983. This conclusion has been based on an unwillingness to infer from legislative silence a congressional intention to abrogate immunities that were both "well established at common law" and "compatible with the purposes of the Civil Rights Act." Owen v. City of Independence. Findings of immunity have thus been "predicated upon a considered inquiry into the immunity historically accorded the relevant official at common law and the interests behind it." Imbler v. Pachtman, 424 U.S. 409, 421 (1976). In Pierson v. Ray, 386 U.S. 547, 555 (1967), for example, we concluded that a police officer would be "excus[ed] from liability for acting under a statute that he reasonably believed to be valid but that was later held unconstitutional, on its face or as applied." And in other contexts we have held, on the basis of "[c]ommon-law tradition . . . and strong public-policy reasons," Wood v. Strickland, 420 U.S. 308, 318 (1975), that certain categories of executive officers should be allowed qualified immunity from liability for acts done on the basis of an objectively reasonable belief that those acts were lawful. See Procunier v. Navarette, 434 U.S. 555 (1978) (prison officials); O'Connor v. Donaldson, 422 U.S. 563 (1975) (superintendent of state hospital); Wood v. Strickland, supra (local school board members); Scheuer v. Rhodes, 416 U.S. 232 (1974) (state Governor and other executive officers). Cf. Owen v. City of Independence, *supra* (no qualified immunity for municipalities).

Nothing in the language or legislative history of §1983, however, suggests that in an action brought against a public official whose position might entitle him to immunity if he acted in good faith, a plaintiff must allege bad faith in order to state a claim for relief. By the plain terms of §1983, two—and only two—allegations are required in order to state a cause of action under that statute. First, the plaintiff must allege that some person has deprived him of a federal right. Second, he must allege that the person who has deprived him of that right acted under color of state or territorial law. See Monroe v. Pape, 365 U.S. 167, 171 (1961). Petitioner has made both of the required allegations. He alleged that his discharge by respondent violated his right to procedural due process, see Board of Regents v. Roth, 408 U.S. 564 (1972), and that respondent acted under color of Puerto Rican law.

Moreover, this Court has never indicated that qualified immunity is relevant to the existence of the plaintiff's cause of action; instead we have described it as a defense available to the official in question. Since qualified immunity is a defense, the burden of pleading it rests with the defendant. See FRCP 8(c) (defendant must plead any "matter constituting an avoidance or affirmative defense"). It is for the official to claim that his conduct was justified by an objectively reasonable belief that it was lawful. We see no basis for imposing on the plaintiff an obligation to anticipate such a defense by stating in his complaint that the defendant acted in bad faith.

Our conclusion as to the allocation of the burden of pleading is supported by the nature of the qualified immunity defense. As our decisions make clear, whether such immunity has been established depends on facts peculiarly within the knowledge and control of the defendant. Thus we have stated that "[i]t is the existence of reasonable grounds for the belief formed at the time and in light of all the circumstances, coupled with good-faith belief, that affords a basis for qualified immunity of executive officers for acts performed in the course of official conduct." Scheuer v. Rhodes, *supra*. The applicable test focuses not only on whether the official has an objectively reasonable basis for that belief, but also on whether "[t]he official himself [is] acting sincerely and with a belief that he is doing right," Wood v. Strickland, *supra*. There may be no way for a plaintiff to know in advance whether the official has such a belief or, indeed, whether he will even claim that he does. The existence of a subjective belief will frequently turn on factors which a plaintiff cannot reasonably be expected to know. For example, the official's belief may be based on state or local law, advice of counsel, administrative practice, or some other factor of which the official alone is aware. To impose the pleading burden on the plaintiff would ignore this elementary fact and be contrary to the established practice in analogous areas of the law.[8]

The decision of the Court of Appeals is reversed, and the case is remanded to that court for further proceedings consistent with this opinion.

It is so ordered.

Mr. Justice REHNQUIST joins the opinion of the Court, reading it as he does to leave open the issue of the burden of persuasion, as opposed to the burden of pleading, with respect to a defense of qualified immunity.

■ NOTES ON AFFIRMATIVE DEFENSES

1. Officer Carlos Gomez brought suit against Superintendent Astol Toledo under §1983. The misconduct allegedly took the form of illegal wiretapping. It looks like a case of retaliatory discharge because plaintiff had testified that other officers had given false testimony in a criminal case. The issue is whether plaintiff was required to allege that defendant acted in "bad faith." Section 1983 does not address this point, but the Court decided almost a century earlier that public servants enjoy qualified immunity in suits under the statute. The question is who bears the burdens of pleading on these matters: How should we answer that?

---

[8] As then Dean Charles Clark stated over 40 years ago: "It seems to be considered only fair that certain types of things which in common law pleading were matters in confession and avoidance—*i.e.*, matters which seemed more or less to admit the general complaint and yet to suggest some other reason why there was no right—must be specifically pleaded in the answer, and that has been a general rule." ABA, Proceedings Institute at Washington and Symposium at New York City on the Federal Rules of Civil Procedure 49 (1939). See also 5 C. Wright & A. Miller, Federal Practice and Procedure §§1270-1271.

2. Almost always, defendants bear not only the burden of *pleading* affirmative defenses, but the burden of persuasion on such defenses at trial. Notice, however, that Chief Justice Rehnquist says in his concurrence that *Gomez* does not decide who bears the burden of persuasion. A few years later, the Court addressed the question of trial burdens in the *Scherer* case, and concluded that *plaintiff* bears the burden of persuasion on at least one point that is important to qualified immunity—whether the right that defendant allegedly infringed was clearly established (if not, defendant was not acting in bad faith). Davis v. Scherer, 468 U.S. 183 (1984). This decision has been broadly read to mean that plaintiff bears the burden of proving that defendant was *not* entitled to immunity. See Swindle v. Livingston Parish School Board, 655 F.3d 386, 400 (11th Cir. 2011) ("plaintiff must demonstrate both that the right the defendant was alleged to have violated was 'clearly established,' and that the defendant acted 'unreasonably' in light of that clearly established law").

3. The stock answer to the question "what happens if the answer fails to raise an affirmative defense?" is that it is waived. See Catelli v. Fleetwood, 842 A.2d 1078, 1081 (R.I. 2004) (failure to plead justification in the form of housing code violations that might excuse nonpayment of rent means that defense was waived). But it is one thing to take this position if defendant files an answer omitting such defenses and goes all the way to trial without mentioning them, quite another to say the defenses are lost forever if, shortly after filing an answer omitting them, defendant tries to remedy the problem. In the first place, FRCP 15 entitles defendants to amend within 21 days after serving their answer, and leave to amend is often granted even if a lot more time has gone by. In the second place, courts are likely to let defendants raise affirmative defenses by appropriate motion. See Federal Marketing Company v. Virginia Impression Products Company, 823 A.2d 513, 526 (D.C. Ct. App. 2003) (failure to raise laches in answer did not waive defense where defendant put plaintiff on notice of defense in summary judgment proceedings). Still, lawyers who omit affirmative defenses cannot *count* on getting permission to do so later, and litigants who wait until late in the game are likely to lose. See Marias Healthcare Services, Inc. v. Turenne, 28 P.3d 491, 494 (Mont. 2001) (raising statute of limitations defense for first time in post-trial memorandum was too late).

4. Suppose defendant makes a pre-answer motion under FRCP 12(b)(6) to dismiss a complaint for failure to state a claim, and the argument is that the complaint is time-barred. Can plaintiff object that the statute of limitations must be raised in the answer, and that the matter cannot be decided now because the answer has not been filed and one cannot tell whether defendant will waive the defense? See Tucker v. State Farm Mutual Automobile Ins. Co., 53 P.3d 947, 950 (Utah 2002) (if complaint shows on its face that suit is time-barred, the matter may be raised on motion under Rule 12(b)(6)).

5. Note that FRCP 8(c) provides a list of affirmative defenses that is exemplary rather than exhaustive. What else belongs on the list? See, e.g., FTC v. A.

E. Staley Mfg. Co., 324 U.S. 746, 759 (1945) (good-faith defense under Robinson-Patman Act); Randall's Food Markets, Inc. v. Johnson, 891 S.W.2d 640, 646 (Tex. 1995) (truth is an affirmative defense in a private suit alleging slander).

5. Getting to the Merits—Bringing Counterclaims Against the Plaintiff

Rule 13 provides for counterclaims, which are usually claims by defendants against plaintiffs, although the Rule is framed in broader language, and it also covers, for example, claims that *plaintiffs* might have against impleaded third-party defendants who bring claims against plaintiffs under Rule 14.

Under Rule 13(b), a defendant in a suit *may* make any claim against the plaintiff who brought the suit. When any such claim arises out of the same transaction or occurrence as *plaintiff's* claim, the message of Rule 13(a) is that defendant *must* do so (with certain exceptions). The reason can be easily seen: Once again there are probably efficiencies if a defendant brings against plaintiff any claim that the defendant might have, as opposed to bringing a separate suit (one lawsuit is more efficient than two), but for claims *unrelated* to plaintiff's claim we want to give defendant a choice whether to pursue the matter now or not.

Consider a paradigm case: Arnold sues Beth for personal injuries and property damage sustained in an accident in which he was driving one car and she another. If Beth too sustained injuries or suffered damage to her car, she must make an appropriate counterclaim. Rule 13(a) does not say what happens if someone in her position fails to make such a counterclaim, but the implication is that the claim is lost, and FRCP 13 is understood as having this consequence.

Counterclaims and Subject Matter Jurisdiction. In suits in state court, for the most part there is no problem with subject matter jurisdiction. One exception arises when a claimant sues in a state court of limited jurisdiction (typically small claims or county court), and plaintiff's jurisdictionally proper complaint is met with a counterclaim that exceeds the limit. In this situation, one possibility is to refuse to hear the counterclaim (and make an exception to the rule *requiring* defendant to advance a counterclaim). Another is to allow removal of the suit to a court that can hear both claim and counterclaim. See, e.g., Cal. Code Civ. Proc. §116.390 (setting up removal procedure). Finally, it seems clear that a defendant can pursue a counterclaim that exceeds the jurisdictional maximum of the court if defendant waives any right to recover more than that maximum.

In federal court, the matter is more complicated. The supplemental jurisdiction statute, 28 USC §1367, contains no "carveout" for counterclaims introduced into suits under FRCP 13. Since §1367(a) creates supplemental jurisdiction for all claims that are part of the same "case or controversy," most if not all compulsory counterclaims are likely covered, in federal question and diversity cases alike, because such counterclaims arise out of the same "transaction or occurrence" as plaintiff's claim. Thus if a Vermont plaintiff sues a New York defendant for injuries arising out of a car accident, and if defendant brings a counterclaim for $50,000 for damages to his car, there is supplemental jurisdiction even though the counterclaim does not satisfy the jurisdictional minimum.

It is harder to say whether supplemental jurisdiction reaches counterclaims that are *not* compulsory—that do *not* arise out of the "same transaction or occurrence" as the plaintiff's claim. Arguably, "same transaction or occurrence" in FRCP 13(a) means the same thing as same "case or controversy" in §1367(a), which suggests that there is no supplemental jurisdiction over permissive counterclaims. If so, and if a Vermont plaintiff sues a New York defendant in federal court on grounds of diversity, alleging that defendant delivered faulty goods under a contract, and if the New York defendant brings a counterclaim alleging that the Vermont plaintiff breached an unrelated contract for other goods and services several years earlier, the counterclaim is permissive. If it sought $50,000 (less than the minimum in diversity cases), there would be no supplemental jurisdiction.

Suffice it to say that the matter remains somewhat in limbo. See, e.g., Jones v. Ford Motor Credit Co., 358 F.3d 205 (2d Cir. 2004) (counterclaims by finance company for amounts due on loan satisfied "same case or controversy" standard, in suit alleging race discrimination in lending, even though they did not satisfy same transaction standard of FRCP 13 and were not compulsory; supplemental jurisdiction statute "displaced" earlier doctrine that permissive counterclaim requires independent jurisdiction) (context is class suit in which counterclaims might make class treatment impracticable).

Express Exceptions. There are two express exceptions to the compulsory counterclaim rule in FRCP 13(a). The first says a counterclaim need not be brought, even if otherwise compulsory, if the claim was pending elsewhere when the action was commenced. The second says a counterclaim need not be brought, even if otherwise compulsory, if the suit rested on an "attachment or other process" that did not establish "personal jurisdiction" over the defendant.

These exceptions are probably less important than they appear:

With respect to the first, if by chance Beth sued Arnold for personal injuries and property damage arising out of their accident, and she filed *her* suit before he filed *his,* then in his (second) suit she need not bring as a counterclaim the same claims that she already brought in her own suit. If both suits are pending in the same state, however, it is likely that Arnold's claims against Beth are compulsory counterclaims in her suit, and for that reason (if for no other) Arnold is not likely to file a second suit. A few states, such as Illinois and New York, do not have compulsory counterclaim rules, and in those states counterclaims are always permissive. See, e.g., 735 Ill. Comp. Stat. 5/2-608 (any claim by defendant against plaintiff "may be pleaded"); N.Y. CPLR §3019 (a counterclaim "may be any cause of action" brought by defendant against plaintiff). In our example, if Beth sued Arnold in Illinois, and Arnold later sued Beth in Indiana, which has a compulsory counterclaim rule similar to FRCP 13(a), pretty clearly Beth need not file a counterclaim and can continue to pursue relief in her Illinois suit.

With respect to the second exception, recall the decision in the *Shaffer* case (Chapter 3C1), where the Court abolished *quasi-in-rem* type 2 jurisdiction, of the sort that was involved in the early cases of *Pennoyer* and *Harris,* in which seizure of property unrelated to the claim was a "jurisdictional hook" that forced defendant to appear or risk losing the property. *Shaffer* left room for some "pure" *in rem* suits, such as probate proceedings and quiet title actions, where it might be that property supports limited jurisdiction over the defendant but not full *in personam* jurisdiction, and in such a case the compulsory counterclaim rule does not apply.

Procedural Complications. Toward the end of this course, you will encounter "preclusion doctrines" that go under the more common names of *res judicata* and *collateral estoppel* (Chapter 14, infra). Simplifying for a moment, the doctrine of *res judicata* holds that the parties are bound by a final judgment, and that each claimant must *in one lawsuit* bring *all the claims* that could be brought in connection with the transaction or occurrence giving rise to the suit. In most jurisdictions, that would mean that Arnold, if he sues Beth, must seek recovery for property damage resulting from the accident *and* his own personal injuries, in one suit rather than two. If he sues for property damage and leaves out the claim for personal injuries, he cannot later sue for them; if he sues for personal injuries and leaves out the claim for property damage, he cannot later sue for property damage.

Again simplifying for a moment, the doctrine of *collateral estoppel* holds that any issue that is actually litigated and finally determined in one suit, if it is essential to the judgment, is binding on the parties in later suits. On our facts, if Arnold sues Beth, and if the case is tried and if Beth has raised the affirmative defense of contributory negligence and offers proof that Arnold was negligent, and if the jury returns a verdict awarding full recovery to Arnold based on findings that Beth was negligent and that Arnold was not, this judgment might prevent Beth from prevailing in a later suit for her own personal injuries or property damage arising out of the accident *even in the absence of* a compulsory counterclaim rule. The reason is that Beth might be collaterally estopped, in her own suit, from claiming that Arnold was negligent or that she was free of negligence. See Restatement Second, Judgments §22, Comment c (where the same facts "constitute a ground of defense" and also "a ground for a counterclaim" and defendant raises those facts by way of defense but not as a counterclaim, and plaintiff prevails, rules of issue preclusion apply, and these "normally preclude relitigation, in a second proceeding between the parties, of issues determined in the first proceeding").

Interestingly, then, part of what is accomplished by a compulsory counterclaim rule is also accomplished, at least sometimes, by the doctrine of *collateral estoppel*. Generally, however, the doctrine of *res judicata* does not require Beth, if she *defends a claim against her* by claiming (and proving) that Arnold was himself negligent in the accident, to bring her own claim for recovery. While *res judicata* requires Arnold to bring all his claims at once (or lose those that he omits), the same doctrine does not require Beth to bring her own counterclaims for recovery even though she *defends against his* claim on the basis that he was negligent. See Restatement Second, Judgments §22, Comment d (where defendant raises facts "as a defense but not as a counterclaim" and prevails, she "is not precluded" from bringing a later suit based on those facts). Still, the compulsory counterclaim rule requires Beth to bring her claims arising out of the accident, thus adding something to what the preclusion doctrines impose.

Common Law Exception. In one setting, a compulsory counterclaim rule is seen as unfair—"reverse party" suits in which a party who is or may be violating the rights of another (the "more natural defendant") "jumps the gun" and becomes plaintiff in a suit for declaratory judgment seeking judicial approval of his interests or behavior. Then the defendant in the declaratory judgment suit files a "reactive" suit as plaintiff seeking damages or other relief ("coercive relief"), and the question arises whether the "new" plaintiff should have raised his claim as a compulsory counterclaim in the declaratory judgment suit. Essentially, we have A versus B in the declaratory judgment suit and B versus A in a coercive suit. Here courts sometimes refuse to apply the compulsory counterclaim rule, and let the second suit proceed. See Allan Block Corp. v. County Materials Corp., 512 F.3d 912 (7th Cir. 2008) (failing to file compulsory counterclaim "does normally preclude its being made the subject of another lawsuit," but if defendants had to make counterclaims in declaratory judgment suits, the latter "would become devices for thwarting" defendant's right to choose a forum; FRCP 13(a) is "not independent" of the common law of *res judicata*, which lets plaintiff split a declaratory judgment claim from a damage claim and bring different suits; FRCP 13(a) "is in effect a procedural implementation of that doctrine," and it "does not specify the consequences" of failing to bring a counterclaim; those consequences are defined by *res judicata*).

The *Allan Block* case in effect says that FRCP 13(a) does not *itself* specify the consequence of failing to bring a compulsory counterclaim, and leaves this matter to the common law of *res judicata*, including the related doctrine of *collateral estoppel*. If so, a new problem appears: Not only in *declaratory judgment* suits, but in *all* suits, the question whether failing to bring a counterclaim forecloses another suit is a function of common law. But those common law doctrines *themselves* defer to FRCP 13(a). *Allan Block* reaches a defensible conclusion, but at the risk of making the obligation to bring a compulsory counterclaim in *any* suit unenforceable.

VALLEY VIEW ANGUS RANCH v. DUKE ENERGY FIELD SERVICES

United States Court of Appeals for the Tenth Circuit
497 F.3d 1096 (10th Cir. 2007)

Before HARTZ, EBEL and O'BRIEN, Circuit Judges.

O'BRIEN, Circuit Judge.

[Valley View Angus Ranch, a 450-acre spread in Oklahoma, sued Duke Energy Field Services, alleging that Duke damaged the ranch when its gas line leaked, discharging condensate. Valley View claimed that this leak polluted soils and groundwater, and it sought damages on theories of trespass, nuisance, and unjust enrichment. Federal jurisdiction rested on diversity of citizenship. The trial court granted Duke's motion for summary judgment on the ground that Valley View's claims were barred by litigation in a suit that Duke had previously filed against Valley View in Oklahoma state court.

In the prior Oklahoma state court suit, Duke sought injunctive relief on the ground that it had a right to enter Valley View ranch to install monitoring wells, and that Valley View had refused access to its property (Valley View claimed that Duke did not reply to its request to learn the location of the monitoring wells that Duke proposed to dig, for the purpose of enabling Duke to investigate the claimed leaks more closely). In addition, Duke sought damages for alleged violation of its easement. Valley View claimed that Duke had committed trespass. Duke filed a motion for partial summary judgment, which the court granted on ground that Duke did have an easement, and the case went to trial on the question whether Valley View violated its duties under the easement and whether Duke had sustained damages. The jury found in favor of Duke, and awarded damages of $1,800. There was no appeal, and judgment became final.]

Duke ... argues [that] Valley View is barred from raising its federal claims because, under Oklahoma's compulsory counterclaim statute, they should have been raised as counterclaims in the state court action. Under Oklahoma's statute, a pleading must "state as a counterclaim any claim which at the time of serving the pleading the pleader has against any opposing party, if it arises out of the transaction or occurrence that is the subject matter of the opposing party's claim and does not require for its adjudication the presence of third parties of whom the court cannot acquire jurisdiction." Okla. Stat. Ann. tit. 12, §2013(A).[10] "Failure to plead a compulsory counterclaim prevents a party from bringing a later independent action on that claim." Oklahoma Gas & Elec. Co. v. Dist. Court, Fifteenth Judicial Dist., Cherokee County, 784 P.2d 61, 64 (Okla. 1989).

. . .

---

[10] Recognizing the text of the Oklahoma compulsory counterclaim rule is identical to the text of FRCP 13(a), Oklahoma courts have looked to federal law for guidance in applying the Oklahoma statute.

For a counterclaim to be compulsory under §2013(A), it must arise out of the "same transaction and occurrence" as the subject matter of the opposing party's claim. *Oklahoma Gas and Electric.* Thus, in order for Valley View's claim to be considered compulsory, Valley View's nuisance and trespass claims must arise out of the "same transaction and occurrence" as Duke's breach of easement claim. "Rather than attempt to define the terms 'transaction' and 'occurrence' precisely, most courts . . . have preferred to suggest standards by which the compulsory or permissive nature of specific counterclaims may be determined. . . ." Fox v. Maulding, 112 F.3d 453, 457 (10th Cir. 1997) (interpreting Oklahoma law). Such factors include: "(1) Are the issues of fact and law raised by the claim and counterclaim largely the same? (2) Would res judicata bar a subsequent suit on defendants' claim absent the compulsory counterclaim rule? (3) Will substantially the same evidence support or refute plaintiffs' claims as well as defendants' counterclaim? and (4) Is there a logical relation between the claim and the counterclaim?" *See also* Charles Alan Wright, Arthur R. Miller & Mary Kay Kane, 6 Federal Practice and Procedure §1410 (listing same factors).

. . .

. . . The *Fox* factors weigh heavily against the conclusion Valley View's federal claims were compulsory counterclaims in the state court action. First, . . . Valley View's claims are not barred by claim preclusion [because they do not involve the same evidence, factual issues, and legal issues]. Second, the issues of fact and law are likely to be very different; the development of fact and law on Valley View's claims would focus on the cause and extent of the leak and whether the alleged pollution resulting therefrom exceeded the norms established by nuisance and trespass law, whereas the development of fact and law on Duke's claim would focus on the existence of an easement and how Duke was denied access. Duke's argument on this point—the operative event underlying both actions was Duke causing the pipeline leak—exaggerates the significance of a single factual similarity. [Third, "the same evidence does not support or refute the principal claim and the purported counterclaims."] Finally, the only logical connection between the parties' claims is: they concern events (namely, the alleged damages caused by the *pipeline leak* and the subsequent *denial of access* to the pipeline to fix that leak) occurring at the same place, albeit at different times. This nexus, however, is too attenuated. [Hence] Valley View's trespass and nuisance claims are not properly categorized as compulsory counterclaims.[14]

---

[14] Because we have determined Valley View's claims would not be barred by the doctrine of claim preclusion or by the counterclaim statute, we find it unnecessary to address Valley View's argument regarding the applicability of the counterclaim rule in cases where the primary claim seeks injunctive relief and the hearing on the preliminary injunction is considered with the trial on the merits.

The district court improperly granted summary judgment to Duke on the basis of claim preclusion and the compulsory counterclaim statute.

[In other parts of its opinion, the court here concludes that Valley View's claims in this case are not barred by either issue preclusion, commonly called "res judicata," or claim preclusion, commonly called "collateral estoppel." The court also concludes that Valley View's claims in this case should not be barred by the somewhat looser doctrine that blocks a litigant in one suit from bringing another suit in which the effect could be to nullify the judgment in the initial suit.]

The judgment of the district court is REVERSED and the case is REMANDED for further proceedings consistent with this opinion.

LETOURNEAU v. HICKEY

Supreme Court of Vermont
807 A.2d 437 (2002)

AMESTOY, C.J., DOOLEY, MORSE, JOHNSON and SKOGLUND, JJ.

Plaintiffs Laurent and Alicia Letourneau appeal the superior court's orders granting defendant Charles Hickey summary judgment on plaintiffs' legal malpractice claim, granting defendants Michael and Susan Judd summary judgment on plaintiffs' slander claim, and summarily denying plaintiffs' motion for relief from a judgment in a prior lawsuit involving the Letourneaus and the Judds. We affirm.

The present case arises out of an earlier lawsuit involving a boundary dispute. The Letourneaus and Judds are neighbors who own adjacent agricultural property. The Letourneaus tapped maple trees on land claimed by both parties. The Judds sued the Letourneaus in 1998, seeking a declaration of the boundary line between the parties' properties. Charles Hickey represented the Letourneaus in that case. Following a two-day hearing, the trial court awarded the Judds title to the disputed property. In its May 1999 decision, the court rejected the Letourneaus' adverse possession claim, but determined that the Letourneaus had acquired a prescriptive profit to harvest maple sap from trees in the disputed area. No appeal was taken from that decision. When the Letourneaus failed to pay attorney Hickey for his legal services, he brought a collection action against them and obtained a default judgment in October 1999.

In February 2001, the Letourneaus filed a complaint against attorney Hickey and the Judds, alleging that attorney Hickey had committed legal malpractice during his representation of them in the boundary dispute case, and that Michael Judd had slandered them during his testimony in that case. Further, based on their malpractice claim, the Letourneaus sought relief from the judgment entered against them. In two separate decisions, the superior court granted summary judgment to attorney Hickey and the Judds. The court ruled that the Letourneaus had waived their right to bring the malpractice claim by failing to raise it as a compulsory counterclaim in the collection action. With respect to the slander claim, the court ruled that the allegedly slanderous testimony was privileged, and that, in any case, the Letourneaus had failed to provide evidence of any actual harm. The court also denied the Letourneaus' motion for relief from judgment without explanation in a motion reaction form. On appeal, the Letourneaus argue that the superior court erred by granting summary judgment to attorney Hickey and the Judds, and abused its discretion by dismissing their motion for relief from judgment without holding a hearing or making findings.

In their first claim of error, the Letourneaus argue that the compulsory counterclaim rule of VRCP 13(a) does not apply to bar their malpractice claim because the judgment against them in the prior collection action was by default. [The court quotes VRCP 13(a), which is substantially identical with FRCP 13(a)(1).]

Generally, a counterclaim is compulsory if it bears a "logical relationship" to the opposing party's earlier claim. Stratton v. Steele, 472 A.2d 1237, 1239 (Vt. 1984). Claims have a logical relationship with each other if the same aggregate set of facts serves as the basis for both claims, and the facts upon which the first claim arises triggers additional legal rights in the defendant that would otherwise remain dormant. We have stated that issue and claim preclusion provide the doctrinal support for this rule. See In re Cent. Vt. Pub. Serv. Corp., 769 A.2d 668, 673 (Vt. 2001) (res judicata applies to compulsory counterclaims). The reporter's notes indicate that Rule 13(a) merely identifies what types of claims are compulsory, and that a defendant who fails to assert such a claim is precluded from a later independent action "not by the rule itself, but by way of waiver or estoppel arising from the failure to plead." Reporter's Notes, VRCP 13.

The Letourneaus do not dispute that their malpractice claim is logically related to the collection action for purposes of Rule 13, but rather rely on another comment in the reporter's notes stating that "a defendant who defaults prior to answer or who submits to a consent judgment is not barred [from raising a compulsory counterclaim], because estoppel should not operate in such circumstances." In the Letourneaus' view, their malpractice action is not barred because the judgment in the collection action was by default. The Letourneaus point out that the comment in the reporter's notes, although merely advisory, is reinforced by the language of Rule 13 providing that a "pleading" must include compulsory counterclaims. According to the

Letourneaus, Rule 13 does not apply because they never filed a pleading in the collection action.

As noted, this Court has indicated that res judicata is the theoretical basis for Rule 13(a), while the reporter's notes refer to waiver and estoppel. The more flexible basis of waiver and estoppel gives courts the discretion to allow litigants in later independent actions, under certain circumstances, to raise what would otherwise be compulsory counterclaims from prior actions. See 6 Charles Alan Wright, Arthur R. Miller & Mary Kay Kane, Federal Practice and Procedure §1417, at 133-34 (2d ed. 1990) [Wright & Miller]. For example, waiver and estoppel might not be applied to bar an otherwise compulsory counterclaim where the parties resolved their dispute by way of a consent judgment acknowledging the absence of the counterclaim, where the court granted the defendant's motion to dismiss before an answer was due, or where the defendant did not knowingly refrain from asserting the counterclaim, such as when an insurance company controls the defense of the first action in the name of a defendant who wants to bring a later action.

None of those circumstances exist here. The Letourneaus attempted to evade service in the collection action, and were finally served only after the superior court granted attorney Hickey's request to tack a copy of the summons and complaint to their residence. Despite being served, they failed to file an answer to the complaint, but later filed several pleadings seeking to overturn the resulting default judgment. Approximately twenty-one months later, the Letourneaus filed an independent malpractice action. Rule 13 was not intended to protect defaulting litigants under such circumstances. This is not a situation where the Letourneaus had no realistic opportunity to file their counterclaim in the prior action, or where the parties voluntarily agreed to a judgment without the counterclaim.

Irrespective of whether the doctrinal underpinning of the compulsory counterclaim rule is res judicata or waiver and estoppel, "courts have given default judgments full effect and have held that a [compulsory] counterclaim omitted from an action that terminates in a default judgment will be barred from any subsequent suits." 6 Wright & Miller §1417. Indeed, in a case involving facts similar to the instant matter, the court stated that it would be "hard to imagine a clearer compulsory counterclaim to a complaint for failure to pay legal fees than a legal malpractice claim stemming from the handling of the litigation for which fees are sought." Law Offices of Jerris Leonard, P.C. v. Mideast Sys., Ltd., 111 F.R.D. 359, 361 (D.D.C. 1986). There, the court held that the defendant was barred from bringing the malpractice claim in a later action, even though the earlier action had resulted in a default judgment. *Id.* at 362 ("The fact that a party declines to appear does not prevent the default judgment from being set up as res judicata against it, barring subsequent counterclaims."); see Cianciolo v. Lauer, 819 S.W.2d 726, 727 (Ky. Ct. App. 1991) ("when one is duly summonsed and suffers a default, he not only loses his right to defend in that litigation, but also his right to assert in an independent action a claim deemed to have been a compulsory counterclaim" under Rule 13).

[The court also rejects the claim of the Letourneaus that Michael Judd was guilty of slander in testifying in the first trial that the Judd's parents receive maple syrup from the Letourneaus, but that the parents "weren't really happy" with the syrup because Letourneau "used to use rubber tires" for heat and that "a lot of times the syrup would taste like rubber tires." The Letourneaus claimed that this testimony was libel "per se" because it impugned "their live-lihood" and that the testimony was "not pertinent to the litigation." The reviewing court rejects these claims, invoking the principle that testimony given in litigation is privileged, and that a libel claim can succeed only if the words "were not pertinent to the matter then in progress" and were "spo-ken maliciously." The "pertinency" standard requires only a "good faith" belief that the statement has "some reasonable relation or reference to the subject of inquiry," which standard was satisfied even if "consideration" for the Letour-neaus' use of the property was not relevant.

The court also affirms the dismissal of the Letourneaus' claim for relief from the earlier judgment as "totally lacking in merit," and the trial judge was not obligated to hold an evidentiary hearing on this claim.]

Affirmed.

■ NOTES ON COUNTERCLAIMS

1. For reasons explored in the introductory material prior to *Valley View,* a compulsory counterclaim rule seems like a good idea. In the paradigm case described there, where Beth and Arnold are involved in litigation stemming from a car accident, it makes sense to require both parties to litigate all issues relating to the accident in a single suit. Much the same seems true in contract litigation, where parties to an agreement wind up in dispute over their rights and obligations and one sues the other. Still, implementing the rule can be challenging, as *Valley View* illustrates. Duke Energy brought the first suit, and Valley View brought the second. In deciding whether Valley View should have counterclaimed in Duke Energy's suit, the question is whether Valley View's claim for trespass and nuisance arises out of the same "transaction or occur-rence" as Duke Energy's claim for improperly denying access to the pipeline. What should be the answer?

2. *Valley View* concludes that there were two transactions or occurrences, not one. There was Valley View's alleged obstruction when Duke Energy sought access, and the earlier trespass when the pipeline leaked. In effect, the judge took a "time and space" approach to the question whether there are two transactions or only one. See also Wigglesworth v. Teamsters Local Union No. 592, 68 F.R.D. 609 (E.D. Va. 1975) (in suit against union alleging violations of rights of members, arising from acts by union officials in denying plaintiff's rights of free speech at meeting, union counterclaimed for damages from plaintiff's statements in press conference saying union was "dominated by the 'Mafia'" and ran "fixed" elections; counterclaim was *not* compulsory; it was "predicated on events which are in no wise part of the transactions or occurrences which gave rise to plaintiff's claim") (hence court lacked jurisdiction over counterclaim). Does this "time and space" approach make sense?

3. *Valley View* suggests four different "standards" for interpreting the "transaction" requirement in FRCP 13(a): Are the issues of law or fact largely the same? Would *res judicata* bar a later suit on a claim that defendant failed to raise in the action? Do plaintiff's claims and defendant's counterclaim involve largely the same evidence? Is the counterclaim "logically related" to plaintiff's claim?

(a) The first and third standards, based on same or overlapping issues and same or overlapping evidence, may be unrealistic because defendants don't always know, when preparing and filing their answer, what issues or evidence will be important. See 6 Wright & Miller, Federal Practice and Procedure §1410 (1994 & Supp. 2009) (criticizing the standards on this ground).

(b) The second standard, which incorporates by reference the *res judicata* doctrine, is unsatisfactory for reasons indicated above: The modern law of *res judicata* leaves to the rules and statutes governing procedure the extent of preclusion for not raising counterclaims.

(c) The "logical relation" standard has the greatest flexibility, but is also the vaguest of the four. It enjoys the endorsement of an early Supreme Court opinion in the *Moore* case. There plaintiff advanced an antitrust claim based on defendant's refusal to provide tickertape service, and the counterclaim asserted that plaintiff was stealing quotations and using them in a "bucket shop" operation (basically a fraudulent scheme). The Court concluded that the counterclaim was compulsory under a rule requiring defendants to bring counterclaims arising out of "the transaction which is the subject matter of the suit" (a standard similar to the one in FRCP 13(a)):

> "Transaction" is a word of flexible meaning. It may comprehend a series of many occurrences, depending not so much upon the immediateness of their connection as upon their logical relationship. The refusal to furnish the quotations is one of the links in the chain which constitutes the transaction upon which appellant here bases its cause of action. It is an important part of the transaction constituting the subject-matter of the counterclaim. It is the one circumstance without which neither party would have found it necessary to seek relief. Essential facts alleged by appellant enter into and constitute in part the cause of action set forth in the counterclaim. That they are not precisely identical, or that the counterclaim embraces additional allegations, as, for example, that appellant is unlawfully getting the quotations, does not matter. To hold otherwise would be

to rob this branch of the rule of all serviceable meaning, since the facts relied upon by the plaintiff rarely, if ever, are, in all particulars, the same as those constituting the defendant's counterclaim.

See Moore v. New York Cotton Exchange, 270 U.S. 593 (1926). *Moore* indicates, doesn't it, that the key in applying the rule is to be pragmatic? Hence the fact that a counterclaim contains new issues, not found in the complaint, or calls for evidence beyond what plaintiff might present, does not matter, does it?

4. Isn't it clear that Duke Energy's claim for obstructing the easement would lead to consideration of the pipeline leak and raise the question whether defendant behaved reasonably in resisting Duke Energy's attempt to enter? Doesn't this fact mean at least that the issues and the evidence raised by the complaint and the counterclaim overlap? Isn't it clear that there is a "logical relation" between the claim for obstruction and the counterclaim for trespass?

5. In *Letourneau*, lawyer Charles Hickey had sued his former clients Laurent and Alicia Letourneau for legal fees. Hickey had represented them as defendants in the suit by Michael and Susan Judd. When a lawyer represents *plaintiffs*, fees often depend on success: If the plaintiffs prevail and collect money, generally the lawyer has no trouble getting paid. But when he represents *defendants* who are not making claims for money, he must make other arrangements, as by charging a "retainer" in advance. Apparently, Hickey did not have such an arrangement. Hickey was not entirely successful in the prior suit, but did get something for his clients: They lost the claim that they owned the land, but won a "prescriptive profit" that entitled them to harvest maple syrup.

6. Hickey obtained a default judgment against the Letourneaus within five months after the Judd suit. It is not clear whether the Letourneaus were represented by a new lawyer when Hickey sued them, but failing to answer put them in default. Why do you suppose they did not defend that suit?

7. In their new suit, the Letourneaus have a lawyer, and they're seeking recovery against Hickey for malpractice, the Judds for slander, and they also want "relief from the judgment" in the Judds' prior suit. The court denied all three claims. Why did the court dismiss the malpractice claim? The first sentence of Vermont Rule 13(a) is substantially identical to FRCP 13(a)(1). Doesn't the language suggest that a claim is lost only if it is compulsory *and* is omitted from an answer in a prior suit? How does the court handle this issue? If the Letourneaus did not retain counsel when Hickey sued them, is it fair to throw out their malpractice claim for procedural reasons now? Compare McKnight v. Dean, 270 F.3d 513 (7th Cir. 2001) (under Wisconsin law, counterclaim is compulsory only if it would nullify judgment in prior action or impair rights established thereby; since attorney in prior suit would be entitled to fees even if he committed malpractice, client's claim for malpractice was not a compulsory counterclaim in prior suit for fees) (malpractice claim fails anyway).

8. Suppose Hickey's answer in the present suit had denied malpractice but had not raised the prior failure by the Letourneaus to assert their claim in Hickey's suit. See FRCP 8(c) and Plus v. Meramec Valley Bank, 81 S.W.3d 528, 534 (Mo. 2002) (defense that plaintiff's claim is barred by compulsory counterclaim rule is itself an affirmative defense that must be pleaded or it is waived).

9. Paraphrasing FRCP 13(a), a counterclaim is compulsory only if defendant "has" the claim "at the time of" serving the answer. See Stone v. Department of Aviation, 453 F.3d 1271 (10th Cir. 2006) (after City sued Stone in state court, in effort to set aside an order by Career Service Authority reinstating Stone after he was fired, Stone sued City in federal court under Americans with Disabilities Act; Stone was *not* barred by state counterclaim rule from bringing this federal claim, as he had not received right-to-sue letter when City brought state suit; counterclaim rule covers only those claims that exist at time of filing answer, and Stone did not yet have right to sue).

6. Failure to Answer: Default

Recall from the *Letourneau* case that the consequence of not defending a suit is that defendant loses by default. Obviously, the system cannot operate effectively if defendants could ignore a suit, and failing to defend leads first to a "default" and finally to a "default judgment." The matter is regulated in FRCP 55 and 60(b).

First, notice that under FRCP 55(a) the court clerk "must enter" the default of a defendant who "has failed to plead or otherwise defend." In its simplest application, defendant fails to file and serve an answer within the allotted time. Plaintiff alerts the clerk, who enters defendant's default.

The next step is to obtain judgment, which the clerk can enter on behalf of the plaintiff if the suit is "for a sum certain" or "a sum that can be made certain by computation" *and if* the defendant "has been defaulted for not appearing" and is "neither a minor nor an incompetent person." The best example of a suit for a "sum certain" is one seeking recovery on a promissory note or lease, in which the amount owing can be readily computed by examining the note or lease and doing simple computations. The Rule contemplates that plaintiff will assist the clerk by supplying an affidavit "showing the amount due," and presumably indicating as well that the defendant is *not* a minor or incompetent person.

In other cases, plaintiff "must apply to the court" for a default judgment—in cases, that is, where the claim is *not* for a sum certain, as is true whenever plaintiff sues for personal injuries, for breach of other kinds of contracts, or for most other forms of damage recovery. If defendant "has appeared" in the action, then under FRCP 55(b)(2) plaintiff must serve her with "written notice of the application at least 7 days before the hearing." In Charles Hickey's original suit, his claim was *not* for a sum certain. Even though lawyers charge clients by the hour, Hickey would have been expected to ask *the judge* to enter a default judgment: A lawyer's bill is seldom merely a function of hours times rate (lawyers usually charge more for "good results" and less for neutral or unfavorable outcomes), and Hickey would have been expected to justify his bill to the court. Such hearings bear some resemblance to a trial, but they are better understood as a judicial inquiry seeking assurance that the facts justify entry of judgment for the plaintiff. Well-pleaded facts are taken as true insofar as they determine basic questions of liability, and a defendant who is in default is not entitled to try to refute such facts. Courts sometimes take testimony, but they need not do so. Defendants can, however, contest the fact and amount of damages, and on this point a default hearing is in effect a trial. See generally Wright & Miller, Federal Practice and Procedure §2688 (3d ed.).

Relief from Default. Routinely, defendants who neglect the matter of defending themselves at the outset regret this choice in the end, and seek relief from default, or from a default judgment. Typically, courts are more generous in granting relief from a default than from a default judgment. Consider the following description of the standards that apply in these settings:

> We review for abuse of discretion the district court's granting of a motion to vacate a default judgment. We review a motion to vacate a default judgment under the stricter standards of Rule 60(b) rather than under the more lax standards governing a motion to vacate the entry of default under Rule 55(c). Waifersong, Ltd. Inc. v. Classic Music Vending, 976 F.2d 290, 292 (6th Cir. 1992) ("But once the court has determined damages and a judgment has been entered, the district court's discretion to vacate the judgment is circumscribed by public policy favoring finality of judgments and termination of litigation. Rule 60(b) reflects this public policy by requiring greater specificity from a moving party before a court will set aside a default judgment.").
>
> The Federal Rules of Civil Procedure require a defendant to serve an answer within twenty days of being served with a summons and complaint [now it is 21 days—ED.]. FRCP 12(a)(1)(A). Rule 55 permits the clerk to enter a default when a party fails to defend an action as required. The court may then enter a default judgment. FRCP 55(b)(1). A party against whom a default judgment has been entered may petition the court to set aside the default judgment under Rules 55(c) and 60(b) for good cause, and upon a showing of mistake, or any other just reason. The seminal case in this circuit on Rule 60(b) motions to vacate default judgments is United Coin Meter Co., Inc. v. Seaboard Coastline R.R., 705 F.2d 839 (6th Cir. 1983). In *United Coin Meter* we noted that Rule 60(b) is to be applied "equitably and liberally" in considering motions to vacate defaults and default judgments, and that the same factors that control a motion to vacate an entry of default under Rule 55(c) are also applicable in determining whether to vacate a default judgment: (1) whether the opposing party would be prejudiced; (2) whether the proponent had a meritorious claim or defense; and (3) whether the proponent's culpable conduct led to the default.

In *Waifersong*, we made it clear that a party seeking to vacate a default judgment under Rule 60(b)(1) must demonstrate first and foremost that the default did not result from his culpable conduct. That burden may be carried, we said, only by meeting the requirements of Rule 60(b)(1), that is, by "demonstrat[ing] that his default was the product of mistake, inadvertence, surprise, or excusable neglect." Only if the moving party makes this showing may the district court proceed to consider the other *United Coin Meter* factors. Other cases have affirmed the more stringent inquiry courts must pursue when vacating a default judgment as opposed to an entry of default.

We recognize that the district court did not consider the *United Coin Meter* factors in the order that *Waifersong* requires. Nonetheless, although the court did not consider first whether St. Paul had demonstrated that the default was not due to its culpable conduct, the court's finding on that issue is clearly sufficient to support its considering the other two factors. First, St. Paul demonstrated that its default was not the result of culpable conduct, but of mistake or, at worst, excusable neglect. St. Paul's counsel did not simply ignore the pleading deadlines, but repeatedly checked with the office of the district court clerk to determine whether service had been effected upon St. Paul and mistakenly relied upon the information obtained from the clerk. Neither St. Paul nor its counsel was willful in failing to respond timely, and the failure to file an answer timely resulted from an honest mistake. . . . Second, as we shall develop more fully below, St. Paul had a meritorious defense. And third, [plaintiff] Abt was not prejudiced by the vacation of the default judgment. St. Paul moved to vacate this judgment immediately upon discovering the default, and that motion was filed less than 30 days after the date the answer to the complaint was due. We have often reiterated the principle that "trials on the merits are favored in federal courts," and that "any doubt should be resolved in favor of the petition to set aside the judgment so that cases may be decided on their merits." *United Coin Meter*. We have therefore held that "mere delay in satisfying a plaintiff's claim, if it should succeed at trial, is not sufficient prejudice to require denial of a motion to set aside a default judgment."

In fact, Abt's arguments are somewhat disingenuous. As the district court pointed out, Abt's attorneys had been in frequent touch with St. Paul's attorneys prior to the initiation of this suit, but elected not to notify them of the filing of the lawsuit, the entry of default or the default judgment.

This is clearly not one of those "most extreme cases" where the default judgment is the result of deliberate, willful, conduct. *United Coin Meter*. Instead, this case presents an appropriate instance for the district court to exercise its discretion to "achieve substantial justice" through the liberal application of Rule 60(b). Blois v. Friday, 612 F.2d 938, 940 (5th Cir. 1980). We hold that the district court did not abuse its discretion in vacating the default judgment.

Weiss v. St. Paul Fire and Marine Ins. Co., 283 F.3d 790, 794 (6th Cir. 2002).

In *Weiss*, the defaulting party was an insurance carrier that declined to defend a breach-of-patent suit against its insured, on the ground that the policy did not cover this form of liability. Later sued for attorneys' fees expended in defending the patent suit, St. Paul found itself in default because its lawyers apparently believed they had no duty to file an answer until plaintiff had filed proof of service with the court. In fact, the contrary is true: Under FRCP 4(l)(3), failing to make proof of service "does not affect the validity of the service." But defendant had received its copy of the complaint by certified mail, so it is possible that the lawyers thought their client had not been served at all, and were checking with the court to see whether proof of service had been filed because they thought the period for answering the complaint would only commence on date of service, and proof of service would supply the date. Inexplicably, the court clerk repeatedly told the lawyers that proof of service had not been filed, even though it *was* filed on September 9, 1992, 15 days after the complaint was filed. In reversing the default judgment, the reviewing court stresses that defense lawyers made an "honest mistake," and that lawyers for the plaintiff had been "in frequent touch" with the defense lawyers (they were trying to settle), but did not reveal that they had filed suit or taken the default judgment.

■ NOTES ON OBTAINING AND CHALLENGING DEFAULT JUDGMENTS

1. Where defendant defaults by failing to appear, the first step is to enter the default under FRCP 55(a). What for? What if defendant files an answer or motion *after* default is entered? See Multiple Resort Ownership Plan, Inc. v. Design-Build-Manage, Inc., 45 P.3d 647, 651 (Wyo. 2002) (entry of default forecloses answer).

2. One possible explanation of the lawyers' conduct in *Weiss* was that they thought service of process had not yet been effected. If that had been right, would it have mattered? Compare O.J. Distributing, Inc. v. Hornell Brewing Co., 340 F.3d 345, 352 (6th Cir. 2003) (if service is improper, court must set aside default, regardless whether defendant satisfies three-factor standard) and Borer v. Lewis, 91 P.3d 375 (Colo. 2004) (must show by clear and convincing evidence that default judgment must be set aside; standard satisfied on showing that defendant had not been served with summons and complaint) with O'Brien v. R.J. O'Brien & Associates, Inc., 998 F.2d 1394 (7th Cir. 1993) (refusing to set aside default 18 months after defective service; summons contained "glaring defects" in referring to defendant by wrong name, failing to say how long defendant had to reply, and using facsimile copy that lacked court seal; in initial submission, defendant contended that it had never been served, but it should not have relied on court clerk; it had actual knowledge of suit and raised defects in service by later motion).

3. In *Weiss,* as in most default cases, it is defendant's failure to "appear" that leads to the default. What does "appear" mean? Courts disagree on the question whether "appearing" requires a filing in court. Compare Lindblom v. Prime Hospitality Corp., 90 P.3d 1283 (Nev. 2004) (in guest's personal injury suit against hotel, defendant participated in settlement talks, which was an appearance under Rule 55(b)(2); default judgment without three-day notice to defendant was void) and Cales v. Wills, 569 S.E.2d 479, 486 (W. Va. 2002) (appearance includes "any communication to an opposing party," whether written or oral, that "demonstrates either an interest in the pending litigation, or actual notice of the litigation") and Estes v. Ashley Hospitality, Inc., 679 N.W.2d 469 (S.D. 2004) (letter to plaintiff did not constitute answer because it was not filed, but did constitute an appearance, and defendant was entitled to notice before default judgment) with Brown v. Lange, 21 P.2d 822, 825 (Alaska 2001) (rejecting idea that appearance can happen "without a presentation or submission of some sort to the court," and concluding that phone call leaving message asking plaintiff's attorney "when he was going to court" was not appearance; defense not entitled to notice of hearing on application for default judgment). Which approach is better—one that counts as an "appearance" any effort by the defendant to defend or one requiring a court filing? Whatever it is, making an "appearance" can be critical. See Chang v. Berc, 64 P.3d 948, 951 (Haw. 2003) (although ordered to attend hearing on application for injunction against harassment, defendant did not; court found that she was in default and entered injunction; defense lawyer was there, ready to present evidence and move forward; court could not take defendant's default).

4. Suppose a defendant *has* appeared, as might happen if defendant files a motion, but that defendant has defaulted in some other way, as by failing to file an answer. In such cases, plaintiff must serve "written notice of the application [for a default judgment] at least 7 days before the hearing." If plaintiff fails to file the notice, would defendant be entitled to set aside the judgment? Compare Valley Heating & Cooling, Inc. v. Bernard/Pocasset Investment Group, L.L.C., 779 A.2d 647 (R.I. 2001) (default judgment entered without notice to defendant who had appeared is void, and should be set aside) with In re Genesys Data Technologies, Inc., 18 P.3d 895 (Haw. 2001) (failure to give notice does not make default judgment void; defense knew about hearing and could challenge amount there).

5. Under FRCP 60(b), a defendant may set aside a default judgment for "excusable neglect," as happened in *Weiss.* Consider these accounts of that concept:

(a) Misinformation from the Clerk's Office. In *Weiss,* the court clerk misinformed the defense on the question whether proof of service had been filed, supporting the finding of excusable neglect. See also Rappleyea v. Campbell, 884 P.2d 126 (Cal. 1994) (relieving defendants of default judgment for more than $200,000 where they were misled by clerk on amount of filing fee; clerk returned answer, which was refiled eight days late, after default).

(b) Mistakes by Insurance Carriers. This element appeared in *Weiss* too. See also Coslett v. Weddle Brothers Construction Co., 798 N.E.2d 859 (Ind. 2003) (in suit against contractor for negligent delay in constructing bridge, defendant forwarded complaint to its carrier, which returned it with

notification that the policy didn't cover this claim; meanwhile, court had entered judgment by default; trial court properly granted relief from the judgment for excusable neglect).

(c) *Unfamiliarity with Legal System.* Sometimes, defendants unfamiliar with the system try in some convincing way to respond, but fall short on a misunderstanding. See Sun Mountain Sports, Inc. v. Gore, 85 P.3d 1286 (Mont. 2004) (pro se defendant, sued in Montana and served in Texas on March 22, was entitled to relief from default judgment for excusable neglect; she filed answer on April 8, but it was returned for failure to pay filing fees; without notice, plaintiff entered defendant's default on April 16, and obtained judgment the next day; defendant acted promptly to hire counsel in Montana, who moved to set aside the judgment and dismiss for lack of jurisdiction on June 13; default was not willful, and reflected excusable neglect). Compare R.C. Associates v. Centex General Contractors, 810 A.2d 242, 244 (R.I. 2002) (refusing to lift default judgment where defendant corporation delayed more than five months in hiring local counsel).

(d) *Personal Emergencies.* See Colton Lumber Co. v. Siemonsma, 561 N.W.2d 871, 874 (S.D. 2002) (court erred in refusing to extend time to answer; defendant was changing residence at time of service, and selling home; he spent much of the 30 days out of state on business, and promptly met attorney on return, moving for extension of time three days after answer was due; court should have granted extension of time); Cook v. Rowland, 49 P.3d 262, 264 (Alaska 2002) (finding good cause to set aside default judgment where defendant had been served "within two weeks of suffering multiple serious gunshot wounds," leading to "extensive medical treatment," heavy medication, and confinement allowing "minimal contact with the outside world") (and prospect of "serious criminal charges"!).

(e) *Mistakes on Time Allowed for Response.* This excuse is often advanced, but it seldom succeeds. See, e.g., Multiple Resort Ownership Plan, Inc. v. Design-Build-Manage, Inc., 45 P.3d 647, 651 (Wyo. 2002) (refusing to set aside default judgment where defendant believed, on basis of conversation with plaintiff's lawyer, that he had indefinite extension of time to answer; local rule requires court's permission for extensions); Tschida v. Rowe, 74 P.3d 1043, 1045 (Mont. 2003) ("mistake" does *not* include failure of plaintiff's lawyer to answer defendant's counterclaim within ten days as required by rules; default judgment for defendant on counterclaim stands).

(f) *Confusion Introduced by Presence of Multiple Parties.* See Upper Plains Contracting Inc. v. Pepsi Americas, 656 N.W.2d 323, 327 (S.D. 2003) (soft drink company, sued by contractor for driving on fresh-poured concrete roadway, relieved from default for failure to answer, where "mistake" was excusable because company believed it need not answer until driver was served as codefendant).

6. In default cases (although not in others), FRCP 54(c) says recovery "must not differ in kind from, or exceed in amount" what plaintiff seeks in the prayer. What is the idea here? Should this limit apply when defendants have a chance to appear in a hearing? See In re Genesys Data Technologies, supra, 18 P.3d at 895 (awarding more than amount in prayer does not make judgment void; defense had notice and could challenge amount in hearing).

(a) Where a hearing is required before judgment by default may be entered, is there anything to be "tried" or "determined?" See Webster v. Perrotta, 774 A.2d 68 (R.I. 2001) (default does not concede amount or measure of damages alleged, and does not give plaintiff "carte blanche to recover for every harm ever sustained"); KPS Associates, Inc. v. Designs by FMC, Inc., 318 F.3d 1, 18 (1st Cir. 2003) (court erred in refusing to inquire into damages after entering default for failing to appear; citing discrepancies between body of complaint and amount in *ad damnum* clause, and arithmetic errors in plaintiff's affidavit, reviewing court remands for hearing on damages; court can enter judgment without requiring proof of damages only in "limited situations," where there can be no reasonable dispute as to amount).

(b) What does the hearing look like? Can the defendant call witnesses and present evidence? If so, what's the difference between a hearing on a default judgment and a trial on the merits? See Digital Broadcast Corp. v. Rosenman & Colin, LLP, 847 A.2d 384, 386 n.4 (D.C. Ct. App. 2004) (in hearing to determine damages, defense is entitled to present evidence in mitigation of damages and cross-examine plaintiff's witnesses); Allstate Ins. Co. v. Green, 794 So. 2d 170, 176 (Miss. 2001) (hearing to determine damages after default is "subject to all the normal rules of evidence and proof"). Is it possible for a plaintiff to emerge empty-handed from such a hearing? See Anheuser-Busch, Inc. v. Philpot, 317 F.3d 1264 (11th Cir. 2003) (in defamation case, court entered defendant's default but then correctly entered judgment against plaintiff, after hearing where plaintiff's expert testified but failed to show that plaintiff was damaged by defendant's conduct).

7. Unless defendant has completely given up, a default judgment favoring plaintiff is likely to be met by a defense motion to set the judgment aside. If defendant succeeds, *generally* the case goes forward and plaintiff cannot take an appeal because lifting the default judgment is not a final order. See 28 USC §1291 (authorizing appeals only from "final decisions"). See also Epting v. Precision Paint & Glass, 110 S.W.3d 747, 749 (Ark. 2003) (order setting aside default judgment and paving way for trial is not final and cannot be appealed). In *Weiss*, plaintiff took an appeal *not* from the order lifting the default judgment, but from a decision awarding summary judgment for defendant, which *is* a final order. Sometimes, defendants decide it is useless to seek relief from the trial court. Since a default judgment is final, they may choose to appeal directly rather than seeking relief by motion. See Pecarsky v. Galaxiworld.com Ltd., 249 F.3d 167 (2d Cir. 2001) (instead of making motion in trial court under FRCP 60(b), defense may appeal default judgment; appellate court considers same factors that trial judge would consider; judgment set aside here, as defendant in complicated securities fraud case was faced with need to find new counsel and trial court gave defendant less than a week to do so).

D PLAINTIFF'S RESPONSE TO THE DEFENDANT

In many if not most cases, a complaint and an answer are the beginning and end of the pleadings. Rule 7 authorizes courts to require plaintiff to reply to answers, but courts seldom do so. (Recall from the Notes on Stating Claims in Section B, supra, that courts sometimes order plaintiffs to reply to answers raising defense of qualified governmental immunity.) Ordinarily, however, plaintiffs do not respond to denials and averments in an answer, nor to affirmative defenses.

Putting aside cases where plaintiffs amend complaints, and cases where defendants bring in additional parties, against whom plaintiffs now file additional claims, there are a handful of common situations where plaintiffs *do* file pleadings that respond to the defendant.

First, in the federal system and many states, plaintiff must file "an answer to a counterclaim designated as a counterclaim." See FRCP 7(a). A moment's reflection will probably lead you to understand the reasons for phrasing the Rule this way: Affirmative defenses and counterclaims can look very much alike. Both introduce new matter, and involve affirmative allegations rather than denials. If plaintiffs had to respond to every "counterclaim" (rather than every counterclaim "designated" as such), they would err on the side of filing replies to anything that a court might later construe as a counterclaim, in fear that not responding would constitute an admission. See FRCP 8(b)(6) ("if a responsive pleading is required" and an allegation is not denied, then it is "admitted").

Second, under FRCP 12(f) the plaintiff may make a motion to strike to dispose of any "insufficient defense" or any "redundant, immaterial, impertinent, or scandalous matter." While the plaintiff does not have to make such motions, and can leave such matters to be resolved at trial, a successful motion to strike can clear up uncertainty and enhance plaintiff's bargaining position. See, e.g., Faulconer v. Wysong and Miles Co., 574 S.E.2d 688, 691 (N.C. 2002) (in employee's breach of contract suit for retirement benefits, striking "commercial impossibility" defense because it could not apply); Roberts v. Consolidation Coal Co., 539 N.E.2d 478, 495 (W. Va. 2000) (in workers' compensation proceedings, striking "contributory negligence/deliberate intention defense" because it "has no basis in the controlling statutes"); Mayes v. Paxton, 437 S.E.2d 66, 69 (S.C. 1993) (in motorcyclist's suit against driver of car, striking defense allegations that cyclist was not wearing a helmet, which did not constitute contributory negligence).

E ┃ THE OBLIGATION TO BE TRUTHFUL: SANCTIONS UNDER FRCP 11

Modern decisions like *Swierkiewicz* stress the tradition that pleadings are less important than they once were, and that the system strives to get to the merits. On the other hand, decisions like *Twombly* and *Tellabs* once again place greater demands on lawyers in preparing the complaint that initiates a lawsuit.

Beginning in the 1980s, another countermovement began, in the belief that bringing a lawsuit had gotten too easy, and that lax pleading standards were helping frivolous suits survive long enough to generate unwarranted expense to the system and to other litigants and lawyers. The result was a series of amendments adding teeth to FRCP 11. That provision had long said that the signature of a lawyer certified that he had read the pleading, that "to the best of [the lawyer's] knowledge, information, and belief" there was good ground for it and it was not being used for delay, but the obligation to be truthful was seldom enforced.

Amended in 1983 and then again 1987 and 1993, FRCP 11 became more elaborate, seeking actually to discourage careless pleading and groundless claims. Under FRCP 11(a) as we have it today, signing a complaint certifies, *inter alia*, that the lawyer believes, "after an inquiry reasonable under the circumstances," that claims and defenses "and other legal contentions" are "warranted by existing law or by a nonfrivolous argument" for a change in the law, *and* that the allegations and contentions have "evidentiary support" or "are likely" to have such support after investigation or discovery. Violating the Rule can lead to sanctions in the form of "reasonable attorney's fees" and other expenses, which courts can impose on parties or lawyers, including law firms that are responsible for work done by a "partner, associate, or employee." It is sometimes said that old Rule 11 required only a "pure heart," but under new Rule 11 a "pure heart" does not excuse an "empty head."

Read FRCP 11 all the way through. Notice these points: Sanctions can be sought by motion or on the court's initiative, but there are differences. Especially important is the "safe harbor" concept, under which a party seeking sanctions must *serve* a motion 21 days before *filing* it, during which time the other side may withdraw or correct a claim or position already taken, thus avoid sanctions. Notice too that *court*-initiated sanctions must proceed through a "show cause" hearing in which the party may try to justify her behavior, but there is *no* safe harbor. Sanctions may include "nonmonetary" measures, as well as a fine, penalty or costs, attorneys' fees, and other expenses.

FRCP 11(a) is specific in describing the obligation of lawyers. Under the prevailing view, this obligation is sometimes summed up by saying that lawyers are expected to be "objectively reasonable" in the claims and positions they advance. This standard clearly applies in connection with *party*-initiated sanctions under FRCP 11(c)(2), but it is possible that *court*-initiated sanctions under FRCP 11(c)(3) require misconduct that is more serious. Both avenues lead to sanctions for behavior described in FRCP 11(a), and nothing suggests more than one standard, but the ACN says that court-initiated sanctions are available for misconduct that is "akin to contempt of court," and this language is sometimes taken as an indication that the behavior must be more serious. See Kaplan v. DaimlerChrysler, A.G., 331 F.3d 1251, 1255 (11th Cir. 2003) (court-initiated sanctions under FRCP 11 require "a higher standard"); In re Pennie & Edmonds, 323 F.3d 86, 89 (2d Cir. 2003) (court-initiated sanctions under FRCP 11 are available only in "more egregious circumstances"). As you are about to discover, courts can *also* act on the basis of "inherent authority," applying a "bad faith" standard that clearly *does* require more serious misconduct than the "objectively unreasonable" standard would require.

Lawyers and judges recognize that FRCP 11 is in tension with our faith in justice produced by advocacy. In one opinion, Judge Berzon put it this way:

> The application of Rule 11 is a task that requires sensitivity to two competing considerations. On the one hand, the perception underlying the Rule is that on occasion attorneys engage in litigation tactics so vexatious as to be unjustifiable even within the broad bounds of our adversarial system, and that neither the other parties nor the courts should have to abide such behavior or waste time and money coping with it. On the other hand, both the Rule itself and our application of the Rule recognize that our system of litigation is an adversary one, and that presenting the facts and law as favorably as fairly possible in favor of one's client is the nub of the lawyer's task. Judges therefore should impose sanctions on lawyers for their mode of advocacy only in the most egregious situations, lest lawyers be deterred from vigorous representation of their clients.

United National Ins. Co. v. R&D Latex Corp., 242 F.3d 1102, 1115 (9th Cir. 2001).

FRCP 11 is not the only provision authorizing sanctions for abuse of the litigation process. At least three other sanction regimes are available, and still other provisions allow sanctions in certain cases. Thus there are sanction provisions in FRCP 16 (pretrial process) and FRCP 37 (discovery). Here are the three major sanction regimes for abuse of the litigation process in federal courts:

(1) *Attorney Sanction Statute.* Under 28 USC §1927, courts can penalize an attorney who "multiplies the proceedings . . . unreasonably and vexatiously" by requiring the attorney "to satisfy personally the excess costs, expenses, and attorneys' fees reasonably incurred because of such conduct."

(2) *PSLRA.* Congress added sanction provisions in the Private Securities Litigation Reform Act in the 1980s. Where it applies (suits under federal securities law asserting fraud and related violations), the PSLRA requires courts to make findings on compliance with FRCP 11. It also provides that sanctions under FRCP 11(b) are mandatory rather than discretionary, and creates a

presumption favoring award of the full amount of attorneys' fees for violations. See 15 USC §78u-4(c).

(3) *Inherent Authority.* Courts have what is called "inherent authority" to deal with abuses of the litigation process. You might think that with so many Rules and statutes, there is no room for broader powers. In 1991, however, the Supreme Court decided that federal courts retain inherent power to sanction parties and lawyers for misconduct. See Chambers v. NASCO, 501 U.S. 32, 49 (1991) (approving sanctions for taking frivolous appeal from judgment awarding specific performance; "nothing in the other sanctioning mechanisms" warrants conclusion that federal court cannot resort to "inherent power" to award attorneys' fees for misconduct; a court is not "forbidden" to resort to its inherent power simply because the conduct "could also be sanctioned" under Rule or statute). In *Chambers,* the Court contemplated sanctions for "bad faith" misconduct, a standard that envisions a greater culpability than the "objective misconduct" standard that courts apply under FRCP 11: To merit sanctions under the court's "inherent" power, a lawyer must know or be chargeable with knowledge that he's doing something wrong.

Consider the account by Judge Newman of the Second Circuit, describing the problems raised by sanctions, and adjustments that may be necessary:

> Any regime of sanctions for a lawyer's role in the course of representing a client inevitably has implications for the functioning of the adversary process. If the sanction regime is too severe, lawyers will sometimes be deterred from making legitimate submissions on behalf of clients out of apprehension that their conduct will erroneously be deemed improper. On the other hand, if the sanction regime is too lenient, lawyers will sometimes be emboldened to make improper submissions on behalf of clients, confident that their misconduct will either be undetected or dealt with too leniently to matter. The 1993 amendments to Rule 11 strike a sensible balance between these extremes by making a lawyer sanctionable for an objectively unreasonable submission and at the same time affording the lawyer a "safe harbor" opportunity to reconsider and withdraw a submission challenged by an adversary.
>
> However, when a lawyer's submission, unchallenged by an adversary, is subject to sanction by a court, the absence of a "safe harbor" opportunity to reconsider risks shifting the balance to the detriment of the adversary process. The risk is that lawyers will sometimes withhold submissions that they honestly believe have plausible evidentiary support for fear that a trial judge, perhaps at the conclusion of a contentious trial, will erroneously consider their claimed belief to be objectively unreasonable. This risk is appropriately minimized, as the Advisory Committee contemplated, by applying a "bad faith" standard to submissions sanctioned without a "safe harbor" opportunity to reconsider. A vigorous adversary process is better served by avoiding the inhibiting effect of an "objectively unreasonable" standard applied to unchallenged submissions, and letting questionable evidence be tested with cross-examination and opposing evidence than by encouraging lawyers to withhold such evidence. It is better to apply a heightened mens rea standard to unchallenged submissions and take the slight risk with respect to such submissions that, on occasion, a jury

will give unwarranted weight to a few submissions that a judge would consider objectively unreasonable than to withhold from the jury many submissions that are objectively reasonable but that cautious lawyers dare not present.

In re Pennie & Edmonds, 323 F.3d 86, 91 (2d Cir. 2003) (reversing sanctions awarded by trial judge against defense lawyers *sua sponte* after plaintiff prevailed in summary judgment, for letting defendant submit false affidavit in opposition, where judge agreed that defense lawyers acted in "subjective good faith").

METHODE ELECTRONICS, INC. v. ADAM TECHNOLOGIES, INC.

United States Court of Appeals for the Seventh Circuit
371 F.3d 923 (2004)

KANNE, EVANS, and WILLIAMS, Circuit Judges.

TERENCE T. EVANS, Circuit Judge.

The parties before us, who are in the electronic connector business, have been involved in a number of disputes in Delaware state courts and one in the United States District Court for the District of New Jersey. The latter resulted in a settlement and an exclusive licensing agreement. When Methode Electronics, Incorporated sought a finding that the licensing agreement was breached, it chose not to return to court in New Jersey, but rather it came to the Northern District of Illinois seeking a temporary restraining order. In its verified complaint, signed by attorney Terrence P. Canade and verified by James F. McQuillen, executive vice-president of Methode, Methode alleged that venue was proper in the Northern District of Illinois. In the eyes of the district judge, the Honorable John F. Grady, that turned out not to be true. Sanctions were imposed against both attorney Canade and Methode. Methode appeals, contending that the sanctions were improperly imposed.

As to the underlying lawsuit, it is enough to say that from 1987 to 1993 Methode owned all the stock of Adam Technologies, Inc. (Adam Tech), a New Jersey corporation with its principal place of business in New Jersey. Under the settlement in the federal district court in New Jersey, Methode was to sell to Vincent DeVito all of its shares in Adam Tech as well as the Adam Tech trade name and trademarks and a large amount of inventory. Under a separate license agreement, Methode obtained an exclusive right to market the remaining Adam Tech products it had on hand; in addition, Adam Tech and DeVito would do nothing to interfere with Methode's exclusive license. The claim in the present lawsuit is that less than a day after the licensing agreement was signed, Adam Tech and DeVito began to undermine Methode's rights by issuing a press release to Methode's customers which announced that "Adam Tech will be accepting orders and opportunities for more than 5,000,000 connectors stocked at its Union, NJ facility." It was in response to this press release that Methode filed the present case. However, as Adam Tech and DeVito point out, the settlement agreement also expressly provided that "nothing shall prevent Mr. DeVito or his designee, during the period of the License Agreement, from selling inventory that Methode delivers pursuant to this Settlement Agreement."

The allegation in the verified complaint which gives rise to the order for sanctions is found in paragraph 19, which states:

> Adam Tech and/or Mr. DeVito issued the Press Release to Methode distributors and customers throughout North America, including distributors and customers in this District.

The verified complaint was filed on May 2, 2003, and 3 days later, on the 5th, Harold Hoffman, the attorney for Adam Tech and DeVito, sent Canade a letter pursuant to Rule 11 advising him that Illinois was not an appropriate forum for the action and that Adam Tech's conduct as alleged in the complaint was permissible under the settlement agreement. Hoffman stated that if Methode proceeded with this case in Illinois, he would seek sanctions under FRCP 11. Despite the letter, McQuillen advised Canade to proceed with Methode's motion for a temporary restraining order. Canade filed the motion and set it for hearing on May 7. Adam Tech and DeVito challenged the allegation that venue was proper in the Northern District of Illinois and disclosed the portion of the settlement agreement that authorized DeVito to sell inventory delivered by Methode during the exclusivity period of the license agreement.

Discussing the latter fact during the hearing, Judge Grady said that Methode had omitted "relevant information that the court should have been given." The judge was, however, more interested in, and annoyed by, the venue allegations. He was concerned with the venue allegations because "if [the court] lacked venue, [it] would in no event grant a temporary restraining order. It would instead ... grant defendants' request that the case be transferred to the District of New Jersey, where venue was clearly proper and where the court was already familiar with the parties and the background of their disputes."

On behalf of Adam Tech and DeVito, attorney Hoffman orally moved for sanctions, requesting that they be awarded costs incurred as a result of being improperly haled into court in Illinois. A briefing schedule was set on the motion.

The next day, the judge entered an order stating that he would delay transferring the case to New Jersey until he had ruled on the motion for sanctions. He then issued a rule "to show cause why [Canade and Methode] should not be held to have violated Rule 11(b)(3) in regard to paragraph 19" of the complaint. A briefing schedule was set on the rule. On May 9, Methode filed a notice of voluntary dismissal of the case without prejudice pursuant to FRCP 41(a).

The rule to show cause remained pending. Discovery confirmed that the venue allegation lacked an evidentiary basis. The press release was not sent directly to entities in the Northern District of Illinois. It only reached Illinois indirectly. Two of Methode's customers, each of which maintain branches in the Northern District, received copies of the press release outside of Illinois, and they were the ones who forwarded copies to those branch offices in Illinois. After considerable examination of the issue, the judge issued an order saying that the venue allegation not only lacked evidentiary support but was intentionally false and that Methode's conduct in advancing it was "intentionally deceptive." He found that neither Adam Tech nor DeVito sent the press release into the district. The order further stated that "this was not a question of mere negligence," but rather an effort to deceive the court. Pursuant to Rule 11(c)(2), the judge imposed sanctions against Methode: a fine of $10,000 payable to the court and half the defendants' attorney fees and expenses, which would be determined later. The same sanction was assessed against attorney Canade. The attorney fees were later stipulated to be $45,000.

In its appeal, Methode contends that Judge Grady erred in awarding attorney fees, costs, and a fine as a sanction because Adam Tech and DeVito did not comply with Rule 11's safe-harbor provisions. Methode also contends that it was error to award sanctions because there is no evidence in the record to support the holding.

We review the grant of sanctions with deference because of the familiarity of the trial court with the relevant proceedings. The imposition of sanctions, under either Rule 11 or the court's inherent power, is reviewed for an abuse of discretion. *Jimenez v. Madison Area Tech. Coll.*, 321 F.3d 652 (7th Cir. 2003).

We reject the claim that there was no evidence in the record to support the holding that Paragraph 19 was false. The record is clear that almost as the verified complaint was being filed, McQuillen told Canade that he did not know whether the press release had been sent to Illinois. Less than 90 minutes before the complaint was filed, Canade sent an e-mail to McQuillen, attaching a draft of the complaint and requesting that McQuillen provide anecdotes to support the allegations in paragraph 19. No anecdotes were provided, supporting an inference that none were available. At his deposition, McQuillen testified that when he signed the verified complaint he did not know whether anyone in the Northern District of Illinois had been sent a copy of the press release:

> Q. Now, sir, on May 2nd before you signed the Verified Complaint at around 3:00 P.M., or somewhere between 3:00 and 4:00 P.M., did you know if the press release had been sent to branch offices in Illinois?
> A. No.

Methode's other claim is that the district court did not have authority to award attorney fees and expenses on a rule to show cause under Rule 11.

Related is the claim that Adam Tech and DeVito did not file a motion as Rule 11 requires, nor did they comply with Rule 11(c)(1)(A)—that is, provide a 21-day "safe harbor." Methode is partly right.

Rule 11 requires that a motion "shall be made separately from other motions or requests and shall describe the specific conduct alleged to violate" the rule. The motion must be served on the opposing party but "shall not be filed with or presented to the court unless within 21 days after service of the motion (or such other period as the court may prescribe), the challenged paper, claim, defense, contention, allegation, or denial is not withdrawn or appropriately corrected." Alternatively, the court may, on its own initiative, "enter an order describing the specific conduct" that appears to violate the rule and "directing an attorney, law firm, or party to show cause" why it has not violated the rule.

It can be argued that Adam Tech and DeVito did not file a separate motion, although their attorney moved for sanctions at the close of the hearing on the request for a temporary restraining order. Methode emphasizes that, in any case, Adam Tech and DeVito did not comply with the safe-harbor provisions of Rule 11. Therefore, the argument goes, the only basis for the award of sanctions is a rule to show cause on the court's own initiative. Methode points out that the problem with the order is that Rule 11 does not authorize the award of attorney fees when the court is acting on its own motion. The rule provides that the sanction may consist of directives of a nonmonetary nature, an order to pay a penalty into court, or, if imposed on motion and warranted for effective deterrence, an order directing payment to the movant of some or all of the reasonable attorneys' fees and other expenses incurred as a direct result of the violation.

We agree with Methode that, if the sanction is imposed on the court's own motion, attorney fees cannot be awarded. We have previously ruled that Rule 11(c)(2) "allows the imposition of attorneys' fees against a party only if the sanctions were initiated by motion" and that it would be an abuse of discretion for a judge to impose sanctions *sua sponte,* pursuant to Rule 11(c)(1)(B). Divane v. Krull Elec. Co., 200 F.3d 1020, 1030 (7th Cir. 1999).

But the record in this case is open to interpretation. We could conclude that Adam Tech and DeVito were in substantial compliance with Rule 11; or we could find that it was impossible for them to comply with Rule 11; or we could determine that Methode waived its right to a 21-day safe harbor.

For example, it is relatively clear that Adam Tech and DeVito did what they could to comply with Rule 11. They sent a "heads-up" letter to Methode. This is exactly what the commentary to the rule suggests a party should do: "In most cases, however, counsel should be expected to give informal notice to the other party, whether in person or by a telephone call or letter, of a potential violation before proceeding to prepare and serve a Rule 11 motion." When Methode proceeded with the hearing, it, in effect, rejected the warning.

And at that point, Adam Tech and DeVito had no opportunity to file their motion and were prevented by the speed of events from granting a 21-day period to withdraw the allegation. They argue, with some basis, that what Methode did when it proceeded with the hearing was to waive the right to the 21-day period.

Then, when the judge chose to proceed on a rule to show cause, the case proceeded on that basis. Under Rule 11 there is no problem with proceeding on the judge's own initiative by a rule to show cause. As we said, the problem is that, under the rule, if he proceeds without a motion from the parties, a judge is without authority to award attorney fees. Even though there may be a basis in this case for finding substantial compliance with the rule, or that Methode waived its rights to the 21-day safe-harbor provision, we will not decide those issues. Rather, we are convinced that this was a proper case for the exercise of the court's inherent power to control the proceedings before it. And, of course, we can affirm "a grant of sanctions on any basis supported by the record and the law." *Divane,* 200 F.3d at 1026.

Rule 11 has not robbed the district courts of their inherent power to impose sanctions for abuse of the judicial system. In Chambers v. NASCO, Inc., 501 U.S. 32, 49 (1991), the Court was quite clear that "the inherent power of a court can be invoked even if procedural rules exist which sanction the same conduct." The Court stated that there was "no basis for holding that the sanctioning scheme of the statute and the rules displaces the inherent power to impose sanction for . . . bad-faith conduct. . . ." Even before *Chambers* we recognized the inherent power of the district courts. *See* G. Heileman Brewing Co. v. Joseph Oat Corp., 871 F.2d 648 (7th Cir. 1989) (en banc). We have, however, continued to make clear that there is a "need to be cautious when resorting to inherent powers to justify an action, particularly when the matter is governed by other procedural rules. . . ." Kovilic Constr. Co. v. Missbrenner, 106 F.3d 768, 772-73 (7th Cir. 1997).

The case before us today illustrates the wisdom of retaining the inherent power of the courts. As in many cases involving a request for preliminary relief, blind adherence to the procedures in Rule 11 is not possible. Events often move too fast to allow strict compliance with the rule. To repeat, Adam Tech and DeVito had sent a letter warning of their intention to move for sanctions if the case remained in Illinois. Methode decided to proceed with its motion for a temporary restraining order by scheduling a hearing 2 days after the letter was sent. The case was filed and voluntarily dismissed, all within 7 days. Short as it was, that time period was long enough for Adam Tech and DeVito to have to appear at a hearing in Illinois, thus incurring the attorney fees and costs at issue here. The judge certainly acted wisely in trying to sort out what was going on.

In order to sanction a party under its inherent power, a court must provide notice of its intention to impose sanctions and give the party an opportunity to respond. Sanctions can then be imposed if the court finds that the party "acted in bad faith, vexatiously, wantonly, or for oppressive reasons...." *Chambers,* 501 U.S. at 33. Judge Grady provided notice and gave Methode an opportunity to respond. He also carefully considered the conduct, examining affidavits, briefs, and McQuillen's deposition testimony. He then found that when McQuillen signed the complaint, he did not know whether any copies of the press release had been sent into the Northern District. He found not only that Methode's venue allegations were false, but that Methode's conduct in advancing them was intentionally deceptive. He recognized that Methode had filed a verified complaint with the explicit allegation that venue was proper in Illinois because a less definite allegation (acknowledging that while it did not have evidentiary support for an allegation that venue was proper in Illinois but that it hoped to develop evidence regarding venue during discovery) would have meant that the temporary restraining order would not have been issued. He said, "[T]his was not a question of mere negligence. It was an effort to deceive the court as to the existence of venue, so that Methode could litigate the case in a forum that was convenient to it, however inconvenient to defendants, and possibly even obtain preliminary injunctive relief." Judge Grady acted well within his authority in ordering a sanction of attorney fees and costs, as well as the fine payable to the court. The order imposing sanctions is AFFIRMED.

■ NOTES ON SANCTIONING LAWYERS AND CLIENTS FOR MISCONDUCT DURING LITIGATION

1. Note that *Methode* unblinkingly awards sanctions for taking a position that is not connected to the merits. The question is whether there is a basis to lay venue in Illinois, and the court thinks plaintiff's lawyer Terrence Canade did something wrong. FRCP 11 is broad enough to apply, and *Methode* recognizes that courts also have inherent power. See also Retail Flooring Dealers of America, Inc. v. Beaulieu of America, LLC, 339 F.3d 1146, 1150 (9th Cir. 2003) (defense sought sanctions for suing in federal court when there was no basis for subject matter jurisdiction) (denied only because motion was filed too late). Federal courts can impose sanctions even if they lack subject matter jurisdiction to entertain the suit itself. See Willy v. Coastal Corp., 503 U.S. 131, 136 (1992) (in case removed from state to federal court, lack of subject matter jurisdiction precludes further litigation, but "does not automatically wipe out all proceedings") (sanction sustained); Perpetual Securities, Inc. v. Tang, 290 F.3d 132, 139 (2d Cir. 2002) (although lacking subject matter jurisdiction, court could award sanctions under FRCP 11).

2. In some respects, *Methode Electronics* is too facile. The opinion reaches wide-ranging and provocative conclusions with little explanation. Is the problem that the case is just too easy? It looks as though Terrence Canade, acting on behalf of James F. McQuillen as vice president of Methode, laid venue in Illinois on the basis of misinformation because Adam Technologies did *not* distribute the press release in Illinois. It "only reached Illinois indirectly" when customers of Methode's forwarded copies to Illinois offices. Before filing, Canade asked McQuillen for "anecdotes to support the allegations" that the release was sent to Illinois, but none were forthcoming. Within days after filing, defendants wrote Canade that he had made a mistake and venue could not be laid in Illinois, but five days later Canade went forward with a hearing on a TRO. To add insult to injury, it is at least arguable that defendant was within its rights in sending out the press release, since defendant retained the right to sell "inventory that Methode delivers." Arguably, both Canade and Methode (lawyer and client) were unreasonable to file in Illinois, and perhaps there was no valid claim at all.

3. But wait a minute. Consider some of the holes in this opinion:

(a) FRCP 11 says a "motion" for sanctions must be "made separately" from other motions. "Motion" contemplates a written document, with a title and caption and identifying information that is to be served "at least 14 days before" a hearing, see FRCP 6(c). Defendant sent a letter to Canade (not a motion), saying that defendant "would seek sanctions." The letter did not purport to provide notice of a hearing. *Methode* brushes this point aside (it can be "argued" that defendants "did not file a separate motion"). Why does FRCP 11 require sanction motions to be made "separately"?

(b) Under FRCP 11(c)(2), wasn't Methode entitled to a 21-day safe harbor? The court says it "could determine" that Methode "waived its right" to a safe harbor. How? By going forward on the application for a TRO? Where does it say that one loses the right to the safe harbor by continuing with the case for several days? The court says the defense was "prevented by the speed of events from granting a 21-day [safe harbor] period." Is this fact an excuse for denying a safe harbor? Compare Retail Flooring Dealers of America, Inc., supra, 339 F.3d at 1146, 1150 (defense sought sanctions for suing in federal court that lacked subject matter jurisdiction; motion was served after case was dismissed; plaintiff had no opportunity to withdraw, so motion violated safe harbor provision and sanctions could not be imposed).

(c) The trial court "chose to proceed on a rule to show cause," which apparently means that defendant's motion doesn't count, and we have a court-initiated sanction. But the sanction is attorneys' fees, and FRCP 11(c) says fees can only be awarded "if imposed on motion and warranted for effective deterrence." See Norsyn v. Desai, 351 F.3d 825, 831 (8th Cir. 2003) (FRCP 11 lets court award costs and attorneys' fees, but "that sword may only be wielded upon the request of the opposing party"). Wait a minute. Apparently, that doesn't matter because we aren't even in Rule 11 anymore.

According to the reviewing court, this case morphed into an inherent power case, so the court doesn't need a rule or statute.

(d) Was there "bad faith"? If a court proceeds on the basis of inherent power, it must find bad faith. Reading between the lines, McQuillen must have told Canade that the press release appeared in Illinois, so Canade thought he could sue in Illinois. See 28 USC §1392(b) (in diversity case, venue may be laid in a district where "a substantial part of the events . . . giving rise to the claim occurred"). Maybe defendants did not send the release to Illinois, but it got there. Even if McQuillen was in "bad faith" if he learned the truth before the complaint was filed, was Canade in bad faith when McQuillen didn't answer his query?

(e) Is it so clear that McQuillen and Canade did anything wrong in filing in Illinois? Does it really *matter* whether defendant sent the release to Illinois or someone else brought it? See, e.g., Bates v. C&S Adjusters, Inc., 980 F.2d 865 (2d Cir. 1992) (in debtor's suit alleging violation of Debt Collection Practices Act, venue could be laid in New York where dunning letter was delivered, even though defendant mailed it to plaintiff's Pennsylvania address and did not know plaintiff had moved or that letter would be forwarded) (applying language for federal question cases using same wording as provision for diversity cases).

4. What do you think of a system that combines elaborate provisions on sanctions with "inherent" powers to do the same thing? Consider these points:

(a) On the one hand, it seems sensible to recognize that FRCP 11 does not cover the ballpark of misconduct in litigation. It covers representations to the court ("signing, filing, submitting, or later advocating"), which is broad. But it is easy to think of misconduct that this language does not reach. See, e.g., First Bank of Marietta v. Hartford Underwriters Ins. Co., 307 F.3d 501, 516 (6th Cir. 2002) (sanctions under FRCP 11 apply to "pleadings and papers," require "objectively unreasonable conduct," and can address only expenses "directly caused"; sanctions imposed under inherent powers can address such matters as withholding evidence, consequences thereof, violating discovery orders, and extending proceedings).

(b) On the other hand, does it make sense to use the concept of "inherent power" to get around restrictions and requirements in FRCP 11? See Perpetual Securities, Inc. v. Tang, 290 F.3d 132, 141 (2d Cir. 2002) (where motion was not properly made, court could award sanctions on its own, but not monetary sanctions like attorneys' fees or costs); Radcliffe v. Rainbow Construction Co., 254 F.3d 772, 789 (9th Cir. 2001) (motion seeking attorneys' fees did not comply with safe harbor requirement; court could not treat it as court-initiated; safe harbor would be "meaningless" if noncompliant motion could be "converted automatically into a court-initiated motion"). But see First Bank of Marietta v. Hartford Underwriters Ins. Co., 307 F.3d 501, 519 (6th Cir. 2002) (invoking inherent power in sustaining award of attorneys' fees against bank suing insurance carrier for losses resulting from bank employee's acts in increasing line of credit beyond borrower's capacity to repay; bank

failed to satisfy condition precedent by filing proof of loss; sanctions against bank were appropriate despite failure to provide safe harbor).

(c) Does a court considering sanctions have to look first to FRCP 11 and the various statutes, or can it simply invoke its inherent authority even if the matter is covered by one of these provisions? In its landmark decision on inherent authority, the Court seemed to blow both hot and cold. See Chambers v. NASCO, 501 U.S. 32, 46 (1991) (court is not "forbidden" to utilize inherent power simply because conduct "could also be sanctioned under the statute or the Rules," but court "ordinarily should rely on the Rules rather than the inherent power" and use the latter if "neither the statute nor the Rules are up to the task"). Compare Montrose Medical Group Participating Savings Plan v. Bulger, 243 F.3d 773 (3d Cir. 2001) (before using inherent power, court should consider whether sanctions under rule or statute are "up to the task") with First Bank of Marietta v. Hartford Underwriters Ins. Co., 307 F.3d 501, 513-514 (6th Cir. 2002) (court may resort to inherent authority even if it has not considered whether conduct could be sanctioned under rules or statutes).

5. In *Methode,* Terrence Canade apparently took his client's word that the press release circulated in Illinois. Must a lawyer investigate what her client says? If the lawyer cannot find confirmation, does that mean she cannot move forward on her client's behalf? Not surprisingly, there are no hard and fast answers: One court commented that FRCP 11 requires the lawyer to conduct "reasonable inquiry" to uncover both "factual" and "legal" bases of a claim. Whether an inquiry is reasonable "may depend on factors such as whether counsel had to rely on a client for factual information, or whether the attorney depended on forwarding counsel or another member of the bar." See Coonts v. Potts, 316 F.3d 745, 753 (8th Cir. 2002) (plaintiff claimed "excessive force" in violation of Fourth Amendment, but claimant "kicked, hit, and attempted to bite" officers who were seizing property, and "destroyed the television by throwing an object through the screen"; inquiry leading to suit under §1983 was unreasonable). But another court concluded, in connection with a citizen's suit alleging that the Forest Service violated a statute in permitting expansion of ski area, that the attorney for the government could rely on "technical expertise" of the Service in arguing that building storage ponds was practically impossible. See Dubois v. United States Department of Agriculture, 270 F.3d 77, 82 (1st Cir. 2001) (reliance on client was reasonable even if mistaken).

6. Sanction awards can be *very* costly. See, e.g., Christian v. Mattel, Inc., 286 F.3d 1118, 1127 (9th Cir. 2002) (in suit against toy maker alleging that "Barbie Doll" designs infringed plaintiff's patent, sanctioning attorney for plaintiff in amount of $500,000 because claim was "legally and factually frivolous" inasmuch as Barbie Dolls were "a prior-created work" that "cannot infringe a later-created one"); Tropf v. Fidelity National Title Ins. Co., 289 F.3d 929, 940 (6th Cir. 2002) (approving sanctions against plaintiff in form of "costs and fees" of $14,000 and injunction against filing similar suits in federal court, in part because plaintiffs brought "at least five lawsuits related to the same transactions" and "repeatedly lost" and "unreasonably and vexatiously multiplied" proceedings by filing "countless motions" when under-lying action had no merit); Lee v. First Lenders Insurance Services, 236 F.3d 443 (8th Cir. 2001) (awarding sanctions of $15,000 under §1927 against law firm that filed class suit and pursued discovery for a year and a half, only to drop suit without explanation; rejecting claim that sanctions could only be awarded under FRCP 11 for frivolous complaint, reviewing court says discovery and motion practice forced defendants to incur additional costs, and this conduct could be sanctioned).

7. To be sure, reviewing courts sometimes reverse sanction awards as going too far. See, e.g., Kaplan v. DaimlerChrysler, A.G., 331 F.3d 1251, 1254 (11th Cir. 2003) (in suit against German automaker, disapproving court-initiated sanctions on defendant for filing motion in limine to exclude "derogatory statements" referring to "Nazis" and "concentration camps," and so forth; sanctions can only be imposed for conduct akin to contempt, and motion may have been "overkill" but was not akin to contempt; judge accepted late motions, and it was "not outlandish" to think that plaintiff's counsel "might subtly if not overtly prey on juror biases"); Hunter v. Earthgrains Company Bakery, 281 F.3d 144 (4th Cir. 2002) (reversing sanction suspending attorney from practice for stating frivolous claim; in light of mandatory arbitration clause in collective bargaining agreement, judge thought claim alleging fraud and discrimination could not be advanced in lawsuit; although counsel claimed that arbitration clause could only block right to sue if it specifically covered discrimination claims, and position had been rejected in earlier case from this Circuit, other Circuits had held that arbitration clause could not block members from suing; plaintiff's lawyer was entitled to try to persuade this court to "correct the error" as she perceived it, and if unsuccessful "she might then have sought relief in the Supreme Court on the basis of the circuit split").

8. As reflected in the remarks by Judges Berzon and Newman quoted before *Methode,* overuse of sanctions threatens the vitality of the adversary system. There is a risk that a prevailing party will try to make victory even sweeter by arguing that the loser not only had a bad case, but made claims or advanced positions that were absolutely groundless. And cases like *Kaplan* (note 7, supra) show that protective motions can *themselves* generate sanction motions—in other words, sanction motions are simply a tool in an arsenal that lawyers use to beat up their adversaries. Occasional opinions recognize that losing a case, even on an early motion challenging the complaint, does not mean the loser should pay, and sometimes even frivolous cases should not generate sanctions. See Tahfs v. Proctor, 316 F.3d 584, 595 (6th Cir. 2003) (dismissing complaint for failure to state claim for relief under §1983, but refusing sanctions and warning that if sanctions could be awarded in such cases, then "almost any complaint dismissed under Rule 12(b)(6)" leads to sanctions); Oxford Asset Management, Ltd. v. Jaharis, 297 F.3d 1182, 1195 (11th Cir. 2002) (claim with evidentiary support was not frivolous even though rejected because defendant was not subject to the alleged duty; sanctions are not appropriate). Judges who impose serious sanctions are expected to

conduct hearings that comport with due process, and not to rely on extra-record information or hearsay that party to be sanctioned cannot meet or rebut. See Vollmer v. Publishers Clearing House, 248 F.3d 698, 710 (7th Cir. 2001) (reversing award of $50,000 in attorneys' fees against counsel who sought to intervene in support of class members; court considered extra-record information provided by lawyers for plaintiff class, including newspaper article describing lawyers for intervenors as "professional objectors"; court could consider past conduct, but offending party must have "full and fair opportunity to respond"); Topalian v. Ehrman, 3 F.3d 931, 936-937 (5th Cir. 1993) (to justify award of $300,000 against lawyer, court must make findings describing conduct, expenses caused by violation, whether costs or expenses were reasonable and whether remedy is the "least severe sanction adequate to achieve the purpose" of FRCP 11).

9. Suppose you recognize that your client's claim may be barred by the statute of limitations. Under FRCP 8(e), this matter and other affirmative defenses must be raised by answer or they are waived. Is a lawyer acting in an "objectively reasonable" fashion if she files a complaint knowing that a defense based on the statute of limitations should prevail, if raised? See White v. General Motors Corp., 908 F.2d 675, 682 (10th Cir. 1990) (reasonable attorney's prefiling investigation includes "determining whether any obvious affirmative defenses bar the case," but attorney can file "if she has a colorable argument as to why an otherwise applicable affirmative defense is inapplicable," as may happen if "the limitation was tolled for part of the period," but argument "must be nonfrivolous" and she runs risk of sanctions if her response to an affirmative defense is unreasonable).

10. Suppose defendant files a motion to dismiss, and serves (but does not file) a motion for sanctions for advancing a groundless claim. Suppose the motion to dismiss is heard 20 days later and the court grants it. Suppose that a week later (27 days after serving the motion for sanctions) defendant *files* the motion for sanctions. Can the court grant sanctions, or does the dismissal "cut short" the 21-day safe harbor provided by FRCP 11, so sanctions cannot be given? Does it matter whether the court allows leave to amend when it grants the motion to dismiss? See Truesdell v. Southern California Permanente Medical Group, 293 F.3d 1146 (9th Cir. 2002) (plaintiff "had the full 21-day period" inasmuch as movant waited 27 days before filing motion for sanctions, and as a practical matter plaintiff "had the full safe-harbor period" because court "dismissed the complaint *with leave to amend*").

F **DISMISSALS OF LAWSUITS**

Once suit is filed, a plaintiff may have second thoughts. If things go badly at the outset, she may conclude that abandoning the venture would be wiser than pursuing it. Then the question arises whether she can walk away but retain the option of pursuing the remedy again at a later time, in the same court or another.

Notice that FRCP 41(a)(1) lets a plaintiff dismiss a suit before defendant serves an answer or motion for summary judgment, and even *after* such events the parties may agree by stipulation to a dismissal, in which case the dismissal is ordinarily "without prejudice," meaning that plaintiff can file the suit later on. Doing so, however, carries costs. Under FRCP 41(d), if plaintiff dismisses a suit and brings a second one that includes "the same claim against the same defendant," the court in the second suit may order plaintiff to pay "costs of that previous action." In any event, plaintiff only has two times to get it right. If she dismisses a second suit, after having once dismissed the same claim, the second dismissal "operates as an adjudication on the merits," which means the claim is foreclosed. In common parlance, it is a dismissal "with prejudice" and plaintiff cannot file a third suit.

Notice too that if defendant has answered or filed a motion for summary judgment, it is too late for plaintiff to dismiss the suit while retaining the option to sue, unless defendant agrees. Finally, notice that FRCP 41(b) authorizes the court to dismiss a suit for failure by the plaintiff "to prosecute" or otherwise "to comply with [the] rules or a court order," and that with some exceptions such dismissal "operates as an adjudication on the merits," meaning again that a later suit is foreclosed. The exceptions are for dismissals for "lack of jurisdiction, for improper venue, or for failure to join a party under rule 19" (dismissals on these grounds do not foreclose another action).

A dismissal with prejudice for failure to prosecute is a harsh sanction, and the fear arises that this measure penalizes the client for shortcomings of the lawyer. There is, of course, the possibility of a malpractice suit, but this remedy is distinctly second best, and has the effect of making enemies out of friends and introducing a new dispute. In theory, at any rate, a client is responsible for choosing his lawyer, and mistakes and misconduct by the lawyer may be attributed to the client. More than 50 years ago, the Court approved dismissal of a suit with prejudice where a lawyer misbehaved in a way that could justify dismissal under FRCP 41. See Link v. Wabash Railroad Co., 370 U.S. 626 (1962) (court could dismiss with prejudice for want of prosecution, where plaintiff's counsel did not attend pretrial conference).

MAREX TITANIC, INC. v. WRECKED AND ABANDONED VESSEL

United States Court of Appeals for the Fourth Circuit
2 F.3d 544 (1993)

Before HALL, Circuit Judge, SPROUSE, Senior Circuit Judge, and MICHAEL, District Judge for the Western District of Virginia, sitting by designation.

HALL, Circuit Judge:

Marex Titanic, Inc. ["Marex"], appeals the district court's judgment awarding Titanic Ventures exclusive salvage rights to the Titanic. Because we conclude that the district court had no authority to vacate Marex's notice of voluntary dismissal, we reverse.

I

On April 15, 1912, the RMS Titanic sank in the North Atlantic Ocean approximately 400 miles off the Newfoundland coast. In 1985, a joint French/American expedition discovered the ship's remains at a depth of approximately 12,000 feet. In 1987, Titanic Ventures (a private American corporation) and The Institute of France for the Research and Exploration of the Sea [IFREMER] (a French governmental organization) conducted a joint salvage operation that recovered 1,800 artifacts from the wreck site. Although additional scientific and photographic dives were conducted, at the time this action came before the district court, Titanic Ventures and IFREMER were the only salvors to have worked on the wreck.

On August 7, 1992, Marex—which had never conducted any salvage operations on the ship—filed this action seeking to be named the sole and exclusive owner of any objects recovered from the Titanic or, alternatively, that it be granted a salvage award. In order to establish the court's jurisdiction, Marex's Ralph White deposited with the court two objects (a piece of metal and a prescription bottle) taken from the wreck.[1] Marex represented to the court that all competing salvage claims had been abandoned.

Based on Marex's representations, on August 12, 1992, the district court issued a warrant of arrest, which Marex was required to publish within 10 days. Notice of the arrest was published on September 23, 1992, 32 days late, and one day after the Marex ship had begun sailing toward the Titanic.

On September 23, 1992, Titanic Ventures' lawyers entered a special appearance seeking to vacate the warrant of arrest. Titanic Ventures argued that Marex had obtained the warrant through factual misrepresentations and that the court should dismiss the case in deference to the French Government's prior exercise of jurisdiction. On September 28, 1992, Titanic Ventures moved for a preliminary injunction to preclude Marex from salvaging the ship.

On September 29, 1992, the district court began hearings on the matter. After several of Titanic Ventures' witnesses had testified, the court issued a temporary restraining order barring Marex from salvaging the wreck until further order. On September 30, the hearing continued, and additional witnesses were heard.

---

[1] According to Titanic Ventures, White smuggled these objects from the ship while working as a member of a prior filming expedition.

As the facts unfolded, the district court made no secret of its feeling that Marex had misled the court in the initial hearing held on August 12, 1992. Marex realized the way the wind was blowing, and, on October 1, 1992, (after three days of hearings) filed a "Notice of Voluntary Dismissal" pursuant to FRCP 41(a)(1)(i). Although Marex came within the Rule's term—Titanic Ventures had not yet served Marex with an answer or a motion for summary judgment—the district court relied on Harvey Aluminum, Inc. v. American Cyanamid Co., 203 F.2d 105 (2d Cir.) (Rule 41(a)(1)(i) dismissal may be denied if parties have argued the merits and substantial evidence has been introduced), cert. denied, 345 U.S. 964 (1953), to "vacate" Marex's notice of dismissal, stating, "it just hasn't gone well for you so now you want to dismiss the case."

On October 2, 1992, Titanic Ventures sought to intervene in Marex's action and filed an "intervening complaint," asking that it be declared the Titanic's exclusive salvor. The district court allowed the intervention and ruled in Titanic Venture's favor by vacating Marex's earlier warrant, which the court found had been obtained through false testimony; granting Titanic Ventures the exclusive right to salvage the wreck; and permanently enjoining Marex "from taking any action towards salvaging . . . the vessel."

On October 16, 1992, Marex filed a motion for reconsideration. Following the district court's denial of this motion, Marex filed this appeal.

II

Although the parties have argued numerous issues in this appeal, we shall confine our discussion to whether the district court violated FRCP 41(a)(1)(i) when it vacated Marex's notice of voluntary dismissal. Our interpretation of Rule 41's scope is a question of law subject to de novo review.

"'We give the Federal Rules of Civil Procedure their plain meaning.' Pavelic & LeFlore v. Marvel Entertainment Group, 493 U.S. [120, 123] (1989). As with a statute, our inquiry is complete if we find the text of the Rule to be clear and unambiguous." Business Guides v. Chromatic Communications Ent., 498 U.S. 533, 540-41 (1991). Accordingly, we turn to the Rule itself [the court quotes FRCP 41(a)].

As the Rule's text makes plain, the universe of plaintiff-initiated, voluntary dismissals is broken into two categories. If the plaintiff files a notice of dismissal before the adverse party serves it with "an answer or a motion for summary judgment," the dismissal is available as a matter of unconditional right, see Matthews v. Gaither, 902 F.2d 877, 880 (11th Cir. 1990), and is self-executing, i.e., it is effective at the moment the notice is filed with the clerk and no judicial approval is required. See FRCP 41 ("an action may be dismissed by the plaintiff without order of the court" (emphasis supplied)); see also cases collected at 5 James Wm. Moore, et al., Moore's Federal Practice

¶ 41.02[2], at 41-17 nn.6, 7 (2d ed. 1992) [hereinafter Moore's], and 9 Charles A. Wright & Arthur R. Miller, Federal Practice and Procedure §2363, at 159 n.43 (1971) [hereinafter Wright & Miller]; American Cyanamid Co. v. McGhee, 317 F.2d 295, 297 (5th Cir. 1963).[2]

If the plaintiff fails to act before the Rule's "point of no return," Winterland Concessions Co. v. Smith, 706 F.2d 793, 795 (7th Cir. 1983), the penalty is that dismissal must be sought under Rule 41(a)(2). For the plaintiff seeking to dismiss without prejudice, this route is far less preferable, because the granting of the motion is within the court's discretion rather than as a matter of right. FRCP 41(a)(2) (dismissal is granted only upon "order of the court and upon such terms and conditions as the court deems proper."); Moore's, at 41-48.

Despite Rule 41(a)(1)(i)'s [now FRCP 41(a)(1)(A)(i)—ED.] plain language, Titanic Ventures seeks to protect its favorable result by arguing that we should endorse the district court's reliance on the Second Circuit's heavily criticized[3] *Harvey Aluminum* exception to Rule 41(a).[4] Admittedly, we cited *Harvey Aluminum* with approval in Armstrong v. Frostie Co., 453 F.2d 914, 916 (4th Cir. 1971).[5] However, this citation does not control our decision today. *Armstrong* merely relied on *Harvey Aluminum* for the principle that Rule 41 was designed to permit an early disengagement of the parties—an

---

[2] In *American Cyanamid*, the court stated: "Rule 41(a)(1) is the shortest and surest route to abort a complaint when it is applicable. So long as plaintiff has not been served with his adversary's answer or motion for summary judgment he need do no more than file a *notice* of dismissal with the Clerk. That document itself closes the file. There is nothing the defendant can do to fan the ashes of that action into life and the court has no role to play. This is a matter of right running to the plaintiff and may not be extinguished or circumscribed by adversary or court. There is not even a perfunctory order of the court closing the file. Its alpha and omega was the doing of the plaintiff alone."

[3] See [cases rejecting *Harvey* and] Wright & Miller §2363 (most courts have refused to apply *Harvey* and have reached the result the language of the rule seems to require).

[4] In Harvey Aluminum v. American Cyanamid Co., 203 F.2d 105 (2d Cir. 1953), the district court held several days of hearings on the plaintiff's motions for injunctive relief and considered the merits of the plaintiff's claim, stating that the plaintiff's chances of success were "remote, if not completely nil." Before the court issued its final ruling, the plaintiff filed a notice of dismissal. The court vacated the notice and denied the injunction on the merits. The Second Circuit affirmed, stating: "The purpose of this rule is to facilitate voluntary dismissals, but to limit them to an early stage of the proceedings before issue is joined. [These hearings were extensive and] the merits of the controversy were squarely raised and the district court in part based its denial of the injunction on its conclusion that the plaintiffs' chance of success on the merits was small. Consequently, although the voluntary dismissal was attempted before any paper labeled "answer" or "motion for summary judgment" was filed, a literal application of Rule 41(a)(1) to the present controversy would not be in accord with its essential purpose of preventing arbitrary dismissals after an advanced stage of a suit has been reached."

[5] In *Armstrong*, the defendant filed an answer and a motion for summary judgment, but the plaintiff's original complaint was dismissed. The plaintiff filed an amended complaint and before the defendant could answer, a notice of dismissal. This Court upheld the district court's refusal to dismiss the action, stating: "Rule 41(a)(1)(i) [now FRCP 41(a)(1)(A)(i)—ED.] is designed to permit a disengagement of the parties at the behest of the plaintiff only in the early stages of a suit, before the defendant has expended time and effort in the preparation of his case. *See* [*Harvey Aluminum*]. . . . Frostie satisfied both the letter and the spirit of the rule by filing an answer and a motion for summary judgment [to the original complaint]."

unexceptional proposition with which any court or commentator would agree. With the issue squarely before us, we reject the *Harvey Aluminum* exception to the plain meaning of Rule 41(a)(1)(i)'s [now FRCP 41(a)(1)(A)(i)—ED.] text.

Admittedly, one can question the wisdom of allowing a party, through adroit lawyering, to dismiss a case in order to avoid an unfavorable decision on the merits after the court has considered the evidence. It is especially tempting to force the plaintiff to take its medicine in a case like this, where the plaintiff's behavior has been so dissembling, if not downright fraudulent.[6]

However, "'Our task is to apply the text, not to improve upon it.'" *Business Guides*, 498 U.S. 533, 549 (1991). When Marex filed its notice of dismissal, Titanic Ventures had not filed an answer or a motion for summary judgment and under Rule 41(a)(1)(i) [now FRCP 41(a)(1)(A)(i)—ED.] the action was terminated and the district court's interlocutory orders were vacated. See In re Piper Aircraft Distribution Systems Antitrust Litigation, 551 F.2d 213, 219 (8th Cir. 1977) (The voluntary dismissal "carrie[d] down with it previous proceedings, and orders in the action, and all pleadings, both of plaintiff and defendant, and all issues, with respect to plaintiff's claim."). Although Titanic Ventures could possibly have initiated a new, independent civil action, the district court had no discretion to allow Titanic Ventures to intervene in the defunct action filed by Marex. Therefore, the district court's judgment is reversed.

■ NOTES ON DISMISSALS, VOLUNTARY AND OTHERWISE

1. Marex Titanic brought what is in substance an *in rem* suit in admiralty, and the "warrant of arrest" issued by the court on proof that plaintiff retrieved several objects from the Titanic amounted to a formal act by which the court asserted jurisdiction to resolve the question of salvage rights. On the day that Marex Titanic "published" the writ (notice to the world), lawyers for Titanic Ventures appeared and turned the tables on plaintiff, seeking to establish that it (not Marex Titanic) had exclusive rights to salvage the Titanic, and to enjoin Marex Titanic (which had launched an expedition to begin salvage work) from going forward. In this setting, Marex dismissed the suit, but the judge "vacated" the dismissal and found in favor of Titanic Ventures. Why should plaintiff have a right to dismiss a complaint once without losing the right to sue again? Why did the judge try to stop Marex Titanic from dismissing

---

[6] Even if the plaintiff has dismissed the action under Rule 41(a)(1)(i) [now FRCP 41(a)(1)(A)(i)—ED.], the majority of courts hold that the district court may still impose sanctions under FRCP 11. *See* Matthews v. Gaither, 902 F.2d 877, 880 (11th Cir. 1990) (collects cases).

without prejudice? Why does the reviewing court ultimately find in favor of Marex Titanic?

2. In the *Armstrong* case, cited in *Marex Titanic,* plaintiff's complaint was met by an answer and motion for summary judgment. The court dismissed the complaint for failing to state a claim, with leave to amend. Plaintiff amended, and defendant moved again to dismiss, but plaintiff filed a voluntary dismissal, which the court vacated. Plaintiff appealed, and the reviewing court held that plaintiff could not dismiss, even though no answer to the amended complaint, and no motion for summary judgment, had been filed. Does *Armstrong* adopt the *Harvey Aluminum* approach that the court rejects in *Marex Titanic*? Although courts often cite *Harvey Aluminum* with approval, few actually apply it. Most hold, as *Marex Titanic* does, that *Harvey Aluminum* is contrary to the plain meaning of FRCP 41. See 9 Wright & Miller, Federal Practice and Procedure §2363 (2004).

3. Where a complaint fails to state a claim for relief and is dismissed on motion pursuant to FRCP 12(b)(6), the dismissal fits FRCP 41(b): It is a dismissal for failure "to comply with these rules." In short, such a dismissal is "on the merits," and a second lawsuit should fail. Of course, it is for this reason that plaintiffs usually seek (and courts usually grant) leave to amend if a complaint fails to state a claim. See Stewart v. U.S. Bancorp, 297 F.3d 953, 958 (9th Cir. 2002) (dismissal for failure to state a claim because federal law preempted plaintiff's state law claim operated as adjudication on the merits, precluding later suit; plaintiff should have amended rather than file new action).

4. Suppose plaintiff moves to dismiss without prejudice, and the court grants the motion, but requires plaintiff to pay attorneys' fees to the defense. Can plaintiff appeal? See Ortega Trujillo v. Banco Central del Ecuador, 379 F.3d 1298 (11th Cir. 2004) (no; voluntary dismissal without prejudice, awarded to plaintiff on his request, is not appealable; requirement imposed as condition "amounts to some degree of prejudice to his action," but imposing such condition "does not amount to the type of 'legal prejudice' which would entitle a plaintiff to appeal the grant of the dismissal he obtains") (plaintiff did not seek to "withdraw" motion, which "could make a difference"). See also Marshall v. Kansas City Southern Railway Co., 378 F.3d 495 (5th Cir. 2004) (voluntary dismissal without prejudice is not an appealable order, and one cannot use this device "as an end-around the final judgment rule to convert an otherwise nonfinal—and thus nonappealable—ruling into a final decision appealable under §1291) (plaintiff could not use this device to appeal decision remanding case to state court for lack of diversity).

5. As FRCP 41(b) reflects, failure to prosecute is a common ground for dismissal (normally with prejudice). What factors, apart from passage of time, should a court consider in deciding whether to dismiss on this ground? See Modrow v. JP Foodservice, Inc., 656 N.W.2d 389 (Minn. 2003) (whether delay is prejudicial to defendant; whether it is excusable) (error to dismiss with prejudice). See also Pomales v. Celulares Telefonica, Inc., 342 F.3d 44

(1st Cir. 2003) (dismissing with prejudice a sexual harassment and discrimination suit for failure to prosecute, after plaintiff's lawyer withdrew and was not replaced in four months); Aura Lamp & Lighting, Inc. v. International Trading Corporation, 325 F.3d 903, 908 (7th Cir. 2003) (approving dismissal with prejudice for want of prosecution where plaintiff failed to sign pleadings, "repeatedly missed court-imposed deadlines for both discovery and motion practice, ignored agreed extensions," failed to amend complaint to cure jurisdictional defect for several months being ordered to do so, and "asked permission to propound discovery" beyond court-ordered cut-off date).

6. A number of states have statutes or rules that provide for dismissal of suits if not brought to trial within five years of filing. See, e.g., Cal. Code Civ. Proc. §§583.310 and 583.360 (suit shall be "brought to trial" within five years after it was "commenced," and suit "shall be dismissed" if it "is not brought to trial" within five years); Nev. RCP, Rule 41(e) (suit shall be dismissed unless it "is brought to trial within five years" after being filed, except where parties stipulate in writing that time may be extended); La. Code Civ. Proc., Art. 561 (suit is "abandoned when the parties fail to take any step in its prosecution or defense" for three years). Apparently, these statutes envision dismissal with prejudice, which is what happens when a federal court dismisses for nonprosecution under FRCP 41. But see Ga. Code §9-2-60 (suit in which "no written order is taken for a period of five years shall automatically stand dismissed with costs to be taxed against the party plaintiff," but if plaintiff "recommences the action within six months," then "the renewed action shall stand upon the same footing" as the original). Suppose a court dismisses a case with prejudice for nonprosecution. Can plaintiff seek reinstatement of the case? See Covington v. Smith, 582 S.E.2d 756, 768 (W. Va. 2003) (yes; under state rule requiring dismissal of case inactive for one year or more but allowing reinstatement, plaintiff here was entitled to reinstate; plaintiff showed of good cause; plaintiff tried to get his former lawyer to move on the case and hired new counsel when these efforts failed).

7. The Supreme Court has held that a voluntary dismissal with prejudice, by agreement of the parties as part of settlement, means the action is over. Hence the trial court lacks jurisdiction to enter enforcement orders if one of the parties fails to perform the settlement. Kokkonen v. Guardian Life Ins. Co. of America, 511 U.S. 375 (1994). It does not follow, of course, that a settlement agreement cannot be enforced: Failing to perform the obligations of a settlement agreement is a breach of contract that can support a new suit even if *res judicata* would block another suit on the underlying claim. The Court in *Kokkonen* indicated that enforcement orders might be entered after a dismissal by stipulation, if the order of dismissal embodies the settlement contract by agreement of the parties. The Court also suggested that enforcement orders are possible when a court dismisses if the dismissal is conditioned on performing the settlement.

G **AMENDING PLEADINGS**

FRCP 15 addresses the matters of amending and supplementing pleadings. Plaintiffs may amend complaints "once as a matter of course" in the first 21 days after filing (or within 21 days after an answer is filed, or a preliminary motion, whichever is earlier). Otherwise, they must obtain court permission, which courts should "freely give when justice so requires," meaning as a practical matter that plaintiffs may count on being able to amend in the early going of lawsuits.

Somewhat more challenging is the question whether an amended complaint can "relate back" to the date of filing. Under FRCP 3 an action is "commenced" when filed, and "commencement" is the act that tolls the statute of limitations in most jurisdictions (it stops ticking; if time had not run out when suit was "commenced," it won't expire while the action is pending, no matter how much time elapses). The matter is complicated by the fact that the law of many states allows filing to toll the statute of limitations only if the summons and complaint are *served* within a limited time (like 60 days) after filing. The "relation back" doctrine makes it possible for plaintiff to amend without running the risk that filing a new action would lead to dismissal: If the amendment requires no permission, the amended complaint is treated as if it had been filed when the original complaint was filed; when permission is required, the result is the same, except that special limits sometimes apply, which we will explore.

1. Entitlement and Permission

Even though the clear thrust of FRCP 15 is that courts are to be generous in allowing amendments, no lawyer can *count* on getting permission to amend, particularly if the suit has been going for several years.

In Johnson v. Methodist Medical Centers, 10 F.3d 1300 (7th Cir. 1993), for example, the court dismissed a mother's malpractice suit on behalf of her 14-year-old daughter Wanda Johnson, who suffered severe brain damage while delivering a baby at Methodist Medical Center (Wanda Johnson was now in her twenties, but "functions at less than an eight-year-old level"). The original complaint, filed on March 18, 1988 (almost six years after events), made claims against Methodist Medical Center on the theory that the Center was liable in respondeat superior for conduct by Drs. Thompson and Doughty, who ministered to Wanda. On June 16, 1989, plaintiff filed an amended complaint (with court permission) adding Dr. O'Connor and other unnamed residents, alleging that Methodist was negligent in failing (1) to use antibiotics, (2) to obtain proper blood cultures, (3) to recognize Wanda's pelvic infection, (4) to recognize "disseminated intravascular coagulation" (a bleeding disorder),

(5) to obtain an assessment of Wanda*'s* "pelvic size and capacity," (6) to have an internal pressure catheter or gauge available, and (7) to identify her infectious diseases. On November 27, 1991, Methodist filed a motion for summary judgment, with affidavits indicating that these claims lacked merit.

On January 13, 1992, plaintiff sought to file another amended complaint naming members of the nursing staff, this time alleging 11 negligent acts, including (1) failures of communication between nurses and doctors, (2) failure of nurses promptly to communicate to Dr. Thompson and residents that Wanda*'s* membranes had ruptured, (3) failure to communicate that the fetal monitor strips were improperly calibrated, (4) failure to chart the rupture of the membranes, (5) failure to report to Dr. Thompson and residents a decrease in the variability of fetal monitor strips, (6) negligently discontinuing fetal heart monitor, (7) negligent performance of unnecessary examinations, (8) introduction of bacteria into the cervix, (9) failure to obtain clinical evaluation of Wanda's labor, (10) negligently providing morphine, and (11) failure properly to evaluate vital signs. The amended complaint also would have added seven allegations of negligence specifically by the Hospital. The trial court denied the amendment, and granted Methodist's motion for summary judgment. The reviewing court affirmed:

> Plaintiff's attorney argued . . . that the proposed complaint's specific allegations were made to meet the summary judgment motion. In answering the court's question of why an amended complaint had not been filed earlier, plaintiff's attorney answered that he did not feel it was necessary to make specific allegations in a complaint. While unnecessary, plaintiff's attorney believed the specific allegations would make the issues clearer for everyone.
>
> At a subsequent hearing on Methodist's summary judgment motion, and in the following written order, the district court noted that plaintiff's attorney failed to provide a valid explanation for why the complaint was not amended earlier. The court decided that four years after commencement of the action was too late to amend the complaint.
>
> The district court concluded that the proposed complaint goes beyond the scope of the second amended complaint. Plaintiff herself acknowledges that "[t]hese allegations [of Methodist's negligence as exposed in plaintiff's experts' depositions by mid-September 1991] were not encompassed by the Second Amended Complaint." The proposed complaint brings in additional actors (*e.g.* the nursing staff), who took alleged actions (or inactions) that are distinct from the allegations raised in the second amended complaint (*e.g.* failure to communicate).
>
> As we view it, plaintiff chose to rest her claims against Methodist on the alleged negligence of the doctors, on the theory that they were Methodist's agents, and otherwise claimed very precise failures of Methodist's employees. When confronted by Methodist's motion for summary judgment, plaintiff realized that she would lose based on the specific claims contained in the second amended complaint. She therefore asked for leave to add a large number of new

specific claims. The choice to leave these claims out of the pleadings for so long a time after plaintiff must have known of them, suggests a doubt about being able to prove these failures or, if proved, that they caused Wanda's injuries.

Plaintiff asserts that Methodist would not be prejudiced if she is allowed to amend her complaint. We do not agree. First, the preceding complaints made very specific allegations, thus focusing the issues narrowly; it was not unreasonable for Methodist to be taken by surprise by the proposed complaint's new allegations. Second, Methodist moved for summary judgment based on the allegations contained in the second amended complaint, which if granted (as here), removes Methodist from this action. Third, it seems likely that Methodist, as it contends, would have to engage in substantial additional discovery and thus be prejudiced if plaintiff's proposed complaint were accepted. If amendment were permitted, Methodist's success in defeating all the claims in the second amended complaint would not end the lawsuit, and it would have to engage in a new contest on different issues—four years after the action was started.

There must be a point at which a plaintiff makes a commitment to the theory of its case. Here, the proposed complaint attempts to add a whole new theory of the case four years after this action was commenced, with no explanation as to why amendment did not take place sooner, except perhaps that plaintiff's attorney felt it was not necessary. But plaintiff had chosen to plead specific negligent acts and omissions in her second amended complaint, and preceding complaints. She did not merely allege that Methodist's agents and employees were negligent, but rather that certain Methodist agents and employees were negligent by reason of specific acts or omissions.

Dr. Zatuchni was first contacted by plaintiff with respect to this case in 1990; Mr. Nellis was contacted in October 1990. Presumably plaintiff's attorneys were informed of their experts' opinions before the experts were deposed in August and September 1991. However, even if we accept plaintiff's assertion that she had no knowledge of the new allegations until the summer 1991 depositions, plaintiff did not move to amend her complaint at that time, but instead only sought to do so when faced with the likelihood that Methodist's motion for summary judgment would succeed.

We conclude that the district court did not abuse its discretion when it denied plaintiff's motion for leave to file a third amended complaint.

Johnson v. Methodist Medical Centers, 10 F.3d 1300, 1303-1304 (7th Cir. 1993).

Surely *Johnson* sends an important message. There are limits, aren't there? What did plaintiff's lawyer do wrong? Has justice been served? Or is it just that "the system" has been vindicated?

2. Relation Back

Consider a case where plaintiff's aim in seeking leave to amend is to add a new defendant, where it appears that the suit could not proceed against the defendant originally named in the complaint.

Civic Park, Spearfish, South Dakota

In a park similar to this one, in Spearfish, South Dakota, Dawn Hedel-Ostrowski apparently fell when a swing that she was using broke. Spearfish is located on the western edge of the state in the northern Black Hills, about 80 miles from Mount Rushmore, 70 miles from the Crazy Horse Memorial, and 25 miles from Devil's Tower (located in Wyoming). Reportedly scenes in *Dances with Wolves* were filmed nearby.

HEDEL-OSTROWSKI v. CITY OF SPEARFISH

Supreme Court of South Dakota
679 N.W.2d 491 (2004)

MEIERHENRY, Justice.

The trial court granted City of Spearfish and Keith Hepper's motion for summary judgment. The trial court found that Dawn Hedel-Ostrowski's (Hedel-Ostrowski) negligence claim against the City and the negligence and nuisance claims against Hepper were barred by the statute of limitations. The trial court further dismissed Hedel-Ostrowski's nuisance claim against the City. We affirm.

FACTS

Hedel-Ostrowski accompanied her two children to a Spearfish city park on September 18, 1999. Hedel-Ostrowski fell when the swing she was using broke. The fall caused nerve damage in her lower leg. She retained counsel and timely submitted a claim against the City of Spearfish for her injuries. The City denied her claim. Subsequently, she was referred to another attorney who failed to pursue her claim in court.[1] She then retained a third attorney who commenced an action on her behalf during September 2002. The complaint named the City, Miracle Recreation Company, Playpower, Inc., and Cameron Holdings Corp. as defendants.

---

[1] The attorney to whom she was referred was temporarily suspended from practicing law approximately two years after agreeing to represent Hedel-Ostrowski.

Hedel-Ostrowski filed a Motion to Amend Complaint on November 7, 2002 to add Keith Hepper (Hepper), head of Spearfish Parks and Recreation, as a defendant. The Amended Complaint also added a claim for nuisance against the City in addition to her initial negligence claim. The City filed a Motion for Summary Judgment claiming the negligence action was barred by SDCL 9-24-5 which requires commencement of an action against a municipality within two years of the occurrence. The City also filed a Motion for Summary Judgment claiming that the negligence action against Hepper was barred by the three year statute of limitations in SDCL 15-2-14(3) and that the nuisance action against the City should be dismissed for failure to state a claim. The trial court granted Hedel-Ostrowski's Motion to amend. The trial court, however, granted summary judgment to the City and Hepper dismissing the negligence and nuisance claims.

. . .

The trial court found Hedel-Ostrowski's claims against Hepper were untimely. The parties disagree which statute of limitations applies to the claim against Hepper. Hepper argues that the two-year statute of limitations in SDCL 9-24-5 applies because he was an employee of the City.[2] Hedel-Ostrowski argues that the statute does not apply to individual employees and asserts that the three-year statute of limitations in SDCL 15-2-14 applies.[3] The trial court found that even if the three-year statute of limitations were applicable, Hedel-Ostrowski's claims were untimely, thus barring suit against Hepper. The trial court determined that the only way that Hedel-Ostrowski's claim against Hepper could be resurrected was by allowing the amended complaint to relate back to the date of the original complaint pursuant to [SDRCP 15(c)]. The trial court, however, determined that the requirements of [SDRCP 15(c)] were not met because there was no showing of mistake or question of identity of the proper party to sue. The trial court did not err in this analysis.

The chronology of events starts with the injury on September 18, 1999. The date the statute of limitations expired against the City . . . was September 18, 2001. Almost a year after the statute had run on September 12, 2002, Hedel-Ostrowski filed suit against the City. The three year statute of limitations . . . expired on September 18, 2002. On November 7, 2002, Hedel-Ostrowski moved to amend the complaint to add Hepper as a party and to add the nuisance claim against the City. Hepper was not served with the Summons and Amended Complaint until February 21, 2003.

---

[2] SDCL 9-24-5 provides: "Any action for recovery of damages for personal injury or death caused by the negligence of a municipality must be commenced within two years from the occurrence of the accident causing the injury or death.

[3] SDCL 15-2-14(3) provides in part: "Except where, in special cases, a different limitation is prescribed by statute, the following civil actions other than for the recovery of real property can be commenced only within three years after the cause of action shall have accrued: . . . (3) An action for personal injury."

Hedel-Ostrowski asserts that her claims against Hepper should be allowed under [SDRCP 15(a) and (c)][4] because they "relate back" to the date of her original pleading dated September 12, 2002, thereby tolling the statute of limitations. In determining if an amendment to a complaint relates back under Rule 15(c), we rely on a three-prong analysis. We recently outlined the requirements:

> (1) the claim asserted in the amended complaint "arose out of the conduct, transaction, or occurrence set forth . . . in the original pleading";
>
> (2) the new defendant "has received such notice of the institution of the action that he will not be prejudiced in maintaining his defense on the merits"; and
>
> (3) the new defendant "knew or should have known that, but for a mistake concerning the identity of the proper party, the action would have been brought against him."

Sjoland v. Carter, 664 N.W.2d 48, 52 (S.D. 2003). The parties agree that requirements one and two were met. They disagree on whether the third requirement was met. The trial court found that because Hedel-Ostrowski did not omit Hepper as a party because of "a mistake concerning [his] identity [as a] proper party," the requirements of [SDRCP 15(c)] were not satisfied.

Generally an amended pleading naming a new party in a lawsuit does not relate back under Rule 15(c). In Moore v. Michelin Tire Co. Inc., 603 N.W.2d 513 (S.D. 1999), this Court affirmed the trial court's finding that "[Rule 15(c)] does not allow for adding new parties to a pending action after the statute of limitation has expired." In *Moore,* the plaintiffs had named some defendants but used John Doe pleadings for another. It was not until after the statute of limitations had run that they attempted to substitute the name of the party for John Doe. We said, "'for all practical purposes all defendants specifically unnamed are not yet parties to a suit and, if added later, are considered new parties to the litigation. Therefore, amendments to a complaint that add new parties do not relate back'" (quoting Thomas v. Process Equipment Corp., 397 N.W.2d 224, 226 (Mich. App. 1986)). In the present case, Hedel-Ostrowski did not use John Doe pleadings.

---

[4] [The court quotes SDRCP 15(a) and (c), which are similar to FRCP 15(a) and (c). SDRCP 15(c) tracks the federal language in stating that an amendment changing parties to a suit relates back "to the date of the original pleading" if the claim in the amended pleading "arose out of the conduct, transaction or occurrence set forth or attempted to be set forth in the original pleading" and if the new party "received such notice of the institution of the action that [the new party] will not be prejudiced in maintaining his defense on the merits," and "knew or should have known that, but for a mistake concerning the identity of the proper party, the action would have been brought against [the new party]." Under SDRCP 15(c), the new party must receive such notice "within the period provided by law for commending the action against him." This differs from the *federal* language requiring the new party to receive notice "within the time period provided by Rule 4(m) for service of the summons and complaint."—ED.]

Relation back was also denied in *McCloud v. Andersen*, 485 N.W.2d 799 (S.D. 1992). In that case, the plaintiff failed to name the defendant's insurer before the statute of limitations expired. The plaintiff knew the insurer's identity prior to the running of the statute of limitations. This Court determined that the plaintiff had "simply ignored or failed to respond in a reasonable fashion to notice that State Farm was a potential defendant." We held that "Rule 15(c) should not be applied to assist [plaintiff's] lack of diligence."

Hedel-Ostrowski argues that because Hepper admitted he had notice of the suit before the statute of limitations ran, Rule 15 applies.[5] Whether Hepper had notice is, however, only part of the requirement. The party must have known that "but for a mistake concerning [his] identity, the action would have been brought against him." Hedel-Ostrowski attempts to use the relate back rule to add a defendant who she simply failed to identify as a potential defendant before the running of the statute of limitations. In *McCloud* we said, "Rule 15(c) was never intended to assist a plaintiff who ignores or fails to respond in a reasonable fashion to notice of a potential party, nor was it intended to permit a plaintiff to engage in piecemeal litigation." *Id.* (quoting *Kilkenny v. Arco Marine, Inc.*, 800 F.2d 853, 857 (9th Cir. 1986)).

Hedel-Ostrowski claims that adding Hepper as a party should be allowed because he was omitted as a party because of a mistake. She relies on a West Virginia case which allowed relation back because of a mistake of law. *Brooks v. Isinghood*, 213 W. Va. 675, 584 S.E.2d 531 (W. Va. 2003). In *Brooks,* the plaintiff's complaint alleged "that the City, through certain employees acting within the scope of their employment with the City, acted recklessly and in willful disregard of the safety of Mr. Brooks." The plaintiff, however, had omitted naming individual employees as defendants. Plaintiff's attorney claimed a mistake of law based on the language of W. Va. Code, 29-12A-1 to 18.[6] He "believed he could not name the individual employees." In contrast, Hedel-Ostrowski makes no assertion that she believed that she was not lawfully able to name Hepper in her original complaint. Nor does Hedel-Ostrowski's attorney point to any statutory language that led him to believe Hepper could not be named. Hedel-Ostrowski has failed to make a sufficient showing under Rule 15(c) for the claims against Hepper to relate back to the original pleading. The trial court did not err in concluding that the claims

[5] The original complaint made the following allegations generally including the City's employees: "It was the duty of the Defendant, City of Spearfish and its employees and servants, to install reasonably safe recreational equipment at the park and to maintain said equipment in a reasonably safe condition so that any person using the same would be protected from injury." The Amended Complaint merely inserted the name of Keith Hepper as follows: "It was the duty of the Defendants, Keith Hepper and City of Spearfish and its employees and servant...."

[6] The relevant part of the West Virginia Code is: "(b) Suits instituted pursuant to the provisions of this article shall name as defendant the political subdivision against which liability is sought to be established. *In no instance may an employee of political subdivision acting within the scope of his employment be named as defendant.*" W. Va. Code §29-12A-13(b) (1986) (emphasis added).

against Hepper were barred by the statute of limitations. In light of our ruling, we need not address whether the two or three year statute of limitations applies since both had expired.

[The court concludes that plaintiff has no claim against the City for nuisance, rejecting plaintiff's claim that placing a swing in a park without posting a notice about a weight restriction constituted a public nuisance. The court quotes a state statute indicating that "[n]othing which is done or maintained under the express authority of a statute can be deemed a nuisance," and concludes that since the City of Spearfish is authorized by statute to "establish, improve, maintain and regulate public parks," it is exempt from nuisance claims.]

We affirm.

GILBERTSON, Chief Justice, and SABERS, KONENKAMP, and ZINTER, Justices, concur.

■ NOTES ON THE RELATION BACK DOCTRINE

1. In a passage edited out of the opinion, *Hedel-Ostrowski* states that the claim against the City is barred by S.D. Codified Laws §§21-10-2 and 9-38-1 (the former provides that nothing done by a City "under the express authority of a statute" can be a nuisance; the latter authorizes Cities to establish "public parks"). These provisions implement a form of sovereign immunity. In modern terms, sovereign immunity can be justified on the ground that it is better for citizens to suffer inconveniences and even injuries than for government to be impeded by lawsuits. This protective doctrine has been scaled back or abrogated in most states, and is often the subject of detailed statutory regulation. Typically, one may sue public agencies (states, cities, other political subdivisions) for "proprietary torts," which include negligent driving in official vehicles or nuisance in maintaining park facilities (as alleged in *Hedel-Ostrowski*), but not for injuries resulting from the exercise of "discretionary functions," like failing to enact a building code that might have prevented a fire. Typically, modern statutes require that claimants first notify the governmental body (so the matter can be worked out), and often they require prompt notice.

2. Does *Hedel-Ostrowski* present a situation in which it seems wise to block suits against the City? Consider Epstein, Torts §22.7 (1999) (state statutes "recognize liability for garden-variety torts arising out of automobile accidents, medical malpractice, and premises liability, subject in the last case to the uneasiness, shared by private landowners, of having to either warn or patrol wide swaths of public property, which may become dangerous because of natural conditions and forces"). Is the risk of injury from playground equipment so obvious, and potentially so burdensome if the City is liable for a swing that breaks or is defective, that it is better to force users to bear the risks than to push the City to stop supplying playground equipment in public areas?

3. Sovereign immunity does not always immunize individual agents of the sovereign. The statute construed in *Hedel-Ostrowski* states, in effect, that public parks cannot be nuisances, which might block claims against Keith Hepper as well as claims against the City of Spearfish. But public employees do not always enjoy the same immunity as the entity they work for, which may explain the effort plaintiff made in *Hedel-Ostrowski* to amend the complaint to add Keith Hepper as defendant.

4. If plaintiff wants an amendment to relate back to the original filing date, and wants to add a defendant, the court says she must satisfy three conditions (really four if one counts the "timeliness" requirement, see note 6 below).

(a) Same Transaction. First, the amended complaint must allege claims arising out of the same "conduct, transaction, or occurrence" as the one alleged (or "attempted" to be alleged) in the original complaint. Both FRCP 15 and the South Dakota Rule have this requirement. Everyone agrees that the requirement is satisfied here. What if the original complaint alleged that the stairs in a building were improperly designed (because treads and risers were not within the accepted norms for stairs) but the amended complaint named a new party *and* alleged that those in charge of the building did not properly clean or maintain the staircase? See Swartz v. Gold Dust Casino, 91 F.R.D. 543 (D. Nev. 1981) (treating plaintiff's fall on the staircase as the relevant transaction and allowing relation back).

(b) Notice. Second, the person to be added as defendant must receive "notice" that is adequate and timely. The "adequacy" element means that the party to be added ("the new party") must learn of the suit in a way that conveys to him that the intent was to include him in the suit originally, so he is not "prejudiced" in his defense. The "timely" element means that he received notice *either* within the time allowed by the applicable statute of limitations (as the South Dakota Rule says) *or* within the time allowed by the applicable statute of limitations *plus* the time allowed for service of the summons and complaint (as the Federal Rule says). In *Hedel-Ostrowski,* the original complaint was filed on September 12, 2002 (six days before the three-year statute would run).

(c) Knowledge of Mistake. Third, the original failure to name the party to be added must be the product of "mistake" that the new party "knew or should have known" about. It's pretty obvious that not naming Keith Hepper as defendant was a strategic error, since Dawn Hedel-Ostrowski can't sue the City. How does the court approach the question of mistake, and why was this requirement *not* satisfied here? The court says this case differs from the West Virginia decision in *Brooks,* where plaintiff didn't name the employee because the statute said an employee was not to be "named as defendant" (despite the

statute, *Brooks* concluded that in some circumstances the employee *could be named* as defendant). Didn't Hedel-Ostrowski's lawyer make a similar mistake? What else could it be? *Hedel-Ostrowski* is not alone in construing mistake narrowly. See also Schwindel v. Meade County, 113 S.W.3d 159, 169 (Ky. 2003) (in personal injury suit arising out of fall in bleachers at softball game, denying leave to add county agents to suit originally naming only county and school board; "there was no mistake" in choosing the original defendants); Garland v. Sherwin, 804 A.2d 354, 356 (Me. 2002) (conscious choice to sue one defendant rather than another is not a mistake under Rule 15(c); relation back does not apply). What is the point of requiring plaintiff to prove her failure to name the defendant was the product of a "mistake," anyway?

5. Suppose the reason for adding a new defendant is that plaintiff cannot serve the original defendant and decides that another is a more promising target. If the newly named defendant had notice of the original suit within the limitations period, does the amendment satisfy the requirement that the original pleading was the product of "mistake"? See Rivers v. American Commerce Insurance Co., 836 A.2d 200 (R.I. 2003) (no; claimant originally named other driver, but couldn't serve him; although insurance carrier had received a copy of the complaint within the limitations period, amendment still did not relate back because plaintiff "made no mistake about the proper parties to the action").

6. Consider what we might call the "timeliness" requirement that the court in *Hedel-Ostrowski* does not discuss. On the day when Dawn Hedel-Ostrowski served the complaint on the City of Spearfish (town of about 12,000 people), it's likely that Keith Hepper did not see or read or pay attention to the document. It likely went straight to the lawyer whom the City retains to handle such matters, and that lawyer would likely have gotten in touch with Mr. Hepper to find out what was going on with the swings in the park. Mr. Hepper would likely know something about the incident, since Ms. Hedel-Ostroski already filed a claim against the City. What we learn from the opinion, however, is that Hepper had notice of the suit that SDRCP 15(c) requires—he "received such notice of the institution of the action" that he "would not be prejudiced" in defending on the merits, and he got notice before the statute of limitations had run. Under SDCCP 15(c), the party to be named in the amended complaint should receive notice "within the period provided by law for commencing the action against him." Assuming that the statute of limitations allows three years for claims against him, he should have notice by September 17, 2002. The complaint was filed five days before then, and if it was served on the City on that day, then the lawyer likely had notice that day too, or at most a day or two later. If the lawyer promptly contacted Hepper, then Hepper too had timely notice. It is sometimes possible to argue that notice to the lawyer is notice to the client. Compare Garvin v. City of Philadelphia, 354 F.3d 215, 222 (3d Cir. 2003) (notice to attorney was *not* notice to later-named defendants whom attorney then represented, at least where attorney had not previously represented defendants similar to those now to be added) with Singletary v. Pennsylvania Dep't of Corrections, 266 F.3d 186, 196 (3d Cir. 2001) ("shared attorney" method of imputing notice to defendant named by amendment rests on "the notion that, when an originally named party and the party who is sought to be added are represented by the same attorney, the attorney is likely to have communicated to the latter party that he may very well be joined in the action"). Why, when a complaint is amended to name a new defendant on account of a "mistake" made in the original complaint, does the rule require the new defendant to have notice within the period prescribed by the statute of limitations? FRCP 15(c) frames this requirement slightly differently—under the federal language, the new defendant must have notice "within the time period provided by Rule 4(m) for serving the summons and complaint" (120 days after filing). What explains this difference?

7. Courts disagree on the question whether naming "John Doe" defendants can entitle a claimant to add names later and take advantage of the relation back doctrine. Compare Garrett v. Fleming, 362 F.3d 692, 696 (10th Cir. 2004) (substituting named defendants for "John Doe" defendants "amounted to adding a new party" and was not a matter of "mistake" under FRCP 15) with *Singletary*, 266 F.3d at 186, 200 (noting that most courts conclude that substituting named defendant for "John Doe" defendants cannot qualify for relation back under the "mistake" doctrine, but that binding Third Circuit authority allows relation back to apply in this situation, if all the requirements of FRCP 15(c) are met).

CHAPTER 8

Shaping the Suit: Joinder of Claims and Parties

INTRODUCTION

This chapter examines foundational issues relating to lawsuits: Who can sue? What shape can the suit take? Are there claims or parties that *must be* in the suit?

We focus primarily on the way that the Federal Rules handle these topics. As noted earlier, these Rules have been remarkably successful and are the basis for similar rules in 25 states plus the District of Columbia (see Chapter 7, footnote 3). Even Code states often follow procedural conventions similar to those in the Rules.

Recall from Chapters 1 and 4 that federal courts have *limited* jurisdiction. The significance of this point, in the setting of the rules governing joinder of claims and parties, arises from the requirements of "complete diversity" and "amount in controversy." Sometimes the Rules invite or require the addition of parties and claims that would conflict with these restrictions on federal subject matter jurisdiction. The framers were aware of this possibility, and Rule 82 says the Rules "do not extend or limit" district court jurisdiction or venue.

Recall from Chapter 4 the supplemental jurisdiction statute, 28 USC §1367. In federal question cases, federal courts have supplemental jurisdiction over all claims that are "so related" to federal claims that they "form part of the same case or controversy" under Article III of the Constitution. This language approximates the phrase coined by Justice Brennan in defining pendent jurisdiction before the matter was regulated by statute—*Gibbs* said pendent jurisdiction reached all claims arising out of "a common nucleus of operative fact." See United Mine Workers v. Gibbs, 383 U.S. 715, 725 (1966). *Both* these phrases—"same case or controversy" and "common nucleus of operative fact"—seem in turn to approximate the concept often found in the Civil Rules describing claims arising out of the same "transaction or occurrence." As a rule of thumb, it is fair to say that in federal question cases there is jurisdiction over all *additional* claims that enter a case under the Civil Rules that arise out of the same transaction as the main claim.

Recall also from Chapter 4, however, that the supplemental jurisdiction statute is less generous in diversity cases. Again the beginning point is §1367(a), which says federal courts have jurisdiction over claims "so related" to a claim satisfying the standard for diversity jurisdiction that the additional claims "form part of the same case or controversy," but *this* time we must watch for "carveouts" in §1367(b), which *deny* supplemental jurisdiction in certain situations.

Oversimplifying for a moment, the most important places in diversity suits in which supplemental jurisdiction does *not* exist (or might not exist), are these three:

First, the statute does not modify the "complete diversity" rule in diversity cases. Hence a New York plaintiff cannot join a Pennsylvania plaintiff in a diversity suit against a citizen of New York—even if FRCP 20 would allow such joinder because both claims arise out of the "same transaction" or "occurrence." And a New York plaintiff suing a defendant from Pennsylvania cannot name another defendant who is a citizen of New York—even if FRCP 20 would otherwise allow such joinder because the claim against the second New Yorker arises out of the same "transaction" or "occurrence" as the claim against the Pennsylvanian.

The *Exxon* case (Chapter 4C2, supra), however, held that §1367 *does* confer supplemental jurisdiction over claims by additional plaintiffs in diversity suits that do not satisfy the amount-in-controversy requirement. If two New Yorkers sue a Pennsylvanian in a diversity case and one plaintiff seeks more than the minimum (more than $75,000), there is supplemental jurisdiction over the claims by the second New Yorker against the same Pennsylvania defendant even if they do not satisfy the minimum (second New Yorker seeks only $50,000).

Second, the statute *declines* to extend supplemental jurisdiction in diversity cases over parties that must be added under FRCP 19 ("indispensable parties"). If a citizen of Colorado brings a diversity suit against a citizen of Arizona, and if plaintiff can only prosecute this claim if a second Colorado citizen is added as defendant, the case must be dismissed. (This matter is examined in connection with FRCP 19, below.)

Third, there is room to doubt whether there is supplemental jurisdiction in diversity cases over counterclaims that are permissive but not compulsory. Recall from Chapter 7C5 that supplemental jurisdiction extends to compulsory counterclaims (those arising out of the same "transaction or occurrence"), but probably not to *all* permissive counterclaims, even if it covers some of them.

A STATUS; PROBLEMS OF ELIGIBILITY

It comes as no surprise that not everyone with a legal problem or question can bring suit, and not everyone may be sued—persons who cannot sue or be sued are said to lack "capacity" to bring or defend lawsuits. Children apart (more on this subject below), issues of capacity are rare. More common are issues relating to standing: One must have "standing" to sue, meaning, among other things, that one has suffered some particular harm that is not suffered generally by everyone. Another matter affecting eligibility to sue, related to the idea of standing, goes under the rubric "real party in interest," which means that the party actually entitled to the relief being sought must sue in his or her own name, with important exceptions.

1. Standing to Sue

To sue, a person must have standing. This doctrine is a subcategory in a cluster of doctrines relating to "justiciability," and it envisions one who has suffered a specific harm that is special or different from harm suffered by the population in general.

Justiciability customarily refers to three main ideas:

(1) Actual Controversy. Under Article III of the Constitution, federal courts decide "cases or controversies." That is to say, federal courts do not answer "legal questions" or give "advisory opinions." If the head of the Federal Aviation Administration wants to know whether he can (or must) bar peanuts as food served on passenger airplanes on account of severe (even fatal reactions) some people have to peanuts, he cannot submit a formal question to a court asking its opinion about his authority or obligations on this matter.

State courts observe a similar limit on justiciability. Even where state constitutions do not track Article III, similar ideas about justiciability appear. See State ex rel. Wright v. Oklahoma Corp. Comm'n, 170 P.3d 1024 (Okla. 2007) ("justiciable controversy" means "a lively case or controversy between antagonistic demands," not those that are "merely speculative," which seek a "prohibited advisory opinion"); Ferreiro v. Philadelphia Indemnity Insurance Co., 928 So. 2d 374, 376 (Fla. App. 2006) (to satisfy standing requirement, plaintiff must show that "a case or controversy exists" between plaintiff and defendant).

(2) Ripeness. A court should decide only questions that are current, so resolution will affect parties in what they're doing or soon will do. In 2003, for example, the Court declined to decide whether the Contract Disputes Act of 1978 applies to agreements between National Parks and concessioners on providing services in national parks (running lodges, selling gasoline and food-stuffs, operating guest ranches, and so forth). The Park Service had conducted a process leading to adoption of a rule that "binding written agreements" between the Director of the Service and concessioners "are not contracts" under the statute. Concessioners, with a nonprofit trade association, sued the Director seeking declaratory relief, arguing that their contracts entitled them to a "preferential right of renewal," under which each would have the right "to match the best bid" made by a competitor.

The D.C. Circuit Court thought the case satisfied the "ripeness" standard, which relates to "the fitness of the issues for judicial decision" and the "hardship to the parties" that would result from delay. Courts can "defer judgment if intervening circumstances" are likely to obviate the need for decision, but this case was ripe because "a loss of opportunity to compete is an injury in fact," and plaintiffs were within the "zone of interests" protected by the National Parks Omnibus Management Act of 1998. See Amfac Resorts, L.L.C. v. U.S. Department of the Interior, 142 F. Supp. 54 (D.D.C. 2001), aff'd, 282 F.3d 818 (D.C. Cir. 2002).

The Supreme Court disagreed. It concurred in viewing ripeness as having to do with fitness for decision and hardship on parties, but it concluded that the Service did not have jurisdiction to administer the Contract Disputes Act (the task belongs with "agency contracting officers and boards of contract appeals, as well as the Federal Court of Claims" and other federal courts). The regulation adopted by the Service was a "general statement of policy" that did not create "adverse effects of a strictly legal kind." The regulation "does not affect a concessioner's primary conduct," as it remains "free to conduct its business as it sees fit." Nor is the case fit for review, even though it presents a legal question about final agency action, because "further factual development" would make it easier to appraise the issues. See National Park Hospitality Ass'n v. Department of Interior, 538 U.S. 803 (2003).

(3) Standing. This doctrine implements ideas about separation of powers among the executive, legislative, and judicial branches, and is crucial in defining and limiting the judicial function. The Court has spoken of standing as arising from the "case or controversy" requirement and the separation of powers doctrine, which derives from the framework of government set up by the Constitution.

The Court admits that its decisions on standing have been less than pellucid. See, e.g., Valley Forge Christian College v. Americans United for Separation of Church and State, 454 U.S. 464, 475 (1982) (we have not defined standing "with complete consistency," and it "cannot be reduced to a one-sentence or one-paragraph definition"); Flast v. Cohen, 392 U.S. 83, 129 (1968) (standing is a "word game played by secret rules") (Justice Harlan, dissenting). The Court has also said that standing is a "complicated specialty of federal jurisdiction," see United States ex rel. Chapman v. Federal Power Commission, 345 U.S. 153, 156 (1953), prompting an astute observer to retort that the Court knows that federal standing law is "too complex" for federal courts to apply "consistently." States, he concluded, have been more realistic in adopting the "simple proposition that those who are in fact adversely affected" can sue. See 3 K.C. Davis, Administrative Law Treatise 217 (1958).

With those caveats in mind, we should tread gingerly in attempting a description. Standing is understood as requiring three things: First, there must be a claimant who suffered injury or is at imminent risk of injury of a sort that is peculiar to him or her, not shared by everyone in the population. Second, there must be a direct causal connection between defendant's conduct and the injury. Third, the injury must be redressable—something that a court can repair by an order or judgment that prevents or compensates for the injury. Beyond these points, the Court has spoken of "prudential" concerns rooted in sound judicial administration, identifying three additional factors: First, a claimant must assert her own rights, not the rights of another. Second, being a taxpayer or citizen is not enough to confer standing on claims challenging government action. Third, the claimant must be within the zone of interests addressed by the statute or constitutional clause. See Wright, Law of Federal Courts §13 (6th ed. 2003).

Fortunately, issues of standing are confined, as a practical matter, to "public law" litigation, such as institutional reform suits, challenges to the legality or constitutionality of laws or regulations, and challenges to administrative decisions, as exemplified in Kleissler v. United States Forest Service, 157 F.3d 964 (3d Cir. 1998) (Section G, infra). "In theory," Professor Wright has said, standing is *not* limited to such cases and can arise in contract and tort cases too, where the plaintiff "must satisfy the court that he is the real party in interest," but in practice these suits are always brought by someone who was "harmed by the supposed wrong, and standing to sue is self-evident." Wright, supra.

2. Capacity to Sue and Be Sued (FRCP 17)

Practically any adult can sue or be sued: For the most part, personal characteristics do not create or defeat capacity to sue. Thus married persons can sue or be sued without joining spouses,[1] and convicted felons can sue (at least if they are not incarcerated). Also partnerships and corporate entities can sue or be sued (also governmental entities).

Minors lack capacity to sue or be sued. Typical statutes set the age of majority at 18 years, as is true in Colorado, for example. See Colo. Rev. Stat. §13-22-101 ("every person, otherwise competent, shall be deemed to be of full age at the age of eighteen years" for purpose of entering into contracts, managing property, and bringing suit or being sued). This disability,

---

[1] Long ago married women could not sue, nor black Americans or Native Americans. The shadow of such rules, relics of the past, is still visible in provisions noting the abolition of the old restrictions. See, e.g., Colorado Rule 17(b) (a married woman "may sue and be sued in all matters the same as though she were sole").

however, means less than it might seem: A child may sue (and less often may be sued) through a representative, and FRCP 17(c) recognizes that a child who does not have a "guardian" or other representative with fiduciary responsibilities (like a parent) may sue through "a next friend" or "guardian ad litem" (guardian for the suit) whom the court appoints "as it deems proper for the protection of the infant or incompetent person."

Incompetent persons also lack the necessary capacity to sue or be sued (a category that may include insane persons or persons who, for whatever reason, lack the ability to make important decisions for themselves). Here too, they can sue (or less often be sued) through guardians appointed by the court.

Capacity issues are rare, so litigants need not allege anything about "the capacity of a party to sue or be sued" under FRCP 9(a), which adds that litigants also need not allege "the authority of a party to be sued in a representative capacity," or even "the legal existence of an organized association of persons." A complaint may need to touch on these matters, however, to show that a court has jurisdiction: FRCP 8(a) requires complaints in civil suits in federal courts to include "a short and plain statement of the ground for the court's jurisdiction," and FRCP 17(a) recognizes that this requirement acknowledges that something about the claimant must be alleged "to show the jurisdiction of the court." Thus it is not necessary to allege that "Mary Martin is an adult" or "of sound mind," but it may be necessary to allege that she is a "citizen of Illinois" to show that her citizenship is diverse from the named defendant, alleged to be a "citizen of Ohio," which must be shown to establish diversity jurisdiction in a federal court. (In state courts, customarily jurisdictional matters need not be alleged.)

Convicted felons may sue or be sued, although "civil death" statutes in some states prevent incarcerated prisoners from bringing suit. Federal courts have not allowed these statutes to block prisoner suits seeking to vindicate constitutional rights under 42 USC §1983. See, e.g., Almond v. Kent, 459 F.2d 200 (4th Cir. 1972).

Not surprisingly, capacity to sue or be sued is determined by the law of the person's domicile, and the capacity of a corporation is determined by the law of the chartering state. See FRCP 17(b). "Domestication" statutes require corporations doing business in the state to appoint a local agent for service of process, to file bylaws and articles of incorporation, and to pay yearly fees, and most such statutes provide that failing to comply bars a corporation from bringing claims in the courts of the state. See Notes on Domestication Statutes (Chapter 3B1, supra). Federal courts honor such statutes in diversity suits. See Woods v. Interstate Realty Co., 337 U.S. 535 (1949) (Chapter 6A2, supra).

3. Real Party in Interest—In General (FRCP 17)

The real party in interest rule seeks to assure that the person or entity bringing a claim is one entitled to enforce it. Hence FRCP 17(a) says every suit "must be prosecuted in the name of the real party in interest." Being sure the claimant is entitled to advance the claim helps guard against the possibility that a defendant will be sued later by someone else, so FRCP 17(a) implements concerns similar to those of the compulsory joinder provision (FRCP 19 requires joinder of one whose absence brings a "substantial risk" that someone in the suit will incur "double, multiple, or otherwise inconsistent obligations").

This provision does not always ensure that the "real" beneficiary of a suit is the one who sues. Trusts, for example, are set up so care can be taken in managing money or other property in the best interests of a beneficiary, who may be a minor or someone else who might not be able to manage things, or to ensure that the property or money is used in a way that comports with the wishes of the settlor. In such situations, as FRCP 17(b) envisions, "a trustee of an express trust" is the real party in interest who may sue to enforce the rights of the trust itself.

The same idea applies to (a) executors, whose usual job is to carry out the wishes of a testator in managing the estate, (b) administrators, whose usual job is to handle an estate left by someone who died without a will, (c) guardians, who are usually court-appointed persons who care for someone who cannot care for himself (because of youth or old age or mental or physical infirmity), and (d) bailees, who usually hold property temporarily for another, as is true of companies that store goods for safekeeping without having title. Bailees were included, according to the ACN to FRCP 17(b), to "preserve the admiralty practice" under which the owner or master of a vessel can sue for damages to cargo, but "bailee" is broader and reaches other situations. See Bradley v. St. Louis Terminal Warehouse Co., 189 F.2d 818 (8th Cir. 1951) (warehouse company could sue trustee of bankrupt former owner of goods, who had sold them; plaintiff was holding goods on behalf of bank, to which goods were pledged as collateral on loan to bankrupt).

4. Real Party in Interest—Insured Parties (FRCP 17)

One might think the principle in FRCP 17 would require insurance carriers to be named as parties in litigation in many situations where, in practice, they are *not* so named and their role remains hidden from view.

Subrogation and Cooperation. Most insurance policies covering injury to persons or loss of property contain "subrogation" clauses, under which the carrier "steps into the shoes of" the insured after paying for her losses (less a deductible and subject to a maximum). They also contain "cooperation" clauses, under which the insured agrees to help the carrier if litigation ensues, and to accept representation by a lawyer chosen and compensated by the carrier. If losses or injuries for which the carrier has paid were caused by another's tortious conduct, and if the tortfeasor has money or carries insurance against liability, then suing the tortfeasor may be worthwhile.

Hence the carrier who paid the injured party may want to sue, and subrogation and cooperation clauses enable the carrier to do so.

To make the situation concrete, suppose Amy drives a car and carries insurance covering damage or loss of her car and medical expenses if she is injured, and her carrier is Atlantic Casualty. Suppose Ben also drives a car, and carries insurance covering liability, and his carrier is Pacific Auto. (Usually, both drivers have "comprehensive" coverage reaching their own losses and medical expenses, and also their own tort liability.) If Amy and Ben collide and Amy is injured and suffers damage to her car, Atlantic pays her losses and becomes "subrogated" to her right to sue Ben. If it would be worthwhile to sue—Atlantic will have tried to persuade Pacific to reimburse Atlantic for what it paid Amy—then Atlantic can sue.

In this situation, Atlantic and Pacific are likely to have the most at stake. Amy has been paid, and Ben—unless he is wealthy—will not likely be asked to pay a penny out of pocket even if he is at fault. One might think Atlantic would sue Pacific (the suit would be styled "Atlantic v. Pacific"). In most jurisdictions, however, that is not so. *Despite* the "real party in interest" rule, Amy will be the plaintiff and Ben will be the defendant (the suit is styled "Amy v. Ben"). The carriers will hire the lawyers, and Amy and Ben will cooperate in litigating.

Making Insurance Coverage Invisible. Why do we do things this way? Basically, insurance carriers go to great length to remain invisible, and the law accommodates their interests. From the perspective of Pacific (Ben's insurer), being invisible is preferable because the carrier does not want a jury (even a judge, in a bench trial) to be extravagant in awarding a high amount simply because Ben won't be hurt and a "deep pocket" institution like Pacific can afford it without "hurting anyone." From the perspective of Atlantic (Amy's insurer), being invisible is preferable because Amy as an individual who suffered injury and loss is a more sympathetic claimant, and a jury (or judge) is likely to award more to her than to Atlantic. See, e.g., Krohn v. New Jersey Full Insurance Underwriters Association, 720 A.2d 640, 642 (N.J. Super. App. Div. 1998) (efforts by lawyers to make jury aware of "irrelevant and prejudicial facts surrounding insurance coverage" have long been criticized; probative value of information on insurance is outweighed by risk of prejudice, as jurors "may recklessly award damages based upon the perceived 'deep pocket' of the carrier").

In such a suit, where Amy and Ben are the parties but recovery will be paid by (and go to) an insurance carrier, the role of insurance remains hidden. In the voir dire process by which juries are picked, questionnaires will ask potential jurors about their association or experiences with insurers, and those who work for or express negative attitudes about insurance can be excluded "for cause" (as you will see in Chapter 12). And the Rules of Evidence block proof of insurance, if offered to show negligence or due care. It is a strange and ironic fact that *sometimes* the existence of insurance arguably proves "due care" on the theory that one who obtains liability coverage is acting responsibly, hence is more likely to be careful, and *sometimes* the same point arguably proves "negligence," because one who purchases insurance no longer has to worry about causing damage (insurance is a "license to be careless"). FRE 411 blocks both these arguments.

At least some decisions let insurance carriers hide their roles *even when they can be sued directly*. If, for example, Amy wins a judgment against Ben, and if his carrier refuses to pay, Amy *can* sue Pacific Auto directly. In this setting, courts sometimes let the carrier keep from the jury the fact that it is an insurance company. See Bardis v. First Trenton Insurance Co., 971 A.2d 1062 (N.J. 2009) (plaintiff sued its own carrier under an uninsured motorist clause because the tortfeasor's coverage was insufficient; plaintiff's claim was "contractual," but it "has little to do with the contract of insurance and everything to do with the accident," and only the "happenstance" of minimal coverage brought the carrier into court).

Collateral Source Doctrine. One might ask why, if Amy has been paid for her losses and injuries, she has any claim against Ben? Can't he reduce his exposure by the amount that Amy collected? The answer is generally no. Under the "collateral source" doctrine, payments that Amy collects from Atlantic do *not* offset claims she can prove against Ben. The idea is that Amy should "have the benefit of her own thrift." She paid for the Atlantic policy and collected, and she should not have to "share with the wrongdoer" the recovery made possible by her insurance.

Not all carriers who pay for property losses and medical expenses bring suits against alleged tortfeasors. The carriers may not consider it worthwhile, and often—particularly in the setting sketched above in which Amy and Ben are the principal actors—carriers can work out liability issues among themselves. Atlantic and Pacific may agree, for example, that Ben's negligence caused the accident, and Pacific will reimburse Atlantic for payments that Atlantic makes to Amy. This system enables carriers to reassess rate structures, perhaps leading to an increase in premiums for Ben (or cancellation).

Insurance Doesn't Cover Everything. One element has been left out: If Amy suffered property loss and injuries, she has claims for "pain and suffering" that her insurance does not cover, and perhaps for economic loss (lost wages or future loss of economic opportunity on account of disability), also not covered by insurance. Hence she has an incentive to sue, and to seek a lawyer of her own choosing. The prospect of large recovery for pain and suffering, and perhaps lost wages or economic opportunities, can make Amy's case attractive to a lawyer, who might keep as much as half of any verdict won on her behalf, in our contingent fee system.

■ NOTES ON INSURED PARTIES

1. Isn't the silence of FRCP 17 on insurance carriers surprising? Doesn't the general principle in FRCP 17(a) suggest that Atlantic should be the plaintiff after it pays for Amy's losses and expenses, at least to the extent that these are included in the suit? In the *Aetna* case, decided a decade after the Civil Rules took effect, the Supreme Court said that indeed an insurance carrier *should* sue in its own name. *Aetna* was a consolidated appeal of three cases involving claims by carriers against the government, brought under the Federal Tort Claims Act, for personal injuries caused allegedly caused by government agents. In one, the carrier paid the claim of a federal employee under the workers' compensation law. In another, the insured was a private party allegedly injured by the negligence of a Forest Service employee driving a government vehicle. In the third, two carriers paid parts of losses sustained by the owner of property damaged by fire through the negligence of a government employee. The Court addressed the question whether the carriers should or could sue in their own name:

> FRCP 17(a) . . . provides that "Every action shall be prosecuted in the name of the real party in interest," and of course an insurer-subrogee, who has substantive equitable rights, qualifies as such. If the subrogee has paid an entire loss suffered by the insured, it is the only real party in interest and must sue in its own name. If it has paid only part of the loss, both the insured and insurer (and other insurers, if any, who have also paid portions of the loss) have substantive rights against the tortfeasor which qualify them as real parties in interest.
>
> In cases of partial subrogation the question arises whether suit may be brought by the insurer alone, whether suit must be brought in the name of the insured for his own use and for the use of the insurance company, or whether all parties in interest must join in the action. Under the common law practice rights acquired by subrogation could be enforced in an action at law only in the name of the insured to the insurer's use, as was also true of suits on assignments. Mr. Justice Stone characterized this rule as "a vestige of the common law's reluctance to admit that a chose in action may be assigned, (which) is today but a formality which has been widely abolished by legislation." Aetna Life Ins. Co. v. Moses, 287 U.S. 530, 540 (1933). . . . FRCP 17(a) was taken almost verbatim from Equity Rule 37. No reason appears why such a practice should now be required in cases of partial subrogation, since both insured and insurer "own" portions of the substantive right and should appear in the litigation in their own names.
>
> Although either party may sue, the United States, upon timely motion, may compel their joinder. Both are "necessary" parties. FRCP 19(b). The pleadings should be made to reveal and assert the actual interest of the plaintiff, and to indicate the interests of any others in the claim. Additional parties may be added at any stage of the proceedings, on motion of the United States, upon such terms as may be just.

United States v. Aetna Casualty & Surety Co., 338 U.S. 366, 380-381 (1949). *Aetna* suggests, doesn't it, that in federal court the carrier is the real party in interest insofar as it paid the claims of the insured and has been subrogated to her rights?

2. Some states construe their real party in interest rule the same way that *Aetna* interpreted FRCP 17. See, e.g., Broadnax v. Griswold, 17 So. 3d 656 (Ala.

Civ. App. 2008) (under insurance policy, payment of full compensation divested the insured of right to recover damages and made insurer the real party in interest). Despite *Aetna,* however, the prevailing rule in state courts is that a carrier, when subrogated to the claims of its insured after paying for the latter's losses, is *not* the real party in interest. See, e.g., Spectra Audio Research, Inc. v. Chon, 880 N.Y.S.2d 612 (N.Y. App. Div. 2009) (subrogation lets insurer stand in shoes of insured in seeking indemnification from third parties whose wrongdoing caused loss reimbursed by insurer, but suit can be brought in name of insured as an "exception" to the real party in interest rule). In New York, where *Spectra* was decided, the matter is codified. See McKinney's CPLR §1004 (insured person who has executed for a carrier "either a loan or subrogation receipt, trust agreement, or other similar instrument" may "sue or be sued" without joining carrier).

3. What about insurance carriers as *defendants?*

(a) The prevailing view is that an injured party has no claim against a tortfeasor's liability carrier: The person who caused the injury is the insured, not the carrier. Hence the law of most states does not let a claimant sue the tortfeasor's carrier "directly." It is different if the claimant obtains a judgment against the insured and the carrier refuses to pay because (for example) it claims that the policy was not in effect or does not cover the accident. Then a judgment-holding claimant can sue the carrier, and some states have statutes authorizing such suits. See, e.g., Ala. Code §27-23-2 (if judgment against the insured is not "satisfied within 30 days," claimant "may proceed against" the carrier). Reportedly, most states recognize this right. See, e.g., Norton v. Belarus Machinery of USA, Inc., 2005 WL 1501452 (M.D. Ala. 2005) (most states allow suits against the carrier after claimant obtains judgment against the insured).

(b) The real party in interest rule might be read to mean that liability carriers, particularly if they will pay a judgment, are the real party in interest on the defense side. Note, however, FRCP 17(a) says only that suits "must be prosecuted in the name of the real party in interest," suggesting that the concept applies to plaintiffs alone. Two states (Wisconsin and Louisiana) have "direct action" statutes authorizing injured claimants to sue carriers without first having sued (or obtained judgment against) the tortfeasor. See La. Stat. Ann. §22:1269 (injured persons "have a right of direct action against the insurer" and may sue "the insurer alone" or both the insurer and the insured); Wis. Stat. Ann. §632.33 (insurer is liable, up to policy limits, to "the persons entitled to recover against the insured" for death or personal injury or property damage, regardless whether liability is "presently established or is contingent"). A few states allow direct actions on the theory that claimants are third-party beneficiaries of insurance contracts. See Wachovia Insurance Services, Inc. v. Toomey, 994 So. 2d 980 (Fla. 2008).

(c) For purposes of the *Erie* doctrine (Chapter 6), state law allowing or not allowing direct actions is substantive, so selecting a federal rather than a state forum should not affect the matter. See, e.g., NAP, Inc. v. Shuttletex, Inc.,

112 F. Supp. 2d 369, 373 (S.D.N.Y. 2000) (state statute allowing suit against carrier only if claimant first obtains judgment against the insured is "substantive" under *Erie*).

(d) Recall that after abandoning *quasi-in-rem* type 2 jurisdiction in *Shaffer*, where the presence of property was a "jurisdictional hook" to force defendant to appear where the property is located, the Court refused to let plaintiff use attachment to forge a "judicially created" direct action statute. See Rush v. Savchuk, 444 U.S. 430 (1980) (in suit against Indiana motorist, claimant could not obtain jurisdiction by attaching liability policy in Minnesota) (described in Chapter 3C4, supra, in the Notes on General Jurisdiction, in note 4, after the *Goodyear* case).

5. Immunities from Suit

Various forms of immunity from suit are available, primarily to public officials and entities. Rule 8's list does not include "immunity," but usually it is viewed as an affirmative defense, so not raising it can waive it. Usually, defendants bear the burden of persuasion, but recall *Gomez* (Chapter 7C4, supra), where Justice Rehnquist agreed that immunity is an affirmative defense but said the burden of persuasion is another matter. See also note 3 in the Notes on Affirmative Defenses, set out after *Gomez*, citing cases indicating that some burdens relating to immunity fall on plaintiff, others on defendant.

The doctrine of sovereign immunity that came to America from England is the source of various forms of immunity today—as a matter of common law, in constitutional provisions, and sometimes in statutes or statutory interpretation. These doctrines are complex, and are examined in other courses (Federal Courts, Local Government, Constitutional Law). What follows is a brief account of important features that litigators need to know.

Federal Institutional Immunities. The United States cannot be sued unless Congress consents, but there are two vital limitations or exceptions:

First, litigants can seek injunctive relief against federal officials to keep them from acting in excess of their authority or implementing an unconstitutional statute. See Larson v. Domestic & Foreign Commerce Corp., 337 U.S. 682 (1949). Under *Larson*, however, acting with the authority conferred by a valid statute is a defense even if the conduct is otherwise tortious. Federal courts have jurisdiction because suits against federal officers fit the "arising under" statute in advancing claims under federal law, and can be brought under 28 USC §1331. See also 28 USC §1346 (conferring jurisdiction in federal courts over suits against the United States). In 1976, in an effort to resolve confusion arising from the limits stated or implied in *Larson*, Congress enacted a statute formally waiving sovereign immunity for suits seeking injunctive relief against federal officers. See 5 USC §702.

Second, the *Bivens* doctrine allows damage claims against federal officers for acting in violation of Fourth Amendment rights (forbidding "unreasonable searches and seizures"). See Bivens v. Six Unknown Named Agents of the Federal Bureau of Narcotics, 403 U.S. 388 (1971) (allowing damage claims arising out of illegal drug raid). Recall that 42 USC §1983 authorizes suits against *state* officials who violate constitutional rights. At least in the area of Fourth Amendment violations, *Bivens* accomplishes something similar for citizens injured by *federal* officials.

Perhaps the largest area of consent to suits against the United States embraces tort claims arising out of negligent misconduct by federal agents. Under the Federal Tort Claims Act (enacted in 1946), claimants can sue in federal court for damages arising out of everything from malpractice in VA Hospitals to negligent operation of government vehicles. See 28 USC §§2674-2678. The Act incorporates the law of the state where the conduct took place, and in this sense state tort law is woven into the fabric of federal law. The Act has limitations: Punitive damage claims are not allowed; attorneys' fees are limited to 25 percent of a judgment or 20 percent of settlement; judges (not juries) decide the cases; suit under the statute bars other claims against the agent in question; relief may be had for negligence, but not on theories of strict liability or for most intentional torts. And the statute recognizes a major exception for "discretionary functions," which shields the government against claims stemming from policy choices by officials. Another critical exception, recognized in cases but not expressly provided by statute, covers injuries arising during military service. See Feres v. United Sates, 340 U.S. 135 (1950).

Beyond the vast area covered by the Federal Tort Claims Act, many statutes authorize monetary recovery against the government, and jurisdiction is for the most part vested in the Court of Federal Claims, which hears cases involving suits for tax refunds, taking of private property for public use, claims involving military personnel, and suits by government contractors.

State Institutional Immunities. Under the Eleventh Amendment, federal courts cannot hear suits against states. Although the wording suggests only that federal courts cannot hear suits brought against a state by a citizen of another state, the Amendment has been interpreted to bar suit in federal court by persons from any state against a state. See Hans v. Louisiana, 134 U.S. 1 (1890).

Importantly, the Eleventh Amendment does *not* bar federal suits by the United States against a state, nor suits by one state against another, nor suits against cities or municipalities, although the status of suits against state agencies is in disarray, and sometimes suits are allowed, but sometimes not. In another important wrinkle, the "stripping" doctrine established more than a century ago in Ex Parte Young, 209 U.S. 123 (1908), means that the Eleventh Amendment does not bar suit against a state *officer*. Such a suit does *not* count as a suit against a state, so long as the plaintiff is seeking what amounts to injunctive relief, although the contrary is true if plaintiff seeks monetary relief that would be paid out of the state treasury. The "stripping" doctrine takes its name from the fact that in such a suit the state is "stripped" of its immunity, because the officer *is* the state for purposes of constitutional commands (no "state" shall deprive a person of due process or equal protection) but is *not* the state for purposes of the Eleventh Amendment. Essentially, this doctrine lets citizens sue to block or correct behavior by state officers and institutions that would violate federal law or the Constitution.

The doctrine of *Ex Parte Young* paves the way for federal courts to award injunctive relief against states, but not damages. Of course injunctive relief can lead to higher costs: If, for example, a federal court orders a state to improve its welfare system, it may cost the state more money, but the Court has concluded that this fact does not stand in the way, so long as the relief asks for future compliance, as opposed to payments for past shortcomings. See Edelman v. Jordan, 415 U.S. 651 (1974). Also Eleventh Amendment immunity does not protect state officials from being sued for damages in federal court. Recall Carey v. Piphus, 435 U.S. 247 (1978) (Chapter 1B), which illustrates this principle in a suit seeking damages and injunctive relief against school officials under §1983. More recently, you have learned that such officials may have qualified immunity defenses, see Chapter 7B1 and 7C4, supra, but these can be overcome in appropriate cases. States often reimburse or indemnify officials against whom money damages are awarded, and sometimes state law requires such reimbursement, but this fact does not mean that a damage award entered against a state official violates Eleventh Amendment immunity. See, e.g., Chestnut v. Lowell, 305 F.3d 18 (1st Cir. 2002).

Notable as well is the fact that Eleventh Amendment immunity can be overridden by statute when Congress acts under powers conferred by the Fourteenth Amendment (authorizing "appropriate" federal legislation to "enforce" the amendment). See Fitzpatrick v. Bitzer, 427 U.S. 445 (1978) (allowing damage recovery against state under Title VII of Civil Rights Act of 1964 for discrimination in employment). Under *Fitzpatrick,* the Court has held that 42 USC §1988, which allows the award of attorney fees to prevailing plaintiffs to in suits to enforce rights of equality, overrides Eleventh Amendment immunity, when such fees are incurred in seeking injunctive relief. See Hutto v. Finney, 437 U.S. 678 (1978).

Congressional power to override Eleventh Amendment immunity is limited. First, there must be a clear statement in the legislation itself, so §1983, the all-important statute authorizing suits against persons acting "under color of state law" for violating federal rights, does *not* override Eleventh Amendment immunity. See Quern v. Jordan, 440 U.S. 332 (1979) (§1983 "does not explicitly and by clear language indicate on its face an intent to sweep away the immunity of the States," so it does not). Second, Congress can override Eleventh Amendment immunity authorizing damage recovery against states to enforce rights already recognized by courts, but cannot create new rights in this way or expand existing rights. See City of Boerne v. Flores, 421 U.S. 507 (1997). See generally the discussion of these matters in Erwin Chemerinsky, Federal Jurisdiction, §§7.4-7.7 (5th ed. 2007).

When claimants sue cities or state agencies, however, they cannot recover damages on the theory that applies in suits against private companies. In *that* setting, the question is whether the tortfeasor was acting within the scope of his duties, or (if not) whether the entity should be liable for failure properly to control or curb his conduct (we speak of "respondeat superior"). A claimant suing a city or agency for damages under §1983, however, must show that the conduct in question executed a "policy or custom" of the city. Congress did not, the Court concluded in *Monell,* intend to hold municipalities liable under §1983 "on a *respondeat superior* theory," but wanted to limit municipal liability to cases where a person acted "pursuant to official municipal policy," thus "caused a constitutional tort." Monell v. Department of Social Services of City of New York, 436 U.S. 658, 691 (1978).

Personal Immunities. State and federal officials enjoy personal immunities from liability. Indeed, *because* of exceptions to institutional immunities, *personal* immunities become even more important.

Sometimes officials have "absolute" immunity. The President is absolutely immune from civil liability for actions performed in his capacity as chief executive, see Nixon v. Fitzgerald, 457 U.S. 751 (1982), although *not* during his time in office for civil liability incurred before taking office, see Clinton v. Jones, 520 U.S. 681 (1997). Also blessed with "absolute immunity" are judges performing judicial acts, state legislators, Senators and Representatives and their staffs in performing legislative functions, prosecutors performing prosecutorial duties, and police and law enforcement officers testifying in court (not liable in damages even for perjury).

More common are "qualified" immunities that protect state and federal actors performing discretionary functions in good faith. In its decision in *Harlow,* the Court described the standard in these terms: "[O]fficials performing discretionary functions generally are shielded from liability for civil damages insofar as their conduct does not violate clearly established statutory or constitutional rights of which a reasonable person would have known." See Harlow v. Fitzgerald, 457 U.S. 800, 818 (1982).

B JOINDER OF CLAIMS

Under FRCP 18(a), a party may join "as many claims as it has against an opposing party." This provision authorizes a plaintiff suing one defendant to join in the suit as many different claims as he chooses, regardless of whether they are related in any way.

There is no limit on the *kind* or *number* of claims that may be joined: If Pilsner sues Davis for breach of a contract to install sidewalks, Pilsner may join a claim for battery arising out of a fight in a local watering hole that has no connection with the contract claim. The idea is not so much that it is efficient to try disparate claims together, but that it is better for opposing parties to settle all their differences at once. More often than not, the claims that one plaintiff has against another are related, and one reason to bring all the claims that the plaintiff's lawyer can think of is that the proof might support recovery on one claim but not another (and the statute of limitations for one claim may differ from that for another claim). See, e.g., Great Plains Federal Savings and Loan Association v. Dabney, 846 P.3d 1088 (Okla. 1993) (bank's claim against law firm alleging breach of contract was timely even if claim in tort alleging malpractice would have been barred).

Notice that FRCP 18 covers not only claims that a *plaintiff* may bring against a *defendant,* but claims that other parties may add. If Pilsner sues Davis and Elson for breach of contract to install sidewalks, Davis may have a claim against Elson arising out of the same transaction (installing sidewalks). In this situation, FRCP 13(g) allows one defendant to bring a claim against another defendant (these are called "crossclaims"). If Davis brings this claim against Elson, then Davis may *also* bring a claim against Elson for libel even if it has no other connection to the suit.

Permissive versus Voluntary? Three rules speak explicitly of joining claims, all in permissive terms. Rule 18 says the plaintiff "may join" all the claims she has against the defendant; Rule 13(g) says a defendant "may" bring claims against codefendants (if they arise out of the same "transaction or occurrence" that plaintiff sued on); Rule 14(a) says a defendant "may" bring claims against a nonparty "who is or may be liable" for whatever the defendant might owe the plaintiff. To be sure, Rule 13(a) contains a "compulsory" element: A defendant "must" bring against the plaintiff any counterclaim that defendant has against the plaintiff if it arises (once again) out of the same "transaction or occurrence" as plaintiff's claim. But Rule 13(b) speaks again in permissive terms: A defendant "may" bring any *other* counterclaim she has against the plaintiff, which means that counterclaims are compulsory if they arise out of the same transaction, but otherwise are permissive.

In a sense, joining *claims* is usually permissive, as far as the Rules are concerned. In a real way, however, this appearance is misleading: You will see in Chapter 14 that the doctrine of *res judicata*, not codified in the Rules, has real impact here. Oversimplifying slightly, this doctrine means that a party who brings one claim and *could* bring another claim arising out of the same transaction may be foreclosed from bringing the other claim later if she does not bring it the first time.

C JOINDER OF PARTIES

1. Permissive (FRCP 20)

Under Rule 20, claimants may join as plaintiffs if "they assert any right to relief jointly, severally, or in the alternative," so long as their claims arise out of "the same transaction, occurrence, or series of transactions" and they raise "any question of law or fact" common to other claims in the suit. Similarly, defendants may be joined in a suit if claims are asserted against them "jointly, severally, or in the alternative," and if they arise out of "the same transaction, occurrence, or series of transactions or occurrences" and if they raise "any question of law or fact" that is common to other claims in the suit.

Ciba Plant, McIntosh, Alabama

The Ciba Plant in McIntosh, Alabama that was the subject of the suit described in the *Fisher* case became part of BASF in a merger occurring in 2008. According to its website in 2012, the plant employs 451 persons and makes "antioxidants to preserve plastics," chemicals used to stabilize colors in furniture and automobile coatings, "tinuvins" that "absorb damaging ultraviolet light in automotive finishes, photographic inks and outdoor stains," and "stibenics" that serve as "optical brighteners in laundry detergents." McIntosh, Alabama is a small town in the western part of the state about 44 miles north of Mobile, with 244 inhabitants, according to the 2000 Census.

FISHER v. CIBA SPECIALTY CHEMICALS CORPORATION

Southern District of Alabama
245 F.R.D. 539 (S.D. Ala. 2007)

WILLIAM H. STEELE, United States District Judge.

This matter comes before the Court on Defendants' Motion to Sever. The Motion has been briefed and is ripe for disposition at this time.

This action involves claims brought by five individual plaintiffs who own property in or around Washington County, Alabama alleging diminution in value to their real estate caused by environmental contamination from a nearby chemical manufacturing facility that is or has been owned at various times by defendants. Plaintiffs contend that their properties are contaminated by DDT emanating from Ciba's McIntosh plant. [The case was originally filed as a class suit, but the court denied class certification because, *inter alia*, plaintiffs did not show that common questions predominated.] In the wake of that ruling, the plaintiffs have continued to prosecute their individual causes of action on state-law theories of negligence, conspiracy, strict liability, trespass, nuisance, intentional misrepresentation, negligent misrepresentation, fraud and fraudulent concealment, constructive fraud, and punitive/exemplary damages, as well as a federal claim under the Racketeer Influenced and Corrupt Organizations Act, 18 USC §§1961 *et seq.* As reflected in the Fourth Amended Class Action Complaint filed on October 30, 2006, all five plaintiffs (Jessie Fisher, Arlean Reed, Barbara Byrd, Ronald McIntyre and Sharon Greer) assert the same claims against the same defendants on the same legal theories.

On April 27, 2007, defendants filed a Motion to Sever, pursuant to FRCP 20 and 21, seeking to splinter the trial of these proceedings (which is slated for the August 2007 trial term) into five separate trials, one for each plaintiff. Defendants ground their Motion on assertions that a common trial would be inefficient and prejudicial.[2] Plaintiffs oppose the Motion, arguing that severing the plaintiffs' essentially identical claims would effect great inefficiency, undue delay and undue expense, while also burdening the Court with presiding over a largely similar trial five times in a row.

Defendants' Motion is filed pursuant to FRCP 20(b), which provides that courts "may order separate trials or make other orders to prevent delay or prejudice," and FRCP 21, which provides that "[a]ny claim against a party may be severed and proceeded with separately" [a 2007 amendment changed the language slightly—Ed.].[3]

The determination of whether to grant a motion to sever is left to the discretion of the trial court. See Alexander v. Fulton County, Ga., 207 F.3d 1303, 1324 n.16 (11th Cir. 2000) ("The trial court likewise has discretion

---

[2] Defendants also argue in their Motion that severance is warranted because plaintiffs never moved for consolidation and this Court never entered an order consolidating the five cases. But this argument turns the posture of this case on its head. The five plaintiffs here did not bring five separate cases; to the contrary, they brought a single integrated lawsuit. Nothing in the Federal Rules of Civil Procedure would obligate them to seek permission from the Court to consolidate their claims; after all, plaintiffs' claims are already consolidated on the face of the pleadings. Rather, the onus is on defendants to seek severance of the various plaintiffs' claims if defendants believe that such claims were soldered together improperly or that some undue prejudice or inefficiency would result from trying them en masse. . . .

[3] Defendants do not proceed under Rule 42(b); therefore, the Court will not consider that procedure here. See McDaniel v. Anheuser-Busch, Inc., 987 F.2d 298, 304 (5th Cir. 1993) (explaining that Rule 21 motions and Rule 42(b) motions "are distinct and preferably should be treated as such," even though they are often commingled in the caselaw).

under Rule 20(b) to order separate trials 'to prevent delay or prejudice.'"). Among the factors considered in exercising that discretion include whether the claims arise from the same transaction or occurrence, whether they present some common question of law or fact, whether severance would facilitate settlement or judicial economy, and the relative prejudice to each side if the motion is granted or denied. See, e.g., Disparte v. Corporate Executive Bd., 223 F.R.D. 7, 12 (D.D.C. 2004) (severance of plaintiffs' claims turns on considerations of whether claims arise from same transaction or occurrence, whether claims present some common question of law or fact, whether settlement of claims or judicial economy would be facilitated, whether prejudice would be avoided if severance were granted, and whether different witnesses and documentary proof are required for the separate claims); Donato v. Fitzgibbons, 172 F.R.D. 75, 85 (S.D.N.Y. 1997) ("A court may order separate trials for three reasons: to avoid prejudice, to provide for convenience, or to expedite the proceedings and economize the use of resources."). In considering whether to order separate trials of any claims or issues, "the paramount consideration must remain a fair and impartial trial to all litigants through a balance of benefits and prejudice." Medtronic Xomed, Inc. v. Gyrus ENT LLC, 440 F. Supp. 2d 1333, 1334 (M.D. Fla. 2006).

In assessing whether severance is appropriate under Rules 20 and 21, one factor is whether the claims arise from the same transaction. The Eleventh Circuit has opined that the term "transaction is a word of flexible meaning" that "may comprehend a series of many occurrences, depending not so much upon the immediateness of their connection as upon their logical relationship." *Alexander,* 207 F.3d at 1323. Likewise, for purposes of the commonality element, the *Alexander* panel stressed that "Rule 20 does not require that *all* questions of law and fact raised by the dispute be common, but only that *some* question of law or fact be common to all parties."

At the class certification stage, the Court has already found in this case that common issues do not predominate over individual-specific issues pursuant to Rule 23(b)(3). But the Rule 20 inquiry is distinct from that under Rule 23, and a ruling against the plaintiffs on the latter in no way suggests (much less mandates) a like outcome with respect to the former. Stated differently, there is no predomination prerequisite for joinder of multiple plaintiffs' claims, and Rule 20 contemplates a much lower threshold for allowing plaintiffs' claims to proceed to trial together than is required by Rule 23 for class certification. The touchstone of the Rule 20 joinder/severance analysis is whether the interests of efficiency and judicial economy would be advanced by allowing the claims to travel together, and whether any party would be prejudiced if they did. The Court now turns to that inquiry.

Defendants articulate four different grounds for their contention that severance of each plaintiff's claims from each other plaintiff's claims for trial purposes is appropriate. In particular, defendants argue that (i) plaintiffs' claims do not arise from the same transaction or occurrence; (ii) plaintiffs will rely on individualized evidence to prove their claims; (iii) defendants will invoke individual-specific defenses; and (iv) a common trial will be prejudicial to defendants.

The first three of defendants' contentions logically should be considered together, because they all are fundamentally challenges to the efficiency of trying all five plaintiffs' claims in a single trial. As the Order denying class certification spelled out in exhaustive detail, the evidence at trial will undoubtedly include both a core nucleus of common issues (*e.g.*, whether and when Ciba created DDT wastes; whether, when and how those wastes may have migrated offsite; the pathways of that migration; the characteristics and impacts of those chemicals on property values; whether Ciba misled the public concerning DDT contamination; whether Ciba manipulated government regulators on that point; whether Ciba conspired with others to avoid cleaning up the contamination; etc.)[4] and a vector of plaintiff-specific issues (*e.g.*, whether plaintiff's property is contaminated with DDT, whether that contamination came from Ciba, whether plaintiff's claims are timely, the extent to which plaintiff's property declined in value, whether plaintiff relied on defendants' alleged fraudulent misrepresentations, whether plaintiff suffered injury as a result of such reliance, whether plaintiff's reliance was to his or her detriment, etc.).

Plainly, to conduct a single joint trial would be a strategy marked by both efficiencies, inasmuch as the issues of common proof need only be presented and decided once, and inefficiencies, inasmuch as there will be a certain degree of unique evidence and argument as to each plaintiff's claims that is not germane to the other plaintiffs' claims. What the Court must do, then, is to weigh and balance the efficiencies of trying all five plaintiffs' claims together against the inefficiencies of trying all five plaintiffs' claims together. Not surprisingly, each side advocates that the scales tip in a different direction. After careful consideration of the respective arguments of counsel, the Court is persuaded that, while neither approach is optimal, the interests of efficiency would be best served by keeping the plaintiffs' claims together for trial in their present consolidated posture. The Court anticipates that there will be substantial overlapping background evidence for all plaintiffs' claims concerning the environmental history and activities of the Ciba plant, and the

---

[4] These commonalities are sufficient to satisfy the flexible definition of "transaction" employed for Rule 20 purposes. Contrary to defendants' position, plaintiffs' evidence of the creation and migration of DDT wastes from Ciba's McIntosh facility supports a conclusion that plaintiffs' claims all arise from the same transaction and occurrence, given the "logical relationship" of the "series of many occurrences" that gives rise to those claims. *Alexander,* 207 F.3d at 1323. Likewise, the shared issues outlined above unquestionably constitute the requisite common questions of law or fact necessary to support joinder under Rule 20. To the extent that defendants maintain that the five plaintiffs are misjoined in this lawsuit, then, that argument fails.

interactions of Ciba with the media, government regulators, and alleged co-conspirators. Moreover, plaintiffs have argued, and defendants have not disputed, that it is probable that the same roster of nine expert witnesses (three for plaintiffs and six for defendants), all of whom live out of state, will be called to testify with respect to each plaintiff's claims. To require these nine experts (not to mention counsel, many of whom live in Texas and Louisiana) to travel to Mobile, Alabama five times in quick succession (or to sit and wait in a hotel for days on end) to testify in five different trials would be financially foolhardy and needlessly wasteful of the parties' economic resources, potentially even rendering these trials cost-prohibitive.[5] Moreover, if these nine experts would be testifying to substantially similar, partially overlapping opinions in each of these five trials, the attendant drag on the efficient administration of justice would be considerable, as this Court would be subjected to something akin to a judicial *Groundhog Day*. Under the specific circumstances of this case, it appears far preferable from a judicial economy standpoint to hear all of the evidence once, including both common and plaintiff-specific facts, in a single trial proceeding than to hear the common evidence five times, with plaintiff-specific testimony being confined to each plaintiff's individual trial. Accordingly, the Court finds that considerations of efficiency and delay do not militate in favor of a Rule 21 severance.[6]

Defendants also maintain that a joint trial would be "extremely prejudicial" to them.[7] This objection is apparently threefold, to wit: (a) a multiplicity of plaintiff-specific facts will confuse the jury; (b) to the extent that one plaintiff's claims are stronger than the others' evidence as to that plaintiff may unfairly taint the jury as to the other plaintiffs' claims; and (c) consolidation for trial will allow plaintiffs to "bolster their individually weak cases by a suggestion that contamination is widespread." None of these considerations are persuasive. As an initial matter, the risk of jury confusion in determining which facts attach to which plaintiffs appears minimal. Federal juries are routinely asked to parse facts that are relevant to particular claims or

[5] To illustrate the point, the aggregated hourly rate of these nine expert witnesses approaches $3,000, which equals or exceeds the county-assessed property values of four of the five plaintiffs' property at issue herein.
[6] Defendants decry plaintiffs' efficiency arguments, maintaining that "[e]conomy is a particularly illusory justification when Plaintiffs' counsel have indicated they may file as many as 2000 additional cases involving McIntosh residents alleging personal or property injuries due to alleged contamination." This assertion confuses the issue. The question before the Court is whether the claims of these five plaintiffs (and no others) should be tried collectively or separately. Whatever future intentions plaintiffs' counsel may or may not have concerning as yet unfiled lawsuits on behalf of other persons is utterly irrelevant and will not be considered.
[7] Defendants even go so far as to assert that a joint trial would violate their Seventh Amendment right to a trial by jury. Of course, even if all five plaintiffs' claims are tried together, those claims will still be tried to a jury, with appropriate limiting instructions as to evidence relevant to the claims of one plaintiff but not to others. The Court is unaware of any authority for the proposition that the joinder of multiple plaintiffs' claims in such circumstances is tantamount to a Seventh Amendment violation, and defendants have cited none. . . .

particular parties, and are able to do so without difficulty so long as counsel presents the evidence in a cogent, orderly fashion that makes clear which evidence attaches to which particular claims or defenses. Furthermore, defendants' "taint" argument disregards the ready availability of limiting instructions (should counsel draft and propose same) designed specifically to circumscribe the uses for which particular evidence may be considered, as well as pattern charges stressing that the claims and defenses of each party must be considered separately and independently from those of each other party.[8] There is no reason to believe that a jury would be unwilling or unable to follow such instructions in this case; therefore, defendants' protestations of prejudice are misplaced.

Finally, as for defendants' stated concern that the joinder of plaintiffs' claims in one trial might give rise to a suggestion that contamination from the Ciba plaint is widespread, the Court fully anticipates that plaintiffs' evidence—whether presented in one trial or five trials—will be that the alleged contamination is, in fact, widespread. Thus, this "suggestion" will be before the jury in plaintiffs' evidentiary submission at trial, irrespective of whether severance is granted.

In short, the Court finds that defendants have failed to make a showing of prejudice sufficient to justify the heavy burden that would be visited on the litigants and this Court alike by virtue of the proposed fragmentation of the plaintiffs' claims into five overlapping trials.

There are unquestionably common issues of fact and law linking all five plaintiffs' claims of diminution in property value from alleged DDT contamination on their properties arising from activities at Ciba's chemical manufacturing plant in McIntosh, Alabama, and all such claims clearly arise from the same transaction or occurrence for Rule 20 purposes. As such, plaintiffs' joinder of all of their claims into one lawsuit was proper. Those claims may be severed from one another under Rule 21 in the Court's discretion based on considerations of efficiency, judicial economy and prejudice. Here, if plaintiffs' claims are disaggregated into five separate, repetitive jury trials, the expense to the parties and the drain on scarce judicial resources will be considerable, perhaps even enormous. By contrast, the risk of prejudice to defendants arising from the cumulative presentation of all

---

[8] For example, Section 6.2 of the Basic Instructions of the Eleventh Circuit Pattern Jury Instructions reads, in part, "When more than one claim is involved, and when more than one defense is asserted, you should consider each claim and each defense separately." This pattern charge could readily be adapted to address defendants' concern. Similarly, a charge such as the following could be given: "Although there are [five] plaintiffs in this action, it does not follow from that fact alone that if one plaintiff is entitled to recover, [the others] are entitled to recover. The defendant is entitled to a fair consideration as to each plaintiff, just as each plaintiff is entitled to a fair consideration of that plaintiff's claim against the defendant." Federal Jury Practice and Instructions (5th ed.) §103.13. An instruction along these lines would alleviate any reasonable concern that defendants might harbor on this point.

plaintiffs' evidence in a single trial proceeding is remote. Contrary to defendants' position, nothing in this arrangement would infringe on their Seventh Amendment right to trial by jury. Whatever risk of prejudice might exist is satisfactorily attenuated by the availability of limiting instructions and jury charges to ensure that the jury does not use any admitted evidence for any improper purpose. For all of these reasons, in the discretion of the Court, the Motion to Sever is denied. The claims of all five plaintiffs will be tried concurrently, before a single jury, in the August 2007 trial term.

■ NOTES ON PERMISSIVE JOINDER OF PARTIES

1. Suppose the five claimants each owned homes located near the Ciba plant in McIntosh, Alabama (a town of about 250 people 45 miles north of Mobile in the southwest corner of the state), and they sued Ciba because its newly built parking lot was insufficient to accommodate the cars of its employees, who were parking in plaintiffs' neighborhood, depriving residents of parking spots. Would joinder be proper? Would it matter whether plaintiffs sought damages or an injunction?

2. Obviously, the term "series" of transactions or occurrences, as we find it in FRCP 20, could embrace almost anything. Suppose, for example, three homeowners purchase insurance covering fire loss from the same company, and their homes burn in separate fires. Suppose the carrier refuses to pay all three claims. Can the three homeowners join in a single lawsuit against the carrier? See Sieron v. Hanover Fire and Casualty Insurance Co., 485 F. Supp. 2d 954 (S.D. Ill. 2007) (such claims raise common questions of law and fact, but "do not arise out of the same transaction, occurrence, or series of transactions or occurrences"). See also Ex Parte Novartis Pharmaceuticals Corp., 975 So. 2d 297 (Ala. 2007) ("series of transactions" has flexible meaning, but requires more than similar goods used for similar purpose; claims against companies were not "links in the same chain" where State does not allege conspiracy or concerted action; consumer who buys boat, car, and tractor and finances purchases through separate lenders cannot sue all of them in one suit because claims "do not arise from the same transaction"). How does *Fisher* construe "transaction" or "occurrence," or "series of transactions or occurrences"?

3. Rule 20 also contains a "common question" requirement. What function does it serve? How does the court handle it? Does the stress on overlapping evidence serve as a proxy for the common question requirement? Under FRCP 23(a), class actions are proper only if they involve common questions (all class actions must raise "questions of law or fact common to the class") and class suits under FRCP 23(b)(3) can go forward only if common questions "predominate." Why doesn't rejecting a class suit under FRCP 23(b)(3) also lead to severing the claims?

4. Rule 20(b) authorizes "separate trials" and other measures to "protect a party against embarrassment, delay, expense, or other prejudice." What prejudice does Ciba fear? The Rules of Evidence generally do not allow use of "other acts" to prove what a *person* did on a particular occasion. See FRE 404 (with some exceptions, evidence of character "is not admissible for the purpose of proving action in conformity therewith on a particular occasion"). On the other hand, FRE 407 authorizes evidence of the "routine practice of an organization" to prove its conduct on a particular occasion. If evidence of what Ciba did to one parcel were inadmissible as proof of what it did to another parcel, that would support a claim of prejudice to Ciba arising out of a joint trial, wouldn't it? Could Ciba be prejudiced even if such proof *were* admissible and could be used in this way?

5. *Fisher* is firm on the point that all five claims are to be tried together. It would be possible under FRCP 20, wouldn't it, to maintain the five claims as a single lawsuit but conduct separate trials if the claims do not settle? See FRCP 42(b) (court may order separate trials of "claims, crossclaims, counterclaims, or third-party claims" brought in a single suit). It is also possible to go in the opposite direction: Under FRCP 42(a), if each of the five claimants in *Fisher* had filed separate suits, the court could "join for hearing or trial" all of the claims. Between FRCP 20 and FRCP 42, it is possible to split a single suit into multiple trials or combine different suits (if pending in the same court) for a single trial.

2. Compulsory (FRCP 19)

Rule 19 addresses the subject of compulsory joinder: What parties *must join* as claimants in a suit or *be joined* as defending parties in order to have a viable suit? In a sense, Rule 19 is about what it takes to have a "whole" lawsuit. Transactions giving rise to conflicting claims or rights are infinitely varied. If one party involved in such transactions sues another, we do not always wind up with a dispute that can be resolved in a satisfactory manner. One piece of a larger matrix of disagreement and conflict may not be adequate in size or shape to enable a court to do much good, and proceeding without others involved in the transaction might be unfair to the others or to parties in the suit.

What Does "Indispensable" Mean? What Does "Necessary" Mean? The compulsory joinder concept came in for early criticism, on the ground that it rested on unworkable categories, but even more profoundly on the ground that it hobbled courts in cases where absent parties could not be included on account of jurisdictional limitations. Much of the blame was laid at the feet of the Supreme Court for its decision in Shields v. Barrow, 58 U.S. 130 (1854), which recognized the categories of "necessary," meaning parties who had to be joined if possible, and "indispensable," meaning parties who were *so essential* that the court could not act without them. If an absent party was in the latter category, the suit had to be dismissed if he could not be joined because there was no *in personam* jurisdiction over him (as would happen if he were beyond reach of service of process, or lacking minimum contacts) or no subject matter jurisdiction (as would happen in a diversity suit if he was needed as a defendant but his citizenship was the same as that of a plaintiff, so his presence would violate the complete diversity rule).

Unfortunately, the categories of "necessary" and "indispensable" parties could not be applied reliably. In an influential article, Professor John Reed called for abandonment of these labels. He argued that FRCP 19 should be rewritten in functional terms, and complained about the "fallacy" that the absence of a party deprives the court of power to act with respect to the parties before it. See John Reed, *Compulsory Joinder of Parties in Civil Actions,* 55 Mich. L. Rev. 327, 330 (1957). See also Geoffrey Hazard, *Indispensable Party: The Historical Origin of a Procedural Phantom*, 61 Colum. L. Rev. 1254, 1255 (1961). In response to such criticism, FRCP 19 was rewritten in 1968, when it took its present form.

As rewritten, Rule 19 does not use the term "indispensable." More importantly, the Rule speaks functionally, inviting a two-part inquiry. First, the court is to decide whether the absent party should be joined under Rule 19(a). If the answer is yes but the party cannot be joined, the court is to move to a second inquiry: Are the factors that led to a decision that the absent party should be joined *so compelling* that the suit should be dismissed if he cannot be? The message is that the court should try its best to go forward without someone who cannot be joined, and should only dismiss in an extreme situation. In effect, Rule 19 takes largely the approach that Professor Reed advanced. Still, Rule 19 is a forbidding and difficult rule, even in its reworked form, and decisions applying it are among the most difficult to understand.

First Inquiry: Who Must Be Joined? Rule 19(a) provides three criteria to help figure out who must be included, and the underlying concepts are easily stated. First is the matter of "complete relief," and the question is whether the court can provide an adequate remedy if the absent party is not joined. Second is the matter of prejudice to an absent party, and the question is whether "as a practical matter" the interests of that party will be adversely affected if the suit goes forward without it. Third is the matter of prejudice to parties already in the suit, and the question is whether they will be at risk of "incurring double, multiple, or otherwise inconsistent obligations" if the suit goes forward without the absent party.

In considering the complete relief criterion, it would be plausible to require a claimant to include as defendants all who might be liable for plaintiff's injuries. Sometimes, naming fewer than all means that a claimant cannot recover every dollar of damages: Tort liability in ordinary negligence actions usually is proportional to the degree of fault or causation, so a defending party who is only 60 percent responsible is liable for only 60 percent of the damages. Sometimes, naming fewer than all defendants does not prevent a claimant from getting a judgment for every dollar, but not naming other parties still means that a victorious plaintiff has fewer assets against which a favorable judgment may be enforced. Most courts, however, view the "complete relief" criterion as *not* standing in the way in either of these cases. Most say this criterion requires only that the court be able to grant complete relief *as measured by the parties already in the suit.* See General Refractories Co. v. First State Ins. Co., 500 F.3d 306, 313 (3d Cir. 2007) (under state law, if multiple insurance policies are "triggered for an indivisible loss," the insured may select the policy on which to sue; even if liability is several and not joint, claimant may obtain complete relief in a suit against one of the severally liable parties); MasterCard International Inc. v. Visa International Service Ass'n, Inc., 471 F.3d 377, 386 (2d Cir. 2006) (FRCP 19(a)(1) "is concerned only with those who are already parties").

In considering prejudice to absent parties, we confront a paradox: Non-parties can never be "bound," so one can argue that no absent party can *ever* be adversely affected by a judgment. FRCP 19, however, embodies the conviction that even absent persons or entities can be adversely affected in ways that count enough to require their presence. In a 1989 decision, the Supreme Court held that white firefighters in Birmingham, Alabama must have a chance to challenge a consent decree entered in a class suit brought on behalf of black firefighters, since the decree put in place a program that had an impact on hiring and promotion. The opinion implied that white firefighters should have been made parties, rejecting arguments that it was up to them to intervene, and not up to the plaintiffs to include them. See Martin v. Wilks, 490 U.S. 755 (1989).

Second Inquiry: Can the Court Proceed Without the Missing Party? Rule 19(b) applies when a court under FRCP 19(a) has identified someone who should be in the suit but "cannot be made a party." In this circumstance, courts consider (1) "the extent" to which a judgment rendered *without* the missing party would be "prejudicial" to that party or to those already in the suit, (2) whether this prejudice could be "lessened or avoided" by "shaping" the relief, including "protective provisions," or taking "other measures," (3) whether a judgment rendered without the missing party will really be adequate, and (4) whether plaintiff will have "an adequate remedy" if the suit is dismissed because the absent party cannot be joined.

Perhaps the most common reason a missing party cannot be joined is that the court cannot exercise jurisdiction over it. In one Georgia case involving an attempt to clear title to waterfront property, the court could not proceed without the Tennessee Valley Authority, which "operates and exercises dominion over" the lake, and the TVA is a federal entity that can only be sued in federal court. See Dixon v. Cole, 589 S.E.2d 94 (Ga. 2003). In many suits in federal court that proceed on the basis of diversity jurisdiction, a party that should be joined would destroy diversity, and therefore cannot be joined. In almost all such cases, plaintiff has an alternative, which is to sue in state court. At least sometimes, this alternative counts. See Poulos v. Nicolaides, 241 Fed. Appx. 25 (3d Cir. 2007) (dismissing contract suit for failure to name obligor; plaintiff could sue in state court).

Fewer cases apply FRCP 19(b) than 19(a). In a case that reached the Supreme Court, a car accident spawned multiple suits, and going forward in federal court without some of claimants (who could not be joined for jurisdictional reasons) might have resulted in depleting the resources provided by insurance before other claimants could obtain judgments. The Court concluded that the chance of prejudice to the missing party was remote, and execution on judgments could be deferred until other claimants won or lost, thus avoiding a finding that they were indispensable. See Provident Tradesmen's Bank & Trust Co. v. Patterson, 390 U.S. 102 (1968). Before dismissing because an absent party who cannot be joined is indispensable, a court must consider seriously the factors in FRCP 19(b).

Raising the Issue. Recall that FRCP 12(b) includes "failure to join a party under Rule 19" among defenses that can be raised by answer or pre-answer motion. Recall too that FRCP 12(h)(2) says failing to join "a person required by Rule 19(b)" may be raised in any pleading, by motion for judgment, "or at trial," and it is clear that *unlike* more fragile defenses (like improper venue), *this* defense is not lost by failing to include it in a motion or answer, and it can be raised late in the game. Indeed, there was a tradition of labeling the defense of failing to join an indispensable party as "jurisdictional," but FRCP 12 does not go that far.

This defense can be raised at trial, even at the end of trial. Once a court has rendered a judgment, however, a party who raises this defense has a steeper hill to climb if the hope is to set aside the judgment. The various calculations called for by Rule 19 are very much affected by the fact that the time and energy of the parties and the court have been expended and a result has been reached. See Merrill Lynch & Co. v. Allegheny Energy, Inc., 500 F.3d 171 (2d Cir. 2007) (in contract suit, even if S was "paradigmatic indispensable party," defendant agreed that S was dispensable by failing to argue the contrary at trial, "and its subsequent failure to raise the point sufficiently" on appeal, means that plaintiff's interest in preserving the judgment "may only be overborne by greater contrary considerations than those that would be required at an earlier stage").

Some Easy Cases. Sometimes FRCP 19 operates in a straightforward way to achieve a constructive result. In a Nebraska case, for example, two brothers held title to a farm as tenants in common, and one died (Robert). His surviving brother Raymond sued Robert's personal representative, alleging that the two had decided that title was to be transferred to Raymond, but that Robert died before the deed could be executed. The residuary devisees named in Robert's will, who would inherit Robert's title (his half interest as tenant in common), sought to intervene, but the court would not let them in. On appeal, the reviewing court held that the residuary devisees were not only entitled to intervene, but were indispensable parties whom the court should have included in the suit on its own initiative. See Ruzicka v. Ruzicka, 635 N.W.2d 528 (Neb. 2001). And in a West Virginia case, Retail Design won an injunction requiring the Department of Transportation to close an access road that would have led to a parcel being developed by One-Gateway for a big box store, but the reviewing court found that One-Gateway was indispensable because disposition of the action would impair its ability to protect its interest. See State ex rel. One-Gateway v. Johnson, 542 S.W.2d 894 (W. Va. 2000).

Must All Tortfeasors Be Joined as Defendants? Must All Claimants Join in Tort Cases as Plaintiffs? The short answer to both questions is no. It is easy to imagine that the answer to both questions should be yes, so let's think about it.

The driver of a car who is injured in an accident involving two other cars might be required to join both the other drivers. (For that matter, if there are claims that manufacturing defects in a car caused the accident, joinder of the manufacturers might be required, and perhaps the seller of the car too.) Arguably, naming only one alleged tortfeasor means the claimant cannot get complete relief: A judgment against only one could be executed only against that one, and if there are not enough assets to cover the judgment, plaintiff cannot collect all that he is due. More saliently, in a system in which each tortfeasor is liable only for the portion of the damages that corresponds to his proportion of fault, the problem of complete relief becomes starker (claimant can only get 50 percent recovery if he sued only a tortfeasor who is 50 percent responsible). One might add that naming only one tortfeasor might result in imposing a larger share of liability on him than would happen if multiple defendants were named: Even if each is *in theory* liable only proportionately, a jury with only one visible party to blame might impose a larger share of liability on that party, which is prejudice caused to the named defendant by the absence of other responsible parties. Note, however, that FRCP 19 speaks not in terms of mere "prejudice" to parties already named, but in terms of "incurring double, multiple, or inconsistent obligations," and being liable for more than one's fair share does not seem to satisfy this stronger language. See Janney Montgomery Scott, Inc. v. Shepard Niles, Inc., 11 F.3d 399, 412 (3d Cir. 1993) (failing to join co-obligor might result in higher liability for defendant, but forcing it to "bear the whole loss . . . is not the equivalent of double liability" and is not prejudice).

In any event, it is settled law in most places that claimants in tort cases need not name all tortfeasors. "Complete relief" means relief that is complete between the named parties, and the fact that a single named defendant can bring in the fault of others by way of limiting his own liability is considered protection enough. Equally important, courts take the view that plaintiffs should be allowed to choose to sue any responsible party and should not be restricted by FRCP 19. (Where a tortfeasor named as defendant is entitled to contribution or indemnity from another tortfeasor, she can bring such a party in by impleader under FRCP 14.) See Temple v. Synthes Corp., 498 U.S. 5, 7 (1990) (patient implanted with "plate and screw device" in lower spine could sue manufacturer of device, and need not name doctor and hospital; "it is not necessary for all joint tortfeasors to be named as defendants in a single lawsuit"). Some jurisdictions, however, depart from this pattern and require plaintiffs to join all alleged tortfeasors. See, e.g., Samuelson v. McMurtry, 962 S.W.2d 473, 475-476 (Tenn. 1998) (alleged tort-feasors must plead comparative fault as affirmative defense, and statute allows plaintiffs additional time to name others; "where the separate, independent negligent acts of more than one tortfeasor combine to cause a single, indivisible injury, all tortfeasors must be joined" unless joinder is prohibited by other law; here separate independent acts by doctor and others caused a single injury).

Just as it is easy to imagine a rule requiring joinder of tortfeasors as defendants, it is easy to imagine a rule requiring joinder of claimants as plaintiffs. After all, if we let one claimant pursue the tortfeasors without others, the one who sues might exhaust assets or insurance coverage, leaving other claimants nothing on which to realize their claims. One can also argue that a tortfeasor sued by one of several claimants cannot get "complete relief," at least in the sense that a single judgment for or against him leaves him subject to further claims. Allowing separate suits might, in addition, lead to inconsistent adjudications, sending at best "mixed messages" on the question whether defendant's conduct was tortious. Finally, not enforcing joinder encourages multiplicity of actions, wasting resources.

Despite these arguments, additional tort claimants are neither necessary nor indispensable parties. See Grove v. Pfister, 110 P.3d 275, 280 (Wyo. 2005) (front passenger need not join rear passenger in suit against driver; doing otherwise would "render meaningless the distinction between permissive and compulsory joinder," even though one reason for it is to prevent multiplicity of suits); 7 Wright & Miller, Federal Practice and Procedure §1623 (liability of joint tortfeasors is joint and several; FRCP 19 does not alter "long-standing practice of not requiring the addition of joint tortfeasors," and if several suits arise out of one accident "the complaining parties need not be joined in suits brought by the others").

Must All Co-obligees Join as Claimants in Contract Cases? Must Co-obligors All Be Joined as Defendants? The short answer to the first question is yes, and the short answer to the second is no.

Consider first the joinder of co-obligees as plaintiffs. Suppose Murphy agrees to buy a yacht company from Dickson and Davis, but Murphy backs out. Suppose Dickson sues Murphy in federal court on the basis of diversity jurisdiction, but Davis does not join as plaintiff (one of two obligees has brought the suit, but the other has not joined). Going forward could lead to later problems for Murphy or Davis. Without Davis, Dickson might obtain judgment against Murphy that would fully discharge his obligations, and Davis would receive nothing. In the language of FRCP 19(a)(1)(B), going forward without Davis might "impair or impede" his ability to protect his interests. Or Murphy might wind up compensating Dickson and then discover that Davis has brought a second suit for the same dollars. In the language of FRCP 19(a)(1)(B), Murphy faces a "substantial risk of incurring double" liability. See Dickson v. Murphy, 202 Fed. Appx. 578 (3d Cir. 2006) (absent sellers are indispensable; their presence would destroy diversity; suit must be dismissed).

Consider now the joinder of co-obligors as defendants. Suppose, on facts like those sketched above, the *sellers* back out: Murphy is ready to proceed, but Dickson and Davis have decided they can get a better price from someone else. Murphy brings suit against Dickson alone, leaving Davis out. If Murphy were seeking specific performance, which required Dickson and Davis to sign a deed to real property, perhaps Murphy *would* be required to name both. A deed signed by one of two owners of a piece of property would not convey title, and "complete relief" could not be granted. But if Murphy sought only damages, it would matter little or not at all that he named Dickson but not Davis. Dickson is *not* put to the risk of incurring double or multiple liability simply because Davis is missing. And Davis is *not* likely to suffer prejudice because he has been left out. In this situation, joining co-obligors as defendants is not required. See In re Olympic Mills Corp., 477 F.3d 1, 10 (1st Cir. 2007) ("co-obligors are generally not indispensable parties in contract suits that do not involve reformation, cancellation, rescission or otherwise challenge the validity of the contract").

MASTERCARD INTERNATIONAL, INC. v. VISA INTERNATIONAL SERVICE ASS'N, INC.

United States Court of Appeals for the Second Circuit
471 F.3d 377 (2d Cir. 2006)

Before MINER, POOLER, and KATZMANN, Circuit Judges.

POOLER, Circuit Judge.

[MasterCard sued Federation Internationale de Football Association (FIFA), the governing body of soccer and organizer of the World Cup tournaments. MasterCard claimed it had a contract with FIFA (the MasterCard Contract) that gave it the "first right to acquire" exclusive sponsorship rights in its category in World Cup events in 2010 and 2014. MasterCard alleged that it served as official sponsor of World Cup events in 1994, 1998, 2002, and 2006, and that these events are the most viewed sporting events in the world, drawing a cumulative audience of 28.8 billion viewers from more than 200 countries in 2002.

Under the MasterCard contract, plaintiff claimed, FIFA cannot offer these sponsorship rights to any other entity in its product category without first giving MasterCard the opportunity to purchase the rights on comparable terms. MasterCard alleged that FIFA offered it "exclusive sponsorship rights for all FIFA competitions between 2007 and 2014, including the 2010 and 2014 World Cups."

While negotiating these matters with MasterCard, FIFA also negotiated with Visa over the same rights. On March 30, 2006, MasterCard learned that FIFA had decided to finalize an agreement with Visa, and a week later FIFA wrote a letter to MasterCard confirming that it had granted Visa "exclusive sponsorship rights to FIFA competitions, including the World Cup, through 2014" (the Visa Contract). On April 20, 2006, MasterCard filed suit in federal court in New York for breach of contract and an injunction barring FIFA from "consummating, effectuating or performing" the Visa Contract and ordering FIFA to perform its alleged duties under the MasterCard Contract. MasterCard sought a preliminary injunction, and a hearing was set for September 18.

In the meantime, Visa was in communication with FIFA, and Visa sent a letter to the court saying it was a "necessary and indispensable party" because of its entitlement to the FIFA sponsorship rights. For this reason, Visa asked that the suit be dismissed: Since both MasterCard and Visa are incorporated in Delaware, Visa argued that it could not be joined (doing so would destroy jurisdiction). The court construed Visa's letter as a motion to dismiss under FRCP 19, and held a hearing on September 21, after which it denied the motion. The court concluded that Visa's presence was unnecessary in the dispute between MasterCard and FIFA, and that even if MasterCard won, Visa could sue FIFA for breach of the Visa Contract. Also Visa did not participate in the negotiations between MasterCard and FIFA, so it could add nothing to the suit. Visa also tried to intervene in the suit under FRCP 24, but the court denied this motion as well. The trial court stayed the proceedings to allow time for Visa to take an appeal.

The reviewing court comments that Visa "should not have been allowed to file a motion to dismiss" because it was not a party, and that Visa should have filed a motion to intervene (which in substance it did by the letter). Still, the trial court could consider the question whether Visa was indispensable because this matter may be considered "sua sponte even if it is not raised by the parties to the action."

Although denying a motion to dismiss for failure to join an indispensable party is not ordinarily appealable (it does not fit the collateral order doctrine that sometimes allows interlocutory appeals), still the denial of a motion to intervene *is* ordinarily appealable, and a court reviewing the disposition of such a motion may also review issues that are "inextricably intertwined" with that motion.]

We review the district court's failure to join a party under Rule 19 only for abuse of discretion. "A district court 'abuses' or 'exceeds' the discretion accorded to it when (1) its decision rests on an error of law (such as application of the wrong legal principle) or a clearly erroneous factual finding, or (2) its decision—though not necessarily the product of a legal error or clearly erroneous factual finding—cannot be located within the range of permissible decisions." Jonesfilm v. Lion Gate Int'l, 299 F.3d 134, 139 (2d Cir. 2002) (internal quotation marks omitted) (quoting Zervos v. Verizon New York, Inc., 252 F.3d 163, 169 (2d Cir. 2001)). [The court quotes FRCP 19(a).] Visa contends that it fits within all three of these categories. We disagree.

A party is necessary under Rule 19(a)(1) [now 19(a)(1)(A)—ED.] only if in that party's absence "complete relief cannot be accorded *among those already parties.*" FRCP 19(a)(1) (emphasis added). Visa's absence will not prevent the district court from granting complete relief between MasterCard and FIFA. Visa argues that without it in the case, MasterCard can receive only partial relief because Visa still holds contractual rights to the sponsorship rights and will file suit against FIFA to enforce the Visa Contract. While there is no question that further litigation between Visa and FIFA, and perhaps Master-Card and Visa, is inevitable if MasterCard prevails in this lawsuit, Rule 19(a)(1) is concerned only with those who are already parties. MasterCard can obtain complete relief *as to FIFA* without Visa's presence in the case. If MasterCard prevails and is granted its requested relief, FIFA will be enjoined from awarding the sponsorship rights to another party, including Visa. This will resolve the dispute between MasterCard and FIFA, and Visa's presence is unnecessary to decide those questions. Thus, Visa is not a necessary party under Rule 19(a)(1).[6]

We find no abuse of discretion in the district court's conclusion that Visa was not a necessary party under Rule 19(a)(2)(i) [now 19(a)(1)(B)(1)—ED.]. Visa claims that because MasterCard seeks to enjoin FIFA from performing the Visa Contract, its interests are clearly implicated and it is therefore entitled to appear in this litigation. Visa relies primarily on this court's decision in Crouse-Hinds Co. v. InterNorth, Inc., 634 F.2d 690 (2d Cir. 1980), which it characterizes as controlling here. In *Crouse-Hinds,* the defendant asserted a counterclaim alleging that a proposed merger between the plaintiff and a third party, Belden, was unfair under the business judgment rule because it lacked any legitimate business purpose and was entered into solely to defeat the defendant's tender offer.

---

[6] In addition, there is no dispute that complete relief can be granted without Visa's presence if FIFA prevails in the underlying lawsuit.

The counterclaim sought to enjoin the merger. On appeal of the district court's grant of a preliminary injunction, this court noted its disagreement with the district court's conclusion that Belden was not a necessary party to the action because "Belden's rights [under the merger agreement] would clearly be prejudiced if the relief sought by InterNorth were to be granted."

Visa's reliance on this case is misplaced. In *Crouse-Hinds*, the actual contract involving the absent third party was the basis of the claim. The counterclaim specifically challenged the validity of the merger agreement and sought to set aside that agreement. If the defendant prevailed on this counterclaim, the merger agreement would be deemed invalid, which would presumably affect Belden's ability to then sue for breach of that agreement or invoke any of the protections in that agreement. Thus, non-party Belden was faced with the possibility of having its contract terminated in its absence. In contrast, in this case, while the Visa Contract may be affected by this litigation, it is not the contract at issue in MasterCard's lawsuit. The underlying litigation involves the MasterCard Contract and whether MasterCard had a right of first refusal to the World Cup sponsorship rights. Even if MasterCard prevails and receives the relief it seeks, that does not render the Visa Contract invalid. It means that FIFA likely has breached the warranty provision of that contract, and Visa has the right to sue FIFA for that breach.

Furthermore, in *Crouse-Hinds*, because the absent non-party was a party to the contract at issue, its ability to protect its interest in that contract would have been seriously impaired if it were not made a party to the action. This places the absentee non-party in *Crouse-Hinds* in a distinctly different position from Visa, whose contract with FIFA is not at issue here. As the district court correctly found, Visa's ability to protect its interest in its contract with FIFA will not be impaired if is not joined here. The primary flaw in Visa's argument is that it has construed Rule 19(a)(2)(i) [now 19(a)(1)(B)(i)—ED.] to extend to any party whose interests would be impaired or impeded by a litigation. This overlooks a key element of the definition of "necessary" party under Rule 19(a)(2)(i) [now 19(a)(1)(B)(i)—ED.]. It is not enough . . . for a third party to have an interest, even a very strong interest, in the litigation. Nor is it enough for a third party to be adversely affected by the outcome of the litigation. Rather, necessary parties . . . are only those parties whose ability to protect their interests would be impaired *because of* that party's absence from the litigation. *See* FRCP 19(a)(2) [now 19(a)(1)(B)—ED.] (defining necessary party as one with an "interest relating to the subject of the action and is so situated that the disposition of the action *in the person's absence* may . . . as a practical matter impair or impede the person's ability to protect that interest" (emphasis added)). Thus, while Visa may have an interest that would be impaired by the outcome of this litigation, Visa still does not qualify as a necessary party under Rule 19(a)(2)(i) because the harm Visa may suffer is not *caused by* Visa's absence from this litigation. Any such harm would result from FIFA's alleged conduct in awarding Visa sponsorship rights it could not legally give. We would be significantly broadening both Rule 19(a)(2)(i) [now 19(a)(1)(B)(i)—ED.] and the principle discussed in *Crouse-Hinds* if we found that because the outcome of this case may impact a separate contract involving a different party, that finding would transform the action into "an action to set aside a lease or a contract." *Crouse-Hinds* involved an actual action to set aside a contract; here we have an action that could in the future impact a third party's rights under a separate contract. We, therefore, do not find *Crouse-Hinds* controlling here and decline to broaden its scope to reach the facts before us, particularly since doing so would read a key element out of the text of Rule 19(a)(2)(i) [now 19(a)(1)(B)(i)—ED.].

Visa also relies on several cases that recite the general proposition that a party who claims title to a piece of property that is the subject of an action has sufficient interest in the action to justify compulsory joinder, and urges us to follow that reasoning here. Visa attempts to characterize this case as if it were a proceeding to determine the rightful owner of a piece of property to which MasterCard and Visa have competing claims. While we have held in cases involving this factual scenario that all claimants to the property at issue are necessary parties to the action, *see, e.g.,* Brody v. Village of Port Chester, 345 F.3d 103, 117-19 (2d Cir. 2003) (holding that in action by property owner to recover land taken by eminent domain, current titleholder to land might be necessary party if district court were to restore land to plaintiff); Kulawy v. United States, 917 F.2d 729, 736 (2d Cir. 1990) (holding that in an action to quiet title by aggrieved tax payer against government seeking to recover automobiles sold to satisfy tax lien, purchasers of automobiles were necessary parties), we do not find this reasoning applicable here. In *Brody* and *Kulawy,* the district courts were required to determine who among several parties had title to a piece of property. Thus, the district court could not grant the relief sought—declaring the plaintiff the titleholder—in the absence of the current or competing titleholders to that piece of property. As MasterCard correctly notes, the MasterCard-FIFA dispute is not an *in rem* proceeding between competing claimants with the district court tasked with deciding who has superior rights to a piece of property. The district court only need decide whether MasterCard has a right of first refusal under its prior contract with FIFA. While this has the *effect* of determining who will get the sponsorship rights, that does not transform this case into an in rem proceeding nor does it place Visa in the same position as MasterCard as a competing claimant. Unfortunately for Visa, there is nothing it can do about the fact that MasterCard's prior contractual rights with FIFA may preclude FIFA's ability to grant the sponsorship rights to Visa. Visa's problems here are due to FIFA's alleged actions, not Visa's absence from this litigation. Nor will its absence prevent Visa from seeking the only remedy available to it if MasterCard indeed has a right of first refusal to the sponsorship rights: Visa can sue FIFA for breach of the warranty provision in the Visa Contract. For these reasons, we find the district court properly rejected Visa's contention that it is a necessary party under Rule 19(a)(2)(i) [now 19(a)(1)(B)(i)—ED.].

The district court's conclusion that Visa does not satisfy Rule 19(a)(2)(ii) [now 19(a)(1)(B)(ii)—ED.] is also not an abuse of discretion. Visa presents us with the following scenario: MasterCard prevails in the underlying lawsuit and is granted injunctive relief that prohibits FIFA from performing its obligations under the Visa Contract; Visa then sues FIFA for breach of the warranty provision in the Visa Contract seeking specific performance; Visa prevails and is granted specific performance requiring FIFA to perform its obligations under the Visa Contract. According to Visa, the possibility exists that FIFA could be under court order to perform the Visa Contract and under court order not to perform the Visa Contract, and this potential for inconsistent obligations renders Visa a necessary party to this litigation. Once again, Visa is ignoring a critical element in Rule 19(a)(2)(ii) [now 19(a)(1)(B)(ii)—ED.]: the substantial risk of inconsistent obligations must be *caused by* the nonparty's absence in the case. FIFA's risk of multiple obligations to different parties is not a result of Visa's absence in this lawsuit; it is the result of FIFA allegedly breaching its contract with MasterCard and awarding Visa sponsorship rights it was contractually prohibited from granting. Visa's presence in this lawsuit will not remedy that fact. Whether Visa is or is not a party in the underlying lawsuit, FIFA and Visa will litigate *their* dispute under *their* contract later on down the road if MasterCard prevails here. Visa cannot relitigate and undo a finding in this case that the MasterCard Contract contains a right of first refusal or that FIFA breached its contract with MasterCard since these issues admittedly have nothing to do with Visa.

We are also not persuaded that the scenario envisioned by Visa, in which the court below enjoins FIFA from performing the Visa Contract while a subsequent court orders FIFA to perform the Visa Contract, presents a "substantial risk" of inconsistent obligations, as required by Rule 19(a)(2)(ii) [now 19(a)(1)(B)(ii)—ED.]. It is difficult to believe that a subsequent tribunal faced with a party under a prior court-ordered injunction will nevertheless order that party to perform the very obligations a prior court has prohibited it from performing. While Visa is correct that *it* will not be bound by any injunction entered in the underlying litigation in its absence, FIFA is certainly bound by any such injunction and a subsequent proceeding will have to recognize and respect the injunction ordered by the district court in this case. It is worth noting that FIFA, the party supposedly facing this grave predicament, has not advanced the argument that it would be prejudiced by Visa's absence from this case. FIFA never raised the Rule 19 defense before the district court, it did not join in Visa's motion below, and it has not participated in any way in the proceedings before this court. If FIFA actually believed it would suffer prejudice if Visa is not a party in this case, it surely would have had something to say on this point.

For these reasons, we cannot say that the district court's conclusion that Visa is not a necessary party under Rule 19(a)(2)(ii) [now 19(a)(1)(B)(ii)—ED.] was an abuse of discretion. Having found that Visa satisfies none of the three criteria for compulsory joinder, we affirm the district court's decision that Visa is not a necessary party under Rule 19(a).

The district court also found that even assuming Visa were a necessary party, it was not indispensable under Rule 19(b). Since we affirm the district court's conclusion that Visa is a not a necessary party, we need not discuss whether the district court properly found that Visa was not an indispensable party. See Viacom Int'l, Inc. v. Kearney, 212 F.3d 721, 724 (2d Cir. 2000) ("If a party does not qualify as necessary under Rule 19(a), then the court need not decide whether its absence warrants dismissal under Rule 19(b)."). Accordingly, we reject the challenge to the district court's subject matter jurisdiction over the underlying action.

[The trial court also properly denied Visa's motion to intervene under FRCP 24. Citing the "overlapping language" in FRCP 19(a)(1)(B)(i) and 24(a)(2), both of which contemplate an absent party having an interest relating to the subject of the action, the court says that these provisions "mirror each other." Since Visa did not satisfy FRCP 19(a)(1)(B)(i), it also does not satisfy FRCP 24(a)(2). Moreover, Visa's application to intervene was untimely.]

For the foregoing reasons, we dismiss the appeal originally filed by Visa of the district court's Rule 19 Order, reject Visa's argument that the district court lacks subject matter jurisdiction because Visa is a necessary and indispensable party, affirm the district court's Rule 24 Order, vacate the stay previously granted by this court, and remand the matter to the district court.

■ NOTES ON NECESSARY AND INDISPENSABLE PARTIES

1. On the question of "complete relief," *MasterCard* says the focus is relief that can be awarded among those who are already in the suit. Hence the fact that the court could not, for example, enjoin Visa from advertising itself as "the official card of the 2010 and 2014 World Cup" does not matter. Can MasterCard obtain complete relief, even against FIFA, in a suit that does not include Visa? The reviewing court says that if MasterCard gets what it seeks, the court will enjoin FIFA from awarding sponsorship rights to Visa. Can that happen in a suit that does not include Visa?

2. On the question whether proceeding without Visa would be prejudicial to Visa—would "impair or impede" its ability to protect its interests as envisioned by FRE 19(a)(1)(B)(i)—the court makes three arguments.

(a) First, the suit involves the MasterCard contract, not the Visa contract, and the missing party (Visa) is not a party to the contract. Hence *Crouse-*

Hinds does not control: There the defendant tried to prevent a plaintiff from performing a contract between it and Belden (a nonparty). Is this argument convincing?

(b) Second, it is "not enough" that Visa has even a "very strong interest" in the litigation, or that the interest would be "adversely affected" by the outcome. To satisfy this prong of FRCP 19, it is necessary to show that harm to the absent party is "caused by" its absence. Here harm to Visa would be caused by "FIFA's alleged conduct" in granting Visa some rights that "it could not legally give." Under what circumstances, then, can *absence from a lawsuit* harm the absent party?

(c) Third, property cases are unlike the situation in *MasterCard*. In *Brody*, the "current titleholder" had to be joined in a suit to recover land taken by eminent domain. In *Kulawy*, a taxpayer seeking to recover automobiles sold satisfy a tax lien had to join those who purchased the automobiles at the government's sale. But *MasterCard* is not an *in rem* proceeding—not a suit where the court must decide "who has superior rights to a piece of property." Instead, the case requires only a decision whether plaintiff has a right of first refusal. Is *this* persuasive?

3. On the question whether moving forward without Visa would be prejudicial to FIFA—whether, in the words of FRCP 19(a)(1)(B)(ii), proceeding in that way would leave FIFA "subject to a substantial risk of incurring double, multiple, or otherwise inconsistent obligations"—the court again finds that the criterion is not satisfied. As Visa argued, plaintiff might get an injunction blocking FIFA from honoring its commitment to Visa, and Visa might then seek specific performance in a second suit and prevail. Doesn't this possibility raise the risk of *one* judgment forbidding FIFA from awarding sponsorship rights to Visa and another *requiring* FIFA to do so? Again the court offers an answer: If this unhappy result eventuates, it isn't the *absence* of Visa that causes it, but FIFA's own behavior in "breaching its contract with MasterCard," and Visa's *presence* in the suit (if it were joined) would not "remedy that fact." Even if there *are* two suits, the court finds it "difficult to believe" that a later court, faced with the fact that the court in this suit enjoined FIFA from going forward with Visa, would then order FIFA to do the opposite. Are *these* arguments convincing? If a second court would never behave that way, what is the meaning of the language in FRCP 19 that envisions such a possibility?

4. *MasterCard* is not alone in giving narrow construction to FRCP 19 in a contract setting involving conflicting contract rights. In the *Helzberg* case that arose in Iowa, Valley West as operator of a shopping mall contracted to allow Helzberg Diamonds to operate the only jewelry store, but then leased another space to Lord's Jewelers. Helzberg sued Valley West in Missouri, but could not join Lord's because it was not subject to jurisdiction there. The Eighth Circuit took an approach that differed slightly from that of the Second Circuit in *MasterCard*. The Eighth Circuit thought Lord's should have been joined under FRCP 19(a) "if feasible" because an injunction would impair or impede its ability to protect its interest. But looking at FRCP 19(b) to decide whether the risk of prejudice to Lord's was so great that the case should be dismissed, the Eighth Circuit answered in the negative, allowing the case to continue. If an injunction issued, and Valley West tried to terminate the lease with Lord's, the court thought Lord's would "retain all of its rights" under that lease so it would not be prejudiced "in a way contemplated by Rule 19(b)." Nor would its absence prejudice Valley West: If the dispute led to two suits, one leading to judgment requiring Valley West to terminate the arrangement with Lord's and the other requiring Valley West to honor the arrangement, "any inconsistency in those obligations will result from Valley West's voluntary execution of two Lease Agreements which impose inconsistent obligations rather than from Lord's absence." See Helzberg's Diamond Shops, Inc. v. Valley West Des Moines Shopping Center, 564 F.2d 816, 819 (8th Cir. 1977).

5. Sometimes courts *do* find that a suit cannot continue because someone's absence creates an intolerable risk of "double" or "multiple" liability for someone already in the suit, or "inconsistent obligations." In an employment discrimination suit against a power district on Navaho Nation lands, for example, plaintiff claimed that the district's agreement with the Nation to give preferential treatment to Navaho tribe members violated the district's obligations under antidiscrimination law. The district claimed that it could not be sued unless the Navaho Nation were joined. See Dawavendewa v. Salt River Project Agricultural Improvement and Power District, 276 F.3d 1150, 1158-1162 (9th Cir. 2002) (going forward without Navaho Nation "threatens to leave [defendant] subject to a substantial risk of incurring multiple or inconsistent obligations," but Nation cannot be joined because of sovereign immunity; suit must be dismissed). In a suit alleging that the Postal Department discriminated against plaintiff on account of age, two other applicants for the position had to be joined. See Evans v. Potter, 215 F.R.D. 571, 574 (D.S.D. 2003) (only one of three applicants could be awarded the position, so all must be before the court; allowing "more than one of the claimants to recover a full damages award with respect to the single position would subject the Defendant to inconsistent obligations," and this risk is "substantial" in this case, as all three have actions pending) (absent defendant can be joined, as there is good jurisdiction).

 IMPLEADER

Impleader is used for claims that a defendant wishes to bring against an outsider, not yet named as a party, where defendant claims the third party should pay part or all of what the court decides that defendant owes to the plaintiff. Often a defendant who impleads such a third party is seeking to enforce rights of indemnification, subrogation, or contribution. Often such claims rest on alleged breach of warranty or common law doctrine allowing contribution among joint tortfeasors to achieve proportional levels of liability. In a suit brought by the purchaser of vinyl window louvers for use in public schools in Hawaii, for example, defendant seller impleaded the manufacturer, contending that any problems in the louvers reflected a breach of warranty and seeking contribution for sums for which the seller might be found liable to the buyer. See SCD RMA, LLC. v. Farsighted Enterprises, Inc., 59 F. Supp. 2d 1141, 1148 (D. Haw. 2008).

Rule 14 lets defendant implead a third party who "is or may be liable" to defendant for all or part of plaintiff's claim. Thus it permits what is called an "accelerated" determination of liability: In theory, the third party does not owe anything to defendant at the moment when impleader is filed, because liability is contingent on plaintiff's success on the original claim. In federal courts, impleader taking advantage of this accelerated feature can go forward even if state law would not allow it until after entry of judgment against the defendant. In other words, the acceleration feature is a matter of procedure, on which federal law controls. See Ohio Savings Bank v. Manhattan Mortgage Co., 455 F. Supp. 247, 254 (S.D.N.Y. 2006) (it does not matter that state law does not enforce contribution until the original defendant has paid more than his share; state rule is procedural, and federal courts in diversity cases apply federal procedural law).

It is of course another matter if state law does not allow recovery against the third party at all. Here state law controls. See Neal v. 21st Mortgage Corp., 601 F. Supp. 2d 828 (S.D. Miss. 2009) (denying impleader; whether defendant can recover from impleaded third-party defendant is determined by state law, which does not allow a tortfeasor who is sued to recover from a tortfeasor who has *not* been sued).

It is settled that federal courts have supplemental jurisdiction over impleader claims under FRCP 14. It does not matter whether the third party defendant is a citizen of the same state as the defendant or of the same state as the plaintiff, or whether the amount sought meets the jurisdictional minimum. See Grimes v. Mazda North American Operations, 355 F.3d 566, 571-573 (6th Cir. 2004) (supplemental jurisdiction applies to proper third-party claims).

Impleader is often called "derivative" because the right to implead "derives" from defendant's potential liability to the plaintiff, and the impleader claim itself is contingent on plaintiff's winning against the defendant. When defendant impleads a third party on a derivative claim under FRCP 14, it is open to the defendant (now called third-party plaintiff) to join additional claims it may have against the impleaded third-party defendant, even if these are not derivative claims, and even though they could not be brought alone under FRCP 14. The reason is that FRCP 18 governs not the rights of *plaintiff* to join in a single suit all claims she may have against the defendant, but the rights of "a party asserting a claim," specifically including a one asserting a "third-party" claim. See Lehman v. Revolution Portfolio LLC, 166 F.3d 389, 393 (1st Cir. 1999) ("absolutely no reason why" defendant could not append "independent claim" to other impleader claims).

YELIN v. CARVEL CORP.

Supreme Court of New Mexico (1995)
893 P.2d 450

FROST, Justice.

Defendants-Appellants, Kenneth and Jacqueline Yelin (the Yelins), appeal from the district court's order dismissing their third-party complaint against Third-Party-Defendant-Appellee, Carvel Corporation (Carvel). The district court held that the third-party complaint was improperly filed under SCRA 1986, 1-014(A) [which is substantially similar to FRCP 14(a)]. We affirm.

Carvel is in the business of licensing individuals to manufacture and sell ice cream and frozen dessert products under the Carvel name. In December 1986 the Yelins entered into a franchise agreement with Carvel to sell ice cream products in Albuquerque. As part of the agreement, Carvel's wholly owned subsidiary, Franchise Stores Realty Corporation, leased retail space in Albuquerque from George Doolittle and Jeanette Doolittle Ingram (the Doolittles). Franchise Stores Realty Corporation then assigned its entire interest in the lease to the Yelins as owners of the franchise. The term of the lease was for a period of nine years and ten months, beginning on February 1, 1987, and its provisions included payments for rent, taxes, insurance, and other miscellaneous charges. The Yelins operated the Carvel franchise for approximately 3 1/2 years. Over the course of this period, however, the franchise lost money, and, ultimately, the Yelins were forced to close the business.

In September 1991 the Doolittles filed suit against the Yelins for breach of the lease agreement. The Doolittles claimed that the Yelins breached the lease by failing to continue to operate their business at the leased premises, and by failing to pay rent and their proportionate share of taxes, insurance, and other costs. The Yelins, in turn, filed a third-party complaint against Carvel seeking to recover, in addition to other damages, all amounts adjudged against them in the Doolittles' suit. The Yelins claim that Carvel's negligent misrepresentations induced them to enter the franchise agreement and that Carvel breached the terms of the franchise agreement by failing to provide advertising and necessary supplies on a timely basis. The Yelins argue that Carvel's failures and wrongful conduct interfered with their ability to make a profit and thereby precluded them from fulfilling their obligations under the lease agreement.

Carvel moved to dismiss the third-party complaint on the grounds that it was improper under SCRA 1-014(A), which governs third-party practice. The district court granted the motion to dismiss, finding that Carvel's potential liability to the Yelins was not dependent on the outcome of the Doolittles' suit. The Yelins now appeal the dismissal.

The issue on appeal is whether the Yelins may properly implead Carvel. . . . SCRA 1-014(A) allows a defendant to implead "a person not a party to the action who is or may be liable to him for all or part of the plaintiff's claim against him." This Court has consistently interpreted this requirement to mean that the third party's potential liability must be derivative of or dependent upon the outcome of the primary claim against the defendant. See also 6 Wright et al., Federal Practice and Procedure §1446 (2d ed. 1990) (noting that the secondary or derivative liability notion is central to impleader); United States v. Joe Grasso & Son, Inc., 380 F.2d 749, 751 (5th Cir. 1967) (noting that FRCP require derivative liability).

Traditionally, we have held that derivative or secondary liability to the defendant, on the basis of indemnity, contribution or some similar theory, is essential for maintaining a third-party action. . . . Thus, we note that although SCRA 1-014 should be interpreted liberally to facilitate judicial economy, "it was not intended to be used to resolve every controversy between the defendant and a third-party which may have some relationship with the transaction at issue in the original complaint." Yates Exploration, Inc. v. Valley Improvement Ass'n, 773 P.2d 350, 353 (N.M. 1989).

The only question in this appeal is whether Carvel's potential liability is derivative of or independent from the Doolittles' main claim against the Yelins. The Yelins argue that a defendant sued for breach of contract has a right of implied indemnity against a third person whose wrong caused the defendant's breach. They claim that Carvel's wrongful conduct and breach of the franchise agreement made it impossible for them to fulfill their obligations under the lease agreement and that Carvel's actions give rise to a claim for implied indemnity.

New Mexico courts have allowed an action for indemnification in several situations. See Amrep Southwest, Inc. v. Shollenbarger Wood Treating, Inc., 893 P.2d 438, 441-42 (N.M. 1995). Traditional indemnification is based on an independent, preexisting legal relationship, and the right to indemnification typically arises from an express or implied contract. New Mexico courts have also held that indemnification can arise by operation of law to prevent an inequitable result. Consequently, we have applied equitable indemnity in cases involving vicarious or derivative liability, "as when an employer must pay for the negligent conduct of its employee under the doctrine of respondeat superior or when a person is directed by another to do something that appears innocent but is in fact wrongful." *Id.* We have also applied indemnification principles "in both negligence and strict liability cases involving persons in the chain of supply of a product, and in breach of warranty cases." *Id.* In addition, this Court recently recognized the theory of proportional indemnification, which applies when both a defendant and a third party would be concurrently liable to the plaintiff but, because of the plaintiff's choice of remedy, the liability is placed only on the former and cannot be prorated between the wrongdoers. The Yelins' indemnity claim, however, does not implicate any of these designated theories; nor do the underlying facts of this case fall within one of the aforementioned situations in which we have applied indemnity principles in order to avoid inequitable results.

· · ·

The Yelins' claim for indemnity is much closer to the claim the court in Southeast Mortgage Co. v. Mullins, 514 F.2d 747 (5th Cir. 1975), rejected as improper under FRCP 14, the federal counterpart to SCRA 1-014. In *Southeast Mortgage,* the Department of Housing and Urban Development (HUD) helped the defendant, Mullins, take out a loan to purchase a home. After Mullins defaulted on the loan and the mortgage company instituted foreclosure proceedings against Mullins, she attempted to implead HUD. Mullins alleged that HUD had violated the National Housing Act by failing to enforce certain regulations thereby causing the foreclosure proceeding. The court noted,

> The sole connection between the [main claim and the third-party claim] is the contention that, but for HUD's failure to adopt and enforce adequate regulations, there would have been no foreclosure proceedings.
>
> The suggestion that a separate and independent claim can be made the proper subject of a third party complaint because, but for the violation of duty alleged the main claim would not have matured, has been rejected by this and other courts.

After examining two related cases, the court concluded:

> The common thread running through these cases, and our own, is that the right or duty alleged to have been violated in the third party complaint does not emanate from the main claim but exists wholly independent of it. In each, the nexus with the principal action is not that it establishes the right to relief, but merely the need for relief.

National Bank of Canada v. Artex Industries, Inc., 627 F. Supp. 610 (S.D.N.Y. 1986), also addressed the issue before us. In *Artex,* the plaintiff bank paid a supplier on defendant Artex's behalf and then mistakenly credited the payment back to Artex's account. The bank then sued Artex for return of the mistaken payment. Artex impleaded Seaport, the corporation for whom it had acquired the supplies, claiming that Seaport had not paid Artex an outstanding balance on the construction contract. The *Artex* court found that the "minimal overlap" between the main claim and the disputes involved in the third-party claim was insufficient to allow the latter to stand. "The outcome of the third-party claim must be contingent on the outcome of the main claim, and here Seaport's liability to Artex under their contract involves many issues unconnected with NBC's claim for the return of a mistaken payment." The court dismissed the impleader claim without prejudice as improper under FRCP 14.

The court in AAA Excavating, Inc. v. Francis Construction, Inc., 678 S.W.2d 889, 894 (Mo. Ct. App. 1984), similarly dismissed defendant's claim for indemnity that was based on third-party defendant's alleged negligent misrepresentation. In *AAA Excavating,* the excavating company brought suit against the general contractor for unpaid work. The contractor, in turn, impleaded a consultant who the contractor claimed was negligent in performing soil samples and compaction tests. The contractor argued that it was unable to pay AAA Excavating because it had spent the funds on other repairs necessitated by the consultant's misrepresentations regarding soil stability. The court dismissed the claim, noting, "If a third party plaintiff could proceed and recover against the third party defendant even if the third party plaintiff were to win in the suit brought by the plaintiff the petition would not be covered by [the rules governing third-party practice]." The court held: "Regardless of the outcome of AAA Excavating's claim, defendant will still have a claim against [third-party defendant] for all of its claimed damages.... Defendant's claim is in no way dependent upon the disposition of plaintiff's petition against defendant."[1]

In the case at bar, the Yelins' claim against Carvel also involves the resolution of many issues legally and factually unconnected with the Doolittles' claim, and similarly is not contingent upon the outcome. The Yelins are asserting a claim against Carvel for the amounts they are alleged to owe the Doolittles, as items of damage for Carvel's alleged wrongful conduct and misrepresentations which induced the Yelins to enter into the lease. This is not really a claim that the third-party defendant is liable for the rent due from the Yelins; it is a claim that is independent of the lease itself.

The Yelins maintain that their claim against Carvel is derivative of the Doolittles' claim because the main claim will determine whether the Yelins have been damaged by Carvel's actions. However, this argument mistakes the nature of derivative liability. The only effect resolution of the Doolittles' claim might have on the Yelins' claim will be to establish the amount of a portion of the damages that Carvel may owe if they are found to be liable to the Yelins. Carvel's actual liability is entirely separate from the Yelins' breach of the lease agreement. If the Yelins' allegations against Carvel are found to be true, the Yelins would be entitled to recover damages for breach of contract or

---

[1] See also United States v. Olavarrieta, 812 F.2d 640, 642-43 (11th Cir. 1987) (holding that under Florida law defendant's claim against third party for fraud and breach of contract in failing to award defendant a J.D. degree was independent of plaintiff's suit for repayment of defendant's student loans), *cert. denied,* 484 U.S. 851; Rozelle v. Connecticut Gen. Life Ins. Co., 471 F.2d 29, 30 (10th Cir. 1972) (finding that "[t]he obligation of [defendant] to pay was not conditioned upon the actions of the [third-party defendants]," and that resolution of the main claim "did not . . . preclude [defendant] from recovery of any damage which he might have sustained if able to show wrongdoing in the exercise of [third-party defendants] reserved timber rights."), *cert. denied,* 411 U.S. 921; Jobe v. King, 629 P.2d 1031, 1033 (Ariz. App. 1981) (dismissing as too tenuous to support indemnity under Rule 14(a) defendant's third-party claim alleging that neighbor's wrongful act made it financially impossible for defendant to pay rent); Robertson v. TWP, Inc., 656 P.2d 547, 551 (Wyo. 1983) (finding that third-party defendant's alleged wrongful acts were too remote a cause of defendant's injury to form the basis for indemnity). But see Bear Creek Planning Comm. v. Title Ins. & Trust Co., 211 Cal. Rptr. 172, 178 (Cal. App. 1985) (noting that under California law, implied contractual indemnity is based upon the premise that a contractual obligation carries an implied promise to indemnify for foreseeable damages resulting to the indemnitee from the indemnitor's improper performance), *disapproved on other grounds,* 791 P.2d 290 (1990).

misrepresentation regardless of whether the Doolittles recover against the Yelins. Thus, while the Yelins' claim against Carvel may be transactionally related to the Doolittles' main claim, it is not derivative of that claim and is not the proper subject of a third-party complaint. In addition, the presence of Carvel as a party in this matter would complicate rather than simplify resolution of the issues involved. See *Yates Exploration.*

Accordingly, the district court properly dismissed the third-party complaint for failing to demonstrate derivative liability as required under SCRA 1-014. Indeed, "[t]o refuse to dismiss a third-party complaint which did not meet the standards of Rule 1-014 . . . would be an abuse of discretion." *Id.* We note that the Yelins are still free to pursue their claims against Carvel in a separate action if they so choose.

For the foregoing reasons, we affirm the judgment of the trial court.

BACA, C.J., and RANSOM and MINZNER, JJ., concur.

FRANCHINI, Justice (dissenting).

I respectfully dissent. The trial court appears to have confused the proof of liability requirement. That court dismissed the Yelins' third-party claim on the premise that all of Carvel's potential third-party liability to the Yelins was not premised on the first-party liability established by proof of the breach of lease. Our rules do not require that. Joinder simply requires that the first-party defendant allege that a third-party is liable to him for "part of the plaintiff's claim." SCRA 1-014(A). Any additional third-party claims are entertained by reason of judicial economy and are collateral to the claim that satisfied the joinder requirement.

The business's failure undisputedly was the direct cause of the breach of the lease, thus the claim is both transactionally related to and derivative of the major first-party claim. In my opinion it is not, as the majority suggests, "entirely separate from the Yelins' breach of the lease agreement." The jury can determine to what degree or percentage, if any, Carvel caused the business's failure and the resulting inability to pay the rents due under the lease. Obviously, if the Doolittles fail to prove that the Yelins were liable for damages for breach of the lease, the Yelins' third-party allegations of damages based on liability under the lease would also fail. The Yelins satisfied the requirement of stating facts sufficient to show that Carvel had "potential liability to the defendant which is . . . dependent upon the resolution of the main claim." *Yates Exploration,* 773 P.2d at 354. Unlike the defendant in *Yates Exploration,* the Yelins have established a substantive basis for relief that is transactionally connected to the first-party claim.

The cases cited by the opinion are all factually distinguishable. I respectfully submit that this case is not "closer to" *Southeast Mortgage.* There, the defendant did not allege that the third-party defendant's negligence caused her to breach her contract—she simply alleged that HUD failed to provide limitations to keep the first-party plaintiff from suing her for breach of contract in the first place. Thus, she did not properly allege facts showing that HUD was liable for part of the mortgagee's claim against her.

In *Artex* the suit was for return of a mistaken payment, not for breach of a contract. The defendant could not allege any acts by a third party that had anything to do with the mistake, thus its claim against the third-party defendant was not transactionally related. Likewise, the defendants in *AAA Excavating, Olavarrieta, Jobe,* and *Robertson* could not show that the alleged wrongful acts were transactionally related.

In this case, Carvel was originally primarily liable for the lease and the Doolittles' claim against the Yelins was based on the assignment of the lease to them. The Yelins asserted that the lease assignment was obtained by Carvel's fraudulent and negligent misrepresentations and that the original lease was obtained for the sole purpose of inducing individuals to enter into franchise agreements with Carvel. The Yelins further alleged that the Doolittles knew that performance of the lease depended upon fulfillment of Carvel's obligations under the franchise. In its answer brief Carvel claims that the Yelins did not allege that Carvel is primarily liable. However, it seems to me that the Yelins' claims that the assignment was void *ab initio* because of fraud does give rise to the possibility that Carvel could be found primarily liable under the original lease. I believe the trial court improperly dismissed the Yelins' claims against Carvel. I would reverse the trial court.

■ NOTES ON IMPLEADER

1. What theory of recovery do the Doolittles advance against Kenneth and Jacqueline Yelin? What theory of recovery do the Yelins advance against Carvel? If the claim against Carvel has merit, Carvel should be liable for any foreseeable damages proximately caused by its conduct, shouldn't it? Wouldn't these include unpaid rent on the lease from the Doolittles? Why does the majority conclude that the impleader was improper? The majority says the Yelins' claim is "separate and independent" from plaintiff's claim, and not "derivative." Is that right? The majority describes similar cases, where impleader was not allowed. See also Mattes v. ABC Plastics, Inc., 323 F.3d 695 (8th Cir. 2003) (borrower who obtained guarantee from SBA cannot go into default on lease and then, when sued for rent, implead SBA on ground that it failed to reveal contamination on the parcel; there is "no coherent legal theory" under which SBA could be liable to lessee; guaranteeing a loan does not cause the guarantor to be liable on lease separate from loan itself); Gabbidon v. King, 610 N.E.2d 321 (Mass. 1993) (parents sue landlord alleging that lead contamination harmed five-year-old; landlord cannot implead Director of Lead Poisoning Prevention program on ground that regulations are unlawful; landlord does not allege that Director is directly or derivatively liable for plaintiff's injuries).

2. Judge Franchini argues in dissent that the damage allegedly suffered by the Yelins (their "business's failure") was "the direct cause of the breach" of their lease from the Doolittles, hence that the Yelins' claim was "both transactionally related to and derivative of" the Doolittle's claim. Is he right? For a case allowing impleader on parallel facts, see Magnet Bank, F.S.B. v. Barnette, 419 S.E.2d 696, 698 (W. Va. 1992) (bank sues borrower for unpaid balance on loan secured by borrower's rights under lease; landlord had become insolvent and bankruptcy court voided lease because it had not been recorded; borrower could then implead attorney who failed to record lease; under "purely factual analysis," borrower's claim against attorney derived from original loan, as solvency of security constituted a "substantial interest" of Bank and was "of equal importance" to borrowers, who had right to claim that if security agreement had been "validated by a timely recording of the lease, their personal liability would have been at least diminished, if not offset, by the security").

3. In tort cases, common law tradition long held that if the negligence of more than one tortfeasor proximately caused the injuries sued upon, then all tortfeasors were "jointly and severally" liable. "Jointly" means each is liable for the full damages caused by all. It does not follow that plaintiff could recover full damages from more than one defendant ("double" or "multiple" recovery). It meant only that plaintiff could obtain a judgment for all her damages against each and every defendant, and could then recover full damages by executing judgment partly against some or all or in full against any one. "Severally" meant that one or more tortfeasors could be sued even if others were not. See Temple v. Synthes Corp., 498 U.S. 5, 7 (1990) ("it is not necessary for all joint tortfeasors to be named as defendants in a single lawsuit").

(a) This system encourages a defendant sued in tort to implead others that the defendant believes to be jointly responsible, or partly responsible, for injuries sustained by plaintiff. See, e.g., Arroyo Lopez v. Hospital Dr. Dominguez, Inc., 262 F.R.D. 93 (D.P.R. 2009) (in parents' wrongful death suit against doctors alleging negligent failure to treat or stabilize child, doctors could implead hospital as alleged joint tortfeasor on claim that hospital's negligence contributed to child's death). Strategically, it is less than optimal to implead others: Impleader does not require defendant to admit responsibility toward plaintiff, but a defendant who impleads a third party is, if he denies negligence, put in the awkward position of saying "I didn't do anything wrong, but if I did, it's really more the other guy's fault."

(b) In this system, if one of several alleged tortfeasors settles with the claimant in separate negotiations, he risks losing his right to seek reimbursement or indemnity from others. See Charleston Area Medical Center, Inc. v. Parke-Davis, 614 S.E.2d 15 (W. Va. 2005) (hospital cannot recover against drug maker after settling claim by patient's estate for $2.5 million; hospital claimed

labeling on drug that caused death was misleading and defective; tortfeasor who negotiates settlement before suit is filed cannot seek contribution from another tortfeasor who was not apprised of or party to negotiations). In contract cases, similar risks appear. See Carpetland of Northwest Arkansas, Inc. v. Howard, 803 S.W.2d 512, 513-514 (Ark. 1991) (indemnitee on implied covenant for indemnification cannot recover on showing liability, but must show that he has incurred substantial loss; voluntary payment does not extinguish indemnitee's claim, but recovery is subject to proof of liability and reasonableness of amount of settlement; here indemnitee made no showing of reasonableness of settlement and cannot recover).

(c) In this system, suppose one of several alleged tortfeasors settles a claim, and the claimant then sues others. If the latter claim that the settling tortfeasor is liable for a portion of plaintiff's total damages and the jury agrees, can the court credit the judgment against nonsettling defendants with the amount paid in settlement? See Young v. Latta, 589 A.2d 1020 (N.J. 1991) (yes; fact that defendants did not implead settling tortfeasors did not stand in the way).

4. Does failure to file a third-party claim foreclose a tortfeasor, against whom judgment is entered in favor of a claimant, from filing a separate suit against another tortfeasor for contribution? Compare Howell v. Luckey, 518 S.E.2d 873 (W. Va. 1999) (yes; litigating in one suit avoids multiple suits and inconsistent verdicts and promotes judicial economy) with St. Paul Insurance Co. v. Hayes, 676 A.2d 510, 512 (Me. 1996) (defendant loses no rights by waiting to bring independent suit for indemnification after liability to claimant has been determined) and Uniform Contribution Among Tortfeasors Act §3(a) (whether or not judgment is entered in suit against two or more tortfeasors, "contribution may be enforced by separate action"). Which approach is sounder, that of *Howell* or of *St. Paul Insurance* and the Uniform Act? If a third-party entitlement to indemnity arises as a matter of contract law, which rule should prevail, the one requiring defendant to bring the impleader or the one allowing separate suit? See Janney Montgomery Scott, Inc. v. Shepard Niles, Inc., 11 F.3d 399, 423 (3d Cir. 1993) (in contract suit, one claiming contribution or indemnity may implead absent party, but is not required to; if it does not implead, it can bring separate action).

5. Where "joint" liability has been displaced by proportional liability, joint tortfeasors are theoretically liable only to the extent that negligence caused the damage. If substantive principles limit liability of tortfeasors this way, can one who is named as defendant implead others for indemnity or contribution? See Cooney v. Molis, 640 A.2d 527, 530 (R.I. 1994) (no; Rule 14 allows defendants to implead only third-party defendants "who are or may be liable to the defendants").

6. Can a court deny impleader if it would delay litigation already in process? Compare State of West Virginia ex rel. Thrasher Engineering, Inc. v. Fox, 218 S.E.2d 481 (W. Va. 2005) (in suit by public service district and property owners against designer of vacuum sewage collection system, denying the latter's motion to implead Department of Environmental Protection that approved design; third-party defendants argued that impleader would prejudice them and plaintiffs because of undue delay; defendant waited 15 months before filing third-party claim, and further discovery would be necessary) and Weyerhaeuser Co. v. Wells, 593 So. 2d 1010, 1013 (Miss. 1992) (in worker's suit, blocking building owner's attempt to implead employer on basis of contract of indemnity; adding third-party complaint might bring "unnecessary prejudice" to plaintiff, as original complaint set forth "simple claim of negligence," and indemnity "would have been a much more complicated issue" as validity of indemnification agreement was more complicated; exclusivity of workers' compensation remedy would come into dispute) with State ex rel. Leung v. Sanders, 584 S.E.2d 203 (W. Va. 2003) (in malpractice suit, court erred in preventing doctor from impleading another doctor who had treated plaintiff previously; discovery was far from complete, and case could not have been ready for trial on scheduled date and would have had to be moved even without impleader).

7. If a defendant claims that someone else is responsible for the damages claimed, and in effect that plaintiff has sued the wrong party, can defendant implead the other under FRCP 14? See United States v. Bailey, 516 F. Supp. 2d 998, 1019-1020 (D. Minn. 2007) (no; "defendant may not use Rule 14 to implead a third-party defendant who may have liability to the plaintiff *instead* of the defendant or in addition to the defendant," and instead Rule 14 lets defendant implead a third party "only if that third party will be liable to the *defendant* if the defendant is found liable to the plaintiff"); Watergate Landmark Condominium Unit Owners' Ass'n v. Wiss, 117 F.R.D. 576, 578 (E.D. Va. 1987) (third-party claim is not appropriate where defendant says, in effect, "It was him, not me").

E COUNTERCLAIMS AND CROSSCLAIMS

Recall from Chapter 7C, where you read *Valley View Ranch* and *Letourneau*, that Rule 13 provides for counterclaims. These are usually claims by defendants against plaintiffs, but the Rule is broader, and it also covers, for example, claims that *plaintiffs* might have against impleaded third-party defendants, if the latter have brought claims against plaintiffs under Rule 14. Counterclaims are divided between compulsory (arising out of the same "transaction or occurrence") and permissive (all others). As you learned, classifying a counterclaim as compulsory or permissive affects both questions of waiver or forfeiture (not bringing a compulsory counterclaim waives or forfeits the right to bring the claim in a new suit) and subject matter jurisdiction (supplemental jurisdiction almost surely applies to compulsory counterclaims, but not necessarily to permissive ones). We need not dwell longer on this subject here.

Crossclaims. Rule 13 also provides for crossclaims, and these are relatively unproblematic. Under Rule 13(g), coparties—usually defendants—"may" make claims against one another if they arise "out of the transaction or occurrence" that gave rise to the suit or "relates to any property that is the subject matter" of the suit. The Rule is permissive rather than mandatory. A moment's reflection suggests the reason: It is likely to be more efficient to adjudicate all claims arising out of a single transaction or occurrence in one suit as opposed to many, but the framers of the Rules thought we should not *require* defendants to make crossclaims, as they did not choose the time or place of suit.

The supplemental jurisdiction statute, 28 USC §1367, contains no "carve-outs" for claims by one coparty against another under FRCP 13(g), so there is supplemental jurisdiction over such claims if they are part of the same "case or controversy" under §1367(a). They are likely to satisfy this criterion by arising "out of the transaction or occurrence" or relating to property that is the "subject matter" of the main claim. Thus if an Indiana plaintiff brings a diversity suit against four citizens of Kentucky, the latter may make claims against one another arising out of the same transaction even though they are all co-citizens of Kentucky and even if the amount they are claiming does not exceed $75,000.

F   INTERPLEADER

The interpleader device allows somebody who holds property to which others lay claim, or owes money without being sure whom he should pay, to enlist the aid of a court in answering such questions.

In the most common situation for which interpleader is designed, a person covered by life insurance has died and uncertainties have arisen as to the right beneficiary. Sometimes, a spouse with life insurance goes through a divorce and remarries, and steps are taken to name the new husband or wife as beneficiary, but are botched in some way, or not carried to completion. After the death of the insured, his or her first and second spouses step forward to claim the proceeds, and the carrier interpleads the two. Similar confusion arises in myriad situations involving life insurance or retirement assets. See, e.g., Sun Life Assurance Co. of Canada v. Sampson, 556 F.3d 1 (1st Cir. 2009) (interpleader by life insurance company after death of insured wife; question was whether surviving husband was entitled to proceeds, or whether he and wife's three children were entitled to equal shares); Metropolitan Life Ins. Co. v. Parker, 436 F.3d 1109 (9th Cir. 2006) (interpleader suit to resolve conflicting claims to retirement assets, pressed by decedent's widow, his ex-wife, and a son born to a third woman five months after decedent's death).

In an infamous case once read by law students, a dispute arose between a daughter in California and her father in Pennsylvania over the "surrender value" of a policy on the father's life. The carrier filed an interpleader in state court in Pennsylvania, and the court awarded the value of the policy to the father, deciding that there had been no assignment. Meanwhile, the daughter sued the carrier in California, obtaining a judgment awarding her the value of the policy. The Court decided that the daughter was not bound by the Pennsylvania judgment because she was not subject to jurisdiction there, and affirmed the judgment, so the carrier in effect "paid twice." See New York Life Ins. Co. v. Dunlevy, 241 U.S. 518 (1916).

Dunlevy was a wakeup call for the insurance industry, and Congress soon enacted the federal interpleader statute, authorizing interpleader in any case in which the stake exceeds $500 and in which claimants come from more than one state. Venue may be laid where any claimant resides, and service of process runs nationwide. In a case like *Dunlevy,* assuming the value of the policy exceeds $500, the carrier could interplead father and daughter in either Pennsylvania or California. See generally 28 USC §§1335 (basic interpleader provision), 1397 (venue in statutory interpleader cases) and 2361 (nationwide service of process).

In the federal system, there is also "Rules interpleader," because FRCP 22 authorizes interpleader suits. Rules interpleader differs from statutory interpleader in four respects that count in cases brought in federal court on the basis of state law (most interpleader cases rest on state law): First, Rules interpleader requires complete diversity between stakeholder and all claimants. Second, Rules interpleader is subject to ordinary venue rules, which means that in cases where the stakeholder is the plaintiff (usually the way it happens), venue may not automatically be laid where any claimant resides. (Under 28 USC §1391(a), venue may be laid where a defendant lives only if all other defendants live in the same state; otherwise venue may be laid where "a substantial part of the events or omissions giving rise to the claim occurred," or a "substantial part of the property" is situated, or where any defendant is subject to jurisdiction if there is no other district where the suit may be brought.) Third, the amount in controversy must exceed the jurisdictional minimum (more than $75,000). Fourth, defendants may be brought into court only if the relevant state long-arm statute reaches them and they satisfy the "minimum contacts" standard.

A moment's reflection may lead you to conclude that there is only one situation in which Rules interpleader in federal court in cases based on state law provides something that statutory interpleader does not—the case where all claimants are from one state. (Statutory interpleader is unavailable, interpleader can proceed under FRCP 22 if the amount exceeds $75,000, requirements of venue and personal jurisdiction are met, and stakeholder is diverse from claimants.)

STATE FARM FIRE & CASUALTY CO. v. TASHIRE

Supreme Court of the United States
386 U.S. 523 (1967)

Mr. Justice FORTAS delivered the opinion of the Court.

Early one September morning in 1964, a Greyhound bus proceeding northward through Shasta County, California, collided with a southbound pickup truck. Two of the passengers aboard the bus were killed. Thirty-three others were injured, as were the bus driver, the driver of the truck and its lone passenger. One of the dead and 10 of the injured passengers were Canadians; the rest of the individuals involved were citizens of five American States. The ensuing litigation led to the present case, which raises important questions concerning administration of the interpleader remedy in the federal courts.

The litigation began when four of the injured passengers filed suit in California state courts, seeking damages in excess of $1,000,000. Named as defendants were Greyhound Lines, Inc., a California corporation; Theron Nauta, the bus driver; Ellis Clark, who drove the truck; and Kenneth Glasgow, the passenger in the truck who was apparently its owner as well. Each of the individual defendants was a citizen and resident of Oregon. Before these cases could come to trial and before other suits were filed in California or elsewhere, petitioner State Farm Fire & Casualty Company, an Illinois corporation, brought this action in the nature of interpleader in the United States District Court for the District of Oregon.

In its complaint State Farm asserted that at the time of the Shasta County collision it had in force an insurance policy with respect to Ellis Clark, driver of the truck, providing for bodily injury liability up to $10,000 per person and $20,000 per occurrence and for legal representation of Clark in actions covered by the policy. It asserted that actions already filed in California and others which it anticipated would be filed far exceeded in aggregate damages sought the amount of its maximum liability under the policy. Accordingly, it paid into court the sum of $20,000 and asked the court (1) to require all claimants to establish their claims against Clark and his insurer in this single proceeding and in no other, and (2) to discharge State Farm from all further obligations under its policy—including its duty to defend Clark in lawsuits arising from the accident. Alternatively, State Farm expressed its conviction that the policy issued to Clark excluded from coverage accidents resulting from his operation of a truck which belonged to another and was being used in the business of another. The complaint, therefore, requested that the court decree that the insurer owed no duty to Clark and was not liable on the policy, and it asked the court to refund the $20,000 deposit.

Joined as defendants were Clark, Glasgow, Nauta, Greyhound Lines, and each of the prospective claimants. Jurisdiction was predicated upon 28 USC §1335, the federal interpleader statute, and upon general diversity, of citizenship, there being diversity between two or more of the claimants to the fund and between State Farm and all of the named defendants.

An order issued, requiring the defendants to show cause why they should not be restrained from filing or prosecuting "any proceeding in any state or United States Court affecting the property or obligation involved in this interpleader action, and specifically against the plaintiff and the defendant Ellis D. Clark." Personal service was effected on each of the American defendants, and registered mail was employed to reach the 11 Canadian claimants. Defendants Nauta, Greyhound, and several of the injured passengers responded, contending that the policy did cover this accident and advancing various arguments for the position that interpleader was either impermissible or inappropriate in the present circumstances. Greyhound, however, soon switched sides and moved that the court broaden any injunction to include Nauta and Greyhound among those who could not be sued except within the confines of the interpleader proceeding.

When a temporary injunction along the lines sought by State Farm was issued by the United States District Court for the District of Oregon, the present respondents [passengers on bus, or their representatives—ED.] moved to dismiss the action and, in the alternative, for a change of venue—to the Northern District of California, in which district the collision had occurred. After a hearing, the court declined to dissolve the temporary injunction, but continued the motion for a change of venue. The injunction was later broadened to include the protection sought by Greyhound, but modified to permit the filing—although not the prosecution—of suits. The injunction, therefore, provided that all suits against Clark, State Farm, Greyhound, and Nauta be prosecuted in the interpleader proceeding.

On interlocutory appeal [under 28 USC §1292(a)(1), which authorizes such appeals from the grant of permanent injunctions—ED.], the Court of Appeals for the Ninth Circuit reversed. The court found it unnecessary to reach respondents' contentions relating to service of process and the scope of the injunction, for it concluded that interpleader was not available in the circumstances of this case. It held that in States like Oregon which do not permit "direct action" suits against insurance companies until judgments are obtained against the insured, the insurance companies may not invoke federal interpleader until the claims against the insured, the alleged tortfeasor, have been reduced to judgment. Until that is done, said the court, claimants with unliquidated tort claims are not "claimants" within the meaning of §1335, nor are they "persons having claims against the plaintiff" within the meaning of FRCP 22. In accord with that view, it directed dissolution of the temporary injunction and dismissal of the action. Because the Court of Appeals' decision on this point conflicts with those of other federal courts, and concerns a matter of significance to the administration of federal interpleader, we granted certiorari. Although we reverse the decision of the Court of Appeals upon the jurisdictional question, we direct a substantial modification of the District Court's injunction for reasons which will appear.

I

Before considering the issues presented by the petition for certiorari, we find it necessary to dispose of a question neither raised by the parties nor passed upon by the courts below. Since the matter concerns our jurisdiction, we raise it on our own motion. The interpleader statute, 28 USC §1335, applies where there are "Two or more adverse claimants, of diverse citizenship...." This provision has been uniformly construed to require only "minimal diversity," that is, diversity of citizenship between two or more claimants, without regard to the circumstance that other rival claimants may be cocitzens. The language of the statute, the legislative purpose broadly to remedy the problems posed by multiple claimants to a single fund, and the consistent judicial interpretation tacitly accepted by Congress, persuade us that the statute requires no more. There remains, however, the question whether such a statutory construction is consistent with Article III of our Constitution, which extends the federal judicial power to "Controversies ... between citizens of different States ... and between a State, or the Citizens thereof, and foreign States, Citizens or Subjects." In Strawbridge v. Curtiss, 3 Cranch 267 (1806), this Court held that the diversity of citizenship statute required "complete diversity": where cocitizens appeared on both sides of a dispute, jurisdiction was lost. But Chief Justice Marshall there purported to construe only "The words of the act of congress," not the Constitution itself. And in a variety of contexts this Court and the lower courts have concluded that Article III poses no obstacle to the legislative extension of federal jurisdiction, founded on diversity, so long as any two adverse parties are not cocitizens. Accordingly, we conclude that the present case is properly in the federal courts.

II

We do not agree with the Court of Appeals that, in the absence of a state law or contractual provision for "direct action" suits against the insurance company, the company must wait until persons asserting claims against its insured have reduced those claims to judgment before seeking to invoke the benefits of federal interpleader. That may have been a tenable position under the 1926 and 1936 interpleader statutes. These statutes did not carry forward the language in the 1917 Act authorizing interpleader where adverse claimants "may claim" benefits as well as where they "are claiming" them. In 1948, however, in the revision of the Judicial Code, the "may claim" language was restored. Until the decision below, every court confronted by the question has concluded that the 1948 revision removed whatever requirement there might previously have been that the insurance company wait until at least two claimants reduced their claims to judgments. The commentators are in accord.

Considerations of judicial administration demonstrate the soundness of this view which, in any event, seems compelled by the language of the present statute, which is remedial and to be liberally construed. Were an insurance company required to await reduction of claims to judgment, the first claimant to obtain such a judgment or to negotiate a settlement might appropriate all or a disproportionate slice of the fund before his fellow claimants were able to establish their claims. The difficulties such a race to judgment pose for the insurer, and the unfairness which may result to some claimants, were among the principal evils the interpleader device was intended to remedy.

III

The fact that State Farm had properly invoked the interpleader jurisdiction under §1335 did not, however, entitle it to an order both enjoining prosecution of suits against it outside the confines of the interpleader proceeding and also extending such protection to its insured, the alleged tortfeasor. Still less was Greyhound Lines entitled to have that order expanded so as to protect itself and its driver, also alleged to be tortfeasors, from suits brought by its passengers in various state or federal courts. Here, the scope of the litigation, in terms of parties and claims, was vastly more extensive than the confines of the "fund," the deposited proceeds of the insurance policy. In these circumstances, the mere existence of such a fund cannot, by use of interpleader, be employed to accomplish purposes that exceed the needs of orderly contest with respect to the fund.

There are situations, of a type not present here, where the effect of interpleader is to confine the total litigation to a single forum and proceeding. One such case is where a stakeholder, faced with rival claims to the fund itself, acknowledges—or denies—his liability to one or the other of the claimants. In this situation, the fund itself is the target of the claimants. It marks the outer limits of the controversy. It is, therefore, reasonable and sensible that interpleader, in discharge of its office to protect the fund, should also protect the stakeholder from vexatious and multiple litigation. In this context, the suits sought to be enjoined are squarely within the language of 28 USC §2361 . . . [quoting statute].

But the present case is another matter. Here, an accident has happened. Thirty-five passengers or their representatives have claims which they wish to press against a variety of defendants: the bus company, its driver, the owner of the truck, and the truck driver. The circumstance that one of the prospective defendants happens to have an insurance policy is a fortuitous event which should not of itself shape the nature of the ensuing litigation. For example, a resident of California, injured in California aboard a bus owned by a California corporation should not be forced to sue that corporation anywhere but in California simply because another prospective defendant carried an insurance policy. And an insurance company whose maximum interest in the case cannot exceed $20,000 and who in fact asserts that it has no interest at all, should not be allowed to determine that dozens of tort plaintiffs must be compelled to press their claims—even those claims which are not against the insured and which in no event could be satisfied out of the meager insurance fund—in a single forum of the insurance company's choosing. There is nothing in the statutory scheme, and very little in the judicial and academic commentary upon that scheme, which requires that the tail be allowed to wag the dog in this fashion.

State Farm's interest in this case, which is the fulcrum of the interpleader procedure, is confined to its $20,000 fund. That interest receives full vindication when the court restrains claimants from seeking to enforce against the insurance company any judgment obtained against its insured, except in the interpleader proceeding itself. To the extent that the District Court sought to control claimants' lawsuits against the insured and other alleged tortfeasors, it exceeded the powers granted to it by the statutory scheme.

We recognize, of course, that our view of interpleader means that it cannot be used to solve all the vexing problems of multiparty litigation arising out of a mass tort. But interpleader was never intended to perform such a function, to be an all-purpose "bill of peace."[17] Had it been so intended, careful provision would necessarily have been made to insure that a party with little or no interest in the outcome of a complex controversy should not strip truly interested parties of substantial rights—such as the right to choose the forum in which to establish their claims, subject to generally applicable rules of jurisdiction, venue, service of process, removal, and change of venue. None of the legislative and academic sponsors of a modern federal interpleader device viewed their accomplishment as a "bill of peace," capable of sweeping dozens of lawsuits out of the various state and federal courts in which they were brought and into a single interpleader proceeding. . . .

---

[17] There is not a word in the legislative history suggesting such a purpose. And Professor Chafee, upon whose work the Congress heavily depended, has written that little thought was given to the scope of the "second stage" of interpleader, to just what would be adjudicated by the interpleader court. See Chafee, Broadening the Second Stage of Federal Interpleader, 56 Harv. L. Rev. 929, 944-945 (1943). We note that in Professor Chafee's own study of the bill of peace as a device for dealing with the problem of multiparty litigation, he fails even to mention interpleader. See Chafee, Some Problems of Equity 149-198 (1950). In his writing on interpleader, Chafee assumed that the interpleader court would allocate the fund "among all the claimants who get judgment within a reasonable time. . . ." Chafee, The Federal Interpleader Act of 1936: II, 45 Yale L.J. 1161, 1165 (1936). See also Chafee, 49 Yale L.J., at 420-421.

[W]e hold that the interpleader statute did not authorize the injunction entered in the present case. Upon remand, the injunction is to be modified consistently with this opinion.

The judgment of the Court of Appeals is reversed, and the case is remanded to the United States District Court for proceedings consistent with this opinion.

It is so ordered.

[The dissenting opinion of Justice Douglas is omitted.]

■ NOTES ON INTERPLEADER

1. *Tashire* is remembered as much for its discussion of the complete diversity issue as for its holding about interpleader. On the diversity matter, the question was whether Chief Justice John Marshall was construing only the diversity statute in *Strawbridge* when he concluded that "complete diversity" was required. The other possibility was that *Strawbridge* sheds light on the clause in the Constitution that authorizes diversity jurisdiction. In *Strawbridge*, Marshall referred to the "words of the act of congress," by which he meant the statute now codified as 28 USC §1332(a)(1). But the statute uses the same words as Article III §2 of the Constitution: Both refer to suits "between citizens of different states." Before *Tashire*, nobody knew whether *Strawbridge* (which enjoyed almost the status of the tablets of Moses because Marshall was the author) illuminated only the meaning of the statute or *also* the meaning of Article III §2.

(a) In *Tashire*, why did the diversity question arise? The problem identified by the Court was that the 33 surviving passengers and two estates of passengers killed in the accident were named as defendants in State Farm's interpleader suit. We are told that twenty-three passengers and one estate were citizens of five different states. More than one apparently haled from California (where suits had been filed against Greyhound), and there was considerable "overlap" in citizenship among them. In statutory interpleader suits, the citizenship of the claimants is what counts for jurisdictional purposes: Each is viewed as a plaintiff suing all the others in their efforts to win the money that is at stake. If complete diversity were required, the suit could not go forward because (at the very least) there was more than one Californian in the mix of claimants.

(b) The parties did not see any problem with jurisdiction and the Court raised this issue on its own. The Court announces its conclusion on what Marshall meant in *Strawbridge*, which had been decided 161 years earlier. How did the Court know what he meant? Is there a room in the Court

with a secret phone by which the Justices sitting in 1967 could contact Justice Marshall (or his ghost)? If that were possible, would it be the right way to interpret *Strawbridge*?

(c) What difference would it make if both the Constitution and the statute required complete diversity? The constitutional language defines federal "judicial Power." What is implied about what Congress could or could not do if the Court had decided that Marshall had meant that the *Constitution* required complete diversity?

(d) Recall from Chapter 4 that Congress expanded federal jurisdiction in certain mass accident cases (in which "at least 75 natural persons have died" in an accident "at a discrete location"), where minimal diversity suffices. See 28 USC §1369. And in the Class Action Fairness Act, codified in large part as 28 USC §1332(d), Congress similarly provided that minimal diversity suffices, as you will soon see. And of course the interpleader statute applied in *Tashire* also provides for jurisdiction where there is minimal diversity among claimants, so long as the amount at stake exceeds $500. See 28 USC §1335(b).

2. Why can't State Farm use interpleader to force claimants to litigate in federal court in Oregon? (It's *not* for lack of subject matter jurisdiction.) Why did Greyhound, which initially opposed State Farm's attempt to use interpleader, change its position and make common cause with State Farm? If passengers from California and Oregon had sued Greyhound in California state court, could Greyhound have responded by using the interpleader device? The answer is no, and *Tashire* is the place to find the answer. Do you see why?

3. Sometimes, it is clear that a single piece of property is at issue, that there are multiple claims to it, and that the property must go to one of the claimants. In the *Samaniego* case, for example, the government confiscated championship boxing belts belonging to Roberto Duran, the Panamanian champion in the 1970s. The belts had been in the possession of Luis Gonzalez Baez, a Miami businessman who tried to sell them to people who turned out to be undercover FBI agents for $200,000. Duran claimed his brother-in-law, Bolivar Iglesias, had stolen the belts from Duran's house, hence that Baez was dealing in stolen property and the belts should be returned, but Baez claimed the belts had not been stolen. The government brought an interpleader suit, naming Duran and Baez, and the two of them fought it out. The jury decided the belts had been stolen and returned them to Duran. See United States v. Samaniego, 345 F.3d 1280 (11th Cir. 2003) (affirming).

G INTERVENTION

So far we've looked at rules prescribing what *parties* may do in sculpting a lawsuit. FRCP 20 talks about plaintiffs joining the suit, and plaintiffs joining defendants. Rule 20 prescribes options (the verb is "may") and limits (parties can be joined only if the "same transaction" and "common question" standards are met). FRCP 19 addresses the question whether certain parties *must* be in a suit (the verb is "must"), and *usually* this command imposes obligations on plaintiffs. Who *must* plaintiffs name as defendants (or sometimes as additional plaintiffs)?

FRCP 24 comes at questions of party joinder from a different direction: Who can come to the court, knock on the door (so to speak), and get into a suit uninvited? Putting aside the references in FRCP 24 to intervenors who have special statutory rights (there are few such statutes), the answer is given in terms that should sound familiar because they resemble the terms in FRCP 19 ("necessary and indispensable parties" provision): An outsider is an intervenor as of right if he claims "an interest relating to the property or transaction" in suit and is "so situated" that the outcome of the suit might "as a practical matter impair or impede" the outsider's ability to protect his interest, "unless existing parties adequately represent that interest." An outsider is a "permissive" intervenor if he has a "claim or defense that shares with the main action a common question of law or fact."

Here is a place where the supplemental jurisdiction statute includes some "carveouts." In diversity cases, there is *no* supplemental jurisdiction over "claims by plaintiffs against persons made parties under Rule 24," and *no* supplemental jurisdiction "over claims by persons . . . seeking to intervene as plaintiffs under Rule 24," if exercising jurisdiction would be "inconsistent with" 28 USC §1332 (basic diversity statute). There are subtleties in this language, but suffice it to say that intervenors in diversity cases must usually satisfy the complete diversity and amount-in-controversy requirements, which means they can intervene as parties-plaintiff only if they are diverse from all the defendants or as parties-defendant only if they are diverse from all the plaintiffs, and if they bring claims for relief they must normally satisfy the jurisdictional minimum.

KLEISSLER v. UNITED STATES FOREST SERVICE

United States Court of Appeals for the Third Circuit
157 F.3d 964 (3d Cir. 1998)

WEIS, Circuit Judge

The district court denied a request for intervention by local governmental bodies and business concerns in litigation brought by environmentalists to restrict logging activities in a National Forest. We conclude that the proposed intervenors established a threat to their interests from the suit and a reasonable doubt whether the government agency would adequately represent those concerns. Accordingly, we reverse the district court's order and remand for further proceedings.

Plaintiffs are six Pennsylvania and Ohio residents and an Indiana organization committed to environmental preservation. They filed suit against the United States Forest Service ("Service") asserting that the agency had violated statutory requirements in approving two projects that permitted substantial tree cutting in the Allegheny National Forest. Plaintiffs requested an injunction barring implementation of the proposed measures, halting all logging activity, and suspending or canceling contracts for logging in the forest. In addition, plaintiffs sought a declaration that approval of the projects was arbitrary, capricious, and not in conformity with the law.

Through the National Forest Management Act of 1976, Congress authorized the Secretary of Agriculture to develop land and resource plans that are used as a guide to all resource activities in a national forest, including timber harvesting. See 16 USC §1604. The process is described in some depth in Ohio Forestry Association v. Sierra Club, 523 U.S. 726 (1998) and need not be detailed here. The statute also imposes procedural obligations on the Secretary to ensure that environmental interests will be considered in the plan.

In 1997, the Service, as the Secretary's designee, approved the Minister Watershed Project and the South Branch Willow Creek Project, both covering areas within the Allegheny National Forest in Northwestern Pennsylvania. The projects called for substantial tree harvesting through "even-aged management." This process, in general terms, contemplates clearing designated areas of all trees, rather than focusing on individual trees within the given tract, the latter being far more costly and time-consuming for timber companies. In launching the projects, the Service concluded that they were consistent with the resource plan and would not create a significant environmental impact within the forest.

The plaintiffs' complaint alleges that the projects violate the National Environmental Policy Act (NEPA), 42 USC §4332, because of the lack of an environmental impact statement and, among other things, the failure to consider more environmentally-protective alternatives. The complaint also alleges several violations of the National Forest Management Act, including an objection to even-aged management and the "landscape corridor approach," which endorses the even-aged timber-cutting philosophy.

A motion for leave to intervene was filed by a number of area school districts located near the Allegheny National Forest, including Ridgway, Bradford, Kane, Johnsonburg, and Smethport. In addition, six townships—Cherry Grove, Hamilton, Hamlin, Highland, Wetmore, and Jones—sought intervention.

The school districts and municipalities asserted an interest in the suit because they receive funds from receipts of logging operations in the forest. By statute, the federal government disburses twenty-five percent of the gross amounts received from the forest to the Commonwealth of Pennsylvania at the end of each fiscal year. In turn, the Commonwealth forwards these sums to counties where the forest is situated, which then pass the money on to local municipalities and school districts for the benefit of public schools and roads. During the ten years preceding the filing of this suit, the federal government disbursed, on average, in excess of $4 million per year to the Commonwealth. Elimination of logging contracts would deprive the localities of this resource.

Joining the motion for leave to intervene were Brookville Wood Products, Inc., Northeast Hardwoods, Ridgway Lumber Co., Payne Forest Products, Inc., Spilka Wood Products Co., and Allegheny Hardwood Utilization Group, Inc. Payne and Spilka have existing contracts to cut timber as part of the Minister Watershed Project. Ridgway was the successful bidder on a contract under the South Branch Willow Creek Project, but the Service has withheld awarding the contract pending the outcome of this litigation. Brookville Wood Products and Northeast Hardwoods are also lumber companies that generate most of their income from contracts with the Service. Allegheny Hardwood is a nonprofit corporation whose members hold existing sales contracts with the Service and expect to bid on future timber sales contracts that would be affected by this litigation.

The district court reviewed the prerequisites for intervention as set out in FRCP 24(a)(2) and denied the motion as to all applicants except Payne and Spilka. In those two instances, the court determined that intervention was justified because existing contract rights would be threatened if plaintiffs prevailed.

The court observed that the other applicants had interests of "an economic nature based on expectation." Although those "interests are very important, the court is compelled to conclude based on the case law that they are not the type of protectable interests that justify intervention as of right under Rule 24(a)(2)." The court also denied permissive intervention under Rule 24(b)(2). All of the unsuccessful applicants have appealed.

I

During the pendency of this appeal, the district court entered summary judgment for defendants on most claims asserted by plaintiffs with respect to the two projects because of the failure to exhaust administrative remedies. The district court is presently considering whether claims challenging the landscape corridor approach as a management philosophy should suffer a similar fate.

Plaintiffs have secured a certification under FRCP 54(b) and are appealing the adverse district court ruling. Because that order and any future adverse action on the remaining claim might be reversed by this Court or the Supreme Court, the applicants' ability to participate remains a viable issue. This appeal consequently is not moot.

II

... We have interpreted Rule 24(a)(2) to require proof of four elements from the applicant seeking intervention as of right: first, a timely application for leave to intervene; second, a sufficient interest in the litigation; third, a threat that the interest will be impaired or affected, as a practical matter, by the disposition of the action; and fourth, inadequate representation of the prospective intervenor's interest by existing parties to the litigation. Mountain Top Condo. Ass'n v. Dave Stabbert Master Builder, Inc., 72 F.3d 361, 365-66 (3d Cir. 1995); Development Fin. Corp. v. Alpha Hous. & Health Care, Inc., 54 F.3d 156, 161-62 (3d Cir. 1995); United States v. Alcan Alum., Inc., 25 F.3d 1174, 1181 (3d Cir. 1994); Brody v. Spang, 957 F.2d 1108, 1115 (3d Cir. 1992); Harris v. Pernsley, 820 F.2d 592, 596 (3d Cir. 1987). We will reverse a district court's determination on a motion to intervene as of right if the court has abused its discretion by applying an improper legal standard or reaching a conclusion we are confident is incorrect. The parties to this appeal do not dispute the timeliness of the motion for leave to intervene, so we move on to consider the other elements.

To justify intervention as of right, the applicant must have an interest "relating to the property or transaction which is the subject of the action" that is "significantly protectable." Donaldson v. United States, 400 U.S. 517, 531 (1971). That observation, however, has not led to a "precise and authoritative definition" of the interest that satisfies Rule 24(a)(2). *Mountain Top Condo*; see also Conservation Law Foundation v. Mosbacher, 966 F.2d 39, 41 (1st Cir. 1992) ("no bright line of demarcation exists"). Some courts treat the "interest" test as a pragmatic process that qualifies as many concerned parties as is compatible with efficiency. Others reject interests that are "speculative." Often the determination of whether an interest is significantly protectable is "colored to some extent" by the "practical impairment" inquiry. *Conservation Law Foundation.*

The nebulous nature of the standard is apparent from our precedents. Old Colony Trust Co. v. Penrose Industries Corp., 387 F.2d 939, 941 (3d Cir. 1968), held that in a declaratory judgment action over the commercial reasonableness of the sale price of collateral, a "would-be purchaser" did not have an adequate interest for intervention. On the other hand, in EEOC v. AT&T, 506 F.2d 735, 741-42 (3d Cir. 1974), a union was permitted to intervene to contest a proposed consent decree between the government and an employer that could have affected the terms of a collective bargaining agreement.

In *Harris*, the court denied intervention to a district attorney in a suit brought to alleviate overcrowding and other conditions in the local penal institution. We observed that the district attorney did not administer the prison and that a consent decree placing a ceiling on the prison population would only tangentially affect his ability to prosecute. By contrast, *Alcan*

Aluminum held that an adequate interest for intervention had been established where a right of contribution for expenses incurred in cleaning up a hazardous waste site could have been jeopardized by a proposed consent decree.

Brody involved a suit to enjoin religious speech. A group of students and parents sought to intervene in opposition to plaintiffs. We concluded that the proposed intervenors had no interest in litigating the merits of the school's policies, but to the extent a remedy fashioned in a decree might infringe on their First Amendment rights, the parents and students could be eligible for participation in the suit. We also commented on "our policy preference which, as a matter of judicial economy, favors intervention over subsequent collateral attacks."

In *Alpha Housing,* the sole member of a nonprofit corporation sought to intervene to protect the continued viability and tax exempt status of the corporation. We accepted the plaintiffs' concession that these interests were significant enough to support intervention. Finally, in *Mountain Top Condominium,* we concluded that the intervenors' interest in the disposition of a specific fund was sufficient to justify intervention even though they could not challenge the merits of another party's claim to the fund.

This brief review of our jurisprudence does not yield a pattern that will easily support or defeat intervention in all circumstances. Rather, the variety of factual situations and their resolution demonstrate our adherence to the elasticity that Rule 24 contemplates when compared to the rigidity of earlier practice. See Cascade Natural Gas Corp. v. El Paso Natural Gas Co., 386 U.S. 129, 133-34 (1967).

A leading treatise explains that pragmatism is a substantial factor that must be considered: "The central purpose of the 1966 amendment was to allow intervention by those who might be practically disadvantaged by the disposition of the action and to repudiate the view, [under the former rule], that intervention must be limited to those who would be legally bound as a matter of res judicata." 7C Wright, Miller & Kane, Federal Practice and Procedure: Civil 2d §1908, at 301 (1986).

Phraseology such as "mere economic interests," for example, has been used but has not proved decisive in practice,[1] nor have concepts such as "mere expectancies" or "indefiniteness" been particularly helpful in identifying the nature of the interest required. We have more often relied on pragmatic

---

[1] That phrase and others like it were mentioned in *Mountain Top Condominium* and *Alcan Aluminum.* The concept was explored in New Orleans Public Service, Inc. v. United Gas Pipe Line Co., 732 F.2d 452, 464-66, 470 (5th Cir. 1984) (en banc). The issue in *NOPSI* was the remoteness of the interest of the city as a regulatory agency in a breach of contract suit brought by a public utility against one of its gas suppliers. It was not the fact that the city's interest was financial in nature that disqualified it, but rather, because its interest was too attenuated from that of the utility. The city failed to show that it possessed any interest recognized by substantive law.

considerations such as the benefits derived from consolidation of disputes into one proceeding. Those considerations, however, should not prevail if the focus of the litigation would be unduly dissipated or case management would become exceptionally complex.

Our survey of the law in other Circuits, particularly as applied in environmental litigation, provides some helpful background. In Sierra Club v. Espy, 18 F.3d 1202 (5th Cir. 1994), the case upon which the district court principally relied, plaintiffs challenged certain management practices of the Service in Texas forests. The Court of Appeals for the Fifth Circuit concluded that two trade groups whose members included the "major purchasers and processors" of timber had an interest sufficient to satisfy Rule 24(a). In that case, some member companies had interests in existing timber contracts.

In Sierra Club v. Glickman, 82 F.3d 106 (5th Cir. 1996) (per curiam), a trade association representing farmers sought intervention in a suit to cut off federal subsidies to those who pumped water from an aquifer. Plaintiffs contended that over-pumping threatened endangered species and public health. The court concluded that the suit "potentially" interfered with the intervenors' contract rights by disrupting their access to irrigation water.

Similarly, intervention was permitted by the Court of Appeals for the First Circuit in *Conservation Law Foundation*, where plaintiffs and a government agency agreed on a consent decree that set timetables for the establishment of a government plan that would impair the business of commercial fisheries. As targets of a regulatory plan ultimately aimed at reducing over-fishing, the commercial fisheries alleged an interest that supported intervention.

Some decisions, however, adopt a more mechanical approach when evaluating the relevant interests. In Portland Audubon Society v. Hodel, 866 F.2d 302 (9th Cir. 1989), for example, the Court of Appeals for the Ninth Circuit held that an economic interest in protecting a continuous supply of timber was insufficient to warrant intervention in a NEPA case by a trade group and various timber companies. Following Wade v. Goldschmidt, 673 F.2d 182 (7th Cir. 1982) (per curiam), *Portland Audubon* held that in a suit to compel an agency to follow NEPA, only governmental bodies may be defendants. . . .

These cases seem to suggest that NEPA suits are *sui generis* because "only the government" can comply with that statute. We are reluctant to endorse a narrow approach that makes the onus of compliance the litmus test for intervention. Such a wooden standard minimizes the flexibility and spirit of Rule 24 as interpreted in *Cascade Natural Gas.*

The reality is that NEPA cases frequently pit private, state, and federal interests against each other. Rigid rules in such cases contravene a major premise of intervention—the protection of third parties affected by pending litigation. Evenhandedness is of paramount importance.

The expansion of standing by statute and case law has enabled "private attorneys general" and "public interest" groups to call governmental agencies to task in litigation. These efforts, though often well-intentioned, sometimes concentrate on narrow issues that are of significant concern to plaintiffs but have an immediate and deleterious effect on other individuals and entities. Rather than barring access to these parties, Rule 24 allows the court to give them the opportunity to present their positions. . . .

The convergence of conservation and timber interests that has occurred in this case confirms that the categorical approach can be too inflexible. Protecting timber interests has been an express Congressional policy since the establishment of the national forest system through the Organic Administration Act of 1897. That policy was affirmed in the Multiple-Use Sustained-Yield Act of 1960, and reaffirmed in the National Forest Management Act of 1976. The National Forest Management Act also blends logging and environmental interests by requiring land management plans to be drafted "under the principles of the Multiple-Use Sustained-Yield Act" and "in accordance with" NEPA.

Under these circumstances, we think that the decision of the Court of Appeals for the Fifth Circuit in *Espy* represents a more realistic approach in permitting intervention. Timber companies have direct and substantial interests in a lawsuit aimed at halting logging or, at a minimum, reducing the efficiency of their method of timber-cutting.

Adequacy of interest alone, however, is not enough to grant intervention. Because Rule 24(a) envisions a separate inquiry into whether the government or other existing parties will adequately advocate the applicant's interest, courts must be careful not to blur the interest and representation factors together.

The burden of establishing inadequacy of representation by existing parties varies with each case. A government entity charged by law with representing a national policy is presumed adequate for the task, particularly when the concerns of the proposed intervenor, e.g., a "public interest" group, closely parallel those of the public agency. In that circumstance, the "would-be intervenor [must make] a strong showing of inadequate representation." Mausolf [v. Babbit], 85 F.3d [1295,] at 1303 [(8th Cir. 1995)]. But the presumption notwithstanding, when an agency's views are necessarily colored by its view of the public welfare rather than the more parochial views of a proposed intervenor whose interest is personal to it, the burden is comparatively light. *Conservation Law Foundation*; accord *Mausolf* ("when the proposed intervenors' concern is not a matter of 'sovereign interest,' there is no reason to think the government will represent it").

This overview demonstrates that Rule 24 demands flexibility when dealing with the myriad situations in which claims for intervention arise. Nonetheless, the polestar for evaluating a claim for intervention is always whether the proposed intervenor's interest is direct or remote. Due regard for efficient conduct of the litigation requires that intervenors should have an interest that is specific to them, is capable of definition, and will be directly affected in a substantially concrete fashion by the relief sought. The interest may not be remote or attenuated. The facts assume overwhelming importance in each decision.

Counseled by these appellate opinions, we assess the case before us. The relief sought by plaintiffs, i.e., an injunction to bar logging (at least until such time as the NEPA process is completed) would have an immediate, adverse financial effect on the school districts and municipalities. That result is not speculative, intangible or unmeasurable, especially when, as other courts have observed, NEPA compliance actions can take years.

The school districts and municipalities have direct interests in this litigation because state law commands the Commonwealth, through its political subdivisions, to forward to them federal grant money generated through timber harvesting each year, money that they will lose, at least temporarily and perhaps permanently, if plaintiffs are successful in this lawsuit. To suspend the flow of revenue to the school districts and municipalities for even a limited period of time would affect spending for essential school activities and public projects. We are persuaded that the interests jeopardized, which are protected by state law, are direct, substantial and of adequate public interest as to justify intervention. In these sparsely populated areas with limited tax bases, the impairment caused by curtailing revenue provided through logging activity would be significant.

Turning to the private-party applicants, the district court cited *Espy* for the proposition that only those timber companies with existing contracts had an interest that would support intervention. From our point of view, *Espy* states a rule of inclusion for evaluating interests under Rule 24(a)(2), but should not be read to exclude similar, contract-related interests of the type implicated here.

Ridgway Lumber had more than a mere expectancy of obtaining a contract in the future. It was already a successful bidder, and from all that appears in the record, would now be a party to a remunerative contract for logging but for the institution of this litigation. Realistically, Ridgway has as strong an economic stake in the outcome of this litigation as do Spilka and Payne, which were permitted to intervene.

Brookville Wood Products and Northeast Hardwoods may not have received contracts under the projects challenged by plaintiffs, but the district court found that they are "very dependent on timber contracts with the [Service] to cut timber" in the Forest and "their continued existence may be jeopardized" if plaintiffs prevail. In addition, like the other timber companies, they have a considerable stake in ensuring that the landscape corridor approach to forest management remains in place. Congress has designated our national forests for multiple uses, but it has also emphasized that those uses are "not in derogation of" timber harvesting. 16 USC §528. This statement of policy, when viewed in light of the district court's finding that a victory for plaintiffs could destroy their business, satisfies us that Brookville and Northeast Hardwoods have a substantial interest, directly related to and threatened by this litigation, that meets the requirements of Rule 24(a).

Allegheny Hardwood falls within the category of those trade associations representing threatened businesses granted intervention in such cases as *Glickman, Espy,* and *Conservation Law Foundation.* We find the rulings in those cases persuasive and applicable to Allegheny Hardwood.

Therefore, we conclude that the interests of the private-party applicants are direct, not remote. In other words, they have more than mere attenuated economic interests because, as we have outlined, their longstanding dependence on contractual relations with the Service is unique to them.

Although plaintiffs assert that the proposed intervenors' interests are adequately protected by the government defendant, the district court found otherwise with respect to Payne and Spilka. The court pointed out that in a companion case the agency chose not to appeal an adverse ruling in connection with timber sales in other projects in the Allegheny National Forest. Consequently, that litigation gave legitimate pause to the lumber companies' confidence in adequate representation by the Service.

In addition, the government represents numerous complex and conflicting interests in matters of this nature. The straightforward business interests asserted by intervenors here may become lost in the thicket of sometimes inconsistent governmental policies. Although it is unlikely that the intervenors' economic interest will change, it is not realistic to assume that the agency's programs will remain static or unaffected by unanticipated policy shifts.

Plaintiffs contend that whatever the doubts about the vigor of the government's representation, Payne and Spilka's interests are aligned with those of the proposed intervenors. We disagree. It does not strain the imagination to conjure up situations in which Payne and Spilka may face the irresistible temptation to work out settlements that benefit themselves and not the other, competing timber companies. Compromises of that nature might also harm the school districts and municipalities, which have interests inextricably intertwined with, but distinct from, those of the timber companies.

In Solid Waste Agency [v. United States Army Corps of Engineers, 101 F.3d 503 (7th Cir. 1996)], the Court of Appeals for the Seventh Circuit discussed the value of a "wait and see" approach in which proposed intervenors would file a conditional application with the understanding that the district court would defer consideration until requested to do so. Such a procedure may work in some cases, but on balance, intervenors and the public interest in efficient handling of litigation are better served by prompt action on intervention motion. The early presence of intervenors may serve to prevent errors from creeping into the proceedings, clarify some issues, and perhaps contribute to an amicable settlement. Postponing intervention in the name of efficiency until after the original parties have forged an agreement or have litigated some issues may, in fact, encourage collateral attack and foster inefficiency. In other words, the game may already be lost by the time the intervenors get to bat in the late innings.

III

We conclude that in the circumstances of this case, the motion for leave to intervene should have been granted. Each applicant has a significantly protectable interest in the transaction that may be jeopardized by the lawsuit. None of the existing parties will adequately represent their interests. Although there are a number of intervenors, we are confident that the very able district judge will effectively handle any case-management problems that may arise. Accordingly, we will reverse the order denying intervention and remand the case to the district court for further proceedings consistent with this Opinion.

BECKER, Chief Judge, concurring.

[The majority's analytical framework "departs from the doctrinal view" of this Circuit and "will create mischief," opening the area to an amorphous "I know it when I see it" approach. The majority adopts a "flexible" and "balanced and blending" approach, but has taken pragmatism too far. The hardest question relates to the nature of the intervenor's interest, and the starting point is the *Donaldson* case, holding that the interest must be "significantly protectable." Judge Becker quotes *Harris, Mountain Top, Old Colony Trust* cases, agreeing with outcome reached by the majority in allowing all the intervenors to get in to the case.]

A more difficult case is presented with respect to proposed intervenors Brookville Wood Products, Inc. and Northeast Hardwoods. Neither of these companies has an existing contract for cutting timber in the ANF, nor have they successfully bid on a contract which would have been consummated but for the present litigation. However, the district court found that these companies "generate the majority of their revenues from timber contracts with the [Forest Service] to cut timber in the Allegheny National Forest" and that they "are very dependent on [these] timber contracts." I understand this finding, in light of the record, to mean that these companies have consistently been successful bidders in ANF logging contracts, that it is only an accident of timing that they do not have contracts at this juncture, and that—particularly given the remoteness of the area in which the companies operate—they are very likely to secure contracts in the near future if logging contracts are there to be bid (which will depend on the outcome of this litigation). In evaluating the interest of the companies without existing contracts, it is apparent that it is not an "actual" interest, but neither is it speculative. Under these circumstances, I cannot say that the majority is wrong when it finds that these companies also have the sufficient interest to meet our requirements for intervention as of right.

Finally, the government intervenors have an actual, direct interest in this litigation by virtue of their statutory right to a portion of the proceeds from contracts between logging companies and the Forest Service. The local governments are effectively limited partners with the named defendant in this case, having no control over the formation of the logging contracts but a vested right to a portion of the proceeds therefrom. Without this piggybacking on the named defendants, I would question whether the municipalities have a sufficient interest to intervene, solely based on their loss of revenue from reduced tax receipts. The majority is not clear about this distinction, emphasizing the "limited tax bases" of the municipalities in question. In my view, it is only the statutory right to logging proceeds that gives the municipalities here a sufficient interest to intervene and to protect that interest from interference that could arise from this litigation.

As noted above, the majority does not clearly draw the line between interests sufficient for intervention under Rule 24(a)(2) and those not sufficient. To better illustrate where I believe this line is drawn, I consider the proposed intervention of hypothetical parties to the present case. The logging companies to whom we grant intervention today purchase supplies from other companies for the products they need to carry out their timber-cutting business. If the logging companies' contracts with the Forest Service are suspended or canceled, the supply companies could suffer a loss of business as the logging companies no longer need purchase supplies for timber-cutting. In addition, the logging companies employ workers who use their wages to purchase products and services in local establishments, such as gas stations, grocery stores, etc. Assume one of these establishments is a diner frequented by logging company employees. When the logging companies' contracts with the Forest Service are disrupted by this litigation, these employees may be laid off or their wages reduced. With less income, they might gather at the diner with less frequency. The diner clearly will suffer an economic harm, formally (if not directly) caused by the present litigation. The same would be true of local municipalities if they did not have [sic; had?] the statutory right to a portion of the logging contract proceeds; they too would suffer an economic harm caused indirectly by the present litigation.

If the logging supply companies or the local diner were to petition for intervention as of right, should the district court find their interest sufficient to warrant intervention under Rule 24(a)(2)? I believe the majority's "elastic" approach at once gives the district court little guidance in answering this question, and gives it license to do whatever it wants. In contrast, I think it is clear that neither the Rule nor our prior jurisprudence in this area would permit the supply company or the diner to intervene as of right. While both of these businesses likely will suffer an economic harm from the litigation, in terms of both the nature and the reality of the interest, this harm is both too contingent and too remote from the litigation itself to be a legally cognizable interest sufficient for intervention under Rule 24(a)(2).

Unlike the logging companies and the local governments, which suffer an immediate, direct harm when the logging contracts are suspended—even if they somehow can replace their canceled contracts or lost revenue from some other source—the diner and supply company suffer any loss only down the line, after the logging companies have reduced their workers' wages or stopped ordering logging supplies. Further, such losses that the diner or supply company may suffer are not grounded in a legal right—contractual, property, or statutory—which is related to the litigation at hand. See, e.g., Forest Conservation Council v. United States Forest Serv., 66 F.3d 1489, 1495-97 (9th Cir. 1995) (only "tangible, concrete rights protected by" statute or contract constitute a sufficient interest under Rule 24(a)(2); purely economic injuries, pecuniary losses, or frustrated financial expectations are not sufficient interests).[4]

. . .

[This litigation could "practically impair the interests of all the proposed intervenors" if the court granted the injunctive relief requested by the plaintiffs. The interests of the logging companies have interests in contracts "either existing or certain to be entered into in the near future (absent the litigation)," and an injunction that "suspends, cancels, or prevents" future Forest Service contracts "will directly and immediately affect this interest." Local governments would also "immediately lose the income" to which those contracts entitle them.]

The only hope of preventing impairment would be if the proposed intervenors filed their own suit and argued that the Forest Service has acted in compliance with the relevant statutes and that, therefore, no injunction should issue. However, a contrary determination in the present case would have a *stare decisis* effect on this potential future litigation, leaving the proposed intervenors without legal recourse to protect their interests. . . .

In sum, I believe that an increasingly clear, if flexible, standard has developed in our Rule 24(a)(2) case law, which we should adhere to in this case and in future intervention situations, and which requires a searching analysis of each of the elements required for intervention as of right. I also believe that this jurisprudence, while not necessarily followed in the majority opinion, leads to the same result. I therefore concur in the judgment granting intervention to all of the proposed intervenors.

[4] The same analysis holds for municipalities without a piggyback right who may suffer losses when the citizens (lumber company employees) or businesses (logging companies, supply companies, local establishments) within their communities have less income and pay fewer taxes. Unlike the actual municipalities and school districts at issue here, local governments without a direct statutory right to a share of the proceeds from logging contracts have neither the tangible interest nor the direct link to the litigation necessary for intervention under Rule 24(a)(2).

■ **NOTES ON INTERVENTION**

1. Plaintiffs in *Kleissler* are people from Pennsylvania and Ohio and "an Indiana organization committed to environmental preservation." They want to halt planned logging activities in Allegheny National Forest, and contracts for such work (existing and future). Plaintiffs claim an environmental impact statement was required, and that the Forest Service failed to consider "more environmentally-protective measures." The statute directs agencies to adopt a "systematic, interdisciplinary approach" that will assess environmental impacts "along with economic and technical considerations," and describe "adverse environmental effects which cannot be avoided," taking into account the relationship between "short-term use" and "long-term productivity." See 32 USC §4332. In short, *Kleissler* is the quintessential "public law" suit, where equitable relief is sought on the basis of broad-textured multifaceted standards, and claimants purport to seek wiser implementation of the values set out in the law. Apart from "doing good" in the sense just described, what kinds of interest are plaintiffs asserting?

2. The would-be intervenors in *Kleissler* are school districts and municipalities, on the one hand, and wood-producing companies who conduct logging operations, on the other. What kinds of interests are they asserting?

3. Why does an organization "committed to environmental preservation" have standing? Why do people in Pennsylvania and Ohio have standing? In a landmark decision, the Court held that "aesthetic, conservational, and recreational" interests may justify standing, see Sierra Club v. Morton, 405 U.S. 727, 738 (1972) (but plaintiff lacked standing here because it failed to allege that it or its members would be affected by the challenged action), and in various other decisions the Court has approved standing for environmental groups. See, e.g., Friends of the Earth, Inc. v. Laidlaw Environmental Services (TOC), 528 U.S. 167 (2000) (applying statute authorizing citizen suits to enforce clean water standards).

4. It is actually not clear whether intervenors must have standing—whether they must be persons or entities who could sue (or be sued) in order to qualify as intervenors. The would-be intervenors in *Kleissler* are *defending* the Forest Service policy permitting logging, which means that they are not bringing "claims for relief" themselves. Does it make sense to let someone enter a case as an intervenor when he or she is not advancing a claim and has not been named as a defendant? Does such a person have standing to be a party? Compare San Juan County v. United States, 503 F.3d 1363, 1372 (10th Cir. 2007) (intervenors need not have standing to sue) with Massolf v. Babbitt, 85 F.3d 1295, 1301 (8th Cir. 1996) ("a federal case is a limited affair, and not everyone with an opinion is invited to attend") (intervenors must have standing). What difference does it make that such a person is (or is not) allowed to intervene and become a party to the suit? Couldn't such a person simply file an amicus brief?

5. As noted above, FRCP 24 resembles FRCP 19. Under FRCP 19, one must be joined if she "claims an interest" relating to the subject of the suit, and going forward without her would "as a practical matter impair or impede" her ability to protect that interest. Under FRCP 24, however, such a person cannot *enter* the suit as intervenor *if* someone already in the suit "adequately represent[s] that interest." It sounds, doesn't it, as though a person might be someone who must be joined in the suit under FRCP 19 (if a party raises the issue, or if the court does), but that this same person might *not* be allowed to intervene if she "knocked on the door" and tried to get in under FRCP 24? Suffice it to say that appearances (and the language of the provisions) are deceiving. In fact "interest" in FRCP 24 is more broadly construed than "interest" in FRCP 19. In short, outsiders might be allowed to intervene in a suit under FRCP 24 even though their joinder would not be required under FRCP 19. See Smuck v. Hobson, 408 F.2d 175 (D.C. Cir. 1969) ("occasions upon which a petitioner should be allowed to intervene under Rule 24 are not necessarily limited to those situations when the trial court should compel him to become a party under Rule 19"). Putting aside the question whether the language of the two provisions can be reconciled to this result, does the result make sense?

6. What does "interest" mean in FRCP 24? Here as in the area of standing, the Supreme Court has spoken to the matter many times, and in widely varying voices. Consider these decisions:

(a) In Cascade Natural Gas Corp. v. El Paso, 386 U.S. 129 (1967), the Court adopted an expansive definition of interest. There El Paso Natural Gas had been ordered to divest itself of its interest in Pacific Northwest Pipeline Company. Three would-be intervenors sought to participate in the case, and the Court found that all were intervenors as of right. The State of California could intervene, to ensure that Pacific Northwest could emerge "as an effective competitor." Southern California Edison could intervene, as an "industrial user of natural gas," to ensure that competition in supplying gas remained vigorous. And Cascade Natural Gas could intervene, as a utility that used the services of Pacific Northwest and clearly wanted those services to continue. The Court approved intervention for all three, in an opinion that construed "interest" in broad economic terms.

(b) In Donaldson v. United States, 400 U.S. 517 (1971), the Court held that a taxpayer could not intervene in an IRS summons enforcement proceeding seeking employment and compensation records of the taxpayer's former employer. The taxpayer's "interest," the Court said, was in trying to "counter and overcome" the willingness of the employer to cooperate with the IRS, which is not the interest contemplated by FRCP 24. That provision contemplates a "significantly protectable interest," which the taxpayer might have if he claimed a privilege or claimed abuse of process, but any such interest could be asserted "in any subsequent trial."

(c) In Trbovich v. United Mine Workers, 404 U.S. 582 (1972), the Court let a union member intervene in an action brought by the Secretary of Labor to set aside a union election for violations of the Labor-Management Reporting and

Disclosure Act. The Court accepted the proposition that the member's interest "in democratic elections" justified intervention. *Trbovich* did not cite *Donaldson.*

(d) Given the decisions in *Cascade, Donaldson,* and *Trbovich,* what should a court do in the following situation? A utility sues a natural gas supplier, seeking rescission of a rate increase on ground that it violates its contract with the supplier. The City of New Orleans seeks to intervene, to argue on behalf of utility users that the rise in gas prices is illegal because it infringes the right of the City to set utility rates. (The City, joined by several would-be ratepayer-intervenors, also alleges that the rise in rates will have adverse impacts on them.) Should intervention be allowed because, under cases like *Cascade Natural Gas* and *Trbovich,* it suffices that the intervenors are affected indirectly by the transaction in litigation, or should intervention be denied because, under cases like *Donaldson,* the intervenors lack a legally protectable interest? See New Orleans Public Service, Inc. v. United Gas Pipe Line, 732 F.2d 452, 465-467 (5th Cir. 1984) (denying intervention; intervenors must have a "direct" and "substantial" and "legally protectable" interest, which means "something more than an economic interest," and *Donaldson* requires instead an interest that "substantive law recognizes as belonging to or being owned by the applicant," and intervention is subject to the "prudential standing requirement") (*Trbovich* was different because the intervenor was "within the zone of interests" protected by the statute, and there is no similar "public law question" in this suit on a private contract; *Cascade* is different too because antitrust law involved in that case accords to states "substantive rights to be free of antitrust injury to its general economy). Did the court get it right?

CLASS ACTIONS

Everyone has heard of class actions: There's even a movie starring Gene Hackman entitled *Class Action* (1991). Class actions conjure up images of lawyers bringing economically powerful defendants to heel on behalf of many people who could not obtain justice any other way. Class action lawsuits, however, are not for the faint-hearted or the inexperienced lawyer: They are costly to finance and hard to bring to conclusion. One or more courses in law school are largely devoted to this subject.

1. A Special Joinder Device, or Something Else?

Conventionally, class suits are thought to be a special joinder mechanism, and it is for this reason that the relevant provision (FRCP 23) is in Article IV under the heading "Parties," along with Rules governing joinder of claims and parties in ordinary litigation.

Arguably, however, class suits belong in a stand-alone category. The reason is that members of classes other than the "named plaintiff" or "standard bearer," who appears in court as class representative, are not "parties" in the usual sense, and they lack many attributes of parties. (We focus on *plaintiff* class suits. FRCP 23 also contemplates *defendant* classes, but these are rare.) To begin with, class members do not ordinarily appear in the suit, although they can ask to intervene. They are *probably* not subject to the usual *party* discovery devices, at least not to the same extent as ordinary parties, and here we mean mostly written interrogatories. And class members cannot *prevent* the lawyer for the class from settling their claims, although they can object to proposed settlements.

On the other hand, class members are, in theory and often in reality, bound by judgments in class suits. In service of that end, FRCP 23 sets out criteria designed to ensure that the interests of class members are adequately represented.

2. The Approach of FRCP 23: The Certification Process

Although it has been often amended since it was promulgated in its present form in 1966, FRCP 23 has remained much the same Rule in important ways. It was in 1966 that the Advisory Committee decided to change radically the shape of class suits: Prior to that time, members of plaintiff classes could take advantage of a favorable judgment but were not bound by an unfavorable judgment. In this sense, the older version of the Rule was understood as a kind of "one-way intervention," and a big reason for revising the Rule was to remove this feature.

Since 1966, FRCP 23 has required courts to "certify" class suits. The effect of certifying is to transform a suit from one that can involve and bind only named parties (named plaintiff and defendants) into one that also involves and can bind class members. Certification proceeds at "an early practicable time" under FRCP 23(c)(1)(A), and the reason for acting promptly is to put everyone on notice—court, parties, class members, lawyers—of the nature of the suit so they can act appropriately. It is necessary to be a little bit cautious here, however, because FRCP 23(c)(1)(C) also provides that certification orders may be "altered or amended" in ways that can exclude persons previously in the class or add persons not previously included. In a sense, then, certification decisions are tentative and subject to revision. But when class members have been notified, certification is supposed to mean something: Reliance interests build up, and certification decisions are not lightly made or easily changed.

The task of certification involves taking a preliminary look at the suit to see whether the requirements for class treatment are satisfied. Under FRCP 23(a), every suit that is to proceed as a class action must satisfy four threshold requirements: Numerosity (so many people in the class that joining them all is "impracticable"); common questions of law or fact (a standard that is common to other joinder provisions, including FRCP 18 and 19, which you have already looked at); typicality (named plaintiff's claims must be "typical" of claims of class members); adequate representation (named plaintiff must "fairly and adequately protect" interests of the class). As you will soon see, "adequate representation" is a key element in class actions, and one that rests on constitutional notions of due process, as the Court decided in the *Hansberry* case (Section H4, infra).

In the *Wal-Mart* case in 2011, the Supreme Court had before it a purported nationwide class suit alleging that a giant retailer discriminated against women. In a 5-4 decision, the Court disapproved class treatment because the common question requirement was not satisfied. (We look further at *Wal-Mart* in the Notes following the *Allen* case in Section H5, infra). *Wal-Mart* shed important light on the certification process:

> The class action is "an exception to the usual rule that litigation is con-ducted by and on behalf of the individual named parties only." Califano v. Yama-saki, 442 U.S. 682, 700-701 (1979). In order to justify a departure from that rule, "a class representative must be part of the class and 'possess the same interest and suffer the same injury' as the class members." East Tex. Motor Freight System, Inc. v. Rodriguez, 431 U.S. 395, 403 (1977) (quoting Schlesinger v. Reservists Comm. to Stop the War, 418 U.S. 208, 216 (1974)). Rule 23(a) ensures that the named plaintiffs are appropriate representatives of the class whose claims they wish to litigate. The Rule's four requirements—numerosity, commonality, typi-cality, and adequate representation—"effectively 'limit the class claims to those fairly encompassed by the named plaintiff's claims.'" General Telephone Co. of Southwest v. Falcon, 457 U.S. 147, 156 (1982) (quoting General Telephone Co. of Northwest v. EEOC, 446 U.S. 318, 330 (1980)).
>
> . . .
>
> Rule 23 does not set forth a mere pleading standard. A party seeking class certification must affirmatively demonstrate his compliance with the Rule—that is, he must be prepared to prove that there are *in fact* sufficiently numerous parties, common questions of law or fact, etc. We recognized in *Falcon* that "sometimes it may be necessary for the court to probe behind the pleadings before coming to rest on the certification question," and that certification is proper only if "the trial court is satisfied, after a rigorous analysis, that the pre-requisites of Rule 23(a) have been satisfied" ("[A]ctual, not presumed, confor-mance with Rule 23(a) remains . . . indispensable"). Frequently that "rigorous analysis" will entail some overlap with the merits of the plaintiff's underlying claim. That cannot be helped. "'[T]he class determination generally involves con-siderations that are enmeshed in the factual and legal issues comprising the plaintiff's cause of action.'" *Falcon* (quoting Coopers & Lybrand v. Livesay, 437 U.S. 463, 469 (1978)). Nor is there anything unusual about that consequence: The necessity of touching aspects of the merits in order to resolve preliminary mat-ters, *e.g.,* jurisdiction and venue, is a familiar feature of litigation.

> In this case, proof of commonality necessarily overlaps with respondents' merits contention that Wal-Mart engages in a *pattern or practice* of discrimination. That is so because, in resolving an individual's Title VII claim, the crux of the inquiry is "the reason for a particular employment decision," Cooper v. Federal Reserve Bank of Richmond, 467 U.S. 867, 876 (1984). Here respondents wish to sue about literally millions of employment decisions at once. Without some glue holding the alleged *reasons* for all those decisions together, it will be impossible to say that examination of all the class members' claims for relief will produce a common answer to the crucial question *why was I disfavored.*

Wal-Mart Stores, Inc. v. Dukes, 131 S. Ct. 2541, 2551-2552 (2011). In short, the certification decision requires the court and the parties to roll up their sleeves and get into the facts and theories of the case, and it is *not* something that can be undertaken just by looking at the complaint.

3. The Approach of FRCP 23: Four Types of Class Suits

The hallmark of the 1966 amendment was not only its introduction of a certification requirement, but its abandonment of the formalism embodied in the prior version of the Rule, which had authorized class suits to enforce "joint or common" rights, and sometimes "several" rights. Courts had to draw distinctions based largely on property and contract law, which proved mystifying and unworkable. Part of the new functionality in the modern Rule involves the four basic requirements in FRCP 23(a) (numerosity, and so forth). The new functionality extends as well into the four different types of class suits authorized by the Rule:

(1) "Incompatible Standards" Class Suits. Under FRCP 23(b)(1)(A), a class suit may be brought if individual suits would "create a risk" of "inconsistent or varying adjudications" that would set up "incompatible standards of conduct" for the party opposing the class (usually defendants). Notice the resemblance to the criterion in FRCP 19 that requires joinder of parties if, in their absence, someone already in the suit would be put to the risk of "incurring double, multiple, or otherwise inconsistent obligations." The approach of FRCP 23 is to involve essential outsiders by means of class treatment, while the approach of FRCP 19 is to insist on joining them as parties.

An example from the distant past illustrates this kind of class suit. In Supreme Tribe of Ben Hur v. Cauble, 255 U.S. 356 (1921), a few members of a fraternal society (which provided an early form of life insurance), acting on behalf of all, sued the Society to enjoin a certain use of its funds. The court entered a decree setting out the rights and obligations of the Society with respect to members, and the Supreme Court concluded that the decree was binding on all. Here is a case where defendant's obligation was to treat members equally and fairly, and separate member suits would have brought risks of differing and conflicting decrees.

(2) "Limited Fund" Class Suits. Under FRCP 23(b)(1)(B), a class suit may be brought if separate suits by members of the class would "as a practical matter" dispose of the interests of other members or "would substantially impair or impede their ability to protect their interests." Notice the resemblance to another concept in FRCP 19, requiring joinder of parties if going forward without them would "as a practical matter impair or impede" their ability to "protect" their "interests." Again the approach of FRCP 23 is to involve them by class treatment, and the approach of FRCP 19 is to insist on joining them.[2]

One example of such a suit (litigated under a state counterpart to FRCP 23) is State Department of Revenue v. Andrade, 23 P.3d 58 (Alaska 2001), in which a legal alien living in Alaska challenged the constitutionality of the Permanent Fund Dividend payable to Alaskans out of state tax collections, on ground that the fund excluded them because they "could not legally form an intent to remain in Alaska indefinitely based on their immigrant status." Such a case can go forward under FRCP 23(b)(2)(B) because the fund is finite (taxes collected and dedicated to this purpose), and individual suits seeking shares of it would affect what others might receive. In another case brought under FRCP 23(b)(2)(B), investors seeking to save a failing company provided a cash infusion of $600,000 that was misused by executives, and the court approved a class suit for investors, treating what was left of the money as "property held in constructive trust by reason of fraud," noting that no claimant sought "full recovery" in "ordinary tort liability," asking only to recover from the fund. See Dickinson v. Burnham, 197 F.2d 973, 980 (2d Cir. 1952).

Because class suits under FRCP 23(b)(1) do not carry "opt-out rights" (nor do class suits brought under FRCP 23(b)(2)), lawyers seeking to reach global settlements in massive class suits have sometimes sought to stretch the limited fund concept, but in the *Ortiz* case in 2001 the Supreme Court refused to go along. *Ortiz* brings to the fore a feature of many modern class suits, and you will see this feature again when you read *Amchem* (Section H8, infra): *Ortiz* was put together with no intention of going to trial, but rather to get court approval of settlement. Asbestos makers would set up a trust fund, financed partly by insurance, and the argument was that the case fit FRCP 23(b)(2) because claims exceeded the ability to pay. The Court rejected this undertaking for many reasons: First, it thought the estimate of assets was speculative, largely because it rested on guesses

---

[2] The first two types of class suits have something in common with interpleader. Like the "incompatible standards" class suit, interpleader helps save a party (the stakeholder) from multiple or inconsistent obligations; like the "limited fund" class suit, interpleader assures that claimants recover what they should.

about the outcome of other litigation that would determine the extent of insurance liability. Second, in traditional limited fund suits "the whole of the inadequate fund" was used to pay claimants, but the proposal in *Ortiz* let asbestos makers retain most of their net worth. Third, claimants were not receiving equitable treatment: The settlement left in place side agreements settling other claims on terms more favorable than those available to the class, and class members with highly varied claims were treated alike, with inadequate "structural protections." The settlement was especially inadequate for claimants not yet manifesting ailments. See Ortiz v. Fibreboard Corp., 527 U.S. 815 (1999).

Long before *Ortiz*, courts had stretched the limited fund concept in a different way. In tort cases arising out of exposure to toxic substances or use of products sold nationally, the notion grew up that multiple punitive damage awards could "overpunish" defendants. In order to cap punitive damage claims, it was thought that limited fund class suits could establish the appropriate amount, determine liability, and distribute the resultant "fund" among claimants. Trial courts occasionally certified class treatment, but often these decisions were reversed on appeal for various reasons, including lack of a "true" limit on such liability. See, e.g., In re Northern District of California "Dalkon Shield" IUD Products Liability Litigation, 521 F. Supp. 1188 (N.D. Cal. 1981), *rev'g* 693 F.2d 847 (9th Cir. 1982). In light of modern decisions recognizing that the Constitution does limit punitive liability in some way, some modern decisions approve certification of limited fund classes in this context, see In re Exxon Valdez, 270 F.3d 1215 (9th Cir. 2001). *Ortiz,* however, raised new questions, and the area remains controversial.[3]

(3) "Unfair Treatment" Class Suits. Under FRCP 23(b)(2), a class suit may seek "injunctive" or "declaratory" relief when defendant has "acted or refused to act on grounds generally applicable to the class." This provision covers two kinds of suits that are common in modern litigation, particularly in federal court. One is the discrimination suit, which classically involves claims that employment practices violate Title VII of the Civil Rights Act of 1964, or equal protection (where the statutory authority for suit is 42 USC §1983). These suits often raise claims of ethnic or racial discrimination, and more recently discrimination based on gender, age, disability, religion, sexual orientation, and other factors. The *Wal-Mart* case was one such suit, although class treatment failed there because the majority thought the common question requirement could not be satisfied in a nationwide suit. See *Wal-Mart Stores,*

---

[3] See generally Laura J. Hines, *Obstacles to Determining Punitive Damages in Class Actions*, 36 Wake Forest L. Rev. 889 (2001); Richard Nagareda, *Punitive Damage Class Actions and the Baseline of Tort*, 36 Wake Forest L. Rev. 943 (2001); Joan Steinman, *Managing Punitive Damages: A Role for Mandatory "Limited Generosity" Classes and Antisuit Injunctions?*, 36 Wake Forest L. Rev. 1043 (2001); Sheila Scheuerman, *Two Worlds Collide: How the Supreme Court's Recent Punitive Damages Decisions Affect Class Actions*, 60 Baylor L. Rev. 880 (2008).

supra, at 2541. You will see an example of a successful suit in this setting in the *Allen* case, infra.

The other kind of suit that often fits this category is the institutional reform suit, which classically involves challenges to prison conditions, and now many more kinds of institutions and their practices. See, e.g., Pierce v. County of Orange, 526 F.3d 1190 (9th Cir. 2008) (class suit achieving changes in jail conditions for pretrial detainees under §1983). It is this kind of suit that successfully challenged the use of racial preferences in college admissions at the University of Michigan, see Gratz v. Bollinger, 539 U.S. 244 (2003).

(4) "Common Question" Class Suits. Under FRPC 23(b)(3), a class suit can seek money damages if it satisfies the central criterion requiring that common questions of law or fact "predominate" and if a class suit would be "superior to other available methods," taking into account the interests of class members in controlling their cases, the extent of other litigation involving the same controversy, the relative merits of "concentrating" the suit in one place, and—especially important—"likely difficulties in managing" the suit. A salient feature of this kind of class suit is that class members are entitled to notice and an opportunity to "opt out" after the class has been certified.

It is the common question class suit that most captures popular imagination, and has proved attractive to plaintiffs' lawyers because of the prospect of huge fees awarded out of judgment or settlement, and most terrifying to defendants because of the possibility of huge liability. When it comes to suits seeking damage recovery in amounts that are too small per claimant to support separate suits ("negative value" suits), class litigation may be the only way that recovery is possible.

In the last 30 years, claimants have brought many common question class suits in situations in which potential recovery per class member is high enough to justify individual suits. *Especially* in this setting, courts applying FRCP 23(b)(3) are supposed to engage in a "rigorous analysis" of the factors justifying this kind of suit. See Vega v. T-Mobile USA, Inc., 564 F.3d 1256, 1269 (11th Cir. 2009) (reversing order certifying class in suit by former employees seeking commissions on sales of prepaid cellular telephone accounts, for failing to conduct "rigorous analysis" to ensure that FRCP 23's requirements are satisfied).

Hybrid Class Suits. Rule 23 contemplates the possibility of classwide treatment for part of a suit, but not the whole suit. In the words of Rule 23(c)(4), "an action may be brought or maintained as a class action with respect to particular issues." Hence it is sometimes possible to determine "liability" on a classwide basis while leaving decisions on "damages" to be determined claimant by claimant (in effect, in "individual suits") later. You will see this feature in the *Allen* and *Madison* cases (Sections H4 and H5, infra).

4. The Fundamental Challenge: Ensuring Adequate Representation

Now we go back in time, and look at the landmark decision in the *Hansberry* case, decided long before the 1966 reforms of Rule 23. It is *Hansberry* that set up, as the constitutional standard of due process, what is probably the single most important element in any proper class suit—adequate representation of class members.

Earl B. Dickerson

In the suit against the Hansberry family leading to the appeal and the famous decision in the *Hansberry* case, a prominent African-American attorney named Earl B. Dickerson (1891-1986) represented the defendants. Not only did he represent them in the state courts, but he argued the case before the Supreme Court as well, where he prevailed. Dickerson earned a bachelor's degree from the University of Illinois, served as an enlisted man in the United States Army during World War I, and became the first African-American graduate of the University of Chicago Law School in 1920. He engaged in private practice and became active in politics and civil rights, serving on the Chicago City Council (the first African American to hold that post) and on the board of the NAACP. He also served as president of the Chicago Urban League and the National Lawyers Guild.

HANSBERRY v. LEE

United States Supreme Court
311 U.S. 32 (1940)

Mr. Justice STONE delivered the opinion of the Court.

The question is whether the Supreme Court of Illinois, by its adjudication that petitioners in this case are bound by a judgment rendered in an earlier litigation to which they were not parties, has deprived them of the due process of law guaranteed by the Fourteenth Amendment.

Respondents brought this suit in the Circuit Court of Cook County, Illinois, to enjoin the breach by petitioners of an agreement restricting the use of land within a described area of the City of Chicago, which was alleged to have been entered into by some five hundred of the land owners. The agreement stipulated that for a specified period no part of the land should be "sold, leased to or permitted to be occupied by any person of the colored race," and provided that it should not be effective unless signed by the "owners of 95 per centum of the frontage" within the described area. The bill of complaint set up that the owners of 95 per cent of the frontage had signed; that respondents are owners of land within the restricted area who have either signed the agreement or acquired their land from others who did sign and that petitioners Hansberry, who are Negroes, have, with the alleged aid of the other petitioners and with knowledge of the agreement, acquired and are occupying land in the restricted area formerly belonging to an owner who had signed the agreement.

To the defense that the agreement had never become effective because owners of 95 per cent of the frontage had not signed it, respondents pleaded that that issue was res judicata by the decree in an earlier suit. Burke v. Kleiman, 277 Ill. App. 519 (1934). To this petitioners pleaded, by way of rejoinder, that they were not parties to that suit or bound by its decree, and that denial of their right to litigate, in the present suit, the issue of performance of the condition precedent to the validity of the agreement would be a denial of due process of law guaranteed by the Fourteenth Amendment. It does not appear, nor is it contended that any of petitioners is the successor in interest to or in privity with any of the parties in the earlier suit.

The circuit court, after a trial on the merits, found that owners of only about 54 per cent of the frontage had signed the agreement, and that the only support of the judgment in the *Burke* case was a false and fraudulent stipulation of the parties that 95 per cent had signed. But it ruled that the issue of performance of the condition precedent to the validity of the agreement was res judicata as alleged and entered a decree for respondents. The Supreme Court of Illinois affirmed. We granted certiorari to resolve the constitutional question.

The Supreme Court of Illinois, upon an examination of the record in Burke v. Kleiman, found that that suit, in the Superior Court of Cook County, was brought by a landowner in the restricted area to enforce the agreement which had been signed by her predecessor in title, in behalf of herself and other property owners in like situation, against four named individuals who had acquired or asserted an interest in a plot of land formerly owned by another signer of the agreement; that upon stipulation of the parties in that suit that the agreement had been signed by owners of 95 per cent of all the frontage, the court had adjudged that the agreement was in force, that it was a covenant running with the land and binding all the land within the described area in the hands of the parties to the agreement and those claiming under them including defendants, and had entered its decree restraining the breach of the agreement by the defendants and those claiming under them, and that the appellate court had affirmed the decree. It found that the stipulation was untrue but held, contrary to the trial court, that it was not fraudulent or collusive. It also appears from the record in Burke v.

Kleiman that the case was tried on an agreed statement of facts which raised only a single issue, whether by reason of changes in the restricted area, the agreement had ceased to be enforceable in equity.

From this the Supreme Court of Illinois concluded in the present case that Burke v. Kleiman was a "class" or "representative" suit and that in such a suit "where the remedy is pursued by a plaintiff who has the right to represent the class to which he belongs, other members of the class are bound by the results in the case unless it is reversed or set aside on direct proceedings"; that petitioners in the present suit were members of the class represented by the plaintiffs in the earlier suit and consequently were bound by its decree which had rendered the issue of performance of the condition precedent to the restrictive agreement res judicata, so far as petitioners are concerned. The court thought that the circumstance that the stipulation in the earlier suit that owners of 95 per cent of the frontage had signed the agreement was contrary to the fact as found in the present suit did not militate against this conclusion since the court in the earlier suit had jurisdiction to determine the fact as between the parties before it and that its determination, because of the representative character of the suit, even though erroneous, was binding on petitioners until set aside by a direct attack on the first judgment.

State courts are free to attach such descriptive labels to litigations before them as they may choose and to attribute to them such consequences as they think appropriate under state constitutions and laws, subject only to the requirements of the Constitution of the United States. But when the judgment of a state court, ascribing to the judgment of another court the binding force and effect of res judicata, is challenged for want of due process it becomes the duty of this Court to examine the course of procedure in both litigations to ascertain whether the litigant whose rights have thus been adjudicated has been afforded such notice and opportunity to be heard as are requisite to the due process which the Constitution prescribes. Western Life Indemnity Co. v. Rupp, 235 U.S. 261, 273 (1914).

It is a principle of general application in Anglo-American jurisprudence that one is not bound by a judgment in personam in a litigation in which he is not designated as a party or to which he has not been made a party by service of process. Pennoyer v. Neff, 95 U.S. 714 (1877). A judgment rendered in such circumstances is not entitled to the full faith and credit which the Constitution and statute of the United States, 28 USC §687 [now 28 USC §1738], prescribe, and judicial action enforcing it against the person or property of the absent party is not that due process which the Fifth and Fourteenth Amendments requires.

To these general rules there is a recognized exception that, to an extent not precisely defined by judicial opinion, the judgment in a "class" or "representative" suit, to which some members of the class are parties, may bind members of the class or those represented who were not made parties to it. Smith v. Swormstedt, 57 U.S. 288 (1853); Royal Arcanum v. Green, 237 U.S. 531 (1915); Hartford L. Ins. Co. v. Ibs, 237 U.S. 662 (1915); Hartford Life Ins. Co. v. Barber, 245 U.S. 146 (1917); Supreme Tribe of Ben-Hur v. Cauble, 255 U.S. 356 (1921); cf. Christopher v. Brusselback, 302 U.S. 500 (1938).

The class suit was an invention of equity to enable it to proceed to a decree in suits where the number of those interested in the subject of the litigation is so great that their joinder as parties in conformity to the usual rules of procedure is impracticable. Courts are not infrequently called upon to proceed with causes in which the number of those interested in the litigation is so great as to make difficult or impossible the joinder of all because some are not within the jurisdiction or because their whereabouts is unknown or where if all were made parties to the suit its continued abatement by the death of some would prevent or unduly delay a decree. In such cases where the interests of those not joined are of the same class as the interests of those who are, and where it is considered that the latter fairly represent the former in the prosecution of the litigation of the issues in which all have a common interest, the court will proceed to a decree.

It is evident that the considerations which may induce a court thus to proceed, despite a technical defect of parties, may differ from those which must be taken into account in determining whether the absent parties are bound by the decree or, if it is adjudged that they are, in ascertaining whether such an adjudication satisfies the requirements of due process and of full faith and credit. Nevertheless there is scope within the framework of the Constitution for holding in appropriate cases that a judgment rendered in a class suit is res judicata as to members of the class who are not formal parties to the suit. Here, as elsewhere, the Fourteenth Amendment does not compel state courts or legislatures to adopt any particular rule for establishing the conclusiveness of judgments in class suits, nor does it compel the adoption of the particular rules thought by this court to be appropriate for the federal courts. With a proper regard for divergent local institutions and interests, this Court is justified in saying that there has been a failure of due process only in those cases where it cannot be said that the procedure adopted, fairly insures the protection of the interests of absent parties who are to be bound by it.

It is familiar doctrine of the federal courts that members of a class not present as parties to the litigation may be bound by the judgment where they are in fact adequately represented by parties who are present, or where they actually participate in the conduct of the litigation in which members of the class are present as parties, or where the interest of the members of the class, some of whom are present as parties, is joint, or where for any other reason the relationship between the parties present and those who are absent is such as legally to entitle the former to stand in judgment for the latter.

In all such cases, so far as it can be said that the members of the class who are present are, by generally recognized rules of law, entitled to stand in judgment for those who are not, we may assume for present purposes that such procedure affords a protection to the parties who are represented though absent, which would satisfy the requirements of due process and full faith and credit. Nor do we find it necessary for the decision of this case to say that, when the only circumstance defining the class is that the determination of the rights of its members turns upon a single issue of fact or law, a state could not constitutionally adopt a procedure whereby some of the members of the class could stand in judgment for all, provided that the procedure were so devised and applied as to insure that those present are of the same class as those absent and that the litigation is so conducted as to insure the full and fair consideration of the common issue. We decide only that the procedure and the course of litigation sustained here by the plea of res judicata do not satisfy these requirements.

The restrictive agreement did not purport to create a joint obligation or liability. If valid and effective its promises were the several obligations of the signers and those claiming under them. The promises ran severally to every other signer. It is plain that in such circumstances all those alleged to be bound by the agreement would not constitute a single class in any litigation brought to enforce it. Those who sought to secure its benefits by enforcing it could not be said to be in the same class with or represent those whose interest was in resisting performance, for the agreement by its terms imposes obligations and confers rights on the owner of each plot of land who signs it. If those who thus seek to secure the benefits of the agreement were rightly regarded by the state Supreme Court as constituting a class, it is evident that those signers or their successors who are interested in challenging the validity of the agreement and resisting its performance are not of the same class in the sense that their interests are identical so that any group who had elected to enforce rights conferred by the agreement could be said to be acting in the interest of any others who were free to deny its obligation.

Because of the dual and potentially conflicting interests of those who are putative parties to the agreement in compelling or resisting its performance, it is impossible to say, solely because they are parties to it, that any two of them are of the same class. Nor without more, and with the due regard for the protection of the rights of absent parties which due process exacts, can some be permitted to stand in judgment for all.

It is one thing to say that some members of a class may represent other members in a litigation where the sole and common interest of the class in the litigation, is either to assert a common right or to challenge an asserted obligation. Smith v. Swormstedt; Supreme Tribe of Ben-Hur v. Cauble. It is quite another to hold that all those who are free alternatively either to assert rights or to challenge them are of a single class, so that any group merely because it is of the class so constituted, may be deemed adequately to represent any others of the class in litigating their interests in either alternative. Such a selection of representatives for purposes of litigation, whose substantial interests are not necessarily or even probably the same as those whom they are deemed to represent, does not afford that protection to absent parties which due process requires. The doctrine of representation of absent parties in a class suit has not hitherto been thought to go so far. Apart from the opportunities it would afford for the fraudulent and collusive sacrifice of the rights of absent parties, we think that the representation in this case no more satisfies the requirements of due process than a trial by a judicial officer who is in such situation that he may have an interest in the outcome of the litigation in conflict with that of the litigants.

The plaintiffs in the *Burke* case sought to compel performance of the agreement on behalf of themselves and all others similarly situated. They did not designate the defendants in the suit as a class or seek any injunction or other relief against others than the named defendants, and the decree which was entered did not purport to bind others. In seeking to enforce the agreement the plaintiffs in that suit were not representing the petitioners here whose substantial interest is in resisting performance. The defendants in the first suit were not treated by the pleadings or decree as representing others or as foreclosing by their defense the rights of others, and even though nominal defendants, it does not appear that their interest in defeating the contract outweighed their interest in establishing its validity. For a court in this situation to ascribe to either the plaintiffs or defendants the performance of such functions on behalf of petitioners here, is to attribute to them a power that it cannot be said that they had assumed to exercise, and a responsibility which, in view of their dual interests it does not appear that they could rightly discharge.

Reversed.

Mr. Justice McREYNOLDS, Mr. Justice ROBERTS and Mr. Justice REED concur in the result.

■ NOTES ON *HANSBERRY* AND THE PROBLEM OF ADEQUATE REPRESENTATION

1. When Carl and Nannie Hansberry and their daughter Lorraine moved into 6140 South Rhodes Avenue, they were not the first black Americans in the neighborhood. The same broker on the sale to the Hansberry family had arranged a sale to another black buyer, in both cases disguising the fact that the buyers were black. Indeed, many black Americans had moved to adjacent areas in South Chicago. When Anna Lee and others sued the Hansberry family (and others who allegedly conspired to violate the covenant), Earl

Dickerson represented the defendants. After what seemed to the Hansberry family to be a pyrrhic victory, they moved to another neighborhood. Ultimately, Carl Hansberry emigrated to Mexico, but died there of a sudden ailment a year later. Lorraine Hansberry became a playwright, and her play *A Raisin in the Sun* (first performed in 1959) told a story of a black family living in an apartment on the South Side trying to decide whether to move to a white neighborhood in which residents intimidate black neighbors and try to dissuade blacks from coming at all. Dickerson and the Hansberry family hoped for a judgment that racial covenants are invalid. The Court had struck down racially restrictive zoning ordinances, see Buchanan v. Warley, 245 U.S. 60 (1917), but its earlier decision in The Civil Rights Cases, 109 U.S. 3 (1883), had held that the Fourteenth Amendment only bars racial discrimination by governments, not by individuals. Eight years after *Hansberry,* the Court held that private racial covenants cannot be enforced in courts. See Shelley v. Kraemer, 334 U.S. 1 (1948). See generally Jay Tidmarsh, *The Story of* Hansberry: *The Rise of the Modern Class Action*, in Civil Procedure Stories 233 (Kevin Clermont, 2d ed. 2008).

2. As a matter of real property and contract law, one who owns real estate can sell it and create restrictions or burdens that are enforceable against buyers and their successors. If Amy owns adjacent parcels Redacre and Greenacre, she can convey title in Greenacre to Carl while reserving her right to drive over part of Greenacre to get from Redacre to a public road. Such a burden binds Carl and later owners of Greenacre: If Carl conveys title to Dora, she is bound too. And successors in the ownership of Redacre can enforce the same rights: If Amy conveys her title in Redacre to Bob, he can enforce the covenants against Carl as long as he owns Greenacre, or Dora if she has bought Greenacre from Carl. Covenants "running with the land" stay in place unless otherwise altered.

3. Plaintiffs in *Hansberry* did *not* merely argue that Hansberry and other defendants were bound by a covenant. Plaintiffs argued that they were bound by the judgment in Burke v. Kleiman, 277 Ill. App. 519 (1934). If a racial covenant is enforceable, as appeared to be true at the time, what did plaintiffs hope to gain by arguing that defendants were bound by the judgment in *Burke*?

4. Suppose a neighborhood covenant says roofs must be of "cedar shake shingles," and Frank (an owner subject to the covenant) puts up a roof made of concrete tiles (these can be made to look like wooden shakes). Suppose Ellen, who lives next to Frank, sues him, and he argues that the covenant is obsolete because new studies show that wooden shake roofs are a fire hazard (they are now barred in many communities). In *Hansberry,* defendants argued this point. See Burke v. Kleiman, 277 Ill. App. 519 (1934) ("conditions have so changed in the restricted area" that enforcing the covenant "would be inequitable and a hardship"). That is a pretty good argument, isn't it? Obsolescence is the most common way to put an end to covenants that have outlived their usefulness.

5. Much is made of the observation in *Hansberry* that Isaac Kleiman and the other defendants in *Burke* signed a "false and fraudulent" stipulation agreeing that "95 per cent of the frontage" had signed, which was the prerequisite to binding the neighborhood. (A prior original covenant, or perhaps a local law, must have set that figure: Absent such covenant or law, nobody would be bound by a covenant who hadn't signed it.) In a modern study of the question whether enough people had signed to pass the 95 percent threshold, Professor Tidmarsh concluded that as much as 96.6 percent of the frontage had signed, or as little as 71.4 percent. In *Hansberry* this point was disputed. Ambiguities in wording, uncertainty about geographical coverage, and discrepancies in signatures raised issues. See Tidmarsh, supra. Given these facts, should one conclude that the defense lawyers in *Burke* didn't fight hard enough, and failed adequately to represent those interested in striking down the covenants? If the defense in *Burke* had put up only token opposition to the covenants, why did they appeal when they lost at trial? Isn't it understandable, given the difficulties surrounding the 95 percent requirement, that defendants chose to agree that the covenant had taken effect and instead attacked it as unenforceable because of changed conditions? Winning just because too few people had signed would not end racial covenants, which is what Dickerson and his clients wanted.

6. What is the most important point made in *Hansberry*? Isn't it that nobody is bound by a judgment unless he or she is a party or a member of a class in a suit brought as such, and was "adequately represented"? Apparently, *Burke* was a class suit, brought by Ida Burke "on behalf of herself and on behalf of all other property owners" covered by the covenant. When Burke won, and the judgment concluded that the covenant was enforceable, wasn't everyone in the neighborhood bound—at least if the judgment is valid? Wouldn't it follow, then, that anyone who showed up later would be bound to a covenant whose validity was reinforced by a judgment?

7. The Court comments in *Hansberry* that the neighborhood covered by the covenant contains at least two classes—those who wanted to enforce it and those who wanted to resist it. Hence the judgment won by a class of enforcers could not bind resisters. In dictum at the end, *Hansberry* suggests a solution: Plaintiffs in *Burke* could have "designate[d]" defendants as representatives of a "class," by which the Court means covenant resisters. Then we would have a bilateral class suit—a class of covenant enforcers suing a class of covenant resisters.

(a) Recalling from note 4, supra, the neighborhood dispute over a covenant requiring cedar shake shingles, we can imagine a class suit being brought in order to resolve the matter. We're supposing that Ellen wants to enforce the covenant, but Frank resists it, having put up a concrete tile roof. Ellen might sue on behalf of a class comprised of "everyone who wants cedar shake shingles on roofs in the neighborhood," naming Frank as representative of a class comprised of "everyone who doesn't want cedar shake shingle roofs." If this case were litigated and if Frank were to lose,

presumably the covenant would be not only enforceable, but would now have the added strength provided by a court judgment binding covenant resisters, including those who acquire property in the neighborhood later on.

(b) Why should it make a difference, in terms of binding newcomers, whether Frank was sued as representative of a class rather than as an individual? Note that FRCP 23 requires the judge to ensure that parties acting on behalf of a class adequately represent the class, but courts have no similar obligation to ensure that individual parties are adequately represented by their lawyers.

(c) When *Burke* and *Hansberry* were litigated in the 1930s, procedural conventions relating to class suits did not include certification proceedings, and FRCP 23 did not exist. In today's world, a judge would ascertain that both Ellen and Frank adequately represented their respective classes, and would either certify or refuse to certify the classes. If the judge did certify a bilateral class suit and grew uneasy later, the certification order could be "altered or amended." Do these safeguards explain why it matters, in terms of binding a class of covenant resisters, whether Frank is sued as an individual or as representative of a class?

8. Not surprisingly, given *Hansberry,* conflicts within a purported class can stand in the way of certification or settlement approval. See Amchem Products v. Windsor, 521 U.S. 591 (1977) (disapproving proposed global settlement of asbestos claims because class embraced people with present symptoms and ailments and people who had not yet manifested symptoms; their interests differed); Danvers Motor Co. v. Ford Motor Co., 543 F.3d 141, 138 (3d Cir. 2008) (disapproving certification of car dealerships challenging automaker's incentive program because of "diversity and conflict" within class); Langbecker v. Electronic Data Systems Corp., 476 F.3d 299, 315 (5th Cir. 2007) (intraclass conflicts may negate adequacy of representation, making certification improper).

9. Broadly understood, doesn't *Hansberry* hold that when it is claimed in a later suit that a party (call her "Smith") is bound by an earlier judgment where her interests were represented by someone else, Smith can try to show that she should *not* be bound because her interests were *not* adequately represented? If Smith, who was not a *party* to the prior suit (she was a class member), can only be bound if the interests of her class were adequately represented, then in the second proceeding the court would be looking *a second time* at same issues that the first court already examined, under modern procedures. The first court assured adequate representation for the class. The second court, when a class member claims that she was not adequately represented, looks *again* at the same thing. See, e.g., Pelt v. Utah, 539 F.3d 1271, 1284-1285 (10th Cir. 2008) (two prior class suits did not bind Navajo beneficiaries of trust fund managed by state; prior suits were dismissed for failure to prosecute; counsel for plaintiffs failed vigorously to pursue and protect beneficiaries' interests; determination in original suits that standard bearers adequately represented class, "even though correct when made, may not be correct at later stages," and court adjudicating a class action cannot "predetermine the res judicata effect of its own judgment," which can only be determined in a later suit). *Pelt* and other cases read *Hansberry* this way, putting in place what we might call the "Second Look Doctrine" (*two courts examine adequacy of representation*).

10. There are reasons to doubt that a bilateral class could have "solved the problem" in *Hansberry:* First, defendant classes are rare. Unlike plaintiff classes, defendants designated as class representatives are drafted into this role. Often they resist it, and courts are reluctant to force defendants to shoulder this burden. Second, classes defined by "attitude" or "state of mind" are rare, and courts are uneasy about such definitions. Third, while courts sometimes recognize classes of people who have not yet appeared, such classes too are rare, and it is not so clear that plaintiff in *Hansberry* could have sued a class comprised of "everyone who might show up some day and want to resist the covenant." Fourth, the Court was uneasy about enforcing a racial covenant. Apparently, it was not ready in 1940 to reach the conclusion it reached eight years later in *Shelley,* but the dictum at the end of the opinion is probably designed not so much to show how to enforce a racial covenant as to engage in what we might call "constructive speculation" about solutions to problems that arise from conflicts within classes.

5. The "Unfair Treatment" Class Suit Under FRCP 23(b)(2)

It turns out that discrimination suits against employers were not the paradigm case in the minds of the framers in 1966 as they came up with FRCP 23(b)(2)—they were thinking about desegregation suits against public institutions. But vastly expanded litigation under the Civil Rights Act of 1964, usually in the employment context, is now the most common form of unfair treatment class litigation.

In institutional reform litigation under FRCP 23(b)(2), significant challenges arise when the remedy requires courts not merely to order changes in procedures, staffing, or rules, but involves courts in day-to-day supervision. See, e.g., Shook v. Board of County Commissioners of County of El Paso, 543 F.3d 597 (10th Cir. 2008) (in suit alleging inadequate mental health care for jailed inmates, plaintiffs sought orders directing officials not to use restraints, pepper spray, or Tasers in circumstances posing "substantial risk of serious harm" to prisoners; practice is to be enjoined "by reference to circumstances that vary among class members," and different injunctions are required to establish appropriate behavior for different groups; "classwide relief may be difficult to come by").

Note again that FRCP 23(b)(2) does not provide for opt-out rights, so members of a class certified under this provision are not entitled to withdraw.

The same is true in classes certified under FRCP 23(b)(1), where the explanation is easily found: Classwide treatment is necessary because individual suits would *inevitably* affect class members or create difficulty for defendants.

What is the explanation for making "unfair treatment" class suits under FRCP 23(b)(2) mandatory? It is often said that classes certified under FRCP 23(b)(2) can be mandatory, because they have special unity or cohesiveness and the remedy is equitable in nature, rather than focused on money damages. See In re St. Jude Medical, Inc., 425 F.3d 1116, 2212 (8th Cir. 2008) (primary relief must be equitable or injunctive, and "even greater cohesiveness" is required). Indeed, *lack* of such unity can be a reason to refuse certification, and the absence of opt-out rights sometimes persuades courts not to permit class treatment, see McClain v. Lufkin Industries, 519 F.3d 264, 283 (5th Cir. 2008) (certification under (b)(2) blocks opting out and sacrifices members' rights to pursue significant remedies, so "it is too high a price"). More often, however, courts comment that opt-out rights can be allowed after all in suits certified under (b)(2) when special reasons appear, see In re Monumental Life Ins. Co., 365 F.3d 408, 416 (5th Cir. 2004) (remanding with instruction to consider possibility of opt-out rights). But see In re Allstate Ins. Co., 400 F.3d 505, 508 (7th Cir. 2005) (efforts to "restructure" (b)(2) suits by providing opt-out rights "would be complicated and confusing—unnecessarily so").

ALLEN v. INTERNATIONAL TRUCK AND ENGINE CORP.

United States Court of Appeals for the Seventh Circuit
358 F.3d 469 (2004)

Before BAUER, EASTERBROOK, and KANNE, Circuit Judges.

EASTERBROOK, Circuit Judge.

Plaintiffs are 27 current or former employees at the Indianapolis plant of International Truck & Engine Corp., which used to be called Navistar International Corporation. They contend that white employees at the plant evinced pervasive hostility toward, and harassment of, their black co-workers, and that, when black employees complained, the plant's top supervisors told them that nothing would be done, and their best option was to quit. Plaintiffs seek both financial and equitable relief; they also want to be certified as representatives of a class of the plant's current and former black employees, some 350 in number during the period covered by the complaint. The district judge found that all requirements of FRCP 23(a) have been satisfied but declined to allow plaintiffs to represent others similarly situated: The presence of individual claims made class treatment of damages imprudent, and the seventh amendment rendered class treatment of the equitable theories improper. Plaintiffs have filed a petition under Rule 23(f) seeking interlocutory review of this decision. The parties' comprehensive submissions show not only that immediate review would promote the development of the law governing questions that have escaped resolution on appeal from final decisions, but also that the district court committed an error best handled by a swift remand. It is better to act summarily on this interlocutory matter than to delay the proceedings during full-dress appellate review.

After concluding that Rule 23(a)'s requirements had been met, the district court turned to the two pertinent subsections of Rule 23(b). Although the plaintiffs' allegations fit Rule 23(b)(2), which deals with situations in which "the party opposing the class has acted or refused to act on grounds generally applicable to the class, thereby making appropriate final injunctive relief or corresponding declaratory relief with respect to the class as a whole," the statutory authorization in 1991 of damages recoveries for employees in Title VII cases has complicated what used to be an almost automatic class certification in pattern-or-practice cases. See General Telephone Co. v. Falcon, 457 U.S. 147 (1982). The difficulty is that employees may prefer to litigate damages claims on their own behalf, and may have a constitutional entitlement to do so, while class certification under Rule 23(b)(2) usually means that class members will not be allowed to opt out. Jefferson v. Ingersoll International Inc., 195 F.3d 894 (7th Cir. 1999), holds that Rule 23(b)(2) may not be used, even in a pattern-or-practice suit, unless persons with significant damages claims are allowed to opt out of the class to the extent that the litigation concerns financial relief. The district judge concluded that employees' financial stakes are too high to be called incidental to equitable relief, and that opt-out rights therefore must be extended. Although this conclusion did not foreclose certification under Rule 23(b)(3)—or perhaps hybrid certification under Rule 23(b)(2) with opt-out confined to damages issues, a possibility suggested by *Jefferson*—the judge thought that neither step would be prudent because the employees' injuries are dissimilar. Some may have been exposed to pervasive harassment and suffered great distress; others may have seen or heard little of the offensive material. This meant, the judge wrote, that "issues common to the class as a whole are subordinate to the specific circumstances surrounding each individual Plaintiffs' [sic] claim for compensatory and punitive damages."

That left the possibility of a class certified under Rule 23(b)(2) for equitable relief only, with the 27 individual plaintiffs pursuing damages for their own accounts. Here the district court found the seventh amendment to be a stumbling block. Factual issues common to damages and equitable claims must be tried to a jury, whose resolution of factual matters will control. See Dairy Queen, Inc. v. Wood, 369 U.S. 469, 479 (1962); Beacon Theatres, Inc. v. Westover, 359 U.S. 500 (1959). The judge wrote: "Given the individual and case-specific issues relative to Plaintiffs' hostile work environment claims, the court finds that pursuing this course would result in confusion and be overly burdensome to the resources of the court system." Other district judges within this circuit have reached contrary conclusions, and so far we have not had occasion to address this subject.

It is hard to see why management of a class certified under Rule 23(b)(2) for prospective relief alone would be any more difficult than management of a suit with 27 individual plaintiffs seeking both legal and equitable relief. In either event, a jury trial must be held, and factual matters bearing on both damages and injunctive relief must be presented to that body. Even if the judge were to hold 27 separate damages trials, each of the 27 plaintiffs would be entitled to present evidence about the plant-wide environment in order to show entitlement to an injunction. The district judge did not explain how even one trial, with 27 plaintiffs, could be easier to manage than a class proceeding; and if the judge contemplated 27 trials, then a class proceeding looks even better by comparison. What is more, handling equitable issues on a classwide basis would solve a problem sure to bedevil individual proceedings: How is it feasible to draft and enforce an injunction that will bear on these 27 plaintiffs alone, and *not* on the other 323 black employees? Unless it is possible to prepare such relief—and we do not see how it could be, or why a court should try—then the equitable aspects of the litigation are classwide whether the judge certifies a class action or not. (The need for, if not inevitability of, classwide treatment when injunctive relief is at stake is what Rule 23(b)(2) is about.) Formal certification has two benefits over the informal approach: first, class certification obliges counsel (and the representative plaintiffs) to proceed as fiduciaries for all 350 employees, rather than try to maximize the outcome for these 27 at the potential expense of the other 323; second, certification will entitle counsel to attorneys' fees representing the gains (if any) achieved by all employees, and not just the named plaintiffs.

Certifying a class for injunctive purposes, while handling damages claims individually, does not transgress the seventh amendment. Just as in a single-person (or 27-person) suit, a jury will resolve common factual disputes, and its resolution will control when the judge takes up the request for an injunction. International Truck will enjoy its jury trial right either way; and once *one* jury (in individual or class litigation) has resolved a factual dispute, principles of issue preclusion can bind the defendant to that outcome in future litigation consistently with the seventh amendment. See Parklane Hosiery Co. v. Shore, 439 U.S. 322 (1979); cf. Blonder-Tongue Laboratories, Inc. v. University of Illinois Foundation, 402 U.S. 313 (1971). The other 323 employees' right to jury trial can be protected in either or both of two ways: By offering them the opportunity to opt out, or by denying them (in any later damages proceedings) both the benefits and the detriments of issue and claim preclusion. See Lytle v. Household Manufacturing, Inc., 494 U.S. 545 (1990); Premier Electrical Construction Co. v. National Electrical Contractors Ass'n, Inc., 814 F.2d 358 (7th Cir. 1987). Thus a class proceeding for equitable relief vindicates the seventh amendment as fully as do individual trials, is no more complex than individual trials, yet produces benefits compared with the one-person-at-a-time paradigm. The district court erred in concluding that seventh amendment concerns foreclose certification of a class under Rule 23(b)(2).

Whether full class treatment of damages issues would be manageable is too fact-sensitive, and too much of a judgment call, to warrant interlocutory review in this court. But because this litigation will proceed as a class action for equitable relief, it would be prudent for the district court to reconsider whether at least some of the issues bearing on damages—such as the existence of plant-wide racial animosity, which collectively "constitute[s] one unlawful employment practice," National Railroad Passenger Corp. v. Morgan, 536 U.S. 101 (2002)—could be treated on a class basis (with opt-out rights under Rule 23(b)(3) or a hybrid Rule 23(b)(2) certification) even if some other issues, such as assessment of damages for each worker, must be handled individually. (The employer's contention that even partial class certification is inappropriate because workers may have *liked* being called "nigger" and "jungle bunny," chuckled when other workers posted cartoons of black men being lynched and displayed nooses in the workplace, or at least not minded such things, strains credulity. Still, questions about subjective reactions also could be isolated for individual treatment if evidence demonstrates that insults and threats rolled off the backs of some workers.)

The order of the district court is vacated, and the case is remanded with instructions to certify a class under Rule 23(b)(2) for equitable matters and to reconsider the extent to which damages matters also could benefit from class treatment.

■ NOTES ON "UNFAIR TREATMENT" CLASS SUITS

1. Notice that the Seventh Circuit entertains an appeal in *Allen* from a trial court order refusing to certify the class. Normally, "interlocutory orders"—those that are not the "final order" in the case—cannot be appealed. Instead the litigant who wants review of such an order must wait until the end of the suit to appeal. Before FRCP 23(f) was adopted, allowing appeals from orders "granting or denying" class certification in the discretion of the Court of Appeals, such orders were not considered final judgments even though orders denying certification were often the "death knell" of class suits. See Coopers & Lybrand v. Livesay, 437 U.S. 463 (1978) (refusing to allow appeal under "collateral order" doctrine and declining to adopt "death knell" theory treating denial of certification as a final judgment). You can see how important this avenue of review is for plaintiffs in the *Allen* case.

2. In some ways, *Allen* is perfect for at least partial resolution as a class suit: The class is manageable (350 persons), the suit involves a single location, and the claim is that company policies allowed or encouraged a hostile work-place, hence that injunctive relief was appropriate—precisely the kind of suit envisioned in FRCP 23(b)(2). This provision is well suited to claims resting on a "disparate impact" theory (policies impacting a protected group more negatively than others, and not reasonably job-related). In "unfair treatment" cases, where the claim is that the employer intentionally discriminated against members of a protected group, class litigation under FRCP 23(b)(2) may be appropriate if plaintiffs can prove a "pattern or practice" of discrimination, but such cases have tougher sledding if they claim that individual employment decisions were discriminatory. But even here, anecdotal proof may establish discrimination in individual cases, and enough individual instances can show the "pattern or practice" justifying class litigation. What sort of injunctive relief should the trial court fashion in the *Allen* case if plaintiffs prove racial harassment?

3. Originally, the 1964 Civil Rights Act did not authorize recovery of ordinary damages, like those from injury to reputation or mental trauma, but did authorize recovery of "back pay" (money that claimant would have gotten if she had been hired or promoted) and "front pay" (money that claimant would get in the future if he or she had not left or had not been fired, where it is impracticable to return to the job). Since 1991, the Civil Rights Act has authorized recovery of ordinary damages (note the comment in *Allen* that the amendment "complicated" matters).

(a) It was once the case that damage claims seeking back pay could be brought as 23(b)(2) suits, as courts often held that this relief was "incidental" and figuring the amount was a "ministerial" task, at least if the main reason for the suit was to win injunctive relief, see Thorn v. Jefferson-Pilot Life Ins. Co., 445 F.3d 311, 331 (4th Cir. 2006). The Court's 2011 decision in *Wal-Mart* cast doubt on this approach: There all nine Justices agreed, on the facts, that back pay could not be awarded. See *Wal-Mart Stores*, supra, at 2541 (expressing "serious doubt" whether monetary relief is proper in (b)(2) suit; it is not "where (as here) the monetary relief is not incidental to the injunctive or declaratory relief").

(b) How about awarding front pay in a (b)(2) suit? See Eubanks v. Billington, 110 F.3d 87, 92 (D.C. Cir. 1997) (mentioning both front pay and back pay as relief allowed in 23(b)(2) suits). *Wal-Mart* appears to cast doubt on such an award in this setting too. Is front pay really incidental and ministerial? Can it be described as equitable relief? See Pollard v. E.I. du Pont de Nemours & Co., 532 U.S. 843 (2001) (treating front pay award under Title VII as equitable relief) and Gilliland v. Missouri Athletic Club, 273 S.W.3d 516, 524 (Mo. 2009) (front pay is equitable remedy that is "an offshoot of the court's equitable power to grant reinstatement," which can be awarded where employer-employee relationship "cannot be repaired through reinstatement"); Brooks v. Lexington-Fayette Urban County Housing Authority, 231 S.W.3d 790, 805 (Ky. 2004) (whether to award front pay, and if so how much is for judge to decide, not jury).

(c) When 23(b)(2) discrimination suits seek damages as well as injunctive relief, the ACN to FRCP 23 implies that the right question is whether the suit "relates exclusively or predominantly" to money damages. In addition to *Wal-Mart,* see Reeb v. Ohio Department of Rehabilitation and Correction, 435 F.3d 639, 651 (6th Cir. 2006) (because of "individualized nature" of compensatory damages sought under Title VII, these claims predominate and cannot be sought in (b)(2) class suit); Allison v. Citgo Petroleum Corp., 151 F.3d 402, 415 (5th Cir. 1998) (monetary relief predominates unless "incidental to requested injunctive or declaratory relief," meaning that damages "flow directly from liability to the class *as a whole,*" and damages recovered in (b)(2) class suits "should at least be capable of computation by means of objective standards" and not "intangible, subjective differences") (damage claims were *not* incidental; they turned on "psychological or medical evidence" and rested on "emotional and other intangible injuries" that required individual relief).

4. In *Allen,* the damage claims were also problematic from the standpoint of jury trial entitlement. Invoking the decisions in *Beacon Theatres* (Chapter 12A1, infra), *Allen* says a jury must decide the basic questions on which injunctive relief and damage recovery turn—was there racial harassment in the workplace that the company did not address? The jury's resolution of these questions would "control" the balance of the suit. (You will discover that this reading of *Beacon Theatres* is probably correct.) If the jury found in favor of plaintiffs, the judge would decide whether to issue an injunction and what it should say, and the jury would decide damages. (If the jury decided for *defendant* on claims of harassment, the case would be over.) The claim for injunctive relief, the court says, is enough by itself to justify classwide treatment: What point is being made here? Does this argument explain why 23(b)(2) suits do not normally carry opt-out rights?

5. In a class suit tried to a jury that includes damage claims, questions of manageability become important. The judge thought that trying to a jury the damage claims of 323 black employees would be difficult or impossible, and this fact had a lot to do with the refusal to certify. How does the reviewing court reply? If the judge decided on remand to try "all liability issues" to a jury and if the jury came out in favor of the class, what would happen next? The court says questions surrounding "full class treatment of damage issues" are "too fact-sensitive" to be reviewed. What should the trial court do on remand if it concludes that "full class treatment" of such issues *cannot* be undertaken?

6. Recall that FRCP 23(a) requires "common questions" in *all* class suits, but few if any purported class suits were seen as failing in this respect. In its 2011 decision in *Wal-Mart,* a 5-4 majority of the Court put new rigor into this requirement, in a nationwide employment discrimination suit under FRCP 23(b)(2).

> The crux of this case is commonality—the rule requiring a plaintiff to show that "there are questions of law or fact common to the class." Rule 23(a)(2). That

language is easy to misread, since "[a]ny competently crafted class complaint literally raises common 'questions.'" Nagareda, Class Certification in the Age of Aggregate Proof, 84 N.Y.U. L. Rev. 97, 131-132 (2009). For example: Do all of us plaintiffs indeed work for Wal-Mart? Do our managers have discretion over pay? Is that an unlawful employment practice? What remedies should we get? Reciting these questions is not sufficient to obtain class certification. Commonality requires the plaintiff to demonstrate that the class members "have suffered the same injury," General Telephone Co. of Southwest v. Falcon, 457 U.S. 147, 157 (1982). This does not mean merely that they have all suffered a violation of the same provision of law. Title VII, for example, can be violated in many ways—by intentional discrimination, or by hiring and promotion criteria that result in disparate impact, and by the use of these practices on the part of many different superiors in a single company. Quite obviously, the mere claim by employees of the same company that they have suffered a Title VII injury, or even a disparate-impact Title VII injury, gives no cause to believe that all their claims can productively be litigated at once. Their claims must depend upon a common contention—for example, the assertion of discriminatory bias on the part of the same supervisor. That common contention, moreover, must be of such a nature that it is capable of classwide resolution—which means that determination of its truth or falsity will resolve an issue that is central to the validity of each one of the claims in one stroke.

> What matters to class certification . . . is not the raising of common "questions"—even in droves—but, rather the capacity of a classwide proceeding to generate common *answers* apt to drive the resolution of the litigation. Dissimilarities within the proposed class are what have the potential to impede the generation of common answers.

Nagareda, *supra*, at 132.

. . .

This Court's opinion in *Falcon* describes how the commonality issue must be approached. . . . First, if the employer "used a biased testing procedure to evaluate both applicants for employment and incumbent employees, a class action on behalf of every applicant or employee who might have been prejudiced by the test clearly would satisfy the commonality and typicality requirements of Rule 23(a)." Second, "[s]ignificant proof that an employer operated under a general policy of discrimination conceivably could justify a class of both applicants and employees if the discrimination manifested itself in hiring and promotion practices in the same general fashion, such as through entirely subjective decisionmaking processes." We think that statement precisely describes respondents' burden in this case. The first manner of bridging the gap obviously has no application here; Wal-Mart has no testing procedure or other companywide evaluation method that can be charged with bias. The whole point of permitting discretionary decisionmaking is to avoid evaluating employees under a common standard.

The second manner of bridging the gap requires "significant proof" that Wal-Mart "operated under a general policy of discrimination." That is entirely absent here. Wal-Mart's announced policy forbids sex discrimination, and as the District Court recognized the company imposes penalties for denials of equal employment opportunity. The only evidence of a "general policy of discrimina-tion" [that] respondents produced was the testimony of Dr. William Bielby, their sociological expert. Relying on "social framework" analysis, Bielby testified that Wal-Mart has a "strong corporate culture," that makes it "'vulnerable'" to "gender bias." He could not, however, "determine with any specificity how regularly stereo-types play a meaningful role in employment decisions at Wal-Mart. At his depo-sition Dr. Bielby conceded that he could not calculate whether 0.5 percent or 95 percent of the employment decisions at Wal-Mart might be determined by stereo-typed thinking." The parties dispute whether Bielby's testimony even met the stan-dards for the admission of expert testimony under FRE 702 and our *Daubert* case, see Daubert v. Merrell Dow Pharmaceuticals, Inc., 509 U.S. 579 (1993). The District Court concluded that *Daubert* did not apply to expert testimony at the certification stage of class-action proceedings. We doubt that is so, but even if properly con-sidered, Bielby's testimony does nothing to advance respondents' case. "[W]hether 0.5 percent or 95 percent of the employment decisions at Wal-Mart might be deter-mined by stereotyped thinking" is the essential question on which respondents' theory of commonality depends. If Bielby admittedly has no answer to that question, we can safely disregard what he has to say. It is worlds away from "sig-nificant proof" that Wal-Mart "operated under a general policy of discrimination."

Wal-Mart Stores, supra, at 2541 (also recognizing that giving discretion to super-visors can support a discrimination claim, but not all such systems yield common questions; most such managers select "sex-neutral, performance-based criteria," while others may choose criteria that have "disparate impact," and yet others may engage in "intentional discrimination," but claimants have not shown that managers here exercise discretion "in a common way" and the statistical evidence does not suggest discrimination provable on a classwide basis). Obvi-ously, *Wal-Mart* was very much affected in its outcome by the size of the class (nationwide, hundreds of thousands of employees in thousands of stores): *Wal-Mart* would not block classwide treatment of cases like *Allen*, would it?

6. The "Common Question" Class Suit Under FRCP 23(b)(3)

The framers of Rule 23(b)(3) apparently had in mind the small-claim consumer-driven class suit,[4] such as the *Daar* case in California, in which plaintiff for a class of cab riders claimed the cab company had overcharged users. This case reached the California Supreme Court shortly after FRCP 23 was amended. See Daar v. Yellow Cab, 433 P.2d 732 (Cal. 1967) (approving class treatment and expressing preference for system in which claimants come forward with personal claims, with unpaid balance to go to the state, but leaving matter up to

---

[4] Martin H. Redish, Wholesale Justice, Constitutional Democracy and the Problem of the Class Action Lawsuit 41 (2009) (committee had in mind "small-claim consumer class actions in which no one class member would have a sufficient interest to litigate an individual claim").

court). *Daar* settled under terms in which the cab company agreed to lower its rates until the prior overcharges were "paid back" to future users. See Natalie A. DeJarlais, Note, *The Consumer Trust Fund: A Cy Pres Solution to Undistributed Funds in Consumer Class Actions*, 38 Hastings L.J. 729, 738 (1987).

In the ACN accompanying FRCP 23(b)(3), the framers cited other kinds of cases. One was securities fraud cases, where the ACN comments that *some* fraud cases may be suited to classwide adjudication if "perpetrated on numerous persons by the use of similar misrepresentations" despite the need for "separate determination" of damages. Other such cases, however, would not lend themselves to class treatment if there is "material variation" among representations or "kinds or degrees of reliance." Investor fraud cases have fared well as modern forms of classwide adjudication under FRCP 23(b)(3). The framers also commented that antitrust cases "may or may not" lend themselves to classwide adjudication.

Edward Percy Moran, Battle of New Orleans

When schoolchildren visited the Chalmette National Battlefield in January 2007 to watch a reenactment of the Battle of New Orleans, they were witnesses to an annual commemoration, with costumes, maneuvers, and cannon firings. That battle occurred on January 8, 1815, a week after a peace treaty had been signed ending the War of 1812 (word had not yet reached New Orleans), but Jackson won the day, and his victory started him along the road leading to the presidency 15 years later. The war, which was the second armed conflict between Britain and the new American republic within a generation, grew out of trade disputes, American territorial ambitions in Canada, fears that Britain was encouraging a separate Indian nation, and incidents on the high seas involving impressment of American sailors to serve in the British navy. Andrew Jackson was a slaveholder, and he and others had attacked and killed American Indians during frontier conflicts in Alabama, Tennessee, and elsewhere. Modern historians give Jackson's presidency mixed reviews, although "Jacksonian Democracy" characterizes the American generation between the election of 1828 and the Civil War. On the negative side were his staunch opposition to the Bank of the United States (economists think shutting down the bank was a mistake that benefitted nobody) and the implementation of his Indian removal policy that led to what has been called the "Trail of Tears," in which thousands died of starvation and disease. On the positive side were Jackson's successful opposition to the "nullification" movement championed by John C. Calhoun (Jackson's own Vice President), and progress toward broadening public participation in government, in which Jackson deeply believed (property qualifications had already been largely abolished, and during his presidency voting rights expanded).

MADISON v. CHALMETTE REFINING, L.L.C.

United States Court of Appeals for the Fifth Circuit
637 F.3d 551 (5th Cir. 2011)

EDITH BROWN CLEMENT, Circuit Judge:

This is an interlocutory appeal under Rule 23(f) of the Federal Rules of Civil Procedure. Defendant-Appellant Chalmette Refining, L.L.C., appeals the district court's order certifying a class alleging claims arising out of a petroleum coke dust release from its refinery. For the following reasons, we REVERSE the district court's order granting class certification and REMAND this case for further proceedings.

FACTS AND PROCEEDINGS

On January 12, 2007, a number of schoolchildren, chaperoned by parents and teachers, participated in a historical reenactment at the Chalmette National Battlefield, "the site along the Mississippi River where Andrew Jackson gave the British their comeuppance." Douglas Brinkley, The Wilderness Warrior: Theodore Roosevelt and the Crusade For America 414 (2009). Adjacent to the battlefield is the Chalmette Refinery. In the early afternoon, the Chalmette Refinery released an amount of petroleum coke dust that Plaintiffs-Appellees (hereinafter, "Plaintiffs"), attendees and parents of attendees of the reenactment, allege migrated over the battlefield. Plaintiffs filed suit, seeking to sue on behalf of themselves and all other individuals who were exposed to the coke dust on the battlefield. They sought a variety of damages, including personal injury, fear, anguish, discomfort, inconvenience, pain and suffering, emotional distress, psychiatric and psychological damages, evacuation, economic damages, and property damages.[2]

The district court allowed the parties to conduct discovery on the issue of class certification, "[a]s it is encouraged to do." Gene & Gene, L.L.C. v. BioPay, L.L.C., 624 F.3d 698, 703 n.3 (5th Cir. 2010). Chalmette Refining deposed each of the five named class representatives; Plaintiffs apparently conducted no discovery. Plaintiffs then moved for class certification under Rule 23(b)(3), asserting that this lawsuit is a type of action where "questions of law or fact common to class members predominate over any questions affecting only individual members, and that a class action is superior to other available methods for fairly and efficiently adjudicating the controversy." FRCP 23(b)(3). The proposed class consisted of

---

[2] Plaintiffs also alleged that some individuals would require continued medical monitoring and attempted to form a class to recover for these costs. The district court denied Plaintiffs' request for certification of a medical monitoring class. That aspect of the district court's order is not on appeal.

all persons entities (sic) located at the Chalmette National Battlefield in St. Bernard Parish, Louisiana, in the early afternoon of Friday, January 12, 2007 and who sustained property damage, personal injuries, emotional, mental, or economic damages and/or inconvenience or evacuation as a result of the incident.

Chalmette Refining opposed the motion.

Over two years later, the district court held a hearing on the motion to certify the class. At the conclusion of that hearing, and without any evidence being introduced, the district court orally granted Plaintiffs' motion. Fourteen days later, and although the district court had not yet issued a written order, Chalmette Refining petitioned this court for permission to take an interlocutory appeal pursuant to Rule 23(f). We granted the petition. Two months later, and although it had already granted Plaintiffs' motion, the district court issued a written order again granting Plaintiffs' motion. The written order relied on the reasons stated during the class certification hearing and offered supplemental analysis. The district court later stayed proceedings pending the resolution of this appeal. *See* FRCP 23(f).

DISCUSSION

I. RULE 23

Rule 23(a) requires four prerequisites in order to certify a class action. [The court cites numerosity, common question, typicality, and adequate representation.] "In addition to these prerequisites, a party seeking class certification under Rule 23(b)(3) must also demonstrate both (1) that questions common to the class members predominate over questions affecting only individual members, and (2) that class resolution is superior to alternative methods for adjudication of the controversy." Feder v. Electric Data Sys. Corp., 429 F.3d 125, 129 (5th Cir. 2005). The district court found that Plaintiffs satisfied all of these requirements.

II. STANDARD OF REVIEW

We review the district court's decision to certify a class for an abuse of discretion. "The decision to certify is within the broad discretion of the [district] court, but that discretion must be exercised within the framework of [R]ule 23." Castano v. American Tobacco Co., 84 F.3d 734, 740 (5th Cir. 1996) (citing Gulf Oil Co. v. Bernard, 452 U.S. 89, 100 (1981)).

III. ANALYSIS

"Recognizing the important due process concerns of both plaintiffs and defendants inherent in the certification decision, the Supreme Court requires district courts to conduct a rigorous analysis of Rule 23 prerequisites." Unger v. Amedisys Inc., 401 F.3d 316, 320-21 (5th Cir. 2005) (citing General

Telephone Co. v. Falcon, 457 U.S. 147, 161 (1982)). Where the plaintiff seeks to certify a class under Rule 23(b)(3), the Rules demand "a close look at the case before it is accepted as a class action." Amchem Products, Inc. v. Windsor, 521 U.S. 591 (1997). "[W]e stress that it is the party seeking certification who bears the burden of establishing that the requirements of Rule 23 have been met." Bell Atlantic Corp. v. AT&T Corp., 339 F.3d 294, 301 (5th Cir. 2003) (citing O'Sullivan v. Countrywide Home Loans, Inc., 319 F.3d 732, 737-38 (5th Cir. 2003)).

Although class certification hearings "should not be mini-trials on the merits of the class or individual claims . . . going beyond the pleadings is necessary, as a court must understand the claims, defenses, relevant facts, and applicable substantive law in order to make a meaningful determination of the certification issues." *Unger* (citing *Castano*). The "close look" demanded by *Amchem* requires examination of both "the parties' claims and evidence." *Id.* "The plain text of Rule 23 requires the court to 'find,' not merely assume, the facts favoring class certification." *Id.*

. . .

The crux of this appeal lies in the legal basis for and sufficiency of evidence supporting the district court's findings of superiority and predominance under Rule 23(b)(3). Before certifying a class under Rule 23(b)(3), a court must determine that "questions of law or fact common to the members of the class predominate over any questions affecting only individual members and that a class action is superior to other available methods for fairly and efficiently adjudicating the controversy." Determining whether the plaintiffs can clear the predominance hurdle set by Rule 23(b)(3) requires district courts to consider "how a trial on the merits would be conducted if a class were certified." Sandwich Chef of Texas, Inc. v. Reliance Nat'l Indemnity Ins. Co., 319 F.3d 205, 218 (5th Cir. 2003). This, in turn, "entails identifying the substantive issues that will control the outcome, assessing which issues will predominate, and then determining whether the issues are common to the class," a process that ultimately "prevents the class from degenerating into a series of individual trials." *O'Sullivan.* Determining whether the superiority requirement is met requires a fact-specific analysis and will vary depending on the circumstances of any given case. *See* 7AA Wright, Miller & Kane, Federal Practice & Procedure §1783 (3d ed. 2005).

In Steering Committee v. Exxon Mobil Corp., 461 F.3d 598, 600 (5th Cir. 2006), this court found no abuse of discretion and affirmed a district court's denial of class certification in a case arising out of a fire at Exxon's Baton Rouge chemical plant. We noted that "the district court found that 'individual issues surrounding exposure, dose, health effects, and damages will dominate at the trial' [and] [t]he district court concluded that 'one set of operative facts would not establish liability and that the end result would be a series of individual mini-trials which the predominance requirement is intended to prevent.'" Chalmette Refining argues that this case is nearly identical to *Steering Committee* and, as such, the class certification decision should be reversed. Chalmette Refining also relies heavily on an advisory committee note to Rule 23(b)(3), which has been cited numerous times by this court as highlighting the "relationship between predominance and superiority in mass torts." *See* Castano v. American Tobacco Co., 84 F.3d 734, 745 n.19 (5th Cir. 1996). According to the note:

> A "mass accident" resulting in injuries to numerous persons is ordinarily not appropriate for a class action because of the likelihood that significant questions, not only of damages but of liability and defenses to liability, would be present, affecting the individuals in different ways. In these circumstances an action conducted nominally as a class action would degenerate in practice into multiple lawsuits separately tried.

ACN to FRCP 23(b)(3).

The district court determined that Rule 23(b)(3)'s predominance requirement was satisfied because "there is one set of operative facts that [will] determine liability. Plaintiffs were either on the battlefield and exposed to the coke dust or they were not. This case only deals with actual exposure and not fear of exposure. This class deals with a narrow window of exposure, in a narrow area, and to a narrow group of individuals." We hold that the district court abused its discretion by failing to afford its predominance determination the "rigorous analysis" that Rule 23 requires.

The district court did not meaningfully consider how Plaintiffs' claims would be tried, as *Unger* requires. The two cases relied upon by the district court in conducting its conclusory inquiry are instructive. In Watson v. Shell Oil, 979 F.2d 1014, 1016 (5th Cir. 1992), this court affirmed a district court's decision to certify a class of over 18,000 plaintiffs seeking damages stemming from an explosion at a Shell plant. Whether *Watson* has survived later developments in class action law—embodied in *Amchem* and its progeny—is an open question, but even in *Watson*, the district court had "issued orders detailing a four-phase plan for trial." That plan allowed the district court to adjudicate common class issues in the first phase and then later adjudicate individualized issues in other phases. In Turner v. Murphy Oil USA, Inc., 234 F.R.D. 597, 601 (E.D. La. 2006), the district court granted class certification to a class of plaintiffs who suffered damages resulting from a post-Hurricane Katrina oil storage tank spill. Critical to the court's predominance inquiry was the fact that "Plaintiffs submitted a proposed trial plan to the Court. The plan provides for a three-phase trial." "[T]he Court believes that the existence of a trial plan, and the potential for bifurcation of the issues of liability and damages, will address the Defendant's concern that individualized inquiries will be needed to determine damage amounts in these cases."

In stark contrast to the detailed trial plans in *Watson* and *Turner*, the district court simply concluded that "[t]he common liability issues can be tried in a single class action trial with any individual issues of damages reserved for individual treatment." The district court failed to consider whether this case could be "streamlined using other case management tools, including narrowing the claims and potential plaintiffs through summary judgment, [or] facilitating the disposition of the remaining plaintiffs' claims through issuance of a *Lone Pine*[3] order." *Steering Comm.* Indeed there was no "analysis or discussion regarding how it would administer the trial." Robinson v. Texas Automobile Dealers Ass'n, 387 F.3d 416, 425-26 (5th Cir. 2004).

The court failed to identify "the substantive issues that will control the outcome, assess[ ] which issues will predominate, and then determin[e] whether the issues are common to the class." *Bell Atlantic.* Absent this analysis, "it was impossible for the court to know whether the common issues would be a 'significant' portion of the individual trials," *Castano,* much less whether the common issues predominate. The opinion is also silent as to the relevant state law that applies to Plaintiffs' claims and what Plaintiffs must prove to make their case. The district court characterized the issue of liability as "Plaintiffs were either on the battlefield and exposed to the coke dust or they were not," but this oversimplifies the issue. Chalmette Refining correctly notes that, even among the named class representatives, significant disparities exist, in terms of exposure, location, and whether mitigative steps were taken. As in *Steering Committee,* "primary issues left to be resolved would turn on location, exposure, dose, susceptibility to illness, nature of symptoms, type and cost of medical treatment, and subsequent impact of illnesses on individuals."

We must reverse because, "[i]n its certification order, the [district] court did not indicate that it [had] seriously considered the administration of the trial. Instead, it appears to have adopted a figure-it-out-as-we-go-along approach that *Castano* criticized and that other Fifth Circuit cases have not endorsed." *Robinson.* By failing to adequately analyze and balance the common issues against the individualized issues, the district court abused its discretion in determining that common issues predominated and in certifying the class. We do not suggest that class treatment is necessarily inappropriate. As Chalmette Refining acknowledged at oral argument, class treatment on the common issue of liability may indeed be appropriate. But our precedent demands a far more rigorous analysis than the district court conducted.

---

[3] "*Lone Pine* orders, which derive their name from Lore v. Lone Pine Corp., 1986 WL 637507 (N.J. Sup. Ct. Nov. 18, 1986), are pre-discovery orders designed to handle the complex issues and potential burdens on defendants and the court in mass tort litigation by requiring plaintiffs to produce some evidence to support a credible claim." *Steering Committee.*

CONCLUSION

The district court's class certification order is REVERSED and this case is REMANDED to the district court for further proceedings.

[The dissenting concurring opinion by Judge DENNIS is omitted.]

■ NOTES ON "COMMON QUESTION" CLASS SUITS

1. As you can see by reading *Madison*, one major hurdle in (b)(3) classes is the predominance requirement, which adds something to the "common question" requirement that FRCP 23(a)(2) imposes for *all* class suits. See Amchem Products, Inc. v. Windsor, 521 U.S. 591, 623-624 (1997) (even if FRCP 23(a)(2) is satisfied "the predominance criterion is far more demanding"). In one oft-quoted formulation, common questions predominate if they have "a direct impact" on claims of all members in proving liability that is "more substantial than the impact of individualized issues." See, e.g., Sacred Heart Health Systems, Inc. v. Humana Military Healthcare Services, Inc., 601 F.3d 1159, 1170 (11th Cir. 2011). Recall *Wal-Mart's* description of the common question standard that *all* class suits must meet under FRCP 23(a)(2)—what matters is questions that can generate "common answers" for class members (see note 6 in Notes on "Unfair Treatment" Class Suits in Section H5, supra). Presumably, "exposure" to coke dust is a common question affecting every claimant in *Madison*. Or is that many individual questions? If it *is* a common question, does it predominate?

2. There are other hurdles, especially the "superiority" requirement mentioned in *Madison*. In connection with these "twin" requirements (superiority and predominance), FRCP 23(b)(3) lists four "matters" pertinent to the inquiry—the interests of class members in "individually controlling" their own cases, "extent and nature" of related litigation, "desirability or undesirability" of concentrating claims in the forum, and "likely difficulties in managing a class action." Among these four, "manageability" is most often mentioned.

(a) Doesn't it seem that the reviewing court's concern in *Madison* over a "trial plan" is a way of addressing manageability (hence superiority)? In the *Turner* case, cited in *Madison*, plaintiffs were property and business owners seeking recovery for damages sustained after oil spilled from a storage tank as a result of Hurricane Katrina. Plaintiffs proposed a three-phase trial, in which issues of statutory strict liability and negligence would be tried first (along with individual damages for the class standard bearers), then liability for punitive damages, and then damages for class members. See Turner v. Murphy Oil USA, Inc., 234 F.R.D. 597, 606 (E.D. La. 2006). Does this model seem plausible in *Madison*?

(b) Watson, also cited in *Madison*, involved an explosion at a refinery, with resultant injuries and property loss in the community. There the court certified a class and planned a four-phase trial. Phase 1 would address "common issues of liability." Phase 2 would "determine compensatory damages in 20 fully-tried sample plaintiff cases" and "establish the ratio" of punitive to actual damages (assuming that Phase 1 found liability for punitive damages). Phase 3 would address "issues unique to each [class member's] compensatory damages claims, e.g., injury, causation, and quantum," and would include "trials in waves of five," gathered in accordance with factors like location and extent and nature of damages, which would produce data on which the balance of claims could be settled. Phase 4 would involve a computation and award of punitive damages, if any. See Watson v. Shell Oil Co., 979 F.2d 1014, 1018 (5th Cir. 1992). See also Jenkins v. Raymark Industries, Inc., 782 F.2d 468 (5th Cir. 1986) (landmark case approving certification of common questions in asbestos mass exposure case). Does this model seem plausible in *Madison*?

3. Suppose defendant in *Madison* claims that ailments allegedly stemming from the January 12 outing actually predated it, or had other causes. Do such defenses count in assessing predominance? In a case cited in *Madison*, the Fifth Circuit said yes. See Gene and Gene LLC v. BioPay LLC, 541 F.3d 318 (5th Cir. 2008) (in suit alleging violation of Telephone Consumer Protection Act, based on "fax blasting" of commercial messages, defense claimed it not only purchased databases including contact information but it "culled fax numbers from other sources," and that recipients had consented to a "significant number" of the faxes; regardless whether consent is handled as an element of the claim or an affirmative defense, it counts in predominance inquiry; absent generalized proof of consent, predominance standard could not be satisfied).

4. As the court notes in *Madison*, the 1966 ACN accompanying revised FRCP 23 said "mass accident" cases are "ordinarily *not* appropriate" for class treatment because of multiple questions relating to damages, liability, and defenses to liability that would affect individual claimants "in different ways," leading to "multiple lawsuits separately tried." Times seem to have changed: Such cases have proven *very tempting* to plaintiffs' lawyers, who file many purported class actions advancing claims arising out of mass accidents. Moreover, a prominent participant in the 1966 revisions of FRCP 23 reportedly changed his mind. See Herbert B. Newberg, Newberg on Class Actions §17.06 (4th ed. 2010), quoting the late Professor Charles A. Wright, a noted commentator on procedure and author of an authoritative treatise, as saying he "thought then" that the comment in the ACN was true, but that "I am profoundly convinced now that that is untrue," and that the judicial system "is simply not going to be able to cope with the challenge of [the] mass repetitive wrong" *unless* it can employ the class action device.

5. "Mass accident" (the term used in the ACN) and "mass repetitive wrong" (Professor Wright's term) may not mean quite the same thing, and the two terms both seem to overlap with a third descriptive term—"mass exposure." All three seem fitting in *Madison*. What happened there looks like a "mass accident" in the sense of involving a single release of "coke dust" from defendant's refinery. Arguably, that event was also a "repetitive wrong" because it affected many people. And it involved "mass exposure" because class members apparently breathed and were otherwise affected by the coke dust, which might carry consequences not immediately known (plaintiffs sought "medical monitoring" as well as damages). Many cases testing the parameters of FRCP 23 fall into these categories:

(a) *Mass Accident Cases.* Compare Watson v. Shell Oil Co., 979 F.2d 1014, 1018 (5th Cir. 1992) (approving class treatment in refinery explosion case) (see note 2, supra) with Steering Committee v. Exxon Mobil Corp., 461 F.3d 598 (5th Cir. 2006) (refusing to certify (b)(3) class in suit arising out of damages from fire in chemical plant, citing differences in exposure, injury, and treatment among class members).

(b) *Mass Exposure Cases.* The framers of FRCP 23 probably did *not* foresee "mass exposure" cases, like those relating to asbestos (once used as insulating material, especially in ships but also in buildings; also used in automobile brakes), Agent Orange (defoliant used during the Vietnam War), and Bendectin (anti-nausea pill taken by pregnant women), but these have become prominent features of the class action landscape. In the next section, you will look at *Amchem*, which raised the question of "settlement classes" in this context. See Amchem Products, Inc. v. Windsor, 521 U.S. 591 (1997). Compare Gates v. Rohm and Haas Co., 655 F.3d 255 (3d Cir. 2011) (refusing to certify common question class in suit alleging property damage caused by release of toxic chemicals) with Gintis v. Bouchard Transportation Co., 596 F.3d 64 (1st Cir. 2010) (remanding common question class suit arising out of oil spill allegedly contaminating shoreline, for further consideration of predominance and superiority requirements).

(c) *Product Defect Cases.* See In re Zurn Pex Plumbing Products Liability Litigation, 644 F.3d 604 (8th Cir. 2011) (certifying common question class suit against makers of polyethylene plumbing systems alleging defects in brass fittings); Daffin v. Ford Motor Co., 458 F.3d 549 (6th Cir. 2006) (certifying (b)(3) class comprised of Ohio residents who own or lease 1999 or 2000 Mercury Villagers, seeking damages from defective throttle assembly causing accelerator to stick).

(d) *Service Torts or Violations.* See Stearns v. Ticketmaster Corp., 655 F.3d 1013 (9th Cir. 2011) (remanding for further consideration a putative class suit on behalf of consumers alleging that entertainment ticket sellers violated state consumer protection statutes, unfair competition law, and federal statute); Randleman v. Fidelity National Title Insurance Co., 646 F.3d 347 (6th Cir. 2011) (refusing to certify common question class of Ohio borrowers who refinanced home mortgages alleging that insurer charged excessive premium on title insurance; common questions did not predominate).

(e) Others. See, e.g., Shahriar v. Smith & Wollensky Restaurant Group, Inc., 659 F.3d 234 (2d Cir. 2011) (certifying (b)(3) class suing under Fair Labor Standards Act, alleging that employers required employees to share tips with ineligible employees); Behrend v. Comcast Corp., 655 F.3d 182 (3d Cir. 2011) (certifying common question class in suit by consumers of cable television services alleging antitrust violations).

6. In *Madison,* the court faults the trial judge for not conducting a "rigorous analysis" aimed at determining whether the prerequisites of FRCP 23(b)(3) are satisfied, particularly those relating to "predominance" and "superiority." What did he fail to do in *Madison* that should now be done? Suppose plaintiffs offer expert testimony (or affidavits) that "exposure to coke dust from defendant's plant was uniform over Chalmette Battlefield," and that exposure "had similar toxic effects on exposed persons, causing immediate respiratory distress and raising the risk of predictable diseases." Suppose defendants offer expert testimony (or affidavits) that "exposure over the Battlefield varied, and risks from such exposure depend on one's health, age, and other individual factors." Should the court *decide,* on such evidence, which expert is right, for purposes of deciding whether common questions predominate? In the *Hydrogen Peroxide* case, the reviewing court said yes: It was "erroneous" for the judge to think he was "barred from weighing" expert testimony: "Weighing conflicting expert testimony at the certification stage is not only permissible; it may be integral to the rigorous analysis Rule 23 demands." Just because the court "weighs" expert testimony in deciding whether to certify, however, does not mean the factfinder is bound if the case goes to trial: "[F]indings with respect to class certification do not bind the ultimate factfinder on the merits." In re Hydrogen Peroxide Antitrust Litigation, 552 F.3d 305, 322-324 (3d Cir. 2008).

7. Is "rigorous analysis" necessary to protect defendants from blackmail? Consider the ACN to the 1998 amendments to FRCP 23, which says class certification "may force a defendant to settle rather than incur the costs of defending a class action and run the risk of potentially ruinous liability." See also Newton v. Merrill Lynch, Pierce, Fenner & Smith, Inc., 259 F.3d 154, 167 n.8 (3d Cir. 2001) (certifying a large class "may place acute and unwarranted pressure on defendants to settle," which is "a factor we weigh in our certification decision"). Should courts go even further than *Hydrogen Peroxide* and *Madison* suggest, by performing a preliminary appraisal of the merits? Notice in *Madison* the court's suggestion in footnote 3 that a *Lone Pine* order would help by requiring plaintiffs to "produce some evidence to support a credible claim." See generally Robert G. Bone & David S. Evans, *Class Certification and the Substantive Merits,* 31 Duke L.J. 1251, 1328 (2002) (error costs from mistaken grants of certification exceed error costs from mistaken denials; courts should "conduct a merits review as part of every certification decision," on basis of precertification discovery, to "help deter frivolous suits by controlling abuse of the settlement leverage [that] certification creates").

8. Is the required analysis also necessary to protect claimants from being bound by judgments in suits in which their interests were not represented? For an illuminating discussion of the role of judges in class certification decisions, as illustrated in *Madison* and *Hydrogen Peroxide,* see Richard Marcus, *Reviving Judicial Gatekeeping of Aggregation: Scrutinizing the Merits on Class Certification,* 79 Geo. Wash. L. Rev. 324 (2011) (citing statistics indicating that the rate of certification is falling, but this fact "tells us little about whether that effect is a good thing," and the conversation seems to be "frozen in the impasse" of claims that class suits amount to "legalized theft" as against claims that class suits are "remarkable instances of social and economic justice").

9. One of the more controversial aspects of (b)(3) suits involves the development of a remedy generally called "fluid recovery." When, for example, a defendant has overcharged or otherwise damaged each member of a large class in some small amount—the typical "negative value" class suit—it may be impossible to get relief to the very persons injured. In the *Daar* case described at the beginning of this section, for example, the court ordered taxi companies to lower the fares they charged until they had "paid back" what they illegally collected before. Fluid recovery can take at least four different forms:

(a) Most familiar is "price reduction," as happened in *Daar*. Here plaintiff proves that defendant overcharged members of the public—and the class is *defined* as customers who have incurred overcharges—and the remedy is to create a "fund" to be distributed to users of the services or purchasers of the goods in the form of "undercharges" until the "fund" is depleted. This approach eliminates the red tape that would bind up any effort to repay each overcharged consumer the amount right for him or her, and takes away the problem of moral hazard. One drawback is that one cannot even hope the repayment will go to the right people. Should this objection be taken seriously? Suppose a service provider in a competitive market is ordered to cut charges for future users: If consumers that would otherwise purchase the service from someone else are drawn to defendant by the reduced charges, can this be fair to competitors? See Democratic Central Committee of District of Columbia v. Washington Metropolitan Area Transit Commission, 84 F.3d 451, 455-456 (D.C. Cir. 1996) (citing "inability to predict or control its effect on a market," court says this approach is most appropriate if defendant is a monopoly).

(b) In the "escheat model," defendant pays the amount of the judgment to a government entity to augment either the general fund or funds allocated to an agency that serves or aids the group comprising the class. In the *Democratic Central Committee* case, cited above, the court took this approach in a seeking "excessive fares collected" by the DC Transit Commission from bus riders.

(c) In the "consumer trust fund" approach, defendant pays the amount of the judgment to a court-appointed trustee or board that creates "an

organization through which it finances projects beneficial to the injured consumers and those similarly situated," or in the alternative pays the amount of
the judgment "to an existing organization to support new and ongoing projects." See *Democratic Central Committee,* supra, at 451, 456.

  (d) A fourth model involves "claimant fund sharing." Under this
approach, defendant pays the money to a court administrator or to a trust,
and compensation goes to "all who submit legitimate claims," but class members who do not come forward receive nothing, and other claimants may well
receive more than their share ("a windfall"). See *Democratic Central Committee,* supra, at 456.

7. Opt-Out Rights and Notice

Rule 23(c) says that in common question suits—those certified under
(b)(3)—the court "must direct to class members the best notice that is practicable," including "individual notice to all members who can be identified
through reasonable effort."

  The notice must state "clearly and concisely" and in "plain, easily understood language" the nature of the suit, definition of the class, and the claims,
issues, or defenses. It must also state that a class member "may enter an
appearance" through a lawyer if he or she "so desires," that the court will
"exclude from the class any member who requests exclusion" (providing information on "time and manner" for requesting exclusion), and that the court
must advise everyone that a judgment binds members of the class who do not
request exclusion.

  In an early case construing this provision, the Supreme Court held that
plaintiff must bear the cost of notice, and that the requirement of giving
"individual notice" to identifiable members means what it suggests—personal
notice, typically by mail. See Eisen v. Carlisle & Jacqueline, 417 U.S. 156 (1982).
Eisen involved claims on behalf of a class of six million investors for alleged
overcharges in brokerage commissions, and the value of the standard bearer's
claim was estimated at $75, which may have been typical across the class. The
trial court thought that 2.25 million members could be identified, but plaintiff's lawyer was unwilling to finance the costs of notice to such a group.
Hence the judge decided to require individual notice to members of the
class who had engaged in ten or more trades during the period, plus sample
notice to 5,000 others selected at random. After a preliminary inquiry into the
merits, the court concluded that plaintiff was likely to prevail, and on that
ground the court ordered defendant to bear the cost of notice.

  The Supreme Court disapproved this approach. It read FRCP 23 as requiring individual notice to all identifiable class members, alluding to Mullane v.
Central Hanover Bank & Trust Co., 339 U.S. 306 (1950) (Chapter 3D, supra),
which held as a matter of due process that plaintiffs had to give notice "reasonably calculated, under all the circumstances, to apprise interested parties

of the pendency of the action." Recall that *Mullane* was a suit in which a bank sought a judgment that would have exonerated it from liability for managing mutual funds over the year, and the interested parties were the owners or beneficiaries of the funds (the court had appointed guardians to look after their interests). In citing *Mullane, Eisen* might be understood to mean that it is not just FRCP 23 that requires such notice, but the Constitution as well. Suffice it to say that this point remains unresolved.

Perhaps equally important, *Eisen* did not agree that cost of notice could be put on the defendant. See Eisen v. Carlisle & Jacqueline, 417 U.S. 156, 177 (1982) (standard bearer "must bear the cost of notice to the members of his class"). As if to drive home the point, the Court decided several years later that plaintiffs could not use the discovery process to shift to defendants the cost of identifying members of a plaintiff class. See Oppenheimer Fund, Inc. v. Sanders, 339 U.S. 306 (1978).

Eisen also disapproved the process followed by the trial court in deciding to charge defendants the costs of notice. Nothing in the "language or history" of FRCP 23 justifies a preliminary inquiry into the merits, which would allow the standard bearer to "secure the benefits of a class action without first satisfying the requirements," and which is "directly contrary" to language in the Rule that then required certification resolved "as soon as practicable" (now it says "at an early practicable time"). The Court quoted a 1971 Circuit Court decision saying the question in deciding whether to certify a class is *not* whether claimants "will prevail on the merits," but whether FRCP 23 is satisfied. A preliminary inquiry into the merits may, moreover, cause "substantial prejudice" to a defendant because it proceeds without "traditional rules and procedures" that govern trial, and a "tentative" finding "may color" the case, and put defendant to an "unfair burden." See Eisen v. Carlisle & Jacqueline, 417 U.S. 156, 177-178 (1982).

■ NOTES ON OPT-OUT RIGHTS, NOTICE, AND PRELIMINARY HEARINGS

1. Why allow opting out in common question class suits? *Hansberry* holds that adequate representation is the key to binding members of a plaintiff class, and FRCP 23 *requires* adequate representation in all class suits. Isn't that enough?

2. As the Rule is set up, a purported class member is "in unless she gets out." Doing nothing means she is in. Should it be done this way, or would it be better to have an "opt in" mechanism (one is "only in if she chooses to be"). In the *Shutts* case, the Supreme Court rejected an argument, advanced in a class action in state court, that distant members of the plaintiff class (over whom the court might not have jurisdiction, absent consent), could not be viewed as being in the class unless they "opted in." See Phillips Petroleum v. Shutts, 472

U.S. 797, 821-822 (1985) (described and quoted in Section H7, infra). Prior to 1966, FRCP 23 was an opt-in rule. Consider these arguments:

(a) Few people with small claims will pursue their rights. If they get notice that someone has brought suit and they might recover, few would invest time or energy to figure out what is going on, or fill out a form for what seems like a distant prospect of a small recovery. If the Rule required people to opt in, few would. Their rights would go unvindicated; misconduct would go uncorrected; the cost to society in wrongful charges or illegal prices or behavior would not be redressed; defendants would keep ill-gotten gains and continue unlawful behavior. See Deborah Hensler, et al., Class Action Dilemmas: Pursuing Public Goals for Private Gain 66 (2000).

(b) Ours is a nation of individual freedom, whose strength lies in maximizing possibilities for advancement by individual initiative. Our approach to civil justice expresses these ideals in an adversary system that rests on the idea that people who have suffered harm because of misconduct by others can vindicate their rights if they choose. One observer argues that an opt-out system should not be used in a class suit for recoveries that are so trivial that class members would not make claims for recovery even if the suit settles or goes to trial and verdict in their favor:

> [The opt-out procedure] creates a framework for litigation that threatens to undermine the essential premises of the private compensatory model of adjudication . . . [under which] the substantive law simultaneously proscribes the specified behavior . . . and vests in the victims . . . the individual right to sue the wrongdoer in order to be made whole. None of the laws in question draws any distinction between individual and class injuries. To the contrary, they do nothing more than vest compensatory rights in individual victims. . . . [Because Rule 23] transforms individual victims into class members solely on the basis of their failure to remove themselves from the class, . . . it virtually invites the creation of a class in which, as a practical matter, numerous class members have not only not actually assented to suit, but are completely unaware that they are even suing.
>
> . . .
>
> Adopting an inference of inclusion in the class on the basis of purely passive behavior on the part of the absent class members has the effect of creating a "faux" class, which does not truly represent aggregation of willing plaintiffs as much as a comatose grouping of absent class members who know little or nothing of the proceeding and are unlikely to pursue whatever relief the proceeding makes available to them on an individual basis. As a result, the class proceeding is often transformed into a bounty hunter action in which the only interested parties are the class attorneys, thus effectively transforming the underlying substantive law into something other than what it purports to be—namely, a compensatory remedial action.

Martin H. Redish, Wholesale Justice, Constitutional Democracy and the Problem of the Class Action Lawsuit 36, 132, 169-170 (2009).

3. Does *Eisen* keep a court from imposing cost of notice on defendants if liability is established? Some courts think not. See Hunt v. Imperial Merchant Services, Inc., 560 F.3d 1137 (9th Cir. 2009) (after awarding partial summary judgment for class on claims under Fair Debt Collection Act, then certifying classes under (b)(2) and (b)(3), court could order defendant to pay cost of notice to class; *Eisen* does not bar shifting costs after plaintiffs achieve success on merits).

4. How many people who get notice of a class suit in which they will be included (unless they opt out) understand what is going on? One observer learned that at least some recipients of such a notice in a class suit were confused. The suit sought damages on an antitrust theory from drug companies on behalf of antibiotics purchasers. The notice generated these responses:

> Dear Sir:
> I received your pamphlet on drugs, which I think will be of great value to me in the future. Due to circumstances beyond my control I will not be able to attend this class at the time prescribed on your letter due to the fact that my working hours are from 7:00 until 4:30.

> Dear Sir:
> Our son is in the Navy, stationed in the Caribbean some place. Please let us know exactly what kind of drugs he is accused of taking. From a mother who will help if properly informed. A worried mother, Jane Doe

> Dear Attorney General:
> Holy greetings to you in Jesus name. I received a card from you and I don't understand it, and my husband can't read his. Most of the time all I buy is olive oil for healing oil after praying over it, it is anointed with God's power and ain't nothing like dope.

See Deborah Rhode, *Class Conflicts in Class Actions,* 34 Stan. L. Rev. 1183, 1235 (1982) (quoting Horne & King, *I Am Sorry, But I Cannot Attend Your Class Action,* Va. L. Weekly, Feb. 4, 1972). Can the problem be solved by ensuring, as FRCP 23(c)(1)(B) tries to do, that the notice is written "clearly and concisely" and "in plain, easily understood language"?

5. For years, the language in *Eisen* criticizing the judge for conducting a preliminary hearing into the merits was taken to mean that judges must resolve certification issues without even referring to substantive issues. But recall the *Madison* case in the prior section, which exemplifies the modern approach endorsed in In re Hydrogen Peroxide Antitrust Litigation, 552 F.3d 305, 307 (3d Cir. 2008). Recall as well the language in *Wal-Mart* quoted in Section H2, supra. See also In re Initial Public Offering Securities Litigation, 471 F.3d 24 (2d Cir. 2006) (*Eisen* does not excuse court from deciding whether FRCP 23's requirements are satisfied; *Eisen* precludes consideration of the merits "only when a merits issue is unrelated to a Rule 23 requirement," but court has "considerable discretion to limit both discovery and the extent of a hearing" on certification issues to avoid letting a Rule 23 hearing become "a protracted mini-trial of substantial portions" on the underlying claims).

8. Jurisdiction and Choice-of-Law Issues

In class suits, issues of jurisdiction abound. It is less important for you to learn the history than for you to learn where we are, and to examine some of the questions that remain.

***In Personam* Jurisdiction.** The question whether a court in a plaintiff class suit has jurisdiction over the defendant is resolved as it is resolved in individual suits. In state courts, the answer turns on the long-arm statute and the limits of due process under cases that began with *International Shoe* (Chapter 3B, supra). In federal court, plaintiff class suits asserting state law claims are similarly subject to state long-arm statutes and due process. In plaintiff class suits asserting federal claims, brought mostly in federal court, jurisdictional reach is less certain, as is true of individual federal question suits: Whether there is nationwide jurisdiction may turn on the underlying statute or on resolving a question that courts usually avoid, which is whether the reach of federal court authority is subject to similar constitutional limits to those that apply to state courts.

Suits on behalf of a plaintiff class raise one question unique to class suits, which is how and to what extent a forum obtains jurisdiction over absent members of the plaintiff class. Class members are not defendants, and not even parties in the full sense of the term, and yet they can be bound by a judgment or settlement and they stand to lose or gain. The Supreme Court addressed this matter in the *Shutts* case in 1985. *Shutts* was a class suit brought in state court in Kansas, on behalf of the owners of royalty interests in natural gas wells operated by Phillips Petroleum Company. Plaintiff Irl Shutts was a Kansas resident, and he sought to represent royalty owners around the country (members of the class are found in all 50 states and the District of Columbia) holding interests in wells located in Kansas, Oklahoma, Texas, Wyoming, and 11 other states. The claim was that Phillips was underpaying interest on royalties that it withheld after increases in natural gas prices were implemented but before they were approved by the Federal Power Commission. One question was whether the Kansas court had jurisdiction over class members living elsewhere. The Court concluded in the affirmative:

> The burdens placed by a State upon an absent class-action plaintiff are not of the same order of magnitude as those it places upon an absent defendant. An out-of-state defendant summoned by a plaintiff is faced with the full powers of the forum State to render judgment *against* it. The defendant must generally hire counsel and travel to the forum to defend itself from the plaintiff's claim, or suffer a default judgment. The defendant may be forced to participate in extended and

often costly discovery, and will be forced to respond in damages or to comply with some other form of remedy imposed by the court should it lose the suit. The defendant may also face liability for court costs and attorney's fees. These burdens are substantial, and the minimum contacts requirement of the Due Process Clause prevents the forum State from unfairly imposing them upon the defendant.

. . .

In sharp contrast to the predicament of a defendant haled into an out-of-state forum, the plaintiffs in this suit were not haled anywhere to defend themselves upon pain of a default judgment. As commentators have noted, from the plaintiffs' point of view a class action resembles a "quasi-administrative proceeding, conducted by the judge." 3B J. Moore & J. Kennedy, Moore's Federal Practice ¶ 23.45[4.-5] (1984); Kaplan, Continuing Work of the Civil Committee: 1966 Amendments to the Federal Rules of Civil Procedure (I), 81 Harv. L. Rev. 356, 398 (1967).

A plaintiff class in Kansas and numerous other jurisdictions cannot first be certified unless the judge, with the aid of the named plaintiffs and defendant, conducts an inquiry into the common nature of the named plaintiffs' and the absent plaintiffs' claims, the adequacy of representation, the jurisdiction possessed over the class, and any other matters that will bear upon proper representation of the absent plaintiffs' interest. See, *e.g.,* Kan. Stat. Ann. §60-223 (1983); FRCP 23. Unlike a defendant in a civil suit, a class-action plaintiff is not required to fend for himself. The court and named plaintiffs protect his interests. Indeed, the class-action defendant itself has a great interest in ensuring that the absent plaintiff's claims are properly before the forum. In this case, for example, the defendant sought to avoid class certification by alleging that the absent plaintiffs would not be adequately represented and were not amenable to jurisdiction.

The concern of the typical class-action rules for the absent plaintiffs is manifested in other ways. Most jurisdictions, including Kansas, require that a class action, once certified, may not be dismissed or compromised without the approval of the court. In many jurisdictions such as Kansas the court may amend the pleadings to ensure that all sections of the class are represented adequately.

Besides this continuing solicitude for their rights, absent plaintiff class members are not subject to other burdens imposed upon defendants. They need not hire counsel or appear. They are almost never subject to counterclaims or cross-claims, or liability for fees or costs.[2] Absent plaintiff class members are not subject to coercive or punitive remedies. Nor will an adverse judgment typically bind an absent plaintiff for any damages, although a valid adverse judgment may extinguish any of the plaintiff's claims which were litigated.

Unlike a defendant in a normal civil suit, an absent class-action plaintiff is not required to do anything. He may sit back and allow the litigation to run its course, content in knowing that there are safeguards provided for his protection.

---

[2] Petitioner places emphasis on the fact that absent class members might be subject to discovery, counterclaims, cross-claims, or court costs. Petitioner cites no cases involving any such imposition upon plaintiffs, however. We are convinced that such burdens are rarely imposed upon plaintiff class members, and that the disposition of these issues is best left to a case which presents them in a more concrete way.

In most class actions an absent plaintiff is provided at least with an opportunity to "opt out" of the class, and if he takes advantage of that opportunity he is removed from the litigation entirely. This was true of the Kansas proceedings in this case. The Kansas procedure provided for the mailing of a notice to each class member by first-class mail. The notice, as we have previously indicated, described the action and informed the class member that he could appear in person or by counsel, in default of which he would be represented by the named plaintiffs and their attorneys. The notice further stated that class members would be included in the class and bound by the judgment unless they "opted out" by executing and returning a "request for exclusion" that was included in the notice.

Phillips Petroleum v. Shutts, 472 U.S. 797, 821-822 (1985).

Subject Matter Jurisdiction: Conventional Class Suits. In state courts, class suits are brought in courts of general jurisdiction (typically district or superior courts). Such suits are not usually within the jurisdiction of small claims courts or other courts of limited or specialty jurisdiction.

In the federal system, issues of subject matter jurisdiction arise most often in class suits asserting state law claims. Here we must distinguish between "conventional" class suits and those covered by the Class Action Fairness Act, which covers basically "national class suits" where the Act expands federal jurisdiction and sets up what some call a preference for litigation in federal court (taken up separately below).

The citizenship of standard bearers counts in applying the "complete diversity" requirement of §1332, and citizenship of class members does not count. Thus a standard bearer from North Carolina may sue a defendant who is a citizen of South Carolina, even if the class includes citizens of South Carolina, and such a suit can proceed even if the standard bearer is the *only* claimant diverse from the defendant. The amount-in-controversy requirement for diversity suits is satisfied if the standard bearer claims more than the minimum—more than $75,000. If this condition is satisfied, it does not matter that claims of class members are smaller. This is the conclusion indicated by the decision in *Exxon*, which relied on the supplemental jurisdiction statute (28 USC §1367), and this outcome may have been the unintended consequence of a drafting error. See Exxon Mobil Corp. v. Allapattah Services, Inc., 545 U.S. 546 (2005) (Chapter 4C2, supra). The result in *Exxon* was earth-shaking for diversity class suits, because prior doctrine held that *every member* of a plaintiff class in a diversity suit had to seek more than the minimum. See Zahn v. International Paper Co., 414 U.S. 291 (1973). (*Exxon* appears to indicate that, in class suits in which multiple standard bearers represent related classes, only one standard bearer must satisfy the jurisdictional minimum in her own personal claim, and of course none of the class members need satisfy the minimum. But this precise question did not arise in *Exxon:* One of the cases on review was a class suit, but it seems to have involved only one standard bearer.)

Subject Matter Jurisdiction: CAFA Suits. The long and complicated Class Action Fairness Act of 1995 (CAFA) vastly expanded diversity jurisdiction in large multistate class suits, and added regulations of some aspects of settlements.

In enacting CAFA, Congress found that class suits are "an important and valuable part of the legal system," but the concept of diversity jurisdiction was being "undermined" by interpretations that were "keeping cases of national importance out of federal courts." Hence CAFA amended 28 USC §1332 (basic diversity jurisdiction statute) by adding subsection (d). Ignoring details for a moment, the major change is in authorizing federal jurisdiction on the basis of minimal diversity (any standard bearer being diverse from any defendant even if not diverse from other defendants and even if another standard bearer is not diverse from any defendant) where the aggregate amount in controversy exceeds $5 million. Even before CAFA, it did not matter that members of a class were not diverse from defendants, but CAFA went much further. After *Exxon,* it didn't matter whether class members sought less than the minimum, but CAFA went even further in providing that *no* claimant had to satisfy the minimum, so long as the class as a whole sought more than $5 million.

CAFA includes a provision authorizing removal from state court of any suit that could originally have been brought in federal court under CAFA, regardless whether any defendant is a citizen of the forum state. 28 USC §1453.

There are qualifications that reduce the apparent expansion introduced by CAFA. Most important are three provisions designed to prevent or discourage federal jurisdiction in suits that are more "local" even though they satisfy the basic CAFA standards (minimal diversity and aggregate claims exceeding $5 million). First, a discretionary provision says federal courts may decline jurisdiction if "more than one-third but less than two-thirds" of class members are citizens of the same state as "primary defendants." See §1332(d)(3) (in exercising this discretion, the court should consider whether the claims "involve matters of national or interstate interest" and certain other factors). Second, a strict exception says that federal courts "shall decline" jurisdiction if "greater than two-thirds" of the class are citizens of the same state as one of the major defendants (with criteria identifying such defendants) and the suit was filed in that state and most injuries occurred there. Third, "carveouts" implement the Eleventh Amendment (barring federal jurisdiction in suits against states) and weed out smaller suits: Thus CAFA jurisdiction does not extend to class suits in which "primary defendants" are state officials or other governmental entities "against whom the district court may be foreclosed from ordering relief." And CAFA jurisdiction does not extend to suits in which the proposed class has fewer than 100 persons. See 28 USC §1332(d)(5). There are other carveouts, most importantly removing jurisdiction from securities suits, and suits relating to "internal affairs or governance of a corporation." See 28 USC §1332(d)(8).

We are about to look at class suits that are filed with the intent and expectation of settlement. Before looking at these, we should pause to recognize that many class suits—even those filed *without* expectation of settlement—do settle. Sometimes defendants have seen settlements as a business opportunity. So-called coupon settlements are those in which defendant agrees, in effect, to give class members special prices or deals ("coupons") on future purchases. But many coupons do not offer much (and are not "cashed in"), and coupon settlements may provide illusory benefits. See Figueroa v. Sharper Image Corp., 517 F. Supp. 2d 1292, 1302 (S.D. Fla. 2007) (such settlements "often do not provide meaningful compensation" and "fail to disgorge ill-gotten gains," requiring class members "to do future business with the defendant in order to receive compensation"); Christopher Leslie, *The Need to Study Coupon Settlements in Class Action Litigation*, 18 Geo. J. Legal Ethics 1395, 1396-1397 (2005).

In enacting CAFA, Congress found that class members often "receive little or no benefit" from "coupons or other awards of little or no value," while lawyers collect high fees. To remedy the situation, CAFA includes a provision stating that the fee award, to the extent it rests on coupon settlements, shall be "based on the value to the class members of the coupons that are [actually] redeemed," as opposed to the overall (theoretical) value of all coupons issued or made available. See 28 USC §1712(a). The same statute tells courts to appraise proposed coupon settlements and allow them only on the basis of written findings that they are "fair, reasonable, and adequate for class members." See 28 USC §1712(e).

For scholarly commentary on CAFA, see Stephen B. Burbank, *The Impact of the Class Action Fairness Act on the Federal Courts: An Empirical Analysis of Filings and Removals*, 156 U. Pa. L. Rev. 1723 (2008); Judith Resnik, *Lessons in Federalism from the 1960s Class Action Rule and the 2005 Class Action Fairness Act: "The Political Safeguards" of Aggregate Translocal Actions*, 156 U. Pa. L. Rev. 1919 (2008); Edward F. Sherman, *Class Actions After the Class Action Fairness Act of 2005*, 80 Tul. L. Rev. 1593 (2006).

9. Settlement and "Settlement Classes"

Now we turn to class suits filed long after negotiations have led the parties to agreement on settlement terms. Such suits are sometimes filed simply for the purpose of obtaining a judgment and judicial approval: A big difference between individual and class suits is that the latter cannot be settled without court approval. Another difference is that class members may not all agree that a settlement is "fair," and FRCP 23(e) contemplates that they are to receive notice of a proposed settlement and given a chance to object.

In the *Amchem* case set out below, the Court examined a settlement of enormous proportions, far larger than the run-of-the-mill class suit. *Amchem*, like the *Ortiz* case before it (Section H2, supra), was a suit filed with no intent of going to trial. The parties had reached agreement beforehand, and the role of the court was to approve—or not—a settlement that would bind parties and class members.

AMCHEM PRODUCTS, INC. v. WINDSOR
Supreme Court of the United States
521 U.S. 591 (1997)

Justice GINSBURG delivered the opinion of the Court.

This case concerns the legitimacy under FRCP 23 of a class-action certification sought to achieve global settlement of current and future asbestos-related claims. The class proposed for certification potentially encompasses hundreds of thousands, perhaps millions, of individuals tied together by this commonality: Each was, or some day may be, adversely affected by past exposure to asbestos products manufactured by one or more of 20 companies. Those companies, defendants in the lower courts, are petitioners here.

The United States District Court for the Eastern District of Pennsylvania certified the class for settlement only, finding that the proposed settlement was fair and that representation and notice had been adequate. That court enjoined class members from separately pursuing asbestos-related personal-injury suits in any court, federal or state, pending the issuance of a final order. The Court of Appeals for the Third Circuit vacated the District Court's orders, holding that the class certification failed to satisfy Rule 23's requirements in several critical respects. We affirm the Court of Appeals' judgment.

I

A . . .

. . .

[The Panel on Multidistrict Litigation] transferred all asbestos cases then filed, but not yet on trial in federal courts to a single district, the United States District Court for the Eastern District of Pennsylvania; pursuant to the transfer order, the collected cases were consolidated for pretrial proceedings before Judge Weiner. The order aggregated pending cases only; no authority resides in the MDL Panel to license for consolidated proceedings claims not yet filed.

B

After the consolidation, attorneys for plaintiffs and defendants formed separate steering committees and began settlement negotiations. . . . Although the

MDL Panel order collected, transferred, and consolidated only cases already commenced in federal courts, settlement negotiations included efforts to find a "means of resolving . . . future cases."

. . .

To that end, [counsel for the Center for Claims Resolution, a consortium of 20 former asbestos manufacturers and petitioner in this case] approached the lawyers who had headed the Plaintiffs' Steering Committee . . . and a new round of negotiations began; that round yielded the mass settlement agreement now in controversy. At the time, the former heads of the Plaintiffs' Steering Committee represented thousands of plaintiffs with then-pending asbestos-related claims—claimants the parties to this suit call "inventory" plaintiffs. CCR indicated in these discussions that it would resist settlement of inventory cases absent "some kind of protection for the future."

Settlement talks thus concentrated on devising an administrative scheme for disposition of asbestos claims not yet in litigation. In these negotiations, counsel for masses of inventory plaintiffs endeavored to represent the interests of the anticipated future claimants, although those lawyers then had no attorney-client relationship with such claimants.

Once negotiations seemed likely to produce an agreement purporting to bind potential plaintiffs, CCR agreed to settle, through separate agreements, the claims of plaintiffs who had already filed asbestos-related lawsuits. In one such agreement, CCR defendants promised to pay more than $200 million to gain release of the claims of numerous inventory plaintiffs. After settling the inventory claims, CCR, together with the plaintiffs' lawyers CCR had approached, launched this case, exclusively involving persons outside the MDL Panel's province—plaintiffs without already pending lawsuits.[3]

C

The class action thus instituted was not intended to be litigated. Rather, within the space of a single day, January 15, 1993, the settling parties—CCR defendants and the representatives of the plaintiff class described below—presented to the District Court a complaint, an answer, a proposed settlement agreement, and a joint motion for conditional class certification.[4] The complaint identified nine lead plaintiffs, designating them and members of their families as representatives of a class comprising all persons who had not filed an asbestos-related lawsuit against a CCR defendant as of the date the class

---

[3] It is basic to comprehension of this proceeding to notice that no transferred case is included in the settlement at issue, and no case covered by the settlement existed as a civil action at the time of the MDL Panel transfer.

[4] Also on the same day, the CCR defendants filed a third-party action against their insurers, seeking a declaratory judgment holding the insurers liable for the costs of the settlement. The insurance litigation, on which implementation of the settlement is conditioned, is still pending in the District Court.

action commenced, but who (1) had been exposed—occupationally or through the occupational exposure of a spouse or household member—to asbestos or products containing asbestos attributable to a CCR defendant, or (2) . . . [had a] spouse or family member [who] had been so exposed. Untold numbers of individuals may fall within this description. All named plaintiffs alleged that they or a member of their family had been exposed to asbestos-containing products of CCR defendants. More than half of the named plaintiffs alleged that they or their family members had already suffered various physical injuries as a result of the exposure. The others alleged that they had not yet manifested any asbestos-related condition. The complaint delineated no subclasses; all named plaintiffs were designated as representatives of the class as a whole.

. . .

A stipulation of settlement accompanied the pleadings; it proposed to settle, and to preclude nearly all class members from litigating against CCR companies, all claims not filed before January 15, 1993, involving compensation for present and future asbestos-related personal injury or death. An exhaustive document exceeding 100 pages, the stipulation presents in detail an administrative mechanism and a schedule of payments to compensate class members who meet defined asbestos-exposure and medical requirements. The stipulation describes four categories of compensable disease: mesothelioma; lung cancer; certain "other cancers" (colon-rectal, laryngeal, esophageal, and stomach cancer); and "non-malignant conditions" (asbestosis and bilateral pleural thickening). Persons with "exceptional" medical claims—claims that do not fall within the four described diagnostic categories—may in some instances qualify for compensation, but the settlement caps the number of "exceptional" claims CCR must cover.

For each qualifying disease category, the stipulation specifies the range of damages CCR will pay to qualifying claimants. Payments under the settlement are not adjustable for inflation. Mesothelioma claimants—the most highly compensated category—are scheduled to receive between $20,000 and $200,000. The stipulation provides that CCR is to propose the level of compensation within the prescribed ranges; it also establishes procedures to resolve disputes over medical diagnoses and levels of compensation.

Compensation above the fixed ranges may be obtained for "extraordinary" claims. But the settlement places both numerical caps and dollar limits on such claims.[6] The settlement also imposes "case flow maximums," which cap the number of claims payable for each disease in a given year.

---

[6] Only three percent of the qualified mesothelioma, lung cancer, and "other cancer" claims, and only one percent of the total number of qualified "non-malignant condition" claims can be designated "extraordinary." Average expenditures are specified for claims found "extraordinary"; mesothelioma victims with compensable extraordinary claims, for example, receive, on average, $300,000.

Class members are to receive no compensation for certain kinds of claims, even if otherwise applicable state law recognizes such claims. Claims that garner no compensation under the settlement include claims by family members of asbestos-exposed individuals for loss of consortium, and claims by so-called "exposure-only" plaintiffs for increased risk of cancer, fear of future asbestos-related injury, and medical monitoring. "Pleural" claims, which might be asserted by persons with asbestos-related plaques on their lungs but no accompanying physical impairment, are also excluded. Although not entitled to present compensation, exposure-only claimants and pleural claimants may qualify for benefits when and if they develop a compensable disease and meet the relevant exposure and medical criteria. Defendants forgo defenses to liability, including statute of limitations pleas.

Class members, in the main, are bound by the settlement in perpetuity, while CCR defendants may choose to withdraw from the settlement after ten years. A small number of class members—only a few per year—may reject the settlement and pursue their claims in court. Those permitted to exercise this option, however, may not assert any punitive damages claim or any claim for increased risk of cancer. Aspects of the administration of the settlement are to be monitored by the AFL-CIO and class counsel. Class counsel are to receive attorneys' fees in an amount to be approved by the District Court.

D

On January 29, 1993, as requested by the settling parties, the District Court conditionally certified, under FRCP 23(b)(3), an encompassing opt-out class. The certified class included persons occupationally exposed to defendants' asbestos products, and members of their families, who had not filed suit as of January 15. Judge Weiner appointed Locks, Motley, and Rice as class counsel, noting that "[t]he Court may in the future appoint additional counsel if it is deemed necessary and advisable." At no stage of the proceedings, however, were additional counsel in fact appointed. Nor was the class ever divided into subclasses. In a separate order, Judge Weiner assigned to Judge Reed, also of the Eastern District of Pennsylvania, "the task of conducting fairness proceedings and of determining whether the proposed settlement is fair to the class." Various class members raised objections to the settlement stipulation, and Judge Weiner granted the objectors full rights to participate in the subsequent proceedings.[7]

---

[7] These objectors, now respondents before this Court, include three groups of individuals with overlapping interests, designated as the "Windsor Group," the New Jersey "White Lung Group," and the "Cargile Group." Margaret Balonis, an individual objector, is also a respondent before this Court. Balonis states that her husband, Casimir, was exposed to asbestos in the late 1940's and was diagnosed with mesothelioma in May 1994, after expiration of the opt-out period. The Balonises sued CCR members in Maryland state court, but were charged with civil contempt for violating the Federal District Court's antisuit injunction. Casimir Balonis died in October 1996.

In preliminary rulings, Judge Reed . . . approved the settling parties' elaborate plan for giving notice to the class. The court-approved notice informed recipients that they could exclude themselves from the class, if they so chose, within a three-month opt-out period.

Objectors raised numerous challenges to the settlement. They urged that the settlement unfairly disadvantaged those without currently compensable conditions in that it failed to adjust for inflation or to account for changes, over time, in medical understanding. They maintained that compensation levels were intolerably low in comparison to awards available in tort litigation or payments received by the inventory plaintiffs. And they objected to the absence of any compensation for certain claims, for example, medical monitoring, compensable under the tort law of several States. Rejecting these and all other objections, Judge Reed concluded that the settlement terms were fair and had been negotiated without collusion. He also found that adequate notice had been given to class members, and that final class certification under Rule 23(b)(3) was appropriate.

. . .

Strenuous objections had been asserted regarding the adequacy of representation, a Rule 23(a)(4) requirement. Objectors maintained that class counsel and class representatives had disqualifying conflicts of interests. In particular, objectors urged, claimants whose injuries had become manifest and claimants without manifest injuries should not have common counsel and should not be aggregated in a single class. Furthermore, objectors argued, lawyers representing inventory plaintiffs should not represent the newly formed class.

Satisfied that class counsel had ably negotiated the settlement in the best interests of all concerned, and that the named parties served as adequate representatives, the District Court rejected these objections. Subclasses were unnecessary, the District Court held, bearing in mind the added cost and confusion they would entail and the ability of class members to exclude themselves from the class during the three-month opt-out period. Reasoning that the representative plaintiffs "have a strong interest that recovery for *all* of the medical categories be maximized because they may have claims in *any,* or several categories," the District Court found "no antagonism of interest between class members with various medical conditions, or between persons with and without currently manifest asbestos impairment." Declaring class certification appropriate and the settlement fair, the District Court preliminarily enjoined all class members from commencing any asbestos-related suit against the CCR defendants in any state or federal court.

The objectors appealed. The United States Court of Appeals for the Third Circuit vacated the certification, holding that the requirements of Rule 23 had not been satisfied.

. . .

IV

We granted review to decide the role settlement may play, under existing Rule 23, in determining the propriety of class certification. The Third Circuit's opinion stated that each of the requirements of Rule 23(a) and (b)(3) "must be satisfied without taking into account the settlement." That statement, petitioners urge, is incorrect.

We agree with petitioners to this limited extent: Settlement is relevant to a class certification. The Third Circuit's opinion bears modification in that respect. But, as we earlier observed, the Court of Appeals in fact did not ignore the settlement; instead, that court homed in on settlement terms in explaining why it found the absentees' interests inadequately represented. The Third Circuit's close inspection of the settlement in that regard was altogether proper.

Confronted with a request for settlement-only class certification, a district court need not inquire whether the case, if tried, would present intractable management problems, see FRCP 23(b)(3)(D), for the proposal is that there be no trial. But other specifications of the Rule—those designed to protect absentees by blocking unwarranted or overbroad class definitions—demand undiluted, even heightened, attention in the settlement context. Such attention is of vital importance, for a court asked to certify a settlement class will lack the opportunity, present when a case is litigated, to adjust the class, informed by the proceedings as they unfold. See Rule 23(c), (d).

And, of overriding importance, courts must be mindful that the Rule as now composed sets the requirements they are bound to enforce. Federal Rules take effect after an extensive deliberative process involving many reviewers: a Rules Advisory Committee, public commenters, the Judicial Conference, this Court, the Congress. See 28 USC §§2073, 2074. The text of a rule thus proposed and reviewed limits judicial inventiveness. Courts are not free to amend a rule outside the process Congress ordered, a process properly tuned to the instruction that rules of procedure "shall not abridge . . . any substantive right." §2072(b).

Rule 23(e), on settlement of class actions, reads in its entirety: "A class action shall not be dismissed or compromised without the approval of the court, and notice of the proposed dismissal or compromise shall be given to all members of the class in such manner as the court directs." [FRCP 23(e) still contains this language, but additional clauses were later added, spelling out procedures for approving settlement in more detail.—ED.] This prescription was designed to function as an additional requirement, not a superseding direction, for the "class action" to which Rule 23(e) refers is one qualified for certification under Rule 23(a) and (b). Subdivisions (a) and (b) focus court attention on whether a proposed class has sufficient unity so that absent members can fairly be bound by decisions of class representatives.

That dominant concern persists when settlement, rather than trial, is proposed.

The safeguards provided by the Rule 23(a) and (b) class-qualifying criteria, we emphasize, are not impractical impediments—checks shorn of utility—in the settlement-class context. First, the standards set for the protection of absent class members serve to inhibit appraisals of the chancellor's foot kind—class certifications dependent upon the court's gestalt judgment or overarching impression of the settlement's fairness.

Second, if a fairness inquiry under Rule 23(e) controlled certification, eclipsing Rule 23(a) and (b), and permitting class designation despite the impossibility of litigation, both class counsel and court would be disarmed. Class counsel confined to settlement negotiations could not use the threat of litigation to press for a better offer, see Coffee, Class Wars: The Dilemma of the Mass Tort Class Action, 95 Colum. L. Rev. 1343, 1379-1380 (1995), and the court would face a bargain proffered for its approval without benefit of adversarial investigation.

Federal courts, in any case, lack authority to substitute for Rule 23's certification criteria a standard never adopted—that if a settlement is "fair," then certification is proper. Applying to this case criteria the rulemakers set, we conclude that the Third Circuit's appraisal is essentially correct. Although that court should have acknowledged that settlement is a factor in the calculus, a remand is not warranted on that account. The Court of Appeals' opinion amply demonstrates why—with or without a settlement on the table—the sprawling class the District Court certified does not satisfy Rule 23's requirements.

A

We address first the requirement of Rule 23(b)(3) that "[common] questions of law or fact ... predominate over any questions affecting only individual members." The District Court concluded that predominance was satisfied based on two factors: class members' shared experience of asbestos exposure and their common "interest in receiving prompt and fair compensation for their claims, while minimizing the risks and transaction costs inherent in the asbestos litigation process as it occurs presently in the tort system." The settling parties also contend that lying at the settlement's fairness is a common question, predominating over disparate legal issues that might be pivotal in litigation but become irrelevant under the settlement.

The predominance requirement stated in Rule 23(b)(3), we hold, is not met by the factors on which the District Court relied. The benefits asbestos-exposed persons might gain from the establishment of a grand-scale compensation scheme is a matter fit for legislative consideration, but it is not pertinent to the predominance inquiry. That inquiry trains on the legal or factual questions that qualify each class member's case as a genuine controversy, questions that preexist any settlement.[18]

The Rule 23(b)(3) predominance inquiry tests whether proposed classes are sufficiently cohesive to warrant adjudication by representation. The inquiry appropriate under Rule 23(e), on the other hand, protects unnamed class members "from unjust or unfair settlements affecting their rights when the representatives become fainthearted before the action is adjudicated or are able to secure satisfaction of their individual claims by a compromise." But it is not the mission of Rule 23(e) to assure the class cohesion that legitimizes representative action in the first place. If a common interest in a fair compromise could satisfy the predominance requirement of Rule 23(b)(3), that vital prescription would be stripped of any meaning in the settlement context.

The District Court also relied upon this commonality: "The members of the class have all been exposed to asbestos products supplied by the defendants. . . ." Even if Rule 23(a)'s commonality requirement may be satisfied by that shared experience, the predominance criterion is far more demanding. Given the greater number of questions peculiar to the several categories of class members, and to individuals within each category, and the significance of those uncommon questions, any overarching dispute about the health consequences of asbestos exposure cannot satisfy the Rule 23(b)(3) predominance standard.

The Third Circuit highlighted the disparate questions undermining class cohesion in this case:

> Class members were exposed to different asbestos-containing products, for different amounts of time, in different ways, and over different periods. Some class members suffer no physical injury or have only asymptomatic pleural changes, while others suffer from lung cancer, disabling asbestosis, or from mesothelioma. . . . Each has a different history of cigarette smoking, a factor that complicates the causation inquiry.
>
> The [exposure-only] plaintiffs especially share little in common, either with each other or with the presently injured class members. It is unclear whether they will contract asbestos-related disease and, if so, what disease each will suffer. They will also incur different medical expenses because their monitoring and treatment will depend on singular circumstances and individual medical histories.

Differences in state law, the Court of Appeals observed, compound these disparities (citing Phillips Petroleum Co. v. Shutts, 472 U.S. 797, 823 (1985)).

---

[18] In this respect, the predominance requirement of Rule 23(b)(3) is similar to the requirement of Rule 23(a)(3) that "claims or defenses" of the named representatives must be "typical of the claims or defenses of the class." The words "claims or defenses" in this context—just as in the context of Rule 24(b)(2) governing permissive intervention—"manifestly refer to the kinds of claims or defenses that can be raised in courts of law as part of an actual or impending law suit." Diamond v. Charles, 476 U.S. 54, 76-77 (1986) (O'Connor, J., concurring in part and concurring in judgment).

No settlement class called to our attention is as sprawling as this one. Predominance is a test readily met in certain cases alleging consumer or securities fraud or violations of the antitrust laws. Even mass tort cases arising from a common cause or disaster may, depending upon the circumstances, satisfy the predominance requirement. The Advisory Committee for the 1966 revision of Rule 23, it is true, noted that "mass accident" cases are likely to present "significant questions, not only of damages but of liability and defenses of liability, . . . affecting the individuals in different ways." And the Committee advised that such cases are "ordinarily not appropriate" for class treatment. But the text of the Rule does not categorically exclude mass tort cases from class certification, and District Courts, since the late 1970's, have been certifying such cases in increasing number. The Committee's warning, however, continues to call for caution when individual stakes are high and disparities among class members great. As the Third Circuit's opinion makes plain, the certification in this case does not follow the counsel of caution. That certification cannot be upheld, for it rests on a conception of Rule 23(b)(3)'s predominance requirement irreconcilable with the Rule's design.

B

Nor can the class approved by the District Court satisfy Rule 23(a)(4)'s requirement that the named parties "will fairly and adequately protect the interests of the class." The adequacy inquiry under Rule 23(a)(4) serves to uncover conflicts of interest between named parties and the class they seek to represent. See General Telephone Co. of Southwest v. Falcon, 457 U.S. 147, 157-158, n.13 (1982). "[A] class representative must be part of the class and 'possess the same interest and suffer the same injury' as the class members." East Tex. Motor Freight System, Inc. v. Rodriguez, 431 U.S. 395, 403 (1977) (quoting Schlesinger v. Reservists Comm. to Stop the War, 418 U.S. 208, 216 (1974)).[20]

As the Third Circuit pointed out, named parties with diverse medical conditions sought to act on behalf of a single giant class rather than on behalf of discrete subclasses. In significant respects, the interests of those within the single class are not aligned. Most saliently, for the currently injured, the critical goal is generous immediate payments. That goal tugs against the interest

---

[20] The adequacy-of-representation requirement "tend[s] to merge" with the commonality and typicality criteria of Rule 23(a), which "serve as guideposts for determining whether . . . maintenance of a class action is economical and whether the named plaintiff's claim and the class claims are so interrelated that the interests of the class members will be fairly and adequately protected in their absence." General Telephone Co. of Southwest v. Falcon, 457 U.S. 147, 157, n.13 (1982). The adequacy heading also factors in competency and conflicts of class counsel. Like the Third Circuit, we decline to address adequacy-of-counsel issues discretely in light of our conclusions that common questions of law or fact do not predominate and that the named plaintiffs cannot adequately represent the interests of this enormous class.

of exposure-only plaintiffs in ensuring an ample, inflation-protected fund for the future.

The disparity between the currently injured and exposure-only categories of plaintiffs, and the diversity within each category are not made insignificant by the District Court's finding that petitioners' assets suffice to pay claims under the settlement. Although this is not a "limited fund" case certified under Rule 23(b)(1)(B), the terms of the settlement reflect essential allocation decisions designed to confine compensation and to limit defendants' liability. For example, ... the settlement includes no adjustment for inflation; only a few claimants per year can opt out at the back end; and loss-of-consortium claims are extinguished with no compensation.

The settling parties, in sum, achieved a global compromise with no structural assurance of fair and adequate representation for the diverse groups and individuals affected. Although the named parties alleged a range of complaints, each served generally as representative for the whole, not for a separate constituency. . . .

C

Impediments to the provision of adequate notice, the Third Circuit emphasized, rendered highly problematic any endeavor to tie to a settlement class persons with no perceptible asbestos-related disease at the time of the settlement. Many persons in the exposure-only category, the Court of Appeals stressed, may not even know of their exposure, or realize the extent of the harm they may incur. Even if they fully appreciate the significance of class notice, those without current afflictions may not have the information or foresight needed to decide, intelligently, whether to stay in or opt out.

Family members of asbestos-exposed individuals may themselves fall prey to disease or may ultimately have ripe claims for loss of consortium. Yet large numbers of people in this category—future spouses and children of asbestos victims—could not be alerted to their class membership. And current spouses and children of the occupationally exposed may know nothing of that exposure.

Because we have concluded that the class in this case cannot satisfy the requirements of common issue predominance and adequacy of representation, we need not rule, definitively, on the notice given here. In accord with the Third Circuit, however, we recognize the gravity of the question whether class action notice sufficient under the Constitution and Rule 23 could ever be given to legions so unselfconscious and amorphous.

V

The argument is sensibly made that a nationwide administrative claims processing regime would provide the most secure, fair, and efficient means of compensating victims of asbestos exposure. Congress, however, has not adopted such a solution. And Rule 23, which must be interpreted with fidelity to the Rules Enabling Act and applied with the interests of absent class members in close view, cannot carry the large load CCR, class counsel, and the District Court heaped upon it. As this case exemplifies, the rulemakers' prescriptions for class actions may be endangered by "those who embrace [Rule 23] too enthusiastically just as [they are by] those who approach [the Rule] with distaste." C. Wright, Law of Federal Courts 508 (5th ed. 1994).

For the reasons stated, the judgment of the Court of Appeals for the Third Circuit is *Affirmed.*

Justice O'CONNOR took no part in the consideration or decision of this case.

Justice BREYER, with whom Justice STEVENS joins, concurring in part and dissenting in part.

. . .

I

First, I believe the majority understates the importance of settlement in this case. Between 13 and 21 million workers have been exposed to asbestos in the workplace—over the past 40 or 50 years—but the most severe instances of such exposure probably occurred three or four decades ago. This exposure has led to several hundred thousand lawsuits, about 15% of which involved claims for cancer and about 30% for asbestosis. About half of the suits have involved claims for pleural thickening and plaques—the harmfulness of which is apparently controversial. (One expert below testified that they "don't transform into cancer" and are not "predictor[s] of future disease.") Some of those who suffer from the most serious injuries, however, have received little or no compensation. These lawsuits have taken up more than 6% of all federal civil filings in one recent year, and are subject to a delay that is twice that of other civil suits.

Delays, high costs, and a random pattern of noncompensation led the Judicial Conference Ad Hoc Committee on Asbestos Litigation to transfer all federal asbestos personal-injury cases to the Eastern District of Pennsylvania in an effort to bring about a fair and comprehensive settlement. It is worth considering a few of the Committee's comments. See Judicial Conference Report 2 ("'Decisions concerning thousands of deaths, millions of injuries, and billions of dollars are entangled in a litigation system whose strengths have increasingly been overshadowed by its weaknesses.' The ensuing five years have seen the picture worsen: increased filings, larger backlogs, higher costs, more bankruptcies and poorer prospects that judgments—if ever obtained—can be collected" (quoting Rand Corporation Institute for Civil Justice)); *id.,* at 13 ("The transaction costs associated with asbestos litigation are an unconscionable burden on the victims of asbestos disease." "[O]f each asbestos litigation dollar, 61 cents is consumed in transaction costs.... Only 39 cents were paid to the asbestos victims" (citing Rand finding)); *id.,* at 12 ("Delays also can increase transaction costs, especially the attorneys' fees paid by defendants at hourly rates. These costs reduce either the insurance fund or the company's assets, thereby reducing the funds available to pay pending and future claimants. By the end of the trial phase in [one case], at least seven defendants had declared bankruptcy (as a result of asbestos claims generally").

Although the transfer of the federal asbestos cases did not produce a general settlement, it was intertwined with and led to a lengthy year-long negotiation between the cochairs of the Plaintiff's Multi-District Litigation Steering Committee (elected by the Plaintiff's Committee Members and approved by the District Court) and the 20 asbestos defendants who are before us here. These "protracted and vigorous" negotiations led to the present partial settlement, which will pay an estimated $1.3 billion and compensate perhaps 100,000 class members in the first 10 years.

. . .

Second, the majority, in reviewing the District Court's determination that common "issues of fact and law predominate," says that the predominance "inquiry trains on the legal or factual questions that qualify each class member's case as a genuine controversy, questions that preexist any settlement." I find it difficult to interpret this sentence in a way that could lead me to the majority's conclusion. If the majority means that these pre-settlement questions are what matters, then how does it reconcile its statement with its basic conclusion that "settlement is relevant" to class certification, or with the numerous lower court authority that says that settlement is not only relevant, but important?

Nor do I understand how one could decide whether common questions "predominate" in the abstract—without looking at what is likely to be at issue in the proceedings that will ensue, namely, the settlement. Every group of human beings, after all, has some features in common, and some that differ. How can a court make a contextual judgment of the sort that Rule 23 requires without looking to what proceedings will follow? Such guideposts help it decide whether, in light of common concerns and differences, certification will achieve Rule 23's basic objective—"economies of time, effort, and expense." ACN to FRCP 23(b)(3). As this Court has previously observed, "sometimes it may be necessary for the court to probe behind the pleadings before coming to rest on the certification question." General Telephone Co. of Southwest v. Falcon. [Settlement may] "add a great deal of information to the court's inquiry and will often expose diverging interests or common issues that were not evident or clear from the complaint" and courts "can and should" look to it to enhance the "ability ... to make informed certification decisions." In re Asbestos Litigation, 90 F.3d 963, 975 (5th Cir. 1996).

. . .

Of course, as the majority points out, there are also important differences among class members. Different plaintiffs were exposed to different products for different times; each has a distinct medical history and a different history of smoking; and many cases arise under the laws of different States. The relevant question, however, is *how much* these differences matter in respect to the legal proceedings that lie ahead. Many, if not all, toxic tort class actions involve plaintiffs with such differences. And the differences in state law are of diminished importance in respect to a proposed settlement in which the defendants have waived all defenses and agreed to compensate all those who were injured.

These differences might warrant subclasses, though subclasses can have problems of their own. "There can be a cost in creating more distinct subgroups, each with its own representation. . . . [T]he more subclasses created, the more severe conflicts bubble to the surface and inhibit settlement. . . . The resources of defendants and, ultimately, the community must not be exhausted by protracted litigation." Weinstein, Individual Justice in Mass Tort Litigation, at 66. Or these differences may be too serious to permit an effort at group settlement. This kind of determination, as I have said, is one that the law commits to the discretion of the district court—reviewable for abuse of discretion by a court of appeals. I believe that we are far too distant from the litigation itself to reweigh the fact-specific Rule 23 determinations and to find them erroneous without the benefit of the Court of Appeals first having restudied the matter with today's legal standard in mind.

Third, the majority concludes that the "representative parties" will not "fairly and adequately protect the interests of the class." Rule 23(a)(4). It finds a serious conflict between plaintiffs who are now injured and those who may be injured in the future because "for the currently injured, the critical goal is generous immediate payments," a goal that "tugs against the interest of exposure-only plaintiffs in ensuring an ample, inflation-protected fund for the future."

I agree that there is a serious problem, but it is a problem that often exists in toxic tort cases. And it is a problem that potentially exists whenever a single defendant injures several plaintiffs, for a settling plaintiff leaves fewer assets available for the others. With class actions, at least, plaintiffs have the consolation that a district court, thoroughly familiar with the facts, is charged with the responsibility of ensuring that the interests of no class members are sacrificed.

But this Court cannot easily safeguard such interests through review of a cold record. "What constitutes adequate representation is a question of fact that depends on the circumstances of each case." 7A Wright, Miller, & Kane, Federal Practice and Procedure §1765, at 271. That is particularly so when, as here, there is an unusual baseline, namely, the "'real and present danger'" described by the Judicial Conference Report above. The majority's use of the lack of an inflation adjustment as evidence of inadequacy of representation for future plaintiffs is one example of this difficulty. An inflation adjustment might not be as valuable as the majority assumes if most plaintiffs are old and not worried about receiving compensation decades from now. There are, of course, strong arguments as to its value. But that disagreement is one that this Court is poorly situated to resolve.

Further, certain details of the settlement that are not discussed in the majority opinion suggest that the settlement may be of greater benefit to future plaintiffs than the majority suggests. The District Court concluded that future plaintiffs receive a "significant value" from the settlement due to a variety of its items that benefit future plaintiffs, such as: (1) tolling the statute of limitations so that class members "will no longer be forced to file premature lawsuits or risk their claims being time-barred"; (2) waiver of defenses to liability; (3) payment of claims, if and when members become sick, pursuant to the settlement's compensation standards, which avoids "the uncertainties, long delays and high transaction costs [including attorney's fees] of the tort system"; (4) "some assurance that there will be funds available if and when they get sick," based on the finding that each defendant "has shown an ability to fund the payment of all qualifying claims" under the settlement; and (5) the right to additional compensation if cancer develops (many settlements for plaintiffs with noncancerous conditions bar such additional claims). For these reasons, and others, the District Court found that the distinction between present and future plaintiffs was "illusory."

. . .

Fourth, I am more agnostic than is the majority about the basic fairness of the settlement. The District Court's conclusions rested upon complicated factual findings that are not easily cast aside. It is helpful to consider some of them, such as its determination that the settlement provided "fair compensation . . . while reducing the delays and transaction costs endemic to the asbestos litigation process" and that "the proposed class action settlement is superior to other available methods for the fair and efficient resolution of the asbestos-related personal injury claims of class members." Indeed, the settlement has been endorsed as fair and reasonable by the AFL-CIO (and its Building and Construction Trades Department), which represents a "'substantial percentage'" of class members, and which has a role in monitoring implementation of the settlement. I do not intend to pass judgment upon the settlement's fairness, but I do believe that these matters would have to be explored in far greater depth before I could reach a conclusion about fairness. And that task, as I have said, is one for the Court of Appeals.

Finally, I believe it is up to the District Court, rather than this Court, to review the legal sufficiency of notice to members of the class. The District

Court found that the plan to provide notice was implemented at a cost of millions of dollars and included hundreds of thousands of individual notices, a wide-ranging television and print campaign, and significant additional efforts by 35 international and national unions to notify their members. Every notice emphasized that an individual did not currently have to be sick to be a class member. And in the end, the District Court was "confident" that Rule 23 and due process requirements were satisfied because, as a result of this "extensive and expensive notice procedure," "over six million" individuals "received actual notice materials," and "millions more" were reached by the media campaign. Although the majority, in principle, is reviewing a Court of Appeals' conclusion, it seems to me that its opinion might call into question the fact-related determinations of the District Court. To the extent that it does so, I disagree, for such findings cannot be so quickly disregarded. And I do not think that our precedents permit this Court to do so.

II

The issues in this case are complicated and difficult. The District Court might have been correct. Or not. Subclasses might be appropriate. Or not. I cannot tell. And I do not believe that this Court should be in the business of trying to make these fact-based determinations. That is a job suited to the district courts in the first instance, and the courts of appeals on review. But there is no reason in this case to believe that the Court of Appeals conducted its prior review with an understanding that the settlement could have constituted a reasonably strong factor in favor of class certification. For this reason, I would provide the courts below with an opportunity to analyze the factual questions involved in certification by vacating the judgment, and remanding the case for further proceedings.

■ NOTES ON SETTLEMENT AND SETTLEMENT CLASSES

1. Justice Ginsburg notes that the Judicial Panel on Multidistrict Litigation (JPML) had consolidated pending cases for pretrial in the Eastern District of Pennsylvania, and that lawyers for the Center for Claims Resolution (CCR)—a consortium representing asbestos industry defendants—approached plaintiffs' steering committee lawyers with a proposal for "global" settlement—one that would resolve not only all *pending* claims, but all claims that might arise. How can lawyers for a class represent claimants they can only imagine?

2. The proposed settlement set aside $200 million for "inventory plaintiffs" (those with pending suits that had been transferred to Pennsylvania). *That* settlement was off the table: At issue in *Amchem* was the fairness of a settlement of claims that *had not been filed*—claims by clients who may never have spoken to a lawyer. As the Court comments in footnote 3, "no transferred case" was included in the proposed settlement, and "no case covered by the settlement" reviewed here even "existed as a civil action" when the lawyers gathered. In short, the gathering of the pending suits became the occasion for defendants to "buy peace" with the world. What dangers does this situation portend? See John Coffee, *Class Wars: The Dilemma of the Mass Tort Class Action*, 95 Colum. L. Rev. 1343, 1354 (1995) ("suspect settlements" may arise if defendants "shop for favorable settlement terms" by contacting lawyers for claimants or "inducing them to compete against each other," which can "develop into a reverse auction, with the low bidder among the plaintiffs' attorneys winning the right to settle").

3. Apart from the difficulty of representing future claimants, do you suppose the willingness of "their lawyers" to agree to a settlement was affected by the fact that these lawyers had already won a $200 million settlement in the cases they had filed? In 2003, FRCP 23(e) was amended to add language requiring parties seeking approval of a settlement to "file a statement identifying any agreement made in connection with" it. How should the Court think about the fact that the settlement offered for its approval, which Justice Breyer in his concurrence appraises at $1.3 billion, was negotiated by lawyers who separately agreed on a $100 million settlement for pending claims? Objectors claimed that "compensation levels" were "intolerably low" when compared with the inventory settlements.

4. For "settlement classes," filing a lawsuit is more or less a formality. In *Amchem*, the only "adversary proceedings" went forward in the other cases (those covered by "inventory settlements"), and the lawyers who worked out the deal embodied in the proposed global settlement acted on information they developed in negotiations. Since asbestos litigation had been going on for many years, and had been often studied, commented on, and analyzed, the lawyers had lots of data. But the purpose of the suit was to get a judicial "good housekeeping seal of approval" on the settlement that had been already worked out and there was no threat of litigation. Absent such a threat, do claimants have a bargaining posture that is likely to lead to a fair deal? Note Justice Ginsburg's comment in *Amchem* that if litigation is "impossible," then "both class counsel and court" are "disarmed."

5. In *Amchem*, the opinion for the Third Circuit that rejected the settlement was written by the late Judge Edward R. Becker, who was a giant among judges. He thought that even in settlement class suits, all the basic requirements of FRCP 23(a) and (b) must be satisfied. Justice Ginsburg deals gently and respectfully with Becker's conclusion, but says it "bears modification" on this point: The fact of settlement *is* relevant to certification because problems of manageability are not important. Still, the "fairness" inquiry demanded by FRCP 23(e) does not "eclips[e]" the other certification requirements, especially predominance and fair representation. What problems arise in *Amchem* with respect to the predominance standard? What problems arise with respect to representation? The Court says the parties reached a "global compromise with no structural assurance" of adequate representation. What does "structural assurance" mean?

6. The Court comments that the standard bearers "sought to act on behalf of a single giant class rather than on behalf of discrete subclasses." Would subclassing help? What objection do Justices Breyer and Stevens, who would uphold the proposed settlement, raise about subclassing?

7. Notice the complex and imaginative provisions in the settlement: In various categories, specific recoveries are proposed; persons with "extraordinary" claims can seek higher recoveries than those set forth on a schedule (ranging from $20,000 to $200,000); even the timing of payouts was set. And in settlement class suits, at least where filing and proposed settlement happen at once (as in *Amchem*), class members receive the "opt out" notice at the same time, and can look at the settlement as they decide. (In other cases, where the opt-out period has passed at the time of settlement, FRCP 23(e)(4) lets courts require "a new opportunity to request exclusion.") In its opinion rejecting the settlement, the Third Circuit commented that future claimants would want "sturdy back-end opt-out rights," see Georgine v. Amchem Products, Inc., 83 F.3d 610, 630-631 (3d Cir. 1996), and Justice Ginsburg is sympathetic, criticizing the settlement because "only a few claimants per year can opt out at the back end." When proposed settlements let class members opt out, what problems arise for defendants? If you were a defense lawyer, how would you deal with them?

8. One of the most difficult tasks for lawyers is to decide how much less than "full value" a case is worth if it is settled rather than fought through to the end. A plaintiff's lawyer, thinking his client's damages are fairly valued at $800,000, must decide whether to accept a much lower sum (like $200,000) rather than go to trial. If the lawyer thinks he has a 50/50 chance of prevailing at trial, presumably a settlement of $400,000 or more is in his client's best interest. How can a lawyer really know whether his chances are 50/50 as opposed to 25/75? And the lawyer's thinking would likely be affected by the number of hours he's sunk into the case and the time he expects trial to take—insofar as he acts in *his own* best interest, the lawyer will be tempted to recommend accepting a lower settlement than the odds of prevailing would indicate, if his fee is to come out of the award (he's taken the case on a contingency) or if his client must "prevail" in order to take advantage of a fee-shifting statute. In the context of class actions, this matter is even more difficult, and courts appraising settlements are right in the middle of such "judgment calls." See generally International Union v. General Motors Corp., 497 F.3d 615, 631 (6th Cir. 2007) (in appraising classwide settlement, court should consider "(1) the risk of fraud or collusion; (2) the complexity, expense and likely duration of the litigation; (3) the amount of discovery engaged in by the parties; (4) the likelihood of success on the merits; (5) the opinions of class counsel and class representatives; (6) the reaction of absent class members; and (7) the public interest").

10. Is There Such a Thing as Trying to Do Too Much?

In a class suit brought on behalf of tens of millions of cigarette smokers seeking $800 *billion*, the theory of recovery was fraud, and the claim was that cigarette makers falsely represented that smoking "light" cigarettes was healthier than smoking "regular" cigarettes. The Second Circuit reversed a trial court order certifying a class: "Not every wrong can have a legal remedy," the reviewing court opined, "at least not without causing collateral damage to the fabric of our laws." See McLaughlin v. American Tobacco Company, 522 F.3d 215, 219 (2d Cir. 2008).

In a different way, lawyers have stretched the criteria in Rule 23, arguably trying to do more than can reasonably be done. In *Amchem*, a big problem was that the settlement included both exposure-only and ailing people; in *Eisen*, the class was too large and recovery was too small to allow for the required individual notice; in *Wal-Mart*, there were no salient common questions in a suit challenging nationwide employment practices in thousands of Wal-Mart stores.

In two other respects that often appear, lawyers have arguably tried to do too much with class suits, leading to judicial disapproval. One involves suits requiring application of the laws of many states; the other involves suits asking courts to resolve, all at once, many claims with which courts have little experience.

Too Many Different Laws. The *Shutts* litigation (Section H8, supra) illustrates a suit requiring application of the laws of many different states. Recall that the claims in *Shutts* involved royalty holders living in all 50 states and the District of Columbia, having interests in wells located in Kansas, Oklahoma, Texas, Wyoming, and 11 other states. The Kansas court decided to apply Kansas law to all the claims because otherwise the suit would be hard or impossible to manage. The Supreme Court rejected this approach:

> The Kansas class-action statute, like those of most other jurisdictions, requires that there be "common issues of law or fact." But while a State may . . . assume jurisdiction over the claims of plaintiffs whose principal contacts are with other States, it may not use this assumption of jurisdiction as an added weight in the scale when considering the permissible constitutional limits on choice of substantive law. It may not take a transaction with little or no relationship to the forum and apply the law of the forum in order to satisfy the procedural requirement that there be a "common question of law." The issue of personal jurisdiction over plaintiffs in a class action is entirely distinct from the question of the constitutional limitations on choice of law; the latter calculus is not altered by the fact that it may be more difficult or more burdensome to comply with the constitutional limitations because of the large number of transactions which the State proposes to adjudicate and which have little connection with the forum.
>
> Kansas must have a "significant contact or significant aggregation of contacts" to the claims asserted by each member of the plaintiff class, contacts

"creating state interests," in order to ensure that the choice of Kansas law is not arbitrary or unfair. Given Kansas' lack of "interest" in claims unrelated to that State, and the substantive conflict with jurisdictions such as Texas, we conclude that application of Kansas law to every claim in this case is sufficiently arbitrary and unfair as to exceed constitutional limits.

Phillips Petroleum v. Shutts, 472 U.S. 797, 821-822 (1985) (rejecting claims that class members chose Kansas law by not opting out, and noting that "the expectation of the parties" is an element in fairness, and that there is no indication that royalty holders elsewhere anticipated that Kansas law would control). Concerns relating to choice of law were also an element in the *Amchem* decision (Section H8, supra), which describes the holding of the Third Circuit disapproving the settlement in that case, in part because the parties paid insufficient attention to variations in the laws of the 50 states (citing the decision in *Shutts*).

Novel Claims. The *Rhone-Poulenc* case illustrates the attempted use of the class action to resolve, all at once, claims with which courts have little experience. In that case, plaintiffs sought to represent a nationwide class of 20,000 hemophiliacs who contracted AIDS after receiving transfusions that included "blood solids" manufactured by defendants. The theories underlying the claims were that defendants, even before it was discovered that heat treatment could kill the AIDS virus, should have screened more carefully for hepatitis B, because doing so would also prevent the spread of the AIDS virus ("serendipity theory"), and that defendants delayed in screening donors when they learned about AIDS in the 1980s. The Seventh Circuit reversed an order certifying the class:

> Three concerns, none of them necessarily sufficient in itself but cumulatively compelling, persuade us [that the judge committed an abuse of discretion in certifying a class].
>
> The first is a concern with forcing these defendants to stake their companies on the outcome of a single jury trial, or be forced by fear of the risk of bankruptcy to settle even if they have no legal liability, when it is entirely feasible to allow a final, authoritative determination of their liability for the colossal misfortune that has befallen the hemophiliac population to emerge from a decentralized process of multiple trials, involving different juries, and different standards of liability, in different jurisdictions; and when, in addition, the preliminary indications are that the defendants are not liable for the grievous harm that has befallen the members of the class. These qualifications are important. In most class actions—and those the ones in which the rationale for the procedure is most compelling—individual suits are infeasible because the claim of each class member is tiny relative to the expense of litigation. That plainly is not the situation here. A notable feature of this case, and one that has not been remarked upon or encountered, so far as we are aware, in previous cases, is the demonstrated great likelihood that the plaintiffs' claims, despite their human appeal, lack legal merit. This is the inference

from the defendants' having won 92.3 percent (12/13) of the cases to have gone to judgment. Granted, thirteen is a small sample and further trials, if they are held, may alter the pattern that the sample reveals. But whether they do or not, the result will be robust if these further trials are permitted to go forward, because the pattern that results will reflect a consensus, or at least a pooling of judgment, of many different tribunals.

For this consensus or maturing of judgment the district judge proposes to substitute a single trial before a single jury instructed in accordance with no actual law of any jurisdiction—a jury that will receive a kind of Esperanto instruction, merging the negligence standards of the 50 states and the District of Columbia. One jury, consisting of six persons (the standard federal civil jury nowadays consists of six regular jurors and two alternates), will hold the fate of an industry in the palm of its hand. This jury, jury number fourteen, may disagree with twelve of the previous thirteen juries—and hurl the industry into bankruptcy. That kind of thing can happen in our system of civil justice (it is not likely to happen, because the industry is likely to settle—whether or not it really is liable) without violating anyone's legal rights. But it need not be tolerated when the alternative exists of submitting an issue to multiple juries constituting in the aggregate a much larger and more diverse sample of decision-makers. That would not be a feasible option if the stakes to each class member were too slight to repay the cost of suit, even though the aggregate stakes were very large and would repay the costs of a consolidated proceeding. But this is not the case with regard to the HIV-hemophilia litigation. Each plaintiff if successful is apt to receive a judgment in the millions. With the aggregate stakes in the tens or hundreds of millions of dollars, or even in the billions, it is not a waste of judicial resources to conduct more than one trial, before more than six jurors, to determine whether a major segment of the international pharmaceutical industry is to follow the asbestos manufacturers into Chapter 11.

Matter of Rhone-Poulenc v. Rohrer, 51 F.3d 1293, 1299-1300 (7th Cir. 1995).

■ NOTES ON "SUPERSIZED" CLASS SUITS

1. On the choice-of-law issue, *Shutts* invoked the *Allstate* case, which rejected a due process challenge to the application of Minnesota law in a suit filed in Minnesota involving a fatal car-motorcycle crash in Wisconsin. The people in the accident lived in Wisconsin (decedent lived there in a town close to the Minnesota border), but afterward decedent's widow moved to Minnesota. She sued the carrier that insured decedent's three cars, and the question was whether she could "stack" coverages to get $45,000 for her husband's death, rather than $15,000. (Minnesota law allowed stacking; Wisconsin law did not.) The Supreme Court approved application of Minnesota law, but said that there are constitutional limits beyond which a state could not go in applying its own law to occurrences elsewhere: "[F]or a State's substantive law to be selected in a constitutionally permissible manner, that State must have a significant contact or significant aggregation of contacts, creating state interests, such that choice of its law is neither arbitrary nor fundamentally unfair." Allstate Insurance Co. v. Hague, 449 U.S. 302, 312 (1981) (stressing that decedent was working in Minnesota at time of accident, even though he lived across the border in Wisconsin; the insurance carrier was doing business in Minnesota; decedent's widow had moved to Minnesota at the time of the suit).

(a) The Court has not developed a constitutional choice-of-law jurisprudence on issues of choice of law that is anywhere near as expansive as the jurisprudence governing personal jurisdiction. Many fewer cases deal with constitutional restrictions on choice of law, and *Allstate* illustrates the proposition that the Court has given the states leeway on choice of law. Remember that state choice-of-law principles govern in diversity cases under *Klaxon*, and these are largely matters of state common law. See Klaxon Co. v. Stentor Elec. Mfg. Co., 313 U.S. 487 (1941) (described in the Notes on *Erie's* First 20 Years in Chapter 6A2, supra).

(b) Still, choice-of-law rules are important in class actions involving claims that are geographically disbursed as in the *Shutts* case. Doesn't *Shutts* itself stand importantly for the proposition that the needs of the court or parties in managing a class suit do not justify shortcutting or overlooking choice-of-law issues? Since *Shutts,* many purported nationwide class suits have failed in large measure because choice-of-law issues raised management problems. Recall that "the likely difficulties in managing a class action" count in "common question" class actions under FRCP 23(b)(3). See, e.g., Castano v. American Tobacco Co., 84 F.3d 734, 740 (5th Cir. 1996) (decertifying purported nationwide class of nicotine-addicted people on fraud theories, because court failed adequately to consider choice-of-law issues in applying predominance requirement); In Matter of Bridgestone/Firestone, Inc., 288 F.3d 1012 (7th Cir. 2002) (decertifying purported nationwide class of SUV owners claiming abnormally high tire failure rate; choice-of-law issues made suit unmanageable).

(c) The *Rhone-Poulenc* decision disapproved an attempt to overcome choice-of-law problems by giving an instruction purporting to consolidate different state laws. See Rhone-Poulenc v. Rohrer, 51 F.3d 1293, 1300 (7th Cir. 1995) (decrying "Esperanto instruction" merging negligence standards of 50 states, calling it an invitation to decide "under a legal standard that does not actually exist anywhere in the world" and offering this observation: "[O]ne wonders what the Supreme Court thought it was doing in the *Erie* case when it held that it was *unconstitutional* for federal courts in diversity cases to apply federal general common law").

2. If *Rhone-Poulenc* proceeded to a classwide adjudication of the rights of hemophiliacs against makers of blood solids, a single court (perhaps a single jury) would resolve the issues for everyone at once, in a single gulp (so to speak). But common law does not normally spring full blown into existence out of the experience of a single case: The "life of the law," as Justice Holmes famously remarked, "has not been logic, but experience." See O.W. Holmes, The Common Law 1 (1881). Doesn't "experience" suggest a gradual accumulation of understanding through repeated encounters with similar situations?

(a) In 1996, the Advisory Committee considered amending FRCP 23(b)(3) to add language authorizing courts to consider not only the "extent" and "nature" of "related litigation" in applying the superiority requirement, but also the "maturity" of such claims. See Preliminary Draft of Proposed Amendments, 167 F.R.D. 523, 559 (1997). This proposal was not adopted. Should it have been?

(b) Without such language, can a court consider this factor in ruling on certification motions? Compare Castano v. American Tobacco Co., 84 F.3d 734, 747 (expressing concern that a mass tort "cannot be properly certified without a prior track record of trials from which the district court can draw the information necessary to make the predominance and superiority analysis required by rule 23," and that certifying such cases brings "a higher than normal risk that the class action may not be superior to individual adjudication"), with Klay v. Humana, Inc., 382 F.3d 1241, 1272 (11th Cir. 2004) (rejecting "immature tort" doctrine and commenting that there is "no reason why" courts "cannot make the necessary determinations under Rule 23 based on the pleadings and whatever evidence has been gathered through discovery"). In its third edition, the Manual for Complex Litigation commented that "fairness may demand that mass torts with few prior verdicts or judgments be litigated first in smaller units . . . until general causation, typical injuries, and levels of damages become established." See Manual for Complex Litigation (Third) §33.26 (1997)—but the fourth edition drops this comment. See Manual for Complex Litigation (Fourth) (2004).

11. Finality of Class Action Judgments: A Look Back

We started our study of class actions by looking at *Hansberry.* To get at *Hansberry*'s procedural significance, we put aside racial covenants and imagine a suit brought to enforce a covenant that could be valid today, like a commitment to use cedar shake shingles on roofs of houses. Under today's class action standards, we can imagine such a suit going forward as a class action. It could be brought under FRCP 23(b)(2) on behalf of a class of homeowners against noncompliant neighbors, seeking an injunction directing them to replace their roofs with cedar shake shingles.

The propriety of such a suit did not arise directly in *Hansberry,* which addressed the question whether a judgment could bind members of the class in later litigation. On its facts, *Hansberry* concluded in the negative as a matter of due process, but it also said that a judgment could bind absent class members if they were adequately represented in the prior suit. Tantalizingly, *Hansberry* suggested that *if* the first suit had been a bilateral class suit, the problem (which was that the covenant resisters had not been adequately represented) might be solved. Recall our example in which Ellen sues Frank, in a bilateral class suit by covenant enforcers in the neighborhood (Ellen as standard bearer) against covenant resisters (Frank as standard bearer).

Supposing that Ellen wins, we might then imagine another resident of the neighborhood (call her Francis) who puts up a roof that violates the covenant, or a newcomer who purchase a house in the neighborhood and does the same thing (call him Felix). And we might imagine another resident who brings suit to enforce the covenant (call her Elisa) and claims the benefit of the judgment in Ellen's suit, or even a newcomer to the neighborhood (call her Emily).

Are these possible defendants bound by the judgment? We mean now Francis, who lived in the neighborhood at the time of the suit, and Felix, who bought a house in the neighborhood later. And can these possible plaintiffs take advantage of the judgment? We mean Elisa, who lived in the neighborhood, and Emily, who later bought a house there. *Hansberry* bears on the former questions, indicating that Francis and even Felix may be bound *if* their interests were adequately represented by Frank in Ellen's suit. *Hansberry* does not bear particularly on the latter question (whether Elisa or Emily can sue on Ellen's judgment).

Recall that *Hansberry* implicitly refused to consider the possibility that the Hansberry family might have been adequately represented by the defendant Kleiman. Why not? At least Kleiman took a position congenial to the Hansberry family in arguing *against* the covenant. Implicitly, *Hansberry* indicates that the Hansberry family cannot be represented by a defendant sued as an individual and not as standard bearer for a defendant class. Expressly, *Hansberry* indicates that even *if* the Hansberry family had been members of a class on whose behalf the first suit was litigated, the second court can inquire into the question of adequate representation—taking what we have called a "second look." Going back to the cedar shake shingle example, Francis and Felix might be bound if they are members of a class of covenant resisters whose interests were represented by Frank in the first suit, but *not* if the first suit had been brought against Frank as an individual, and not as standard bearer for a defendant class. And even if Frank *did* represent a class of covenant resisters, the court in the second suit must inquire into the adequacy of Frank's representation of Francis and Felix, and can find that they are bound only if Frank adequately represented them.

■ NOTES ON *HANSBERRY* AND COLLATERAL REVIEW OF JUDGMENTS IN CLASS SUITS

1. Chapter 14 of this book takes up the binding effect of judgments. Suffice it to say that it is always the court in a second (or later) suit that has to decide what effect to give a judgment in a first (or earlier) suit. Of course, that happened in *Hansberry* too: The Illinois court (and ultimately the United States Supreme Court) had to decide, in the suit brought by Anna Lee against members of the Hansberry family, whether the latter were bound by the judgment reached in the earlier suit brought by Burke against Kleiman.

(a) You will also learn that in *ordinary* suits the second court's inquiry is limited. Ignoring complications and details that we will talk about in Chapter 14, the second court asks whether the issues or claims litigated in the first suit are the same as those in the second, whether the party to be bound was a party in the first suit, and whether the first court had good jurisdiction—and even *this* question drops away if jurisdiction was actually *litigated* (or might have been) in the first suit. If these and related questions are answered in the affirmative, someone who was a party in the first suit and is a party in the second suit is usually *bound* by the judgment in the first suit.

(b) Hansberry indicates that when the question is whether a class member is bound by a judgment in the first suit, the role of the second court is different. It must consider the adequacy of representation in the first suit: *This question* does not normally arise in ordinary suits, where the question is whether someone who was actually *a party* in the prior suit is bound by the judgment. See, e.g., Stephenson v. Dow Chemical Co., 273 F.3d 249, 257-258 (2d Cir. 2001) (under *Hansberry,* members of a class in an earlier suit may collaterally attack, in second suit, the judgment rendered in the earlier suit, on question of adequate representation there), *aff'd in part and vacated in part,* Dow Chemical Co. v. Stephenson, 539 U.S. 111 (2001)).

(c) In Chapter 14, you will also consider who can enforce judgments from prior suits—whether people like Elisa and Emily can enforce a judgment won by someone like Ellen, which is a question that *Hansberry* does not address.

2. Under modern class action procedure, it is not as clear as it once was that members of a class in one suit may raise such collateral attacks in a second suit, *if* matters of adequate representation were litigated and resolved in the first suit. Compare Restatement (Second) of Judgments §42, comment b (1982) (notice to class members is "an invitation to dispute the propriety" of certifying a class, but such notice "does not foreclose the notified party from later contesting the adequacy of the representation and on that basis avoiding the conclusive effect of a judgment") with Principles of the Law of Aggregate Litigation §3.14 (2010) (normal vehicle for challenging settlement of aggregate suit is "direct appeal," and judgment embodying settlement in class suit cannot be challenged in later suit except on ground that the first court lacked jurisdiction or "failed to make the necessary findings of adequate representation, or failed to afford class members reasonable notice and opportunity to be heard"). For an argument *favoring* the position taken in the 2010 Principles, see Samuel Issacharoff & Richard Nagareda, *Class Settlements Under Attack,* 156 U. Pa. L. Rev. 1649 (2008) (arguing that jurisdiction in class suits raising issues connected with national markets "cannot turn on some vestigial notion of territoriality," and that failure to object in a class suit can waive the right to object later). For a strong objection to that view, see Patrick Woolley, *The*

Jurisdictional Nature of Adequate Representation in Class Litigation, 79 Geo. Wash. L. Rev. 410 (2011) (arguing that class members can be bound on theories of waiver, if they fail to appear in the suit, only if they are subject to *minimum contact* jurisdiction and served with summonses). Who has the better of this argument, and why?

CHAPTER 9

Pretrial Discovery

A | PHILOSOPHY AND DILEMMAS OF MODERN DISCOVERY

Liberal pretrial discovery is the solution devised by modern procedure to the problem of preparing attorneys and parties for trial: Let each side be fully informed on the facts, the witnesses to be called, and the documents and other proof to be offered. Then lawyers will be more effective in presenting relevant information, testing and challenging it, and trials will perform better in resolving disputes and arriving at the truth.

Specifically, expanded discovery can help focus the issues—a task once performed at the pleading stage, which required particularity and detail. The optimism that attended the adoption of liberal discovery stemmed from the belief that the older practice of crystallizing the issues at the pleading stage had failed. Recall that FRCP 8 did away with "cause of action" in favor of "claim for relief," and stressed brevity and clarity rather than detail. Reduced reliance on pleadings went hand in hand with increased use of discovery and the gradual adoption and elaboration of pretrial procedures.

To paraphrase the Court's optimism in the *Hickman* case shortly after adopting the modern regime, discovery helps the parties learn about sources of information and ascertain facts, so trials need not be "carried on in the dark," and lawyers and parties can come to trial with the "fullest possible knowledge of the issues and facts." Equally important, "[n]o longer can the time-honored cry of 'fishing expedition' serve to preclude a party from inquiring into the facts underlying his opponent's case." Hickman v. Taylor, 329 U.S. 495, 507 (1947) (Section E, infra). The world has changed, and the optimism has disappeared. The problem is that discovery has become expensive. Even though many if not most cases involve modest or minimal discovery (sometimes none at all), it is also true that many cases bring huge discovery costs. There seem to be at least three reasons:

First, attorneys have found that discovery can be used tactically, to drive up costs and delay settlement or trial. Discovery can also be a strategic weapon, making litigation *so* costly that settlement is the only possible outcome. Even worse, discovery has become, in many cases, not a means to an end, but an end in itself.

Second, the invention of computers, the proliferation of electronically stored information (ESI), and the pace and sophistication of technology have put stresses on part of the discovery system—production of documents. Discovery rules were crafted for a world where records were written on paper and existed in finite quantities. Now the technology of ESI has vastly increased the quantity of recorded information: We have email, internet postings, instant messaging, Facebook, Twitter, recorded voice messages, and "metadata" (partially hidden and partially visible data recording access and changes to data). Such information did not exist in the past, or could only be accessed by asking people what they remembered. The presence of computers affects discovery in another way: Lawyers work with computers too, which can be used in discovery, and this fact means that even more information is generated that may itself be discoverable, like drafts of documents and communications with witnesses or clients (although usually these are privileged and beyond the reach of discovery).

Third, the scope of litigation has expanded, and issues have become complex. Litigation takes up such matters as reforming prisons and other institutions; protecting the environment; examining the practices of the insurance industry, banks, brokerages, and other financial institutions, not to mention issues relating to product safety and toxic exposure. Often such cases require expertise and invite detailed examination of transactions, events, and the gathering of huge amounts of data through discovery.

For these reasons, the optimism of *Hickman* has been replaced by complaints and laments about lawyer conduct. Consider this appraisal by a seasoned federal jurist:

> . . . Unlike a majority of District Judges who routinely relegate discovery disputes to Magistrate Judges, this court has always heard and decided its own discovery matters. After seventeen years on the bench, the undersigned has concluded that, despite the best efforts of Congress, the Advisory Committee on Civil Rules and other similar bodies, litigation expenses continue to rise, often due to ever-increasing discovery demands and ensuing discovery disputes.[2] As Judge Patrick Higginbotham has observed, "The discovery beast has yet to be tamed."[3]
>
> Additionally, refereeing contentious discovery disputes is, in my view, perhaps the most unwelcome aspect of a trial judge's work. For example, United

---

[2] *See, e.g.,* James S. Kakalik, et al., Just Speedy and Inexpensive? An Evaluation of Judicial Case Management Under the Civil Justice Reform Act, Rand Inst. 1 (1996) (concluding that Congress's landmark legislation [—] the 1991 Civil Justice Reform Act [—] "had little effect on time to disposition, litigation costs, and attorneys' satisfaction and views on the fairness of case management").

[3] Patrick E. Higginbotham, So Why Do We Call Them Trial Courts?, 55 SMU L. Rev. 1405, 1417 (2002).

States District Judge Wayne Alley once vented his displeasure with discovery battles in the following order:

> Defendant's Motion to Dismiss or in the Alternative to Continue Trial is denied. If the recitals in the briefs from both sides are accepted at face value, neither side has conducted discovery according to the letter and spirit of the Oklahoma County Bar Association Lawyer's Creed. This is an aspirational creed not subject to enforcement by this Court, but violative conduct does call for judicial disapprobation at least. If there is a hell to which disputatious, uncivil, vituperative lawyers go, let it be one in which the damned are eternally locked in discovery disputes with other lawyers of equally repugnant attributes.

Krueger v. Pelican Prod. Corp., C/A No. 87-2385-A (W.D. Okla. Feb. 24, 1989).

Resolving contentious discovery disputes is especially difficult in those cases (and there are many) where both sides have behaved badly. Judges often find themselves in a position similar to NFL referees, who have to peel the players off of each other in an effort to find the player in the middle who started the melee. The answer is not always clear and the decision of what sanction, if any, to impose is especially difficult where there is a degree of fault on both sides.

Also, numerical inflation appears to be setting in. In past years, discovery battles typically involved "thousands of documents." Recently, however, one attorney suggested to me at a discovery hearing that, including the request for electronic mail communications, a production request was "likely to exceed one million pages." Further, the parties often overreach in their discovery requests[5] and stonewall interrogatories from their opponents.[6] Hardball discovery, which is still a problem in some cases,[7] is costly to our system and consumes an inordinate amount of judicial resources.[8]

In addition, this court's own firsthand observation of discovery expenditures in civil litigation yields the inescapable conclusion that litigants expend enormous amounts of money on discovery in cases that do not even make it to trial. A recent case on this court's docket is illustrative. Twin City Fire Ins. Co. v. Ben Arnold-Sunbelt Beverage Co., 336 F. Supp. 610 (D.S.C. 2004), involved two female employees who had sued their corporation for sexual harassment in state court. The claimed harassment involved one corporate officer who allegedly groped and inappropriately touched the two employees in the privacy of his

---

[5] As one court colorfully observed: Even if one is entitled to embark on a fishing expedition, one must at least use "rod and reel, or even a reasonably sized net[; not] drain the pond and collect the fish from the bottom." In re IBM Peripheral EDP Devices Antitrust Litigation, 77 F.R.D. 39, 42 (N.D. Cal. 1977).

[6] I have presided over one discovery dispute where the defendant's attorney objected to an interrogatory, which essentially sought the names of witnesses, on the grounds that it was burdensome and oppressive, while at the same time propounding an identically-worded question in his own interrogatories.

[7] I hasten to add that not all civil disputes involve extensive discovery requests or hardball discovery tactics. In many cases, litigants and their attorneys behave professionally throughout the litigation.

[8] I have, on occasion, attempted to avoid duplication of effort by requiring a party to disclose to me if there were prior rulings on discoverability by other judges in cases involving essentially identical claims. Such efforts are usually unsuccessful. I am typically told that litigants have no way of retrieving or assimilating discovery rulings by other judges in related litigation.

office, with no third party witnesses. The claims asserted in the cases were all state law claims for assault and battery, intentional infliction of emotional distress, and the like. There were no complicated Title VII claims or other unique issues in either of the cases—the cases presented a pure swearing contest involving no more than three potential eyewitnesses (the two victims and the defendant). The cases eventually settled prior to trial. The controversy made its way to this court's docket in a declaratory judgment action brought by the insurance companies who refused to provide a defense. In that case, which only involved state law claims, the defense team spent a staggering $1.5 million to engage in discovery prior to settling the cases.

Network Computing Services Corp. v. Cisco Systems, Inc., 223 F.R.D. 392 (D.S.C. 2004) (opinion by Chief Judge Joseph F. Anderson, Jr.).

B PHASES OF DISCOVERY

Under FRCP 26, discovery goes forward in four phases. The first two occur early in the litigation process, the latter two following at a more measured pace:

First, the parties meet and discuss the case, explore possible settlement, and either make their first disclosures ("automatic" discovery, discussed next) or arrange for those disclosures to occur. They also "discuss any issues about preserving discoverable information" and then "develop a proposed discovery plan." This meeting is to occur 21 days before the first pretrial scheduling conference, which itself is to occur within the first four months (timing set up in FRCP 16 is more detailed). See FRCP 26(f).

Second, the parties are to conduct the first phase of "automatic discovery" required by FRCP 26(a)(1), to include the following:

> ➤ providing name and contact information of "each individual likely to have discoverable information" along with a description of the subject matter, if the disclosing party might use such person "to support its claims or defenses" (but not people who might be called "solely for impeachment");
> ➤ providing a copy or description of documents, electronically stored data, and tangible things that the disclosing party has in its "possession and control" that it "may use to support its claims or defenses" (but not "solely for impeachment");
> ➤ providing "a computation of each category of damages" claimed by the disclosing party, along with "evidentiary material" on which the computations are based (unless "privileged or protected from disclosure");
> ➤ providing for inspection and copying "any insurance agreement" that covers all or part of any judgment in the suit.

Rule 37(c) puts teeth in the automatic discovery obligations by providing that one who "fails to provide information or identify a witness" under Rule 26(a) "is not allowed to use that information or witness" unless the failure was "substantially justified" or "harmless." In short, not cooperating in automatic discovery can have consequences.

Third, the parties conduct their own discovery, using five devices: Depositions (FRCP 30 and 32), interrogatories (FRCP 33), production of documents (FRCP 34), requests for admissions (FRCP 36), and physical or mental examinations of opposing parties (FRCP 35). This phase can be conveniently dubbed "party driven" discovery.

Fourth, in a deferred phase of "automatic discovery," the parties disclose the identities of expert witnesses, and supply written reports, which must be "prepared and signed" by each expert, setting out complete statements of the opinions that each is to express, the "basis and reasons" for them, and the "data or other information" on which those opinions rest. These reports are to include "exhibits" that may be used to "summarize or support" such opinions, as well as statements of the "qualifications" of the expert (with "a list of all publications" she has authored in the last ten years) and a "list of all other cases" in which she has testified as an expert and a statement of "the compensation to be paid" in this case. These disclosures are to go forward "at least 90 days before the date set for trial," or at such earlier time as the parties may agree or the court may order. See FRCP 26(a)(2).

Throughout all phases, the parties are under a continuing obligation to "supplement" or "correct" disclosure or response on learning that "in some material respect" the disclosure or response was "incomplete or incorrect," at least if the "additional or corrective information" has not been made known to the other parties "during the discovery process or in writing." The court may also order supplemental or corrective disclosure or responses. See FRCP 26(e).

■ NOTES ON CONFERRAL REQUIREMENTS AND AUTOMATIC DISCOVERY

1. The duty to confer applies not only to the early meeting, but to later disputes over discovery. A party who wants a court order "compelling discovery" under FRCP 37(a) must include a certification that it "has in good faith conferred or attempted to confer" with the resisting side, and the purpose is to avoid the need for court action. Similarly, a motion for sanctions, if a party fails to obey a court order, triggers an obligation to confer. What is the message? You saw Judge Anderson's comments, quoted above. Now consider this view:

[T]here must be a change in culture among litigation lawyers. The last 30 years have seen truculence, gamesmanship, and a supreme rule of "volunteer nothing." Because of the new complexity and volume of information, however, the game theory underlying much of litigation has changed. Litigators must collaborate far more than they have in the past, particularly concerning the discovery of information systems. If they do not, they act against their own self-interest.

George L. Paul & Jason R. Baron, *Information Inflation: Can the Legal System Adapt?*, 13 Rich. J.L. & Tech. 10 (2007).

2. The duty to make "automatic discovery" is narrower than one might expect. Automatic discovery obliges a party to produce names of witnesses and descriptions of documents that the party "may use to support its claims or defenses," *not* the names of every witness and *not* descriptions of every document that might support *other parties'* claims or defenses. In this sense, automatic discovery is more limited than the party-driven discovery that proceeds later. Why is automatic discovery limited in this way? See Justice Scalia's comments, dissenting from the original version of the automatic discovery device, which obliged lawyers automatically to turn over various information "relevant to disputed facts alleged with particularity." Justice Scalia said this mechanism "does not fit comfortably within the American judicial system" because it puts on lawyers the obligation to disclose information damaging to their clients, acting "on their own initiative" and thus bringing an "intolerable strain" in light of their "ethical duty to represent their clients and not to assist the opposing side." See Amendments to Federal Rules of Civil Procedure, 146 F.R.D. 401, 511 (1993) (Justice Scalia, dissenting statement, joined by Justice Thomas and, on the discovery issue, by Justice Souter). Does the narrowed version in today's rule, which (apart from a damage computation and insurance information) covers only material that the disclosing party "may use to support its claims or defenses," answer Justice Scalia's objection?

3. Automatic discovery includes a "computation of each category of damages." In many tort cases, "medical specials" are damages that can be computed on the basis of hospital, doctor, and laboratory bills. "Pain and suffering" is harder to calculate, and recall from Chapter 2A2 that courts take a dim view of "per diem" arguments that ask juries "how much one day of pain" should be worth in dollars. What is expected in such categories is a rough estimate, and it is doubtful that plaintiffs should be responsible for surveying verdicts and binding themselves to whatever those cases yielded.

(a) In other cases—one thinks of antitrust suits and patent litigation, where damages can include lost business opportunities—calculation of damages is more difficult, and courts must give claimants a chance to develop the relevant materials and "computation[s]."

(b) Often the difficulty for claimants is that the information necessary to comply with this request must itself be discovered from the other side. In such settings, courts excuse claimants from the obligation to produce such information early. See, e.g., Gillum v. ICF Emergency Management Services,

L.L.C., 2009 WL 1458200 (M.D. La. 2009) (cannot expect claimant seeking damages for age discrimination in employment to compute damages because defendant failed to provide him, and an expert who would work with the data, "all of the information needed" to make computations; plaintiff could compute some damages, like lost wages, on its own based on information "within its possession or control"). See also 1993 ACN to FRCP 26(a) (one "would not be expected to provide a calculation of damages which, as in many patent infringement actions, depends on information in the possession of another party or person").

4. Relevant information about insurance is subject to automatic discovery even though proof of insurance is generally inadmissible at trial. See Evidence Rule 411 (proof of insurance is not admissible on question whether a party "acted negligently or otherwise wrongfully"). Most states have followed the federal lead in including insurance as part of pretrial discovery. See Thomas v. Oldfield, 279 S.W.3d 259, 264 (Tenn. 2009) (45 states allow discovery of liability insurance by rule or statute and three others construe their law similarly, and joining the majority on this point). Why should insurance be discoverable, given that it is seldom admissible at trial?

(a) Should claimants also be allowed to discover the net worth of the defendant, and details about defendant's assets? Uniformly, courts say no. Grosec v. Panther Transportation, Inc., 251 F.R.D. 162, 165 (M.D. Pa. 2008) ("a case is about the events that gave rise to it, not about the wealth of the individuals involved"). The rule is otherwise in domestic relation cases where division of marital assets is in issue. See McMahon v. McMahon, 718 N.Y.S.2d 353 (N.Y. App. Div. 2001) (noting exchange of net worth statements in divorce action). If insurance coverage is ordinarily discoverable, why not information about net worth and assets, and even annual income?

(b) In cases involving claims for punitive damages, such discovery is allowed, and net worth may be proved at trial. Why? See, e.g., Transportation Insurance Co. v. Moriel, 879 S.W.2d 10, 29 (Tex. 1994) (net worth is "relevant in determining the proper amount of punitive damages, and therefore may be subject to pretrial discovery"). In some states, however, claimants seeking punitive damages must make out a prima facie case before discovery of net worth can go forward, see, e.g., McBurney v. The GM Card, 869 A.2d 586, 592 (R.I. 2005) (before delving into defendant's private financial information, plaintiff must make a prima facie showing in evidentiary hearing that there is a viable claim for punitive damages), and some states address the matter by statute, see, e.g., Cal. Civ. Code §3295 (defendant may obtain order barring proof of its financial condition until plaintiff has made out a "prima facie case" of liability for punitive damages; no discovery can go forward along these lines until plaintiff shows "substantial probability" of prevailing on such claims); S.D. Codified Laws §21-1-4.1 (before discovery on punitive damage claims can go forward, court must find, in hearing on basis of "clear and convincing evidence," that there is "reasonable basis" to

believe defendant engaged in "willful, wanton or malicious conduct"). What is the purpose of such requirements?

 SCOPE OF DISCOVERY

FRCP 26(b)(1) describes the scope of discovery in broad terms: Discovery may delve into "any nonprivileged matter that is relevant to any party's claim or defense," and we are told for good measure that this definition embraces "the existence, description, nature, custody, condition, and location of any documents or other tangible things," and also the "identity and location" of persons having relevant knowledge—eyewitnesses and others.

This description of scope applies to the various devices used during the party-driven phase of discovery, and thus covers, for example, the questions that can be asked in depositions, requests for documents, and the scope of interrogatories.

To be sure, the description can be changed—either narrowed (which often happens) or expanded (which rarely happens). On the matter of narrowing discovery, the opening phrase of FRCP 26(b)(1) says the scope of discovery can be "limited by court order." This phrase is a reference to FRCP 26(c)(1), under which a court may issue a "protective order" to prevent or reduce "annoyance, embarrassment, oppression, or undue burden or expense." The Rule also says courts may impose conditions on discovery of material comprising "a trade secret, or other confidential research, development, or commercial information." The usual condition is that the party who obtains it may not reveal it to others, or may reveal it "only in a specific way," and this language contemplates orders that block a party from sharing such material with those who might use it to damage or compete with the disclosing party. It is even possible for courts to order lawyers for parties seeking such information not to share it with their own clients.

On the matter of expanding discovery, Rule 26(b)(1) says the court may, for "good cause," allow discovery of "any matter relevant to the subject matter" of the suit. This provision carries forward the definition of scope of discovery that Rule 26 had on adoption in 1938. The narrower "default" language in the present rule—discovery can go into "any nonprivileged matter that is relevant to any party's claim or defense"—was intended to limit discovery and responds to complaints that discovery is too expensive and is out of hand.

Finally, it is worth repeating that the scope of automatic discovery is narrower than the scope of party-driven discovery. Thus automatic discovery reaches documents that the disclosing party "may use in support of its claims or defenses," and witnesses that the disclosing party may call "in support of its claims or defenses."

■ PROBLEM 9-A. Underhood Fire in the Mercury

On Tuesday evening, July 20, 2012, Frank and Nora Pierce were driving their 2008 Mercury Grand Marquis in heavy traffic on the Jack Nicklaus Freeway in Columbus, Ohio, when a fire broke out under the hood. Distracted by the smoke, Nora failed to brake when traffic in front of her slowed to a near stop, and plowed into the back of a truck. Frank Pierce died in the accident, and Nora suffered serious spinal cord injuries.

Nora Pierce consults a product liability lawyer named Donald Schrader, who talks to her about the accident. He learns the nature of her injuries, and learns that Frank had been a risk analyst at Nationwide Mutual in Columbus, and earned a good salary.

Schrader asks a technician to examine what's left of the Mercury, which was placed in storage after being towed. Based on what the technician tells him, fortified by research into "underhood fires" in Ford-made cars, Schrader concludes that the fire was caused by a faulty speed control deactivation switch (SCDS) that turns off the cruise control when pressure is applied to the brakes, and he learns that the problem relates to the "kapton seal" that is supposed to prevent hot oil from coming into contact with electrical connections in the mechanism. The switch is made by Indiana Instruments.

Schrader agrees to represent Nora Pierce. He files suit seeking recovery for her injuries, and recovery for the estate of Frank Pierce, in Federal District Court. She is named as plaintiff in the count seeking recovery for her own injuries, and as plaintiff and executor of the Estate of Frank Pierce in the other count. Named as defendants are Ford and Indiana Instruments. Jurisdiction rests on diversity of citizenship. Ford is a Delaware corporation with principal place of business in Michigan, and Indiana Instruments is a Delaware corporation with principal place of business in Indiana.

The complaint alleges claims in negligence, breach of warranty, and strict liability. Nora alleges "injuries to her spine and neck, resulting in multiple surgeries, continuing pain and disability, and extreme discomfort and anxiety." She also seeks recovery for loss of "the companionship and support, financial as well as personal and emotional," stemming from the death of Frank Pierce. As executor of his estate, Nora seeks recovery for his wrongful death, including "pain and suffering that Pierce experienced in the accident that took his life," and "losses of the enjoyment of living," and "financial losses in the form of lifetime earnings that were cut off by his death."

During automatic discovery, Nora turned over her own medical records reflecting treatment for her injuries, and a computation of damages based in part on estimates of Frank's likely earnings at Nationwide Mutual.

(1) In Nora's deposition, Ed Rifkin as counsel for Ford asks Nora whether she "has seen or consulted a psychiatrist or psychologist or coun-selor during the past three years," and she says she "saw a psychologist for a period of six months about two years ago." She identifies the psy-chologist as Amy Maris of Maris Clinic. When asked why she consulted Dr. Maris, Nora replies that "it was to treat for depression arising out of the death of my mother." Rifkin seeks to question Nora further about her treat-ment, but on Schrader's advice she declines to reply. Later Rifkin gets a subpoena directing Dr. Maris to produce "all records relating to consulta-tions with Nora Pierce for the previous five years." Dr. Maris telephones Donald Schrader and tells him about the subpoena, and he moves to quash, arguing that "discovery of the substance of any conversations between Nora Pierce and Dr. Maris is irrelevant, would violate the privacy of my client, and is improper because such information is within the psy-chotherapist-patient privilege."

(2) On behalf of Ford, Rifkin seeks production of "federal income tax returns" for Frank Pierce for the tax years 1999-2009. On behalf of Nora Pierce, Schrader objects that this request is "beyond the scope of legiti-mate discovery, and again unnecessarily invasive of the privacy interests of Nora Pierce."

(3) On behalf of Nora Pierce, Schrader asks Ford to produce "all reports of, and claims arising out of, accidents in motor vehicles manufactured by Ford between 2002 and 2012 caused, or suspected or believed to have been caused, by underhood fires." On behalf of Ford, Rifkin objects that this request is "overbroad in covering vehicles other than Mercury Marquis cars made in 2008 where the cause is suspected or believed to have been the SCDS."

(4) On behalf of Nora Pierce, Schrader seeks from Ford and Indiana Instruments "drawings and design and manufacture data relating to the SCDS and the kapton seal." On behalf of Ford and Indiana (who joins with Ford), Rifkin objects that "the request seeks information covered by the trade secrets privilege in FRCP 26(c)(1)(G)."

How should the court rule on these various discovery disputes, and why?

■ NOTES ON THE SCOPE OF DISCOVERY

1. When parties object that discovery is going too far afield, arguments over relevancy often focus on the question whether the matter being sought is rele-vant and could be used at trial. It is probably reasonable, and certainly inevitable, that objecting parties would argue such points. Consider the following:

(a) FRE 401 defines relevancy. Evidence is relevant if it has "any ten-dency" to make a fact that is "of consequence" in the action "more or less

probable than it would be without the evidence." Under FRE 402, relevant evidence is admissible unless excludable under some other Rule, or statute or the Constitution. Importantly, FRE 403 adds that even relevant evidence may be excluded for "unfair prejudice" or other reasons, especially waste of time, confusing issues, or misleading the jury. You will learn in the Evidence course that these provisions set a standard weighted in favor of admissibility.

(b) Rule 26 does *not* require the matter being discovered to be admissible at trial, *and* it is commonly said that ideas of relevancy expressed in FRCP 26 are *more liberal* and not *more restrictive,* than the idea of relevancy in FRE 401-403.

2. How is whatever Nora Pierce said to Dr. Maris, or the latter's opinion or diagnosis, relevant? What other considerations should affect the court in ruling on the objections raised by Nora Pierce? Consider the following:

(a) Federal courts apply state privilege law in diversity cases under FRE 501, and Ohio recognizes a psychotherapist-patient privilege. You will learn in Evidence that putting one's psychological condition in issue usually waives this privilege. Should one take the view that Nora Pierce put her psychological condition in issue by seeking damages for pain and suffering on account of her injuries and her husband's death? Compare In re Sims, 534 F.3d 117, 134 (2d Cir. 2008) (in civil rights suit by state prisoner against corrections officer alleging excessive force, claimant did not waive psychotherapist-patient privilege by claiming emotional distress) with Griffin-El v. Beard, 2009 WL 678700 (E.D. Pa. 2009) (where plaintiff claimed emotional distress, suffering, and humiliation, defense could discover evidence relating to medical, psychological, psychiatric, or counseling records). If no privilege applies, should disclosure be ordered, or does FRCP 26(c)(1) provide an additional basis for protection?

(b) What steps, short of blocking discovery altogether, could Schrader ask the court to take for Nora Pierce with respect to information on psychological counseling? See Bell v. Columbia St. Mary's, Inc., 2009 WL 187935 (E.D. Wis. 2009) (granting motion to seal report containing psychological evaluation of plaintiff" because of the "potentially embarrassing nature of the information"). Is this step adequate?

3. How about Frank Pierce's income tax returns? Are they relevant to claims or defenses? Not surprisingly, one cannot usually get from the IRS a tax return filed by another. See 26 USC §6103. The ACN to the 1970 amendments to FRCP 26, which added language on protective orders that is still in the Rule, comments that a party's tax return "is not privileged," but that courts "have recognized that interests in privacy may call for a measure of extra protection." How should Schrader argue this point? Does it matter that Nationwide Mutual (where Pierce had been employed) has an office in Columbus, and could be asked to provide information?

4. Should Ford have to turn over "reports of, and claims arising out of," accidents in Ford-made vehicles caused by underhood fires? If there were

multiple causes of such fires, would that affect your answer? What is encom-
passed by this request?

(a) Assuming similarity to the accident in suit, courts allow discovery
along these lines. Compare In re Cooper Tire & Rubber Co., 568 F.3d 1180
(10th Cir. 2009) (in suit against tire maker arising out of fatal auto accident,
allowing discovery of "other complaints or suits" under "relaxed" requirement
of "substantial similarity," including information on other kinds of tires) and
Preston v. Montana Eighteenth Judicial District Court, Gallatin County, 936
P.2d 814, 819 (Mont. 1997) (in suit against maker of pneumatic roofing nailer
that discharged nail into head of roofer when he accidentally bumped its tip,
plaintiff could discover similar injuries caused by same alleged defect in other
models made by defendant) with Acoba v. General Tire, Inc., 986 P.2d 268, 298
(Haw. 1999) (authorizing limited discovery of prior accidents involving tire
rim base, but disapproving request for information on "all inquiries, investigations, responses or other correspondence relating to the safety" of product;
relevancy was "outweighed by the burden placed on Firestone," if it had to
produce "names of every individual and every related document for every
lawsuit and claim filed, as well as every correspondence made regarding
the safety" of the tire rim base).

(b) Product liability cases are not the only ones in which defendants
are asked about similar incidents. See, e.g., Richardson v. State, 130 P.3d 634
(Mont. 2006) (84-year-old invitee attending water aerobics class in pool at
state college, injured in fall on concrete floor of locker room, was entitled
to information about "any other falls occurring anywhere within" the facility
"at any time"); French v. Hawaii Pizza Hut, Inc., 99 P.3d 1046 (Haw. 2004) (in
discrimination suit, plaintiff could discover records of medical leaves,
employee transfers, and sales volumes for five-year period, which were relevant to claim that defendant "failed to adequately accommodate [plaintiff's]
disability upon her return from medical leave"). Still, courts balk at requests
for information about incidents that are too dissimilar from the events in
litigation, and balk at requests that are too diffuse or global in scope.
See Ex parte Vulcan Materials Co., 992 So. 2d 1252 (Ala. 2008) (request for
emails relating to defendant's knowledge of other litigation was too broad;
requests should be "closely tailored" to claims; nationwide discovery is too
broad, and must be subject to "reasonable temporal limitations") (one request
related to all litigation in state in past five years; others were "international" or
had no temporal restriction); Ex parte Orkin, Inc., 960 So. 2d 635, 641 (Ala.
2006) (in fraud suit, plaintiff was not entitled to discover "all corporate
representative depositions in cases regarding fraud and termite treatment"
and Alabama customer files of Orkin from 1978 to 2002; Orkin said it had
23,000 active termite-service customers in Alabama, that files were not stored
in central location, that production would require review in 12 locations in
5 states; discovery about nonparty customers does not correlate to issues;
plaintiffs can discover materials necessary to fraud claims, but broad request
should not be allowed on "unsubstantiated hypothesis that a search of records

related to nonparties might uncover fact patterns similar to their own," and 24-year period was too long); Diggs v. Novant Health, Inc., 628 S.E.2d 851, 865-866 (N.C. App. 2006) (in suit by patient whose esophagus was perforated during gall bladder surgery, refusing request for statistical reports on infection control during 1996-2000; infection was "internal" and came from "leaking esophagus, not from infection of her incision or other source in the hospital").

5. In product liability cases, plaintiffs like Nora Pierce often seek from defendants like Indiana Instruments specifications on the design and manufacture of the allegedly defective item. Such material can be critical, and discovery is routinely allowed. See, e.g., In re Cooper Tire & Rubber Co., supra, at 1180, 1194 (in suit against tire maker arising out of fatal auto accident, rejecting claim of trade secrets protection). Protective measures are sometimes taken. See Smith v. BIC Corp., 869 F.2d 194, 200 (3d Cir. 1989) (should restrict dissemination of information on design, safety, and quality turned over during discovery in product liability case). Sometimes discovery is denied altogether, see Laffitte v. Bridgestone Corp., 674 S.E.2d 154, 478 (S.C. 2009) (in suit against tire maker, denying discovery into "skim stock formula," as there may be reasonable alternatives) (citing NTSB report stressing that performance studies can examine defect without relying on chemical analysis), accord Bridgestone Americas Holding, Inc. v. Mayberry, 878 N.E.2d 189, 196 (Ind. 2007).

6. In suits raising issues of employee misconduct, should claimants be entitled to discover personnel files? See Regan-Touhy v. Walgreen Co., 526 F.3d 641 (10th Cir. 2008) (plaintiff, treated for genital herpes, claimed that defendant's employees told others, including ex-husband, about her condition, and sought personnel files of person suspected of releasing information; request was overbroad and not reasonably calculated to lead to discovery of admissible evidence; personnel files "often contain sensitive personal information, just as pharmacy files do, and it is not unreasonable to be cautious about ordering their entire contents disclosed willy-nilly") (requests for all email from employee, and all communication between her and her employer were also overbroad; personnel files are not "categorically out-of-bounds," and "more narrowly targeted request" for documents indicating disciplinary action would be different).

D DISCOVERY DEVICES

There are five mechanisms for obtaining discovery: depositions under FRCP 30 (see also FRCP 32), interrogatories under FRCP 33, production of documents under FRCP 34, physical and mental examination under FRCP 35, and admissions under FRCP 36. Far and away the most important are depositions, interrogatories, and document production.

Most of these mechanisms can only be used to get information from *parties*, not from third persons who are outsiders to the litigation. Thus interrogatories, production of documents, admissions, and physical and mental examinations can be used only against parties. Nonparties, however, can be required to produce documents in a different way: They can be subpoenaed to produce under FRCP 45, so documents in the hands of nonparties are also subject to discovery (we speak of subpoenas "duces tecum"). And of course depositions can be taken of parties and nonparties alike.

Most of these mechanisms are attorney-driven and do not require court permission. Only physical and mental examinations require a motion.

1. Depositions

Depositions are the most common form of modern discovery, and they go forward in most suits of substantial size or importance.

The Scene. Usually, a deposition is taken in the office or conference room of the attorney who requested (or "noticed") it, and usually the only people who attend are the attorneys for the parties in the suit, the witness, and a court reporter. In the simplest two-party lawsuit, that means four people, but suits with many parties may have many lawyers, and sometimes assistants or secretaries attend as well.

The witness is sworn (the reporter takes care of this detail), and generally the party who requested the deposition goes first in asking questions. The witness answers, and the reporter makes a verbatim transcript. When the first lawyer is finished, the other lawyer (or other lawyers) can ask questions. In the typical case, where plaintiff takes the deposition of the defendant or defendant takes the deposition of the plaintiff, the questioners have agendas at cross purposes, and often the job of the second lawyer is to help the witness qualify, refute, or clarify whatever concessions or admissions the initial lawyer got. Unlike trials, where the initial examination (the "direct") sets the parameters, and later questioning ("cross-examination") is limited to the subject matter of the direct, depositions provide every lawyer a chance to ask questions on any aspect of the case—anything relevant to "claims and defenses" in the suit.

Utility of Depositions. Taking depositions serves three critical functions. First, depositions "preserve testimony" because they generate a permanent memorial of what a witness says under oath, and if the witness dies or is unavailable at trial, often the deposition is itself admissible. We consider this point further below.

Second, depositions tie a witness to a version of events. It is not quite right to say that one is "bound" by what one says in a deposition. Even a plaintiff or defendant who gives a deposition in her own case (usually noticed by the other side) can testify differently at trial. *Still*, the deposition can be used to challenge ("impeach") a witness who changes her story. Moreover, if the deposition was false, or if a party changes her story because she acquires additional information, the obligation to "supplement" or "correct" comes into play. See FRCP 26(e). So, at least, a deposition makes it much harder for witnesses, especially parties in a suit, to change their stories, and depositions force witnesses (especially *parties*, who have something immediately at stake) to think and speak carefully, which in itself tends to assure that their stories will not change.

Third, depositions provide information that can be invaluable. The lawyer on one side can talk to her client, and to nonparty witnesses (if they are willing), but cannot ethically approach a client on the other side represented by another lawyer. If a plaintiff—and really we are talking about her lawyer—wants to find out what happened, one source of information is the client on the other side. In finding out what he has to say, plaintiff's lawyer will also learn how he will testify if he takes the stand. The same is true of defendant's lawyer, who wants to find out what she can from plaintiff, and learn what kind of witness he will be. Depositions are the best way to learn such information.

Use at Trial. In the Evidence course you will learn that an out-of-court statement is hearsay if offered to prove the matter asserted—or as lawyers usually say, "the truth of the matter asserted." See FRE 801. Out-of-court statements include just about everything that is said about a case before trial, including statements in the form of deposition testimony. If Nora said in her deposition that she "was going about 65 when I saw the traffic slowing down ahead of me," and if her statement were offered to prove she was driving that speed, it is hearsay.

There are many hearsay exceptions, under which out-of-court statements are admissible even though they *are* hearsay, but two are important here. First, anything a party says, with important exceptions that we need not consider now, is admissible *against that party*. These are what we call "admissions." See FRE 801(d)(2). Hence defendants in Nora's wrongful death suit can offer in evidence Nora's statement that she was going 65 at the time of the accident. That statement could be offered against her whether it was made on the street to a friend, or in a deposition taken in the case itself.

Second, the "former testimony" exception allows the use of *all* deposition testimony (assuming it is relevant and not excludable under some other rule) if the person who gave the deposition is "unavailable" as a witness at trial. If, for example, an eyewitness saw the accident in which Nora's car ran into the truck and gave a deposition describing the accident, then any party—Nora, Ford Motor Company, Indiana Instruments—can offer that deposition at trial if the witness has in the meantime become unavailable to testify. See FRCP 32(a)(4), which codifies the "former testimony" exception as it applies to depositions, and defines what unavailable to testify means. See also FRE 804(b)(1), which codifies the "former testimony" exception more broadly.

Finally, it is worth noting that depositions can *always* be used at trial if the deponent takes the stand and testifies in a manner that departs from the deposition. Lawyers refer to this use of prior statements as one among many kinds of "impeachment" of witnesses. See FRCP 32(a)(2), which says that "any party" may use a deposition to "contradict or impeach" the testimony given at trial by the deponent as a witness.

■ **PROBLEM 9-B. "Did You Consult a Lawyer About a Divorce?"**

In the suit by Nora Pierce, on her own behalf and as executor, Ed Rifkin as counsel for defendant Ford notices the deposition of Nora Pierce, to take place in Rifkin's office in Columbus, Ohio 35 days hence, on August 23 at 10 A.M. At Donald Schrader's request, as counsel for Nora Pierce, the deposition is put over until December 12 at 10 A.M.

On the appointed day and hour, Schrader and Pierce arrive at Rifkin's office. The reporter is there, and the deposition begins. Rifkin questions Pierce about the accident, asking how fast she was going when she became aware that traffic ahead was slowing down ("I think I was going about 65"), what lane she was in ("We were in the left-hand lane overtaking a slower car"), and what happened when she applied the brakes ("I saw smoke coming out of the hood, and the pedal wasn't holding or slowing down the car").

Then Rifkin questions Pierce about her marriage ("I see you've made a claim for loss of consortium, so I have to ask some questions about your relationship to your husband"). He brings out that Nora and Frank had been married for twelve years, that they have two children, and Rifkin then asks "did you consult a lawyer about a divorce last year?" and "were you aware that your husband was seeing another woman?" and "isn't it the case that you and he were considering ending your marriage?" As these questions progress, Schrader voices objections: "I don't see what this has to do with the case," and "these questions are insulting and hurtful to my client," and "this innuendo is baseless and irresponsible." In the end, however, Schrader tells Nora "these questions should never have been asked, but go ahead and answer them anyway, as best you can."

When Nora's deposition is concluded, Schrader tells Rifkin "I would like to take the deposition of Rodney Sheer, who is apparently the man in charge of safety testing at Ford in Dearborn, who knows what testing was done on Mercury Marquis automobiles. When could you make him available in Columbus?" They discuss the matter, but Rifkin declines to commit to producing Rodney Sheer, and the matter is left unresolved. In further conversation, Ed Rifkin tells Donald Schrader that Rifkin "has spoken to

Sylvia Moss, a resident of Pittsburgh who was in her own car at the accident scene that day," and Rifkin says he wants to take her deposition on behalf of Ford. This matter too is left unresolved.

Did Schrader do the right thing in objecting to Rifkin's questions to Nora Pierce about her marriage? What did Rifkin hope to gain? Were the questions proper? If Rifkin won't agree to get Ford to send Rodney Sheer from Dearborn to Columbus, what can Schrader do? Can Rifkin take the deposition of Sylvia Moss? If so, what does Rifkin have to do? Look closely at FRCP 30(a) and (b), and FRCP 45(a)(2) and (c)(3).

■ NOTES ON THE MECHANICS AND PRACTICALITIES OF DEPOSITIONS

1. How does a deposition get set up? Look at FRCP 30(a) and (b), which say that a party may take the deposition of a witness by giving notice. Is there any difference between deposing the adverse party and deposing a nonparty witness? Look at FRCP 30(b), 30(g), and 45(a). When Donald Schrader called Ed Rifkin and asked to reschedule Nora's deposition, why did Rifkin cooperate? Did he have to? What could Schrader do if Rifkin refused to reschedule? While the text of these provisions leaves some doubt whether a subpoena is required, the intended meaning is that a subpoena is not necessary when one litigant deposes another. The contrary is true, however, and a subpoena *is* necessary, when a litigant deposes a nonparty witness. See 8A Wright & Miller, Federal Practice and Procedure §2112 (explaining these points).

(a) Consider Schrader's proposed deposition of Rodney Sheer, the Ford design engineer in Dearborn. FRCP 30(b)(6) authorizes a party to depose a corporation or organization, and to describe in the "notice or subpoena" the subject of the deposition, in which case the corporation or organization "must then designate one or more officers, directors, or managing agents" to testify. Sheer does not fit these categories: He is not a defendant, and is not an "officer, director, or managing agent." His deposition is *not* the deposition of a party, and a subpoena is required. Which court issues it, the federal court in Ohio where the suit is pending, or the federal court in Michigan? Where can the deposition be held? Read carefully FRCP 45(a). Regardless what these provisions *require*, why might Ford agree to send Sheer from Michigan to Ohio to be deposed?

(b) You know from Chapter 3 that Ford is likely subject to jurisdiction in Ohio, in the Pierce suit. Under FRCP 30(b)(6), Ford itself could be deposed by having to produce an officer, director, or managing agent. Probably, that would not happen here, as none of the officers, directors, or managing agents of Ford would have useful information, but in another case such a deposition might be important. If Ford can be sued in Ohio, does it follow that Ford must

produce an officer, director, or managing agent to be deposed in Ohio? What if Ford were *plaintiff* in a suit in Ohio? On these points, the Rules do not provide an answer, but the *custom* is to expect out-of-state plaintiffs to make themselves available in the forum state (or in the case of organizations, their officer, director, or managing agent), and in the case of out-of-court defendants the custom is for the plaintiff to go to them for depositions. See Wright & Miller, supra, §2112 ("normal rule" is that plaintiff must "make himself or herself available for examination" where suit is brought because "plaintiff has selected the forum").

(c) What about Rifkin's proposed deposition of Pennsylvania resident Sylvia Moss, a nonparty? If Rifkin subpoenas her, where can she be made to appear? Look at FRCP 45(a) and (c). Which court issues the subpoena? If Schrader wanted to object to the proposed deposition and move to quash the subpoena on ground that it is unduly burdensome, where would he file his objection? See FRCP 26(c)(1) (protective orders to be sought "on matters relating to a deposition, in the court for the district where the deposition will be taken"). And see FRCP 45(c)(2) (with respect to subpoenas, "issuing court" may "quash or modify" or issue orders "compelling production or attendance").

2. On the surface, depositions are disarmingly simple procedures. The lawyers, witness, and court reporter (whose presence the party taking the deposition arranges in advance) assemble at the appointed time and place, and the lawyers ask questions. If the hours drag on, the parties can agree on breaks, or a longer adjournment for lunch, and the deposition can continue into the evening if everyone agrees, or resume the next morning or at some other mutually agreeable time.

(a) Consider now the preparation that the parties undertake. What should Rifkin do to prepare? How about Schrader? Commonly, lawyers representing clients who are to be "deposed" arrange time to talk with them in advance. Lawyers call the process of witness preparation "woodshedding" or sometimes "sandpapering." The most common advice: "Don't answer questions that aren't being asked." Why is this advice given?

(b) What else should Schrader tell Nora Pierce? You will likely take a course in legal ethics, where you will learn that lawyers *cannot* counsel their clients to perjure themselves, and indeed cannot knowingly let their clients testify untruthfully, and must take immediate steps to correct an untruthful answer if they know, based on prior conversations, that the client is being untruthful.

3. You will learn in the Evidence course that ordinarily one cannot offer proof of a person's "character" in order to prove conduct on a particular occasion, with some exceptions in criminal cases (where defendants can offer proof of "good character" to help establish their innocence). In general, proof of conduct (or misconduct) outside of the immediate acts or events in litigation is excluded, again with exceptions. When "character itself" is in issue because it is "an essential element" in a claim, however, proof of relevant behavior is generally admissible. See FRE 405. Does Nora Pierce's claim for loss of companionship (often called "consortium") put in issue the character of her husband? Does it put in issue the nature of her relationship with Frank Pierce? See St. Clair v. Eastern Air Lines, Inc., 279 F.2d 119, 121 (2d Cir. 1961) (in wrongful death suit "personal habits and qualities" of decedent are relevant in determining earning ability); Price v. County of San Diego, 165 F.R.D. 614, 622 (S.D. Cal. 1996) (claim for loss of consortium "places information regarding the marital relationship at issue," as the "character" of the relationship is "relevant to the issue of damages for the loss of care, comfort and society" and the "mental or emotional state of the relationship," including "affection or dislike, happiness or unhappiness" affects damages).

4. Recall from Chapter 1D2 that the profession suffers mightily from the feeling in the bar that many lawyers are rude and uncivil. And recall the Professional Standards adopted by the Seventh Circuit in 1991, which include a commitment to "treat all other counsel, parties, and witnesses in a civil and courteous manner," and *not* to "reflect the ill feelings of our clients" in dealings with others. Depositions are one place where lawyers on opposite sides come face to face, and rude behavior and obstructionism come to the surface. See, e.g., Redwood v. Dobson, 476 F.3d 462, 469-470 (7th Cir. 2007) (lawyer D's questions "ventured so far beyond the pale" that objection by the other side was inevitable; D's conduct was "shameful" and "mutual enmity does not excuse the breakdown of decorum" that occurred; court "should have used its authority to maintain standards of civility and professionalism") (censuring three lawyers for "conduct unbecoming a member of the bar" and admonishing a fourth); GMAC Bank v. HTFC Corp., 248 F.R.D. 182 (E.D. Pa. 2008) (describing "spectacular failure" of deposition process and addressing the question "how to rein in incivility by counsel," and describing "hostile, uncivil and vulgar conduct" that resulted in "impeding, delaying and frustrating fair examination," and quoting vile and crude language, such as "go get fucked," by both lawyers and clients) (imposing monetary sanctions on offending lawyers).

(a) Perhaps lawyers behave as illustrated in *Redwood* and *GMAC* because they work under stress. But that is not sufficient excuse, and it is possible that something else is going on: Some argue that the profession has deteriorated and there is no sense of honor among practitioners, perhaps because lawyers who encounter each other in a case will likely never see each other again. Perhaps there are simply personal failings: One can sympathize with the question "Didn't your parents teach you better?" But suppose *none* of those explanations is right: Are there tactical reasons for such behavior? What might they be? How can they be countered?

(b) The exchange between Rifkin and Schrader in Problem 9-B does not hold a candle to the behavior in *Redwood* and *GMAC*, does it? Indeed, Schrader's complaint is a mild objection. Rifkin's questions imply that he has found out something, don't they? Could he ask such questions even if he has *no* basis for them? Assuming that he does have a basis, are they proper? Why or why not? If they *are* proper, is there any explanation for the fact that

Schrader objected? Look at FRCP 30(c)(2). If Schrader *failed to object,* would he lose the right to object to Ford's use of Nora's answers at trial? See FRCP 32(d)(2)(A).

5. In many respects, depositions are the "Cadillac" of discovery devices, particularly when compared to other common kinds of discovery (interrogatories and requests for documents). See Mill-Run Tours, Inc. v. Khashoggi, 124 F.R.D. 547, 549-550 (S.D.N.Y. 1989) (citing reasons why oral depositions should not be "routinely replaced" by the interrogatory format, which "does not permit the probing follow-up questions necessary in all but the simplest litigation," and does not allow counsel to "observe the demeanor of the witness and evaluate his credibility in anticipation of trial") (interrogatories are also less desirable because they "provide an opportunity for counsel to assist the witness in providing answers so carefully tailored that they are likely to generate additional discovery disputes"); National Life Ins. Co. v. Hartford Accident and Indemnity Co., 615 F.2d 595, 600 n.5 (3d Cir. 1980) (citing "spontaneity of the responses" as the reason to prefer oral depositions); Greenberg v. Safe Lighting, Inc., Insertia Switch Division, 24 F.R.D. 410, 411 (S.D.N.Y. 1959) ("advantages of oral examination far outweigh the advantages of written interrogatories").

2. Interrogatories

Interrogatories are written questions that one party propounds for another party to answer. Rule 33 provides for these, and this device (unlike depositions) can be used *only* to obtain information from other parties in the suit.

As a practical matter, attorneys are involved (and play the primary role) both in writing interrogatories and answering them, although the *party* to whom interrogatories are addressed is the one who must answer them, and who must sign the answers, which are to be "in writing under oath." If the responding party thinks an interrogatory is improper, her *attorney* raises objection and signs the objection itself. See FRCP 34(b).

Despite the praise for oral depositions, are there areas in which interrogatories are more useful? Consider, for example, whether a deposition or interrogatory would be a better way to obtain information on the net worth of a company or the salary earned by a decedent on whose behalf a wrongful death claim is advanced. Why might interrogatories work better in such cases?

In at least some areas where interrogatories would work well, the obligation of automatic discovery makes interrogatories unnecessary. Thus the parties exchange names and identifying information relating to witnesses as part of automatic discovery. But automatic discovery obliges each party only to reveal witnesses that the party might call in support of its case, and does *not* reach witnesses that a party might know about that it does not expect to call, so at least some information relating to witnesses may remain to be brought to light through interrogatories. Can you think of other areas in which interrogatories are likely to be particularly useful?

Finally, consider the use of interrogatories to get at what happened in accidents or during surgery or in the workplace. Do you think interrogatories could be useful in getting a defendant to admit to negligence or malpractice, or to concede that untoward things occurred in the workplace? Why or why not?

Use in Evidence. Recall from the discussion of depositions that hearsay is an out-of-court statement offered to prove the truth of the matter asserted. Interrogatories (really "interrogatory answers"), like deposition testimony, are out-of-court statements, hence hearsay if offered at trial to prove what they assert. If Nora Pierce answered an interrogatory by saying "I was going about 65 when I saw the traffic slowing down ahead of me," and if this statement were offered in evidence to prove she was driving that speed at the time, it is hearsay.

Once again, almost always an answer to an interrogatory qualifies as an "admission" under FRE 801(d)(2), which makes it admissible *against the party who made that answer.* Unlike deposition testimony, however, an answer to an interrogatory does *not* fit the "former testimony" exception. As a practical matter, then, interrogatory answers can usually be offered *against* the offering party, but not on her behalf.

■ PROBLEM 9-C. "Describe Every Accident"

In Nora Pierce's suit against Ford Motor Company and Indiana Instruments, recall that she seeks recovery for "injuries to her spine and neck," which led to surgeries, "continuing pain and disability, and extreme discomfort." Ford (through its lawyer Ed Rifkin) has propounded the following interrogatories to Nora Pierce:

7. Over the period from July 20, 2002 through July 20, 2012, describe every automobile or vehicular accident in which you were involved as driver. Provide date and location, describe cause and severity. Identify others in the same automobile or motor vehicle, and describe in detail the injuries you sustained, if any.

8. For every accident described in your answer to Question 7, state whether you received a traffic citation, and indicate its type or nature, and state the fine or other punishment imposed.

9. For every accident described in your answer to Question 7, state whether claims were made against you or against liability insurance covering you or the automobile or motor vehicle, and whether any lawsuits were filed against you or the liability insurance carrier. Identify the parties making such claims, and set forth the amount paid to any such claimant or the amount of

any judgment entered in any such suits against you or the liability insurance carrier.

10. To the extent not covered in Question 7, describe every automobile or vehicular accident in which you were involved in any way, occurring between July 20, 2002 and July 20, 2012, and describe in detail how the accident occurred, and any injuries you sustained.

11. To the extent not covered by your answer to Question 7, describe any and all injuries or ailments you experienced in the period beginning July 20, 2002 and ending at the present time, and identify all doctors involved in treating or diagnosing such ailments and injuries, including names and addresses and related contact information.

On behalf of Nora Pierce, Donald Schrader crafts the following Answers and Objections, which Nora Pierce and Donald Schrader sign, she under oath as the person making the Answers and he as author of the Objections, in the manner contemplated by FRCP 33(b).

7. On February 19, 2005, at the intersection of West Lane Avenue and North Star Road in Columbus, I was driving the Mercury Marquis and was involved in an intersection collision with another car, but no injuries resulted from that accident. On Thursday August 23, 2009, while I was driving eastward on Interstate 70 outside Effingham, Illinois, in our Mercury Grand Marquis with my husband Frank as passenger, there was a collision between us and a pickup truck as I was changing lanes and the vehicles bumped together and swerved, and I sustained minor abrasions and was hospitalized briefly but released the same day.

8. Plaintiff objects to this question because the accidents described in Answer 7 occurred in totally different situations at times that were three and seven years before the accident in issue here, and any citations are irrelevant to the issues in this case.

9. In the intersection collision in Columbus on February 19, 2005, we made a claim against the other driver's insurance, and they paid about $3,000 for repairs to our Mercury. For the accident in Illinois on August 23, 2009, the owner of the pickup truck made a claim against our insurance and the matter was settled on that basis. I don't know how much was paid out or the name of the person in the pickup truck. I know of no lawsuits arising out of either accident.

10. Other than the accidents described in Answer 7, I was a passenger in the right front seat of a car driven by my husband Frank Pierce, when we were struck from behind on March 17, 2008 at the intersection of East Fifth Avenue and North High Street in Columbus while our car was stationary. I sustained what the doctor called a mild whiplash injury or neck sprain, and was hospitalized briefly but released later the same day.

11. Plaintiff objects to this interrogatory as intrusive, burdensome, overbroad, and indeterminate. Ailments that Nora Pierce may or may not suffer are irrelevant to claims for personal injuries made here. Minor injuries that Nora Pierce suffered in accidents in 2005, 2008, and 2009 are described above.

Invoking FRCP 37, Ed Rifkin moves for an order compelling further answers to Interrogatories 8 and 11, and seeks costs of making the motion. In opposition, Donald Schrader reiterates his objection to Question 8 on grounds that any traffic citations that might or might not have been issued to Nora Pierce in different situations three and seven years previously are irrelevant. He also reiterates his objection that other "ailments" are irrelevant. How should the court rule, and why?

■ NOTES ON USE AND LIMITATIONS OF INTERROGATORIES

1. Even in proper areas of inquiry, responding parties often object that interrogatories are unduly "burdensome" and too broad or vague. Consider the task of the lawyer drafting interrogatories: What leads a lawyer like Ed Rifkin in the Problem to be overbroad? What leads a lawyer like Donald Schrader to object on this ground? See, e.g., Info-Hold, Inc. v. Sound Merchandising, Inc., 538 F.3d 448, 457-458 (6th Cir. 2008) (defendant objected that question about other services that "relate to the on-hold messaging industry" was "vague and ambiguous" as well as "overly broad" and "unduly burdensome," which put on plaintiff the burden to "clarify" or obtain court order directing defendant to answer). Read FRCP 37(a), and consider the costs and benefits of making motions to compel further responses to interrogatories.

2. Accident litigation almost always leads defense lawyers to ask about prior accidents. The aim is typically threefold:

(a) One purpose is to determine whether the claimed injuries were really caused by the accident in suit. On this point, consider the objection of Nora Pierce to Interrogatory 11. Is inquiry into prior ailments relevant? With respect to injuries, are her answers describing the three prior accidents adequate? See Rivers v. Solley, 177 P.3d 270 (Ariz. 2008) (dismissing claims because of plaintiff's failure to disclose prior accident just 16 days before the one in issue, which caused similar injuries and physical complaints); Davidson v. Slater, 914 A.2d 282, 295 (N.J. 2007) ("defendants routinely will inquire during discovery about a plaintiff's prior injuries"); Shroades v. Food Lion, Inc., 530 S.E.2d 456, 459 (W. Va. 1999) ("it is difficult to imagine evidence more probative as to liability than a prior injury caused by the same mechanism," in this case a runaway shopping cart; in addition to "the obvious impact on the claimant's credibility, such evidence could have also completely changed the expert medical testimony in this case with regard to causation").

(b) Another purpose is find out whether a party is careless and accident-prone, hence more likely to be at fault in the case at hand. Here the prospect of success is low. Again the Evidence Rules usually exclude such proof. See Evidence Rules 404-405, which bar proof of prior negligence to

prove negligence on the occasion in question. See Sparks v. Gilley Trucking Co., 992 F.2d 50, 52-53 (4th Cir. 1993) (in suit arising out of car accident, reversible error to admit evidence that plaintiff received speeding tickets on unrelated occasions). Should plaintiff have to answer Interrogatory 8 about prior citations? Suppose at trial Nora Pierce took the stand and testified that she is "always a careful driver." You will learn in Evidence that such testimony might "open the door" to proving prior acts of negligence. Should this possibility be enough to justify Interrogatory 8? See Atkinson v. Atcheson, Topeka & Santa Fe Ry. Co., 197 F.2d 244, 245 (10th Cir. 1952) (where plaintiff testifies that she is a careful driver, defendant could bring out on cross that she was in the wrong lane in a two-car accident). Rule 26 does not say, in so many words, that evidence that might impeach a witness is discoverable. Note that Rule 26(a) *exempts* evidence that "would be used solely for impeachment" from the obligations of automatic discovery. If impeaching evidence is exempt from automatic discovery, is it nevertheless implicitly covered by the wider concept of relevance in FRCP 26(b)(1) governing party-driven discovery? See Wright & Miller, supra, §2015 (discovery of information usable to impeach a witness for the other side is "commonly allowed," but "the very range of materials" that might have impeachment value is so broad that it "strains the outer limits" of reasonable boundaries; limiting discovery of impeaching material to what is "otherwise relevant" is too narrow; test should be whether the matter "actually will produce admissible evidence").

(c) The third purpose, somewhat indirectly served by asking about prior accidents, is to find out whether plaintiff is a chronic litigant. Courts seldom allow proof along these lines, perhaps because few people fit this category, but sometimes proof of this sort is admitted. See Outley v. New York, 837 F.2d 587, 591-595 (2d Cir. 1988) (sometimes such proof can indicate a pattern of "fraudulent conduct," but there was insufficient proof of that here).

3. In an effort to prevent abuse, FRCP 33 limits the number of interrogatories that "a party may serve on any other party" to "no more than 25," which includes "all discrete subparts." See also Mississippi Rule 33(a) (each party may serve as many as 30 interrogatories, but each "shall consist of a single question"); Payne v. Whitten, 948 So. 2d 427 (Miss. 2007) (interrogatory asking "how the accident occurred" and "the basis of any claim of a contributing cause" violated rule limiting each interrogatory to "a single question").

4. "Contention interrogatories" can help the parties, especially defendants in negligence suits, flesh out claims that are often stated in general terms in the pleadings. Thus one party can ask another to "state all the facts" supporting a claim for negligence, or a defense to a negligence claim. How are contention interrogatories different from more typical interrogatories, such as those set out Problem 9-C, above?

(a) Recall that Form 11 allows a plaintiff to allege negligence in conclusory fashion, at least in the setting of auto accident litigation, to avoid forcing her to commit to a single theory at the outset, allowing discovery to develop what really happened. Doesn't it make sense, then, to let

defendants "nail things down" during discovery? Or should this matter wait until still later, when the parties hold their final pretrial conference? See, e.g., Hartsfield v. Gulf Oil Corp., 29 F.R.D. 163, 164 (E.D. Pa. 1962) (approving interrogatories asking plaintiff to "state in detail the facts or information supporting" various claims of negligence; it is now settled that interrogatories can obtain "a specification of the facts upon which a claim of negligence is founded").

(b) Discovery is often a lengthy process. Contention interrogatories, if asked early in the process, could defeat the purpose of letting parties plead generally, couldn't they? See 0_2 Micro International Ltd. v. Monolithic Power Systems, Inc., 467 F.3d 1355, 1365-1366 (9th Cir. 2006) (answers to contention interrogatories "are often postponed until the close of discovery" or they can be "amended as a matter of course" during discovery).

(c) Contention interrogatories may be less than fully effective in narrowing issues. One reason is that answers to interrogatories, even if admissible, are not *binding* in the sense of foreclosing a party from taking a different position. Perhaps for this reason, courts are sometimes reluctant to allow such interrogatories control the positions later taken at trial. See, e.g., Moore v. Computer Associates International, Inc., 2009 WL 2870213 n.4 (D. Ariz. 2009) (contention interrogatories can narrow and sharpen issues, but "do not limit the party's ability to make an argument in future proceedings").

(d) Plaintiffs can also use contention interrogatories to get the other side to "flesh out" defenses. See, e.g., Campbell v. Washington, 2009 WL 577599 (W.D. Wash. 2009) (can ask defendant to "identify facts" supporting defense that plaintiff failed to state claim on which relief can be granted); Grinnel Corp. v. Palms 211 Ocean Blvd., Ltd., 924 So. 2d 887 (Fla. App. 2006) (plaintiff can ask defendant to state "all facts supporting" various denials and affirmative defenses).

(e) Contention interrogatories can be useful in other contexts than negligence suits. See, e.g., Skaff v. Meridien North America Beverly Hills, LLC, 506 F.3d 832, 842 (9th Cir. 2007) (in suit under Americans with Disabilities Act, defendant asked by interrogatory "to detail the barriers" that plaintiff encountered in hotel; defense could properly ask "what barriers [plaintiff] had encountered, where they were in the hotel, when he encountered them, what he did about it, whether any person was present when he encountered the barriers, and, for each barrier, what damages he claimed to have suffered") (opinion describes answers, and points out that defendant could have sought to compel more complete answers if it considered plaintiff's answers to be conclusory).

5. As noted above, answers to interrogatories are often admissible against the answering party. Also important, motions for summary judgment can rest in whole or in part on interrogatory answers. See FRCP 56(c)(2) (summary judgment may be entered if the pleadings and affidavits, as well as "materials in the record," which include "interrogatory answers," show there is "no genuine issue as to any material fact" and that the movant is entitled to judgment). Still, answers to interrogatories may be excludable, even when offered against the answering party, as happens if they reveal prior accidents, which usually cannot be used to prove negligence on the occasion. And while the answering party may use her own answers to support her motion for sum-mary judgment, she cannot use them *at trial* against the other side because they are "hearsay" that do not fit the admissions doctrine when the answering party offers them.

6. Note that FRCP 33(d) lets a party reply to an interrogatory by offering to allow the information seeker to review and copy relevant records, if the answer "may be determined in that way," where "the burden of deriving or ascertaining the answer will be substantially the same for either party." This option is tempt-ing, but is not quite as useful as may appear. Courts usually require responding parties to direct inquiring parties to documents that *contain the answer*, and they cannot simply offer to make all their records available. See Ak-Chin Indian Community v. United States, 85 Fed. Cl. 397, 403 (Fed. Cl. 2009) ("a broad reference to a set of documents does not meet the specificity requirement").

3. Requests for Production and Inspection

The request for production is the main way to obtain documentary evidence, including electronically stored information (ESI). In many suits, such material is critical, and many documents or data collections can be used in evidence at trial because they fit major exceptions to the hearsay doctrine—the business records exception, covering such things as doctor and hospital records, bill-ings and invoices, and the public records exception, covering such things as records of government disbursements. See FRE 803(6) and (8).

Rule 34 was drafted in an era that we have left behind, when "production of documents" meant that the discovering party would go to the place where paper documents were stored, and could inspect and read them and select some to be copied. Since then, we have had two revolutions. First was the advent of the modern office copier in the 1960s, which made it more economical—even from the standpoint of the party disclosing documents—to make physical copies of paper documents and send them to the information seeker. Second was the advent of electronic data storage, which has, at least since the 1980s, played an ever-larger role in storing information that once existed only on paper. Now information generated by business and government, and for that matter by individuals in their personal lives, exists *only* as ESI.

Hence modern document discovery has more and more become discovery of ESI, and "producing" such material is a matter of "downloading" and transmit-ting it to the information seeker. Of course, the transmission itself is electronic—ESI is sent to the information seeker by means of internet connections, or sometimes stored on media like flash drives that can be easily delivered to the information seeker. So important and so prevalent is such discovery, espe-cially in "big ticket" complex litigation, that "e-discovery" figures prominently in the professional vocabulary, and major law firms have departments of techni-cians, lawyers, and paralegals who specialize in the area. See generally Richard Marcus, *The Electronic Lawyer*, 58 DePaul L. Rev. 263 (2009).

Many documents, including ESI, that would be likely candidates of requests for production under FRCP 34, are now already produced during automatic discovery, which obliges every party to produce "a copy" or "a description by category and location" of relevant material. In this case, as in the case of automatic discovery of witnesses and identifying information about them, the obligation extends only to material of this sort that the party "may use to support its claims or defenses." That leaves out *other* such material, which can still be discovered through requests for production under FRCP 34.

Production of documents is a device that is sometimes abused. Usually, complaints are directed against the requesting party, but producing parties sometimes misbehave too. See, e.g., Garcia v. Berkshire Life Ins. Co. of America, 569 F.3d 1174, 1181 (10th Cir. 2009) (dismissing suit against insurer for disability payments where plaintiff "was herself culpable" for submitting fabrications "carefully constructed to look like authentic documents," in the form of letters "made to look as though they were printed on authentic letterhead" and emails that were "spliced together so as to appear accurate," and "fax banners were added to documents to disguise their origin"). Today, the most common claims of abuse involve requests for production of ESI, and the most common area of dispute involves ESI. This subject is examined separately in Section H, infra.

4. Physical and Mental Examination

Among the less-used discovery devices is the physical or mental examination of a party (or a person in the "custody" or "control" of a party), which may be done under court order on a showing of "good cause" under FRCP 35.

In a 1964 decision that put this provision to the test, a court ordered examinations of the driver of a bus that crashed into the back of a tractor-trailer truck while the two vehicles were going the same direction on a four-lane divided highway. Reportedly, the lights on the rear of the trailer were visible for half- to three-quarters of a mile, and the bus driver himself said that he saw them for a period of 10 to 15 seconds before the collision. Still he did not slow down or move to the left-hand lane. In the collision, several people were seriously injured, and the bus driver (Schlagenhauf) had been involved in a similar accident before. On these facts, the owner of the truck (the injured parties sued Greyhound, the bus driver, and the truck owner) got a court order requiring Schlagenhauf to undergo what turned out to be four different examinations—by specialists in internal medicine, ophthalmology, neurology, and psychiatry (the original order actually required him to undergo *nine* examinations, apparently in error, and it was later corrected).

The bus driver successfully sought review of this order by writ of mandamus (unusual in itself), and challenged FRCP 35 on many grounds. He argued that the court lacked power to order such an examination, that FRCP 35 did not apply to a defendant (apparently on the theory that he does not put his own condition in issue, thus differing from plaintiffs seeking recovery for injuries), that FRCP 35 does not authorize an examination at the behest of one who is "not a party" in relation to the person to be examined (apparently a reference to the fact that the truck company had not made a claim against the bus driver, although the plaintiffs had), and that the Rule cannot apply unless good cause is shown. The Court rejected all but the last challenge:

> Schlagenhauf did not assert his mental or physical condition either in support of or in defense of a claim. His condition was sought to be placed in issue by other parties. Thus . . . Rule 35 required that these parties make an affirmative showing that petitioner's mental or physical condition was in controversy and that there was good cause for the examinations requested. This, the record plainly shows, they failed to do.
>
> The only allegations in the pleadings relating to this subject were the general conclusory statement in [the truck owner's] answer to the crossclaim that "Schlagenhauf was not mentally or physically capable of operating" the bus at the time of the accident and the limited allegation in National Lead's cross-claim that, at the time of the accident, "the eyes and vision of . . . Schlagenhauf was (sic) impaired and deficient."
>
> The attorney's affidavit attached to the petition for the examinations provided: That . . . Schlagenhauf, in his deposition . . . admitted that he saw red lights for 10 to 15 seconds prior to a collision with a semi-tractor trailer unit and yet drove his vehicle on without reducing speed and without altering the course thereof; [and That] The only eye-witness to this accident known to this affiant . . . testified that immediately prior to the impact between the bus and truck that he had also been approaching the truck from the rear and that he had clearly seen the lights of the truck for a distance of three-quarters to one-half mile to the rear thereof; [and That] Schlagenhauf has admitted in his deposition . . . that he was involved in a (prior) similar type rear end collision.
>
> This record cannot support even the corrected order which required one examination in each of the four specialties of internal medicine, ophthalmology, neurology, and psychiatry. Nothing in the pleadings or affidavit would afford a basis for a belief that Schlagenhauf was suffering from a mental or neurological illness warranting wide-ranging psychiatric or neurological examinations. Nor is there anything stated justifying the broad internal medicine examination.
>
> The only specific allegation made in support of the four examinations ordered was that the "eyes and vision" of Schlagenhauf were impaired. Considering this in conjunction with the affidavit, we would be hesitant to set aside a visual examination if it had been the only one ordered. However, as the case must be remanded to the District Court because of the other examinations ordered, it would be appropriate for the District Judge to reconsider also this order in light of the guidelines set forth in this opinion.
>
> The Federal Rules of Civil Procedure should be liberally construed, but they should not be expanded by disregarding plainly expressed limitations. The "good cause" and "in controversy" requirements of Rule 35 make it very apparent that sweeping examinations of a party who has not affirmatively put into issue his own mental or physical condition are not to be automatically ordered merely because the person has been involved in an accident—or, as in this case, two accidents—and a general charge of negligence is lodged. Mental and physical

examinations are only to be ordered upon a discriminating application by the district judge of the limitations prescribed by the Rule. To hold otherwise would mean that such examinations could be ordered routinely in automobile accident cases. The plain language of Rule 35 precludes such an untoward result.

Accordingly, the judgment of the Court of Appeals is vacated and the case remanded to the District Court to reconsider the examination order in light of the guidelines herein formulated and for further proceedings in conformity with this opinion.

Schlagenhauf v. Holder, 379 U.S. 104, 119-122 (1964).

Justice Black minced no words in a spirited dissent:

> I think this record plainly shows that there was a controversy as to Schlagenhauf's mental and physical health and that "good cause" was shown for a physical and mental examination of him, unless failure to deny the allegations amounted to an admission that they were true. While the papers filed in connection with this motion were informal, there can be no doubt that other parties in the lawsuit specifically and unequivocally charged that Schlagenhauf was not mentally or physically capable of operating a motor bus at the time of the collision, and that his negligent operation of the bus caused the resulting injuries and damage. [Justice Black recites the basic facts, stressing that conditions were good, that the lights of the truck were visible and Schlagenhauf admitted seeing them and having been involved in a similar accident before, and that he did not deny the suggestions that "mental and physical health and his eyes and vision were impaired and deficient."] In a collision case like this one, evidence concerning very bad eyesight or impaired mental or physical health which may affect the ability to drive is obviously of the highest relevance. It is equally obvious, I think, that when a vehicle continues down an open road and smashes into a truck in front of it although the truck is in plain sight and there is ample time and room to avoid collision, the chances are good that the driver has some physical, mental or moral defect. When such a thing happens twice, one is even more likely to ask, "What is the matter with that driver? Is he blind or crazy?"

379 U.S. 104, at 122-123.

■ NOTES ON COURT-ORDERED EXAMINATIONS

1. Had the Court approved the four court-ordered examinations in *Schlagenhauf*, would claimants routinely ask for such examinations of persons charged with negligence, as evidence that their employer should be viewed as responsible for putting them in positions that could lead to accidents? In a footnote, the Court cited statistics indicating that in 1964 nearly 10,000 cases were filed that involved personal injuries arising out of auto accidents, and that there were more than 11 *million* such accidents involving almost 20 million drivers. Justice Douglas concurred, but would have denied the examinations rather than inviting reconsideration. He was as vigorous in *opposing* the examinations as Justice Black was in favoring them:

> I do not suppose there is any licensed driver of a car or a truck who does not suffer from some ailment, whether it be ulcers, bad eyesight, abnormal blood pressure, deafness, liver malfunction, bursitis, rheumatism, or what not. If he or she is turned over to the plaintiff's doctors and psychoanalysts to discover the cause of the mishap, the door will be opened for grave miscarriages of justice. When the defendant's doctors examine plaintiff, they are normally interested only in answering a single question: did plaintiff in fact sustain the specific injuries claimed? But plaintiff's doctors will naturally be inclined to go on a fishing expedition in search of anything which will tend to prove that the defendant was unfit to perform the acts which resulted in the plaintiff's injury. And a doctor for a fee can easily discover something wrong with any patient—a condition that in prejudiced medical eyes might have caused the accident. Once defendants are turned over to medical or psychiatric clinics for an analysis of their physical wellbeing and the condition of their psyche, the effective trial will be held there and not before the jury. There are no lawyers in those clinics to stop the doctor from probing this organ or that one, to halt a further inquiry, to object to a line of questioning. And there is no judge to sit as arbiter. The doctor or the psychiatrist has a holiday in the privacy of his office. The defendant is at the doctor's (or psychiatrist's) mercy; and his report may either overawe or confuse the jury and prevent a fair trial.

379 U.S. 104, 125. Who's right here—the majority, Justice Black, or Justice Douglas? What should the trial court do on remand?

2. The more likely subjects for court-ordered physical or mental exams are parties advancing claims for injuries. Usually, such parties seek treatment and voluntarily make their records available—and for the most part they would be discoverable anyway. Suppose, however, that defending parties are not satisfied with such material. Here four points that merit consideration:

(a) First, the parties have considerable incentive to agree to physical examinations—plaintiffs because they would rather select the doctor or doctors to conduct such examinations, and defendants because they might lose a motion to compel. In its present form, FRCP 35(b)(6) makes parts of the rule applicable to examinations undertaken by stipulation: The parties are to share the examiners' reports and "reports of all earlier examinations" on the same condition, and delivering such reports to the other side entitles either party to obtain similar reports from the other side. When an examined party requests or obtains such a report from the other side, she "waives any privilege" for "testimony about all examinations of the same condition."

(b) Second, by putting her physical condition in issue, a claimant is usually said to waive protections otherwise accorded by the physician-patient privilege, even without requesting a report on a court-ordered examination or one done by stipulation, and there is little chance that the material in any underlying doctor's reports could be kept out of evidence or guarded from discovery.

(c) It is another matter with psychiatric records, as you saw in the Notes on Scope of Discovery, supra. See also Stuff v. Simmons, 838 N.E.2d

1096, 1103 (Ind. 2005) (in suit arising out of accident in which defendant rear-ended plaintiff, refusing request for neuropsychological examination of plaintiff; "standard request for [damages from] pain and suffering and emotional distress" in personal injury claim would not put claimant's mental condition in controversy; that would only happen if claimant alleges "a mental injury that exceeds the common emotional reaction to an injury or loss," and ordering such an examination "would open the door to involuntary mental examinations in virtually every soft tissue injury case"); Gepner v. Fujicolor Processing, Inc. of Sioux Falls, 637 N.W.2d 681, 689 (N.D. 2001) (mental evaluation can be ordered under Rule 35 when plaintiff (1) pleads a specific claim for intentional or negligent infliction of emotional distress; (2) pleads specific mental or psychiatric injury or disorder; (3) claims unusually severe emotional distress; (4) offers expert testimony to support a claim of emotional distress; or (5) concedes her mental condition is in controversy).

5. Requests for Admission

The fifth and last discovery device is requests for admission under Rule 36. In a sense, this mechanism is not discovery at all. The requesting party is not really seeking evidence or information, but is trying to narrow the issues, in a manner that resembles contention interrogatories. Perhaps more important, the response of a party to a request to admit does not simply produce evidence or a substitute for evidence that can be *used* against the party at trial, but is *binding* (unless the party obtains relief from what he has admitted). In the words of FRCP 36(b), a matter admitted under this provision "is conclusively established" unless the court permits a party to withdraw it.

In other words, a response to a request to admit is like the answer that a defendant files (and like a complaint that plaintiff files). Just as an answer (and to some extent a complaint) binds the party who files it to the things he admits or fails to deny, so a response to a request to admit binds the party. These are "judicial" admissions, as opposed to the "personal" admissions that occur when a party gives deposition testimony or answers an interrogatory (where what the party says is *admissible* against the party, but does not prevent him or her from taking a different tack at trial).

Although a response to a request to admit has the effect of a "judicial" admission that removes issues from consideration at trial, FRCP 36 softens the blow by providing that admissions under this provision "cannot be used against the party in any other proceeding." See FRCP 36(b). This provision encourages parties formally to make admissions under the Rule, rather than backing away from doing so because they could come back to haunt the maker later on.

Like other discovery devices, requests for admissions can be abusive. See, e.g., Haley v. Harbin, 933 So. 2d 261 (Miss. 2005) (250 requests for admission, directed to doctor and taking up 33 pages, along with interrogatories asking for 1,802 responses and taking 117 pages of printout, were "grossly excessive in number, unduly burdensome, and oppressive," and many were confusing and ambiguous) (vacating and remanding).

E WORK PRODUCT PROTECTION

Among the most important rights of a lawyer who does litigation—and *this* right does indeed belong to the lawyer rather than his client—is the right to keep the fruits of his own labor, undertaken in preparation for litigation, and perhaps just as importantly his own creative thinking. Thus the lawyer has the right *not* to turn such things over to adversaries, at least most of the time.

The Court's landmark decision in the *Hickman* case was handed down two generations ago, in 1947, when the Civil Rules made no mention of "work product." Read *Hickman* now. In the Notes after the opinion, you will encounter the provisions now in FRCP 26 that were added in an effort to codify the work product doctrine.

Justice Robert H. Jackson (1892-1954)

More famous than Justice Murphy's majority opinion in *Hickman* is the concurrence by Justice Jackson, which shows an acute appreciation of the situation of lawyers litigating cases. Justice Jackson was self-trained, not attending college and having only a year in law school. He studied as an apprentice in a law office, passed the bar at age 21, and was the last person appointed to the Supreme Court without a law degree. He served for 13 years (1941-1954), but took time away when he became Chief Counsel for the United States during the trial of high-ranking Nazi leaders at Nuremberg. Jackson authored the Court's opinion in *Mullane* (Chapter 3D1, supra), and also the opinion in Wickard v. Filburn, 317 U.S. 111 (1942), which is famous for its *very* expansive interpretation of congressional power under the Commerce Clause. Jackson is perhaps best remembered for coining memorable phrases and for his concurring opinion in the *Youngstown Steel* case, where he laid out in systematic fashion his view of presidential power, in a statement that is much admired and frequently cited today. See Youngstown Steel & Tube Co. v. Sawyer, 343 U.S. 579, 634 (1952) (Jackson,

concurring). Here are some of his pronouncements: "The naïve assumption that prejudicial effects can be overcome by instructions to the jury all practicing lawyers know to be unmitigated fiction." Krulewitch v. United States, 336 U.S. 440, 453 (1949) (Jackson, concurring). "There is danger that, if the Court does not temper its doctrinaire logic with a little practical wisdom, it will convert the constitutional Bill of Rights into a suicide pact." Terminiello v. City of Chicago, 337 U.S. 1, 37 (Jackson, dissenting).

HICKMAN v. TAYLOR

United States Supreme Court
329 U.S. 495 (1947)

Mr. Justice MURPHY delivered the opinion of the Court.

This case presents an important problem under the Federal Rules of Civil Procedure as to the extent to which a party may inquire into oral and written statements of witnesses, or other information, secured by an adverse party's counsel in the course of preparation for possible litigation after a claim has arisen. Examination into a person's files and records, including those resulting from the professional activities of an attorney, must be judged with care. It is not without reason that various safeguards have been established to preclude unwarranted excursions into the privacy of a man's work. At the same time, public policy supports reasonable and necessary inquiries. Properly to balance these competing interests is a delicate and difficult task.

On February 7, 1943, the tug "J.M. Taylor" sank while engaged in helping to tow a car float of the Baltimore & Ohio Railroad across the Delaware River at Philadelphia. The accident was apparently unusual in nature, the cause of it still being unknown. Five of the nine crew members were drowned. Three days later the tug owners and the underwriters employed a law firm, of which respondent Fortenbaugh is a member, to defend them against potential suits by representatives of the deceased crew members and to sue the railroad for damages to the tug.

A public hearing was held on March 4, 1943, before the United States Steamboat Inspectors, at which the four survivors were examined. This testimony was recorded and made available to all interested parties. Shortly thereafter, Fortenbaugh privately interviewed the survivors and took statements from them with an eye toward the anticipated litigation; the survivors signed these statements on March 29. Fortenbaugh also interviewed other persons believed to have some information relating to the accident and in some cases he made memoranda of what they told him. At the time when Fortenbaugh secured the statements of the survivors, representatives of two of the deceased crew members had been in communication with him. Ultimately claims were presented by representatives of all five of the deceased; four of the claims, however, were settled without litigation. The fifth claimant, petitioner herein, brought suit in a federal court under the Jones Act on November 26, 1943, naming as defendants the two tug owners, individually and as partners, and the railroad.

One year later, petitioner filed 39 interrogatories directed to the tug owners. The 38th interrogatory read: "State whether any statements of the members of the crews of the Tugs 'J.M. Taylor' and 'Philadelphia' or of any other vessel were taken in connection with the towing of the car float and the sinking of the Tug 'John M. Taylor.' Attach hereto exact copies of all such statements if in writing, and if oral, set forth in detail the exact provisions of any such oral statements or reports."

Supplemental interrogatories asked whether any oral or written statements, records, reports or other memoranda had been made concerning any matter relative to the towing operation, the sinking of the tug, the salvaging and repair of the tug, and the death of the deceased. If the answer was in the affirmative, the tug owners were then requested to set forth the nature of all such records, reports, statements or other memoranda.

The tug owners, through Fortenbaugh, answered all of the interrogatories except No. 38 and the supplemental ones just described. While admitting that statements of the survivors had been taken, they declined to summarize or set forth the contents. They did so on the ground that such requests called "for privileged matter obtained in preparation for litigation" and constituted "an attempt to obtain indirectly counsel's private files." It was claimed that answering these requests "would involve practically turning over not only the complete files, but also the telephone records and, almost, the thoughts of counsel."

In connection with the hearing on these objections, Fortenbaugh made a written statement and gave an informal oral deposition explaining the circumstances under which he had taken the statements. But he was not expressly asked in the deposition to produce the statements. The District Court for the Eastern District of Pennsylvania, sitting en banc, held that the requested matters were not privileged. The court then decreed that the tug owners and Fortenbaugh, as counsel and agent for the tug owners forthwith "Answer Plaintiff's 38th interrogatory and supplemental interrogatories; produce all written statements of witnesses obtained by Mr. Fortenbaugh, as counsel and agent for Defendants; state in substance any fact concerning this case which Defendants learned through oral statements made by witnesses to Mr. Fortenbaugh whether or not included in his private memoranda and produce Mr. Fortenbaugh's memoranda containing statements of fact by witnesses or to submit these memoranda to the Court for determination of those portions which should be revealed to Plaintiff." Upon their refusal, the court adjudged them in contempt and ordered them imprisoned until they complied.

The Third Circuit Court of Appeals, also sitting en banc, reversed the judgment of the District Court. It held that the information here sought was part of the "work product of the lawyer" and hence privileged from discovery under the Federal Rules of Civil Procedure. The importance of the problem, which has engendered a great divergence of views among district courts, led us to grant certiorari.

[The Supreme Court addresses two preliminary questions—one relating to the discovery provision that could justify holding Fortenbaugh and his clients in contempt, the other relating to the matter of attorney-client privilege.

On the first point, the Court says that the materials in question were in Fortenbaugh's possession, that Hickman used interrogatories, and that the trial court in its contempt order invoked both FRCP 33 on interrogatories and FRCP 34 on requests for production. Since those provisions allow discovery only from *parties,* not their *lawyers,* the Court of Appeals thought the basis of the contempt order had to be found elsewhere, and it invoked the provision on depositions, then found in FRCP 26. But the Court concludes that FRCP 26 was not involved. Nor could FRCP 34 be the basis for contempt, since Hickman had not filed a motion to compel production, which FRCP 34 then required. (Years later it was amended to delete the requirement of a court order.) Moreover, FRCP 33 on interrogatories could not be the basis for contempt: Interrogatories cannot be directed to counsel for a party, and *documents* were being sought, not information. The tug company could not refuse to answer interrogatories by claiming that only its lawyer has the information, but that is not what Fortenbaugh and the company were doing. So the order was flawed in holding the tug owners in contempt "for failure to produce that which was in the possession of their counsel," and in holding Fortenbaugh in contempt "for failure to produce that which he could not be compelled to produce" under FRCP 33 or 34. Hickman could have taken Fortenbaugh's deposition in conjunction with a subpoena duces tecum under FRCP 45. Still, the Court concludes, it is "unnecessary and unwise to rest our decision upon this procedural irregularity."

The Court then concludes that the materials in issue "fall outside the scope" of the attorney-client privilege, which "does not extend to information which an attorney secures from a witness while acting for his client in anticipation of litigation." Nor does it reach "memoranda, briefs, communications and other writings prepared by counsel for his own use," nor yet "writings which reflect an attorney's mental impressions, conclusions, opinions or legal theories."]

But the impropriety of invoking that privilege does not provide an answer to the problem before us. Petitioner has made more than an ordinary request for relevant, non-privileged facts in the possession of his adversaries or their counsel. He has sought discovery as of right of oral and written statements of witnesses whose identity is well known and whose availability to petitioner appears unimpaired. He has sought production of these matters after making the most searching inquiries of his opponents as to the circumstances surrounding the fatal accident, which inquiries were sworn to have been answered to the best of their information and belief. Interrogatories were directed toward all the events prior to, during and subsequent to the sinking of the tug. Full and honest answers to such broad inquiries would necessarily have included all pertinent information gleaned by Fortenbaugh through his interviews with the witnesses. Petitioner makes no suggestion, and we cannot assume, that the tug owners or Fortenbaugh were incomplete or dishonest in the framing of their answers. In addition, petitioner was free to examine the public testimony of the witnesses taken before the United States Steamboat Inspectors. We are thus dealing with an attempt to secure the production of written statements and mental impressions contained in the files and the mind of the attorney Fortenbaugh without any showing of necessity or any indication or claim that denial of such production would unduly prejudice the preparation of petitioner's case or cause him any hardship or injustice. For aught that appears, the essence of what petitioner seeks either has been revealed to him already through the interrogatories or is readily available to him direct from the witnesses for the asking.

The District Court, after hearing objections to petitioner's request, commanded Fortenbaugh to produce all written statements of witnesses and to state in substance any facts learned through oral statements of witnesses to him. Fortenbaugh was to submit any memoranda he had made of the oral statements so that the court might determine what portions should be revealed to petitioner. All of this was ordered without any showing by petitioner, or any requirement that he make a proper showing, of the necessity for the production of any of this material or any demonstration that denial of production would cause hardship or injustice. The court simply ordered production on the theory that the facts sought were material and were not privileged as constituting attorney-client communications.

In our opinion, neither Rule 26 nor any other rule dealing with discovery contemplates production under such circumstances. That is not because the subject matter is privileged or irrelevant, as those concepts are used in these rules. Here is simply an attempt, without purported necessity or justification, to secure written statements, private memoranda and personal recollections prepared or formed by an adverse party's counsel in the course of his legal duties. As such, it falls outside the arena of discovery and contravenes the public policy underlying the orderly prosecution and defense of legal claims. Not even the most liberal of discovery theories can justify unwarranted inquiries into the files and the mental impressions of an attorney.

Historically, a lawyer is an officer of the court and is bound to work for the advancement of justice while faithfully protecting the rightful interests of his clients. In performing his various duties, however, it is essential that a lawyer work with a certain degree of privacy, free from unnecessary intrusion by opposing parties and their counsel. Proper preparation of a client's case demands that he assemble information, sift what he considers to be the relevant from the irrelevant facts, prepare his legal theories and plan his strategy without undue and needless interference. That is the historical and the necessary way in which lawyers act within the framework of our system of jurisprudence to promote justice and to protect their clients' interests. This work is reflected, of course, in interviews, statements, memoranda, correspondence, briefs, mental impressions, personal beliefs, and countless other tangible and intangible ways—aptly though roughly termed by the Circuit Court of Appeals in this case as the "Work product of the lawyer." Were such materials open to opposing counsel on mere demand, much of what is now put down in writing would remain unwritten. An attorney's thoughts, heretofore inviolate, would not be his own. Inefficiency, unfairness and sharp practices would inevitably develop in the giving of legal advice and in the preparation of cases for trial. The effect on the legal profession would be demoralizing. And the interests of the clients and the cause of justice would be poorly served.

We do not mean to say that all written materials obtained or prepared by an adversary's counsel with an eye toward litigation are necessarily free from discovery in all cases. Where relevant and non-privileged facts remain hidden in an attorney's file and where production of those facts is essential to the preparation of one's case, discovery may properly be had. Such written statements and documents might, under certain circumstances, be admissible in evidence or give clues as to the existence or location of relevant facts. Or they might be useful for purposes of impeachment or corroboration. And production might be justified where the witnesses are no longer available or can be reached only with difficulty. Were production of written statements and documents to be precluded under such circumstances, the liberal ideals of the deposition-discovery portions of the Federal Rules of Civil Procedure would be stripped of much of their meaning. But the general policy against invading the privacy of an attorney's course of preparation is so well recognized and so essential to an orderly working of our system of legal procedure that a burden rests on the one who would invade that privacy to establish adequate reasons to justify production through a subpoena or court order. That burden, we believe, is necessarily implicit in the rules as now constituted.

Rule 30(b) [now FRCP 26(c)—ED.], as presently written, gives the trial judge the requisite discretion to make a judgment as to whether discovery should be allowed as to written statements secured from witnesses. [This reference is to the material on protective orders, which was moved from FRCP 30(b) to FRCP 26(c) in 1970.—ED.] But in the instant case there was no room for that discretion to operate in favor of the petitioner. No attempt was made to establish any reason why Fortenbaugh should be forced to produce the written statements. There was only a naked, general demand for these materials as of right and a finding by the District Court that no recognizable privilege was involved. That was insufficient to justify discovery under these circumstances and the court should have sustained the refusal of the tug owners and Fortenbaugh to produce.

But as to oral statements made by witnesses to Fortenbaugh, whether presently in the form of his mental impressions or memoranda, we do not believe that any showing of necessity can be made under the circumstances of this case so as to justify production. Under ordinary conditions, forcing an attorney to repeat or write out all that witnesses have told him and to deliver the account to his adversary gives rise to grave dangers of inaccuracy and untrustworthiness. No legitimate purpose is served by such production. The practice forces the attorney to testify as to what he remembers or what he saw fit to write down regarding witnesses' remarks. Such testimony could not qualify as evidence; and to use it for impeachment or corroborative purposes would make the attorney much less an officer of the court and much more an ordinary witness. The standards of the profession would thereby suffer.

Denial of production of this nature does not mean that any material, non-privileged facts can be hidden from the petitioner in this case. He need not be unduly hindered in the preparation of his case, in the discovery of facts or in his anticipation of his opponents' position. Searching interrogatories directed to Fortenbaugh and the tug owners, production of written documents and statements upon a proper showing and direct interviews with the witnesses themselves all serve to reveal the facts in Fortenbaugh's possession to the fullest possible extent consistent with public policy. Petitioner's counsel frankly admits that he wants the oral statements only to help prepare himself to examine witnesses and to make sure that he has overlooked nothing. That is insufficient under the circumstances to permit him an exception to the policy underlying the privacy of Fortenbaugh's professional activities. If there should be a rare situation justifying production of these matters, petitioner's case is not of that type.

We fully appreciate the widespread controversy among the members of the legal profession over the problem raised by this case. It is a problem that rests on what has been one of the most hazy frontiers of the discovery process. But until some rule or statute definitely prescribes otherwise, we are not justified in permitting discovery in a situation of this nature as a matter of unqualified right. When Rule 26 and the other discovery rules were adopted, this Court and the members of the bar in general certainly did not believe or contemplate that all the files and mental processes of lawyers were thereby opened to the free scrutiny of their adversaries. And we refuse to interpret the rules at this time so as to reach so harsh and unwarranted a result.

We therefore affirm the judgment of the Circuit Court of Appeals.
Affirmed.

Mr. Justice JACKSON, concurring. . . .

The primary effect of the practice advocated here would be on the legal profession itself. But it too often is overlooked that the lawyer and the law office are indispensable parts of our administration of justice. Law-abiding people can go nowhere else to learn the ever changing and constantly multiplying rules by which they must behave and to obtain redress for their wrongs. The welfare and tone of the legal profession is therefore of prime consequence to society, which would feel the consequences of such a practice as petitioner urges secondarily but certainly. . . .

Counsel for the petitioner candidly said on argument that he wanted this information to help prepare himself to examine witnesses, to make sure he overlooked nothing. He bases his claim to it in his brief on the view that the Rules were to do away with the old situation where a law suit developed into "a battle of wits between counsel." But a common law trial is and always should be an adversary proceeding. Discovery was hardly intended to enable a learned profession to perform its functions either without wits or on wits borrowed from the adversary.

The real purpose and the probable effect of the practice ordered by the district court would be to put trials on a level even lower than a "battle of wits." I can conceive of no practice more demoralizing to the Bar than to require a lawyer to write out and deliver to his adversary an account of what witnesses have told him. Even if his recollection were perfect, the statement would be his language permeated with his inferences. Everyone who has tried it knows that it is almost impossible so fairly to record the expressions and emphasis of a witness that when he testifies in the environment of the court and under the influence of the leading question there will not be departures in some respects. Whenever the testimony of the witness would differ from the "exact" statement the lawyer had delivered, the lawyer's statement would be whipped out to impeach the witness. Counsel producing his adversary's "inexact" statement could lose nothing by saying, "Here is a contradiction, gentlemen of the jury. I do not know whether it is my adversary or his witness who is not telling the truth, but one is not." Of course, if this practice were adopted, that scene would be repeated over and over again. The lawyer who delivers such statements often would find himself branded a deceiver afraid to take the stand to support his own version of the witness's conversation with him, or else he will have to go on the stand to defend his own credibility—perhaps against that of his chief witness, or possibly even his client.

Every lawyer dislikes to take the witness stand and will do so only for grave reasons. This is partly because it is not his role; he is almost invariably a poor witness. But he steps out of professional character to do it. He regrets it; the profession discourages it. But the practice advocated here is one which would force him to be a witness, not as to what he has seen or done but as to other witnesses' stories, and not because he wants to do so but in self-defense.

And what is the lawyer to do who has interviewed one whom he believes to be a biased, lying or hostile witness to get his unfavorable statements and know what to meet? He must record and deliver such statements even though he would not vouch for the credibility of the witness by calling him. Perhaps the other side would not want to call him either, but the attorney is open to the charge of suppressing evidence at the trial if he fails to call such a hostile witness even though he never regarded him as reliable or truthful. . . .

Mr. Justice FRANKFURTER joins in this opinion.

■ NOTES ON WORK PRODUCT PROTECTION

1. Let us skip the part of *Hickman* that says the attorney-client privilege does *not* apply to statements by crew members to Samuel Fortenbaugh, lawyer for the tugboat company. We will consider this point in connection with the *Upjohn* case, coming up next, which deals with the attorney-client privilege. Let us look instead at the work product protection that the Court crafts. First of all, what did plaintiffs want from Fortenbaugh?

2. Up until now, you have been looking at a discovery system designed to allow one side to discover from the other everything that might be relevant—using the term "relevant" in its broadest sense—and holding back from discovery only such material as might be burdensome or privileged or overly invasive of the privacy of the other side. The efforts of lawyers, which for the most part their clients pay for in the long run, are considerable. Now all of a sudden we are concerned about the lawyers. Why?

3. Twice the Court says the tugboat company—which means as a practical matter Samuel Fortenbaugh acting on its behalf—must answer "searching interrogatories" about what happened. The Court adds that "full and honest answers" to such interrogatories "would necessarily have included all pertinent information," and that *nobody* says (plaintiff "makes no suggestion, and we cannot assume") that the tug owners or Fortenbaugh were "incomplete or dishonest" in their answers. And again, the Court says the answers "serve to reveal the facts in Fortenbaugh's possession to the fullest possible extent consistent with public policy." Really? Are you convinced? What does "consistent with public policy mean" if the answers are "full and complete"?

4. The Court in *Hickman* takes pains to say the protection of work product is not absolute. Does *Hickman* recognize "degrees" of protection? Are there differences, for example, between oral and written statements by eyewitnesses? How about "thoughts" or "theories" of the attorney? See Commissioner of Revenue v. Comcast Corp., 901 N.E.2d 1185, 1202 (Mass. 2009) (courts disagree whether "opinion" work product is absolutely protected, or merely receives "heightened" protection; even if not absolute, disclosure is required "only in rare or 'extremely unusual' circumstances," and Commissioner did not satisfy standard in seeking house counsel's communications with outside tax accountants on sale of stock under antitrust judgment). What does it take to overcome work product protection?

5. Now look at FRCP 23(b)(3). Adopted in 1970, this provision was designed to codify *Hickman.*

(a) As set out in FRCP 23(b)(3), work product protection applies to "documents and tangible things" that are "prepared in anticipation of trial." Does this language match the scope of work product protection developed in *Hickman*? Note also that FRCP 23(b)(3)(B) indicates that *if* a court orders disclosure of work product, it "must protect against disclosure of the mental impressions, conclusions, opinions, or legal theories of a party's attorney or other representative." Does this phrase *expand* work product protection? Is *all* such material embraced by the phrase "document and tangible things"? See In re Seagate Technology, 497 F.3d 1360, 1376 (Fed. Cir. 2007) (*Hickman's* work product doctrine was "partially codified" in FRCP 26, but courts continue to apply *Hickman* to nontangible matters; otherwise the doctrine would protect files, but "attorneys themselves would have no work product objection" to depositions); State ex rel. Rogers v. Cohen, 262 S.W.3d 648, 652 (Mo. 2008) (work product protection covers "documents or tangible things," and also "mental impressions" that receive "complete protection").

(b) Notice that work product protection in FRCP 26(b)(3) reaches documents and tangible things prepared in anticipation of litigation or for trial by the "attorney" for a party, and more generally by "its representative," which includes a "consultant, surety, indemnitor, insurer, or agent." Does *Hickman* reach trial preparation material produced by the efforts of such other people? Does it reach material produced through the efforts of investigators working for a party's attorney? Who else does FRCP 26(b)(3) embrace? See, e.g., Henderson v. Newport County Regional Young Men's Christian Association, 966 A.2d 1242 (R.I. 2009) (in suit against nonprofit alleging that it negligently hired and supervised gymnastics coach who inappropriately touched athlete, report prepared by risk abuse management company, when defense counsel asked defendant's board to review "staff policies and procedure" in anticipation of potential litigation, was within work product protection; it is not necessary for litigation to have been commenced; work product "encompasses any material gathered in anticipation of litigation," whether or not the attorney prepared it; rationale is to prevent one attorney from "freeloading" on adversary's work) (plaintiff did not show substantial need).

6. How imminent must the prospect of litigation be? See Compton v. Safeway, Inc., 169 P.3d 135, 137 (Colo. 2007) (in deliveryman's suit for trip-and-fall injury on defendant's premises, recorded statements by employees to store's risk management and loss control department, taken a month after the accident when plaintiff's lawyer contacted the store and said it was responsible, were not work product; there was no "substantial probability of imminent litigation," and statements were taken in ordinary course of business; litigation did not become probable until a month later when Safeway denied claim) (Safeway is not independently insured, but owns company that insures it).

   7. What facts in *Hickman* cut *against* allowing the sought-after discovery? Under FRCP 26(b)(3), what facts would count, in another case, in favor of discovery? In discussing "substantial need," which is the term used in FRCP 26(b)(3) to describe the showing that justifies production despite the work product doctrine, the ACN comments that courts should consider whether, "even if [the information seeker] obtains the information by independent means," it may not be "the substantial equivalent" of what he seeks in discovery. The ACN comment also alludes to a witness who gave "a fresh and contemporaneous account in a written statement" but is available to the information seeker "only a substantial time thereafter."

   (a) Courts do not always think passage of time suffices to overcome work product protection, particularly if the information seeker has not tried other channels. Compare Duffy v. Wilson, 289 S.W.3d 555 (Ky. 2009) (in suit arising out of death of high school football player after practice, work product included statements taken by insurance adjuster from school personnel; insurer was investigating circumstances to defend litigation or claims; fact that statements were made "more closely in time" to the death than "any statements obtainable now" did not overcome protection; plaintiffs "made no attempt to take depositions," and witnesses were still available; death occurred on July 19, 2006; interviews happened on August 1 and 2; suit was filed in January 2007; motions to obtain interviews happened on August 1 and 2, a year after interviews) with Cardenas v. Jerath, 180 P.3d 415 (Colo. 2008) (in suit against hospital arising out of birth of child with neurological injuries, defense lawyer investigated circumstances of birth, and hospital did not conduct "routine factual investigation" of its own; since "factual information concerning the medical care" was essential to plaintiff's case, and hospital did not do its own investigation, and since four years had elapsed, memory of labor and delivery nurse may "differ from the contemporaneous sense impressions" she provided to lawyer shortly thereafter, plaintiff showed substantial hardship and was entitled to lawyer's report).

   (b) One who talks to a lawyer is entitled to get his own statement from the lawyer without making a showing of substantial need. See FRCP 26(b)(3)(C). Why? If any surviving crew member had brought suit, what does this provision suggest to his lawyer?

F   ATTORNEY-CLIENT PRIVILEGE

Discovery has always exempted material covered by "privilege," and far and away the most important privilege—or at least the one most often invoked in this setting—is the privilege covering confidential communications between attorneys and their clients.

As you will see when you read the *Upjohn* decision, FRE 501 provides that federal courts apply *state* privilege rules if state law supplies the rule of decision, which means for the most part "diversity cases." Otherwise federal courts apply federal privilege law. The latter is a matter of "common law interpreted in light of reason and experience." Behind this mild language lurks a larger drama: The framers of the Evidence Rules thought privilege law was "procedural" for *Erie* purposes, and they proposed to narrow many privileges, particularly the two spousal privileges (one covering confidential communications between spouses, the other covering spousal testimony). On both points, Congress disagreed, and FRE 501 was the result. See generally 2 Mueller & Kirkpatrick, Federal Evidence §5:1 (3d ed. 2007) (also describing struggle provoked by proposed state secrets privilege and congressional reactions).

While work product protection belongs to the lawyer, the attorney-client privilege belongs to the client. Since most inquiries that might disclose privileged material are directed to the lawyer, however, it is the lawyer who usually claims the privilege on his client's behalf (in most cases, the lawyer is ethically obliged, and presumptively entitled, to do so). Usually communications between lawyer and client in private settings are presumed to be confidential, but in less common situations where communications occur in public, or where the client intends later disclosure, the privilege does not apply.

In general, privileges must be claimed in timely fashion or they are lost. Recall that the scope of discovery, as defined in FRCP 26(b)(1), includes "nonprivileged matter," which means that privileged matter is not discoverable. Hence privilege claims often arise during discovery. As amended in 1993, FRCP 26(b)(5) says that a party who claims that material is privileged must "expressly make the claim" and "describe the nature" of privileged material "in a manner that" enables the court to decide the issue—although the claimant may do so "without revealing" the privileged matter itself. Also claims of privilege are to be discussed in the initial discovery conference. See FRCP 26(e)(2).

Among the most intractable issues in applying the privilege, perhaps two loom largest. One is its scope when the client is a corporation or other entity, and on this point the framers of the Rules of Evidence made the decision that the topic was too hot to handle, so they proposed a detailed rule governing attorney-client privilege but did not resolve this issue. The second intractable issue involves conduct that waives the privilege, and this matter is addressed—at least in part—by a "clawback" provision that was added to FRCP 26(b)(5)(B) in 2006, and by FRE 502, which Congress enacted in 2007. We turn to these matters now.

Jeremy Bentham

Jeremy Bentham was an English utilitarian philosopher (1748-1832) and a bit of a curmudgeon (at his request, his body was dissected after his death in a public anatomy lecture, and his skeleton was stored in a wooden cabinet called the "auto-icon," padded out so that it appears that the man himself is seated in a chair behind a glass pane, still kept at University College London). Among lawyers, he is remembered for his scathing critique of the attorney-client privilege, asking "wherein will consist the mischief" if such a privilege were not recognized? His answer: "The [client] by the supposition is guilty, and if not, by the supposition there is nothing to betray; let the law advisor say everything he has heard," and the client "cannot have anything to fear from it." And abolishing the privilege would keep the guilty person from getting "quite so much assistance from his law advisor . . . as he may at present." See Bentham, Rationale of Judicial Evidence, 301-304 (1827). An early twentieth-century commentator, John Henry Wigmore (a giant in the field of American Evidence law, who died in 1943), gave grudging support to the privilege, but he narrowed it as much as he could, and later Charles T. McCormick (another giant in the field) mostly agreed with Wigmore but was slightly more generous in recognizing privacy concerns. You will see that the Court in *Upjohn* is more sympathetic to the privilege. How would you answer Bentham's charges, or do you find yourself sympathizing with him?

UPJOHN COMPANY v. UNITED STATES

United States Supreme Court
449 U.S. 383 (1981)

Justice Rehnquist delivered the opinion of the Court.

We granted certiorari in this case to address important questions concerning the scope of the attorney-client privilege in the corporate context and the applicability of the work-product doctrine in proceedings to enforce tax summonses. With respect to the privilege question the parties and various *amici* have described our task as one of choosing between two "tests" which have gained adherents in the courts of appeals. We are acutely aware, however, that we sit to decide concrete cases and not abstract propositions of law. We decline to lay down a broad rule or series of rules to govern all conceivable future questions in this area, even were we able to do so. We can and do, however, conclude that the attorney-client privilege protects the communications involved in this case from compelled disclosure and that the work-product doctrine does apply in tax summons enforcement proceedings.

I

Petitioner Upjohn Co. manufactures and sells pharmaceuticals here and abroad. In January 1976 independent accountants conducting an audit of one of Upjohn's foreign subsidiaries discovered that the subsidiary made payments to or for the benefit of foreign government officials in order to secure government business. The accountants, so informed petitioner, Mr. Gerard Thomas, Upjohn's Vice President, Secretary, and General Counsel. Thomas is a member of the Michigan and New York Bars, and has been Upjohn's General Counsel for 20 years. He consulted with outside counsel and R. T. Parfet, Jr., Upjohn's Chairman of the Board. It was decided that the company would conduct an internal investigation of what were termed "questionable payments." As part of this investigation the attorneys prepared a letter containing a questionnaire which was sent to "All Foreign General and Area Managers" over the Chairman's signature. The letter began by noting recent disclosures that several American companies made "possibly illegal" payments to foreign government officials and emphasized that the management needed full information concerning any such payments made by Upjohn. The letter indicated that the Chairman had asked Thomas, identified as "the company's General Counsel," "to conduct an investigation for the purpose of determining the nature and magnitude of any payments made by the Upjohn Company or any of its subsidiaries to any employee or official of a foreign government." The questionnaire sought detailed information concerning such payments. Managers were instructed to treat the investigation as "highly confidential" and not to discuss it with anyone other than Upjohn employees who might be helpful in providing the requested information. Responses were to be sent directly to Thomas. Thomas and outside counsel also interviewed the recipients of the questionnaire and some 33 other Upjohn officers or employees as part of the investigation.

On March 26, 1976, the company voluntarily submitted a preliminary report to the Securities and Exchange Commission on Form 8-K disclosing certain questionable payments. A copy of the report was simultaneously submitted to the Internal Revenue Service, which immediately began an investigation to determine the tax consequences of the payments. Special agents conducting the investigation were given lists by Upjohn of all those interviewed and all who had responded to the questionnaire. On November 23, 1976, the Service issued a summons pursuant to 26 USC §7602 demanding production of:

> All files relative to the investigation conducted under the supervision of Gerard Thomas to identify payments to employees of foreign governments and any

political contributions made by the Upjohn Company or any of its affiliates since January 1, 1971 and to determine whether any funds of the Upjohn Company had been improperly accounted for on the corporate books during the same period. The records should include but not be limited to written questionnaires sent to managers of the Upjohn Company's foreign affiliates, and memorandums or notes of the interviews conducted in the United States and abroad with officers and employees of the Upjohn Company and its subsidiaries.

The company declined to produce the documents specified . . . on the grounds that they were protected from disclosure by the attorney-client privilege and constituted the work product of attorneys prepared in anticipation of litigation. On August 31, 1977, the United States filed a petition seeking enforcement of the summons under 26 USC §§7402(b) and 7604(a) in the United States District Court for the Western District of Michigan. That court adopted the recommendation of a Magistrate who concluded that the summons should be enforced. Petitioners appealed to the Court of Appeals for the Sixth Circuit which rejected the Magistrate's finding of a waiver of the attorney-client privilege, but agreed that the privilege did not apply "[t]o the extent that the communications were made by officers and agents not responsible for directing Upjohn's actions in response to legal advice . . . for the simple reason that the communications were not the 'client's.'" The court reasoned that accepting petitioners' claim for a broader application of the privilege would encourage upper-echelon management to ignore unpleasant facts and create too broad a "zone of silence." Noting that Upjohn's counsel had interviewed officials such as the Chairman and President, the Court of Appeals remanded to the District Court so that a determination of who was within the "control group" could be made. In a concluding footnote the court stated that the work-product doctrine "is not applicable to administrative summonses issued under 26 USC §7602."

II

Federal Rule of Evidence 501 provides that "the privilege of a witness . . . shall be governed by the principles of the common law as they may be interpreted by the courts of the United States in light of reason and experience." The attorney-client privilege is the oldest of the privileges for confidential communications known to the common law. Its purpose is to encourage full and frank communication between attorneys and their clients and thereby promote broader public interests in the observance of law and administration of justice. The privilege recognizes that sound legal advice or advocacy serves public ends and that such advice or advocacy depends upon the lawyer's being fully informed by the client. As we stated last Term in Trammel v. United States, 445 U.S. 40, 51 (1980): "The lawyer-client privilege rests on the need for the advocate and counselor to know all that relates to the client's reasons for seeking representation if the professional mission is to be carried out." And in Fisher v. United States, 425 U.S. 391, 403 (1976), we recognized the purpose of the privilege to be "to encourage clients to make full disclosure to their attorneys." This rationale for the privilege has long been recognized by the Court, see Hunt v. Blackburn, 128 U.S. 464, 470 (1888) (privilege "is founded upon the necessity, in the interest and administration of justice, of the aid of persons having knowledge of the law and skilled in its practice, which assistance can only be safely and readily availed of when free from the consequences or the apprehension of disclosure"). Admittedly complications in the application of the privilege arise when the client is a corporation, which in theory is an artificial creature of the law, and not an individual; but this Court has assumed that the privilege applies when the client is a corporation, and the Government does not contest the general proposition.

The Court of Appeals, however, considered the application of the privilege in the corporate context to present a "different problem," since the client was an inanimate entity and "only the senior management, guiding and integrating the several operations, . . . can be said to possess an identity analogous to the corporation as a whole." The first case to articulate the so-called "control group test" adopted by the court below, Philadelphia v. Westinghouse Electric Corp., 210 F. Supp. 483, 485 (E.D. Pa.), *petition for mandamus and prohibition denied sub nom.* General Electric Co. v. Kirkpatrick, 312 F.2d 742 (3d Cir. 1962), *cert. denied,* 372 U.S. 943 (1963), reflected a similar conceptual approach:

> Keeping in mind that the question is, Is it the corporation which is seeking the lawyer's advice when the asserted privileged communication is made?, the most satisfactory solution, I think, is that if the employee making the communication, of whatever rank he may be, is in a position to control or even to take a substantial part in a decision about any action which the corporation may take upon the advice of the attorney, . . . then, in effect, *he is (or personifies) the corporation* when he makes his disclosure to the lawyer and the privilege would apply. (Emphasis supplied.)

Such a view, we think, overlooks the fact that the privilege exists to protect not only the giving of professional advice to those who can act on it but also the giving of information to the lawyer to enable him to give sound and informed advice. The first step in the resolution of any legal problem is ascertaining the factual background and sifting through the facts with an eye to the legally relevant. See ABA Code of Professional Responsibility, Ethical Consideration 4-1:

> A lawyer should be fully informed of all the facts of the matter he is handling in order for his client to obtain the full advantage of our legal system. It is for the lawyer in the exercise of his independent professional judgment to separate the relevant and important from the irrelevant and unimportant. The observance of the ethical obligation of a lawyer to hold inviolate the confidences and secrets of his client not only

facilitates the full development of facts essential to proper representation of the client but also encourages laymen to seek early legal assistance.

See also Hickman v. Taylor, 329 U.S. 495, 511 (1947).

In the case of the individual client the provider of information and the person who acts on the lawyer's advice are one and the same. In the corporate context, however, it will frequently be employees beyond the control group as defined by the court below—"officers and agents . . . responsible for directing [the company's] actions in response to legal advice"—who will possess the information needed by the corporation's lawyers. Middle-level- and indeed lower-level-employees can, by actions within the scope of their employment, embroil the corporation in serious legal difficulties, and it is only natural that these employees would have the relevant information needed by corporate counsel if he is adequately to advise the client with respect to such actual or potential difficulties. This fact was noted in Diversified Industries, Inc. v. Meredith, 572 F.2d 596 (CA8 1978) (en banc):

> In a corporation, it may be necessary to glean information relevant to a legal problem from middle management or non-management personnel as well as from top executives. The attorney dealing with a complex legal problem "is thus faced with a 'Hobson's choice.' If he interviews employees not having 'the very highest authority,' their communications to him will not be privileged. If, on the other hand, he interviews *only* those employees with the 'very highest authority,' he may find it extremely difficult, if not impossible, to determine what happened."

The control group test adopted by the court below thus frustrates the very purpose of the privilege by discouraging the communication of relevant information by employees of the client to attorneys seeking to render legal advice to the client corporation. The attorney's advice will also frequently be more significant to noncontrol group members than to those who officially sanction the advice, and the control group test makes it more difficult to convey full and frank legal advice to the employees who will put into effect the client corporation's policy. See, *e.g.*, Duplan Corp. v. Deering Milliken, Inc., 397 F. Supp. 1146, 1164 (D.S.C. 1974) ("After the lawyer forms his or her opinion, it is of no immediate benefit to the Chairman of the Board or the President. It must be given to the corporate personnel who will apply it").

The narrow scope given the attorney-client privilege by the court below not only makes it difficult for corporate attorneys to formulate sound advice when their client is faced with a specific legal problem but also threatens to limit the valuable efforts of corporate counsel to ensure their client's compliance with the law. In light of the vast and complicated array of regulatory legislation confronting the modern corporation, corporations, unlike most individuals, "constantly go to lawyers to find out how to obey the law," Burnham, The Attorney-Client Privilege in the Corporate Arena, 24 Bus. Law. 901,

913 (1969), particularly since compliance with the law in this area is hardly an instinctive matter, see, *e.g.,* United States v. United States Gypsum Co., 438 U.S. 422, 440-441 (1978) ("the behavior proscribed by the [Sherman] Act is often difficult to distinguish from the gray zone of socially acceptable and economically justifiable business conduct").[2] The test adopted by the court below is difficult to apply in practice, though no abstractly formulated and unvarying "test" will necessarily enable courts to decide questions such as this with mathematical precision. But if the purpose of the attorney-client privilege is to be served, the attorney and client must be able to predict with some degree of certainty whether particular discussions will be protected. An uncertain privilege, or one which purports to be certain but results in widely varying applications by the courts, is little better than no privilege at all. The very terms of the test adopted by the court below suggest the unpredictability of its application. The test restricts the availability of the privilege to those officers who play a "substantial role" in deciding and directing a corporation's legal response. Disparate decisions in cases applying this test illustrate its unpredictability. Compare, *e.g.,* Hogan v. Zletz, 43 F.R.D. 308, 315-316 (N.D. Okl. 1967), *aff'd in part sub nom.* Natta v. Hogan, 392 F.2d 686 (10th Cir. 1968) (control group includes managers and assistant managers of patent division and research and development department), with Congoleum Industries, Inc. v. GAF Corp., 49 F.R.D. 82, 83-85 (E.D. Pa. 1969), *aff'd,* 478 F.2d 1398 (3d Cir. 1973) (control group includes only division and corporate vice presidents, and not two directors of research and vice president for production and research).

The communications at issue were made by Upjohn employees[3] to counsel for Upjohn acting as such, at the direction of corporate superiors in order to secure legal advice from counsel. As the Magistrate found, "Mr. Thomas consulted with the Chairman of the Board and outside counsel and thereafter conducted a factual investigation to determine the nature and extent of the questionable payments *and to be in a position to give legal advice to the company with respect to the payments.*" (Emphasis supplied.) Information, not available from upper-echelon management, was needed to supply a

---

[2] The Government argues that the risk of civil or criminal liability suffices to ensure that corporations will seek legal advice in the absence of the protection of the privilege. This response ignores the fact that the depth and quality of any investigations, to ensure compliance with the law would suffer, even were they undertaken. The response also proves too much, since it applies to all communications covered by the privilege: an individual trying to comply with the law or faced with a legal problem also has strong incentive to disclose information to his lawyer, yet the common law has recognized the value of the privilege in further facilitating communications.

[3] Seven of the eighty-six employees interviewed by counsel had terminated their employment with Upjohn at the time of the interview. Petitioners argue that the privilege should nonetheless apply to communications by these former employees concerning activities during their period of employment. Neither the District Court nor the Court of Appeals had occasion to address this issue, and we decline to decide it without the benefit of treatment below.

basis for legal advice concerning compliance with securities and tax laws, foreign laws, currency regulations, duties to shareholders, and potential litigation in each of these areas. The communications concerned matters within the scope of the employees' corporate duties, and the employees themselves were sufficiently aware that they were being questioned in order that the corporation could obtain legal advice. The questionnaire identified Thomas as "the company's General Counsel" and referred in its opening sentence to the possible illegality of payments such as the ones on which information was sought. A statement of policy accompanying the questionnaire clearly indicated the legal implications of the investigation. The policy statement was issued "in order that there be no uncertainty in the future as to the policy with respect to the practices which are the subject of this investigation." It began "Upjohn will comply with all laws and regulations," and stated that commissions or payments "will not be used as a subterfuge for bribes or illegal payments" and that all payments must be "proper and legal." Any future agreements with foreign distributors or agents were to be approved "by a company attorney" and any questions concerning the policy were to be referred "to the company's General Counsel." This statement was issued to Upjohn employees worldwide, so that even those interviewees not receiving a questionnaire were aware of the legal implications of the interviews. Pursuant to explicit instructions from the Chairman of the Board, the communications were considered "highly confidential" when made, and have been kept confidential by the company.[5] Consistent with the underlying purposes of the attorney-client privilege, these communications must be protected against compelled disclosure.

The Court of Appeals declined to extend the attorney-client privilege beyond the limits of the control group test for fear that doing so would entail severe burdens on discovery and create a broad "zone of silence" over corporate affairs. Application of the attorney-client privilege to communications such as those involved here, however, puts the adversary in no worse position than if the communications had never taken place. The privilege only protects disclosure of communications; it does not protect disclosure of the underlying facts by those who communicated with the attorney:

> [T]he protection of the privilege extends only to *communications* and not to facts. A fact is one thing and a communication concerning that fact is an entirely different thing. The client cannot be compelled to answer the question, "What did you say or write to the attorney?" but may not refuse to disclose any relevant fact within his knowledge merely because he incorporated a statement of such fact into his communication to his attorney.

---

[5] See Magistrate's opinion: "The responses to the questionnaires and the notes of the interviews have been treated as confidential material and have not been disclosed to anyone except Mr. Thomas and outside counsel."

Here the Government was free to question the employees who communicated with Thomas and outside counsel. Upjohn has provided the IRS with a list of such employees, and the IRS has already interviewed some 25 of them. While it would probably be more convenient for the Government to secure the results of petitioner's internal investigation by simply subpoenaing the questionnaires and notes taken by petitioner's attorneys, such considerations of convenience do not overcome the policies served by the attorney-client privilege. As Justice Jackson noted in his concurring opinion in Hickman v. Taylor: "Discovery was hardly intended to enable a learned profession to perform its functions . . . on wits borrowed from the adversary."

Needless to say, we decide only the case before us, and do not undertake to draft a set of rules which should govern challenges to investigatory subpoenas. Any such approach would violate the spirit of FRE 501. While such a "case-by-case" basis may to some slight extent undermine desirable certainty in the boundaries of the attorney-client privilege, it obeys the spirit of the Rules. At the same time we conclude that the narrow "control group test" sanctioned by the Court of Appeals, in this case cannot, consistent with "the principles of the common law as . . . interpreted . . . in the light of reason and experience," FRE 501, govern the development of the law in this area.

III

Our decision that the communications by Upjohn employees to counsel are covered by the attorney-client privilege disposes of the case so far as the responses to the questionnaires and any notes reflecting responses to interview questions are concerned. The summons reaches further, however, and Thomas has testified that his notes and memoranda of interviews go beyond recording responses to his questions. To the extent that the material subject to the summons is not protected by the attorney-client privilege as disclosing communications between an employee and counsel, we must reach the ruling by the Court of Appeals that the work-product doctrine does not apply to summonses issued under 26 USC §7602.[6]

The Government concedes, wisely, that the Court of Appeals erred and that the work-product doctrine does apply to IRS summonses. This doctrine was announced by the Court over 30 years ago in Hickman v. Taylor. . . . The "strong public policy" underlying the work-product doctrine was reaffirmed recently in United States v. Nobles, 422 U.S. 225, 236-240 (1975), and has been substantially incorporated in Federal Rule of Civil Procedure 26(b)(3).

---

[6] The following discussion will also be relevant to counsel's notes and memoranda of interviews with the seven former employees should it be determined that the attorney-client privilege does not apply to them. See n.3, *supra*.

... While conceding the applicability of the work-product doctrine, the Government asserts that it has made a sufficient showing of necessity to overcome its protections. The Magistrate apparently so found. The Government relies on the following language in *Hickman*:

> We do not mean to say that all written materials obtained or prepared by an adversary's counsel with an eye toward litigation are necessarily free from discovery in all cases. Where relevant and nonprivileged facts remain hidden in an attorney's file and where production of those facts is essential to the preparation of one's case, discovery may properly be had.... And production might be justified where the witnesses are no longer available or can be reached only with difficulty.

The Government stresses that interviewees are scattered across the globe and that Upjohn has forbidden its employees to answer questions it considers irrelevant. The above-quoted language from *Hickman*, however, did not apply to "oral statements made by witnesses ... whether presently in the form of [the attorney's] mental impressions or memoranda." As to such material the Court did "not believe that any showing of necessity can be made under the circumstances of this case so as to justify production.... If there should be a rare situation justifying production of these matters petitioner's case is not of that type." Forcing an attorney to disclose notes and memoranda of witnesses' oral statements is particularly disfavored because it tends to reveal the attorney's mental processes.[8]

Rule 26 accords special protection to work product revealing the attorney's mental processes. The Rule permits disclosure of documents and tangible things constituting attorney work product upon a showing of substantial need and inability to obtain the equivalent without undue hardship. This was the standard applied by the Magistrate. Rule 26 goes on, however, to state that "[i]n ordering discovery of such materials when the required showing has been made, the court shall protect against disclosure of the mental impressions, conclusions, opinions or legal theories of an attorney or other representative of a party concerning the litigation." Although this language does not specifically refer to memoranda based on oral statements of witnesses, the *Hickman* court stressed the danger that compelled disclosure of such memoranda would reveal the attorney's mental processes. It is clear that this is the sort of material the draftsmen of the Rule had in mind as deserving special protection. See ACN to 1970 Amendment ("The subdivision ... goes on to protect against disclosure the mental impressions, conclusions, opinions, or legal theories ... of an attorney or other

---

[8] Thomas described his notes of the interviews as containing "what I considered to be the important questions, the substance of the responses to them, my beliefs as to the importance of these, my beliefs as to how they related to the inquiry, my thoughts as to how they related to other questions. In some instances they might even suggest other questions that I would have to ask or things that I needed to find elsewhere."

representative of a party. The *Hickman* opinion drew special attention to the need for protecting an attorney against discovery of memoranda prepared from recollection of oral interviews. The courts have steadfastly safeguarded against disclosure of lawyers' mental impressions and legal theories . . .").

Based on the foregoing, some courts have concluded that *no* showing of necessity can overcome protection of work product which is based on oral statements from witnesses. Those courts declining to adopt an absolute rule have nonetheless recognized that such material is entitled to special protection.

We do not decide the issue at this time. . . . The notes and memoranda sought by the Government here, however, are work product based on oral statements. If they reveal communications, they are, in this case, protected by the attorney-client privilege. To the extent they do not reveal communications, they reveal the attorneys' mental processes in evaluating the communications. As Rule 26 and *Hickman* make clear, such work product cannot be disclosed simply on a showing of substantial need and inability to obtain the equivalent without undue hardship.

While we are not prepared at this juncture to say that such material is always protected by the work-product rule, we think a far stronger showing of necessity and unavailability by other means than was made by the Government or applied by the Magistrate in this case would be necessary to compel disclosure. . . .

Accordingly, the judgment of the Court of Appeals is reversed, and the case remanded for further proceedings.

It is so ordered.

[The concurring opinion by Chief Justice Burger is omitted.]

■ NOTES ON ATTORNEY-CLIENT PRIVILEGE IN THE CORPORATE SETTING

1. In *Upjohn*, what was the government seeking and why?

2. The Court says it is not trying "to lay down a broad rule or series of rules" to govern the privilege matter, and later the Court says FRE 501 requires a "case-by-case" approach and it was deciding "only the case before us." These comments hint at the drama behind FRE 501 and the statute enacted by Congress, which requires that changes in *privilege* rules (but not *other* Rules of Evidence) to be *enacted* by Congress in order to take effect (Rules in other areas can be changed by the usual rulemaking process, with Court approval and notification of Congress, *unless* Congress intervenes to block such changes). See 28 USC §2074(c) (any rule "creating, abolishing, or modifying an evidentiary privilege shall have no force or effect unless approved by Act of Congress").

3. For corporate and organizational clients, courts have considered at least four possible approaches, but the two extremes never garnered much support. One extreme would deny all protection of the privilege to corporate clients, and the other would extend the privilege to everyone employed by the corporation who speaks with a lawyer. What remains are intermediate positions, of which the two most common are the so-called control group standard and some variant of the "subject matter" standard. On what grounds does *Upjohn* criticize the "control group" standard?

(a) Bearing in mind the warning that the Court was deciding only the case before it, what criteria determine the reach of the privilege in the corporate setting? One apparent criterion requires a purpose to obtain legal advice—but *this* requirement applies to *all* applications of the privilege, and hardly counts as a special limit for corporate clients. What do you make of the notion that the employees spoke to the lawyer at the request of upper-echelon management? What do you make of the reference to maintaining secrecy *within the corporation*? What would be entailed in this step?

(b) At the heart of *Upjohn* is the notion that whoever speaks to the lawyer, the privilege applies only if the spokesperson talks about something in the "subject matter" of his duties. A notion close to this one emerged more than ten years earlier in a decision by the Seventh Circuit in the *Harper & Row* case, which the Court in *Upjohn* cited in another connection (in a passage edited from the opinion above). See Harper & Row Publishers, Inc. v. Decker, 423 F.2d 487, 491-492 (7th Cir. 1970), *aff'd by equally divided Court,* 400 U.S. 348 (1971). Does *Upjohn*'s version of the privilege solve the problem of vagueness, on which ground the Court criticizes the "control group" standard?

(c) Recall the *Hickman* decision, which indicated that statements by surviving crew members to the lawyer Fortenbaugh were *not* privileged. If Fortenbaugh had talked to the captain who had charge of the helm at the time, and the captain said the tug collided with a barge, would the *Upjohn* approach suggest that the attorney-client privilege applies? What if Fortenbaugh talked to the galley cook, and asked him to describe what happened? If the answers differ, does the difference make sense?

(d) Ironically, given *Upjohn*'s warnings that the Court was deciding only the case before it, the decision has had widespread impact, not only among federal courts where it is authoritative, but in influencing state law as well. To begin with, the National Conference of Commissioners on Uniform State Laws modified its own version of the rule governing the attorney-client privilege in order to codify *Upjohn*. See Uniform Rule 503 (1986) (defining client to include "corporation" and defining representative of a client whose communications can be privileged as including any person who "makes or receives a confidential communication while acting in the scope of employment"), and a number of states have followed suit by amending their own rules. See, e.g., Texas Rule 503; Vermont Rule 503 (both following Uniform

Rule 502). See also Oregon Evidence Code §503 (differing in wording from the Uniform Rule, but similarly broad in reach). Others states have moved in the same direction by court decision, see, e.g., Keefe v. Bernard, 774 N.E.2d 663 (Iowa 2009); Alliance Construction Solutions, Inc. v. Department of Corrections, 54 P.3d 861 (Colo. 2002); Lexington Public Library v. Clark, 90 S.W.2d 53, 59 (Ky. 2002); Southern Bell Tel. & Tel. Co. v. Deason, 632 So. 2d 1377 (Fla. 1994); Samaritan Foundation v. Goodfarb, 862 P.2d 870 (Ariz. 1993).

(e) Other states, however, still follow the control group standard. See, e.g., Consolidation Coal Co. v. Bucyrus-Erie Co., 432 N.E.2d 240 (Ill. 1982); Leer v. Chicago, Minneapolis, St. Paul and Pacific Railway Co., 308 N.W.2d 305 (Minn. 1981). See also E.I. du Pont de Nemours & Co. v. Forma-Pack, Inc., 718 A.2d 1129 (Md. 1998) (continuing to avoid the question).

4. *Upjohn* accepts the view that the privilege applies not only to individuals, but to corporate or organizational clients, but this view has not gone unchallenged. One form of argument stresses that corporations are heavily regulated, and risk criminal sanctions for violating regulatory rules, so even *without* a privilege corporations will seek legal assistance because they *must.* Note the Court's response in footnote 2. Is this attack on the corporate privilege simply an argument that we don't need a privilege at all because *nobody* can go without a lawyer when one needs to sue or has been sued?

(a) Professor Stephen Saltzburg advances a similar argument in a more elaborate way. He says lawyers will talk to witnesses like the crew members in *Hickman* even *without* protection, pointing out that work product claims can be overcome by showing good cause. And corporate employees are willing to talk with lawyers simply because they are told to do so, and they do not own or control the privilege (it is up to high-ranking officers whether to claim the privilege). See Stephen J. Saltzburg, *Corporate and Related Attorney-Client Privilege Claims: A Suggested Approach*, 12 Hofstra L. Rev. 279, 303-304 (1984) (*Upjohn's* broad privilege gives corporations "the best of two worlds," as their attorneys "have an advantage over other lawyers in securing statements" because corporations "exert a coercive influence" to get employees to talk and, once the corporation obtains their statements, "it freely uses them in any manner it chooses while simultaneously claiming a privilege" to block others from using them). Professor Saltzburg would not deny privilege protection to corporate clients, but would allow it only where agents would also have their own personal privilege in speaking with the lawyer. See also Elizabeth Thornburg, *Sanctifying Secrecy: The Mythology of the Corporate Attorney-Client Privilege*, 69 Notre Dame L. Rev. 157 (1993) (for similar reasons, arguing that privilege should be abolished in this setting; attacking as "myths" the arguments that corporate clients need the privilege to encourage employees to speak with lawyers, or that lawyers need it to encourage them to inquire into facts; privacy interests, which might justify the privilege for individual clients, cannot apply to corporate clients; privilege is socially costly because it must be litigated and hides relevant information).

(b) Consider these arguments. Let us agree that it really is the corporation, rather than employees, that owns the privilege. See, e.g., Commodity Futures Trading Commission v. Weintraub, 471 U.S. 343, 348 (1985) (power to waive corporation's privilege "rests with the corporation's management," to be exercised by officers and directors). Does it follow that narrowing or abolishing the privilege in the corporate setting would have no impact (or negligible impact) on the willingness of corporations to seek legal advice, or on efforts that lawyers would make to obtain information? How often do you think a corporation, after encouraging employees to talk confidentially with counsel, would turn over to the other side the information thus provided or would use it to discipline or fire employees? Often, or seldom? Is that the way modern corporations, with human resource departments or functionally similar officers, discipline or fire employees? Do you think employees who talked to Fortenbaugh were likely to get fired or disciplined? How about Upjohn employees who talked to Girard Thomas?

5. Privilege law has long experienced a chilly reception among academic commentators and courts.

(a) Two giants of the twentieth century were critical of privileges, arguing essentially that they shut out the light, and that their value was unproved. Hence their treatises construed even the attorney-client privilege (the most settled of all of them) in the narrowest possible way, to make it hard for privilege claimants to prevail. See generally 8 Wigmore on Evidence §2291 (McNaughton rev. 1961) (benefits of attorney-client privilege are "indirect and speculative" while "its obstruction is plain and concrete," and it is "an obstacle to the investigation of the truth" and "ought to be strictly confined"); McCormick on Evidence §87 (6th ed. 2006) (quoting Wigmore, but adding that "considerations of privacy" play a role and noting that the attorney acts as "fighter" for his client, and the privilege is "integrally related to an entire code of professional conduct" that could not be altered without changing "the underlying ethical system").

(b) In trying to narrow the privilege, Wigmore listed eight requirements: (1) It applies only when "legal advice" is sought; (2) it applies only when the advice is sought from a "legal adviser in his capacity as such"; (3) it reaches communications "relating to that purpose"; (4) the communication must be "made in confidence"; (5) the communication must be made "by the client"; (6) if so, the communication is "permanently protected" at "his instance"; (7) the privilege protects against disclosure by the client or the lawyer; and (8) it applies unless waived. See Wigmore, supra, §2292. On many points, Wigmore is right: The privilege does apply only when a client seeks legal advice, and the communications must relate to that purpose. These hurdles are easily vaulted, and as a practical matter the points of difficulty arise when lawyers are consulted for personal or business or financial advice. And it is true that the privilege covers only confidential statements (point 4 on the list), but this condition is readily satisfied, and the presence of law office functionaries (secretaries, clerks, paralegals, or experts that the

lawyer retains in order to represent the client effectively) does not defeat a privilege claim. Most courts say the privilege is *not* limited to statements "by the client" (point 5), but extends to statements by the lawyer. It is true that the privilege applies at the "instance" of the client (point 6), but the lawyer can claim the privilege for the client, and the lawyer is *presumed* to be authorized and is *ethically obliged* to do so. Finally, the reference to protecting only against disclosure by the client or lawyer (point 7) incorporates, among other things, Wigmore's opinion that the privilege cannot block disclosure by eavesdroppers. The modern attitude on this point, however, is more sympathetic to the privilege claimant if he has taken reasonable steps to protect the confidentiality of the communication. See Mueller & Kirkpatrick, Evidence §§5.9-5.29 (4th ed. 2009). See also FRCP 26(b)(5) (allowing party who produces privileged matter to "notify" the recipient, who is then obliged to "return, sequester, or destroy" the matter and cannot "use or disclose" it until the privilege claim is resolved); FRE 502 (in cases of accidental disclosure in discovery, claimant does *not* lose protection of privilege if she had taken reasonable steps to guard against disclosure and takes reasonable steps after disclosure to rectify the error).

(c) The author of this work thinks the privilege is critical to our system and makes a real contribution to the administration of justice. See Mueller & Kirkpatrick, Evidence §5.8 (4th ed. 2009) (without privilege, "any client would be deterred from seeking legal assistance in the first instance, or at least inhibited from making full and candid disclosure," so attorneys "would be deprived of the factual information necessary to provide effective legal representation") (privilege "helps lawyers provide the legal advice, and render legal services that are needed if clients are to assert their rights effectively").

(d) In reaching your own conclusion, ask yourself some questions: In a world in which the privilege exists, what do lawyers say to clients—and to agents or employees of clients, like the people to whom the lawyer in *Upjohn* spoke? In a world in which the privilege was taken away or did not apply (because it is limited by something like the "control group" standard rejected by *Upjohn*), what would lawyers be obliged to say—if they have any sense of decency—to clients and others to whom they spoke?

6. The *Upjohn* standard can enlarge the scope of protection afforded by the privilege beyond what the control group standard would provide. See, e.g., The St. Luke Hospitals, Inc. v. Kopowski, 160 S.W.3d 771, 776 (Ky. 2005) (in malpractice suit against hospital for death of newborn, statements by nurses to risk management officer, made at behest of hospital's attorney, were privileged under KRE 503, which embodies subject matter standard; they are immune from discovery; privilege differs from work product in that privileged communications are not discoverable even when information is "essential to the underlying case and cannot be obtained from another source").

7. In footnote 3 of *Upjohn,* the Court left open the question whether the privilege extends to "former employees" interviewed about "questionable payments" they might have been involved in. Modern decisions conclude that the corporation's privilege *does* extend to conversations with people who used to work for the company and now speak to the corporation's lawyer about their work. See, e.g., In re Allen, 106 F.3d 582, 605-606 (4th Cir. 1997) (*Upjohn* analysis "applies equally to former employees"); Denver Post Corp. v. University of Colorado, 739 P.2d 874, 880-881 (Colo. App. 1987) (applying *Upjohn* to interviews between university counsel and former employees) (but University waived privilege). Ethical rules bar lawyers from speaking *ex parte* with parties on the other side of a lawsuit who are represented by other lawyers. If the privilege extends to employees and *former employees* of a corporate party, does it follow that a lawyer on the other side cannot contact them *ex parte*? See Niesig v. Team I, 558 N.E.2d 1030 (N.Y. 1990) (extent of privilege in *Upjohn* is "an entirely different subject" from question whether corporate employee is a "party" for purpose of ethical rule barring *ex parte* communication; for the latter purpose, corporate party includes "corporate employees whose acts or omissions in the matter under inquiry are binding on the corporation," being "in effect, the corporation's 'alter ego,'" plus those whose acts or omissions are "imputed to the corporation for purposes of its liability," and "employees implementing the advice of counsel," but all others "may be interviewed informally").

8. Under FRCP 26(b)(5), a party claiming a privilege in discovery must do so "expressly" and "describe the nature of the documents, communications, or tangible things" being withheld. It won't do simply to hold back material to which a privilege attaches. This "express" claim can stop short of "revealing" the matter covered by the privilege, but yet it is to "enable other parties to assess the claim." Courts may conduct *in camera* examinations of documents claimed to be privileged, but privilege claimants must help by generating "privilege logs" describing the material claimed to be privileged and explaining reasons. Here is how the Colorado Supreme Court describes it:

> A privilege log identifies the document and explains why it should not be disclosed. One of the purposes for requiring the party resisting discovery to file a privilege log is to reduce the need for in camera inspections of documents. If, after reviewing the privilege log, the party seeking discovery still contends the privilege or other basis for nondisclosure does not apply, and the parties cannot resolve the dispute informally, the party resisting discovery may request in camera inspection of the documents listed on the privilege log. During the in camera inspection, the trial court [applies] the appropriate balancing test, and makes its decision requiring or restricting disclosure.

DeSantis v. Simon, 209 P.3d 1069, 1074 (Colo. 2009) (doctor did not have privilege to refuse to produce records of disciplinary proceedings against him resulting in suspension of his license).

(a) On the burdens shouldered by objecting parties, see AAB Joint Venture v. United States, 75 Fed. Cl. 432, 447 (Fed. Cl. 2007) (defense described author and addressee, and gave brief description of documents; this

"conclusory statement" did not satisfy burden for claiming privilege; defendant "must set forth objective facts" to show that requirements of privilege are met); Burlington Northern & Santa Fe Ry. Co. v. District Court, 408 F.3d 1142 (9th Cir. 2005) ("boilerplate objections or blanket refusals" in response to a request for production do not suffice; even so, there is no *per se* rule that failing to produce a privilege log within the 30 days allowed to respond to production request waives privilege; court should consider "degree to which" objection or privilege claim enables court and opposition to evaluate claim, timeliness of objection, and accompanying information, magnitude of request for production, and other circumstances that may make it "unusually easy" or "unusually hard" to respond: "These factors should be applied in the context of a holistic reasonableness analysis, intended to forestall needless waste of time and resources, as well as tactical manipulation of the rules and the discovery process. They should not be applied as a mechanistic determination of whether the information is provided in a particular format. Finally, the application of these factors shall be subject to any applicable local rules, agreements or stipulations among the litigants, and discovery or protective orders.") (footnote says that "in discovery-intensive litigation" compiling privilege log in 30 days may be "exceedingly difficult," and litigants seeking discovery may abuse rule by propounding "exhaustive and simultaneous" requests; litigants may secure appropriate agreement or protective order).

9. A significant difficulty for privilege claimants is that claims and defenses advanced in the suit may waive the privilege. See In re EchoStar Communications Corp., 448 F.3d 1294, 1302 (Fed. Cir. 2006) (in connection with claim for willful patent infringement, advice-of-counsel defense waives privilege for communications, including documentary communications like opinion letters and memoranda; defense also waives work product protection for communication between lawyer and client, but not for documents analyzing law, facts, trial strategy, which reflected attorney's mental impressions not given to client). See also Richard Marcus, *The Perils of Privilege: Waiver and the Litigator*, 84 Mich. L. Rev. 1605 (1986).

10. Another significant difficulty for privilege claimants is that the pressures of discovery can make it not only costly, but sometimes difficult or even impossible, to examine every requested document to determine whether it contains privileged matter or work product. In recognition of this fact, a "claw-back" provision was added to FRCP 26 in 2006. See FRCP 26(b)(5)(B) (allowing a party claiming privilege or work product protection to notify the other side that information turned over during discovery is subject to such a claim, and explaining "the basis" for the claim; upon such notice, the other side must "promptly return, sequester, or destroy the specified information and any copies" and must not "use or disclose" it until the claim is resolved). Implicitly, this clawback provision assumes that production of privileged matter or work product does not *necessarily* waive privilege or work product claims. FRE 502, enacted by Congress in 2007, makes this point expressly:

Disclosure in a federal proceeding "does not operate as a waiver" in that proceeding if it is "inadvertent" and the claimant "took reasonable steps to prevent disclosure" and then "took reasonable steps to rectify the error" (citing FRCP 26(b)(5)(B)). FRE 502 also addresses related issues (any waiver extends to "undisclosed" matter only if the waiver was "intentional" and the undisclosed matter concerns "the same subject matter" and "ought in fairness" to be considered along with what was disclosed). Finally, FRE 502 attempts to reconcile *Erie* issues when disclosures that might constitute waiver occur in federal or state court and the question is what effect to give to such conduct in the other system.

11. It may be worth noting that most American courts extend the privilege to "house counsel" of corporate entities, as in *Upjohn* itself—that is to say, the privilege extends to communications with lawyers regularly employed by the corporation who act in their professional capacity as lawyers. In contrast to American and British practice, the European Union does *not* recognize the privilege in this setting. See Azko Nobel Chemicals Ltd and Akros Chemicals Ltd v. European Commission (2010) (privilege rules applied by EU differ from those of some Member States; communications are privileged only if made for purposes and in the interests of the client's rights and defenses by an independent lawyer, meaning one not connected to client in an employment relationship).

G   DISCOVERY OF EXPERTS

Beginning in 1993, FRCP 26 required litigants to turn over, without even being asked, the identity of any expert witness who is to testify at trial, as well as "a written report" that the expert has "prepared and signed," if he is "retained or specially employed" to testify in the case, or employed by a party with duties that "regularly involve giving expert testimony." This obligation can be seen as part of "automatic" discovery, although it proceeds later in the case, because it takes a while for lawyers to find and make arrangements with experts, and their identities and roles in a case are not known at the beginning. This requirement is elaborate: The report must contain a "complete statement" of opinions and underlying "reasons" as well as "the data or other information" and "exhibits that will be used to summarize or report" the opinions, along with a statement of the expert's qualifications, a list of cases in which she has testified in the last four years, and a statement of her compensation in this case. See FRCP 26(b)(2).

This disclosure regime reflects modern litigation, where experts play important roles. Requiring disclosure of the expert's involvement in prior suits represents an attempt to balance work product protection—it is understood that finding experts, making the arrangements, and bringing them "up to speed" involves considerable effort by lawyers—with the need of the other side to be able to prepare to counter and cross-examine. The fear is that trial lawyers cannot prepare for the latter task if they are in the dark about the expected testimony, so considerable advance disclosure is necessary.

■ PROBLEM 9-D. What Experts Did You Consult?

In defending the suit brought by Nora Pierce against Ford and Indiana Instruments, Ed Rifkin looks for experts who could testify that the speed control deactivation switch (SCDS) and its kapton seal are well designed, functional, and not unreasonably dangerous.

Naturally, Rifkin begins by contacting engineers who work for Ford, but he also casts about for independent experts. Both inside the Ford organization and outside it, Rifkin finds educated and experienced potential witnesses, all of whom have advanced degrees and expertise on issues likely to arise in the case. Rifkin contacts them. He has obtained from Indiana Instruments design drawings and manufacturing specifications, and has obtained from Ford the test data on the device, and he provides this material to each expert or makes sure that each has access to it.

First, Rifkin talks to Dr. Gina Nye, who works as a design engineer for Ford. She participated in the design and testing of Mercury Marquis automobiles, and worked on the design of the SCDS and similar electronic components related to cruise control mechanisms in the Ford family of cars. She explains the function and design of the SCDS and tells Rifkin that she doesn't think the SCDS had anything to do with the underhood fire. She ventures the opinion that the fire may have started because oil was spilled on the manifold in a recent lubrication and it caught fire when the car was driven at speed on the freeway on a hot day. Rifkin decides that Nye would be a good witness, asks her to prepare a report, and Ford agrees to release her from duties in order to help with the defense of Ford, and to testify in the case.

Second, Rifkin talks to Michael Overby, a consulting automotive engineer in an engineering firm who is familiar with the function and design of many different SCDS units. For a preliminary fee of $2,800, Overby agrees to examine the designs and specifications and give Rifkin a "preliminary read." Ten days later Overby calls and offers his opinion that the SCDS was "basically a variation of a design that is standard in the industry," and that this design has a good safety record. He explains the functions of the unit and says he doubts that it could get hot enough to start an underhood fire. Rifkin decides that Overby would be a good witness, and hires him to prepare a report on his conclusions. For an additional $4,000 fee, Overby does so, and agrees to testify and consult on an hourly basis thereafter.

Third, Rifkin talks with Dr. Dennis Padget, another independent engineering consultant who has his own firm. For a preliminary fee of $2,600, he examines the documentation and contacts Rifkin. He tells Rifkin he can see how the fire may have started, but thinks that it had "nothing to do with the SCDS," and agrees with Nye's conclusion that the fire likely resulted from oil left on the manifold after lubrication. Padget agrees to help Rifkin in preparing the defense. At Rifkin's request, Padget writes a report, including detailed findings and the basis for them, as well as information about his education and career. Rifkin sees that he has testified in many product liability cases, always for the defense, and Rifkin decides to use Padget's help but not to call him as a witness.

Fourth, Rifkin speaks to Dr. Linsey Quinn, a professor of design engineering, who charges a preliminary fee of $2,400 to "spend a few hours examining the designs and specifications." A few days later Quinn telephones Rifkin and they talk the matter over. Quinn tells Rifkin that she thinks there are "obvious flaws" in the design, and that the risk would be that the switch would overheat under stress, and its proximity to an oil line presents "a serious risk of fire." Rifkin thanks her for her opinion and tells Quinn that Rifkin does not think he will need her services. At Rifkin's request, Quinn writes a brief report in the form of a letter, and Rifkin pays her fee, which has grown to $3,600 (the $2,400 for the initial consultation and examination of documents and $1,200 more for the brief report).

The following issues emerge:

(1) Rifkin turns over to Schrader the reports of Dr. Nye and Michael Overby. Schrader notices their depositions, and subpoenas them. Rifkin objects and moves to quash the subpoenas and notices of deposition. Can Schrader take these depositions? Does he have to make some special showing? Does he have to compensate Pierce and Overby for their time in preparing their reports? For their time in being deposed?

(2) Does Rifkin have to identify Dennis Padget and Linsey Quinn, and turn over their reports?

(3) Schrader has heard about Rifkin's contacts with Dennis Padget and Linsey Quinn through "back channels." He notices their depositions and serves them with subpoenas, but Rifkin objects and moves to quash the subpoenas and notices of deposition. What kind of showing, if any, must Schrader make to go forward? If the depositions are allowed, does Schrader have to compensate Padget and Quinn for the time they've already spent? For the time the deposition takes?

■ NOTES ON DISCLOSURE OF EXPERTS

1. Looking at FRCP 26(b)(4), you see that it both authorizes and limits discovery conducted by one party about experts contacted by the other side. The language envisions two kinds of experts—those who will testify at trial and those who will not (whose function is largely to consult and help the lawyer understand technical issues). In fact, however, it is easy to think of five categories of experts, three of which are not expressly contemplated in the Rules. Let us consider all five categories:

(a) Experts Who Are to Testify at Trial. For specially retained experts who are to testify (Gina Nye and Michael Overby in the Problem), a special report is required—and every such expert must *sign* the report—and the report must be turned over to the other side even if it is not asked for. Why? *After* the report is produced, can the other side take the expert's deposition? If so, what must the discovering party be prepared to pay? Look carefully at FRCP 26(b)(4). Why does the Rule do what it does here?

(b) Experts Who Consult But Are Not to Testify. For specially retained experts who are *not* to testify—and Dennis Padget in the Problem fits this category—there is no need to provide a report to the other side. Why not? For such experts, the other side can take depositions only on application to the court showing "extraordinary circumstances." Why such a stiff requirement? What must the discovering party pay this time? Why does FRCP 26(b)(4) do what it does in this situation?

(c) Experts Informally Consulted. Not mentioned in FRCP 26(b)(4) are experts who are consulted preliminarily, as in the case of Linsey Quinn, but who play no further role. If you are wondering whether Ed Rifkin has an obligation to make known to Donald Schrader the fact that Rifkin has located someone whom Donald Schrader would like to know about, the answer is probably not. See, e.g., Ager v. Jane C. Stormont Hospital & Training School for Nurses, 622 F.3d 496, 501 (10th Cir. 1980) ("no provision in the rules" covers an expert "informally consulted," and they "cannot be discovered or deposed"). Why?

(d) Experts Who Participate in (or Observe) Events. Also not mentioned in FRCP 26(b)(4) are experts who testify or consult but who also participate in events. If, for example, an accident injures occupants of a car and a physician driving by stops and assumes a Good Samaritan role, she becomes a witness to whatever she observes as she ministers to an injured person. In a later lawsuit, could she refuse to testify unless she was compensated? Even if she's asked questions about the nature of the injuries that only a physician could answer? No, she cannot refuse to answer. She is an ordinary witness, and the fact that her training and experience provide insights that other passers-by would not have makes no difference. See ACN to FRCP 26 (1970) (expert who acquires information as "an actor or viewer with respect to the transactions or occurrences . . . should be treated as an ordinary witness"). Consider Gina Nye: Isn't she a bit like the physician who stops at an accident

scene, in that Nye also has knowledge relating to the case—she knows about the testing of the Mercury Marquis automobile—that she acquired by participating in relevant events? See Vance v. Marion General Hospital, 847 N.E.2d 1229 (Ohio App. 2006) (in suit against hospital and doctors alleging failure properly to treat cardiac emergency, resulting in necrosis of hand requiring amputation performed by L, a nonparty, plaintiff subpoenaed L, who moved to quash unless he received $2,500; court ordered deposition to proceed, and L sought $8,000 because he had to clear a day from his schedule; court awarded $1,500, and plaintiff appealed; reviewing court approves award as a "reasonable compromise" between amount initially requested by L, which was $2,500, and amount offered by plaintiff, which was $500 plus $350/hour). In amendments to FRCP 26 adopted in 2010, this kind of expert is obliquely recognized in Rule 26(b)(2)(C), which says that the automatic disclosure requirement includes a statement of "the subject matter" of her expected testimony, and "a summary of the facts or opinions" expected from the witness.

(e) Unaffiliated Experts. Sometimes, a research scientist undertakes a study that yields information that would be useful in lawsuits, but the scientist has no connection with the parties or the events or transactions in litigation. Such a person may qualify as an expert, but is outside the contemplation of FRCP 26(b)(4). It is rare for parties to subpoena such persons rather than seeking to hire them, as common sense suggests that they are more likely to be helpful if hired and compensated than if "drafted" and dragged into the suit involuntarily. Courts disagree on how to handle such matters. Compare Wright v. Jeep Corp., 547 F. Supp. 871 (D. Mich. 1982) (subpoena served on professor at University of Michigan who had studied and published paper dealing with On-Road Crash Experience of Utility Vehicles; administration of justice "required testimony of all persons unless reasons are established to the contrary," and FRCP 26(b)(4) does not apply; there is no privilege and no constitutional exemption, and fact that testifying is a burden does not excuse witness; parties to "submit proposals to the Court to lessen the burden" on the witness and "compensate him adequately") with Buchanan v. American Motors Corp., 697 F.2d 151 (6th Cir. 1983) (quashing subpoena directed to same professor). In 1991, FRCP 45 was amended to say that a subpoena may be quashed or modified if it requires disclosure of an "unretained expert's opinion or information that does not describe specific occurrences in dispute and results from the expert's study that was not requested by a party."

2. Let's reconsider the testifying expert—the first category, where discovery is fullest. The report turned over to the other side includes not only a "complete statement of all opinions" to which the witness will testify, and the "data" and "other information" that she considered, and "any exhibits" to be used at trial, and a statement of the qualifications of the expert and a "list of all other cases" in which she has testified in the past four years, and a "statement of the compensation" she expects for preparing and testifying. Why can the other side also depose such experts?

3. Consider the kinds of information that might be used at trial to impeach the expert. See, e.g., Noffke v. Perez, 178 P.3d 1141 (Alaska 2008) (can require defense expert to turn over tax returns; expert was not fortuitously brought in as treating physician, but was a business providing services knowing that suit is going forward; returns could show proportion of income expert earns by testifying that bears on bias; returns produced under protective order); Primm v. Isaac, 127 S.W.3d 630 (Ky. 2004) (during discovery, litigant may ask doctor about number of examinations he performed for employers, insurance companies, and other defendants in previous year, as compared to number of patients treated, and charge for each examination and for depositions; litigant is not entitled to tax records; court would not "preclude discovery" of such material, which may be required if party can demonstrate that additional information is necessary); Wrobleski v. de Lara, 727 A.2d 930, 938 (Md. 1999) (can ask whether expert "earns a significant portion or amount" of income from testifying, and amount and proportion of income derived from this source in recent past; expert is not to be harassed through "wholesale rummaging" into personal and financial records; court should tightly control process; deriving substantial income from testifying does not mean expert is not "honest, accurate, and credible," but is "a factor" for trier of fact to consider); Elkins v. Syken, 672 So. 2d 517 (Fla. 1996) (expert may be asked about compensation for pending case, what kind of work she usually does when hired by lawyers—i.e., whether she testifies for plaintiff or defendants—and what portion of her time or work is devoted to litigation, which can be "a fair estimate" based on hours or percentage of income or number of medical examinations she performs in a year; she may be required to identify each case in which she has testified for a reasonable period, normally three years, but production of 1099 tax forms may be required only on "the most unusual or compelling circumstance" and expert may not be required "to compile or produce nonexistent documents"); Plitt v. Griggs, 585 So. 2d 1317 (Ala. 1991) (requiring plaintiff's medical expert to identify accountant who prepared tax return, which might lead to information on amount of income derived from testifying for plaintiffs in malpractice suits).

4. Consider the consulting expert. What "exceptional circumstances" would justify taking his deposition? See, e.g., Willis v. Central Mutual Insurance Co., 2009 WL 1787679 (W.D. La. 2009) (in accident suit in which child allegedly suffered head or brain injuries, requiring plaintiff's neuropsychologist to turn over data gathered shortly after accident; defense doctor submitted affidavit indicating that "testing more proximal to the incident" was "especially relevant" in providing "baseline for comparison of other neurological test results") (defense was seeking only this data, not seeking to depose expert); Caribbean I Owners' Association, Inc. v. Great American Insurance Co. of New York, 2009 WL 499500 (S.D. Ala. 2009) (in suit arising out of hurricane damage, extraordinary circumstance justified defense discovery of plaintiff's consulting expert, who had examined building before it was damaged; condition "before and after" the hurricane was a "central issue" and "prehurricane condition" is not something that can be duplicated).

5. Suppose a party designates a testifying expert, turns over the reports, and then changes the designation to nontestifying or consulting expert? Most courts say such a change is permissible, and the other side can take the expert's deposition after the redesignation only by satisfying the exceptional circumstances standard. See R.C. Olmstead, Inc. v. CU Interface, LLC, 2009 WL 3049877 (N.D. Ohio 2009); In re Shell Oil Refinery, 132 F.R.D. 437, 440 (E.D. La. 1990). But see Hartford Fire Ins. Co. v. Transgroup Express, Inc., 2009 WL 2252179 (N.D. Ill. 2009) (can depose resdesignated expert *without* satisfying exceptional circumstances standard).

6. How should courts deal with the expert who is informally consulted? It is commonplace for lawyers in Rifkin's position to try to reach an understanding with an expert to the effect that she will not contact the other side, in case she thinks the other side has the better case, and an agreement not to do so might even be included in any informal letter agreement between a lawyer and an expert like Linsey Quinn. See Sowders v. Lewis, 241 So. 3d 319, 323 (Ky. 2007) (in malpractice suit, plaintiff's counsel contacted Dr. B and asked him to review the case; affidavit said counsel gave Dr. B some work product material; Dr. B opined that there was no violation of standard of care; thereafter defense called Dr. B, who told defense that he'd reviewed case for plaintiff; when defense notified plaintiff that it was calling Dr. B, plaintiff sought order disqualifying Dr. B from testifying; reviewing court issues writ of mandamus compelling exclusion of Dr. B; "unduly narrow interpretation" of work product will make lawyers reluctant to disclose confidential information to nontestifying consultant; a finding that he reviewed the case for the opposing party and gave an opinion is enough to disqualify him; "litigation experts understand this rule and it is not difficult to comply with").

7. When an expert is not merely involved in assisting a litigant during the suit or presenting expert testimony, she may be beyond the limits of work product, hence open to broader discovery by the other side. See, e.g., In re Long Branch Manufactured Gas Plant, 907 A.2d 438, 443-445 (N.J. Super. 2005) (in suit alleging environmental pollution, ordering discovery of nontestifying expert who made public statements defending company; consulting expert who acts in "different capacities" and plays "additional role" beyond helping in lawsuit may be outside "protective shield" of work product; acting in "different capacities" may make her an "actor" or "ordinary witness") (work product did not apply; discovering party did not need to show good cause to make discovery).

8. Perhaps not surprisingly, failing to produce the required reports by experts who are to testify can have drastic consequences. See, e.g., Reese v. Herbert, 527 F.3d 1253 (11th Cir. 2008) (awarding summary judgment for defense in suit alleging excessive force; plaintiff was more than two months late in disclosing, and then revealed name of expert but not required reports; court could disallow expert's affidavit in ruling on summary judgment); Banks v. Hill, 978 So. 2d 663 (Miss. 2008) (failure to disclose experts in personal injury case merited order excluding their testimony). As you can imagine, courts do not *automatically* bar testimony by experts for failure to comply with discovery requirements. See, e.g., Trattler v. Citron, 182 P.3d 674 (Colo. 2008) (in malpractice suit, plaintiff's failure to disclose testifying history of her expert doctors did not require exclusion of testimony, but only exclusion of prior testifying experience; whether also to exclude testimony depends on "nature and severity" of violation of duty; defense knew about plaintiff's experts, and testifying history was not "central to the case"). A modern West Virginia decision came up with a list of factors to be considered in this connection, including (1) prejudice or surprise to party against whom testimony is offered, (2) ability of that party to cure prejudice, (3) bad faith or willfulness of proponent, and (4) practical importance of the testimony. See West Virginia Department of Transportation, Division of Highways v. Parkersburg Inn, Inc., 2008 WL 4867412 (W. Va. 2008) (in connection with inn's claim for business losses due to rerouting of highway, excluding claimant's expert testimony on damages; expert had been listed as witness but not as expert; DOH was prejudiced and surprised; witness had indicated that he was not going to provide expert testimony; there was no way of curing problem; inn's failure may not have been in bad faith or willful, but did show gross negligence; inn had other expert testimony on same point). See also Young v. Interstate Hotels and Resorts, 906 A.2d 857 (D.C. 2006) (whether to allow expert testimony improperly left off pretrial discovery statement turns on whether (1) admitting testimony would "incurably surprise or prejudice" opponent, (2) excluding would incurably prejudice proponent, (3) proponent's failure was inadvertent or willful, (4) impact admitting the testimony on orderliness and efficiency of trial; and (5) impact of excluding it on completeness of information before court or jury) (no showing of bad faith, but claimant was "not diligent in managing this litigation by ascertaining his theory of the case and identifying an appropriate expert," as appellant had seven months to find expert after learning that one was required, and "apparently did nothing" and did not "provide any reasons for his failure").

9. The duty to supplement responses made during discovery, see FRCP 26(e), extends to materials that a party will use in presenting expert testimony. See, e.g., Hartel v. Pruett, 2008 WL 4879223 (Miss. 2008) (in malpractice suit, defense asked for articles to be used during presentation of plaintiff's expert testimony; plaintiff said it would provide list; articles were disclosed six days before trial, and court blocked plaintiff from using them under Rule 803(18); reviewing court approves, holding that plaintiffs should have supplemented their response earlier).

■ **PROBLEM 9-E. "Produce All Correspondence"**

Susan and Brad Finley bring a malpractice suit in state court against surgeon Jeff Conlon, after their six-year-old child Sara suffered partial paralysis of the right side of her face as a result of an operation to remove a growth on her neck.

In discovery, Nina Gould as counsel for plaintiffs lists Dr. Mary Kern as an expert whom Gould expects to call as a witness, and produces Dr. Kern's report explaining why the surgery by Dr. Conlon involved negligence and why it caused partial paralysis.

Nina Gould obtains the complete medical records of the hospital relating to Sara Finley, and takes the deposition of Dr. Conlon.

As counsel for Dr. Conlon, Mark Hodges serves on Mary Kern a subpoena duces tecum, advising her that Hodges intends to depose her in this matter and requesting "all correspondence to or from Nina Gould or anyone else relating to the case."

On behalf of the Finleys, Nina Gould moves to quash the subpoena in part and seeks a protective order exempting from production "all correspondence from me to Dr. Mary Kern" and barring Hodges from questioning Kern "on any conversations she may have had with me as counsel for Susan and Brad Finley." Gould says she did indeed write to Mary Kern, and claims that "this letter reflects my work product" because it "points out my theory of the case and highlights passages in the deposition of Dr. Conlon that support our claim." Gould also says she "conferred by phone and in person with Mary Kern several times," and says these conversations "discussed the facts and my theories supporting our malpractice claim."

Invoking the state's Rule 26 (identical to FRCP 26), Hodges argues that "disclosure to an expert who is expected to testify constitutes waiver of work product protection."

How should the court rule, and why?

■ **NOTES ON THE "WOODSHEDDING" OF EXPERTS, AND ON IMPEACHMENT**

1. Reportedly, it comes as a shock to European legal analysts that lawyers in this country can prepare witnesses to testify, but it is standard operating procedure for American lawyers. Witness preparation ("woodshedding" or "sandpapering") is a routine function of litigating lawyers, undertaken with both experts and lay witnesses. With experts, such preparation is important because lawyers want them to be more familiar with the facts than they would be if left to their own devices. Even more important, most observers think that expertise is *not* "neutral" or "nonpartisan," and an expert can be most helpful if he knows the theory that the lawyer is pursuing. (Indeed, consulting experts usually help shape those theories.)

(a) When a lawyer prepares an expert to testify, the lawyer is likely to do what Gould did—showing the expert relevant records and highlighting facts or theories the lawyer considers important. Often there has already been full discovery of documents, and depositions have been taken, and the other side has in its hands everything that the lawyer hiring the expert has. In this setting, then, what is claimed to be work product is not so much "raw" or "factual" data, but rather the lawyer's *selection* and *suggested interpretation* of such facts or data.

(b) Regardless whether disclosure is required in cases like the one in Problem 9-E, one can expect that the cross-examiner in a deposition of an expert like Mary Kern (whom plaintiffs intend to call) will ask, "Have you spoken with plaintiff's lawyer about this case?" and "Did plaintiff's lawyer show you any letters, memoranda, or other documentary material? The question "goes to bias or influence," as you will see in the Evidence course— bias meaning a possible predisposition to see the facts a certain way. And such a question is undoubtedly proper.

(c) If you were Nina Gould, how would you prepare Mary Kern for such questions? Bearing in mind that she must be truthful, what kinds of things would you want her to say when asked about such preparatory sessions?

2. Notice that FRCP 26(a)(2) requires "automatic" disclosure of reports "signed and prepared" by Mary Kern, and this disclosure requirement includes "data or other information" that she considered in forming her "opinions." There is nothing wrong, however, with Mary Kern stating in such a report *the facts* on which she relies *without also saying* that she depended on Gould in selecting those facts, which means that even a report complying with FRCP 26(a)(2) does not necessarily disclose the substance of communications between Mary Kern and Nina Gould. Note, however, the following language in the ACN accompanying the 1993 amendment to FRCP 26, which strengthened the reporting requirement:

> The report is to disclose the data and other information considered by the expert and any exhibits or charts that summarize or support the expert's opinions. Given this obligation of disclosure, litigants should no longer be able to argue that materials furnished to their experts to be used in forming their opinions—whether or not ultimately relied upon by the expert—are privileged or otherwise protected from disclosure when such persons are testifying or being deposed.

In light of this language, a leading treatise announces this conclusion: "At least with respect to experts who testify at trial, the disclosure requirements of Rule 26(a)(2), adopted in 1993, were intended to pretermit further discussion and mandate disclosure despite privilege." See 8 Wright, Miller & Marcus, Federal Practice and Procedure §2016.2 (3d ed.).

3. Whether or not this conclusion is correct, courts have struggled with this issue. The language of the Rule and the ACN *could be read* otherwise, as leaving untouched matters of privilege and work product, or as requiring disclosure only of "facts" and not "opinions" held by the lawyer or "theories" suggested by the lawyer. Most modern decisions, however, accept the view that sharing work product with witnesses who are to testify waives all protection for everything the attorney shares with the expert.

(a) Here is a good expression of the prevailing modern view:

> Strong public policy considerations support a construction of Rule 26(a)(2) favoring broad disclosure. A bright-line rule promotes efficiency, fairness, and the truth seeking process. Requiring trial courts to review every expert communication in camera to determine the appropriate degree of disclosure, on the other hand, simply foments needless discovery battles, undercuts the truth seeking principles of the rules of civil procedure, and wastes scarce judicial resources.
>
> A bright-line rule preserves judicial economy by obviating the need for a judge to consider whether counsel's communications to retained experts contain work product. It also frees trial courts from the burdensome task of sifting through volumes of documents to separate "factual work product" from "opinion work product"—a compromise approach struck by some jurisdictions.
>
> A bright-line approach also gives parties notice of precisely which materials will be discoverable in every case, thereby reducing the number of discovery disputes. "Without a clear and uniform rule to indicate the consequences of disclosure, the litigator must repeatedly face the frustrating decision whether to disclose protected documents to the expert, and ultimately he must choose either to gamble that the court will not order discovery of work product documents disclosed to the expert or to play it safe and forego the benefits of disclosure." Lee Mickus, *Discovery of Work Product Disclosed to a Testifying Expert Under the 1993 Amendments to the Federal Rules of Civil Procedure,* 27 Creighton L. Rev. 773, 774-775 (1994). Thus, the adoption of a bright-line rule "actually preserves opinion work product in that there is no lingering uncertainty as to what documents will be disclosed. Counsel can easily protect genuine work product by simply not divulging it to the expert." Karn v. Rand, 168 F.R.D. 663, 641 (N.D. Ind. 1996). Concomitantly, a bright-line rule promotes fairness among litigants by subjecting all parties who retain experts to the same disclosure requirements.
>
> Perhaps most importantly, a bright-line disclosure rule advances the truth seeking function of the discovery rules. This court has emphasized the primacy of this objective in the discovery context, holding that the Colorado Rules of Civil Procedure are to be liberally construed to effectuate their truth seeking purpose.
>
> If an adverse party is to determine the extent to which the expert's opinion has been shaped or influenced by the version of the facts selected and presented by the counsel retaining the expert, she must have access to the documents or materials that the expert considers. Without such access, the opposing party will be unable to conduct a full and fair cross-examination of the expert.

A bright-line rule's promotion of the truth seeking function of discovery does not compromise the strong policies underlying the work product doctrine. The work product doctrine is intended to permit an attorney to prepare her case by distinguishing relevant from irrelevant facts, testing novel legal theories, and deliberating over tactics and strategy. These objectives are not undermined by a bright-line rule because divulging opinion work product to a testifying expert "does not result in counsel developing new legal theories or in enhancing the conducting of a factual investigation. Rather, the work product either informs the expert as to what counsel believes are relevant facts, or seeks to influence him to render a favorable opinion." *Karn,* supra, 168 F.R.D. at 640.

Moreover, Rule 26(b)(4)(B) provides that an attorney may consult on a confidential basis with as many non-testifying experts as she deems necessary to develop legal theories and to test their scientific viability. When she does so, the attorney is "free to think dispassionately, reliably, and creatively both about the law and the evidence in the case and about which strategic approaches are likely to be in [her] client's best interests." Intermedics, Inc. v. Ventritex, Inc., 139 F.R.D. 384, 392 (N.D. Cal. 1991) (making this point under the pre-1993 Rules). Additionally, "[a]n attorney wishing to maintain the protection afforded by the work product doctrine can choose to provide the expert with all relevant facts instead of directing the expert's attention to certain facts and instead of including opinions and conclusions drawn by the attorney." Lamonds v. Gen. Motors Corp., 180 F.R.D. 302, 306 (W.D. Va. 1998).

Gall v. Jamison, 44 P.3d 233, 239-240 (Colo. 2002). See also Regional Airport Authority of Louisville v. LFG, LLC, 460 F.3d 697 (6th Cir. 2006) (adopting "bright-line" rule adopted by "overwhelming majority" of courts requiring disclosure of "all documents, including attorney opinion work product, given to testifying experts"); In re Pioneer Hi-Bred International, Inc., 238 F.3d 1370, 1375-1376 (Fed. Cir. 2001) (disclosure to testifying expert waives privilege and work product protection; it is assumed that "privileged or protected material will be made public"); State ex rel. Tracy v. Dandurand, 30 S.W.3d 831, 835 (Mo. 2000) (one may discover by deposition facts and opinions to which expert will testify, and probe basis of opinions; expert must produce materials he has reviewed, and these cannot be withheld under claim that he did not rely on them).

(b) The other side of the issue continues to find support in modern decisions. One court put it this way:

The central inquiry on cross examination of an expert witness . . . is not the question of if and to what extent the expert was influenced by counsel; rather it is this: what is the basis for the expert's opinion? Cross examination on the adequacy and reliability of the stated basis of the expert's opinion can be conducted effectively absent a line of questioning on counsel's role in assisting the expert.

Nexxus Products Co. v. CVS New York, Inc., 188 F.R.D. 7, 10-11 (D. Mass. 1999) (protecting from discovery "core work product" that lawyer shares with expert promotes "unconstrained communications" and better serves truth-seeking function of trial process). Here is how another court put it:

> We find compelling the rationale of those courts that effective cross-examination on the issue of the basis of an expert's opinion nonetheless may be conducted without revealing the mental impressions, conclusions, opinions, or legal theories of an attorney. The adversarial system continues to place a check upon the bias of testifying expert witnesses absent such disclosure, for their testimony is subject to impeachment by the contrary testimony of experts for the opposing party or other contrary authorities. Moreover, we agree with these federal courts that any value that may result from revealing how an attorney has influenced a testifying expert does not override the strong policy against disclosure of attorneys' innermost thought processes. The need to protect such opinion work product was made apparent in *Hickman,* is codified in our rules, and has been reiterated by this Court on a number of occasions. We do not intend to diminish this strong policy today.
>
> The very essence of trial preparation and strategy is that an attorney must take facts, sift them, decide what is relevant and what is not, develop theories based on applicable law, and prepare his or her client's witnesses accordingly. Without the ability to protect their own conclusions and theories from discovery, attorneys may not be able to fully and confidently prepare expert witnesses for their clients' trials. Permitting full disclosure of everything revealed to expert witnesses might hamper the trial preparation process because attorneys would be reluctant to reveal their mental impressions, legal theories, trial tactics, and strategies to testifying experts. In our opinion, it is the disclosure of just such information that Rule 26(b)(3)'s dictation of the work-product privilege was intended to prevent.

Crowe Countryside Realty Associates Co., LLC v. Novare Engineers, Inc., 891 A.2d 838, 846-847 (R.I. 2006) (judge may "examine communications exchanged between attorneys and testifying experts" and make "independent determinations about their classification as factual or opinion work product," an approach that strikes the right "balance" between "protecting an attorney's opinion" as contemplated in *Hickman* and "permitting full disclosure of the factual bases" as contemplated by Rule 26).

(c) Which views do you find most persuasive, those articulated in *Gall, Regional Airport Authority, Pioneer Hi-Bred* and *Dandurand,* or those in *Nexxus* and *Crowe*? See also In re Christus Spohn Hospital Kleberg, 222 S.W.3d 434 (Tex. 2007) (on learning of upcoming suit for death of plaintiff's daughter, hospital's internal investigator prepared a "Confidential Communication Prepared in Anticipation of Litigation," summarizing interviews with employees and correspondence with counsel; paralegal sent this to hospital's expert witness on standard-of-care issues, Nurse Kendra Menzies; paralegal was from California, and thought the material would still be privileged; nurse did not list them as documents she reviewed, but plaintiff tried to depose her about them; hospital claimed work product protection, invoking "snap-back provision" which allows return of inadvertently transmitted documents; Texas rule

requires disclosure of all facts known by expert regardless "when and how" acquired, including all documents or reports "provided to, reviewed by, or prepared by or for the expert" in anticipation of testimony; expert witness occupies "unique place in our adversarial system," and appears to juries as "objective authority figure more knowledgeable and credible than the typical lay witness," so juries rely more on experts; also they are "unfettered by firsthand-knowledge requirements," so expert "paints a powerful image on the litigation canvas," and usually the hiring attorney "selects the materials that will provide color and hue": "Just as a purveyor of fine art must examine the medium used in order to distinguish masterpiece from fake, a jury must understand the pallet from which the expert paints to accurately assess the testimony's worth. Given the importance that expert testimony can assume, the jury should be aware of documents and tangible things provided to the expert that might have influenced the expert's opinion. In terms of determining what effect documents provided to an expert had in shaping the expert's mental impressions and opinions, the attorney's intent in producing the documents is irrelevant.").

4. How do experts like Mary Kern prepare the reports that FRCP 26(a)(2) requires the party to turn over to the other side? If your instinct is that the lawyer—in our example, Nina Gould—has something to do with it, you are right. Not always, but often lawyers help in drafting efforts, and it is more than possible that lawyers take the laboring oar. Suppose such a report goes through many drafts, and the lawyer makes suggestions that "nudge" the report in some direction and the expert has ideas that go in other directions. Ultimately, of course, the expert must sign the report—remember that FRCP 26(a)(2) requires a report "prepared and signed" by the expert. If the idea behind requiring disclosure of work product that was considered by an expert in preparing the report is to enable the other side to test and cross-examine, should prior drafts be discoverable? The substance of the conversations between expert and lawyer?

(a) This issue has proved contentious, and many decisions require production of draft reports. See, e.g., Elm Grove Coal Co. v. Director, 480 F.3d 278 (4th Cir. 2007) (physicians expected to testify prepared reports; one "admitted that he had not written 'every word' of his report," and that attorney "provided him with certain documents," and another said that counsel "provided him with relevant documents and summaries"; these experts could not be "properly and fully cross-examined" without draft reports; fact that lawyer "participated in" preparation "does not bar use of the expert's opinion, or necessarily even impeach" reliability, but it does have potential "impact on the weight" that such opinions deserve, and the "interplay between testifying experts and the lawyers who retained them" should be "fair game for cross-examination"); Krisa v. Equitable Life Assurance Society, 196 F.R.D. 254, 256-257 (M.D. Pa. 2000) (preliminary and draft reports of testifying expert are not covered by work product).

(b) Other decisions say, in effect, "enough is enough" and deny requests for drafts. See, e.g., In re Teleglobe Communications Corp., 392 B.R. 561 (Bankr. D. Del. 2008) (need not produce expert "draft reports," as expert "does not really

'consider' prior drafts in forming his opinion") (these are "simply preliminary iterations"); Alder v. Shelton, 778 A.2d 1181, 1190-1192 (N.J. Super. 2001) (decisions denying discovery of draft reports rest on "need to encourage a close and collaborative effort between the expert and the retaining attorney," in belief that requiring disclosure "puts too prominent a focus on the mechanics of the production of an expert's report rather than focusing on the basis of the expert's opinion," and these decisions "have common sense on their side") (experts "usually destroy their draft reports," so draft reports "are available only from the unwary or careless expert or in odd circumstances like the present case").

5. In light of these developments, the Civil Rules Advisory Committee proposed an amendment that took effect in December 2010. The amendment cut back on required disclosures. Partly, the underlying purpose was to reject decisions requiring production of draft reports. With respect to draft reports, the amendment did two things:

(a) First, amended FRCP 26(b)(2) requires expert reports to reflect "facts or data," not "data or other information" as the pre-amendment Rule said. The new language reduces the degree to which the disclosure obligation includes communications with the lawyer. The ACN says this language should "alter the outcomes" in cases requiring "disclosure of all attorney-expert communications and draft reports." The ACN also says the new language stop shorts of requiring disclosure of "theories and mental impressions of counsel." As was true before, amended FRCP 26(b)(2) still requires disclosure of facts or data "considered by" the expert, not simply those on which he "relies."

(b) Second, the amendment added language extending work product protection to "drafts" of reports that are required to be disclosed, and "communications between" the expert and the lawyer, *except* to the extent such communications deal with "compensation" or identify "facts or data that the party's attorney provided and that the expert considered" in forming his opinions or that identify "assumptions that the party's attorney provided and that the expert relied upon." See FRCP 26(b)(4)(C).

H   E-DISCOVERY

The advent of computers, and their universal use and enormous capacities, have had a huge impact on discovery. ESI is the shorthand term for "electronically stored information," and the quantity of such information has multiplied exponentially. Today almost all business litigation and many other suits involve discovery of ESI. Today ESI means not just files in computers operated by litigants, but information on websites and stored in cellphones and similar mechanisms, including emails, "tweets," Facebook postings, and instant messaging records.

1. Nature of the Beast

The Rules were drafted in the age of paper records, and electronic data storage had been a fact of life for more than ten years when the Rules were amended in 2006 to deal expressly (if modestly) with issues that come with discovery of ESI. Here is a summary of the changes:

> ➤ Under FRCP 16(b)(3)(B), the pretrial scheduling order is to "provide for the disclosure of electronically stored information";
> ➤ Under FRCP 26(a)(1)(A), the automatic discovery process involves describing not only documents, but "electronically stored information" that the producing party has and "may use" at trial to support claims or defenses;
> ➤ Under FRCP 26(b)(2)(B), a party need not produce electronically stored information "from sources that the party identifies as not reasonably accessible," although production of such material may be ordered on motion unless the other side shows that it is not reasonably accessible "because of undue burden or cost";
> ➤ Under FRCP 26(f)(3)(C), the discovery plan assembled by the parties is to cover "electronically stored information, including the form or forms in which it should be produced";
> ➤ Under FRCP 34(b), a party seeking discovery of ESI may "specify the form or forms" in which it is to be produced, and the responding party may object; the amended provision goes on to state that a party producing ESI "must produce it in a form or forms in which it is ordinarily maintained or in a reasonably usable form or forms," and "need not produce the same electronically stored information in more than one form."
> ➤ Under FRCP 37(e), a party may not be sanctioned (absent "extraordinary circumstances") for failing to produce ESI that has been "lost as a result of the routine, good-faith operation of an electronic information system.
> ➤ Under FRCP 45(d), a person responding to a subpoena seeking ESI that does not "specify a form" for the material "must produce it in a form or forms in which it is ordinarily maintained or in a reasonably usable form or forms," and the producing party need not produce ESI "in more than one form" and need not produce ESI that is "not reasonably accessible because oif undue burden or cost" (but issues surrounding such points can be resolved by a court, and discovery can be ordered on a showing of "good cause" subject to conditions that a court may impose).

Now look at this excerpt from the Third Circuit's opinion in the *Race Tires America* case, to get a picture of e-discovery in a modern "big case."

RACE TIRES AMERICA v. HOOSIER RACING TIRE CORP.

United States Court of Appeals for the Third Circuit
674 F.3d 158 (3d Cir. 2012)

Vanaskie, Circuit Judge.

[Race Tires America (RTA), a tire supplier, brought this antitrust suit against Hoosier and Dirt Motor Sports (DMS), alleging antitrust violations arising out of the adoption of a "single tire rule" for certain motor sports. RTA estimated that total damages, before trebling under the statute, exceeded $30 million. Ultimately, defendants won summary judgment, and sought to recover costs of e-discovery under FRCP 54(d), in the amount of $365,000. FRCP 54(d) traditionally covers fees of the court clerk or marshal, fees for printed or recorded transcripts necessarily acquired for use in the case, fees and disbursements for printing and witnesses, fees for making copies of materials, docket fees, and compensation for court-appointed experts, interpreters, and the like. The court *rejects* most of the application for costs, and describes the discovery that went forward.]

As would be expected in a case of this nature and magnitude, the parties engaged in extensive discovery of ESI. The Case Management Order ("CMO"), issued by the District Court in January of 2008, directed the parties to attempt to agree upon a list of keyword search terms, with a party's use of such terms carrying a presumption that it had fulfilled its "obligation to conduct a reasonable search." The CMO further provided that, unless native file format was "reasonably necessary to enable the other parties to review those files," ESI was to "be produced in 'Tagged Image File Format,'" accompanied by "[a] cross reference or unitization file, in standard format (e.g. Opticon, Summation DII, or the like) showing the Bates number of each page and the appropriate unitization of the documents."[2] The CMO further identified specific metadata fields that had to be produced if reasonably available.[3] Finally, the CMO directed the parties to produce "[a]n extracted text file or searchable

---

[2] The native file format is the "file structure defined by the original creating application," such as a document created and opened in a word processing application. The Sedona Conference, *The Sedona Conference Glossary: E-Discovery & Digital Information Management* 35 (Sherry B. Harris et al. eds., 3d ed. 2010). Tagged Image File Format ("TIFF") is "[a] widely used and supported graphic file format[ ] for storing bit-mapped images, with many different compression formats and resolutions." *Id.* TIFF "[i]mages are stored in tagged fields, and programs use the tags to accept or ignore fields, depending on the application." Unitization is "[t]he assembly of individually scanned pages into documents." *Id.*

[3] Metadata is "[d]ata typically stored electronically that describes characteristics of ESI, found in different places in different forms." The Sedona Conference, supra note 2, at 34. While "[s]ome metadata, such as file dates and sizes, can easily be seen by users[,] other metadata can be hidden or embedded and unavailable to computer users who are not technically adept." For example, in this case, the District Court ordered the parties to produce "metadata fields associated with each electronic document . . . where reasonably available," including, in part, the fields of "BegDoc," "EndDoc," "BegAttach," "EndAttach," "Author," "BCC,"

version . . . for each electronic document in a document level text file (except for any file produced in native format)."[4]

Hoosier and DMS each retained separate vendors to assist with the production of ESI.[5] Specifically, DMS retained Capital City Consulting ("CCC"), a North Carolina firm, and Hoosier retained Preferred Imaging and Xact Data Discovery. Based upon the vendors' invoices, RTA categorized the activities conducted by the vendors as follows: (1) preservation and collection of ESI; (2) processing the collected ESI; (3) keyword searching; (4) culling privileged material; (5) scanning and TIFF conversion; (6) optical character recognition ("OCR") conversion; and (7) conversion of racing videos from VHS format to DVD format.[6]

In total, Hoosier produced 430,733 pages of ESI, and DMS produced 178,413 documents in electronic format. In addition, ten DVDs of racing videos were produced. Hoosier paid its electronic discovery vendors, Preferred Imaging and Xact Data Discovery, more than $125,000. DMS claims to have incurred more than $240,000 in charges from CCC.

[The court concludes that 28 USC §1920, which authorizes recovery of "costs of making copies" necessary in the suit does *not* include most charges by vendors for their services, apart from "the conversion of native files to TIFF" and "the scanning of documents to create digital duplicates." The court awards the defense $20,083.51 in discovery costs.]

■ NOTES ON E-DISCOVERY IN THE TWENTY-FIRST CENTURY

1. The CMO in *Race Tires America*, generated on the basis of work done by lawyers meeting as required by Rules 16 and 26, was filled with details: Not only did the parties agree on search terms to be used by the producing party in responding to discovery requests, but they agreed as well on the form in

---

"CC," "Company," "Custodian Name," "Date Created," "Date Last Modified," and "Edit Time." Allowing discovery of these metadata fields permitted the parties to seek information that may not have been available in the documents' text.

[4] An extracted text file is a file containing text taken from an original electronic document. *See* Sedona Conference, *supra* note 2, at 12 (defining "[d]ata [e]xtraction").

[5] Electronic discovery has spawned much more than "[a] cottage industry." Hopson v. City of Baltimore, 232 F.R.D. 228, 239 n.32 (D. Md. 2005) (quoting T. Delaney, *E-Mail Discovery: The Duties, Danger and Expense,* 46 Fed. Lawyer 42, 44 (Jan. 1999)). For the year 2009, electronic discovery vendors had revenues equaling approximately $2.8 billion. *See* Arin Greenwood, *Law Practice: A New View, Part 2: E-Discovery Changes Have Some Seeing a Career in Document Review,* 97 A.B.A. J. 27, 27 (2011) (citing George Socha & Tom Gelbmann, *2010 Socha-Gelbmann Electronic Discovery Survey* (2010)).

[6] OCR is "[a] technology process that translates and converts printed matter on an image into a format that a computer can manipulate . . . and, therefore, renders that matter text searchable." Sedona Conference, *supra* note 2, at 37.

which the data would be produced. The order went so far as to address the standard of care required of the disclosing party: Complying with stipulated search strategies yields a "presumption" that the disclosing party has done what is expected. That implies that more might be required, doesn't it, since compliance isn't conclusive proof of an adequate response?

2. Much of the work was so technical that it wasn't carried out by client or lawyer, but by consulting firms in the business of dealing with electronic data during litigation. The task they performed was not small: It involved more than 600,000 documents and fees of $365,000. Of course, that wasn't the end of it: Lawyers or paralegals for the producing party normally spend time on the material before it's turned over to the other side, because they too need to know what they're turning over, what it might mean, and whether some of the material should be withheld because—despite having been picked up by the search—it isn't relevant or might be privileged.

3. The opinion refers frequently to the Sedona Conference, which describes itself as a nonprofit organization founded by an antitrust lawyer in 1997 and "dedicated to the advanced study of law and policy in the areas of antitrust law, complex litigation, and intellectual property rights." Its published reports on e-discovery and other cutting edge topics are helpful and informative, and often cited by courts, as in *Race Tires America.*

4. The coming of e-discovery put a premium on cooperation among lawyers during required consultations. See, e.g., Beard Research, Inc. v. Kates, 981 A.2d 1175, 1187 (Del. Ch. 2009) (absent "affirmative steps," some ESI will be "lost during the course of litigation through routine business practices or otherwise," which are realities that "counsel strongly in favor of early and, if necessary, frequent communications among counsel for opposing litigants to determine how discovery of ESI will be handled," and if lawyers do not take such steps the court "is not likely to be sympathetic when, for example, one party later complains that stringent measures were not instituted voluntarily by her adversary to ensure that no potentially relevant information was lost"); Trusz v. UBS Realty Investors LLC, 2010 WL 3583064 (D. Conn. 2010) (counsel agree on search terms; issues raised by motion could have been resolved if counsel had *actually* conferred; counsel must hold "an *in person conference*") (threatening to appoint magistrate judge to determine issues, with costs taxed as she may direct).

5. The 2006 amendments to the Civil Rules are process-oriented: They contain important provisions (directing parties to cover ESI in their plan, allowing the requesting party to specify "form" while allowing the producing party to object, and expressly relieving parties from the burden of producing ESI that is not "reasonably accessible"). But the Rule leaves much to the wise discretion of trial judges, and does not speak of cost allocation or offer details on distinguishing between accessible and inaccessible data. You are about to see the efforts of one trial judge to fill in these and other gaps.

2. Who Pays? How Much Is Discoverable? What About Retaining Data? What If Data Is Lost?

Race Tires America raises one issue relating to payment of expenses—are e-discovery costs recoverable by the prevailing party as part of costs? But it does not address the question whether the requesting party can be burdened *during discovery* with the costs incurred by the other side, and this issue arises often in the context of e-discovery. Also not discussed in *Race Tires America* is the extent to which a party can be asked to dig up data that is not readily accessible on an online server. Finally, the ephemeral nature of ESI, coupled with the increasing sophistication of "record retention" policies, which really means "record destruction procedures," has brought to the fore a new set of questions: How much data must be preserved, and what should happen when data is lost?

A series of five opinions by a federal trial court in the *Zubulake* litigation (a hard-fought sex discrimination case) made District Judge Shira Scheindlin a leading figure in the law of e-discovery. The following discussion and questions make frequent reference to four of her opinions in that case (others dealt with different matters). At the end of the day, the plaintiff Laura Zubulake reportedly won a verdict against defendant UBS, based on her claims of sex discrimination, in excess of $29 million (published reports indicate that the parties settled privately thereafter for an undisclosed sum).

A Starting Point: Who Pays? Long before e-discovery appeared, the Supreme Court set the "default rule," which is that each side pays its own costs. In other words, the disclosing party pays the cost of finding the information requested by the other side, and the requesting party pays its costs of making inquiry and dealing with the results. See Oppenheimer Fund v. Sanders, 437 U.S. 340, 358 (1978) (under discovery rules, "the presumption is that the responding party must bear the expense of complying with discovery requests," although he may "invoke the district court's discretion under Rule 26(c)" to prevent undue burden or expense, which can include "orders conditioning discovery on the requesting party's payment of the costs"). Many published opinions, including those in the *Zubulake* case, have unhesitatingly applied this principle to e-discovery. See, e.g., Dahl v. Bain Capital Partners, LLC, 655 F. Supp. 2d 146 (D. Mass. 2009) (applying *Oppenheimer* presumption, but suggesting that "costs can be shifted if the responding party identifies the source of the requested documents as not reasonably accessible because of an undue burden or cost").

Under a regime in which each side bears its own costs, it is not surprising that *Race Tires America* arose: Defendants recognized that they could not seek costs as discovery proceeded, so they tried to recover them at the end of the case, with limited success. One of the most promising ways of shifting costs involves arguments that the data being sought is not readily accessible, which leads to our next topic.

How Much Is Discoverable? Sometimes connected with questions of relevance, but sometimes wholly apart, is the question of accessibility of ESI. It is one thing to ask one to produce data that can be retrieved from an online server, quite another to ask a party to produce data that is not readily accessible. In *Zubulake I,* the court identified five categories of ESI: active online data, near-line data, offline storage/archives, backup tapes, and erased, fragmented, or damaged data. The court commented that the first three categories "are typically identified as accessible," and the last two are inaccessible.[1]

Another prominent decision on e-discovery came in the *McPeek* litigation. Both *McPeek* and *Zubulake* involved discrimination claims, and in each case plaintiff sought emails among colleagues that might disclose behavior and attitudes supporting the claims (Laura Zubulake claimed sex discrimination based on her being a woman; Steven McPeek claimed sexual harassment by male supervisor and retaliation when he complained). In each case, defendant produced emails responsive to plaintiff's request, and in each case plaintiff sought additional emails that could only be recovered from backup tapes, with some difficulty and expense. In each case, the trial court faced the question whether to permit additional discovery from these hard-to-access media, and who should pay for it.

In *McPeek,* Judge Facciola was troubled at burdening the government with all costs because it is not a "profit-making entity," in which incurring these costs "would yield the same 'profit' that other foregone economic activity would yield," and also because the government must "insist that its [own] employees do the restoration" of the backed up data (to protect against public disclosure), so the function of the agency will suffer "to the detriment of the taxpayers." Invoking the principle of "marginal utility," the court concluded that "the more likely it is that the backup tape contains information that is relevant to a claim or defense, the fairer it is that the government agency search at its own expense." The court was also troubled by the fact that ordering the producing party to bear all expense provides the other side with "a gigantic club with which to beat [the producing party] into settlement." The

---

[1] Online storage means material stored on magnetic disk during "the very active stages" of its life, when it is accessed frequently and can be retrieved quickly. Near-line data refers to "material stored in a robotic storage device" that uses "robotic arms" for access and retrieval, in which access speeds can be very high or very low. Offline storage refers to data stored on "removable optical disk" or other media, where retrieval requires "manual intervention" and access speeds may entail minutes or hours or even days. Backup tapes include devices that read and write data sequentially, often compressing the data so as to store more of it, and reading these sources may entail going through much extraneous material, and is much more time consuming and expensive. Erased, fragmented, or damaged data includes larger blocks that are broken up so as to accommodate new data, as well as data that have been damaged or erased, in which case "significant processing" is required. See Zubulake v. UBS Warburg LLC, 217 F.R.D. 309, 318-319 (S.D.N.Y. 2003) (*Zubulake I*).

court ordered defendant to search for emails from a certain computer for a one-year period, to document the time and money spent, and to return with arguments about further efforts at retrieval and allocation of expenses. McPeek v. Ashcroft, 202 F.R.D. 31, 34-35 (D.D.C. 2001); later opinion, 212 F.R.D. 33 (D.C. 2003) (declining to order further discovery because backup tapes covering other periods were unlikely to yield useful information).

The *Zubulake* litigation became more complicated, but it too involved initial restoration of some backed up data, with the idea of revisiting the matter to decide how much further to go and how to allocate costs. *Zubulake I* ordered defendant UBS (a Swiss-based global financial institution) to produce all relevant emails from its online and near-line data, and emails from five backup tapes selected by plaintiff, all at its own expense. See *Zubulake I*, at 324.

Who Pays (Revisited)? In compliance with the court's directive in *Zubulake I*, defendant produced some 600 discrete emails, and it asked the court to shift to plaintiff the costs of restoring relevant emails from 72 additional backup tapes. UBS had spent $11,524 in retrieving the data from the five backup tapes, so projected costs for the remaining 72 tapes would be $165,954. The court concluded that the emails already produced were indeed relevant, and revealed "a hostile relationship between Chapin and Zubulake," but none of those emails provided "direct evidence of discrimination" because they did not suggest that "dislike of Zubulake" was related to gender.

Zubulake I had endorsed a seven-factor test to resolve the cost-shifting problem. This test requires courts to consider (1) the extent to which the discovery request is tailored to obtain relevant material, (2) the availability of such information elsewhere, (3) total cost of production compared to amount in controversy, (4) total cost of production compared to resources available to each side, (5) relative ability of each party to control costs, and incentive to do so, (6) importance of the issues, and (7) relative benefits to the parties from obtaining the information. The first two factors, the court concluded in *Zubulake I*, are the most important (and they are essentially the "marginal utility" standard of *McPeek*). See *Zubulake I*, supra, at 324. In *Zubulake III*, the court again applied the seven-factor test, and concluded that UBS should pay 75 percent of those costs of retrieving relevant emails from the remaining 72 backup tapes and that Zubulake should pay 25 percent. See Zubulake v. UBS Warburg, 216 F.R.D. 280, 287-291 (S.D.N.Y. 2003) (*Zubulake III*).

Retaining Data; Consequence of Losing Data. While doing the restoration required by *Zubulake III*, UBS discovered that some backup tapes covering months and persons connected with the case were missing, and that certain relevant emails had been deleted from the online servers after the dispute had arisen (although they were preserved on backup tapes), leading plaintiff to return to court seeking sanctions. The court's opinion in *Zubulake IV* addressed these matters.

Zubulake IV decided that the duty to preserve data arises when litigation can be anticipated. In this case, the duty arose before suit was filed, when Zubulake had lodged charges with the EEOC, at which time "almost everyone associated with [her] recognized the possibility that she might sue." While a party at risk of being sued need not preserve "every shred of paper, every email or electronic document, and every backup tape," such a party "must not destroy unique, relevant evidence," and must preserve every document in existence or created thereafter (including emails on backup tapes) so as to preserve "a complete set of relevant documents." It can continue any regular process of destroying "inaccessible backup tapes" usually maintained only for purposes of recovery from disaster, but it should put in place a "litigation hold" for relevant material, and should preserve even backup tapes of documents connected with "key players" in the suit. See Zubulake v. UBS Warburg, 220 F.R.D. 212, 215-218 (S.D.N.Y. 2003) (*Zubulake IV*).

In a still later opinion, the court added that counsel has important responsibilities to ensure compliance with the duty to retain data: Counsel "must issue a 'litigation hold' at the outset of litigation or whenever litigation is reasonably anticipated," reissuing this directive periodically "so that new employees are aware of it." Second, counsel should "communicate directly with the 'key players' in the litigation." Third, counsel should "instruct all employees to produce electronic copies of their relevant active files" and ensure that "all backup media" is "identified and stored in a safe place." See Zubulake v. UBS Warburg, 229 F.R.D. 422, 332-434 (S.D.N.Y. 2004) (*Zubulake V*).

UBS did not do all it should, leading to this question: What should be the consequences of "spoliation"? The court considered three possible options: First, ordering the noncompliant party to bear a higher proportion of the costs of making discovery (UBS was already to bear 75 percent of its costs in retrieving the information requested but the remaining 25 percent of its costs had been shifted to plaintiff because she was seeking information that was inaccessible); second, an instruction inviting the jury to draw an adverse inference, from the fact that possibly relevant material had been lost, that this material would have supported the other side; third, shifting to the noncompliant party the additional costs incurred by the other side in pursuing further discovery trying to find out what the lost data might contain or suggest. In *Zubulake V,* the court took all three steps: UBS had failed to do all it should to preserve data (UBS personnel "continued to delete relevant emails"), and UBS "acted willfully in destroying potentially relevant information." Hence the court ordered UBS to bear the full costs of restoring the remaining 72 backup tapes, and promised an adverse inference instruction to the jury, and the court ordered UBS to pay *plaintiff's* costs for deposing key witnesses about information that might be on the lost material. See *Zubulake V,* supra, at 422.

■ NOTES ON E-DISCOVERY, DATA PRESERVATION, COSTS, AND SPOLIATION

1. The opinions in *Zubulake* terrify many lawyers. No lawyer was sanctioned there, but UBS lawyers were faulted for not doing enough even though they told their client to preserve data. And the court imposed costs on UBS, approved far-reaching discovery, and pledged to give the spoliation inference instruction. See generally Robert A. Weninger, *Electronic Discovery and Sanctions for Spoliation: Perspectives from the Classroom*, 61 Cath. U. L. Rev. 775 (2012) (useful discussion of issues surrounding spoliation and sanctions); Dan H. Willoughby, Jr., Rose Hunter Jones, and Gregory R. Antine, *Sanctions for E-Discovery Violations: By the Numbers*, 60 Duke L.J. 789 (2010) (sanctions for e-discovery violations have risen in the last ten years). The reported $29 million verdict may have proved the wisdom behind the comment in *Zubulake IV* that "an adverse inference instruction often ends litigation" because it is "too difficult a hurdle for the spoliator to overcome" and has "*in terrorem* effect." *Zubulake IV*, supra, at 219. Still, the *Zubulake* opinions reflect the decisions of one trial judge in one case. How authoritative can they be? They are influential, but are not binding elsewhere and do not enjoy the imprimatur of the Court of Appeals or the Supreme Court. *Most* opinions that we have on e-discovery issues come from district courts, and many are "not reported" (they appear in electronic sources and may be cited, but carry less weight than published opinions).

2. Does *Zubulake* adequately deal with the "gigantic club" problem noted in *McPeek*, which sometimes is described as a "perverse incentive" problem? See, e.g., Covad Communications Co. v. Revonet, Inc., 258 F.R.D. 5, 16 (D.C. Cir. 2009) (new technologies can be outcome determinative, "often at significant expense," and putting all costs on producing party "may create a perverse incentive" for the other side "to dispense with reason and restraint and unleash every new technology under the sun to try and find information that supports the requesting party's claims").

3. Is there any alternative to putting counsel in charge of ensuring that clients preserve ESI when litigation comes into view? Courts sometimes order use of "forensic imaging" to preserve content of computer memories. See, e.g., *Covad Communications Co.*, supra, at 5, 9 (in suit claiming that defendant hired to conduct sales and marketing campaign sold to others data belonging to plaintiff, ordering creation of forensic images of defendant's drives and computers to preserve information); Ameriwood Industries, Inc. v. Liberman, 2006 WL 3825291 (E.D. Mo. 2006) (ordering defendant to permit plaintiff's expert to make "mirror images" of defendant's computer memories). Should claims by one side that the other failed adequately to turn over ESI suffice as the basis to resort to forensic imaging? See John B. v. Goetz, 531 F.3d 448, 460 (6th Cir. 2008) (granting mandamus relief from order requiring defendants to allow plaintiff's expert, accompanied by deputy U.S. Marshals, to make images of hard drives and other devices; "mere skepticism that an opposing party has not produced all relevant information is not sufficient to warrant drastic electronic discovery measures"). See also New Hampshire Ball Bearings, Inc. v. Jackson, 969 A.2d 351, 360 (N.H. 2009) (forensic imaging can be ordered, but it can be so broad and intrusive that courts have been cautious, and without a showing of "relevance and need" courts disallow the drastic measure of letting one party "image all of an opponent's electronic media").

4. As reflected in the description of *Zubulake*, the court initially refused plaintiff's request for an adverse inference instruction. The court said that such an instruction is warranted only if (a) the party in question had control over the evidence and an obligation to preserve it, (b) the destruction went forward with a "culpable state of mind," and (c) the destroyed evidence was "relevant" and could be taken as proof that would support a claim or defense advanced by the other side. If evidence is destroyed "in bad faith" ("intentionally or willfully"), this fact alone demonstrates relevance. When plaintiff first asked for the instruction, there was no problem on the first and second points: UBS was in control and was "culpable," but plaintiffs did not convince the court that the lost emails would show sex discrimination, and UBS was not shown to have acted "in bad faith." See *Zubulake IV*, supra, at 220-221. In the end, however, when it came out that people at UBS deleted emails (one being "irretrievably" lost), and lost backup tapes, and failed to produce others that had been requested, the court concluded that indeed UBS had acted willfully and agreed to the adverse inference instruction. See *Zubulake V*, supra, at 427-436. Is the court on the right track here?

I   DISCOVERY SANCTIONS

You will see when you read FRCP 37 all the way through—and you should do that now—that the Rule sets up the possibility of serious sanctions for "failure" of a party to comply with discovery obligations. Among them are orders directing that certain facts "be taken as established" ("establishment preclusion" blocking the party at fault from proving designated matters), or prohibiting the party at fault from "supporting or opposing designated claims or defenses," or "striking pleadings," or "staying further proceedings" until the party does what it is supposed to do, or "dismissing the action" or "rendering a default judgment," or "treating as contempt" the conduct of the party at fault.

All these are unpleasant consequences—consequences that, if visited on a party for failing to make discovery, may produce an acute sense of embarrassment on the lawyer's part when she is obliged to tell her client what has happened, at least if it is her fault. Sometimes the fault is with a party: If a lawyer tells her client that an interrogatory requires certain information, which the client must dig up and supply, and if the client won't cooperate, the fault may lie with the client. Of course, the lawyer needs to warn the client what might happen, and of course, it may be possible to get more time. See, e.g., FRCP 34(h), allowing 30 days to reply to interrogatories, and providing that the parties may stipulate to "longer time" (or, less often, "shorter" time), and also that the court may order the time to be increased or (less often) decreased.

The main road to sanctions involves making a motion for a court order compelling discovery. Under FRCP 37(b)(4), "an evasive or incomplete disclosure, answer or response *must* be treated as a failure to disclose, answer or respond" for purposes of FRCP 37(a). And so the main relief is an order requiring the nonperforming party to cure the problem—by providing further answers or documents, for example. Note that the motion papers must include a "certification" that the movant "has in good faith conferred or attempted to confer with" the other side in an effort to get what is wanted "without court action." Finally, note that a party who obtains a court order for further discovery is also entitled to its "reasonable expenses" in making the motion, including attorneys' fees, but that losing the motion can result in an award of fees to the other side.

Sanctions vary in severity—an order "staying further proceedings" until the derelict party follows directions and answers or replies or produces documents, for example, is less consequential than an order "dismissing the action." Not surprisingly, in selecting among the various sanctions, a court considers such things as the seriousness of the failure, the importance of the information, the time that the party has had to comply, and the efforts that the party has (or has not) made to do what is required.

■ NOTES ON DISCOVERY SANCTIONS

1. The Supreme Court has given conflicting signals. On the one hand, the decision in *Hovey* held that a court cannot strike an answer and enter judgment against a defendant *simply as punishment* for disobeying an order. See Hovey v. Elliott, 167 U.S. 409 (1897). On the other hand, in *Hammond* the Court sustained the power of a court to strike an answer and enter judgment by default against a defendant that failed to obey an order to produce "books and papers" of the company and the witnesses, distinguishing *Hovey* on the ground that the failure to produce *here* supported an inference that the defense lacked merit, see Hammond Packing Co. v. State of Arkansas, 211 U.S. 322, 350-351 (1912). It is one thing, the Court seemed to say, to enter an order removing issues or claims or defenses simply as a means of punishing a party, quite another to enter such an order where disobedience is itself probative evidence against the noncompliant party.

2. The Court has spoken to other aspects of discovery sanctions.

(a) In *Société Internationale*, a Swiss holding company sued the Attorney General to recover property seized by the United States under the Trading with the Enemy Act during World War II, and the Court ordered plaintiff to

produce banking records of one of its clients in Switzerland. Plaintiff produced some records after obtaining permission from the Swiss government, but not all of them. The Court refused to conclude that plaintiff lacked "control" over the documents under FRCP 34, stressing that it was in a "most advantageous position to plead with its own sovereign for relaxation of penal laws or for adoption of plans which will at the least achieve a significant measure of compliance with the production order." The Court also concluded that FRCP 37 allows sanctions for "failure" to make discovery, and that "willfulness or good faith" do not affect "noncompliance," and are relevant only in selecting a remedy. In this case, it could not be said that failure to produce reflected "willfulness, bad faith, or any fault," as opposed to "inability" to do so. Hence dismissal was too severe. See Société Internationale pour Participations Industrielles et Commerciales v. Rogers, 357 U.S. 197 (1958).

(b) In *National Hockey League*, the Court approved dismissal of an antitrust suit when plaintiff didn't answer interrogatories as ordered. The Court stressed that the trial judge had made detailed findings of fact, and the Circuit Court had not taken issue with them. Hence "the most severe" sanction must be available, "not merely to penalize," but "to deter those who might be tempted" to do the same thing. In view of plaintiff's "flagrant bad faith" and "callous disregard" of responsibilities, dismissal was appropriate. See National Hockey League v. Metropolitan Hockey Club, Inc., 427 U.S. 639, 643 (1976).

3. Between them, *Société Internationale* and *National Hockey League* suggest that a trial court has wide discretion in applying FRCP 37, that it can impose sanctions not only to secure compliance but to deter future noncompliance, that fault or culpability is relevant in selecting remedies, and that noncompliance alone ("failure" to make discovery, to use the term in FRCP 37) can merit sanctions. It is harder to say what degree of fault is required, if any, for various sanctions, and how to assess fault. One notable attempt appeared in the *Cine Forty-Second Street* case, where the Second Circuit approved a sanction barring proof of damages in an antitrust suit that also sought injunctive relief, on a finding that plaintiff was grossly negligent in failing, after repeated directives by a magistrate, to produce information on the subject. The court said that if a party makes "good faith efforts" but is "thwarted by circumstances beyond his control," as might happen because the documents are located in a foreign country and a statute of that country makes disclosure a crime, then "an order dismissing the complaint" would violate due process. "Fault," the court wrote, "must at least cover gross negligence of the type present in this case." See Cine Forty-Second Street Theatre Corp. v. Allied Artists Picture Corp., 602 F.2d 1062, 1067 (2d Cir. 1979).

(a) Today *most* if not all the information sought in *Cine Forty-Second Street* would be produced at the outset, during "automatic discovery" under FRCP 26(a)(1)(A)(iii).

(b) Be sure you understand, by reading FRCP 37, that the issues resolved by the court in *Cine Forty-Second Street* can arise today under FRCP 26 and 37 and can be resolved the same way.

4. Suppose defendant in an accident case involving claims for a back injury asks plaintiff by interrogatory, "Were you in a skiing accident within a six-month period prior to the accident in issue in this case, and if so, describe the injuries you suffered in that skiing accident." Suppose plaintiff answers, "I was in a skiing accident in Alta, Utah, three months before the accident in issue, but I wasn't hurt very bad." That answer is inadequate. Suppose defendant goes to court (after trying to get more by conferring with plaintiff's lawyer) and asks for an order striking his personal injury allegations, invoking FRCP 37(b)(2)(A)(iii) (authorizing an order "striking pleadings in whole or in part"). Suppose plaintiff opposes this motion, correctly pointing out that defendant "didn't get an order requiring me to do more than I already did," but that defendant points out correctly that FRCP 37(d)(1)(A)(ii) allows a court to order such sanctions as striking a pleading if the other side "fails to serve its answers" after being "properly served" with interrogatories *and* that FRCP 37(a)(4) says that "an evasive or incomplete" answer "must be treated as a failure" to answer. Plaintiff should *not* win this argument, but you need to look at the cited provisions carefully to figure out why. Do that now.

5. The coming of e-discovery can combine with the sanction scheme in FRCP 37 to produce staggering results. Remember the *Zubulake* case (described in Section H, supra). Another memorable example is a fraud suit against Morgan Stanley for misrepresenting the financial condition of Sunbeam Corporation in merger talks with Coleman Holdings, where the judge concluded that defendant failed properly to produce electronic records and had continued overwriting data for more than a year while falsely certifying that it had complied with discovery orders. As a sanction, the court entered partial summary judgment, gave an adverse inference instruction, and shifted to defendant the burden of disproving plaintiff's claim of fraud. In the end, a jury awarded plaintiff $604 million in compensatory damages and $850 million in punitive damages. See Coleman (Parent) Holdings, Inc. v. Morgan Stanley & Co., 20 So. 3d 952 (Fla. App. 2009).

CHAPTER 10

Pretrial Management

INTRODUCTION

Back in 1938 when the Rules were promulgated, Rule 16 began life as a small provision that allowed district judges to hold pretrial conferences. Amended in 1983 and again in 1993, Rule 16 is now a major provision that builds on an initial planning conference that lawyers must attend (see FRCP 26(f)) and requires courts to enter a "scheduling order" that limits "the time to join other parties, amend the pleadings, complete discovery, and file motions" (FRCP 16(b)).

At least as important as the elaborate provisions in FRCP 16 is the philosophy and judicial mindset behind them. Judges are leaders and managers rather than simply arbiters, umpires, or decision makers, and judges are to establish timelines—or better yet, get the parties to agree on timelines—that will control the rest of the lawsuit. Recall from the *Malone* case (Chapter 1F) that judges go *much* further than setting timelines: In *Malone,* the judge demanded that plaintiff's counsel prepare a list of questions and expected answers for every witness, and dismissed the case with prejudice when compliance was not forthcoming.

Let's look more closely at pretrial procedures, and pick up some important points about these procedures as envisioned in FRCP 16:

➤ Trial courts "must" issue scheduling orders governing amendments to pleadings, joinder of parties, discovery, and pretrial motions (FRCP 16(b)).
➤ Trial courts "may" order parties and counsel to attend pretrial conferences; whether or not to do so is discretionary (FRCP 16(a)).
➤ Topics for discussion at any conference include formulating and simplifying issues, obtaining admissions and stipulations, avoiding

unnecessary proof and limiting expert testimony, identifying witnesses and documents, settling the case, and considering the possibility of separate trials for some claims or issues (FRCP 16(c)).

➤ Trial courts may hold a "final pretrial conference" to formulate a trial plan that will "facilitate the admission of evidence" (FRCP 16(e)).

➤ Trial courts may issue an order "reciting the action taken" in any pretrial conference, which "controls the course of the action unless the court modifies it" (FRCP 16(e)).

➤ Trial courts may sanction a party or lawyer who fails to appear at a pretrial or scheduling conference or is "unprepared to participate" or who "does not participate in good faith" or who "fails to obey a scheduling or other pretrial order," or may tax such attorney or party for "reasonable expenses" ("including attorney fees") caused by noncompliance with the Rule (Rule 16(f)).

A | MODERN PRETRIAL MANAGEMENT—DOES IT WORK?

Concerns over judicial efficiency underlie the modern approach to pretrial, and something more besides: Parties operating in an adversary system, in today's regulated society where litigation has increased exponentially while judicial resources have not kept up, cannot be expected to move efficiently from initial phases toward trial. Judge William Schwarzer, a long-time advocate of active managerial judging, put it this way: Discovery is "conducted so aggressively and abusively that it frustrates the objectives of the Federal Rules," and "adversarial techniques are generally counterproductive" in discovery and pretrial, as it is hard for a lawyer "to let her witness give damaging testimony at a deposition" or to "produce a smoking gun document," and adversarial techniques "are not conducive to nonconfrontational approaches" that can narrow issues or expedite litigation. See William W. Schwarzer, *The Federal Rules, the Adversary Process, and Discovery Reform*, 50 U. Pitt. L. Rev. 703, 714 (1989).

In classic articles, the late Professor Abram Chayes was even more emphatic about the importance of judges as managers, and about the forces that brought us to this place. See Abram Chayes, *The Role of the Judge in Public Law Litigation*, 89 Harv. L. Rev. 1281 (1976); *Public Law Litigation and the Burger Court*, 96 Harv. L. Rev. 4 (1981). Faced with "a growing body of legislation designed explicitly to modify and regulate basic social and economic arrangements" (see Role of the Judge at 1288), lawsuits came to look very different from traditional litigation—now suits involve more parties, relief includes more injunctions and ongoing judicial supervision, and the work of courts is less connected with resolving private disputes than with "vindicat[ing] public policies" (see Public Law Litigation at 4). Hence the judge is "the dominant figure in organizing and guiding the case, and he draws for support not only on the parties and their counsel, but on a wide range of outsiders—masters, experts, and oversight personnel" (see Role of the Judge at 1284).

These developments have not gone without criticism. In another classic article, Professor Judith Resnik offered a sharp critique of what she called—in a term that has stuck—"managerial judging." Pointing out that "few institutional constraints inhibit judges" during the pretrial phase—because pretrial rulings cannot be appealed, and review at the end of the case is highly deferential—she expressed doubt that this development actually increases efficiency, and pointed out that merely improving the rate of disposition of cases does not show that justice has been improved. Perhaps more important, taking on this role "expands the opportunities" for abuse of power while bringing judges into frequent informal contact with litigators invites "growth of personal bias." And increased involvement give judges "stakes" in the cases they manage, in which traditional "due process" values of "accuracy of decisionmaking" and "adequacy of reasoning" and "quality of adjudication" play second fiddle to "speed, control, and quantity" of dispositions. See Judith Resnik, *Managerial Judges*, 96 Harv. L. Rev. 374, 427-434 (1982).

Professor Tidmarsh offers what is perhaps the most pointed criticism of managerial judging, in an article whose main focus is what Professor Richard Marcus calls the "liberal ethos" in which the central aim of procedural rules is to arrive at a judgment "on the merits," and in which Rules are framed in open-textured functional provisions. It was Roscoe Pound who in 1906 delivered a speech on "The Causes of Popular Dissatisfaction with the Administration of Justice," whose target was the technicality of then-existing procedural law and excessive partisanship that he viewed as the result. In the following passage, Professor Tidmarsh argues that the looseness built into the Rules, and one might say particularly Rule 16, has huge impacts on outcomes:

> One of the appeals of Pound's view is the apparent neutrality of his "on the merits" principle; value determinations are left to the substantive law, of which the judge is a disinterested but enthusiastic expositor. Because it takes no sides on the outcomes of specific disputes, Pound's procedural system seems to be one on which partisans can agree. But the claim of neutrality is a chimera. Differing case management practices, in which judges are given wide (indeed, Pound-like) discretion to choose procedures to manage litigation, can deliver widely different expected outcomes. . . . Contrary to Pound's rose-colored view, there is no such thing as a baseline "neutral procedure." Put differently, in a world with omniscient judges, there is no need of procedure; but, in a world without omniscient judges, "on the merits" resolutions do not exist independently of the procedures used to obtain the result. The procedures used help to define what the merits are; "on the merits" has no meaning or significance apart from a given procedural system. The decision between competing procedural rules is often a decision between competing outcomes—between the groups we choose to favor and those we do not. Therefore, judicial discretion

carries the inherent risk that individual judges will shape procedural rules to achieve desired outcomes. Procedure is not devoid of politics.

Jay Tidmarsh, *Pound's Century, and Ours*, 81 Notre Dame L. Rev. 513, 533-534 (2006).

> There are indications that active judicial management in pretrial proceedings has had positive impact. Still, evidence for such improvements is hard to come by, and the only point on which there seems to be universal agreement is that setting firm deadlines *early* in the process does increase efficiency and reduce costs.[1]

Richard L. Marcus, *Reining in the American Litigator: The New Role of American Judges*, 27 Hastings Int'l & Comp. L. Rev. 3 (2003) (doubting that judicial management unduly constrains lawyers in discovery; acknowledging that judicial management "can force a lawyer to do more work than would be done otherwise" and drive up costs, but suggesting that judicial management may also improve "quality" of litigation; noting the criticism that judicial management leads to undue formality, but suggesting that informal resolution of differences "often saves time and money").

■ NOTES ON PRETRIAL

1. One criticism of the pretrial management model is that it takes judges away from the task of judging. See, e.g., Judge Patrick E. Higginbotham, *The Present Plight of the United States District Courts*, 60 Duke L.J. 745, 747 (2010) (federal judges now operate "more like administrative agencies" than trial courts, and in the disappearance of actual trials "we are witnessing the death of an institution whose structure is as old as the Republic"); Stephen N. Subrin, *Uniformity in Procedural Rules and the Attributes of a Sound Procedural System: The Case for Presumptive Limits*, 49 Ala. L. Rev. 79, 100-101 (1997) (judges became managers of necessity: "This is not what it meant to be a wise judge for the past three millennium," and judges "should not be reduced to being efficiency experts trying to curtail run-away cases and provoke settlements"). Consider whether the distracting effect of managerial judging is worth this cost. What else can we do? Have less regulation? More courts? Smaller lawsuits?

---

[1] Congress got into the act with the Civil Justice Reform Act of 1990, ordering federal courts to experiment with case management, and they did so with new vigor. Two RAND studies, however, concluded that the experiment had little positive impact. See James S. Krakalik et al., An Evaluation of Judicial Case Management Under the Civil Justice Reform Act 54-57 (1996) (reporting that early case management might actually increase costs); James S. Krakalik et al., *Discovery Management: Further Analysis of the Civil Justice Reform Act Evaluation Data*, 39 B.C. L. Rev. 613, 652-654 (1998) (case management increases costs initially, but achieves efficiencies as case moves forward).

2. Another criticism of pretrial management is that it is ill-suited for "smaller" or "simpler" cases. In at least some state systems, this concern has led to a simplified pretrial process in smaller cases, or to "tracking systems" designed for particular kinds of cases. See, e.g., Stephen N. Subrin, *The Limitations of Transsubstantive Procedure: An Essay on Adjusting the "One Size Fits All" Assumption*, 87 Denv. U. L. Rev. 377 (2010) (selecting some cases for "a special, simplified track on a case-size basis" makes "the most sense" while preserving "transsubstantivity" because it includes cases resting on a "wide range of substantive laws"); Colorado Rule 16.1 (in cases involving claims not exceeding $100,000, simplified pretrial procedures apply unless one or more parties elects otherwise; providing for expanded automatic discovery, exchanges of trial exhibits, and limiting testimony by witnesses whose depositions have not been taken).

3. What about the criticism that managerial judging is too much subject to judicial discretion? Compare Robert G. Bone, *Who Decides? A Critical Look at Procedural Discretion*, 28 Cardozo L. Rev. 1961, 1996-2000 (2007) (criticizing reliance on discretion, which makes judge into a "strategic player" whose behavior brings "social costs" despite doing "everything she can to further legitimate procedural policies and goals") and Tidmarsh, supra, at 513, 537 (discretionary procedure leads to lack of uniformity and to "delay, expense, and uncertainty") with Marcus, supra (although constraints on judges "have waned in the era of managerial judging," their area of discretion is "largely divorced from the underlying substance," and we are not seeing many claims that judges are "using their procedural discretion to advance their substantive preferences").

4. Professor Thornburg points out that judges enjoy tremendous discretion in managing trials too. You will consider the Rules of Evidence, which are major and detailed provisions governing proof at trial, when you take the Evidence course. Many of these do indeed accord a wide measure of discretion. See Elizabeth Thornburg, *The Managerial Judge Goes to Trial*, 44 U. Rich. L. Rev. 1261, 1324 (2010) (pointing out that judges have discretion in scheduling trial, shaping and ordering the proceedings, and making trial plans; judges can influence the selection of juries, admit or exclude evidence and control its format, decide the format for jury verdict, and they have the power to order new trials or not, depending on their view of the outcome; managerial judging "threatens both distributive and procedural justice," and allows "inconsistency that affects outcomes and neutrality").

B PRETRIAL ORDERS: INCENTIVIZING AND SANCTIONING LITIGANTS

Recall that under FRCP 16(e) the final pretrial order "controls" the suit thereafter. In perhaps the most important application of this language, claims, defenses, or issues that never appeared previously may enter the case and go forward to trial, *and* claims, defenses, or issues that *did* appear earlier can drop from the case.[2]

Recall the liberality authorized by FRCP 15 for amending pleadings (Chapter 7G). Parties may amend without permission if they act quickly, and thereafter they can amend by permission. If a party who omitted a claim or defense in pleadings could count on raising such omitted matter in pretrial statements, it would take the pressure off parties to get it right the first time, and there would be no point in FRCP 15's provision requiring permission to amend after the initial period has passed. Understanding this point, courts do not always let parties add forgotten claims, defenses, or issues to pretrial statements.[3]

Lest you think that pretrial orders are anything to be trifled with, or that courts are shy in coming down on lawyers who shirk what courts conceive to be their duties, read the *FM Industries* case and think about the message it delivers.

FM INDUSTRIES, INC. v. CITICORP CREDIT SERVICES, INC.

United States Court of Appeals for the Seventh Circuit
614 F.3d 335 (2010)

Before Easterbrook, Chief Judge, and Wood and Tinder, Circuit Judges.

Easterbrook, Chief Judge.

FM Industries sued Citicorp Credit Services for copyright infringement. The copyrighted work is computer software—"The Ultimate Collection and Network Software" or TUCANS—designed to help lawyers to collect debts and lenders to monitor how its lawyers are doing. The suit also named the Law Offices of Ross Gelfand, LLC, contending that it continued using the software after Citicorp dropped its license and told outside lawyers to stop using TUCANS. (There were still more defendants, whose dismissal is no longer contested.) The "copying" in question is the transfer of software

---

[2] In re Net-Velazquez, 625 F.3d 34, 40 (1st Cir. 2010) (in bankruptcy proceedings, bank failed "to pursue or even raise" defense of payment by mistake "at any point subsequent to its answer," and joint pretrial report did not mention it; Rules are set up "to winnow the issues presented by the pleadings as a case progresses," and resulting order is intended to shape trial, so claims or defenses omitted from it are "waived, whether or not properly raised in the pleadings"); Robinson v. McNeil Consumer Healthcare, 615 F.3d 861, 872 (7th Cir. 2010) (refusing to allow amendment to pretrial order to let plaintiff reinstate implied warranty claim; "plaintiff dropped the ball" and if fault was lawyer's, plaintiff may have a remedy against him); Friedman & Friedman, Ltd. v. Tim McCandless, Inc., 606 F.3d 494 498 (8th Cir. 2010) ("unpled affirmative defense identified in the pretrial order is no exception to the rule that issues identified in the pretrial order supersede the pleadings").

[3] See, e.g., Cruz v. Safford, 579 F.3d 840, 844 (7th Cir. 2007) (refusing to allow prisoner to add pendent state law claim for assault and battery in pretrial order; these claims had not been raised before, and parties had already gone far in the case; defendant had not researched or prepared these matters).

from a computer's hard disk to its random access memory, without the permission of the copyright proprietor. Citicorp licensed the TUCANS program, but FM Industries contends that Citicorp did not pay the agreed price and induced its outside debt-collection lawyers to go on using the program (thus making extra copies in computers' memory) after the license expired.

The district court dismissed FM Industries' request for damages because it failed to register the copyright until 2007. "Statutory damages" are available only for infringement after registration, and then only if the registration occurred within three months of the work's publication (2004 for this version of TUCANS). 17 USC §412. FM Industries never tried to show actual damages. That left questions about prospective relief. Defendants contended that Michael Friedman (FM Industries' president and principal shareholder) owns the copyright, . . . [which] would imply that the suit must be dismissed under FRCP 17(a), because not filed in the name of the real party in interest. Defendants also maintained that no infringement was ongoing or in prospect. The district judge concluded that material disputes prevented summary judgment on those questions and set the case for trial.

Ownership matters not only under Rule 17 but also because it affects who is entitled to damages. Friedman had filed for bankruptcy and wanted to keep any copyright recovery away from his creditors, prominent among which was Citicorp. FM Industries never did produce a contemporaneous document showing a transfer of ownership to itself, and the district judge was understandably suspicious of an affidavit that Friedman executed while this suit, and his bankruptcy, were under way.

Trial never occurred. Local rules require the parties to cooperate to produce a pretrial order. Northern District of Illinois Local Rule 16.1 Appendix ("Standing Order Establishing Pretrial Procedure") Instruction 6. The plaintiff's lawyer is supposed to produce a draft, which serves as the basis of discussion and modification. Wayne D. Rhine, the principal counsel for FM Industries, did not complete this task on time. When he finally produced a draft, it was egregiously noncompliant. (The problem here, and in much else that went wrong with the case, is that Rhine allowed Friedman, a nonlawyer, to draft many of the papers that were filed over Rhine's name. Rhine insists that he did not simply rent out his law license but instead reviewed and edited the documents before filing them. We accept that representation, but it also means that Rhine, who resumed legal practice in 2006 after 24 years as a judge of the Circuit Court of Cook County, Illinois, bears the responsibility for amateurish and absurd filings.)

Defendants' lawyers noted the problems, which Rhine promised to fix. But by the date set for the parties to present the joint pretrial order to the court, Rhine had not provided a revision incorporating defendants' contributions. Instead he presented a new draft based on the original deficient one and omitting the defendants' corrections and proposals, despite Rhine's promise to include them. The district judge reminded Rhine of the need to do his duties and warned him that failure would lead to dismissal for want of prosecution. Defense counsel drafted a pretrial order and asked Rhine to suggest modifications. Instead Rhine again tendered a woefully defective product that reflected the work of Friedman rather than anyone who knew what he was doing. Defendants protested; Rhine promised to do better. But at the next status conference in the district court there was no pretrial order to consider. The judge gave up and on May 6, 2008, dismissed the remaining claims for want of prosecution.

Next Rhine filed a motion asking the judge to reconsider and reinstate the claims originally set for trial. While the parties debated the propriety of relieving FM Industries of the adverse decision, defendants continued to request that Rhine prepare a draft pretrial order. By July 23, 2008, when the judge denied the motion to reinstate the dismissed claims, Rhine *still* had not submitted a draft in anything remotely like the form required and had not begun the process of consultation needed to get from the plaintiff's initial draft to the final joint pretrial order. Rhine's failure to act even with the benefit of this additional time was the district judge's main reason for denying the motion.

Dismayed by what had happened, the district court then ordered FM Industries to pay defendants' legal fees under 17 USC §505. The judge also concluded that Rhine had vexatiously multiplied the proceedings and is liable for attorneys' fees under 28 USC §1927. The judge made a further award under §1927 against William T. McGrath, a copyright specialist who Rhine had engaged to assist him. McGrath had signed only five of FM Industries' plentiful filings, but the judge deemed him fully responsible—perhaps more so than Rhine, a newcomer to copyright litigation. FM Industries was ordered to pay approximately $750,000 in attorneys' fees under §505. The tab for the two lawyers was smaller, because the district judge deemed only a subset of the filings sanctionable under §1927. They were held jointly and severally responsible for $35,000. A separate order directed Rhine to pay an additional $2,694.60.

FM Industries no longer contests the district judge's conclusion that it is not entitled to damages. But it says that the judge should have granted partial summary judgment in its favor on the question whether it owns and is entitled to enforce the copyright. That subject is no longer relevant, however, nor does it matter whether the judge should have given FM Industries more time for discovery. Even if the evidence establishes that Friedman transferred the copyright to FM Industries, triable questions remained about whether any defendant was infringing the copyright. So the judge could not have entered summary judgment in FM Industries' favor. And the reason this case did not get to trial is that Rhine bollixed the job of preparing the pretrial order. All other subjects fall out of the picture.

Now represented by different counsel, FM Industries says that pretrial orders aren't all that important and that errors in their preparation shouldn't lead to dismissal. But FRCP 16(f)(1)(B) says that, when a party is unprepared to participate in the pretrial conference, a judge may use any of the sanctions mentioned in FRCP 37(b)(2)(A)(ii)-(vii). Subsection (v) in this list authorizes "dismissing the action or proceeding in whole or in part." That's what the judge did. (Contrast Smith v. Chicago School Reform Board of Trustees, 165 F.3d 1142 (7th Cir. 1999), which reversed a judge for using the sanction specified in Rule 37(b)(2)(A)(i), which is omitted from the authorization in Rule 16(f)(1)(B).)

It is not as if the judge acted precipitately. Rhine's failures were of both commission (bizarre drafts) and omission (producing nothing when a new draft was required, and not using defendants' drafts as the basis for his own proposals). The judge warned Rhine that failure to produce an appropriate draft and cooperate in negotiation would lead to dismissal. The warning did not work. And the real end did not come until, 11 weeks after the dismissal for want of prosecution, Rhine *still* had not produced a plausible draft pretrial order. A district judge need not wait forever. Eventually a plaintiff's failure to cooperate in the prosecution of its own suit leads to dismissal. The sanction must be proportional to the delict, but the problem with the pretrial order was just the straw that broke the camel's back. There were many more deficiencies, which surely influenced the dismissal order as well as the substantial awards of attorneys' fees.

Long before dismissing this suit for want of prosecution, the district judge had concluded that FM Industries and its lawyers were playing games, engaged in extortion, or both. They demanded statutory damages of $15 billion, although 17 USC §504(c)(2) provides that, even for willful infringement, the award cannot exceed $150,000. The theory seems to have been that this limit applies per copy made, and that as computers are very good at copying data, and may move software instructions around in random access memory, every computer using the TUCANS software made multiple copies daily. This is the same flavor of argument that a former judge in the District of Columbia made in support of his demand for $65 million from a laundry that supposedly lost one pair of pants. That claim failed, see Pearson v. Chung, 961 A.2d 1067 (D.C. App. 2008), and was widely lampooned. The defendants pointed out that the statutory limit under §504(c) is per copyright ("any one work" is the statutory language) rather than per copy, as well as the fact that the delayed registration made statutory damages unavailable. Rhine and his client were undeterred and filed a blizzard of paper, to which defendants had to respond.

That's not all—and not even the worst of it. Although Rhine never produced a plausible draft of a pretrial order, and exceeded many other time limits in the litigation, when defendants missed *one* discovery deadline, and by a single day, FM Industries moved for sanctions. It wanted cash compensation for the injury caused by this delay. How much? It demanded $815 million! The defendants and the district judge were not amused, but defendants had to devote substantial time (and thus expense) to responding, because if the judge were prepared to award even a tiny fraction of the request the outlay would be considerable.

FM Industries served extensive discovery demands on several law firms that are not parties to the suit but work as outside counsel for Citicorp in collecting debts. Rhine did not pay any attention to FRCP 45, which tells litigants how to obtain information from nonparties. Nor did Rhine notice that the right venue for nonparty discovery is a court with personal jurisdiction over each entity. A federal district court's subpoena power in most civil litigation runs only within its district (or 100 miles from its courthouse, if that is farther). See Rule 45(b)(2)(B). After serving blunderbuss demands without regard to the rules, forcing the recipients to incur legal expenses to learn what obligations they had (none, as it turns out), FM Industries simply walked away when informed that all of the demands that it had served were ineffectual. It did not follow up with proper subpoenas.

This was extortionate discovery, the kind a litigant undertakes when it hopes to be paid to go away and spare opponents the expense of vindicating their rights. FM Industries' attempt to force Charles Prince, then the chairman of Citigroup's board of directors, and Sanford Weill, his predecessor, to submit to depositions, even though they had nothing to do with Citicorp's use of TUCANS, is further evidence that FM Industries and its lawyers were engaged in an abuse of legal process.

There is more, but extending this recitation would not serve much purpose.

As for attorneys' fees: None of the appellants questions the reasonableness of the amounts. They contend only that the district judge should not have awarded any fees at all. Yet a defendant that prevails in copyright litigation is presumptively entitled to fees under §505. Damages and equitable relief encourage copyright proprietors to enforce their rights, whether or not they get attorneys' fees too. A defendant who prevails in copyright litigation vindicates the public's interest in the use of intellectual property, but without an award of fees the prevailing defendant has only losses to show for the litigation. Defendants in this suit incurred substantial expense to beat back a series of preposterous claims ($15 billion in statutory damages indeed!) and are entitled to be made whole. Not that FM Industries is apt to pay, but defendants are entitled to what they can collect from any unencumbered assets they can find. (Defendants stand in line behind FM Industries' secured creditors.)

Rhine contends that he did not "multiply" the proceedings, and therefore should not have been sanctioned under §1927, but the district court's award is sound. This litigation was marked by excessive and unnecessary filings that richly deserve the label vexatious. Rhine's objections are quibbles. He contends, for example, that he did not demand $15 billion in damages—a stupendous figure that led defendants to generate far more paper, and endure higher legal bills, than any plausible claim would have warranted. No, Rhine insists, all he did was demand that defendants and the court use a formula that worked out to $15 billion. The fact that the phrase "$15 billion" does not appear in a complaint is irrelevant. A complaint that demands $150,000 (the statutory cap) times 100,000 (the complaint's estimate of the number of times computers copied the software into random access memory) is demanding $15 billion. Even lawyers can multiply two numbers. And the fact that this sum is, in the words of Rhine's appellate brief—he is representing himself and testing the adage that a lawyer who does this has a fool for a client—"one prayer for relief, out of many, and based on certain possible scenarios" does not help. One other prayer "out of many" was for statutory damages of $7.2 million ($150,000 times 48, the number of outside law firms that used the software), which is no more tenable than $15 billion. Another demand was for $235 million in actual damages, which plaintiff never attempted to prove and now has abandoned. No more need be said about the award against Rhine.

McGrath, by contrast, did not sign the complaint, demand $815 million as a discovery sanction, insist that Sanford Weill appear for a deposition, foul up the process of preparing a pretrial order, or take any of the other steps that led to the sanction against Rhine. True, he filed an appearance for FM Industries and signed five papers, but the district court did not find that any of those five vexatiously multiplied the proceedings. Indeed, neither the magistrate judge (who recommended sanctions) nor the district judge identified a single thing that McGrath did wrong. He seems to have been sanctioned for making the mistake of agreeing to help a careless lawyer (Rhine) who put his name to frivolous and malicious documents drafted by a self-interested layman (Friedman), and then not reviewing all of the documents that Friedman prepared for Rhine's signature. But of course McGrath was not engaged as a second-tier reviewer of Friedman's scribbling; he was engaged to help Rhine get his bearings in copyright law. That McGrath failed at this task does not make him responsible for documents that bear Rhine's name but not his own.

Liability under §1927 is direct, not vicarious. At oral argument defendants contended that McGrath could be held liable because he did not prevent Rhine from filing unreasonable and vexatious documents. Well, McGrath was not hired to do that, and no lawyer undertakes such a role for free. Section 1927 does not require every lawyer who files an appearance to review and vet every paper filed by every other lawyer. Neither the text of §1927, nor any decision of which we are aware, imposes on any lawyer a duty to supervise or correct another lawyer's work. Nor did the district court give this as a reason for the award against McGrath. We appreciate that the judge was disgusted by the behavior of FM Industries and its counsel, but personal responsibility remains essential to an award of sanctions under §1927.

The decision awarding sanctions against McGrath is reversed. All of the district court's other decisions are affirmed.

■ NOTES ON THE PRETRIAL PROCESS

1. Recall Judge Schwarzer's argument that adversarial techniques are "counterproductive" during discovery and pretrial. Does *FM Industries* support his argument? If the facts recited by the court are correct, it is hard to believe that Wayne Rhine was not acting strategically—avoiding the assigned task of drafting an appropriate pretrial order and persisting in submitting material that the court had rejected—characterized by Judge Easterbrook as "egregiously noncompliant" and perhaps drafted by the lawyer's client. Notice the other criticisms uppermost in Judge Easterbrook's mind—the high damage demand ($15 billion), the fact that *plaintiffs* sought sanctions when defendants were a day late in discovery, and the fact that plaintiff filed discovery demands that did not comply with the Rules. Do these points show the judge had lost objectivity when it came to the issue at hand—should failure to produce a pretrial order lead to dismissal with prejudice—or do they show that plaintiff richly deserved this severe sanction?

2. Suppose important claims, issues, or defenses are *omitted* from a pretrial order. FRCP 16(b)(3) contemplates that pretrial scheduling orders may be modified "only for good cause" and with the court's consent, and FRCP16(e) contemplates that pretrial orders can be modified. Also, FRCP 16(f) says "a final pretrial order" can be amended after the final conference "to prevent manifest injustice." If a party seeks modification of a pretrial order to include something that was omitted, what kind of showing must it make? See Meaux Surface Protection, Inc. v. Fogleman, 607 F.3d 161, 167 (5th Cir. 2010) (court considers explanation for failure, importance of amendment, potential prejudice in allowing amendment, and availability of continuance to cure prejudice) (letting plaintiff amend to seek lost profits, without which plaintiff had no claim; trial court allowed amendment to prevent substantial injustice, a "watertight" finding; prejudice was minor).

CHAPTER 11

Summary Judgment, and a Look at Burdens

INTRODUCTION

Sometimes a lawsuit proceeds past the pleading stage and through discovery, and one or all parties conclude that there is no doubt about the facts. Or it may happen that one party concludes—or all parties may agree—that there is simply no evidence that can prove a critical point. If indeed the facts are clear and certain, or there is no proof of a critical point, the case should not go to trial because there is nothing for a factfinder to do—no "facts to be found," no conflict among witnesses to resolve. Hence we need a mechanism that lets a court enter judgment summarily, awarding recovery or denying it. That mechanism is the motion for summary judgment, which is authorized by FRCP 56.

Motions to Dismiss Compared. Summary disposition is available at the pleading stage as well. Recall that a motion under FRCP 12(b) can lead to dismissal if the complaint fails to state a claim. Although it happens less often, a motion for judgment on the pleadings under FRCP 12(c) can lead to victory for *either* side—plaintiff can win if defendant's answer does not deny the charging allegations or offer any other defenses, and defendant can win if the pleadings show that plaintiff cannot recover. What is the difference between such preliminary motions and the motion for summary judgment? The answer is that the former scrutinizes *the pleadings* to see whether they adequately allege claims or defenses, while the summary judgment motion scrutinizes evidence of *facts* to see whether, in the words of FRCP 56(a), there is any "genuine dispute as to any material fact."

It's obvious what a court looks at to resolve motions brought under FRCP 12(b)—the pleadings. It is less obvious what a court looks at to determine whether the facts are subject to "genuine dispute." If you parse FRCP 56(c), you will see that courts look at affidavits provided by the parties—that is to say, sworn written statements that ordinarily require the seal of a notary.[1] Courts also look at material generated in discovery—depositions, documents, admissions, interrogatory answers. Conspicuously *missing* from the list in FRCP 56(c) is "pleadings," and it is commonly said that a motion for summary judgment "pierces the pleadings" because a party *seeking* summary judgment cannot just point to her complaint or answer and say "I'm entitled to judgment because I alleged or denied X and Y and Z," and a party *resisting* summary judgment cannot just point to *her* complaint or answer and say the motion should be denied on that basis.

An Example. Suppose Lincoln General issued supplemental liability insurance coverage (SLI) in the amount of $1 million on a car that Raymond rented from Traveler Rental, and Raymond drove the car under the influence of methamphetamines. Suppose that when he saw the blinking lights of a patrol car signaling him to stop, he fled in what became a high-speed chase ending in a collision with a car driven by Brandon, leading to his death. Raymond has demanded that Lincoln defend a tort suit brought by Brandon's estate, but Lincoln thinks it has no responsibility because of Raymond's bad behavior. Lincoln seeks a declaratory judgment that its SLI does not apply because of an exclusion reaching use of the car "in a race or similar contest" or "for any illegal purpose" or while the driver is "under the influence of alcohol or drugs." After discovery, Lincoln moves for summary judgment. If all agree as to what happened, there is no factual issue. One might argue about other things: Is the exclusion void as violating public policy? If not, it seems that Lincoln should have judgment. See, e.g., Bailey v. Lincoln General Insurance Co., 2011 WL 2150759 (Colo. 2011) (approving summary judgment for Lincoln; exclusions did not violate public policy).

A Simple Matter? From one perspective, motions for summary judgment are simple matters: A party makes a motion, claiming that the evidence is one-sided or there is no evidence of some point critical to the other side; the court searches the record, including affidavits and discovery documents, and resolves the issue.

But it is not so simple: For one thing, summary judgment motions invite a look at the allocation of burdens, meaning which side has to prove what? And if the parties produce affidavits and discovery documents to show what the evidence is, how much evidence is enough? What if affidavits or discovery information comes from witnesses who might, if they testified at trial, be

---

[1] A "jurat" ("she swore" in Latin), is the notary's signed-and-sealed statement that the "affiant" (maker of the affidavit) appeared before the notary and swore or committed under penalty of perjury to the truthfulness of the affidavit itself.

disbelieved? Are summary judgment motions appropriate where the critical issue is something vague and arguably subjective, like knowledge or intent? Behind these questions is the fear that the summary judgment mechanism infringes the right to a jury trial. Judges and lawyers sometimes denigrate summary judgment as "trial by affidavit," in contrast with a "real trial" in which witnesses appear and testify, to be scrutinized and believed or disbelieved.

A   BURDENS OF PROOF: A FIRST LOOK

We speak of "burdens" in procedure because courts act only when parties ask them to do so and, as we usually say, "prove their case." Hence *allocating* burdens and *defining* their extent are critical.

Oversimplifying for a moment, normally plaintiff bears the burdens at the beginning of a lawsuit, because *plaintiff* is the one who wants the court to do something. Thus, as you saw in Chapter 7, plaintiff bears the burden of pleading a claim for relief. The idea of burdens also lies behind orders that emerge from pretrial conferences, which set out the "issues" to be tried and aim to avoid "unnecessary proof and cumulative evidence" (FRCP 16), as you saw in Chapter 10.

Plaintiff bears the burdens at trial too, where we speak of the burden of proof. These burdens are "given teeth" in jury instructions, which are quite specific about who bears what burden, and in this sense burdens shape trials. When the proof is in, post-trial motions raise the question whether enough evidence has been presented, and in this sense these motions test the performance of the parties in carrying their burdens (see Chapter 12C1).

Now we must look at burdens in more detail. The reason is that summary judgment motions are affected by burdens: For one thing, *any time* court action is precipitated by party request (motion), we must consider whether the movant has done what must be done to advance the request. More importantly, a summary judgment motion goes to the heart of the case: Such a motion can terminate proceedings by leading to "judgment on the merits" that has the same effect as judgment after trial. Hence the fortunes of the parties should be resolved in this setting in light of what would be expected of them if the case went to trial.

1. Burdens of Production and Persuasion

"Burden of proof," it turns out, is an imprecise term that embraces two related but different concepts that come into play in a trial. One is the burden of producing evidence (burden of production); the other is the burden of persuasion.

Burden of Production. To say a party bears the burden of producing evidence is to say she runs the risk of losing automatically (on motion for judgment as a matter of law, before or after verdict) if she does not offer sufficient evidence to enable a reasonable person to find in her favor. At the outset, usually the party who bears the burden of persuasion also bears the burden of production. If Agnes sues Burt for personal injuries arising from a car accident, for example, she bears the burden of producing evidence of Burt's negligence. If she carries the burden, she is assured that the trier will consider and weigh her evidence, a benefit most visible in a jury-tried case.

Success in carrying the burden of production does not necessarily shift that burden to the adversary. If Agnes offers sufficient evidence to support a finding that Burt was negligent, the trier of fact ordinarily remains free to reject her proof. Hence the burden of production does not pass to Burt, and he might win even if he produces no counterproof, though the risk that the trier will find against him may be higher if he stands silent rather than offering credible counterproof.

If the party bearing the burden of production carries it very well, however, the burden does shift to her opponent. That means he can lose automatically if he does not offer rebuttal evidence. Jurisdictions vary in defining proof that shifts the burden of production to the opponent. "Cogent and compelling" can serve as a convenient shorthand for proof of this quality, and it is evidence that is so persuasive that a reasonable jury could not reject it: It makes sense to say that proof of this quality shifts the burden of production to the other side because a reasonable jury *must* accept such proof unless it is answered or rebutted in some way. (Testimonial proof cannot have this burden-shifting effect if a reasonable person could disbelieve the witnesses.) Agnes might shift the burden to Burt by offering unequivocal testimony by neutral observers that Burt rear-ended her car while she was stopped at the intersection for a red light, if Burt fails to make any headway in discrediting the witnesses on cross or otherwise. Burt must offer *some* counterproof—like evidence that he did not run into Agnes, or did so only because *he* was struck by another car. Failing to produce counterproof puts him at risk of a partial judgment as a matter of law on negligence, leaving only damages to be determined by the jury.

Burden of Persuasion. To say a party bears the burden of persuasion (or risk of nonpersuasion) is to say she can win only if the evidence persuades the trier that the facts exist that are necessary if she is to prevail. Ordinarily, that means she wins only if, on the basis of the evidence, those facts seem more likely true than not. Perhaps because this burden operates at the end of trial, courts say it never "shifts." Usually, it is actually mentioned only in jury trials, in argument and instructions.

Elements in These Burdens. Parties need not produce evidence on every element that might bear on liability, any more than they must plead them. The best reason to ignore many potential elements is that ordinarily they do not affect outcome. As Professor Cleary put it, requiring plaintiff in a contract suit "to establish the existence or nonexistence . . . of every concept treated in Corbin and Williston" would be burdensome, and would force the lawsuit to cover "unnecessary territory." See Edward Cleary, *Presuming and Pleading: An Essay on Juristic Immaturity*, 12 Stan. L. Rev. 5, 7 (1959). Thus, evidence sufficient to enable the trier to find agreement, consideration, performance, breach, and damages normally satisfies the burden of production in a contract suit. In the absence of defense evidence, plaintiff prevails if the trier is persuaded on these points. Yet the right to recover might turn on matters such as the fulfillment of conditions, legality of the agreement or contemplated performance, modification of terms, waiver, estoppel, or accord and satisfaction. If such issues are raised (normally defendant must do so), the outcome might turn on how they are resolved.

Allocating Burdens. On any particular point, ordinarily burdens of pleading, producing evidence, and persuading the trier of fact are all cast on the same party. Unfortunately, modern textwriters give confusing signals on the relationship between the pretrial burden of pleading and the trial burdens, implying that one burden impels the others, but disagree as to which is in the driver's seat.[2] And (as is true of the burden of pleading) it is easy enough to discern the custom on such matters, but hard to explain *why* the burdens are allocated as they are, or to come up with rules of general application. It turns out that burdens of persuasion at trial are allocated by reference to the same four concerns that apply to burdens of pleading that you saw in Chapter 7: That is to say, burdens are allocated to serve substantive policy, to recognize what is most probably true, to place them on the party most likely to have access to the necessary proof, and to help resolve cases where definitive proof is unavailable.

Weight of the Burdens. In civil cases, burdens of production and persuasion are related: The first requires a party to produce sufficient evidence to permit reasonable persons on the jury to find the point with the requisite measure of certainty, as defined by the burden of persuasion. The second means, in most civil actions, proof by a preponderance—that is, evidence that persuades the jury that the points to be proved are more likely so than not.[3]

---

[2] Compare McCormick on Evidence §337, at 509 (J. Strong 5th ed. 1999) (usually "the party who has the burden of pleading a fact will have the burdens of producing evidence and of persuading the jury of its existence") with J. Cound, J. Friedenthal, A. Miller & J. Sexton, Civil Procedure Cases and Materials 527 (8th ed. 2001) (burden of pleading an issue "usually is assigned to the party who has the burden of producing evidence on that issue at trial").

[3] In some civil actions (suits for fraud or reformation of a contract), the party bearing those burdens can prevail only on the basis of "clear and convincing evidence," which seems to enhance both burdens. In assorted other special cases, similar heavy burdens are imposed. See, e.g., Addington v. Texas, 441 U.S. 418 (1979) (in civil commitment proceedings, due process requires burden of persuasion "equal to or greater than" clear and convincing standard).

2. The Football Field Analogy

The effect of burdens can be illustrated by imagining a football field, in which there are three important areas. One is the area between the near goal line and the twenty-yard line; another is the larger area between the two twenties; third is the area between the far twenty and the far goal line. Now imagine a game between plaintiff Paula and defendant David. If Paula has the ball, and on fourth down she is stopped shy of her own twenty, we can say her proof is "insufficient" and she should lose automatically. If she makes it out to the vast middle area (between the twenties), we say her proof is "sufficient," and it is up to the factfinder to decide whether she wins or not. If she gets the ball beyond David's twenty, we say her proof is "cogent and compelling" and she wins automatically.

Of course, the game doesn't stop after one series of plays. If David gets the ball and advances toward midfield (between the twenties), then again it is up to the factfinder to decide. If he stops short of his own twenty, he loses automatically (his proof is insufficient, or hers is cogent and compelling). If he gets beyond Paula's twenty, he wins automatically.

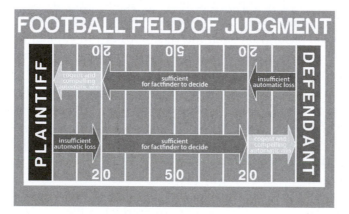

The analogy has limits, but is useful in several ways: First, it may help you visualize the differences between insufficient, sufficient, and cogent and compelling evidence. Second, you can see that the factfinder (usually juries, but a similar idea applies to judges in bench-tried cases) has leeway in deciding what the evidence proves—we speak of juries "weighing" the evidence and of the "discretion" of judges to decide the facts in bench-tried cases. Thus in the vast sixty-yard space between the twenties, the question whether Paula or David should prevail—Paula because she's gotten beyond midfield, or David because we end up closer to Paula's goal than his—is up to the factfinder. And the illustration makes the intuitively congenial point that ending up shy of one's own twenty means trouble, while reaching a point beyond the opponent's twenty means that scoring is almost inevitable.

3. Burdens and Summary Judgment: Three Paradigm Situations

Motions for summary judgment are made in three different situations that affect the manner of their resolution. The following descriptions are oversimplified in assuming that plaintiffs bear the burdens of production and persuasion, and defendants do not—which is usually true, but not always.

(1) Plaintiff's Motion. When plaintiff moves for summary judgment, it is understood that she must make her case by offering what we have called cogent and compelling evidence of the elements in her claim. In a contract case, for example, the usual elements are (a) agreement, (b) plaintiff's performance, (c) defendant's failure to perform, and (d) resultant damages (see Chapter 7B3, supra). If plaintiff establishes these points by proof of this quality, *and if defendant offers nothing in defense* (no proof, for example, that defendant did perform, or that conditions for defendant's performance did not obtain), plaintiff is entitled to summary judgment. Often *partial* summary judgment is appropriate, see FRCP 56(g) (court may enter an order stating that some "material fact" is not in dispute and "treating the fact as established"). In our contract suit, the court might determine liability and leave damages for trial.

(2) Defense Motion ("The Facts Are on My Side"). Sometimes, a defendant seeks summary judgment by arguing that the critical facts are known, and defendant must prevail. In Tim's suit against E&E Repair, for example, plaintiff claimed he was injured when a truck owned by his employer rolled backward after being parked and struck him. E&E had been asked to repair the parking brake, but it advised Tim's employer that it was unable to repair the brake and it still did not work. E&E was entitled to summary judgment. See Lindsley v. E&E Automotive & Tire Service, Inc., 241 P.3d 880 (Alaska 2010). In such a simple case, the motion is unproblematic.

(3) Defense Motion ("Plaintiff Has No Evidence"). Sometimes defense motions for summary judgment rest not on the proposition that the facts are known and there is no liability, but on the proposition that plaintiff has no proof of a critical fact. In a suit against Best Buy, for example, where Tina claimed she fell and broke her ankle in the store on account of improper waxing and floor maintenance, Best Buy won summary judgment on a showing that Tina's only proof of causation was projected testimony by an engineer who had inspected the floor three years later, which could not suffice to prove negligence. See Kieffer v. Best Buy, 14 A.3d 737 (N.J. 2011). Again, in such a simple case the motion is unproblematic.

As you can imagine, defendants more often move for summary judgment than plaintiffs, as in the second and third situations. Note that in these cases, the movant would not bear the burdens of production or persuasion at trial, so one may plausibly ask whether the movant should have any burden at all in making the motion: Must the movant establish the absence of proof by some elaborate means, or can it simply make the motion and force *plaintiff* to come up with proof?

B SUMMARY JUDGMENT: THE *ADICKES* AND *CELOTEX* CASES

Now we turn to two classic Supreme Court decisions on defense motions for summary judgment—in the *Adickes* case in 1970 and the *Celotex* case in 1986. Both construe FRCP 56, which has changed in the meantime, but the decisions illustrate different attitudes toward the motion, and both cases could plausibly come out the same way today, under the present language in Rule 56.

Kress Store, Hattiesburg, Mississippi

Sit-in demonstrations, such as the one that gave rise to the *Adickes* case, began as early as the 1930s, and they were to become important in the movement for racial equality that led to passage of the Civil Rights Act of 1964. Already in 1948 President Truman had issued an executive order requiring equality of treatment in the military, and in 1954 the Supreme Court had declared in *Brown* that segregation in public schools violates the Equal Protection Clause. See Brown v. Board of Education, 347
U.S. 483 (1954). In the next year, Rosa Parks famously refused to relinquish her seat at the front of the bus in Montgomery, Alabama. But segregation remained a fact of American life, and it took the civil rights movement, led by Martin Luther King, Jr. and others, to create the political conditions necessary to the passage in1964 of the Civil Rights Act. Integral to this movement were sit-ins and marches. President Kennedy gave important speeches aligning himself and his administration with the movement for racial equality, but he died from an assassin's bullet some nine months before Congress acted. The sit-in that gave rise to the *Adickes* case occurred in August 1964, just a month after President Johnson had signed the Civil Rights Act, and it was but one such event in a long chain of similar ones: Notable similar actions had already occurred in retail establishments in North Carolina (the Woolworth's store in Greensboro), in Kentucky (the Nashville sit-ins), and elsewhere. In 1965, Congress enacted the Voting Rights Act, and in 1968 President Johnson signed amendments extending the reach of the Civil Rights Act.

ADICKES v. S.H. KRESS & COMPANY

United States Supreme Court
398 U.S. 144 (1970)

Mr. Justice HARLAN delivered the opinion of the Court.

[Sandra Adickes was a white woman from New York serving as a volunteer teacher in a Freedom School for black children in Hattiesburg, Mississippi. In August 1964 she went with six students to the public library, where the librarian asked them to leave, and later called the chief of police, who came and told them that the library was closed, ordering them to leave. They then went to the Kress store to eat lunch.

The complaint alleged that after the group sat down, a policeman entered and saw Ms. Adickes with her students. A waitress took the students' orders but refused to serve Ms. Adickes because she was "in the company of Negroes." According to the complaint, the group left the store, but on reaching the sidewalk, the officer who saw them in the store arrested Ms. Adickes on a "groundless charge of vagrancy."

Under §1983, plaintiff must prove that Kress deprived her of a right secured by the Constitution, and acted under color of law. Since Kress is the defendant (not a state official), Adickes can recover only if she can show that "a Kress employee, in the course of employment, and a Hattiesburg policeman somehow reached an understanding to deny Miss Adickes service . . . or to cause her subsequent arrest" because she was a white person in the company of black persons.]

We now proceed to consider whether the District Court erred in granting summary judgment on the conspiracy count. In granting respondent's motion, the District Court simply stated that there was "no evidence in the complaint or in the affidavits and other papers from which a 'reasonably minded person' might draw an inference of conspiracy." Our own scrutiny of the factual allegations of petitioner's complaint, as well as the material found in the affidavits and depositions presented by Kress to the District Court, however, convinces us that summary judgment was improper here, for we think respondent failed to carry its burden of showing the absence of any genuine issue of fact. Before explaining why this is so, it is useful to state the factual arguments, made by the parties concerning summary judgment, and the reasoning of the courts below.

In moving for summary judgment, Kress argued that "uncontested facts" established that no conspiracy existed between any Kress employee and the police. To support this assertion, Kress pointed first to the statements in the deposition of the store manager (Mr. Powell) that (a) he had not communicated with the police,[8] and that (b) he had, by a prearranged

---

[8] [Powell said he knew the police chief, and that the arresting officer Ralph Hillman came to the store "maybe every day," but on the occasion in question Powell didn't see any police in or near the store, and he denied calling them or agreeing with any official to deny Ms. Adickes the use of the library or arranging to refuse service in the Kress store or asking any official to arrest Ms. Adickes.—ED.]

tacit signal,[9] ordered the food counter supervisor to see that Miss Adickes was refused service only because he was fearful of a riot in the store by customers angered at seeing a "mixed group" of whites and blacks eating together.[10] Kress also relied on affidavits from the Hattiesburg chief of police,[11] and the two arresting officers,[12] to the effect that store manager Powell had not requested that petitioner be arrested. Finally, Kress pointed to the statements in petitioner's own deposition that she had no knowledge of any communication between any Kress employee and any member of the Hattiesburg police, and was relying on circumstantial evidence to support her contention that there was an arrangement between Kress and the police.

Petitioner, in opposing summary judgment, pointed out that respondent had failed in its moving papers to dispute the allegation in petitioner's complaint, a statement at her deposition,[13] and an unsworn statement by a Kress employee,[14] all to the effect that there was a policeman in the store at the time of the refusal to serve her, and that this was the policeman who subsequently arrested her. Petitioner argued that although she had no knowledge of an agreement between Kress and the police, the sequence of events created a substantial enough possibility of a conspiracy to allow her to proceed to trial, especially given the fact that the noncircumstantial evidence of the conspiracy could only come from adverse witnesses. Further, she submitted an affidavit specifically disputing the manager's assertion that the situation in the store at the time of the refusal was "explosive," thus creating an issue of fact as to what his motives might have been in ordering the refusal of service.

We think that on the basis of this record, it was error to grant summary judgment. As the moving party, respondent had the burden of showing the

---

[9] [Powell said the signal was a nod of his head, and that his arrangement with Ms Baggett (the food supervisor) involved an understanding that she was to serve anyone, unless he shook his head no. This arrangement was designed to ward off violence because "there was quite a lot" of violence in Hattiesburg directed toward white people in the company of black people.—ED.]

[10] [Powell said that shortly after noon there were 75 to 100 people in the store, and the lunch counter was nearly full. He describes people beginning to "mill around the store" and "coming over towards the lunch counter," with "real sour looks on their faces," and "they looked like a frightened mob," and there were 25 to 30 people looking in from outside, and it looked to Powell "like one person could have yelled 'Let's get them,'" which would "cause this group to turn into a mob."—ED.]

[11] [The chief, who was not present, said he had not arranged with Powell to arrest anyone, and had never discussed arresting Ms. Adickes.—ED.]

[12] [Officers Boone and Hillman, in identical language, said that the arrest was made "on the public streets" of Hattiesburg, and was "an officer's discretion arrest," and neither had consulted with Powell. Nobody in Kress asked that the arrest be made, and nobody was consulted prior to the arrest.—ED.]

[13] [Ms. Adickes testified that one of her students saw a policeman in the store, and two students testified in depositions to like effect.—ED.]

[14] [An unsworn statement by Kress "check-out girl" Irene Sullivan said Officer Hillman came into the store about noon.—ED.]

absence of a genuine issue as to any material fact, and for these purposes the material it lodged must be viewed in the light most favorable to the opposing party. Respondent here did not carry its burden because of its failure to foreclose the possibility that there was a policeman in the Kress store while petitioner was awaiting service, and that this policeman reached an understanding with some Kress employee that petitioner not be served.

It is true that Mr. Powell, the store manager, claimed in his deposition that he had not seen or communicated with a policeman prior to his tacit signal to Miss Baggett, the supervisor of the food counter. But respondent did not submit any affidavits from Miss Baggett, or from Miss Freeman, the waitress who actually refused petitioner service, either of whom might well have seen and communicated with a policeman in the store. Further, we find it particularly noteworthy that the two officers involved in the arrest each failed in his affidavit to foreclose the possibility (1) that he was in the store while petitioner was there; and (2) that, upon seeing petitioner with Negroes, he communicated his disapproval to a Kress employee, thereby influencing the decision not to serve petitioner.

Given these unexplained gaps in the materials submitted by respondent, we conclude that respondent failed to fulfill its initial burden of demonstrating what is a critical element in this aspect of the case—that there was no policeman in the store. If a policeman were present, we think it would be open to a jury, in light of the sequence that followed, to infer from the circumstances that the policeman and a Kress employee had a "meeting of the minds" and thus reached an understanding that petitioner should be refused service. Because "(o)n summary judgment the inferences to be drawn from the underlying facts contained in (the moving party's) materials must be viewed in the light most favorable to the party opposing the motion," United States v. Diebold, Inc., 369 U.S. 654, 655 (1962), we think respondent's failure to show there was no policeman in the store requires reversal.

... [R]espondent argues that it was incumbent on petitioner to come forward with an affidavit properly asserting the presence of the policeman in the store, if she were to rely on that fact to avoid summary judgment. Respondent notes in this regard that none of the materials upon which petitioner relied met the requirements of Rule 56(e).[19]

This argument does not withstand scrutiny, however, for both the commentary on and background of [FRCP 56(e)] conclusively show that it was not intended to modify the burden of the moving party under Rule 56(c) to show

---

[19] [Ms. Adickes's statement describing what the student said was hearsay, as was the unsworn statement by the "check-out girl" and FRCP 56(c) states that "reliance on allegations in the complaint is not sufficient." The requirements for affidavits, previously found in FRCP 56(e), have been moved to FRCP 56(c)(4), but are substantially identical to what they were before.—ED.]

initially the absence of a genuine issue concerning any material fact. The ACN on [FRCP 56(e)] states that the [changes introduced in 1963] were not designed to "affect the ordinary standards applicable to the summary judgment." And [the ACN] stated that "(w)here the evidentiary matter in support of the motion does not establish the absence of a genuine issue, summary judgment must be denied even if no opposing evidentiary matter is presented." Because respondent did not meet its initial burden of establishing the absence of a policeman in the store, petitioner here was not required to come forward with suitable opposing affidavits.

If respondent had met its initial burden by, for example, submitting affidavits from the policemen denying their presence in the store at the time in question, Rule 56(e) would then have required petitioner to have done more than simply rely on the contrary allegation in her complaint. To have avoided conceding this fact for purposes of summary judgment, petitioner would have had to come forward with either (1) the affidavit of someone who saw the policeman in the store or (2) an affidavit under Rule 56(f) explaining why at that time it was impractical to do so. Even though not essential here to defeat respondent's motion, the submission of such an affidavit would have been the preferable course for petitioner's counsel to have followed. As one commentator has said:

> It has always been perilous for the opposing party neither to proffer any countering evidentiary materials nor file a 56(f) affidavit. And the peril rightly continues (after the amendment to Rule 56(e)). Yet the party moving for summary judgment has the burden to show that he is entitled to judgment under established principles; and if he does not discharge that burden then he is not entitled to judgment. No defense to an insufficient showing is required.

6 J. Moore, Federal Practice 56.22(2), pp. 2824 2825 (2d ed. 1966).

[The Court discusses "state action" at length, and concludes, *inter alia*, that Adickes can satisfy this requirement if she shows that Kress "refused her service because of a state-enforced custom of segregating the races in public restaurants."]

[Justice Marshall took no part in the decision. Justice Black concurs in a separate opinion. Justice Brennan separately concurs and dissents.]

■ NOTES ON *ADICKES* AND CONCERN TO PROTECT PLAINTIFFS

1. In *Adickes,* the defense claims "the facts are on my side" (second situation described in the introductory comments). The critical point, on which plaintiff's claim depends, is official involvement in the refusal to serve Sandra

Adickes and her students at the lunch counter—in effect a "conspiracy," or perhaps "consciously parallel behavior" between the store and the police. What does the defense offer in support of the proposition that there was *no* official involvement? Do the materials presented by Kress suffice to prove "absence of conspiracy"? Why or why not?

2. The Court says Kress didn't "carry its burden" as moving party because it did not "foreclose the possibility" of official involvement. Doesn't foreclosing the possibility sound like producing evidence that no reasonable person could reject—like satisfying the cogent and compelling standard? Should the burden on a *defendant* moving for summary judgment be *that* heavy?

3. What can be said in favor of the *Adickes* approach? Does the language in *today's* FRCP 56(a) support putting a burden on defendant? Note that it says summary judgment is to be granted "if the movant shows" there is no genuine dispute: Does the quoted phrase mean *every* movant (plaintiff or defendant, whether or not he would bear a trial burden) must bear a particular burden in moving for summary judgment? (When *Adickes* was decided, FRCP 56 said a party could move for summary judgment "with or without supporting affidavits," but it also spoke of motions "properly made and supported." Even though this language has changed, it seems that *Adickes* could be decided the same way today.)

4. Consider plaintiff's proof: We have a statement by a Kress employee that Officer Hillman had been in the store that day. We have two student depositions of like effect. We also have Sandra Adickes's testimony that one of her students told her she saw a policeman in the store. Forget for a moment the matter of "form," and assume that we have affidavits by the employee and the student to which Sandra Adickes referred in her deposition: Would all this evidence suffice to prove that Kress and the police acted together—conspiring or engaging in consciously parallel behavior?

5. Consider defendant's proof in *Adickes:* We have statements by Powell and arresting officers Hillman and Boone that there was no understanding between the officers and the store. Would this evidence *suffice* as the basis to find that there was no conspiracy or consciously parallel behavior? Would a reasonable factfinder (judge or jury) *have* to reach that conclusion on these statements? Notice the dictum in *Adickes*—the Court's statement toward the end of the opinion that if Kress had submitted affidavits by the officers "denying their presence in the store at the time," then *plaintiff* would have come forward with counterproof (proof contradicting this claim and placing a police officer in the store).

6. Professor Currie roundly criticized *Adickes,* arguing that the Court was wrong *both* in requiring defendant to "foreclose the possibility" that police were in the store *and* in commenting that affidavits by the officers stating that they were not in the store would have *required* the court to award judgment to defendant unless plaintiff came up with counterproof. See David Currie, *Thoughts on Directed Verdicts and Summary Judgments*, 45 U. Chi. L.

Rev. 72, 76 (1977) (*Adickes's* holding "confines the summary judgment procedure so narrowly as to impair its effectiveness"; its dictum that an "uncontroverted affidavit denying the conspiracy allegations" would require "the opposite result" expands summary judgment so far as "to threaten the right to a jury trial"). Was he right?

CELOTEX CORPORATION v. CATRETT

Supreme Court of the United States
477 U.S. 317 (1986)

Justice REHNQUIST delivered the opinion of the Court.

The United States District Court for the District of Columbia granted the motion of petitioner Celotex Corporation for summary judgment against respondent Catrett because the latter was unable to produce evidence in support of her allegation in her wrongful-death complaint that the decedent had been exposed to petitioner's asbestos products. A divided panel of the Court of Appeals for the District of Columbia Circuit reversed, however, holding that petitioner's failure to support its motion with evidence tending to *negate* such exposure precluded the entry of summary judgment in its favor. This view conflicted with that of the Third Circuit in In re Japanese Electronic Products, 723 F.2d 238 (3d Cir. 1983), *rev'd on other grounds sub nom.* Matsushita Electric Industrial Co. v. Zenith Radio Corp., 475 U.S. 574 (1986). We granted certiorari to resolve the conflict, and now reverse the decision of the District of Columbia Circuit.

Respondent commenced this lawsuit in September 1980, alleging that the death in 1979 of her husband, Louis H. Catrett, resulted from his exposure to products containing asbestos manufactured or distributed by 15 named corporations. Respondent's complaint sounded in negligence, breach of warranty, and strict liability. Two of the defendants filed motions challenging the District Court's *in personam* jurisdiction, and the remaining 13, including petitioner, filed motions for summary judgment. Petitioner's motion, which was first filed in September 1981, argued that summary judgment was proper because respondent had "failed to produce evidence that any [Celotex] product . . . was the proximate cause of the injuries alleged within the jurisdictional limits of [the District] Court." In particular, petitioner noted that respondent had failed to identify, in answering interrogatories specifically requesting such information, any witnesses who could testify about the decedent's exposure to petitioner's asbestos products. In response to petitioner's summary judgment motion, respondent then produced three documents which she claimed "demonstrate that there is a genuine material factual dispute" as to whether the decedent had ever been exposed to petitioner's asbestos products. The three documents included a transcript of a deposition of the decedent, a letter from an official of one of the decedent's former employers whom petitioner planned to call as a trial witness, and a letter from an insurance company to respondent's attorney, all tending to establish that the decedent had been exposed to petitioner's asbestos products in Chicago during 1970-1971. Petitioner, in turn, argued that the three documents were inadmissible hearsay and thus could not be considered in opposition to the summary judgment motion.

In July 1982, almost two years after the commencement of the lawsuit, the District Court granted all of the motions filed by the various defendants. The court explained that it was granting petitioner's summary judgment motion because "there [was] no showing that the plaintiff was exposed to the defendant Celotex's product in the District of Columbia or elsewhere within the statutory period." Respondent appealed only the grant of summary judgment in favor of petitioner, and a divided panel of the District of Columbia Circuit reversed. The majority of the Court of Appeals held that petitioner's summary judgment motion was rendered "fatally defective" by the fact that petitioner "made no effort to adduce *any* evidence, in the form of affidavits or otherwise, to support its motion." According to the majority, Rule 56(e) of the Federal Rules of Civil Procedure, and this Court's decision in Adickes v. S.H. Kress & Co., 398 U.S. 144, 159 (1970), establish that "the party opposing the motion for summary judgment bears the burden of responding *only after* the moving party has met its burden of coming forward with proof of the absence of any genuine issues of material fact." The majority therefore declined to consider petitioner's argument that none of the evidence produced by respondent in opposition to the motion for summary judgment would have been admissible at trial. The dissenting judge argued that "[t]he majority errs in supposing that a party seeking summary judgment must always make an affirmative evidentiary showing, even in cases where there is not a triable, factual dispute" (Bork, J., dissenting). According to the dissenting judge, the majority's decision "undermines the traditional authority of trial judges to grant summary judgment in meritless cases."

We think that the position taken by the majority of the Court of Appeals is inconsistent with the standard for summary judgment set forth in FRCP 56(c). Under Rule 56(c), summary judgment is proper "if the pleadings, depositions, answers to interrogatories, and admissions on file, together with the affidavits, if any, show that there is no genuine issue as to any material fact and that the moving party is entitled to a judgment as a matter of law." In our view, the plain language of Rule 56(c) mandates the entry of summary judgment, after adequate time for discovery and upon motion, against a party who fails to make a showing sufficient to establish the existence of an element essential to that party's case, and on which that party will bear the burden of proof at trial. In such a situation, there can be "no genuine issue as to any material fact," since a complete failure of proof concerning an essential element of the non-moving party's case necessarily renders all other facts immaterial. The moving party is "entitled to a judgment as a matter of law" because the nonmoving party has failed to make a sufficient showing on an essential element of her case with respect to which she has the burden of proof. "[T]h[e] standard [for granting summary judgment] mirrors the standard for a directed verdict under FRCP 50(a). . . ." Anderson v. Liberty Lobby, Inc., 477 U.S. 242, 250 (1986).

Of course, a party seeking summary judgment always bears the initial responsibility of informing the district court of the basis for its motion, and identifying those portions of "the pleadings, depositions, answers to interrogatories, and admissions on file, together with the affidavits, if any," which it believes demonstrate the absence of a genuine issue of material fact. But unlike the Court of Appeals, we find no express or implied requirement in Rule 56 that the moving party support its motion with affidavits or other similar materials *negating* the opponent's claim. . . . [R]egardless of whether the moving party accompanies its summary judgment motion with affidavits, the motion may, and should, be granted so long as whatever is before the district court demonstrates that the standard for the entry of summary judgment, as set forth in Rule 56(c), is satisfied. One of the principal purposes of the summary judgment rule is to isolate and dispose of factually unsupported claims or defenses, and we think it should be interpreted in a way that allows it to accomplish this purpose.[5]

[The Court construes then-existing Rule 56 as authorizing summary judgment, regardless whether the moving party presents affidavits or similar material. Under the Rule, the opposing party must "go beyond the pleadings" and submit "her own affidavits" or similar material showing that "there is a genuine issue for trial."]

We do not mean that the nonmoving party must produce evidence in a form that would be admissible at trial in order to avoid summary judgment. Obviously, Rule 56 does not require the nonmoving party to depose her own witnesses. Rule 56(e) permits a proper summary judgment motion to be opposed by any of the kinds of evidentiary materials listed in Rule 56(c), except the mere pleadings themselves, and it is from this list that one would normally expect the nonmoving party to make the showing to which we have referred.

The Court of Appeals in this case felt itself constrained, however, by language in our decision in Adickes v. S.H. Kress & Co., 398 U.S. 144 (1970). There we held that summary judgment had been improperly entered in favor of the defendant restaurant in an action brought under 42 USC

---

[5] See Louis, Federal Summary Judgment Doctrine: A Critical Analysis, 83 Yale L.J. 745, 752 (1974); Currie, Thoughts on Directed Verdicts and Summary Judgments, 45 U. Chi. L. Rev. 72, 79 (1977).

§1983. In the course of its opinion, the *Adickes* Court said that "both the commentary on and the background of the 1963 amendment conclusively-show that it was not intended to modify the burden of the moving party . . . to show initially the absence of a genuine issue concerning any material fact." We think that this statement is accurate in a literal sense, since we fully agree with the *Adickes* Court that the 1963 amendment to Rule 56(e) was not designed to modify the burden of making the showing generally required by Rule 56(c). It also appears to us that, on the basis of the showing before the Court in *Adickes,* the motion for summary judgment in that case should have been denied. But we do not think the *Adickes* language quoted above should be construed to mean that the burden is on the party moving for summary judgment to produce evidence showing the absence of a genuine issue of material fact, even with respect to an issue on which the nonmoving party bears the burden of proof. Instead, as we have explained, the burden on the moving party may be discharged by "showing"—that is, pointing out to the district court—that there is an absence of evidence to support the nonmoving party's case.

. . .

Respondent commenced this action in September 1980, and petitioner's motion was filed in September 1981. The parties had conducted discovery, and no serious claim can be made that respondent was in any sense "railroaded" by a premature motion for summary judgment. Any potential problem with such premature motions can be adequately dealt with under Rule 56(f), which allows a summary judgment motion to be denied, or the hearing on the motion to be continued, if the nonmoving party has not had an opportunity to make full discovery.

In this Court, respondent's brief and oral argument have been devoted as much to the proposition that an adequate showing of exposure to petitioner's asbestos products was made as to the proposition that no such showing should have been required. But the Court of Appeals declined to address either the adequacy of the showing made by respondent in opposition to petitioner's motion for summary judgment, or the question whether such a showing, if reduced to admissible evidence, would be sufficient to carry respondent's burden of proof at trial. We think the Court of Appeals with its superior knowledge of local law is better suited than we are to make these determinations in the first instance.

The Federal Rules of Civil Procedure have for almost 50 years authorized motions for summary judgment upon proper showings of the lack of a genuine, triable issue of material fact. Summary judgment procedure is properly regarded not as a disfavored procedural shortcut, but rather as an integral part of the Federal Rules as a whole, which are designed "to secure the just, speedy and inexpensive determination of every action." FRCP 1. Before the shift to "notice pleading" accomplished by the Federal Rules, motions to dismiss a complaint or to strike a defense were the principal tools by which factually insufficient claims or defenses could be isolated and prevented from going to trial with the attendant unwarranted consumption of public and private resources. But with the advent of "notice pleading," the motion to dismiss seldom fulfills this function any more, and its place has been taken by the motion for summary judgment. Rule 56 must be construed with due regard not only for the rights of persons asserting claims and defenses that are adequately based in fact to have those claims and defenses tried to a jury, but also for the rights of persons opposing such claims and defenses to demonstrate in the manner provided by the Rule, prior to trial, that the claims and defenses have no factual basis.

The judgment of the Court of Appeals is accordingly reversed, and the case is remanded for further proceedings consistent with this opinion.

It is so ordered.

Justice WHITE, concurring.

I agree that the Court of Appeals was wrong in holding that the moving defendant must always support his motion with evidence or affidavits showing the absence of a genuine dispute about a material fact. I also agree that the movant may rely on depositions, answers to interrogatories, and the like, to demonstrate that the plaintiff has no evidence to prove his case and hence that there can be no factual dispute. But the movant must discharge the burden the Rules place upon him: It is not enough to move for summary judgment without supporting the motion in any way or with a conclusory assertion that the plaintiff has no evidence to prove his case.

A plaintiff need not initiate any discovery or reveal his witnesses or evidence unless required to do so under the discovery Rules or by court order. Of course, he must respond if required to do so; but he need not also depose his witnesses or obtain their affidavits to defeat a summary judgment motion asserting only that he has failed to produce any support for his case. It is the defendant's task to negate, if he can, the claimed basis for the suit.

Petitioner Celotex does not dispute that if respondent has named a witness to support her claim, summary judgment should not be granted without Celotex somehow showing that the named witness' possible testimony raises no genuine issue of material fact. It asserts, however, that respondent has failed on request to produce any basis for her case. Respondent, on the other hand, does not contend that she was not obligated to reveal her witnesses and evidence but insists that she has revealed enough to defeat the motion for summary judgment. Because the Court of Appeals found it unnecessary to address this aspect of the case, I agree that the case should be remanded for further proceedings.

Justice Brennan, with whom The Chief Justice and Justice Blackmun join, dissenting.

This case requires the Court to determine whether Celotex satisfied its initial burden of production in moving for summary judgment on the ground that the plaintiff lacked evidence to establish an essential element of her case at trial. I do not disagree with the Court's legal analysis. The Court clearly rejects the ruling of the Court of Appeals that the defendant must provide affirmative evidence disproving the plaintiff's case. Beyond this, however, the Court has not clearly explained what is required of a moving party seeking summary judgment on the ground that the nonmoving party cannot prove its case.[1] This lack of clarity is unfortunate: district courts must routinely decide summary judgment motions, and the Court's opinion will very likely create confusion. For this reason, even if I agreed with the Court's result, I would have written separately to explain more clearly the law in this area. However, because I believe that Celotex did not meet its burden of production under Federal Rule of Civil Procedure 56, I respectfully dissent from the Court's judgment.

I

Summary judgment is appropriate where the Court is satisfied "that there is no genuine issue as to any material fact and that the moving party is entitled to a judgment as a matter of law." FRCP 56(c). The burden of establishing the non-existence of a "genuine issue" is on the party moving for summary judgment. This burden has two distinct components: an initial burden of production, which shifts to the nonmoving party if satisfied by the moving party; and an ultimate burden of persuasion, which always remains on the moving party. The court need not decide whether the moving party has satisfied its ultimate burden of persuasion[2] unless and until the Court finds that the moving party has discharged its initial burden of production. *Adickes*; 1963 ACN on FRCP 56(e).

The burden of production imposed by Rule 56 requires the moving party to make a prima facie showing that it is entitled to summary judgment. The manner in which this showing can be made depends upon which party will

---

[1] It is also unclear what the Court of Appeals is supposed to do in this case on remand. Justice White—who has provided the Court's fifth vote—plainly believes that the Court of Appeals should reevaluate whether the defendant met its initial burden of production. However, the decision to reverse rather than to vacate the judgment below implies that the Court of Appeals should assume that Celotex has met its initial burden of production and ask only whether the plaintiff responded adequately, and, if so, whether the defendant has met its ultimate burden of persuasion that no genuine issue exists for trial. Absent some clearer expression from the Court to the contrary, Justice White's understanding would seem to be controlling.

[2] The burden of persuasion imposed on a moving party by Rule 56 is a stringent one. Summary judgment should not be granted unless it is clear that a trial is unnecessary, Anderson v. Liberty Lobby, Inc., 477 U.S. 242, 255 (1986), and any doubt as to the existence of a genuine issue for trial should be resolved against the moving party, *Adickes*. In determining whether a moving party has met its burden of persuasion, the court is obliged to take account of the entire setting of the case and must consider all papers of record as well as any materials prepared for the motion. . . .

bear the burden of persuasion on the challenged claim at trial. If the *moving* party will bear the burden of persuasion at trial, that party must support its motion with credible evidence—using any of the materials specified in Rule 56(c)—that would entitle it to a directed verdict if not controverted at trial. Such an affirmative showing shifts the burden of production to the party opposing the motion and requires that party either to produce evidentiary materials that demonstrate the existence of a "genuine issue" for trial or to submit an affidavit requesting additional time for discovery.

If the burden of persuasion at trial would be on the *non-moving* party, the party moving for summary judgment may satisfy Rule 56's burden of production in either of two ways. First, the moving party may submit affirmative evidence that negates an essential element of the nonmoving party's claim. Second, the moving party may demonstrate to the Court that the nonmoving party's evidence is insufficient to establish an essential element of the non-moving party's claim. If the nonmoving party cannot muster sufficient evidence to make out its claim, a trial would be useless and the moving party is entitled to summary judgment as a matter of law.

Where the moving party adopts this second option and seeks summary judgment on the ground that the nonmoving party—who will bear the burden of persuasion at trial—has no evidence, the mechanics of discharging Rule 56's burden of production are somewhat trickier. Plainly, a conclusory assertion that the nonmoving party has no evidence is insufficient. Such a "burden" of production is no burden at all and would simply permit summary judgment procedure to be converted into a tool for harassment. Rather, as the Court confirms, a party who moves for summary judgment on the ground that the nonmoving party has no evidence must affirmatively show the absence of evidence in the record. This may require the moving party to depose the nonmoving party's witnesses or to establish the inadequacy of documentary evidence. If there is literally no evidence in the record, the moving party may demonstrate this by reviewing for the court the admissions, interrogatories, and other exchanges between the parties that are in the record. Either way, however, the moving party must affirmatively demonstrate that there is no evidence in the record to support a judgment for the nonmoving party.

If the moving party has not fully discharged this initial burden of production, its motion for summary judgment must be denied, and the Court need not consider whether the moving party has met its ultimate burden of persuasion. Accordingly, the nonmoving party may defeat a motion for summary judgment that asserts that the nonmoving party has no evidence by calling the Court's attention to supporting evidence already in the record that was overlooked or ignored by the moving party. In that event, the moving party must respond by making an attempt to demonstrate the inadequacy of this evidence, for it is only by attacking all the record evidence allegedly supporting the nonmoving party that a party seeking summary judgment satisfies Rule 56's burden of production.[3] Thus, if the record disclosed that the moving party had overlooked a witness who would provide relevant testimony for the nonmoving party at trial, the Court could not find that the moving party had discharged its initial burden of production unless the moving party sought to demonstrate the inadequacy of this witness' testimony. Absent such a demonstration, summary judgment would have to be denied on the ground that the moving party had failed to meet its burden of production under Rule 56.

. . .

The opinion in *Adickes* has sometimes been read to hold that summary judgment was inappropriate because the respondent had not submitted affirmative evidence to negate the possibility that there was a policeman in the store. The Court of Appeals apparently read *Adickes* this way and therefore required Celotex to submit evidence establishing that plaintiff's decedent had not been exposed to Celotex asbestos. I agree with the Court that this reading of *Adickes* was erroneous and that Celotex could seek summary judgment on the ground that plaintiff could not prove exposure to Celotex asbestos at trial. However, Celotex was still required to satisfy its initial burden of production.

II

I do not read the Court's opinion to say anything inconsistent with or different than the preceding discussion. My disagreement with the Court concerns the application of these principles to the facts of this case.

Defendant Celotex sought summary judgment on the ground that plaintiff had "failed to produce" any evidence that her decedent had ever been exposed to Celotex asbestos. Celotex supported this motion with a two-page "Statement of Material Facts as to Which There is No Genuine Issue" and a three-page "Memorandum of Points and Authorities" which asserted that the plaintiff had failed to identify any evidence in responding to two sets of interrogatories propounded by Celotex and that therefore the record was "totally devoid" of evidence to support plaintiff's claim.

Approximately three months earlier, Celotex had filed an essentially identical motion. Plaintiff responded to this earlier motion by producing

---

[3] Once the moving party has attacked whatever record evidence—if any—the nonmoving party purports to rely upon, the burden of production shifts to the nonmoving party, who must either (1) rehabilitate the evidence attacked in the moving party's papers, (2) produce additional evidence showing the existence of a genuine issue for trial as provided in Rule 56(e), or (3) submit an affidavit explaining why further discovery is necessary as provided in Rule 56(f). Summary judgment should be granted if the nonmoving party fails to respond in one or more of these ways, or if, after the nonmoving party responds, the court determines that the moving party has met its ultimate burden of persuading the court that there is no genuine issue of material fact for trial.

three pieces of evidence which she claimed "[a]t the very least ... demonstrate that there is a genuine factual dispute for trial": (1) a letter from an insurance representative of another defendant describing asbestos products to which plaintiff's decedent had been exposed; (2) a letter from T.R. Hoff, a former supervisor of decedent, describing asbestos products to which decedent had been exposed; and (3) a copy of decedent's deposition from earlier workmen's compensation proceedings. Plaintiff also apparently indicated at that time that she intended to call Mr. Hoff as a witness at trial.

Celotex subsequently withdrew its first motion for summary judgment.[5] However, as a result of this motion, when Celotex filed its second summary judgment motion, the record *did* contain evidence—including at least one witness—supporting plaintiff's claim. Indeed, counsel for Celotex admitted to this Court at oral argument that Celotex was aware of this evidence and of plaintiff's intention to call Mr. Hoff as a witness at trial when the second summary judgment motion was filed. Moreover, plaintiff's response to Celotex' second motion pointed to this evidence—noting that it had already been provided to counsel for Celotex in connection with the first motion—and argued that Celotex had failed to "meet its burden of proving that there is no genuine factual dispute for trial."

On these facts, there is simply no question that Celotex failed to discharge its initial burden of production. Having chosen to base its motion on the argument that there was no evidence in the record to support plaintiff's claim, Celotex was not free to ignore supporting evidence that the record clearly contained. Rather, Celotex was required, as an initial matter, to attack the adequacy of this evidence. Celotex' failure to fulfill this simple requirement constituted a failure to discharge its initial burden of production under Rule 56, and thereby rendered summary judgment improper.[6]

This case is indistinguishable from *Adickes.* Here, as there, the defendant moved for summary judgment on the ground that the record contained no evidence to support an essential element of the plaintiff's claim. Here, as there, the plaintiff responded by drawing the court's attention to evidence that was already in the record and that had been ignored by the moving party. Consequently, here, as there, summary judgment should be denied

---

[5] Celotex apparently withdrew this motion because, contrary to the assertion made in the first summary judgment motion, its second set of interrogatories had not been served on the plaintiff.

[6] If the plaintiff had answered Celotex' second set of interrogatories with the evidence in her response to the first summary judgment motion, and Celotex had ignored those interrogatories and based its second summary judgment motion on the first set of interrogatories only, Celotex obviously could not claim to have discharged its Rule 56 burden of production. This result should not be different simply because the evidence plaintiff relied upon to support her claim was acquired by Celotex other than in plaintiff's answers to interrogatories.

on the ground that the moving party failed to satisfy its initial burden of production.[7]

[The dissenting opinion by Justice Stevens is omitted.]

■ NOTES ON THE COURT'S NEW STANDARD

1. In *Celotex*, the defense claims that "plaintiff has no evidence" (the case resembles the third situation described in the introductory material). The critical point, on which plaintiff's case depends, is Louis Catrett's exposure to asbestos products made or distributed by Celotex. The trial court awarded summary judgment to Celotex, but the D.C. Court of Appeals reversed in a split opinion, in which the majority concluded that defendant did not carry its burden of "coming forward with proof of the absence of any genuine issue." See Catrett v. Johns-Manville Sales Corp., 756 F.2d 181, 184 (D.C. Cir. 1985).

(a) On this question, the Supreme Court disagrees. *Celotex* says the moving party only "bears the initial responsibility," of "informing" the court of the basis for the motion and "identifying" parts of the record that show the absence of a genuine issue. Was the Court applying the *Adickes* standard? Professor Shapiro says *Celotex* "managed to gut [*Adickes*] without overruling it." See David Shapiro, *The Story of* Celotex: *The Role of Summary Judgment in the Administration of Civil Justice*, in Civil Procedure Stories 359, 373 (Kevin M. Clermont, ed.) (2d ed. 2008). Is he right?

(b) In concurrence, Justice White says it is "not enough" to seek summary judgment "without supporting the motion" or by "a conclusory assertion" that plaintiff has no evidence. In dissent, Justice Brennan concludes that Celotex did *not* carry its burden of production, and was obliged to deal with evidence of exposure in the record. The Court *remands* the case. Is Justice White closer to Justice Brennan on the burden that the *movant* must carry than to the Court's opinion? In footnote 1, Brennan points out that White is the "fifth vote," so his view is "controlling" on the movant's burden. On remand, should the D.C. Circuit rule again that Celotex did not carry its burden as moving party?

---

[7] Although Justice White agrees that "if [plaintiff] has named a witness to support her claim, summary judgment should not be granted without Celotex somehow showing that the named witness' possible testimony raises no genuine issue of material fact," he would remand "[b]ecause the Court of Appeals found it unnecessary to address this aspect of the case." However, Celotex has admitted that plaintiff had disclosed her intent to call Mr. Hoff as a witness at trial before Celotex filed its second motion for summary judgment. Under the circumstances, then, remanding is a waste of time.

(c) On remand, the same panel again found that summary judgment was improper, but this time *not* because Celotex failed to carry its burden. The majority concluded that Justice White's opinion did *not* leave room to fault Celotex for failing to carry its burden as moving party ("Justice White did, after all, join the opinion of the majority"). See Catrett v. Johns-Manville Sales Corp., 826 F.2d 33, 40 (D.C. Cir. 1987). The reason why Celotex still lost is taken up in notes 7-8, below.

2. Three views have emerged on the burden that defendants should carry in making motions for summary judgment:

(a) The most generous view holds that burdens in moving for summary judgment should mirror trial burdens—that a defendant who would have no burden at trial should have no burden in moving for summary judgment. Recall Professor Currie's criticism of *Adickes,* and see David Currie, *Thoughts on Directed Verdicts and Summary Judgments,* 45 U. Chi. L. Rev. 72, 79 (1977) (moving for summary judgment "puts an opposing party with the burden of proof to the task of producing evidence sufficient to sustain a favorable verdict"). In their treatise, Professors Brunet and Redish agree. They argue that "it makes little practical sense" to withhold from the trial court information that would tell it that one side or the other will be entitled to judgment as a matter of law at trial. The rigorous approach associated with *Adickes* and Professor Moore (quoted in *Adickes*) prevents the court "from examining the sufficiency of the nonmovant's evidence unless the movant effectively shifts the burden of production," which "artificially" prevents the court from "learning that a trial is unnecessary." See Brunet & Redish, Summary Judgment: Federal Law and Practice §5:3 (3d ed. 2006) (Currie's position is "the most persuasive of the conceivable alternatives," and Rule 11 sanctions will "deter summary judgment motions intended solely to harass nonmovants").

(b) An intermediate view holds that a moving party who does not bear the burden of persuasion at trial should still demonstrate that the other side lacks sufficient proof or produce sufficient evidence that the facts favor the movant. Such a movant must

> support his motion with some affidavits or other materials showing or at least suggesting the nonexistence of an essential element of the opposing party's case. . . . The degree of persuasiveness with which he must show or suggest this nonexistence in order to compel the opposing party to respond at his peril is the crucial issue. Before that question is reached, however, several important corollaries can be derived simply from the conclusion that the moving party faces some burden. First, if he fails to discharge the burden, his motion fails, even though the opposing party makes no response. Second, if he discharges this burden, he should be deemed to have established the nonexistence of the essential element in question unless the opposing party responds adequately. Ordinarily the motion must then be granted. Third, the opposing party will be required to respond only with respect to those essential elements of the claim upon which the moving party has discharged his burden.

See Martin Louis, *Federal Summary Judgment Doctrine: A Critical Analysis,* 83 Yale L.J. 745, 750 (1974).

(c) The most rigorous view is associated with *Adickes* itself, and with Professor William Moore, quoted in *Adickes.* Under this view, even a defending party who moves for summary judgment must conclusively show that judgment must be given for defendant—in effect, offering "cogent and compelling evidence" that the facts favor the defendant.

(d) Which of these views best describes the position of the Court as it emerged in *Celotex*?

3. Like *Adickes,* the opinion in *Celotex* stresses language no longer in FRCP 56 (we no longer have language stating that movants may proceed "with or without affidavits," or implying that the opposing party need only come forward to meet a motion that has been "properly made and supported"). In its present wording, FRCP 56(a) authorizes summary judgment if the movant "shows that there is no genuine issue," and FRCP 56(c) says a party asserting that a fact is beyond dispute "must support the assertion" by "citing to particular parts" of the record or by "showing that the materials cited do not establish the absence or presence of a genuine dispute, or that an adverse party cannot produce admissible evidence to support the fact." While the new wording departs from the old, there is nothing in the new wording, is there, that rejects the *Celotex* approach?

4. After *Celotex,* it is fair to say that federal courts are not of one mind in their approach to summary judgment. Some equate *Celotex* with the most generous approach. See, e.g., Silverman v. Board of Education, City of Chicago, 637 F.3d 719 (7th Cir. 2011) (must enter summary judgment against party who fails to make showing sufficient to establish element essential to its case, on which it bears the burden at trial) (quoting *Celotex*). More common are decisions approving summary judgment for defendants while at least paying lip service to the proposition that defendants as moving parties have a burden to carry. See, e.g., Cotroneo v. Shaw Environmental & Infrastructure, Inc., 639 F.3d 186, 191 (5th Cir. 2011) (movant must establish that there are no genuine issues of material fact; then burden shifts to opposing party); AFL-CIO v. City of Miami, 637 F.3d 1178, 1186 (11th Cir. 2011) (moving party must "demonstrate that no genuine issue of material fact exists"); Rivera-Colon v. Mills, 635 F.3d 9, 12 (1st Cir. 2011) ("moving party must show entitlement to judgment as a matter of law"); Napier v. Laurel County, Kentucky, 636 F.3d 218, 225 (6th Cir. 2011) (defendants moved for summary judgment on a defense, so "it was their burden to show that there was an absence of evidence to support the nonmoving party's case") (defense met this burden; plaintiff offered no rebuttal). Occasional decisions seem more serious about putting burdens on defendants as movants. See Maydak v. United States, 630 F.3d 166, 181-182 (D.C. Cir. 2010 (if burden of persuasion at trial rests on party opposing motion, movant may satisfy FRCP 56's burden of production by submitting affirmative evidence negating essential element in opponent's claim or demonstrating that opponent's evidence is insufficient) (quoting Brennan's dissent in *Celotex*).

5. State courts too are split in their approaches. As in the federal system, some read *Celotex* as endorsing the generous approach. See, e.g., Farr v. Gulf Agency, 2011 WL 2420844 (Ala. 2011) (when basis of summary judgment is failure of opponent's proof, movant's burden is limited to informing court of basis); Burton v. Twin Commander Aircraft LLC, 2011 WL 1314031 (Wash. 2011) (when defendant "satisfies the initial burden of establishing the absence of a material fact issue," inquiry shifts to plaintiff; motion should be granted if plaintiff fails to make sufficient showing). Others reject *Celotex* (an option available for state courts but not federal courts) and insist that defendants bear a real burden in seeking summary judgment. See, e.g., Winegrad v. New York University Medical Center, 476 N.E.2d 642 (N.Y. 1985) (movant "must make a prima facie showing of entitlement to judgment as a matter of law, tendering sufficient evidence to eliminate any material issues," and failing to do so "requires denial of the motion, regardless of the sufficiency of the opposing papers") ("bare conclusory allegations" that doctors "did not deviate from good and acceptable medical practices, with no factual relationship to the alleged injury" did not entitle defense to summary judgment); Visingardi v. Tirone, 193 So. 2d 601 (Fla. 1966) (unless record shows absence of causal relationship, plaintiff opposing summary judgment motion is under no obligation to prove cause) (reversing summary judgment for plaintiff); Webster v. Marthin Memorial Medical Center, Inc., 57 So. 3d 896 (Fla. App. 2011) (following *Visingardi*); Jarboe v. Landmark Community Newspapers of Indiana, Inc., 644 N.E.2d 118 (Ind. 1994) (state summary judgment procedure "abruptly diverges" from federal practice, where movant "is not required to negate an opponent's claim," and "need only inform the court of the basis of the motion and identify relevant portions of the record" showing absence of genuine issue; then burden rests on opponent "to make a showing sufficient to establish the existence of each challenged element" on which it bears the burden of proof; Indiana "does not adhere to *Celotex* and the federal methodology"); Steelvest, Inc. v. Scansteel Service Center, Inc., 807 S.W.2d 476, 481-482 (Ky. 1991) (in federal practice, movant need not "produce evidence showing the absence of a genuine issue," but only to "show that there is an absence of evidence," but in Kentucky the movant "must convince the court, by the evidence of record, of the nonexistence of an issue of material fact").

6. *Celotex* is one of a now-famous "trilogy" of decisions by the Court handed down in 1986. The first of the three was Matsushita Electric Indus. Co. v. Zenith Radio Corp., 475 U.S. 574 (1986), which involved Zenith's antitrust claim against Japanese television manufacturers, alleging that they conspired to set prices artificially low in order to drive American manufacturers out of the market. Defendants should have prevailed in their motion for summary judgment, the Court concluded, because they carried their burden in making the motion, and plaintiffs had to "do more than simply show that there is some metaphysical doubt as to the material facts," and must "come forward with more persuasive evidence" in cases where "factual context renders [their] claim implausible." Decided the same day as *Celotex*, the third case was Anderson v. Liberty Lobby, Inc., 477 U.S. 242 (1986), where plaintiffs sued for libel and had to prove "actual malice" by "clear and convincing" evidence because they were public figures and the First Amendment applies to the speech in question. In *Anderson*, the Court said that the standard for summary judgment motions "mirrors the standard" that applies in post-trial motions for judgment as a matter of law, and that courts may throw out a claim when plaintiff's proof is "merely colorable" and "not significantly probative."

(a) This summary judgment trilogy is highly influential. See Adam Steinman, *The Irrepressible Myth of* Celotex: *Reconsidering Summary Judgment Burdens Twenty Years After the Trilogy*, 53 Wash. & Lee L. Rev. 81 (2006) (trilogy has had "a profound impact on federal litigation," *Celotex* and *Anderson* having been cited "more than any other" Supreme Court decisions "by a staggering margin").

(b) Everyone reads *Celotex* as making summary judgment easier to get. Some praise this development. See, e.g., Martin H. Redish, *Summary Judgment and the Vanishing Trial: Implications of the Litigation Matrix*, 57 Stan. L. Rev. 1329 (2005) (*Celotex* rejects "judicial imposition" of the "unjustifiably prohibitive burden" on the movant that *Adickes* had imposed, and most courts "wisely read" *Celotex* as imposing "virtually no burden at all on the movant" if she would have none at trial).

(c) Others see in *Celotex* an alteration in the balance of power that favors defendants. See, e.g., Samuel Issacharoff & George Loewenstein, *Second Thoughts About Summary Judgment*, 100 Yale L.J. 73 (1990) (expanded summary judgment raises costs to plaintiffs, lowers settlement value, transfers wealth from plaintiffs to defendants); Jeffrey Stempel, *A Distorted Mirror: The Supreme Court's Shimmering View of Summary Judgment, Directed Verdict, and the Adjudication Process*, 49 Ohio St. L.J. 95 (1988) (criticizing increased availability of summary judgment as failing to achieve efficiencies and permitting final disposition on basis of "incomplete, possibly inadequate, or sometimes fraudulent" records).

7. As noted above, the D.C. Circuit again ruled against Celotex on remand, but for a different reason. This time the majority thought plaintiff had produced enough evidence of exposure to Celotex products containing asbestos to justify going to trial. The most important item was the Hoff letter, to which every opinion in the case refers. Hoff was an officer in a company that employed Catrett in 1971, and his letter said that during that time Catrett's duties were "to supervise and train crews in the application of Firebar Fireproofing." Firebar was an asbestos-containing product made by Panacon, and Celotex had acquired Panacon and assumed its rights and liabilities. See Catrett v. Johns-Manville Sales Corp., 826 F.2d 33 (D.C. Cir. 1987).

8. What material counts in summary judgment motions in deciding whether there is a "genuine issue" of "material fact"? In colloquial terms, the best answer is, "something pretty close to evidence that would be admitted at trial." Under FRCP 56, affidavits and depositions given in the case can be used, and such materials are in effect "precursors" or "images" of testimony: We can be reasonably confident that affiants (witnesses who make affidavits) and deponents would appear in person at trial and testify in the manner indicated by their affidavits or depositions.

(a) Shouldn't plaintiff have gotten an affidavit or deposition from Mr. Hoff? The dissenting judge on remand in the D.C. Circuit stressed this point ("the Hoff letter is inadmissible hearsay").

(b) Recall that Louis Catrett gave a deposition before he died (it's mentioned in the majority opinion and by Justice Brennan in dissent). In the opinion by the D.C. Court of Appeals on remand, we are told that Catrett "recounted his use of an asbestos product named Firebar." Why doesn't this item count? In fact, why isn't it decisive? (Recall that Louis Catrett had died, and his widow was pursuing his claim: Obviously, Catrett satisfied the "unavailability" criterion that makes depositions, taken in the suit in which they are offered, admissible in evidence.)

(c) When there are indications in the record that proof of an important fact exists, but the proof has not been cast in the form of an affidavit or deposition testimony, is awarding summary judgment for the other side unduly punitive? Should Celotex have dealt with the Hoff letter in some way, or with the Catrett deposition? Is that what Justice Brennan was arguing? See Steinman, supra (where discovery materials reveal identities of witnesses, defendant as moving party must depose them and show why they would not prove the critical point; where record reveals information supporting the point that is the "substantial equivalent" of documents mentioned in FRCP 56, this information counts in favor of the opponent; hence the Hoff letter counts as the substantial equivalent of Catrett's discovery answers).

9. Recall that the Court in *Celotex* said the party resisting summary judgment need *not* "produce evidence in a form that would be admissible at trial." On the other hand, the Court also said that neither side can rely on "mere pleadings," and it is commonplace for courts to reject "mere hearsay," as the dissenting judge in the opinion on remand in *Celotex* wanted to do. You have not yet taken Evidence, but you understand that out-of-court statements offered to prove what they assert are hearsay, that hearsay is generally inadmissible unless it fits some exception, *and* that affidavits are hearsay (if offered to prove the matter asserted) and are not admissible (there is no exception for affidavits). As Professor Duane points out, *technically* the question in summary judgment is not "what are the facts," but "is there a genuine issue" *about* the facts, so *technically* an affidavit or something like the Hoff letter is not offered to prove facts. Why then prefer an affidavit over a letter? Because an affidavit is the most reliable proof of what a witness will testify to if called? See James Duane, *The Four Greatest Myths About Summary Judgment*, 52 Wash. & Lee L. Rev. 1523, 1535, 1539-1540 (1995) (in ruling on summary judgment, court is "neither permitted nor required" to draw conclusions "about what happened," which would entail a hearsay use of affidavits, but to decide "what will happen at trial," and affidavits are "the best available evidence" of what one "can reasonably expect the affiant to say under oath or affirmation on the witness stand"). *Despite* this fact, courts usually reject "second layer" hearsay, like deposition testimony by Sandra Adickes describing what her student said about a police officer being in the store. Courts want the critical statement to be cast in the form of a deposition or affidavit.

CHAPTER 12

Trial and After: Entitlement to a Jury; Impaneling Juries; Post-Trial Challenges

INTRODUCTION: CIVIL JURIES IN HISTORICAL PERSPECTIVE

Juries had been part of the English legal system for more than six hundred years when the Constitution was adopted in 1789. Historians credit the Normans with introducing juries to England after the conquest in 1066, but modern research suggests that juries predated this event and were used in Anglo-Saxon England as early as the seventh century.

In their earliest forms, juries were not the factfinding bodies of today: The Normans used juries to compile the Domesday book, which was an inventory of real and personal property in England put together for the purpose of what we would call "tax collection" today. But in about 1179, King Henry II employed juries in a manner close to our modern understanding when he included them in his newly instituted form of action titled "novel disseisin" (a remedy by which a person forced from his property could reclaim it). The common law writ system that began after the conquest went hand in hand with development of civil juries.

In the writ system, the sheriff would summon "twelve free and lawful men of the neighborhood" to "make recognition concerning it." As the last phrase suggests, these fact-declaring juries were to come to the proceedings already having relevant knowledge. Thus they were both witnesses and factfinders, operating differently from the modern jury. See Carl Stephenson & Frederick Markham, Sources of English Constitutional History 83 (1937) (setting forth Assize of Novel Disseisin); 1 Frederick Pollock & Frederic William Maitland,

History of English Law Before the Time of Edward I 146 (2d ed. 1968) (describing jury role) (hereinafter "Pollock & Maitland"); 2 Pollock & Maitland 120 (by thirteenth century, trial by jury is centerpiece of English civil procedure).

Well prior to the sixteenth and seventeenth centuries when English colonists began coming to America, English juries in civil cases had moved closer to being factfinders. In 1215, the Lateran Council had voiced the opposition of the church to trial by duel or ordeal, which increased pressure to develop another mechanism to resolve civil disputes. It came to be understood that juries were to reach unanimity, which suggests that they were not merely to act on whatever knowledge they already had, but to reach a decision based on experience and reason. The process of "attaint," in which jurors had been imprisoned for reaching false verdicts, had disappeared, which suggests again that jurors were no longer regarded as men who were to say what they already knew. By the early 1500s, juries in England were asked decide on the basis of what they heard in court. See generally Theodore Plucknett, A Concise History of the Common Law 129-130 (5th ed. 1956); 2 Pollock & Maitland 624-628 (describing functions of civil juries in thirteenth century and forward); John P. Dawson, A History of Lay Judges 118-129 (1960) (English kings, already in the twelfth century, were drawn to juries because there were not enough experienced judicial officers to develop facts by interrogating witnesses, but juries continued, for "a full 500 years from its organization in the thirteenth century," to perform a mixed function of providing and judging evidence).

In colonial America, civil juries were a feature of the landscape in Virginia by 1624, and were included in the Massachusetts Body of Liberties in 1641. In 1734, a colonial jury refused to convict journalist John Peter Zenger of seditious libel for accusing William Crosby (colonial governor of New York) with corruption, misfeasance, and usurping the right to jury trial. The jury was instructed to convict if it believed Zenger wrote the articles (which was established), but the jury acquitted Zenger anyway: The verdict helped establish that the press can criticize the government, and showed that juries can defend personal liberties. Prior to the constitutional convention in 1776, all the colonies embraced trial by jury. The role of juries was a focal point in other political skirmishes in New York, and jurors in Massachusetts became instruments of resistance to the crown when they refused to be sworn by a judge who accepted a royal salary. The right to a jury trial became an issue during disputes over the Intolerable Acts in the 1770s, and drew attention in the First Continental Congress in 1774. In paragraph 19, the Declaration of Independence lists denial of "the benefits of trial by jury" among the grievances justifying the break with England, and other drafters included the right of jury trial in the constitutions of the 13 original states. For an account of these matters, see Stephan Landsman, *The Civil Jury in America: Scenes from an Unappreciated History*, 44 Hastings L.J. 579, 595 and passim (1993) (struggle over jury trial entitlement was "an important aspect of the fight for American independence and served to help unite the colonies").

The matter of jury trial received almost no attention in the Constitutional Convention in Philadelphia in 1787. As adopted (before the first ten amendments setting out the Bill of Rights were added), the Constitution guaranteed only the right to jury trial in criminal cases, making no mention of jury trials in civil cases. The matter of civil juries was raised late, and opponents argued (and kept arguing during ratification) that drafting a provision to embody this guarantee would be too difficult because juries are not used in *all* civil cases and the line between those tried to juries and those tried to judges is sometimes hard to draw. Opponents of the Constitution (antifederalists) stressed the omission of a guarantee of a jury in civil cases, and Hamilton replied that "liberty" did not depend on civil juries, and that they were useful only as an antidote to judicial corruption. See Federalist No. 83, at 561-563 (Cook ed., 1960) (omitting the protection does not abolish juries in civil cases; the institution "will remain precisely in the same situation in which it is placed by the state constitutions"). Professor Landsman, in the account cited above, explains the omission by suggesting that the overwhelming concern was to fashion a more effective national government, and the framers had in mind "a series of provocative events" in which North Carolina and Rhode Island "shamelessly manipulated their currencies to assist debtors" and Massachusetts taxpayers "began an open revolt against payment of the state's debts" (Shay's Rebellion):

> This background may help to explain how the civil jury, which had been the most popular vehicle of courtroom justice in the period leading up to and including the Revolution, came to be ignored by the drafters of the Constitution in 1787. The delegates who drafted a new plan of government were, for the most part, creditor-oriented nationalists. They were deeply troubled by recent events in the country and were committed to creating a strong national government that would put an end to the threat of anarchy. They spent most of their time and energy fashioning the executive and legislative branches of this new, stronger central government.

Landsman, supra, at 597-598 (framers thought juries "should play only a modest part in the governance" of the new nation; juries were less necessary because judges were no longer controlled by the British; a counterweight against unjust laws was no longer needed, as the new nation would be a democracy; juries bring drawback of being biased against creditors).

The ratification debates in the colonies included vigorous discussion of the absence of a jury trial entitlement in federal court in civil cases. The fear was that out-of-state creditors could sue local citizens in federal court, thus avoiding the jury trial that would be guaranteed in state suits between local citizens. This situation would lead to oppression, particularly if the only power of review resided in a national Supreme Court located (as the colonists assumed) in Philadelphia. The upshot of ratification debates was an understanding that what we know as the Bill of Rights (the first ten amendments, including the Seventh Amendment's guarantee of jury trial in civil cases) would be submitted by the new national Congress to the states for adoption. James Madison, serving as a member of the House of Representatives, introduced and sponsored the measure that became the Bill of Rights, which took effect on December 15, 1791 when Virginia became the eleventh state to approve it (the number of states now having increased to 14 when Vermont joined the union, 11 approvals were needed). For the details of this story, see Charles W. Wolfram, *The Constitutional History of the Seventh Amendment*, 57 Minn. L. Rev. 639, 679-703 (1973); Edith Guild Henderson, *The Background of the Seventh Amendment*, 30 Harv. L. Rev. 289 (1966).

Who Serves on Juries? The quick answer today is that jurors are selected from voter registration lists, and laws relating to service draw no distinctions on the basis of gender, age, ethnicity, or race. Noncitizens and convicted felons are excluded. Of course, there are exemptions that enable people to be excused from service, and various restrictions let parties challenge persons who should not serve as jurors on account of attitudes or connection with the case.

Perhaps not surprisingly given the nation's history, jury service was not always a universal duty or opportunity. Thus black Americans did not serve on juries in earlier centuries, particularly in parts of the country where they were most numerous, not only because of slavery but because of statutes and practices designed to keep them from serving. In 1880, the Court held that this exclusion violates the Equal Protection Clause, but blacks continued to be excluded, at least in the South, and things only began to change in the 1960s with the coming of the civil rights movement.[1] Indeed, it was not until 1986 that a major barrier to black participation on juries was removed: Then the Court held that prosecutors could not utilize peremptory challenges (letting lawyers remove some potential jurors without giving a reason) to exclude black jurors on account of race, and the principle was later broadened to reach civil cases. Some state statutes go further still in restricting the use of peremptory challenges.[2]

Women did not serve on juries in earlier centuries. Beginning in Wyoming in 1870, various Western states admitted women to jury duty, but almost a century passed before the right to serve was accorded to men and women on the same terms (by the middle of the last century, most differences took the form of exemptions accorded to women automatically or because of

---

[1] See Strauder v. State of West Virginia, 100 U.S. 303 (1880) (state statute barring black Americans from juries violates Equal Protection Clause). See also 8 USC §44 (no citizen is disqualified for service in state or federal court "on account of race, color, or previous condition of servitude"), enacted in 1875 and now embodied in 18 USC §243 (creating criminal penalties for official who "excludes or fails to summon" someone for jury duty in violation of the general principle). See also Powers v. Ohio, 499 U.S. 400 (1991) (defendant may object to race-based exclusion of jurors without sharing same race as excluded persons).
[2] See Batson v. Kentucky, 476 U.S. 79 (1986) (barring prosecutorial use of peremptories to exclude potential black jurors for reasons of race); Edmonson v. Leesville Concrete Co., 500 U.S. 614 (1991) (principle applies in civil cases); Georgia v. McCollum, 505 U.S. 42 (1992) (principle applies to defendants in criminal cases).

motherhood or domestic situation).[3] Drawing on holdings relating to race, the Court has adopted a principle barring use of peremptory challenges to exclude on account of gender, and some state statutes reach further to prevent misuse of the peremptory challenge.[4]

On another front, the Court has held that juries should be "drawn from a cross-section of the community," which "does not mean" that *every* jury must represent "all the economic, social, religious, racial, political and geographical groups," but does mean that prospective jurors must be selected "without systematic and intentional exclusion of any of these groups." Hence officials must recognize that eligible jurors "are to be found in every stratum of society," and that competence is "an individual rather than a group or class matter." Thiel v. Southern Pacific Co., 328 U.S. 217, 220 (1948). In *Thiel*, a man who had "jumped out of the window of a moving train" sued for damages, arguing that the railroad should have known that he was "out of his normal mind" and should not have let him board the train or should have placed him under guard. His case was tried to a jury, which found for the railroad, and plaintiff appealed on the ground that his jury was drawn from a panel that included "mostly business executives" or people "having the employer's viewpoint," which gave too much representation to that group and discriminated against "other occupations and classes," especially employees and "those in the poorer classes." The commissioner and court clerk in *Thiel* testified that they "deliberately and intentionally" excluded wage earners and used the city directory to find prospective jurors. The clerk testified that he would not include, for example, a longshoreman in the jury pool: When such a person says he "is working for $10 a day and cannot afford to work for four [statutory rate for jury duty], the Judge has never made one of those men serve." There was further evidence that businessmen and their wives constituted at least half of the jury list. The Supreme Court rejected this approach:

> [T]he general principles underlying proper jury selection clearly outlaw the exclusion practiced on this instance. Jury competence is not limited to those who earn

---

[3] See Hearings on S.J. Resolution 61, Subcommittee on Constitutional Amendments, Senate Committee on the Judiciary, 91st Cong., 2d Sess. 725-727 (1970) ("there is no distinction between males and females as to the basic qualifications" for jury service; 26 states recognize no exemptions for women, but may require "some affirmative act" or "a determination made by the body listing potential jurors" before service is allowed; 23 states have "specific exemptions or excuses for women or for female-dominated professions or categories"; one state has laws putting it in one or the other category, but which one can't be determined); Joanna L. Grossman, *Women's Jury Service: Right of Citizenship or Privilege of Difference*, 46 Stan. L. Rev. 1115, 1136-1137 (1994) (describing evolution of women's participation on juries; reporting that it was not until 1968 that women could serve as jurors in all 50 states). On the Wyoming experience, see Grace R. Hebard, *The First Woman Jury*, 7 J. Am. Hist. 1293 (1913). See also Taylor v. Louisiana, 419 U.S. 522 (1975) (invalidating Louisiana scheme requiring women to register to serve on juries; violates representative sample requirement).

[4] See J.E.B. v. Alabama ex rel. T.B., 511 U.S. 127 (1994) (state, in paternity action on behalf of mother, could not use peremptory challenge to exclude men). See also Cal. Code Civ. Proc. §231.5 (may not use peremptory challenge for reasons of "race, color, religion, sex, national origin, sexual orientation, or similar grounds").

their livelihood on other than a daily basis. One who is paid $3 a day may be as fully competent as one who is paid $30 a week or $300 a month. In other words, the pay period of a particular individual is completely irrelevant to his eligibility and capacity to serve as a juror. Wage earners, including those who are paid by the day, constitute a very substantial portion of the community, a portion that cannot be intentionally and systematically excluded in whole or in part without doing violence to the democratic nature of the jury system. Were we to sanction an exclusion of this nature we would encourage whatever desires those responsible for the selection of jury panels may have to discriminate against persons of low economic and social status. We would breathe life into any latent tendencies to establish the jury as the instrument of the economically and socially privileged. That we refuse to do.

It is clear that a federal judge would be justified in excusing a daily wage earner for whom jury service would entail an undue financial hardship. But that fact cannot support the complete exclusion of all daily wage earners regardless of whether there is actual hardship involved. Here there was no effort, no intention, to determine in advance which individual members of the daily wage earning class would suffer an undue hardship by serving on a jury at the rate of $4 a day. All were systematically and automatically excluded. In this connection it should be noted that the mere fact that a person earns more than $4 a day would not serve as an excuse. Jury service is a duty as well as a privilege of citizenship; it is a duty that cannot be shirked on a plea of inconvenience or decreased earning power. Only when the financial embarrassment is such as to impose a real burden and hardship does a valid excuse of this nature appear. Thus a blanket exclusion of all daily wage earners, however well-intentioned and however justified by prior actions of trial judges, must be counted among those tendencies which undermine and weaken the institution of jury trial.

Thiel v. Southern Pacific Co., 328 U.S. 217, 222-224 (1948).

For many years, voter registration lists have served as the basis for drawing juries, in both state and federal court. In the federal system, the statutory scheme expresses the purpose of assuring random selection of juries "from a fair cross section of the community," and contemplates the use of "voter registration lists or the lists of actual voters." See generally 28 USC §§1861-1878.

 A   ENTITLEMENT TO JURY TRIAL

The Seventh Amendment says the right to trial by jury "shall be preserved," but only in "suits at common law," and it provides that "no fact tried by a jury" shall be "re-examined" in any way other than "according to the rules of the common law." Recall that the Seventh Amendment applies in federal courts, not state courts.

State constitutional provisions, statutes, or rules guarantee jury trial entitlement in civil cases in all 50 states. Almost from their beginning as colonies, the original 13 states recognized the right to jury trials in civil cases. Today the laws of all 50 States—usually the relevant guarantee is found in the state constitution—protect the right to a jury trial in civil damage suits. See, e.g., Cal. Const., Art. I §16 ("Trial by jury is an inviolate right and shall be secured to all," but in civil cases there can be fewer than 12 jurors if the parties agree); N.Y. Const., Art. I §2 (where trial by jury "has heretofore been guaranteed by constitutional provision," it shall remain "inviolate forever," but in civil cases the legislature may permit verdicts to rest on five-sixths of the jurors).

In ensuing sections, we examine trial by jury in three important dimensions.

First, we take up the scope of jury trial entitlement. The language in the Seventh Amendment saying the right to jury trial shall be "preserved" seems to embody a *historical* standard. Our right to a jury trial in civil cases rests on *practice* that existed some time in the past, and presumably the reference is to 1789 when the Seventh Amendment was presented to Congress, or 1791, when it was ratified. We also have words of limitation: The Seventh Amendment applies in "suits at common law," not *other* civil suits, which means there is no jury trial entitlement in suits in equity, although you are about to learn that drawing the line between these two categories is challenging.

Second, we take up practical problems in operating a jury system: Who can serve? How are jurors selected and impaneled?

Third, we take up mechanisms that restrict the authority of juries: judgments as a matter of law under FRCP 50, and new trials, which can be awarded, *inter alia*, when verdicts are "against the weight of the evidence." These devices implicate another clause in the Seventh Amendment—the "Re-examination" Clause—but courts have found that these control mechanisms are consistent with the Seventh Amendment and state jury trial guarantees.

1. Beginnings of the Modern Era: End of Historical Test

The common law writ system that began in post-conquest England was remarkably successful, but did not prove adequate for all situations, and a competing judicial system called the Court of Chancery grew up in London beginning in the thirteenth century. Over the next two centuries, this court undertook to administer a system of justice that supplemented the common law writ system.

The Chancellor offered remedies that the common law writ system did not offer, particularly injunctive relief and decrees of specific performance of contracts. Common law courts awarded only relief in the form of damages. Another major difference was that common law courts used juries and the Chancellor did not. Not surprisingly, the two systems clashed in England, but they continued to function as separate systems through the adoption of the Constitution in this country in 1787.

In the Seventh Amendment, "suits at common law" was understood as a reference to suits descending from the common law writ system, in contrast to suits tried in Chancery. The understanding was that the Seventh Amendment entitled parties to trial by jury in suits "at law" (seeking monetary relief), but not suits "in equity" (seeking injunctive relief, restitution, specific performance, or reformation of contract). American courts and judges were *not* divided between "equitable" courts and courts "at law" in the manner that obtained in England, where Chancery was in London and the common law courts were all over the realm, and the judges and court facilities were different. In American courts, however, there were still actions at law with jury trial entitlement, and actions in equity without jury.

There are three problems in taking the distinction between actions at law and actions in equity as the basis for deciding whether there is a right to trial by jury. First, historical practices were not static, but changing, and it is sometimes hard to say whether a particular suit would carry a jury trial right in 1789. Second, remedies in American courts have evolved since 1789, and applying a historical test becomes harder. Third, adoption of the Federal Rules in 1938 formally put an end to suits at law and suits in equity. Rule 2 says there is "one form of action," and that is "the civil action." This "merger of law and equity" creates what might be the single biggest modern difficulty in deciding the scope of the right to jury trial: Indeed, it seems fair to say that the *only* remaining distinction between law and equity is that the jury trial attaches to suits at law and not to suits in equity.

■ PROBLEM 12-A. "You Didn't Tell Us He Had Been Sick"

Ann and Stewart Stillman purchased from Provident Insurance Company a term policy insuring Stewart Stillman's life for $100,000. Three months later Stewart Stillman died from lung cancer.

In federal court on the basis of diversity jurisdiction, Provident sues Ann Stillman, as beneficiary under the policy, seeking a declaratory judgment that the policy is not binding because Stewart Stillman made "material misrepresentations of fact" in purchasing the policy, "knowing that he was suffering from an ailment that was likely to be, and was in fact, terminal, while representing that he was healthy." The complaint alleges that Provident "required Stewart Stillman to undergo a physical examination," but Stillman and his doctor "conspired to hide and disguise Stillman's true condition, and misrepresented that Stillman was healthy."

Ann Stillman denies the charging allegations in Provident's complaint, and wants to collect $100,000 under the terms of the policy.

(A) How would this situation play out prior to the merger of law and equity? (The Notes below will help you think about this question.)

(B) How would this situation play out *after* the merger of law and equity but *before* the decision in *Beacon Theatres,* which you are about to read? (Again the Notes below will help you think about this question.)

■ NOTES ON THE HISTORICAL APPROACH

1. The facts of Problem 12-A parallel the *American Life* case, which reached the Supreme Court in 1937—one year before the adoption of the Federal Rules, and consequently a year before the merger of law and equity in federal courts. In *American Life,* the carrier brought suit in equity to rescind a life insurance policy that had been issued three months before the death of the insured, on the ground that the applicants had misrepresented the health of the insured. The beneficiaries then brought their own suit at law to collect the proceeds of the policy. In the carrier's suit, the beneficiaries moved to dismiss, arguing that issues of fraud could be resolved as a defense to the claim on the policy in the suit at law. The carrier sought an injunction blocking the suit at law. Before the court could rule, the parties stipulated that the suit in equity could go forward first. The carrier prevailed, but lost in the Tenth Circuit Court of Appeals, where the reviewing court concluded that the carrier had "an adequate remedy at law." The Supreme Court disagreed with the Tenth Circuit, although it agreed that fraud is "provable as a defense in an action at law upon the policy." But awaiting suit by the beneficiaries was an option "fraught with peril" for the carrier. The reason is that an "incontestability" clause allowed only two years from date of issuance to rescind the policy for fraud. Even though the beneficiaries sued promptly (before the two-year period had run), the suit in equity should have gone forward: "[T]he settled rule is that equitable jurisdiction existing at the filing of a bill [as a complaint in equity was called] is not destroyed because an adequate legal remedy may have become available thereafter. . . . A court has control over its own docket. In the exercise of sound discretion it may hold one lawsuit in abeyance to abide the outcome of another, especially where the parties and issues are the same, . . . but [the beneficiaries] gave that possibility away [by the stipulation]." American Life Insurance Co. v. Stewart, 300 U.S. 203, 215 (1937).

2. Let's consider now the proper handling of the Provident/Stillman litigation in a pre-merger world (prior to 1938). Provident's would be a "suit in equity," brought on the equity side of the federal court, subject to the Rules of Equity.

(a) Stillman, if she wanted to try to a jury her claim for $100,000, would file her own suit against Provident (an action "at law"), and demand a jury trial. In Provident's suit, Stillman would seek a stay or make a motion to dismiss, arguing that Provident could raise the issue of fraud as a defense

in Stillman's suit, pointing out that "fraud in the inducement" had "crept into law" (in suits at law, common law judges were recognizing this matter as a defense).

(b) In its equity suit, Provident would oppose the motion that Stillman made, and seek an injunction blocking her suit. Provident would point out that once a suit in equity was brought in the Court of Chancery in England, the Chancellor would take his step, issuing an injunction ordering a beneficiary not to pursue her suit at law on the policy, to allow time to resolve issues of fraud in the inducement and rescission in the carrier's suit in equity. If the Chancellor upheld the contract and rejected the claim of fraud, he would dismiss the suit, and then the beneficiary's suit at law could go forward. (Under some conditions, although probably not this one, the Chancellor might even invoke the "equitable cleanup" doctrine and decide damage claims connected to the transaction in issue.)

(c) Doesn't *American Life* indicate that things should go very much the way that Provident wants?

3. Now let's consider the proper handling of the Provident/Stillman litigation in a post-merger world (after 1938), before the decision in *Beacon Theatres* (which you are about to read). There would be only one proceeding: Provident's suit would be a "civil action" (not a "suit in equity").

(a) In Provident's suit, Stillman would file a counterclaim for $100,000, and might demand a jury trial of all questions, arguing that a jury can resolve Provident's issues because fraud in the inducement had "crept into law" as a defense to a contract claim.

(b) Provident would move to strike Stillman's demand for a jury trial, and ask the judge to resolve all the issues. There would be no need for an injunction because Stillman would not file a second suit. Instead, Provident would ask for a sequencing order that would act like an injunction, under which the court would resolve the fraud claim first. If that claim were rejected, the judge might empanel a jury to hear Stillman's claim for $100,000, or conceivably decide that claim too, under the equitable cleanup doctrine.

(c) If the merger of law and equity doesn't change the jury trial entitlement, doesn't *American Life* indicate that things should go very much as Provident wants? (You are about to read the *Beacon Theatres* case, where you will see that the Court has another idea about jury trial entitlement in a post-merger world.)

4. The question whether the judge could decide Stillman's claim of money damages for breach of contract in a pre-merger world—or in a post-merger world if the court adheres closely to historic practice—is harder to answer. In England, and in the United States before the merger of law and equity, a plaintiff could sometimes bring a suit in equity that would lead to an award of damages. Under the "equitable clean-up doctrine," a court in equity could refuse, for example, a decree requiring specific performance of a contract, and award damages instead. But it is not so clear that this doctrine could apply on these facts because damages are not included either in Provident's claim for rescission or in Stillman's defense that the policy is valid, and the obligation to bring counterclaims in a suit in equity in a pre-merger world did not reach counterclaims *at law*. The "equitable cleanup" doctrine brought other problems, including vagueness, possibilities for abuse (plaintiff could bring an equitable claim that he couldn't hope to win and seek damages in a setting in which the other side could not demand a jury), and risks that for *both* parties (plaintiff might not know whether he could win equitable relief, and lose the right to a jury trial on damage issues; defendant could be held hostage to plaintiff's choice of equitable versus legal suit). For a sympathetic treatment of the clean-up doctrine, which nevertheless expresses the hope that it can be abandoned, see Leo Levin, *Equitable Clean-Up and the Jury: A Suggested Orientation*, 100 Univ. Pa. L. Rev. 320, 321-322, 353 (1951) (clean-up doctrine rested on sound consideration that plaintiff entitled to both equitable and legal remedies "needed relief from the burden of two days in court," and on consideration of litigant who "legitimately but vainly sought" equitable relief; clean-up doctrine avoided "procedural inequities" that were "inherent" in divided system; merging law and equity has been a "boon," and one may hope for reformulation of constitutional entitlement to a jury trial that will "avoid, or limit, the backward glance" that incorporates clean-up doctrine in defining scope of entitlement).

Justice Hugo Black (1886-1971)

Justice Hugo Black, whose opinion in the *Beacon Theatres* case you are about to read, served on the court for 34 years (1937-1971). He was a fierce advocate for the incorporation of the Bill of Rights into the Due Process Clause of the Fourteenth Amendment. A major doctrinal shift, this development had the effect of holding states to the same standards as the federal government (previously, it was understood that the Bill of Rights applied only against the federal government). Justice Black was a defender of the freedom of juries to decide cases as they saw fit, and you will read his dissenting opinion in the *Galloway* case later in this chapter. In *Beacon Theatres*, Justice Black and the majority saw a chance to expand jury trial entitlement in civil cases. Justice Black was known for his stress on textualism. You saw his dissent in *International Shoe* (Chapter 3B1, supra), where he thought it was clear that due process allowed Washington to exercise jurisdiction, and he viewed the new "minimum contacts" standard as displacing due process with something else. He was also known for his vigorous defense of individual rights, and for his sense of judicial restraint: He had much in common with Justice Douglas, but feuded with him on the question whether the Bill of Rights includes a right of privacy (Douglas saying yes, Black saying no). Unlike other strict constructionists, however, Black took an expansive view of federal legislative power while paradoxically defending state prerogatives, contributing to the development of the doctrine of abstention, which you encountered in the *Pennzoil* case (Chapter 6C, supra).

BEACON THEATRES, INC. v. WESTOVER

Supreme Court of the United States
359 U.S. 500 (1959)

Mr. Justice BLACK delivered the opinion of the Court.

Petitioner, Beacon Theatres, Inc., sought by mandamus to require a district judge in the Southern District of California to vacate certain orders alleged to deprive it of a jury trial of issues arising in a suit brought against it by Fox West Coast Theatres, Inc. The Court of Appeals for the Ninth Circuit refused the writ, holding that the trial judge had acted within his proper discretion in denying petitioner's request for a jury. We granted certiorari because "Maintenance of the jury as a factfinding body is of such importance and occupies so firm a place in our history and jurisprudence that any seeming curtailment of the right to a jury trial should be scrutinized with the utmost care." Dimick v. Schiedt, 293 U.S. 474 (1935).

Fox had asked for declaratory relief against Beacon alleging a controversy arising under the Sherman Antitrust Act, 15 USC §§1, 2, and under the Clayton Act, 15 USC §15, which authorizes suits for treble damages against Sherman Act violators. According to the complaint Fox operates a movie theatre in San Bernardino, California, and has long been exhibiting films under contracts with movie distributors. These contracts grant it the exclusive right to show "first run" pictures in the "San Bernardino competitive area" and provide for "clearance"—a period of time during which no other theatre can exhibit the same pictures. After building a drive in theatre about 11 miles from San Bernardino, Beacon notified Fox that it considered contracts barring simultaneous exhibitions of first-run films in the two theatres to be overt acts in violation of the antitrust laws. Fox's complaint alleged that this notification, together with threats of treble damage suits against Fox and its distributors, gave rise to "duress and coercion" which deprived Fox of a valuable property right, the right to negotiate for exclusive first-run contracts. Unless Beacon was restrained, the complaint continued, irreparable harm would result. Accordingly, while its pleading was styled a "Complaint for Declaratory Relief," Fox prayed both for a declaration that a grant of clearance between the Fox and Beacon theatres is reasonable and not in violation of the antitrust laws, and for an injunction, pending final resolution of the litigation, to prevent Beacon from instituting any action under the antitrust laws against Fox and its distributors arising out of the controversy alleged in the complaint. Beacon filed an answer, a counterclaim against Fox, and a cross-claim against an exhibitor who had intervened. These denied the threats and asserted that there was no substantial competition between the two theatres, that the clearances granted were therefore unreasonable, and that a conspiracy existed between Fox and its distributors to manipulate contracts and clearances so as to restrain trade and monopolize first-run pictures in violation of the antitrust laws. Treble damages were asked.

Beacon demanded a jury trial of the factual issues in the case as provided by FRCP 38(b). The District Court, however, viewed the issues raised by the "Complaint for Declaratory Relief," including the question of competition between the two theatres, as essentially equitable. Acting under the purported authority of Rules 42(b) and 57, it directed that these issues be tried to the court before jury determination of the validity of the charges of antitrust violations made in the counterclaim and crossclaim. A common issue of the "Complaint for Declaratory Relief," the counterclaim, and the crossclaim was the reasonableness of the clearances granted to Fox, which depended, in part, on the existence of competition between the two theatres. Thus the effect of the action of the District Court could be, as the Court of Appeals believed, "to limit the petitioner's opportunity fully to try to a jury every issue which has a bearing upon its treble damage suit," for determination of the issue of clearances by the judge might "operate either by way of res judicata or collateral estoppel so as to conclude both parties with respect thereto at the subsequent trial of the treble damage claim."

The District Court's finding that the Complaint for Declaratory Relief presented basically equitable issues draws no support from the Declaratory Judgment Act, 28 USC §§2201, 2202; FRCP 57. That statute, while allowing prospective defendants to sue to establish their nonliability, specifically preserves the right to jury trial for both parties. It follows that if Beacon would have been entitled to a jury trial in a treble damage suit against Fox it cannot be deprived of that right merely because Fox took advantage of the availability of declaratory relief to sue Beacon first. Since the right to trial by jury applies to treble damage suits under the antitrust laws, and is, in fact, an essential part of the congressional plan for making competition rather than monopoly the rule of trade, the Sherman and Clayton Act issues on which Fox sought a declaration were essentially jury questions.

Nevertheless the Court of Appeals refused to upset the order of the district judge. It held that the question of whether a right to jury trial existed was to be judged by Fox's complaint read as a whole. In addition to seeking a declaratory judgment, the court said, Fox's complaint can be read as making out a valid plea for injunctive relief, thus stating a claim traditionally cognizable in equity. A party who is entitled to maintain a suit in equity for an injunction, said the court, may have all the issues in his suit determined by the judge without a jury regardless of whether legal rights are involved. The court then rejected the argument that equitable relief, traditionally available only when legal remedies are inadequate, was rendered unnecessary in this case by the filing of the counterclaim and cross-claim which presented all the issues necessary to a determination of the right to injunctive relief. Relying on American Life Ins. Co. v. Stewart, 300 U.S. 203, 215 (1937), decided before the enactment of the Federal Rules of Civil Procedure, it invoked the principle that a court sitting in equity could retain jurisdiction even though later a legal remedy became available. In such instances the equity court had discretion to enjoin the later lawsuit in order to allow the whole dispute to be determined in one case in one court. Reasoning by analogy, the Court of Appeals held it was not an abuse of discretion for the district judge, acting under FRCP 42(b), to try the equitable cause first even though this might, through collateral estoppel, prevent a full jury trial of the counterclaim and cross-claim which were as effectively stopped as by an equity injunction.

. . .

The basis of injunctive relief in the federal courts has always been irreparable harm and inadequacy of legal remedies. At least as much is required to justify a trial court in using its discretion under the Federal Rules to allow claims of equitable origins to be tried ahead of legal ones, since this has the same effect as an equitable injunction of the legal claims. And it is immaterial, in judging if that discretion is properly employed, that before the Federal Rules and the Declaratory Judgment Act were passed, courts of equity, exercising a jurisdiction separate from courts of law, were, in some cases, allowed to enjoin subsequent legal actions between the same parties involving the same controversy. This was because the subsequent legal action, though providing an opportunity to try the case to a jury, might not protect the right of the equity plaintiff to a fair and orderly adjudication of the controversy. Under such circumstances the legal remedy could quite naturally be deemed inadequate. Inadequacy of remedy and irreparable harm are practical terms, however. As such their existence today must be determined, not by precedents decided under discarded procedures, but in the light of the remedies now made available by the Declaratory Judgment Act and the Federal Rules.

Viewed in this manner, the use of discretion by the trial court under Rule 42(b) to deprive Beacon of a full jury trial on its counterclaim and crossclaim, as well as on Fox's plea for declaratory relief, cannot be justified. Under the Federal Rules the same court may try both legal and equitable causes in the same action. FRCP 1, 2, 18. Thus any defenses, equitable or legal, Fox may have to charges of antitrust violations can be raised either in its suit for declaratory relief or in answer to Beacon's counterclaim. On proper showing, harassment by threats of other suits, or other suits actually brought, involving the issues being tried in this case, could be temporarily enjoined pending the outcome of this litigation. Whatever permanent injunctive relief Fox might be entitled to on the basis of the decision in this case could, of course, be given by the court after the jury renders its verdict. In this way the issues between these parties could be settled in one suit giving Beacon a full jury trial of every antitrust issue. By contrast, the holding of the court below while granting Fox no additional protection unless the avoidance of jury trial be considered as such, would compel Beacon to split his antitrust case, trying part to a judge and part to a jury.[10] Such a result, which involves the postponement and subordination of Fox's own legal claim for declaratory relief as well as of the counterclaim which Beacon was compelled by the Federal Rules to bring, is not permissible.

Our decision is consistent with the plan of the Federal Rules and the Declaratory Judgment Act to effect substantial procedural reform while retaining a distinction between jury and nonjury issues and leaving substantive rights unchanged. Since in the federal courts equity has always acted only when legal remedies were inadequate, the expansion of adequate legal remedies provided by the Declaratory Judgment Act and the Federal Rules necessarily affects the scope of equity. Thus, the justification for equity's deciding legal issues once it obtains jurisdiction, and refusing to dismiss a case, merely because subsequently a legal remedy becomes available, must be re-evaluated in the light of the liberal joinder provisions of the Federal Rules which allow legal and equitable causes to be brought and resolved in one civil action. Similarly the need for, and therefore, the availability of such equitable remedies as Bills of Peace, Quia Timet and Injunction must be reconsidered in view of the existence of the Declaratory Judgment Act as well as the liberal joinder provision of the Rules. This is not only in accord with the spirit of the Rules and the Act but is required by the provision in the Rules that "(t)he right of trial by jury as declared by the Seventh Amendment to the Constitution or as given by a statute of the United States shall be preserved ... inviolate."[16]

If there should be cases where the availability of declaratory judgment or joinder in one suit of legal and equitable causes would not in all respects protect the plaintiff seeking equitable relief from irreparable harm while affording a jury trial in the legal cause, the trial court will necessarily have to use its discretion in deciding whether the legal or equitable cause should be tried first. Since the right to jury trial is a constitutional one, however, while no similar requirement protects trials by the court, that discretion is very narrowly limited and must, wherever possible, be exercised to preserve jury trial. As this Court said in Scott v. Neely, 140 U.S. 106 (1891): "In the Federal courts this (jury) right cannot be dispensed with, except by the assent of the parties entitled to it; nor can it be impaired by any blending with a claim, properly cognizable at law, of a demand for equitable relief in aid of the legal action, or during its pendency." This longstanding principle of equity dictates that only under the most imperative circumstances, circumstances which in

---

[10] Since the issue of violation of the antitrust laws often turns on the reasonableness of a restraint on trade in the light of all the facts, it is particularly undesirable to have some of the relevant considerations tried by one factfinder and some by another.

[16] FRCP 38(a). In delegating to the Supreme Court responsibility for drawing up rules, Congress declared that "such rules shall not abridge, enlarge or modify any substantive right and shall preserve the right of trial by jury as at common law and as declared by the Seventh Amendment to the Constitution." 28 USC §2072. [The Court quotes the Preservation Clause of Seventh Amendment.]

view of the flexible procedures of the Federal Rules we cannot now anticipate, can the right to a jury trial of legal issues be lost through prior determination of equitable claims. As we have shown, this is far from being such a case.

Respondent claims mandamus is not available under the All Writs Act, 28 USC §1651. Whatever differences of opinion there may be in other types of cases, we think the right to grant mandamus to require jury trial where it has been improperly denied is settled.

The judgment of the Court of Appeals is reversed.

Mr. Justice FRANKFURTER took no part in the consideration or decision of this case.

Mr. Justice STEWART, with whom Mr. Justice HARLAN and Mr. Justice WHITTAKER concur, dissenting.

There can be no doubt that a litigant is entitled to a writ of mandamus to protect a clear constitutional or statutory right to a jury trial. But there was no denial of such a right here. The district judge simply exercised his inherent discretion, now explicitly confirmed by the Federal Rules of Civil Procedure, to schedule the trial of an equitable claim in advance of an action at law. Even an abuse of such discretion could not, I think, be attacked by the extraordinary writ of mandamus. In any event no abuse of discretion is apparent in this case.

The complaint filed by Fox stated a claim traditionally cognizable in equity. That claim, in brief, was that Beacon had wrongfully interfered with the right of Fox to compete freely with Beacon and other distributors for the licensing of films for first-run exhibition in the San Bernardino area. The complaint alleged that the plaintiff was without an adequate remedy at law and would be irreparably harmed unless the defendant were restrained from continuing to interfere—by coercion and threats of litigation—with the plaintiff's lawful business relationships.

The Court of Appeals found that the complaint, although inartistically drawn, contained allegations entitling the petitioner to equitable relief. That finding is accepted in the prevailing opinion today. If the complaint had been answered simply by a general denial, therefore, the issues would under traditional principles have been triable as a proceeding in equity. Instead of just putting in issue the allegations of the complaint, however, Beacon filed pleadings which affirmatively alleged the existence of a broad conspiracy among the plaintiff and other theatre owners to monopolize the first-run exhibition of films in the San Bernardino area to refrain from competing among themselves, and to discriminate against Beacon in granting film licenses. Based upon these allegations, Beacon asked damages in the amount of $300,000. Clearly these conspiracy allegations stated a cause of action triable as of right by a jury. What was demanded by Beacon, however, was a jury trial not only of this cause of action, but also of the issues presented by the original complaint.

Upon motion of Fox the trial judge ordered the original action for declaratory and equitable relief to be tried separately to the court and in advance of the trial of the defendant's counter-claim and cross-claim for damages. The court's order, which carefully preserved the right to trial by jury upon the conspiracy and damage issues raised by the counterclaim and cross-claim, was in conformity with the specific provisions of the Federal Rules of Civil Procedure.[3] Yet it is decided today that the Court of Appeals must compel the district judge to rescind it.

Assuming the existence of a factual issue common both to the plaintiff's original action and the defendant's counterclaim for damages, I cannot agree that the District Court must be compelled to try the counterclaim first.[4] It is, of course, a matter of no great moment in what order the issues between the parties in the present litigation are tried. What is disturbing is the process by which the Court arrives at its decision—a process which appears to disregard the historic relationship between equity and law.

I

The Court suggests that "the expansion of adequate legal remedies provided by the Declaratory Judgment Act ... necessarily affects the scope of equity." Does the Court mean to say that the mere availability of an action for a declaratory judgment operates to furnish "an adequate remedy at law" so as to deprive a court of equity of the power to act? That novel line of reasoning is at least implied in the Court's opinion. But the Declaratory Judgment Act did not "expand" the substantive law. That Act merely provided a new statutory remedy, neither legal nor equitable, but available in the areas of

---

[3] [Justice Stewart quotes FRCP 42(b), which authorizes courts to order separate trials for various claims brought in a single suit.] The ACN to Rule 39 states that, "When certain of the issues are to be tried by jury and others by the court, the court may determine the sequence in which such issues shall be tried." This language was at one time contained in a draft of the Rules, but was deleted because "the power is adequately given by Rule 42(b). . . ." Moore's Federal Practice (2d ed.) §39.12, n.8. See also Rule 57, which provides, *inter alia*, that "The court may order a speedy hearing of an action for a declaratory judgment and may advance it on the calendar." [The phrase "and may advance it on the calendar" is no longer in FRCP 57.—Ed.]

[4] It is not altogether clear at this stage of the proceedings whether the existence of substantial competition between Fox and Beacon is actually a material issue of fact common to both the equitable claim and the counterclaim for damages. The respondent ingeniously argues that determination in the equitable suit of the issue of competition between the theatres would be determinative of little or nothing in the counterclaim for damages. [The argument stresses that Fox's claim for injunctive and declaratory relief raises the question whether Fox and Beacon are in competition with each other, while Beacon's counterclaim raises the question whether Beacon and other exhibitors are conspiring in restraint of trade. Failing to prove conspiracy would make it unnecessary to decide the question of competition, and *proving* conspiracy would make it unnecessary to prove competition in order to recover, although an absence of competition would depress any damage claim.—Ed.]

both equity and law. When declaratory relief is sought, the right to trial by jury depends upon the basic context in which the issues are presented. If the basic issues in an action for declaratory relief are of a kind traditionally cognizable in equity, e.g., a suit for cancellation of a written instrument, the declaratory judgment is not a "remedy at law." If, on the other hand, the issues arise in a context traditionally cognizable at common law, the right to a jury trial of course remains unimpaired, even though the only relief demanded is a declaratory judgment.

Thus, if in this case the complaint had asked merely for a judgment declaring that the plaintiff's specified manner of business dealings with distributors and other exhibitors did not render it liable to Beacon under the antitrust laws, this would have been simply a "juxtaposition of parties" case in which Beacon could have demanded a jury trial.[7] But the complaint in the present case, as the Court recognizes, presented issues of exclusively equitable cognizance, going well beyond a mere defense to any subsequent action at law. Fox sought from the court protection against Beacon's allegedly unlawful interference with its business relationships—protection which this Court seems to recognize might not have been afforded by a declaratory judgment, unsupplemented by equitable relief. The availability of a declaratory judgment did not, therefore, operate to confer upon Beacon the right to trial by jury with respect to the issues raised by the complaint.

II

The Court's opinion does not, of course, hold or even suggest that a court of equity may never determine "legal rights." For indeed it is precisely such rights which the Chancellor, when his jurisdiction has been properly invoked, has often been called upon to decide. Issues of fact are rarely either "legal" or "equitable." All depends upon the context in which they arise. . . .

It has been an established rule "that equitable jurisdiction existing at the filing of a bill is not destroyed because an adequate legal remedy may have become available thereafter."[8] American Life Ins. Co. v. Stewart, 300 U.S. 203 (1937). It has also been long settled that the District Court in its discretion may order the trial of a suit in equity in advance of an action at law between the same parties, even if there is a factual issue common to both. [Justice Stewart quotes language from the *American Life* decision stressing that a

---

[7] "Transposition of parties" would perhaps be a more accurate description. A typical such case is one in which a plaintiff uses the declaratory judgment procedure to seek a determination of nonliability to a legal claim asserted by the defendant. The defendant in such a case is, of course, entitled to a jury trial.

[8] The suggestion by the Court that "This was because the subsequent legal action, though providing an opportunity to try the case to a jury, might not protect the right of the equity plaintiff to a fair and orderly adjudication of the controversy" is plainly inconsistent with many of the cases in which the rule has been applied.

court "has control over its own docket," and "may hold one lawsuit in abeyance" while another is tried, especially where "the parties and the issues are the same."][9]

III

The Court today sweeps away these basic principles as "precedents decided under discarded procedures." It suggests that the Federal Rules of Civil Procedure have somehow worked an "expansion of adequate legal remedies" so as to oust the District Courts of equitable jurisdiction, as well as to deprive them of their traditional power to control their own dockets. But obviously the Federal Rules could not and did not "expand" the substantive law one whit.

Like the Declaratory Judgment Act, the Federal Rules preserve inviolate the right to trial by jury in actions historically cognizable at common law, as under the Constitution they must. They do not create a right of trial by jury where that right "does not exist under the Constitution or statutes of the United States" [citing FRCP 39(a), which contained this phrase at the time—this language was later deleted from the Rule—Ed.]. Since Beacon's counterclaim was compulsory under the Rules, see Rule 13(a), it is apparent that by filing it Beacon could not be held to have waived its jury rights.[12] But neither can the counterclaim be held to have transformed Fox's original complaint into an action at law.[13]

The Rules make possible the trial of legal and equitable claims in the same proceeding, but they expressly affirm the power of a trial judge to determine the order in which claims shall be heard. Rule 42(b). Certainly the Federal Rules were not intended to undermine the basic structure of equity jurisprudence, developed over the centuries and explicitly recognized in the United States Constitution. . . .

■ NOTES ON THE DAWN OF THE MODERN APPROACH

1. In thinking about *Beacon Theatres*, a good starting point is to ask why Beacon would be entitled to a jury trial in a suit under the Sherman Act, which forbids combinations or conspiracies "in restraint of trade" and authorizes

---

[9] It is arguable that if a case factually similar to American Life Ins. Co. v. Stewart were to arise under the Declaratory Judgment Act, the defendant would be entitled to a jury trial. See footnote 7[, supra].

[12] This is not, of course, to suggest that the filing of a permissive "legal" counterclaim to an "equitable" complaint would amount to a waiver of jury rights on the issues raised by the counterclaim.

[13] Determination of whether a claim stated by the complaint is triable by the court or by a jury will normally not be dependent upon the "legal" or "equitable" character of the counterclaim. There are situations, however, such as a case in which the plaintiff seeks a declaration of invalidity or noninfringement of a patent, in which the relief sought by the counterclaim will determine the nature of the entire case.

suits where plaintiffs can recover treble damages. Can a suit under a statute be a suit "at common law" under the Seventh Amendment? The Court treats as given that antitrust suits carry a right to trial by jury, but is coy on the question whether this right applies because of the Seventh Amendment or because Congress created the right in the statute itself (right to jury trial is "an essential part of the congressional scheme"). Years later, in Curtis v. Loether, 415 U.S. 189 (1974), the Court decided that suits under Title VIII of the Civil Rights Act of 1968 (fair housing provisions) carry a right to a jury trial. The opinion addresses the question to which the Court only assumed an answer in *Beacon Theatres*. In *Curtis*, defendant landlord claimed a right to trial by jury, perhaps thinking a jury would be less sympathetic than a judge to a claim of racial discrimination. The Court invoked a modern-sounding principle set out in a decision handed down more than a century earlier in Parsons v. Bedford, 3 Pet. 433, 446-447 (1983), which said the Seventh Amendment preserves the right to jury trial not only in "old and settled" common law proceedings, but also in suits "in which *legal* rights were to be ascertained." In *Curtis*, the Court concluded that the jury trial entitlement "does apply to actions enforcing statutory rights" when they are "legal" in nature, as is true when they seek damages in a suit that "sounds basically in tort." The Court has reiterated this position. See Tull v. United States, 481 U.S. 412, 417 (1987) (cases "analogous to" suits at law carry jury trial right, including causes of action created by "congressional enactment"); Chauffeurs, Teamsters & Helpers, Local No. 391 v. Terry, 494 U.S. 558, 654 (1990) (jury trial right "extends to causes of action created by Congress").

2. The judge in *Beacon Theatres* decided to hear Fox's claim for injunctive relief before he entertained Beacon's antitrust claim. Recall from the Notes following Problem 12-A that if the suit had been brought in England centuries ago, or in pre-merger federal court in America, the federal judge in Fox's suit could issue an injunction blocking Beacon from filing a federal antitrust suit (or prosecuting the suit if it had already been filed). By analogy, a federal judge in a merged system might simply resolve all the issues relating to injunctive relief first (without jury) and then try to a jury issues of damages. Of course, a decision to enjoin Beacon Theatres might pre-empt a damage claim, but that shouldn't matter: The reason would be that Beacon is not entitled to claim damages because the judge decided critical points adversely to Beacon. The Court in *Beacon Theatres* turned its back on this approach, didn't it? Thus it turned its back on the *American Life* case that had been decided 22 years earlier (*American Life* is described in the Notes after Problem 12-A, supra, and in Justice Stewart's dissent in *Beacon Theatres*). Why does the Court depart from tradition so decisively?

(a) Perhaps one reason is an aversion to procedural "gamesmanship" that might reduce entitlement to a jury trial. Beacon "cannot be deprived" of its jury trial right, the Court says, "merely because Fox took advantage of the availability of declaratory relief" to sue first.

(b) Another reason is that the world has changed, and the Court is concerned that modern developments might reduce the dimensions of jury trial entitlement. In other words, the historical approach seems less and less tenable, and steps need to be taken to protect jury trial entitlement. Look for passages in *Beacon Theatres* that tell us that these changes count. Notice the reference to "precedents decided under discarded procedures." What does the Court mean in this passage? Notice Justice Stewart's reaction: Neither the Declaratory Judgment Act nor the Rules affect jury trial entitlement. The Court seems to be saying otherwise, doesn't it?

3. The problem that came up in *Beacon Theatres* was destined to arise. For one thing, the Seventh Amendment points *both* toward historical practice as key in determining the extent of entitlement to a jury trial (by saying the right shall be "preserved") *and* toward the *nature of the case* as key (by saying the right is preserved in "suits at common law"). *Beacon Theatres* resolves the tension between these standards by stressing that it is the latter criterion that counts, doesn't it? See, e.g., John McCoid, *Procedural Reform and the Right to Jury Trial: A Study of Beacon Theatres, Inc. v. Westover,* 116 U. Pa. L. Rev. 1, 11 (1967) (if *Beacon Theatres* means that right to a jury trial is constitutionally secured, "at its core must be the view that the command of the Seventh Amendment is one of adherence to a principle rather than to a particular set of results," and the principle turns on "the distinction between law and equity jurisdiction").

4. In *Beacon Theatres,* how important is it that there were issues common to the legal and equitable claims? Look at the Court's footnote 10 and accompanying text. But notice two things: First, the issues raised by the claim for injunctive relief and the counterclaim for damages don't overlap as much as might appear. It is true that a decision on the reasonableness of the clearances bears on the question whether Fox can stop Beacon from threatening suit, and on the question whether Beacon can recover damages. But this issue would not by itself determine either party's right to relief. To be entitled to an injunction, Fox would have to prove harassment, not simply talk about a suit or the reasonableness of the clearances; to be entitled to damages, Beacon would have to show that it actually suffered in its business, not just unreasonableness of the clearances. Second, the stress on the changed world has broader implications than would be indicated by extending jury trial entitlement to issues common to equitable and legal claims.

5. Three years after *Beacon Theatres,* the Court handed down a decision that appeared to abolish the equitable clean-up doctrine. The owner of the Dairy Queen franchise sued a franchisee for an accounting, arguing that defendant failed to pay sums required by the franchise agreement. Defendant claimed the parties had entered into a "novation" (substituting a different obligation for the original, and perhaps a different obligor), and demanded a jury trial. The court thought no jury was required, either because the suit was purely equitable or because legal issues raised by the defense were "incidental" to an equitable suit. The Supreme Court disagreed: The question is whether the action "contains legal issues," not whether issues triable to a judge are "incidental" to equitable issues, "for no such rule may be applied in the federal courts." Plaintiff's claim for money damages could not be construed as equitable merely because plaintiff sought an "accounting" rather than "damages." If the accounts on which the claim depends are so complicated that "only a court of equity can satisfactorily unravel them," it does not follow that these issues are for a judge. Under FRCP 53(b), the court can "appoint masters to assist the jury in those exceptional cases where the legal issues are too complicated for the jury adequately to handle alone." Dairy Queen v. Wood, 369 U.S. 469, 471, 477-478 (1962). To what extent is the holding of *Dairy Queen* already implicit in *Beacon Theatres*? In taking the view that the suit in *Beacon Theatres* was "essentially equitable," wasn't the judge in *Beacon Theatres* applying the equitable clean-up doctrine, and didn't the Court—without coming right out and saying it—already implicity conclude that this approach is no longer acceptable?

6. After *Beacon Theatres* and *Dairy Queen,* how should the court handle a suit like the one described in Problem 12-A (patterned after the *American Life Insurance* case)? How should it handle *Beacon Theatres*? *Dairy Queen*?

7. *Beacon Theatres* should not be taken to mean that a trial court cannot *ever* decide equitable issues that might foreclose later suits at law. Suppose, for example, plaintiff seeks reformation of a contract and damages for breach of the reformed agreement. If the contract calls for defendant to sell plaintiff 1,000 gallons of "turpentine" and plaintiff sues to reform the agreement to specify 1,000 gallons of "mineral spirits," then to recover damages because defendant delivered turpentine instead of mineral spirits, a judge would decide the equitable claim for reformation. If the judge granted this relief, plaintiff could seek damages for breach. If the judge refused to reform the contract, the damage claim would be foreclosed. Thus judges sometimes resolve equitable issues that dispose of legal claims. On a narrow reading of *Beacon Theatres,* there is no violation of the right to jury trial because the issues in the equitable claim (was a mistake made? should the contract be reformed?) are not the same as the issues in the legal claim (did defendant breach the contract? was plaintiff damaged?). But even under a broad reading of *Beacon Theatres,* in which changes in procedure expand jury trial entitlement, there is no reason to think *Beacon Theatres* requires the judge to turn over to a jury the traditional equitable issues raised by reformation claims.

8. Although *Beacon Theatres* and *Dairy Queen* apply the Seventh Amendment and are not binding on state courts interpreting their own right to trial by jury in civil cases in their own systems, the opinions have been influential in state jurisprudence. Rules, statutes, or constitutional provisions in many states resemble the Seventh Amendment in using words like "preserve" or "remain inviolate" (suggesting retention of something already in existence). For decisions following *Beacon Theatres,* see, e.g., Mundhenke v. Holm, 2010 WL 3172172 (S.D. 2010) ("the incidental claim rule" is abrogated in South Dakota to the extent that it is inconsistent with *Beacon Theatres* and *Dairy*

Queen); Onvoy, Inc. v. Allete, Inc., 736 N.W.2d 611, 617 (Minn. 2007) (agreeing with *Beacon Theatres* that jury should make "factual findings that are common to both claims at law and claims for equitable relief," and that these are binding on the trial court in deciding the equitable claims); Blea v. Fields, 120 P.3d 430, 433 (N.M. 2005) (similar to *Onvoy*). In some states, the right to a jury trial is broader than in the federal system. See, e.g., Stukey v. Stephens, 295 P.2d 973 (Ariz. 1931) (under Arizona law either party "is entitled as a matter of right" to a jury trial "in equity as well as in law cases," although juries in equity cases are "advisory") (Arizona constitutional provision says right to jury trial "shall remain inviolate").

2. Growing Pains: Jury Trials in the Administrative State

Not long after *Beacon Theatres* and *Dairy Queen*, the Court's effort to distance itself from pure historicism encountered new challenges in cases involving administrative agencies and what came to be called "public rights."

The leading decision is Katchen v. Landy, 382 U.S. 323 (1966). There a creditor brought suit in bankruptcy court against a trustee in bankruptcy, seeking money allegedly owed by the bankrupt. The trustee sought to recoup sums already paid to the creditor, on the ground that they constituted a "voidable preference" (payment made shortly before bankruptcy, which can be disallowed and recovered for the bankrupt estate, to prevent one creditor from recovering a disproportionate amount). The creditor argued that *if* the trustee had sued to recover the alleged preference, the suit would be heard in federal district court where the creditor was entitled to a jury trial, and that the result should not change because the preference issue arose in bankruptcy. Not so, the Court concluded. Bankruptcy courts "are essentially courts of equity" that "proceed in summary fashion" to secure prompt and effective resolution of bankruptcy matters. While the creditor "might be entitled to a jury trial on the issue of preference if he presented no claim in the bankruptcy proceedings," it is different "when the same issue arises as part of the process of allowance and disallowance of claims, [where] it is triable in equity." If the creditor were entitled to a jury trial here, bankruptcy proceedings would have to be "suspended . . . , with all the delay and expense that course would entail," which is not "consistent with the equitable purposes of the Bankruptcy Act nor with the rule of *Beacon Theatres* and *Dairy Queen*, which is itself an equitable doctrine."

Three important things happened in *Katchen*: First, the Court applied its new approach to jury trial entitlement in the context of administrative machinery set up by statute. Second, the Court appeared to have forgotten that it had abolished—or apparently abolished—the equitable clean-up doctrine in *Dairy Queen* four years earlier, invoking that doctrine in substance if not in name. Third, the Court appeared willing to allow for a *contraction* in jury trial entitlement on account of modern procedural developments.

Four other decisions shed light—and let us admit that they sow some confusion too—on what we might call the *Katchen* doctrine:

(1) *Atlas Roofing.* Here the Court held that an employer fined for violations of workplace safety rules did not have a right to a jury trial on the propriety of the fine, and upheld the statutory scheme in which the employer had to appear before an administrative law judge to argue that the fine was improper. In cases where "public rights" are in issue—cases where the government "sues in its sovereign capacity to enforce public rights" created by statute—Congress may assign "the factfinding function and initial adjudication" to an administrative forum. The Court distinguished "private tort, contract, and property cases" as "not at all implicated" in its holding. See Atlas Roofing Co. v. Occupational Safety and Health Review Commission, 430 U.S. 442, 450, 458 (1977).

(2) *Jones & Laughlin Steel.* This case arose long before *Katchen* (and before *Beacon Theatres* and *Dairy Queen*), and *later* the Court interpreted this decision in light of its new approach. In *Jones & Laughlin Steel*, the Court approved use of a federal district court, sitting without jury, to enforce an NLRB order requiring Jones & Laughlin to reinstate employees and pay back wages. In what might be described as an exercise in historical revisionism, the Court reconstructed *Jones & Laughlin* in Curtis v. Loether, 415 U.S. 189, 194 (1974), saying that *Jones & Laughlin* stands for the proposition that the right to a jury trial is "generally inapplicable in administrative proceedings," where such a right would be "incompatible with the whole concept of administrative adjudication" and "substantially interfere" with agency enforcement. See NLRB v. Jones & Laughlin Steel Corp., 301 U.S. 1 (1937).

(3) *Granfinanciera.* In this complicated decision, the question was whether a bankruptcy court, where the judge lacks life tenure and operates without jury, could adjudicate a claim by the trustee to recover from a creditor of the bankrupt a fraudulent transfer (payment to one creditor made with intent to defraud others) that the creditor got from the bankrupt. The Court was split, and the sprawling opinions take up more than 60 pages. The majority acknowledged that *Atlas Roofing* lets Congress assign to agencies the responsibility to adjudicate "public rights" without jury, but held that Congress "lacks the power to strip" the jury trial right from parties contesting "matters of private right." Justice Brennan for the majority asserted that recovering a fraudulent transfer is "more accurately characterized as [asserting] a private than a public right," and that "actions to recover preferential or fraudulent transfers were often brought at law in 18th-century England." Justice White, author of *Katchen*, filed a strong dissent. He argued that Congress in revising the Bankruptcy Code had channeled disputes over preferences and fraudulent transfers into "core" bankruptcy proceedings, and Congress can entrust such matters to "specialized forums and tribunals." Granfinanciera, S.A. v. Nordberg, 492 U.S. 33 (1989).

(4) *Langenkamp.* Finally, a year after *Granfinanciera,* the Court seemed to recognize the confusion it had sown, and granted review in the *Langenkamp* case. There, creditors filed a claim against the bankrupt estate, and the trustee sued in bankruptcy court to recover voidable preferences. Understandably thinking that *Granfinanciera* meant creditors had a right to a jury trial, the Tenth Circuit so held. Not so, the Supreme Court decided in a per curiam opinion. By filing in bankruptcy court, creditors subjected themselves to the bankruptcy court's equitable power. The trustee's claim for a preference is "part of the claims-allowance process which is triable only in equity." Langenkamp v. Culp, 498 U.S. 42 (1990).

■ NOTES ON JURY TRIAL ENTITLEMENT IN THE ADMINISTRATIVE STATE

1. Consider the elements that appear important in the *Katchen* doctrine: They include (a) an administrative mechanism involving a forum other than an Article III court, (b) a specialized focus on matters like bankruptcy, workplace safety, or labor and employment regulation, and (c) enforcement of "public" rights. These are not ingredients that define equity jurisprudence, and yet this category must somehow fit in the universe envisioned in the Seventh Amendment and *Beacon Theatres,* in which everything is either law (or "common law") or equity.

(a) Why assign decisionmaking to an administrative mechanism (agency or bankruptcy court)? Bankruptcy court resembles a court of law because a judge presides and the Rules of Evidence apply, see FRE 1101(a), but bankruptcy judges do not enjoy life tenure (federal judges in District Courts, Courts of Appeal, and the Supreme Court have life tenure). In federal agencies, adjudicatory proceedings, like the ones leading to the fine imposed in *Atlas Roofing* and reinstatement and back pay orders in *Jones & Laughlin,* are presided over by Administrative Law Judges, and proceedings are governed by the Administrative Procedure Act, see especially 5 USC §§554 and 556 (describing agency adjudicatory procedure). Administrative Law Judges lack life tenure too.

(b) How does one distinguish "public" from "private" rights? Does "public" refer to regulatory measures enforced by agencies that protect health and safety, like the workplace safety rules, as *Atlas Roofing* suggests? Do they *exclude* ordinary tort claims, as *Atlas Roofing* said? In *Granfinanciera,* the Court claimed to "adhere" to that vision, but said Congress may "fashion causes of action that are closely *analogous* to common-law claims and place them beyond the ambit of the Seventh Amendment by assigning their resolution to a forum in which jury trials are unavailable." It added

that the "the Federal Government need not be a party for a case to revolve around 'public rights.'"

2. It has long been understood that the OSHA statute does not create a private right in employees to sue their employers for injuries incurred on the job, see Russell v. Bartley, 494 F.2d 334 (6th Cir. 1974), but sometimes OSHA violations affect tort suits for negligence arising from workplace accidents, see Fuszek v. Royal King Fisheries, Inc., 98 F.3d 514 (9th Cir. 1996) (OSHA violation precludes reduction in seaman's recovery in Jones Act suit against operator of fishing vessel).

(a) Suppose Congress enacted a provision saying that "employees may sue employers for negligence resulting in workplace injuries, and violations of safety standards set under this Act shall be prima facie evidence of negligence, all such claims to be adjudicated by the Occupational Health and Safety Administration" (where juries are unavailable). Would this provision be constitutional?

(b) Could Congress pass a similar provision specifying that claims should be tried in federal District Court, in a bench trial "without jury"?

(c) Suppose Congress decides that auto accident litigation is clogging civil dockets and that disputes over common issues of negligence could be resolved better and more efficiently by an Automobile Accident Tribunal (AAT). It enacts legislation requiring such claims to be brought before the AAT, to be finally resolved by hearing examiners. Or Congress does something similar with respect to medical malpractice claims, perhaps deciding that "panels of medical specialists" should decide such claims. Can such provisions determine jury trial entitlement?

3. Further Growing Pains: The Issue-by-Issue Approach

In Ross v. Bernhard, 396 U.S. 531 (1970), the Court decided that what had theretofore been viewed as a single claim had to be subdivided into separate elements in order to accord proper scope to the jury trial entitlement.

Ross was a derivative suit, which was historically viewed as a suit in equity, but plaintiffs demanded a jury trial.[5] The Court held that these are "dual nature" lawsuits, partly equitable and partly legal. In the former category, a derivative suit raises the question whether plaintiffs are entitled to sue at all, which turns on whether they owned stock at the relevant time and whether

---

[5] You've seen derivative suits before. See, e.g., Shaffer v. Heitner, 433 U.S. 186 (1977) (Chapter 3C1); Cohen v. Beneficial Industrial Loan Corp., 337 U.S. 541 (1949) (note 7(b) in the Notes on *Erie's* First 20 Years, Chapter 6A2). Still, a word of explanation may help: Generally, derivative suits are brought by shareholders in a corporation, usually against managers, and usually the claim is that they enriched themselves at the cost of the corporation in breach of their fiduciary duty to shareholders. Any recovery goes to the corporation, making shareholders whole by increasing the value of the entity. See FRCP 23.1.

they demanded that the managers bring suit for the corporation themselves. (One reason to let shareholders bring such suits is that managers may disagree on the wisdom of suing, particularly if they themselves are the wrong-doers! But derivative suits are sometimes brought against others, and in any event managers should have the first "say" on the question whether to sue.) In the latter category is the claim for damages itself ("the merits of the corporation's claim").

In *Ross*, the Court concluded that entitlement to a jury turns on "the nature of the issue to be tried rather than the character of the overall action." Stressing that plaintiffs were seeking "money damages" and that they alleged "breach of contract" as well as "gross negligence," the Court concluded that the corporation's claim was "at least in part, a legal one." Under *Beacon Theatres*, "there is a right to a jury trial on the legal claims which must not be infringed either by trying the legal issues as incidental to the equitable ones" or by "court trial of a common issue existing between the claims."

Justice Stewart, who dissented in *Beacon Theatres*, was flabbergasted. Beginning with the point that plaintiff's "right to get into court at all is conceded to be equitable," Stewart argued that courts and commentators agree that derivative suits are equitable and are "unitary" and do not involve litigation in which a party brings a claim that is concededly legal and a claim that is concededly equitable. Derivative suits, he argued, were not "originally viewed" as suits to enforce "a corporate cause of action," but as equitable suits permitted "only against the managers" to enforce fiduciary duties—"the right of a beneficiary" to recover from "an unfaithful fiduciary." Perhaps more importantly, there are "no such things as inherently 'legal issues' or inherently 'equitable issues,'" but "only factual issues" which "'like chameleons . . . take their color from surrounding circumstances'" (quoting Fleming James, *The Right to a Jury Trial in Civil Actions*, 72 Yale L.J. 655 (1963)).

■ NOTES ON STRESSES IN THE NEW STANDARD

1. *Ross* is not the first decision implying that right to a jury trial attaches to "legal issues," as opposed to "legal claims" or "legal suits," but *is* the first to take this position decisively where this move seems essential to the judgment. (Already in *Dairy Queen*, the Court said that the "sole question" was whether the suit "contains legal issues," but there the point wasn't critical: The damage claim sounded in common law, and the question was whether the "accounting" element could result in denying a jury trial on damages under the clean-up doctrine.) Isn't Justice Stewart right in saying that there is no such thing as an "inherently" legal or equitable issue? In *Terry*, which you are soon to read, the Court seemed to treat as undecided the question whether the Seventh Amendment demands an issue-by-issue inquiry. See Chauffeurs, Teamsters & Helpers, Local No. 391 v. Terry, 494 U.S. 558, 570 n.6 (1990) (whether Seventh Amendment "requires an examination of the nature of each element of a typical claim is not presented" because the claim here is "not typical," but consists of "discrete issues that would normally be brought as two claims").

2. The majority characterizes the second part of a derivative suit as "legal." The corporation's claim for fraud can be characterized as a claim at law that carries a jury trial entitlement, but isn't it more realistic to characterize derivative suits as claiming breach of fiduciary duty, which is traditionally equitable? Writing after *Beacon Theatres* and before *Ross*, Professor McCoid anticipated that derivative suits would be viewed as equitable because the "trust relationship" is central, and a shareholder sues as "representative" of shareholders. See McCoid, supra, at 1, 22 (but acknowledging that "representative" suits were treated as suits at law in context of class actions).

3. Consider class actions: In *Ross*, the majority drew on the proposition that Courts of Appeal have decided that class action plaintiffs "may obtain a jury trial on any legal issues," citing FRCP 23 as a procedural advance of the sort to which the Court alluded in *Beacon Theatres* that removed procedural impediments to a jury trial, and thus created new circumstances in which the jury trial entitlement attaches. See *Ross*, 396 U.S. at 541. See also Ortiz v. Fibreboard Corp., 527 U.S. 815, 846 (1999) (settled among lower courts that class action plaintiffs may obtain jury trials on legal issues). And see 42 USC §1981a (entitling plaintiffs suing for intentional workplace discrimination to seek compensatory damages, in addition to back pay, and extending jury trial entitlement).

4. In *Ross*, the majority indicated with approval that the lower federal courts have extended jury trial entitlement to claims brought by intervenors "on any legal issues," and also to interpleader suits, and "numerous courts and commentators have now come to the conclusion that the right to a jury should not turn on how the parties happen to be brought into court." See *Ross*, 396 U.S. at 542 n.15.

5. *Ross* confirms the idea at the heart of *Beacon Theatres*, which is that the jury trial entitlement expands with the evolution of procedure. *Katchen* showed that jury trial entitlement sometimes *shrinks* with procedural innovation, and other cases allowed procedural evolution to shrink or cut back on jury trial entitlement:

(a) In Parklane Hosiery v. Shore, 439 U.S. 322 (1979), the Court addressed the question whether plaintiff, who had not been party to a prior suit, could take advantage of a judgment in that suit, to bind the defendant under the doctrine of "collateral estoppel" (or "issue preclusion"). The government had brought an enforcement suit that concluded that Parklane violated the Securities Exchange Act by committing fraud. There was no jury trial right, and the government prevailed. Then Shore brought a class suit on behalf of persons who bought or sold stock during the period of the fraud, and the question was whether the company was bound by the earlier judgment. Under the traditional common law rule, the answer was no: Plaintiff could not invoke issue preclusion because of the "mutuality rule," under which

only a party who had *been* a party to the prior suit could invoke issue preclusion. (The party *against whom* preclusion is sought *had to have been* a party in the prior suit: It would usually violate due process to bind someone who had not been a party in the prior suit.) But *if* preclusion applied, the company would be bound by a judgment handed down in a bench-tried case without the jury trial option. The Court did not hesitate to reject tradition: The right to a jury trial, the majority held, is basically "neutral" and "quite unlike" imposing on a party the duty to defend in an inconvenient forum. Chief Justice Rehnquist dissented, suggesting that the framers of the Constitution would be "amazed" that the use of juries is "neutral," suggesting that the outcome in a jury-tried case might be different, and noting that a jury must be assembled in the second suit to determine damages anyway. (You will read *Parklane* in Chapter 14.)

(b) In a later case on strange facts, the question was whether a decision by a judge of certain equitable issues was binding on parties after the judge *erroneously* dismissed their legal claims. No, the Court held in Lytle v. Household Manufacturing, Inc., 494 U.S. 545 (1990). In this situation, the Seventh Amendment means the parties are not bound on those issues common to their equitable and (erroneously dismissed) legal claims. In *Lytle*, the judge erred in dismissing claims under 42 USC §1981 (barring racial discrimination in contractual relationships), where there is an entitlement to a jury trial. Then the judge resolved related claims under Title VII of the Civil Rights Act, where precedent indicated that there was no jury trial right. The case was *not* governed by *Parklane*. It would be "anomalous" to say a district court cannot deny a jury trial by resolving an equitable issue first (as *Beacon Theatres* indicates), but then let a court "accomplish the same result by erroneously dismissing the legal claim" and resolving the remaining issues itself.

4. A Footnote Out of Nowhere: Complex Cases and the Right to Jury Trial

Ross became famous for a footnote that might have been the harbinger of a revolutionary shift in jury trial rights. To end the suspense, the revolution didn't happen and there is no indication that it will, but the footnote is often discussed, and it merits a detour. In footnote 10 in *Ross,* the Court said:

> [T]he "legal" nature of an issue is determined by considering, first, the pre-merger custom with reference to such questions; second, the remedy sought; and, third, the practical abilities and limitations of juries. Of these factors, the first, requiring extensive and possibly abstruse historical inquiry, is obviously the most difficult to apply. See James, Right to a Jury Trial in Civil Actions, 72 Yale L.J. 655 (1963).

Ross v. Bernhard, 396 U.S. 531, 738 n.10 (1970). It is the third factor—"the practical abilities and limitations of juries"—that drew particular attention, because it suggested that the scope of the constitutional right might be subject to a limit for peculiarly complex cases.

The Court has backed away from any notion of a "complex case" exception. It did so, fittingly enough, in footnotes in two later cases. In Tull v. United States, 481 U.S. 412, 418 n.4 (1987), the Court cited *Ross* and its reference to "the practical limitations of a jury," but said these considerations are not "an independent basis for extending [sic] the right to a jury trial." And two years later, in Granfinanciera v. Nordberg, 492 U.S. 33, 42 n.4 (1989), the Court said the reference in *Ross* to "the practical abilities and limitations of juries" carries a narrower meaning than one might imagine: That reference, the Court said in *Granfinanciera*, "appears" to relate to the *Katchen* decision—that is, "the practical abilities and limitations of juries" counts in deciding (again in the words of the *Granfinanciera* footnote) "whether Congress has permissibly entrusted the resolution of certain disputes to an administrative agency or specialized court of equity, and whether jury trials would impair the functioning of the legislative scheme."

5. An Awkward Accommodation (The So-Called Two-Pronged Standard)

However much one might want to divorce the question of jury trial entitlement from history, it seems impossible—and probably undesirable—to get away from historical inquiries altogether. After all, one aspect of legal doctrines that seems almost inherent in the very *idea* of law is that it should carry through from one case to another, and legal doctrines should be stable enough so people can plan and decide how to live their lives. In the Seventh Amendment, and in the commands of many state provisions, jury trial entitlement has an additional claim to the importance of historical inquiry because of words like "preserve" and "retain inviolate."

CHAUFFEURS, TEAMSTERS & HELPERS, LOCAL NO. 391 v. TERRY

Supreme Court of the United States
494 U.S. 558 (1990)

Justice MARSHALL delivered the opinion of the Court [in which Chief Justice REHNQUIST concurs, along with Justices BRENNAN, WHITE, BLACKMUN, and STEVENS], except as to Part III-A [in which Chief Justice REHNQUIST and Justices WHITE and BLACKMUN concur].

This case presents the question whether an employee who seeks relief in the form of backpay for a union's alleged breach of its duty of fair representation has a right to trial by jury. We hold that the Seventh Amendment entitles such a plaintiff to a jury trial.

I

McLean Trucking Company and the Chauffeurs, Teamsters, and Helpers Local No. 391 (Union) were parties to a collective-bargaining agreement that governed the terms and conditions of employment at McLean's terminals. The 27 respondents were employed by McLean as truckdrivers in bargaining units covered by the agreement, and all were members of the Union. In 1982 McLean implemented a change in operations that resulted in the elimination of some of its terminals and the reorganization of others. As part of that change, McLean transferred respondents to the terminal located in Winston-Salem and agreed to give them special seniority rights in relation to "inactive" employees in Winston-Salem who had been laid off temporarily.

[Plaintiffs filed a grievance with the Union contesting the order of layoffs and of recalls and challenging the company's policy of stripping seniority rights from laid-off drivers. The Grievance Committee ordered the company to recall plaintiffs who were laid off, to lay off certain inactive drivers, and to recognize special seniority rights until inactive drivers were recalled. The company recalled plaintiffs, but later recalled inactive employees and let them regain seniority rights. This move resulted, after another round of layoffs, in according plaintiffs lower priority than inactive drivers, and led plaintiffs to suffer further layoffs. Plaintiffs filed another grievance, but the Committee held that the company was not in violation of the earlier decision. Plaintiffs sued in federal court, alleging that the company had violated the collective bargaining agreement and that the Union breached its duty of fair representation. The company went bankrupt, and claims against it were dismissed, along with all claims for injunctive relief. What remained were claims for compensatory damages against the Union. Plaintiffs demanded a jury, and the Union moved to strike the demand. The District Court denied the motion to strike, and the Court of Appeals affirmed, holding that plaintiffs were entitled to a jury trial under the Seventh Amendment.]

II

The duty of fair representation is inferred from unions' exclusive authority under the National Labor Relations Act (NLRA) to represent all employees in a bargaining unit. Vaca v. Sipes, 386 U.S. 171, 177 (1967). The duty requires a union "to serve the interests of all members without hostility or discrimination toward any, to exercise its discretion with complete good faith and honesty, and to avoid arbitrary conduct." A union must discharge its duty both in bargaining with the employer and in its enforcement of the resulting collective-bargaining agreement. Thus, the Union here was required to pursue respondents' grievances in a manner consistent with the principles of fair representation.

Because most collective-bargaining agreements accord finality to grievance or arbitration procedures established by the collective-bargaining agreement, an employee normally cannot bring a §301 action against an employer unless he can show that the union breached its duty of fair representation in its handling of his grievance. DelCostello v. Teamsters, 462 U.S. 151, 163-164 (1983). Whether the employee sues both the labor union and the employer or only one of those entities, he must prove the same two facts to recover money damages: that the employer's action violated the terms of the collective-bargaining agreement and that the union breached its duty of fair representation.

III

We turn now to the constitutional issue presented in this case—whether respondents are entitled to a jury trial. . . .

To determine whether a particular action will resolve legal rights, we examine both the nature of the issues involved and the remedy sought. "First, we compare the statutory action to 18th-century actions brought in the courts of England prior to the merger of the courts of law and equity. Second, we examine the remedy sought and determine whether it is legal or equitable in nature." Tull v. U.S., 481 U.S. 412, 417-418 (1987) (citations omitted). The second inquiry is the more important in our analysis. Granfinanciera, S.A. v. Nordberg, 492 U.S. 33, 42 (1989).[4]

A

An action for breach of a union's duty of fair representation was unknown in 18th-century England; in fact, collective bargaining was unlawful. We must therefore look for an analogous cause of action that existed in the 18th century to determine whether the nature of this duty of fair representation suit is legal or equitable.

[The Union claims that the suit most resembles an action to vacate an arbitration award, which was an equitable claim in the eighteenth century.

---

[4] Justice Stevens' analysis emphasizes a third consideration, namely whether "the issues [presented by the claim] are typical grist for the jury's judgment." This Court, however, has never relied on this consideration "as an independent basis for extending the right to a jury trial under the Seventh Amendment." Tull v. United States, 481 U.S. 412, 418, n.4 (1987). We recently noted that this consideration is relevant only to the determination "whether Congress has permissibly entrusted the resolution of certain disputes to an administrative agency or specialized court of equity, and whether jury trials would impair the functioning of the legislative scheme." Granfinanciera v. Nordberg, 492 U.S., at 42, n.4. No one disputes that an action for breach of the duty of fair representation may properly be brought in an Article III court; thus, the factor does not affect our analysis.

But the arbitration analogy is "inapposite" because "no grievance committee" has considered the claims against the Union here.]

The Union next argues that respondents' duty of fair representation action is comparable to an action by a trust beneficiary against a trustee for breach of fiduciary duty. Such actions were within the exclusive jurisdiction of courts of equity. This analogy is far more persuasive than the arbitration analogy. Just as a trustee must act in the best interests of the beneficiaries, a union, as the exclusive representative of the workers, must exercise its power to act on behalf of the employees in good faith. Moreover, just as a beneficiary does not directly control the actions of a trustee, an individual employee lacks direct control over a union's actions taken on his behalf.

The trust analogy extends to a union's handling of grievances. In most cases, a trustee has the exclusive authority to sue third parties who injure the beneficiaries' interest in the trust, including any legal claim the trustee holds in trust for the beneficiaries. The trustee then has the sole responsibility for determining whether to settle, arbitrate, or otherwise dispose of the claim. Similarly, the union typically has broad discretion in its decision whether and how to pursue an employee's grievance against an employer. Just as a trust beneficiary can sue to enforce a contract entered into on his behalf by the trustee only if the trustee "improperly refuses or neglects to bring an action against the third person," Restatement (Second) of Trusts, *supra*, §282(2), so an employee can sue his employer for a breach of the collective-bargaining agreement only if he shows that the union breached its duty of fair representation in its handling of the grievance.

Respondents contend that their duty of fair representation suit is less like a trust action than an attorney malpractice action, which was historically an action at law . . . [but] we find that, in the context of the Seventh Amendment inquiry, the attorney malpractice analogy does not capture the relationship between the union and the represented employees as fully as the trust analogy does.

The attorney malpractice analogy is inadequate in several respects. Although an attorney malpractice suit is in some ways similar to a suit alleging a union's breach of its fiduciary duty, the two actions are fundamentally different. The nature of an action is in large part controlled by the nature of the underlying relationship between the parties. Unlike employees represented by a union, a client controls the significant decisions concerning his representation. Moreover, a client can fire his attorney if he is dissatisfied with his attorney's performance. This option is not available to an individual employee who is unhappy with a union's representation, unless a majority of the members of the bargaining unit share his dissatisfaction. Thus, we find the malpractice analogy less convincing than the trust analogy.

Nevertheless, the trust analogy does not persuade us to characterize respondents' claim as wholly equitable. The Union's argument mischaracterizes the nature of our comparison of the action before us to 18th-century forms of action. As we observed in Ross v. Bernhard, 396 U.S. 531 (1970), "The Seventh Amendment question depends on the nature of the *issue* to be tried rather than the character of the overall action" (finding a right to jury trial in a shareholder's derivative suit, a type of suit traditionally brought in courts of equity, because plaintiffs' case presented legal issues of breach of contract and negligence). As discussed above, to recover from the Union here, respondents must prove both that McLean violated §301 by breaching the collective-bargaining agreement and that the Union breached its duty of fair representation.[6] When viewed in isolation, the duty of fair representation issue is analogous to a claim against a trustee for breach of fiduciary duty. The §301 issue, however, is comparable to a breach of contract claim—a legal issue.[7]

Respondents' action against the Union thus encompasses both equitable and legal issues. The first part of our Seventh Amendment inquiry, then, leaves us in equipoise as to whether respondents are entitled to a jury trial.

B

Our determination under the first part of the Seventh Amendment analysis is only preliminary. In this case, the only remedy sought is a request for compensatory damages representing backpay and benefits. Generally, an action for money damages was "the traditional form of relief offered in the courts of law." Curtis v. Loether, 415 U.S. 189, 196 (1974). This Court has not, however, held that "any award of monetary relief must *necessarily* be 'legal' relief." *Ibid.* (emphasis added). Nonetheless, because we conclude that the remedy respondents seek has none of the attributes that must be present before we will find an exception to the general rule and characterize damages as equitable, we find that the remedy sought by respondents is legal.

First, we have characterized damages as equitable where they are restitutionary, such as in "action[s] for disgorgement of improper profits," *Tull, supra,*

---

[6] The dissent characterizes this opinion as "pars[ing] legal elements out of equitable claims." The question whether the Seventh Amendment analysis requires an examination of the nature of each element of a typical claim is not presented by this case. The claim we confront here is not typical; instead, it is a claim consisting of discrete issues that would normally be brought as two claims, one against the employer and one against the union. Had the employer remained a defendant in this action, the dissent would surely agree that the §301 claim against the employer was a separate claim. The Seventh Amendment analysis should not turn on the ability of the plaintiff to maintain his suit against both defendants, when the issues in the suit remain the same even when he can sue only the union. Consideration of the nature of the two issues in this hybrid action is therefore warranted.

[7] In United Parcel Service, Inc. v. Mitchell, 451 U.S. 56 (1981), we found a §301 action against the employer more analogous to a suit to set aside an arbitration award than to a breach of contract suit because the employee, to overturn the grievance committee's decision, had to prove that the union violated its duty of fair representation. In that case, we analyzed the action as a whole; in this case, however, the Seventh Amendment requires that we treat each issue separately. When considered by itself, the §301 issue is closely analogous to a breach of contract claim.

481 U.S. at 424. The backpay sought by respondents is not money wrongfully held by the Union, but wages and benefits they would have received from McLean had the Union processed the employees' grievances properly. Such relief is not restitutionary.

Second, a monetary award "incidental to or intertwined with injunctive relief" may be equitable. *Tull, supra.* See, *e.g.,* Mitchell v. Robert DeMario Jewelry, Inc., 361 U.S. 288, 291-292 (1960) (District Court had power, incident to its injunctive powers, to award backpay under the Fair Labor Standards Act; also backpay in that case was restitutionary). Because respondents seek only money damages, this characteristic is clearly absent from the case.[8]

The Union argues that the backpay relief sought here must nonetheless be considered equitable because this Court has labeled backpay awarded under Title VII, of the Civil Rights Act of 1964, 42 USC §2000e *et seq.,* as equitable. See Albemarle Paper Co. v. Moody, 422 U.S. 405, 415-418 (1975) (characterizing backpay awarded against employer under Title VII as equitable in context of assessing whether judge erred in refusing to award such relief). It contends that the Title VII analogy is compelling in the context of the duty of fair representation because the Title VII backpay provision was based on the NLRA provision governing backpay awards for unfair labor practices, 29 USC §160(c) ("[W]here an order directs reinstatement of an employee, back pay may be required of the employer or labor organization"). We are not convinced.

The Court has never held that a plaintiff seeking backpay under Title VII has a right to a jury trial. Assuming, without deciding, that such a Title VII plaintiff has no right to a jury trial, the Union's argument does not persuade us that respondents are not entitled to a jury trial here. Congress specifically characterized backpay under Title VII as a form of "equitable relief." 42 USC §2000e-5(g) ("[T]he court may ... order such affirmative action as may be appropriate, which may include, but is not limited to, reinstatement or hiring of employees, with or without back pay ..., or any other equitable relief as the court deems appropriate"). Congress made no similar pronouncement regarding the duty of fair representation. Furthermore, the Court has noted that backpay sought from an employer under Title VII would generally be

---

[8] Both the Union and the dissent argue that the backpay award sought here is equitable because it is closely analogous to damages awarded to beneficiaries for a trustee's breach of trust. Such damages were available only in courts of equity because those courts had exclusive jurisdiction over actions involving a trustee's breach of his fiduciary duties.

The Union's argument, however, conflates the two parts of our Seventh Amendment inquiry. Under the dissent's approach, if the action at issue were analogous to an 18th-century action within the exclusive jurisdiction of the courts of equity, we would necessarily conclude that the remedy sought was also equitable because it would have been unavailable in a court of law. This view would, in effect, make the first part of our inquiry dispositive. We have clearly held, however, that the second part of the inquiry—the nature of the relief—is more important to the Seventh Amendment determination. The second part of the analysis ... requires consideration of the general types of relief provided by courts of law and equity.

restitutionary in nature, in contrast to the damages sought here from the Union. Thus, the remedy sought in this duty of fair representation case is clearly different from backpay sought for violations of Title VII.

Moreover, the fact that Title VII's backpay provision may have been modeled on a provision in the NLRA concerning remedies for unfair labor practices does not require that the backpay remedy available here be considered equitable. The Union apparently reasons that if Title VII is comparable to one labor law remedy it is comparable to all remedies available in the NLRA context. Although both the duty of fair representation and the unfair labor practice provisions of the NLRA are components of national labor policy, their purposes are not identical. Unlike the unfair labor practice provisions of the NLRA, which are concerned primarily with the public interest in effecting federal labor policy, the duty of fair representation targets "'the wrong done the individual employee.'" Electrical Workers v. Foust, 442 U.S. 42, 49 n.12 (1979) (quoting Vaca v. Sipes, 386 U.S., at 182, n.8) (emphasis deleted). Thus, the remedies appropriate for unfair labor practices may differ from the remedies for a breach of the duty of fair representation, given the need to vindicate different goals. Certainly, the connection between backpay under Title VII and damages under the unfair labor practice provision of the NLRA does not require us to find a parallel connection between Title VII backpay and money damages for breach of the duty of fair representation.

We hold, then, that the remedy of backpay sought in this duty of fair representation action is legal in nature. Considering both parts of the Seventh Amendment inquiry, we find that respondents are entitled to a jury trial on all issues presented in their suit.

IV

On balance, our analysis of the nature of respondents' duty of fair representation action and the remedy they seek convinces us that this action is a legal one. Although the search for an adequate 18th-century analog revealed that the claim includes both legal and equitable issues, the money damages respondents seek are the type of relief traditionally awarded by courts of law. Thus, the Seventh Amendment entitles respondents to a jury trial, and we therefore affirm the judgment of the Court of Appeals.

It is so ordered.

Justice BRENNAN, concurring in part and concurring in the judgment.

I agree with the Court that respondents seek a remedy that is legal in nature and that the Seventh Amendment entitles respondents to a jury trial on their duty of fair representation claims. I therefore join Parts I, II, III-B, and IV of the Court's opinion. I do not join that part of the opinion which reprises the particular historical analysis this Court has employed to determine whether a claim is a "Sui[t] at common law" under the Seventh Amendment, *ante,* because I believe the historical test can and should be simplified.

The current test, first expounded in Curtis v. Loether, 415 U.S. 189, 194 (1974), requires a court to compare the right at issue to 18th-century English forms of action to determine whether the historically analogous right was vindicated in an action at law or in equity, and to examine whether the remedy sought is legal or equitable in nature. However, this Court, in expounding the test, has repeatedly discounted the significance of the analogous form of action for deciding where the Seventh Amendment applies. I think it is time we dispense with it altogether. I would decide Seventh Amendment questions on the basis of the relief sought. If the relief is legal in nature, *i.e.,* if it is the kind of relief that historically was available from courts of law, I would hold that the parties have a constitutional right to a trial by jury—unless Congress has permissibly delegated the particular dispute to a non-Article III decisionmaker and jury trials would frustrate Congress' purposes in enacting a particular statutory scheme.

I believe that our insistence that the jury trial right hinges in part on a comparison of the substantive right at issue to forms of action used in English courts 200 years ago needlessly convolutes our Seventh Amendment jurisprudence. For the past decade and a half, this Court has explained that the two parts of the historical test are not equal in weight, that the nature of the remedy is more important than the nature of the right. Since the existence of a right to jury trial therefore turns on the nature of the remedy, absent congressional delegation to a specialized decisionmaker, there remains little purpose to our rattling through dusty attics of ancient writs. The time has come to borrow William of Occam's razor and sever this portion of our analysis.

We have long acknowledged that, of the factors relevant to the jury trial right, comparison of the claim to ancient forms of action, "requiring extensive and possibly abstruse historical inquiry, is obviously the most difficult to apply." Ross v. Bernhard, 396 U.S. 531, 538, n.10 (1970). Requiring judges, with neither the training nor time necessary for reputable historical scholarship, to root through the tangle of primary and secondary sources to determine which of a hundred or so writs is analogous to the right at issue has embroiled courts in recondite controversies better left to legal historians. For example, in *Granfinanciera, S.A., supra,* decided last Term, both Justice White, in dissent, and I, writing for the Court, struggled with the question whether an equity court would have heard the suit that was comparable to the modern statutory action at issue....

To be sure, it is neither unusual nor embarrassing for members of a court to disagree and disagree vehemently. But it better behooves judges to disagree within the province of judicial expertise. Furthermore, inquiries into the appropriate historical analogs for the rights at issue are not necessarily susceptible of sound resolution under the best of circumstances. As one scholar observes: "[T]he line between law and equity (and therefore between jury and non-jury trial) was not a fixed and static one. There was a continual process of borrowing by one jurisdiction from the other; there were less frequent instances of a sloughing off of older functions. . . . The borrowing by each jurisdiction from the other was not accompanied by an equivalent sloughing off of functions. This led to a very large overlap between law and equity." James, Right to a Jury Trial in Civil Actions, 72 Yale L.J. 655, 658-659 (1963).

In addition, modern statutory rights did not exist in the 18th century, and even the most exacting historical research may not elicit a clear historical analog.[5] The right at issue here, for example, is a creature of modern labor law quite foreign to Georgian England. Justice Stewart recognized the perplexities involved in this task in his dissent in Ross v. Bernhard, *supra*, albeit drawing a different conclusion. "The fact is," he said, "that there are, for the most part, no such things as inherently 'legal issues' or inherently 'equitable issues.' There are only factual issues, and, 'like chameleons [they] take their color from surrounding circumstances.' Thus, the Court's 'nature of the issue' approach is hardly meaningful." I have grappled with this kind of inquiry for three decades on this Court and have come to the realization that engaging in such inquiries is impracticable and unilluminating.

To rest the historical test required by the Seventh Amendment solely on the nature of the relief sought would not, of course, offer the federal courts a rule that is in all cases self-executing. Courts will still be required to ask which remedies were traditionally available at law and which only in equity. But this inquiry involves fewer variables and simpler choices, on the whole, and is far more manageable than the scholasticist debates in which we have been engaged. Moreover, the rule I propose would remain true to the Seventh Amendment, as it is undisputed that, historically, "[j]urisdictional lines [between law and equity] were primarily a matter of remedy." McCoid, Procedural Reform and the Right to Jury Trial: A Study of *Beacon Theaters, Inc. v. Westover*, 116 U. Pa. L. Rev. 1 (1967). See also Redish, Seventh Amendment Right to Jury Trial: A Study in the Irrationality of Rational Decision Making, 70 Nw. U. L. Rev. 486, 490 (1975) ("In the majority of cases at common

---

[5] See also McCoid, Procedural Reform and the Right to Jury Trial: A Study of *Beacon Theaters, Inc. v. Westover*, 116 U. Pa. L. Rev. 1, 2 (1967) ("[C]omplications stem from historical shifts and overlapping jurisdiction. Moreover, the careful historian encounters difficulty in applying the fruits of his study to contemporary civil litigation involving subject matter and procedural patterns unused, and sometimes unknown, in 1791") (footnotes omitted).

law, the equitable or legal nature of a suit was determined not by the substantive nature of the cause of action but by the remedy sought").[7]

. . .

What Blackstone described as "the glory of the English law" and "the most transcendent privilege which any subject can enjoy," 3 W. Blackstone, Commentaries, was crucial in the eyes of those who founded this country. The encroachment on civil jury trial by colonial administrators was a "deeply divisive issue in the years just preceding the outbreak of hostilities between the colonies and England," and all 13 States reinstituted the right after hostilities ensued. Wolfram, The Constitutional History of the Seventh Amendment, 57 Minn. L. Rev. 639, 654-655 (1973). "In fact, '[t]he right to trial by jury was probably the only one universally secured by the first American constitutions.'" *Id.*, at 655 (quoting L. Levy, Freedom of Speech and Press in Early American History—Legacy of Suppression 281 (1963 reprint)). Fear of a Federal Government that had not guaranteed jury trial in civil cases, voiced first at the Philadelphia Convention in 1787 and regularly during the ratification debates, was the concern that precipitated the maelstrom over the need for a bill of rights in the United States Constitution.

. . .

We can guard this right and save our courts from needless and intractable excursions into increasingly unfamiliar territory simply by retiring that prong of our Seventh Amendment test which we have already cast into a certain doubt. If we are not prepared to accord the nature of the historical analog sufficient weight for this factor to affect the outcome of our inquiry, except in the rarest of hypothetical cases, what reason do we have for insisting that federal judges proceed with this arduous inquiry? It is time we read the writing on the wall, especially as we ourselves put it there.

Justice Stevens, concurring in part and concurring in the judgment.

Because I believe the Court has made this case unnecessarily difficult by exaggerating the importance of finding a precise common-law analogue to the duty of fair representation, I do not join Part III-A of its opinion. Ironically, by stressing the importance of identifying an exact analogue, the Court has diminished the utility of looking for any analogue.

As I have suggested in the past, I believe the duty of fair representation action resembles a common-law action against an attorney for malpractice more closely than it does any other form of action. Of course, this action is not

---

[7] [Justice Brennan comments that some "advocate abolishing the historical test altogether," but says "I am not among them." He and Justice Kennedy differ "in our evaluations of which historical test provides the more reliable results." The first prong of the current test "requires courts to measure modern statutory actions against 18th century English actions" that are "so remote in form and concept" that there is no real comparison, and the attempted comparison amounts to "the manufacture of a legal fiction." By contrast, focusing on the nature of the relief is "more manageable" and "more reliably grounded in history."—Ed.]

an exact counterpart to a malpractice suit. Indeed, by definition, no recently recognized form of action—whether the product of express congressional enactment or of judicial interpretation—can have a precise analogue in 17th- or 18th-century English law. Were it otherwise the form of action would not in fact be "recently recognized."

But the Court surely overstates this action's similarity to an action against a trustee. Collective bargaining involves no settlor, no trust corpus, and no trust instrument executed to convey property to beneficiaries chosen at the settlor's pleasure. Nor are these distinctions reified matters of pure form. The law of trusts originated to expand the varieties of land ownership in feudal England, and evolved to protect the paternalistic beneficence of the wealthy, often between generations and always over time. Beneficiaries are protected from their own judgment. The attorney-client relationship, by contrast, advances the client's interests in dealings with adverse parties. Clients are saved from their lack of skill, but their judgment is honored. Union members, as a group, accordingly have the power to hire, fire, and direct the actions of their representatives—prerogatives anathema to the paternalistic forms of the equitable trust.[2]

Equitable reasoning calibrated by the sophisticated judgment of the jurist, the accountant, and the chancellor is thus appropriately invoked when the impact of a trustee's conduct on the future interests of contingent remaindermen must be reviewed. However, the commonsense understanding of the jury, selected to represent the community, is appropriately invoked when disputes in the factory, the warehouse, and the garage must be resolved. In most duty of fair representation cases, the issues, which require an understanding of the realities of employment relationships, are typical grist for the jury's judgment. Indeed, the law defining the union's duty of fair representation has developed in cases tried to juries. . . .

As the Court correctly observed in *Curtis,* "in an ordinary civil action in the district courts, where there is obviously no functional justification for denying the jury trial right, a jury trial must be available if the action involves rights and remedies of the sort typically enforced in an action at law." As I had occasion to remark at an earlier proceeding in the same case, the relevant historical question is not whether a suit was "specifically recognized at common law," but whether "the nature of the substantive right asserted . . . is analogous to common law rights" and whether the relief sought is "typical of an action at law." Rogers v. Loether, 467 F.2d 1110, 1116-1117 (7th Cir. 1972). Duty of fair representation suits are for the most part ordinary civil actions

---

[2] Indeed, to make sense of the trust analogy, the majority must apparently be willing to assume that the union members, considered collectively, are both beneficiary and settlor, and that the settlor retains considerable power over the corpus, including the power to revoke the trust. That is an odd sort of trust.

involving the stuff of contract and malpractice disputes. There is accordingly no ground for excluding these actions from the jury right.

In my view, the evolution of this doctrine through suits tried to juries, the useful analogy to common-law malpractice cases, and the well-recognized duty to scrutinize any proposed curtailment of the right to a jury trial "with the utmost care," provide a plainly sufficient basis for the Court's holding today. I therefore join its judgment and all of its opinion except for Part III-A.

Justice KENNEDY, with whom Justice O'CONNOR and Justice SCALIA join, dissenting.

This case asks whether the Seventh Amendment guarantees the respondent union members a jury trial in a duty of fair representation action against their labor union. The Court is quite correct, in my view, in its formulation of the initial premises that must govern the case. Under *Curtis*, the right to a jury trial in a statutory action depends on the presence of "legal rights and remedies." To determine whether rights and remedies in a duty of fair representation action are legal in character, we must compare the action to the 18th-century cases permitted in the law courts of England, and we must examine the nature of the relief sought. See *Granfinanciera*. I agree also with those Members of the Court who find that the duty of fair representation action resembles an equitable trust action more than a suit for malpractice.

I disagree with the analytic innovation of the Court that identification of the trust action as a model for modern duty of fair representation actions is insufficient to decide the case. The Seventh Amendment requires us to determine whether the duty of fair representation action "is more similar to cases that were tried in courts of law than to suits tried in courts of equity." Tull v. United States, 481 U.S. 412, 417 (1987). Having made this decision in favor of an equitable action, our inquiry should end. Because the Court disagrees with this proposition, I dissent.

I

Both the Union and the respondents identify historical actions to which they find the duty of fair representation action most analogous. The Union contends that the action resembles a traditional equitable suit by a beneficiary against a trustee for failing to pursue a claim that he holds in trust. In other words, the Union compares itself to a trustee that, in its discretion, has decided not to press certain claims. The respondents argue that the duty of fair representation action resembles a traditional legal malpractice suit by a client against his lawyer for mishandling a claim. They contend that the Union, when acting as their legal representative, had a duty to press their grievances.

Justice Marshall, speaking for four Members of the Court, states an important and correct reason for finding the trust model better than the malpractice analogy. He observes that the client of an attorney, unlike a union member or beneficiary, controls the significant decisions concerning his litigation and can fire the attorney if not satisfied. Put another way, although a lawyer acts as an agent of his client, unions and trustees do not serve as agents of their members and beneficiaries in the conventional sense of being subject to their direction and control in pursuing claims. An individual union member cannot require his union to pursue a claim and cannot choose a different representative. See 29 USC §159(a) (1982 ed.) (making the union elected by the employees in a bargaining unit the exclusive representative); Vaca v. Sipes, 386 U.S. 171, 177 (1967) (allowing a union to exercise discretion in fulfilling its duty of fair representation). A trustee, likewise, may exercise proper discretion in deciding whether to press claims held in trust, and in general does not act as an agent of his beneficiaries. . . .

Further considerations fortify the conclusion that the trust analogy is the controlling one here. A union's duty of fair representation accords with a trustee's duty of impartiality. The duty of fair representation requires a union "to make an honest effort to serve the interests of all of [its] members, without hostility to any." Ford Motor Co. v. Huffman, 345 U.S. 330, 337 (1953). This standard may require a union to act for the benefit of employees who, as in this case, have antithetical interests. Trust law, in a similar manner, long has required trustees to serve the interests of all beneficiaries with impartiality.

A lawyer's duty of loyalty is cast in different terms. Although the union is charged with the responsibility of reconciling the positions of its members, the lawyer's duty of loyalty long has precluded the representation of conflicting interests. A lawyer, at least absent knowing waiver by the parties, could not represent both the respondents and the senior laidoff workers as the Union has done in this case.

The relief available in a duty of fair representation action also makes the trust action the better model. To remedy a breach of the duty of fair representation, a court must issue an award "fashioned to make the injured employee whole." Electrical Workers v. Foust, 442 U.S. 42, 49 (1979). The court may order an injunction compelling the union, if it is still able, to pursue the employee's claim, and may require monetary compensation, but it cannot award exemplary or punitive damages. This relief parallels the remedies prevailing in the courts of equity in actions against trustees for failing to pursue claims.

These remedies differ somewhat from those available in attorney malpractice actions. Because legal malpractice was a common-law claim, clients sued their attorneys for breach of professional obligations in the law courts. No one maintains that clients could obtain from these courts the injunctive relief offered in duty of fair representation actions. The evidence suggests that compensatory damages in malpractice cases resembled the monetary relief now awarded in duty of fair representation actions. Yet, as a historical matter, juries did have the authority to award exemplary damages in at least some tort actions. Although the parties have not cited any punitive damages award in an attorney malpractice action prior to 1791, courts have awarded such damages since the 19th century.

For all these reasons, the suit here resembles a trust action, not a legal malpractice action. By this I do not imply that a union acts as a trustee in all instances or that trust law, as a general matter, should inform any particular aspects of federal labor law. Obvious differences between a union and a trustee will exist in other contexts. I would conclude only that, under the analysis directed by our precedents, the respondents may not insist on a jury trial. When all rights and remedies are considered, their action resembles a suit heard by the courts of equity more than a case heard by the courts of law. From this alone it follows that the respondents have no jury trial right on their duty of fair representation claims against the Union.

II

The Court relies on two lines of precedents to overcome the conclusion that the trust action should serve as the controlling model. The first consists of cases in which the Court has considered simplifications in litigation resulting from modern procedural reforms in the federal courts. Justice Marshall asserts that these cases show that the Court must look at the character of individual issues rather than claims as a whole. The second line addresses the significance of the remedy in determining the equitable or legal nature of an action for the purpose of choosing the most appropriate analogy. Under these cases, the Court decides that the respondents have a right to a jury because they seek money damages. These authorities do not support the Court's holding.

A

In three cases we have found a right to trial by jury where there are legal claims that, for procedural reasons, a plaintiff could have or must have raised in the courts of equity before the systems merged. [Justice Kennedy describes the decisions in *Beacon Theatres, Dairy Queen,* and *Ross.*]

These three cases responded to the difficulties created by a merged court system. They stand for the proposition that, because distinct courts of equity no longer exist, the possibility or necessity of using former equitable procedures to press a legal claim no longer will determine the right to a jury. Justice Marshall reads these cases to require a jury trial whenever a cause of action contains legal issues and would require a jury trial in this case because the respondents must prove a breach of the collective-bargaining agreement as one element of their claim.

I disagree. The respondents, as shown above, are asserting an equitable claim. Having reached this conclusion, the *Beacon, Dairy Queen,* and *Ross* cases are inapplicable. Although we have divided self-standing legal claims from equitable declaratory, accounting, and derivative procedures, we have never parsed legal elements out of equitable claims absent specific procedural justifications. Actions which, beyond all question, are equitable in nature may involve some predicate inquiry that would be submitted to a jury in other contexts. For example, just as the plaintiff in a duty of fair representation action against his union must show breach of the collective-bargaining agreement as an initial matter, in an action against a trustee for failing to pursue a claim the beneficiary must show that the claim had some merit. But the question of the claim's validity, even if the claim raises contract issues, would not bring the jury right into play in a suit against a trustee.

Our own writing confirms the consistency of this view with respect to the action before us. We have not deemed the elements of a duty of fair representation action to be independent of each other. Proving breach of the collective-bargaining agreement is but a preliminary and indispensable step to obtaining relief in a duty of fair representation action. We have characterized the breach-of-contract and duty issues as "inextricably interdependent" and have said that "[t]o prevail against either the company or the Union, . . . [employee-plaintiffs] must not only show that their discharge was contrary to the contract but must also carry the burden of demonstrating breach of duty by the Union." DelCostello v. Teamsters, 462 U.S. 151, 164-165 (1983) (internal quotation marks omitted). The absence of distinct equitable courts provides no procedural reason for wresting one of these elements from the other.

B

The Court also rules that, despite the appropriateness of the trust analogy as a whole, the respondents have a right to a jury trial because they seek money damages. The nature of the remedy remains a factor of considerable importance in determining whether a statutory action had a legal or equitable analog in 1791, but we have not adopted a rule that a statutory action permitting damages is by definition more analogous to a legal action than to any equitable suit. In each case, we look to the remedy to determine whether, taken with other factors, it places an action within the definition of "Suits at common law."

[Justice Kennedy distinguishes three prior decisions in which the fact of damage recovery featured strongly in the conclusion that jury trial rights attached. In *Curtis,* damage recovery supported the conclusion that a discrimination suit is analogous to a tort suit, but here damage recovery does not justify a conclusion that suing for breach of fiduciary duties is a tort suit. In *Tull,* the fact of damage recovery helped choose between two competing ways of characterizing an environmental pollution suit (public nuisance or action in debt), but here the breach-of-trust analogy is more persuasive than the only alternative (malpractice). In *Granfinanciera,* the presence of monetary relief was critical in interpreting jury trial entitlement in a suit going forward in a statutory scheme, but in this setting the presence of monetary relief does not carry similar weight, in light of the fact that courts of equity could and did award damages in similar suits.]

III

The Court must adhere to the historical test in determining the right to a jury because the language of the Constitution requires it. The Seventh Amendment "preserves" the right to jury trial in civil cases. We cannot preserve a right existing in 1791 unless we look to history to identify it. Our precedents are in full agreement with this reasoning and insist on adherence to the historical test. No alternatives short of rewriting the Constitution exist. See F. James, Civil Procedure §8.5, p 352 (1965) ("For good or evil, both the constitutio[n] and the charters of the merged procedure embody the policy judgment, quite deliberately made, to leave the extent of jury trial about where history had come to place it"). If we abandon the plain language of the Constitution to expand the jury right, we may expect Courts with opposing views to curtail it in the future.

It is true that a historical inquiry into the distinction between law and equity may require us to enter into a domain becoming less familiar with time. Two centuries have passed since the Seventh Amendment's ratification, and the incompleteness of our historical records makes it difficult to know the nature of certain actions in 1791. The historical test, nonetheless, has received more criticism than it deserves. Although our application of the analysis in some cases may seem biased in favor of jury trials, the test has not become a nullity. We do not require juries in all statutory actions. The historical test, in fact, resolves most cases without difficulty.

I would hesitate to abandon or curtail the historical test out of concern for the competence of the Court to understand legal history. We do look to history for the answers to constitutional questions. Although opinions will differ on what this history shows, the approach has no less validity in the Seventh Amendment context than elsewhere.

If Congress has not provided for a jury trial, we are confined to the Seventh Amendment to determine whether one is required. Our own views respecting the wisdom of using a jury should be put aside. Like Justice Brennan, I admire the jury process. Other judges have taken the opposite view. See, *e.g.,* J. Frank, Law and the Modern Mind 170-185 (1931). But the judgment of our own times is not always preferable to the lessons of history. Our whole constitutional experience teaches that history must inform the judicial inquiry. Our obligation to the Constitution and its Bill of Rights, no less than the compact we have with the generation that wrote them for us, do not permit us to disregard provisions that some may think to be mere matters of historical form.

IV

Because of the employer's bankruptcy, the respondents are proceeding only against the Union in the suit before us. In a typical duty of fair representation action, however, union members may sue both their union and their employer. The Union argues that a duty of fair representation action against an employer also would have an equitable character because it resembles another trust action entertained in the courts of equity. It contends that, if a trustee fails to pursue a claim according to his duty, the beneficiary may join the trustee and the third party in one action and assert in his own name both the claim of breach of fiduciary duty and the claim against the third party. In this case, we do not have to determine the correctness of this analogy, nor must we decide whether *Beacon, Dairy Queen,* or *Ross* would require a jury trial in a suit against an employer. I would deny a jury trial to the respondents here, but would leave these other questions for a later time. Because the Court has reached a different result, I dissent.

■ NOTES ON AN AWKWARD STANDARD

1. *Terry* begins by announcing what has come to be the modern standard, or test, which involves a two-pronged inquiry: (1) Was there a jury trial entitlement in a case that presents the closest historical analogy to the present case? (2) Is the nature of the remedy legal or equitable?

(a) Notice how *Terry* treats the standard as settled. This two-pronged approach is visible in some earlier cases. See Tull v. United States, 481 U.S. 412, 417-418 (1987); Granfinanciera v. Nordberg, 492 U.S. 33, 42 (1989). It is even arguable that this two-pronged approach already made its appearance three years after *Beacon Theatres* in Ross v. Bernhard, 396 U.S. 531 (1970), where the Court in its famous footnote 10 (quoted in Section 12B4, supra) said the question whether an "issue" was "legal" or "equitable" is determined by considering "pre-merger custom" and "the remedy sought."

(b) Assuming this two-pronged approach *is* the way to assess claims of jury trial entitlement, what can one say about a test in which the second part is "more important" than the first—one should ask about analogies to historical practice, but the nature of the remedy sought is the more important inquiry?

(c) Justice Brennan thinks it is time to scrap this prong, and that courts should not be asked undertake historical research that may not yield an answer. Still, Justice Brennan says, courts must ask "which remedies were traditionally available at law and which only in equity." Why should courts ask that if the only thing that counts is the nature of the remedy?

2. Looking at historical analogies, who has the better argument here?

(a) Justice Marshall (writing in Part III-B for himself, Chief Justice Rehnquist, and Justices White and Blackmun) thinks the suit against the union resembles a suit by a beneficiary against a trustee for breach of fiduciary duty, *but* this analogy is not persuasive because the question is "the nature of the issue" rather than the "overall action." Not surprisingly, Justice Marshall cites *Ross*. Wait a minute: Can we really draw analogies between issues as opposed to remedies? *Then* the Court comments that the "§301 issue" is "comparable to a breach of contract claim," which makes it legal, leaving the Court "in equipoise" on the first inquiry. (The reference is to §301 of the LMRA, which provides that suits "for violation of [collective bargaining] contracts" may be brought in federal court.) Is it persuasive to view this suit as a mixed legal and equitable claim—legal in being a suit in contract, equitable in being a suit to enforce fiduciary duties?

(b) Justice Stevens thinks the trust analogy is *not* the closest one, and the suit is closer to a malpractice or a contract action. He also thinks the majority has insisted on "an exact analogue," which by definition would not exist or there would be no need to draw analogies in the first place. Are these views persuasive?

(c) Justices Kennedy, O'Connor, and Scalia in dissent think the trust analogy *is* indeed the closest (agreeing with Marshall and the three who stood with him) *and* should be viewed as "controlling." The duty of "fair representation" is like the trustee's "duty of impartiality." It is *not*, Justice Kennedy argues, like a lawyer's "duty of loyalty" because a lawyer cannot represent "conflicting interests" (unions must act for the benefit of employees who have "antithetical interests"). Even if a "contract" element arises (union's duty to plaintiffs is contractual), it is only "a preliminary but indispensable step" in bringing the fair representation claim.

3. Looking at the second prong, is the remedy sought by plaintiffs in *Terry* legal or equitable? Here the majority has easier sledding, doesn't it? (In Part IIIB, which addresses this point, Justice Marshall writes for himself and five others.) After all, plaintiffs seek money damages, and a suit seeking *that* remedy is usually (and classically) a suit at law. The union's best chance to characterize this remedy as equitable is to stress that it resembles "back pay," which the Court has characterized as an equitable remedy. Why doesn't this argument carry the day? Justice Kennedy, for the three dissenters, is on the defensive here: Damage claims are not *always* legal, and courts of equity "could and did award" monetary relief in breach of trust suits. Who has the better of this part of the argument?

6. Modern Era Reconsidered: Is It Really That Complicated?

It is no exaggeration to say that the 30 or so decisions by the Supreme Court in the time since the decision in *Beacon Theatres* have left the federal law of jury trial entitlement muddled.

Before despairing, however, bear in mind this fact: Often a case falls clearly on one side of the divide or another. Thus, on the one hand, ordinary tort suits, seeking recovery for personal injuries and pain and suffering based on negligence or product liability, or on intentional torts (as in libel suits), are suits at law and there is a jury trial entitlement. And on the other hand, usually suits seeking injunctive relief, specific performance, or reformation of contract are equitable. Suits to rescind a contract are obsolete. In most jurisdictions, a party rescinds by announcing the fact, leaving the matter of breach to be litigated if another party sues. If the suit involves damage claims, the suit is legal and a jury trial right attaches, but if the suit seeks specific performance, it is a suit at equity. If it seeks both damages for breach and specific performance, then in jurisdictions following *Beacon Theatres* the common issues are tried by judge and jury, and the jury awards damages (or not) and the judge awards specific performance (or not), but the judge is bound by the jury's decision on common issues.

B   SELECTING AND MANAGING JURIES

The selection and seating of juries are steps in litigation to which lawyers pay the closest attention. In urban areas, private companies do background research on the persons summoned for jury duty and provide lawyers with this information (for a price). Lawyers zealously guard their rights to exercise challenges, in hope of seating a jury before which they feel they have the best chance of winning.

When jurors are seated, and the trial actually begins, lawyers know their opening statements can be critical in shaping perceptions toward the evidence that is to come. Hence each lawyer devotes considerable attention to this moment, and chooses her words carefully, in hope that jurors will see the case as she frames it. In phrases likely to occur over and over again, the lawyer tells jurors that "the evidence will show" the facts that she lays out carefully. Opening statements are emphatically *not* arguments, however, and a lawyer who goes beyond her own version of the facts by suggesting that the other side's witnesses are not to be believed or seeking to refute in advance testimony expected from the other side will be rebuked by the judge, on objection by the other side and perhaps even without the need to object. Most lawyers conclude that opening statements are best *understated* rather than *inflated*, lest juror expectations be raised beyond what the proof will support.

During trial, jurors are expected to be, for the most part, passive observers. Beginning in the 1980s and 1990s, however, reform movements began to experiment with allowing juries to do more than just sit through trials. In the twenty-first century, juries usually have their own binders with exhibits and instructions, and can take notes, and sometimes ask questions of witnesses.

When the trial ends, the last words that juries hear in the federal system are instructions from the trial judge. In most state systems, the last words are arguments from lawyers. Both these matters receive the closest attention from lawyers as well: Under FRCP 51(a), lawyers are expected to submit to the court (and serve on other parties) suggested instructions, and at the end of the case (after "the close of the evidence") lawyers may request additional instructions ("on issues that could not reasonably have been anticipated") or may even file late requests ("untimely" ones) for instructions. The court is obliged to inform the parties in advance what instructions will be given, so the parties have "opportunity to object" outside the jury's presence.

Closing statements give lawyers their last chance to connect with the jury. Here they can sum up and make a believable story out of the evidence that the jury has heard. Here they echo ideas from their opening remarks. Here is the time for argument—now they *can* explain why the other side's witnesses are wrong or should not be believed.

1. How Many? Must All Agree? (Usually 12; Usually Yes)

Before turning to the selection and seating of jurors, we should pause for a moment to consider the *number* of jurors who sit to decide civil cases.

In a series of opinions, the Supreme Court approved modern experiments using juries of fewer than 12 people. The Court's views on these matters affect jury trials in federal courts, where the usual rule is that civil juries are comprised of 6 persons—FRCP 48 provides that juries shall have "at least 6 and no more than 12 members." Local Rules in many districts either specify a number (like 6, 8, or 12) or allow parties to stipulate to the number (so long as it is at least 6).

The states can make different choices on this score (recall that the Seventh Amendment does not apply to state courts). Most retain the long-standing custom that juries are comprised of 12 people (in a 1998 study, 28 states were in this camp). But most states no longer require civil juries to reach unanimous verdicts. Most of the other 22 states have reduced the size of juries in civil cases (usually authorizing juries of six people), and about half of these require unanimity, while the others allow verdicts to be reached by majority.[6]

2. Who Can Serve? (Juror Qualifications)

Statutes in all states and the federal system spell out the qualifications for jury service. Universally (or nearly so), statutory or constitutional provisions say that each juror must (a) be a citizen of the United States, (b) be able to read and speak and understand English, and (c) have sufficient mental and physical capability to render satisfactory service. In addition, in almost all jurisdictions one can serve as a juror only if he or she (d) has attained the age of 18 years (some states set other minima, like 19 or 21 years), (e) satisfies a residency requirement (some statutes require residency for as long as a year; some simply require residency or specify other minimum periods) and (f) has not been convicted of a felony (some states disqualify persons with *any* criminal conviction, or refine the list of disqualifying convictions in various other ways).

In various ways, most statutes describing juror qualification make exception for people suffering mental ailments. Many statutes, because they are antiquated, are vague and sometimes even primitive on this point. In Michigan, for example, jurors must be "in possession of their natural faculties, not infirm or decrepit," see Mich. Comp. Laws Ann. §928.204, while North Carolina specifies that persons serving as jurors must not have been "adjudged non compos mentis." N.C. Gen. Stat. Ann. §9.3.

Statutes commonly disqualify persons for jury service who are related to a party or an attorney involved in trying the case, or who have certain legal connections to a party. See, e.g., Ala. Code §12-16-150(11) (disqualifying from civil jury any person "related by consanguinity within the ninth degree or by affinity within the fifth degree . . . to any attorney in the case to be tried"); Ga. Code Ann. §15-12-135 (persons are disqualified if "related by consanguinity or affinity to any party . . . within the sixth degree as computed

---

[6] The following survey reflects a 1998 study, and summarizes rules relating to jury size and the degree of agreement required for a verdict in the "biggest" civil cases (leaving out courts of limited jurisdiction and smaller cases): These 9 states require 12-member juries and unanimous verdicts: Alabama, Delaware, Georgia, New Hampshire, North Carolina, Oklahoma, Rhode Island, Tennessee, Vermont. These 19 states require 12-person juries but allow less-than-unanimous verdicts as indicated by the fractions: Alaska (5/6), Arkansas (3/4), California (3/4); Hawaii (5/6); Idaho (3/4); Kansas (5/6), Kentucky (3/4), Louisiana (5/6), Massachusetts (5/6), Mississippi (3/4), Missouri (3/4), Montana (2/3), Nebraska (5/6), Nevada (3/4), New Mexico (5/6), Oregon (3/4), Pennsylvania (5/6), Texas (5/6), South Dakota (5/6). These 11 states allow 6-person juries, but require unanimous verdicts: Colorado, Connecticut, District of Columbia, Florida, Illinois (12-member jury may be demanded), Indiana, Kansas, Maryland, North Dakota (requires 9 jurors in some cases), West Virginia, Wyoming. The following 11 states allow juries of 6 (except as otherwise indicated) and nonunanimous verdicts: Arizona (8 jurors, 3/4), Iowa (8 jurors, 7/8 after 6 hours of deliberation), Maine (8 jurors, 3/4), Michigan (5/6), Minnesota (5/6), New Jersey (5/6; 12-member jury may be demanded); Ohio (8-member jury, 3/4), New York (5/6), Utah (8 jurors, 3/4), Washington (5/6), Wisconsin (5/6).

according to the civil law"); Mont. Code Ann. §25-7-223 (disqualifying anyone who stands "in the relation of guardian and ward" or "employer and employee" or "principal and agent" with a party, or who is "a partner in business" or "surety on any bond or obligation" with either party).

It seems too obvious for words that persons having an economic interest in the outcome should not serve as jurors, and statutes disqualify such persons by listing categories or groupings of people who would have such interest. The Montana statute serves as an example: It disqualifies anyone who is a "debtor" or "creditor" of either party (although one is *not* disqualified "by reason of current bills of gas, water, electricity, or telephone" or because he or she is "a depositor of funds with a bank, savings and loan institution, credit union, or similar financial institution"). See Mont. Code Ann. §25-7-223. And see Doe v. Wal-Mart Stores, Inc., 558 S.E.2d 663, 670 (W. Va. 2001) (in suit claiming that Wal-Mart was responsible for sexual assault in parking lot, court should have excluded a woman who owned stock in Wal-Mart whose husband was also employed by Wal-Mart).

Sometimes state provisions seek to ensure that jurors have good character. See, e.g., Mich. Comp. Laws Ann. §928.204 (jurors must be "of good character, integrity and sound judgment, well informed in and conversant with the English language").

Most states include provisions that do not on their face disqualify people from jury service, but allow them to be excused. Common are provisions allowing members of the armed forces to be excused, and, less commonly, a mother who is breast-feeding a baby. See, e.g., 38 Okla. Stat. Ann. §28(E)(2) (breast-feeding mother is exempt from jury service on request).

The Supreme Court has weighed in on these matters on numerous occasions. Consider this pronouncement:

> It has long been accepted that the Constitution does not forbid the States to prescribe relevant qualifications for their jurors. The States remain free to confine the selection to citizens, to persons meeting specified qualifications of age and educational attainment, and to those possessing good intelligence, sound judgment, and fair character. "Our duty to protect the federal constitutional rights of all does not mean we must or should impose on states our conception of the proper source of jury lists, so long as the source reasonably reflects a cross-section of the population suitable in character and intelligence for that civic duty."

Carter v. Jury Commission of Greene County, 396 U.S. 320, 332-333 (1970) (refusing to strike provision in Alabama statute requiring persons of "good character and sound judgment").

■ NOTES ON JUROR QUALIFICATIONS

1. Should persons convicted of crimes be disqualified from jury service? See, e.g., Brian Kalt, *The Exclusion of Felons from Jury Service*, 53 Am. U. L. Rev.

65, 149 (2003) (felony exclusion results in disqualifying 13 million people, including about 30 percent of black men; felony exclusion is "probably acceptable under current constitutional law," and some felons should be excluded, but "casting out every felon in every case, forever, is excessive").

2. Suppose one is seated on a jury after failing to reveal a disqualifying fact on *voir dire*? Should the loser get a new trial? Without showing prejudice? See Jackson v. State of Alabama State Tenure Commission, 405 F.3d 1276, 1288-1289 (11th Cir. 2005) (awarding new trial where court seated convicted felon; she failed to reveal conviction despite "direct questioning," and nondisclosure was dishonest rather than inadvertent); Marquez v. City of Albuquerque, 399 F.3d 1216, 1224 (10th Cir. 2005) (losing party entitled to new trial on showing that juror failed to answer honestly a material question on *voir dire* that would have provided a valid basis for a challenge for cause); Keibler-Thompson Corp. v. Steading, 907 So. 2d 435 (Ala. 2005) (awarding new trial to defendant in steelworker's negligence suit that led to verdict awarding $500,000 because court seated juror who did not satisfy residency requirement; she did not respond when asked whether she lived in county) (jury rolls indicated that she lived in another county, and in fact she did); Proudfoot v. Dan's Marine Service, Inc., 558 S.E.2d 298 (W. Va. 2001) (awarding new trial where juror had been convicted of a felony, which she concealed on jury qualification form and *voir dire*).

3. How Are They Chosen? (Judges and Lawyers; *Voir Dire* and Challenges)

In civil suits, selecting a jury involves summoning venire members to court and, in most jurisdictions, asking them to fill out forms that determine whether they are competent to serve. They must say, for example, whether they live in the county or district from which the jury is to be drawn, whether they understand English, and whether they have been convicted of a felony. Usually, voter registration lists supply names and addresses of people who are summoned, and courts have programs that assure prospective jurors that they will have to serve only for a single day (and won't have to return multiple times) unless they are selected to serve, in which case they may have to return to court for as long as the suit is tried.

When a case is ready for trial, the clerk sends a panel of venire members to the courtroom. What comes next is "*voir dire*" (literally "to speak the truth," from Latin "*verum*" meaning truth and "*dicere*" meaning speak), and ultimately the exercise of challenges to excuse venire members from service. There are two kinds of challenge (for cause and peremptory), and different methods for exercising these challenges (the strike system and the panel system), examined in ensuing sections.

In the federal system and most states, the judge does the lion's share of *voir dire*. The Rule says the judge may allow the parties or their lawyers—and we're talking about lawyers—to conduct *voir dire*, or to ask additional questions when the judge is through, but often the lawyers are given little opportunity to do so. See FRCP 47(a) (court "may permit" parties or lawyers to examine prospective jurors "or may itself do so"). The federal Rule (many state counterparts have similar language) admonishes courts to "permit the parties or their attorneys" to make further inquiry, but often the lawyers wind up not asking any questions—the language of the Rule requires the court only to allow further inquiry that the court "considers proper" and goes on to say that the court "must itself" ask additional questions submitted by the parties so long as the court "considers [such questions] proper." In some states, lawyers have the right to conduct *voir dire*, and the right to do so is highly prized, although the number of states that follow this tradition has shrunk considerably over the last 50 years.[7]

In civil suits, each side can exercise challenges "for cause," which means either that a venire member does not meet the qualifications or that the person is biased or prejudiced (a ground of challenge once dubbed "for favor"). In most jurisdictions, including the federal system, each side can also exercise what is known as "peremptory" challenges, removing a juror without giving a reason.

■ NOTES ON *VOIR DIRE* AND EXERCISE OF CHALLENGES

1. Why do lawyers prize the right to conduct *voir dire* personally? The tradition of direct attorney participation in *voir dire* is much stronger in state than in federal court. Compare, e.g., Csiszer v. Wren, 614 F.3d 866 (8th Cir. 2010) (brushing off claim that judge should not have conducted entire *voir dire*; he "invited each attorney to approach the bench during *voir dire* to suggest additional areas of inquiry") with Leone v. Goodman, 773 P.2d 342, 222-223 (Nev. 1989) (judge may limit supplemental *voir dire* questions by attorney, but may not preclude *all* attorney participation) (reversing).

2. What objections do you think trial lawyers raise about court-conducted *voir dire*? What objections do *judges* raise about lawyer-conducted *voir dire*? See, e.g., Grover v. Boise Cascade Corp., 860 A.2d 851, 858 (Me. 2004) (open-ended *voir dire* "runs the risk that it will be employed less to assess the qualifications of prospective jurors, and more to influence and predispose prospective jurors to a party's point of view") (attorney introduced "key principles of law" and established rapport with jury, which are not purposes of *voir dire*); Harold v. Corwin, 846 F.2d 1148, 1152 (8th Cir. 1988) (judges

---

[7] See, e.g., Colo. RCP 47(a)(3) (judge questions jurors on qualifications; parties or counsel "shall be permitted to ask . . . additional questions"); Tenn. RCP 47.01 (court "shall permit the parties or their attorneys to conduct the examination"); Wyo. RCP 47(c) (attorneys or pro se party "shall be entitled to conduct the examination of prospective jurors").

ask "allegedly neutral, flat and nonpenetrating questions," and then lawyers lack information needed for peremptory challenges; any busy judge "must candidly admit" to knowing "far less of a given case" than lawyers, who should participate) (concurring opinion by Judge Lay). And see Lane Goldstein, Trial Technique (3d ed. 2010) (two goals of *voir dire* are to "prepare the jury to be receptive" to lawyer's theory and to get jurors to like him, so they "will believe him," and a "friendly attitude" and impression of fairness help "foster a bond" between lawyer and jurors that is "essential to selling them on the case").

3. In theory, *voir dire* does not introduce evidence: It's just questions asked by judges or lawyers. But lawyers load questions with hints about the case or the parties that jurors will likely remember. See Owens v. Mississippi Farm Bureau Casualty Insurance Co., 910 So. 2d 1065, 1077 (Miss. 2005) (defense made jury aware on *voir dire* that plaintiffs were members of country club, traveled to Europe and elsewhere, and supported Republican politicians) (pretrial motion might have led to this information "coming before the jury in a more benign manner," but questions were "reasonably calculated to learn information about jurors, and possible contacts, affiliations and beliefs" that bear on peremptory challenges).

4. Should lawyers be allowed to ask prospective jurors about their attitudes toward "tort reform" or "personal injury plaintiffs" or "pain and suffering" or "malpractice suits"? Compare Mody v. Center for Women's Health, P.C., 998 A.2d 327 (D.C. 2010) (in malpractice case, declining to ask whether potential jurors had heard of "medical liability insurance" crisis, where judge asked more generally whether they or relatives or friends had been involved in malpractice suit, and whether they had "such strong feelings" about healthcare providers that they would have difficulty being fair) with Babcock v. Northwest Memorial Hospital, 767 S.W.2d 705, 709 (Tex. 1989) (litigants should have "broad latitude" on *voir dire*, to discover bias or prejudice so peremptory challenges may be intelligently exercised) (reversing judgment for provider in malpractice case because plaintiff was not allowed to ask about "lawsuit" or "liability insurance" crisis). Compare Chlopek v. Federal Insurance Co., 499 F.3d 692 (7th Cir. 2007) (need not ask about attitudes toward tort reform; in product liability suit, not allowing *voir dire* questions about propriety of damage claims "in light of the assault on the civil jury system conducted by many politicians") and Landon v. Zorn, 884 A.2d 142, 147 (Md. 2005) (rejecting question asking whether any member of panel had "preconceived opinion or bias in favor of, or against, plaintiffs in personal injury cases in general and medical malpractice cases in particular" as this general question did not get at any "specific reason for disqualification and exclusion") (*Borkoski* case, infra, arose in setting in which discovery uncovered advertising campaign by insurance carriers) and Borkoski v. Yost, 594 P.2d 688 (Mont. 1979) (approving questions asking whether prospective jurors were aware of a "national campaign by leading insurance companies [to persuade people] large jury verdicts are in fact paid by the general public and constitute 'windfalls' to recipients").

5. Suppose suit is brought on behalf of a grievously injured person. Should she be required to be in court during *voir dire* so defendant can assess the reaction of potential jurors? See Irvin v. Smith, 31 P.3d 934 (Kan. 2001) (malpractice suit on behalf of girl who was 16 at time of trial, suffering from brain injury and neurological impairment requiring that she be fed by a tube and, due to premature birth, suffering from hydrocephalus that required "VP shunt" extending from brain to abdomen; court told plaintiff that girl had to be present during *voir dire*, so defense could assess reaction of potential jurors, or she could not appear during trial).

6. Should lawyers be allowed on *voir dire* to explore attitudes or beliefs that might suggest reasons to exercise peremptory challenges, as opposed to more particularized disqualifying facts or information? Compare Moday v. Center for Women's Health, P.C., 998 A.2d 327, 333 (D.C. 2010) (purpose of *voir dire* is to enable parties to make effective use of peremptory challenges) with *Landon*, supra (*voir dire* does *not* encompass questions designed to elicit information in aid of exercising peremptory challenges).

7. Suppose that during *voir dire* a prospective juror indicates possible bias. Suppose, for example, that when asked by plaintiff's lawyer whether she can be fair in a medical malpractice case, she says, "I think too many people expect doctors to be able to cure anything and everything, and nobody can help some patients because they're too sick or too badly injured." Suppose the trial judge then intervenes:

> Q (trial judge): Well, do you think you can decide the case on the evidence and the law?
> A (prospective juror): Oh yes, I would definitely expect to do that.
> Q: So you think you can be fair to both sides in this case?
> A: Yes, I would be fair to both sides.

Trial judges often interrupt *voir dire* to ask such "curative" questions. Why? Wouldn't *any* juror say yes to such questions? Does a positive response neutralize prior expressions of bias? Consider O'Dell v. Miller, 565 S.E.2d 407 (W. Va. 2002) (in the face of inconclusive or vague statement on *voir dire* indicating possible bias, further probing is appropriate; once juror makes a clear statement indicating prejudice or bias, she is disqualified as a matter of law and cannot be rehabilitated by "questioning, later retractions, or promises to be fair") (former patient of defendant doctor and current client of law firm representing him should have been disqualified; awarding new trial). Compare Crail Creek Associates, LLC v. Olson, 187 P.3d 667, 672 (Mont. 2008) (in suit against contractor, prospective juror "consistently stated she felt she had made up her mind" and was "inclined to favor contractors," and court's questioning about fairness did not rehabilitate) (new trial granted) with Ford Motor Co. v. Gibson, 659 S.E.2d 346, 353 (Ga. 2008) (court rehabilitated three prospective jurors who "expressed an initial distrust of corporations in general" but all "unequivocally stated that they did not have a particular bias against defendants") and Lewis v. Voss, 770 A.2d 996 (D.C. 2001) (judge should have excused juror who had read book about frivolous lawsuits and had "very unpleasant" experience as defendant and thought tort system "might benefit from an overhaul" and that people in this country "tend to assign blame" or look to others for help when they get into "a tough situation") (judge asked whether she would treat plaintiff's witnesses differently and she said, "No, I don't think so, No," but that did not show she could be impartial). And see Caroline Crocker & Margaret Bull Kovera, *The Effects of Rehabilitative* Voir Dire *on Juror Bias and Decision Making*, 34 J.L. Hum. Behav. 212 (2010) (in mock jury experiment, rehabilitative *voir dire* did lessen "negative impact of juror bias on verdicts").

8. Failing to ask on *voir dire* about potential disqualifying information waives the argument that a juror should have been disqualified. See Holland v. Brandenberg, 627 So. 2d 867, 870 (Ala. 1993) (conviction for offense involving moral turpitude is automatic disqualification, but failing to ask about it on *voir dire* waived objection). Suppose a court uses a questionnaire to ask about disqualifying information and, because potential jurors check boxes indicating that there are no disqualifying facts, the lawyers do not pursue further inquiries. Must lawyers raise points covered by such forms by pursuing the matters on *voir dire*? See Wingate by Carlisle v. Lester E. Cox Medical Center, 853 S.W.2d 912 (Mo. 1993) (plaintiff's lawyer prepared questionnaire, got court's approval, and jurors filled it out; one checked "no" when asked whether he had been sued, which was false; attorney did not pursue it on *voir dire*; attorneys are "obligated to examine" juror qualifications and cannot rely on "court custom" in use of questionnaires). See also State v. Kelly, 606 A.2d 786, 788 (Me. 1992) (in eviction suit, defense lawyer learned during deliberations that jury foreman's father and grandfather were game wardens who often visited disputed land, and that grandfather refused to testify; lawyer said nothing, thus waived objection).

9. Should trial lawyers be allowed to ask jurors how they would vote if a particular point was proved? In a product liability claim against an automaker arising out of the death of a four-year-old child sitting in the front passenger seat without a seatbelt, plaintiff's lawyer sought to ask whether proof of these points would cause jurors to find against the plaintiff. The Texas Supreme Court said no. See Hyundai Motor Co. v. Vasquez, 189 S.W.3d 743, 752-753 (Tex. 2006) (improper to ask what verdict would be if certain facts were proved; *voir dire* is designed to determine whether jurors are fair and impartial, as opposed to biased or prejudiced; it is not designed to uncover attitudes about evidence; such questions seek "to skew the jury by pre-testing their opinions").

10. Should *voir dire* be limited in the interests of protecting potential jurors from embarrassment? One modern court offered this comment:

> Jurors—poorly paid conscripts who play an important role in the American system of justice—have a right not to be humiliated; questions about their personal

appearance, a subject about which most people are sensitive—questions such as "Why is your hair so long?" "Why are you so fat (or so thin)?" "Why are your shirt tails hanging out?" "Are you making a political statement by wearing black lipstick and a ring through your nose?"—should therefore be avoided unless necessary to allay reasonable concerns about a juror's impartiality.

Anderson v. Griffin, 397 F.2d 515, 519 (7th Cir. 2005) (disapproving questions designed to get at racial attitudes; race was not an issue; insufficient ground to suspect racism). See also Tyus v. Urban Search Management, 102 F.3d 256, 262 (7th Cir. 1966) (judge should not have asked whether prospective juror lived in public housing, which was not pertinent; inappropriate for judge to ask about racial composition of residence, perhaps implying that public housing is "plagued by racial problems," as question was "stigmatizing" to prospective juror and may have stigmatized plaintiff).

11. In order to show that juror made a false statement on *voir dire*, an appellant must show that she was asked for information that she failed to give. See, e.g., Spiece v. Garland, 197 S.W.3d 594 (Mo. 2006) (jurors were asked about involvement in personal injury suits; that did not oblige juror to reveal that she had been involved in slip-and-fall accident resulting in insurance settlement, even though she retained attorney, and that she had been involved in car accident leading to claim for property damage; these facts did not show that she filed suit).

4. For-Cause Challenges

Let us consider now challenges for cause.

We can begin at the point where a group of venire members has arrived in the courtroom. It may consist of 20 to 30 persons, or even more (depending on how many members are available, on the nature of the case and the anticipated difficulty in assembling a jury, which may be high if the case is expected to take a long time and jury may be sequestered). When the system works smoothly, the group is more than enough to assemble a jury of the required size for the case.

The next step is to allow each side to exercise challenges for cause. Courts usually follow the strike system or the panel system, which are described below. But first, consider the process for a moment. Suppose the lawyer for plaintiff or defendant personally says, "I challenge Mrs. Dobson for cause on account of the views that she expressed toward personal injury litigation, with our thanks for coming here and being willing to serve." Might not this act by itself affect remaining members of the venire who are ultimately seated on the jury? In part because of this risk, many courts follow systems making it less likely that those who serve will know who is responsible for actions excusing other members of the venire.

Strike System. Most federal courts and some state systems use a strike system in which judges and lawyers question the group. When the questioning is done, the lawyers approach the bench for a whispered conference ("sidebar") or the court calls a recess. The court then asks each side whether it wishes to challenge members of the venire for cause. If so, the challenging lawyer states his reasons, and the lawyer on the other side can respond. The whispered conference or recess ends; the judge announces the venire members who are excused; venire members in the required number are seated (and usually an alternate or two), being called in alphabetical order (beginning with A or with L or going backwards from Z, but following a sequence with a random factor). See Thomas Mauet, Trials: Strategies, Skills, and the New Powers of Persuasion §3.10, p. 64 (2d ed. 2009).

Panel System. In this system, used in many states, the judge calls venire members in the required number to sit in the jury box (again following some sequence turning on the alphabet but with a random factor). This time judges and lawyers question only the jurors in the box (the "panel"). Then lawyers exercise challenges. In many states, challenges are again exercised by means of sidebar conference or recess, where the court resolves issues and announces the names of members who are excused. In many other states, lawyers personally exercise their own challenges, taking turns: At the appropriate moment, the lawyer says something like this: "Plaintiff would like to excuse Mr. Jones from serving on this jury, and we thank you for taking time to be here today." If any dispute arises as to the propriety of this challenge, or the court doubts its propriety, the lawyers are asked to approach the bench and the matter is resolved in a sidebar conference or a recess. Under this approach, obviously members of the venire learn which side challenged which persons, and if a challenge for cause is unsuccessful, the lawyer may be tempted to use a peremptory challenge to remove the person, rather than risking that she will serve with hostile feelings. See Mauet, supra, §3.10, p. 65.

Can Remove Unqualified Persons. Of course, challenges for cause can remove venire members who are not qualified to serve—if it is discovered on *voir dire* that a prospective juror is related to a litigant, or does not live in the area, she can be removed for cause. As indicated above, failing to meet eligibility requirements can lead to new trials on what almost seem to be technicalities.

Many More Reasons. For-cause challenges can remove jurors for many more reasons than count as bare-bones jury qualifications. Prejudice in various forms, or even life experiences that suggest attitudes that could prove hostile to the cause of one of the parties, can justify removal for cause.

■ NOTES ON CHALLENGING POTENTIAL JURORS FOR CAUSE

1. Attitudes count as possible "bias" when they relate specifically to the kinds of parties in the suit or to the claims being advanced, and the question is not whether the juror's attitude is "right" or "wrong," but whether it is a "view" connected with the parties or issues in the case:

(a) In suits raising questions about the health effects of cigarette smoking, attitudes and experiences of friends and family members may count as bias. See Scott v. American Tobacco Co., 814 So. 2d 544 (La. 2002) (in class suit alleging that cigarette companies concealed use of nicotine, court should have excluded for cause (a) one whose brother who smoked and suffers from a heart condition, who said she didn't like smoking; (b) one whose father was a long-time smoker who would like to see him get help to quit; (c) one who had an uncle and mother who smoke and whose father died from heart disease and was a former smoker; and (d) one who had an adult son who smoked in high school, whose mother and brother and sister are smokers and whose mother suffers bronchitis).

(b) In suits alleging "police brutality," attitudes toward police may count as bias. See Butler v. City of Camden, 352 F.3d 811 (3d Cir. 2008) (in suit alleging excessive force, failing to question jurors about law enforcement bias was error; jurors may accord "special deference" to testimony by officers; when such testimony is expected, jurors should be questioned on this subject); Darbin v. Nourse, 664 F.3d 1109, 1114-1115 (9th Cir. 1981) (inquiry into attitudes toward police is "necessary in order to probe for bias associated with the identity and relationship of the parties and the nature of the controversy") (reversing judgment favoring sheriff).

(c) In suits raising employment issues, attitudes of a small employer on the venire may count as bias. See Thompson v. Altheimer & Gray, 248 F.3d 621, 622 (7th Cir. 2001) (when asked if "something about this kind of lawsuit" would incline potential juror to favor one party or another, she said she owned a business and had owned others, and her experience would "cloud" her judgment because she was "constantly faced with people that want various benefits or different positions" and was concerned that denying such requests can lead to suits; she thought some people sue "just because they don't get something they want," but these attitudes were *not* bias; they reflect belief that is undoubtedly true; question was whether belief would "impede her in giving due weight to the evidence," which was not adequately explored) (court should have ascertained whether juror could be fair, but did not; in employment discrimination suit, awarding plaintiff a new trial).

(d) In medical malpractice suits, attitudes of doctors or lawyers who represent doctors may count as bias if they are members of the venire. See Murphy v. Miller, 671 S.E.2d 714, 716-717 (W. Va. 2008) (court should have excused dentist who had been involved in what he called a "frivolous" suit that settled; he indicated on questionnaire that frivolous malpractice suits

"cost everyone except the attorneys" and expressed "specific hesitation" to award damages for anything less than deliberate act); Hafi v. Baker, 164 S.W.3d 383 (Tex. 2005) (lawyer said he would want to be impartial and would do his best to be objective; he agreed that he would "tend to look at it more from [the defense] perspective," but these answers "reflect more of an attempt to 'speak the truth' so that the examining counsel could intelligently exercise peremptory challenges," and not genuine bias).

(e) Sometimes attitudes toward lawyers and tort litigation count as bias. See Black v. SCX Transportation, Inc., 648 S.E.2d 610 (W. Va. 2007) (awarding new trial to plaintiff in asbestos case; court let doctor sit on jury despite saying it would be hard to award damages because of his bias against "personal injury lawyers" and against damages "predicated on anything other than pure objective science") (doctor also indicated bias about asbestos suits because many issues are not about science).

2. Commonly, members of the venire are asked whether they (or relatives) have been involved in litigation (often the question excludes domestic relation suits—divorce, support, child custody—apparently on the theory that experiences in this arena don't color attitudes toward other suits). What is the purpose of such questions? See Neumann v. Arrowsmith, 164 P.3d 116, 120-121 (Okla. 2007) (in medical malpractice suit, losing plaintiff showed that juror had been unsuccessful plaintiff in prior suit for interference with contract; juror mentioned involvement in auto accident case, but not the other case; false answers on voir dire deprive parties of opportunity to "delve deeper into the juror's qualifications, including possible prejudice") (new trial); West v. Holley, 103 P.3d 708, 714 (Utah 2004) (in auto accident suit, venire member W did not speak up when asked whether she had been involved in personal injury case, but another juror's affidavit quoted W as saying she had been sued several times on personal injury claims, and she voiced strong feelings and opinions against awarding general damages; presumption of bias applied) (error to deny plaintiff's challenge for cause); Roberts ex rel. Estate of Roberts v. Tejada, 814 So. 2d 334 (Fla. 2002) (remanding for hearing about jurors, who did not reveal involvement in suits on *voir dire*; there is "no *per se* rule that involvement in any particular prior legal matter is or is not material," but lawyers "must be able to explore the potential impact" of prospective juror's litigation history).

3. Past or existing relationships between members of the venire and a party can indicate potential bias:

(a) In malpractice suits, people who are or have been patients of the doctor or hospital or clinic being sued are often excluded. Should this concern extend to their relatives? See Bowman ex rel. Bowman v. Perkins, 135 S.W.3d 399 (Ky. 2004) (should have removed for cause juror who was in ongoing patient relationship with defendant doctor) (new trial); Allen v. Brown Clinic, PLLP, 531 F.3d 568, 572 (8th Cir. 2008) (court removed four out of ten jurors having doctor/patient relationships with clinic, but seated three; one had no relation with doctor being sued; second cousin of another venire member was

doctor at clinic; another venire member had cousin married to defendant doctor's brother-in-law; each agreed to be fair and impartial) (seating them).

(b) In a suit against a city, county, or political subdivision, should citizens or constituents be removed? Are they too likely to worry that liability could have an impact on their taxes? See Wilson v. Morgan, 477 F.3d 326, 346-347 (6th Cir. 2007) (rejecting such a claim in prisoner's suit for false arrest and imprisonment).

4. Should racial attitudes count? Even if the case does not raise racial issues or create apparent situations where such attitudes might operate? Even without indication that racial biases are at work? See Anderson v. Griffin, 397 F.3d 515 (7th Cir. 2005) (disallowing *voir dire* questions to jurors suspected of being "skinheads," where plaintiff was black but case lacked racial issues; skinhead generally refers to "fierce racists, often neo-Nazi in ideology, who shave their heads," and jurors had "shaven heads or very close-cropped hair," and were questioned about "background, education, and so forth, including what newspapers or magazines they read and what clubs or other organizations they belonged to," but nothing in answers suggested that they were skinheads, and they had no visible tattoos). The Supreme Court has considered this matter in the criminal context. Compare Ham v. South Carolina, 409 U.S. 524, 526-527 (1973) (in drug trial in state court, defendant known for work on civil rights issues was entitled to have potential jurors questioned on racial prejudice) with Ristaino v. Ross, 424 U.S. 589, 595 (1976) (fact that defendants in armed robbery trial were black while victim was white did not require, as constitutional matter, that venire members be questioned on racial attitudes; right to impartial jury "generally can be satisfied by less than an inquiry into a specific prejudice feared by the defendant").

5. Should lack of education constitute a ground for challenge? Some states have moved in this direction. See, e.g., Fla. RCP 1.431(c)(3) (when civil action by nature "requires a knowledge of reading, writing, and arithmetic, or any of them," prospective juror who "does not possess the qualifications" is excludable for cause).

6. What if a trial court erroneously strikes a *qualified* juror? See Lockley v. CSX Transportation, Inc., 2010 WL 3191777 (Pa. Super. Ct. 2010) (erroneously striking qualified juror does not give rise to presumption of prejudice).

7. Are there certain relationships between a potential juror and a party that should result in automatic disqualification? See Hall v. Banc One Management Corp., 873 N.E.2d 290 (Ohio 2007) (in sex discrimination suit against bank and corporate officers, court should have excused for cause prospective juror who was father of two sons working for bank) (statute precludes jury service by parent of children employed by party; plaintiff gets new trial); Mikesinovich v. Reynolds Memorial Hospital, Inc., 640 S.E.2d 560 (W. Va. 2006) (in suit against hospital arising from slip-and-fall while patient was assisted by nurse in moving from bed to wheelchair, court should have dismissed for cause a juror married to hospital employee who served in same location in same job classification as nurse) (new trial); Caterpillar,

Inc. v. Sturman Industries, Inc., 387 F.3d 1358 (7th Cir. 2004) (in trade secrets dispute, judge should have dismissed spouse of plaintiff's employee) (new trial); Kim v. Walls, 563 S.E.2d 847, 849 (Ga. 2002) (in wrongful death suit against physician, court should have excused for cause a nurse who worked in same hospital and had worked with defendant previously in hospital's emergency room) (rejecting *per se* rule, but noting that nurse "expressed partiality in favor of the defendant"); Montesi v. Montesi, 529 S.W.2d 720, 724 (Tenn. App. 1975) (in divorce action, awarding new trial to husband when juror failed to speak up when asked whether he knew any of the parties, and he had served as juror in husband's prior criminal trial resulting in conviction for murdering first wife)(!). But see Cruz v. Jordon, 357 F.3d 269, 270-271 (2d Cir. 2004) (in prisoner's suit alleging improper medical care, refusing to disqualify juror who worked for Department of Corrections; no presumption of bias; juror did not work in facility where claim arose); CSX Transportation, Inc. v. Dansby, 659 So. 2d 35, 39 (Ala. 1995) (employee is not automatically disqualified; better rule is that if employer challenges for cause one of its own employees, it must make a showing of bias or prejudice). Consider relationships that are more tangential. See Wade v. Chengappa, 532 S.W.2d 37, 40-41 (W. Va. 1999) (potential juror L in malpractice suit had "tangential relationship" with defendant doctor's wife, who "in her backup physician role" prescribed medicine by phone for L and treated members of L's family; in this close case, judge properly ascertained that L could serve without bias or prejudice) (plaintiff lost); Toyota Motor Corp. v. McLaurin, 642 S.W.2d 351, 357-359 (Miss. 1994) (in product liability case leading to verdict for plaintiff, court seated eight jurors who had been represented by plaintiff's lawyer or had family members represented by him, including six who "regarded [plaintiff's lawyer] as their lawyer and would go to him if they needed an attorney") (in "sparsely populated" county, plaintiff's lawyer was well known, and "any gathering of people" would probably include some who had been represented by him, or had relatives whom he had represented; court might enlarge venire).

8. Suppose a trial court refuses, at the request of the party who eventually loses, to disqualify a venire member for cause and this person serves as juror in the deliberations leading to the verdict. What kind of showing must the movant make? Here is the description adopted by the Ohio Supreme Court on this point:

> [T]o obtain a new trial in a case in which a juror has not disclosed information during *voir dire*, the moving party must first demonstrate that a juror failed to answer honestly a material question on *voir dire* and that the moving party was prejudiced by the presence on the trial of a juror who failed to disclose material information. To demonstrate prejudice, the moving party must show that an accurate response from the juror would have provided a valid basis for a for-cause challenge. We also hold that in determining whether a juror failed to answer honestly a material question on *voir dire* and whether that nondisclosure

provided a basis for a for-cause challenge, an appellate court may not substitute its judgment for the trial court's judgment unless it appears that the trial court's attitude was unreasonable, arbitrary, or unconscionable.

Grundy v. Dhillon, 900 N.E.2d 153, 164 (Ohio 2008).

5. Peremptory Challenges

Let us now consider peremptory challenges.

Unlike challenges for cause, the number of peremptory challenges is limited. In the federal system, where six-member juries are usually used, each side gets three peremptories. See 28 USC §1870 (in civil cases, "each party shall be entitled to three peremptory challenges"). But see Kalams v. Giacchetto, 842 A.2d 1100, 1112 (Conn. 2004) (judge could allow each side eight instead of four peremptories in sound exercise of discretion). State practice varies: Reportedly, the highest number of peremptories allowed, among states that use twelve-member juries, is eight, but most such states allow four or fewer. In a handful of states, six strikes are allowed, and a few states allow five, and one state allows eight per side.[8]

We begin at the point where a group of venire members has arrived in the courtroom, and for-cause challenges have been exercised to the point where the venire members that remain (or those in the jury box) are qualified to serve. The next step is to allow each side to exercise peremptory challenges. In this process, courts usually follow the approach they take with for-cause challenges—either the strike or the panel system. Again there is concern that jurors ultimately seated may resent lawyers who exercise peremptory challenges, although presumably there is less risk because lawyers need not state (or even hint at) reasons: The lawyer can simply say, "We wish to excuse Mr. Hanson, with our thanks for coming here this morning willing to serve on this jury."

Strike System. Most federal courts and some state systems use the strike system for peremptories. Each side exercises peremptories by crossing out the names of venire members remaining on the list (not excused for cause). Either the parties work from the same list, passing it back and forth, or each works from its own. (The former approach lets the parties know something about which jurors the other side does not want. The latter can result in duplicate strikes, excluding fewer members.) When peremptory strikes have been exercised, the jury is assembled by calling venire members to sit in the jury box (again following a sequence that involves alphabetical

---

[8] See Cortez ex rel. Estate of Puentes v. HCCI-San-Antonio, Inc., 159 S.W.3d 87, 90 n.1 (Tex. 2005) (summarizing 1998 DOJ Study).

order and some random factor). See Mauet, supra, §3.10, p. 67 (this system is standard in federal courts and "more states" are following it).

Panel System. In this system, used in many states, the judge calls the venire members to sit in the jury box. Lawyers exercise peremptory challenges, either in open court or by approaching the bench, one lawyer at a time. As members are removed from the box, new venire members are summoned, questioned, and for-cause challenges are resolved, and again the parties exercise peremptory challenges until they are exhausted or the parties are satisfied. See Mauet, supra.

Not Constitutionally Required. In criminal cases, the Supreme Court has said there is no constitutional right to peremptory challenges. See Gray v. Mississippi, 481 U.S. 648, 663 (1987); Ross v. Oklahoma, 487 U.S. 81 (1988). *Gray* and *Ross* involved the death penalty, and it is hard to imagine that the Court would reject a constitutional basis for peremptories there while finding such a basis in civil cases.

■ NOTES ON PEREMPTORY CHALLENGES

1. Professor Babcock once argued that the peremptory challenge "serves functions that the challenge for cause could never fill," and she identified two such functions. The first is "didactic," in that the peremptory challenge "teaches the litigant, and through him the community, that the jury is a good and proper mode for deciding matters and that its decision should be followed because in a real sense the jury belongs to the litigant" who "chooses it." Second and more provocatively, she argued that the peremptory challenge "avoids trafficking in the core of truth in most common stereotypes," making it unnecessary to articulate the underlying idea. She went on to say that "there are cases that, for example, most middle-aged civil servants would be unable to decide on the evidence." Barbara A. Babcock, *Voir Dire: Preserving "Its Wonderful Power,"* 27 Stan. L. Rev. 545, 552 (1975). Suppose you could find out, for example, that one prospective juror "spent most weekends watching football or basketball or baseball games on TV," that another was a "fitness freak who runs 40 miles a week and works out all the time," that another was "laid off because of an injury at work and now collects disability payments," that another is a "practicing Scientologist" or "orthodox Jew" or "Baptist lay minister," and that yet another "owns an office supply store," and that another is a "nurse in an elder clinic." Does knowledge of such points yield insights that have some "core of truth" that bear on whether a person should serve on a jury in, say, a suit for employment discrimination or product liability?

(*a*) In Batson v. Kentucky, 476 U.S. 79 (1986), the Court held that prosecutors cannot strike jurors on racial grounds, and later the Court extended the principle to both sides in civil cases. See Edmonson v. Leesville Concrete Co., 500 U.S. 614 (1991) (principle applies to civil litigants). Later still, the

Court extended the *Batson* principle to gender-based challenges. See J.E.B. v. Alabama ex rel. T.B., 511 U.S. 127 (1994). Consider this description of the procedure to be followed when a party claims that the other side has violated this principle:

> It is well settled that a civil litigant's exercise of a peremptory jury challenge on account of race violates the equal protection rights of the prospective juror and that the opposing party has standing to object in order to raise the excluded person's rights. When a party challenges the exercise of a peremptory challenge on equal protection grounds, that party bears the burden of proving intentional discrimination by the opposing party. The Supreme Court has delineated a burden-shifting procedure for courts to follow in analyzing a claim of purposeful discrimination in the jury selection process. The party raising the equal protection challenge must first establish a prima facie case of purposeful discrimination in the selection process considering all of the "relevant circumstances, including whether there has been a pattern of strikes against members of a particular race." *Edmonson*. Once a prima facie case of discrimination is established, the burden shifts to the party whose conduct is challenged to come forward with a nondiscriminatory explanation for the use of the challenge. To satisfy this burden, the party need offer only a legitimate reason for exercising the strike, i.e., one that does not deny equal protection; the reason need not be worthy of belief or related to the issues to be tried or to the prospective juror's ability to provide acceptable jury service. The trial court must then decide whether the party challenging the selection process has proven that intentional discrimination was a substantial or motivating factor in the decision to exercise the strike. If the court concludes, or the party admits, that the strike has been exercised in part for a discriminatory purpose, the court must consider whether the party whose conduct is being challenged has demonstrated by a preponderance of the evidence that the strike would have nevertheless been exercised even if an improper factor had not motivated in part the decision to strike. If so, the strike stands.

Jones v. Plaster, 57 F.3d 417, 420-421 (4th Cir. 1995) (black deputy sued white sheriff for discrimination; defendant did not reappoint plaintiff after he campaigned for defendant's electoral opponent; defense struck all four black potential jurors; on challenge by plaintiff, court disallowed strikes, but let defendant strike one later) (remanding to determine whether defense had nondiscriminatory motive).

(b) The bar against race-based challenges applies not only in cases that raise issues of discrimination, but elsewhere too. See, e.g., Zakour v. UT Medical Group, Inc., 215 S.W.3d 763, 773-775 (Tenn. 2007) (in malpractice suit alleging that defendant failed to diagnose plaintiff's breast cancer, awarding plaintiff a new trial; defendant used six out of seven peremptories to strike women, including the only African Americans; in response to plaintiff's *Batson* challenge, defense said one black woman was dismissed because she had "difficulty remembering" verdict in civil case in which she had served and had family history of cancer; in response to gender-based *Batson* challenge, defendants said women were excused on basis of "experience and body mechanics"; record did not support claim that one challenged juror had history of cancer, and court questioned seriousness of claim about failed memory as basis to exclude; lawyers routinely exclude on account of "body language during *voir dire*," but answering *Batson* challenge requires specific descriptions) (citing, as examples of body language that can ward off *Batson* challenge, scowling at lawyers, facial expressions indicating disinterest or hostility; sitting with arms crossed, refusal to make eye contact).

(c) Does the bar against race-based challenges conflict with peremptory challenges to such a degree that they should be abolished? Several scholars think so, including Professor Babcock, who had second thoughts about her observation, quoted in note 1, on the virtue of not "trafficking in the core truth in most common stereotypes." Eighteen years later she wrote that "even though no words were spoken," still "tides of racial passion swept through the courtroom," and "the silence harbored thoughts worse than those that might have been said." Barbara A. Babcock, *A Place in the Palladium: Women's Rights and Jury Service*, 61 U. Cin. L. Rev. 1139, 1147 (1993). See also Nancy Marder, *Justice Stevens, the Peremptory Challenge, and the Jury*, 74 Fordham L. Rev. 1683, 1713 (2005) (judges call for abolishing peremptory challenges because *Batson* failed to end race-based challenges; taking this course would require expanding for-cause challenges, because peremptories would no longer serve as backup; acceptable reasons to challenge for cause might have to reach, for example, not only venire members who *say* they cannot be impartial, but those who "cannot satisfy the appearance of impartiality due to some individual action"). Justice Breyer would abolish peremptories. See Miller-El v. Dretke, 545 U.S. 231, 269-270 (2005) (peremptory challenges "seem increasingly anomalous in our judicial system," where they cannot rest on race or gender; some courts extend similar principles to peremptories based on religious affiliation; yet "use of race- and gender-based stereotypes in the jury-selection process seems better organized than ever before" and jury guide tells lawyers to undertake "demographic analysis" assigning points to characteristics like "age, occupation, and marital status" as well as race and gender) (Breyer, concurring). Was Professor Babcock right the first time, or the second time?

(d) The Court has insisted that peremptories are compatible with *Batson*. See Holland v. Illinois, 493 U.S. 474, 478-482 (1990) (rejecting white defendant's claim that prosecutor's exclusion of all blacks deprived him of constitutional rights; racial groups cannot be excluded from venire, and race-based exclusion from jury is impermissible, but requirement of impartiality does not bar peremptory challenges).

2. Modern judges and scholars have attacked peremptories from yet other perspectives.

(a) One attack rests on the view that peremptory challenges undermine respect for the judicial process. See Morris Hoffman, *Peremptory Challenges Should Be Abolished: A Trial Judge's Perspective*, 64 U. Chi. L. Rev. 809,

854, 858 (1997) (they reflect "deep distrust of prospective jurors wholly inconsistent with the trust we repose in sitting jurors" and send a message to "vast numbers of prospective jurors" challenged in this way who "hold no hidden biases" while devaluing both "the ability of jurors to set those biases aside" and "curative effect of deliberations") (people eliminated "for no reason, or for goofy reasons, get angry" and leave thinking that "the rest of the trial process must be just as bizarre and irrational"). But see Mary Rose, *A* Voir Dire *of* Voir Dire: *Listening to Jurors' Views Regarding the Peremptory Challenge*, 78 Chi.-Kent L. Rev. 1061, 1098 (2003) (based on interviews with more than 200 persons called for North Carolina criminal trials, author concludes that excused jurors are "cognizant of the adversarial interests behind peremptory decisions" and are "generally at peace" with selection practices; if peremptories harmed those who are excused, "it was difficult to find it").

(b) Another attack rests on the view that peremptory challenges result in excluding valuable viewpoints. See Marder, supra, at 1683, 1713-1723 (they deprive juries of "members of groups who can offer different perspectives that might not be shared by other members," such as those whose "outsider status" make them "willing to question traditional assumptions"; black men are more likely to be skeptical of police witnesses than white men; eliminating peremptories helps institution of jury serve what de Tocqueville saw as educational function by ensuring that citizens are treated "with respect" and not eliminated except for "legitimate reason") (getting rid of peremptories would bring "broader swath" of community that better approximates its judgment and reassures it that verdict is fair). See also Roger Allan Ford, *Modeling the Effects of Peremptory Challenges on Jury Selection and Jury Verdicts*, 17 Geo. Mason L. Rev. 377, 421-422 (2010) (peremptories "systematically increase the representation of jurors near the median of the jury pool," and reduce "internal ideological and demographic diversity" to the end that each jury "has more in common than before," while making different juries even more "dissimilar") (these findings "cast significant doubt" on argument that peremptory challenges help create more impartial juries than those selected at random); Nancy S. Marder, *Beyond Gender: Peremptory Challenges and the Roles of the Jury*, 73 Tex. L. Rev. 1041 (1995). Do you agree with these points?

3. Do these attacks smack too much of the academy? Does the "gut instinct" of lawyers merit more respect? Consider this description of peremptory challenges:

> A lawyer might be utterly convinced that a member of the jury venire would vote against his client no matter what the evidence showed, and yet his belief might be based on a hunch that he could not articulate as a ground for a challenge for cause. He might [even] be more eager to strike that juror than one who had an evident bias . . . , for he might think he could overcome the hurdle posed by that bias more readily than he could persuade the stubborn but not demonstrably biased juror.

Thompson v. Altheimer & Gray, 248 F.3d 621, 622 (7th Cir. 2001) (reversing judgment for defendant in discrimination suit for error in refusing to strike juror for cause). Is it really a *value* to have people on juries who hold outlier views? Consider Holland v. Illinois, 493 U.S. 474, 484 (peremptory challenges enable "each side to exclude those jurors it believes will be most partial toward the other side," thus "'eliminat[ing] the extremes of partiality on both sides'") (quoting *Batson*).

4. Sorting out questions of prejudice to a party if a judge errs in refusing to strike a member of the venire for cause has proved difficult. The fact that a party faced with an erroneous refusal to strike for cause can sometimes use a peremptory challenge complicates the inquiry:

(a) In federal courts, a losing party whose for-cause challenge was erroneously overruled can obtain a new trial if the person who should have been removed actually sat on the jury, even if that party could have used a peremptory challenge to cure the problem. See Wright & Miller, Federal Practice and Procedure §384 (criminal defendant "can allow a juror to sit" after his challenge for cause has been rejected in error "and win reversal on appeal if the appellate court agrees that the challenged juror should have been stricken"); *Thompson*, supra, at 621 (same rule applies in civil case).

(b) Many state courts take the opposite position, holding that a losing litigant *cannot* get a new trial if she had a peremptory challenge that she could have used to exclude a juror who should have been removed for cause. See, e.g., Adkins v. Sanders, 871 So. 2d 732, 741 (Miss. 2004) (cannot refrain from exercising all peremptories, then complain of error in refusing to strike juror for cause); Shepherd v. Ledford, 962 S.W.2d 28, 34 (Tex. 1998) (similar).

(c) Which rule is better?

(d) Suppose the losing litigant *does* use a peremptory to remove someone who should have been removed for cause. Can he win a new trial because the error deprived him of a peremptory against someone else who sat on the jury? In federal courts, the Supreme Court answered this question in the negative. See United States v. Martinez-Salazar, 428 U.S. 304 (2000) (nobody claimed that judge "deliberately misapplied the law" to force defendants to use peremptory challenges, and nobody served on jury who should have been excluded for cause); Walzer v. St. Joseph State Hospital, 231 F.3d 1108, 1111 (8th Cir. 2000) (same rule applies in civil cases).

(e) Again many state courts take the opposite view, holding that a losing litigant who used a peremptory to remove someone whom the court seated in error after overruling a challenge for cause *can* win a new trial because the peremptory was unavailable to remove others. See Reff-Conlin's Inc. v. Fireman's Fund Ins. Co., 45 P.3d 863 (Mont. 2002) (verdict loser used peremptory to remove juror who should have been excluded for cause, thus wound up with fewer peremptories than other side) (new trial); Doe v. Wal-Mart Stores, Inc., 558 S.E.2d 663, 670 (W. Va. 2001) (similar); Denver City Tramway Co. v. Kennedy, 117 P. 167 (Colo. 1911) (similar). See also Merritt v. Evansville-Vanderburgh School Corp., 765 N.E.2d 1232, 1235 (Ind. 2002)

(can obtain new trial on exhausting peremptories and striking one who should have been excluded for cause if appellant shows she "would have used that peremptory to strike another juror").

(f) Again, which approach is better?

5. What if a court awards more peremptory challenges to one party than to another? See Cerrano v. Yale-New Haven Hospital, 904 A.2d 149, 164 (Conn. 2006) (judge awarded prevailing plaintiff in medical malpractice case additional peremptories; losing party who complains must exhaust all its own peremptories and request additional ones; must also show that failing to award more resulted in objectionable juror serving on panel) (affirming judgment for plaintiff).

6. Should we further restrict peremptories by barring challenges resting on factors like disabilities and religion? What *other* kinds of peremptory challenge should be barred? See, e.g., Robert W. Gurry, *The Jury Is Out: The Urgent Need for a New Approach in Deciding When Religion-Based Peremptory Strikes Violate the First and Fourteenth Amendments*, 18 Regent U. L. Rev. 91 (2005).

C CONTROLLING JURIES: JUDGMENT AS A MATTER OF LAW AND NEW TRIALS

While it is true that juries, when impaneled to decide civil cases, have considerable power and authority, it is also true that we do not put our entire trust in juries, and the system has many means of controlling what they do.

For example, we have Rules of Evidence. A major reason for these is to prevent juries from hearing things we do not trust them to deal with in an appropriate manner: Thus we exclude hearsay evidence—basically testimony describing what someone else said about the acts, events, or conditions in litigation, offered to prove that those acts or events occurred or the conditions existed. We do so because of concerns over trustworthiness and because we think juries cannot appropriately evaluate statements by persons that they do not see and hear. We also exclude character evidence—proof that a person is a careless driver, for example, if offered to prove action reflecting that character, such as careless driving on the occasion. See FRE 404, 405, and 801-803. These Rules are complicated, and there are exceptions and subtleties that you will study in a course devoted to that subject.

Also judges "instruct" juries on the law, and on various aspects of their behavior. These instructions try to confine juries to considering the evidence in the case, and direct the attention of juries to the applicable legal standards.

Our focus here is on two major jury control mechanisms—motions for judgment as a matter of law and motions for a new trial. What we now call judgment as a matter of law (or "JMAL") was formerly known as directed verdict or judgment notwithstanding the verdict (or the Latin equivalent "judgment non obstante veredicto" or "j.n.o.v.," or sometimes "JNOV"). This matter is governed by FRCP 50, but this rather long rule is devoted mostly to procedural details and complexities that arise when—as commonly happens—a litigant moves *in the alternative* for judgment as a matter of law or a new trial. The heart of the JMAL motion involves appraising the sufficiency of the evidence, a fact that is almost hidden from view if you read the text of FRCP 50 (which you should definitely do).

The motion for a new trial is also governed by a provision in the Rules, but the framers "punted" in crafting FRCP 59: In addition to covering some procedural details, FRCP 59 simply says a new trial in a jury case may be granted "for any reason for which a new trial has heretofore been granted in an action at law in federal courts." Slightly different language covers bench trials. Beneath this language, hidden from view, are a host of issues that we will examine.

1. Judgment as a Matter of Law

Consider this device: Essentially, the movant claims, by making a motion "at any time before the case is submitted to the jury," that there is not sufficient evidence to enable a reasonable jury to find in favor of the other side ("a reasonable jury would not have a legally sufficient evidentiary basis"). See FRCP 50.

The Rule is cast in neutral terms, so both plaintiffs and defendants may make such motions, but in practice it is almost always defendants who move for judgment as a matter of law. For a rare instance where plaintiff won judgment as a matter of law, see Wheeler v. Bennett, 849 S.W.2d 952 (Ark. 1993) (defendant driver struck plaintiff in intersection; defendant admitted running stop sign and that plaintiff did nothing to cause accident; court could direct verdict for plaintiff on liability). Obviously, the appropriate time for a defendant to make such a motion is at the close of the plaintiff's case, or perhaps later, during or at the end of the defense case. Notice in FRCP 50(b) that a party who makes such a motion may "file a renewed motion" seeking judgment as a matter of law if the trial court denied an earlier motion. In effect, the movant may seek judgment as a matter of law *before* the case goes to the jury, and a movant who has taken this step may (if the court does not grant the motion) seek the same remedy again if the jury retires and returns a verdict for the other side. So, in the usual case, a defendant makes the initial motion after plaintiff rests, or perhaps during or after the defense case, and then (if the court denies the motion) the defense makes the motion again if the jury returns an adverse verdict.

The concept of "sufficient evidence" is often illustrated by the football field analogy that you saw in Chapter 11 on Summary Judgment. For the plaintiff, we say that "sufficient evidence" means he has gotten out past his own twenty-yard line but is short of defendant's twenty-yard line (plaintiff has sufficient evidence if he manages to get somewhere between the two twenties). If plaintiff is short of his own twenty, his evidence is insufficient and he is vulnerable to a JMAL motion. If his proof is so strong that he is beyond his opponent's twenty—and in practice we rarely see such a case—then *plaintiff* might win a JMAL motion.

The JMAL device rests on the faith that a judge can examine the proof and decide whether a reasonable jury could find for the party opposing the JMAL motion. In theory, the judge does not "weigh evidence" or "act like a juror," but instead decides whether the evidence is *sufficient* to enable a reasonable person to find for one side rather than the other. JMAL motions raise issues similar to summary judgment motions, except that summary judgment motions are decided on affidavits and discovery—images of the proof that is to come at trial—while JMAL motions are resolved by assessing the evidence *actually produced* at trial.

GALLOWAY v. UNITED STATES

Supreme Court of the United States
319 U.S. 372 (1943)

Mr. Justice RUTLEDGE delivered the opinion of the Court.

Petitioner [Joseph Galloway] seeks benefits for total and permanent disability by reason of insanity he claims existed May 31, 1919. On that day his policy of yearly renewable term insurance lapsed for nonpayment of premium.[1]

The suit was filed June 15, 1938. At the close of all the evidence the District Court granted the Government's motion for a directed verdict. Judgment was entered accordingly. The Circuit Court of Appeals affirmed. Both courts held the evidence legally insufficient to sustain a verdict for petitioner. He says this was erroneous and, in effect, deprived him of trial by jury, contrary to the Seventh Amendment.

[Galloway's argument is] that his case as made was substantial [and] the courts' decisions to the contrary were wrong, and therefore their effect has been to deprive him of a jury trial. . . . Upon the record and the issues as the parties have made them, the only question is whether the evidence was sufficient to sustain a verdict for petitioner. On that basis, we think the judgments must be affirmed.

---

[1] The contract was issued pursuant to the War Risk Insurance Act and insured against death or total permanent disability. [The statute provides that any impairment of "mind or body" that "renders it impossible for the disabled person to follow continuously any substantially gainful occupation" is total disability, which is in turn defined to mean a disability that is "reasonably certain" to continue for life.—ED.]

I

Certain facts are undisputed. Petitioner worked as a longshoreman in Phila-delphia and elsewhere prior to enlistment in the Army November 1, 1917.[3] He became a cook in a machine gun battalion. His unit arrived in France in April, 1918. He served actively until September 24. From then to the following January he was in a hospital with influenza. He then returned to active duty. He came back to the United States, and received honorable discharge April 29, 1919. He enlisted in the Navy January 15, 1920, and was discharged for bad conduct in July. The following December he again enlisted in the Army and served until May, 1922, when he deserted. Thereafter he was carried on the Army records as a deserter.

In 1930 began a series of medical examinations by Veterans' Bureau phy-sicians. On May 19 that year his condition was diagnosed as "Moron, low grade; observation, dementia praecox, simple type." In November, 1931, further exam-ination gave the diagnosis, "Psychosis with other diseases or conditions (organic disease of the central nervous system-type undetermined)." In July, 1934, still another examination was made, with diagnosis: "Psychosis manic and depressive insanity incompetent; hypertension, moderate; otitis media, chronic, left; varicose veins left, mild; abscessed teeth roots; myocarditis, mild."

Petitioner's wife, the nominal party in this suit, was appointed guardian of his person and estate in February, 1932. Claim for insurance benefits was made in June, 1934, and was finally denied by the Board of Veterans' Appeals in January, 1936. This suit followed two and a half years later.

Petitioner concededly is now totally and permanently disabled by reason of insanity and has been for some time prior to institution of this suit. It is conceded also that he was sound in mind and body until he arrived in France in April, 1918.

The theory of his case is that the strain of active service abroad brought on an immediate change, which was the beginning of a mental breakdown that has grown worse continuously through all the later years. Essential in this is the view it had become a total and permanent disability not later than May 31, 1919.

The evidence to support this theory falls naturally into three periods, namely, that prior to 1923; the interval from then to 1930; and that following 1930. It consists in proof of incidents occurring in France to show the begin-nings of change; testimony of changed appearance and behavior in the years immediately following petitioner's return to the United States as compared with those prior to his departure; the medical evidence of insanity accumu-lated in the years following 1930; and finally the evidence of a physician, given largely as medical opinion, which seeks to tie all the other evidence together

---

[3] The record does not show whether this employment was steady and continuous or was spotty and erratic. But there is no contention petitioner's behavior was abnormal before he arrived in France in April, 1918.

as foundation for the conclusion, expressed as of 1941, that petitioner's disability was total and permanent as of a time not later than May of 1919.

Documentary exhibits included military, naval and Veterans' Bureau records. Testimony was given by deposition or at the trial chiefly by five witnesses. One, O'Neill, was a fellow worker and friend from boyhood; two, Wells and Tanikawa, served with petitioner overseas; Lt. Col. Albert K. Mathews, who was an Army chaplain, observed him or another person of the same name at an Army hospital in California during early 1920; and Dr. Wilder, a physician, examined him shortly before the trial and supplied the only expert testimony in his behalf. The petitioner also put into evidence the depositions of Commander Platt and Lt. Col. James E. Matthews, his superior officers in the Navy and the Army, respectively, during 1920-22.

[Wells and Tanikawa, who were with Galloway in France, described his aberrant behavior—"hollering, screeching, swearing," being "nervous" and "irritable" and falsely screaming that "the Germans are coming." O'Neill testified that Galloway was "a wreck" when he came home in 1919, "compared to what he was when he went away" and that Galloway was "unbalanced" and suffered from "crying spells" and alternating "normal behavior and nonsensical talk." According to O'Neill, Galloway described himself as "Doctor Jekyll and Mr. Hyde," and his difficulties persisted for a period of five years, although O'Neill admitted on cross-examination that he could not estimate how many times he had seen Galloway during this period.]

Lt. Col. (Chaplain) Mathews said he observed a Private Joseph Galloway, who was a prisoner for desertion and a patient in the mental ward at Fort MacArthur Station Hospital, California, during a six weeks period early in 1920. The chaplain's testimony gives strong evidence the man he observed was insane. However, there is a fatal weakness in this evidence. In his direct testimony, which was taken by deposition, the chaplain said he was certain that the soldier was petitioner. When confronted with the undisputed fact that petitioner was on active duty in the Navy during the first half of 1920, the witness at first stated that he might have been mistaken as to the time of his observation. Subsequently he reasserted the accuracy of his original statement as to the time of observation, but admitted that he might have been mistaken in believing that the patient-prisoner was petitioner. In this connection he volunteered the statement, "Might I add, sir, that I could not now identify that soldier if I were to meet him face to face, and that is because of the long lapse of time." The patient whom the witness saw was confined to his bed. The record is barren of other evidence, whether by the hospital's or the Army's records or otherwise, to show that petitioner was either patient or prisoner at Fort MacArthur in 1920 or at any other time.

Commander Platt testified that petitioner caused considerable trouble by disobedience and leaving ship without permission during his naval service in the first half of 1920. After "repeated warnings and punishments, leading to court martials," he was sentenced to a bad conduct discharge.

Lt. Col. James E. Matthews (not the chaplain) testified by deposition which petitioner's attorney interrupted Dr. Wilder's testimony to read into evidence. The witness was Galloway's commanding officer from early 1921 to the summer of that year, when petitioner was transferred with other soldiers to another unit. At first Colonel Matthews considered making petitioner a corporal, but found him unreliable and had to discipline him. Petitioner "drank considerably," was "what we called a Bolshevik," did not seem loyal, and "acted as if he was not getting a square deal." The officer concluded "he was a moral pervert and probably used narcotics," but could not secure proof of this. Galloway was court martialed for public drunkenness and disorderly conduct, served a month at hard labor, and returned to active duty. At times he "was one of the very best soldiers I had," at others undependable. He was physically sound, able to do his work, perform close order drill, etc., "very well." He had alternate periods of gaiety and depression, talked incoherently at times, gave the impression he would fight readily, but did not resent orders and seemed to get along well with other soldiers. The officer attributed petitioner's behavior to alcohol and narcotics and it occurred to him at no time to question his sanity.

Dr. Wilder was the key witness. He disclaimed specializing in mental disease, but qualified as having given it "special attention." He first saw petitioner shortly before the trial, examined him "several times." He concluded petitioner's ailment "is a schizophrenic branch or form of praecox." Dr. Wilder heard the testimony and read the depositions of the other witnesses, and examined the documentary evidence. Basing his judgment upon this material, with inferences drawn from it, he concluded petitioner was born with "an inherent instability," though he remained normal until he went to France; began there "to be subjected to the strain of military life, then he began to go to pieces." In May, 1919, petitioner "was still suffering from the acuteness of the breakdown. . . . He is going down hill still, but the thing began with the breakdown. . . ." Petitioner was "definitely insane, yes, sir," in 1920 and "has been insane at all times, at least since July, 1918, the time of this episode on the Marne"; that is, "to the point that he was unable to adapt himself. I don't mean he has not had moments when he could not perform some routine tasks," but "from an occupational standpoint . . . he has been insane." He could follow "a mere matter of routine," but would have no incentive, would not keep a steady job, come to work on time, or do anything he didn't want to do. Dr. Wilder pointed to petitioner's work record before he entered the service and observed: "At no time after he went into the war do we find him able to hold any kind of a job. He broke right down." He explained petitioner's enlistment in the Navy and later in the Army by saying, "It would have been no trick at all for a man who was reasonably conforming to get into the Service."

However, the witness knew "nothing whatever except his getting married" about petitioner's activities between 1925 and 1930, and what he knew of them between 1922 and 1925 was based entirely on O'Neill's testimony and a paper not of record here. Dr. Wilder at first regarded knowledge concerning what petitioner was doing between 1925 and 1930 as not essential. "We have a continuing disease, quite obviously beginning during his military service, and quite obviously continuing in 1930, and the minor incidents don't seem to me—" Counsel for the government interrupted to inquire, "Well, if he was continuously employed for eight hours a day from 1925 to 1930 would that have any bearing?" The witness replied, "It would have a great deal." Upon further questioning, however, he reverted to his first position, stating it would not be necessary or helpful for him to know what petitioner was doing from 1925 to 1930: "I testified from the information I had."

II

This, we think, is the crux of the case and distinguishes it from the cases on which petitioner has relied.[8] His burden was to prove total and permanent disability as of a date not later than May 31, 1919. He has undertaken to do this by showing incipience of mental disability shortly before that time and its continuance and progression throughout the succeeding years. He has clearly established incidence of total and permanent disability as of some period prior to 1938, when he began this suit.[9] For our purposes this may be taken as medically established by the Veterans' Bureau examination and diagnosis of July, 1934.[10]

---

[8] None of them exhibits a period of comparable length as to which evidence is wholly lacking and under circumstances which preclude inference the omission was unintentional.

[9] He has not established a fixed date at which contemporaneous medical examination, both physical and mental, establishes totality and permanence prior to Dr. Wilder's examinations in 1941. Dr. Wilder testified that on the evidence concerning petitioner's behavior at the time of his discharge in 1919, and without reference to the testimony as to later conduct, including O'Neill's, he would reserve his opinion on whether petitioner was then "crazy"—"I wouldn't have enough—."

[10] The previous examinations of 1930 and 1931 show possibility of mental disease in the one case and existence of psychosis with other disease, organic in character but with type undetermined, in the other. These two examinations without more do not prove existence of total and permanent disability; on the contrary, they go far toward showing it could not be established then medically.

The 1930 diagnosis shows only that the examiner regarded petitioner as a moron of low grade, and recommended he be observed for simple dementia praecox. Dr. Wilder found no evidence in 1941 that petitioner was a moron. The 1931 examination is even less conclusive in one respect, namely, that "psychosis" takes the place of moronic status. Dr. Wilder also disagreed with this diagnosis. However, this examination first indicates existence of organic nervous disease. Not until the 1934 diagnosis is there one which might be regarded as showing possible total and permanent disability by medical evidence contemporaneous with the fact.

But if the record is taken to show that some form of mental disability existed in 1930, which later became total and permanent, petitioner's problem remains to demonstrate by more than speculative inference that this condition itself began on or before May 31, 1919 and continuously existed or progressed through the intervening years to 1930.

To show origin before the crucial date, he gives evidence of two abnormal incidents occurring while he was in France, one creating the disturbance before he came near the fighting front, the other yelling that the Germans were coming when he was on guard duty at the Marne. There is no other evidence of abnormal behavior during his entire service of more than a year abroad.

That he was court martialed for these sporadic acts and bound and gagged for one does not prove he was insane or had then a general breakdown in "an already fragile mental constitution," which the vicissitudes of a long-shoreman's life had not been able to crack.

To these two incidents petitioner adds the testimony of O'Neill that he looked and acted like a wreck, compared with his former self, when he returned from France about a month before the crucial date, and O'Neill's vague recollections that this condition continued through the next two, three, four or five years.

O'Neill's testimony apparently takes no account of petitioner's having spent 101 days in a hospital in France with influenza just before he came home. But, given the utmost credence, as is required, it does no more than show that petitioner was subject to alternating periods of gaiety and depression for some indefinite period after his return, extending perhaps as late as 1922. But because of its vagueness as to time, dates, frequency of opportunity for observation, and specific incident, O'Neill's testimony concerning the period from 1922 to 1925 is hardly more than speculative.

We have then the two incidents in France followed by O'Neill's testimony of petitioner's changed condition in 1919 and its continuance to 1922.[11] ... Then follows a chasm of eight years. The only evidence we have concerning this period is the fact that petitioner married his present guardian at some time within it, an act from which in the legal sense no inference of insanity can be drawn.

---

[11] Chaplain Mathews' testimony would be highly probative of insanity existing early in 1920, if petitioner were sufficiently identified as its subject. However, the bare inference of identity which might otherwise be drawn from the mere identity of names cannot be made reasonably in view of its overwhelming contradiction by other evidence presented by petitioner and the failure to produce records from Fort MacArthur Hospital or the Army or from persons who knew the fact that petitioner had been there at any time. The omission eloquently testifies in a manner which no inference could overcome that petitioner never was there. The chaplain's testimony therefore should have been stricken, had the case gone to the jury, and petitioner can derive no aid from it here. ...

This period was eight years of continuous insanity, according to the inference petitioner would be allowed to have drawn. If so, he should have no need of inference. Insanity so long and continuously sustained does not hide itself from the eyes and ears of witnesses.[13] The assiduity which produced the evidence of two "crazy" incidents during a year and a half in France should produce one during eight years or, for that matter, five years in the United States.

Inference is capable of bridging many gaps. But not, in these circumstances, one so wide and deep as this. Knowledge of petitioner's activities and behavior from 1922 or 1925 to 1930 was peculiarly within his ken and that of his wife, who has litigated this cause in his and presumably, though indirectly, in her own behalf. His was the burden to show continuous disability. What he did in this time, or did not do, was vital to his case. Apart from the mere fact of his marriage, the record is blank for five years and almost blank for eight. For all that appears, he may have worked full time and continuously for five and perhaps for eight, with only a possible single interruption.

No favorable inference can be drawn from the omission. It was not one of oversight or inability to secure proof. That is shown by the thoroughness with which the record was prepared for all other periods, before and after this one, and by the fact petitioner's wife, though she married him during the period and was available, did not testify. The only reasonable conclusion is that petitioner, or those who acted for him, deliberately chose, for reasons no doubt considered sufficient (and which we do not criticize, since such matters including tactical ones, are for the judgment of counsel) to present no evidence or perhaps to withhold evidence readily available concerning this long interval, and to trust to the genius of expert medical inference and judicial laxity to bridge this canyon.

In the circumstances exhibited, the former is not equal to the feat, and the latter will not permit it. No case has been cited and none has been found in which inference, however expert, has been permitted to make so broad a leap and take the place of evidence which, according to all reason, must have been at hand. To allow this would permit the substitution of inference, tenuous at best, not merely for evidence absent because impossible or difficult to secure, but for evidence disclosed to be available and not produced. This would substitute speculation for proof. Furthermore, the inference would be more plausible perhaps if the evidence of insanity as of May, 1919, were stronger than it is, such for instance as Chaplain Mathews' testimony would have furnished if it could be taken as applying to petitioner. But, on this record, the

---

[13] [The Court says the "only attempt" to explain the absence of proof for 1922-1930 is a suggestion in plaintiff's brief that one who is insane "would absent himself" from others for "fear of apprehension and punishment," that only Galloway would know what was going on during that period, and that his insanity at the time of trial explains why no proof could be offered. The Court finds this "explanation" to be "obviously untenable," suggesting that his wife was "obviously available" to testify. The Court also wonders out loud how he could have been insane for so long while "absenting himself from persons who could testify" to this point.—ED.]

evidence of insanity as of that time is thin at best, if it can be regarded as at all more than speculative.

Beyond this, there is nothing to show totality or permanence. These come only by what the Circuit Court of Appeals rightly characterized as "long-range retroactive diagnosis." That might suffice, notwithstanding this crucial inference was a matter of opinion, if there were factual evidence over which the medical eye could travel and find continuity through the intervening years. But eight years are too many to permit it to skip, when the bridgeheads (if the figure may be changed) at each end are no stronger than they are here, and when the seer first denies, then admits, then denies again, that what took place in this time would make "a great deal" of difference in what he saw. Expert medical inference rightly can do much. But we think the feat attempted here too large for its accomplishment.

. . .

III

What has been said disposes of the case as the parties have made it. For that reason perhaps nothing more need be said. But objection has been advanced that, in some manner not wholly clear, the directed verdict practice offends the Seventh Amendment.

It may be noted, first, that the Amendment has no application of its own force to this case. The suit is one to enforce a monetary claim against the United States. It hardly can be maintained that under the common law in 1791 jury trial was a matter of right for persons asserting claims against the sovereign. Whatever force the Amendment has therefore is derived because Congress in the legislation cited, has made it applicable. Even so, the objection made on the score of its requirements is untenable.

If the intention is to claim generally that the Amendment deprives the federal courts of power to direct a verdict for insufficiency of evidence, the short answer is the contention has been foreclosed by repeated decisions made here consistently for nearly a century. More recently the practice has been approved explicitly in the promulgation of the Federal Rules of Civil Procedure. *Cf.* Rule 50. The objection therefore comes too late.

Furthermore, the argument from history is not convincing. It is not that "the rules of the common law" in 1791 deprived trial courts of power to withdraw cases from the jury, because not made out, or appellate courts of power to review such determinations. The jury was not absolute master of fact in 1791. Then as now courts excluded evidence for irrelevancy and relevant proof for other reasons. The argument concedes they weighed the evidence, not only piecemeal but in toto for submission to the jury, by at least two procedures, the demurrer to the evidence and the motion for a new trial. The objection is not therefore to the basic thing, which is the power of the court to withhold cases from the jury or set aside the verdict for insufficiency of the evidence. It is rather to incidental or collateral effects, namely, that the directed verdict as now administered differs from both those procedures because, on the one hand, allegedly higher standards of proof are required and, on the other, different consequences follow as to further maintenance of the litigation. Apart from the standards of proof, the argument appears to urge that in 1791, a litigant could challenge his opponent's evidence, either by the demurrer, which when determined ended the litigation, or by motion for a new trial which if successful, gave the adversary another chance to prove his case; and therefore the Amendment excluded any challenge to which one or the other of these consequences does not attach.

The Amendment did not bind the federal courts to the exact procedural incidents or details of jury trial according to the common law in 1791, any more than it tied them to the common-law system of pleading or the specific rules of evidence then prevailing.[22] Nor were "the rules of the common law" then prevalent, including those relating to the procedure by which the judge regulated the jury's role on questions of fact, crystalized in a fixed and immutable system. On the contrary, they were constantly changing and developing during the late eighteenth and early nineteenth centuries.[23] In 1791 this process already had resulted in widely divergent common-law rules on procedural matters among the states, and between them and England. And none of the contemporaneous rules regarding judicial control of the evidence going to juries or its sufficiency to support a verdict had reached any precise, much less final, form. In addition, the passage of time has obscured much of the procedure which then may have had more or less definite form, even for historical purposes.

This difficulty, no doubt, accounts for the amorphous character of the objection now advanced, which insists, not that any single one of the features criticized, but that the cumulative total or the alternative effect of all, was embodied in the Amendment. The more logical conclusion, we think, and the one which both history and the previous decisions here support, is that

---

[22] The rules governing the admissibility of evidence, for example, have a real impact on the jury's function as a trier of facts and the judge's power to impinge on that function. Yet it would hardly be maintained that the broader rules of admissibility now prevalent offend the Seventh Amendment because at the time of its adoption evidence now admitted would have been excluded.

[23] E.g., during the eighteenth and nineteenth centuries, the nonsuit was being transformed in practice from a device by which a plaintiff voluntarily discontinued his action in order to try again another day into a procedure by which a defendant could put in issue the sufficiency of the plaintiff's evidence to go to the jury, differing from the directed verdict in that respect only in form. The nonsuit, of course, differed in consequence from the directed verdict, for it left the plaintiff free to try again.

Similarly the demurrer to the evidence practice was not static during this period as a comparison of [certain English cases] and the American practice on the demurrer to the evidence reveals. Nor was the conception of directing a verdict entirely unknown to the eighteenth century common law. While there is no reason to believe that the notion at that time even approximated in character the present directed verdict, the cases serve further to show the plastic and developing character of these procedural devices during the eighteenth and nineteenth centuries.

the Amendment was designed to preserve the basic institution of jury trial in only its most fundamental elements, not the great mass of procedural forms and details, varying even then so widely among common-law jurisdictions.

Apart from the uncertainty and the variety of conclusion which follows from an effort at purely historical accuracy, the consequences flowing from the view asserted are sufficient to refute it. It may be doubted that the Amendment requires challenge to an opponent's case to be made without reference to the merits of one's own and at the price of all opportunity to have it considered. On the other hand, there is equal room for disbelieving it compels endless repetition of litigation and unlimited chance, by education gained at the opposing party's expense, for perfecting a case at other trials. The essential inconsistency of these alternatives would seem sufficient to refute that either or both, to the exclusion of all others, received constitutional sanctity by the Amendment's force. The first alternative, drawn from the demurrer to the evidence, attributes to the Amendment the effect of forcing one admission because another and an entirely different one is made,[28] and thereby compels conclusion of the litigation once and for all. The true effect of imposing such a risk would not be to guarantee the plaintiff a jury trial. It would be rather to deprive the defendant (or the plaintiff if he were the challenger) of that right; or, if not that, then of the right to challenge the legal sufficiency of the opposing case. The Amendment was not framed or adopted to deprive either party of either right. It is impartial in its guaranty of both. To posit assertion of one upon sacrifice of the other would dilute and distort the full protection intended. The admitted validity of the practice on the motion for a new trial goes far to demonstrate this.[29] It negatives any idea that the challenge must be made at such a risk as the demurrer imposed. As for the other alternative, it is not urged that the Amendment guarantees another trial whenever challenge to the sufficiency of evidence is sustained. That argument, in turn, is precluded by the practice on demurrer to the evidence.

. . .

---

[28] By conceding the full scope of an opponent's evidence and asserting its insufficiency in law, which is one thing, the challenger must be taken, perforce the Amendment, also to admit he has no case, if the other's evidence is found legally sufficient, which is quite another thing. In effect, one must stake his case, not upon its own merit on the facts, but on the chance he may be right in regarding his opponent's as wanting in probative content. If he takes the gamble and loses, he pays with his own case, regardless of its merit and without opportunity for the jury to consider it. To force this choice and yet deny that afforded by the directed verdict would be to imbed in the Constitution the hypertechnicality of common-law pleading and procedure in their heyday.

[29] Under that practice the moving party receives the benefit of jury evaluation of his own case and of challenge to his opponent's for insufficiency. If he loses on the challenge, the litigation is ended. But this is not because, in making it, he is forced to admit his own is insufficient. It is rather for the reasons that the court finds the opposite party's evidence is legally sufficient and the jury has found it outweighs his own. There is thus no forced surrender of one right from assertion of another. On the other hand, if the challenger wins, there is another trial. But this is because he has sought it, not because the Amendment guarantees it.

Accordingly, the judgment is
Affirmed.

Mr. Justice BLACK, with whom Mr. Justice DOUGLAS and Mr. Justice MURPHY concur, dissenting.

. . .

The Court here re-examines testimony offered in a common law suit, weighs conflicting evidence, and holds that the litigant may never take this case to a jury. The founders of our government thought that trial of fact by juries rather than by judges was an essential bulwark of civil liberty. For this reason, among others, they adopted Article III, §2 of the Constitution, and the Sixth and Seventh Amendments. Today's decision marks a continuation of the gradual process of judicial erosion which in one hundred fifty years has slowly worn away a major portion of the essential guarantee of the Seventh Amendment.

. . .

The principal method by which judges prevented cases from going to the jury in the Seventeenth and Eighteenth Centuries was by the demurrer to the evidence, under which the defendant at the end of the trial admitted all facts shown by the plaintiff as well as all inferences which might be drawn from the facts, and asked for a ruling of the Court on the "law of the case." This practice fell into disuse in England in 1793. The power of federal judges to comment to the jury on the evidence gave them additional influence. The right of involuntary non-suit of a plaintiff, which might have been used to expand judicial power at jury expense was at first denied federal courts.

As Hamilton had declared in The Federalist, the basic judicial control of the jury function was in the court's power to order a new trial.[8] In 1830, this Court said: "The only modes known to the common law to re-examine such facts, are the granting of a new trial by the court where the issue was tried, or to which the record was properly returnable; or the award of a venire facias de novo, by an appellate court, for some error of law which intervened in the proceedings." Parsons v. Bedford, supra, 3 Pet. 433, 448 (1830). That retrial by a new jury rather than factual reevaluation by a court is a constitutional right of genuine value was restated as recently as Slocum v. New York Life Insurance Co., 228 U.S. 364 (1913).

A long step toward the determination of fact by judges instead of by juries was the invention of the directed verdict. In 1850, what seems to have been the first directed verdict case considered by this Court, Parks v. Ross, 11 How. 362, 374 (1850), was presented for decision. The Court held that the directed verdict serves the same purpose as the demurrer to the evidence, and that since there was "no evidence whatever" on the critical issue in the case, the

---

[8] A method used in early England of reversal of a jury verdict by the process of attaint which required a review of the facts by a new jury of twenty-four and resulted in punishment of the first jury for its error, had disappeared. Plucknett, A Concise History of the Common Law (2d ed.), 121.

directed verdict was approved. The decision was an innovation, a departure from the traditional rule restated only fifteen years before in Greenleaf v. Birth, 1835, 9 Pet. 292, 299 (1835), in which this Court had said: "Where there is no evidence tending to prove a particular fact, the court(s) are bound so to instruct the jury, when requested; but they cannot legally give any instruction which shall take from the jury the right of weighing the evidence and determining what effect it shall have."

This new device contained potentialities for judicial control of the jury which had not existed in the demurrer to the evidence. In the first place, demurring to the evidence was risky business, for in so doing the party not only admitted the truth of all the testimony against him but also all reasonable inferences which might be drawn from it; and upon joinder in demurrer the case was withdrawn from the jury while the court proceeded to give final judgment either for or against the demurrant. Imposition of this risk was no mere technicality; for by making withdrawal of a case from the jury dangerous to the moving litigant's cause, the early law went far to assure that facts would never be examined except by a jury. Under the directed verdict practice the moving party takes no such chance, for if his motion is denied, instead of suffering a directed verdict against him, his case merely continues into the hands of the jury. The litigant not only takes no risk by a motion for a directed verdict, but in making such a motion gives himself two opportunities to avoid the jury's decision; for under the federal variant of judgment notwithstanding the verdict, the judge may reserve opinion on the motion for a directed verdict and then give judgment for the moving party after the jury was formally found against him. In the second place, under the directed verdict practice the courts soon abandoned the "admission of all facts and reasonable inferences" standard referred to, and created the so-called "substantial evidence" rule which permitted directed verdicts even though there was far more evidence in the case than a plaintiff would have needed to withstand a demurrer.

The substantial evidence rule did not spring into existence immediately upon the adoption of the directed verdict device. For a few more years federal judges held to the traditional rule that juries might pass finally on facts if there was "any evidence" to support a party's contention. The rule that a case must go to the jury unless there was "no evidence" was completely repudiated in Schuylkill and Dauphin Improvement Co. v. Munson, 14 Wall. 442, 447 (1871), upon which the Court today relies in part. There the Court declared that "some" evidence was not enough—there must be evidence sufficiently persuasive to the judge so that he thinks "a jury can properly proceed." The traditional rule was given an ugly name, "the scintilla rule," to hasten its demise. For a time traces of the old formula remained, . . . but the new spirit prevailed. . . . The same transition from jury supremacy to jury subordination through judicial decisions took place in State courts.

Later cases permitted the development of added judicial control.[17] New and totally unwarranted formulas, which should surely be eradicated from the law at the first opportunity, were added as recently as 1929 in Gunning v. Cooley, 281 U.S. 90 (1929), which, by sheerest dictum, made new encroachments on the jury's constitutional functions. There it was announced that a judge might weigh the evidence to determine whether he, and not the jury, thought it was "overwhelming" for either party, and then direct a verdict. *Cf.* Pence v. United States, 316 U.S. 332, 340 (1942); Gunning v. Cooley, 281 U.S. 90, 94 (1930), [which] also suggests quite unnecessarily for its decision, that "When a plaintiff produces evidence that is consistent with an hypothesis that the defendant is not negligent, and also with one that he is, his proof tends to establish neither." This dictum, which assumes that a judge can weigh conflicting evidence with mathematical precision and which wholly deprives the jury of the right to resolve that conflict, was applied in Pennsylvania Railroad Co. v. Chamberlain, 288 U.S. 333 (1933). With it, and other tools, jury verdicts on disputed facts have been set aside or directed verdicts authorized so regularly as to make the practice commonplace while the motion for directed verdict itself has become routine.

. . .

The story thus briefly told depicts the constriction of a constitutional civil right and should not be continued. . . .

The call for the true application of the Seventh Amendment is not to words, but to the spirit of honest desire to see that Constitutional right preserved. Either the judge or the jury must decide facts and to the extent that we take this responsibility, we lessen the jury function. . . .

[Justice Black concludes, on the basis of a lengthy discussion, that there was sufficient evidence that Joseph Galloway was totally and permanently disabled no later than May 31, 1919, to support a jury verdict in his favor.]

■ NOTES ON JMAL MOTIONS AND THE SUFFICIENCY CONCEPT

1. In *Galloway,* the federal statutory claim for recovery on a war risk insurance policy carried a right to a jury trial, and the Court applied the constitutional standard because Congress incorporated it into the statute. The case never actually went to a jury: The trial court granted the government's motion for a directed verdict (now we would say JMAL) *without* obtaining a verdict.

---

[17] One additional device was the remittitur practice which gives the court a method of controlling jury findings as to damages. Arkansas Valley Land & Cattle Co. v. Mann, 130 U.S. 69 (1889).

(a) What are the advantages and drawbacks in granting such a motion without sending the case to a jury first? Is there an appreciable savings in time? Is something gained by the fact that there is no actual *verdict* to set aside if the motion is granted in advance? Consider the fact that a court that grants a JMAL motion *without* first obtaining a verdict might be reversed on appeal: If the appellate court, instead of agreeing with the judge as happened in *Galloway*, had disagreed and told the judge that there *was* sufficient evidence (as Justice Black and the dissenters thought), what happens then?

(b) What are the advantages and drawbacks if a court grants a JMAL motion *after* a verdict is returned? If the jury returned a verdict favoring Joseph Galloway (and Freda, who sued on his behalf), granting the JMAL motion for the government would make graphic the court's view that the jury behaved unreasonably, wouldn't it? Suppose the court took this course, and plaintiff then appealed from the judgment and prevailed because the reviewing court agreed with Justice Black and the dissenters in *Galloway* that there was, after all, sufficient evidence to justify an award for the plaintiff. What would happen then? Would delaying a ruling have saved time?

(c) If one supposes that a trial takes five days, and deliberations take one day, it is possible to work out the relative risks and benefits of granting JMAL motions and the "percentage" of times that a trial court must be *correct* in ruling on such motions if we are to achieve efficiency. On this supposition, granting a JMAL motion for defendant *before* the case goes to deliberations saves a day if the trial judge is right, but costs six days (five for a new trial, one for deliberations) if she is wrong. The indicated conclusion is that a trial judge should grant such a motion only if she is *very likely* to get it right.

2. The critical question was whether Joseph Galloway was totally disabled as of May 31, 1919. The legal standard defines total disability as being too impaired "to follow continuously any gainful occupation" and a finding of total disability can rest on the conclusion that it is "reasonably certain" that an existing disability will continue for life. We know that Galloway was disabled in 1938 when his wife Freda brought suit. We have testimony by at least six witnesses (boyhood friend John O'Neill, colleagues in arms Wells and Tanaka, Chaplain Mathews, Commander Platt, Colonel Matthews) describing experiences with Galloway during the early period (1919-1923). Why aren't these witnesses enough?

3. The Court is troubled by the gap in Dr. Wilder's knowledge between 1925 and 1930 (11-15 years before he examined Galloway), and by the lack of evidence about Galloway between 1922 and 1930. The Court even tweaks the plaintiff—getting married, which apparently happened in 1919, is "an act from which in the legal sense no inference of insanity can be drawn"! What is going on here? Isn't it understandable that plaintiff would focus on the early years, given the critical date of May 1919? Isn't it understandable that Galloway's expert would testify on the basis of his examination of Galloway, which happened about 20 years later, because that's when Freda Galloway decided to sue?

4. A perennial problem for courts and litigants, as for historians, is the absence of direct evidence on the point of interest. Unable to find anything better, litigants offer circumstantial evidence (historians base arguments on similar evidence), which *by definition* means evidence that can be interpreted or explained in different ways. If it seems that either inference is possible, or to put it another way, that two or more explanations are *equally* plausible, should the jury be allowed to decide which interpretation to adopt?

(a) In a suit arising out of the death of a brakeman who fell from one of two strings of freight cars moving on one track in a railyard sorting operation, three eyewitnesses testified that the strings did *not* collide, but one testified that he saw one string gaining on the other and then turned away and then heard a crash, whereupon he looked again and saw the strings moving together. There was considerable commotion and noise, and the lone witness who thought the strings collided was 900 feet from the place where the body was recovered and almost in line with the track (he saw the crash from only a slight 3-degree angle). The Court thought there was "no direct evidence" of a crash that could have caused the fall and death: The case was one "where proven facts give equal support to each of two inconsistent inferences," so judgment must go "as a matter of law" against the one "upon whom rests the necessity of sustaining one of these inferences." See Pennsylvania Railroad Co. v. Chamberlain, 288 U.S. 333, 339 (1933) (if "several inferences" are "equally consistent with all the facts," there is "no evidence" on which to rest a verdict; a witness cannot "resolve the doubt as to which of two equally justifiable inferences" is correct by "drawing a conclusion").

(b) Recall the *Lavender* decision from Chapter 1E, where switchman Haney was found dead in a railyard, having been struck on the head by a blunt instrument. Plaintiff's theory was that he was hit by a mail hook protruding from a car that could swing as the car moved, and defendant's theory was that Haney was killed by an assailant ("many hoboes and tramps frequented the area at night"), and the Court held that the case should go to a jury: When "fair-minded" people "may draw different inferences," the Court wrote, "a measure of speculation and conjecture is required," and if an "evidentiary basis" exists, it does not matter that a court "might draw a contrary inference or feel that another conclusion is more reasonable."

(c) Can *Lavender* be reconciled with *Chamberlain*? If juries decide where competing inferences seem equally likely, does it follow that we give juries cases that cannot be rationally decided? Hence (as *Lavender* indicates) juries engage in speculation and conjecture? How should we understand *Galloway*, which says that giving the case to the jury "would substitute speculation for proof"? See William V. Dorsaneo, *Reexamining the Right to Trial by Jury*, 45 SMU L. Rev. 1695, 1708-1709 (2001) ("without expressly overruling or repudiating" the rule in *Chamberlain*, *Lavender* embraced a "reasonable basis in the record" standard under which juries can decide cases where reasonable

minds could differ, and courts take cases from juries only if there can be but one reasonable conclusion on the evidence).

5. There may be ways to extricate ourselves from at least some such dilemmas. Three are especially worthy of note:

(a) First, it is sometimes possible to shift or manipulate burdens of persuasion to ameliorate problems caused by lack of proof. In the famous case of Summers v. Tice, 199 P.2d 1 (1948), the California Supreme Court concluded that if two hunters negligently fired guns in the vicinity of the plaintiff, who was injured by a bullet from one of them, both defendants can be viewed as wrongdoers, and each can be burdened with proving that he was not responsible. See Restatement (Second) of Torts §433B (1965) (normally, burden of proof is on plaintiff, but where conduct by two or more actors is "tortious" and harm was caused by only one, but there is "uncertainty" as to which actor caused the harm, "the burden is upon each such actor to prove that he has not caused the harm").

(b) Second, courts sometimes develop roadmaps to deal with recurrent problems of circumstantial evidence, based on statutory mandates and considerations of policy. Recall the *Swierkiewicz* case from Chapter 7B1, where the question was whether the burden of *pleading* intentional discrimination should track trial burdens (the answer was no; pleading burdens need not track trial burdens). The trial burdens were mapped out in McDonnell Douglas Corp. v. Green, 411 U.S. 792, 802 (1973), where the Court said that one claiming intentional discrimination in a Title VII case must "carry the initial burden" of proving "(i) that he belongs to a racial minority; (ii) that he applied and was qualified for a job for which the employer was seeking applicants; (iii) that, despite his qualifications, he was rejected; and (iv) that, after his rejection, the position remained open and the employer continued to seek applicants from persons of complainant's qualifications." Proving these points raises a "presumption" of intentional discrimination, which means that a plaintiff who proves those foundational points wins automatically, as a matter of law, if defendant fails to offer proof of nondiscriminatory motive. See Texas Department of Community Affairs v. Burdine, 450 U.S. 248, 255 (1981) (if trier of fact "believes the plaintiff's evidence, and if the employer is silent in the face of the presumption, the court must enter judgment for the plaintiff because no issue of fact remains"). Still later, the Court held that if defendant *does* come forward with evidence of nondiscriminatory motive, the case can still go to the jury, but plaintiff no longer wins "automatically." The jury may consider and even reject the defendant's explanation, and the very fact of offering a false explanation constitutes *additional* evidence of discrimination. See St. Mary's Honor Center v. Hicks, 509 U.S. 502, 511 (1993) ("disbelief" in reasons offered by defendant, particularly if "accompanied by a suspicion of mendacity" may, together with elements in *McDonnell Douglas* prima facie case, "suffice to show intentional discrimination").

(c) Third, and related to the approach in *St. Mary's Honor Center* and *Galloway,* courts often take the position that destroying or failing to produce

available evidence raises a presumption that the missing evidence would be unfavorable. See, e.g., Davis v. Wal-Mart Stores, Inc., 774 So. 2d 84, 88 (La. 2000) (in suit by customer injured when wooden Santa Claus fell from shelf and struck her on the head, defense "failed to explain why they neither photographed the shelf nor the statue itself," and trial court could find that this failure warranted use of presumption that the evidence "would have been detrimental to the defendant's case in accordance with the court's instructions"); Felix v. Gonzalez, 87 S.W.3d 574, 580 (Tex. App. 2002) ("intentional spoliation of evidence raises a presumption that the evidence would have been unfavorable," and "unintentional spoliation or the failure to produce evidence within a party's control raises a rebuttable presumption that the missing evidence would be unfavorable").

6. Descriptions of the standard to be applied in ruling on a motion for judgment as a matter of law abound. Here is one of the better ones:

> Judgment as a matter of law may be granted only if, when viewing the evidence in the light most favorable to the nonmoving party, there is "no legally sufficient evidentiary basis" for a reasonable jury to find for the nonmoving party and there is "only one conclusion that can reasonably be drawn from the evidence." The nonmoving party is entitled to the benefit of every reasonable inference from the evidence, and we must be cognizant that "it is the responsibility of the jury (and not the judge) to weigh the evidence and to pass upon the credibility of the witnesses." Although the nonmoving party is "entitled to the benefit of all logical inferences, the jury may not be allowed to engage in idle speculation."

Washington Metropolitan Area Transit Authority v. Barksdale-Showell, Inc., 965 A.2d 16, 24 (D.C. 2009). See also Monahan v. GMAC Mortgage Corp., 893 A.2d 298, 303 (Vt. 2005) (where evidence "supports multiple reasonable inferences," it is "for the jury to choose among them").

7. Courts sometimes use the term "substantial" evidence in describing the sufficiency standard. In *Galloway*, Justice Black argued that "any" evidence supporting the point to be proved should be viewed as "sufficient," and he complained that the "substantial" evidence standard came with the directed verdict motion as a further attempt to reduce the authority of juries. Most courts using the term "substantial" in this context, however, define "substantial evidence" the same way that one would define "sufficient evidence." See, e.g., Crawford County v. Jones, 232 S.W.3d 433, 437 (Ark. 2006) ("substantial" evidence "goes beyond suspicion or conjecture and is sufficient to compel a conclusion one way or the other," but in determining whether there is substantial evidence, court views "the evidence and all reasonable inferences arising therefrom in the light most favorable" to party opposing motion); Davis v. Microsoft Corp., 70 P.3d 126, 131 (Wash. 2003) (substantial evidence means "that character of evidence which would convince an unprejudiced thinking mind of the truth of the fact" and as evidence sufficient to "persuade a fair-minded, rational person of the truth of a declared premise"). See also Ala. Code §12-21-12 ("substantial evidence" is required in civil actions, meaning "evidence of such quality and weight that reasonable and fair-minded persons in the exercise of impartial judgment might reach different conclusions as to the existence of the fact sought to be proven"). One prominent source has concluded that in this setting the two terms appear to mean the same thing. See 9B Wright & Miller, Federal Practice and Procedure (Civil) §2524. Justice Black is right on at least one point—the term "scintilla" is used to discredit the notion that "any" evidence is sufficient. See, e.g., Anderson v. Liberty Lobby, Inc., 477 U.S. 242, 251 (1986) ("formerly" courts were satisfied with "what is called a scintilla of evidence," but no longer); Ala. Code §12-21-12 ("scintilla rule of evidence is hereby abolished in all civil actions," *and* "a scintilla of evidence is insufficient to permit submission of an issue of fact to the trier of facts")(!).

8. In the federal system and most states, a court decides whether to enter judgment as a matter of law by considering all the evidence, giving generous construction to proof offered by the party *opposing* the motion and *not* resolving credibility issues. When it comes to evidence offered by the *moving* party, courts often say it counts only if the jury would be "required to believe it." Very little evidence fits this category. Juries do *not*, for example, have to believe testimony by "interested" witnesses who are connected with a party. Juries do not even have to believe "disinterested" testimony if it is open to doubt, as it almost always is, or has been impeached or contradicted by other proof. But juries probably *do* have to accept unequivocal testimony by multiple disinterested witnesses whose credibility has *not* been called into question, and whose evidence is *not* contradicted. In the federal system, the Supreme Court described the proper approach in these terms:

> The Courts of Appeals have articulated differing formulations as to what evidence a court is to consider in ruling on a Rule 50 motion. Some decisions have stated that review is limited to that evidence favorable to the nonmoving party, while most have held that review extends to the entire record, drawing all reasonable inferences in favor of the nonmovant.
>
> On closer examination, this conflict seems more semantic than real. Those decisions holding that review under Rule 50 should be limited to evidence favorable to the nonmovant appear to have their genesis in Wilkerson v. McCarthy, 336 U.S. 53 (1949). In *Wilkerson*, we stated that "in passing upon whether there is sufficient evidence to submit an issue to the jury we need look only to the evidence and reasonable inferences which tend to support the case of" the nonmoving party. But subsequent decisions have clarified that this passage was referring to the evidence to which the trial court should give credence, not the evidence that the court should review. In the analogous context of summary judgment under Rule 56, we have stated that the court must review the record "taken as a whole." Matsushita Elec. Industrial Co. v. Zenith Radio Corp., 475 U.S. 574, 587 (1986). And the standard for granting summary judgment "mirrors" the standard for judgment as a matter of law, such that "the inquiry under each is the same." Anderson v. Liberty Lobby, Inc., 477 U.S. 242, 250-251(1986); see also

Celotex Corp. v. Catrett, 477 U.S. 317, 323 (1986). It therefore follows that, in entertaining a motion for judgment as a matter of law, the court should review all of the evidence in the record.

In doing so, however, the court must draw all reasonable inferences in favor of the nonmoving party, and it may not make credibility determinations or weigh the evidence. Lytle v. Household Mfg., Inc., 494 U.S. 545, 554-555 (1990); Liberty Lobby, Inc., supra; Continental Ore Co. v. Union Carbide & Carbon Corp., 370 U.S. 690, 696 (1962). "Credibility determinations, the weighing of the evidence, and the drawing of legitimate inferences from the facts are jury functions, not those of a judge." *Liberty Lobby,* supra. Thus, although the court should review the record as a whole, it must disregard all evidence favorable to the moving party that the jury is not required to believe. That is, the court should give credence to the evidence favoring the nonmovant as well as that "evidence supporting the moving party that is uncontradicted and unimpeached, at least to the extent that that evidence comes from disinterested witnesses."

Reeves v. Sanderson Plumbing Products, Inc., 530 U.S. 133, 149-150 (2000). An influential treatise endorses this "all the evidence" approach. See Wright & Miller, supra, §2529 ("correct rule" is that court in ruling on JMAL motion "may consider all of the evidence favorable to the position of the party opposing the motion . . . as well as any unfavorable evidence that the jury is required to believe"); East Texas Medical Center Regional Healthcare System v. Lexington Insurance Co., 575 F.3d 520, 525 (5th Cir. 2009) (in ruling on JMAL motion, court considers "all the evidence presented at trial in the light most favorable to the nonmoving party," disregarding "evidence favorable to the moving party that the jury is not required to believe").

9. Some states do appear to follow a more stringent rule, insisting that courts look *only* at evidence offered by the party opposing the motion. See Mills v. CSX Transport, Inc., 300 S.W.3d 627, 632 (Tenn. 2009) (take strongest legitimate view of evidence favoring opposing party and discard all countervailing evidence); Youree v. Eshaghoff, 256 S.W.3d 551, 554 (Ark. App. 2007) (appellate court "will only consider evidence favorable to [the party opposing the motion]").

2. New Trial Motions: Errors and Second Chances; Remittitur and Additur

Few trials make it from beginning to end without mistakes: In part, we must chalk this fact up to the complexity of law; in part, we must chalk it up to human fallibility. While even parties who lose on the merits after trial experience some level of satisfaction in the fact that they *have been heard* and their grievance has been considered (and presumably taken seriously), still there are few litigants who actually "don't care about the money," and those who lose are likely to think that things went wrong and the court or jury made a mistake.

Everyone knows that judgments rendered by trial courts can be appealed, but it is less commonly understood that litigants can ask trial courts to correct themselves. The mechanism designed for this purpose is the motion for a new trial under FRCP 59. The material on appeals (Chapter 13) examines the fact that appellate courts make corrections that stand at one remove from "getting the right outcome." The job of the appellate court is *not* to be sure that the facts were found right or that conflicts in proof were correctly resolved. Rather, the job of the appellate court (and of lawyers who frame and present the issues and arguments) is to detect errors and decide whether they counted in some way—whether they likely affected the judgment or outcome.

Motions for a new trial serve a similar function: A litigant who is dissatisfied with the judgment, and who thinks an error was committed, can move for a new trial on this ground. There are four kinds of error that are most often advanced as reasons for reversal on appeal, and these can also be brought forward in motions for a new trial, heard in the first instance by the trial judge: (1) errors in admitting or excluding evidence; (2) errors in jury instructions; (3) errors in giving a case to a jury when there is only one reasonable outcome; and (4) misconduct by one of the participants in the trial—lawyer, witness, party, jury, court clerk or bailiff, or judge—that might have affected the verdict. Any of these grounds can support giving the verdict loser a second chance.[9]

New trial motions can be made for other reasons as well.

Perhaps most importantly, a party dissatisfied with a verdict can move for a new trial on the ground that the verdict is "against the weight of the evidence." This claim comes closer than any other to arguing that the aggrieved party should get relief simply because the jury "got it wrong." The argument is *not* that some kind of error or mistake was made, but that the jury did not adequately credit the moving party's proof, or gave too much credence to opposing proof, or perhaps decided the case on the basis of improper considerations, like bias or prejudice, or even randomly and mindlessly. See Weida v. Kegarise, 849 N.W.2d 1147, 1152 (Ind. 2006) (in new trial motion, judge "acts as juror rather 'than a mere umpire' and fulfills the judicial role having 'ke[pt] his eyes and ears open to what was going on during the trial [in order to] pass upon the purely legal questions

---

[9] In judge-tried cases, there will not be errors in jury instructions, but the judge can "get the law wrong" in the "findings and conclusions" required by FRCP 52, which is a similar kind of error. Also it can be said that errors in admitting or excluding evidence seldom generate reversals in judge-tried cases, in part because judges are presumed to know what evidence they can rely on and what evidence they cannot rely on, and a lawyer for the winning side who prepares the findings and conclusions will take care, whenever possible, *not* to rely on evidence that the other side has objected to. And in judge-tried cases there can be no error in giving a case to a jury when the evidence is such that only one decision is reasonable, but a judge *can* make a mistake in deciding a case on insufficient evidence.

involved in the case, as well as determine the weight and sufficiency of the evidence'"); Conte v. General Housewares Corp., 215 F.3d 628, 637 (6th Cir. 2000) (in ruling on new trial motion, court may compare opposing proofs and weigh evidence); DLC Management Corp. v. Town of Hyde Park, 1263 F.3d 124, 134 (2d Cir. 1998) (court may grant new trial "even if there is substantial evidence supporting the jury's verdict" and judge "is free to weigh the evidence himself, and need not view it in the light most favorable to the verdict winner").

Still, trial judges and reviewing courts are uncomfortable when judges "second guess" juries, and the cases quoted above contain language cautioning judges not to interfere freely with the work of juries. Courts also disagree on the question whether, in ruling on new trial motions, the judge can "act like a thirteenth juror." Note the suggestion in the *Weida* case that judges can do so. But one modern court phrased its cautionary warnings in language that specifically cautions judges *not* to act like jurors:

> [A] district court considering a motion for a new trial . . . may not substitute its own judgment for that of the jury, or act as a thirteenth juror when the evidence is such that different persons would naturally and fairly come to different conclusions, but may set aside a jury verdict when, in considering and weighing all the evidence, the court's judgment tells it the verdict is wrong because it is manifestly against the weight of the evidence.

Gisvold v. Windbreak, Inc., 730 N.W.2d 597, 601 (N.D. 2007). See also Molski v. M.J. Cable, Inc., 481 F.3d 724, 729 (9th Cir. 2007) (may grant new trial only if verdict is contrary to "clear weight of the evidence" or "based upon false or perjurious evidence" or to prevent "miscarriage of justice"); Farrior v. Waterford Board of Education, 277 F.3d 633, 634 (2d Cir. 2002) (verdict is against the weight of the evidence "if and only if the verdict is seriously erroneous or a miscarriage of justice") (per curiam).

We turn now to the most common kind of argument that a verdict should be set aside and a new trial granted—the argument that a damage award is so high that it is beyond reason. Typically, the moving party claims the jury was carried away by emotion, passion, prejudice, or bias in doing what it did. Perhaps unsurprisingly, courts in this situation have come up with a device called "*remittitur*," which means simply that the judge, if he thinks the jury award *is* too high, can suggest that the claimant accept something less. Mechanically, the court then *denies* the defense motion for a new trial *if* the plaintiff accepts the lesser sum. If she does, judgment in the lesser sum is entered.

You may be wondering whether the opposite "mistake" happens—whether juries ever set damage awards too low. The answer is yes, but seemingly less often. When it *does* happen, plaintiff can move for a new trial, and courts have come up with the same scheme to shortcut things: A court can *deny* a plaintiff's new trial motion *on condition that* defendant agree to a judgment in a greater amount than the jury awarded. If she agrees, then judgment in the greater amount is entered. We use the term "*additur*" to describe this technique.

In federal courts, *additur* does not exist. A venerable decision by the Supreme Court in Dimick v. Schiedt, 293 U.S. 474 (1935), concluded on the basis of history that while *remittitur* is consistent with the "Re-examination Clause" of the Seventh Amendment, *additur* is not. Unlike the approach taken to the "Preservation" Clause of the Seventh Amendment, where the Court in the *Beacon Theatres* line *departed* from historical practices, and unlike the approach in *Galloway* to the Preservation Clause, where the Court was again willing to depart from historical practice, the Court in *Dimick* closed the door to an updated construction. In an unfortunate phrase embodying the most empty kind of formalistic logic, the Court buttressed its conclusion by saying that *additur* is different from *remittitur* because *additur* represents "a bald addition of something which in no sense can be said to be included in the verdict," but *remittitur* in contrast "has the effect of merely lopping off an excrescence"(!).

In most states, the additur device is available.[10] Recall that the Seventh Amendment does not apply to states, and they are free in civil cases to accord the right to trial by jury in civil cases in whatever way their laws provide. See Baudanza v. Comcast of Massachusetts I, Inc., 912 N.E.2d 458, 463-464 (Mass. 2009) (finding no ground for distinguishing between additur and remittitur, as a matter of state constitutional law); Reid v. Hindt, 976 A.2d 125, 131 (Del. 2009) (additur and remittitur cannot be distinguished in reason or logic, and both "do not violate the right to trial by jury").

■ PROBLEM 12-B. Danielle's Weakened Arm

Through her mother and guardian Meryl Fuller, Danielle Fuller brings suit in state court against Ocean Vista Hospital (OVH) and Doctors Carol Harper (a second-year resident at OVH), Eric Burns (another second-year resident), and Debra Cramer, the attending physician and obstetrician on duty. Plaintiffs demand a jury trial.

---

[10] In a 2010 survey, the author found cases in 19 states approving additur, and most rejecting *Dimick* (California, Delaware, Florida, Illinois, Louisiana, Maryland, Massachusetts, Minnesota, Nevada, New Jersey, New Mexico, New York, Ohio, North Carolina, Rhode Island, Tennessee, Utah, Vermont, and Washington). Cases in 20 more states use additur and assume its validity (Alabama, Alaska, Arizona, Colorado, Connecticut, Georgia, Idaho, Indiana, Iowa, Maine, Michigan, Mississippi, Missouri, New Hampshire, North Dakota, South Carolina, South Dakota, West Virginia, Wisconsin, and Wyoming). Cases in nine states plus the District of Columbia disapprove additur or say it is unavailable (Arkansas, DC, Kansas, Kentucky, Montana, Nebraska, Oklahoma, Pennsylvania, Texas, and Virginia). Two states (Hawaii and Oregon) seem to leave the matter unresolved.

Meryl Fuller went to OVH at 4 A.M. on June 25, 2007, experiencing labor pain. Harper examined Ms. Fuller at 4 P.M. and found that her labor was progressing well. At 10 P.M., however, Harper again examined Ms. Fuller and found that her cervix had stopped dilating, probably because of fetal pelvic disproportion—the mother's pelvis cannot accommodate the size of the baby. There were no signs of stress in the baby, however, and Dr. Harper decided that she should perform a caesarian (or c-section). Harper told Dr. Burns to monitor Ms. Fuller while Harper performed another c-section. After examining the charts and the fetal monitor, Dr. Burns decided that a c-section was no longer appropriate because the baby was experiencing a reduced heart rate and variability in the beat, indicating an impaired oxygen supply. At 10:45 P.M., Fuller was fully dilated and the baby's head was at the vaginal opening, and Dr. Burns summoned Dr. Cramer to the operating room as attending physician, but she was engaged in another delivery and could not come.

At 11 P.M., Dr. Burns delivered Danielle himself, although recognizing that she would be large and that conventional delivery brought a risk of shoulder dystocia, which can result from delivering a baby whose shoulder becomes stuck against the mother's pubic bone, obstructing its passage through the birth canal, as was happening here. Dr. Burns freed Danielle by changing Ms. Fuller's position, by pressing on her pubic bone, and by enlarging the incision to expand her vaginal opening. Danielle was injured in the birth process, emerging with an atrophied and partially paralyzed arm.

Plaintiff presents expert testimony that choosing conventional delivery rather than a c-section was a departure from accepted medical standards. The long 18-hour labor and position and size of the baby indicated a c-section, and the fetal monitor readings did not justify conventional delivery. Defendant presents testimony that the original decision to resort to a c-section was right, but that when Danielle began to move through the birth canal, the necessity for surgical delivery disappeared, and the "environmental insult" indicated by fetal monitor readings, which could include things like compression of the umbilical cord or the baby's head, indicated that the wisest course was to deliver as quickly as possible, and that Dr. Burns' actions in doing so conformed to accepted medical practice.

There is evidence that Danielle has paralysis of some of her arm muscles, and weakening of others. Also there is evidence that she has limited motion of her right arm, and cannot move her right hand, thumb, or fingers, although she can hold light objects placed in her hand. Expert testimony indicates that her condition is not expected to improve. The jury is shown a video made for trial, "A Day in the Life of Danielle Fuller," who is four years old at the time of trial. There is testimony that Danielle is disappointed and frustrated with her disability, and that she needs assistance with tasks that require two hands, such as washing herself and combing her hair. She is doing well in school, but has difficulty with writing simple letters.

Additional testimony indicates that Danielle is bright and self-confident, and has learned to speak both English and French, but that she may experience serious limitations as an adult because most jobs require two hands, and that she will be unable to perform tasks required of many careers.

The jury returns a verdict in the amount of $1 million for medical and related expenses (counseling and related special expenses necessitated by Danielle's condition) and $24 million in general damages for Danielle plus $5 million in general damages for her mother.

Defendants file a motion for a new trial or, in the alternative, for remittitur. Announcing that she is "staggered by the size of the verdict for general damages," the trial judge concludes that the amounts are "excessive." She advises the parties that she intends to deny the motion for a new trial on condition that Danielle (through her guardian) accept a remittitur reducing the general verdict to from $24 to $8 million, and that Meryl Fuller accept a remittitur from $5 million to $500,000.

(A) If Danielle and Meryl Fuller refuse to accept the remitted amounts, a new trial will proceed. Should they be able to seek immediate review of the order?

(B) If defendants OVH and the doctors are not satisfied with the suggested new amounts, and think they are *still* excessive, should *they* be able to appeal?

(C) Suppose Danielle and Meryl Fuller do accept the remitted amounts, and judgment is entered accordingly. *Now* there is no doubt that defendants can appeal, because *now* we have a final judgment. But can *plaintiffs* appeal after having accepted the lowered amount?

(D) What standard should the trial court use in deciding whether the verdict is excessive? *Is* an award of $24 million excessive for Danielle Fuller? Is $5 million excessive for Meryl Fuller?

(E) If the trial court believes that on these facts the *most* that a jury could reasonably award to Danielle Fuller is $12 million and the *least* that a jury could reasonably award is $4 million, should the trial judge be able to select $8 million as the appropriate amount? Or should she be required either to choose the *highest* plausible amount ($12 million) or the *lowest* plausible amount ($4 million)?

■ NOTES ON REMITTITUR AND ADDITUR

1. On the matter of plaintiffs' appeal (Question A), the material on appeal (Chapter 13) will tell you that the federal system and most states follow variations of the "final judgment rule," and appeals cannot be taken from nonfinal ("interlocutory") orders. An order granting a new trial motion is a classic example of a nonfinal order. The trial judge retains jurisdiction and the case is ongoing.

(a) In accord with this rule, it is settled in the federal system that an order granting a new trial unless plaintiff agrees to a remittitur is not final. If plaintiff refuses, the order takes effect and the case must be tried again. See Kelly v. Moore, 376 F.2d 481, 483 (5th Cir. 2004) (order granting a new trial is interlocutory, not final, and is generally not appealable); Herold v. Burlington Northern, Inc., 761 F.2d 1241, 1249 (8th Cir. 1985) (order granting new trial after refusal to accept remittitur is interlocutory and ordinarily not appealable).

(b) Consider the matter from plaintiffs' perspective. Danielle and Meryl Fuller can only avoid another trial, where it is possible that they will come away with nothing or with substantially less, if they agree to the remittitur and give up much of what the jury awarded. If they think the award is reasonable and supported by evidence, they will want to appeal the judge's order.

(c) Some states make an exception to the final judgment rule and let plaintiff appeal a remittitur case, although others agree with the federal approach. Compare Rhode Island Managed Eye Care, Inc. v. Blue Cross & Blue Shield, 996 A.2d 684 (R.I. 2010) (plaintiff can appeal order denying defense motion for new trial unless plaintiff agrees to forgo award for lost profits) and Canterino v. The Mirage Casino-Hotel, 16 P.3d 415 (Nev. 2001) (entertaining plaintiff's appeal from order awarding new trial after refusing to accept remittitur) with *Baudanza*, supra, at 458, 464 (order granting new trial subject to remittitur is nonfinal; appeal must await judgment after new trial in event remittitur is declined).

2. On the matter of defense appeals from remittitur orders (Question B), bear in mind that a defendant might consider the remitted amount to be *still* far too high. The hospital and the doctors might think that giving Danielle $8 million and her mother $500,000 is unreasonable. Like plaintiffs, defendants too may object to what the trial judge has done, and may want an appeal if they cannot persuade the judge to propose an even greater reduction in the award. In most jurisdictions, only *plaintiff* may object in remittitur cases, by refusing to agree to a judgment requiring it to accept less, although some take the view that *both* parties can object, reasoning that a small remittitur can err in failing adequately to help defendant and that a small additur can err in failing adequately to help plaintiff. In these jurisdictions, the result is that a new trial must be ordered unless both sides agree to the altered amount suggested by the court. See Waste Management, Inc. v. Mora, 940 So. 2d 1105, 1109 (Fla. 2006) ("party adversely affected" by proposed remittitur or additur may appeal, which means both parties; "only when the parties agree with the trial court's amount of remittitur or additur will the remittitur or additur be enforced in lieu of a new trial"); Dedeaux v. Pellerin Laundry, Inc., 947 So. 2d 900, 908 (Miss. 2007) ("grant of an additur or remittitur shall take effect only if accepted by all the parties," and if any does not agree each "shall have the right to either demand a new trial on damages, or appeal the order asserting an abuse of discretion on the part of the trial judge"); Allsup's Convenience Stores, Inc. v. North River Insurance Co., 976 P.2d 1, 8 (N.M. 1998) (plaintiff may accept remittitur under protest and appeal). See also Hilb, Rogal & Hamilton Co. v. Beiersdoerfer, 33 So. 3d 557 (Ala. 2009) (plaintiff and defendant cross-appeal from trial court's order remitting award) (court erred in declining to give plaintiff the option of a new trial).

3. On the matter of plaintiff taking an appeal after agreeing to a remittitur or defendant taking an appeal after agreeing to an additur (Question C), most jurisdictions say no. The choice for plaintiffs is to accept the remittitur or decline it, and for defendants the choice is to accept an additur or decline it, but accepting the court's suggestion waives a right to appeal. See Donovan v. Penn Shipping Co., 429 U.S. 648, 649 (1977) ("plaintiff cannot appeal the propriety of a remittitur order to which he has agreed") (per curiam); *Baudanza*, supra, at 458, 464 ("a defendant accepting an additur order pursuant to rule 59(a), as well as a plaintiff accepting a remittitur order under the same rule, may not appeal from that order once judgment has entered"); Dalton v. Herold, 934 P.2d 649, 650 (Utah 1997) (defendant can refuse an additur and prefer a new trial, but he "may not appeal from an additur that he has accepted"). In some jurisdictions, however, plaintiff may accept a remitter under protest and appeal, and defendant may accept an additur under protest and appeal. See, e.g., Va. Code Ann. §8.01-383.1 (plaintiff who accepts remittitur "under protest" may appeal "as in other actions"). And many jurisdictions allow a consenting party to appeal if *the other side* appeals. See, e.g., Miss. Code Ann. §11-1-55 (if additur or remittitur is accepted "and the other party perfects a direct appeal, then the party accepting the additur or remittitur shall have the right to cross appeal for the purpose of reversing the action of the court in regard to the additur or remittitur"); Wash. Rev. Code §4.76.030 (similar).

4. How can courts second-guess juries where damages cannot be computed mathematically or measured with precision (Question D)? In deciding whether remittitur is appropriate, or additur, courts address this matter as though the question is whether the jury award is supported by the evidence. But usually the evidence is unquantified and unquantifiable, and it seems that the only way to arrive at a figure is to bring experience and common sense to bear and hope for the best. Difficulties such as these are acute not only in cases like the Problem, where the question is how to compensate someone for a lifetime disability, but in wrongful death cases (where the question is how to quantify the value of a life to a surviving spouse, parent, child, or sibling), but in everyday cases in which the question is how to compensate a person for pain and suffering stemming from physical injury or emotional trauma.

   (a) In search of other ways to describe situations where remittitur or additur might be appropriate, courts often comment that verdicts are entitled to deference and that the judge is not to act as a "thirteenth juror." The

decisions speak of verdicts so high or low that they "shock the conscience," and awards that are "disproportionate," and they cite indicators that the jury was motivated by passion and prejudice, or acted in haste or carelessly. See, e.g., Chilson v. Allstate Insurance Co., 979 A.2d 1078, 1984 (Del. 2009) (citing "extraordinary size" of award, "brevity of the deliberations" raising concern over "jury's diligence" and over "bias, passion, prejudice, or other improper motive") (approving remittitur); Earlington v. Anastasi, 976 A.2d 689, 697 (Conn. 2009) (relevant question is whether verdict is within limits of what is fair and reasonable or whether it shocks the conscience); Dilone v. Anchor Glass Container Corp., 755 A.2d 818 (R.I. 2000) (additur raises jury award for pain and suffering from $50,000 to $100,000; judge said jury's award "shocks my conscience" and was "grossly inadequate).

(b) Are verdicts in other cases helpful in gauging the reasonableness of an award? Compare Jasper v. H. Nizam, Inc., 764 N.W.2d 751, 772 (Iowa 2009) ("rough parameters of a range" of what is reasonable for pain and suffering can be gleaned from other like cases) with Wal-Mart Stores, Inc. v. Tucker, 120 S.W.3d 61, 69 (Ark. 2003) (cannot "rely on awards made in other cases in determining whether an award of damages is excessive," and such comparisons are unsatisfactory "not only because the degree of injury is rarely the same, but also because the dollar no longer has its prior value") ("more poignantly stated, our determination of whether a jury verdict is excessive is made on a case-by-case basis").

(c) Would it be sensible to approach these problems by setting a ratio that relates awards for "special damages" (mostly medical expenses or "economic damages" that can be objectively measured in various ways) and awards for pain and suffering (that are more subjective)? Some courts set such ratios: See Estate of Jones v. Phillips ex rel. Phillips, 992 So. 2d 1131, 1150 (Miss. 2008) (approving award of $5 million, "a large verdict" that was "just over eleven times special damages," court cites cases approving awards in ratios between 4 and 41 times special damages, and finds award reasonable) (denying request for remittitur).

(d) Should a verdict awarding recovery for medical expenses on account of injury but denying recovery for pain and suffering be viewed as inadequate as a matter of law? See Wichers v. Hatch, 745 A.2d 789 (Conn. 2000) (after minor accident, plaintiff did not go to doctor or seek medical help; he went home for lunch and returned to work that afternoon, but that evening consulted a chiropractor whom he had been seeing for seven years; jury awarded $3,377 for medical expenses and nothing for pain or suffering; court abandons older *per se* rule that award of economic damages with no award for noneconomic damages was inadequate as a matter of law; award should be "tested in light of the circumstances," and decision whether award is reasonable must be made "not on the assumption that the jury made a mistake, but, rather, on the supposition that the jury did exactly what it intended to do") (additur improper).

5. Deciding whether to set remittitur (or for that matter additur) at the *top* or at the *bottom* of the permissible range has itself proved challenging (Question E). Three different approaches are visible in the cases:

(a) Under a "maximum adjustment" approach, a court might set a remittitur at the *lowest* reasonable amount (smallest sum supported by evidence), and set an additur at the *highest* reasonable amount (highest sum supported by evidence). In favor of this approach, one might say that if defendant (in a remittitur situation) is entitled to another trial, the shortcut represented by the remittitur is consistent with this right only if plaintiff accepts a reduced sum that matches the best outcome a defendant could hope for in another trial. Similarly, one might say that if plaintiff (in an additur situation) is entitled to another trial, the shortcut represented by the additur is consistent with this right only if defendant agrees to pay an increased sum that matches the best outcome a plaintiff could hope for in another trial. What is the problem with this approach? Some older opinions endorse it. See Swanson v. Schultz, 270 N.W.43, 46 (Wis. 1936) ("to protect the party obliged to pay against a judge's assessment of damages," court should set remittitur at "the lowest amount" that the evidence could justify).

(b) Under a "minimum adjustment" approach, a court might set a remittitur at the *highest* reasonable amount (highest sum supported by evidence) and set an additur at the *lowest* reasonable amount (lowest sum supported by evidence). In favor of this approach, one might say that this use of these shortcuts is the best way to honor the original verdict, which (in the remittitur situation) conveys the message that the jury prefers the highest possible award, and (in the additur situation) conveys the message that the jury prefers the lowest possible award. What is the problem, perhaps more theoretical than real, with this approach? Some courts endorse this approach. See, e.g., Travis Lumber Co. v. Deichman, 2009 WL 1423542 (Ark. 2009) ("we allow a remittitur down to the most liberal amount that we would approve if the jury had returned a verdict"); *Jasper,* supra, at 751, 777 ("only the excess of the award is remitted," so remittitur should set award to the highest amount supported by the record); Jastram ex rel. Jastram v. Kruse, 962 A.2d 503, 512 (N.J. 2008) (set remittitur to highest figure that could be supported by the evidence); Fertile ex rel. Fertile v. St. Michael's Medical Center, 779 A.2d 1078, 1089 (N.J. 2001) ("remitting the award to the highest figure that could be supported by the evidence is the most analytically solid approach"); Haynes v. Golub Corp., 692 A.2d 377, 384 (Vt. 1997) ("size of the remittitur is the amount needed to eliminate the excess damages").

(c) Given the problems presented by the maximum and minimum approaches, would it be better just to "cut the baby in half" by setting the amount (either remittitur or additur) somewhere in the middle of the permissible range? Does this approach nod adequately in the direction of the party whose entitlement to another trial may be denied if the other side accepts what the court puts out there, while also respecting the original verdict by not going to the opposite extreme? See Alfano v. Insurance Center of Torrington,

525 A.2d 1338, 1342 (Conn. 1987) (amount of remittitur "rests largely within the discretion of the trial court"); D'Annolfo v. Stoneham Housing Authority, 378 N.E.2d 971, 979 (Mass. 1978) (judge need not use remittitur to take away "only so much of the amount of the verdict as exceeds the maximum," and can remit as much of the damages as the court considers excessive).

6. Consider these attempts to apply the remittitur device in connection with compensation for mental anguish: Besler v. Board of Education of West Windsor-Plainsboro Regional School District, 993 A.2d 805, 826 (N.J. 2010) (in suit against basketball coach for verbally harassing high school girl on team, award of $100,000 to her father was excessive; purpose was to compensate for mental anguish when he was not allowed to speak at school board meeting; such high damages for emotional distress "must be based on more than *de minimis* mental anguish, or fleeting embarrassment, or mere shock and bewilderment") (father was "deeply upset and humiliated," but award is "so clearly excessive that it constitutes 'a miscarriage of justice'" likely resulting from "evidential spillover" from daughter's case); *Jasper*, supra, at 751, 772 (Iowa 2009) (damages from pain and suffering are by nature "highly subjective" and cannot be "easily calculated in economic terms," but award "is not without boundaries," and can be "limited to a reasonable range" derived from evidence; in wrongful discharge suits, "upper range of emotional-distress damages increases as the nature of the wrongful conduct ... becomes more egregious, and the emotional distress ... becomes more severe and persistent," and length of employment, compatibility of worker in job, age, and employment skills, and span of time needed to find another job relate to amount of damages) (trial court to offer remittitur reducing recovery from $100,000 to $50,000); Kmart Corp. v. Kyles, 723 So. 2d 572, 578 (Ala. 1998) (authorizing "stricter scrutiny" of award for mental anguish where victim offers "little or no direct evidence" of degree of suffering; plaintiff did not testify, in third trial of claim of malicious prosecution for shoplifting, because cross-examination in earlier trials had revealed arrest and incarceration; there she testified that she "went crazy" and was "too embarrassed to shop" and feared being accused again of shoplifting and attempted suicide and sought care in psychiatric hospital) (ordering court to offer plaintiff remittitur reducing $90,000 award to $15,000, and reducing compensatory damages from $100,000 to $15,000).

7. How does one measure damages for wrongful death? Consider Hyrcza v. West Penn Allegheny Health System, Inc., 978 A.2d 961, 980 (Pa. Super. 2009) (approving more than $7 million for death of 60-year-old woman on basis of testimony on her "enormous contribution" to lives of seven children and husband) (verdict was "admittedly large," but it was a "very tragic case" in which decedent suffered "significant pain and suffering" for several days while dying in hospital).

8. Would it be better to approach the subject of controlling jury excesses by statute? Unsatisfied with judicial attempts to limit the generosity of juries with respect to noneconomic damages, many states enacted statutory damage caps. Some courts, however, have decided that this approach is unconstitutional because the statutes infringe on the judicial function and the right to a jury trial. See Atlanta Oculoplastic Surgery, P.C. v. Nestlehutt, 691 S.E.2d 218, 224 (Ga. 2010) (statute capping noneconomic damages at $350,000 violates state constitutional right to jury trial; cap differs from remittitur, which is "a corollary of the courts' constitutionally derived authority to grant new trials"); Lebron v. Gottlieb Memorial Hospital, 930 N.E.2d 895 (Ill. 2010) (statute capping noneconomic damages in malpractice suits at $1 million violates separation of powers clause in state constitution). Others courts have upheld them. See Arbino v. Johnson & Johnson, 880 N.E.2d 420 (Ohio 2007) (on certified question from federal court, stating that statutory cap on recovery for noneconomic damages is constitutional); Phillips v. Mirac, Inc., 685 N.W.2d 174 (Mich. 2004) (approving statutory damage cap for personal injury or death in suits against car rental companies).

9. Are there times when remittitur is not the right response to a jury award that seems excessive? See *Chilson*, supra, at 1078, 1084 ("in minutes" jury awarded $2 million verdict that "shocked the trial court's conscience," as such an award "may indicate jury bias, passion, prejudice, or some other improper motive," in which remittitur is inadequate remedy) (new trial on all issues); Pellicer ex rel. Pellicer v. St. Barnabas Hospital, 974 A.2d 1070 (N.J. 2009) (setting aside verdict against hospital and medical providers for $71 million, including $50 million for pain and suffering, after four-month-old infant with spina bifida was accidentally disconnected from respirator with resulting severe brain damage; ordinarily, reviewing court relies on trial courts and their "feel of the case," but "when the magnitude of the verdict is 'historic' or enormous," appellate court must engage in "careful and searching review") (verdict "far exceeded even plaintiffs' counsel's time-unit argument, with its 'thirty-nine-million minutes' appeal"; new trial on liability and damages); Gilbert v. DaimlerChrysler Corp., 685 N.W.2d 391, 401-402 (Mich. 2004) (award of $21 million, mostly for emotional distress, was "the largest amount ever awarded for a single-plaintiff sexual harassment claim," 70 times larger than could be won under federal law; plaintiff was made the object of an obscene cartoon by name in a depiction of her performing a lewd act on named coworker; plaintiffs who experience harassment "in its most aggressive form—unwanted touching and persistent, predatory sexual advances" have received "far less in compensatory damages," and this verdict exceeded "by leaps and bounds" verdicts in similar cases) (remanding for new trial).

10. Like remittitur, additur (although deployed far less often) can have a significant effect. See *Baudanza*, supra, at 458, 466 (driver injured in accident when defendant's truck struck his car in intersection; verdict of $193,273 matched plaintiff's medical bills; judge denied new trial motion on condition that defendant consent to additur of $200,000 for pain and suffering, which was reasonable in light of "extensive and painful injuries"); Pucket v. Verska, 158 P.3d 937 (in malpractice case, jury awarded $92,720 in economic damages and $50,000 in noneconomic damages; court could grant additur raising economic damages to $289,971 and noneconomic damages to $400,000); Dilone v. Anchor Glass Container Corp., 755 A.2d 818 (R.I. 2000) (where jury returned verdict of $25,000 for medical expenses and $50,000 for pain and suffering, after plaintiff suffered lacerations in right wrist, causing loss of feeling in thumb, index finger, middle finger, and half of ring finger, leading to three surgeries and extensive therapy and "permanent impairment rating of thirty-nine percent of the upper extremity, or twenty-three percent whole body impairment," approving additur of $100,000 for pain and suffering). See also Reid v. Hindt, 976 A.2d 125, 131 (Del. 2009) (*defendant* moved for additur in amount of $2,500 after plaintiff won verdict indicating liability but awarding no damages; court *rejects* claim by plaintiff that she should be asked whether she agrees; additur gave her more than judgment on verdict). Additur is sometimes found inappropriate. See, e.g., Columbus Regional Healthcare Systems v. Henderson, 652 S.E.2d 522, 524-525 (Ga. 2007) (jury award of no damages on one claim may indicate "inconsistent or contradictory" verdict, in which case new trial may be appropriate, but additur would substitute court's finding for jury's and add something not in verdict); Smedberg v. Detlef's Custodial Service, Inc., 940 A.2d 674, 677 n.2 (Vt. 2007) (additur not appropriate where verdict is "internally inconsistent or suggests a compromise").

3. A Procedural Jungle: Combined Motions Under FRCP 50 and 59

At the end of a jury trial when the evidence is in, it is common for one or both parties to seek judgment as a matter of law. Defendants almost always make such motions—plaintiffs make them less often—and if the court denies the motion, submits the case to the jury, and enters judgment on the verdict, the losing party often *renews* the motion for judgment as a matter of law.

Recall that one can seek judgment as a matter of law after the verdict has been returned (and judgment entered on it) *only if* one previously sought judgment as a matter of law at the close of the evidence. On the timing of these motions, FRCP 50 sets limits: The initial motion must be made after the other side "has been fully heard," see FRCP 50(a)(1), and "before the case is submitted to the jury," see FRCP 50(a)(2). Rule 50 contemplates not only the possibility of entering *judgment* as a matter of law, but the possibility of simply "resolv[ing]" an issue against one party or another, see FRCP 50(a)(1)(A).

The renewed motion, if the first motion is denied, must be made "no later than 28 days after the entry of judgment" or (if the motion takes up an issue that was not "decided by a verdict") "no later than 28 days after the jury was discharged." See FRCP 59(b).

In passing, it should be noted that there is a "technical" reason to require a pre-verdict motion for judgment as a matter of law as a *precondition* for making a post-verdict motion, and a functional reason as well. The "technical" reason, at least in the federal system, is that the Supreme Court held in an early case that the directed verdict (predecessor of JMAL) was unconstitutional under the Seventh Amendment because it was unknown at common law. See Slocum v. New York Life Ins. Co., 228 U.S. 364 (1913). Years later, the Court decided that if a court *reserved its ruling* on a pre-verdict motion for a directed verdict, it could enter judgment for the movant after the jury returned its verdict. See Baltimore & Carolina Line, Inc. v. Redman, 295 U.S. 654 (1935). The later-adopted Rule 50(b) states that a court that *denies* a pre-verdict JMAL motion "is considered to have submitted" the case to the jury "subject to the court's later deciding the legal questions raised by the motion," which means *Slocum* is effectively eclipsed, but the pre-verdict motion is crucial in preserving the right to a post-verdict JMAL.

The *functional* reason to require a pre-verdict motion is that *if* the problem is that the party opposing the motion has neglected to prove some point critical to her case, the court can let her reopen and present the missing proof. Thus a plaintiff who sues a defendant for the negligent accident caused by the driver of a company truck, if she forgets to prove that the driver worked for the defendant and was acting within the scope of her employment, may be allowed to reopen and prove these points (if she has the evidence). If the matter arises for the first time after the verdict is entered, it is too late for such a cure.

It is not only judgment as a matter of law that the verdict loser seeks after judgment has been entered on the verdict, but also a *new trial*. This double-barreled effort to seek relief is contemplated in FRCP 50, which addresses the procedural complexities of these combined motions in detail. Read FRCP 50 all the way through.

■ PROBLEM 12-C. "I Had to Stop for Those Sheep!"

Westbound on I-70 in the Colorado Rockies close to Georgetown, Colleen McCallum slowed her Chevrolet Malibu from a speed of 65 miles per hour to a speed of 10 miles per hour as she saw what turned out to be six bighorn sheep in the roadway ahead. At this point, I-70 is a four-lane divided highway, and westbound travel climbs toward a steep grade rising above Georgetown en route to Silver Plume, Dillon, Vail, and points west. As McCallum slowed, she was struck from behind by a Subaru Outback driven by Donald Hass, also driving westbound. "I had to stop for those sheep," McCallum later complains to the highway patrolman, "and that guy just plowed into the back of my car."

McCallum sues Hass in state district court in Denver, seeking recovery for loss of her car (the accident "totaled" the Malibu) and for personal injuries and pain and suffering. Hass (a citizen of Kansas) removes the suit to Federal District Court on the basis of diversity, and files an answer and counterclaim seeking recovery for his own property loss (his Outback was totaled too) and personal injuries.

During her case-in-chief, McCallum testifies that she slowed for the bighorn sheep that were in the right-hand lane, and she did not move to the left-hand passing lane because "a big 18-wheeler in the passing lane was gaining fast on me." On cross-examination by counsel for Hass, McCallum agrees that "I decelerated quickly because I could see that the animals were moving slowly and I wasn't at all sure that they'd get out of my way."

During the defense case, Hass testified that he had been traveling in the left-hand passing lane just before the accident, and was behind a Watkins Freight Carrier 18-wheel truck/trailer rig when a car behind him blinked its lights indicating a desire to pass. Hass pulled into the right-hand lane, and then saw what turned out to be McCallum's car "almost stopped dead" in front of him. Hass braked sharply but couldn't stop before hitting McCallum's car. Eyewitness accounts, including statements by the driver of the Watkins truck and drivers of two cars that were behind Hass on the highway, corroborate the accounts of McCallum and Hass. So does the accident report prepared by a highway patrol officer who arrived minutes after the accident.

At the close of the evidence, McCallum moved for judgment as a matter of law on liability, medical specials, and replacement value of the Malibu (which would leave, for the jury to decide, only damages for her pain and suffering). Her lawyer argues thus: "There is no dispute about the cause of this accident, or about medical specials or replacement cost of the Malibu. On the issue of liability, we have a case of negligence *per se*: Mr. Hass struck my client from behind, which means he was too close when he changed lanes or was going too fast. That is negligence pure and simple, and there is nothing for a jury to decide. A following vehicle must keep a safe distance behind a lead vehicle and travel at a safe speed, and the fact that Mr. Hass could not stop when he moved from the passing lane back into the right-hand lane means he was going too fast or entered the lane too close to my client's car. The accident was his fault, and no reasonable jury could find otherwise."

"Not so," replies counsel for Hass, "my client was abiding by the rules of the road, not speeding or doing anything improper, and he could not have expected to encounter an almost-stopped vehicle when he returned from the passing lane to the right-hand lane to let another motorist by. There is no evidence that my client was negligent, and indeed Ms. McCallum created the dangerous condition that led to the accident by slowing almost to a stop in the right-hand lane. She should have pulled off to the side of the road, and didn't, and the accident was her fault. At least the question must go to the jury."

The court denies plaintiff's motion, and submits the case to the jury, telling it to determine causation and degree of fault for each driver and, if it finds that one of the two is solely at fault or more at fault than the other, to determine the amount of damages for the party without fault or with lesser fault. The jury finds that McCallum was 40 percent at fault and that Hass was 60 percent at fault. The verdict states that McCallum suffered $12,000 in property damages (replacement value of the Malibu), $55,600 in medical specials, and $140,000 in pain and suffering, which comes to a total of $207,600. The court enters judgment favoring McCallum in accord with the verdict for $124,560 (reducing the jury award to 60 percent of the totals).

In timely fashion, Colleen McCallum renews her motion for judgment as a matter of law, and in the alternative she asks the court to grant a new trial.

(A) What standard must McCallum satisfy in order to win judgment as a matter of law? What standard must she satisfy to win a new trial? What arguments does she make to satisfy these standards?

(B) In opposing McCallum's motions, Hass defends the decision to give the case to the jury: How does he argue this point? How does he oppose McCallum's request for a new trial?

(C) Suppose that the judge denies both motions and allows judgment on the verdict to stand. McCallum can appeal, arguing that the court erred and should have awarded the JMAL or a new trial. Can an appellate court award the JMAL for McCallum?

(D) Suppose again that the judge denies both motions and McCallum takes an appeal from the judgment on the jury verdict. Hass will again argue (as he did in opposing McCallum's motions before the trial judge, in Question B) that giving the case to the jury was right and a new trial is not appropriate. Can Hass *also* seek a new trial, in case the appellate court thinks McCallum should have judgment as a matter of law for the full $207,640?

(E) Suppose now that the trial judge decides that McCallum is right after all, that running into someone from behind is negligence *per se*, and that McCallum is entitled to her full damages as a matter of law. The judge sets aside the judgment on the verdict and enters a JMAL for McCallum in the unreduced amount of $207,600. Now what happens to McCallum's alternative motion for a new trial?

(F) Suppose once again that the trial judge enters JMAL for McCallum in the unreduced amount of $207,600, and *denies* McCallum's alternative motion for a new trial. *Hass* can take an appeal from the JMAL. Again he will defend the judgment on the verdict, and the trial court's original rulings on McCallum's motion. What can McCallum do? Can she cross-appeal and urge the appellate court to grant a new trial in case it sets aside the JMAL?

■ NOTES ON COMBINED MOTIONS FOR JMAL AND NEW TRIAL

1. On the standard for judgment as a matter of law (Question A), recall the *Galloway* case. In *Galloway,* the defendant was the moving party. In Problem 12C, plaintiff is the moving party. Recall from *Galloway* that a directed verdict motion (now JMAL) tests the "sufficiency" of the evidence. When defendant makes the motion, she usually argues that there is not sufficient evidence on which a jury could base a verdict for the plaintiff. When plaintiff makes the motion, the argument is still about "sufficiency," but from the opposite side. There is not "sufficient" evidence to justify a verdict for the defendant, or to put it more positively, the evidence favoring the plaintiff is so strong—what we have called "cogent and compelling"—that no reasonable jury could reject it. While "sufficiency" is an accepted term, and courts are accustomed to appraising evidence in reaching conclusions that it is either sufficient (so the case goes to the jury) or insufficient (so JMAL is appropriate), there is no uniform term for evidence that is so strong that a reasonable jury must accept it. "Cogent and compelling" is as good as any, and is the term we have used to carry that meaning.

2. The combined motions for JMAL and new trial make two related arguments. First, there is "insufficient evidence" to justify a verdict for Donald Hass, or (to put it the other way) the evidence favoring McCallum is "cogent and compelling." Second, a verdict for Hass is "against the weight of the evidence." In a sense, the two arguments are variations on a theme: If the evidence is *insufficient* to justify a verdict for Hass (or one that reduces McCallum's recovery), then a verdict for Hass (or one that reduces McCallum's recovery) must be *against the weight* of the evidence.

3. The job of the party opposing alternative motions for JMAL or a new trial is, in one sense, made easier by the fact that the jury has rejected the moving party's position (Question B). The jury thought McCallum was partly responsible for what happened, and it is this view that Hass defends. Hass argues that there *is* enough evidence to permit a jury to find as it did, that McCallum's proof is *not* "cogent and compelling," and that the evidence supports the conclusion that the jury reached. And Hass argues that there is no reason for a new trial: The verdict is not "against the weight of the evidence."

4. When a verdict loser—or in McCallum's case the party dissatisfied with a verdict in the belief that it should have been more favorable, as a matter of law—appeals from a judgment after the trial court denies its motion for a JMAL, or a new trial, an appellate court can, if it agrees with appellant, order entry of judgment as a matter of law itself (Question C). See Neely v. Martin K. Eby Construction Co., 386 U.S. 317, 321-322 (1967) ("there is no greater restriction on the province of the jury when an appellate court enters [JMAL] than when a trial court does," hence "no constitutional bar," and courts of appeal can take this step). Indeed, courts of appeal commonly say that they review a grant or denial of a motion for JMAL *de novo,* meaning that it is a pure matter of law and the trial court's opinion is not entitled to deference. See, e.g., Howard v. Missouri Bone and Joint Center, Inc., 615 F.3d 991, 995 (8th Cir. 2010) ("we review de novo the district court's denial of a motion for judgment as a matter of law"); Anaya-Burgos v. Lasalvia-Prisco, 607 F.3d 269, 274 (1st Cir. 2010) (similar).

5. A judge's decision to grant or deny a new trial motion, where the moving party argues that a verdict is against the weight of the evidence, is reviewed under a highly deferential "abuse of discretion" standard. Reviewing a decision *denying* a motion for a new trial has always seemed more problematic than reviewing a decision *granting* a new trial, if only because the former could lead to an appellate directive throwing out a jury verdict—a directive from a court that did not hear the testimony or see the witnesses. Finally, in 1996 the Court decided that an appellate court *can,* consistent with the Seventh Amendment, order a new trial where the trial judge has denied such a motion. See Gasperini v. Center for Humanities, Inc., 518 U.S. 415, 435 (1996) (in connection with motion seeking new trial because verdict is excessive, "appellate review for abuse of discretion is reconcilable with the Seventh Amendment as a control necessary and proper to the fair administration of justice") (you read *Gasperini* in Chapter 6A6 on the role of state law in defining what is excessive in diversity cases). Still, it is rare to find appellate courts ordering new trials on such grounds when the trial court has denied such motions. Indeed, courts still sometimes say that rulings on such motions are unreviewable, and it is clear that trial judges can be reversed only for abuse of discretion. See, e.g., Jocks v. Tavernier, 316 F.3d 128, 137 (2d Cir. 2003) (court's decision that verdict is not against the weight of the evidence "is not reviewable on appeal because of Seventh Amendment concerns"); Dailey v. Societe Generale, 108 F.3d 451, 458 (2d Cir. 1997) (where district court denies motion for a new trial on ground that verdict is against the weight of the evidence, "such a ruling is not reviewable on appeal").

6. Rule 50 treats in detail the situation presented by the Problem, describing possibilities that arise in ruling on alternative motions for JMAL or new trial. If the judge denies McCallum's motion for JMAL, then enters judgment on the verdict (for a sum that McCallum considers too small because it was reduced to account for her supposed negligence in stopping for the bighorn sheep), McCallum can appeal from the judgment on the jury verdict. In this situation, FRCP 50(e) states that the "prevailing party," meaning the verdict winner (or the party defending the verdict, who is Hass in the Problem) can "assert grounds entitling it to a new trial" if the appellate court concludes that the JMAL should have been granted (Question D). Thus Hass can ask the appellate court, even if it thinks McCallum should have won judgment as a matter of law, to order a new trial instead. See, e.g., Cone v. West Virginia Pulp & Paper Co., 330 U.S. 212, 214 (1947) (circumstances "might lead the trial court to believe that a new trial rather than a final termination of the trial stage of the controversy would better serve the ends of justice").

(a) Does the fact that the jury put part of the blame on McCallum, favoring Hass to that extent and returning a verdict that Hass now defends, give force to his argument that a new trial is preferable to judgment in McCallum's favor for all she seeks? Does it make sense, once a case has been tried and the jury has returned a verdict, to give the verdict winner a second chance to "mend his hold" on the verdict, perhaps by presenting more evidence (or doing a better job) in a second trial?

(b) Does it make sense for an *appellate court* to rule, in the first instance, on a new trial request by verdict winner (in our case Hass, as the party defending the verdict as preferable to the JMAL)? In *Neely,* the Court recognized that a reviewing court might prefer to remand so the trial court could consider this request first, and in the *Iacurci* case a year later the Court reinforced this idea. See *Neely,* supra, at 317, 323-324 (appellate court "may prefer that the trial judge pass first upon the appellee's new trial suggestion"); Iacurci v. Lummus Co., 387 U.S. 86, 88 (1967) (Court of Appeals erred in directing entry of JMAL for defense; the case "should have been remanded to the trial judge, who was in the best position to pass upon the question of [plaintiff's right to a] new trial in light of the evidence, his charge to the jury, and the jury's verdict and interrogatory answers"). In *Iacurci,* the jury had answered only one of five questions favorably to plaintiff, and had not replied to the other four, which were read as negative findings. Thirty years later, the Court backed away from *Iacurci,* holding that the appellate court could direct entry of JMAL for the defendant, in a case in which the reviewing court held that the trial judge erred in admitting expert testimony for plaintiff because it did not satisfy the standard for scientific evidence. See Weisgram v. Marley Co., 528 U.S. 440, 455-457 (2000) (parties understood standard for scientific evidence, so it is "implausible to suggest" that they would "initially present less than their best expert evidence" and plaintiff "offered no specific grounds for a new trial") (appellate courts may enter JMAL where, "on excision of testimony erroneously admitted, there remains insufficient evidence to support the jury's verdict"). See also Gasser v. District of Columbia, 442 U.S. 758, 766 (D.C. Cir. 2006) (plaintiff was on notice before close of evidence that his expert's testimony on alleged disabilities was insufficient) (directing JMAL for defense and not remanding to consider plaintiff's new trial request).

(c) The question whether a reviewing court may in the first instance deny a motion for a new trial by the verdict winner (or one like Hass, who defends the verdict) is a vexing one. In a still later case, the Court again implied that trial courts should resolve such matters first. See Unitherm Food Systems, Inc. v. Swift-Eckrich, Inc., 546 U.S. 394 (2006) (where defendant made pre-verdict JMAL motion but *failed* to renew motion after trial,

appellate court could not award JMAL; deciding between JMAL and new trial for verdict winner calls first for an appraisal by the judge "who saw and heard the witnesses and has the feel of the case").

7. If the judge, after sending the case to the jury and then receiving a verdict that discounts McCallum's recovery, *agrees* with McCallum when she renews her JMAL motion, what should the judge do about McCallum's alternative motion for a new trial (Question E)? Rule 50(c)(1) says that in this situation the judge "must also conditionally rule" on her new trial motion. What does this provision mean, and why it in the Rule? Hint: If the trial court awards judgment as a matter of law and the other side appeals and the reviewing court *reverses* what the trial judge did, would the moving party likely want a new trial or prefer to restore the verdict? If the judge believes, as he would if he entered judgment for McCallum as a matter of law, that the evidence and the law support only one reasonable result, wouldn't the judge also think that what the jury did was against the weight of the evidence, hence that a new trial should be awarded? *Usually,* courts that grant JMAL *also* grant the alternative new trial motion, although not always. Rule 50(c)(1) says "granting the motion for a new trial" does not affect the "finality" of the JMAL, which means that the party disadvantaged by the JMAL (Hass, in the Problem) can appeal. Rule 50(c)(2) goes on to say that if the reviewing court reverses the JMAL, "the new trial must proceed unless the appellate court orders otherwise." See also *Neely,* supra, at 317, 323 (FRCP 50 contemplates that the appellate court "will review on appeal both the grant of [JMAL] and, if necessary, the trial court's conditional disposition of the motion for a new trial," which "necessarily includes" power in the appellate court "to grant or deny a new trial in appropriate cases"). As examined in note 8, below, grants or denials of new trial motions, when the ground is that the verdict is against the weight of the evidence, are *almost* unreviewable, which is to say that almost always the trial court's decision on this point is affirmed.

8. If the trial court enters JMAL for McCallum but denies the alternative new trial motion and Hass appeals, McCallum may want to ask the reviewing court to grant a new trial (Question F). In the appeal, Hass will argue that giving the case to the jury was the right thing to do, and that the verdict is not against the weight of the evidence. McCallum must worry about the possibility that the reviewing court will conclude that the JMAL was entered in error and will order the trial judge to enter judgment on the verdict (for the reduced sum). In that case, McCallum might prefer to have a new trial, in which she could hope to convince a new jury that she was not at fault, or at least that her fault was 10 percent or 20 percent rather than 40 percent. FRCP 50(c)(2) deals with this situation, and provides that McCallum as "appellee" may "assert error" in the judge's ruling that denied her new trial motion.

(a) Why might a trial court *grant* a JMAL but *deny* the new trial motion made by the party who is unhappy with the verdict—in effect, giving the moving party the larger victory (JMAL) while *refusing* the smaller victory

(a new trial)? In most cases, a court that awards a JMAL also does grant the new trial motion—again, if the court thinks there is "insufficient evidence" to support what the jury did, or that the evidence for doing something else is "cogent and compelling," then ordinarily the trial court also thinks that what the jury did is "against the weight of the evidence," so a new trial is warranted.

(b) Sometimes, however, questions raised by the alternative motions for JMAL or a new trial involve mixed legal and factual issues. In the Problem, the trial judge might think "there is no way that the driver of a lead car struck from behind can be negligent, regardless what she does." If that becomes the basis for the JMAL, the judge might also think, "if the reviewing court decides that I'm wrong, and that indeed the driver of the lead car *can* be negligent, then there's nothing wrong with the verdict." Then the appropriate thing, from the judge's perspective, is to *grant* the JMAL and *deny* the alternative new trial motion.

(c) The *reviewing* court, however, might think "the judge was wrong, and the lead driver *can* be partly at fault, but in this case 40 percent is excessive, given the evidence." Hence the JMAL must be thrown out, but plaintiff should have another chance at a trial in which the jury assigns a lower level of fault to her.

4. New Trial Motions Based on Misconduct by Jurors (and Sometimes Others)

Once a jury has rendered its verdict, losing parties sometimes conclude that their loss may have been caused by misbehavior on the part of jurors, and sometimes by other persons connected with the trial—court personnel, for example, like the bailiff or even the judge, or witnesses, or the opposing party.

It is easy to imagine things that jurors might do that should not happen during deliberations: Suppose it turns out that a jury decides not to award recovery to a plaintiff because "it will only drive up insurance rates for everyone," or (to take a very different possibility) a jury decides to award recovery because "insurance will pay for it anyhow." Or suppose a jury agrees that everyone will vote the way a majority votes, "just so we don't have to come back tomorrow" (committing to a verdict that fewer than all, or fewer than the required number, agree to). What if a juror visits an accident scene and then reports to the jury what the scene looks like?

It has long been the rule that many forms of jury misbehavior are (and should be) out of bounds when it comes to challenging a verdict. Thus FRE 606(b) bars the use of affidavits or testimony by jurors on "any matter or statement occurring . . . during . . . deliberations," and also bars juror testimony or affidavits to show "the effect of anything" on the mind of any juror or to show juror's "mental processes," *but* juror testimony or affidavits *may be used* to show (1) "extraneous prejudicial information" improperly brought to the jury's attention, (2) "outside influence" improperly brought to bear on any juror, or (3) "a mistake in entering the verdict onto the verdict form." Consider these limits and exceptions in connection with the following problem.

William Murray, First Earl of Mansfield (1705-1793)

Like much American law, the rule expressed in FRE 606(b) came here from England. It emerged from a laconic ruling in 1785 by the Court of King's Bench, where Lord Mansfield said a court "cannot receive" affidavits by jurors alleging that the jury, "being divided in their opinion, tossed up," in reaching a verdict for the plaintiff (a reference to a coin toss or similar resort to chance). Such affidavits reveal conduct by jurors amounting to "a very high misdemeanor," so a court must derive its knowledge of what happened in the jury room "from some other source" (like one who saw the transaction "through a window"). See Vaise v. Delaval, 99 E.R. 944 (King's Bench 1785). The Supreme Court picked up this rule in Dorr v. Pacific Ins. Co., 20 U.S. 581, 604 (1822) (juror affidavits "cannot be admitted to impeach [a] verdict") (citing *Vaise*). The rule was captured in a broader Latin expression "allegans suam turpitudibnem non est audiendus" (loosely, "one may not be heard to allege one's own misbehavior"), see Underhill v. Van Cortlandt, 2 Johns Ch. 339 (N.Y. 1817). This expression too is associated with Lord Mansfield, who employed a similar idea in inventing another principle that made its way into American law—a spouse cannot deny the legitimacy of a child born during the marriage. See Scanlon v. Walshe, 31 A.498 (Md. 1895), tracing statutory presumption of legitimacy to Lord Mansfield in Goodright v. Moss, 98 E.R. 1257 (Kings Bench 1777) ("it is a rule, founded in decency, morality, and policy, that they shall not be permitted to say after marriage, that they have had no connection, and therefore that the offspring is spurious"). We have adopted both these principles, but the underlying reasons have changed: The Notes after Problem 12-D raise the question why we don't admit juror affidavits. What modern reasons might we give in support of the second rule? Lord Mansfield is also credited with a pathbreaking ruling that limited slave trafficking in England. See Somersett's Case, 20 How. St. Tr. 1 (1772).

■ PROBLEM 12-D. "I Think It Was His Parents' Fault"

In June 2010, 14-year-old Jeffrey Morgan was operating a tractor-style home lawnmower made by the LawnCare Company. On request by his father, Irving Morgan, who paid Jeffrey $50 for performing this household chore every week during the summer, Jeffrey was mowing the large 4,000-square-foot rectangular lawn surrounding their home in Topeka, Kansas. Jeffrey had previously operated this mower for some 30 hours over 2 years.

On the occasion in question, ten-year-old Tom Green was riding on the mower with Jeffrey, standing on the left foot platform and holding on to the back of the seat and to the hood of the engine to keep his balance. The Morgans and the Greens were next-door neighbors, and at the time Tamira Green was at home, although she had not heard the sound of the lawnmower and did not know that Jeffrey was mowing the Morgan's lawn. Jeffrey was watching the left front wheel of the mower in order to keep it aligned with the edge of the uncut grass when he saw out of the corner of his eye Tom's four-year-old brother David Green, who was playing with Jeffrey's younger brother and sister in an area of the Morgan yard with a swing set and inflatable pool.

Jeffrey saw that David was ten feet in front of the mower in the cut section of grass retrieving an inflatable ball that had rolled away from the play area. Jeffrey shouted "watch out" in hope of getting David to change directions and to warn Tom to brace himself, immediately released the power lever and applied the brake, and also turned the mower sharply to the right. The left front wheel of the mower went over David's foot, however, and he fell away from the mower and kicked at it, but in the process both feet went beneath the mower shield and came into contact with the rotating blades, severely injuring both his feet.

On David's behalf, his parents George and Tamira Green sued LawnCare, alleging that a defect in design prevented Jeffrey from being able to stop the mower in time and that the blade shield was inadequate to protect bystanders from the kind of accident that happened here. LawnCare maintained that the accident resulted from the negligence of Jeffrey Morgan, Tom Green, Tamira Green, and Irving Morgan.

The case went to trial, and members of the venire were asked on *voir dire* whether "they, or anyone in their immediate families, had sustained any serious injury at home or on the farm or at work that had resulted in disability or prolonged pain and suffering." Only one member raised his hand, and he was eventually excused after additional questioning.

After several hours of deliberation, the jury returned a verdict that David Green had sustained damages in the amount of $14,000, and assigned responsibility for the accident as follows: 0 percent on LawnCare, 20 percent on Jeffrey Morgan, 45 percent on Irving Morgan, and 35 percent on Tamira Green. In accord with the verdict, the judge entered judgment that David should recover nothing.

Plaintiff's lawyer was shocked by the low verdict. On inquiry, he received the following information relating to the jury:

(A) From his client George Green (father of David and Tom), he learned that Juror 1 (Don Payton, who served as foreman), had a son who had been injured by an exploding truck tire, resulting in long convalescence and disfigurement in his torso.

(B) Juror 2 said everyone agreed that "finding liability in cases like this would only encourage lawyers to bring suits and drive up the costs of products for everyone because a few fools hurt themselves, and that was the basis of the verdict."

(C) Juror 3 said that during deliberations another juror told everyone that "he had a friend who owns a LawnCare mower," that Juror 3 had borrowed it twice when his mower was in the shop, and "the design of the LawnCare is about as safe as you could make it," and "you just can't make these things so safe that people won't get hurt if they behave really stupidly."

(D) Juror 4 said "every day the jury ordered and drank four pitchers of beer at lunch," and three jurors "passed out joints, and smoked them too."

(E) Juror 5 said that during deliberations the jury "discussed insurance" and agreed that plaintiff "probably recovered his medical costs from insurance already," and that defendant "probably carried insurance that would cover liability."

(F) Juror 6 and 7 said that after several hours of discussion that "wasn't getting anywhere," they agreed that each would "write down on a slip of paper the amount we thought plaintiff should recover, and then just divide by 12," and "that's how we came out with $14,000 in damages.

Plaintiff moves for a new trial. He argues that Don Payton's failure to disclose on *voir dire* the injury suffered by his son amounted to a lie. He argues as well that the points to which the other jurors would testify, described in items B-F above, constitute "jury misconduct that is serious and prejudicial." Should plaintiff be allowed to establish these points, and do they entitle him to a new trial?

■ NOTES ON SETTING ASIDE VERDICTS FOR MISCONDUCT

1. Why should we limit juror testimony or affidavits as FRE 606(b) does? See Mueller & Kirkpatrick, Evidence §6.10 (5th ed. 2012) (restrictions on impeaching verdicts rest on four grounds; first, "to keep jurors from being harassed by the losing party in efforts to snatch victory from the jaws of defeat by turning up facts that might show misconduct serious enough to set aside the verdict"; second, "to guard the privacy of deliberations in the interest of encouraging full and frank discussions"; third, to avoid undermining finality of verdicts; fourth, to avoid tempting jurors into "tampering with the process" by persuading those who were reluctant to agree that their own consent "rested on false or impermissible considerations"). Do these considerations justify the rule?

2. Failing to disclose material information when asked on *voir dire* can entitle the losing litigant to a new trial. See Grundy v. Dhillon, 900 N.E.2d 153 (Ohio 2008). Consider this point in connection with the affidavit of George Green as proof that Don Payton, jury foreman, had a son who suffered the injury described above.

(a) One question raised by this proof is whether it is even covered by FRE 606(b). Notice that FRE 606(b) bars proof by juror testimony or affidavit, and the literal language does *not* bar proof by means of statements by outsiders based on other sources of information.

(b) Another question is whether FRE 606(b) bars proof that a juror lied on *voir dire*. Rule 606(b) seems to apply to proving matters or statements occurring "during deliberations." Payton's response on *voir dire* occurred *before* deliberations began. Most courts say that FRE 606(b) does *not* bar proof that a juror did not respond truthfully on *voir dire*. See Levinger v. Mercy Medical Center, Nampa, 75 P.3d 1202, 1207 (Idaho 2003) (state counterpart to FRE 606 does not bar juror affidavits revealing dishonesty on *voir dire*) (but motion did not identify basis for claiming false answer or show that juror could have been removed for cause).

(c) A third question is whether it should matter that a juror, or someone in his immediate family, sustained a serious injury in an accident that led to disability or prolonged pain. Is it a problem that such a juror may develop an "attitude" toward the legal system, or makers of products, or toward healthcare providers that would undetectably infect his capacity to evaluate claims by others arising out of such accidents? Consider these comments by the Supreme Court in a similar case:

> This Court has long held that "'[a litigant] is entitled to a fair trial but not a perfect one,' for there are no perfect trials." Brown v. United States, 411 U.S. 223, 231-232 (1973), quoting Bruton v. United States, 391 U.S. 123, 135 (1968), and Lutwak v. United States, 344 U.S. 604, 619 (1953). Trials are costly, not only for the parties, but also for the jurors performing their civic duty and for society which pays the judges and support personnel who manage the trials. It seems doubtful that our judicial system would have the resources to provide litigants with perfect trials, were they possible, and still keep abreast of its constantly increasing case load. Even this straightforward products liability suit extended over a three-week period.
>
> We have also come a long way from the time when all trial error was presumed prejudicial and reviewing courts were considered "citadels of technicality." Kotteakos v. United States, 328 U.S. 750, 759 (1946). The harmless error rules adopted by this Court and Congress embody the principle that courts should exercise judgment in preference to the automatic reversal for "error" and ignore errors that do not affect the essential fairness of the trial. . . .
>
> To invalidate the result of a three-week trial because of a juror's mistaken, though honest response to a question, is to insist on something closer to

perfection than our judicial system can be expected to give. A trial represents an important investment of private and social resources, and it ill serves the important end of finality to wipe the slate clean simply to recreate the peremptory challenge process because counsel lacked an item of information which objectively he should have obtained from a juror on *voir dire* examination. . . . We hold that to obtain a new trial in such a situation, a party must first demonstrate that a juror failed to answer honestly a material question on *voir dire*, and then further show that a correct response would have provided a valid basis for a challenge for cause. The motives for concealing information may vary, but only those reasons that affect a juror's impartiality can truly be said to affect the fairness of a trial.

McDonough Power Equipment, Inc. v. Greenwood, 464 U.S. 548, 552-553 (1984) (*voir dire* protects right to impartial jury by exposing "possible biases, both known and unknown," and bias can lead to excusing for cause; hints of bias "not sufficient to warrant challenge for cause" may help parties exercise peremptory challenges; juror apparently thought son's broken leg was not the kind of injury covered by the question; another juror reported that son had once caught his finger in a bike chain, and another failed to respond, but further questioning brought out that her husband had been injured in a machinery accident; jurors are not necessarily "experts in English usage" and may be "uncertain as to the meaning of terms which are relatively easily understood" by lawyers) (*if* plaintiff had known about injury sustained by foreman's son and failed then to follow up with additional questions, plaintiff would have waived claim of error).

(*d*) Should it matter whether Don Payton's false response on *voir dire* was an intentional effort to conceal or cover up information? In *McDonough,* Chief Justice Rehnquist described a juror's answer as "mistaken" but "honest." See also Johnson v. McCullough, 306 S.W.3d 551, 557 (Mo. 2010) (unintentional nondisclosure does not warrant new trial unless prejudice resulted; prejudice is *presumed* if nondisclosure was intentional; juror M remained silent when panel was asked whether anyone had been involved in lawsuit; question was clear, and triggered M's duty to disclose multiple debt collection suits against her and suit for personal injuries) (granting new trial in malpractice suit that led to judgment for defendant).

3. Consider the attitudes reflected by Juror 2's affidavit (item B), which exhibits hostility toward plaintiffs' verdicts of product liability. Verdicts based on such attitudes do *not* reflect legal standards that jurors are to apply. If venire members expressed such attitudes on *voir dire*, they might be excluded for cause. But not all courts invite questions on *voir dire* that probe such attitudes. If a juror signs an affidavit (or would testify) that the verdict rested on such considerations, should we permit the attack? Would such proof show "extraneous prejudicial information" or "outside influence"? See, e.g., Martinez v. Food City, Inc., 658 F.2d 369, 372 (5th Cir. 1981) (rejecting proof that juror said during deliberations that defendant "should be taught a lesson").

4. Does the fact that Juror 3 (item C) had experience with LawnCare mowers that he shared during deliberations show the trial was unfair? Is what Juror 3 said to the others "extraneous prejudicial information" under FRE 606(b), hence provable in support of a new trial motion? See Bethea v. Springhill Memorial Hospital, 833 So. 2d 1, 7-8 (Ala. 2002) (in product liability suit alleging that plaintiff's child suffered brain damage from improper use of Pitocin, juror shared with others her experience with this drug, telling them she didn't think it could have such effects, which persuaded another to change his mind; cannot prove this point in support of new trial motion; not "extraneous prejudicial information").

5. Does Juror 4's affidavit (item D) about imbibing alcohol during trial or smoking marijuana reveal misconduct that is ground for setting aside a verdict? Does it reflect "extraneous prejudicial information" or "outside influence" under FRE 606(b)? See Tanner v. United States, 483 U.S. 107 (1987) (refusing to set aside fraud conviction where defense counsel reported phone call from juror saying that several jurors "consumed alcohol during the lunch breaks" which caused them "to sleep through the afternoons," and where counsel also received "unsolicited visit" from juror who said jury was "on one big party," drinking one to three pitchers of beer during recesses, and that jurors had mixed drinks and wine, and jurors regularly smoked marijuana during trial; alcohol and drug use represents "no more an 'outside influence' than a virus, poorly prepared food, or a lack of sleep").

(a) FRE 606(b) bars juror affidavits or testimony on occurrences "during . . . deliberations." Does this provision also bar proof of juror behavior *during trial*? Dissenters in *Tanner* argued that it was "undisputed" that FRE 606(b) does not apply to "matters occurring before or after deliberations." Didn't they have a point?

(b) *Should* we allow testimony by jurors on matters occurring during trial but *before* deliberations? See *Grundy*, supra, at 153, 163 (Ohio Rule similar to FRE 606(b) prohibits inquiry into conduct throughout trial, during presentation of evidence and trial itself that might influence juror's mind, emotions, or mental processes during deliberations). Do these broad applications of FRE 606(b) mean lying on *voir dire* also cannot be proved by juror testimony or affidavits? Most courts *allow* such proof (note 1, above).

(c) What if plaintiff could get Aggie Smythe, a waitress in the restaurant where the jurors ate lunch during deliberations, to testify that they imbibed alcohol or smoked marijuana? Would such testimony avoid the concerns of *Tanner*?

6. Consider Juror 5's affidavit (item E) describing conversations about insurance. It is a bedrock principle in American law that jurors should not consider that a judgment against a defendant might be paid by insurance, or that plaintiff might already have recovered damages by collecting insurance. Also, the *fact* of insurance cannot be taken as proving or supporting an inference of negligence or due care. See FRE 411 (insurance may not be used to suggest that one "acted negligently or otherwise wrongfully," but may be used for other limited purposes, like proving "agency, ownership, or control, if controverted, or bias or prejudice of a witness").

(a) Most courts let parties ask "the insurance question" somehow before a jury is seated. See, e.g., St. Louis University v. Geary, 321 S.W.3d 282 (Mo. 2009) (parties have right to know whether venire members have an interest in the outcome; court must first approve question on insurance, which should only be asked once and should not be the first or last question); State ex rel. Nationwide Mutual Insurance Co. v. Karl, 664 S.E.2d 667, 673 (W. Va. 2008) (rule against proving insurance does not block *voir dire* asking whether prospective juror is associated with counsel representing nonparty insurance carrier, defending in name of other driver involved in accident); Jenks v. Bertelsen, 86 P.3d 24 30 (Mont. 2004) (reversible error for one party to mention another's liability insurance during *voir dire*, when counsel repeatedly injects insurance with such force that the jury could scarcely miss the point); Atkins v. Stratmeyer, 600 N.W.2d 891, 896 (S.D. 1999) (can ask about insurance on *voir dire*); Smith v. District Court in and for the Fourth Judicial District, 907 P.3d 611, 612 (Colo. 1995) (even though mentioning it on *voir dire* might lead jury to infer that insurance is involved, still question is allowable because "it tends to reveal possible interest or bias").

(b) Does this effort to keep jurors from knowing about the role of insurance, when coupled with the fact that the parties may ask about insurance before jurors are seated, make sense? Would you be surprised to learn that most courts hold that FRE 606(b) bars proof that jurors considered such matters during deliberations?

7. What's wrong with "quotient verdicts" (described in the statements by Jurors 6 and 7 in item F), if anything? Does FRE 606(b) allow proof that the jury employed this method to determine damages? See, e.g., Lake v. D&L Lagley Trucking, Inc., 233 P.3d 589 (Wyo. 2010) (FRE 606(b) and identical state counterpart do not permit showing that jury reached quotient verdict). Suppose the jury decided liability by flipping a coin? Is a "chance" verdict better, or worse?

8. Suppose a jury increases an award because it assumes the lawyer will charge 40 percent of recovery as fees and thinks plaintiff will have to pay 25 percent in taxes. Could a defendant prove these points by means of testimony or an affidavit by a juror? See Jimmy Day Plumbing & Heating, Inc. v. Smith, 964 So. 2d 1, 9 (Ala. 2007) (no; such discussions do not reflect "outside information").

9. Suppose a jury returns a verdict in a personal injury case awarding $696,000 in noneconomic damages, $440,000 in economic damages, and $1,136,000 in damages for physical impairment. If defendant, noticing that the first two figures when added together come to same amount as the third figure, and learns from jurors that the intent was that the third line reflect the total, rather than a separate item of recovery, can juror affidavits prove the point? See Stewart ex rel. Stewart v. Rice, 47 P.3d 316 (Colo. 2002) (under state Rule 606(b), answer is no).

(a) When *Stewart* was decided, FRE 606(b) (and the Colorado counterpart) contained two exceptions (one for "extraneous prejudicial information," another for "outside influence"). Now both contain a third exception—allowing juror affidavits or testimony to prove that "there was a mistake in entering the verdict onto the verdict form." Would this provision change the outcome in *Stewart*?

(b) One way of avoiding errors in reporting verdicts is to poll the jury after the verdict is announced. In cases like *Stewart,* if each juror says the verdict, as reported on the form, is correct and each concurs in it, should this fact matter if a juror affidavit later asserts that the third line was supposed to be the total?

D BENCH TRIALS: JUDGES AS FACTFINDERS

In civil cases tried to the judge without a jury (bench-tried cases), the judge acts in a dual role, resolving issues of law, including matters of procedure and evidence, and also resolving questions of fact.

To encourage care and transparency, FRCP 52(a) requires the judge, in any case tried without a jury, to "find the facts specially and state its conclusions of law separately." Although reviewing courts encourage trial judges to do what this provision obviously contemplates—to prepare findings and conclusions personally—in fact it is common for the prevailing party to prepare the findings and conclusions. Reviewing courts complain about this practice, but in muted tones that almost encourage trial judges to keep doing the very thing being complained about:

> We, too, have criticized courts for their verbatim adoption of findings of fact prepared by prevailing parties, particularly when those findings have taken the form of conclusory statements unsupported by citation to the record. We are also aware of the potential for overreaching and exaggeration on the part of attorneys preparing findings of fact when they have already been informed that the judge has decided in their favor. Nonetheless, our previous discussions of the subject suggest that even when the trial judge adopts proposed findings verbatim, the findings are those of the court and may be reversed only if clearly erroneous.

Anderson v. City of Bessemer City, N.C., 470 U.S. 564, 572 (1985). See also In re Las Colinas, Inc., 426 F.2d 1005, 1008-1009 (1st Cir. 1970) (asking counsel to submit findings and conclusions is "well established as a valuable aid to decision making," but there is "a clash of interests" between judicial efficiency and the "right of losing counsel to be assured that his position has been thoroughly considered"; when party-prepared findings "wind up as the court's opinion," the court's thought process "may be cast in doubt") (reviewing court praises judge's "reputation for conscientiousness," while expressing the wish that "appearance [should] reflect the actuality"!); Roberts v. Ross, 344 F.2d 747, 751 (3d Cir. 1965) (expressing strong disapproval of practice of announcing decision and asking winning party to prepare findings and conclusions because it "flies in the face of the spirit and purpose, if not the letter, of Rule 52(a)," which is to require the judge "to formulate and articulate his findings of fact and conclusions of law" so that the judge himself is "satisfied that he has dealt fully and properly with all the issues in the case before he decides it and so that the parties involved and this court on appeal may be fully informed as to the bases of his decision," and findings prepared by counsel do not serve that function adequately; they may even induce a reviewing court to find error because they are "inadequate" to support the decision or are "loaded down with argumentative overdetailed partisan matter").

E   EXTRAORDINARY RELIEF: MOTIONS UNDER FRCP 60(b); EQUITABLE PROCEEDINGS; RESISTING VOID JUDGMENTS IN NEW ACTIONS

There are other ways to seek relief from a judgment. Mostly we're now talking about challenges brought long after the time limit for motions for a new trial or judgment as a matter of law has expired (28 days), and after the time for appeal has run (FRAP 4 allows 30 days from entry of judgment to file notice of appeal).

Most important among these other ways are motions under FRCP 60(b), but we should note as well that sometimes judgments are challenged by an independent suit in equity, and that a judgment may be challenged as "void" in another court if defendant did not appear in the original suit and the court lacked jurisdiction over her. To these three mechanisms we now turn.

Rule 60(b) Motions—In General. Motions under FRCP 60(b) are made in the court that rendered the judgment being challenged, and must be made by a party to the original suit. In the federal system, the court that rendered the original judgment has jurisdiction to entertain such a motion—subject matter jurisdiction need not be established anew.

Although FRCP 60(b) does not say so, obtaining relief requires the moving party to show that he acted promptly, that he has a meritorious claim or defense, and that setting aside the judgment will not be prejudicial to the opposing party. See, e.g., Aikens v. Ingram, 652 F.3d 496, 501 (4th Cir. 2011) (rejecting motion by plaintiff in prior suit to set aside judgment dismissing his case, brought against superiors in the National Guard alleging that they illegally intercepted his emails while he was on active duty). Perhaps equally important, relief under FRCP 60(b) cannot involve relitigation of matters previously adjudicated. See James, Hazard & Leubsdorf, Civil Procedure §12.15

(5th ed. 2001) (and the ground advanced now must not have been available as a basis for appeal from the judgment).

Rule 60(b) lists five grounds of relief, and puts a limit of one year from entry of judgment for challenges advancing any of the first three grounds.

Rule 60(b)(1)—Mistake, Excusable Neglect. The first listed ground of relief, subject to the one-year time limit, is "mistake, inadvertence, surprise, or excusable neglect." This ground is often invoked by a defendant seeking relief from a default judgment, and in this setting generally the "merits" were not previously litigated. For this reason, courts are more likely to be generous in awarding relief than they are in connection with any of the other grounds.

Even here, however, relief is far from automatic. Parties are expected to attend to business, and default judgments are one consequence of failing to do so. If they could be lifted as a matter of course, the threat of default would not achieve its purpose in conveying to parties the need to cooperate in proceedings. See, e.g., Franchise Holding II, LLC v. Huntington Restaurants Group, 375 F.3d 922 (9th Cir. 2004) (refusing relief to commercial lender who failed to pay loans, leading to suit and default judgment for more than $27 million).

In this situation, both FRCP 55 and FRCP 60(b) authorize defendants to apply for relief, and courts treat the two rules as setting equivalent standards. In *Franchise Holding*, the court set out the requirements, which define "excusable neglect" (or "mistake" or "inadvertence," which mean about the same thing). Thus *Franchise Holding* asked whether defendant acted promptly, whether he advanced an adequate defense on the merits, and whether lifting the default would be prejudicial to plaintiff. In *Franchise Holding*, the borrower claimed it had relied on a "side agreement" that plaintiff would take no further steps while settlement talks went forward. The court was unpersuaded because plaintiff had written a letter warning defendant that it was prepared to move forward and because defendant failed to advance arguments defending its position. See also Brandt v. American Bankers Ins. Co. of Florida, 653 F.3d 1108, 1111 (9th Cir. 2011) (where defendant seeks relief from default judgment under FRCP 60(b)(1), court considers prejudice to plaintiff, whether defendant has a meritorious defense, and whether defendant's culpable conduct led to the default).

Rule 60(b)(2)—"Newly Discovered Evidence." The second ground of relief, again subject to the one-year time limit, is "newly discovered evidence" that the moving party could not have discovered "with reasonable diligence" before. Because the Rules provide opportunities for discovery, and parties are expected to prosecute claims and defenses with vigor, courts are more skeptical than one might imagine when confronted with motions on this ground. It is understood that the moving party must show that the evidence was discovered after trial, that it is not merely "cumulative" of other evidence, nor merely "impeaching," and that it would be admissible and would likely change the outcome. See, e.g., Dronsejko v. Thornton, 632 F.3d 658 (10th Cir. 2011).

One decision that granted relief on this ground involved a dispute between surviving siblings over $400,000 that the decedent had left in the custody of a third person to turn over to one of his siblings on his death. The trial court had awarded the full sum to one sibling on testimony that decedent intended her to get the full sum, but the other sibling won relief on the basis of a signed document, discovered after trial, where decedent and the third person acknowledged that the money was to go into decedent's estate. See In re Estate of Fournier, 966 A.2d 885 (Me. 2009).

Far more common, however, are decisions denying relief because the "new" evidence is viewed as cumulative, or merely "impeaching." See Pirdair v. Medical Center Hospital of Vermont, 800 A.2d 438 (Vt. 2002) (additional evidence about accuracy of testimony on CAT scan image, "while potentially helpful, would be cumulative") (and does not justify relief from judgment). Perhaps most often, courts conclude that the movant would have uncovered the evidence before if she had been diligent. See, e.g., Raby Construction, LLP v. Orr, 594 S.E.2d 478 (S.C. 2004) (refusing to set aside judgment for contractor in lien enforcement proceeding against restaurant owner, despite testimony that manual ledgers produced by contractor were not as accurate as computer records; restaurant owner could have taken deposition of witness; due diligence would have uncovered this evidence).

Rule 60(b)(3)—"Fraud, Misrepresentation, Misconduct." The third ground of relief under FRCP 60(b), again subject to the one-year time limit, is "fraud" or "misrepresentation" or "misconduct" by an opposing party. Courts once distinguished between "intrinsic" and "extrinsic" fraud, the former embracing things like perjured testimony and the latter embracing things like misrepresentations causing lawyers to fail in crucial duties, such as appearing at trial or filing documents. Courts awarded relief on the latter ground but not the former. FRCP 60(b)(3) abolishes the distinction, however, allowing relief on both grounds.

Courts also subscribe to the idea that "fraud on the court" is the most serious kind of misconduct, and that it more readily justifies relief from a judgment: As the phrase suggests, fraud on the court is described as conduct that does not merely prejudice the opposition, but also harms the integrity of the judicial process, sometimes because of the personal involvement of lawyers or court personnel. See, e.g., United States v. Estate of Stonehill, 660 F.3d 415, 444 (9th Cir. 2011) (nondisclosure of evidence is not fraud on the court, nor is perjury by a party or witness, unless an attorney or other court officer is party to it; fraud on the court usually involves "a scheme by one party to hide a key fact from the court and the opposing party"); In re Golf 255, Inc., 652 F.3d 806, 809 (7th Cir. 2011) (fraud on the court consists of acts that "defile the court" or are "perpetrated by officers of the court," such as lawyers, so "the judicial machinery cannot perform in the usual manner its impartial task of adjudging cases") (quoting Moore's Federal Practice and earlier authorities).

Rule 60(b)(4)—"Void Judgment." The fourth ground of relief under FRCP 60(b), and this ground of attack is *not* subject to the one-year limit, is that the judgment is "void." Recall that one option, if a person is sued in a distant forum that lacks jurisdiction over her—let us say an Oregon defendant is sued in Florida—is to stay home and *not* travel to the court, nor hire a lawyer to appear on her behalf there. If the suit goes to judgment, the Oregon defendant can appear later in the court that rendered the judgment and move to set it aside for lack of jurisdiction over the person. Thus our Oregon defendant can go to Florida and make a motion for relief from the judgment, on the ground that Florida lacked jurisdiction over her.

Unlike most other grounds for relief under FRCP 60(b), this one is not subject to judicial discretion, and the moving party need not show that she has a valid defense or that a trial would result in a different outcome. As in the example of the Oregon defendant sued in Florida, challenges to a void judgment usually involve claims that the court lacked jurisdiction over the person of the moving party. Occasionally, relief is awarded on the ground that the court lacked subject matter jurisdiction, at least if the matter is particularly clear (it is usually said that a "mere error" on this point is not enough to set aside a judgment).

Rule 60(b)(5)—"Satisfied, No Longer Equitable." The fifth ground of relief, also not subject to the one-year limit, is that the judgment has been "satisfied, released, or discharged," or rests on a prior judgment that was itself "reversed or vacated" or that the judgment should not be applied "prospectively" because doing so is "no longer equitable." See, e.g., BUC International Corp. v. International Yacht Council, Ltd., 517 F.3d 1271 (11th Cir. 2008) (allowing relief from judgment to reflect payments received by plaintiff in settlement with joint tortfeasor).

In an important decision in the *Agostini* case in 1997, the Supreme Court ruled in favor of relief from a judgment on the ground that the law on which it rested had been undermined by later developments. The case involved a petition by New York City for relief from a permanent injunction issued 12 years earlier barring assignment of public school teachers to provide remedial education in parochial schools, pursuant to a federal mandate requiring such education for eligible students. Although a prior decision, on which the injunction rested, had been questioned in separate opinions by a majority of Justices, it had not been overruled. Rejecting arguments that granting relief here would "encourage litigants to burden the federal courts with a deluge of Rule 60(b)(5) motions" based on arguments that the law has changed (or should), the Court concluded that this suit involved a request to vacate an injunction "in light of a bona fide, significant change in the law."

See Agostini v. Felton, 521 U.S. 203, 239-240 (1997) (but intervening changes "rarely constitute the extraordinary circumstances required for relief").

Rule 60(b)(6)—"Any Other Reason." Obviously, this "catchall" is designed for the unexpected—the case where powerful reasons appear for setting aside a judgment that are not captured in the list set out in FRCP 60(b)(1)-(5). Because it is actually hard to imagine a reason that is *not* captured in that list, modern decisions stress that fitting this catchall category is not a matter of *avoiding* the categories in the list, but a matter of showing some especially compelling reason to award relief, something *more* extraordinary than the categories in the list. See, e.g., Comment, *Rule 60(b): Survey and Proposal for General Reform*, 60 Cal. L. Rev. 531, 559-560 (1972) ("every conceivable ground for relief arguably comes within the first three subdivisions," so the better approach is to interpret subdivision (6) as requiring "equitable reasons *in addition* to those enumerated").

In the *Klapprott* and *Ackermann* cases, both arising shortly after World War II and involving judgments cancelling naturalization certificates, the Supreme Court reached seemingly conflicting results, although arguably establishing that a party could not obtain relief under FRCP 60(b)(6) unless the situation was *not* covered by FRCP 60(b)(1)-(5). In *Klapprott*, the moving party attacked a judgment four years after it was rendered, arguing that he was in jail at the time and unable to protect his citizenship. In *Ackermann*, the moving party attacked the earlier judgment four years later, alleging that he lacked money at the time and was in detention. The Supreme Court awarded relief in *Klapprott*, on the ground that the movant's situation was not mere "neglect" under FRCP 60(b)(1). Hence FRCP 60(b)(6) applied and he was excused from the one-year limit. In *Ackermann*, the Court came out the other way, concluding that movant made a "voluntary, deliberate, free, untrammeled choice" not to appeal. See Klapprott v. United States, 366 U.S. 942 (1949); Ackermann v. United States, 340 U.S. 193, 197 (1950). In a third case from the same period, again involving denaturalization proceedings, Judge Learned Hand initially excused the moving party for not acting sooner (he allowed 17 years to elapse) because he had gone to Greece in 1929 to bring his family to this country, and had been advised that his wife was too ill to return, and was delayed further by the war. Judge Hand found that the movant was guilty of "excusable neglect," but ruled that relief was available under subdivision (6) anyway. After the decisions in *Klapprott* and *Ackermann* were called to Judge Hand's attention, he changed his mind and concluded that the 17-year delay was not "excusable neglect" after all, but was the product of "forcible obstacles," which brought clause (6) into play! United States v. Karahalias, 205 F.2d 331, 334 (2d Cir. 1953).

Independent Equitable Action. It remains possible to bring an equitable suit to set aside a judgment, although such suits are rare. It is commonly said that courts do not "relitigate" issues that were finally determined in a prior suit between the same parties, although independent actions are sometime brought by outsiders to the original suit, who are not technically "bound" by the prior judgment but might be adversely affected by it. It is also usually said that relief under FRCP 60(b), if available, should be sought first, and that making a motion under that provision and losing are grounds for dismissing an equitable suit too. See generally Wright & Miller, Federal Practice and Procedure §2868.

In one such suit, brought 12 years after a federal court entered judgment on the basis of settlement, awarding to the government title to certain land on Horn Island in the Gulf of Mexico, an alleged title holder sued to set aside the judgment, on the basis of a deed preserved in the National Archives, by which the Spanish Governor of the Island granted title to plaintiff's predecessor in interest prior to the Louisiana Purchase. Although plaintiff had asked the government in the prior suit for information relating to title, the government had not produced this deed. The Court of Appeals set aside the earlier judgment, but the Supreme Court reversed, concluding that an independent action in equity can set aside a prior judgment only "to prevent a grave miscarriage of justice," and the government's earlier failure to make a thorough search of its records did not satisfy this standard. See United States v. Beggerly, 524 U.S. 38, 47 (1998) (adding that allowing such a suit would undermine the one-year time limit in FRCP 60(c)(1) for suits to set aside a judgment for fraud).

Resisting Enforcement of Void Judgments. Recall that defendant has the option of not appearing in a distant forum if she is convinced that the forum lacks jurisdiction over her. If suit is brought in such a forum, and defendant elects not to appear, and also decides not to go later to the forum and make a motion under FRCP 60(b)(4) for relief from the judgment, another option is simply to resist a second suit, brought by the judgment holder against the defendant, to obtain a judgment on the original judgment.

In the example mentioned above, an Oregon defendant can decline to appear in the Florida suit and, if the plaintiff in the Florida suit brings a second action in Oregon to obtain an Oregon judgment based on the Florida judgment, the Oregon defendant can appear and advance the same argument—that the Florida court lacked jurisdiction, so the Florida judgment is not entitled to full faith and credit in Oregon. See U.S. Const., Art. IV §1. On the supposed facts, the Florida judgment is "void for lack of jurisdiction," and the fact that the matter was not "actually litigated" in Florida (because defendant did not appear) means that it can be decided anew by the second court. You encountered this matter when you read the *Compagnie des Bauxites* case (Chapter 3E, supra).

CHAPTER 13

Appellate Review

INTRODUCTION

In the federal system and all but nine states, a litigant who loses a case tried in a court having jurisdiction over large claims (meaning federal district courts and state courts of general jurisdiction) can appeal to an intermediate appellate court (in the other states, appeals go to the state supreme court).[1]

Thus in the federal system a litigant who loses in the federal district court can appeal to the relevant circuit court of appeals—so the loser of a suit filed in the Federal District Court for the Southern District of New York can appeal the judgment to the Second Circuit Court of Appeals (embracing federal districts in Connecticut, New York, and Vermont). In state systems, a litigant who loses in a court of general jurisdiction[2] can appeal the judgment to what is usually called the state court of appeals[3]—so the loser in Texas District Court in San Antonio can appeal to the Texas Court of Appeals (technically Fourth Court of Appeals; Texas has 14 appellate districts). Typically, courts of appeal sit in panels of three, and typically seven justices constitute the state supreme court. There are, however, departures from this pattern: For example, the court of appeals in New York sits in panels of five, and in Wyoming the state supreme court consists of five justices.

In both state and federal courts, the loser at trial has one appeal "as of right," meaning that if she appeals from a final judgment entered by the federal district court or a state trial court of general jurisdiction, the reviewing court *will* take and ultimately rule on the appeal. As you will soon see, appellants are expected

---

[1] The states of Maine, Maryland, Montana, Nevada, New Hampshire, Rhode Island, South Dakota, Vermont, and Wyoming do not have intermediate appellate courts. The same is true in the District of Columbia.
[2] Often these are district courts, but nomenclature is not uniform. See Chapter 1, footnote 6 for a description of the more common names.
[3] Again nomenclature is not uniform. Thus we have the "Illinois Appellate Court," "Massachusetts Appeals Court," "Oklahoma Court of Civil Appeals," and "New York Supreme Court, Appellate Division." But mostly we see courts like "Arizona Court of Appeals," and "California Court of Appeals."

to turn square corners in exercising their right to obtain review, however, and a slip-up, such as failing to file a notice of appeal in timely fashion, can be fatal, leading to dismissal on what is commonly called "jurisdictional" grounds.

In both the federal system and states with intermediate appellate courts, a litigant who loses her first appeal can take another. In federal litigation, that means appealing from the Circuit Court of Appeals to the United States Supreme Court. In state litigation, that means appealing to the state supreme court. But this level of review is discretionary (except in states lacking intermediate appellate courts), and the highest court can (usually does) decline to entertain the appeal.

The litigant who comes out on the losing end after the case has been heard by the highest court of a state can seek review in the United States Supreme Court. Not every state supreme court decision, however, can be reviewed by the United States Supreme Court. To simplify the matter, which is more complicated than the following statement reveals, the Supreme Court can review state court judgments when potentially dispositive issues of federal law are involved, which includes issues of federal statutory law, the Constitution, and (rarely) federal common law.

Recall from your study of federal subject matter jurisdiction and the decision in the *Mottley* case that the Supreme Court had jurisdiction to review the decision by the Kentucky Supreme Court. The Mottleys *originally* sued in federal court, but the Supreme Court held, in the case that you read, that the federal district court lacked jurisdiction to hear their claim because it arose under state contract law. See Louisville & Nashville Railroad Company v. Mottley, 211 U.S. 149 (1908) (Chapter 4B2, supra). But when the Mottleys sued again in state court and again won a judgment (this time one that was affirmed by the Kentucky Supreme Court), the Supreme Court took the case a second time and ruled that the Act of Congress that made it illegal for the railroad to continue to honor its agreement to let the Mottleys ride its trains without charge was valid. The federal district court lacked jurisdiction to *try* the case initially because it was not an "arising under" case for purposes of trial court jurisdiction, but the Supreme Court had jurisdiction to review the Kentucky judgment because it *was* an "arising under" case for purposes of Supreme Court jurisdiction. See generally 28 USC §1257 (defining Supreme Court jurisdiction to review decisions by the "highest court" of any state).

A   REASONS FOR APPELLATE REVIEW; SCOPE AND MECHANICS

1. Why Have Appellate Review? Is This Mechanism Worth It?

It may seem to you that the answers to these questions are obvious. We have appellate review to correct mistakes that trial courts make, and it *is* worthwhile to review trial court decisions because it is important to get the right outcomes. These gut level responses are partly right, but are not the end of the story.

Consider the fact that appellate review does *not* for the most part take up the question whether the judge or jury decided the facts correctly. Consider too that reversals of civil judgments are unusual. The percentage of civil judgments that lead to appeal is small, and the reversal rate is small. Of course the relevant figures vary over time and place (and by judge and category of case), but good rules of thumb include an appeal rate of 5-10 percent and a reversal rate of 20 percent or lower (sometimes much lower).[4] Out of a hundred cases that go to trial and judgment, then, one can expect maybe one or two reversals after review on appeal.

Consider too that maintaining a system of appellate courts is costly, and appeals consume time and money. Consider as well that the Supreme Court has never found that the right to appeal a judgment is guaranteed as an element of due process under the Constitution. See McKane v. Durston, 153 U.S. 684, 687 (1894) (in criminal case, commenting that due process does not include a right of appellate review). If civil appeals don't correct mistakes in factfinding, and if appeals are infrequent and seldom change outcome, is the civil appeal process still worth it?

■ NOTES ON THE VALUE OF APPELLATE REVIEW

1. To begin with, correcting error is only part of what appellate review is all about. It is no accident that you read hundreds (maybe thousands) of appellate opinions in getting a legal education, nor is it accidental that lawyers rely heavily on law revealed in appellate opinions in giving legal advice. In short, the function of appeals is not only to correct error but to make (or at least clarify) law. For many academic commentators, the law-making function eclipses the error-correcting function. For one version of this view, see Owen Fiss, *Against Settlement*, 93 Yale L.J. 1073 (1984) (complaining that the "dispute-resolution story trivializes the remedial dimensions of lawsuits and mistakenly assumes judgment to be the end of the process," and arguing that adjudication "uses public resources" and involves "public officials" whose job "is not to maximize the ends of private parties, nor simply to secure the peace, but to explicate and give force to the values embodied in authoritative texts such as the Constitution and statutes"). Some think appellate judges actually focus more on making law than on correcting

[4] See, e.g., Report of the Director, Administrative Office of U.S. Courts, Judicial Business of the United States Courts, Table B-5 (2010) (reversal rate is 12 percent in private party civil litigation in year ending September 30, 2010).

errors. Consider this account by a judge in the Ninth Circuit Court of
Appeals:

> [N]ot all cases are created equal. Most judicial work is routine and dull, involving
> issues that are of no consequence to anyone other than the parties. Only a few
> cases raise difficult and interesting issues—the kind of issues that make for an
> important judicial opinion. When lawyers seek appointment to judicial office,
> they generally think of the interesting cases as the core of judicial work; none
> I know seeks judicial office so he can spend his days, nights, weekends and hol-
> idays slogging through an unending stack of routine, fact-intensive and largely (in
> the grand scheme of things) inconsequential cases.
>
> Human nature being what it is, there is a strong tendency to devote a dis-
> proportionate amount of judicial time to the big cases and to give short shrift to
> the small ones. There's actually a lot to be said for this. Preparing a precedential
> opinion requires a significant amount of time because such an opinion not only
> decides the dispute between the parties, but also sets the course of the law for
> innumerable cases to come. So you are justified in spending most of your time on
> the big cases, because you really do have a serious responsibility: A rushed and
> sloppy opinion can cause major problems for a lot of people down the road.

Alex Kozinski, *The Real Issues of Judicial Ethics*, 32 Hofstra L. Rev. 1097–1098,
(2004) (adding, as if in afterthought, that "small cases, too, have a legitimate
claim to a fair share of judicial time and attention") (!). See also Paul D. Carrington, *The Function of the Civil Appeal: A Late-Century View*, 38 S.C. L. Rev.
411, 424 (1987) (intermediate appellate courts "emulate the Supreme Court by
giving emphasis to their own creative roles as lawmakers," and they give
"diminishing attention to the seemingly less gratifying work of error correction"). Could it also be that appellate judges are more doctrinaire, hence more
prone to spend time on law making? See Christopher R. Drahozal, *Judicial
Incentives and the Appeals Process*, 51 SMU L. Rev. 469-486 (1998) (postulating
that "stronger relationships between judicial decisions and ideology" are to be
found among appellate judges than among trial judges).

2. Some have argued that congestion in appellate dockets has crippled
the error-correcting function. Consider this description:

> Today, the circuit courts hear oral argument and conduct meaningful face-to-
> face conferences in only half of the cases, with a resultant loss of visibility and
> collegial input. Many cases get very little personal attention from the judges.
> Most of the research and opinion drafting are the bureaucratic task of dozens of
> staff attorneys, who seldom confer with the judges who are the titular authors
> of the opinions. Only a third of the courts' opinions are published; the
> remainder exist in a quasi-precedential netherworld, vastly reducing judicial
> accountability.

William M. Richman & William L. Reynolds, *Elitism, Expediency, and the New
Certiorari: Requiem for the Learned Hand Tradition*, 81 Cornell L. Rev. 273, 341

(1996) (courts give full attention only to "significant cases," meaning those "brought by wealthy, powerful, or institutional litigants," while "routine" or "trivial" cases get less attention). In the article quoted in the prior note, Professor Carrington suggests that the increased caseload, which has come without increases in judgeships, "has led the intermediate courts to abandon the amenities of procedure that enabled them to assure that errors were being corrected and that individual fates were being given the attention formerly expected," and that correcting error "takes time that circuit judges no longer feel [that] they have." See Carrington, supra, at 424-425. Professor Burbank suggests that federal judges may *like* the fact that their dockets are too crowded to allow full effort on every appeal. See Steven B. Burbank, *Judicial Accountability to the Past, Present and Future: Precedent, Politics and Power*, 28 U. Ark. Little Rock L. Rev. 19, 32 (2005) (judges may oppose expansion of the judiciary because of their "desire to mimic the Supreme Court by functionally creating a discretionary docket" in which some cases get short shrift; focus is "issues rather than cases," and selection of issues goes "according to the judges' desire to maximize opportunities to exercise creativity or power or both").

3. Suppose it is true, as many have pointed out, that the cases that go to trial and appeal are the hardest ones, where the law does not provide a definitive answer—that's why they are litigated rather than settled. If these are cases in which there is something to be said for each side, and an outcome favoring one rather than another is not obviously right, does this fact make the error-correcting function harder to exercise? See Chad M. Oldfather, *Error Correction*, 85 Ind. L.J. 49, 50-52 (2010) ("architecture of the American appellate process" rests on formalistic or mechanical notion of law, and our belief that law is often "indeterminate" conflicts with this approach; judges should not adopt "case-focused conception" of review, where goal is to achieve appropriate outcome, but "issue-based conception," in which appellate court serves a "derivative dispute resolution function").

4. Does a system in which a litigant dissatisfied with the result has one appeal as of right encourage trial judges to do better work at an acceptable price?

(a) Professor Harlon Dalton has argued that the threat of correction on appeal does not help much, and that it brings certain drawbacks:

> [T]here is reason to question the intuitively appealing notion that the threat of reversal induces trial judges to self-correct. Some judges just don't take the threat seriously, because the ratio of reversals to total cases is so small, because they view reversals as inevitable or arbitrary, or because they think it inappropriate to concern themselves with what might happen on appeal. . . .
>
> [E]ven if appeal of right does promote self-correction by trial judges, any consequent gain in accuracy may be more than offset by harm done to the trial court as an institution. The more we underscore the fact that trial courts are

hierarchically inferior to appellate courts, the more we feed the notion that they are inferior in other ways as well. Furthermore, the specter of appeal induces passivity in some judges, blunts or misdirects the creativity of others, distorts fact-finding and law-choosing, undermines common law doctrinal development, promotes doctrinal vagueness, encourages jurisprudential sleight of hand, imperils candor, imposes on the parties (as well as the system) additional costs and delays, and imposes on the losing party psychic costs whenever negative facts about her are embellished by the trial judge in an effort to render the opinion appeal-proof.

Harlon Dalton, *Taking the Right to Appeal (More or Less) Seriously*, 95 Yale L.J. 62, 92-93 (1985) (suggesting that appellate review of right should be discarded in many cases and retained in certain others).

(b) Professor Carrington argues that an appellate system strengthens the administration of justice in other ways:

> The appeal [as of right] does serve to incorporate the trial judge into the institutional scheme, diffusing the judge's authority and depersonalizing her responsibility. The prospect of appellate review probably constrains judges more than they like to think, and more than we would like them to think, because even the court of appeals would not want district judges to become singlemindedly attentive to higher authority. More important in my view, however, is the signal sent to the litigants by the recognition of the right of appeal, which does shape their perception of the fairness of the proceeding and the power or prerogative of the trial judge. We send the wrong message to a litigant when we tell him that he is depending on the reactions of a single judge whose decisions will be reviewed by higher authority only as an act of grace. The idea of law is that the individual judge is accountable for the principled exercise of power. Discretionary accountability may look to the skeptic very much like no accountability at all.

Carrington, supra, at 411, 431.

5. Suppose we did away with, or sharply reduced, the possibility of review in civil cases. Would we expect less satisfactory results from trial judges? Consider these comments about the craft of judging, offered from an academic perspective:

> The trial judge is in a unique position of authority over the day-to-day actions of individuals. It is his everyday duty to make decisions which may deprive a man of his fortune or his livelihood, or require him to perform or refrain from action, or cause him to be imprisoned or put to death. Megalomania is an occupational hazard of the judicial office. . . . The judge responsible for making primary decisions must necessarily make a heavy investment of time and interest in particular disputes and individuals that come before him; his limited perspective and his limited opportunity for reflection make it impossible for him to coordinate successfully with his colleagues. Vanity and pride of opinion are additional obstacles;

even very sensitive, intelligent, and self-disciplined judges must be troubled at times by their own involvements of ego. By providing supervision, we keep the various decision makers operating within an institutional framework. Remoteness of the reviewer from the firing line of trial can assure greater objectivity for the institutional process. By employing a larger group of decision makers than can be efficiently employed at the primary level, we bring a broader base of values into operation so that the personal dimension of decisions is diminished. The process of review permits a larger number of decisions to be harmonized under the aegis of a single authority. Moreover, review spreads the responsibility for decisions more broadly. Thus the mistakes may be more bearable to the individuals affected, and the judicial office is made a tolerable employment for men of ordinary sensitivity. Review is, therefore, essential to the goal of law.

Paul D. Carrington, *Crowded Dockets and the Courts of Appeals: The Threat to the Function of Review and the National Law*, 82 Harv. L. Rev. 542, 550-551 (1960).

6. Despite some of the comments quoted above, it seems widely to be recognized that the *first* responsibility of an intermediate court of appeals is to correct error. See Blum v. 1st Auto & Casualty Ins. Co., 786 N.W.2d 78 (Wis. 2010) (main function of intermediate appellate court is "error correcting," but it also engages in "law defining and law development"); Hulsey v. Pride Restaurants, LLC, 367 F.3d 1238, 1243 (11th Cir. 2004) (appellate review of district court decisions is largely an error-correcting function); Whipple v. State, 431 So. 2d 1011, 1014 (Fla. App. 1983) (courts of appeal "engage primarily in the so-called error-correcting function to insure that every litigant receives a fair trial"). In keeping with those comments, and in contrast with intermediate appellate courts, state supreme courts conceive their main role in terms of declaring the law. See, e.g., Farmer v. Baldwin, 205 P.3d 87, 94 (Or. 2009) (supreme court primarily uses its discretionary authority to take on significant issues of law, not "mere error correction"); Bradley v. State, 235 S.W.3d 808 (Tex. Crim. App. 2007) (supreme court is not a court of "error correction," which would "re-do that which the court of appeals has already done," and focus instead is "legal ramifications and ripple effect" of lower court's opinion).

7. Does a system of appellate review favor defendants? One modern empirical study of state court cases suggests that it does. The study concluded that reversal rates for jury trials in defense appeals exceeded reversal rates for bench trials in plaintiff appeals (for defendant appeals, reversal rate was 41.5 percent; for plaintiff appeals, reversal rate was 21.5 percent). See Theodore Eisenberg & Michael Heise, *Plaintiphobia in State Courts? An Empirical Study of State Court Trials on Appeal*, 38 J. Legal Stud. 121 (2009) (citing evidence that trial judges and juries "act in comparable ways when confronted with comparable cases," authors conclude that pro-plaintiff bias in juries cannot account for the discrepancy in reversal rates, hence that "appellate court misperceptions about jurors' bias toward plaintiffs" is the likely explanation) (but noting that "selection bias" in cases that get appealed might account, at least in part, for the discrepancy).

2. Scope of Review

If appellate review does not involve an examination of what happened at trial to see whether the trial court got the facts right or wrong, what *does* it involve? The answer is that appellate review asks whether legal mistakes occurred, or whether someone involved in the trial engaged in misconduct that might have affected the outcome. To be sure, such mistakes *might well lead to* the wrong outcome: If a court tells a jury that defendant is liable only if he was "grossly negligent," and if the jury returns a verdict for the defendant because it thinks he was *negligent* but not *grossly* negligent, the legal mistake produced the wrong outcome. If the case is retried to a new jury, it may well come to pass that the new jury will get it right.

Mostly, however, a review process that focuses on *legal* errors serves only *indirectly* to get the right result. Rules of Evidence, for example, lead to the exclusion of much hearsay, and allow certain kinds of attack on the credibility of witnesses, but not others. We think and hope these Rules, when applied correctly, produce outcomes that are more likely to be right than we would experience if we did not apply the Rules, but we cannot be sure. Hearsay that was correctly excluded might have been right, and impeachment that was allowed might persuade a jury to reject testimony that is correct. In short, most reviews for trial error are not directly connected to right results. The reviewing court does not "second guess" the factfinders (judge or jury).

(1) Legal Mistakes: Errors in Admitting or Excluding Evidence. Perhaps the most common legal mistake that a trial court can make is to admit evidence that should be excluded or exclude evidence that should be admitted.

It bears emphasis that *lawyers* bear the lion's share of responsibility to *prevent* such mistakes. Under Evidence Rule 103, a party wishing to exclude evidence offered by another must object, usually before the evidence is offered. And a party wishing to *introduce* evidence must call the witnesses or present the document or image, and must make an offer of proof if the other side raises objection, and such an offer entails an explanation describing the evidence and explaining why it should be admitted. These mechanisms help ensure that mistakes are avoided and that the court has a chance to get the ruling right. So when an appeal is taken, arguing that mistakes were made, it is already the case that the court and lawyers have done their best to avoid the mistake in the first place.

(2) Legal Mistakes: Error in Law Application (Instructions and Conclusions). A second kind of common legal mistake at trial is misstating or misapplying the law. In jury-tried cases, the governing legal principles are given to the jury in the form of instructions, and in bench-tried cases the judge makes findings of fact and conclusions of law, where the applicable legal principles are set out.

Again, the lion's share of responsibility rests with the parties to get these matters right. Under FRCP 51, the parties are expected to prepare and propose jury instructions, and a party who is unhappy with any instruction is required to object "on the record, stating distinctly the matter objected to and the grounds" (objections must be stated before instructions are given). In judge-tried cases, typically the prevailing party prepares "findings of fact and conclusions of law" that the judge adopts, and errors in legal standards may be found there. See FRCP 52.

(3) Legal Mistakes: Giving a Case to a Jury When There Is Only One Reasonable Outcome. Recall from Chapter 12C1, supra, that evidence can be insufficient or (less often) overwhelming. Motions for judgment as a matter of law raise such points, and if a trial court *denies* such a motion and gives a case to a jury, *and if* the jury does the wrong thing and a court enters judgment on the verdict anyway, this legal mistake can be corrected by taking an appeal. Doing the "wrong thing" would be, for example, finding for a plaintiff who has offered insufficient evidence. Recall that such points are raised by motion for judgment as a matter of law under FRCP 50. Recall too that a party who seeks such a judgment *must* make the motion before the case is submitted to the jury and, if the trial court denies the motion and submits the case to the jury, the moving party *must* in effect *repeat* the motion by making it again after the verdict has been returned and judgment has been entered on the verdict.

In judge-tried cases, a similar issue can be raised by moving to dismiss or (rarely) asking the court simply to enter judgment for the moving party. A judgment against the moving party can be reversed on appeal if the appellate court believes that the trial judge (in a bench trial) simply could not reasonably find against the moving party, committing what can be called "clear error."

(4) Legal Mistakes: Other Kinds of Procedural Errors. Other procedural errors too can be raised and corrected on appeal. You looked at cases in Chapter 3 where judgments were thrown out because the trial court lacked jurisdiction over the defendant. In the *Kulko* case, a husband got a California judgment in a divorce case thrown out for lack of jurisdiction; in *Asahi*, a maker of tire valves from Japan got a California judgment in favor of a tire maker from China thrown out for lack of jurisdiction. Similar things can happen when a court lacks subject matter jurisdiction: Recall the *Mottley* case, where a federal judgment against a railroad was thrown out because the case did not "arise under" federal law.

(5) Misconduct. Everyone involved in the trial of a lawsuit is capable of misbehavior that can result in a reversal. If, for example, jurors do independent research on the matters in litigation, visiting an accident scene without the court's permission and supervision or by doing internet research by means of personal computers or other electronic devices, judgments can be set aside. If court personnel, such as clerk or bailiff or even the judge, misbehave by pressuring the jurors or (in judge-tried cases) doing independent research into the facts, judgments may be set aside. If witnesses misbehave, as might happen if one violates a court order not to talk to other witnesses or not to listen to other witnesses as they testify, judgments may be set aside. And if the parties or their lawyers misbehave, by bribing or threatening or cajoling witnesses or jurors, verdicts may be set aside on these grounds too. Recall FRE 606(b) and Problem 12-D ("I Think It Was His Parents' Fault") in Chapter 12C4, which examines the limits on the use of juror affidavits in raising such points.

Harmless Error Doctrine. It is an article of faith that judgments should not be set aside for errors or misconduct that do not likely affect the outcome of the case. This principle appears in FRCP 61, which states that errors are not ground for a new trial or for setting aside or otherwise disturbing a judgment unless they "affect [a] party's substantial rights." It appears as well in Evidence Rule 103, which says that error may be predicated on a ruling that admits or excludes evidence "only if the error affects a substantial right." These rules embody the "harmless error doctrine," and they mean that reversals may not be had unless a reviewing court thinks it is probable that an error or misconduct affected the outcome. See also 28 USC §2111 (codified version of harmless error principle for federal courts).

Preserving Right of Review. As indicated above, the parties are largely responsible for helping the court avoid errors, and failing to do so means waiving any right to relief by appellate review. Hence the party who prevailed at trial often argues on appeal that the other side waived review by failing to object, or to proffer evidence, or to take other steps (like submitting jury instructions) that are important in "making the record" and "preserving the right to appeal."

While no lawyer can count on it, sometimes reversals may be had for "plain error," meaning a mistake that the appellant (and usually the court and other parties) did not notice or mention. "Plain" error goes by many descriptions, but usually it connotes a mistake that a reviewing court considers obvious and especially serious, and sometimes it is said that plain error must be corrected, even though the appellant did not raise the point at trial in timely fashion, because otherwise the reputation of the court for doing justice would suffer.

3. Obtaining Review: Notice as the Crucial First Step

If a litigant is dissatisfied with the result at trial and wants to appeal, the one singularly important thing she must do is file a timely notice of appeal.

In the easiest situation, a jury returns a verdict or a judge announces a decision, and thereafter judgment is "entered" in the docket book of the court. It is the entry of judgment that starts the appeal clock running. In the federal system, a party dissatisfied with the judgment has 30 days to file notice of appeal with the trial court (the same notice is also served on the other parties). It is the filing of this notice of appeal that is the most critical step in perfecting an appeal: Failing to file timely notice means failing in the appeal. See FRCP 77 and 79 (describing entry of judgment and service of notice of judgment); FRAP 4 (time limit for notice of appeal). See also Ultimate Appliance CC v. Kirby Co., 601 F.3d 414, 416 (6th Cir. 2010) (time for filing notice of appeal runs from entry of judgment, not date when service of judgment is effected).

In the common situation in which a verdict loser makes a timely motion for judgment as a matter of law or a new trial (FRCP 50 and 59)—and "timely" means filing the motion within 28 days after entry of judgment—the time for taking an appeal is tolled until "entry of the order disposing of the last such" motion. If the appellant files notice of appeal *before* the trial court rules on such motions, then the notice "becomes effective" when the court disposes of "the last such remaining motion." FRAP 4(a)(4). See also Moses v. Howard University Hospital, 606 F.3d 789 (D.C. Cir. 2010) (rejecting argument that motion to amend judgment under FRCP 59, filed by trustee in bankruptcy for plaintiff, failed to toll time for plaintiff to appeal; plaintiff filed notice of appeal more than 30 days after entry of judgment but while motion under FRCP 59 was pending; trustee was a "party" for purposes of the motion, which therefore did toll plaintiff's time to appeal; notice of appeal was timely, and took effect when court ruled on motion).

BOWLES v. RUSSELL

Supreme Court of the United States
551 U.S. 205 (2007)

Justice THOMAS delivered the opinion of the Court.

In this case, a District Court purported to extend a party's time for filing an appeal beyond the period allowed by statute. We must decide whether the Court of Appeals had jurisdiction to entertain an appeal filed after the statutory period but within the period allowed by the District Court's order. We have long and repeatedly held that the time limits for filing a notice of appeal are jurisdictional in nature. Accordingly, we hold that petitioner's untimely notice—even though filed in reliance upon a District Court's order—deprived the Court of Appeals of jurisdiction.

I

In 1999, an Ohio jury convicted petitioner Keith Bowles of murder for his involvement in the beating death of Ollie Gipson. The jury sentenced Bowles to 15-years-to-life imprisonment. Bowles unsuccessfully challenged his conviction and sentence on direct appeal.

Bowles then filed a federal habeas corpus application on September 5, 2002. On September 9, 2003, the District Court denied Bowles habeas relief. After the entry of final judgment, Bowles had 30 days to file a notice of appeal. FRAP 4(a)(1)(A); 28 USC §2107(a). He failed to do so. On December 12, 2003, Bowles moved to reopen the period during which he could file his notice of appeal pursuant to Rule 4(a)(6), which allows district courts to extend the filing period for 14 days from the day the district court grants the order to reopen, provided certain conditions are met. See §2107(c).

On February 10, 2004, the District Court granted Bowles' motion. But rather than extending the time period by 14 days, as Rule 4(a)(6) and §2107(c) allow, the District Court inexplicably gave Bowles 17 days—until February 27—to file his notice of appeal. Bowles filed his notice on February 26—within the 17 days allowed by the District Court's order, but after the 14-day period allowed by Rule 4(a)(6) and §2107(c).

On appeal, respondent Russell argued that Bowles' notice was untimely and that the Court of Appeals therefore lacked jurisdiction to hear the case. The Court of Appeals agreed. It first recognized that this Court has consistently held the requirement of filing a timely notice of appeal is "mandatory and jurisdictional." The court also noted that courts of appeals have uniformly held that Rule 4(a)(6)'s 180-day period for filing a motion to reopen is also mandatory and not susceptible to equitable modification. Concluding that "the fourteen-day period in Rule 4(a)(6) should be treated as strictly as the 180-day period in that same Rule," the Court of Appeals held that it was without jurisdiction. We granted certiorari, and now affirm.

II

According to 28 USC §2107(a), parties must file notices of appeal within 30 days of the entry of the judgment being appealed. District courts have limited authority to grant an extension of the 30-day time period. Relevant to this case, if certain conditions are met, district courts have the statutory authority to grant motions to reopen the time for filing an appeal for 14 additional days. §2107(c). FRAP 4 carries §2107 into practice....

It is undisputed that the District Court's order in this case purported to reopen the filing period for more than 14 days. Thus, the question before us is whether the Court of Appeals lacked jurisdiction to entertain an appeal filed outside the 14-day window allowed by §2107(c) but within the longer period granted by the District Court.

A

This Court has long held that the taking of an appeal within the prescribed time is "mandatory and jurisdictional." Griggs v. Provident Consumer

Discount Co., 459 U.S. 56, 61 (1982) (*per curiam*) (internal quotation marks omitted);[2] accord, Hohn v. United States, 524 U.S. 236, 247 (1998); Torres v. Oakland Scavenger Co., 487 U.S. 312, 314-315 (1988); Browder v. Director, 434 U.S. 257, 264 (1978). Indeed, even prior to the creation of the circuit courts of appeals, this Court regarded statutory limitations on the timing of appeals as limitations on its own jurisdiction. See Scarborough v. Pargoud, 108 U.S. 567, 568 (1883) ("[T]he writ of error in this case was not brought within the time limited by law, and we have consequently no jurisdiction"); United States v. Curry, 6 How. 106, 113 (1848) ("[A]s this appeal has not been prosecuted in the manner directed, within the time limited by the acts of Congress, it must be dismissed for want of jurisdiction"). Reflecting the consistency of this Court's holdings, the courts of appeals routinely and uniformly dismiss untimely appeals for lack of jurisdiction. See 15A C. Wright, A. Miller, & E. Cooper, Federal Practice and Procedure §3901, p.6 (2d ed. 1992) ("The rule is well settled that failure to file a timely notice of appeal defeats the jurisdiction of a court of appeals"). In fact, the author of today's dissent recently reiterated that "[t]he accepted fact is that some time limits are jurisdictional even though expressed in a separate statutory section from jurisdictional grants, see, *e.g.,* . . . §2107 (providing that notice of appeal in civil cases must be filed 'within thirty days after the entry of such judgment')." Barnhart v. Peabody Coal Co., 537 U.S. 149, 160 n.6 (2003) (majority opinion of Souter, J., joined by Stevens, Ginsburg, and Breyer, JJ., *inter alios*) (citation omitted).

Although several of our recent decisions have undertaken to clarify the distinction between claims-processing rules and jurisdictional rules, none of them calls into question our longstanding treatment of statutory time limits for taking an appeal as jurisdictional. Indeed, those decisions have also recognized the jurisdictional significance of the fact that a time limitation is set forth in a statute. In Kontrick v. Ryan, 540 U.S. 443 (2004), we held that failure to comply with the time requirement in Federal Rule of Bankruptcy Procedure 4004 did not affect a court's subject-matter jurisdiction. Critical to our analysis was the fact that "[n]o statute . . . specifies a time limit for filing a complaint objecting to the debtor's discharge." Rather, the filing deadlines in the

---

[2] *Griggs* and several other of this Court's decisions ultimately rely on United States v. Robinson, 361 U.S. 220, 229 (1960), for the proposition that the timely filing of a notice of appeal is jurisdictional. As the dissent notes, we have recently questioned *Robinson's* use of the term "jurisdictional." Even in our cases criticizing *Robinson,* however, we have noted the jurisdictional significance of the fact that a time limit is set forth in a statute, and have even pointed to §2107 as a statute deserving of jurisdictional treatment. Additionally, because we rely on those cases in reaching today's holding, the dissent's rhetoric claiming that we are ignoring their reasoning is unfounded.

Regardless of this Court's past careless use of terminology, it is indisputable that time limits for filing a notice of appeal have been treated as jurisdictional in American law for well over a century. Consequently, the dissent's approach would require the repudiation of a century's worth of precedent and practice in American courts. Given the choice between calling into question some dicta in our recent opinions and effectively overruling a century's worth of practice, we think the former option is the only prudent course.

Bankruptcy Rules are "'procedural rules adopted by the Court for the orderly transaction of its business'" that are "'not jurisdictional'" (quoting Schacht v. United States, 398 U.S. 58, 64 (1970)). Because "[o]nly Congress may determine a lower federal court's subject-matter jurisdiction" (citing U.S. Const., Art. III, §1), it was improper for courts to use "the term 'jurisdictional' to describe emphatic time prescriptions in rules of court." See also Eberhart v. United States, 546 U.S. 12 (2005) (*per curiam*). As a point of contrast, we noted that §2107 contains the type of statutory time constraints that would limit a court's jurisdiction.[3] Nor do Arbaugh v. Y & H Corp., 546 U.S. 500 (2006), or Scarborough v. Principi, 541 U.S. 401 (2004), aid petitioner. In *Arbaugh,* the statutory limitation was an employee-numerosity requirement, not a time limit. *Scarborough,* which addressed the availability of attorney's fees under the Equal Access to Justice Act, concerned "a mode of relief . . . ancillary to the judgment of a court" that already had plenary jurisdiction.

This Court's treatment of its certiorari jurisdiction also demonstrates the jurisdictional distinction between court-promulgated rules and limits enacted by Congress. According to our Rules, a petition for a writ of certiorari must be filed within 90 days of the entry of the judgment sought to be reviewed. See this Court's Rule 13.1. That 90-day period applies to both civil and criminal cases. But the 90-day period for civil cases derives from both this Court's Rule 13.1 and 28 USC §2101(c). We have repeatedly held that this statute-based filing period for civil cases is jurisdictional. On the other hand, we have treated the rule-based time limit for criminal cases differently, stating that it may be waived because "[t]he procedural rules adopted by the Court for the orderly transaction of its business are not jurisdictional and can be relaxed by the Court in the exercise of its discretion. . . ." Schacht v. United States, 398 U.S. 58, 64 (1970).

Jurisdictional treatment of statutory time limits makes good sense. Within constitutional bounds, Congress decides what cases the federal courts have jurisdiction to consider. Because Congress decides whether federal courts can hear cases at all, it can also determine when, and under what conditions, federal courts can hear them. Put another way, the notion of "'subject-matter'" jurisdiction obviously extends to "'classes of cases . . . falling within a court's adjudicatory authority,'" *Eberhart, supra* (quoting *Kontrick, supra*), but it is no less "jurisdictional" when Congress prohibits federal courts from adjudicating an otherwise legitimate "class of cases" after a certain period has elapsed from final judgment.

---

[3] At least one federal court of appeals has noted that *Kontrick* and *Eberhart* "called . . . into question" the "longstanding assumption" that the timely filing of a notice of appeal is a jurisdictional requirement. United States v. Sadler, 480 F.3d 932, 935 (9th Cir. 2007). That court nonetheless found that "[t]he distinction between jurisdictional rules and inflexible but not jurisdictional timeliness rules drawn by *Eberhart* and *Kontrick* turns largely on whether the timeliness requirement is or is not grounded in a statute."

The resolution of this case follows naturally from this reasoning. Like the initial 30-day period for filing a notice of appeal, the limit on how long a district court may reopen that period is set forth in a statute, 28 USC §2107(c). Because Congress specifically limited the amount of time by which district courts can extend the notice-of-appeal period in §2107(c), that limitation is more than a simple "claim-processing rule." As we have long held, when an "appeal has not been prosecuted in the manner directed, within the time limited by the acts of Congress, it must be dismissed for want of jurisdiction." *Curry, supra.* Bowles' failure to file his notice of appeal in accordance with the statute therefore deprived the Court of Appeals of jurisdiction. And because Bowles' error is one of jurisdictional magnitude, he cannot rely on forfeiture or waiver to excuse his lack of compliance with the statute's time limitations.

B

Bowles contends that we should excuse his untimely filing because he satisfies the "unique circumstances" doctrine, which has its roots in Harris Truck Lines, Inc. v. Cherry Meat Packers, Inc., 371 U.S. 215 (1962) (*per curiam*). There, pursuant to then-Rule 73(a) of the Federal Rules of Civil Procedure, a District Court entertained a timely motion to extend the time for filing a notice of appeal. The District Court found the moving party had established a showing of "excusable neglect," as required by the Rule, and granted the motion. The Court of Appeals reversed the finding of excusable neglect and, accordingly, held that the District Court lacked jurisdiction to grant the extension. This Court reversed, noting "the obvious great hardship to a party who relies upon the trial judge's finding of 'excusable neglect.'"

Today we make clear that the timely filing of a notice of appeal in a civil case is a jurisdictional requirement. Because this Court has no authority to create equitable exceptions to jurisdictional requirements, use of the "unique circumstances" doctrine is illegitimate. Given that this Court has applied *Harris Truck Lines* only once in the last half century, several courts have rightly questioned its continuing validity. We see no compelling reason to resurrect the doctrine from its 40-year slumber. Accordingly, we reject Bowles' reliance on the doctrine, and we overrule *Harris Truck Lines* and *Thompson* to the extent they purport to authorize an exception to a jurisdictional rule.

C

If rigorous rules like the one applied today are thought to be inequitable, Congress may authorize courts to promulgate rules that excuse compliance with the statutory time limits. Even narrow rules to this effect would give rise to litigation testing their reach and would no doubt detract from the clarity of the rule. However, congressionally authorized rulemaking would likely lead to less litigation than court-created exceptions without authorization. And in all events, for the reasons discussed above, we lack present authority to make the exception petitioner seeks.

III

The Court of Appeals correctly held that it lacked jurisdiction to consider Bowles' appeal. The judgment of the Court of Appeals is affirmed.

It is so ordered.

Justice SOUTER, with whom Justice STEVENS, Justice GINSBURG, and Justice BREYER join, dissenting.

The District Court told petitioner Keith Bowles that his notice of appeal was due on February 27, 2004. He filed a notice of appeal on February 26, only to be told that he was too late because his deadline had actually been February 24. It is intolerable for the judicial system to treat people this way, and there is not even a technical justification for condoning this bait and switch. I respectfully dissent.

I

"'Jurisdiction,'" we have warned several times in the last decade, "'is a word of many, too many, meanings.'" Steel Co. v. Citizens for Better Environment, 523 U.S. 83, 90 (1998) (quoting United States v. Vanness, 85 F.3d 661, 663, n.2 (D.C. Cir. 1996)); Kontrick v. Ryan, 540 U.S. 443, 454 (2004) (quoting *Steel Co.*); Arbaugh v. Y & H Corp., 546 U.S. 500, 510 (2006) (quoting *Steel Co.*); Rockwell Int'l Corp. v. United States, 549 U.S. 457, 467 (2007) (quoting *Steel Co.*). This variety of meaning has insidiously tempted courts, this one included, to engage in "less than meticulous," *Kontrick*, sometimes even "profligate ... use of the term," *Arbaugh*.

In recent years, however, we have tried to clean up our language, and until today we have been avoiding the erroneous jurisdictional conclusions that flow from indiscriminate use of the ambiguous word. Thus, although we used to call the sort of time limit at issue here "mandatory and jurisdictional," United States v. Robinson, 361 U.S. 220, 229 (1960), we have recently and repeatedly corrected that designation as a misuse of the "jurisdiction" label. *Arbaugh, supra* (citing *Robinson* as an example of improper use of the term "jurisdiction"); Eberhart v. United States, 546 U.S. 12, 17-18 (2005) (*per curiam*) (same); *Kontrick, supra* (same).

But one would never guess this from reading the Court's opinion in this case, which suddenly restores *Robinson*'s indiscriminate use of the "mandatory and jurisdictional" label to good law in the face of three unanimous repudiations of *Robinson*'s error. This is puzzling, the more so because our recent (and, I repeat, unanimous) efforts to confine jurisdictional rulings to jurisdiction proper were obviously sound, and the majority makes no attempt to show they were not.

The stakes are high in treating time limits as jurisdictional. While a mandatory but nonjurisdictional limit is enforceable at the insistence of a party claiming its benefit or by a judge concerned with moving the docket, it may be waived or mitigated in exercising reasonable equitable discretion. But if a limit is taken to be jurisdictional, waiver becomes impossible, meritorious excuse irrelevant (unless the statute so provides), and *sua sponte* consideration in the courts of appeals mandatory, see *Arbaugh, supra*. As the Court recognizes, this is no way to regard time limits set out in a court rule rather than a statute, see *Kontrick, supra* ("Only Congress may determine a lower federal court's subject-matter jurisdiction"). But neither is jurisdictional treatment automatic when a time limit is statutory, as it is in this case. Generally speaking, limits on the reach of federal statutes, even nontemporal ones, are only jurisdictional if Congress says so: "when Congress does not rank a statutory limitation on coverage as jurisdictional, courts should treat the restriction as nonjurisdictional in character." *Arbaugh*. Thus, we have held "that time prescriptions, however emphatic, 'are not properly typed "jurisdictional,"'" *id.* (quoting Scarborough v. Principi, 541 U.S. 401, 414 (2004)), absent some jurisdictional designation by Congress. Congress put no jurisdictional tag on the time limit here.

The doctrinal underpinning of this recently repeated view was set out in *Kontrick:* "the label 'jurisdictional' [is appropriate] not for claim-processing rules, but only for prescriptions delineating the classes of cases (subject-matter jurisdiction) and the persons (personal jurisdiction) falling within a court's adjudicatory authority." A filing deadline is the paradigm of a claim-processing rule, not of a delineation of cases that federal courts may hear, and so it falls outside the class of limitations on subject-matter jurisdiction unless Congress says otherwise.[4]

The time limit at issue here, far from defining the set of cases that may be adjudicated, is much more like a statute of limitations, which provides an affirmative defense, see FRCP 8(c), and is not jurisdictional, Day v. McDonough, 547 U.S. 198, 205 (2006). Statutes of limitations may thus be waived, *id.* or excused by rules, such as equitable tolling, that alleviate hardship and unfairness, see Irwin v. Department of Veterans Affairs, 498 U.S. 89, 95-96 (1990).

---

[4] The Court points out that we have affixed a "jurisdiction" label to the time limit contained in §2101(c) for petitions for writ of certiorari in civil cases. *Ante* (citing Federal Election Comm'n v. NRA Political Victory Fund, 513 U.S. 88, 90 (1994); this Court's Rule 13.2). Of course, we initially did so in the days when we used the term imprecisely. The status of §2101(c) is not before the Court in this case, so I express no opinion on whether there are sufficient reasons to treat it as jurisdictional. The Court's observation that jurisdictional treatment has had severe consequences in that context, does nothing to support an argument that jurisdictional treatment is sound, but instead merely shows that the certiorari rule, too, should be reconsidered in light of our recent clarifications of what sorts of rules should be treated as jurisdictional.

Consistent with the traditional view of statutes of limitations, and the carefully limited concept of jurisdiction explained in *Arbaugh, Eberhart,* and *Kontrick,* an exception to the time limit in 28 USC §2107(c) should be available when there is a good justification for one, for reasons we recognized years ago. In Harris Truck Lines, Inc. v. Cherry Meat Packers, Inc., 371 U.S. 215, 217 (1962) (*per curiam*), and Thompson v. INS, 375 U.S. 384, 387 (1964) (*per curiam*), we found that "unique circumstances" excused failures to comply with the time limit. In fact, much like this case, *Harris* and *Thompson* involved district court errors that misled litigants into believing they had more time to file notices of appeal than a statute actually provided. Thus, even back when we thoughtlessly called time limits jurisdictional, we did not actually treat them as beyond exemption to the point of shrugging at the inequity of penalizing a party for relying on what a federal judge had said to him. Since we did not dishonor reasonable reliance on a judge's official word back in the days when we uncritically had a jurisdictional reason to be unfair, it is unsupportable to dishonor it now, after repeatedly disavowing any such jurisdictional justification that would apply to the 14-day time limit of §2107(c). . . .

In ruling that Bowles cannot depend on the word of a District Court Judge, the Court demonstrates that no one may depend on the recent, repeated, and unanimous statements of all participating Justices of this Court. Yet more incongruously, all of these pronouncements by the Court, along with two of our cases, are jettisoned in a ruling for which the leading justification is *stare decisis* ("This Court has long held . . .").

II

We have the authority to recognize an equitable exception to the 14-day limit, and we should do that here, as it certainly seems reasonable to rely on an order from a federal judge.[7] Bowles, though, does not have to convince us as a matter of first impression that his reliance was justified, for we only have to look as far as *Thompson* to know that he ought to prevail. There, the would-be appellant, Thompson, had filed post-trial motions 12 days after the District Court's final order. Although the rules said they should have been filed within 10, FRCP 52(b) and 59(b), the trial court nonetheless had "specifically declared that the 'motion for a new trial' was made 'in ample time.'" *Thompson,* 375 U.S., at 385. Thompson relied on that statement in filing a notice of appeal within 60 days of the denial of the post-trial motions but not within 60 days of entry of the original judgment. Only timely post-trial motions affected the

---

[7] As a member of the Federal Judiciary, I cannot help but think that reliance on our orders is reasonable. See O. Holmes, Natural Law, in Collected Legal Papers 311 (1920). I would also rest better knowing that my innocent errors will not jeopardize anyone's rights unless absolutely necessary.

60-day time limit for filing a notice of appeal, Rule 73(a) (1964 ed.), so the Court of Appeals held the appeal untimely. We vacated because Thompson "relied on the statement of the District Court and filed the appeal within the assumedly new deadline but beyond the old deadline."

Thompson should control. In that case, and this one, the untimely filing of a notice of appeal resulted from reliance on an error by a district court, an error that caused no evident prejudice to the other party. Actually, there is one difference between *Thompson* and this case: Thompson filed his post-trial motions late and the District Court was mistaken when it said they were timely; here, the District Court made the error out of the blue, not on top of any mistake by Bowles, who then filed his notice of appeal by the specific date the District Court had declared timely. If anything, this distinction ought to work in Bowles's favor. Why should we have rewarded Thompson, who introduced the error, but now punish Bowles, who merely trusted the District Court's statement?

Under *Thompson*, it would be no answer to say that Bowles's trust was unreasonable because the 14-day limit was clear and counsel should have checked the judge's arithmetic. The 10-day limit on post-trial motions was no less pellucid in *Thompson*, which came out the other way. And what is more, counsel here could not have uncovered the court's error simply by counting off the days on a calendar. FRAP 4(a)(6) allows a party to file a notice of appeal within 14 days of "the date when [the district court's] order to reopen is entered." See also 28 USC §2107(c)(2) (allowing reopening for "14 days from the date of entry"). The District Court's order was dated February 10, 2004, which reveals the date the judge signed it but not necessarily the date on which the order was entered. Bowles's lawyer therefore could not tell from reading the order, which he received by mail, whether it was entered the day it was signed. Nor is the possibility of delayed entry merely theoretical: the District Court's original judgment in this case, dated July 10, 2003, was not entered until July 28. According to Bowles's lawyer, electronic access to the docket was unavailable at the time, so to learn when the order was actually entered he would have had to call or go to the courthouse and check. Surely this is more than equity demands, and unless every statement by a federal court is to be tagged with the warning "Beware of the Judge," Bowles's lawyer had no obligation to go behind the terms of the order he received.

I have to admit that Bowles's counsel probably did not think the order might have been entered on a different day from the day it was signed. He probably just trusted that the date given was correct, and there was nothing unreasonable in so trusting. The other side let the order pass without objection, either not caring enough to make a fuss or not even noticing the discrepancy; the mistake of a few days was probably not enough to ring the alarm bell to send either lawyer to his copy of the federal rules and then off to the courthouse to check the docket.[9] This would be a different case if the year were wrong on the District Court's order, or if opposing counsel had flagged the error. But on the actual facts, it was reasonable to rely on a facially plausible date provided by a federal judge.

I would vacate the decision of the Court of Appeals and remand for consideration of the merits.

■ NOTES ON TIMELY NOTICE OF APPEAL AND AS "JURISDICTIONAL"

1. Convicted in state court for assault and murder after taking part in an altercation in which he and some friends were seeking revenge for an earlier beating suffered by a relative of one of the friends, Keith Bowles challenged the conviction (which had become final after an unsuccessful appeal) by filing an application in federal court for a writ of habeas corpus. He argued that the statute under which he was convicted violated the Fourteenth Amendment by creating two categories of murder. As reflected in the Court of Appeals opinion, a federal trial judge adopted the findings of a magistrate to whom the application for the writ had been assigned, and denied the application on July 28, 2003. In timely fashion, Bowles filed a petition seeking a new trial under FRCP 50, or an amendment of the judgment under FRCP 52 that would reject the magistrate's findings, but these requests were denied on September 9. Bowles had 30 days to file timely notice of appeal (til October 9). On December 12, Bowles made a motion under FRAP 4, which allows the judge to "reopen the time to file an appeal for a period of 14 days," arguing that he did not receive *notice* of the judgment as required by FRCP 77(d) (clerk to "serve notice" of entry of judgment "immediately"). Apparently, the court agreed that notice had not been served, and reopened the appeal period on February 10, 2004. Inexplicably, however, the trial judge told Bowles's lawyer he had until the 27th (Friday), but the maximum extension could not go beyond February 24 (Tuesday). On February 26 (Thursday), Bowles filed notice of appeal.

2. A habeas corpus petition, although it challenges a *criminal conviction,* is a separate *civil* proceeding, so the Court of Appeals opinion in *Bowles*

---

[9] At first glance it may seem unreasonable for counsel to wait until the penultimate day under the judge's order, filing a notice of appeal being so easy that counsel should not have needed the extra time. But as Bowles's lawyer pointed out at oral argument, filing the notice of appeal starts the clock for filing the record, see FRAP 6(b)(2)(B), 10(b), and 11, which in turn starts the clock for filing a brief, see Rule 31(a)(1), for which counsel might reasonably want as much time as possible. A good lawyer plans ahead, and Bowles had a good lawyer.

(although not the Supreme Court opinion above) cites the relevant civil rules relating to motions for new trials, amending the judgment, and service of notice of the judgment. Hence *Bowles* is properly viewed as a case that sheds light on the attitudes of courts on jurisdictional aspects of filing timely notice of appeal in civil cases.

3. What is the practical difference between a "claims-processing" rule and a "jurisdictional" rule? See Catherine Struve, *Time and the Courts: What Deadlines and Their Treatment Tell Us About the Litigation System*, 59 DePaul L. Rev. 601, 607 (2010) (whether rule is "jurisdictional" counts at least in situations in which opponent "fails to complain" or in which party in violation of deadline offers "an excuse for noncompliance"). Failure to raise a "jurisdictional" limit does not waive the point, and it can be raised by the court itself. And noncompliance with a jurisdictional limit usually cannot be excused—in *Bowles* the noncompliant party had a pretty good excuse (reliance on the court's order), but it didn't count because of the jurisdictional nature of the rule.

4. What do you think of the argument between Justice Thomas for the majority and Justice Souter for the three dissenters? Does the fact that a time limit is *statutory* argue strongly that it is also jurisdictional? In two cases that seemed troublesome for the *Bowles* majority, the Court had "gone the other way" in holding that certain restrictions are not jurisdictional. See Arbaugh v. Y&H Corp., 546 U.S. 500 (2006) (provision in 1964 Civil Rights Act authorizing claims against employers with "fifteen or more employees" is not jurisdictional; numerosity threshold, which defendant first raised after trial before Magistrate Judge, did *not* relate to subject matter jurisdiction; it is located in provision "separate" from jurisdictional provisions); Kontrick v. Ryan, 540 U.S. 443 (2004) (timing provision in Bankruptcy Rules relating to objections that creditors may file is not jurisdictional). How does the Court distinguish these holdings?

5. FRAP 4 is an elaborate provision that sets out the time limits for moving for an extension of time in which to file notice of appeal, and limits the length of the extension. Much the same ground is also covered in 28 USC §2107, but the Rule and the statute use different words, and points of detail relating to time limits can be found in the Rule and not the statute: For example, Rule 4 says that if a party moves for an extension within 30 days after the time for appeal expires, the extension may not "exceed 30 days after the prescribed time [for appeal] or 14 days after the date when the order granting the motion is entered, whichever is later." The *statute* is silent on the length of time that may be granted by way of extension if a motion is filed within 30 days after the time for appeal has run, although the statute *does* provide that if the motion is made thereafter (as happened in *Bowles*), the court may "reopen the time for appeal for a period of 14 days." Does *Bowles* actually mean that *if* the defense had moved to reopen the appeal on October 10 (three days after the time for appeal expired) *and if* the extension went as long as the Rule permits (through November 8, which is 30 days beyond expiration of the time for appeal) *and* if the defendant filed its appeal on November 10 (two days beyond the extended period), the defect would *not* be jurisdictional because the tardy filing would violate FRAP 4 but not 28 USC §2107?

6. Limitation periods are usually statutory too—we refer to "statutes of limitation"—but they are universally treated as matters of affirmative defense. They are "claims-processing rules" that may be waived if not invoked in appropriate fashion. See FRCP 8(e) (defense "must affirmatively state" defense based on "statute of limitations"). See also Menominee Indian Tribe of Wisconsin v. United States, 614 F.3d 519, 524 (D.C. Cir. 2010) (in tribe's suit for reimbursement of medical expenses under contract with government, six-year statutory time limit was claims-processing provision, not jurisdictional; it was subject to equitable tolling while class suit seeking recovery of this money was pending). Does it make sense to treat statutes of limitation one way and statutes limiting time for appeals in a different way? Does it bear on this question that statutes of limitation prevent a claim from being heard, while statutes relating to time for appeal operate only to limit opportunities for review of a claim that has been litigated?

7. Time limits, whether set by rule or by statute, are not magical or even calibrated to accommodate competing interests on some carefully worked out basis. They exist rather as convenient mechanisms to be sure that the judicial system operates in a reasonably prompt manner. Distinguishing between claims-processing rules and jurisdictional rules continues to prove challenging:

(a) Post-*Bowles* appellate decisions treat some statutory limits for appeals as jurisdictional. See, e.g., Henderson v. Shinseki, 589 F.3d 1201 (Fed. Cir. 2009) (120-day statutory limit for veteran to appeal final decision by Board of Veterans' Appeals is jurisdictional and not subject to equitable tolling).

(b) Post-*Bowles* decisions sometimes *reject* claims that time limits found in Rules or common law are jurisdictional, see, e.g., District of Columbia v. Doe, 611 F.3d 888, 896 (D.C. Cir. 2010) (period of limitations for filing suit was not jurisdictional under *Bowles* because it rested on common law, not statute); Advanced Bodycare Solutions, LLC v. Thione International, Inc., 615 F.3d 1352, 1359 (11th Cir. 2010) (FRCP 6 bars court from extending times for filing motions for new trial under FRCP 59 or JMAL under FRCP 50, so tardy motions under the latter did not extend time for appeal under FRAP 4; but FRCP 6 is a claims-processing rule, and failing to object to court's violation of that provision "forfeited" objection to extension of time).

(c) Where a Rule states a time limit that is *not* found in a statute that also sets relevant time limits, doesn't the decision in *Bowles* leave courts at sea? Compare Green v. Drug Enforcement Administration, 606 F.3d 1296, 1301

(11th Cir. 2010) (untimely FRCP 59(e) motion to amend judgment did not toll time for appeal; court has jurisdiction to resolve untimely FRCP 59(e) motion, but FRAP 4 extends time for taking appeal on account of FRCP 59 motions only if they are "timely," and fact that court can entertain untimely motion does not "turn an untimely Rule 59(e) motion into a timely one") with National Ecological Foundation v. Alexander, 496 F.3d 466, 473-475 (6th Cir. 2007) (tardy post-trial motion to amend judgment under FRCP 59(e) extended beginning point of time for filing notice of appeal; "unlike the rule at issue in *Bowles*, Rule 59(e) is a Federal Rule of Civil Procedure promulgated . . . under the Rules Enabling Act").

(d) Sometimes the problem is not whether a time limit for taking an appeal is based on statute or something else, but whether an order is final for the purpose of commencing the period for filing an appeal. See St. Marks Place Housing Co. v. U.S. Department of Housing & Urban Development, 610 F.3d 75 (D.C. Cir. 2010) (district court cannot extend time for taking appeal; court ordered that "this case is closed" but that order "shall not be deemed a final order" until issuance of Memorandum Opinion; time for appeal did not start running; courts "may choose when to decide their cases") (orders "whose finality awaits the issuance of a later opinion should be avoided," but courts need reasonable means to manage loads).

(e) Courts have concluded that the time limits in FRAP 4 for taking appeal are *not* jurisdictional in criminal cases because they "do not have statutory grounding." See, e.g., In re Latture, 605 F.3d 830, 835 (10th Cir. 2010); United States v. Neff, 598 F.3d 320 (7th Cir. 2010).

8. The Court has held that other kinds of statutory requirements are *not* jurisdictional. See, e.g., Reed Elsevier, Inc. v. Muchnick, 130 S. Ct. 1237 (2010) (failing to register copyright before bringing suit for infringement, as required by statute, is not jurisdictional; question is whether statute "clearly states" that requirement is jurisdictional, and it did not; provision is separate from those giving federal courts subject matter jurisdiction; in some circumstances statute expressly allows courts to adjudicate infringement claims involving unregistered works; it would be "at least unusual" to find such exceptions in jurisdictional provisions).

9. *Bowles* has not fared well among academic commentators. See, e.g., Scott Dodson, *Mandatory Rules,* 61 Stan. L. Rev. 1, 8 (2008) (*Bowles* "requires courts to police the deadline *sua sponte*, makes the deadline unsusceptible to waiver, forfeiture, or consent, and allows noncompliance to be raised any time by any party; *Bowles* failed to develop standards for deciding whether rule is jurisdictional, which should turn on whether Congress designated it this way, whether it deals with power of courts or conduct of parties, and what effects of making rule jurisdictional would be); Paul D. Carrington, *A Critical Assessment of the Cultural and Institutional Roles of Appellate Courts* (Book Review), 9 J. App. Prac. & Process 231 (2007) (decrying "brutal result" in *Bowles*, based on "the conclusory declaration" that the time limit for appeals was jurisdictional, in which five Justices "disowned their power to 'create equitable exceptions,' i.e., to do justice even when the mistake was made by a federal district judge and counsel for the state made no objection"). Are you persuaded that it would be wise to make "equitable exceptions" to time limits for appeals? If so, is the fact that the judge made the initial mistake in *Bowles* crucial? In the next case, if the judge got it right but appellant was a day late because of the "press of business," should that be excused too? Are such questions worth litigating, or is a clearcut inflexible rule preferable?

4. Obtaining Review: The Rest of the Process

Given the rigidity of the time requirement for filing notice of appeal, it is a good thing that filing the notice is simple. The work that comes after that is much harder, and so specialized is the enterprise of convincing a reviewing court to reverse a judgment or take some other corrective step that major law firms have departments that do nothing but appellate work.

When a litigant files notice of appeal (and serves the parties), other litigants are given time to decide whether to file notice of cross-appeals. If Marsha has sued Ned and O Company, and the suit has gone to trial with a jury leading to a verdict and then a judgment in in favor of Marsha, it is possible that any of the parties may entertain thoughts of taking an appeal.

For anyone thinking of an appeal, the big question is whether errors at trial likely affected the verdict, or (less often) whether misconduct affected the verdict. If Ned or O Company thinks about an appeal, the questions might be whether the court erred in admitting evidence offered by Marsha, or in excluding evidence offered by Ned or O Company, or whether the jury was properly instructed. Even Marsha might entertain thoughts of an appeal, particularly if she thinks the damage award was far too low. Recall that a litigant unhappy with the results of trial may move for a new trial under FRCP 59, which may result in a new trial on the same grounds that may be advanced on appeal, but without need to take an appeal—especially errors in admitting or excluding evidence or instructing the jury. And recall that a party may seek judgment as a matter of law under FRCP 50, but this argument usually depends on convincing the court that the evidence leaves room for only one reasonable decision.

Appeals involve examination of the trial record. This record consists of three things: One is the papers and exhibits filed in the court. Then there is the transcript of proceedings, meaning generally the verbatim record of trial, and sometimes of motions prior to trial, and of arguments involving counsel and judge, sometimes held in chambers. Finally, there are docket entries kept by the clerk of court, which list the pleadings and motion papers filed in the court. See FRAP 4(a).

An early task for the parties is to designate parts of the record that are important in the appeal. While any part of the record is available to the appellate court—and FRAP 11(a) says that appellant's duties include doing "whatever else is necessary to enable the [trial court] clerk to assemble and forward the record"—the parties are encouraged to agree on an Appendix containing selected parts that bear on the points to be argued on appeal. See FRAP 30(a).

Thereafter the parties prepare and file briefs. Appellant goes first, followed by the other side (appellee). In our example, Ned and O Company are likely appellants, and Marsha is the appellee (and perhaps cross-appellant). The Rules regulate extensively the form to be followed in briefing appeals: Thus the appellate brief must include tables of contents and authorities, including cases and statutes, as well as statements describing the jurisdictional basis for the trial court and the court of appeals. More substantively, appellant must present "a statement of the issues presented for review," a "statement of the case" indicating its "nature" and "the course of proceedings" and the "disposition" below. And of central importance, appellant must state "a summary of the argument" and the argument itself, including the "contentions and the [underlying] reasons," a description of "the applicable standard of review" and a "conclusion." The appellee's answering brief can omit some of the preliminary points if there is no argument about them, but otherwise must contain similar things. See FRAP 28.

There may or may not be oral argument. Any of the parties involved in the appeal may weigh in on the subject by filing a statement arguing for or against holding oral argument, but the court may decide otherwise. See FRAP 34.

■ NOTES ON APPELLATE PROCESS

1. In the example in which Marsha sues Ned and O Company and wins judgment, and defendants appeal, Marsha must decide whether she too should appeal—whether she should file notice of cross-appeal. This question arises when she receives notice of Ned and O Company's appeal even if Marsha would otherwise have been content. How should Marsha (her lawyer) think about this matter?

(a) Suppose Ned and O Company take the position that the judge erred in admitting expert testimony critical to Marsha's case. Marsha will want to defend the decision of the trial judge on this point. She can do this much without filing her own notice of appeal, and her lawyer may decides to stake the case on this position.

(b) Suppose, however, that Marsha (her lawyer) thinks the court erred in *excluding* evidence offered on Marsha's behalf, or *admitting* evidence offered by Ned and O Company, to which she objected. If so, she should file notice of cross-appeal: If Ned and O Company win on *their* appeal, Marsha's lawyer

might preserve the verdict by showing that Marsha would have won anyway if the judge had not made mistakes that benefitted Ned and O Company. More likely, Marsha's lawyer may hope that if the case is to be retried because Ned and O Company prevail, Marsha has a good chance to prevail in a second trial because mistakes in the first trial that helped Ned and O Company will not be made on retrial.

2. From considering the mechanics, you can see that appeals are costly. And you already know that they seldom succeed in reversing judgments. There are many reasons behind this state of affairs.

(a) First, consider the fact that trial errors do not generate reversals or other relief unless the reviewing court thinks they affected outcome. There are many reasons why errors are harmless: If the judge excludes evidence that should have been admitted, the error is likely to be harmless if enough other evidence was admitted to prove the same point; if the judge admits evidence that should have been excluded, the error is likely to be harmless if enough other evidence was admitted to prove the point. In short, many errors are harmless.

(b) Second, a lawyer who seeks reversal must be prepared to show that the trial lawyer did the right thing to "preserve the claim of error." If the trial lawyers for Ned and O Company did not object to Marsha's expert, which means acting in timely fashion and stating grounds, see FRE 103(a)(1), an appeal urging error in admitting the expert's testimony will likely be rejected even *if* the appellate court thinks an error was committed that affected outcome.

(c) Third, the lawyer seeking reversal must show that an error affected the outcome by what amounts to circumstantial arguments. That is to say, the lawyer cannot use affidavits or testimony by jurors, and courts cannot consider what jurors said or thought in deliberations, so these inquiries are by nature "objective" in the sense that the reviewing court must use the record of trial to show what *might have* affected the verdict. See FRE 606(b) (barring use of juror testimony or affidavits to show "any matter or statement occurring" during deliberations or "the effect of anything" upon any juror's "mind or emotions") (with some narrow exceptions), discussed in Chapter 12C4, supra.

B | THE BASIC RULE: ONLY FINAL JUDGMENTS CAN BE APPEALED

Foundational in the law of appellate jurisdiction is the proposition, observed in most states and the federal system, that only "final" judgments may be appealed. Simply stated, the reason behind this principle is that allowing "interlocutory" appeals on a piecemeal basis through the course of suit would be disruptive, time-consuming, costly, and wasteful of resources.

Consider the matter a minute longer: Trial courts make rulings on many issues in any case—on matters like jurisdiction and venue, adequacy of pleadings, joinder of parties, scope and propriety of discovery, empaneling a jury, instructing the jury, admissibility of evidence, and sufficiency of evidence, to list but a few that routinely arise. If every ruling could be appealed, trial courts would find their work often interrupted and subject to long periods of hiatus while appeals were pursued. The time between filing and judgment could expand from a year or more to many years. Wealthy or resourceful litigants could impose costs on their adversaries by taking appeals. And many trial court decisions, if evaluated at the end of the case, can turn out to be insignificant so interlocutory review is unnecessary.

All that being said, it is not all jurisdictions that insist on a finality rule. In New York, for example, appeals from nonfinal orders are routine, and there has in fact been some agitation to reform the procedure of that state for that very reason. See, e.g., Davin Scheffel, *Interlocutory Appeals in New York—Time Has Come for a More Efficient Approach,* 16 Pace L. Rev. 607 (1996) (beginning with comment that in New York "a party may appeal, by right, almost any civil interlocutory order," making New York "one of the most liberal jurisdictions" in this respect).

It is also true that the distinction between jurisdictions that observe the final judgment rule and jurisdictions that allow interlocutory appeals can be overstated. Even those in the former camp allow *some* interlocutory appeals: For example, the writ of mandamus, which involves an "original" proceeding in an appellate court seeking an order directing the trial judge to correct a mistaken ruling, is at least sometimes available even in "final judgment" jurisdictions. And there are other exceptions. In California, for example, a defending party who makes and loses a motion to dismiss for lack of jurisdiction over the person can seek review (indeed *failing* to do so waives the objection). See State Farm General Insurance Co. v. JT's Frames, Inc., 104 Cal. Rptr. 3d 573, 580 (Cal. App. 2010) (endorsing use of mandamus in this setting). In the federal system, however, an order denying a motion to dismiss for lack of jurisdiction generally can't be appealed. See Northern Laminate Sales, Inc. v. Davis, 403 F.3d 14, 23 (1st Cir. 2005).

1. A "Pragmatic" Principle

In the paradigm case, everyone can agree that a judgment that fully disposes of the case is final and appealable. If, for example, plaintiff Abbey sues defendant David, and the case goes to trial leading to judgment in favor of Abbey for $2 million, and if the judgment is "set out in a separate document" and is signed (usually by the court or by the clerk) and entered, all as described in FRCP 58, the judgment is final and may be appealed. The simplicity of this example can vanish, however, in our modern era in which multiple claims and parties are often involved in a single suit. These matters are addressed in FRCP 54(b) (see Section B2, infra.)

The simplest and clearest concept of finality, as illustrated in this example, is indeed commonplace, so finality can be an easy concept to apply. In a few instances, the Court has summed it up in classic phrases: A final judgment "ends the litigation on the merits and leaves nothing for the court to do but execute the judgment." Caitlin v. United States, 324 U.S. 229, 233 (1945). A final judgment is the decision "by which a district court dissociates itself from the case." Swint v. Chambers County Commission, 514 U.S. 35, 42 (1995).

Similarly, one can readily see that many orders entered by a trial judge simply *cannot* normally be counted as final, and would not ordinarily provide ground for appeal as final orders, including (a) denial of a motion for summary judgment, see Zarnow v. City of Wichita Falls, Texas, 614 F.3d 161, 166 (5th Cir. 2010), (b) denial of a motion to dismiss for failure to state a claim, see Kilburn v. Socialist People's Libyan Arab Jamahiriya, 375 F.3d 1123 (D.C. 2004), and (c) denial of motion to dismiss on ground that the chosen forum violated a binding forum selection clause, see Lauro Lines S.R.L. v. Chasser, 490 U.S. 495 (1989).

Even without taking up the challenge of multiple claims and parties in a single suit, however, we encounter many decisions by trial judges (and orders that they make) that are *not* the last thing but are still final in some sense. The Court has long struggled on this account, and has endorsed a "practical not technical" approach to the question whether an order is final and therefore subject to appeal or not. See Cohen v. Beneficial Industrial Loan Corp., 337 U.S. 541, 546 (1949) (Section B2, infra). In several cases, the Court has acknowledged that the question is fraught with difficulty, commenting that whether a ruling is final under 28 USC §1291 "is frequently so close a question that decision of that issue either way can be supported with equally forceful arguments," hence that one cannot "devise a formula to resolve all marginal cases" found within a "twilight zone" of finality. See Gillespie v. United States Steel Corp., 379 U.S. 148, 152 (1964).

QUACKENBUSH v. ALLSTATE INSURANCE COMPANY

Supreme Court of the United States
517 U.S. 706 (1996)

Justice O'Connor delivered the opinion of the Court.

In this case, we consider whether an abstention-based remand order is appealable as a final order under 28 USC §1291, and whether the abstention doctrine first recognized in Burford v. Sun Oil Co., 319 U.S. 315 (1943), can be applied in a common-law suit for damages.

I

Petitioner, the Insurance Commissioner for the State of California, was appointed trustee over the assets of the Mission Insurance Company and its affiliates (Mission companies) in 1987, after those companies were ordered into liquidation by a California court. In an effort to gather the assets of the defunct Mission companies, the Commissioner filed the instant action against respondent Allstate Insurance Company in state court, seeking contract and tort damages for Allstate's alleged breach of certain reinsurance agreements, as well as a general declaration of Allstate's obligations under those agreements.

Allstate removed the action to federal court on diversity grounds and filed a motion to compel arbitration under the Federal Arbitration Act, 9 USC §1 *et seq.* The Commissioner sought remand to state court, arguing that the District Court should abstain from hearing the case under *Burford, supra,* because its resolution might interfere with California's regulation of the Mission insolvency. Specifically, the Commissioner indicated that Allstate would be asserting its right to set off its own contract claims against the Commissioner's recovery under the contract, that the viability of these setoff claims was a hotly disputed question of state law, and that this question was currently pending before the state courts in another case arising out of the Mission insolvency.

The District Court observed that "California has an overriding interest in regulating insurance insolvencies and liquidations in a uniform and orderly manner," and that in this case "this important state interest could be undermined by inconsistent rulings from the federal and state courts." Based on these observations, and its determination that the setoff question should be resolved in state court, the District Court concluded this case was an appropriate one for the exercise of *Burford* abstention. The District Court did not stay its hand pending the California courts' resolution of the setoff issue, but instead remanded the entire case to state court. The District Court entered this remand order without ruling on Allstate's motion to compel arbitration.

After determining that appellate review of the District Court's remand order was not barred by 28 USC §1447(d), and that the remand order was appealable under 28 USC §1291 as a final collateral order, the Court of Appeals for the Ninth Circuit vacated the District Court's decision and ordered the case sent to arbitration. The Ninth Circuit concluded that federal courts can abstain from hearing a case under *Burford* only when the relief being sought is equitable in nature, and therefore held that abstention was inappropriate in this case because the Commissioner purported to be seeking only legal relief. . . .

II

We first consider whether the Court of Appeals had jurisdiction to hear Allstate's appeal under 28 USC §1291, which confers jurisdiction over appeals from "final decisions" of the district courts, and 28 USC §1447(d), which provides that "[a]n order remanding a case to the State court from which it was removed is not reviewable on appeal or otherwise."

We agree with the Ninth Circuit and the parties that §1447(d) interposes no bar to appellate review of the remand order at issue in this case. As we held in Thermtron Products, Inc. v. Hermansdorfer, 423 U.S. 336, 345-346 (1976), . . . "§1447(d) must be read *in pari materia* with §1447(c), so that only remands based on grounds specified in §1447(c) are immune from review under §1447(d)." This gloss renders §1447(d) inapplicable here: The District Court's abstention-based remand order does not fall into either category of remand order described in §1447(c), as it is not based on lack of subject matter jurisdiction or defects in removal procedure.

Finding no affirmative bar to appellate review of the District Court's remand order, we must determine whether that review may be obtained by appeal under §1291. The general rule is that "a party is entitled to a single appeal, to be deferred until final judgment has been entered, in which claims of district court error at any stage of the litigation may be ventilated." Digital Equipment Corp. v. Desktop Direct, Inc., 511 U.S. 863, 868 (1994). Accordingly, we have held that a decision is ordinarily considered final and appealable under §1291 only if it "ends the litigation on the merits and leaves nothing for the court to do but execute the judgment." Catlin v. United States, 324 U.S. 229, 233 (1945). . . .

The application of these principles to the appealability of the remand order before us is controlled by our decision in Moses H. Cone Memorial Hospital v. Mercury Constr. Corp., 460 U.S. 1 (1983). The District Court in that case entered an order under Colorado River Water Conservation Dist. v. United States, 424 U.S. 800 (1976), staying a federal diversity suit pending the completion of a declaratory judgment action that had been filed in state court. The Court of Appeals held that this stay order was appealable under §1291, and we affirmed that determination on two independent grounds.

We . . . concluded that the abstention-based stay order was appealable as a "final decision" under §1291 because it put the litigants "'effectively out of court'" (quoting Idlewild Bon Voyage Liquor Corp. v. Epstein, 370 U.S. 713, 715, n.2 (1962) (*per curiam*)), and because its effect was "precisely to surrender jurisdiction of a federal suit to a state court." These standards do not reflect our oft-repeated definition of finality, but in *Moses H. Cone* we found their application to be compelled by precedent ("*Idlewild's* reasoning is limited to cases where (under *Colorado River*, abstention, or a closely similar doctrine) the object of the stay is to require all or an essential part of the federal suit to be litigated in a state forum").

. . .

The District Court's order remanding on grounds of *Burford* abstention is in all relevant respects indistinguishable from the stay order we found to be appealable in *Moses H. Cone.* No less than an order staying a federal court action pending adjudication of the dispute in state court, it puts the litigants in this case "'effectively out of court,'" *Moses H. Cone* (quoting Idlewild Bon Voyage Liquor Corp. v. Epstein), and its effect is "precisely to surrender jurisdiction of a federal suit to a state court." Indeed, the remand order is clearly more "final" than a stay order in this sense. When a district court remands a case to a state court, the district court disassociates itself from the case entirely, retaining nothing of the matter on the federal court's docket.

. . .

We have previously stated that "an order remanding a removed action does not represent a final judgment reviewable by appeal." Thermtron Products, Inc. v. Hermansdorfer. Petitioner asks that we adhere to that statement and hold that appellate review of the District Court's remand order can only be obtained through a petition for writ of mandamus. To the extent *Thermtron* would require us to ignore the implications of our later holding in *Moses H. Cone,* however, we disavow it. *Thermtron*'s determination that remand orders are not reviewable "final judgments" doubtless was necessary to the resolution of that case (posing the question whether mandamus was the appropriate vehicle), but our principal concern in *Thermtron* was the interpretation of the bar to appellate review embodied in 28 USC §1447(d), and our statement concerning the appropriate procedural vehicle for reviewing a district court's remand order was peripheral to that concern. Moreover, the parties in *Thermtron* did not brief the question, our opinion does not refer to *Catlin* or its definition of "final decisions," and our opinion nowhere addresses whether any class of remand order might be appealable under the collateral order doctrine. Indeed, the only support *Thermtron* cites for the proposition that remand orders are reviewable only by mandamus, not by appeal, is Chicago & Alton Railroad Co. v. Wiswall, 23 Wall. 507 (1875), the superannuated reasoning of which is of little vitality today, compare *id.,* 23 Wall., at 508 (deeming a "writ of error to review what has been done" an inappropriate vehicle for reviewing a court of appeals' "refusal to hear and decide") with *Moses H. Cone,* 460 U.S., at 10-11, n.11 (holding that a stay order is appealable *because* it amounts to a refusal to hear and decide a case).

Admittedly, remand orders like the one entered in this case do not meet the traditional definition of finality—they do not "en[d] the litigation on the merits and leav[e] nothing for the court to do but execute the judgment," *Catlin.* But because the District Court's remand order is functionally indistinguishable from the stay order we found appealable in *Moses H. Cone,* we conclude that it is appealable, and turn to the merits of the Ninth Circuit's decision respecting *Burford* abstention.

[The Court concludes that abstaining under *Burford* was wrong, and affirms the Ninth Circuit decision to send the case to arbitration. Abstention was appropriate in *Burford* in light of "the difficulty of the [state] regulatory issues," the "unified procedures" in Texas, and "the important state interests [that] this system of review was designed to serve." In *Burford,* use of a federal forum "threatened to frustrate the purpose of the complex administrative system that Texas had established," and *Burford* abstention "derives from the discretion historically enjoyed by courts of equity." Here, in contrast, the suit is a damage action that is "not discretionary," and an important federal interest is at stake, namely the interest under the Federal Arbitration Act to enforce arbitration agreements.]

■ NOTES ON "PRACTICAL NOT TECHNICAL" FINALITY

1. What was the California Insurance Commissioner doing in *Quackenbush*? When Allstate removed the case to federal court, what was its aim? In response to removal, the Commissioner invoked the *Burford* abstention doctrine. You've looked at abstention in the Notes on Federal Court Application of State Law (Chapter 6A7, supra), and again in connection with the *Pennzoil* case (Chapter 6C1, supra). Recall that *Burford* endorsed abstention because the case raised state law regulatory questions in the setting of efforts by an agency to implement policy, and the court thought state courts should resolve these first, and federal involvement would endanger state policies. What arguments favor abstention here?

2. In *Quackenbush,* Allstate sought a federal court order compelling arbitration. Instead, the judge remanded to state court, and Allstate appealed. Under the removal statute, an order remanding a case to state court is not appealable, as *Quackenbush* recognizes. See 28 USC §1447(d) (order remanding case to state court from which it was removed "is not reviewable on appeal or otherwise"). Why is the statute necessary? Why doesn't the statute apply in *Quackenbush*? The statute does not address appeals from an order *refusing* to remand. Why doesn't it cover this point?

(a) In Moses H. Cone Memorial Hospital v. Mercury Construction Corporation, 460 U.S. 1 (1983), the Supreme Court held that an order staying a federal suit under the doctrine of *Colorado River* abstention was appealable. *Colorado River* endorsed abstention to allow pending state litigation to go its full course, rather than being interrupted by a federal suit involving the same issues and parties. In *Moses Cone,* a hospital sued a contractor in state court, and the contractor countersued in federal court, seeking (like Allstate in

Quackenbush) an order compelling arbitration. Like the district court in *Quackenbush,* the district court in *Moses Cone* stayed its hand (but invoked *Colorado River* rather than *Burford* abstention). The contractor appealed, and the Court of Appeals found that the abstention order was a final decision that could be appealed, and (like the appellate court in *Quackenbush*) reversed and ordered the case to go to arbitration. In *Moses Cone,* the Supreme Court held that the order staying the suit was a final judgment under 28 USC §1291, hence immediately appealable, and it affirmed the Court of Appeals, resulting in the case going to arbitration. What is the message of *Moses Cone* and *Quackenbush*? Surely it is that invoking an abstention doctrine is an appealable order. Does it make sense to treat such orders as final judgments?

(b) Suppose a federal court *denies* a motion to abstain. Can the disappointed party (the movant) appeal from *this* order? Of course common sense would call out that denying a stay cannot be in any sense "final," and the Supreme Court has taken this position. But arriving at the right answer was harder than you might think: An order denying a stay had been likened to an injunction, and you will see that orders granting or denying or modifying "preliminary" injunctions are appealable. The analogy to the injunction came from the distant past, as it was once the case in English law that the Court of Chancery could enjoin a suit a common law. When law and equity were merged in the United States, the notion arose that an order staying a suit at law so a claim in equity could go forward was in effect an injunction, so it was appealable. But the Court finally said no to this line of thinking, and a refusal to stay a federal suit under an abstention doctrine is now just a nonfinal order that cannot be immediately appealed. See Gulfstream Aerospace Co. v. Mayacamas Corp., 485 U.S. 271 (1988) (also holding that appeal does not lie under the "collateral order" doctrine).

3. In the *Gillespie* case, plaintiff brought suit in federal court on behalf of the estate of a deceased seaman, seeking recovery for his dependent brothers and sisters under the Jones Act (federal statute protecting seamen and families, similar to FELA that operates on behalf of railroaders). She also sought recovery under the Ohio wrongful death and survival statutes. The judge struck the state law claims on the ground that the Jones Act pre-empted state remedies, and struck claims on behalf of the brothers and sisters on the ground that the Jones Act did not authorize such recovery. Plaintiff appealed, and the Court of Appeals exercised jurisdiction. The Supreme Court agreed that the final judgment rule in 28 USC §1291 did not require dismissal. While it was "true that the review of this case by the Court of Appeals could be called 'piecemeal,'" it did not appear that "the cost of trying this case will be greater because the Court of Appeals decided the issues raised instead of compelling the parties to go to trial with them unanswered," and the "eventual costs" would be "less if we now pass on the questions presented" than they would be if the case was sent back without resolving the issues. The claims on appeal were not "formally severable" so as to make the order "unquestionably appealable," but there was "ample reason to view [those] claims as severable in deciding the issue of finality." See Gillespie v. United States Steel Corp., 379 U.S. 148 (1964).

(a) Huh? How's that again? This "piecemeal" review can fit the final judgment concept because trying the case will cost more if the issues are not resolved, and costs will be less if the court passes on them now? Doesn't that mean that every case, once it reaches the court of appeals, should be viewed as fitting the final judgment rule because it is always cheaper (now) to resolve the issues than to go forward at trial with those issues unresolved?

(b) You will see, when you look at FRCP 54(b) (Section C2, infra), that this provision seems tailor-made for situations like *Gillespie,* but FRCP 54(b) requires the judge to certify that there is "no just reason for delay."

(c) *Gillespie* has never been overruled, but it is recognized as an outlier that stands for a rogue principle—that any order disposing of a whole claim can be viewed as final.

4. In the *Brown Shoe* case, the Court considered the finality of a district court decision that defendant violated the antitrust laws and ordered defendant to divest itself of a subsidiary. The Court reserved its right to approve a divestiture plan. Defendant took an appeal that went directly to the Supreme Court under a special provision in the antitrust statute, but this provision incorporates the final judgment standard in 28 USC §1291. The Court held that the decision had "sufficient indicia of finality," noting that "every prayer for relief was passed upon," and that defendant was disputing the propriety of the divestiture order on an "all or nothing" basis, and noting further that divestiture orders require "careful, and often extended, negotiation and formulation" so that delay in reviewing the issues could lead to a "change in market conditions sufficiently pronounced to render impractical or otherwise unenforceable the very plan of asset disposition for which the litigation was held." See Brown Shoe Co. v. United States, 370 U.S. 292, 308-309 (1962).

5. Suppose a suit is brought as a class action, but the court refuses to certify the class and instead strikes the class action allegations. Many such suits are at this point dead in the water: Plaintiff cannot afford to pursue the matter as an individual suit, and suffering a dismissal later for failure to prosecute will not preserve a claim of error (because a court would be right to dismiss if plaintiffs don't move the suit forward, and the ruling on class certification would not be reached). Is the order striking class action allegations final for purposes of appeal under 28 USC §1291? See Coopers & Lybrand v. Livesay, 437 U.S. 463 (1978) (answering in the negative; stressing that an order decertifying or refusing to certify a class "does not of its own force terminate" the suit, rejecting the "death knell" doctrine, and labeling such orders "inherently interlocutory").

(a) If *Coopers & Lybrand* had been decided the other way, would it follow that every order revising the scope or size of the class, if it shrank the class in some way, would be viewed as "final" for purposes of appeal?

(b) The Court in *Coopers & Lybrand* stressed that plaintiffs are free to pursue individual claims, even after an order decertifying or refusing to certify a class, but acknowledged that such rulings "may induce a plaintiff to abandon" individual claims. Would it be better to make the question of finality turn on whether a ruling is likely to result in the suit being dropped?

(c) In 1998, 20 years after *Coopers & Lybrand,* the Court added FRCP 23(f), under which orders "granting or denying" class certification are appealable *if* the court of appeals agrees to hear the case. Does this provision solve the problem? Recall that this provision allowed the appeal in Allen v. International Truck and Engine Corp., 358 F.3d 469 (7th Cir. 1004) (Chapter 8H5, supra).

6. In *Quackenbush,* Allstate took an appeal to the Ninth Circuit, which reversed the district court and remanded the case for arbitration under the federal Arbitration Act, 9 USC §1 et seq. Basically, this statute makes agreements to arbitrate enforceable in federal court, and 9 USC §16 provides that an order "denying an application . . . to compel arbitration" may be appealed. It is something of a mystery why this provision was not applied in this case.

2. Modifying the Concept: "Collateral Order" Appeals

COHEN v. BENEFICIAL INDUSTRIAL LOAN CORP.

Supreme Court of the United States
337 U.S. 541 (1949)

[On the basis of diversity jurisdiction, stockholders brought a derivative suit against managers and directors of Beneficial Industrial Loan Corporation, alleging that defendants had engaged in a conspiracy to enrich themselves at the expense of the corporation, in effect stealing huge sums of money. Plaintiff and an intervenor in the suit owned, between them, 150 shares in the company, just over one-tenth of 1 percent of the outstanding shares. Defendant moved to require plaintiffs to post security for costs, invoking a New Jersey statute that entitled defendants in such suits, when brought by a small percentage of shareholders, to require "security" for "reasonable expenses, including counsel fees." The trial court denied the motion, and defendants appealed. The Court devotes most of the opinion to the question whether such a statute is constitutional, concluding that it is, and to the question whether it applies in federal courts, concluding that it does. At the beginning of the opinion, the Court addresses the question whether the refusal to require security for costs is appealable.]

At the threshold we are met with the question whether the District Court's order refusing to apply the statute was an appealable one. 28 USC §1291 provides, as did its predecessors, for appeal only "from all final decisions of the district courts," except when direct appeal to this Court is provided. . . . It is obvious that, if Congress had allowed appeals only from those final judgments which terminate an action, this order would not be appealable.

The effect of the statute is to disallow appeal from any decision which is tentative, informal or incomplete. Appeal gives the upper court a power of review, not one of intervention. So long as the matter remains open, unfinished or inconclusive, there may be no intrusion by appeal. But the District Court's action upon this application was concluded and closed and its decision final in that sense before the appeal was taken.

Nor does the statute permit appeals, even from fully consummated decisions, where they are but steps towards final judgment in which they will merge. The purpose is to combine in one review all stages of the proceeding that effectively may be reviewed and corrected if and when final judgment results. But this order of the District Court did not make any step toward final disposition of the merits of the case and will not be merged in final judgment. When that time comes, it will be too late effectively to review the present order and the rights conferred by the statute, if it is applicable, will have been lost, probably irreparably. We conclude that the matters embraced in the decision appealed from are not of such an interlocutory nature as to affect, or to be affected by, decision of the merits of this case.

This decision appears to fall in that small class which finally determine claims of right separable from, and collateral to, rights asserted in the action, too important to be denied review and too independent of the cause itself to require that appellate consideration be deferred until the whole case is adjudicated. The Court has long given this provision of the statute this practical rather than a technical construction. Bank of Columbia v. Sweeney, 1 Pet. 567, 569 (1828); United States v. River Rouge Improvement Co., 269 U.S. 411, 414 (1926); Cobbledick v. United States, 309 U.S. 323, 328 (1940).

We hold this order appealable because it is a final disposition of a claimed right which is not an ingredient of the cause of action and does not require consideration with it. But we do not mean that every order fixing security is subject to appeal. Here it is the right to security that presents a serious and unsettled question. If the right were admitted or clear and the order involved only an exercise of discretion as to the amount of security, a matter the statute makes subject to reconsideration from time to time, appealability would present a different question.

JUSTICE SONIA SOTOMAYOR

Justice Sonia Maria Sotomayor was nominated to the Supreme Court in 2009 and confirmed in that year, and she became the first Hispanic (and third female) Justice. (After nomination by President George H.W. Bush, she had served as Judge in the United States District Court for the Southern District of New York; after nomination by President Bill Clinton, she had served as Judge on the Second Circuit.) The opinion in *Mohawk* was her first as Justice of the Supreme Court. In her time on the Second Circuit, Judge Sotomayor had numerous occasions to consider the scope of the "collateral order" doctrine, and had applied it to allow appeals in a handful of cases raising issues of qualified official immunity (see note 4 in the Notes on the Collateral Order Doctrine, following the *Mohawk* case). Although her opinion in *Mohawk* does not make this point, most federal appellate opinions had reached the same conclusion that the Court reached in this case—the collateral order doctrine does *not* apply to rulings overturning claims of attorney-client privilege. For a case that comes out the other way, see In re Teleglobe Communications Corp.,493 F.3d 345 (3d Cir. 2007) (collateral order doctrine does apply to orders overruling claims of privilege). The decision in *Mohawk* has led some courts to decide that the *Perlman* doctrine, under which a privilege holder is sometimes allowed to appeal from an order directed at a third party to produce documents, should be narrowed, at least where the privilege holder is a party to the suit who can appeal at the end. See, e.g., In re Grand Jury, 680 F.3d 328, 341 (3d Cir. 2012) (*Mohawk* may deny a party who is a privilege holder an appeal otherwise available; court "leave[s] for another day" the question whether *Mohawk* "forecloses *Perlman* appeals when the privilege holder is a subject or target of an underlying grand jury investigation").

MOHAWK INDUSTRIES, INC. v. CARPENTER

Supreme Court of the United States
558 U.S. 100 (2009)

Justice SOTOMAYOR delivered the opinion of the Court.

Section 1291 of the Judicial Code confers on federal courts of appeals jurisdiction to review "final decisions of the district courts." 28 USC §1291. Although "final decisions" typically are ones that trigger the entry of judgment, they also include a small set of prejudgment orders that are "collateral to" the merits of an action and "too important" to be denied immediate review. Cohen v. Beneficial Industrial Loan Corp., 337 U.S. 541, 546 (1949). In this case, petitioner Mohawk Industries, Inc., attempted to bring a collateral order appeal after the District Court ordered it to disclose certain confidential materials on the ground that Mohawk had waived the attorney-client privilege. The Court of Appeals dismissed the appeal for want of jurisdiction.

The question before us is whether disclosure orders adverse to the attorney-client privilege qualify for immediate appeal under the collateral order doctrine. Agreeing with the Court of Appeals, we hold that they do not. Post-judgment appeals, together with other review mechanisms, suffice to protect the rights of litigants and preserve the vitality of the attorney-client privilege.

I

In 2007, respondent Norman Carpenter, a former shift supervisor at a Mohawk manufacturing facility, filed suit in the United States District Court for the Northern District of Georgia, alleging that Mohawk had terminated him in violation of 42 USC §1985(2) and various Georgia laws. According to Carpenter's complaint, his termination came after he informed a member of Mohawk's human resources department in an e-mail that the company was employing undocumented immigrants. At the time, unbeknownst to Carpenter, Mohawk stood accused [in the *Williams* case, a pending class suit,] of conspiring to drive down the wages of its legal employees by knowingly hiring undocumented workers in violation of federal and state racketeering laws. Company officials directed Carpenter to meet with the company's retained counsel in the *Williams* case, and counsel allegedly pressured Carpenter to recant his statements. When he refused, Carpenter alleges, Mohawk fired him under false pretenses.

After learning of Carpenter's complaint, the plaintiffs in the *Williams* case sought an evidentiary hearing to explore Carpenter's allegations. In its response to their motion, Mohawk described Carpenter's accusations as "pure fantasy" and recounted the "true facts" of Carpenter's dismissal. According to Mohawk, Carpenter himself had "engaged in blatant and illegal misconduct" by attempting to have Mohawk hire an undocumented worker. The company "commenced an immediate investigation," during which retained counsel interviewed Carpenter. Because Carpenter's "efforts to cause Mohawk to circumvent federal immigration law" "blatantly violated Mohawk policy," the company terminated him.

As these events were unfolding in the *Williams* case, discovery was underway in Carpenter's case. Carpenter filed a motion to compel Mohawk to produce information concerning his meeting with retained counsel and the company's termination decision. Mohawk maintained that the requested information was protected by the attorney-client privilege.

The District Court agreed that the privilege applied to the requested information, but it granted Carpenter's motion to compel disclosure after concluding that Mohawk had implicitly waived the privilege through its representations in the *Williams* case. The court declined to certify its order for interlocutory appeal under 28 USC §1292(b). But, recognizing "the seriousness of its [waiver] finding," it stayed its ruling to allow Mohawk to explore other potential "avenues to appeal . . . , such as a petition for mandamus or appealing this Order under the collateral order doctrine."

Mohawk filed a notice of appeal and a petition for a writ of mandamus to the Eleventh Circuit. The Court of Appeals dismissed the appeal for lack of jurisdiction under 28 USC §1291, holding that the District Court's ruling did not qualify as an immediately appealable collateral order within the meaning of *Cohen*. "Under *Cohen*," the Court of Appeals explained, "an order is appealable if it (1) conclusively determines the disputed question; (2) resolves an important issue completely separate from the merits of the action; and (3) is effectively unreviewable on appeal from a final judgment." According to the court, the District Court's waiver ruling satisfied the first two of these requirements but not the third, because "a discovery order that implicates the attorney-client privilege" can be adequately reviewed "on appeal from a final judgment." The Court of Appeals also rejected Mohawk's mandamus petition, finding no "clear usurpation of power or abuse of discretion" by the District Court. We granted certiorari, to resolve a conflict among the Circuits concerning the availability of collateral appeals in the attorney-client privilege context.

II

A

By statute, Courts of Appeals "have jurisdiction of appeals from all final decisions of the district courts of the United States, . . . except where a direct review may be had in the Supreme Court." 28 USC §1291. A "final decisio[n]" is typically one "by which a district court disassociates itself from a case." *Swint v. Chambers County Comm'n*, 514 U.S. 35, 42 (1995). This Court, however, "has long given" §1291 a "practical rather than a technical construction." As we held in *Cohen*, the statute encompasses not only judgments that "terminate an action," but also a "small class" of collateral rulings that, although they do not end the litigation, are appropriately deemed "final." "That small category includes only decisions that are conclusive, that resolve important questions separate from the merits, and that are effectively unreviewable on appeal from the final judgment in the underlying action." *Swint*.

In applying *Cohen's* collateral order doctrine, we have stressed that it must "never be allowed to swallow the general rule that a party is entitled to a single appeal, to be deferred until final judgment has been entered." Digital Equipment Corp. v. Desktop Direct, Inc., 511 U.S. 863, 868 (1994); see also Will v. Hallock, 546 U.S. 345, 350 (2006) ("emphasizing [the doctrine's] modest scope"). Our admonition reflects a healthy respect for the virtues of the final judgment rule. Permitting piecemeal, prejudgment appeals, we have rec-ognized, undermines "efficient judicial administration" and encroaches upon the prerogatives of district court judges, who play a "special role" in managing ongoing litigation. Firestone Tire & Rubber Co. v. Risjord, 449 U.S. 368, 374 (1981); see also Richardson-Merrell Inc. v. Koller, 472 U.S. 424, 436 (1985) ("[T]he district judge can better exercise [his or her] responsibility [to police the prejudgment tactics of litigants] if the appellate courts do not repeatedly intervene to second-guess prejudgment rulings").

The justification for immediate appeal must therefore be sufficiently strong to overcome the usual benefits of deferring appeal until litigation con-cludes. This requirement finds expression in two of the three traditional *Cohen* conditions. The second condition insists upon "*important* questions separate from the merits." *Swint.* More significantly, "the third *Cohen* question, whether a right is 'adequately vindicable' or 'effectively reviewable,' simply cannot be answered without a judgment about the value of the interests that would be lost through rigorous application of a final judgment require-ment." *Digital Equipment.* That a ruling "may burden litigants in ways that are only imperfectly reparable by appellate reversal of a final district court judgment . . . has never sufficed." Instead, the decisive consideration is whether delaying review until the entry of final judgment "would imperil a substantial public interest" or "some particular value of a high order." *Will.*

In making this determination, we do not engage in an "individualized jurisdictional inquiry." Coopers & Lybrand v. Livesay, 437 U.S. 463, 473 (1978). Rather, our focus is on "the entire category to which a claim belongs." *Digital Equipment.* As long as the class of claims, taken as a whole, can be adequately vindicated by other means, "the chance that the litigation at hand might be speeded, or a 'particular injustic[e]' averted," does not provide a basis for jurisdiction under §1291. *Ibid.* (quoting Van Cauwenberghe v. Biard, 486 U.S. 517, 529 (1988) (alteration in original)).

B

In the present case, the Court of Appeals concluded that the District Court's privilege-waiver order satisfied the first two conditions of the collateral order doctrine—conclusiveness and separateness—but not the third—effective unreviewability. Because we agree with the Court of Appeals that collateral order appeals are not necessary to ensure effective review of orders adverse to the attorney-client privilege, we do not decide whether the other *Cohen* requirements are met.

Mohawk does not dispute that "we have generally denied review of pre-trial discovery orders." *Firestone*; see also 15B C. Wright, A. Miller, & E. Cooper, Federal Practice and Procedure §3914.23 (2d ed. 1992) (hereinafter Wright & Miller) ("[T]he rule remains settled that most discovery rulings are not final").

Mohawk contends, however, that rulings implicating the attorney-client privilege differ in kind from run-of-the-mill discovery orders because of the important institutional interests at stake. According to Mohawk, the right to maintain attorney-client confidences—the *sine qua non* of a meaningful attorney-client relationship—is "irreparably destroyed absent immediate appeal" of adverse privilege rulings.

We readily acknowledge the importance of the attorney-client privilege, which "is one of the oldest recognized privileges for confidential communications." Swidler & Berlin v. United States, 524 U.S. 399, 403 (1998). By assuring confidentiality, the privilege encourages clients to make "full and frank" disclosures to their attorneys, who are then better able to provide candid advice and effective representation. Upjohn Co. v. United States, 449 U.S. 383, 389 (1981). This, in turn, serves "broader public interests in the observance of law and administration of justice."

The crucial question, however, is not whether an interest is important in the abstract; it is whether deferring review until final judgment so imperils the interest as to justify the cost of allowing immediate appeal of the entire class of relevant orders. We routinely require litigants to wait until after final judgment to vindicate valuable rights, including rights central to our adversarial system. In *Digital Equipment*, we rejected an assertion that collateral order review was necessary to promote "the public policy favoring voluntary resolution of disputes." "It defies common sense," we explained, "to maintain that parties' readiness to settle will be significantly dampened (or the corresponding public interest impaired) by a rule that a district court's decision to let allegedly barred litigation go forward may be challenged as a matter of right only on appeal from a judgment for the plaintiff's favor."

We reach a similar conclusion here. In our estimation, postjudgment appeals generally suffice to protect the rights of litigants and assure the vitality of the attorney-client privilege. Appellate courts can remedy the improper disclosure of privileged material in the same way they remedy a host of other erroneous evidentiary rulings: by vacating an adverse judgment and remanding for a new trial in which the protected material and its fruits are excluded from evidence.

Dismissing such relief as inadequate, Mohawk emphasizes that the attorney-client privilege does not merely "prohibi[t] use of protected information at trial"; it provides a "right not to disclose the privileged information in the first place." Mohawk is undoubtedly correct that an order to disclose privileged information intrudes on the confidentiality of attorney-client communications. But deferring review until final judgment does not meaningfully reduce the *ex ante* incentives for full and frank consultations between clients and counsel.

One reason for the lack of a discernible chill is that, in deciding how freely to speak, clients and counsel are unlikely to focus on the remote prospect of an erroneous disclosure order, let alone on the timing of a possible appeal.

Whether or not immediate collateral order appeals are available, clients and counsel must account for the possibility that they will later be required by law to disclose their communications for a variety of reasons—for example, because they misjudged the scope of the privilege, because they waived the privilege, or because their communications fell within the privilege's crime-fraud exception. Most district court rulings on these matters involve the routine application of settled legal principles. They are unlikely to be reversed on appeal, particularly when they rest on factual determinations for which appellate deference is the norm. *See, e.g., Richardson-Merrell* ("Most pretrial orders of district judges are ultimately affirmed by appellate courts."); Reise v. Board of Regents, 957 F.2d 293, 295 (7th Cir. 1992) (noting that "almost all interlocutory appeals from discovery orders would end in affirmance" because "the district court possesses discretion, and review is deferential"). The breadth of the privilege and the narrowness of its exceptions will thus tend to exert a much greater influence on the conduct of clients and counsel than the small risk that the law will be misapplied.[2]

Moreover, were attorneys and clients to reflect upon their appellate options, they would find that litigants confronted with a particularly injurious or novel privilege ruling have several potential avenues of review apart from collateral order appeal. First, a party may ask the district court to certify, and the court of appeals to accept, an interlocutory appeal pursuant to 28 USC §1292(b). The preconditions for §1292(b) review—"a controlling question of law," the prompt resolution of which "may materially advance the ultimate termination of the litigation"—are most likely to be satisfied when a privilege ruling involves a new legal question or is of special consequence, and district courts should not hesitate to certify an interlocutory appeal in such cases. Second, in extraordinary circumstances—*i.e.,* when a disclosure order "amount[s] to a judicial usurpation of power or a clear abuse of discretion," or otherwise works a manifest injustice—a party may petition the court of appeals for a writ of mandamus. Cheney v. United States District Court, 542 U.S. 367, 390 (2004); see also *Firestone*. While these discretionary review mechanisms do not provide relief in every case, they serve as useful "safety valve[s]" for promptly correcting serious errors. *Digital Equipment.*

Another long-recognized option is for a party to defy a disclosure order and incur court-imposed sanctions. District courts have a range of sanctions from which to choose, including "directing that the matters embraced in the order or other designated facts be taken as established for purposes of the action," "prohibiting the disobedient party from supporting or opposing designated claims or defenses," or "striking pleadings in whole or in part." FRCP 37(b)(2)(i)-(iii). Such sanctions allow a party to obtain postjudgment review without having to

---

[2] Perhaps the situation would be different if district courts were systematically underenforcing the privilege, but we have no indication that this is the case.

reveal its privileged information. Alternatively, when the circumstances warrant it, a district court may hold a noncomplying party in contempt. The party can then appeal directly from that ruling, at least when the contempt citation can be characterized as a criminal punishment.

These established mechanisms for appellate review not only provide assurances to clients and counsel about the security of their confidential communications; they also go a long way toward addressing Mohawk's concern that, absent collateral order appeals of adverse attorney-client privilege rulings, some litigants may experience severe hardship. Mohawk is no doubt right that an order to disclose privileged material may, in some situations, have implications beyond the case at hand. But the same can be said about many categories of pretrial discovery orders for which collateral order appeals are unavailable. As with these other orders, rulings adverse to the privilege vary in their significance; some may be momentous, but others are more mundane. Section 1292(b) appeals, mandamus, and appeals from contempt citations facilitate immediate review of some of the more consequential attorney-client privilege rulings. Moreover, protective orders are available to limit the spillover effects of disclosing sensitive information. That a fraction of orders adverse to the attorney-client privilege may nevertheless harm individual litigants in ways that are "only imperfectly reparable" does not justify making all such orders immediately appealable as of right under §1291. *Digital Equipment.*

In short, the limited benefits of applying "the blunt, categorical instrument of §1291 collateral order appeal" to privilege-related disclosure orders simply cannot justify the likely institutional costs. Permitting parties to undertake successive, piecemeal appeals of all adverse attorney-client rulings would unduly delay the resolution of district court litigation and needlessly burden the Courts of Appeals. See Wright & Miller §3914.23, at 123 ("Routine appeal from disputed discovery orders would disrupt the orderly progress of the litigation, swamp the courts of appeals, and substantially reduce the district court's ability to control the discovery process."). Attempting to downplay such concerns, Mohawk asserts that the three Circuits in which the collateral order doctrine currently applies to adverse privilege rulings have seen only a trickle of appeals. But this may be due to the fact that the practice in all three Circuits is relatively new and not yet widely known. Were this Court to approve collateral order appeals in the attorney-client privilege context, many more litigants would likely choose that route. They would also likely seek to extend such a ruling to disclosure orders implicating many other categories of sensitive information, raising an array of line-drawing difficulties.[4]

---

[4] Participating as *amicus curiae* in support of respondent Carpenter, the United States contends that collateral order appeals should be available for rulings involving certain governmental privileges "in light of their structural constitutional grounding under the separation of powers, relatively rare invocation, and unique importance to governmental functions." We express no view on that issue.

C

In concluding that sufficiently effective review of adverse attorney-client privilege rulings can be had without resort to the *Cohen* doctrine, we reiterate that the class of collaterally appealable orders must remain "narrow and selective in its membership." *Will.* This admonition has acquired special force in recent years with the enactment of legislation designating rulemaking, "not expansion by court decision," as the preferred means for determining whether and when prejudgment orders should be immediately appealable. *Swint.* Specifically, Congress in 1990 amended the Rules Enabling Act, 28 USC §2071 *et seq.,* to authorize this Court to adopt rules "defin[ing] when a ruling of a district court is final for the purposes of appeal under section 1291." §2072(c). Shortly thereafter, and along similar lines, Congress empowered this Court to "prescribe rules, in accordance with [§2072], to provide for an appeal of an interlocutory decision to the courts of appeals that is not otherwise provided for under [§1292]." §1292(e). These provisions, we have recognized, "warran[t] the Judiciary's full respect." *Swint.*

Indeed, the rulemaking process has important virtues. It draws on the collective experience of bench and bar, see 28 USC §2073, and it facilitates the adoption of measured, practical solutions. We expect that the combination of standard postjudgment appeals, §1292(b) appeals, mandamus, and contempt appeals will continue to provide adequate protection to litigants ordered to disclose materials purportedly subject to the attorney-client privilege. Any further avenue for immediate appeal of such rulings should be furnished, if at all, through rulemaking, with the opportunity for full airing it provides.

. . .

In sum, we conclude that the collateral order doctrine does not extend to disclosure orders adverse to the attorney-client privilege. Effective appellate review can be had by other means. Accordingly, we affirm the judgment of the Court of Appeals for the Eleventh Circuit.

It is so ordered.

[The concurring opinion of Justice Thomas is omitted.]

■ NOTES ON THE COLLATERAL ORDER DOCTRINE

1. *Cohen* presents what we call the collateral order doctrine as an expression of the "practical rather than technical construction" of the finality concept. *Cohen* is understood as allowing appeals when three criteria are met: An order is appealable if it (a) "conclusively determines" a matter that is (b) "separate from the merits" and (c) cannot be "effectively" reviewed at the end of the suit. In what senses does the ruling satisfy these criteria?

2. *Mohawk* presents the question of attorney-client privilege in a peculiar setting. Norman Carpenter complained to his employer Mohawk about the alleged use of illegal immigrants and got fired. In a pending class suit against Mohawk (*Williams* suit), plaintiffs alleged that Mohawk's practice of hiring undocumented workers was part of a conspiracy to "drive down the wages" of legal employees. Mohawk told Carpenter to talk with the company's "retained counsel" (outside lawyer, not permanently on staff), but Carpenter refused. Later he did talk to a lawyer for the company. According to Carpenter, he was fired because he refused to recant his accusations. When the *Williams* plaintiffs looked into Carpenter's allegations, Mohawk claimed that Carpenter himself tried to get Mohawk to hire illegal workers. Then Carpenter sought "information" in Mohawk's hands "concerning his meeting with" the lawyer Mohawk had retained to defend the class suit. Mohawk invoked the attorney-client privilege, but the court concluded that Mohawk had "waived" the privilege by taking the position in *Williams* that Mohawk did nothing wrong, and that the *Williams* suit rested on Carpenter's own illegal conduct.

(a) Overruling Mohawk's privilege claim might have been the right thing to do. Probably Carpenter satisfied the *Upjohn* "subject matter" standard (Chapter 9F, supra). He was in charge of hourly workers, and was the natural person for a company lawyer to contact in preparing Mohawk's response in *Williams*. But Mohawk's privilege claim is lost if Mohawk advances a defense that relies on the very statements that it seeks to withhold. See generally Mueller & Kirkpatrick, Evidence §5.30 (5th ed. 2012) (advancing claim or defense that puts in issue "the nature of a communication" with the lawyer "impliedly waives any claim of privilege").

(b) Whether the ruling was right or wrong, however, is not the question for purposes of deciding whether an appeal can be heard. Mohawk thought the disclosure order violated its privilege, and sought review. Isn't the ruling on the privilege claim "final" for purposes of the collateral order doctrine? Isn't it "separate from the merits"? Isn't disclosure *itself* damaging (not just *use* of the statement in litigation)? Doesn't it follow that reviewing the matter on appeal after judgment in *Williams* cannot be effective, because the cat is already out of the bag?

(c) In the *Cobbledick* case, cited in *Mohawk* as authority supporting the "practical" approach to finality, the question was whether a nonparty witness, subpoenaed to produce documents before a grand jury, could appeal when the court denied his motion to quash. The answer was no, but the Court said the case is different when the witness "chooses to disobey and is committed for contempt," at which time his case "becomes so severed from the main proceeding as to permit appeal." See Cobbledick v. United States, 309 U.S. 323, 328 (1940). *Cobbledick* stands for the proposition that *even a nonparty witness,* when ordered to disclose as against a claim of privilege (or some other basis for not cooperating), cannot appeal from the order requiring disclosure.

Instead, the witness must *refuse to cooperate* and *then* appeal from the contempt citation. Recall from Hickman v. Taylor, 329 U.S. 495 (1947) (Chapter 9E, supra) that the lawyer Fortenbaugh was ordered to answer questions revealing statements he had gathered from eyewitnesses to the tugboat accident. Fortenbaugh refused to comply and was held in contempt. In this way, Fortenbaugh as a nonparty witness (he *represented* the defendant, but a lawyer is not a party) obtained an appealable order. See generally Richard L. Marcus, *The Story of* Hickman, in Civil Procedure Stories at 323, 336 (2d ed. 2008) (the court held Fortenbaugh and his client in contempt, "to be confined in the Philadelphia County Prison until they complied," but nobody was imprisoned—presumably because the directive was suspended pending appeal; the contempt citation "provided an appealable order permitting immediate appellate review").

(d) It is not entirely clear whether *parties* who are ordered to produce documents or answer questions when a claim of privilege is rejected can, by not complying and being held in contempt, take an appeal. At least in the setting of *civil* contempt citations, where one can get out of jail by complying with the order, it is possible that the *only choice* is to produce (or answer) and appeal in the event of an adverse judgment. See Fox v. Capital Co., 299 U.S. 105, 107 (1936) (party may not appeal civil contempt citation; civil contempt is not a final judgment). In the case of *criminal* contempt citations, where in theory the party remains incarcerated for a fixed period no matter what, or is subjected to a fine no matter what, it would appear that an appeal should lie, but this point is not entirely clear. See generally 2 Mueller & Kirkpatrick, Federal Evidence §5.32 (3d ed. 2007) (discussing review of claims of attorney-client privilege); Wright & Miller, Federal Practice and Procedure §2006 (discussing review of discovery orders).

(e) Mohawk was a *party* in the suit that generated the disclosure order. Hence Mohawk was in the situation of not being sure whether suffering a judgment of contempt would enable an appeal. The company invoked the collateral order doctrine instead, and the Court closed off that mechanism in clear language. Parties in the position of Mohawk have two other options: One is to petition an appellate court for a writ of mandamus directed to the trial judge (taken up in Section B3, infra). The other is to seek the agreement of *both* the trial court and the appellate court to an immediate appeal under 28 USC §1292(b) (taken up in Section C3, infra).

3. The Court in *Mohawk* stresses rulemaking as the process by which the finality of orders for purposes of review are resolved. In 1990, Congress amended the relevant statute to include this subject within the rulemaking powers of the Supreme Court and the Judicial Conference. See 28 USC §2072(c) (Court-promulgated rules "may define when a ruling is final for the purposes of appeal under [28 USC §1291]"). You have seen that the Court in 1998 added language to the class action rule allowing appellate courts to hear appeals from orders "granting or denying" certification. See FRCP 23(f). Even before Congress expanded the rulemaking power, the

Court had provided for interlocutory appeals by Rule. See, e.g., FRCP 54(b) (allowing appeal from judgment on one or more claims if the trial court "expressly determines that there is no just reason for delay"), and we take up this mechanism below (Section C2, infra).

4. The Supreme Court has sent mixed messages on using the collateral order doctrine to appeal rulings denying qualified immunity to public officials. See, e.g., Harlow v. Fitzgerald, 457 U.S. 800 (1982) (officials are entitled to qualified immunity from suit); Mitchell v. Forsyth, 472 U.S. 511, 530 (1985) (defense of qualified immunity is "in part an entitlement not to be forced to litigate," and an order rejecting this defense, "to the extent that it turns on an issue of law, is an appealable 'final decision' within the meaning of 28 USC §1291"); Osborn v. Haley, 549 U.S. 225 (2007) (under statute absolutely immunizing federal employees from tort claims arising out of acts in course of duties, federal court to which case was removed denied certification by Attorney General that employee was acting in course of duties and refused to substitute United States as defendant; collateral order doctrine allowed appeal from this refusal). See also Puerto Rico Aqueduct and Sewer Authority v. Metcalf & Eddy, Inc., 506 U.S. 139 (1993) (allowing collateral order appeal from denial of claim of state sovereign immunity under Eleventh Amendment). Even in cases raising issues relating to official immunity, however, the Court has not always been willing to apply the collateral order doctrine:

(a) In the *Swint* case in 1995 (cited in *Mohawk*), the Court ruled that a county commission, which had invoked the *Mitchell* doctrine as the basis to appeal from the denial of its motion for summary judgment in a civil rights suit, did not fit within *Mitchell*. The Commission had invoked the *Monell* doctrine, which held that municipalities can only be liable under 42 USC §1983 for violations of federal law that occur "pursuant to official governmental policy or custom" (and *not* merely because a municipal agent commits such a violation in the course of duties, which would bring "respondeat superior" liability into play). This defense, the Court decided in *Swint*, does *not* create immunity from suit, but is a "mere defense to liability." See Swint v. Chambers County Commission, 514 U.S. 35, 42-43 (1995) (also ruling was tentative, hence failing that criterion of "collateral order" doctrine).

(b) In another case where the evidence conflicted sharply on the question whether a police officer was present when a constitutional violation occurred (hence potentially liable under §1983), the Court backed away from allowing immediate appeal. See Johnson v. Jones, 515 U.S. 304 (1995) (no appeal from order overruling motions for summary judgment by three defendants on ground of qualified immunity; there was "sufficient circumstantial evidence" that they were present when other defendants beat plaintiff; *Mitchell* allows immediate appeals where qualified immunity turns on issues of law; appeal from decision that there is enough evidence to support a finding is not separate enough from merits to be appealable).

5. In *Harlow* and *Mitchell*, the Court accepted the idea that qualified immunity means a right not even to have to litigate—"an entitlement not to stand trial," the Court called it in *Mitchell.* A moment's reflection suggests that *many other* defenses could be construed this way: Can't a defense based on the statute of limitations, for example, be described as "an entitlement not to stand trial"? Suffice it to say that the Court has steadfastly rejected this characterization in cases not involving official immunity. See, e.g., Lauro Lines S.R.L. v. Chasser, 490 U.S. 495 (1989) (no appeal from order overruling motion to dismiss on ground that plaintiff's chosen forum violated selection clause); Van Cauwenberghe v. Biard, 486 U.S. 517 (1988) (no appeal from denial of motion to dismiss on ground of forum non conveniens); Firestone Tire & Rubber Co. v. Risjord, 449 U.S. 368 (1981) (no appeal from order denying motion to disqualify counsel).

6. The Court has struggled to articulate a principled distinction between the immunity cases and other cases in which a defendant has an arguable "right not to stand trial." Consider these attempts:

(a) In *Digital Equipment,* the trial court dismissed a suit for trademark infringement and unfair competition when the parties settled. Several months later, plaintiff moved to vacate the dismissal and rescind the settlement agreement for misrepresentations of material fact. The court vacated its dismissal, effectively reopening the case, and defendant appealed on the basis of its claim that the settlement gave it a "right not to stand trial altogether," which satisfied the third prong of the collateral order doctrine (cannot be effectively reviewed after final judgment). Acknowledging that this argument exerts "some pull on a narrow analysis," the Court still concluded that the collateral order doctrine does not apply. Experience has taught that "virtually every right that could be enforced appropriately by pretrial dismissal might loosely be described as conferring a 'right not to stand trial,'" but acting on this basis would reduce the final judgment principle in §1291 to a "pretty puny one." The defendant argued that the settlement agreement had a unique feature, which was "an express right not to stand trial," but this fact was not persuasive:

> [S]uch a right by agreement does not rise to the level of importance needed for recognition under §1291. This, indeed, is the bone of the fiercest contention in the case. In disparaging any distinction between an order denying a claim grounded on an explicit constitutional guarantee of immunity from trial and an order at odds with an equally explicit right by private agreement of the parties, [defendant] stresses that the relative "importance" of these rights, heavily relied upon by the Court of Appeals, is a rogue factor. No decision of this Court, [defendant] maintains, has held an order unappealable as "unimportant" when it has otherwise met the three *Cohen* requirements, and whether a decided issue is thought "important," it says, should have no bearing on whether it is "final" under §1291.
>
> If "finality" were as narrow a concept as [defendant] maintains, however, the Court would have had little reason to go beyond the first factor in *Cohen.* And if "importance" were truly aberrational, we would not find it featured so prominently in the *Cohen* opinion itself, which describes the "small class" of immediately appealable prejudgment decisions in terms of rights that are "too

important to be denied review" right away. To be sure, [defendant] may validly question whether "importance" is a factor "beyond" the three *Cohen* conditions or whether it is best considered, as we have sometimes suggested it should be, in connection with the second, "separability," requirement, but neither enquiry could lead to the conclusion that "importance" is itself unimportant. To the contrary, the third *Cohen* question, whether a right is "adequately vindicable" or "effectively reviewable," simply cannot be answered without a judgment about the value of the interests that would be lost through rigorous application of a final judgment requirement.

Digital Equipment Corp. v. Desktop Direct, Inc., 511 U.S. 863, 877-878 (1994). Does the "importance" criterion help distinguish situations where the collateral order doctrine applies from situations where it does not? Does it help enough?

(b) In the *Will* case, plaintiffs included a husband and wife who were forced out of business when Customs agents raided computers in their homes after a credit card stolen from the husband was used to purchase child pornography on the internet. The computers were returned, but stored data that included trade secrets and account files were lost. Plaintiffs sued the government under the Federal Tort Claims Act, but the case was dismissed when the court concluded that the agents acted in the course of detaining goods, which fit a statutory exception to the waiver of sovereign immunity. In the meantime, plaintiffs filed a second suit against individual agents under the *Bivens* doctrine.[5] The Federal Tort Claims Act says that a judgment in a suit brought under it "shall constitute a complete bar to any action by the claimant" against a government employee, and defendants invoked this "judgment bar" in a motion to dismiss. The trial court *denied* the motion on the theory that the dismissal of the Federal Tort Claims suit rested on a procedural ground, so the judgment bar did not come into play. Defendants appealed, and the Court *rejected* their claim that the collateral order doctrine applied:

> Since only some orders denying an asserted right to avoid the burdens of trial qualify, then, as orders that cannot be reviewed "effectively" after a conventional final judgment, the cases have to be combed for some further characteristic that merits appealability under *Cohen;* and as *Digital Equipment* explained, that something further boils down to "a judgment about the value of the interests that would be lost through rigorous application of a final judgment requirement."
>
> Thus, in Nixon v. Fitzgerald, 457 U.S. 731 (1982), we stressed the "compelling public ends," [that were] "rooted in . . . the separation of powers," that would be compromised by failing to allow immediate appeal of a denial of absolute Presidential immunity. In explaining collateral order treatment when a qualified immunity claim was at issue in *Mitchell,* we spoke of the threatened disruption of governmental functions, and fear of inhibiting able people from exercising

---

[5] Bivens v. Six Unknown Named Agents of Fed. Bureau of Narcotics, 403 U.S. 388 (1971) (recognizing implied private right of action against federal officers for violations of constitutional rights).

discretion in public service if a full trial were threatened whenever they acted reasonably in the face of law that is not "clearly established." Puerto Rico Aqueduct and Sewer Authority v. Metcalf & Eddy, Inc., 506 U.S. 139 (1993), explained the immediate appealability of an order denying a claim of Eleventh Amendment immunity by adverting not only to the burdens of litigation but to the need to ensure vindication of a State's dignitary interests. And although the double jeopardy claim given *Cohen* treatment in Abney v. United States, 431 U.S. 651 (1977), did not implicate a right to be free of all proceedings whatsoever (since prior jeopardy is essential to the defense), we described the enormous prosecutorial power of the Government to subject an individual "to embarrassment, expense and ordeal . . . compelling him to live in a continuing state of anxiety" (internal quotation marks omitted); the only way to alleviate these consequences of the Government's superior position was by collateral order appeal.

In each case, some particular value of a high order was marshaled in support of the interest in avoiding trial: honoring the separation of powers, preserving the efficiency of government and the initiative of its officials, respecting a State's dignitary interests, and mitigating the government's advantage over the individual. That is, it is not mere avoidance of a trial, but avoidance of a trial that would imperil a substantial public interest, that counts when asking whether an order is "effectively" unreviewable if review is to be left until later.

Will v. Hallock, 546 U.S. 345, 351-353 (2006). In *Will*, the idea of importance is reformulated in terms of values of "high order," and the examples involve separation of powers, efficiency of government, initiative of public officials, respecting a state's dignitary interests, and "mitigating the government's advantage over the individual." Does the reformulation help? Do the illustrative examples tell us any more? Isn't the list heavily weighted to favor official over private interests?

7. The "collateral order" doctrine is a modification of the finality principle. In situations that fit this doctrine, like appeals from orders rejecting a qualified immunity defense, the 30-day time for appeal begins to run from entry of the order being challenged. See Napoli v. Town of New Windsor, 600 F.3d 168 (2d Cir. 2010).

3. Evading the Concept: Mandamus Review

Mandamus review, as it is usually called, actually involves what is in form a new suit: The aggrieved party commences, in the appellate court, an original proceeding against the judge, and the other party in the suit (the one who gains from the judge's ruling) in effect represents the judge and defends the decision or order being attacked. Mandamus review rests on a thin statutory basis, namely the All Writs Act. See 28 USC §1651 (federal courts "may issue all writs necessary or appropriate in aid of their respective jurisdictions and agreeable to the usages and principles of law"). It is usually said that mandamus review involves the exercise, in advance, of the power of review that would go forward in ordinary cases after final judgment, so it represents an "acceleration" of the exercise of jurisdiction rather than the assumption of new jurisdiction. Mandamus review is discretionary, and the court in which an application is filed may decline to hear the case.

CHENEY v. UNITED STATES DISTRICT COURT

Supreme Court of the United States
542 U.S. 367 (2004)

[Suing under the Federal Advisory Committee Act (FACA), 5 USC App. §2, the Sierra Club and Judicial Watch sought disclosure of records of the National Energy Policy Development Group (NEPDG), which was comprised of federal officials in the Executive Branch, including six cabinet secretaries and many agency heads, chaired by Vice President Richard Cheney. Established in the office of the President, this group was tasked with formulating advice to the President on federal energy policy.

Named as defendants in the suit were Vice President Cheney and other federal officials and agencies participating in NEPDG, as well as NEPDG itself and private parties who allegedly participated in NEPDG deliberations and recommendations.

Defendants all moved to dismiss.

The District Court dismissed claims against the private defendants on the ground that FACA did not create a private cause of action. It dismissed claims against NEPDG because it had been dissolved. FACA's "substantive requirements" could be enforced against agencies under the Administrative Procedure Act, 5 USC §706 (District Court as "reviewing court" may "compel agency action unlawfully withheld or unreasonably delayed"), but it would be "premature" to take up such matter because no final agency action had been taken.

With respect to claims against Vice President Cheney and other officials, the District Court held that plaintiffs could enforce FACA's "substantive requirements" under the Mandamus Act, 28 USC §1361 (district courts "have original jurisdiction of any action in the nature of mandamus to compel an officer or employee of the United States or any agency thereof to perform a duty owed to the plaintiff"). The District Court then *rejected* the claim of the Vice President and other officials that they fit an exemption in FACA for any committee or similar group established or utilized by the President "that is composed wholly of full-time, or permanent part-time, officers or employees of the Federal Government." While plaintiffs did not dispute that the President "appointed only Federal Government officials" to the NEPDG, they alleged that private parties, including lobbyists, attended and participated in nonpublic meetings and were "*de facto* members." Hence plaintiffs "had alleged sufficient facts" to keep Cheney and other officials in the case.

The District Court later approved plaintiffs' discovery plan and denied the government's motion to certify the case for immediate appeal under 28 USC §1292(b) (taken up later in this chapter). The government then sought a writ of mandamus in the District of Columbia Court of Appeals, and the Vice President took an appeal from the District Court's order. The Court of Appeals declined to issue a writ of mandamus, ruling that officials could "guard against intrusion into the President's prerogatives" by asserting claims of executive privilege in response to particular discovery requests. The Court of Appeals also refused the Vice President's interlocutory appeal.]

We now come to the central issue in the case—whether the Court of Appeals was correct to conclude it "ha[d] no authority to exercise the extraordinary remedy of mandamus," on the ground that the Government could protect its rights by asserting executive privilege in the District Court.

The common law writ of mandamus against a lower court is codified at 28 USC §1651(a) [quoting statute]. This is a "drastic and extraordinary" remedy "reserved for really extraordinary causes." Ex Parte Fahey, 332 U.S. 258, 259-260 (1947). "The traditional use of the writ in aid of appellate jurisdiction both at common law and in the federal courts has been to confine [the court against which mandamus is sought] to a lawful exercise of its prescribed jurisdiction." Roche v. Evaporated Milk Assn., 319 U.S. 21, 26 (1943). Although courts have not "confined themselves to an arbitrary and technical definition of 'jurisdiction,'" Will v. United States, 389 U.S. 90, 95 (1967), "*only* exceptional circumstances amounting to a judicial 'usurpation of power,'" or a "clear abuse of discretion," Bankers Life & Casualty Co. v. Holland, 346 U.S. 379, 383 (1953), "will justify the invocation of this extraordinary remedy," *Will.*

As the writ is one of "the most potent weapons in the judicial arsenal," three conditions must be satisfied before it may issue. Kerr v. United States Dist. Court for Northern Dist. of Cal., 426 U.S. 394, 403 (1976). First, "the party seeking issuance of the writ [must] have no other adequate means to attain the relief he desires"—a condition designed to ensure that the writ will not be used as a substitute for the regular appeals process, *Fahey.* Second, the petitioner must satisfy "the burden of showing that [his] right to issuance of the writ is 'clear and indisputable.'" *Kerr* (quoting *Bankers Life*). Third, even if the first two prerequisites have been met, the issuing court, in the exercise of its discretion, must be satisfied that the writ is appropriate under the circumstances. *Kerr* (citing Schlagenhauf v. Holder, 379 U.S. 104, 112, n.8 (1964)). These hurdles, however demanding, are not insuperable. This Court has issued the writ to restrain a lower court when its actions would threaten the separation of powers by "embarrass[ing] the executive arm of the Government," Ex parte Peru, 318 U.S. 578, 588 (1943), or result in the "intrusion by the federal judiciary on a delicate area of federal-state relations," *Will* (citing Maryland v. Soper (No. 1),270 U.S. 9 (1926)).

Were the Vice President not a party in the case, the argument that the Court of Appeals should have entertained an action in mandamus, notwithstanding the District Court's denial of the motion for certification, might present different considerations. Here, however, the Vice President and his co-members on the NEPDG are the subjects of the discovery orders. The mandamus petition alleges that the orders threaten "substantial intrusions on the process by which those in closest operational proximity to the President advise the President." These facts and allegations remove this case from the category of ordinary discovery orders where interlocutory appellate review is unavailable, through mandamus or otherwise. It is well established that "a President's communications and activities encompass a vastly wider range of sensitive material than would be true of any 'ordinary individual.'" United States v. Nixon, 418 U.S. 683, 715 (1974). Chief Justice Marshall, sitting as a trial judge, recognized the unique position of the Executive Branch when he stated that "[i]n no case . . . would a court be required to proceed against the president as against an ordinary individual." United States v. Burr, 25 F. Cas. 187, 192 (No. 14,694) (CC Va. 1807). See also Clinton v. Jones, 520 U.S. 681, 698-699 (1997) ("We have, in short, long recognized the 'unique position in the constitutional scheme' that [the Office of the President] occupies" (quoting Nixon v. Fitzgerald,457 U.S. 731, 749 (1982)) (Breyer, J., concurring in judgment). As United States v. Nixon explained, these principles do not mean that the "President is above the law." Rather, they simply acknowledge that the public interest requires that a coequal branch of Government "afford Presidential confidentiality the greatest protection consistent with the fair administration of justice," and give recognition to the paramount necessity of protecting the Executive Branch from vexatious litigation that might distract it from the energetic performance of its constitutional duties.

These separation-of-powers considerations should inform a court of appeals' evaluation of a mandamus petition involving the President or the Vice President. Accepted mandamus standards are broad enough to allow a court of appeals to prevent a lower court from interfering with a coequal branch's ability to discharge its constitutional responsibilities. See Ex PartePeru, *supra* (recognizing jurisdiction to issue the writ because "the action of the political arm of the Government taken within its appropriate sphere [must] be promptly recognized, and . . . delay and inconvenience of a prolonged litigation [must] be avoided by prompt termination of the proceedings in the district court"); see also Clinton v. Jones, *supra* ("We have recognized that '[e]ven when a branch does not arrogate power to itself . . . the separation-of-powers doctrine requires that a branch not impair another in the performance of its constitutional duties'" (quoting Loving v. United States, 517 U.S. 748, 757 (1996).

[While the Court had held in United States v. Nixon, 418 U.S. 683 (1974), that the President could not avoid a criminal subpoena under a broad claim of executive privilege, the present case is different. Here we have civil litigation, not a criminal prosecution as in the *Nixon* case, where the need for information is "much weightier." Moreover, the present case "is not a routine discovery dispute," and instead involves discovery requests directed to the Vice President and other officials advising the President, where the "autonomy" of the Executive Branch is implicated, as well as its interests in "safeguarding the confidentialities of its communications." Finally, the discovery requests in *Nixon* were tailored to "exacting standards," in contrast to the "overly broad" requests in this case asking for "everything under the sky."]

[Opinions by Justice Stevens, concurring, and by Justices Thomas and Scalia, concurring in part and dissenting in part, and by Justices Ginsburg and Souter, dissenting, are omitted.]

■ NOTES ON MANDAMUS AS A MECHANISM OF INTERLOCUTORY REVIEW

1. In addition to seeking mandamus, the Vice President and other officials took an appeal and invoked the collateral order doctrine. The Court of Appeals concluded that this mechanism was unavailable, and the Court agreed (in a brief passage omitted above). There seem to have been two difficulties:

(a) First, the appeal and petition for mandamus may have been filed too late to satisfy FRAP 4 (allowing 60 days for appeals by government or officer or agency). The Supreme Court notes this point, but concludes that review by mandamus is available, and is not subject to the time limit for ordinary appeals.

(b) Second, the Court of Appeals implied that collateral order review was unavailable because the discovery rulings were nonfinal, and there was no final decision on the question whether FACA applies to a committee comprised entirely of federal officials, reserving decision on the question whether private citizens were *de facto* members of NEPDG, which would bring the statute into play. The Court of Appeals construed the actions of the District Court as requiring production of nonprivileged material and a "privilege log" that would spell out claims of privilege for specific items, which would then be addressed, and perhaps reviewed if privilege claims were overruled. (In the *Nixon* case, cited in *Cheney*, the Court held that the President could claim executive privilege on particular items, and could appeal an order overruling a privilege claim without placing himself "in the posture of disobeying an

order of court merely to trigger" a contempt citation that would provide the more usual procedural mechanism for obtaining review.) The Court of Appeals in *Cheney* also thought the District Court had provided a way for the Vice President and other officials to prove they had responded adequately to discovery, by identifying the information they had produced and showing how it was responsive to discovery requests. Do these aspects of the orders show that they are not sufficiently "final" to satisfy the first criterion of the collateral order doctrine?

2. The opinion in *Cheney* stresses that mandamus review is a "drastic and extraordinary" and "potent" remedy. Hence it is available only if the party seeking relief has "no other adequate means" available, and shows that the right to relief is "clear and indisputable," and in the end relief is still highly discretionary, taking into account what is "appropriate under the circumstances." What persuaded the Court that these conditions were satisfied? How clear can the right to relief be if two Justices and two of the three Judges on the Court of Appeals thought mandamus was inappropriate?

3. In La Buy v. Howes Leather Co., 352 U.S. 249 (1957), the Court approved use of mandamus to compel District Judge La Buy in Chicago to vacate an order referring an antitrust case for trial before a federal master under FRCP 53. Faced with a trial that plaintiffs thought would last six weeks, in a case in which he had conducted hearings on preliminary pleas and motions, Judge La Buy asked the parties to agree to a trial before a master. When he received no response, he appointed a master *sua sponte*. In approving use of the writ to require him to try the case, the Court seemed troubled on three points: First, the Seventh Circuit had issued opinions warning trial judges that the reference practice "does not commend itself" and should be done "seldom" and only in "unusual" circumstances. Second, Judge La Buy had referred eleven cases to masters in six years ("a little cloud may bring a flood's downpour"). Third, he had argued that the cases had "unusual complexity of issues" that threatened his "crowded calendar." But the Court replied that congestion cannot make references "the rule rather than the exception," and that complexity of issues is "an impelling reason for trial before a judge" rather than before "a temporary substitute appointed on an *ad hoc* basis."

4. In Will v. United States, 389 U.S. 90 (1967), the Court *refused* to employ mandamus to correct the actions of a judge in a criminal case in granting a defense discovery request seeking a list of prosecution witnesses. The applicable criminal rule does not authorize discovery of the names of prosecution witnesses, and a federal statute (Jencks Act) bars disclosure of such names prior to trial,[6] so it appears that Judge Will's order was in direct contravention of applicable law. While the Court of Appeals was persuaded to exercise its

---

[6] See Fed. R. Crim. P. 16(b)(2) (defense not entitled to "discovery or inspection of statements made by prospective government witnesses"); 18 USC §3500 ("no statement . . . made by a Government witness or prospective Government witness . . . shall be the subject of subpoena, discovery, or inspection until said witness has testified on direct examination in the trial of the case").

power of mandamus, the Supreme Court was not, and it reversed on the ground that the case was inappropriate for mandamus review. The critical fact was that there was "no evidence . . . concerning [Judge Will's] practice in other cases," so the situation differed from *La Buy*. Should it have counted in *Will* that the government had no other mechanism of obtaining appellate relief? After *Mohawk* (more than 40 years later), the collateral order doctrine would not provide a means of review either.

5. It is worth spending a moment to look at a few cases where the Supreme Court has approved the use of mandamus to review interlocutory orders.

(a) In the *Schlagenhauf* case (described in Chapter 9D4, supra), the Court used mandamus review to strike down the order of a judge, entered without hearing, requiring a bus driver in a suit for personal injuries arising out of an accident in which the bus plowed into a truck stopped at the side of the road, to submit to examinations by specialists in internal medicine, ophthalmology, neurology, and psychiatry.

> It is, of course, well settled, that the writ is not to be used as a substitute for appeal, even though hardship may result from delay and perhaps unnecessary trial. The writ is appropriately issued, however, when there is "usurpation of judicial power" or a clear abuse of discretion.
>
> Here petitioner's basic allegation was lack of power in a district court to order a mental and physical examination of a defendant. That this issue was substantial is underscored by the fact that the challenged order requiring examination of a defendant appears to be the first of its kind in any reported decision in the federal courts under Rule 35, and we have found only one such modern case in the state courts. The Court of Appeals recognized that it had the power to review on a petition for mandamus the basic, undecided question of whether a district court could order the mental or physical examination of a defendant. We agree that, under these unusual circumstances and in light of the authorities, the Court of Appeals had such power.
>
> The petitioner, however, also alleged that, even if Rule 35 gives a district court power to order mental and physical examinations of a defendant in an appropriate case, the District Court here exceeded that power in ordering examinations when petitioner's mental and physical condition was not "in controversy" and no "good cause" was shown, both as expressly required by Rule 35. As we read its opinion, the Court of Appeals reached the "in controversy" issue and determined it adversely to petitioner. It did not, however, reach the issue of "good cause," apparently considering that it was not appropriate to do so on a petition for mandamus.
>
> We recognize that in the ordinary situation where the sole issue presented is the district court's determination that "good cause" has been shown for an examination, mandamus is not an appropriate remedy, absent, of course, a clear abuse of discretion. Here, however, the petition was properly before the court on a substantial allegation of usurpation of power in ordering any examination of a defendant, an issue of first impression that called for the construction and application of Rule 35 in a new context. The meaning of Rule 35's requirements of "in

controversy" and "good cause" also raised issues of first impression. In our view, the Court of Appeals should have also, under these special circumstances, determined the "good cause" issue, so as to avoid piecemeal litigation and to settle new and important problems.

Thus we believe that the Court of Appeals had power to determine all of the issues presented by the petition for mandamus. Normally, wise judicial administration would counsel remand of the cause to the Court of Appeals to reconsider this issue of "good cause." However, in this instance the issue concerns the construction and application of the Federal Rules of Civil Procedure. It is thus appropriate for us to determine on the merits the issues presented and to formulate the necessary guidelines in this area.

Schlagenhauf v. Holder, 379 U.S. 104, 110-112 (1964). Recall that *Schlagenhauf* went on to conclude that the trial court "exceeded [its] power" in ordering examinations without a showing of good cause. It also concluded that FRCP 35 did *not* depend on waiver (which would make it easy for defendants in personal injury suits to obtain court-ordered examinations of plaintiffs), so it can apply to parties that were not seeking recovery for their own injuries. And it reaffirmed that, as limited by the "good cause" requirement, and in cases where physical or mental condition is "in issue," FRCP 35 is "free of constitutional difficulty" and does not violate the restriction in the Rules Enabling Act (28 USC §2072) against enlarging or modifying substantive rights. The Court had already reached similar conclusions 25 years earlier. See Sibbach v. Wilson & Co., 312 U.S. 1 (1941).

(b) In two important modern decisions that you have seen, both addressing the scope of entitlement to a civil jury trial under the Seventh Amendment, the issue reached the Supreme Court by means of petitions for writs of mandamus. See Beacon Theatres, Inc. v. Westover, 359 U.S. 500 (1959) (not commenting on propriety of proceeding this way); Dairy Queen v. Wood, 369 U.S. 469, 472 (1962) (construing *Beacon Theatres* as meaning that courts of appeal should accord mandamus relief "where necessary to protect the constitutional right to trial by jury") (Chapter 12A1, supra). Compare Ross v. Bernhard, 396 U.S. 531 (1970) (question of jury trial entitlement reaches Court on interlocutory appeal under 28 USC §1292(b)); Chauffeurs, Teamsters and Helpers, Local No. 391 v. Terry, 494 U.S. 558 (1990) (similar); Curtis v. Loether, 415 U.S. 189 (1974) (jury trial issue reaches Court on appeal from judgment on the merits).

6. The Court has instructed that mandamus appeals are appropriate when necessary to "confine" a court to a lawful exercise of its jurisdiction or to "compel it to exercise its authority when it has a duty to do so." See, e.g., Roche v. Evaporated Milk Association, 319 U.S. 21, 26 (1943). Thus the Court *rejected* use of mandamus to compel a district court to go forward with a federal question case when it had entered a stay because parallel litigation was pending in state court raising issues identical to those in the federal suit: The case was *not* one in which the district court exceeded its authority, nor one in which it had a duty to go forward because the decision whether to defer "is, in the last analysis, a matter committed to the district court's discretion." See Will v. Calvert Fire Insurance Co., 437 U.S. 655, 664 (1978) (in effect, judge abstained under *Colorado River*, but stayed suit rather than dismissing; if case had been dismissed, appeal could be taken, and reviewing court could have "required such action" as would be just; stay was not equivalent to dismissal, and party seeking federal resolution could urge judge to reconsider). See also Kerr v. U.S. District Court for Northern District of California, 426 U.S. 394, 405 (1976) (rejecting use of mandamus to review decision denying defense motion to quash subpoena seeking prisoner files; trial court did not reject claim of privilege protecting personnel, but invited petitioners to invoke privilege with "the requisite specificity" and seek *in camera* review). Recall Matter of Rhone-Poulenc Rorer Incorporated, 51 F.3d 1293 (1995) (summarized in Chapter 8H10, supra): There the court went out of its way to find that the exercise of jurisdiction in a massive class suit against makers of blood solids was "usurpative," and corrected the trial court by writ of mandamus.

 EXCEPTIONS TO THE FINAL JUDGMENT RULE

1. Orders Relating to Preliminary Injunctions (28 USC §1292(a))

Injunctive relief, in which a court directs a party to do or not do something, has become increasingly commonplace, as courts are often called on to decide what statutes or regulations require (or allow) others to do. In the myriad cases in which such relief is sought, the question often arises whether to await the end of trial before doing anything to require or circumscribe behavior, or whether to act sooner.

Perhaps not surprisingly, courts can often grant immediate short-term relief, and can then decide in a more considered fashion whether or not to grant longer-term interim relief while the case goes forward to trial (or settlement). At the end of the case, when it has been tried or the parties have reached a settlement, the court can then award (or not award) ongoing permanent injunctive relief.

Immediate short-term relief takes the form of a "temporary restraining order" (TRO), which can be entered *ex parte* on application by a party. See FRCP 65 (authorizing court to issue TRO "without written or oral notice" if specific facts appearing in an affidavit or verified complaint "clearly show that immediate and irreparable injury, loss, or damage" will occur otherwise, if the moving party explains in writing that it has made efforts to notify the other side or explains why notice should not be required). Under the Rule, such relief can last only 14 days, and the other side may ask the court to dissolve the order on two days' notice.

Longer-term relief, which can continue all the way through the litigation the same relief originally provided by the TRO, is generally called a "preliminary injunction," and such relief is usually awarded after a hearing and argument in which the party seeking the relief must show a likelihood of prevailing at trial, and the need to do something now rather than waiting. In Alliance for the Wild Rockies v. Cottrell, 632 F.3d 1127 (9th Cir. 2010) (Chapter 2A3, supra), we saw a decision that grappled with one fundamental issue that arises in this setting. The question is whether the key factor of probable success on the merits should be evaluated on a correlative basis with two other key factors (cost to plaintiff if court errs in refusing preliminary injunctive relief, and cost to defendant if court errs in granting injunctive relief), or whether probable success on the merits is an entirely independent factor. If three factors are correlative, the resultant "sliding scale approach" makes preliminary injunctive more often available because a weak showing of likely success on the merits can be overcome by a strong showing on the other two factors. On the other hand, if the factors are independent, a strong showing of likely success on the merits is always required. *Alliance* endorsed the correlative (or "sliding scale") approach. The court then enjoined the forest service to block immediate implementation of conservation measures.

Relief granted after trial on the merits (or settlement presented to the court as the basis for a court order) is ordinarily termed a permanent injunction, and it is part of the final judgment.

Under 28 USC §1292(a)(1), an "interlocutory" order "granting, continuing, modifying, refusing or dissolving" an injunction may be appealed. This provision contemplates appeals from "preliminary injunctions," not from TROs or permanent injunctions.

Here is an illustrative example. Oklahoma enacted a statute dealing with illegal immigration and verification of employment eligibility. The statute required employers to use a state-run program to "verify the work authorization status" of employees. The statute contemplated penalties, financial and otherwise, for employers who failed to satisfy these requirements. The Chamber of Commerce brought suit to block enforcement of the statute, arguing that it was "expressly and impliedly preempted by federal law," and sought an order directing the Governor, Secretary of State, and other officials not to enforce the law. The court granted a preliminary injunction, and the defendants appealed under 28 USC §1292(a)(1). See Chamber of Commerce of United States v. Edmondson, 594 F.3d 742 (10th Cir. 2010) (upholding injunction and concluding that plaintiffs are "likely to succeed on the merits" and that part of the statute is expressly preempted and part is impliedly preempted).

2. Multiple Claims and the Certification Procedure of FRCP 54(b)

Application of the finality concept very easily can become blurred and uncertain. Suppose, for example, that Abbey, Ben, and Carla sue David, Eric, and Fiona.

First, suppose the three defendants move to dismiss for lack of jurisdiction under FRCP 12(b), and David prevails but Eric and Fiona do not (so the claims by three plaintiffs remain pending against two defendants). Does an order dismissing the claims against David amount to a final judgment for purposes of appeal by the three plaintiffs? Pretty clearly, Eric and Fiona do not have an appeal: They are unsuccessful defendants who did not prevail on motions to dismiss, and orders denying their motions cannot by any stretch be viewed as final judgments.

Second, suppose that David, Eric, and Fiona move under FRCP 12(b) to dismiss the plaintiffs' claims for failure to state claims on which relief can be granted, and they prevail as to Abbey, but fail as to Ben and Carla. In most cases, of course, Abbey would be given leave to amend, but suppose she does not (perhaps cannot, consistent with the obligation of truthful pleading) file a complaint that states a claim for relief, and her claims are dismissed. (Under FRCP 41, such a dismissal "operates as an adjudication on the merits," meaning that Abbey is *not* free to start over by filing a new suit.) Does the order dismissing Abbey's complaint amount to a final judgment for purposes of appeal by Abbey? Again, pretty clearly defendants (all three of them) cannot appeal from their *loss* on the motion with respect to Ben and Carla, because losing the argument for dismissal leads to an order denying their motion, which is not a final judgment by any stretch.

The framers of the Civil Rules recognized that with expanded opportunities for joinder of claims and parties, more cases would arise in which deferring to the end the possibility of review would work unwelcome hardships and burden the process unduly. Hence Rule 54(b) was included, which in its present form allows the judge, in any suit involving "more than one claim for relief," to enter a "final judgment" on any such claim, if the judge expressly determines that there is "no just reason for delay." Thus the judge, in dismissing the claims of Abbey, Ben, and Carla against David in the first example above, could determine that there is no just reason for delay, and enter a final judgment in favor of David and against the three plaintiffs, who could appeal. And the judge, in dismissing Abbey's claim against the three defendants, could determine that there is no just reason for delay, and enter final judgment in favor of the three defendants and against Abbey, and Abbey could appeal.

This "certification" process, as the determination described in FRCP 54(b) is usually called, can be viewed as consistent with the final judgment principle. The trial court acts, as the Court commented in Sears, Roebuck & Co. v. Mackey, 351 U.S. 427, 435 (1956), as "dispatcher" by determining "in the first instance" when each "final decision" on one or more but less than all the claims in a suit involving more than one claim is "ready for appeal." This procedure "does not relax the finality required of each decision," but provides "a practical means of permitting an appeal to be taken from one or more final decisions on individual claims." The judgment entered by the district court, and certified for appeal, is "final," even though it is not the last thing in the case.

Without such certification, no appeals would be permitted in the situations described above, so in another sense FRCP 54(b) represents a significant change in the final judgment principle. The Rule itself goes on to say that "any order or other decision" disposing of "fewer than all the claims or the rights and liabilities of fewer than all the parties" does *not* "end the action as to any of the claims or parties." It is clear, moreover, that without the 54(b) certification, no party would have an appeal in either of the situations described above (unless one of the other interlocutory appeal mechanisms were available).

It is worth noting briefly that FRCP 54(b) was not always read generously. Early decisions, when the wording of the Rule was not what it is now, differed over the meaning of the term "final judgment," and interpreted the Rule as authorizing entry of final judgment only when the claim in question was "separate" from any claims that remained pending.

On the question what "final judgment" means, the Second Circuit held, in a prominent case, that a decision against one of two defendants on a summary judgment motion, holding that this defendant had no right to certain funds, was *not* final because title to the funds remained in issue among other parties. See Clark v. Taylor, 163 F.2d 940 (2d Cir. 1940). But ten years later the Court decided that a judgment dismissing claims by an intervenor was final for purposes of review despite the continuation of related claims. See Dickinson v. Petroleum Conversion Corp., 338 U.S. 507, 514 (1950) (when claims by intervenor were dismissed, intervenor was "out of the case," and decree "was not tentative, informal nor incomplete as to it," but the case was "concluded," and what remained was "supervisory jurisdiction" relating to distribution of the award, a matter on which intervenor "no longer had any concern").

On the question whether a "claim" appealed under FRCP 54(b) has to be "separate" from claims that remain pending, courts in the early years thought a claim appealed under FRCP 54 had to rest on different factual bases from claims that remained pending, or had to rest on different theories.

CURTISS-WRIGHT CORPORATION v. GENERAL ELECTRIC COMPANY

Supreme Court of the United States
446 U.S. 1 (1980)

Mr. Chief Justice Burger delivered the opinion of the Court.

FRCP 54(b) allows a district court dealing with multiple claims or multiple parties to direct the entry of final judgment as to fewer than all of the claims or parties; to do so, the court must make an express determination that there is no just reason for delay. We granted certiorari in order to examine the use of this procedural device.

I

From 1968 to 1972, respondent General Electric Co. entered into a series of 21 contracts with petitioner Curtiss-Wright Corp. for the manufacture of components designed for use in nuclear powered naval vessels. These contracts had a total value of $215 million.

In 1976, Curtiss-Wright brought a diversity action in the United States District Court for the District of New Jersey, seeking damages and reformation with regard to the 21 contracts. The complaint asserted claims based on alleged fraud, misrepresentation, and breach of contract by General Electric. It also sought $19 million from General Electric on the outstanding balance due on the contracts already performed.

General Electric counterclaimed for $1.9 million in costs allegedly incurred as the result of "extraordinary efforts" provided to Curtiss-Wright during performance of the contracts which enabled Curtiss-Wright to avoid a contract default. General Electric also sought, by way of counterclaim, to recover $52 million by which Curtiss-Wright was allegedly unjustly enriched as a result of these "extraordinary efforts."

The facts underlying most of these claims and counterclaims are in dispute. As to Curtiss-Wright's claims for the $19 million balance due, however, the sole dispute concerns the application of a release clause contained in each of the 21 agreements, which states that "Seller . . . agree[s] as a condition precedent to final payment, that the Buyer and the Government . . . are released from all liabilities, obligations and claims arising under or by virtue of this order." When Curtiss-Wright moved for summary judgment on the balance due, General Electric contended that so long as Curtiss-Wright's other claims remained pending, this provision constituted a bar to recovery of the undisputed balance.

The District Court rejected this contention and granted summary judgment for Curtiss-Wright on this otherwise undisputed claim. Applying New York law by which the parties had agreed to be bound, the District Court held that Curtiss-Wright was entitled to payment of the balance due notwithstanding the release clause. The court also ruled that Curtiss-Wright was entitled to prejudgment interest at the New York statutory rate of 6% per annum.

Curtiss-Wright then moved for a certification of the District Court's orders as final judgments under FRCP 54(b). . . . The court expressly directed entry of final judgment for Curtiss-Wright and made the determination that there was "no just reason for delay" pursuant to Rule 54(b).

The District Court also provided a written statement of reasons supporting its decision to certify the judgment as final. It acknowledged that Rule 54(b) certification was not to be granted as a matter of course, and that this remedy should be reserved for the infrequent harsh case because of the overload in appellate courts which would otherwise result from appeals of an interlocutory nature. The essential inquiry was stated to be "whether, after balancing the competing factors, finality of judgment should be ordered to advance the interests of sound judicial administration and justice to the litigants."

The District Court then went on to identify the relevant factors in the case before it. It found that certification would not result in unnecessary appellate review; that the claims finally adjudicated were separate, distinct, and independent of any of the other claims or counterclaims involved; that review of these adjudicated claims would not be mooted by any future developments in the case; and that the nature of the claims was such that no appellate court would have to decide the same issues more than once even if there were subsequent appeals.

Turning to considerations of justice to the litigants, the District Court found that Curtiss-Wright would suffer severe daily financial loss from non-payment of the $19 million judgment because current interest rates were higher than the statutory prejudgment rate, a situation compounded by the large amount of money involved. The court observed that the complex nature of the remaining claims could, without certification, mean a delay that "would span many months, if not years."

The court found that solvency of the parties was not a significant factor, since each appeared to be financially sound. Although the presence of General Electric's counterclaims and the consequent possibility of a setoff recovery were factors which weighed against certification, the court, in balancing these factors, determined that they were outweighed by the other factors in the case. Accordingly, it granted Rule 54(b) certification. It also granted General Electric's motion for a stay without bond pending appeal.

A divided panel of the United States Court of Appeals for the Third Circuit held that the case was controlled by its decision in Allis-Chalmers Corp. v. Philadelphia Electric Co., 521 F.2d 360 (1975), where the court had stated:

> In the absence of unusual or harsh circumstances, we believe that the presence of a counterclaim, which could result in a set-off against any amounts due and owing to the plaintiff, weighs heavily against the grant of 54(b) certification.

In *Allis-Chalmers*, the court defined unusual or harsh circumstances as those factors "involving considerations of solvency, economic duress, etc."

In the Third Circuit's view, the question was which of the parties should have the benefit of the amount of the balance due pending final resolution of the litigation. The court held that *Allis-Chalmers* dictated "that the matter remain in status quo when non-frivolous counterclaims are pending, and in the absence of unusual or harsh circumstances." The Court of Appeals acknowledged that Curtiss-Wright's inability to have use of the money from the judgment might seem harsh, but noted that the same could be said for General Electric if it were forced to pay Curtiss-Wright now but later prevailed on its counterclaims.

The Court of Appeals concluded that the District Court had abused its discretion by granting Rule 54(b) certification in this situation and dismissed the case for want of an appealable order; it also directed the District Court to vacate its Rule 54(b) determination of finality. Curtiss-Wright's petition for rehearing and suggestion for rehearing en banc were denied. Four judges dissented from that denial, observing that the case was in conflict with United Bank of Pueblo v. Hartford Accident & Indemnity Co., 529 F.2d 490 (10th Cir. 1976). We reverse.

II

Nearly a quarter of a century ago, in Sears, Roebuck & Co. v. Mackey, 351 U.S. 427 (1956), this Court outlined the steps to be followed in making determinations under Rule 54(b). A district court must first determine that it is dealing with a "final judgment." It must be a "judgment" in the sense that it is a decision upon a cognizable claim for relief, and it must be "final" in the sense that it is "an ultimate disposition of an individual claim entered in the course of a multiple claims action."

Once having found finality, the district court must go on to determine whether there is any just reason for delay. Not all final judgments on individual claims should be immediately appealable, even if they are in some sense separable from the remaining unresolved claims. The function of the district court under the Rule is to act as a "dispatcher." It is left to the sound judicial discretion of the district court to determine the "appropriate time" when each final decision in a multiple claims action is ready for appeal. This discretion is to be exercised "in the interest of sound judicial administration."

Thus, in deciding whether there are no just reasons to delay the appeal of individual final judgments in setting such as this, a district court must take into account judicial administrative interests as well as the equities involved. Consideration of the former is necessary to assure that application of the Rule effectively "preserves the historic federal policy against piecemeal appeals." It was therefore proper for the District Judge here to consider such factors as whether the claims under review were separable from the others remaining to be adjudicated and whether the nature of the claims already determined was such that no appellate court would have to decide the same issues more than once even if there were subsequent appeals.[2]

Here the District Judge saw no sound reason to delay appellate resolution of the undisputed claims already adjudicated. The contrary conclusion of the

---

[2] We do not suggest that the presence of one of these factors would necessarily mean that Rule 54(b) certification would be improper. It would, however, require the district court to find a sufficiently important reason for nonetheless granting certification. For example, if the district court concluded that there was a possibility that an appellate court would have to face the same issues on a subsequent appeal, this might perhaps be offset by a finding that an appellate resolution of the certified claims would facilitate a settlement of the remainder of the claims. See Cold Metal Process Co. v.United Engineering & Foundry Co., 351 U.S. 445, 450 n.5 (1956).

Court of Appeals was strongly influenced by the existence of nonfrivolous counterclaims. The mere presence of such claims, however, does not render a Rule 54(b) certification inappropriate. If it did, Rule 54(b) would lose much of its utility. In Cold Metal Process Co. v. United Engineering & Foundry Co., 351 U.S. 445 (1956), this Court explained that counterclaims, whether compulsory or permissive, present no special problems for Rule 54(b) determinations; counterclaims are not to be evaluated differently from other claims. Like other claims, their significance for Rule 54(b) purposes turns on their interrelationship with the claims on which certification is sought. Here, the District Judge determined that General Electric's counterclaims were severable from the claims which had been determined in terms of both the factual and the legal issues involved. The Court of Appeals did not conclude otherwise.

What the Court of Appeals found objectionable about the District Judge's exercise of discretion was the assessment of the equities involved. The Court of Appeals concluded that the possibility of a setoff required that the status quo be maintained unless petitioner could show harsh or unusual circumstances; it held that such a showing had not been made in the District Court.

This holding reflects a misinterpretation of the standard of review for Rule 54(b) certifications and a misperception of the appellate function in such cases. The Court of Appeals relied on a statement of the Advisory Committee on the Rules of Civil Procedure, and its error derives from reading a description in the commentary as a standard of construction. When Rule 54(b) was amended in 1946, the Notes of the Advisory Committee which accompanied the suggested amendment indicated that the entire lawsuit was generally the appropriate unit for appellate review, "and that this rule needed only the exercise of a discretionary power to afford a remedy in the infrequent harsh case to provide a simple, definite, workable rule." However accurate it may be as a description of cases qualifying for Rule 54(b) treatment, the phrase "infrequent harsh case" in isolation is neither workable nor entirely reliable as a benchmark for appellate review. There is no indication it was ever intended by the drafters to function as such.

In *Sears*, the Court stated that the decision to certify was with good reason left to the sound judicial discretion of the district court. At the same time, the Court noted that "[w]ith equally good reason, any *abuse* of that discretion remains reviewable by the Court of Appeals" (emphasis added). The Court indicated that the standard against which a district court's exercise of discretion is to be judged is the "interest of sound judicial administration." Admittedly this presents issues not always easily resolved, but the proper role of the court of appeals is not to reweigh the equities or reassess the facts but to make sure that the conclusions derived from those weighings and assessments are juridically sound and supported by the record.

There are thus two aspects to the proper function of a reviewing court in Rule 54(b) cases. The court of appeals must, of course, scrutinize the district court's evaluation of such factors as the interrelationship of the claims so as to prevent piecemeal appeals in cases which should be reviewed only as single units. But once such juridical concerns have been met, the discretionary judgment of the district court should be given substantial deference, for that court is "the one most likely to be familiar with the case and with any justifiable reasons for delay." *Sears, supra.* The reviewing court should disturb the trial court's assessment of the equities only if it can say that the judge's conclusion was clearly unreasonable.

Plainly, sound judicial administration does not require that Rule 54(b) requests be granted routinely. That is implicit in commending them to the sound discretion of a district court. Because this discretion "is, with good reason, vested by the rule primarily" in the district courts, *Sears, supra,* and because the number of possible situations is large, we are reluctant either to fix or sanction narrow guidelines for the district courts to follow. We are satisfied, however, that on the record here the District Court's assessment of the equities was reasonable.

One of the equities which the District Judge considered was the difference between the statutory and market rates of interest. Respondent correctly points out that adjustment of the statutory prejudgment interest rate is a matter within the province of the legislature, but that fact does not make the existing differential irrelevant for Rule 54(b) purposes. If the judgment is otherwise certifiable, the fact that a litigant who has successfully reduced his claim to judgment stands to lose money because of the difference in interest rates is surely not a "just reason for delay."

The difference between the prejudgment and market interest rates was not the only factor considered by the District Court. The court also noted that the debts in issue were liquidated and large, and that absent Rule 54(b) certification they would not be paid for "many months, if not years" because the rest of the litigation would be expected to continue for that period of time. The District Judge had noted earlier in his opinion on the merits of the release clause issue that respondent General Electric contested neither the amount of the debt nor the fact that it must eventually be paid. The only contest was over the effect of the release clause on the timing of the payment, an isolated and strictly legal issue on which summary judgment had been entered against respondent.

The question before the District Court thus came down to which of the parties should get the benefit of the difference between the prejudgment and market rates of interest on debts admittedly owing and adjudged to be due while unrelated claims were litigated. The central factor weighing in favor of General Electric was that its pending counterclaims created the possibility of a setoff against the amount it owed petitioner. This possibility was surely not an insignificant factor, especially since the counterclaims had survived a motion to dismiss for failure to state a claim. But the District Court took this into account when it determined that both litigants appeared to be in financially sound condition, and that Curtiss-Wright would be able to satisfy a judgment on the counterclaims should any be entered.

The Court of Appeals concluded that this was not enough, and suggested that the presence of such factors as economic duress and insolvency would be necessary to qualify the judgment for Rule 54(b) certification. But if Curtiss-Wright were under a threat of insolvency, that factor alone would weigh *against* qualifying; that very threat would cast doubt upon Curtiss-Wright's capacity to produce all or part of the $19 million should General Electric prevail on some of its counterclaims. Such a showing would thus in fact be self-defeating.

Nor is General Electric's solvency a dispositive factor; if its financial position were such that a delay in entry of judgment on Curtiss-Wright's claims would impair Curtiss-Wright's ability to collect on the judgment, that would weigh in favor of certification. But the fact that General Electric is capable of paying either now or later is not a "just reason for delay." At most, as the District Court found, the fact that neither party is or will become insolvent renders that factor neutral in a proper weighing of the equities involved.

The question in cases such as this is likely to be close, but the task of weighing and balancing the contending factors is peculiarly one for the trial judge, who can explore all the facets of a case. As we have noted, that assessment merits substantial deference on review. Here, the District Court's assessment of the equities between the parties was based on an intimate knowledge of the case and is a reasonable one. The District Court having found no other reason justifying delay, we conclude that it did not abuse its discretion in granting petitioner's motion for certification under Rule 54(b).[3]

Accordingly, the judgment of the Court of Appeals is vacated, and the case is remanded for proceedings consistent with this opinion.

It is so ordered.

---

[3] We note that FRCP 62(h) allows a court certifying a judgment under Rule 54(b) to stay its enforcement until the entering of a subsequent judgment or judgments. Rule 62(h) also states that the court "may prescribe such conditions as are necessary to secure the benefit thereof to the party in whose favor the judgment is entered." Under this Rule, we assume it would be within the power of the District Court to protect all parties by having the losing party deposit the amount of the judgment with the court, directing the Clerk to purchase high yield government obligations and to hold them pending the outcome of the case. In this way, valid considerations of economic duress and solvency, which do not affect the juridical considerations involved in a Rule 54(b) determination, can be provided for without preventing Rule 54(b) certification. In the instant case, after certifying the judgment as final under Rule 54(b), the District Court granted respondent's motion for a stay of judgment without bond, but only pending resolution of the appeal.

■ NOTES ON APPEALS UNDER FRCP 54(b)

1. Why was there "no just reason for delay" under FRCP 54(b) with respect to Curtiss-Wright's claims for $19 million? In light of the fact that General Electric continued to press its counterclaim for $52 million, does it make sense to award final judgment to Curtiss-Wright? The Third Circuit thought the trial court should *not* have employed the 54(b) procedure by entering final judgment. The effect of doing so, based on the required determination, is to enable the judgment holder to commence execution: Curtiss-Wright could demand that General Electric pay the judgment or take steps to execute (levying against General Electric property). The trial judge granted GE's "motion for a stay without bond pending appeal." What does this mean? If there was "no just reason for delay," why the stay?

2. *Curtiss-Wright* signs on to the view that a court reviewing a 54(b) determination should not "reweigh the equities or reassess the facts," but should ascertain that the conclusions "derived from those weighings and assessments are juridically sound and supported by the record." What does *that* mean?

3. The appellate mechanism created by FRCP 54(b) applies to the disposition of *claims*, not orders or rulings on points narrower than claims. See Reiter v. Cooper, 507 U.S. 258, 265 (1993) (consequence of fact that an "unreasonable-rate claim is technically a counterclaim rather than a defense" is that a defense cannot be "adjudicated separately from the plaintiff's claim," but a counterclaim "can be" and thus can become a "separate final judgment" under FRCP 54(b)); Liberty Mutual Insurance Co. v. Wetzel, 424 U.S. 737, 743 (1976) (in suit alleging that company's employee insurance benefits and maternity leave regulations discriminate against women, finding of liability that did not accord relief did not dispose of claim, and was not appealable under FRCP 54(b)). Suppose General Electric had raised two defenses to Curtiss-Wright's claim for $19 million—one based on the release and another on "accord and satisfaction," meaning that the two had carried out an understanding that compromised the $19 million obligation. Suppose Curtiss-Wright had made a motion to strike the defense based on the release clause, and the court agreed that the release clause did *not* provide a defense and granted the motion. If Curtiss-Wright had then asked the trial judge to determine that there was no just reason to delay and to enter "final judgment rejecting the release clause," would this course be proper under FRCP 54(b)? If the judge *did* take this course, and GE took an appeal and argued that this use of FRCP 54(b) was improper, should the reviewing court be similarly deferential to the trial judge?

4. *Curtiss-Wright* does not discuss the question whether the judgment disposed of one or more "claims," perhaps because nobody raised this issue, and it seems apparent that indeed the judgment would pass whatever test one might devise to distinguish "claims" from other issues. Curtiss-Wright brought suit on the basis of 21 contracts, and the court determined that the matters being resolved were indeed claims that were "separate, distinct, and independent" of other claims, and amounts covered by the judgment were "liquidated and large." As noted in *Curtiss-Wright,* the Court has several times addressed the question of what constitutes a "claim" for purposes of FRCP 54(b):

(a) In *Sears,* cited in *Curtiss-Wright,* plaintiff brought a claim under the antitrust laws for damages to three ventures. Three other counts sought recovery under common law for damages to each venture. The judge dismissed the antitrust claim and one of the common law claims, and entered a FRCP 54(b) certificate for those two claims. Defendant argued that the antitrust claim could not be severed from the common law claims, and the Court acknowledged that the antitrust claim "does rest in part on some of the facts" involved in the two other claims. Still, the "basis of liability" for the antitrust claim was "independent" of the common law basis of the other claims, and "it cannot be well argued" that the certified claims were so "inherently inseparable from, or closely related to" the remaining claims that they could not be severed and entered as judgments subject to immediate appeal. Sears, Roebuck & Co. v. Mackey, 351 U.S. 427, 426 & n.9 (1956).

(b) On the day it decided *Sears,* the Court also decided the *Cold Metal* case, which approved certification of judgment against plaintiff on a contract claim despite a counterclaim "arising in part out of the same transactions" as those that were the subject of the dismissed claim. Cold Metal Process Co. v. United Engineering & Foundry Co., 351 U.S. 445 (1956).

(c) *Sears* and *Cold Metal* mean that a trial court may certify a claim for appeal even if parallel and overlapping claims remain pending, whether brought by plaintiff as in *Sears* or defendant as in *Cold Metal.*

(d) Do the cases mean more? Do they mean that every theory of recovery generates a claim that can be split off from others for certification and immediate appeal? Even if all theories support the same recovery? If plaintiff brings a two-count complaint seeking recovery for emotional distress, alleging in one count that defendant acted intentionally and in another that he acted negligently, could a court dismiss one of these counts and certify the other? Most courts say no: A mere "difference in theories" does *not* constitute multiple claims that can generate a certificate and separate appeals. See Lloyd Noland Foundation, Inc. v. Tenet Health Care Corp., 483 F.3d 773, 781 (11th Cir. 2007) (granting summary judgment for defendants on contractual indemnification did not dispose of claim seeking common law indemnification; no final judgment under FRCP 54(b) on any claim).

(e) Disposition of every claim by or against a single party is probably enough to support certification and separate appeal, see Marseilles Hydro Power, LLC v. Marseilles Land and Water Co., 518 F.3d 459, 463 (7th Cir. 2008) (FRCP 54(b) "authorizes certification when everything having to do with a particular party is wrapped up").

(f) The hardest cases involve disposition of different "counts" or "theories" in claims by one party against another. Here the prevailing approach is

that multiple claims can be present if multiple relief is possible. In the *Marseilles Hydro Power* case, noted just above, the Seventh Circuit put it this way:

> If any loose ends remain with one or the other [party], certification is still appropriate if certain claims have finally been resolved. That requires a somewhat more complex inquiry. If an examination of the record reveals that the claims on appeal are too similar to the issues remaining in the district court, then we would have to conclude that there was no partial final judgment of the sort contemplated by the rule. In such a case, we would have no jurisdiction to entertain the appeal. When a district court invokes Rule 54(b), we have an independent obligation to ensure that its decision on a given claim is indeed a final one. See Curtiss-Wright Corp. v. General Electric Co., 446 U.S. 1, 7-8 (1980). We must also decide whether the district court abused its discretion in determining that there was no just reason for delay. Both questions involve consideration of the factual relation between the issues that have been resolved and those that remain.
>
> There are no bright-line rules for determining whether two claims are separate for Rule 54(b) purposes, but we find some guidance in Amalgamated Meat Cutters & Butcher Workmen v. Thompson Farms Co., 642 F.2d 1065, 1070-71 (7th Cir. 1981). "At a minimum, claims cannot be separate unless separate recovery is possible on each. . . . Hence, mere variations of legal theory do not constitute separate claims. . . . Nor are claims so closely related that they would fall afoul of the rule against splitting claims if brought separately. . . ." This inquiry involves comparing the issues at stake in the appealed claims and those remaining in the district court, Indiana Harbor Belt R.R. Co. v. American Cyanamid Co., 860 F.2d 1441, 1444 (7th Cir. 1988), and determining whether there is a "significant factual overlap," Automatic Liquid Packaging, Inc. v. Dominik, 852 F.2d 1036, 1037 (7th Cir. 1988). In the course of this examination, we bear in mind that the rule defines a class of final judgments, suitable for appeal under 28 USC §1291. The scope of Rule 54(b) must therefore be confined to "situations where one of multiple claims is fully adjudicated—to spare the court of appeals from having to keep relearning the facts of a case on successive appeals." *American Cyanamid.* "[I]f there are different facts (and of course different issues) consideration of the appeals piecemeal rather than all at once will not involve a duplication in the efforts required of the judges to prepare for argument in, and to decide, each appeal." Jack Walters & Sons Corp. v. Morton Bldg., Inc., 737 F.2d 698, 702 (7th Cir. 1984). Even if two claims arise from the same event or occurrence, they may be separable for Rule 54(b) purposes if they rely on entirely different legal entitlements yielding separate recoveries, rather than different legal theories aimed at the same recovery.

Marseilles Hydro Power, LLC v. Marseilles Land and Water Co., 518 F.3d 459, 463-464 (7th Cir. 2008).

5. *Curtiss-Wright* mentions that the trial court, in making the determination under FRCP 54(b), can consider "such factors as whether the claims under review were separable from the others remaining to be adjudicated" and whether multiple appeals would lead to appellate decisions of "the same issues more than once." Where such factors appear, reviewing courts sometimes decline to entertain appeals based on certification under FRCP 54(b). See, e.g., Oklahoma City Urban Renewal Authority v. City of Oklahoma City, 110 P.3d 550, 559 (Okla. 2005) (court erred in certifying appeal under state rule 54(b) because declaratory judgment and *qui tam* claims "arise from the same transactions or occurrences" and are "interrelated and intertwined," having "so much factual overlap" that they are "the functional equivalent of nonseverable claims").

6. Note that the 54(b) procedure requires the would-be appellant to obtain a certificate from the *trial judge.* See Powell v. Cannon, 179 P.3d 799, 807 (Utah 2008) (failure to request 54(b) certificate deprives reviewing court of jurisdiction on appeal, even in case where certification by trial court would have been proper).

3. The Dual Certification Procedure Under §1292(b)

Enacted in 1958, the dual certificate statute authorizes immediate review of any "order" if the district judge certifies that (a) it "involves a controlling question of law," (b) there is "substantial ground for difference of opinion" on the matter, and (c) "an immediate appeal ... may materially advance the ultimate termination of the litigation." Then the Court of Appeals that "would have jurisdiction" in an appeal from a final judgment in the suit "may ... in its discretion" permit an appeal on application made to it within ten days.

This provision amounts to recognition of two important points: First, the final judgment rule is not always optimal in balancing the need for review against considerations of efficiency and fairness. Second, nobody really has any idea how to describe or define cases that should be exceptions. In effect, the statute says "let's ask the trial judge and the reviewing court whether it would be better to let an appeal go forward now, and if they agree that it would be a good idea, let's do it."

Here are some cases where the statutory dual certification mechanism has been used:

(1) In United States v. Stanley, 483 U.S. 669 (1987), James Stanley, an Army Sergeant who volunteered in a program to test the effectiveness of protective clothing and equipment, was given LSD without his knowledge, in an Army project to study its effects on human subjects. He sued under the Federal Tort Claims Act, but the court dismissed the claims under the *Feres* doctrine. See Feres v. United States, 340 U.S. 135 (1950) (Federal Tort Claims Act does not authorize recovery for injuries incident to military service). After appeal, Stanley amended his complaint to state claims under the *Bivens* doctrine. See Bivens v. Six Unknown Named Agents of Fed. Bureau of Narcotics, 403 U.S. 288 (1970) (recognizing implied right to sue federal officers for violations of constitutional rights). Despite the Court's later holding in Chappell v.

Wallace, 462 U.S. 296 (1983), that enlisted military personnel may not recover damages from superior officers for constitutional violations, the court refused to dismiss the *Bivens* claims, apparently believing that *Chappell* did not entirely foreclose them. But it signed a 1292(b) certificate allowing appeal. The Eleventh Circuit accepted the appeal, decided that retaining the case was correct, and then re-examined the prior dismissal of the FTCA claim, concluding that this claim too should be reinstated. The Supreme Court took the appeal and concluded that the trial judge should have dismissed. The Court faulted the Eleventh Circuit for taking up again the FTCA claim: Under the 1292(b) procedure, the *only* question before the reviewing court was the propriety of "an order refusing to dismiss Stanley's *Bivens* claims on the basis of our holding in *Chappell*."

(2) In Marrese v. American Academy of Orthopaedic Surgeons, 470 U.S. 373 (1985) (Chapter 14C1, infra), a federal court hearing a federal antitrust suit refused to dismiss on the basis of a judgment in a state suit brought by the same plaintiff against the same defendants, alleging the same claims, but under *state* law. In the belief that a state court judgment could have no impact on a suit based on federal law that can *only* be brought in federal court, the trial court refused to dismiss. But the court entered a 1292(b) certificate to review the matter, and again the case reached the Supreme Court. (As you will see, the Court decided that state law *does* control the *res judicata* effect of a state judgment, even when it comes to later claims brought under federal law that can only be litigated in federal court.)

(3) In Catalano, Inc. v. Target Sales, Inc., 446 U.S. 643 (1980), a federal court in a class suit by retailers of beer refused to rule that a secret agreement among wholesalers to insist on payment in advance or on delivery (instead of extending interest-free credit for the period allowed by state law) was a *per se* violation of the Sherman Antitrust Act. The court entered a 1292(b) certificate, and the Court of Appeals accepted review and agreed with the ruling of the trial court, whereupon the Supreme Court granted certiorari and reversed, holding that the agreement was indeed a *per se* violation.

(4) In Herbert v. Lando, 441 U.S. 153 (1979), a retired Army officer sued CBS and others for libel after he had accused superior officers of covering up reports of atrocities and war crimes during the Viet Nam conflict, and the trial court denied his request to compel answers relating to defendant's editorial policies, in the belief that the First Amendment shielded defendants from such intrusive discovery. Plaintiff was a public figure, so he had to prove malice in order to recover, and the trial court recognized the difficulties presented if the discovery were curtailed, so it certified the matter for interlocutory appeal, and the case went to the Supreme Court, which decided that the discovery was warranted, and reversed the trial court's determination on this matter.

Applying to the trial court for certification of an order for purposes of appeal seems an ever-present possibility, giving rise to arguments that a party who *fails* to apply for such an order, on suffering an adverse ruling on some point at the trial level, has *waived* the right to predicate error on such a ruling. The Court has *rejected* this argument, however, and failing to apply for a certification does *not* waive rights to urge error if appellate review later goes forward on some other basis. See Caterpillar Inc. v. Lewis, 519 U.S. 61, 74 (1996) (one is not required to "seek permission to take an interlocutory appeal pursuant to 28 USC §1292(b) in order to avoid waiving whatever ultimate appeal right" might exist).

The Court often comments, in cases in which a party sought interlocutory review on some other basis, such as the final judgment principle or the collateral order doctrine, that §1292(b) would be a preferable way to seek review. See Coopers & Lybrand v. Livesay, 437 U.S. 463 (1978) (refusing to entertain appeal from order decertifying class on theory that this order was a final judgment because it was the "death knell" for the suit; noting that the parties did not seek certification under §1292(b), and commenting that this mechanism is preferable in such cases).

The 1292(b) procedure requires the trial court and the reviewing court to agree on allowing the appeal. Sometimes trial courts certify an order, but the reviewing court disagrees and refuses to entertain the appeal. See Deposit Guaranty National Bank v. Roper, 445 U.S. 326 (1980) (under 1292(b), district court certified for appeal a ruling denying motion to certify a class; reviewing court declined review). Ultimately, plaintiffs in *Roper* won a kind of pyrrhic victory, as the Supreme Court held that defendant's offer to pay the individual plaintiff the amount demanded did *not* moot the class suit. The case then proceeded as a class suit, but plaintiff class lost on the merits. See Roper v. Consurve, Inc., 932 F.2d 965 (5th Cir. 1991) (affirming without opinion), *cert. denied,* 502 U.S. 861 (1991).

 ## D APPELLATE REVIEW OF FACTS

As noted at the beginning of this chapter, appellate review seeks to correct errors, like mistakes in jury instructions or admitting or excluding evidence, but *does not* take up the question whether the factfinder (judge or jury) got the facts right.

There are of course reasons for this deference, and two stand out: First, appellate courts are remote from the evidence presented at trial. By comparison, the trial judge and the jury (if any) can see and hear everything firsthand. Hearing a witness tell what he knows, watching the process of direct and cross-examination, seeing *all the evidence* that the parties produce, put the factfinder—whether judge or jury—in a better position to decide where the truth is. Second, in jury-tried cases it is not the responsibility of *any* judge—trial or appellate—to find the facts. Hence the mere fact that the case is tried to a jury suggests that appellate courts should defer, and should not intervene simply because it sees the case differently.

Still, we do not hold the view that trial judges and juries are infallible. We do not put their work beyond reach of *all* appellate scrutiny. One challenge for reviewing courts, then, is to define a standard of review, which can be described in terms of either "degree of deference" or "degree of scrutiny." A high degree of deference means giving trial judges (or juries) lots of leeway, and corresponds to a *low* degree of scrutiny, or less intrusive review. A *low* degree of deference means giving trial judges (or juries) less leeway, and corresponds to a high degree of scrutiny, or more exacting review. Perhaps not surprisingly, different standards apply in different settings. The highest standard involving the least deference and most exacting review is typically described as "*de novo*" review, under which an appellate court can correct the work of a trial court simply because the reviewing court thinks the trial court got it wrong. An intermediate standard involving more deference and less exacting review is described as the "clear error" standard, under which an appellate court can correct the work of a trial court only if the reviewing court is convinced that the trial court was clearly or certainly wrong. The lowest standard, involving the most deference and least exacting review, is typically described in terms of "abuse of discretion," under which an appellate court can correct the work of a trial court only if the reviewing court thinks the trial judge "abused its discretion," which is often equated with doing something arbitrary or capricious.

Reviewing courts have another challenge, which involves separating the function of judge or jury as factfinder from their function in law application: It is one thing to say a trial judge or jury deserves deference in deciding whether a traffic light was red or not, quite another to say a judge or jury deserves deference in deciding, for example, what standard of care a grocery store owes to its patrons. See, e.g., Janis v. Nash Finch Co., 780 N.W.2d 497 (S.D. 2010) (in slip-and-fall suit by patron against supermarket, defining duty owed by store to patron raises question of law, which includes foreseeability in defining extent of duty; whether supermarket breached duty raises question of fact for jury) (reversing summary judgment for defendant).

1. Jury-Tried Cases—The Power to Enter Judgments as a Matter of Law and to Order New Trials

In civil cases tried to juries, recall from Chapter 12 that we have two procedural devices that operate to constrain what juries can do. One involves judgment as a matter of law (JMAL): If the evidence is such that a reasonable jury could find only for the plaintiff or only for the defendant, a JMAL motion can be granted under FRCP 50, and either the case is taken from the jury before it retires to deliberate or, if the jury is allowed to deliberate and return a verdict, a "renewed" JMAL request can be used to reject an irrational verdict.

When a JMAL motion is made, the question is whether there is "sufficient evidence" to take the case to the jury. In the common situation where defendant makes the motion, the argument is that plaintiff has "no evidence" or "insufficient evidence" on a critical point, hence that defendant is entitled to judgment. In the less common situation where plaintiff or claimant makes such a motion, the argument is that the evidence so overwhelmingly favors the plaintiff—what we have called "cogent and compelling" evidence—that no reasonable jury could reject it, hence that judgment should be entered for the plaintiff or claimant.

Recall too that a party who loses after a jury returns a verdict for the other side can seek a new trial under FRCP 59 for errors or because the verdict is "against the weight of the evidence." Here the question is not whether there is sufficient evidence—it is *not* the same question that arises on JMAL motions. Rather, the question is whether, even *though* there is enough evidence to find as the jury found, nevertheless the jury just got it wrong, and the verdict should be set aside and the case retried.

Recall that these motions can be combined, and that for the most part they must be made within 28 days after entry of judgment. The very fact that they may be combined complicates the strategies of parties on appeal: For example, a defendant who loses at trial when a judgment is entered against her on the basis of a jury verdict may move for judgment as a matter of law, and may move, in the alternative, for a new trial. If the judge denies both motions, defendant may appeal, and then *plaintiff* may seek a new trial at the court of appeals in case it is inclined to award judgment as a matter of law to defendant.

■ NOTES ON APPELLATE REVIEW OF JURY FACTFINDING

1. Suppose defendant makes a motion for judgment as a matter of law at the close of the evidence, and the motion is denied and the case goes to a jury, which finds for plaintiff. Defendant renews the motion, in accord with the procedure laid out in FRCP 50, and again it is denied, and judgment is entered on the verdict. Now defendant can appeal and urge error in the trial court's ruling: What standard of review applies? Does an appellate court conduct *de novo* review, or look for "clear error," or is "abuse of discretion" the appropriate standard? In fact, the cases are as one in saying that appellate courts accord essentially *no* deference in this circumstance: A reviewing court decides "*de novo*" whether the evidence sufficed to take the case to the jury. See, e.g., Rocky Mountain Christian Church v. Board of County Commissioners, 613 F.3d 1229 (10th Cir. 2010); Malone v. Lockheed Martin Corp., 610 F.3d 16, 19 (1st Cir. 2010).

2. Of course, *de novo* review masks an important point, which is that the question whether the evidence is sufficient to create a jury question is *itself* a deferential standard. See, e.g., United States ex rel. Miller v. Bill Harbert International Construction, Inc., 608 F.3d 871, 899 (D.C. Cir. 2010) (while "we review [a] decision [to deny a motion for judgment as a matter of law] *de novo,* we 'do not . . . lightly disturb a jury verdict,'" but instead "we 'draw all reasonable inferences in favor of the nonmoving party and . . . may not make credibility determinations or weigh the evidence,'" and we therefore "'disregard all evidence favorable to the moving party [here, the defendants] that the jury is not required to believe,' and will reverse a jury's decision 'only if the evidence and all reasonable inferences that can be drawn therefrom are so one-sided that reasonable men and women could not have reached a verdict in plaintiff[s'] favor'"). In the end, then, appellate courts reviewing decisions denying motions for judgment as a matter of law feel free to correct mistakes by trial judges (review is *de novo*), but still the question is not whether the trial judge or the reviewing court thinks that the jury decided the case right, but whether there was sufficient evidence on which a reasonable person *could* decide the case as the jury did. Does this standard make sense in this situation? Does it make sense for reviewing courts to apply a *de novo* standard here?

2. Judge-Tried Cases—"Clear Error" Review

Recall that in civil cases tried to the judge without a jury (bench-tried cases), the judge has a dual role: He resolves both issues of law, including matters of procedure and evidence, and also questions of fact. Recall too that FRCP 52 requires the trial judge in such cases to "find the facts specially and state . . . conclusions of law separately." See FRCP 52(a).

Of course judgments entered on the basis of such findings and conclusions by a trial judge may be reviewed on appeal for error. A moment's reflection, however, will lead you to conclude that many kinds of errors that are common in cases tried to juries simply do not occur, or are less likely to lead to reversal if they *do* occur, in judge-tried cases. In judge-tried cases, for example, there are no jury instructions, and the closest analogy would be errors in conclusions of law, which reflect mistakes that in a jury-tried case would be embedded in jury instructions. And while judges can make mistakes in admitting or excluding evidence, even in bench trials, it is commonly understood that the judgment in a bench-tried case is almost *never* overturned for errors in *admitting* evidence. The reason is that judges are presumed to have relied only on evidence properly admitted, and are presumed not to have relied on evidence that should not have come into the case.

Consider now one of the more challenging problems of appellate review in judge-tried cases—the review of judge-made findings of fact for "clear error."

PULLMAN-STANDARD v. SWINT

Supreme Court of the United States
456 U.S. 273 (1982)

Justice WHITE delivered the opinion of the Court.

Respondents were black employees at the Bessemer, Ala., plant of petitioner Pullman-Standard (the Company), a manufacturer of railway freight cars and parts. They brought suit against the Company and the union petitioners—the United Steelworkers of America, AFL-CIO-CLC, and its Local 1466 (collectively USW)—alleging violations of Title VII of the Civil Rights Act of 1964, as amended, 42 USC §2000e *et seq.* and 42 USC §1981. As they come here, these cases involve only the validity, under Title VII, of a seniority system maintained by the Company and USW. The District Court found "that the differences in terms, conditions or privileges of employment resulting [from the seniority system] are 'not the result of an intention to discriminate' because of race or color," and held, therefore, that the system satisfied the requirements of §703(h) of the Act. The Court of Appeals for the Fifth Circuit reversed:

> Because we find that the differences in the terms, conditions and standards of employment for black workers and white workers at Pullman-Standard resulted from an intent to discriminate because of race, we hold that the system is not legally valid under section 703(h) of Title VII, 42 USC 2000e-2(h).

We granted the petitions for certiorari filed by USW and by the Company, limited to the first question presented in each petition: whether a court of appeals is bound by the "clearly erroneous" rule of FRCP 52(a) in reviewing a district court's findings of fact, arrived at after a lengthy trial, as to the motivation of the parties who negotiated a seniority system; and whether the court below applied wrong legal criteria in determining the bona fides of the seniority system. We conclude that the Court of Appeals erred in the course of its review and accordingly reverse its judgment and remand for further proceedings.

Title VII is a broad remedial measure, designed "to assure equality of employment opportunities." McDonnell Douglas Corp. v. Green, 411 U.S. 792, 800 (1973). The Act was designed to bar not only overt employment discrimination, "but also practices that are fair in form, but discriminatory in operation." Griggs v. Duke Power Co., 401 U.S. 424, 431 (1971). "Thus, the Court has repeatedly held that a prima facie Title VII violation may be established by policies or practices that are neutral on their face and in intent but that nonetheless discriminate in effect against a particular group." Teamsters v. United States, 431 U.S. 324, 349 (1977) (hereinafter *Teamsters*). The Act's treatment of seniority systems, however, establishes an exception to these general principles. 42 USC §2000e-2(h), provides in pertinent part:

> Notwithstanding any other provision of this subchapter, it shall not be an unlaw- ful employment practice for an employer to apply different standards of

compensation, or different terms, conditions, or privileges of employment pursuant to a bona fide seniority . . . system . . . provided that such differences are not the result of an intention to discriminate because of race.

Under this section, a showing of disparate impact is insufficient to invalidate a seniority system, even though the result may be to perpetuate pre-Act discrimination. In Trans World Airlines, Inc. v. Hardison, 432 U.S. 63, 82 (1977), we summarized the effect of §703(h) as follows: "[A]bsent a discriminatory purpose, the operation of a seniority system cannot be an unlawful employment practice even if the system has some discriminatory consequences." Thus, any challenge to a seniority system under Title VII will require a trial on the issue of discriminatory intent: Was the system adopted because of its racially discriminatory impact?

. . .

[The District Court followed the decision in James v. Stockham Valves & Fittings Co., 559 F.2d 310 (5th Cir. 1977), which held that *Teamsters* requires a consideration of "the totality of the circumstances in the development and maintenance of the system." The District Court considered four factors: (1) whether the system operates to discourage all employees equally from transferring between seniority units (the court concluded that the system was facially neutral and that claims of racial discrimination were unsubstantiated), (2) whether the departmental structure is rational in light of general industry practice (the court found that it was), (3) whether the system had its genesis in discrimination (the court concluded that the system was not related to discriminatory practices), and (4) whether the system was created and maintained "free from any illegal purpose" (the court concluded that the system was not tainted by such purpose).

The Court of Appeals reached the opposite conclusion. On the first point, the Court of Appeals thought the trial court erred in "putting aside qualitative differences between the departments in which blacks were concentrated and those dominated by whites." On the second, it rejected the conclusion that the structure was rational, and thought departments were created in arbitrary fashion. Third, the Court of Appeals thought that the motives of IAM (International Association of Machinists and Aerospace Workers) were relevant and that it had discriminatory intent. On the fourth point, the Court of Appeals recited and did not expressly set aside what the District Court had found. The Court of Appeals then announced its "definite and firm conviction" that the trial court had made a mistake about discriminatory purpose.]

Having rejected the District Court's finding, the court made its own findings as to whether the USW seniority system was protected by §703(h):

> We consider significant in our decision the manner by which the two seniority units were set up, the creation of the various all-white and all-black departments within the USW unit at the time of certification and in the years thereafter,

conditions of racial discrimination which affected the negotiation and renegotiation of the system, and the extent to which the system and the attendant no-transfer rule locked blacks into the least remunerative positions within the company. Because we find that the differences in the terms, conditions and standards of employment for black workers and white workers at Pullman-Standard resulted from an intent to discriminate because of race, we hold that the system is not legally valid under section 703(h) of Title VII, 42 USC §2000e-2(h).

In connection with its assertion that it was convinced that a mistake had been made, the Court of Appeals, in a footnote, referred to the clearly-erroneous standard of Rule 52(a).[14] It pointed out, however, that if findings "are made under an erroneous view of controlling legal principles, the clearly-erroneous rule does not apply, and the findings may not stand." Finally, quoting from East v. Romine, Inc., 518 F.2d 332, 339 (5th Cir. 1975), the Court of Appeals repeated the following view of its appellate function in Title VII cases where purposeful discrimination is at issue:

> Although discrimination *vel non* is essentially a question of fact it is, at the same time, the ultimate issue for resolution in this case, being expressly proscribed by 42 USC §2000e-2(a). As such, a finding of discrimination or non-discrimination is a finding of ultimate fact. [Cites omitted.] In reviewing the district court's findings, therefore, we will proceed to make an independent determination of appellant's allegations of discrimination, though bound by findings of subsidiary fact which are themselves not clearly erroneous.

... [P]etitioners submit that the Court of Appeals made an independent determination of discriminatory purpose, the "ultimate fact" in this case, and that this was error under Rule 52(a). We agree with petitioners that if the Court of Appeals followed what seems to be the accepted rule in that Circuit, its judgment must be reversed.[16]

Rule 52(a) broadly requires that findings of fact not be set aside unless clearly erroneous. It does not make exceptions or purport to exclude certain categories of factual findings from the obligation of a court of appeals to accept a district court's findings unless clearly erroneous. It does not divide facts into categories; in particular, it does not divide findings of fact into those that deal with "ultimate" and those that deal with "subsidiary" facts.

---

[14] In United States v. United States Gypsum Co., 333 U.S. 364, 395 (1948), this Court characterized the clearly-erroneous standard as follows: "A finding is 'clearly erroneous' when although there is evidence to support it, the reviewing court on the entire evidence is left with the definite and firm conviction that a mistake has been committed." We note that the Court of Appeals quoted this passage at the conclusion of its analysis of the District Court opinion.

[16] There is some indication . . . that the Circuit rule with respect to "ultimate facts" is only another way of stating a standard of review with respect to mixed questions of law and fact—the ultimate "fact" is the statutory, legally determinative consideration (here, intentional discrimination) which is or is not satisfied by subsidiary facts admitted or found by the trier of fact. As indicated in the text, however, the question of intentional discrimination under §703(h) is a pure question of fact. . . .

The Rule does not apply to conclusions of law. The Court of Appeals, therefore, was quite right in saying that if a district court's findings rest on an erroneous view of the law, they may be set aside on that basis. But here the District Court was not faulted for misunderstanding or applying an erroneous definition of intentional discrimination. It was reversed for arriving at what the Court of Appeals thought was an erroneous finding as to whether the differential impact of the seniority system reflected an intent to discriminate on account of race. That question, as we see it, is a pure question of fact, subject to Rule 52(a)'s clearly-erroneous standard. It is not a question of law and not a mixed question of law and fact.

The Court has previously noted the vexing nature of the distinction between questions of fact and questions of law. See Baumgartner v. United States, 322 U.S. 665, 671 (1944). Rule 52(a) does not furnish particular guidance with respect to distinguishing law from fact. Nor do we yet know of any other rule or principle that will unerringly distinguish a factual finding from a legal conclusion. For the reasons that follow, however, we have little doubt about the factual nature of §703(h)'s requirement that a seniority system be free of an intent to discriminate.

Treating issues of intent as factual matters for the trier of fact is commonplace. In Dayton Board of Education v. Brinkman, 443 U.S. 526, 534 (1979), the principal question was whether the defendants had intentionally maintained a racially segregated school system at a specified time in the past. We recognized that issue as essentially factual, subject to the clearly-erroneous rule. In Commissioner v. Duberstein, 363 U.S. 278 (1960), the Court held that the principal criterion for identifying a gift under the applicable provision of the Internal Revenue Code was the intent or motive of the donor—"one that inquires what the basic reason for his conduct was in fact." Resolution of that issue determined the ultimate issue of whether a gift had been made. Both issues were held to be questions of fact subject to the clearly-erroneous rule. In United States v. Yellow Cab Co., 338 U.S. 338, 341 (1949), an antitrust case, the Court referred to "[f]indings as to the design, motive and intent with which men act" as peculiarly factual issues for the trier of fact and therefore subject to appellate review under Rule 52.

Justice Black's dissent in *Yellow Cab* suggested a contrary approach. Relying on United States v. Griffith, 334 U.S. 100 (1948), he argued that it is not always necessary to prove "specific intent" to restrain trade; it is enough if a restraint is the result or consequence of a defendant's conduct or business arrangements. Such an approach, however, is specifically precluded by §703(h) in Title VII cases challenging seniority systems. Differentials among employees that result from a seniority system are not unlawful employment practices unless the product of an intent to discriminate. It would make no sense, therefore, to say that the intent to discriminate required by §703(h) may be presumed from such an impact. As §703(h) was construed in *Teamsters*, there must be a finding of actual intent to discriminate on racial grounds on the part of those who negotiated or maintained the system. That finding appears to us to be a pure question of fact.

This is not to say that discriminatory impact is not part of the evidence to be considered by the trial court in reaching a finding on whether there was such a discriminatory intent as a factual matter. We do assert, however, that under §703(h) discriminatory intent is a finding of fact to be made by the trial court; it is not a question of law and not a mixed question of law and fact of the kind that in some cases may allow an appellate court to review the facts to see if they satisfy some legal concept of discriminatory intent.[19] Discriminatory intent here means actual motive; it is not a legal presumption to be drawn from a factual showing of something less than actual motive. Thus, a court of appeals may only reverse a district court's finding on discriminatory intent if it concludes that the finding is clearly erroneous under Rule 52(a). Insofar as the Fifth Circuit assumed otherwise, it erred.

Respondents do not directly defend the Fifth Circuit rule that a trial court's finding on discriminatory intent is not subject to the clearly-erroneous standard of Rule 52(a). Rather, among other things, they submit that the Court of Appeals recognized and, where appropriate, properly applied Rule 52(a) in setting aside the findings of the District Court. This position has force, but for two reasons it is not persuasive.

First, although the Court of Appeals acknowledged and correctly stated the controlling standard of Rule 52(a), the acknowledgment came late in the court's opinion. The court had not expressly referred to or applied Rule 52(a) in the course of disagreeing with the District Court's resolution of the factual issues deemed relevant under James v. Stockham Valves & Fittings Co., 559 F.2d 310 (5th Cir. 1977).[21] Furthermore, the paragraph in which the court finally concludes that the USW seniority system is unprotected by §703(h)

---

[19] We need not, therefore, address the much-mooted issue of the applicability of the Rule 52(a) standard to mixed questions of law and fact—*i.e.*, questions in which the historical facts are admitted or established, the rule of law is undisputed, and the issue is whether the facts satisfy the statutory standard, or to put it another way, whether the rule of law as applied to the established facts is or is not violated. There is substantial authority in the Circuits on both sides of this question. There is also support in decisions of this Court for the proposition that conclusions on mixed questions of law and fact are independently reviewable by an appellate court, *e.g.*, Bogardus v. Commissioner, 302 U.S. 34, 39 (1937); Helvering v. Tex-Penn Oil Co., 300 U.S. 481, 491 (1937); Helvering v. Rankin, 295 U.S. 123, 131 (1935). But cf., Commissioner v. Duberstein, 363 U.S. 278, 289 (1960); Commissioner v. Heininger, 320 U.S. 467, 475 (1943).

[21] In particular, in regard to the second *James* factor—whether the departmental structure was rational or in line with industry practice—the Court of Appeals did not focus on the evidentiary basis for any particular finding of the District Court. It appeared to make an independent examination of the record and arrive at its own conclusion contrary to that of the District Court. Likewise, in dealing with the genesis of the seniority system and whether or not the negotiation or maintenance of the system was tainted with racial discrimination, the Court of Appeals, while identifying what it thought was legal error in failing to consider the racial practices and intentions of IAM, did not otherwise overturn any of the District Court's findings as clearly erroneous.

strongly suggests that the outcome was the product of the court's independent consideration of the totality of the circumstances it found in the record.

Second and more fundamentally, when the court stated that it was convinced that a mistake had been made, it then identified not only the mistake but also the source of that mistake. The mistake of the District Court was that on the record there could be no doubt about the existence of a discriminatory purpose. The source of the mistake was the District Court's failure to recognize the relevance of the racial purposes of IAM. Had the District Court "given the IAM's role in the creation and establishment of the seniority system its due consideration," it "might have reached a different conclusion."

When an appellate court discerns that a district court has failed to make a finding because of an erroneous view of the law, the usual rule is that there should be a remand for further proceedings to permit the trial court to make the missing findings. . . . Likewise, where findings are infirm because of an erroneous view of the law, a remand is the proper course unless the record permits only one resolution of the factual issue. All of this is elementary. Yet the Court of Appeals, after holding that the District Court had failed to consider relevant evidence and indicating that the District Court might have come to a different conclusion had it considered that evidence, failed to remand for further proceedings as to the intent of IAM and the significance, if any, of such a finding with respect to the intent of USW itself. Instead, the Court of Appeals made its own determination as to the motives of IAM, found that USW had acquiesced in the IAM conduct, and apparently concluded that the foregoing was sufficient to remove the system from the protection of §703(h).[23]

Proceeding in this manner seems to us incredible unless the Court of Appeals construed its own well-established Circuit rule with respect to its authority to arrive at independent findings on ultimate facts free of the strictures of Rule 52(a) also to permit it to examine the record and make its own independent findings with respect to those issues on which the district court's findings are set aside for an error of law. As we have previously said, however, the premise for this conclusion is infirm: whether an ultimate fact or not, discriminatory intent under §703(h) is a factual matter subject to the clearly-erroneous standard of Rule 52(a). It follows that when a district court's finding on such an ultimate fact is set aside for an error of law, the court of appeals is not relieved of the usual requirement of remanding for further

---

[23] IAM's discriminatory motivation, if it existed, cannot be imputed to USW. It is relevant only to the extent that it may shed some light on the purpose of USW or the Company in creating and maintaining the separate seniority system at issue in these cases. A discriminatory intent on the part of IAM, therefore, does not control the outcome of these cases. Neither does the fact, if true, that USW acquiesced in racially discriminatory conduct on the part of IAM. Such acquiescence is not the equivalent of a discriminatory purpose on the part of USW.

proceedings to the tribunal charged with the task of factfinding in the first instance.

Accordingly, the judgment of the Court of Appeals is reversed, and the cases are remanded to that court for further proceedings consistent with this opinion.

[Justice Stevens concurred in part. Justices Marshall and Blackmun dissented, arguing that in cases involving documentary evidence the reviewing court is in just as good a position as the trial court, hence that review may be more intrusive. FRCP 52(a) was amended after this decision to include language applying the clear error standard to findings of fact "whether based on oral or other evidence."]

■ NOTES ON "CLEAR ERROR" REVIEW OF JUDGE-FOUND FACTS

1. The "clear error" standard is embodied in FRCP 52(a)(6), which says findings of fact "must not be set aside unless clearly erroneous." This standard applies not only in cases based on live testimony ("oral" evidence), but in cases based on "other evidence," referring to documents. Why should a reviewing court correct the factual findings of a trial judge only if they are "clearly" erroneous? Why not correct them just because the reviewing court thinks they're wrong?

2. Trial judges in bench-tried cases make *both* findings of fact and conclusions of law. As *Swint* says, the clear error standard applies to the former, not to the latter. Why? What standard applies to review of conclusions of law?

3. In *Swint*, the appellate court reviewed a finding of the trial judge that differences in terms of employment stemming from the seniority system did *not* grow out of an intent to discriminate on race or color. Plausibly enough, the approach endorsed in the Fifth Circuit opinion in *James* said this question had to be resolved by considering "the totality of the circumstances" and that four factors are important—whether the seniority system "operates to discourage all employees equally" from transferring among departments, whether the departmental structure is "rational" in light of industry practice, whether the system had its "genesis" in discrimination, and whether there was any "illegal purpose" behind the system. The trial court thought the seniority system in the Pullman plant passed muster by reference to *all* these factors, and the reviewing court disagreed on three of the four, concluding that these showed intentional discrimination.

4. What standard should courts observe in reviewing punitive damage awards? Compare Slovinski v. Elliot, 927 N.E.2d 1221, 1225 (Ill. 2010) (abuse of discretion standard applies to review of decision to reduce punitive damages by means of remittitur) with Perrine v. E.I. du Pont de Nemours and Co., 694 S.E.2d 815, 882 (W. Va. 2010) (circuit court's review of such award *de novo*); Wash. Rev. Code Ann. §4.76.030 (if remittitur is agreed to and opposing party appeals, consenting party is not bound, and reviewing court shall "review de novo the action of the trial court" applying "a presumption that the amount of damages awarded by the verdict of the jury was correct").

5. Most jurisdictions hold that the grant or denial of new trial motion on ground of excessive damages is reviewed for abuse of discretion. See Emberton v. GMRI, Inc., 299 S.W.2d 565, 579 (Ky. 2009) (refusing to order new trial); Mathieu Enterprises, Inc. v. Patsy's Companies, 978 A.2d 481, 483-484 (Vt. 2009) (reversing for improperly ordering remittitur). Here is one court's attempt to explain why such deference is appropriate:

> The "feel of the case" is not just an empty shibboleth—it is the trial judge who sees and hears the witnesses and the attorneys, and who has a first-hand opportunity to assess their believability and their effect on the jury. It is the judge who sees the jurors wince, weep, snicker, avert their eyes, or shake their heads in disbelief. Those personal observations of all of the players is [*sic*] "the feel of the case" to which an appellate court defers. Obviously, insofar as the trial judge's decision rests on "'determination[s] as to worth, plausibility, consistency or other tangible considerations apparent from the face of the record,'" an appellate court need not defer.

Jastram ex rel. Jastram v. Kruse, 962 A.2d 503, 512 (N.J. 2008) (court of appeals had ordered remittitur reducing verdict of $500,000 for pain and suffering to $50,000; reviewing court here restores verdict) (plaintiff suffered back injuries in car accident). But see Earlington v. Anastasi, 976 A.2d 689, 697-698 (Conn. 2009) (ruling on motion to set aside verdict as excessive is entitled to great weight and reasonable presumption of correctness, but this court has "a long history of ordering plaintiffs to accept a remittitur or submit to a new trial," and here an award of $1,588,000 in economic damages was not supported by the record; ordering remittitur to $542,126 or new trial if plaintiff does not accept); Bunch v. King County Department of Youth Services, 116 P.3d 381, 387 (Wash. 2005) (order remitting damage award is reviewed *de novo* "since it substitutes the court's finding on a question of fact," but orders denying remittitur are reviewed for abuse of discretion, "using the substantial evidence, shocks the conscience, and passion and prejudice standard").

CHAPTER 14

Binding Effect of Judgments

INTRODUCTION

The finality doctrines, often lumped together under the heading of *res judicata,* mark a point of transition in the law of procedure. When a suit has gone to judgment, no longer are "doing substantial justice" and "flexibility" the names of the game. Now the system stiffens, in effect, and a hard-nosed attitude sets in. Judgments, once rendered and final, are *very* hard to dislodge in new suits.

Two doctrines are at work here: The classical term "res judicata" and its modern equivalent "claim preclusion," which is preferred in the Restatement (Second) of Judgments (1982), actually describes only one of the two. The idea of *res judicata* (claim preclusion) is that when a case has gone to final judgment on the merits, the parties are bound. There is no more "claim" to be litigated because the *judgment* has taken its place. If a plaintiff sues and wins, her claim "merges" in the judgment, and now she has a judgment but no claim. If she sues and loses, her claim is "barred" by the judgment, and again there is a judgment, but no claim.

In its simplest application, claim preclusion means that if Parson sues Dixon for damage to her car arising out of a traffic accident and the case goes to final judgment, she cannot sue Dixon again for the same damage. Win or lose in the first suit, she is foreclosed from bringing a later suit to add to her recovery (if she won the first time) or to get a second bite at the apple (if she lost the first time). Her original claim is merged in the judgment or barred by it. It does not matter whether the original judgment was wrong, or whether the claimant has new or better ideas about how to litigate her claim. If mistakes were made in the first suit, the time to correct them was then, while the suit was pending, and mechanisms like post-trial motions and appeals are designed for this purpose.

Claim preclusion deals *both* with "what actually happened" *and* with "might have beens" (what could have been pursued in the first suit, even if it wasn't). Hence it is critical for purposes of claim preclusion to know what "claim" means and—without pretending to be definitive—the modern approach is "transactional." Claim preclusion operates, in the words of the Second Restatement, on every claim arising out of "the transaction, or series of connected transactions" that is the subject of a suit. See Restatement (Second) of Judgments §24 (1982).

The second doctrine, classically known as "collateral estoppel," and now often called by the more modern term "issue preclusion," holds that all matters that are finally and necessarily resolved in reaching final judgment are not to be litigated again later, and the parties to the first suit are bound on those matters.

In its simplest application, if Porter sues Davis for violating Porter's patent by marketing device X and loses after a trial on the merits because Davis prevails, as his sole defense, in his contention that the patent is invalid, then Porter will be out of luck if he later sues Davis for a quite separate violation of the same patent when Davis markets device Y. The finding of patent invalidity, which was essential to the first judgment, will block Porter in the second suit from claiming once again that he holds a valid patent.

In contrast to claim preclusion, issue preclusion looks *only at* what was actually decided before, and not at the "might have beens." And the focus of issue preclusion is not "claims," but the narrower element of "issues."

A FINALITY AND REPOSE: BASIC POLICY CONSIDERATIONS

Both claim preclusion and issue preclusion—*res judicata* and *collateral estoppel*—serve a variety of interests.

First, both doctrines serve interests in repose: Once a litigant has had her "day in court," it is important to move on and put behind us the dispute that was resolved in a suit. Defendants should not be "twice vexed" by the same claim, and plaintiffs should not hope for a different and better outcome by suing again. Lawsuits are expensive, time consuming, and distracting, and it is better to have done with a dispute when it has been finally resolved than to continue it, even if mistakes were made or the judgment was wrong. In serving this "policy of repose," doctrines of *res judicata* and *collateral estoppel* (claim preclusion and issue preclusion) complement statutes of limitations, which come at the purpose from another direction (mere passage of time puts disputes to rest).

Second, both claim and issue preclusion serve interests in efficiency: When possible, claims and issues should be resolved once rather than repeatedly. Courts are public institutions of limited resources, and they should not be asked to do redundant work. Litigants too should use resources wisely rather than wastefully.

Third, respect for the judicial system requires respect for the judgments that the system labors to reach. If multiple courts address the same claims and issues and reach conflicting conclusions, or if the result achieved in one lawsuit could be discarded in another, litigants and the general public would lose respect for the work of courts and be less willing to comply with orders and decrees.

On these points, see Parklane Hosiery v. Shore, 439 U.S. 322, 326 (1979) (*res judicata* serves "dual purpose of protecting litigants from the burden of relitigating an identical issue with the same party or his privy and of promoting judicial economy by preventing needless litigation"); Sutliffe v. Epping School District, 584 F.3d 314, 329 (1st Cir. 2009) (*res judicata* is not a "legal technicality," but a doctrine rooted in "essential considerations of fairness and judicial economy"); Creech v. Addington, 281 S.W.3d 363, 376 (Tenn. 2009) ("primary purposes of [claim preclusion] are to promote finality in litigation, prevent inconsistent or contradictory judgments, conserve legal resources, and protect litigants from the cost and vexation of multiple lawsuits").

A moment's reflection will tell you that these laudable aims cannot be fully achieved. If use of asbestos in the shipping and construction industries leads to suits in many states, from Texas to Washington (and California to Virginia), it may be both impossible and undesirable to force all the claims into one suit, and courts in different suits may reach conflicting results on the same questions. Whatever value finality may have, one cannot imagine elevating that value to such a point that a loss by litigant A in a suit against the XYZ Company, which satisfies the court that its warnings about asbestos were adequate, should bind litigant B who was exposed to the same product in another place: Litigant B cannot be bound because it would violate due process to bind him by a judgment in a suit in which he was not a party and to which he had no connection. Recall Hansberry v. Lee, 311 U.S. 32 (1940) (Chapter 8H4, supra).

Perhaps equally important in terms of the limited efficacy of preclusion doctrines is the fact that just figuring out whether they apply takes some doing. It may be more expensive to figure out whether a claim or issue is precluded by another judgment than it would be to litigate the claim or issue in the second suit.

B CLAIM PRECLUSION (*RES JUDICATA*)

It is time to dig deeper. A judgment generally has *res judicata* effect in a later suit if (a) it is final, (b) it is on the merits, (c) it resolves the same claim brought in the later suit (or a claim arising out of the same transaction), and (d) the same parties are involved in both suits.

We are about to consider these elements more closely, but it is worth noting first that *res judicata* or claim preclusion can have very dramatic effect. There is nothing to stop disputes from generating multiple suits. When parallel suits move forward, involving the same claims and parties, the first judgment that is entered has claim preclusive effect, which can lead to summary dismissal of other suits. See, e.g., Giragosian v. Ryan, 547 F.3d 59 (1st Cir. 2008) (owner of gun shop sued first in state court, then in federal court, challenging validity of revocation of permit; state court entered judgment dismissing claims, which had *res judicata* effect and required federal court to dismiss); Restatement of Judgments (Second) §14, Comment a (1982) ("when two actions are pending which are based on the same claim, or which involve the same issue, it is the final judgment first rendered in one of the actions which becomes conclusive in the other action ... , regardless which action was first brought").

Now let us consider the four elements. We then turn to the exceptions (or limits) that have been called into being when treating a prior judgment as conclusive seems the wrong thing to do. Finally, we consider claim preclusion in a federal system: What effect does a judgment in a federal court have in a later state court action, and vice versa? It turns out that *these* questions lead to choice-of-law issues, because *some* law must determine the *res judicata* effect of a judgment. Sometimes the choice is between consulting the law of the jurisdiction where the first judgment was rendered or the law of the jurisdiction where *res judicata* effect is sought. On other occasions, the choice is between applying federal law and state law.

1. Final Judgment

The first requirement (judgment must be "final") has led to variation among courts. For purposes of appellate review and execution (collection or enforcement), a judgment is normally final when "entered," and it is often supposed that this event makes a judgment final for purposes of *res judicata*. But you have seen that finality for purposes of appeal has undergone creative interpretation, and it is probably not the case that being appealable is necessary for purposes of *res judicata*.

Nor does the fact that an appeal is possible mean that the judgment is *not yet* final. Most courts say that a judgment is final for *res judicata* purposes if it could still be appealed, and even if an appeal is pending, and even if post-trial motions seeking a new trial or judgment as a matter of law are pending (or could still be made). The idea is that most such challenges fail, so postponing *res judicata* effect is unnecessary. See Patton v. Klein, 746 A.2d 866, 869 n.6 (D.C. 1999) (rejecting argument that *res judicata* did not apply because appeal in prior action was pending); Restatement (Second) of Judgments §13 (1982). Of course, it is another matter if judgment in the earlier suit has been set aside and a new trial granted, or if an appeal has overturned a judgment, or if judgment as a matter of law has been entered (in which case *that* judgment is the final one for purposes of *res judicata*).

Sometimes the question whether to give a judgment *res judicata* effect can be postponed so appeals or post-trial challenges can be resolved, and there is an obvious benefit to this approach when it is practical. If a second judgment rests on an earlier judgment that *has now been* set aside (first judgment was set aside after the second judgment was entered on the basis of the first judgment), relief from the second judgment may be possible under FRCP 60(b) (allowing relief from a judgment "based on an earlier judgment that has been reversed or vacated").

2. On the Merits

When we speak of judgment "on the merits," the paradigm case is the one that goes to a trial with witnesses and evidence and arguments that lead to deliberations by a jury and a verdict (or deliberations by a judge and a decision). Judgment is then entered, and by all measures we have a judgment "on the merits."

Of course, most civil disputes settle, often without suit being filed, and most suits that are filed settle too. Often terms of settlement require claimants to dismiss "with prejudice," which helps assure *res judicata* effect if a claimant becomes dissatisfied and refiles a dismissed claim, or other claims arising out of the same transaction (settlement agreements are usually drafted broadly to cover all possible claims). See, e.g., Oreck Direct LLC v. Dyson, Inc., 560 F.3d 398, 402-403 (5th Cir. 2009) (suit by one maker of vacuum cleaners against another; prior suit leading to settlement and dismissal with prejudice barred present suit; courts honor express agreement letting parties split claims, but this settlement was a "full and complete" release).

The binding effect of settled suits is particularly important in class actions, which (like other suits) usually settle without trial. See, e.g., Simmermon v. Dryvit Systems, Inc., 953 A.2d 478, 487 (N.J. 2008) (suit against maker of synthetic stucco used to cover houses was barred by *res judicata* effect of judgment entered on basis of settlement in nationwide class suit in Tennessee) (plaintiff claimed he did not get notice of hearings on settlement, but administrator in Tennessee suit found that notice was sent to plaintiff); People ex rel. Spitzer v. Applied Card Systems, Inc., 894 N.E.2d 1 (N.Y. 2008) (judgment against lender based on court-approved settlement of nationwide class action in California barred this suit, brought by state attorney general to recover on behalf of people who were members of class).

The tendency has been to *expand* the reach of *res judicata* to cover dismissals that occur before trial for reasons that might be regarded as "procedural." As you think about Problem 14-A, consider why this expansion has occurred.

■ PROBLEM 14-A. "They're Picking on Me"

Pat Symes purchased a large parcel in Summit County, Colorado, near Breckenridge. On the property are two residential structures and a detached garage. Neighbors Mike Wilson and Dale Barnes hold access easements over the Symes parcel, for ingress and egress, and they engaged a contractor who used a bulldozer, grader, spreader, and compactor to improve the roadway, causing damage to trees and other physical features of the Symes parcel.

Symes complained to Jake Jeffers, the local sheriff, but after investigating the matter he declined to intervene. Thereafter, apparently acting on a report from Jeffers, the County Board of Commissioners notified Symes that she could not use both residences for purposes of habitation, and that she had to repair and remodel the bathroom in one of the structures or it would be ruled uninhabitable.

"They're picking on me," Symes told her lawyer, filling out the details of her interactions with Wilson, Barnes, Sheriff Jeffers, and the Board. In federal court in Colorado, Symes sues Jeffers and the Board under 28 USC §1983. Symes claims that the Board deprived her of property without due process, and that the Board and Sheriff Jeffers violated her equal protection rights by treating her differently because she was an unmarried woman. She joins Wilson and Barnes, against whom she advances trespass claims under state law. Since all three are citizens of Colorado, her lawyer invokes supplemental jurisdiction under 28 USC §1367.

The Board and Sheriff Jeffers move to dismiss for failure to state a claim under FRCP 12(b)(6). The court dismisses the takings claim without granting leave to amend, ruling that the action of the Board in barring use of both residences for habitation was not a taking. The court dismisses the discrimination claim with leave to amend, finding that the allegations were "insufficient on their face to state a claim for discrimination under the facial plausibility standard adopted in the *Iqbal* decision." (The reference is to Ashcroft v. Iqbal, 556 U.S. 662 (2009), described in Chapter 7B2, supra.)

On motion to dismiss for lack of subject matter jurisdiction, brought by Mike Wilson and Dale Barnes, the court dismisses the claims against them, concluding that they are not sufficiently related to the federal claim to be part of the same "case or controversy" under 28 USC §1367(a).

If Pat Symes now files in Colorado state court, naming the same parties and advancing the same claims, should her suit be dismissed on grounds of *res judicata*?

■ NOTES ON *RES JUDICATA* EFFECTS OF DISMISSALS BEFORE TRIAL

1. Historically, dismissal on a demurrer or motion to dismiss for failure to state a claim was viewed as resolving *only* the question whether the complaint was adequate, meaning that plaintiff could file a different complaint without risking dismissal on grounds of *res judicata*. Put another way, dismissal on a demurrer or motion to dismiss was not viewed as a decision "on the merits." Modern courts, however, routinely say that dismissal for failure to state a claim does have *res judicata* effect. You have looked at this matter in Chapter 7C2, supra (especially note 6 in Notes on Motions Attacking the Complaint). And see, e.g., State ex rel. Arcadia Acres v. Ohio Department of Job and Family Services, 914 N.E.2d 170, 175 (Ohio 2009). Does application of *res judicata* in this setting serve the aims of the doctrine, or was the older approach better? How much court time is used when a case is dismissed on such a motion? How many resources of the defense? Does the fact that courts usually grant plaintiff one or two opportunities to amend explain why such dismissals are now viewed as being "on the merits"?

(a) On facts like those in this Problem, a court dismissed the federal takings claims without leave to amend. Should this fact count, when it comes to giving or not giving *res judicata* effect to the judgment? Legnani v. Alitalia Linee Aeree Italiane, 400 F.3d 139 (2d Cir. 2005) (suit under Title VII alleging discrimination and retaliation did not bar later suit claiming retaliatory discharge; first action was pending when plaintiff was discharged; fact that plaintiff tried to amend to add claim for retaliatory discharge, which court refused to allow, had no bearing on *res judicata*).

(b) Since dismissal of the takings claims did not dispose of the whole suit, probably Ms. Symes could not have taken an immediate appeal, although she could appeal at the end if the suit went to a judgment after trial, or if the judge dismissed the whole thing, as she eventually did, for other reasons. If Ms. Symes did *not* take an appeal, how would that cut in terms of according *res judicata* effect?

(c) With respect to the discrimination claim, the court granted leave to amend. Should failing to amend count, if Ms. Symes filed a later suit raising the same claim?

(d) Because a judgment dismissing claims at the pleading stage rests on a "thin" record, it may be hard for defendant in a later suit to prove that the earlier suit advanced claims arising out of the same transaction, but even "bare bones" complaints usually reveal enough to enable a court to decide this point.

2. What about the dismissal of the state law claims for want of jurisdiction? It's subject matter jurisdiction that is the problem, isn't it? See Restatement (Second) of Judgments §20(1)(a) (1982) (judgment for defendant does not bar another suit when it rests on dismissal for lack of jurisdiction, improper venue, or nonjoinder or misjoinder of parties) (1982); Watkins v. Resorts International

Hotel and Casino, Inc., 591 A.2d 592, 600-601 (N.J. 1991) (dismissals based on "procedural inability to consider a case" don't have *res judicata* effect) (mentioning dismissals for lack of capacity to be sued and applying principle to suit dismissed for failure of service of process and lack of standing, even though the latter involves "considerations similar to those involved in a dismissal for failure to state a claim on which relief can be granted" because dismissal for lack of standing involves limits on exercise of jurisdiction and "amounts to a refusal by the court to resolve the matter").

3. What should be the effect of a judgment entered for the defendant on the ground that the statute of limitations bars the suit? Within a single jurisdiction, it is usually said that *res judicata* bars a second suit. Indeed, a judgment rejecting a claim on this ground may bar a second suit raising additional claims based on the same transaction, at least within a single jurisdiction. See, e.g., Ekladrawy v. Fanguard Group, Inc., 584 F.3d 169, 172-173 (3d Cir. 2009) (earlier Title VII suit was dismissed because plaintiff filed more than 180 days after obtaining right-to-sue letter, which is treated as a dismissal based on the statute of limitations; hence claims under §1981 are barred). Usually, however, it is another matter altogether if a suit brought in one state is dismissed as time-barred and plaintiff files in a new state where the suit is *not* time barred. See generally Restatement (Second) of Judgments §19, Comment f (1982) (citing example of suit dismissed as barred by statute of limitations in one state but not in a second state as an instance in which *res judicata* does *not* apply). If the first suit was filed where the claim arose, and it is dismissed as barred by the statute of limitations, it might not help to file in another state with a longer statute, as many states have "borrowing" statutes that apply any shorter statute of limitations that exist where the claim arose. See generally Ibrahim J. Wani, *Borrowing Statutes, Statutes of Limitation and Modern Choice of Law*, 57 UMKC L. Rev. 681 (1989).

4. What about a suit dismissed for failure to prosecute? See FRCP 41(b), under which dismissal for failure to prosecute "or to comply with these rules or a court order" acts as "an adjudication on the merits." And see, e.g., Bragg v. Flint Board of Education, 570 F.3d 775 (6th Cir. 2009) (state suit filed in 2007 was removed to federal court and dismissed under FRCP 41(b) for failure to prosecute; later suit raising new claims arising out of same transaction was barred); Five Star Capital Corp. v. Ruby, 194 P.3d 709 (Nev. 2008) (suit for specific performance was barred by judgment in prior suit dismissing same claim on account of plaintiff's failure to appear at pretrial calendar call). Note the language in FRCP 41(a)(1)(B) indicating that if the plaintiff has *previously and voluntarily* dismissed a suit "based on or including the same claim," then a *new voluntary* dismissal "operates as an adjudication on the merits." And see U.S. Bank National Association v. Gullota, 899 N.E.2d 987 (Ohio 2008) (bank dismissed two foreclosure suits; *res judicata* barred third foreclosure based on same note and mortgage). When you read the *Semtek* case, you will see that the Supreme Court has construed FRCP 41, when a diversity suit has been thrown out on the basis that the claims are barred by the statute of limitations, as blocking an attempt to refile the suit in the same federal court, but not as blocking an attempt to refile elsewhere. Semtek International v. Lockheed Martin Corporation, 531 U.S. 497 (2001) (diversity suit was dismissed as time-barred by a federal court in California; FRCP 41 did not bar filing same suit in state court in Maryland; federal *res judicata* law applies, and incorporates state rule) (Section C2, infra).

5. Dismissal of a suit because plaintiff was not the real party in interest does not bar a later suit. See Gillig v. Nike, Inc., 602 F.3d 1354 (Fed. Cir. 2010) (dismissal for lack of standing or because plaintiff was not real party in interest does not have *res judicata* effect).

3. Same Transaction

Sometimes it is plain that two suits involve claims arising out of the same transaction: If cars collide, for example, and the driver/owner of one sues the driver/owner of the other for property damage, and later sues the same defendant for personal injuries arising out of the same accident, the two suits arise out of the same transaction. If the first suit goes to final judgment and defendant in the second suit raises *res judicata* as a defense, the second suit will be dismissed. As indicated at the beginning of this chapter in the example of Parson suing Dixon, if plaintiff wins the first suit, any claim for personal injuries that she *might have brought* in the original suit is said to have "merged" into her judgment awarding recovery for damage to her car; if she lost the first suit, any claim for personal injuries that she *might have brought* in the original suit is said to be "barred" by the judgment rejecting her claim for damages to her car. In either case, it is customary to say that plaintiff, when she brings her second suit for personal injuries, is improperly trying to split her claims.

Under the "same transaction" standard, claim preclusion forecloses claims for what amounts to the same damages based on new theories that were not advanced in a prior suit. See, e.g., Plunkett v. State, 869 A.2d 1185 (R.I. 2005) (dismissed director of judicial information system claimed discrimination based on age and disability; plaintiff lost earlier suit alleging wrongful termination and claiming that 20-year employment history meant he could be terminated only for cause; *res judicata* bars new claims); Plum Creek Development Co. v. City of Conway, 512 S.E.2d 106 (S.C. 1999) (developer who sought writ of mandamus requiring city to supply water and sewer service could not later sue for damages on account of city's refusal); Drays v. Town of Houlton, 726 A.2d 1257 (Me. 1999) (owner of club featuring nude dancing sued in state court alleging that revocation of "nude activity permit" constituted malicious prosecution, slander, and infliction of emotional distress; *res judicata* barred these claims because plaintiff lost earlier federal suit alleging that revocation violated constitutional rights; state and federal claims arose out of "common nucleus" and were "related in time, space, origin, and motivation" and could "most conveniently be presented in the same trial," differing only in "theories of relief and recovery"); ElGabri v.

Lekas, 681 A.2d 271, 278 (R.I. 1996) (federal suit by one doctor against others alleging antitrust claims for false statements preventing plaintiff from obtaining hospital privileges barred state claims for libel, slander, and infliction of mental distress; "the engines that drove both the state and the federal lawsuits were fueled by the defendant doctors' defamatory remarks and writings effectively and wrongfully precluding [plaintiff's] opportunity to obtain hospital staff privileges").

It bears recollecting that defendant must raise the defense of *res judicata.* It is an affirmative defense under FRCP 8(e) that is waived if not raised affirmatively in the answer. Ordinarily, the matter is then resolved in a motion for judgment on the pleadings. See, e.g., Carr v. Tillery, 591 F.3d 909 (7th Cir. 2010). Accordingly, a pre-answer motion to dismiss under FRCP 12(b)(6) would seem to be the *wrong* way to raise the point (because a later answer failing to raise the defense would waive it), but courts often resolve the issue in a motion to dismiss, on the reasonable assumption that a defendant who asserts the defense in this way is unlikely later to forget to raise it in the answer. See, e.g., Muhammad v. Oliver, 547 F.3d 874, 878 (7th Cir. 2008) (*res judicata* "is not one of the affirmative defenses that Rule 12(b) permits to made by motion rather than in the answer," but "when an affirmative defense is disclosed in the complaint, it provides a proper basis for a Rule 12(b)(6) motion") (*res judicata* bars this suit).

MANICKI v. ZEILMANN

United States Court of Appeals for the Seventh Circuit
443 F.3d 922 (2006)

Before BAUER, POSNER, and MANION, Circuit Judges.

POSNER, Circuit Judge.

Mark Manicki brought a federal civil rights suit (42 USC §1983) that the district judge dismissed as barred by res judicata, precipitating this appeal. Manicki was in his one-year probationary period as a new police officer when he witnessed a fight between two other officers. In the ensuing criminal investigation he told investigators that one of the officers had started the fight. The police chief, defendant Zeilmann, wanted Manicki (or so the latter contends) to tell the investigators that both officers had been equally at fault, in the hope that this would ward off any criminal prosecution of the officer, a favorite of Zeilmann's, whom Manicki had identified as the instigator. When Manicki refused to alter his statement, Zeilmann wrote a letter to the city's board of fire and police commissioners stating that Manicki had failed to perform adequately during his probationary period and should be fired—and the board fired him. In this suit, which is against both Zeilmann and the city, Manicki contends that Zeilmann's letter retaliating against him for telling the investigators the truth violated the First Amendment.

The res judicata issue arose as follows. The board had conducted no hearing before firing Manicki; it had acted solely on the basis of the letter. Manicki sued the board and Zeilmann in an Illinois state court, complaining that he had been fired on the basis of Zeilmann's letter, which had, the suit charged, been "made in retaliation for [Manicki's] acting as a witness in a criminal matter against another police officer and could constitute the criminal offense of Harassment of a Witness.... [The board had] afforded no due process prior to [Manicki's] dismissal" and its decision to dismiss him had been "against the manifest weight of the evidence," "arbitrary and capricious," and "legally erroneous." Manicki acknowledged that a probationary employee ordinarily lacks the kind of interest that entitles him to a predeprivation hearing, but contended that the collective bargaining agreement between the Ottawa police department and the department's employees created such an interest. [Ottawa, Illinois is a town of about 20,000 people located some 70 miles southwest of Chicago.] The state court disagreed and entered judgment in favor of the defendants. That is the judgment the district court ruled bars Manicki's federal suit.

In Krecek v. Board of Police Commissioners, 646 N.E.2d 1314, 1317 (Ill. App. 1995), a case nearly identical to this one, the court held that a judgment determining that the plaintiff didn't have a right to a hearing was not res judicata in her subsequent suit, which charged that her termination was retaliatory, as she would have tried to show had she been given a hearing. But *Krecek* was decided at a time when many Illinois courts applied a "same evidence" test for res judicata. Later the Supreme Court of Illinois made clear that this was not the right test, that a plaintiff is not permitted to slice up his claim into little pieces and make each the subject of a separate lawsuit based on slightly different evidence. River Park, Inc. v. City of Highland Park, 703 N.E.2d 883, 893-94 (Ill. 1998); Durgins v. City of East St. Louis, 272 F.3d 841, 844 (7th Cir. 2001); see also Licari v. City of Chicago, 298 F.3d 664, 667 (7th Cir. 2002) (Illinois law).

But what exactly is a "claim" (or, in an older terminology, a "cause of action")? *River Park* adopted the prevailing definition: it is the "transaction" or (equivalently) the "operative facts" that give rise to the plaintiff's right to obtain legal relief, rather than the particular legal category or theory that shows that the transaction really does entitle him to a legal remedy. There might after all be numerous categories or theories that fit the facts (breach of contract, common law tort, violation of federal civil rights law, etc.), and they should be joined in a single suit rather than parceled out among a set of different suits based on the same facts so that if the plaintiff strikes out on one theory he can try again on another. Such a way of proceeding would impose gratuitous burdens on defendants and on the courts.

But terms like "transaction" and "operative facts" are not self-evident; indeed, it is quite unclear what "operative" is supposed to mean in this popular formulation. Language has its limits, and courts are often better at producing sensible results than at devising helpful verbal formulas. In Herrmann v. Cencom Cable Associates, Inc., 999 F.2d 223, 226 (7th Cir. 1993), we thought it a useful clarification to "suggest that two claims are one for purposes of res judicata if they are based on the same, or nearly the same, factual allegations." This directs attention to the degree of factual overlap between assertedly different claims and hence the appropriateness of trying them together rather than separately.

In the spirit of this approach Manicki argues that there are two separate clusters of facts in this case, the first being the police board's denying him a predeprivation hearing, the subject of the state court suit, and the second (though it came first in time) being the letter by Zeilmann to the board which precipitated Manicki's dismissal and hence the filing of the first suit. But the clusters are not really separate, except in not being simultaneous; together they constitute the circumstances of Manicki's dismissal and "form a convenient trial unit." Mpoyo v. Litton Electro-Optical Systems, 430 F.3d 985, 987 (9th Cir. 2005).

Manicki's dismissal was the collaborative product of Zeilmann and the board. Zeilmann writes the board a letter recommending that it dismiss Manicki, and the board, without bothering to get a response from Manicki, fires him. There were, if Manicki was correct, two constitutional violations—a procedural violation by the board in denying him a predeprivation hearing, and a substantive violation by Zeilmann in maneuvering to get Manicki fired in retaliation for refusing to alter a truthful statement to investigators. But the two violations are based on the same episode, namely the dismissal of Manicki on the basis of Zeilmann's letter, and to make each violation the subject of a separate trial would, because of the extent of the factual overlap, increase the expense of litigation without compensating benefit. In the first case, where Manicki's goal was a hearing before the board, he wanted to present evidence of the retaliatory motive for, and consequent lack of credibility of, Zeilmann's letter to the board. In the second case, which was based squarely on Zeilmann's letter, he wanted to show that it was indeed the letter that had precipitated his dismissal by the board. Moreover, the ultimate relief sought in both cases included reinstatement, and the facts bearing on the appropriateness of that remedy (if Manicki succeeded in establishing liability) would be the same.

This is not to say that the test for res judicata is a genetic one, that is, one based on the two suits' having a common source—Zeilmann's anger at Manicki's refusal to alter his account of the fight. Claims that have too little factual overlap to warrant being forced into a single suit (that is, to warrant being deemed a single "claim" for purposes of res judicata) can nevertheless have the same origin. When an employee complains about discrimination and the employer fires him in retaliation for complaining, the employee's discrimination and retaliation claims can sometimes be litigated separately even though both have a common origin in the discrimination against the employee. There is bound to be evidentiary overlap, but it may be slight, because most discriminating employers do not also retaliate against complaining employees and an employer may (and in fact is likely to) retaliate against an employee who files a groundless complaint. When, however, the same action is charged as both discrimination and retaliation, the evidentiary overlap is so extensive that the plaintiff is forbidden to make each the subject of a separate suit.

Here too, the two claims—due process and retaliation—are tightly bound together, because Manicki wanted a due process hearing so that he could prove retaliation. Imagine if instead Zeilmann had shot Manicki or tossed a Molotov cocktail into his house. No reference to that conduct would be needed to establish that Manicki had been denied a predeprivation hearing to which he was entitled.

Suppose Manicki had won his first case and thus had succeeded in getting a hearing before the board, but the board after the hearing again ruled against him. He could then, if he is right that the judgment in the state court suit was not res judicata, bring a second suit (the suit before us) against Zeilmann complaining about the letter that led to his dismissal (though depending on the ground of the board's action, Zeilmann might have a defense of collateral estoppel). In contrast, if Manicki must join both his legal theories in one suit, then if the court finds that he was dismissed in violation of his constitutional rights it can avoid having to resolve the issue of his right to a hearing; the court would order him reinstated and the issue of a hearing would be moot.

All else aside, Manicki's joining Zeilmann as a defendant in the first suit was a fatal step, though this requires some explaining. Even if a plaintiff's right to relief arises from what is realistically viewed as a single episode, if it is a right against multiple parties—joint tortfeasors, if the right arises under tort law—he needn't join them in one suit, unless there is privity among those parties, Lawlor v. National Screen Service Corp., 349 U.S. 322, 330 (1955), for in that event separate suits against them are treated as the equivalent of separate suits against the same party. "Privity" in this context means that because the parties have by virtue of contract or otherwise identical interests, a claim or defense by one is equivalent to a claim or defense by all. There is no privity between Zeilmann and the board. Both are agents of the city, but their interests diverge. Manicki charges them with different legal violations, and so one or the other defendant could win though the other lost.

Assuming that Zeilmann and the board acted wrongfully, as Manicki charges, they were in effect joint tortfeasors. It was their combined action that did in Manicki. Had Zeilmann not written his letter, the board would not have fired Manicki, and if the board had granted him a hearing it might well have discovered Zeilmann's retaliatory motive and, again, not fired Manicki. But Manicki sued both Zeilmann and the board in the same case, and you cannot sue all your joint tortfeasors in the same case and then when you lose sue one of them separately. That would be taking two bites at the same apple. And if the second suit against Zeilmann is thus barred, the suit cannot be saved by the fact that the city is also named as a defendant. The city's liability is derivative from Zeilmann's, the contention being that either Zeilmann was a policymaker whose actions thus bound the city or that the city ratified his persecution of Manicki.

Manicki argues that the defendants are precluded from invoking res judicata because they failed to warn him, when they learned that he planned to file a second suit, that such a suit would be barred by res judicata. He relies on the rule that "the failure of the defendant to object to the splitting of the plaintiff's claim is effective as an acquiescence in the splitting of the claim." This rule of Illinois law does not govern the purely procedural question of what issues must be raised, and when, in a federal lawsuit. In any event, the cited cases are ones in which, by failing to raise the defense of res judicata in timely fashion, the defendant wasted the time of the plaintiff and the court. There is no duty to warn a prospective adversary of the defenses you will interpose if he carries out his threat to sue you.

AFFIRMED.

■ NOTES ON THE "SAME TRANSACTION" STANDARD

1. Mark Manicki first sued Brian Zeilmann and the board of fire and police commissioners in state court, and later sued the same two defendants in Illinois in federal court. Judge Posner concludes that the "same transaction" standard was satisfied and that Manicki impermissibly split his claims. Didn't the claim that Manicki advanced in the first suit call into question the failure to hold a hearing, while his claim in the second suit challenged his firing? The court comments that the firing came "second in time," because any hearing should have been held first. Should they be viewed as the same transaction?

(a) The Second Restatement says claim preclusion applies to "all rights of the plaintiff to remedies against the defendant with respect to all or any part of the transaction, or series of connected transactions, out of which the action arose." In deciding what "factual grouping" amounts to a "transaction," and what groupings are a "series," a court should operate "pragmatically," and should give weight to "such considerations as whether the facts are related in time, space, origin, or motivation, whether they form a convenient trial unit, and whether their treatment as a unit conforms to the parties' expectations or business understanding or usage." See Restatement (Second) of Judgments §28 (1982).

(b) In *Manicki*, Judge Posner comments (quoting the *Herrmann* case) that two claims are likely to be one if they rest on "the same, or nearly the same, factual allegations." Courts often mention as well that *res judicata* is likely to apply if the second suit rests on the "same evidence" as the first.

Indeed, Judge Posner in *Manicki* remarks that Illinois once applied that standard. For a more recent example, see Powell v. Infinity Ins. Co., 922 A.2d 1073, 1076 (Conn. 2007) (*res judicata* applied because the two suits "grew out of the same transaction or nucleus of facts" and also "entailed the presentation of the same evidence") (and involved infringement of "the same rights"). It seems, however, that the "same evidence" standard is *narrower* than the same transaction standard, see River Park, Inc. v. City of Highland Park, 703 N.E.2d 883, 892 (Ill. 1998) (the "tests are not the same," and same evidence standard is "narrower") (cited in *Manicki*).

(c) Do some of the Restatement factors, supplemented by consideration of the "factual allegations" and "evidence," point toward the conclusion reached in *Manicki*? What does "related" in time or space mean? Was the motivation of the board or the city in firing Manicki "related" to the motivation of Brian Zeilmann in pressuring him? Are the factual allegations "the same, or nearly the same"? Is the evidence the same? With respect to "business usage," the Restatement cites a suit on a "running account," where the creditor is expected to sue for all unpaid items, so failing to include one precludes "further action" to recover it. On the other hand, separate promissory notes could generate separate suits (they are said to be separate obligations). See Restatement (Second) of Judgments §24, Comment d (1982).

(d) In *Manicki*, the court says judges are "better at producing sensible results than at devising helpful verbal formulas." Does the court reach a sensible result?

(e) Rule 18 *allows* plaintiff (she "may join") to include "as independent or alternative claims, as many claims as [she] has against an opposing party." The effect of *res judicata* is to say that plaintiff *must* join claims arising out of the same transaction, in the sense that *not doing so* results in losing them. See, e.g., Harrison v. Chandler-Sampson Insurance, Inc., 891 So. 2d 224, 233 (Miss. 2005) ("res judicata serves as a mandatory device for claim joinder by restricting the claims which a party may refrain from asserting against the opposing party," and the possibility of being later barred from asserting a claim has an *in terrorem* effect and "encourages cautious attorneys to join claims") (quoting Wright & Miller); 66, Inc. v. Crestwood Commons Redevelopment Corp., 998 S.W.2d 32, 43 (Mo. 1999) (*res judicata* "can operate to require joinder of claims arising from the same transaction or occurrence even where the rule on joinder of claims does not require such joinder"). What considerations might incline a lawyer *not* to put into a complaint a count advancing claims based on every theory he might think of?

2. In *Manicki*, Judge Posner engages in a thought experiment, supposing that Manicki won his first case, obtaining a hearing, but the board fired him anyway. Could he sue again? The suggestion is that Manicki could, except for one thing: He had taken the "fatal step" of naming Zeilman in both suits. Apparently, a suit against the board alone would not have foreclosed a later suit against Zeilmann. Why not? Recall that FRCP 20 *lets* a plaintiff join all defendants against whom "any right to relief is asserted" (whether "jointly or severally") that arises out of "the same transaction, occurrence, or series of transactions or occurrences." If *Manicki* is right in saying that plaintiff need not join every joint tortfeasor, then the impact of *res judicata* on permissive joinder of parties under FRCP 20 is different from its impact on joinder of claims under FRCP 18. Recall too that FRCP 19, which *requires* plaintiffs to join defendants under some circumstances, does *not* require plaintiffs to join joint tortfeasors, although a few jurisdictions depart from this practice in order to implement comparative fault theories. See Temple v. Synthes Corp. Ltd., 498 U.S. 5, 7 (1990), and Samuelson v. McMurtry, 962 S.W.2d 473, 475-476 (Tenn. 1998) (both described in Chapter 8C2, supra).

3. Suppose a three-car accident leading to a suit by Driver 1 against Drivers 2 and 3. Suppose Drivers 2 and 3 raise contributory negligence as defenses, but do not bring damage claims against Driver 1. And suppose that Driver 2 could make a negligence claim against Driver 3 but does not. If Driver 1's suit goes to judgment on the merits, and if Drivers 2 and 3 bring separate suits against Driver 1, can Driver 1 raise the defense of claim preclusion? If Driver 1's suit goes to judgment on the merits, and if Driver 2 sues Driver 3, who in turn brings a counterclaim, can either get the other's claim dismissed by invoking claim preclusion?

(a) If Driver 1's suit were brought in federal court, Driver 2 "must state" a counterclaim arising out of the same transaction under FRCP 13(a) (most states have similar rules). Generally common law issue preclusion doctrines do not apply because they defer to the content of applicable civil rules. See Restatement (Second) of Judgments §22 (1982) (if defendant fails to bring a counterclaim, later suit is precluded if counterclaim was "required to be interposed by a compulsory counterclaim statute or rule"). But sometimes civil rules do not bar later claims, even though the situation is one in which allowing defendant to bring a later suit would lead to problems. See, e.g., Martino v. McDonald's System, Inc., 598 F.2d 1079, 1082 (7th Cir. 1979) (fast food franchise sued M and relatives alleging that they violated agreement not to enter into competing business; case settled before defendants answered, and consent judgment was entered; counterclaim rule did not apply because no answer was filed, but M was still precluded from bringing the present suit alleging that franchise agreement violated antitrust law; claim preclusion applies where allowing second suit "would nullify rights established by the prior action") (*res judicata* "preserves the integrity of judgments and protects those who rely on them," and "counterclaim exception" to *res judicata* law should not permit plaintiff to "wage this direct attack" on rights established by first judgment). See also Restatement (Second) of Judgments §22 (1982) (second suit, advancing claim that might have been a counterclaim in prior suit, is barred if "the relationship between the counterclaim [that might have been brought in the prior suit] and the plaintiff's claim [in the prior suit] is such that successful prosecution of the second action would nullify the initial judgment or would impair rights established in the initial action").

(b) If Driver 1's suit were brought in federal court, FRCP 13(g) provides that Drivers 2 and 3 "may state" claims against one another that arise out of the same "transaction" (including a claim that the other "may be liable" if plaintiff prevails), and most states have similar rules. Here too, the custom is to resolve issues of claim preclusion by applying the rule governing these matters, rather than the doctrine of issue preclusion. In other words, under the prevailing view, defendants may bring such claims or defer them and file a later suit.

(c) For counterclaims and cross-claims, the doctrine of claim preclusion *does* apply if any such claim is brought and resolved by final judgment. See, e.g., Restatement (Second) of Judgments §23 (1982) (if defendant interposes a counterclaim and a final judgment is rendered against him on this counterclaim, "the rules of bar are applicable to the judgment"); Kootenai Electric Co-Operative, Inc. v. Lamar Corp., 219 P.3d 440, 446 (Idaho 2009) (in suit by workman injured when billboard touched power line, brought against billboard owner and electric co-operative, the latter cross-claimed against the former for apportionment of liability and fault, but did not seek statutory indemnification; later suit by co-operative for indemnification was barred by *res judicata*; cross-claims are permissive, but defendant who brings cross-claim against a codefendant becomes "adverse as to that claim and the principles of *res judicata* apply"); Getty Oil Co. v. Insurance Co. of North America, 845 S.W.2d 794, 799 (Tex. 1992) (defendant need not assert cross-claim under state rule "simply because it arises from the same subject matter as plaintiff's claim," but one who asserts a cross-claim is plaintiff for purposes of *res judicata*, "and is required to assert all claims against" codefendant arising from subject matter of original cross-claim).

4. The decision in *Manicki* comments that claims having "too little factual overlap" need not be combined, and that an employee who is fired after complaining about discrimination can "sometimes" litigate a discrimination claim in one suit and a retaliatory termination claim in a separate suit. Sometimes it is plain that successive suits involve different transactions, by any reasonable understanding of the term. See McCoy v. Michigan, 369 Fed. Appx. 646 (6th Cir. 2010) (corrections officer claimed race discrimination in his dismissal in June 2004; in state suit in 1999, dismissed in 2000, he claimed discrimination in 1997 termination [he was reinstated]; in federal suit in 2001, dismissed in 2002, he again alleged discrimination, this time based on gender and race, and added a claim for retaliation; third suit was *not* barred by losses in first two; third suit challenged activities occurring from June 2004 on, and "despite everything that may have occurred previously," the origins of the various claims were "simply not the same," *even though* court in first suit had not yet entered judgment when events leading to third suit took place). See also Lundquist v. Rice Memorial Hospital, 238 F.3d 975 (8th Cir. 2001) (judgment in nurse's first suit under Americans With Disabilities Act (ADA), arising out of events prior to January 1997, did not bar suit for discriminatory discharge in violation of ADA, arising out of later events, including her firing in December 1997). Sometimes the opposite is true, and changes between the first and second suit are so slight that claim preclusion should apply. See, e.g., Haag v. United States, 589 F.3d 43 (1st Cir. 2009) (claim that attorney for taxpayer did not receive proper notice from IRS was barred by earlier suit litigating claim that IRS failed to give proper notice to the taxpayer herself).

5. Suppose property is reclassified from agricultural to residential (resulting in higher taxes), and a taxpayer challenges the change in a 1999 suit filed then that extends into 2000. If she loses, can she bring suit challenging the change for the tax year 2000? See Colvin v. Story County Board of Review, 653 N.W.2d 345 (Iowa 2002) (yes; taxes for separate years "do not grow out of the same transaction").

6. Claims arising out of a contract that includes an indemnification provision can yield two suits, one to establish breach and liability, the other to enforce the indemnity obligation. See LaPoint v. AmerisourceBergen Corp., 970 A.2d 185, 193 (Del. Super. 2009) (after suit established liability for breach of contract, plaintiff could bring separate suit for attorneys' fees and costs of litigation in first suit; even under transactional approach, there are two claims; prior to judgment based on breach of contract, nobody could know whether defendant would be in breach of indemnity obligation; while contract is usually a single transaction for purposes of claim preclusion, contractual rights "triggered" after initial suit has been filed are not barred by *res judicata*, which "cannot be given the effect of extinguishing claims which did not even then exist"). Compare Powell v. Infinity Insurance Co., 922 A.2d 1073, 1081 (Conn. 2007) (suit against uninsured motorist carrier for breach of contract barred second suit alleging bad faith failure to honor contract).

7. By longstanding tradition, the reach of *res judicata* used to be defined in terms of "primary rights," and jurisdictions taking this approach generally found that claims for property damage and claims for personal injuries were different and could be advanced in different lawsuits. In a classic exposition of this view, the Ohio Supreme Court had this to say:

> [T]he universally accepted tests for the application of the doctrine of *res judicata* call for a segregation and separate consideration of the legal implications arising from the distinctions of the substantive law applied to the facts in issue. [The most widely accepted test holds as follows:] (1) The evidence to support the two causes of action must be identical; (2) there must be a single right violated; (3) there must be a single act or contract involved; (4) there must be the same findings and judgment involved; and (5) in the case of contracts the consideration must be entire.

Vasu v. Kohlers, Inc., 61 N.E.2d 707, 715 (Ohio 1945) (motorcyclist could sue city once for damages to his motorcycle and separately for personal injuries). Barely 14 years later, however, the Ohio court changed its mind, and decided that a plaintiff injured in an accident cannot split such claims. The court commented that *Vasu* and similar decisions were affected by the fact that an insurance carrier had brought the first suit, as subrogee for the insured owner, and that foreclosing the owner's later suit for personal injuries would be unjust. In other cases, however, personal injury claims should be brought in the same suit as claims for property damages. See Rush v. City of Maple Heights, 147 N.E.2d 599, 606 (Ohio 1958) (there is "no valid reason in these days of code pleading to adhere to the old English rule as to distinctions between injuries to the person and damages to the person's property resulting from a single tort").

(a) Some states still adhere to the "primary rights" approach, notably California, where it may well be that claims for personal injuries can be brought separately from claims for property damage. See Friedman Professional Management Co. v. Norcal Mutual Insurance Co., 15 Cal. Rptr. 3d 359, 367 (Cal. App. 2004) (in suit arising out of surgery that went "horribly wrong," plaintiff could sue separately for malpractice, sexual battery, and invasion of privacy; under "transaction" standard, claims could not be split, but California follows "primary right" standard, under which "the core concept is the harm suffered") (malpractice claim asserted "bodily injury" while claim for sexual battery and invasion of privacy involved harm to plaintiff's "*dignitary* and *privacy* interests" in not being touched by a person without her consent). And see, e.g., Boeken v. Philip Morris USA, Inc., 230 P.3d 342 (Cal. 2010) (applying primary right standard); Brodheim v. Cry, 584 F.3d 1262, 1268 (9th Cir. 2009) (prisoner's federal suit alleging retaliatory chilling of constitutional rights was not barred by prior state suit alleging lack of meaningful review of complaints; California follows "primary rights" standard, and rights asserted here are "distinct" from those asserted in prior state suit).

(b) Illinois once followed yet another standard—asking whether the "same evidence" was involved in the prior suit and a later action. It abandoned this approach, however, in favor of a transactional standard in order to broaden the effects of claim preclusion. See River Park, Inc. v. City of Highland Park, 703 N.E.2d 883, 892 (Ill. 1998) (same evidence test is narrower than transactional test; the former is "tied to the theories of relief asserted by a plaintiff," so claims arising out of the same transaction may be separate "because the evidence needed to support the theories on which they are based differs") ("our approval of the transactional test necessitates a rejection of the same evidence test").

4. Same Parties (and Nonparty Preclusion and the "Privity" Rule)

In most cases where claim preclusion can plausibly be invoked, both the party seeking its protection and the party to be bound were themselves parties to a prior suit leading to judgment. Indeed, it is usually said that claim preclusion applies only if the "same parties" are in both suits. Take a simple example: Priscilla was a passenger in a car driven by David, and a collision occurs that injures people. If Priscilla sues David for her injuries and *loses,* and she later sues David again, he can invoke claim preclusion to block the second suit. Both the party invoking claim preclusion (David) and the party to be bound (Priscilla) were parties to the prior suit. The "same parties" standard is satisfied.

Changes in parties usually mean that claim preclusion cannot apply (the rule usually holds true that the same parties must be involved in both suits). Changes in parties can lead to situations in which an outsider (someone not involved in the first suit) tries to invoke claim preclusion, and to situations in which a party (someone who *was* involved in the first suit) invokes claim preclusion against an outsider (someone not involved in the first suit).

Outsider Invokes Against Party. Suppose Priscilla sues David on account of the automobile accident and loses, and she then sues the manufacturer of David's car. Can the manufacturer (not a party in the first suit) invoke claim preclusion in defense? Usually not, and one reason is that the parties are not the same. Arguably there are better reasons: Priscilla's claims against the manufacturer arose out of a different transaction—manufacture of the vehicle, which happened before the accident. (Even this difference might not save the day for Priscilla, inasmuch as the claim against the manufacturer really turns on the accident—arguably the manufacturer committed no tort just by making a car that was defective. Liability arose—or might arise—when the defect led to accident and injury.)

Party Invokes Against Outsider. Sometimes the reverse occurs. Suppose again that Priscilla sues David and loses, and then Phil, who was a passenger in the same car, sues David for injuries *he* sustained in the accident. Can David invoke claim preclusion in defense against Phil (not a party to the first suit)? Usually not, and one reason is that the parties are not the same. Again, arguably there are better reasons. For one thing, you might instinctively think of the principle, which has been fundamental in American law at least since the *Hansberry* case (Chapter 8H4, supra), that a judgment cannot bind someone who was not a party. Binding a nonparty would violate due process because the party has not had a chance to be heard, has not had his "day in court."[1] Also the claims are also not the same: Priscilla's claim against David is not the same as Phil's claim against David.

Sometimes, however, changes in parties leave room for at least plausible arguments that claim preclusion applies. Sometimes the connection between

---

[1] *Hansberry* recognized that members of a *class* represented adequately in one suit can be barred by judgment in that suit. One problem in *Hansberry* was that the first suit did not purport to bind a *class* of persons interested in striking down racial covenants.

the outsider and a party in the prior suit, whether the outsider is the one *invoking* claim preclusion or the one *to be bound*, is sufficiently close that it becomes plausible to apply preclusion after all. It is commonly said in such cases that the outsider is "in privity" with one who was a party in the prior suit.

TAYLOR v. STURGELL

Supreme Court of the United States
553 U.S. 880 (2008)

Justice Ginsburg delivered the opinion of the Court.

"It is a principle of general application in Anglo-American jurisprudence that one is not bound by a judgment *in personam* in a litigation in which he is not designated as a party or to which he has not been made a party by service of process." Hansberry v. Lee, 311 U.S. 32, 40 (1940). Several exceptions, recognized in this Court's decisions, temper this basic rule. In a class action, for example, a person not named as a party may be bound by a judgment on the merits of the action, if she was adequately represented by a party who actively participated in the litigation. In this case, we consider for the first time whether there is a "virtual representation" exception to the general rule against precluding nonparties. Adopted by a number of courts, including the courts below in the case now before us, the exception so styled is broader than any we have so far approved.

The virtual representation question we examine in this opinion arises in the following context. Petitioner Brent Taylor filed a lawsuit under the Freedom of Information Act seeking certain documents from the Federal Aviation Administration. Greg Herrick, Taylor's friend, had previously brought an unsuccessful suit seeking the same records. The two men have no legal relationship, and there is no evidence that Taylor controlled, financed, participated in, or even had notice of Herrick's earlier suit. Nevertheless, the D.C. Circuit held Taylor's suit precluded by the judgment against Herrick because, in that court's assessment, Herrick qualified as Taylor's "virtual representative."

We disapprove the doctrine of preclusion by "virtual representation," and hold, based on the record as it now stands, that the judgment against Herrick does not bar Taylor from maintaining this suit.

I

The Freedom of Information Act (FOIA) accords "any person" a right to request any records held by a federal agency. 5 USC §552(a) (2006 ed.). No reason need be given for a FOIA request, and unless the requested materials fall within one of the Act's enumerated exemptions, the agency must "make the records promptly available" to the requester. If an agency refuses to furnish the requested records, the requester may file suit in federal court and obtain an injunction "order[ing] the production of any agency records improperly withheld."

The courts below held the instant FOIA suit barred by the judgment in earlier litigation seeking the same records. Because the lower courts' decisions turned on the connection between the two lawsuits, we begin with a full account of each action.

A

The first suit was filed by Greg Herrick, an antique aircraft enthusiast and the owner of an F-45 airplane, a vintage model manufactured by the Fairchild Engine and Airplane Corporation (FEAC) in the 1930's. In 1997, seeking information that would help him restore his plane to its original condition, Herrick filed a FOIA request asking the Federal Aviation Administration (FAA) for copies of any technical documents about the F-45 contained in the agency's records.

To gain a certificate authorizing the manufacture and sale of the F-45, FEAC had submitted to the FAA's predecessor, the Civil Aeronautics Authority, detailed specifications and other technical data about the plane. Hundreds of pages of documents produced by FEAC in the certification process remain in the FAA's records. The FAA denied Herrick's request, however, upon finding that the documents he sought are subject to FOIA's exemption for "trade secrets and commercial or financial information obtained from a person and privileged or confidential," 5 USC §552(b)(4) (2006 ed.). In an administrative appeal, Herrick urged that FEAC and its successors had waived any trade-secret protection. The FAA thereupon contacted FEAC's corporate successor, respondent Fairchild Corporation (Fairchild). Because Fairchild objected to release of the documents, the agency adhered to its original decision.

Herrick then filed suit in the U.S. District Court for the District of Wyoming. Challenging the FAA's invocation of the trade-secret exemption, Herrick placed heavy weight on a 1955 letter from FEAC to the Civil Aeronautics Authority. The letter authorized the agency to lend any documents in its files to the public "for use in making repairs or replacement parts for aircraft produced by Fairchild." Herrick v. Garvey, 298 F.3d 1184, 1193 (10th Cir. 2002) (internal quotation marks omitted). This broad authorization, Herrick maintained, showed that the F-45 certification records held by the FAA could not be regarded as "secre[t]" or "confidential" within the meaning of §552(b)(4).

Rejecting Herrick's argument, the District Court granted summary judgment to the FAA. The 1955 letter, the court reasoned, did not deprive the F-45 certification documents of trade-secret status, for those documents were never in fact released pursuant to the letter's blanket authorization. The court also stated that even if the 1955 letter had waived trade-secret protection, Fairchild had successfully "reversed" the waiver by objecting to the FAA's release of the records to Herrick.

On appeal, the Tenth Circuit agreed with Herrick that the 1955 letter had stripped the requested documents of trade-secret protection. But the Court of Appeals upheld the District Court's alternative determination—*i.e.,* that Fairchild had restored trade-secret status by objecting to Herrick's FOIA request. On that ground, the appeals court affirmed the entry of summary judgment for the FAA.

In so ruling, the Tenth Circuit noted that Herrick had failed to challenge two suppositions underlying the District Court's decision. First, the District Court assumed trade-secret status could be "restored" to documents that had lost protection. Second, the District Court also assumed that Fairchild had regained trade-secret status for the documents even though the company claimed that status only "*after* Herrick had initiated his request" for the F-45 records. The Court of Appeals expressed no opinion on the validity of these suppositions.

B

The Tenth Circuit's decision issued on July 24, 2002. Less than a month later, on August 22, petitioner Brent Taylor—a friend of Herrick's and an antique aircraft enthusiast in his own right—submitted a FOIA request seeking the same documents Herrick had unsuccessfully sued to obtain. When the FAA failed to respond, Taylor filed a complaint in the U.S. District Court for the District of Columbia. Like Herrick, Taylor argued that FEAC's 1955 letter had stripped the records of their trade-secret status. But Taylor also sought to litigate the two issues concerning recapture of protected status that Herrick had failed to raise in his appeal to the Tenth Circuit.

After Fairchild intervened as a defendant,[1] the District Court in D.C. concluded that Taylor's suit was barred by claim preclusion; accordingly, it granted summary judgment to Fairchild and the FAA. The court acknowledged that Taylor was not a party to Herrick's suit. Relying on the Eighth Circuit's decision in Tyus v. Schoemehl, 93 F.3d 449 (8th Cir. 1996), however, it held that a nonparty may be bound by a judgment if she was "virtually represented" by a party.

The Eighth Circuit's seven-factor test for virtual representation, adopted by the District Court in Taylor's case, requires an "identity of interests" between the person to be bound and a party to the judgment. Six additional factors counsel in favor of virtual representation under the Eighth Circuit's test, but are not prerequisites: (1) a "close relationship" between the present

---

[1] Although Fairchild provided documents to the Wyoming District Court and filed an *amicus* brief in the Tenth Circuit, it was not a party to Herrick's suit.

party and a party to the judgment alleged to be preclusive; (2) "participation in the prior litigation" by the present party; (3) the present party's "apparent acquiescence" to the preclusive effect of the judgment; (4) "deliberat[e] maneuver[ing]" to avoid the effect of the judgment; (5) adequate representation of the present party by a party to the prior adjudication; and (6) a suit raising a "public law" rather than a "private law" issue. These factors, the D.C. District Court observed, "constitute a fluid test with imprecise boundaries" and call for "a broad, case-by-case inquiry."

The record before the District Court in Taylor's suit revealed the following facts about the relationship between Taylor and Herrick: Taylor is the president of the Antique Aircraft Association, an organization to which Herrick belongs; the two men are "close associate[s]"; Herrick asked Taylor to help restore Herrick's F-45, though they had no contract or agreement for Taylor's participation in the restoration; Taylor was represented by the lawyer who represented Herrick in the earlier litigation; and Herrick apparently gave Taylor documents that Herrick had obtained from the FAA during discovery in his suit.

Fairchild and the FAA conceded that Taylor had not participated in Herrick's suit. The D.C. District Court determined, however, that Herrick ranked as Taylor's virtual representative because the facts fit each of the other six indicators on the Eighth Circuit's list. Accordingly, the District Court held Taylor's suit, seeking the same documents Herrick had requested, barred by the judgment against Herrick.

The D.C. Circuit affirmed. It observed, first, that other Circuits "vary widely" in their approaches to virtual representation. Taylor v. Blakey, 490 F.3d 965, 971 (2007). In this regard, the D.C. Circuit contrasted the multifactor balancing test applied by the Eighth Circuit and the D.C. District Court with the Fourth Circuit's narrower approach, which "treats a party as a virtual representative only if the party is 'accountable to the nonparties who file a subsequent suit' and has 'the tacit approval of the court' to act on the nonpart[ies'] behalf." *Ibid.* (quoting Klugh v. United States, 818 F.2d 294, 300 (4th Cir. 1987)).

Rejecting both of these approaches, the D.C. Circuit announced its own five-factor test. The first two factors—"identity of interests" and "adequate representation"—are necessary but not sufficient for virtual representation. In addition, at least one of three other factors must be established: "a close relationship between the present party and his putative representative," "substantial participation by the present party in the first case," or "tactical maneuvering on the part of the present party to avoid preclusion by the prior judgment."

Applying this test to the record in Taylor's case, the D.C. Circuit found both of the necessary conditions for virtual representation well met. As to identity of interests, the court emphasized that Taylor and Herrick sought the same result—release of the F-45 documents. Moreover, the D.C. Circuit observed, Herrick owned an F-45 airplane, and therefore had "if anything, a stronger incentive to litigate" than Taylor, who had only a "general interest in public disclosure and the preservation of antique aircraft heritage" (internal quotation marks omitted).

Turning to adequacy of representation, the D.C. Circuit acknowledged that some other Circuits regard notice of a prior suit as essential to a determination that a nonparty was adequately represented in that suit. Disagreeing with these courts, the D.C. Circuit deemed notice an "important" but not an indispensable element in the adequacy inquiry. The court then concluded that Herrick had adequately represented Taylor even though Taylor had received no notice of Herrick's suit. For this conclusion, the appeals court relied on Herrick's "strong incentive to litigate" and Taylor's later engagement of the same attorney, which indicated to the court Taylor's satisfaction with that attorney's performance in Herrick's case.

The D.C. Circuit also found its "close relationship" criterion met, for Herrick had "asked Taylor to assist him in restoring his F-45" and "provided information to Taylor that Herrick had obtained through discovery"; furthermore, Taylor "did not oppose Fairchild's characterization of Herrick as his 'close associate.'" Because the three above-described factors sufficed to establish virtual representation under the D.C. Circuit's five-factor test, the appeals court left open the question whether Taylor had engaged in "tactical maneuvering" (calling the facts bearing on tactical maneuvering "ambigu[ous]").

We granted certiorari to resolve the disagreement among the Circuits over the permissibility and scope of preclusion based on "virtual representation."[3]

II

The preclusive effect of a federal-court judgment is determined by federal common law. See Semtek Int'l Inc. v. Lockheed Martin Corp., 531 U.S. 497, 507-508 (2001). For judgments in federal-question cases—for example, Herrick's FOIA suit—federal courts participate in developing "uniform federal rule[s]" of res judicata, which this Court has ultimate authority to determine and declare.[4] The federal common law of preclusion is, of course, subject to due process limitations. See Richards v. Jefferson County, 517 U.S. 793, 797 (1996).

Taylor's case presents an issue of first impression in this sense: Until now, we have never addressed the doctrine of "virtual representation" adopted (in varying forms) by several Circuits and relied upon by the courts below. Our

---

[3] The Ninth Circuit applies a five-factor test similar to the D.C. Circuit's. See Kourtis v. Cameron, 419 F.3d 989, 996 (9th Cir. 2005). The Fifth, Sixth, and Eleventh Circuits, like the Fourth Circuit, have constrained the reach of virtual representation by requiring, inter alia, the existence of a legal relationship between the nonparty to be bound and the putative representative. See Pollard v. Cockrell, 578 F.2d 1002, 1008 (5th Cir. 1978); Becherer v. Merrill Lynch, Pierce, Fenner, & Smith, Inc., 193 F.3d 415, 424 (6th Cir. 1999); EEOC v. Pemco Aeroplex, Inc., 383 F.3d 1280, 1289 (11th Cir. 2004). The Seventh Circuit, in contrast, has rejected the doctrine of virtual representation altogether. See Perry v. Globe Auto Recycling, Inc., 227 F.3d 950, 953 (7th Cir. 2000).

[4] For judgments in diversity cases, federal law incorporates the rules of preclusion applied by the State in which the rendering court sits. See Semtek Int'l Inc. v. Lockheed Martin Corp., 531 U.S. 497, 508 (2001).

inquiry, however, is guided by well-established precedent regarding the propriety of nonparty preclusion. We review that precedent before taking up directly the issue of virtual representation.

A

The preclusive effect of a judgment is defined by claim preclusion and issue preclusion, which are collectively referred to as "res judicata."[5] Under the doctrine of claim preclusion, a final judgment forecloses "successive litigation of the very same claim, whether or not relitigation of the claim raises the same issues as the earlier suit." New Hampshire v. Maine, 532 U.S. 742, 748 (2001). Issue preclusion, in contrast, bars "successive litigation of an issue of fact or law actually litigated and resolved in a valid court determination essential to the prior judgment," even if the issue recurs in the context of a different claim. By "preclud[ing] parties from contesting matters that they have had a full and fair opportunity to litigate," these two doctrines protect against "the expense and vexation attending multiple lawsuits, conserv[e] judicial resources, and foste[r] reliance on judicial action by minimizing the possibility of inconsistent decisions." Montana v. United States, 440 U.S. 147, 153-154 (1979).

A person who was not a party to a suit generally has not had a "full and fair opportunity to litigate" the claims and issues settled in that suit. The application of claim and issue preclusion to nonparties thus runs up against the "deep-rooted historic tradition that everyone should have his own day in court." *Richards,* 517 U.S., at 798 (internal quotation marks omitted). Indicating the strength of that tradition, we have often repeated the general rule that "one is not bound by a judgment *in personam* in a litigation in which he is not designated as a party or to which he has not been made a party by service of process." *Hansberry,* 311 U.S., at 40. See also, *e.g.,* Richards, 517 U.S., at 798; Martin v. Wilks, 490 U.S. 755, 761 (1989); Zenith Radio Corp. v. Hazeltine Research, Inc., 395 U.S. 100, 110 (1969).

B

Though hardly in doubt, the rule against nonparty preclusion is subject to exceptions. For present purposes, the recognized exceptions can be grouped into six categories.[6]

---

[5] These terms have replaced a more confusing lexicon. Claim preclusion describes the rules formerly known as "merger" and "bar," while issue preclusion encompasses the doctrines once known as "collateral estoppel" and "direct estoppel." See Migra v. Warren City School Dist. Bd. of Ed., 465 U.S. 75, 77, n.1 (1984).

[6] The established grounds for nonparty preclusion could be organized differently. See, *e.g.,* Restatement (Second) of Judgments §§39-62 (1980) (hereinafter Restatement); D. Shapiro, Civil Procedure: Preclusion in Civil Actions 75-92 (2001); 18A C. Wright, A. Miller, & E. Cooper, Federal Practice and Procedure §4448, pp.327-329 (2d ed. 2002) (hereinafter Wright & Miller). The list that follows is meant only to provide a framework for our consideration of virtual representation, not to establish a definitive taxonomy.

First, "[a] person who agrees to be bound by the determination of issues in an action between others is bound in accordance with the terms of his agreement." 1 Restatement (Second) of Judgments §40 (1980) (hereinafter Restatement). For example, "if separate actions involving the same transaction are brought by different plaintiffs against the same defendant, all the parties to all the actions may agree that the question of the defendant's liability will be definitely determined, one way or the other, in a 'test case.'" D. Shapiro, Civil Procedure: Preclusion in Civil Actions 77-78 (2001) (hereinafter Shapiro). See also California v. Texas, 459 U.S. 1096, 1097 (1983) (dismissing certain defendants from a suit based on a stipulation "that each of said defendants . . . will be bound by a final judgment of this Court" on a specified issue).[7]

Second, nonparty preclusion may be justified based on a variety of pre-existing "substantive legal relationship[s]" between the person to be bound and a party to the judgment. Qualifying relationships include, but are not limited to, preceding and succeeding owners of property, bailee and bailor, and assignee and assignor. See 2 Restatement §§43-44, 52, 55. These exceptions originated "as much from the needs of property law as from the values of preclusion by judgment." 18A C. Wright, A. Miller, & E. Cooper, Federal Practice and Procedure §44489 (2d ed. 2002) (hereinafter Wright & Miller).[8]

Third, we have confirmed that, "in certain limited circumstances," a nonparty may be bound by a judgment because she was "adequately represented by someone with the same interests who [wa]s a party" to the suit. *Richards*, 517 U.S., at 798 (internal quotation marks omitted). Representative suits with preclusive effect on nonparties include properly conducted class actions, see *Martin*, 490 U.S., at 762, n.2 (citing FRCP 23), and suits brought by trustees, guardians, and other fiduciaries, see Sea-Land Services, Inc. v. Gaudet, 414 U.S. 573, 593 (1974).

Fourth, a nonparty is bound by a judgment if she "assume[d] control" over the litigation in which that judgment was rendered. *Montana*, 440 U.S., at 154. See also Schnell v. Peter Eckrich & Sons, Inc., 365 U.S. 260, 262, n.4 (1961); Restatement §39. Because such a person has had "the opportunity to present proofs and argument," he has already "had his day in court" even though he was not a formal party to the litigation. *Id.*, Comment *a.*

---

[7] The Restatement observes that a nonparty may be bound not only by express or implied agreement, but also through conduct inducing reliance by others. See Restatement §62. We have never had occasion to consider this ground for nonparty preclusion, and we express no view on it here.

[8] The substantive legal relationships justifying preclusion are sometimes collectively referred to as "privity." See, e.g., Richards v. Jefferson County, 517 U.S. 793, 798 (1996); Restatement §62, Comment *a.* The term "privity," however, has also come to be used more broadly, as a way to express the conclusion that nonparty preclusion is appropriate on any ground. To ward off confusion, we avoid using the term "privity" in this opinion.

Fifth, a party bound by a judgment may not avoid its preclusive force by relitigating through a proxy. Preclusion is thus in order when a person who did not participate in a litigation later brings suit as the designated representative of a person who was a party to the prior adjudication. See Chicago, R.I. & P.R. Co. v. Schendel, 270 U.S. 611, 620, 623 (1926). And although our decisions have not addressed the issue directly, it also seems clear that preclusion is appropriate when a nonparty later brings suit as an agent for a party who is bound by a judgment.

Sixth, in certain circumstances a special statutory scheme may "expressly foreclos[e] successive litigation by nonlitigants . . . if the scheme is otherwise consistent with due process." *Martin*, 490 U.S., at 762, n.2. Examples of such schemes include bankruptcy and probate proceedings and *quo warranto* actions or other suits that, "under [the governing] law, [may] be brought only on behalf of the public at large," *Richards*, 517 U.S., at 804.

III

Reaching beyond these six established categories, some lower courts have recognized a "virtual representation" exception to the rule against nonparty preclusion. Decisions of these courts, however, have been far from consistent. See 18A Wright & Miller §4457, p.513 (virtual representation lacks a "clear or coherent theory"; decisions applying it have "an episodic quality"). Some Circuits use the label, but define "virtual representation" so that it is no broader than the recognized exception for adequate representation. But other courts, including the Eighth, Ninth, and D.C. Circuits, apply multifactor tests for virtual representation that permit nonparty preclusion in cases that do not fit within any of the established exceptions.

The D.C. Circuit, the FAA, and Fairchild have presented three arguments in support of an expansive doctrine of virtual representation. We find none of them persuasive.

A

The D.C. Circuit purported to ground its virtual representation doctrine in this Court's decisions stating that, in some circumstances, a person may be bound by a judgment if she was adequately represented by a party to the proceeding yielding that judgment. But the D.C. Circuit's definition of "adequate representation" strayed from the meaning our decisions have attributed to that term.

In *Richards*, we reviewed a decision by the Alabama Supreme Court holding that a challenge to a tax was barred by a judgment upholding the same tax in a suit filed by different taxpayers. The plaintiffs in the first suit "did not sue on behalf of a class," their complaint "did not purport to assert any claim against or on behalf of any nonparties," and the judgment "did not purport to bind" nonparties. There was no indication, we emphasized, that the court in the first suit "took care to protect the interests" of absent parties, or that the parties to that litigation "understood their suit to be on behalf of absent [parties]." In these circumstances, we held, the application of claim preclusion was inconsistent with "the due process of law guaranteed by the Fourteenth Amendment."

The D.C. Circuit stated, without elaboration, that it did not "read *Richards* to hold a nonparty . . . adequately represented only if special procedures were followed [to protect the nonparty] or the party to the prior suit understood it was representing the nonparty." As the D.C. Circuit saw this case, Herrick adequately represented Taylor for two principal reasons: Herrick had a strong incentive to litigate; and Taylor later hired Herrick's lawyer, suggesting Taylor's "satisfaction with the attorney's performance in the prior case."

The D.C. Circuit misapprehended *Richards*. As just recounted, our holding that the Alabama Supreme Court's application of res judicata to nonparties violated due process turned on the lack of either special procedures to protect the nonparties' interests or an understanding by the concerned parties that the first suit was brought in a representative capacity. See *Richards*, 517 U.S., at 801-802. *Richards* thus established that representation is "adequate" for purposes of nonparty preclusion only if (at a minimum) one of these two circumstances is present.

We restated *Richards'* core holding in South Central Bell Telephone Co. v. Alabama, 526 U.S. 160 (1999). In that case, as in *Richards*, the Alabama courts had held that a judgment rejecting a challenge to a tax by one group of taxpayers barred a subsequent suit by a different taxpayer. In *South Central Bell*, however, the nonparty had notice of the original suit and engaged one of the lawyers earlier employed by the original plaintiffs. Under the D.C. Circuit's decision in Taylor's case, these factors apparently would have sufficed to establish adequate representation. Yet *South Central Bell* held that the application of res judicata in that case violated due process. Our inquiry came to an end when we determined that the original plaintiffs had not understood themselves to be acting in a representative capacity and that there had been no special procedures to safeguard the interests of absentees.

Our decisions recognizing that a nonparty may be bound by a judgment if she was adequately represented by a party to the earlier suit thus provide no support for the D.C. Circuit's broad theory of virtual representation.

B

Fairchild and the FAA do not argue that the D.C. Circuit's virtual representation doctrine fits within any of the recognized grounds for nonparty preclusion. Rather, they ask us to abandon the attempt to delineate discrete grounds and clear rules altogether. Preclusion is in order, they contend, whenever "the relationship between a party and a non-party is 'close enough' to bring the second litigant within the judgment." Courts should make the "close enough" determination, they urge, through a "heavily fact-driven" and "equitable" inquiry. See also FAA Brief, at 22 ("there is no clear test" for nonparty preclusion; rather, an "equitable and fact-intensive" inquiry is demanded (internal quotation marks omitted)). Only this sort of diffuse balancing, Fairchild and the FAA argue, can account for all of the situations in which nonparty preclusion is appropriate.

We reject this argument for three reasons. First, our decisions emphasize the fundamental nature of the general rule that a litigant is not bound by a judgment to which she was not a party. See, *e.g., Richards,* 517 U.S., at 798-799. Accordingly, we have endeavored to delineate discrete exceptions that apply in "limited circumstances." Respondents' amorphous balancing test is at odds with the constrained approach to nonparty preclusion our decisions advance.

Resisting this reading of our precedents, respondents call up three decisions they view as supportive of the approach they espouse. Fairchild quotes our statement in Coryell v. Phipps, 317 U.S. 406, 411 (1943), that privity "turns on the facts of particular cases." That observation, however, scarcely implies that privity is governed by a diffuse balancing test.[9] Fairchild also cites Blonder-Tongue Laboratories, Inc. v. University of Ill. Foundation, 402 U.S. 313 (1971), which stated that estoppel questions turn on "the trial courts' sense of justice and equity." This passing statement, however, was not made with nonparty preclusion in mind; it appeared in a discussion recognizing district courts' discretion to *limit* the use of issue preclusion against persons who *were* parties to a judgment.

The FAA relies on United States v. Des Moines Valley R. Co., 84 F. 40 (8th Cir. 1897), an opinion we quoted with approval in *Schendel,* 270 U.S., at 619-620. *Des Moines Valley* was a quiet title action in which the named plaintiff was the United States. The Government, however, had "no interest in the land" and had "simply permitted [the landowner] to use its name as the nominal plaintiff." The suit was therefore barred, the appeals court held, by an earlier judgment against the landowner. As the court explained: "[W]here the government lends its name as a plaintiff . . . to enable one private person to maintain a suit against another," the government is "subject to the same defenses which exist . . . against the real party in interest." *Des Moines Valley*, the FAA contended at oral argument, demonstrates that it is sometimes appropriate to bind a nonparty in circumstances that do not fit within any of the established grounds for nonparty preclusion. Properly understood, however, *Des Moines Valley* is simply an application of the fifth basis for nonparty preclusion described above: A party may not use a representative or agent to relitigate

---

[9] Moreover, *Coryell* interpreted the term "privity" not in the context of res judicata, but as used in a statute governing shipowner liability. And we made the statement Fairchild quotes in explaining why it was appropriate to defer to the findings of the lower courts, not as a comment on the substantive rules of privity.

an adverse judgment.[10] We thus find no support in our precedents for the lax approach to nonparty preclusion advocated by respondents.

Our second reason for rejecting a broad doctrine of virtual representation rests on the limitations attending nonparty preclusion based on adequate representation. A party's representation of a nonparty is "adequate" for preclusion purposes only if, at a minimum: (1) the interests of the nonparty and her representative are aligned, see *Hansberry*; and (2) either the party understood herself to be acting in a representative capacity or the original court took care to protect the interests of the nonparty. In addition, adequate representation sometimes requires (3) notice of the original suit to the persons alleged to have been represented, see *Richards*.[11] In the class-action context, these limitations are implemented by the procedural safeguards contained in FRCP 23.

An expansive doctrine of virtual representation, however, would "recogniz[e], in effect, a common-law kind of class action." *Tice v. American Airlines, Inc*, 162 F.2d 966, 972 (7th Cir. 1998) (internal quotation marks omitted). That is, virtual representation would authorize preclusion based on identity of interests and some kind of relationship between parties and nonparties, shorn of the procedural protections prescribed in *Hansberry, Richards*, and Rule 23. These protections, grounded in due process, could be circumvented were we to approve a virtual representation doctrine that allowed courts to "create *de facto* class actions at will." *Tice*.

Third, a diffuse balancing approach to nonparty preclusion would likely create more headaches than it relieves. Most obviously, it could significantly complicate the task of district courts faced in the first instance with preclusion questions. An all-things-considered balancing approach might spark wide-ranging, time-consuming, and expensive discovery tracking factors potentially relevant under seven- or five-prong tests. And after the relevant facts are established, district judges would be called upon to evaluate them under a standard that provides no firm guidance. See *Tyus*, 93 F.3d, at 455 (conceding that "there is no clear test for determining the applicability of" the virtual representation doctrine announced in that case). Preclusion doctrine, it should be recalled, is intended to reduce the burden of litigation on courts

---

[10] The FAA urges that there was no agency relationship between the landowner and the United States because the landowner did not control the U.S. Attorney's conduct of the suit. That point is debatable. See United States v. Des Moines Valley R. Co., 84 F. 40, 42-43 (8th Cir. 1897) (the United States was only a "nominal plaintiff"; it merely "len[t]" its name to the landowner). But even if the FAA is correct about agency, the United States plainly litigated as the landowner's designated representative. See *id.* ("The bill does not attempt to conceal the fact that . . . its real purpose is to champion the cause of [the landowner] . . . ."). See also Chicago, R.I. & P.R. Co. v. Schendel, 270 U.S. 611, 618-620 (1926) (classifying *Des Moines Valley* with other cases of preclusion based on representation).

[11] *Richards* suggested that notice is required in some representative suits, *e.g.*, class actions seeking monetary relief. See 517 U.S., at 801 (citing Hansberry v. Lee, 311 U.S. 32 (1940), Eisen v. Carlisle & Jacquelin, 417 U.S. 156 (1974), and Mullane v. Central Hanover Bank & Trust Co., 339 U.S. 306, 319 (1950)). But we assumed without deciding that a lack of notice might be overcome in some circumstances.

and parties. Cf. *Montana.* "In this area of the law," we agree, "'crisp rules with sharp corners' are preferable to a round-about doctrine of opaque standards." Bittinger v. Tecumseh Products Co., 123 F.3d 877, 881 (6th Cir. 1997).

C

Finally, relying on the Eighth Circuit's decision in *Tyus,* the FAA maintains that nonparty preclusion should apply more broadly in "public-law" litigation than in "private-law" controversies. To support this position, the FAA offers two arguments. First, the FAA urges, our decision in *Richards* acknowledges that, in certain cases, the plaintiff has a reduced interest in controlling the litigation "because of the public nature of the right at issue." When a taxpayer challenges "an alleged misuse of public funds" or "other public action," we observed in *Richards,* the suit "has only an indirect impact on [the plaintiff's] interests." In actions of this character, the Court said, "we may assume that the States have wide latitude to establish procedures . . . to limit the number of judicial proceedings that may be entertained."

Taylor's FOIA action falls within the category described in *Richards,* the FAA contends, because "the duty to disclose under FOIA is owed to the public generally." The opening sentence of FOIA, it is true, states that agencies "shall make [information] available to the public." 5 USC §552(a) (2006 ed.). Equally true, we have several times said that FOIA vindicates a "public" interest. The Act, however, instructs agencies receiving FOIA requests to make the information available not to the public at large, but rather to the "person" making the request. §552(a)(3)(A). See also §552(a)(3)(B) ("In making any record available *to a person* under this paragraph, an agency shall provide the record in any [readily reproducible] form or format requested *by the person. . . .*" (emphasis added)). Thus, in contrast to the public-law litigation contemplated in *Richards,* a successful FOIA action results in a grant of relief to the individual plaintiff, not a decree benefiting the public at large.

Furthermore, we said in *Richards* only that, for the type of public-law claims there envisioned, States are free to adopt procedures limiting repetitive litigation. In this regard, we referred to instances in which the first judgment foreclosed successive litigation by other plaintiffs because, "under state law, [the suit] could be brought only on behalf of the public at large."[12] *Richards* spoke of state legislation, but it appears equally evident that *Congress,* in providing for actions vindicating a public interest, may "limit the number of judicial proceedings that may be entertained." It hardly follows, however, that *this Court* should proscribe or confine successive FOIA suits by different requesters. Indeed, Congress' provision for FOIA suits with no statutory

---

[12] Nonparty preclusion in such cases ranks under the sixth exception described above: special statutory schemes that expressly limit subsequent suits.

constraint on successive actions counsels against judicial imposition of constraints through extraordinary application of the common law of preclusion.

The FAA next argues that "the threat of vexatious litigation is heightened" in public-law cases because "the number of plaintiffs with standing is potentially limitless." FOIA does allow "any person" whose request is denied to resort to federal court for review of the agency's determination. 5 USC §552(a)(3)(A), (4)(B) (2006 ed.). Thus it is theoretically possible that several persons could coordinate to mount a series of repetitive lawsuits.

But we are not convinced that this risk justifies departure from the usual rules governing nonparty preclusion. First, *stare decisis* will allow courts swiftly to dispose of repetitive suits brought in the same circuit. Second, even when *stare decisis* is not dispositive, "the human tendency not to waste money will deter the bringing of suits based on claims or issues that have already been adversely determined against others." This intuition seems to be borne out by experience: The FAA has not called our attention to any instances of abusive FOIA suits in the Circuits that reject the virtual-representation theory respondents advocate here.

IV

For the foregoing reasons, we disapprove the theory of virtual representation on which the decision below rested. The preclusive effects of a judgment in a federal-question case decided by a federal court should instead be determined according to the established grounds for nonparty preclusion described in this opinion.

Although references to "virtual representation" have proliferated in the lower courts, our decision is unlikely to occasion any great shift in actual practice. Many opinions use the term "virtual representation" in reaching results at least arguably defensible on established grounds. In these cases, dropping the "virtual representation" label would lead to clearer analysis with little, if any, change in outcomes. See *Tice*, 162 F.3d, at 971 ("[T]he term 'virtual representation' has cast more shadows than light on the problem [of nonparty preclusion].").

In some cases, however, lower courts have relied on virtual representation to extend nonparty preclusion beyond the latter doctrine's proper bounds. We now turn back to Taylor's action to determine whether his suit is such a case, or whether the result reached by the courts below can be justified on one of the recognized grounds for nonparty preclusion.

A

It is uncontested that four of the six grounds for nonparty preclusion have no application here: There is no indication that Taylor agreed to be bound by Herrick's litigation, that Taylor and Herrick have any legal relationship, that Taylor exercised any control over Herrick's suit, or that this suit implicates any special statutory scheme limiting relitigation. Neither the FAA nor Fairchild contends otherwise.

It is equally clear that preclusion cannot be justified on the theory that Taylor was adequately represented in Herrick's suit. Nothing in the record indicates that Herrick understood himself to be suing on Taylor's behalf, that Taylor even knew of Herrick's suit, or that the Wyoming District Court took special care to protect Taylor's interests. Under our pathmarking precedent, therefore, Herrick's representation was not "adequate."

That leaves only the fifth category: preclusion because a nonparty to an earlier litigation has brought suit as a representative or agent of a party who is bound by the prior adjudication. Taylor is not Herrick's legal representative and he has not purported to sue in a representative capacity. He concedes, however, that preclusion would be appropriate if respondents could demonstrate that he is acting as Herrick's "undisclosed agen[t]."

Respondents argue here, as they did below, that Taylor's suit is a collusive attempt to relitigate Herrick's action. The D.C. Circuit considered a similar question in addressing the "tactical maneuvering" prong of its virtual representation test. The Court of Appeals did not, however, treat the issue as one of agency, and it expressly declined to reach any definitive conclusions due to "the ambiguity of the facts." We therefore remand to give the courts below an opportunity to determine whether Taylor, in pursuing the instant FOIA suit, is acting as Herrick's agent. Taylor concedes that such a remand is appropriate.

We have never defined the showing required to establish that a nonparty to a prior adjudication has become a litigating agent for a party to the earlier case. Because the issue has not been briefed in any detail, we do not discuss the matter elaborately here. We note, however, that courts should be cautious about finding preclusion on this basis. A mere whiff of "tactical maneuvering" will not suffice; instead, principles of agency law are suggestive. They indicate that preclusion is appropriate only if the putative agent's conduct of the suit is subject to the control of the party who is bound by the prior adjudication. See Restatement (Second) of Agency §14, p. 60 (1957) ("A principal has the right to control the conduct of the agent with respect to matters entrusted to him.").[13]

B

On remand, Fairchild suggests, Taylor should bear the burden of proving he is not acting as Herrick's agent. When a defendant points to evidence establishing a close relationship between successive litigants, Fairchild maintains, "the burden

---

[13] Our decision in Montana v. United States, 440 U.S. 147 (1979), also suggests a "control" test for agency. In that case, we held that the United States was barred from bringing a suit because it had controlled a prior unsuccessful action filed by a federal contractor. We see no reason why preclusion based on a lesser showing would have been appropriate if the order of the two actions had been switched—that is, if the United States had brought the first suit itself, and then sought to relitigate the same claim through the contractor.

[should] shif[t] to the second litigant to submit evidence refuting the charge" of agency. Fairchild justifies this proposed burden-shift on the ground that "it is unlikely an opposing party will have access to direct evidence of collusion."

We reject Fairchild's suggestion. Claim preclusion, like issue preclusion, is an affirmative defense. See FRCP 8(c); *Blonder-Tongue*, 402 U.S., at 350. Ordinarily, it is incumbent on the defendant to plead and prove such a defense, see Jones v. Bock, 549 U.S. 199 (2007), and we have never recognized claim preclusion as an exception to that general rule, see 18 Wright & Miller §4405, p. 83 ("[A] party asserting preclusion must carry the burden of establishing all necessary elements."). We acknowledge that direct evidence justifying nonparty preclusion is often in the hands of plaintiffs rather than defendants. But "[v]ery often one must plead and prove matters as to which his adversary has superior access to the proof." 2 K. Broun, McCormick on Evidence §337, p.475 (6th ed. 2006). In these situations, targeted interrogatories or deposition questions can reduce the information disparity. We see no greater cause here than in other matters of affirmative defense to disturb the traditional allocation of the proof burden.

. . .

For the reasons stated, the judgment of the United States Court of Appeals for the District of Columbia Circuit is vacated, and the case is remanded for further proceedings consistent with this opinion.

It is so ordered.

■ NOTES ON APPLYING CLAIM PRECLUSION DESPITE CHANGED PARTIES

1. In *Taylor*, claim preclusion was invoked *against* one who was an outsider to the prior suit, who never "had his day in court." In this sense, *Taylor* reaches a conclusion that is hardly surprising. Fittingly, Justice Ginsburg begins her opinion in *Taylor* by invoking the proposition for which *Hansberry* is best known, which is that nonparties are *not* bound. In *Taylor,* Greg Herrick brought the first suit and Brent Taylor brought the second. The two are friends, antique aircraft enthusiasts, "close associates" who worked together in restoring Herrick's F-5 aircraft, and Taylor is president of a club to which Herrick belongs. The two employed the same lawyer, and Herrick turned over to Taylor documents that he got during discovery in his suit. Still it was not shown that Taylor "controlled, financed, participated in, or even had notice of Herrick's earlier suit." On what basis did the District of Columbia Circuit Court find that Taylor's claim in the second suit was barred by Herrick's loss in the first?

2. Is there any reason to think Taylor did (or could have done) anything more or different in the second suit to advance the claim that Herrick had brought before?

3. Justice Ginsburg, who is not noted for being a traditionalist when it comes to the judicial function, spells out six exceptions to the rule against nonparty preclusion and declines the invitation by Sturgell (FAA administrator) to adopt a "balancing" approach as one that "would likely create more headaches than it relieves." Are the headaches worse than those that come with resolving issues of adequate representation in a class suit that went to judgment on the merits?

4. Let us now consider the six exceptions listed by the Court in *Taylor*:

(a) First, parties may agree to be bound by litigation brought by or prosecuted against another. What might persuade a nonparty to be bound by litigation conducted by others? One situation illustrating this exception involves indemnity agreements. If one agrees to hold another harmless in the event of liability, or is bound as an indemnitor to another, the person or entity involved in such agreement or bound in this way may also decide voluntarily to be bound by any judgment ultimately entered against the indemnitee. Thus a company that puts up a bond covering the performance of a builder or electrician may agree to pay any judgment entered against the builder or electrician, simply in order to avoid the necessity of being involved in litigation. See Restatement (Second) of Judgments §40 (1982) (citing indemnification arrangement as an example, but warning in Comment b that an agreement to be bound should be inferred only in "the plainest circumstances").

(b) Second, pre-existing legal relationships, like "succeeding owners of property, bailee and bailor, and assignee and assignor," may lead to judgments involving one party that bind another. Suppose Abe as owner of Blackacre sues George as owner of Greenacre to secure the right to drive over part of Greenacre in going back and forth to Blackacre. Suppose Abe prevails, and George then conveys Greenacre to Helen. It seems right to hold that Helen is bound by George's loss in Abe's suit, at least insofar as the judgment establishes the right of the owner of Blackacre to drive over Greenacre by way of ingress and egress, doesn't it? Is it also right, if Abe *loses* in his suit against George, to say that Bill, if he purchases Blackacre from Abe, is bound? Do similar considerations suggest that a bailor should be bound by judgment against a bailee, or an assignee by judgment against an assignor? This exception is often described by the word "privity," which term also applies to the third and fourth exceptions, described next.[2]

---

[2] See O'Nesti v. DeBartolo Realty Corp., 862 N.E.2d 803 (Ohio 2007) (privity exists when one succeeds to the interest of a party "or had the right to control the proceedings or make a defense" in the prior proceeding; also "interest in the result" or "active participation" may establish privity; the concept may also apply to people who "raise identical legal claims and seek identical rather than individually tailored result," and "mutuality of interest" and "identity of desired result" may support privity; also privity may exist if "a government official is sued in his individual and his official capacity" and "between an association and its individual members" if they are "liable by law for a judgment against the association") (some relationships, however, including "mother and minor child," do not establish privity).

(c) Third, there are "limited circumstances" in which one person adequately represents another, like class suits, and suits by trustees, guardians, and other fiduciaries. What's the difference between such suits and the suit that Greg Herrick brought, where the judgment does *not* bind Brent Taylor?

(d) Fourth, there are cases in which a nonparty assumes control over a suit, and can then be bound by the judgment ultimately rendered. In Montana v. United States, 440 U.S. 147 (1979), cited in *Taylor,* the government required a federal contractor to challenge a Montana gross receipts tax levied against public contractors, on the ground that it discriminated against the government. The case was litigated in Montana state court, which upheld the tax and rejected the challenge. The government then resumed its own challenge to the tax, which it had previously filed in federal court. The case went to the Supreme Court, which found that the government was bound by the contractor's loss in Montana. The interests served by claim and issue preclusion, the Court concluded in *Montana*, are "implicated when nonparties assume control over litigation in which they have a direct financial or proprietary interest," and this fact justifies binding the government by the contractor's loss in *Montana*.

(e) Fifth, there are cases in which a litigant acts as a "proxy" for someone who has previously litigated the same claim. Here the court cites Chicago, Rock Island and Pacific Railway v. Schendel, 270 U.S. 611 (1926), where workers' compensation proceedings were brought in state court by a representative of the estate of a railroader killed in an accident. A separate FELA suit was brought in federal court by the railroader's widow. The Court concluded in *Schendel* that the outcome of the state proceeding was binding on the widow in her later FELA suit.

(f) Sixth, "statutory scheme[s]" sometimes foreclose later suits by non-litigants, such as bankruptcy and probate proceedings. Consider some practical necessities. In bankruptcy, the aim is to resolve finally the claims against a debtor who cannot pay all his debts, which may entail giving the debtor a "new start" in life or (usually in the case of organizational debtors) winding up the affairs of a business by distributing its assets fairly to creditors and putting an end to the business. In probate, the aim is to pay off the debts of the decedent and distribute the remaining property to the heirs or devisees. If bankruptcy and probate proceedings could not finally resolve the affairs of the bankrupt or the estate, they would not succeed in one of their fundamental aims. See Richards v. Jefferson County, 517 U.S. 793, 803-804 (1996) (judgment in suit rejecting challenge to state occupational tax did not bar suit by second taxpayer challenging tax; states may adopt remedial schemes that foreclose successive litigation by nonparties, as in probate and bankruptcy, but scheme must be consistent with due process; where citizen challenges tax as invalid expenditure, such a scheme could be deployed; where citizen claims that tax is invalid as applied to her, she may not be foreclosed by prior suit if she has not received notice and was not represented).

5. Sometimes the operative effect of *res judicata* arising out of a judgment in one suit reaches claims against other parties. See Creech v. Addington, 281 S.W.3d 363 (Tenn. 2009) (investors sued agents and principals for fraud; after judgment for defendants, plaintiffs appealed, but only against principals; judgment favoring agents was final; under "same transaction" standard, dismissal of claims against agents foreclosed litigation of claims against principals); deLeon v. Slear, 616 A.2d 380 (Md. 1992) (where doctor sued hospital alleging defamation by nurses in hospital's employ and lost, *res judicata* barred doctor's second suit against nurses for same alleged defamation). See also Restatement (Second) of Judgments §51 (1982) (if two persons are related in such a way that one is "vicariously responsible for the conduct of the other," and if claimant sues one and loses, his loss bars a claim against the other unless the new claim rests on "grounds that could not have been asserted" in the first suit or judgment in that suit rested on a defense "personal to the defendant"). But see Esquire Trade & Finance, Inc. v. CBQ, Inc., 562 F.3d 516, 520-521 (2d Cir. 2009) (debenture holders sued Socrates Technologies and arrived at settlement and suit was dismissed with prejudice; then debenture holders sued CBQ as purchaser of assets of Socrates; these claims were not barred by *res judicata*; CBQ was not in privity with Socrates, as CBQ purchased assets but did not assume liabilities of Socrates).

6. For a pre-*Taylor* decision applying the doctrine of virtual representation to bar a second suit by persons not parties in the prior suit, see Beahm v. 7 Eleven, Inc., 672 S.E.2d 598 (W. Va. 2008) (on ground that statute of limitations had run, federal court dismissed claims against convenience store alleging that leak from underground gas tank contaminated groundwater under nearby properties; owners of other nearby properties then sue; court dismisses on ground of *res judicata*, invoking virtual representation; "something more than a common interest" is required, and more than injuries caused by a "single wrongful act," but here several plaintiffs sought to join prior suit, and their attorney "advanced substantially the same proof in both cases," and all parties to this suit knew of prior suit and "would have had the same practical opportunity to control the course of the proceedings," relying "not only on the same expert witnesses and expert opinions," but also on "the very same fact witnesses, documents and exhibits").

5. Exceptions to (and Limits of) Claim Preclusion

There are many exceptions to the doctrine of claim preclusion, where courts have decided that splitting claims is permissible.

Prominent among the exceptions is the one that allows the parties to agree to split claims. Thus, for example, plaintiff and defendant may stipulate to dismissal of a claim "without prejudice," leaving plaintiff free to bring the dismissed claim later in another suit. They may find this approach attractive for a variety of reasons, such as saving time and money (from plaintiff's perspective) and putting off a potential obligation (from defendant's perspective).

Similarly, when cases settle, the parties enter into agreements that either do or do not settle various possible claims relating to the matters at hand. Agreements that *fail to address* related claims are likely to be construed as consenting to later suits, so "tacit" agreements can result in splitting claims. See, e.g., Young-Henderson v. Spartanburg Area Mental Health Center, 945 F.3d 770, 775 (4th Cir. 1991) (consent decree specifically addressed claims "raised in the complaint" and expressly did not cover "other charges or claims," which plaintiff could pursue later).

Sometimes "consent" simply means failing to raise the matter as an affirmative defense—filing an answer without raising *res judicata* is in effect constructive consent to claim splitting. See, e.g., Clements v. Airport Authority of Washtoe County, 69 F.3d 321 (9th Cir. 1995) (defendant waived *res judicata* by failing to raise it).

The Restatement (Second) of Judgments (1982) recognizes six exceptions to claim preclusion. First is the situation surveyed above, where the parties agree to allow claim splitting. See Restatement §26(1)(a) (speaking of agreement "in terms or in effect," including acquiescence by the defendant). Second is an exception where the court in the prior suit "expressly reserved" plaintiff's right to sue again. See Restatement §26(1)(b). Third is the so-called jurisdiction exception, where plaintiff could not rely on "a certain theory" or seek "a certain remedy or form of relief" in the first suit because of limitations on "subject matter jurisdiction" or because of restrictions on the authority of the first court "to entertain multiple theories or demands for multiple remedies" in a single suit and plaintiff brings another suit on such theories or for such remedies. See Restatement §16(1)(c). Fourth is an exception for an earlier judgment that is "plainly inconsistent" with "fair and equitable implementation" of a statutory or constitutional scheme, or where "it is the sense of the scheme" that plaintiff should be allowed to split claims. See Restatement §26(1)(d). Fifth is the situation in which "substantive policy" in cases involving "a continuing or recurrent wrong," allows plaintiff to "sue once for the total harm, both past and prospective" or "sue from time to time" for damages incurred to the date of suit. See Restatement §26(1)(e). Sixth is a catchall category for cases where policies favoring preclusion "are overcome for an extraordinary reason," like the "invalidity of a continuing restraint or condition having a vital relation to personal liberty" or the failure of a prior suit "to yield a coherent disposition of the controversy." See Restatement §26(1)(f).

■ **PROBLEM 14-B. "Part of That's Mine"**

Steven Brooks and Shari Thielen entered into a living-together relationship near a small town in New Hampshire in 2005. With Shari's two young daughters from a previous marriage, they moved into a "starter home" on a rustic two-acre parcel that Brooks had purchased for $48,000 in 2003. They and the children lived together for six years, during which time Steven and Shari had jobs and earned money that they put into repairs, improvements, and additions to the home, adding bathrooms, bedrooms, garage, family room, and deck.

When they parted in 2012, Shari Thielen filed suit in small claims court to retrieve certain items of personal property, including a handbuilt hardwood dresser, a computer, a large television set, and other personal items including children's clothes and several beds. She prevailed, and recovered these items.

In 2013, Shari Thielen filed suit in superior court, bringing claims in breach of contract, unjust enrichment, and constructive trust. Lying behind these claims was her contention that improvements on the property had raised its value to $250,000, and her efforts and financial contributions were responsible for at least half its increased value. She sought $101,000 in damages, and asked for a constructive trust so that if the property were sold she would be entitled to that sum from the proceeds.

Brooks invoked *res judicata* as a defense, asserting in his answer that Thielen's claim had merged in the judgment in small claims court. How should the court rule, and why?

■ **NOTES ON EXCEPTIONS TO THE RULE AGAINST CLAIM PRECLUSION**

1. Courts of small claims in New Hampshire are subject to limitations on jurisdiction of two sorts. First, they cannot award judgments for large sums (the limit is $7,000). Second, they cannot adjudicate matters involving title to real estate. See N.H. Rev. Stat. §503:1. Most states limit the jurisdiction of small claims courts in similar ways.

(a) Should the fact that the small claims court could not enter judgment for more than $7,000 affect Shari Thielen? Usually, it is said that one who *chooses* small claims court, as opposed to a court of general jurisdiction, *waives* her right to collect more than the limit allows. If, contrary to the facts in Problem 14-B, Steven had destroyed items that Shari claimed as hers, and if she sought damages, it would make sense, wouldn't it, to say

that in choosing small claims court she waived her right to collect more than $7,000 for these items?

(b) Should the fact that the small claims court could not adjudicate title to property affect Shari Thielen? She could have brought her first suit in superior court, where she could have asked *both* for return of property and for a constructive trust to secure her "fair share" of the increased value of the house and parcel.

(c) Should Shari Thielen's case fit the "jurisdiction" exception described prior to Problem 14-A, set out in Restatement (Second) of Judgments §26(1)(c) (1982) (exception where plaintiff "was unable to rely on a certain theory" or "seek a certain remedy or form of relief" because of limitations on "subject matter jurisdiction"). You will encounter this exception again when you read the *Marrese* case.

2. Suppose Steven and Shari had been married, and when they parted company Shari brought suit to recover personal property in a New Hampshire court of general jurisdiction. Should we recognize an exception for interspousal suits?

(a) Nobody would say that Shari should be precluded from later seeking a divorce even if she had adequate ground for divorce when she filed suit to recover her property, and even if the reason for a divorce was disagreement over the property. One might argue that the "transaction" standard does not reach the matter of dissolution. One might also say that seeking a divorce is always an "extraordinary reason" to depart from the principle of claim preclusion, and an ongoing marriage is a "condition having a vital relation to personal liberty." Hence it fits the catchall exception described above. See Restatement (Second) of Judgments §26, Illustration 8 (1982) (wife who sues husband for separate maintenance based on desertion is not precluded from later seeking a divorce; it is unwise to force her "to demand the most drastic remedy" in first suit, and unwise to block a divorce if she is now "prepared to make the case for it") (offered as illustration of "extraordinary reason" category).

(b) Slightly more difficult are the cases in which the spouses divorce, and later one seeks damages for abuse occurring during the marriage. Should this situation too be exempt from issue preclusion arising from a divorce decree? Some courts allow splitting in this situation, but not all. Compare McNair v. McNair, 856 A.2d 5, 15 (N.H. 2004) (divorce decree does not preclude domestic violence claim) and Simmons v. Simmons, 773 P.2d 602 (Colo. App. 1998) (wife's assault and battery claim was not barred by prior divorce decree in which she did not bring counterclaim) and Delahunty v. Massachusetts Mutual Life Ins. Co., 674 A.2d 1290, 1296 (Conn. 1996) (in dissolution action, court considers conduct of parties, but judgment does not compensate spouse for injuries suffered during marriage; applying claim preclusion here would "create greater problems than it would solve") with Tevis v. Tevis, 400 A.2d 1189 (N.J. 1979) (tort claim, which could have been brought in wife's divorce suit, is barred). See also Dressler v. Morrison, 130 P.3d 978, 981 (Ariz. 2006) (claim preclusion does not bar later claims involving property rights not adjudicated in dissolution decree).

(c) Perhaps equally important, dissolutions of marriage often bring issues relating to children and support obligations that change over time and must be revisited. See, e.g., Restatement (Second) of Judgments §13, Comment c (1982) (while judgment granting continuing relief has *res judicata effect*, changed circumstances may make it "too burdensome or otherwise inapposite," and usually a party may "apply to the rendering court for a modification"); Spiker v. Spiker, 708 N.W.2d 347 (Iowa 2006) (*res judicata* did not bar mother's attempt to modify grandparent visitation decree; fact that law was declared unconstitutional constituted an important change in circumstance).

(d) Even if interspousal suits should not receive quite the same *res judicata* effect as judgments in other suits, they merit *res judicata* effect in many circumstances. See, e.g., McElroy v. Kennedy, 74 P.3d 903 (Alaska 2003) (claim preclusive effect of earlier child support litigation barred father's suit seeking reimbursement of support, based on genetic tests proving he was not the biological father). See also Restatement (Second) of Judgments §31 (dealing with judgments determining status, including divorce, annulment, adoption, revocation of citizenship, appointment of guardian, and other matters).

3. Declaratory judgment suits enable a party to seek the help of a court in sorting out her rights and responsibilities with respect to another party. Thus, for example, the owner of a landlocked parcel might claim to be entitled to drive over her neighbor's adjacent parcel to reach the nearest public thoroughfare. If the neighbor objects and denies that such right exists, the landlocked owner may want to bring a declaratory judgment suit to establish her right. Should she be required at the same time to seek injunctive relief or damages for acts by her neighbor denying passage in the past? The usual answer is no: Under the prevailing rule, one who seeks a declaratory judgment is *not* required also to seek injunctive or other relief, and one who prevails in a declaratory judgment suit may bring a later suit for further relief, "even in an action on the same claim which prompted the [prior] action for a declaratory judgment." See Restatement (Second) of Judgments §33, Comment c (1982). See also Andrew Robinson International, Inc. v. Hartford Fire Insurance Co., 547 F.3d 48 (1st Cir. 2008) (building occupant's suit for declaratory judgment that "lead-laden dust" was *not* excepted from coverage as "pollutant" did not foreclose later suit alleging that insurer's "stonewalling" constituted unfair and deceptive trade practice and seeking treble damages).

(a) Why have this exception? See generally Andrew Robinson International, Inc. v. Hartford Fire Insurance Co., 547 F.3d 48 (1st Cir. 2008) (most jurisdictions favor limited preclusive effect for declaratory judgment suits, which conserves judicial resources and lets courts clarify legal relationships before they are disturbed and thrust into full-blown litigation).

(b) Would it make sense to extend this exception to contract litigation? See, e.g., D'Allessandro v. Wassel, 587 A.2d 724 (Pa. 1991) (prior suit for specific performance did not require plaintiff to join claims in fraud and misrepresentation, which could be advanced later).

(c) Suppose, in our suit by the landlocked owner for a declaration of right to drive over an adjacent parcel, the defending party could bring a claim for trespass. If the trespass claim fits the compulsory counterclaim rule, must it be brought or lost forever? Recall that FRCP 13(b) requires counterclaims arising out of the same transaction to be brought, or they are lost. See Allan Block Corp. v. County Materials Corp., 512 F.3d 912, 916-917 (7th Cir. 2008) (excusing defendant in declaratory judgment suit from filing counterclaim arising out of same transaction; if defendant had to bring such counterclaims, declaratory judgment suits "would become devices for thwarting the choice of forum by the defendant").

(d) The declaratory judgment exception is not as broad as one might imagine. Suppose, for example, the landlocked neighbor *loses* her suit for declaratory relief because the court concludes that she is *not* entitled to pass over her neighbor's parcel to get to the nearest road. Even though *claim* preclusion does not apply, *issue* preclusion ("collateral estoppel") does apply, and a later suit seeking damages or an injunction is likely to be unsuccessful because the issues on which plaintiff must prevail have been resolved.

(e) Should the exception apply if plaintiff seeks not only a declaratory judgment, but additional relief, like an injunction? See, e.g., Sebra v. Wentworth, 990 A.2d 538 (Me. 2010) (in landowner's suit against landlocked neighbor for trespass, landlocked neighbor's prior suit seeking declaratory and injunctive relief barred its counterclaim in this suit seeking easement by necessity; declaratory suit exception did *not* apply; prior suit sought more than declaratory relief). See also Giannone v. York Tape & Label, Inc., 548 F.3d 191 (2d Cir. 2008) (after obtaining declaration that noncompetition covenant was unenforceable, and injunction barring enforcement, plaintiff could not bring new suit for damages based on covenant).

4. The fourth exception, recognized in Restatement (Second) of Judgments §26(1)(d), allows splitting where requiring all claims to be made at once would be inconsistent with the "sense of [a statutory] scheme." To some extent, declaratory judgment suits fit this category, but a more powerful example is the unlawful detainer suit, which allows an owner or landlord to evict a tenant summarily, and in this situation it is usually said that suits for unpaid rent and damage to the premises can be brought later. See, e.g., Jackson v. U.S. Postal Service, 799 F.3d 1018 (5th Cir. 1986) (it is not disputed that if plaintiff's unlawful detainer suit had not been removed, plaintiffs "could have filed a second suit in state court to recover the unpaid rent") (in this removed suit, plaintiff can obtain injunctive relief "on an expedited basis" and can then take up claims for unpaid rent).

5. Consider cases of continuing or recurrent wrongs, which comprise the fifth exception in Restatement (Second) of Judgments §26(1)(e). Where, for example, a contract contemplates an ongoing relationship in which performance produces an obligation on the other side to pay, as might happen where an insurance agent earns commissions for signing customers or obtaining renewals, it is usually said that a claimant may sue for payments due up to the time of filing, and may separately sue thereafter to enforce later-accruing obligations. See, e.g., Wilson v. Western Alliance Corp., 715 P.2d 1344, 1346 (Or. App. 1986) (rule against splitting does not prevent "successive actions for successive breaches" if contract has not been terminated on account of breach). The Restatement cites the example of one who maintains a structure on his land that causes ongoing harm: Here plaintiff "must claim all damages suffered to the time of suit," although some jurisdictions distinguish between "temporary" and "permanent" nuisances, requiring but one suit in the latter category, and putting plaintiff at risk of improperly splitting claims if he misjudges the case and brings several suits. See Restatement (Second) of Judgments §26, Comment h (1982). There are other pitfalls, as courts disagree on plaintiff's obligation if defendant resumes or continues the conduct that gave rise to the suit. In such cases, must plaintiff amend to add new allegations or broaden the suit?

(a) Some cases recognize a duty to amend. See Buck v. Thomas M. Cooley Law School, 597 F.3d 812, 817 (6th Cir. 2010) (after losing state claims based on alleged disabilities, federal claims in federal court were barred even though they occurred after plaintiff filed state claims; state law required her to "supplement her complaint with related factual allegations that develop 'during the pendency of' her state suit or have them barred by res judicata"); Dubuc v. Green Oak Township, 312 F.3d 736, 750-751 (6th Cir. 2006) (victim of ongoing retaliation may file multiple suits; if retaliation persists after the first, *res judicata* would not apply; if further misconduct "occurs before adjudication on the merits of the initial suit," however, claimant "is obliged to amend his or her initial complaint," and cannot "continue to relitigate the same issue" by "merely positing a few additional facts") (if ongoing conduct "is actually the defendant continuing on the same course" that a court previously found proper, later court "must conclude that the plaintiff is simply trying to relitigate the same claim").

(b) Others come out the other way, indicating that plaintiff need not amend to add claims arising out of post-filing behavior, see Smith v. Potter, 513 F.3d 781, 783 (7th Cir. 2008) (*res judicata* "does not bar a suit based on claims that accrue after a previous suit was filed"); Hatch v. Boulder Town Council, 471 F.3d 1142, 1148 (10th Cir. 2006) (state preclusion law only requires plaintiff to include facts known at time of filing; for *res judicata* purposes only those count in deciding whether second suit can be brought); Mitchell v. City of Moore, Oklahoma, 218 F.3d 1190, 1202 (10th Cir. 2000) ("all claims arising from the same employment relationship constitute the same transaction or series of transactions," but claim preclusion "does not necessarily bar plaintiffs from litigating claims based on conduct that occurred after the initial complaint was filed") (plaintiffs have no obligation to expand suits to add claims that did not exist at time of filing).

6. Finally, consider the sixth exception, where some "extraordinary reason" justifies departing from claim preclusion, or where a suit fails to yield "a coherent disposition" of a controversy. In fact, this exception is rare in practice, although the other part of the exception (referring to the invalidity of "a continuing restraint" having a vital relation to personal liberty has traction in the domestic relation cases described above). Consider these situations:

(a) Seven plaintiffs sue a department store for antitrust violations, but lose because the court concludes under current doctrine that the antitrust laws protect commercial interests but not consumer interests. Five plaintiffs appeal, but two others do not and instead file a second suit. The five appellants prevail, and the reviewing court holds that antitrust law has changed and does allow consumers to recover. Should we make an exception to the doctrine of claim preclusion to allow the two nonappealing plaintiffs, who have filed their own second suit, to proceed? See Federated Department Stores, Inc. v. Moitie, 452 U.S. 394 (1981) (rejecting Ninth Circuit's conclusion that "simple justice" requires exception; simple justice is achieved "when a complex body of law developed over a period of years is evenhandedly applied," and *res judicata* "serves vital public interests beyond any individual judge's ad hoc determination of the equities in a particular case"). But see Pierce v. Morrison Mahoney LLP, 897 N.E.2d 562, 573 (Mass. 2008) (declining to accord *offensive* issue preclusive effect on issue that was "essentially legal," where original proceedings involved arbitration and second gave opportunity for appellate court to address the issue) (according *res judicata* effect would inappropriately foreclose opportunity to reconsider issue).

(b) In a classic case, A contracted to sell a farm to B by warranty deed to be signed also by A's wife (her signature releasing dower rights). B went into possession, but A's wife refused to sign. B brought suit against A seeking specific performance in the form of a deed signed by A alone, with allowance for dower rights. A answered and counterclaimed for rescission. The court denied both B's requested relief and A's counterclaim. B remained in possession and refused to make payments. A sued to eject B, who counterclaimed for specific performance, tendering the balance of the price and seeking a deed signed by A alone, with adjustment for dower rights. Both parties invoked *res judicata*. The Illinois Supreme Court concluded that claim preclusion does not apply. See Adams v. Pearson, 104 N.E.2d 267 (Ill. 1952) (in this "unique and nonrecurrent situation," claim preclusion would produce "an unsatisfactory and perhaps inequitable result" and the equities were with B; remanding with direction to enter judgment on B's counterclaim). The Restatement cites *Adams* as authority for §26(a)(1)(f) (exception for judgment that does not yield "a coherent disposition").

(c) In contrast to *Adams* is another classic decision refusing to make an exception to *res judicata* despite a conflicted outcome. In Reed v. Allen, 286 U.S. 191 (1932), an interpleader suit naming D and E as rival claimants to rents due under a lease led to judgment favoring D on the basis of a clause in a will

interpreted as giving D title to the property. D then sued to eject E and prevailed on the basis of the judgment in the interpleader suit. E had taken an appeal in the interpleader suit, and won a reversal. E then sued D, seeking possession of the property. The Supreme Court concluded, however, that E was bound by the judgment in the ejectment suit. The result was that E was entitled to the rent (having won the reversal of the judgment in the interpleader suit), but D was in possession. The Court in *Moitie* cited *Reed* in support of its conclusion that preclusion law is important, and that it justifies allowing claimants who do not appeal from an adverse judgment to continue to be bound by it, even though similarly situated claimants prevail on appeal.

C CLAIM PRECLUSION IN A FEDERAL SYSTEM

In a federal system, we encounter both "vertical" and "horizontal" issues in connection with recognition of judgments. In the vertical dimension, we have issues relating to recognition in federal court of state judgments and recognition in state court of federal judgments. In the horizontal dimension, we have issues relating to recognition, in the courts of one state, of judgments by courts in another state. And both vertical and horizontal issues can appear in a single case, as happens when a federal court in one part of the country is asked to recognize a judgment rendered by a state court in another part of the country.

Both the Constitution and a federal statute bear on these problems. Under Article IV of the Constitution, "Full Faith and Credit shall be given in each State to the public Acts, Records, and judicial proceedings of every other State." (Congress is also given power "by general Laws" to "prescribe the Manner" of recognition.) And 28 USC §1738, carrying out the power conferred by the Constitution, provides that the "judicial proceedings" of every state court "shall have the same full faith and credit in every court" in the United States "as they have by law or usage in the courts of [the rendering] State." In other words, the judgment of a Florida court is entitled to the same "full faith and credit" in a state court in Nebraska or in any other state, and in any federal court anywhere in the country, as the judgment of the Florida court would have in Florida.

You are about to read two cases that can fairly be described as bewildering. But before you venture into the forest and encounter this bewilderment, bear in mind two wonderfully simple points that you might otherwise miss. First, as *Marrese* will tell you, state law determines the claim preclusive effect of a state court judgment. Second, as *Semtek* will tell you, federal law determines the claim preclusive effect of a federal court judgment. Hold on to these points.

1. Effects of State Court Judgments

MARRESE v. AMERICAN ACADEMY OF ORTHOPAEDIC SURGEONS

Supreme Court of the United States
470 U.S. 373 (1985)

Justice O'CONNOR delivered the opinion of the Court.

This case concerns the preclusive effect of a state court judgment in a subsequent lawsuit involving federal antitrust claims within the exclusive jurisdiction of the federal courts. The Court of Appeals for the Seventh Circuit, sitting en banc, held as a matter of federal law that the earlier state court judgments barred the federal antitrust suit. Under 28 USC §1738, a federal court generally is required to consider first the law of the State in which the judgment was rendered to determine its preclusive effect. Because the lower courts did not consider state preclusion law in this case, we reverse and remand.

I

Petitioners are board-certified orthopedic surgeons who applied for membership in respondent American Academy of Orthopaedic Surgeons (Academy). Respondent denied the membership applications without providing a hearing or a statement of reasons. In November 1976, petitioner Dr. Treister filed suit in the Circuit Court of Cook County, State of Illinois, alleging that the denial of membership in the Academy violated associational rights protected by Illinois common law. Petitioner Dr. Marrese separately filed a similar action in state court. Neither petitioner alleged a violation of state antitrust law in his state court action; nor did either petitioner contemporaneously file a federal antitrust suit. The Illinois Appellate Court ultimately held that Dr. Treister's complaint failed to state a cause of action, and the Illinois Supreme Court denied leave to appeal. After the Appellate Court ruled against Dr. Treister, the Circuit Court dismissed Dr. Marrese's complaint.

In March 1980, petitioners filed a federal antitrust suit in the United States District Court for the Northern District of Illinois based on the same events underlying their unsuccessful state court actions. As amended, the complaint alleged that respondent Academy possesses monopoly power, that petitioners were denied membership in order to discourage competition, and that their exclusion constituted a boycott in violation of §1 of the Sherman Act, 15 USC §1. Respondent filed a motion to dismiss arguing that claim preclusion barred the federal antitrust claim because the earlier state court actions concerned the same facts and were dismissed with prejudice.[1] In denying this motion, the District Court reasoned that state courts lack jurisdiction over federal antitrust claims, and therefore a state court judgment cannot have claim preclusive effect in a subsequent federal antitrust suit. Discovery began and respondent refused to allow petitioners access to certain files relating to membership applications. After respondent persisted in this refusal despite a discovery order, the District Court held respondent in criminal contempt.

The judgment of contempt was reversed by a divided panel of the Court of Appeals in an opinion holding that the District Judge had abused his discretion by authorizing discovery of the membership files and also suggesting that the federal action was barred by claim preclusion and that the antitrust claims were groundless. . . .

III

The issue presented by this case is whether a state court judgment may have preclusive effect on a federal antitrust claim that could not have been raised in the state proceeding. Although federal antitrust claims are within the exclusive jurisdiction of the federal courts, the Court of Appeals ruled that the dismissal of petitioners' complaints in state court barred them from bringing a claim based on the same facts under the Sherman Act. The Court of Appeals erred by suggesting that in these circumstances a federal court should determine the preclusive effect of a state court judgment without regard to the law of the State in which judgment was rendered.

The preclusive effect of a state court judgment in a subsequent federal lawsuit generally is determined by the full faith and credit statute, which provides that state judicial proceedings "shall have the same full faith and credit in every court within the United States . . . as they have by law or usage in the courts of such State . . . from which they are taken." 28 USC §1738. This statute directs a federal court to refer to the preclusion law of the State in which judgment was rendered. "It has long been established that §1738 does not allow federal courts to employ their own rules of res judicata in determining the effect of state judgments. Rather, it goes beyond the common law and commands a federal court to accept the rules chosen by the State from which the judgment is taken." Kremer v. Chemical Construction Corp., 456 U.S. 461, 481-482 (1982); see also Allen v. McCurry, 449 U.S. 90, 96 (1980). Section 1738 embodies concerns of comity and federalism that allow the States to determine, subject to the requirements of the statute and the Due Process

---

[1] In this opinion we use the term "claim preclusion" to refer to "res judicata" in a narrow sense, *i.e.,* the preclusive effect of a judgment in foreclosing litigation of matters that should have been raised in an earlier suit. In contrast, we use the term "issue preclusion" to refer to the effect of a judgment in foreclosing relitigation of a matter that has been litigated and decided. See Migra v. Warren City School Dist. Bd. of Ed., 465 U.S. 75, 77, n.1 (1984).

Clause, the preclusive effect of judgments in their own courts. See *Kremer. Cf.* Riley v. New York Trust Co., 315 U.S. 343, 349 (1942) (discussing preclusive effect of state judgment in proceedings in another State).

The fact that petitioners' antitrust claim is within the exclusive jurisdiction of the federal courts does not necessarily make §1738 inapplicable to this case. Our decisions indicate that a state court judgment may in some circumstances have preclusive effect in a subsequent action within the exclusive jurisdiction of the federal courts. Without discussing §1738, this Court has held that the issue preclusive effect of a state court judgment barred a subsequent patent suit that could not have been brought in state court. Becher v. Contoure Laboratories, Inc., 279 U.S. 388 (1929). Moreover, *Kremer* held that §1738 applies to a claim of employment discrimination under Title VII of the Civil Rights Act of 1964, although the Court expressly declined to decide whether Title VII claims can be brought only in federal courts. *Kremer* implies that absent an exception to §1738, state law determines at least the issue preclusive effect of a prior state judgment in a subsequent action involving a claim within the exclusive jurisdiction of the federal courts.

More generally, *Kremer* indicates that §1738 requires a federal court to look first to state preclusion law in determining the preclusive effects of a state court judgment. *Cf.* Haring v. Prosise, 462 U.S. 306, 314 & n.8 (1983); Smith, Full Faith and Credit and Section 1983: A Reappraisal, 63 N.C. L. Rev. 59, 110-111 (1984). The Court's analysis in *Kremer* began with the finding that state law would in fact bar relitigation of the discrimination issue decided in the earlier state proceedings. That finding implied that the plaintiff could not relitigate the same issue in federal court unless some exception to §1738 applied. *Kremer* observed that "an exception to §1738 will not be recognized unless a later statute contains an express or implied repeal." Title VII does not expressly repeal §1738, and the Court concluded that the statutory provisions and legislative history do not support a finding of implied repeal. We conclude that the basic approach adopted in *Kremer* applies in a lawsuit involving a claim within the exclusive jurisdiction of the federal courts.

To be sure, a state court will not have occasion to address the specific question whether a state judgment has issue or claim preclusive effect in a later action that can be brought only in federal court. Nevertheless, a federal court may rely in the first instance on state preclusion principles to determine the extent to which an earlier state judgment bars subsequent litigation. *Cf.* FDIC v. Eckhardt, 691 F.2d 245, 247-248 (6th Cir. 1982) (applying state law to determine preclusive effect on claim within concurrent jurisdiction of state and federal courts). *Kremer* illustrates that a federal court can apply state rules of issue preclusion to determine if a matter actually litigated in state court may be relitigated in a subsequent federal proceeding.

With respect to matters that were not decided in the state proceedings, we note that claim preclusion generally does not apply where "[t]he plaintiff was unable to rely on a certain theory of the case or to seek a certain remedy because of the limitations on the subject matter jurisdiction of the courts...." Restatement (Second) of Judgments §26(1)(c) (1982). If state preclusion law includes this requirement of prior jurisdictional competency, which is generally true, a state judgment will *not* have claim preclusive effect on a cause of action within the exclusive jurisdiction of the federal courts. Even in the event that a party asserting the affirmative defense of claim preclusion can show that state preclusion rules in some circumstances bar a claim outside the jurisdiction of the court that rendered the initial judgment, the federal court should first consider whether application of the state rules would bar the particular federal claim.[2]

Reference to state preclusion law may make it unnecessary to determine if the federal court, as an exception to §1738, should refuse to give preclusive effect to a state court judgment. The issue whether there is an exception to §1738 arises only if state law indicates that litigation of a particular claim or issue should be barred in the subsequent federal proceeding. To the extent that state preclusion law indicates that a judgment normally does not have claim preclusive effect as to matters that the court lacked jurisdiction to entertain, lower courts and commentators have correctly concluded that a state court judgment does not bar a subsequent federal antitrust claim. Unless application of Illinois preclusion law suggests, contrary to the usual view, that petitioners' federal antitrust claim is somehow barred, there will be no need to decide in this case if there is an exception to §1738.[3]

---

[2] Our analysis does not necessarily suggest that the Court of Appeals for the Fourth Circuit erred in its holding in Nash County Board of Education v. Biltmore Co., 640 F.2d 484 (4th Cir. 1981), *cert. denied,* 454 U.S. 878 (1981). The Court of Appeals there applied federal preclusion principles to conclude that a state judgment approving settlement of state antitrust claims barred a subsequent federal antitrust claim. Although our decision today indicates that the Court of Appeals should have looked in the first instance to state law to determine the preclusive effect of the state judgment, the same holding would result if application of state preclusion law suggests that the settlement bars the subsequent federal claim and if there is no exception to §1738 in these circumstances. Cf. 640 F.2d, at 487, n.5 (noting that state law gives preclusive effect to consent judgment). We, of course, do not address those issues here.

[3] The Chief Justice notes that preclusion rules bar the splitting of a cause of action between a court of limited jurisdiction and one of general jurisdiction, and suggests that state requirements of jurisdictional competency may leave unclear whether a state court action precludes a subsequent federal antitrust claim. The rule that the judgment of a court of limited jurisdiction concludes the entire claim assumes that the plaintiff might have commenced his action in a court *in the same system of courts* that was competent to give full relief. See Restatement (Second) of Judgments §24, Comment *g* (1982). Moreover, the jurisdictional competency requirement generally is understood to imply that state court litigation based on a state statute analogous to a federal statute, *e.g.,* a state antitrust law, does not bar subsequent attempts to secure relief in federal court if the state court lacked jurisdiction over the federal statutory claim. *Id.,* §26(1)(c), Illustration 2. Although a particular State's preclusion principles conceivably could support a rule similar to that proposed by the Chief Justice, where state preclusion rules do not indicate that a claim is barred, we do not believe that federal courts should fashion a federal rule to preclude a claim that could not have been raised in the state proceedings.

The Court of Appeals did not apply the approach to §1738 that we have outlined. Both the plurality opinion and an opinion concurring in part express the view that §1738 allows a federal court to give a state court judgment greater preclusive effect than the state courts themselves would give to it. This proposition, however, was rejected by Migra v. Warren City School Dist. Bd. of Ed., 465 U.S. 75 (1984), a case decided shortly after the Court of Appeals announced its decision in the instant case. In *Migra,* a discharged schoolteacher filed suit under 42 USC §1983 in federal court after she prevailed in state court on a contract claim involving the same underlying events. The Federal District Court dismissed the §1983 action as barred by claim preclusion. The opinion of this Court emphasized that under §1738, state law determined the preclusive effect of the state judgment. Because it was unclear from the record whether the District Court's ruling was based on state preclusion law, we remanded for clarification on this point. Such a remand obviously would have been unnecessary were a federal court free to give greater preclusive effect to a state court judgment than would the judgment-rendering State.

We are unwilling to create a special exception to §1738 for federal antitrust claims that would give state court judgments greater preclusive effect than would the courts of the State rendering the judgment. *Cf.* Haring v. Prosise (refusing to create special preclusion rule for §1983 claim subsequent to plaintiff's guilty plea). The plurality opinion for the Court of Appeals relied on Federated Department Stores, Inc. v. Moitie, 452 U.S. 394 (1981), to observe that the doctrine of claim preclusion protects defendants from repetitive lawsuits based on the same conduct, and that there is a practical need to require plaintiffs "to litigate their claims in an economical and parsimonious fashion." We agree that these are valid and important concerns, and we note that under §1738 state issue preclusion law may promote the goals of repose and conservation of judicial resources by preventing the relitigation of certain issues in a subsequent federal proceeding. See *Kremer* (state judgment barred subsequent Title VII action in federal court).

If we had a single system of courts and our only concerns were efficiency and finality, it might be desirable to fashion claim preclusion rules that would require a plaintiff to bring suit initially in the forum of most general jurisdiction, thereby resolving as many issues as possible in one proceeding. See Restatement (Second) of Judgments §24, Comment *g* (1982). The decision of the Court of Appeals approximates such a rule inasmuch as it encourages plaintiffs to file suit initially in federal district court and to attempt to bring any state law claims pendent to their federal antitrust claims. Whether this result would reduce the overall burden of litigation is debatable, and we decline to base our interpretation of §1738 on our opinion on this question.

More importantly, we have parallel systems of state and federal courts, and the concerns of comity reflected in §1738 generally allow States to determine the preclusive scope of their own courts' judgments. See *Kremer, supra;*

Allen v. McCurry; *cf.* Currie, Res Judicata: The Neglected Defense, 45 U. Chi. L. Rev. 317, 327 (1978) (state policies may seek to limit preclusive effect of state court judgment). These concerns certainly are not made less compelling because state courts lack jurisdiction over federal antitrust claims. We therefore reject a judicially created exception to §1738 that effectively holds as a matter of federal law that a plaintiff can bring state law claims initially in state court only at the cost of forgoing subsequent federal antitrust claims. Federated Department Stores, Inc. v. Moitie does not suggest a contrary conclusion. That case did not involve §1738; rather it held that "accepted principles of res judicata" determine the preclusive effect of a federal court judgment.

In this case the Court of Appeals should have first referred to Illinois law to determine the preclusive effect of the state judgment. Only if state law indicates that a particular claim or issue would be barred, is it necessary to determine if an exception to §1738 should apply. Although for purposes of this case, we need not decide if such an exception exists for federal antitrust claims, we observe that the more general question is whether the concerns underlying a particular grant of exclusive jurisdiction justify a finding of an implied partial repeal of §1738. Resolution of this question will depend on the particular federal statute as well as the nature of the claim or issue involved in the subsequent federal action. Our previous decisions indicate that the primary consideration must be the intent of Congress. See *Kremer, supra* (finding no congressional intent to depart from §1738 for purposes of Title VII); *cf.* Brown v. Felsen, 442 U.S. 127, 138 (1979) (finding congressional intent that state judgments would not have claim preclusive effect on dischargeability issue in bankruptcy).

IV

The decisions below did not consider Illinois preclusion law in their discussion of the claim preclusion issue. The District Court relied on federal law to conclude that the state judgments did not bar the claims under the Sherman Act. Similarly, the plurality opinion of the Court of Appeals did not discuss Illinois principles of claim preclusion. Although an opinion concurring in part also concluded that petitioners' antitrust claim was barred as a matter of federal law, it did suggest that this conclusion was consistent with Illinois law. A dissenting opinion vigorously argued that principles of Illinois claim preclusion law did not require dismissal of the federal antitrust claims. Before this Court, the parties have continued to disagree about the content of Illinois preclusion law. We believe that this dispute is best resolved in the first instance by the District Court. *Cf.* Migra v. Warren City School Dist. Bd. of Ed.

Petitioners also urge us to reverse the decision of the Court of Appeals with respect to the contempt order. We specifically declined to grant certiorari on questions related to the discovery order or the subsequent contempt order, and we do not address those issues here.

The judgment of the Court of Appeals is reversed, and the case is remanded for further proceedings consistent with this opinion.

It is so ordered.

Justice BLACKMUN and Justice STEVENS took no part in the consideration or decision of this case.

Chief Justice BURGER, concurring in the judgment.

I agree with the Court's implicit conclusion that the Court of Appeals approached 28 USC §1738 too narrowly and technically by holding it irrelevant on the ground that Illinois law does not address the preclusive effect of a state court judgment on a federal antitrust suit. In the circumstances presented by this case, a fair reading of §1738 requires federal courts to look first to general principles of state preclusion law. Those principles control if they clearly establish that the state court judgment does not bar the later federal action: Only recently, we reaffirmed in Migra v. Warren City School District Board of Education, 465 U.S. 75 (1984), that a federal court is not free to accord greater preclusive effect to a state court judgment than the state courts themselves would give to it.

The Court now remands with directions for the District Court to consider Illinois claim preclusion law, but no guidance is given as to how the District Court should proceed if it finds state law silent or indeterminate on the claim preclusion question. The Court's refusal to acknowledge this potential problem appears to stem from a belief that the jurisdictional competency requirement of res judicata doctrine will dispose of most cases like this.

I cannot agree with the Court's interpretation of the jurisdictional competency requirement. If state law provides a cause of action that is virtually identical with a federal statutory cause of action, a plaintiff suing in state court is able to rely on the same theory of the case and obtain the same remedy as would be available in federal court, even when the plaintiff cannot expressly invoke the federal statute because it is within the exclusive jurisdiction of the federal courts. In this situation, the jurisdictional competency requirement is effectively satisfied. Therefore, the fact that state law recognizes the jurisdictional competency requirement does not necessarily imply that a state court judgment has no claim preclusive effect on a cause of action within exclusive federal jurisdiction.

The states that recognize the jurisdictional competency requirement do not all define it in the same terms. Illinois courts have expressed the doctrine in the following manner: "The principle [of res judicata] extends not only to questions which were actually litigated but also to all *questions* which *could have been raised* or determined." Spiller v. Continental Tube Co., 447 N.E.2d

834, 838 (Ill. 1983) (emphasis added). In the present case, each petitioner could have alleged a cause of action under the Illinois Antitrust Act, in his prior state court lawsuit against respondent. The principles of Illinois res judicata doctrine appear to be indeterminate as to whether petitioners' ability to raise state antitrust claims in their prior state court suits should preclude their assertion of essentially the same claims in the present federal action. This indeterminacy arises from the fact that the Illinois courts have not addressed whether the notion of "questions which could have been raised" should be applied narrowly or broadly. No Illinois court has considered how the jurisdictional competency requirement should apply in the type of situation presented by this case, where the same theory of recovery may be asserted under different statutes. Nor has any Illinois court considered whether res judicata precludes splitting a cause of action between a court of limited jurisdiction and one of general jurisdiction.[3]

Hence it is likely that the principles of Illinois claim preclusion law do not speak to the preclusive effect that petitioners' state court judgments should have on the present action. In this situation, it may be consistent with §1738 for a federal court to formulate a federal rule to resolve the matter. If state law is simply indeterminate, the concerns of comity and federalism underlying §1738 do not come into play. At the same time, the federal courts have direct interests in ensuring that their resources are used efficiently and not as a means of harassing defendants with repetitive lawsuits, as well as in ensuring that parties asserting federal rights have an adequate opportunity to litigate those rights. Given the insubstantiality of the state interests and the weight of the federal interests, a strong argument could be made that a federal rule would be more appropriate than a creative interpretation of ambiguous state law.[4] When state law is

---

[3] Compare Restatement (Second) of Judgments §24, Comment *g*, Illustration 14 (1982):

> In an automobile collision, A is injured and his car damaged as a result of the negligence of B. Instead of suing in a court of general jurisdiction of the state, A brings his action for the damage to his car in a justice's court, which has jurisdiction in actions for damage to property but has no jurisdiction in actions for injury to the person. Judgment is rendered for A for the damage to the car. A cannot thereafter maintain an action against B to recover for the injury to his person arising out of the same collision.

See also 18 C. Wright, A. Miller, & E. Cooper, Federal Practice and Procedure §4412, p. 95 (1981), stating that the "general rule" in state courts is that "[a] second action will not be permitted on parts of a single claim that could have been asserted in a court of broader jurisdiction simply because the plaintiff went first to a court of limited jurisdiction in the same state that could not hear them." The holding in Lucas v. Le Compte, 42 Ill. 303 (1866), is similar to this "general rule," but that holding was based on a construction of an Illinois statute which (a) has been repealed and (b) had a broader preclusive effect than general Illinois res judicata doctrine has. Clancey v. McBride, 169 N.E. 729 (Ill. 1929), involved the same circumstances as the above-quoted illustration from the Restatement. The court resolved the case, however, without reference to the limited jurisdiction of the justice's court, by concluding that injury to the person and injury to property are distinct legal wrongs that can be the subject of separate lawsuits.

[4] By contrast, when a federal court construes substantive rights and obligations under state law in the context of a diversity action, the federal interest is insignificant and the state's interest is much more direct than it is in the present situation, even if the relevant state law is ambiguous.

indeterminate or ambiguous, a clear federal rule would promote substantive interests as well: "Uncertainty intrinsically works to defeat the opportunities for repose and reliance sought by the rules of preclusion, and confounds the desire for efficiency by inviting repetitious litigation to test the preclusive effects of the first effort." 18 C. Wright, A. Miller, & E. Cooper, *supra,* n.3, §4407.

A federal rule might be fashioned from the test, which this Court has applied in other contexts, that a party is precluded from asserting a claim that he had a "full and fair opportunity" to litigate in a prior action. See, *e.g.,* Kremer v. Chemical Construction Corp., 456 U.S. 461, 485 (1982); Allen v. McCurry, 449 U.S. 90, 95 (1980); Montana v. United States, 440 U.S. 147, 153 (1979); Blonder-Tongue Laboratories, Inc. v. University of Illinois Foundation, 402 U.S. 313, 328 (1971). Thus, if a state statute is identical in all material respects with a federal statute within exclusive federal jurisdiction, a party's ability to assert a claim under the state statute in a prior state court action might be said to have provided, in effect, a "full and fair opportunity" to litigate his rights under the federal statute.

The Court will eventually have to face these questions; I would resolve them now.

■ NOTES ON THE PRECLUSIVE EFFECT OF STATE COURT JUDGMENTS

1. State preclusion law determines the effect of a judgment in state court. What could be simpler and more obvious? It would be strange, wouldn't it, if *federal* law determined the effect of a state court judgment? And it would be downright bizarre, wouldn't it, if the law of *some other state* determined the effect of a state court judgment—if, for example, Texas law determined the effect of the judgment of an Illinois state court? So where we end up is sensible: The effect of a judgment is determined by the law of the jurisdiction that rendered the judgment.

2. In a federal system, however, things are not so simple. The question in *Marrese* was what effect a state court judgment should have on a *federal question* claim. This question arises in a federal system because federal and state law can both apply to the same transaction, and because state courts have concurrent jurisdiction over many federal claims. Recall that the "default" rule is that federal claims *can* be brought in state court unless Congress says otherwise (Chapter 4B): Often, then, state courts may—indeed *must*—hear federal question claims. But in *Marrese,* the question which law determines the effect of the Illinois judgment is made harder by the fact that the federal claims in question—the ones sought to be barred by the state court judgment against the plaintiff—are in the small category of claims that *could never be litigated* in state court. Hence the question: Does the judgment against Marrese on his state claims bar his later suit in federal court on federal claims that he could not have raised in the state suit?

(a) The Court doesn't answer this question, does it? The Court *does* say that Illinois law is the place to look for the answer. When the case returns to the Seventh Circuit, and the judge looks to Illinois law for an answer, what do you suppose she will find? Will there be an Illinois decision that a federal antitrust claim is barred by the loss in state court on state law claims?

(b) What *should be* the answer to the question whether Marrese's federal claim is barred by the loss suffered in the first suit?

(c) Chief Justice Burger thinks federal courts should formulate a federal rule to resolve the issue in *Marrese*. Is his argument convincing?

3. Because we are a federal system, in which the courts of each state are independent from the courts of other states, a judgment rendered in one state can become the basis for a suit in another. If, for example, plaintiff in Illinois wins an Illinois judgment against a person from Georgia, the Illinois plaintiff may seek enforcement of the Illinois judgment against property or assets of the defendant in Georgia. Many states allow a streamlined "registration" procedure, under which a judgment winner can register a judgment rendered by a court in another state (the Illinois judgment can be registered in Georgia), in a process that lets the defendant object in the new state that the rendering state lacked jurisdiction. See generally the Uniform Enforcement of Foreign Judgments Act, 13 ULA 261 et seq. (1986) (which has been adopted in 47 states). Other states expect the judgment holder to sue on the original judgment (a more elaborate process), but in either case the new state (Georgia, in our example) ultimately enters its own judgment on the basis of the original judgment (from Illinois, in our example). The new judgment then becomes the basis for levying on local assets of the debtor.

(a) Because debtors might have property in many states, it may even happen that the original judgment becomes the basis for multiple proceedings in other states. If, for example, the debtor has assets in Georgia, Florida, and Texas, the holder of an Illinois judgment might seek recognition of that judgment in the other three states. In our example, if the defendant did not appear in the Illinois suit, he may appear in later suits on the Illinois judgment and contest the jurisdiction of the Illinois court. If he appears in the Georgia suit and prevails on the claim that the Illinois court lacked jurisdiction, then judgment will *not* be entered in Georgia, and the Illinois suit is not entitled to full faith and credit. Suppose the plaintiff then sues in Florida. What should the Florida court do? See Walliser v. Hannig, 2009 WL 5125160 (7th Cir. 2009) (in this suit, plaintiff is barred by the judgment in the second suit, and cannot challenge the determination in that suit that the original judgment is *not* entitled to recognition).

(b) Because the world is an imperfect place, and courts can err, it is possible that Georgia might recognize the Illinois judgment but Florida might

not. If plaintiff then brings a fourth suit in Texas, what should the Texas court do? Follow the Georgia judgment (recognizing the Illinois judgment) or the Florida judgment (refusing recognition)? The answer is, follow the *most recent* decision. See Treinies v. Sunshine Mining Co., 308 U.S. 66 (1940). The rule is, when courts disagree on the recognition of a judgment, the last decision in time prevails. What can be said in favor of this approach? What against? See generally Ruth B. Ginsburg, *Judgments in Search of Full Faith and Credit: The Last-in-Time Rule for Conflicting Judgments*, 82 Harv. L. Rev. 798 (1969).

2. Effects of Federal Court Judgments

SEMTEK INTERNATIONAL v. LOCKHEED MARTIN CORPORATION

Supreme Court of the United States
531 U.S. 497 (2001)

Justice SCALIA delivered the opinion of the Court.

This case presents the question whether the claim-preclusive effect of a federal judgment dismissing a diversity action on statute-of-limitations grounds is determined by the law of the State in which the federal court sits.

I

Petitioner filed a complaint against respondent in California state court, alleging inducement of breach of contract and various business torts. Respondent removed the case to the United States District Court for the Central District of California on the basis of diversity of citizenship, see 28 USC §§1332, 1441, and successfully moved to dismiss petitioner's claims as barred by California's 2-year statute of limitations. In its order of dismissal, the District Court, adopting language suggested by respondent, dismissed petitioner's claims "in [their] entirety on the merits and with prejudice." Without contesting the District Court's designation of its dismissal as "on the merits," petitioner appealed to the Court of Appeals for the Ninth Circuit, which affirmed the District Court's order. Petitioner also brought suit against respondent in the State Circuit Court for Baltimore City, Maryland, alleging the same causes of action, which were not time barred under Maryland's 3-year statute of limitations. Respondent sought injunctive relief against this action from the California federal court under the All Writs Act, 28 USC §1651, and removed the action to the United States District Court for the District of Maryland on federal-question grounds (diversity grounds were not available because Lockheed "is a Maryland citizen," Semtek Int'l, Inc. v. Lockheed Martin Corp., 988 F. Supp. 913, 914 (1997)). The California federal court denied the relief requested, and the Maryland federal court remanded the case to state court because the federal question arose only by way of defense. Following a hearing, the Maryland state court granted respondent's motion to dismiss on the ground of res judicata. Petitioner then returned to the California federal court and the Ninth Circuit, unsuccessfully moving both courts to amend the former's earlier order so as to indicate that the dismissal was not "on the merits." Petitioner also appealed the Maryland trial court's order of dismissal to the Maryland Court of Special Appeals. The Court of Special Appeals affirmed, holding that, regardless of whether California would have accorded claim-preclusive effect to a statute-of-limitations dismissal by one of its own courts, the dismissal by the California federal court barred the complaint filed in Maryland, since the res judicata effect of federal diversity judgments is prescribed by federal law, under which the earlier dismissal was on the merits and claim preclusive. After the Maryland Court of Appeals declined to review the case, we granted certiorari.

II

Petitioner contends that the outcome of this case is controlled by *Dupasseur v. Rochereau*, 21 Wall. 130, 135 (1874), which held that the res judicata effect of a federal diversity judgment "is such as would belong to judgments of the State courts rendered under similar circumstances," and may not be accorded any "higher sanctity or effect." Since, petitioner argues, the dismissal of an action on statute-of-limitations grounds by a California state court would not be claim preclusive, it follows that the similar dismissal of this diversity action by the California federal court cannot be claim preclusive. While we agree that this would be the result demanded by *Dupasseur*, the case is not dispositive because it was decided under the Conformity Act of 1872, which required federal courts to apply the procedural law of the forum State in nonequity cases. That arguably affected the outcome of the case. See Restatement (Second) of Judgments §87, Comment *a*, p. 315 (1980) (hereinafter Restatement) ("Since procedural law largely determines the matters that may be adjudicated in an action, state law had to be considered in ascertaining the effect of a federal judgment").

   Respondent, for its part, contends that the outcome of this case is controlled by FRCP 41(b) [the Court quotes Rule]. Since the dismissal here did not "otherwise specif[y]" (indeed, it specifically stated that it *was* "on the merits"), and did not pertain to the excepted subjects of jurisdiction, venue, or joinder, it follows, respondent contends, that the dismissal "is entitled to claim preclusive effect."

   Implicit in this reasoning is the unstated minor premise that all judgments denominated "on the merits" are entitled to claim-preclusive effect. That premise is not necessarily valid. The original connotation of an "on the merits" adjudication is one that actually "pass[es] directly on the substance of [a particular] claim" before the court. Restatement §19, Comment *a*, at 161. That connotation remains common to every jurisdiction of which we are aware. . . . And it is, we think, the meaning intended in those many statements to the effect that a judgment "on the merits" triggers the doctrine of res judicata or claim preclusion. See, e.g., Parklane Hosiery Co. v. Shore, 439 U.S. 322, 326, n.5, (1979) ("Under the doctrine of res judicata, a judgment on the merits in a prior suit bars a second suit involving the same parties or their privies based on the same cause of action"); Goddard v. Security Title Ins. & Guarantee Co., 92 P.2d 804, 806 (Cal. 1939) ("[A] final judgment, rendered upon the merits by a court having jurisdiction of the cause . . . is a complete bar to a new suit between [the parties or their privies] on the same cause of action" (internal quotation marks and citations omitted)).

But over the years the meaning of the term "judgment on the merits" "has gradually undergone change," R. Marcus, M. Redish, & E. Sherman, Civil Procedure: A Modern Approach 1140-1141 (3d ed. 2000), and it has come to be applied to some judgments (such as the one involved here) that do *not* pass upon the substantive merits of a claim and hence do *not* (in many jurisdictions) entail claim-preclusive effect. [The Court cites cases that treat dismissals as bars to later suits when the dismissals rest on statutes of limitations or failure to state a claim.] That is why the Restatement of Judgments has abandoned the use of the term—"because of its possibly misleading connotations," Restatement §19, Comment *a*, at 161.

In short, it is no longer true that a judgment "on the merits" is necessarily a judgment entitled to claim-preclusive effect; and there are a number of reasons for believing that the phrase "adjudication upon the merits" does not bear that meaning in Rule 41(b). To begin with, Rule 41(b) sets forth nothing more than a default rule for determining the import of a dismissal (a dismissal is "upon the merits," with the three stated exceptions, unless the court "otherwise specifies"). This would be a highly peculiar context in which to announce a federally prescribed rule on the complex question of claim preclusion, saying in effect, "All federal dismissals (with three specified exceptions) preclude suit elsewhere, unless the court otherwise specifies."

And even apart from the purely default character of Rule 41(b), it would be peculiar to find a rule governing the effect that must be accorded federal judgments by other courts ensconced in rules governing the internal procedures of the rendering court itself. Indeed, such a rule would arguably violate the jurisdictional limitation of the Rules Enabling Act: that the Rules "shall not abridge, enlarge or modify any substantive right," 28 USC §2072(b). *Cf.* Ortiz v. Fibreboard Corp., 527 U.S. 815, 842 (1999) (adopting a "limiting construction" of FRCP 23(b)(1)(B) in order to "minimiz[e] potential conflict with the Rules Enabling Act, and [to] avoi[d] serious constitutional concerns"). In the present case, for example, if California law left petitioner free to sue on this claim in Maryland even after the California statute of limitations had expired, the federal court's extinguishment of that right (through Rule 41(b)'s mandated claim-preclusive effect of its judgment) would seem to violate this limitation.

Moreover, as so interpreted, the Rule would in many cases violate the federalism principle of Erie R. Co. v. Tompkins, 304 U.S. 64, 78-80 (1938), by engendering "'substantial' variations [in outcomes] between state and federal litigation" which would "[l]ikely ... influence the choice of a forum," [citing *Hanna* and *York*]. *Cf.* Walker v. Armco Steel Corp., 446 U.S. 740, 748-753 (1980). With regard to the claim-preclusion issue involved in the present case, for example, the traditional rule is that expiration of the applicable statute of limitations merely bars the remedy and does not extinguish the substantive right, so that dismissal on that ground does not have claim-preclusive effect in other jurisdictions with longer, unexpired limitations periods. See Restatement (Second) of Conflict of Laws §§142(2), 143 (1969); Restatement of Judgments §49, Comment *a* (1942). Out-of-state defendants sued on stale claims in California and in other States adhering to this traditional rule would systematically remove state-law suits brought against them to federal court—where, unless otherwise specified, a statute-of-limitations dismissal would bar suit everywhere.[1]

Finally, if Rule 41(b) did mean what respondent suggests, we would surely have relied upon it in our cases recognizing the claim-preclusive effect of federal judgments in federal-question cases. Yet for over half a century since the promulgation of Rule 41(b), we have not once done so.

We think the key to a more reasonable interpretation of the meaning of "operates as an adjudication upon the merits" in Rule 41(b) is to be found in Rule 41(a), which, in discussing the effect of voluntary dismissal by the plaintiff, makes clear that an "adjudication upon the merits" is the opposite of a "dismissal without prejudice" [the Court quotes Rule]. The primary meaning of "dismissal without prejudice," we think, is dismissal without barring the plaintiff from returning later, to the same court, with the same underlying claim. That will also ordinarily (though not always) have the consequence of not barring the claim from *other* courts, but its primary meaning relates to the dismissing court itself. Thus, Black's Law Dictionary (7th ed. 1999) defines "dismissed without prejudice" as "removed from the court's docket in such a way that the plaintiff may refile the same suit on the same claim," and defines "dismissal without prejudice" as "[a] dismissal that does not bar the plaintiff from refiling the lawsuit within the applicable limitations period."

We think, then, that the effect of the "adjudication upon the merits" default provision of Rule 41(b)—and, presumably, of the explicit order in

---

[1] Rule 41(b), interpreted as a preclusion-establishing rule, would not have the two effects described in the preceding paragraphs—arguable violation of the Rules Enabling Act and incompatibility with *Erie*—if the court's failure to specify an other-than-on-the-merits dismissal were subject to reversal on appeal whenever it would alter the rule of claim preclusion applied by the State in which the federal court sits. No one suggests that this is the rule, and we are aware of no case that applies it.

the present case that used the language of that default provision—is simply that, unlike a dismissal "without prejudice," the dismissal in the present case barred refiling of the same claim in the United States District Court for the Central District of California. That is undoubtedly a necessary condition, but it is not a sufficient one, for claim-preclusive effect in other courts.[2]

III

Having concluded that the claim-preclusive effect, in Maryland, of this California federal diversity judgment is dictated neither by Dupasseur v. Rochereau, as petitioner contends, nor by Rule 41(b), as respondent contends, we turn to consideration of what determines the issue. Neither the Full Faith and Credit Clause, U.S. Const., Art. IV, §1, nor the full faith and credit statute, 28 USC §1738, addresses the question. By their terms they govern the effects to be given only to state-court judgments (and, in the case of the statute, to judgments by courts of territories and possessions). And no other federal textual provision, neither of the Constitution nor of any statute, addresses the claim-preclusive effect of a judgment in a federal diversity action.

It is also true, however, that no federal textual provision addresses the claim-preclusive effect of a federal-court judgment in a federal-question case, yet we have long held that States cannot give those judgments merely whatever effect they would give their own judgments, but must accord them the effect that this Court prescribes. See Stoll v. Gottlieb, 305 U.S. 165, 171-172 (1938); Gunter v. Atlantic Coast Line R. Co., 200 U.S. 273, 290-291 (1906); Deposit Bank v. Frankfort, 191 U.S. 499, 514-515 (1903). The reasoning of that line of cases suggests, moreover, that even when States are allowed to give federal judgments (notably, judgments in diversity cases) no more than the effect accorded to state judgments, that disposition is by direction of *this* Court, which has the last word on the claim-preclusive effect of *all* federal judgments [the Court quotes the *Deposit Bank* case]. In other words, in *Dupasseur* the State was allowed (indeed, required) to give a federal diversity judgment no more effect than it would accord one of its own judgments only because reference to state law was *the federal rule that this Court deemed appropriate.* In short, federal common law governs the claim-preclusive effect of a dismissal by a federal court sitting in diversity. See generally R. Fallon, D. Meltzer, & D. Shapiro, Hart and Wechsler's The Federal Courts and the

---

[2] We do not decide whether, in a diversity case, a federal court's "dismissal upon the merits" (in the sense we have described), under circumstances where a state court would decree only a "dismissal without prejudice," abridges a "substantive right" and thus exceeds the authorization of the Rules Enabling Act. We think the situation will present itself more rarely than would the arguable violation of the Act that would ensue from interpreting Rule 41(b) as a rule of claim preclusion; and if it is a violation, can be more easily dealt with on direct appeal.

Federal System 1473 (4th ed. 1996); Degnan, Federalized Res Judicata, 85 Yale L.J. 741 (1976).

It is left to us, then, to determine the appropriate federal rule. And despite the sea change that has occurred in the background law since *Dupasseur* was decided—not only repeal of the Conformity Act but also the watershed decision of this Court in *Erie*—we think the result decreed by *Dupasseur* continues to be correct for diversity cases. Since state, rather than federal, substantive law is at issue there is no need for a uniform federal rule. And indeed, nationwide uniformity in the substance of the matter is better served by having the same claim-preclusive rule (the state rule) apply whether the dismissal has been ordered by a state or a federal court. This is, it seems to us, a classic case for adopting, as the federally prescribed rule of decision, the law that would be applied by state courts in the State in which the federal diversity court sits. See Gasperini v. Center for Humanities, Inc., 518 U.S. 415, 429-431 (1996); Walker v. Armco Steel Corp., 446 U.S., at 752-753; Bernhardt v. Polygraphic Co. of America, 350 U.S. 198, 202-205 (1956); Palmer v. Hoffman, 318 U.S. 109, 117 (1943); Klaxon Co. v. Stentor Elec. Mfg. Co., 313 U.S. 487, 496 (1941); Cities Service Oil Co. v. Dunlap, 308 U.S. 208, 212 (1939). As we have alluded to above, any other rule would produce the sort of "forum-shopping . . . and . . . inequitable administration of the laws" that *Erie* seeks to avoid, *Hanna*, since filing in, or removing to, federal court would be encouraged by the divergent effects that the litigants would anticipate from likely grounds of dismissal.

This federal reference to state law will not obtain, of course, in situations in which the state law is incompatible with federal interests. If, for example, state law did not accord claim-preclusive effect to dismissals for willful violation of discovery orders, federal courts' interest in the integrity of their own processes might justify a contrary federal rule. No such conflict with potential federal interests exists in the present case. Dismissal of this state cause of action was decreed by the California federal court only because the California statute of limitations so required; and there is no conceivable federal interest in giving that time bar more effect in other courts than the California courts themselves would impose.

. . .

Because the claim-preclusive effect of the California federal court's dismissal "upon the merits" of petitioner's action on statute-of-limitations grounds is governed by a federal rule that in turn incorporates California's law of claim preclusion (the content of which we do not pass upon today), the Maryland Court of Special Appeals erred in holding that the dismissal necessarily precluded the bringing of this action in the Maryland courts. The judgment is reversed, and the case remanded for further proceedings not inconsistent with this opinion.

It is so ordered.

■ NOTES ON THE PRECLUSIVE EFFECT OF FEDERAL COURT JUDGMENTS

1. We can begin consideration of *Semtek* by making mirror-image points to the ones with which we began in considering *Marrese*: Federal preclusion law determines the effect of a judgment rendered by a federal court. What could be simpler and more obvious? It would be strange, wouldn't it, if *state* law determined the effect of a federal court judgment? Where we end up is, once again, imminently sensible: The effect of a judgment is determined by the law of the jurisdiction that rendered the judgment (here, federal law).

2. Once again, we must recognize that in a federal system, things are not simple. The question in *Semtek* was what effect the judgment of a federal court should have on a *state law* claim. Such questions arise in a federal system because state and federal law can both apply to the same transaction, and because federal courts can entertain state law claims—in diversity cases, federal courts are in the business of deciding state law claims, although the question whether federal courts will be involved is very much up to the parties. Even when a plaintiff *can* sue in federal court (the amount in controversy and diversity requirements are satisfied), she may still elect to sue in state court. And if a plaintiff does make this choice, a defendant may decide not to remove even if the removal statute would let her do so (as would be true if she is sued in some state other than her domicile).

3. In *Semtek*, plaintiff sued in state court, and defendant removed to federal court and won a dismissal on ground that the statute of limitations had run. Recall that often such dismissals in state court on this ground preclude new suits in other courts of the same state, but generally such dismissals do not preclude relitigation in some other state (see note 3 in Notes on Res Judicata Effects of Dismissals Before Trial in Section B2, supra).

(a) FRCP 41 says dismissals are "on the merits," with three exceptions (these cover dismissals for lack of jurisdiction, improper venue, or failure to join a party under FRCP 19). It is not obvious that any of these exceptions can apply here, although it is sometimes said that dismissals of suits as barred by statutes of limitation are "jurisdictional" (they bar only "the remedy" and not "the right"). The Court in *Semtek*, however, does not apply an exception in FRCP 41. Doesn't this provision, if no exception applies, suggest that the dismissal in federal court in California should block the new suit in Maryland? The Court does not reach this conclusion, does it? Why not?

(b) Although *Semtek* does not rely on FRCP 41 in deciding the effect of the federal court judgment in California, it does conclude that the answer is to be found in federal law—not in FRCP 41, but in "federal common law." And the *content* of federal common law in this context, the Court tells us, is *state* preclusion law. Recall the *Kimbell Foods* case, where the Court concluded that federal law absorbed the content of Texas law in the setting of a contest between private and government lenders over what was left of a bankrupt

borrower's assets. See United States v. Kimbell Foods, Inc., 440 U.S. 715 (1979) (described in Chapter 6B2). Does it make sense to do something similar in *Semtek?* Why?

(c) If, as was argued in *Semtek,* California would not regard a dismissal on ground of the statute of limitations as claim preclusive, then it would seem that a second suit should be allowed to go forward in another state (such as Maryland). If, however, California law did treat dismissal on this ground as claim preclusive, then a second suit in another state should also be barred. But, as we have already seen, usually *state court* dismissals on this ground are *not* viewed as claim preclusive when suit is brought elsewhere. Would *Semtek* lead to the conclusion, then, that a federal judgment in a diversity case based on the running of the statute of limitations would have *greater* claim preclusive effect in another state than a judgment by a state court on that ground would have? Professor Burbank suggests a solution to this problem. See Stephen B. Burbank, Semtek, *Forum Shopping, and Federal Common Law,* 77 Notre Dame L. Rev. 1027, 1049 (2002) (*Semtek* should be interpreted as requiring a court in the second state to accord "the same preclusive effect" to a federal judgment that would be required of a state court judgment under the full faith and credit clause). Does *Semtek* lend itself to this interpretation?

(d) Suppose Abe sues Brenda in federal court in California on the basis of diversity jurisdiction, but Brenda wins a dismissal under FRCP 37 because Abe refuses to make discovery as ordered by the court. Can Carol now bring the same claim in state court in California, or is it barred by *res judicata?* The Court in *Semtek* acknowledges, doesn't it, that sometimes a federal "reference to state law" is inappropriate, if state law is "incompatible with federal interests." And it cites this very example. So we are not to read *Semtek* as meaning that federal preclusion law *invariably* incorporates the state rule, even in diversity cases, are we?

(e) Suppose Carol brings a diversity suit against Don in federal court in New York, and that Don has a claim against Carol arising out of the same transaction. Under FRCP 13(a), Don's claim would be a compulsory counterclaim, but New York does not have a compulsory counterclaim rule. Suppose Carol loses the case after a trial on the merits (for reasons having nothing to do with the claim that Don could have brought but did not). If Don later brings suit against Carol in a California state court advancing the claim that he left out of Carol's New York suit, can Carol defend on the ground that Don has lost his right to bring the claim now? See Allan Block Corp. v. County Materials Corp., 512 F.3d 912 (7th Cir. 2008) (*res judicata* doctrine, not FRCP 13, determines effect of AB's failure as defendant in federal diversity suit to interpose counterclaim; in second suit in federal court, AB, as plaintiff, could bring claim it did not bring in first suit, where plaintiff sought declaratory relief; under *Semtek,* federal *res judicata* law applies, which adopts state rule

as federal law; AB's claim in second suit was not barred because state *res judicata* doctrine did not require AB to file counterclaim in first suit).

(f) Isn't there a legitimate federal interest in regulating the claims that can be and must be brought in federal court, even in diversity cases? Professor Woolley argues that the range of cases in which state law should inform the content of the federal common law of preclusion is actually rather narrow, identifying three broad federal interests: One is an interest in the "integrity of [federal] judicial processes," and another is an interest in "determining the authority of federal judgments," and the third is an interest in "the proper allocation of federal judicial resources." Don't these interests justify requiring Don to bring his claim against Carol when she sues him? See generally Patrick Woolley, *The Sources of Federal Preclusion Law After* Semtek, 72 Univ. Cin. L. Rev. 527, 532, 605-606 (2003) (noting that "many state courts have concluded that federal preclusion law bars assertion of counterclaims that should have been advanced in [an earlier federal suit]," arguing that it is "wrong" to think that the Federal Rules cannot govern the preclusive effects of federal judgments, and concluding that federal interests justify applying a "uniform preclusion rule in this context"). Can you think of other places where federal dismissals of diversity suits should bar later litigation, even in state court, as a matter of uniform federal law rather than as a matter of federal law that incorporates state principles?

D ISSUE PRECLUSION (*COLLATERAL ESTOPPEL*)

We leave claim preclusion and move to what lawyers in the generation of your parents and grandparents called "collateral estoppel"—a term that survives and appears in modern cases and in these pages—and to what the Restatement calls "issue preclusion." We leave the land of "might have beens" and enter the land of "actually litigated and determined."

Equally importantly, we leave the land of "claims" and enter the realm of "issues." What is foreclosed when issue preclusion applies is not a claim, but an issue: To hearken back to the example at the beginning of this chapter, Porter's loss to Davis in a patent suit, on ground that Porter's claimed patent is invalid, will prevent Porter from suing Davis for a different alleged violation of the same patent years later—not because the new claim is foreclosed, but because Porter is bound on the issue of patent validity, which he litigated and lost in the first suit. In the words of the Restatement, when "an issue of fact or law is actually litigated and determined by a valid and final judgment, and the determination is essential to the judgment, the determination is conclusive in a subsequent action between the parties, whether on the same or a different claim." Restatement (Second) of Judgments §27 (1982).

1. "Actually Litigated and Determined"

In the paradigmatic case, "actually litigated" means that the issue was fully examined in a trial on the merits, with witnesses called to testify, and other evidence offered, and that the matter was contested (not stipulated, conceded, or agreed to). "Determined" means the matter was submitted to the trier of fact (judge or jury), and the trier reached a conclusion that was presented by way of verdict or written up as findings and conclusions as contemplated by FRCP 52 (court "must find the facts specially and state its conclusions of law separately," and these may be stated on the record or "in an opinion or a memorandum of decision").

At the opposite extreme is a judgment entered by default. Most courts (although not all) hold that default judgments do not generate issue preclusive effect. See, e.g., In re Sandoval, 232 P.3d 422 (Nev. 2010) (issue preclusion depends on actual litigation, and there are "legitimate reasons" why one might not have taken a prior opportunity to litigate, including lack of knowledge, inconvenient forum, or fact that litigating the issue may be more costly than is worthwhile; hence default judgment does not have issue preclusive effect).

Between these extremes are a host of situations. Most courts say that "actually litigated" embraces many cases falling short of resolution by trial. According to the Restatement, an issue is actually litigated if it is "properly raised, by the pleadings or otherwise, and is submitted for determination, and is determined," which includes issues "submitted and determined on a motion to dismiss for failure to state a claim, a motion for judgment on the pleadings, a motion for summary judgment . . . , a motion for directed verdict, . . . as well as on a judgment entered on a verdict," and a determination may arise on the basis of "a failure of pleading or of proof as well as on the sustaining of the burden of proof." See Restatement (Second) of Judgments §27, Comment d (1982).

Partly because of disagreement on the question whether a point must be "actually litigated," courts disagree on the question whether a plea of guilty in a criminal case can have issue preclusive effect in a later civil case. Judges in criminal proceedings must ascertain that such pleas have a factual basis, and defendants are required to "allocute"—to state publicly in court that they understand their rights and have decided to plead guilty and to state publicly that they are in fact guilty. But guilty pleas are products of the plea bargaining process, and defendants are put under pressure to plead guilty to avoid the risk of punishment greater than the prosecutor usually offers in exchange for a plea. Do these considerations point toward allowing *collateral estoppel* effect or denying it? Compare Bradley Ventures, Inc. v. Farm Bureau Mutual Ins. Co. of Arkansas, 264 S.W.3d 485 (Ark. 2007) (denying *collateral estoppel* effect to guilty plea on charges of "reckless burning") and Mrozek v. Intra Financial Corp., 699 N.W.2d 54 (Wis. 2005) (denying *collateral estoppel* effect to pleas of guilty on securities fraud charges) with Butler v. Mooers, 771 A.2d 1034 (Me.

2001) (according *collateral estoppel* effect to plea of guilty to bank fraud charge), and see generally David Shapiro, *Should a Guilty Plea Have Preclusive Effect?*, 70 Iowa L. Rev. 27 (1984) (arguing against *collateral estoppel* effect for pleas of guilty). You will learn in the Evidence course, and you might consider it relevant here, that guilty pleas are "admissions" by the defendant that are admissible against them in later civil suits under FRE 801(d)(2) *even if* they do not achieve preclusive effect. Evidence of this sort is likely to be pretty convincing, isn't it?

2. "Valid and Final Judgment"

Again the idea here is clear enough in some situations. "Valid" means, at least, a judgment by a court having jurisdiction over the parties and subject matter. Final connotes, at least, a decision that will not be revisited or reconsidered later in the suit, and typically the idea of finality corresponds with the kind of order from which the losing party may take an appeal—in other words, it is the last thing that the court does in the matter.

Recall from your study of jurisdiction—over the person (Chapter 3) and over the subject matter (Chapter 4)—that actually litigating jurisdiction, in proceedings in which the court decides the point, resolves the matter in a way that binds the parties. Recall too that normally subject matter jurisdiction cannot be conferred by consent (although personal jurisdiction *can* be): Even if a defendant fails to object at the outset to a lack of subject matter jurisdiction, the point can be raised by either side any time during pendency of the proceedings, even on appeal. Indeed, an appellate court may address the matter itself, even if none of the parties and no judge previously has raised the point. *But*—and it's a *big* "but"—a court that *decides* that it has subject matter jurisdiction *does* have it, although the matter is of course reviewable on appeal. This "bootstrapping" doctrine expresses an important point: Finality, as protected by the doctrines of claim preclusion and issue preclusion, is even more important, in the case of a decision that a court has jurisdiction, than being "right" about jurisdiction, and even more important than preventing courts from acting when they lack subject matter jurisdiction.

The points developed here were settled many years ago. In the area of jurisdiction over the person, the classic case is Baldwin v. Iowa State Traveling Men's Association, 283 U.S. 522, 524 (1931) (defendant appeared and objected that Missouri state court lacked jurisdiction over the person; trial court resolved the issue against defendant and refused to dismiss; defendant defaulted; judgment was entitled to full faith and credit in Iowa; public policy requires "an end of litigation," and those who contest an issue are "bound by the result" and the matter is "forever settled as between the parties," which doctrine applies whenever one "voluntarily appears, presents his case and is fully heard," at least in the absence of fraud). See also Restatement (Second) of Judgments §10 (1982) (a party may object on grounds of inadequate notice or lack of "territorial jurisdiction," but resolution of such objection "precludes the party who asserted it from litigating" the matter in a later suit).

In the area of subject matter jurisdiction, the rule that the parties are bound is even more rigorous because it is *assumed* that a court resolved the issue of its own subject matter jurisdiction in a way that binds the parties, even if nobody raised the point. The classic case is Des Moines Navigation & R. Co. v. Iowa Homestead Co., 123 U.S. 552 (1887) (after losing earlier suit in federal court, Iowa Homestead filed second suit in state court; defendant pled earlier judgment as bar, but plaintiff urged that prior court lacked subject matter jurisdiction because both parties were Iowa citizens; earlier judgment was "a valid and subsisting prior adjudication" that was "binding on these parties, and a bar to this action"). See also Restatement (Second) of Judgments §12 (1982) (recognizing some exceptions to this doctrine, taken up below); Stoll v. Gottlieb, 305 U.S. 165, 171-172 (every court rendering a judgment "tacitly, if not expressly, determines its own jurisdiction over the parties and the subject matter").

■ NOTES ON VALID AND FINAL JUDGMENTS

1. In rare cases involving subject matter jurisdiction, courts have recognized exceptions to the principle that deciding the case implies that the court also made a decision about subject matter jurisdiction that binds the parties.

(a) Consider a Depression-era case, in which a Wisconsin state court foreclosed a farm while the debtors had a pending petition in bankruptcy aimed at composing and extending their debts. Under federal law, filing the bankruptcy petition put in place a stay of state foreclosure proceedings, but this point was not raised in the Wisconsin proceeding, and the Wisconsin Supreme Court affirmed the foreclosure and rejected a claim that the automatic stay statute was self-executing. The United States Supreme Court took the case and acknowledged that a judgment bears "a presumption of regularity" and is generally not "subject to collateral attack," but stressed that Congress has "plenary" and "exclusive" power over bankruptcy, concluding that Congress intended to block the continuing exercise of state court jurisdiction even if the matter is not "contested" or "even raised." Hence the state court judgment did *not* stand in the way of a second suit, this time brought by the debtors (again in Wisconsin state court) to cancel the sheriff's deed and evict the lenders from the farm. See Kalb v. Feuerstein, 308 U.S. 433 (1940). *Kalb* is widely understood as a decision allowing collateral attack on a judgment for lack of subject matter jurisdiction where the court *clearly* lacked jurisdiction, and letting the judgment stand would defeat important policies.

(b) Consider a case that reached a final judgment resting on a statute conferring jurisdiction that was later declared unconstitutional. The substantive issues resolved in that suit were raised thereafter in another suit. Does the

situation present another instance where we should make exception to the finality that would be produced by doctrines of claim and issue preclusion? See Chicot County Drainage District v. Baxter State Bank, 308 U.S. 371, 375 (1940) (apart from arguments over constitutionality of statute, "all the elements necessary to constitute the defense of *res judicata*" appeared, and those contesting the earlier judgment had the opportunity before to challenge the statute and are "not the less bound by the decree because they failed" to raise the challenge). Recall Federated Department Stores, Inc. v. Moitie, 452 U.S. 394 (1981), described in note 6 in the Notes on Exceptions to the Doctrine of Claim Preclusion in Section 14B5, supra. Does *Moitie* make better sense in light of the earlier decision in *Chicot County*?

2. The Restatement, in an attempt to harmonize the cases, suggests three situations in which subject matter jurisdiction should be open to a second look, even when judgment was entered after the parties appeared and litigated. One is the situation in which the "subject matter of the action was so plainly beyond the court's jurisdiction" that going forward was a "manifest abuse of authority." Second is the situation in which allowing a judgment to stand "would substantially infringe the authority of another tribunal or agency of government." Third is the situation in which the court lacks "capability to make an adequately informed determination" of its own jurisdiction, and "as a matter of procedural fairness" the party opposing enforcement of the judgment "should have opportunity belatedly" to challenge jurisdiction. See Restatement (Second) of Judgments §12 (1982). Perhaps not surprisingly, the Restaters cite *Kalb* in the second category.

3. In connection with issue preclusion, as is also true in with claim preclusion, the question whether a judgment is final has led to some difficulties:

(a) Courts disagree on the question whether a judgment is final while appeal is pending. Compare Rantz v. Kaufman, 109 P.3d 132 (Colo. 2005) (judgment on appeal is not sufficiently final to generate issue preclusive effect) with Baltrusch v. Baltrusch, 130 P.3d 1257, 1275 (Mont. 2006) (judgment was final enough for issue preclusive effect despite pendency of post-trial motions for new trial or JMAL).

(b) A finding or determination can sometimes be viewed as final for purposes of issue preclusion even if no final judgment is entered. See Davis v. Davis, 663 A.2d 499, 503 (D.C. 1995) (in suit seeking declaration that father was entitled to have former wife and children undergo blood testing to determine paternity, plaintiff was precluded by determination in divorce proceedings that he was *not* entitled to blood tests; although plaintiff had dismissed divorce proceedings prior to issuance of final decree, so there was no final judgment subject to appeal, determination was final enough to have issue preclusive effect).

4. Sometimes claims that are dismissed for lack of jurisdiction may nevertheless suffer adverse consequences because other claims, over which jurisdiction exists, go to final judgment that resolves issues critical to the dismissed claims. See Oman v. Davis School District, 194 P.3d 956, 966

(Utah 2008) (electrician fired from job with school district brought suit in federal court alleging claims under §1983 with state law claims, including one for breach of contract; federal court ruled for defendant on §1983 claim on ground that terminating employment did not violate contract, and dismissed state law claims by declining to exercise supplemental jurisdiction; when plaintiff pursued contract claim in state court, claim preclusion did not apply, but issue preclusion did apply; question of breach of contract "was squarely before the federal court, was litigated by the parties, and was necessary to the court's final judgment").

3. "Essential to the Judgment"

A considerable challenge to the doctrine of issue preclusion is the matter of deciding what findings are "essential to" a prior judgment. Let us contemplate this challenge in the context of a problem that illustrates four situations, and an actual case dealing with the fourth (perhaps most difficult) situation.

■ PROBLEM 14-C. "Your Trucks Are Messing Up My Access Road"

Debra Palmer owns Oak Park Gardens, a 12-acre parcel off County Road 34 near Keedysville, Maryland (close to the Antietam Battlefield), and she grows and markets produce (asparagus, broccoli, cauliflower, salad greens, and strawberries). Her parcel has a large frontage on Dogstreet Road. Her neighbor is Frank Drew, who owns a 20-acre parcel called Dawson Farm, on which he breeds and sells horses. Dawson Farm has a short frontage on Dogstreet Road.

A wide access road serves Oak Park Gardens and Dawson Farm, and a second, less convenient and narrower access road serves the Dawson Farm alone. Over several years, Palmer and Drew came to disagreement on the question whether the wide access road lies entirely on Oak Park Gardens or on Dawson Farm, or whether indeed it straddles the two parcels in such way that both Palmer and Drew can use it without encroaching on the other's land. Drew drives heavy trucks towing horse trailers back and forth, which cause more ruts and wear than do the lighter cars and trucks that Palmer uses in coming and going from Oak Park Gardens. Palmer complains to Drew that "your trucks are messing up my access road," and asks him to "drive on your own road," to which Drew replies that "the access road belongs to me, or at least to both of us, and anyway I'm only using the narrow road for my trucks."

In 2008, Palmer brings suit against Drew for trespass, seeking declaratory and injunctive relief and damages. In this suit, the two issues are whether Palmer holds title to the wide access road and whether Drew drove on it. Drew denies that Palmer holds title to the wide access road, and avers that at least half the road is on his parcel; Drew also denies that he drove over the wide access road, and avers that he used only the narrower road on his own parcel. These matters are tried to a jury, and both sides call witnesses and offer other evidence in support of their positions.

In 2011, Palmer again sues Drew, seeking damages for alleged additional trespasses that occurred after judgment had been reached in the 2008 suit.

(A) Assume that the 2008 suit led to a general verdict for Drew, and judgment in his favor that became final. If so, can Drew use the 2008 judgment in the 2011 suit as the basis for issue preclusion against Palmer, to prevent her from litigating again the question of title to the wide access road?

(B) Assume that the 2008 suit led to a general verdict for Palmer, and that judgment was entered in her favor that became final. If so, can Palmer use the 2008 judgment in the 2011 suit as the basis for issue preclusion against Drew, to prevent him from litigating again the question of title to the wide access road?

(C) Assume that the 2008 suit led to a special verdict for Drew, in which a jury found that Palmer holds title to the wide access road but that Drew did not drive on that road. If so, can Palmer use the 2008 judgment in the 2011 suit as the basis for issue preclusion against Drew, to prevent him from litigating again the question of title to the wide access road?

(D) Assume that the first suit led to a special verdict for Drew, in which the jury found that Parker did not own the wide access road and that Drew did not drive on it. If so, can Drew use the 2008 judgment in the 2011 suit as the basis for issue preclusion against Palmer, to prevent her from litigating again the question of title to the wide access road?

■ NOTES ON WHICH FACTS ARE "ESSENTIAL TO THE JUDGMENT"

1. Under supposition (A), can we tell why the jury found in Drew's favor in the 2008 suit? If not, should it matter? See, e.g., Russell v. Place, 94 U.S. 606 (1876) (plaintiff advanced two claims in prior suit for patent infringement and prevailed, but record did not "disclose the nature of the infringement for which damages were recovered," so judgment lacked "that certainty which is essential to its operation as an estoppel"); Dowling v. Finley Associates,

Inc., 727 A.2d 1245, 1251-1252 (Conn. 1999) (general verdict could have rested on failure to prove improper conduct or on finding that claim was barred by statute of limitations; general verdict does not have issue preclusive effect if there is no way to know basis of jury's determination).

(a) Suppose, contrary to the facts in Problem 14-C, that the record of the 2008 trial shows that the only testimony and evidence in the case related to title. Could we then apply issue preclusion to block Palmer from relitigating title? See Wright & Miller, Federal Practice and Procedure §4420 (examining the record often leads to "a process of inference, in which it is taken that an issue was actually decided if its decision was necessary to support the result reached," and the "simple fact" of winning or losing may reveal "all of the issues that would have had to be resolved to support the result"); Stoehr v. Mohamed, 244 F.3d 206, 208 (1st Cir. 2001) (an issue may be "actually decided" even if not expressly decided if it constituted a necessary component of the decision reached).

(b) Suppose the record of prior proceedings is not definitive on the point in question. Can a later court examine the record to deduce what was likely determined and what was not? See Bangert Brothers, Inc. v. Kiewit Western Co., 310 F.3d 1278, 1298 (10th Cir. 2002) (concluding that prior verdict did not include award of prejudgment interest; although one exhibit "referred to interest," plaintiff's experts "did not discuss that element" and counsel did not mention it in closing argument); Hardy v. Johns-Manville Sales Corp., 341 (5th Cir. 1982) (special interrogatories in prior asbestos case were "general and not specifically directed to failure to warn," and jury was instructed only on breach of warranty and strict liability and not on duty to warn; still appellate court on direct review in prior case concluded that verdict "necessarily included" a finding on failure to warn, which was implicit in the verdict).

(c) If the record of the prior proceedings is sparse or nonexistent, applying preclusion law becomes difficult indeed. On the one hand, we have at least a strong tradition of *not* allowing the decision maker, judge or jury, to testify to what was decided. See, e.g., Grip-Pak, Inc. v. Illinois Tool Works, Inc., 694 F.2d 466, 470 (7th Cir. 1982) (courts do not "take evidence from the judge in an earlier suit to find out what his findings really meant," as parties should be able to "rely on what the judgment says in guiding their behavior"), *cert. denied,* 461 U.S. 958; Kazan v. Wolinski, 721 F.2d 911, 915 (3d Cir. 1983) (note from juror to judge in first case could not be used to determine what jury decided). Compare FRE 606(b) (on the matter of validity of a verdict, juror testimony and affidavits are inadmissible, with some narrow exceptions). On the other hand, sometimes courts with nothing else to go on have admitted such testimony. See, e.g., Restatement (Second) of Judgments §27, Comment f (1982) ("extrinsic evidence" can be used to decide what was

determined in prior suit if "pleadings and other materials of record" do not resolve the matter). There is even an early suggestion by the Supreme Court that the question of what was determined in a prior suit may itself be a jury issue in a later suit. See Washington, A.G. Steam Packet Co. v. Sickles, 72 U.S. 580, 593 (1866).

2. Under supposition (B), the general verdict for Palmer in the 2008 suit means, doesn't it, that the jury *must* have found in her favor both on the question of title and on the question whether Drew drove on the wide access road? And aren't both findings essential to the judgment? See Restatement (Second) of Judgments §27, Comment g (1982) (if several issues are litigated, and "a judgment cannot properly be rendered in favor of one party unless all of the issues are decided in his favor, and judgment is given for him, the judgment is conclusive with respect to all the issues").

3. Under supposition (C), the special verdict for Drew includes a finding that Palmer holds title to the wide access road. Is this finding necessary to the judgment? See, e.g., Wilson v. Wilson, 607 P.2d 539, 541-542 (Mont. 1980) (in LW's suit seeking custody of child and dissolution of marriage to KW, prior finding by Indiana court in LW's paternity suit against KW that child was born "out of wedlock" was not entitled to issue preclusive effect; marital relationship was not "an essential or material fact in the paternity suit"); Restatement (Second) of Judgments §27, Illustration 14 (1982) (in A's suit against B for trademark infringement, a judgment in A's prior suit for previous infringements does not preclude relitigation of validity of trademark; in prior suit, court found trademark valid but not infringed; finding of validity was *not* essential to judgment denying A's claim for infringement).

4. Under supposition (D), the special verdict for Drew could rest on *either* of the two findings, could it not? That is, a finding that Parker did not own the wide access road is enough by itself to justify a verdict in favor of Drew, and a finding that Drew did not drive on the wide access road is also enough by itself to justify a verdict in favor of Drew. This situation has proved to be the most challenging for courts to handle. Before considering the matter further, read the *L'Oreal* case.

JEAN ALEXANDER COSMETICS v. L'OREAL USA

United States Court of Appeals for the Third Circuit
458 F.3d 244 (3d Cir. 2006)

RENDELL, Circuit Judge.

[L'Oreal and Jean Alexander Cosmetics engage in a trademark dispute. L'Oreal began using the "Shades EQ" mark in 1988 for hair care products. Two years later, Jean Alexander introduced its "EQ System" mark, which it registered with the Patent and Trademark Office (PTO) in 1993. In 1996, L'Oreal tried to register a "modernized version" of the Shades EQ mark that it had used since 1992, but the examiner rejected the application because the Shades EQ mark was likely to be confused with the EQ System mark.

L'Oreal petitioned Trademark Trial and Appeal Board (TTAB) to cancel Jean Alexander's registration, alleging that L'Oreal had used the Shades EQ mark before Jean Alexander began using the EQ System mark. L'Oreal argued that its two versions of the mark were legal equivalents, hence that they should track the date of original use and achieve priority. Jean Alexander denied both priority and confusion. The parties created an extensive record, including depositions. In June 2001, the TTAB dismissed L'Oreal's petition, holding that the original Shades EQ mark did have priority over the EQ System mark, but that the modernized Shades EQ mark was *not* the equivalent of the original mark and did not have priority.

"[S]olely for the sake of completeness," the TTAB took up the question of confusion, concluding that there was no likelihood of confusion between the marks. It cited testimony by L'Oreal's Assistant VP for Marketing (who said only that there was "some possibility" of confusion), testimony by L'Oreal's former Senior VP for Marketing and Advertising (who said there was "no likelihood" of confusion between the modernized Shades EQ mark and the EQ System mark), and testimony by Jean Alexander's CEO that the public was unlikely to be confused. The TTAB also stressed that neither party offered proof of any actual instances of confusion.

L'Oreal then sought again to register its modernized Shades EQ trademark, and this time the PTO did so. Jean Alexander noticed its opposition, but the TTAB found that issue preclusion barred Jean Alexander's claim. Jean Alexander then sued L'Oreal in District Court alleging trademark infringement, and the District Court dismissed on ground of issue preclusion.]

The District Court had subject matter jurisdiction under 28 USC §1338 and we have appellate jurisdiction under 28 USC §1291.

[A "plenary standard" of review applies to matters of issue preclusion used defensively. There are four requirements for issue preclusion: The identical issue was previously adjudicated; it was actually litigated and determined by a final and valid judgment; the prior determination was necessary to the decision; the party to be precluded was fully represented and had a full and fair opportunity to litigate.]

The dispute in this case centers on whether the TTAB's finding on likelihood of confusion was "necessary" to its decision in the cancellation proceedings. Jean Alexander argues that once the Board concluded that the EQ System mark had priority over the modernized Shades EQ mark, there was no reason for it to analyze likelihood of confusion as to these two marks. To resolve the case at that point, the TTAB needed only to consider whether the original Shades EQ mark, which had priority, was likely to be confused with the EQ System mark.[3] Thus, Jean Alexander contends that the Board's determination that there was no likelihood of confusion as between the EQ System mark and the modernized Shades EQ mark was unnecessary to its 2001 decision and should not be given preclusive effect.

L'Oreal argues that collateral estoppel applies here because both priority of use and likelihood of confusion figured prominently in the cancellation proceedings and both issues were potentially dispositive of the case. L'Oreal urges us to adopt a rule under which preclusive effect is given to a finding that is an alternative ground for a judgment where that finding, standing alone, would have been sufficient to support the judgment. Though an alternative finding may not be strictly necessary to the judgment in the sense that there was another stated basis for the decision, L'Oreal contends that giving such a finding preclusive effect would not compromise the objectives behind the necessity principle.

The requirement that a preclusive finding must have been necessary to a judgment is rooted in principles of fairness. "[P]arties should be estopped only on issues they actually deem important, and not on incidental matters." Lynne Carol Fashions, Inc. v. Cranston Print Works Co., 453 F.2d 1177, 1183 (3d Cir. 1972). Because litigants are likely to view an issue that is necessary to the resolution of a case as important and to litigate it vigorously, it is fair to give such a determination preclusive effect. See Wickham Contracting Co., Inc. v. Board of Education of City of New York, 715 F.2d 21, 28 (2d Cir. 1983) (noting that the necessity rule ensures that "parties to litigation have sufficient notice and incentive to litigate matters in earlier proceedings which may bind them in subsequent matters"). The necessity requirement also ensures that preclusive effect is not given to determinations that did not "receive close judicial attention," Commercial Assocs. v. Tilcon Gammino, Inc., 998 F.2d 1092, 1097 (1st Cir. 1993), or that were unappealable by virtue of being incidental to a decision, see Restatement (Second) of Judgments §27 comment h. See also Pettaway v. Plummer, 943 F.2d 1041, 1044 (9th Cir. 1991) ("The primary purpose of the rule that prior resolution of an issue will have collateral estoppel effect only if it was necessarily decided is to ensure that the finder of fact in the first case took sufficient care in determining the issue."); Hicks v. Quaker Oats Co., 662 F.2d 1158, 1168 (5th Cir. 1981) ("[A]n immaterial issue may not have been afforded the same careful deliberation and analysis as an issue necessary to the judgment ... [and] a decision on an immaterial issue provides the losing party with no incentive to contest an erroneous decision by appeal."); 18 Charles Alan Wright et al., Federal Practice and

---

[3] Had the Board concluded that the original and modernized Shades EQ marks were legal equivalents, it could have tacked the date of first use of the original version onto the modernized version. This would have given the modernized version priority over the EQ System mark and forced the Board to address whether there was a likelihood of confusion between the EQ System mark and the modernized Shades EQ mark.

Procedure §4421, p. 539 (2d ed. 2002) (recounting these "[t]wo common explanations" for the necessity requirement).

There is no question that likelihood of confusion was a central issue in the cancellation proceedings. It was the focus of the parties' pleadings and had been litigated extensively over the course of four years. Reviewing its own decision from 2001, the TTAB noted that this was "not a case where the Board made incidental determinations on an issue which was not before it." Rather, the TTAB believed that likelihood of confusion was an important issue in the case and, in fact, intended its determination that there was no likelihood of confusion to be controlling if its holding on priority were overturned on appeal. Thus, L'Oreal is correct that the finding on likelihood of confusion constituted an alternative ground on which the Board dismissed its petition to cancel.

However, this conclusion does not resolve the question of whether the finding should be given preclusive effect because, as Jean Alexander notes, the case could have been resolved without the Board's determination that there was no likelihood of confusion between the EQ System mark and the modernized Shades EQ mark. We must determine whether a finding that is an alternate, but independently sufficient, basis for a judgment should be deemed necessary to a decision for purposes of collateral estoppel.

"Traditional analysis has viewed [alternative holdings] as presenting a dilemma between two choices—preclusion must be available as to each of the independently sufficient findings, or it must be denied as to all." Wright et al., supra, at §4421, p. 564. Courts that apply collateral estoppel to alternative findings have sidestepped the requirement that the determination be "necessary" to the decision and focused instead on the trustworthiness and practical considerations surrounding the adjudication. Those courts that deny preclusion to independently sufficient findings do so because an alternative holding, by definition, is not "necessary" to a judgment.

The First Restatement of Judgments resolved this dilemma in favor of extending preclusion to each alternative holding. See Restatement of Judgments §68 comment n (1942) ("Where the judgment is based upon the matters litigated as alternative grounds, the judgment is determinative on both grounds, although either alone would have been sufficient to support the judgment."). The Second Restatement, crafted forty years later, adopted the contrary position. It states that "[i]f a judgment of a court of first instance is based on determinations of two issues, either of which standing independently would be sufficient to support the result, the judgment is not conclusive with respect to either issue standing alone." Restatement (Second) of Judgments §27 comment i.

There is no consensus among the courts of appeals as to whether the First or Second Restatement offers the better approach. [The court cites opinions from the Second, Seventh, Ninth, and Eleventh Circuits that generally give preclusive effect to alternative findings. The court cites opinions in the Tenth and Federal Circuits that refuse to give preclusive effect to alternative findings that were each independently sufficient to support a judgment.] We have never chosen between the positions of the First or Second Restatement under the circumstances before us. We will accordingly turn to the arguments in support of each approach.

Applying issue preclusion to independently sufficient alternative findings furthers the basic objectives of the doctrine. "Collateral estoppel . . . has the dual purpose of protecting litigants from the burden of relitigating an identical issue with the same party or his privy and of promoting judicial economy by preventing needless litigation." Parklane Hosiery v. Shore, 439 U.S. 322, 326 (1979). Denying preclusive effect to a finding that would support a court's judgment merely because the case was disposed of on other grounds as well would result in the inefficient use of private and public litigation resources. Courts routinely decide cases on multiple grounds, each of which has been fully litigated and given careful consideration due to their potentially dispositive role in the case. Because the interests that the necessity principle protects are not compromised under these circumstances, it would be curious to conclude that none of these findings were necessary to the judgment for purposes of collateral estoppel. See Restatement of Judgments §68 comment n ("It seems obvious that it should not be held that neither [alternative finding] is material [to a judgment], and hence both should be held to be material.").

In opposition to this position are three arguments against applying collateral estoppel to independently sufficient alternative findings. "First, a determination in the alternative may not have been as carefully or rigorously considered as it would have if it had been necessary to the result, and in that sense it has some of the characteristics of dicta." Restatement (Second) of Judgments §27 comment i. Second, "[s]ince one alternative ground will support the judgment, the losing litigant has little incentive to appeal another ground, even if erroneous." Hicks v. Quaker Oats Co., 662 F.2d 1158, 1168 (5th Cir. 1981); see also Restatement (Second) of Judgments §27 comment i ("[T]he losing party, although entitled to appeal from both determinations, might be dissuaded from doing so because of the likelihood that at least one of them would be upheld and the other not even reached."). Without an "incentive to appeal, the losing litigant will be less likely to consider collateral consequences of the erroneous ground, and this may disadvantage him unfairly later, unless he is particularly prescient." *Hicks*, at 1168.

Finally, to the extent that parties would file "cautionary appeals" to avoid the possible preclusive effects of an alternative holding in future litigation, this would "increas[e] the burdens of litigation on the parties and the courts rather than lightening those burdens." Restatement (Second) of Judgments §27 comment i. Of course, this result is "contrary to the principles of judicial economy which motivated the doctrine of collateral estoppel in the first place." *Hicks*, at 1169.

We are not persuaded by the rationale supporting the position of the Second Restatement. As a general matter, we are unconvinced that courts do, or should be assumed to, give less rigorous consideration to the alternative grounds they voice for their decisions. A determination that is independently sufficient to support a court's judgment is not "incidental, collateral, or immaterial to that judgment," *Hicks*, at 1168, and it is reasonable to expect that such a finding is the product of careful judicial reasoning.

Moreover, because collateral estoppel applies only to issues that were "actually litigated" in prior proceedings, there is little risk that preclusive effect will be given to determinations that the parties did not deem important or that were not subject to evidentiary proof. See Wright et al., supra, at §4419, p. 495 (noting the relationship between the "actual litigation" and "necessary" prongs for collateral estoppel); id. at §4421, p. 545 ("The necessity principle may become mingled with the requirements of actual litigation and actual decision."). For example, in the instant case, the parties focused on the likelihood of confusion in their pleadings and extensively litigated the issue for more than four years. Thus, litigants are adequately protected from the unfairness of giving preclusive effect to a finding that was not "vigorously litigated" or was not a "focus of the court's decision." Commercial Associates v. Tilcon Gammino, Inc., 998 F.2d 1092, 1097 (1st Cir. 1993); see also Williams v. Ward, 556 F.2d 1143, 1154 (2d Cir. 1977) ("The concern that an issue not essential to the prior judgment may not have been afforded the careful deliberation and analysis normally applied to essential issues is a real one in some circumstances, but not . . . where [the prior court] had the substantive issue fully briefed, and discussed its factual basis at length.").

Nor do we believe that the position of the First Restatement increases the risk that preclusion will be applied unfairly against a litigant who failed to appeal a judgment because it was supportable on alternative grounds. This concern is utterly speculative and does not outweigh the systemic interest that courts and litigants have in ensuring that the identical parties receive only "one bite at the apple" on a given issue.

Adopting the Second Restatement's view that preclusive effect should be denied to findings because they are stated in the alternative would significantly weaken the principle that "later courts should honor the first actual decision of a matter that has been actually litigated." Wright et al., supra, at §4416, p. 386. The doctrine of collateral estoppel protects this vital interest of the judicial system. See Southern Pacific Railway v. United States, 168 U.S. 1 (1897) (noting that the "general rule" of issue preclusion "is demanded by the very object for which civil courts have been established"). Litigants often raise multiple issues that are potentially dispositive of a case, and courts routinely address them in the interest of providing a complete and thoroughly reasoned decision. To permit or require relitigation of all alternative findings would eviscerate a great number of judicial determinations that were the products of costly litigation and careful deliberation. Indeed, under the approach of the Second Restatement, the judicial findings in nearly any complex case would be unlikely to preclude subsequent relitigation of the same issues.

Thus, we will follow the traditional view that independently sufficient alternative findings should be given preclusive effect. We recognize that such determinations do not fulfill the necessity requirement for collateral estoppel in a strict sense but, just as we did not "quibbl[e] about the necessity principle'" in the context of declaratory judgments, Henglein v. Colt Industries Operating Corp., 260 F.3d 201, at 212 (3d Cir. 2001) (quoting Wright et al., supra, at §4421, p. 581), neither will we do so in the context of alternative holdings that have been actually litigated and decided. Applying collateral estoppel in such cases does not undermine the interests that the necessity principle protects. We have little difficulty promoting the objectives of the necessity rule rather than requiring its formal fulfillment in situations where those objectives are served and it is equitable to do so. See Raytech Corp. v. White, 54 F.3d 187, 195 n.8 (noting that issue preclusion is equitable in nature); Jack Faucett Assocs., Inc. v. AT&T Co., 744 F.2d 118, 125 (D.C. Cir. 1984) (same); see also National Railroad Passenger Corp. v Pennsylvania Public Utilities Commission, 288 F.3d 519, 525 (3d Cir. 2002) (describing the "equitable exceptions" to collateral estoppel); Restatement (Second) of Judgments §28 (same). Accordingly, we adopt the view of the First Restatement and the other courts of appeals that permit the application of issue preclusion to alternative findings.

We note that at least one commentator has offered a variation on the First Restatement's rule, whereby independently sufficient alternative findings would be given preclusive effect only "if a second court can determine without extended inquiry that a particular finding reflects a careful process of decision." Wright et al., supra, at §4421, p. 580; see also National Satellite Sports, Inc. v. Eliadis, Inc., 253 F.3d 900, 909 (6th Cir. 2001) ("[W]here . . . one ground for the decision is clearly primary and the other only secondary, the secondary ground is not 'necessary to the outcome' for the purposes of issue preclusion."). This approach might work well in circumstances such as those before us, where the same tribunal that made the potentially preclusive finding also concluded later that this finding was necessary to its earlier judgment. However, "it is in the interest of predictability and simplicity for the result of nonpreclusion to be uniform." Restatement (Second) of Judgments §27 comment i. Given that "the question of preclusion will almost always be a close one if each case is to rest on its own particular facts," id., a rule that required case-by-case evaluation and second-guessing of how carefully the first tribunal considered a question would deny the parties the benefit of a "clear rule" and would likely result in a "wasteful expansion of the effort to reconstruct the initial process of decision," Wright et al., supra, at §4421, p. 580. We thus believe that the First Restatement of Judgments articulates a clearer and better rule to be applied in the circumstances before us.

Jean Alexander contends that, regardless of whether we adopt the First Restatement rule, it would be unfair to apply issue preclusion here because Jean Alexander was the prevailing party in the cancellation proceedings and was therefore unable to appeal the TTAB's favorable finding on likelihood of confusion. See Restatement (Second) of Judgments §28(1) (rejecting issue preclusion where "the party against whom preclusion is sought could not, as a matter of law, have obtained review of the judgment in the initial action"). We disagree. Any "party to a [TTAB] proceeding who is dissatisfied with the decision of the Board" may appeal. Trademark Trial and Appeal Board Manual of Procedure §901.01 (2d ed. 2004); see also 15 USC §1071; 37 CFR §2.145. But see Alltrade, Inc. v. Uniweld Prods., Inc., 946 F.2d 622, 626 (9th Cir. 1991) (citing [another case] for proposition that a prevailing party may only appeal the Board's action in needlessly reaching an issue, rather than its erroneous resolution of that issue). More generally, the Supreme Court has held that a prevailing party may appeal "for the purpose of obtaining a review of findings he deems erroneous which are not necessary to support the decree." Electrical Fittings Corp. v. Thomas & Betts Co., 307 U.S. 241, 242 (1939); see also Deposit Guaranty National Bank v. Roper, 445 U.S. 326, 334 (1980) ([A]ppeal may be permitted from an adverse ruling collateral to the judgment on the merits at the behest of the party who has prevailed on the merits, so long as that party retains a stake in the appeal satisfying the requirements of Art[icle] III."). Under this authority, Jean Alexander could have appealed the Board's finding on likelihood of confusion, even as the prevailing party.

Jean Alexander's corollary argument is that, even if it could have appealed the finding, it would have harmed its own interest to do so. "In the context of the [c]ancellation [p]roceeding before the TTAB, Jean Alexander had absolutely no interest in proving that there was likelihood of confusion," as this was a requirement for L'Oreal to prevail. We are unsympathetic to this argument. It was not necessary for Jean Alexander to resist the cancellation petition by denying the likelihood of confusion between its EQ System mark and the modernized Shades EQ mark and raising the issue as an affirmative defense. However, having raised and litigated this specific claim, Jean Alexander cannot now avoid the Board's determination of it because its own interests or the litigation context have changed. See United States v. Webber, 396 F.2d 381, 385-86 (3d Cir. 1968).

We follow the rule of the First Restatement of Judgments and give preclusive effect to the TTAB's alternative holding that there is no likelihood of confusion between L'Oreal's modernized Shades EQ mark and Jean

Alexander's EQ System mark.[5] Because Jean Alexander's claim is barred by the doctrine of collateral estoppel, we will affirm the District Court's order.

Jean Alexander also argues that the District Court should have converted L'Oreal's motion to dismiss into a motion for summary judgment after L'Oreal attached to its motion to dismiss copies of the TTAB's opinions and the parties' pleadings before the TTAB in the cancellation action. However, "[t]o resolve a 12(b)(6) motion, a court may properly look at public records, including judicial proceedings, in addition to the allegations in the complaint." S. Cross Overseas Agencies, Inc. v. Wah Kwong Shipping Group Ltd., 181 F.3d 410, 426 (3d Cir. 1999). Thus, the District Court did not err in this respect.

■ NOTES ON ISSUE PRECLUSIVE EFFECTS OF ALTERNATIVE FINDINGS

1. L'Oreal began the fight over use of competing trademarks that both had "EQ" as a central signifier, but lost before the TTAB. What did L'Oreal want, and why did TTAB rule against the company? Jean Alexander initiated a second round in their dispute, but lost on issue preclusion. On what issue was Jean Alexander precluded?

2. Does *L'Oreal* accept the principle that only issues *essential* to a judgment are given preclusive effect? Is the finding to which the court accords preclusion in *L'Oreal* essential to the conclusion reached by the TTAB? How, if at all, does it differ from the finding that the court made in the first suit described in Problem 14-C, under supposition (D)—the finding that Drew didn't drive on the wide access road and that Palmer does not hold title to the road in a trial resulting in judgment for Drew?

3. *L'Oreal* notes that the First Restatement of Judgments in 1942 took the view that alternative findings merit issue preclusive effect, but the Second Restatement in 1982 comes out the other way. It notes as well a split in the Circuits as between the two views.

(a) In support of the Second Restatement view *against* giving preclusive effect to alternative findings, the court cites the argument that these may not have been "as carefully or rigorously considered" as a finding that is *indispensable* to a judgment. What do you think of that argument? If you chose the law school that you are attending on the basis of geography (it's

---

[5] We also reject Jean Alexander's alternative arguments. First, it has claimed that it lacked a full and fair opportunity to litigate likelihood of confusion because it did not bear the burden of proof on this issue in the cancellation proceedings. We reject this argument out of hand. There is no legal authority for the proposition that a party without the burden of proof does not have the opportunity to litigate an issue and, in any event, Jean Alexander asserted as an affirmative defense to the cancellation action that there was no likelihood of confusion and therefore did bear a burden of proof on the issue.

where you live or want to practice or want to live) and prestige (it had a better reputation than available alternatives), would these reasons be *less fully* considered than a decision based, let us say, *solely* on one or another of those considerations? How does the *L'Oreal* court respond to arguments against according preclusive effect to alternative findings?

(b) Also in support of the Second Restatement view, the court cites the matter of appellate policy, noting that the loser in a suit based on alternative findings (each being sufficient) has less motivation to appeal because success depends on demonstrating errors at trial that are serious enough to set aside *both* (or *all*) necessary findings. Is this argument persuasive? Is it consistent with the view that preclusive effect (whether we're speaking of issue preclusion or claim preclusion) normally attaches at the moment a judgment becomes final, regardless whether the time for appeal has run? Does the outcome in *L'Oreal,* which *rejects* the position of the Second Restatement, encourage "unnecessary" or "wasteful" appeals?

(c) If a professor was fired for plagiarizing, and the judge dismisses his suit on the ground that he did indeed plagiarize and that his complaint failed to state a claim under the applicable statute (which dealt with retaliatory discharge), the Second Restatement approach would say that neither finding merits preclusive effect. Wouldn't claim preclusion block a new suit based on some other theory, such as discrimination? It will often be the case, won't it, that it's unnecessary to choose between giving or withholding issue preclusion in the situation of alternative findings? See Heyliger v. State University and Community College System, 126 F.3d 849, 853-854 (6th Cir. 1997) (in dismissing state retaliation suit, judge found that plaintiff committed plagiarism; finding was not essential, as judgment rested on conclusion that plaintiff failed to allege facts sufficient to suggest retaliation) (no issue preclusive effect, but claim preclusion barred second suit).

(d) For decisions that concur in the approach taken by the Second Restatement in declining to give issue preclusive effect to alternative sufficient findings, see Hicks v. Quaker Oats Co., 662 F.2d 1158, 1168 (5th Cir. 1981) (prior determination on issues of reliance and promissory estoppel were not entitled to issue preclusive effect, as they represented alternative sufficient findings); Herzog v. Lexington Township, 657 N.E.2d 926, 931 (Ill. 1995).

4. Where a judgment resting on two sufficient grounds is appealed, and the reviewing court affirms on the basis of one of the two grounds (but not others), courts are more willing to accord issue preclusive effect to the ground thus affirmed. See, e.g., Stanton v. Schultz, 222 P.3d 303 (Colo. 2010) (in suit against lawyer alleging malpractice, declining to accord issue preclusive effect to conclusion that newly discovered evidence was not ground for a new trial because defendant failed to prove due diligence, the new evidence was merely impeaching, and it would not likely have affected outcome; appellate court affirmed only on ground that defendant did not show due diligence, and only that point can have issue preclusive effect); Beaver v. John Q. Hammons Hotels, L.P., 138 S.W.3d 664 (Ark. 2003) (according preclusive effect to alternative ground of decision that was affirmed on appeal). Even the Second Restatement agrees that in this situation issue preclusion is appropriate. See Restatement (Second) of Judgments §27, Comment o (1982) (losing party has "obtained an appellate decision in the issue").

5. Which should be more important, preclusion policy or appellate policy? Would it be wiser to expand issue preclusion even though it might lead to more appeals, or to constrict issue preclusion to lessen the pressure (or temptation) to appeal? See, e.g., Chase Manhattan Mortgage Corp. v. Moore, 446 F.3d 725 (7th Cir. 2006) (in suit seeking foreclosure and deficiency judgment, bank moved for summary judgment; court denied motion but, on discovering that defendant submitted fake documents as proof that he'd paid mortgage, granted summary judgment for plaintiff, which simply terminated the case; noting "oddity" that bank was *not* appealing and that borrower, who remained in possession and "was not ordered to do or pay anything," *was* seeking review, court comments that in general one can appeal only to challenge an adverse finding that might be issue preclusive later, *but* that if avoiding this effect is the *only* reason to appeal because the party has prevailed, such a finding "*has* no collateral estoppel effect") (court allows appeal because it expects that in any later suit by the bank, borrower would be viewed as precluded on issue of liability).

6. Some courts decline to accord issue preclusive effect to determinations that were not subject to review. See Winters v. Diamond Shamrock Chemical Co., 149 F.3d 387, 395-396 (5th Cir. 1998) (declining to give issue preclusive effect to prior determination that a case could not properly be removed; an order declining to remand a removed case is not reviewable, so issue preclusion is inappropriate).

4. Same Parties and the "Privity" Rule

Traditionally claim preclusion applied only in subsequent litigation between the same parties. In the example given at the beginning of this chapter, where Porter sued Davis for patent infringement and lost on a finding that the patent was invalid (the only issue litigated), the doctrine of issue preclusion blocks Porter from arguing that the patent is valid if he sues Davis for a different violation of the same patent claims. Porter and Davis are parties in both suits.

Courts have long understood that *sometimes* nonparties should be bound on issues resolved in the suit because they stand in a close relationship to a party. If, for example, the patent underlying the claim that Porter brought against Davis were in fact owned by Osborn, who had licensed use of the patent to Porter, and if Osborn had encouraged Porter to sue Davis and had worked with Porter in bringing the unsuccessful suit, a court might find that Osborn too is precluded from litigating new claims against Davis for later violations of the same patent. Usually, courts describe the connection between people like Osborn and Porter in terms of "privity," which is not so much a term of art as an expression of the idea of "sufficient connection to treat someone who was not a party as though she was a party."

■ NOTES ON NONPARTIES "IN PRIVITY WITH" PARTIES

1. One of the classic situations in which nonparties are often found to be in privity with parties is the situation in which the two have simultaneous or successive interests in property. Thus grantors and grantees are often considered to be in privity, and sometimes lessors and lessees, devisors and devisees, and trustees and beneficiaries. For an example, see Modiri v. 1342 Restaurant Group, Inc., 904 A.2d 391 (D.C. 2006) (in first suit, owner TK obtained judgment terminating lease with CH because prostitution was conducted on premises; CH had subleased to BF, who assigned his interest to RG, which sublet part of the premises to MM, who was allegedly responsible for the prostitution; in second suit, RG sued MM for damages arising out of the violation of the lease; MM was in privity with CH, and was therefore bound by the judgment that TK had obtained against CH; privity means that one is so identified with another that the latter represents the same right, so that the latter represents the former's interests; CH sought to defend by showing that MM "was not conducting an illegal business," and MM was asked to testify, and he sent the manager of the business to testify; MM's interests were "aligned with" those of CH); State Farm Casualty Co. v. Fullerton, 118 F.3d 374, 385 (5th Cir. 1997) (husband shot and killed wife and stepdaughter, and pled guilty to murder; in suit by heirs of victims against insurance carrier that provided homeowner's coverage, claimants were precluded on question whether insured committed murder, bringing into play an exclusion for injuries "caused intentionally by or at the direction of the insured") (heirs were in privity with husband because of "derivative nature of their recovery under the policy").

2. The concept of privity includes one who is a successor in interest in ownership rights, so a grantee is usually said to be in privity with his grantor. See, e.g., Watkins v. Peacock, 184 P.3d 210 (Idaho 2008) (as "successors in interest" to the Davises, the Watkins are "their privies" and are entitled to enforce a claim of *res judicata* arising out of a suit between the Watkins and Peacock). See also Wamsley v. Nodak Mutual Insurance Co., 178 P.3d 102, 114 (Mont. 2008) (privity "applies to one whose interest has been legally represented," and "privies" are "those who are so connected in estate or in blood or in law as to be identified with the same interest").

3. What else does privity mean? See Bates v. Township of Van Buren, 459 F.3d 731 (6th Cir. 2006) (topless dancer and owner of bar where she performed were in privity, so his prior suit challenging anti-nudity ordinance barred her later suit challenging the same ordinance).

5. Use of Preclusion by Nonparties and the "Mutuality" Rule

Consider once more the example at the beginning of this chapter, where Porter sued Davis for patent infringement and lost on a finding that the patent was invalid (only issue litigated). Recall that issue preclusion blocks Porter from suing Davis later for a different violation of the same patent claims, and recall, from the most recent iteration of this example in the last section, that Osborn may be precluded on the issue of patent validity too if he owns the patent, as he is in privity with Porter.

Suppose now that Porter brings a third suit, this time against Decker, for violating the same patent claims advanced in the suits against Davis. Under traditional doctrine, the result here is different. Decker was not a party to the prior suit (nor in privity with a party), so Decker could not block Porter from asserting again the validity of the patent. Enshrined in something called the "mutuality rule," the tradition was that only one who would have been bound by a judgment in a prior suit could invoke issue preclusion, and Decker would not have been bound by the judgments in Porter's suits against Davis. Hence Decker could not invoke claim preclusion to put an end to Porter's third suit. There is another way of looking at the mutuality doctrine: The right to benefit from issue preclusion must be "earned," and persons who were not parties to a prior suit, and had nothing directly at stake, have not earned the right to claim the protection of the doctrine.

Not surprisingly, there were situations in which the mutuality doctrine worked mischief. Suppose Amy collides with a truck driven by Ben, who works for Centex Company and is acting within the scope of his employment. Amy sues Ben and loses, and Amy then sues Centex Company on a theory of respondeat superior, but otherwise makes the same claim she brought in her suit against Ben. This situation brings to the fore not only the serious question whether a litigant like Amy should be able to bring more than one suit arising out of a single accident, but the sticky question what to do if Amy were to prevail against Centex after losing against Ben. In theory, a principal or employer who incurs loss because of the negligence or malfeasance of an agent or employee (like Ben) has a right of indemnity against the latter: On our facts, Centex could sue Ben for indemnity, or bring Ben into Amy's suit by impleading him under FRCP 14. In this setting, allowing Amy to litigate her case twice brings the potential embarrassment of inconsistent judgments, *and* the danger that we must choose between protecting Ben from liability to Centex or denying the right of Centex to indemnification. The choice presents a kind of double bind in which both options are unacceptable: Allowing Ben to be liable to Centex has the effect of taking from Ben what he won when he fended off Amy's claim. Denying Centex the right to collect from Ben takes away from Centex its right of indemnity on account of a suit that went to judgment without Centex being able to participate.

In cases like this one, courts long ago retreated from the mutuality rule, and allowed nonparty indemnitees (like Centex in the example described above) to take advantage of issue preclusion to block Amy's second suit. See, e.g., Restatement of Judgments §99 (1942) (where one charged with a tort or breach of contract prevails on the merits, plaintiff cannot bring a new suit "against another responsible for the conduct of such person" based on the same theory); Good Health Dairy Products Corp. v. Emery, 9 N.E.2d 758, 759 (N.Y. 1937) ("where the liability of a principal or master is derivative, a judgment on the merits in favor of the servant or agent from whom the liability is derived may be set up as a defense by the principal or master, although he was not a party to the earlier action"). For a modern example, see Fuentes v. Jednat, 229 P.3d 949 (Wyo. 2010) (after plaintiffs sued drunk driver and won judgment, *res judicata* barred suit against uncle of drunk driver for negligent entrustment; when judgment "includes a determination of the entirety of recoverable damages suffered by the plaintiff for an indivisible injury and provides for their recovery by the plaintiff against one or more of the defendants, payment of the full amount of recoverable damages constitutes a satisfaction of the plaintiff's rights against all tortfeasors").

Two pathbreaking decisions institutionalized an exception to the mutuality rule in allowing what we now call "defensive nonmutual preclusion" (or "nonmutual collateral estoppel used as a shield") without relying particularly on the double bind that appears in the indemnity cases. In Bernhard v. Bank of America, 122 P.2d 892 (Cal. 1942), plaintiff sued Bank of America, claiming that the executor of an estate had wrongfully taken money from the decedent by depositing her checks in his own account in Bank of America. Plaintiff had previously made the same argument in probate court, however, where the executor had filed an accounting, and the same claims that she brought against Bank of America had been determined there. In an opinion for the California Supreme Court, Justice Roger Traynor, a respected jurist, concluded that preclusion should apply if the "identical" issue was litigated before in a case that went to judgment on the merits and the party against whom preclusion is asserted was herself "a party or in privity with a party to the prior adjudication."

Coming later to the game, the United States Supreme Court reached a result similar to *Bernhard* in a patent case. In Blonder-Tongue Laboratories, Inc. v. University of Illinois Foundation, 402 U.S. 313 (1971), the question was whether a plaintiff who brought suit for patent infringement and lost on a finding that the patent was invalid could advance a second claim turning on the validity of the same patent in a new suit against a second alleged infringer. The Court answered in the negative, raising the "broader question" whether a litigant should have "more than one full and fair opportunity for judicial resolution of the same issue." Suggesting that providing more than one opportunity would be a "misallocation of resources" and that it smacked of "Bentham's reference to the gaming table," the Court rejected application of the mutuality doctrine in this setting. While some language in the opinion suggests that it might be limited to patent cases (the Court cited the "inordinate amount of trial time" taken in patent litigation, and the "economic consequences" of patent litigation to consumers and manufacturers), the opinion is widely read and cited for the proposition that the mutuality doctrine should be abandoned, at least when issue preclusion is advanced defensively to block successive claims by plaintiffs against new defendants.

It is worthy of note that states remain free to retain or abolish the mutuality principle. Many states have followed the lead of the Court and done away with the mutuality requirement. See, e.g., Briggs v. Newton, 984 P.2d 1113, 1120 (Alaska 1999); Tofany v. NBS Imaging Systems, Inc., 616 N.E. 1034, 1038 (Ind. 1993). Some states, however, retain the mutuality rule. See, e.g., Rawlings v. Lopez, 591 S.E.2d 691 (Va. 2004).

PARKLANE HOSIERY COMPANY, INC. v. SHORE

Supreme Court of the United States
439 U.S. 322 (1979)

Mr. Justice STEWART delivered the opinion of the Court.

This case presents the question whether a party who has had issues of fact adjudicated adversely to it in an equitable action may be collaterally estopped from relitigating the same issues before a jury in a subsequent legal action brought against it by a new party.

The respondent brought this stockholder's class action against the petitioners in a Federal District Court. The complaint alleged that the petitioners, Parklane Hosiery Co., Inc. (Parklane), and 13 of its officers, directors, and stockholders, had issued a materially false and misleading proxy statement in connection with a merger. The proxy statement, according to the complaint, had violated [various provisions of] the Securities Exchange Act of 1934, 15 USC §§78n(a), 78j(b), and 78t(a), as well as various rules and regulations promulgated by the Securities and Exchange Commission (SEC). The complaint sought damages, rescission of the merger, and recovery of costs.

Before this action came to trial, the SEC filed suit against the same defendants in the Federal District Court, alleging that the proxy statement that had been issued by Parklane was materially false and misleading in essentially the same respects as those that had been alleged in the respondent's complaint. Injunctive relief was requested. After a 4-day trial, the District Court found that the proxy statement was materially false and misleading in the respects alleged, and entered a declaratory judgment to that effect. The Court of Appeals for the Second Circuit affirmed this judgment.

The respondent in the present case then moved for partial summary judgment against the petitioners, asserting that the petitioners were collaterally estopped from relitigating the issues that had been resolved against them in the action brought by the SEC.[2] The District Court denied the motion on the ground that such an application of collateral estoppel would deny the petitioners their Seventh Amendment right to a jury trial. The Court of Appeals for the Second Circuit reversed, holding that a party who has had issues of fact determined against him after a full and fair opportunity to litigate in a nonjury trial is collaterally estopped from obtaining a subsequent jury trial of these same issues of fact. The appellate court concluded that "the Seventh Amendment preserves the right to jury trial only with respect to issues of fact, [and] once those issues have been fully and fairly adjudicated in a prior proceeding, nothing remains for trial, either with or without a jury." Because of an inter-circuit conflict, we granted certiorari.

I

The threshold question to be considered is whether, quite apart from the right to a jury trial under the Seventh Amendment, the petitioners can be precluded from relitigating facts resolved adversely to them in a prior equitable proceeding with another party under the general law of collateral estoppel. Specifically, we must determine whether a litigant who was not a party to a prior judgment may nevertheless use that judgment "offensively" to prevent a defendant from relitigating issues resolved in the earlier proceeding.[4]

A

Collateral estoppel, like the related doctrine of res judicata,[5] has the dual purpose of protecting litigants from the burden of relitigating an identical issue with the same party or his privy and of promoting judicial economy by preventing needless litigation. Blonder-Tongue Laboratories, Inc. v. University of Illinois Foundation, 402 U.S. 313, 328-329 (1971). Until relatively recently, however, the scope of collateral estoppel was limited by the doctrine of mutuality of parties. Under this mutuality doctrine, neither party could use

---

[2] A private plaintiff in an action under the proxy rules is not entitled to relief simply by demonstrating that the proxy solicitation was materially false and misleading. The plaintiff must also show that he was injured and prove damages. Since the SEC action was limited to a determination of whether the proxy statement contained materially false and misleading information, the respondent conceded that he would still have to prove these other elements of his prima facie case in the private action. The petitioners' right to a jury trial on those remaining issues is not contested.

[4] In this context, offensive use of collateral estoppel occurs when the plaintiff seeks to foreclose the defendant from litigating an issue the defendant has previously litigated unsuccessfully in an action with another party. Defensive use occurs when a defendant seeks to prevent a plaintiff from asserting a claim the plaintiff has previously litigated and lost against another defendant.

[5] Under the doctrine of res judicata, a judgment on the merits in a prior suit bars a second suit involving the same parties or their privies based on the same cause of action. Under the doctrine of collateral estoppel, on the other hand, the second action is upon a different cause of action and the judgment in the prior suit precludes relitigation of issues actually litigated and necessary to the outcome of the first action.

a prior judgment as an estoppel against the other unless both parties were bound by the judgment. Based on the premise that it is somehow unfair to allow a party to use a prior judgment when he himself would not be so bound,[7] the mutuality requirement provided a party who had litigated and lost in a previous action an opportunity to relitigate identical issues with new parties.

By failing to recognize the obvious difference in position between a party who has never litigated an issue and one who has fully litigated and lost, the mutuality requirement was criticized almost from its inception. Recognizing the validity of this criticism, the Court in *Blonder-Tongue Laboratories, supra*, abandoned the mutuality requirement, at least in cases where a patentee seeks to relitigate the validity of a patent after a federal court in a previous lawsuit has already declared it invalid. The "broader question" before the Court, however, was "whether it is any longer tenable to afford a litigant more than one full and fair opportunity for judicial resolution of the same issue." The Court strongly suggested a negative answer to that question:

> In any lawsuit where a defendant, because of the mutuality principle, is forced to present a complete defense on the merits to a claim which the plaintiff has fully litigated and lost in a prior action, there is an arguable misallocation of resources. To the extent the defendant in the second suit may not win by asserting, without contradiction, that the plaintiff had fully and fairly, but unsuccessfully, litigated the same claim in the prior suit, the defendant's time and money are diverted from alternative uses—productive or otherwise—to relitigation of a decided issue. And, still assuming that the issue was resolved correctly in the first suit, there is reason to be concerned about the plaintiff's allocation of resources. Permitting repeated litigation of the same issue as long as the supply of unrelated defendants holds out reflects either the aura of the gaming table or "a lack of discipline and of disinterestedness on the part of the lower courts, hardly a worthy or wise basis for fashioning rules of procedure." Kerotest Mfg. Co. v. C-O-Two Co., 342 U.S. 180, 185 (1952). Although neither judges, the parties, nor the adversary system performs perfectly in all cases, the requirement of determining whether the party against whom an estoppel is asserted had a full and fair opportunity to litigate is a most significant safeguard.[10]

---

[7] It is a violation of due process for a judgment to be binding on a litigant who was not a party or a privy and therefore has never had an opportunity to be heard. Blonder-Tongue Laboratories, Inc. v. University of Illinois Foundation, 402 U.S. 313, 329 (1971); Hansberry v. Lee, 311 U.S. 32, 40 (1940).

[10] The Court also emphasized that relitigation of issues previously adjudicated is particularly wasteful in patent cases because of their staggering expense and typical length. Under the doctrine of mutuality of parties an alleged infringer might find it cheaper to pay royalties than to challenge a patent that had been declared invalid in a prior suit, since the holder of the patent is entitled to a statutory presumption of validity.

B

The *Blonder-Tongue* case involved defensive use of collateral estoppel—a plaintiff was estopped from asserting a claim that the plaintiff had previously litigated and lost against another defendant. The present case, by contrast, involves offensive use of collateral estoppel—a plaintiff is seeking to estop a defendant from relitigating the issues which the defendant previously litigated and lost against another plaintiff. In both the offensive and defensive use situations, the party against whom estoppel is asserted has litigated and lost in an earlier action. Nevertheless, several reasons have been advanced why the two situations should be treated differently.[11]

First, offensive use of collateral estoppel does not promote judicial economy in the same manner as defensive use does. Defensive use of collateral estoppel precludes a plaintiff from relitigating identical issues by merely "switching adversaries." Bernhard v. Bank of America Nat. Trust & Savings Assn., 122 P.2d, 892, 895 (Cal. 1942).[12] Thus defensive collateral estoppel gives a plaintiff a strong incentive to join all potential defendants in the first action if possible. Offensive use of collateral estoppel, on the other hand, creates precisely the opposite incentive. Since a plaintiff will be able to rely on a previous judgment against a defendant but will not be bound by that judgment if the defendant wins, the plaintiff has every incentive to adopt a "wait and see" attitude, in the hope that the first action by another plaintiff will result in a favorable judgment. *E.g.,* Nevarov v. Caldwell, 327 P.2d 111, 115 (Cal. App. 1958); Reardon v. Allen, 213 A.2d 26, 32 (N.J. Super. 1965). Thus offensive use of collateral estoppel will likely increase rather than decrease the total amount of litigation, since potential plaintiffs will have everything to gain and nothing to lose by not intervening in the first action.[13]

A second argument against offensive use of collateral estoppel is that it may be unfair to a defendant. If a defendant in the first action is sued for small or nominal damages, he may have little incentive to defend vigorously, particularly if future suits are not foreseeable. The Evergreens v. Nunan, 141 F.2d 927, 929 (2d Cir. 1944); cf. Berner v. British Commonwealth Pac. Airlines, 346 F.2d 532 (2d Cir. 1965) (application of offensive collateral estoppel denied

---

[11] Various commentators have expressed reservations regarding the application of offensive collateral estoppel. Currie, Mutuality of Estoppel: Limits of the *Bernhard* Doctrine, 9 Stan. L. Rev. 281 (1957); Semmel, Collateral Estoppel, Mutuality and Joinder of Parties, 68 Colum. L. Rev. 1457 (1968); Note, The Impacts of Defensive and Offensive Assertion of Collateral Estoppel by a Nonparty, 35 Geo. Wash. L. Rev. 1010 (1967). Professor Currie later tempered his reservations. Civil Procedure: The Tempest Brews, 53 Calif. L. Rev. 25 (1965).

[12] Under the mutuality requirement, a plaintiff could accomplish this result since he would not have been bound by the judgment had the original defendant won.

[13] The Restatement (Second) of Judgments §§88(3) (Tent. Draft No. 2, 1975) provides that application of collateral estoppel may be denied if the party asserting it "could have effected joinder in the first action between himself and his present adversary." [This language was ultimately adopted in Restatement (Second) of Judgments §29(3) (1982).—Ed.]

where defendant did not appeal an adverse judgment awarding damages of $35,000 and defendant was later sued for over $7 million). Allowing offensive collateral estoppel may also be unfair to a defendant if the judgment relied upon as a basis for the estoppel is itself inconsistent with one or more previous judgments in favor of the defendant.[14] Still another situation where it might be unfair to apply offensive estoppel is where the second action affords the defendant procedural opportunities unavailable in the first action that could readily cause a different result.[15]

C

We have concluded that the preferable approach for dealing with these problems in the federal courts is not to preclude the use of offensive collateral estoppel, but to grant trial courts broad discretion to determine when it should be applied.[16] The general rule should be that in cases where a plaintiff could easily have joined in the earlier action or where, either for the reasons discussed above or for other reasons, the application of offensive estoppel would be unfair to a defendant, a trial judge should not allow the use of offensive collateral estoppel.

In the present case, however, none of the circumstances that might justify reluctance to allow the offensive use of collateral estoppel is present. The application of offensive collateral estoppel will not here reward a private plaintiff who could have joined in the previous action, since the respondent

---

[14] In Professor Currie's familiar example, a railroad collision injures 50 passengers all of whom bring separate actions against the railroad. After the railroad wins the first 25 suits, a plaintiff wins in suit 26. Professor Currie argues that offensive use of collateral estoppel should not be applied so as to allow plaintiffs 27 through 50 automatically to recover. [The Court cites tentative draft of Restatement, which had language later adopted in Restatement (Second) of Judgments §29(4) (1982) (nonparty to prior suit cannot invoke issue preclusion if prior determination is "itself inconsistent with another determination of the same issue").—ED.]

[15] If, for example, the defendant in the first action was forced to defend in an inconvenient forum and therefore was unable to engage in full scale discovery or call witnesses, application of offensive collateral estoppel may be unwarranted. Indeed, differences in available procedures may sometimes justify not allowing a prior judgment to have estoppel effect in a subsequent action even between the same parties, or where defensive estoppel is asserted against a plaintiff who has litigated and lost. The problem of unfairness is particularly acute in cases of offensive estoppel, however, because the defendant against whom estoppel is asserted typically will not have chosen the forum in the first action. [The Court cites tentative draft of Restatement, which had language later adopted in Restatement (Second) of Judgments §29, Comment d (1982) (differences in procedure between forum that rendered judgment and forum where judgment is offered for issue preclusive effect may justify denying preclusion; such differences might affect "discovery devices" and "plenary as distinct from summary hearing; also preclusion may be inappropriate where the party against whom the judgment is offered "had no choice, or restricted choice, as to the forum in which the issue was litigated").—ED.]

[16] This is essentially the approach of [the tentative draft of the Restatement], which recognizes that "the distinct trend if not the clear weight of recent authority is to the effect that there is no intrinsic difference between 'offensive' as distinct from 'defensive' issue preclusion, although a stronger showing that the prior opportunity to litigate was adequate may be required in the former situation than the latter." [This language was adopted in Restatement (Second) of Judgments §29, Reporter's Note (1982).—ED.]

probably could not have joined in the injunctive action brought by the SEC even had he so desired.[17] Similarly, there is no unfairness to the petitioners in applying offensive collateral estoppel in this case. First, in light of the serious allegations made in the SEC's complaint against the petitioners, as well as the foreseeability of subsequent private suits that typically follow a successful Government judgment, the petitioners had every incentive to litigate the SEC lawsuit fully and vigorously.[18] Second, the judgment in the SEC action was not inconsistent with any previous decision. Finally, there will in the respondent's action be no procedural opportunities available to the petitioners that were unavailable in the first action of a kind that might be likely to cause a different result.[19]

We conclude, therefore, that none of the considerations that would justify a refusal to allow the use of offensive collateral estoppel is present in this case. Since the petitioners received a "full and fair" opportunity to litigate their claims in the SEC action, the contemporary law of collateral estoppel leads inescapably to the conclusion that the petitioners are collaterally estopped from relitigating the question of whether the proxy statement was materially false and misleading.

II

The question that remains is whether, notwithstanding the law of collateral estoppel, the use of offensive collateral estoppel in this case would violate the petitioners' Seventh Amendment right to a jury trial.

[The Court says that it had recognized, even in the *Beacon Theatres* case, supra Chapter 12, that findings in a judge-tried case could foreclose a later jury trial of the same issues, and that in the *Katchen* case, supra Chapter 12, the Court had recognized that equitable determinations can be made prior to litigation before a jury of legal rights, and that equitable determinations can have preclusive effect. The Court concludes that the Seventh Amendment does not require adherence to the mutuality doctrine.]

---

[17] SEC v. Everest Management Corp., 475 F.2d 1236, 1240 (2d Cir. 1972) ("[T]he complicating effect of the additional issues and the additional parties outweighs any advantage of a single disposition of the common issues"). Moreover, consolidation of a private action with one brought by the SEC without its consent is prohibited by statute. 15 USC §78u(g).

[18] After a 4-day trial in which the petitioners had every opportunity to present evidence and call witnesses, the District Court held for the SEC. The petitioners then appealed to the Court of Appeals for the Second Circuit, which affirmed the judgment against them. Moreover, the petitioners were already aware of the action brought by the respondent, since it had commenced before the filing of the SEC action.

[19] It is true, of course, that the petitioners in the present action would be entitled to a jury trial of the issues bearing on whether the proxy statement was materially false and misleading had the SEC action never been brought—a matter to be discussed in Part II of this opinion. But the presence or absence of a jury as factfinder is basically neutral, quite unlike, for example, the necessity of defending the first lawsuit in an inconvenient forum.

Mr. Justice R<small>EHNQUIST</small>, dissenting.

. . .

In my view, it is "unfair" to apply offensive collateral estoppel where the party who is sought to be estopped has not had an opportunity to have the facts of his case determined by a jury. Since in this case petitioners were not entitled to a jury trial in the Securities and Exchange Commission (SEC) lawsuit. I would not estop them from relitigating the issues determined in the SEC suit before a jury in the private action. I believe that several factors militate in favor of this result.

First, the use of offensive collateral estoppel in this case runs counter to the strong federal policy favoring jury trials, even if it does not, as the majority holds, violate the Seventh Amendment. . . . Today's decision will mean that in a large number of private cases defendants will no longer enjoy the right to jury trial.[20] Neither the Court nor respondent has adverted or cited to any unmanageable problems that have resulted from according defendants jury trials in such cases. I simply see no "imperative circumstances" requiring this wholesale abrogation of jury trials.[21]

Second, I believe that the opportunity for a jury trial in the second action could easily lead to a different result from that obtained in the first action before the court and therefore that it is unfair to estop petitioners from relitigating the issues before a jury. This is the position adopted in the Restatement (Second) of Judgments, which disapproves of the application of offensive collateral estoppel where the defendant has an opportunity for a jury trial in the second lawsuit that was not available in the first action. The Court accepts the proposition that it is unfair to apply offensive collateral estoppel "where the second action affords the defendant procedural opportunities unavailable in the first action that could readily cause a different result." Differences in discovery opportunities between the two actions are cited as examples of situations where it would be unfair to permit offensive collateral estoppel. But in the Court's view, the fact that petitioners would have been entitled to a jury trial in the present action is not such a "procedural opportunit[y]" because "the presence or absence of a jury as factfinder is basically *neutral*, quite unlike, for example, the necessity of defending the first lawsuit in an inconvenient forum."

As is evident from the prior brief discussion of the development of the civil jury trial guarantee in this country, those who drafted the Declaration of

---

[20] The Court's decision today may well extend to other areas, such as antitrust, labor, employment discrimination, consumer protection, and the like, where a private plaintiff may sue for damages based on the same or similar violations that are the subject of government actions.

[21] This is not to say that Congress cannot commit enforcement of statutorily created rights to an "administrative process or specialized court of equity." Curtis v. Loether, 415 U.S. 189, 195 (1974); see Atlas Roofing Co., Inc. v. Occupational Safety & Health Review Comm'n, 430 U.S. 442 (1977); Katchen v. Landy, 382 U.S. 323 (1966); NLRB v. Jones & Laughlin Steel Corp., 301 U.S. 1 (1937).

Independence and debated so passionately the proposed Constitution during the ratification period, would indeed be astounded to learn that the presence or absence of a jury is merely "neutral," whereas the availability of discovery, a device unmentioned in the Constitution, may be controlling. It is precisely because the Framers believed that they might receive a different result at the hands of a jury of their peers than at the mercy of the sovereign's judges, that the Seventh Amendment was adopted. And I suspect that anyone who litigates cases before juries in the 1970's would be equally amazed to hear of the supposed lack of distinction between trial by court and trial by jury. The Court can cite no authority in support of this curious proposition. The merits of civil juries have been long debated, but I suspect that juries have never been accused of being merely "neutral" factors.[23]

Contrary to the majority's supposition, juries can make a difference, and our cases have, before today at least, recognized this obvious fact. Thus, in . . . Byrd v. Blue Ridge Rural Electrical Cooperative, *supra*, 356 U.S. 252 (1958), the Court conceded that "the nature of the tribunal which tries issues may be important in the enforcement of the parcel of rights making up a cause of action or defense. . . . It may well be that in the instant personal-injury case the outcome would be substantially affected by whether the issue of immunity is decided by a judge or a jury." Jurors bring to a case their common sense and community values; their "very inexperience is an asset because it secures a fresh perception of each trial, avoiding the stereotypes said to infect the judicial eye." H. Kalven & H. Zeisel, The American Jury 8 (1966).

The ultimate irony of today's decision is that its potential for significantly conserving the resources of either the litigants or the judiciary is doubtful at best. That being the case, I see absolutely no reason to frustrate so cavalierly the important federal policy favoring jury decisions of disputed fact questions. The instant case is an apt example of the minimal savings that will be accomplished by the Court's decision. As the Court admits, even if petitioners are collaterally estopped from relitigating whether the proxy was materially false and misleading, they are still entitled to have a jury determine whether respondent was injured by the alleged misstatements and the amount of damages, if any, sustained by respondent. Thus, a jury must be impaneled in this case in any event. The time saved by not trying the issue of whether the proxy was materially false and misleading before the jury is likely to be insubstantial. It is just as probable that today's decision will have the result of

---

[23] See, e.g., Hearings on Recording of Jury Deliberations Before the Subcommittee to Investigate the Administration of the Internal Security Act and Other Internal Security Laws of the Senate Committee on the Judiciary, 84th Cong., 1st Sess., 63-81 (1955) (thorough summary of arguments pro and con on jury trials and an extensive bibliography); H. Kalven & H. Zeisel, The American Jury 4 n.2 (1966) (bibliography); Redish, Seventh Amendment Right to Jury Trial: A Study in the Irrationality of Rational Decision Making, 70 Nw. U. L. Rev. 486, 502-508 (1975) (discussion of arguments for and against juries).

coercing defendants to agree to consent orders or settlements in agency enforcement actions in order to preserve their right to jury trial in the private actions. In that event, the Court, for no compelling reason, will have simply added a powerful club to the administrative agencies' arsenals that even Congress was unwilling to provide them.

■ NOTES ON OFFENSIVE NONMUTUAL ISSUE PRECLUSION

1. In cases like *Parklane,* the rubber hits the road: We encounter "offensive nonmutual preclusion" (or "nonmutual collateral estoppel used as a sword"). When Leo Shore brought his class action against Parklane Hosiery and many of its officers and directors, the SEC had not begun its enforcement action. But it would not be surprising if plaintiff's lawyer already knew the SEC was interested, and lawyers take cues from administrative agencies in thinking up their own private suits. When the SEC acted, and won its judgment on claims that the proxy statement was false and misleading, Leo Shore's lawyer may well have thought he'd won a jackpot: He has a class suit, and potentially a swift and decisive weapon with which to claim victory on the central question of liability. All that would remain is proving damages. The question was, could he use the weapon of issue preclusion this way? The trial court said no, but the Second Circuit said yes and the Supreme Court agreed. The Court approves nonmutual offensive issue preclusion, but makes it discretionary with courts. Why the need for "broad discretion"?

2. *Parklane* has led some states to adopt offensive nonmutual collateral estoppel with similar caveats. See, e.g., Exotics Hawaii-Kona, Inc. v. E.I. Dupont De Nemours & Co., 90 P.3d 250, 264 (Haw. 2004) (recognizing doctrine, subject to exceptions if plaintiff could easily have joined first suit, defendant had little incentive to defend, or second suit presented procedural opportunities not available in first) (noting other possible exceptions based on public policy).

3. The Second Restatement, in draft form when *Parklane* was decided, was completed and published three years later. It sets forth a list of exceptions to the nonmutual use of issue preclusion (exceptions potentially applicable both to the defensive and the offensive use of nonmutual estoppel). See Restatement (Second) of Judgments §29 (1982). Several of these exceptions are also noted in *Parklane,* and it's worth taking these up in order:

(a) First, nonmutual preclusion may be inappropriate if it would be "incompatible with an applicable scheme of administering the remedies in the actions involved." Consider the situation of a person employed in a prison laundry who suffered serious brain injuries that may have been caused by an ozone system used in the laundry. If she files a workers' compensation

claim before a state labor commission, but loses because the commission concludes that the evidence does not show a causal connection, should she be bound by issue preclusion if she later sues the company that installed the ozone system? See Gudmundson v. Del Ozone, 232 P.3d 1059 (Utah 2010) (no; workers' compensation scheme is designed to provide simple and speedy relief, and giving adverse finding preclusive effect would present a "vexing dilemma" for claimants, who would have to choose between "simple and immediate relief" and "more complex but potentially more lucrative civil litigation") (also claimant could not name installer in workers' compensation proceedings, and preclusion would "shield third-party defendants" from claims that workers' compensation scheme "expressly preserved"). See Restatement (Second) of Judgments §29(1) (1982).

(b) Second, nonmutual preclusion may be inappropriate if the later forum provides "procedural opportunities" not available in the first suit that "could likely result" in a different outcome. See McIlravy v. North River Ins. Co., 563 N.W.2d 323 (Iowa 2002) (defendant bore burden proving good faith in workers' compensation proceeding, but plaintiff bore burden in this suit alleging bad faith refusal to settle; no collateral estoppel effect on finding of bad faith); Olivieri v. Y.M.F. Carpet, Inc., 897 A.2d 1003 (N.J. 2006) (in civil damage suit alleging that employer fired plaintiff for refusing to give false testimony, employer could relitigate question whether plaintiff had resigned without justification; record did not show that findings by unemployment compensation hearing examiner were based on record; no transcript); Danner v. Dillard Department Stores, Inc., 949 P.2d 680 (Okla. 1997) (plaintiff who had been prosecuted for larceny failed to prove lack of probable cause in preliminary hearing; issue preclusion did not stand in the way of proving this point in civil suit against store; preliminary hearing did not afford full and fair opportunity to litigate; determination rested on false testimony that witness recanted at trial; also fact that customer was present at time of alleged theft was not and could not have been discovered before preliminary hearing). See Restatement (Second) of Judgments §29(2) (1982).

(c) Third, nonmutual preclusion may be inappropriate if the party seeking to take advantage of it "could have effected joinder in the first action." This factor, which is stressed in *Parklane*, is often acknowledged in the cases but seldom actually applied. For a decision that finds this factor decisive, see Hunter v. City of Des Moines, 300 N.W.2d 121 (Iowa 1981) (after two-car accident, Driver 1 sued Driver 2 and also named City, on theory that City was negligent in not removing a pile of snow that obstructed vision; passenger in Driver 1's car brought separate suit against Driver 2 and City; plaintiffs in the two suits resisted attempts to combine them; after one suit resulted in judgment against City, other plaintiff invoked issue preclusion; court concludes that preclusion is inappropriate, as plaintiff could easily have joined other suit). See Restatement (Second) of Judgments §29(3) (1982).

(d) Fourth, nonmutual preclusion may be inappropriate if the earlier determination "was itself inconsistent with another determination of the same issue." See, e.g., Appling v. State Farm Mutual Automobile Insurance Co., 340 F.3d 769, 776 (9th Cir. 2003) (trial court could decline to give preclusive effect to prior determination that termination clause of employment contract required good cause, in view of "several other well-reasoned holdings" to the contrary) (four other decisions come out the other way); Aetna Casualty and Surety Co. v. General Dynamics Corp., 968 F.2d 707 (8th Cir. 1992) (in insurance coverage suit brought by carrier, defendant as insured could not preclude carrier from arguing that "damages" under comprehensive liability policy does not include environmental response costs, on basis of prior judgment; carrier prevailed on this point in two other suits) (treating the defense position as seeking nonmutual offensive preclusion). See Restatement (Second) of Judgments §29(4) (1982).

(e) There are other situations in which nonmutual preclusion is viewed as inappropriate. The Restatement lists these: Nonmutual preclusion may be inappropriate if the prior determination was "affected by relationships among the parties to the first action" that do not appear in the later suit, or the prior determination was apparently based on "a compromise verdict or finding." See Restatement (Second) of Judgments §29(5) (1982). Nonmutual preclusion may be inappropriate if it "complicate[s] determination of the [remaining] issues" in a later suit. See Restatement (Second) of Judgments §29(6) (1982). Nonmutual preclusion may be inappropriate for an "issue of law" and foreclosing a later determination would "inappropriately foreclose opportunity for obtaining reconsideration of the legal rule" that underlay it. See Restatement (Second) of Judgments §29(7) (1982). Finally, nonmutual preclusion may be inappropriate in the presence of "other compelling circumstances." See Restatement (Second) of Judgments §29(8) (1982).

4. Successive damage suits arising out of an accident or in the context of product liability claims are not the only context in which offensive nonmutual estoppel can apply. See, e.g., K.H., Sr. v. R.H., 935 A.228 (D.C. 2007) (in suit against plaintiff's ex-wife seeking custody of child born to her while plaintiff and she were married, trial court erred in failing to apply collateral estoppel on basis of prior proceedings adjudging wife to be guilty of child neglect).

5. For a case abandoning the mutuality requirement in the context of the defensive use of collateral estoppel to block plaintiff from suing a new defendant after losing a prior suit against a different defendant, see Monat v. State Farm Ins. Co., 677 N.W.2d 843 (Mich. 2004) (plaintiff who lost suit against other motorist could not bring suit against carrier who provided coverage for injuries by uninsured motorists) (applying nonmutual estoppel).

6. A dramatic possibility for the use of offensive nonmutual preclusion emerges when a victim of violence or sexual assault brings a civil suit against an assailant who has been criminally convicted for the deed. See, e.g., Doe v. Tobias, 715 N.E.2d 829 (Ind. 1999) (in civil suit by juvenile, defendant's criminal conviction for rape and sexual battery receive issue preclusive effect). Less dramatically, persons convicted of crimes can find that convictions have preclusive effect when the crimes create civil liability for fraud and related torts. See, e.g., Fireman's Fund Ins. Co. v. Stites, 258 F.3d 1016 (9th Cir. 2001) (attorney convicted of RICO violations was precluded from denying fraudulent misconduct when sued for reimbursement by insurance carriers who were the victims of attorney's scheme to drive up legal fees by controlling both sides of lawsuits in which carriers were footing legal bills).

7. As you learned in reading *Marrese* and *Semtek*, state law determines the claim preclusive effect of a state court judgment, and federal law determines the claim preclusive effect of a federal court judgment. It seems that these rules apply to issue preclusion too. Suppose a court in Virginia, which retains the mutuality rule that generally blocks third parties from using issue preclusion against one who was a party in a prior suit, enters a judgment and an outsider seeks to use the judgment in a second state to preclude relitigation of issues. Must the second state honor the rule in Virginia that bars outsiders from making this use of the judgment? Or should the second state apply its own law, allowing nonmutual estoppel when the rendering court would not or denying nonmutual estoppel when the rendering court would allow it? See Rourke v. Amchem Products, Inc., 863 A.2d 926 (Md. 2004) (rendering court should have power to limit effects of its own proceedings, which would be destroyed if court in recognition state could allow nonmutual preclusion when rendering court would not) (denying offensive nonmutual preclusion of Virginia judgment because Virginia retains mutuality rule).

8. Congratulations are in order. The material you have read in this book covers a lot of territory and is as demanding as anything you will encounter in law school. The first chapter commented that procedure is an "alien subject" for students in their first year of legal studies, but that it "rewards study." The author of this book hopes that you agree on the latter point, and believes that encountering the material that comprises this book will have brought you to a new understanding of law, and the world we live in. Many points of detail probably won't stay with you forever—they don't always stay with the author either—but much that you have encountered here will come back to you quickly as you move forward in your education and in the profession. Take a moment and feel good about the work you have done and the journey you have taken, and Good Luck as you proceed.

36	915, 923, 941	52(a)(6)	1247
36(b)	941	53	1219
37	737, 933, 994, 996, 997, 1312	53(b)	1062
37(a)	915, 933, 995	54	1225
37(a)(4)	997	54(b)	1192, 1198, 1211, 1223, 1224, 1225, 1232, 1233, 1234, 1235
37(b)	51		
37(b)(2)(A)	45	54(c)	699, 733
37(b)(2)(A)(iii)	997	54(d)	346, 986
37(b)(4)	995	55	728, 1159
37(c)	915	55(a)	728, 731
37(d)(1)(A)(ii)	997	55(b)(2)	728, 731
37(e)	985	56	21, 1011, 1018, 1023, 1026, 1035, 1038
41	537, 750, 755, 756, 1224, 1256, 1257, 1311	56(a)	1011, 1023, 1035
41(a)(1)	750	56(c)	1012, 1021, 1035
41(a)(1)(A)(i)	753, 754	56(c)(2)	935
41(a)(1)(B)	1256	56(c)(4)	1021
41(b)	750, 755, 1256	56(e)	1021
41(d)	750	56(g)	1017
42	142, 792	57	1057
42(a)	792	58	1191
42(b)	792, 1057	59	22, 551, 552, 553, 1110, 1130, 1175, 1186, 1187, 1188, 1239
45	924, 945, 974	59(b)	1141
45(a)	927, 928	59(e)	1187
45(a)(2)	927	60(b)	559, 728, 732, 734, 1158, 1159, 1160, 1161, 1163, 1253
45(c)	928		
45(c)(2)	928	60(b)(1)-(5)	1162
45(c)(3)	927	60(b)(1)	1159, 1162
45(d)	985	60(b)(2)	1159-1160
47(a)	1093	60(b)(3)	1160-1161
48	1089	60(b)(4)	702, 1161, 1163
50	22, 43, 1047, 1110, 1141, 1142, 1146, 1148, 1173, 1175, 1184, 1186, 1188, 1238, 1239	60(b)(5)	1161-1162
		60(b)(6)	1162
		60(c)(1)	1163
50(a)(1)	1141	61	1174
50(a)(1)(A)	1141	65	105, 118, 605, 1222
50(a)(2)	1141	65(b)	12
50(b)	702, 1110, 1142	77	1175
50(c)(1)	1148	77(d)	1184
50(c)(2)	1148	79	1175
50(e)	1146	82	769
51	22, 1173	Form 3	343
51(a)	1089	Form 9	644
52	1130, 1173, 1184, 1240, 1314	Form 11	644, 658, 667, 674, 934
52(a)	1157, 1158, 1240, 1247		

State Rules of Civil Procedure (RCP)

Ala. RCP

82	450
82(c)	450

Colo. RCP

4(g)	345
8(a)	699
16.1	1003
17(b)	773
47(a)(3)	1093

Fla. RCP

1.431(c)(3)	1101

Ind. Trial Procedure Rule

75	453

Miss. RCP

33(a)	934

Nev. RCP

41(e)	756

Ohio Civil Rule

3(b)(7)	447
4.3	447

Okla. RCP

54(b)	1235

S.D. RCP

15(a)	762
15(c)	762, 766

Tenn. RCP

47.01	1093

Tex. RCP

87(6)	452

Vt. RCP

13(a)	723

Wyo. RCP

47(c)	1093

Federal Rules of Appellate Procedure (FRAP)

4	1158, 1175, 1184, 1185, 1186, 1187
4(a)	1188
4(a)(4)	1175
11(a)	1189
28	1189
30(a)	1189
34	1189
38	531, 532

TABLE OF CITATIONS TO THE RULES OF EVIDENCE

TABLE OF AUTHORITIES

Articles and Reports

Duane, James, *The Four Greatest Myths About Summary Judgment,* 52 Wash. & Lee L. Rev. 1523 (1995), 1038

Ehrenzweig, Albert, *The Transient Rule of Personal Jurisdiction: The "Power" Myth and Forum Conveniens,* 65 Yale L.J. 289 (1956), 173

Eisenberg, Theodore, *Measuring the Deterrent Effect of Punitive Damages,* 87 Geo. L. Rev. 347 (1998), 145

Eisenberg, Theodore, & Michael Heise, *Plaintiphobia in State Courts? An Empirical Study of State Court Trials on Appeal,* 38 J. Legal Stud. 121 (2009), 1171

Elliott, Donald, Twombly *in Context: Why Federal Rule of Civil Procedure 4(b) Is Unconstitutional,* 64 Fla. L. Rev. 895 (2012), 671

Ely, John Hart, *The Irrepressible Myth of* Erie, 87 Harv. L. Rev. 693 (1974), 533, 537

Epstein, Richard A., *Bell Atlantic v. Twombly: How Motions to Dismiss Become (Disguised) Summary Judgments,* 25 Wash. U. J.L. & Pol'y 61 (2007), 671

—————————, *Federal Preemption, and Federal Common Law, in Nuisance Cases,* 102 Nw. U. L. Rev. 551 (2008), 580

Estin, Ann Laquer, *Sharing Governance: Family Law in Congress and the States,* 18 Cornell J.L. & Pub. Pol'y 267 (2009), 283, 285

Fairman, Christopher M., *Heightened Pleading,* 81 Tex. L. Rev. 551 (2002), 647

Field, Martha A., *Sources of Law: The Scope of Federal Common Law,* 99 Harv. L. Rev. 881 (1986), 566, 578

Final Report of the Committee on Civility of the Seventh Federal Judicial Circuit, 143 F.R.D. 441 (1992), 25

Fiss, Owen, *Against Settlement,* 93 Yale L.J. 1073 (1984), 1167

Ford, Roger Allan, *Modeling the Effects of Peremptory Challenges on Jury Selection and Jury Verdicts,* 17 Geo. Mason L. Rev. 377 (2010), 1107

Frankel, Marvin E., *The Search for Truth: An Umpireal View,* 123 U. Pa. L. Rev. 1031 (1975), 27

Freer, Richard D., Erie's *Mid-Life Crisis,* 63 Tul. L. Rev. 1087 (1989), 556

—————————, *Some Thoughts on the State of* Erie *After* Gasperini, 76 Tex. L. Rev. 1637 (1998), 553

Friendly, Henry J., *The Historic Basis of Diversity Jurisdiction,* 41 Harv. L. Rev. 483 (1928), 371, 374

Fullerton, Maryellen, *Constitutional Limits on Nationwide Personal Jurisdiction in the Federal Courts,* 79 Nw. U. L. Rev. 1 (1994), 276

Ginsburg, Ruth B., *Judgments in Search of Full Faith and Credit: The Last-in-Time Rule for Conflicting Judgments,* 82 Harv. L. Rev. 798 (1969), 1305

Goldsmith, Jack, & Steven Walt, Erie *and the Irrelevance of Legal Positivism,* 84 Va. L. Rev. 673 (1998), 499

Green, Craig, *Repressing* Erie's *Myth,* 96 Cal. L. Rev. 595 (2008), 495, 496

Gross, Samuel R., *The American Advantage: The Value of Inefficient Litigation,* 85 Mich. L. Rev. 734 (1987), 30

Grosskopf, Ofer, & Barak Medina, *Remedies for Wrongfully-Issued Preliminary Injunctions: The Case for Disgorgement of Profits,* 32 Seattle U. L. Rev. 903 (2009), 120

Grossman, Joanna L., *Women's Jury Service: Right of Citizenship or Privilege of Difference,* 46 Stan. L. Rev. 1115 (1994), 1045

Gurry, Robert W., *The Jury Is Out: The Urgent Need for a New Approach in Deciding When Religion-Based Peremptory Strikes Violate the First and Fourteenth Amendments,* 18 Regent U. L. Rev. 91 (2005), 1109

Hart, Henry, *The Relations Between State and Federal Law,* 54 Colum. L. Rev. 489 (1954), 585

Hazard, Geoffrey C., *Has the* Erie *Doctrine Been Repealed by Congress?,* 156 U. Pa. L. Rev. 1629 (2008), 552

—————————, *Indispensable Party: The Historical Origin of a Procedural Phantom,* 61 Colum. L. Rev. 1254 (1961), 793

Hebard, Grace R., *The First Woman Jury,* 7 J. Am. Hist. 1293 (1913), 1045

Henderson, Edith Guild, *The Background of the Seventh Amendment,* 30 Harv. L. Rev. 289 (1966), 1044

Higginbotham, Patrick E., *The Present Plight of the United States District Courts,* 60 Duke L.J. 745 (2010), 1002

Hines, Laura J., *Obstacles to Determining Punitive Damages in Class Actions,* 36 Wake Forest L. Rev. 889 (2001), 845

Hoff, Patricia M., *The ABC's of the UCCJEA: Interstate Child Custody Practice Under the New Act,* 32 Fam. L.Q. 267 (1998), 285

1406   *Index*